ENGLISH RECUSANT LITERATURE
1558–1640

Selected and Edited by
D. M. ROGERS

Volume 376

THOMAS WORTHINGTON
An Anker of Christian Doctrine
1622

THOMAS WORTHINGTON

An Anker of Christian Doctrine

1622

The Scolar Press

1978

ISBN 0 85967 465 7

Published and printed in Great Britain by
The Scolar Press Limited, 59-61 East Parade,
Ilkley, Yorkshire and
39 Great Russell Street,
London WC1

AN
ANKER
OF CHRISTIAN
DOCTRINE.

Wherein the moſt principall Points of Catholike
Religion, are proued : by the onely written
Word of G o D.

Not rejecting Diuine, nor Apoſtolicall Traditions ; authentical Councels ; Popes Decrees ; ancient Fathers ; nor other ordinarie Proofes ; but
abſtracting from them in this
Encounter.

For better ſatisfaction of thoſe, who will admit
no other triall of true Religion, but
Scriptures onely.

Auctore T. W. S. T. D. P. A.

Search the Scriptures.   Ioan. 5. verſ. 39.
Did the Word of God procede from you ? Or came it vn-
to you onely ?   1. Cor. 14. v.

Printed at Doway
By *Laurence Kellam*, at the ſigne of the
holy Lambe.

M. DC. XXII.

Permiſſu Superiorum.

APPROBATIO.

Ego infrascriptus testor me hunc librum, quatuor partes continentem, cui titulus præfigitur (An Anker of Christian Doctrine &c.) *legisse, nihilq; in eo Fidei Catholicæ, vel bonis moribus aduersum reperisse. Quinimo præcipua fereq; omnia, Christianæ Doctrinæ capita, solis Sacræ Scripturæ testimonijs, valdè in eo confirmata inueni: vt sic importunitati Nouatorum hujus sæculi (qui nullam aliam auctoritatem in rebus fidei controuersis discutiendis, præter scriptum Dei verbum admittant) abundè satisfiat. Quare eundem magna cum vtilitate, tum Catholicorum, tum ipsorum Aduersariorum, prelo mandari posse judico. In cujus rei fidem, nomen meum subscripsi. Die 23. Aprilis. 1622.*

MATTHÆVS KELLISONVS, S. Th. Doct. &c.

Infrascriptus hunc librum in quatuor partes distributum, ab Authore Anglo nobis familiarissime cognito, Anglicana lingua scriptum; & ab alio ejusdem nationis etiam viro doctissimo, S. Theol. Doctore, supra noninalecta, nec quicquam rectæ fidei, aut moribus aduersum continere deprehensum, imo multis modis legentibus profuturum: amborum judicio nixus dignissimum qui imprimatur, censui. Duaci. Die 23. Aprilis. 1622.

BARTHOLOMÆVS PETRVS Sacræ Th. Doct.
& Duaci Professor.

THE PREFACE
To the right welbeloued Christian Reader.

A L that beare the name of Christians, & seme to haue any Religion at al, doe agree in these three general pointes. First that God creating man *to his owne image & liknes*, a reasonable creature, thereby made him apt to participate eternal glory. Secondly, that notwithstanding mans creation in so perfect estate, the greater part of mankinde falleth into eternal perdition. Because (as our Sauiour testifieth) *Brode is the gate, and large is the way that leadeth to perdition, and many there be that enter by it. And narrow is the gate, & strait is the way, that leadeth to life, & few there are that finde it.* And thirdly that true faith and Religion, is the onely way to life euerlasting. For *without faith, it is impossible to please god.*

2 But the maine controuersy is, whether the Romane Religion, commonly called Catholique, or rather some other, be the right way to saluation? Which question one Martin Luther, about an hundred yeares agoe, raised amongst Christians.. For when he first began to preach his new doctrine, there was no publique pretence of any other Religion in the Christian world, but of that only which the Bishop of Rome beleued and professed. Neither was Luthers doctrine at any time approued in England, nor elswhere, saue only in a smale part of Germany. And amongst many others, King Henry the 8. cofuted him in a learned booke. For which, his great zeale, he receaued of Pope Leo the Tenth, the renowmed title (which his successors stil enioy) to be

Gen. 1. v. 26. 1. Tim. 2. v. 4. Math. 7. v. 13. 14.

Heb. 11. v. 6.

1517.

See *Art. 41.*

1522.

Man was created apt for eternal glory.

Moe are damned then saued.

True Religion is the only way to saluation.

Al Christendome generally professing one Religion ; Luther preached new doctrine.

Which was neuer approued in England.

A 2 called

4

The first breach in England was King Henry his making him self head of the Church.

called, *Defender of the faith*. But fhortly after, when the fame King Henry could not obtaine the Popes cõ-fent to put his wife Queene Catherin from him, and to marry an other, he, with aduife of certaine of his owne fubieĉtes, Cranmer, Cromwel, & fome others, abandoning the Popes authoritie, made him felf fu-preme head of the Church of England, and Ireland, in al fpiritual caufes, mantayning ftil in moft other pointes, the Romane Religion. Yet after his death, 1533.

After which, came in Zuing-lianifme in the time of King Edward.

the Gouerners of his yong fonne, King Edward the Sixt, brought in the doĉtrine of Zuinglius; denying 1548. the Real prefence of Chrift in the Sacrament (which Luther acknowledged) and diuers other new opini-ons, with a new forme of publique prayer. And with-al, they laid alfo the Primacie of the Church, vpon the King a childe, fcarfe tenne yeares of age. Al which 1553.

Queene Mary reftored Ca-tholique Reli-gion. Q. Eli-zabeth abro-gated it againe.

Queene Marie reforming, reftored the Catholique Religion. And fhortly againe, Queene Elizabeth re- 1559. affuming to her felf, the fpiritual fupremacy (which noe others in the world graunt to Lay-men, much leffe to children, or women) abrogated the Catho-lique Rites: and in place thereof, renewed the forme of common prayer, which is now in praĉtife, much like to the former, but not in al pointes the fame, which was in King Edwardes time.

Al the Bifhops, and many o-thers remay-ning Catho-lique, M. Iuel chalenged to try true Religi-on, not onlie by the holie Scriptures, but alfo by the aun-cient Fathers.

3 This being done by force & power of the Queene, and of fuch as confented thereto in Parlament: al the Bifhoppes of the Realme, expreffly difclaming frõ it, not only al the fame Bifhoppes, but alfo many others, afwel of the Clergie, as Laitie, both in worde and faĉt, perfcuering in the Catholique faith: one M. Iohn Iuel, preaching at S. Paules Croffe in Lon-don, with ftrange audacitie, challenged al Romane Catholiques in the world, to trie with him, by way of learning, the truth of Religion, now called into

Aĉt. of Par. An 1. Eliz.

con

controuersie : solemnly promising, that if anie of his
aduersaries, should produce, any one sentence, or any
one word, either of holie Scripture, or of authentical
Councel, or Auncient Father, within the first sixe
hundred yeares of Christ, geuing euident testimonie,
for any one of sundry Articles of the Romane Religion, there by him recited, that then he would recant
his denial thereof, and subscribe to the Romane doctrine.

4 Hereupon diuers learned Catholiques with great
speede, some in brefer, some in larger Treatises, e-
specially Doctor Thomas Harding, in an ample work
clearly proued the same Articles, by abundance of
such irrefragable testimonies of holy Script. approued
Councels, and auncient Fathers, as the chalenger had
demanded : And therefore required him, according
to his so publique promise, for his own soules health
and others by him deluded, to recant his errors, &
to submit himself to the Catholique Church. But he
persisting wilful (though, manie of his folowers, by
Gods grace, vpon this occasion, became firme Catholiques) replied against Doctor Harding, and the rest,
vsing such poore shiftes, friuolous euasions, and false
sleightes, that his owne complices, namely Doctor
Laurence Humfrey, in his Booke, *de praxi Romanæ
Curiæ*, plainly confessed, that his Chalenge was incó-
siderate, ouer large, and could not be mantayned.
And therefore our aduersaries euer since, generally
refuse to trie this cause by any other authorities, then
by the only holie Scriptures. Neither wil they submitte them selues, to the Explications of the auncient Fathers, nor yet stand to the expositions of their
felow Protestantes, further then euery ones owne
spirit liketh. For when they are pressed with any such,
either they appeale to some other of their owne Doc-

tors

He was so có-
futed by Doc-
ter Harding, &
others, that his
felowes say : his
chalenge was
too large.

*The Lord
Copley; Doctor
Richard
Steuens;
M. Williã
Reynolds.
And others
innumera-
ble.*

Generally our
aduersaries re-
fuse al other
tryal, but by
the holy Scrip-
tures only.

tors, on whom they more relye, or if them selues professe to be learned, and be vrged with the Doctrine of others, they wil not stick to say, that whosoeuer doe teach otherwise then them selues, whether they be auncient, or late writers, doe mistake the holy Scriptures. Yea, if they be further charged, that either they, or those others doe erre, because they auouch contrary doctrine, they say plainly, that al doctrine which is contrary to theirs, is contrary to the holy Scriptures. And the forsoth, doe they most friuolously pretende, that we must beleue, the diuine Scriptures, before al humane iudgments: as though any Christian euer doubted therof, whereas the true question is, not betwene the diuine Scriptures, and mens writinges, but which men doe best vnderstand & expound the holy Scriptures? And in very deede, this is the proper difference betwixt our aduersaries and vs, touching this point, that they by the holy Scriptures *only*, we by the same *principally*, professe to be instructed.

The true question is who best vnderstand the holy Script.

Protestantes rely only, Catholiques principally vpō holy Scriptures.

We agree to try Religion with our aduersaries, by the holy Scriptures, onely.

5 Rightly then obseruing wherin the question consisteth; whosoeuer wil learne the true sense of holy Scriptures, and therby know the true Religion, must resolue whether he wil vnderstand them as the auncient Fathers did, whom al later Catholique Doctors doe follow; or as some new Doctors expound them. And then which new Doctors he wil preferr, Protestants, or Puritanes, or what others. Or els, (which is an other new way) without binding him self to one sort or other, he wil be his owne chooser, following which sense him self shal iudge best. To which neweft maner of vnderstading gods word, because many in these daies, are so addicted, that they wil not yeld to any other, we condescend to ioyne this issue with them, to trye the true Religion, by the only

only writen word of god, as eachmans owne iudgment, by the grace which god wil geue him, shal be able to discusse and vnderstand it.

6 And this we doe, as willing to vse al possible means to satisfie al: trusting, that as our endeuour semeth necessary for those which wil admitte none other kind of trial, and for their better information, which think that we preferre any other authoritie before the holy Scriptures: so it may be also profitable to many, as being expedient for the more manifestation of truth (which can neuer be too much knowen) & must nedes be wel accepted of our aduersaries, who so continually prouoke vs to this onely trial; bearing the world in hand, that therein they haue great aduauntage against vs. Here therfore, beloued aduersaries, to the more honour of god, and benefite of soules, & particularly, that you and we may be the sooner accorded, to our mutual comforth, & for the necessarie reduction vnto truth, of whosoeuer are presently in errour, we doe agree to encounter you, not onely *principally*, as we haue continually done, but also with the *onely* short and sharpe weapon of the sacred Textes of gods word, writen in the holy Bible of the old & new Testament. Alwaies presupposing, that reasonable conditions may be obserued on both parties, without preiudice to either of both.

7 As first of al, it is stil to be remembred, that albeit we thus condescend to encounter you, by only holy Scriptures; yet we doe not therby graunt your exclusion of other proofes to be iust or lawful. For we doe hold it certaine, that al Christian Doctrine, can not be expresly, and withal immediatly proued by holy Scriptures only; & that other proofes are both *Article 3.* necessary, & authentical, as we doe vndertake (in due *41.42.* places of this work) to proue, by the expresse writen word

Marginal notes:

Hoping that our endeuour wil be profitable to many; being necessary for the deceaued; and expedient for the more manifestation of truth.

We require reasonable conditions.

1.

First to be stil remembred, that we do not exclude, but abstract from other proofes. And therfore if our aduersaries wil vse others against vs, they must admit the like against them selues.

word of God. But we are content to abstract from them, with this prouiso for your good, that if your selues, vpon tryal of this proposed combate, shal find it necessary to vse other meanes, for proofe of some doctrine which you hold, and can not shew immedi- atly by the holy Scriptures; or, if at least you shal think it needeful to repair to the auncient Expositors, for better vnderstanding the true sense of holy Scrip- tures; we wil be no lesse readie, to returne thereunto with you, then we are in the meane time content for your sakes to abstaine from them. And therefore we wil in this case agree, that you may if you can, either produce approued Traditions, Definitions of authen- tical Councels, Popes Decrees, Vniforme consent of the auncient Fathers and Doctors, General practise of the visible knowen Church, or any other substan- tial proofe, & that you may alledge the cleare iudge- ment of Ecclesiastical Interpreters, of any holy Scrip- ture against vs; so that you wil allow vs to vse the same meanes, that each of vs may indifferently de- fend our selues, and assault the others, with the same kindes of defensiue, and offensiue, armour and wea- pons.

8 In the meane while, so long as you wil needes try this cause by the only holy Scriptures, we must re- quire this second condition, that seeing we refraine for your contentment, from other proofes; you must also be bound and limited to the same. For other- wise, it is vnreasonable, & ouer partial dealing, that whatsoeuer you find in any authentical Councel, Popes decree, auncient Father, or Catholique Doc- tor, which may seeme to make for you, or against vs; should by and by, be taken for a wounding blow ge- uen to vs, and neither the same, when it is rightly ex- planed, nor the like, must touch you at al. Whiles therefore

2.
Whiles our aduersaries wil admit noe o- ther proofe but onlie holie Scriptures; they must also be limited ther vnto.

therefore you debarre vs from al other kindes of
proofe, you muſt alſo containe your ſelues within
the ſame liſtes of holie Scriptures onlie.

9 Neuertheleſſe, the third condition may be, if you
pleaſe (for it wil be as needeful to you as to vs) that
it may ſuffice in ſome ſpecial pointes of Chriſtian Doctrine, to proue the thinges them ſelues which we beleue, by neceſſarie concluſions deduced from the holie Scriptures, though the verie wordes or termes be
not there expreſſed : as the wordes *Trinity*, and *Perſon*, in the ſenſe wherein we vſe them, in profeſſing
our beleefe of three diuine perſons in god. Alſo the
conſubſtantialitie of the ſame perſons. The perpetual Virginitie of the moſt B. Virgin Marie, the Mother of God. The name of Sacrament. And the like.

10 The Fourth condition may likewiſe be, whereto
we ſuppoſe you wil alſo accord, that producing particular textes, for proofe of particular pointes, ſearching the proper and vſual ſignification of the ſacred
wordes, weying the circumſtances of perſons, times,
and places, with the occaſion, intention, & drift of
the Author : we may ſo reguard gods holie worde,
conferring text with text, that we admitte that to be
the true doctrine, which ſhal be proued by the more
euident wordes or ſentences. For that in al reaſonable pleas, eſpecially in religious cauſes, the more
cleare textes, ought to illuſtrate the more obſcure.

In caſe alſo that anie wordes or paſſages, may ſeme
cleare to one partie, and obſcure to the other, then
doth reaſon dictate, to reaſonable perſons, to the louers of truth, and ſtudious of concord, that the moe
places in number, being, or ſeming, of like perſpicu-
ity, or obſcuritie, may iuſtlie preuaile to explcate the
fewer : Stil conſidering, that al and euerie parcel of
holy Scripture, is abſolutlie true, whether we vnder-

B   ſtand

3.
That it may
in this combate
ſuffice to either
partie to proue
the thing it ſelf,
though the
word be not
expreſſed in
the holie Scrip-
tures.

4.
That the more
obſcure textes
may be expli-
cated by the
more cleare.

Or the fewer,
by the more in
number, con-
ſidering that al
are true.

stand it or no ; al being indited by the holie Ghost,
the Spirit of truth.

The holy Bible
is set forth in
English, and
this booke is
also written,
that it may ap-
peare which
Religion is best
grounded in
holie Scrip-
tures .

11 Behold these are the conditions, which seme both
reasonable and requisite in this kinde of trial, vndertaken for their contentment, that desire to be informed, who amongst diuers pretenders of true Religion , are best grouded in the holie Scriptures . For
whose sakes also, & for this verie purpose, the whole
sacred Bible faithfully tranflated into english, is lately set forth, with annotations, gathered especially
out of the commentaries, and other writinges of the
auncient Fathers, and Doctors of the Church .

And now this work is compiled more particularly, of the diuine textes ; agreable indeede, to the same
holie Fathers sense and beleefe : but so connecting
manie concordant places, pertayning to the same
pointes of doctrine , though not al that might be
brought (for that would be too immense) yet so
much as may abundantly suffice, afwel for decision of
the cheifest controuersies, of these times, as also for
confirmation of most other principal articles, and diuine misteries of faith and Religion.

The Summe
of al Christian
doctrine is here
proued, be-
cause manie
pointes of con-
trouersie de-
pend vpon o-
ther Articles .

12 Our reasons, why in this maner, we proue the
whole Catholique doctrine, not onlie in matters at
this time in controuersie, but also in such others as
haue bene in former ages, or may be in future, drawne
into question, are especially these three. First because
there is such connexion amongst manie partes of faith
and Religion, that diuers which are or haue bene,
called into controuersie, can not be fully declared,
without presupposed knowledg of other groundes,
whereon they depend . For example, it behoueth
al men, first to beleue, that God is one in subftance,
and three in persons, before they can be wel instructed, that according to the Catholiqne faith, al the
three

three diuine perfons, are confubftantial, and coeternal. Likewife except we firft confeffe, that God
is omnipotent, it wil be hard or impoffible to beleue
miracles. So we muft beleue that there is a Church,
els we can not know what proprieties, priuiledges,
and power it haith. And fo in many other controuerfies, it auaileth much, to fee the proofes of that
which is confeffed, becaufe by the fame oftentimes,
that which is denied, may either wholly, or in fome
part be proued, and explaned.

13 Secondly we confider, that as we are prefently
encombred with the controuerfies raifed by Luther, Zninglius, Cranmer, Caluin, Knox, Cartwright,
and daily by new, and newer feftaries: fo we may
hereafter (we know not how foone) be put to proue,
any other part of Chriftian Religion, not as yet denied. And therefore it fhal be good, to fee fome
groundes in the holy Scriptures, of al the principal
pointes of our faith.

*Secondlie be-
caufe new er-
rois are ftil
deuifed.*

14 Thirdly by this general proofe, of al Chriftian
doftrine, the diligent Reader may fee, that manie o-
ther greateft mifteries, which our prefent aduerfaries
acknowledg to be true and certaine, are as hard to
be proued by expreffe canonical Scripture, as any of
thofe which they deny. Yea I dare auouch, that the
holie Scriptures, doe more clearly fhew, in plaine
termes, the cheifeft pointes of the Romane doftrine,
denyed by Proteftantes and Puritanes, then anie expreffe wordes doe declare, the true Catholique beleefe againft the Arians, Eunomians, Nouatians, Pelagians, and the like. As therefore diuers auncient
Fathers and Doftors, haue, not onlie confuted the
aduerfaries of truth, liuing in their owne time, and
paffed before them, but likewife haue taught, and
explicated the refidue of Chriftian Religion: fo we,

*Thirdly to
fhew that old
herefies had as
great pretence
of holie Scrip-
ture, as anie
new doftrine
now haith.*

B 2 according

according to our smalest talent, by gods gracious helpe, intende to make this summarie proofe of Catholique Religion, & that by the only writen word of God, as a most firme and sacred Anc̄er of Christian Doctrine, against al impugners thereof, which refusing other Proofes, yet acknowledg the eminent authority of the holy Scriptures.

We folow the method of Catechismus ad Parachos. Diuiding the whole worke into four partes, and euerie part into special Articles.

15 For better ordering the whole work, we deuide it into four partes, and euerie part, into manie particular Articles : after the method of the most authentical Catechisme, directed to al Pastors of the Christian world, by the special ordinance of the late holy Councel of Trent.

In the first part, are contayned manie special Articles of faith, which are breefly comprised in the Apostles Crede. In the second are proued, and explicated, the seauen holie Sacraments; with the dread Sacrifice of the Catholique Church, instituted by Christ. In the third are declared, the ten Commaundements of God. And in the fourth part is shewed, the necessitie and efficacie of praier, especially of our Lords praier, called the *Pater noster.* And of other praiers publique and priuate.

Two verie necessarie considerations.

16 And so to end this Preface as I began, I heartely wish al you that desire to be more confirmed in the way of saluation : and againe I besech you for gods more glory, & your owne soules health, wel to ponder theese two pointes. First, that our immortal soules, after our temporal death, and our bodies also, at the general Resurrection, must either be eternally glorified with al the blessed Angels and other Sainctes in vnspeakable ioyes in the kingdom of heauen : or els eternally damned with the deuils, and al the reprobate in vtter darknesse, and inexplicable torments. Secondly, that as the way to this intollerable

1. Al of mankind must either be saued, or damned eternally.

2. The entrance,

Math. 25.v. 32. Rom. 14.v.10.

rable

Math.
7. *v.* 13.
14. *Luc.*
13. *v.*
23. 24.

tollerable euerlasting miserie, is large, the gate is wyde, and manie doe enter into it : and the way to eternal felicitie, is narrow, the gate is straite, and few doe finde it : Euen so, the entrance into the right way is by true faith and Religion : the progresse therein, is by such meanes as true Religion teacheth vs; and the arriual vnto eternal life, is by perseuering to the end in that due seruice of god, which true re-

progresse, and arriual to eternal life, is only by true Religion.

Math 13.
v. 44. 45.
Is. 64. *v.*
4.
1. *Cor.* 2.
v. 9.

ligion requireth. This true religion, is the hidden treasure which, when you finde, you wil be glad. This is the precious Margarite to be desired of al me. This wil bring vs to those celestial ioyes, which neither mortal eye haith seene, nor eare haith heard, nor heart of man can conceiue. For true Religion

Which of al treasures, is most precious.

Math. 10.
v. 37.
Luc. 14.
v. 33.
Deut. 32.
v. 18.
Pron. 5.
v. 9.
Rom. 8.
v. 17.

therfore, we must principallie imploy our selues, our most diligent studies, our best laboures, and al that we haue. And euer be readie in preparation of mind, rather to lose temporal goodes, landes, libertie, and life, then to leaue the right way of eternal life. That being made to the image of god, we be not iniurious to our Maker, nor cruel to out owne soules : But begin, procede, and perseuer, to serue God rightly. So shal we be heyres of God, and felow-heyres of Christ in his Kingdome which haith none end. To him be al glorie for euer. Amen. 1616

Yours euer in Christ our Lord.

Th. W.

The

THE CONTENTS OF THE
FIRST PART.

ARTICLES Of Faith comprifed in the A-
poftles Crede, and commonly deuided into twelve,
are in particular moe in number . We pur-
pofe here to declare thefe folowing, as
moft principal, To which the
reft may be reduced .

Credo. Faith is neceffary to faluation . Article 1.

Mans witte, nor reach of natural reafon, can not attaine faith : Neither is mans teftimonie fufficient to
affure it, but Gods word onlie . Article · 2.
Gods word is partly writen in the holy Scriptures:
partly knowen and kept by Tradition . Article . 3 .
Some holie Scriptures are hard , and require authentical Interpretation. Article . 4.
True miracles are an affured proofe of faith, or of
other truth, for the which they are wrought . Ar. 5.

In Deum. God is one , and there can not be anie other
God . Article . 6.

Partem. In God is Trinitie of Perfons, the Farher, the
Sonne, and the holie Ghoft . Article . 7 ·

Omnipoten- God is omnipotent. Article . 8.
tem. God knoweth al thinges . Article . 9.
God is abfolute goodnes, and al his actions are
good . Article . 10.
Creatorem Angels, the firft creatures, are (the moft part) in
Cæli . glorie

glorie . Manie are damned .   Article . 11.

Holie Angels by their ministerie and prayers, protect and helpe men . Deuils seeke mens ruine .

Article . 12

Man at first receiued original Iustice, which he lost   Et terræ.
by transgressing Gods commandement : And therby
infected al his progeny with original sinne . Art . 13 .

Mans vnderstanding and free-wil, are weakned by
sinne, but not lost .   Article . 14.

After the fal of man, God promised a Redemer :   Et in Iesum.
who was also foreshewed by manie figures, and by al
the Prophets .   Article . 15.

Our Lord Iesus of Nazareth, is Christ our Rede-   Christum.
mer .   Article . 16.

Our Lord Iesus Christ, is God, the Second Per-   Filium eius.
son of the B . Trinitie .   Article . 17.   Vnicum.

Our Lord Iesus Christ, is truly man.   Article . 18   Dominum.
Nostrum.

Christ our Lord, from the instant of his incarna-   Qui conceptus
tion, had fulnes of grace, knowledge, and power .   est de Spiritu
Article . 19.   Sancto.

Christ our Lord, tooke al mans infirmities, not   Natns.
opposite to perfection .   Article . 20.

The B . Virgin Marie, is the Mother of God, and   Ex Maria Vir-
most excellent of al created persons .   Article , 21.   gine.

Christ our Sauiour, after thirtie yeares priuate life,
preached his Gospel, confirming it diuers waies .

Article . 22.

Christ our Redemer, suffered manie greuous tor-   Passus sub Pon-
ments, death on the Crosse, & was buried. Art . 23.   tio Pilato, cru-
cifixus, mor-
tuus, et sepul-
The   tus.

Descendit ad inferos. The glorious soule of our B . Sauiour, parting fro his bodie, descended into hel.　　Article. 24.

Tertia die refurrexit a mortuis. Our Sauiour Iesus Chrift, rose from death the third day.　　　　　　　　　　Article. 25.

Chrift our Lord, appeared often after his Refurrection. And ordeined diuers thinges perteyning to his Church.　　　　　　　　Article. 26.

Afcendit ad cælos Sedet ad dexteram Dei Pat. omn. Chrift our Lord afcended into heauen, sitteth on the right hand of God.　　　　Article. 27.

Inde vent. eft ludic. viuos et mortuos. Chrift our Lord Wil come in Maieftie, and iudge the world.　　　　　　　　Article, 28.

Credo in Spiritum Sanctum. God the holy Ghoft (with the Father & the Sonne) infpireth and fanctifieth the Church, and the members therof.　　　　　　　Article. 29.

Eccefiam. The vniuerfal Church, confifteth of holy Angels, with other Sainctes in heaue; & the faithful in earth : Of al which, Chrift, as man, is head.　Art. 30.

The Militant Church conteyneth two general mēbers, the Clergie, and Laitie, vnder one vifible head.　　　　　　　　　　　Article, 31.

As wel the Clergie, as laitie, conteyne particular bodies, with feueral heades : al fubordinate, in one whole bodie, to one fupreme vifible head. Art. 32.

The true Church of Chrift, is knowen by fpecial markes : The firft of which, is Vnitie.　Art. 33.

In the old Teftament, there was euer one fupreme vifible head of the Church.　　Article. 34.

Chrift our Sauiour, ordained Sainct Peter, cheife of the Apoftles, and vifible head of the militant Church.　　　　　　　　Article. 35.

Chrift our Sauiour alfo ordained a continual Sucfeffion

cession of S. Peters Supremacie, to the end of this world.   Article . 36 .

The true Church of Christ, is holy.   Art · 37 . Sanctam.

The true Church, is Catholique.   Article . 38 . Catholicam.

The true Church is Apostolique .   Article . 39.

The true Church is perpetual, from the beginning of the world, to the end .   Article . 40,
The true Church of God, euer hath bene, & wil be visible .   Article . 41.
The Church can not erre in doctrine of faith nor of maners .   Article . 42.

In the whole Church is Communion of Sacrifice, Sacraments, Praiers, and other good workes .   Sanctorum cōmunionem.
                                             Article . 43 .
Soules in Purgatorie, doe participate of the Communion of Sainctes, receiuing releefe, by the holy Sacrifice, & other suffrages.   Article . 44 .
No Infidels doe participate of the Communion of Sainctes. Neither is it lawful to communicate with them in practise of Religion .   Article . 45 .
Excommunicate persons, are excluded from the Church, and Communion of Sainctes.   Art . 46,
Whosoeuer fal into mortal sinne, lose the participation of good workes, vntil they be truly penitent .   Article . 47 .

In the Catholique Church, is Remission of sinnes, Remissionem and Iustification by grace.   Article . 48 . peccatorum.
Al mankind shal rise from death, at the day of ge- Carnis resur- neral Iudgement.   Article . 49 . rectionem.
The blessed shal enioy eternal glory according to Vitam eternā
                    C   their

their merites   Article . 50 .

The wicked ſhal be in euerlaſting paine, for their
ſinnes .   Article . 51 .

Amen.   It was foreſhewed, and there haue bene, are, and
wil be, hereſies againſt the true faith . Article . 52 .

Antichriſt the head of al heritikes , is to come
nere the end of this world .   Article . 53 .

The Printer to the benigne Reader .

It may pleaſe you to be aduertiſed , that becauſe
the holie Scriptures , are very much cited in this
Booke, I haue thought it better, with conſent of the
Auctor, not to print them in a diſtinct Character, as
the more ordinarie maner is, but rather to include
them within two ſquadros [ ] And to vſe moſt commonly but one ſorte of letters in the whole worke.
Only interpoſing a cnrſiue letter , in ſome ſpecial
wordes, or ſentences , as more particular occaſion
may require .

AN ANKER
OF CHRISTIAN DOC
TRINE.

WHERIN THE MOST
PRINCIPAL POINTES OF
CATHOLIQVE RELIGION
are proued by the only writen word
of God

Diuided into foure partes.

THE FIRST PART CON
CERNING FAITH.

THE FIRST ARTICLE.

Faith is necessarie to saluation .

AS in al other Artes and sciences ; so most e-
specially in Christiã doctrine, certaine principles are presupposed, and must be admitted
as an assured, true, and firme groundworke, wheron
the rest is founded & built . And the verie first principle is, by consent of al men, which vse discourse of
reason, that there is a God, who created heauen and
earth, and al thinges therin conteyned . An other
principle is, that God made Angels, and men, capable of eternal glorie; and al other creatures, as
wel for the greater ornament of the whole world, as
also (most part of them) to serue the vse of men.
The third principle is, that God hath already established al the good Angels that rightly vsed the excellẽt
giftes, which he gaue them, in eternal glorie, & damned the proude wicked spirites which rebelled against
him

*Principles of
Christian doc-
trine presup-
posed.*

1.
*That there is a
God.*

2.
*Angels & men
were ordained
for eternal
glorie.*

3.
*As som are glo-
rified, & some
damned alrea-
dy; so al shal
come to the
one, or the o-*

*Gen . 1 .
Psal . 145 .
v. 6 .*

C 2

ther of these endes.

him, to eternal paines. And hath likewise alreadie glorified many holy soules, and damned others, and so doth daylie either reward, or punish soules departing from their bodies, that in the end of this world, euery one of mankind, shal either possesse eternal heauenly glory, or eternal hellish paine, both in soules and bodies, according to their diuers and final desertes.

Mat. 16.
v. 27.
Apoc. 22.
v. 12.

2.   These three principles S. Paul breefely compriseth in few wordes saying [He that cometh to God must beleue that he is; and is a rewarder to them that seeke him] A cleare doctrine; First, that there is a God; Secondly, that he rewardeth some; Thirdly, that he rewardeth not al, but them that seeke him; and consequently condemneth those which seeke him not. Wherby the Apostle proueth, that to please God, and to receiue his reward of eternal life, faith is absolutly necessary, because (as he affirmed imme-

Heb. 11.
v. 6.

The necessitie of faith is proued by holie Scriptures.

diatly before) [Without faith, it is impossible to please God] Which principles, albeit al wel instructed Christiãs, wil presently acknowledge: yet for our more confirmation and consolation therin, & further satisfactió to such as doe not perhaps so expresly conceiue the necessitie of faith, before al other meritorious workes: we shal more amply declare the same by many euident testimonies of holy Scriptures, beginning with those which the Apostle alledgeth in the same Chapter.

Ibidem.

The definition of faith.

3   Where he fiirst descibeth faith thus: [Faith is the substance of thinges to be hoped for, the argument of thinges not appearing] The word substance here signifying the ground or fundation supporting other thinges, sheweth, that as a house, temple, castle, or other edifice, can not be made nor stande, without a ground-worke: so without faith there can not be any iustification or saluation, nor true
hope

Heb. 11.
v. 1.

hope of eternal life, which is the reward of them that rightly seeke God, and which al faithful iust persons hope to receiue. So the Apostle proceding to demonstrate by examples, the vse and necessity of this Theological vertue of faith, not only teacheth that [by faith we vnderstand (which without it, the wisest Philosophers could neuer vnderstand) that the worlds were framed by the word of God: that of inuisible thinges visible thinges might be made] but also that faith is the ground of al perfect good workes. For [by faith (saich he) Abel offered a greater host to God then Cain, by which he obtained testimony that he was iust, God geuing testimony to his giftes] which Moyses recordeth by these termes, [Our Lord had respect to Abel and to his giftes, but to Cain and to his giftes, he had not respect] The cause of difference was, by the Apostles doctrine, for that Cain wanted such faith as Abel had. [By faith Enoch was translated, that he should not see death. For before his translation (saith the Apostle) he had testimony, that he had pleased God. But without faith, it is impossible to please God] or as Moyses relateth the same thing. [Enoch walked with God] So doth the holy Ghost by diuine Scriptures, connect these principles together, teaching, that without faith, none can offer grateful giftes to God, none can walke with God, none can please God, none can rightly seeke God, none can receiue the reward of eternal glory. To the verie same effect he citeth more examples saying, [By faith, Noe hauing receiued answer concerning those thinges which as yet were not seene, framed the Arke for the sauing of his house; by the which he condemned the world, and was instituted heire of Iustice which is by faith. By faith Abraham obeyed to goe forth, not knowing whither he went. By faith, he aboade in the lande

v. 2.
v. 3.
Gen. 1.
v. 1. 3.
&c.
Heb. 11.
v. 4. &c.

Gen. 4.
v. 4. 5.

Gen. 5.
v. 22.

Gen. 6.
v. 14.

Gen. 12.
v. 14.

Examples of faith in the old Testament.

Abel.

Enoch.

Noe.

Abraham.

C 3   of pro

of promiſe as in a ſtrange lande, dwelling in cotages Ch. 15:
with Iſaac and Iacob, the Coheires of the ſame pro- v. 6.
miſe. By faith, Abraham offered Iſaac when he was Ch. 22.
tempted, and his only begotten did he offer; who v. 3.
had receiued the promiſes (to whom it was ſaid that
in Iſaac, ſhal ſeede be called to thee) accompting,
that God is able to raiſe vp, euen from the dead:]
And more to this purpoſe doth the Apoſtl adde,
(who though he be very breefe, yet we wil be more
Sara: Iſaac: breefe in ſo cleare a matter) [By faith, Sara, Iſaac,
Iacob: Ioſeph: Iacob, Ioſeph, Moyſes, and his parentes; alſo Ra-
Moyſes. &c. hab, Barac, Gedeon, Iephte, Samſon, Daniel, Samuel, and the other Prophets, did, and ſuffered merue- Heb. 11.
lous great thinges, wrought iuſtice, were needy, in v. 33. &c.
diſtreſſe, afflicted, of whom the world was not worthie.

4   But as al theſe were approued by the teſtimony of
faith: ſo others were reproued and reiected for wāt
of faith. Which defect the Royal Prophet Dauid
Lacke of faith taxeth in the multitude of the Iewes when they were Pſal. 77.
is damnable e- in the deſert [They tempted God in their hartes, v. 19 21.
ſpecially in they ſaid: Can God prepare a table in the deſert? 22.
thoſe that once Therefore (ſaith he) our Lord heard, & made delay;
beleued. and fyre was kindled in Iacob, and wrath aſcended
Proued by the vpon Iſrael. Becauſe they beleued not in God, nor
Prophets. hoped in his ſaluation. They beleued not his mer-
Dauid. uelous workes. And their daies failed in vanity, and v. 32. 33.
their yeares in haſt] for being aboue ſix hūdred thou- Nū. 1. v.
ſand men able to beare armes, when they parted frō 46. Ch.
Egypt, they were kept in the deſert the ſpace of four- 26. v. 65.
tie yeares, where al dyed, except only two (Ioſue &
Caleb) in puniſhment for their ſinnes, which eſpecially proceded of incredulitie. Some failing at one
time, ſome at an other, vpon diuers occaſions, but neuer al together, for ſome were ſtil faithful and iuſt,
as the ſame Prophet Dauid ſignifieth ſaying of ſome:
                                                    They

Pf. 105.
v. 12.
v. 25.

[They beleued Gods wordes, & they fang his praife]
And againe; [They did not beleue his word, and they
murmured in their Tabernacles.] Likewife Ifaias
the Prophet teftifieth the neceffitie of faith, & actual beleefe, for receiuing particular benefites at Gods
handes, faying to the King and people of Iuda, in
diftreffed ftate, when they feared to be oppreffed, by
the Kinges of Ifrael and Syria [If you wil not beleue, you fhal not be permanent.] And in general,
forfhewing the fcarfitie of beleuers among the Iewes
when Chriftes Gofpel fhould be preached, faying,
[Who hath beleued our hearing?] becaufe manie of
them would heare, and few belcue [for the heart of
this people (faith our Sauiour) is waxed groffe, and
with their eares, they haue heauily heard.] Of al
fuch, God by the mouth of his Prophet Micheas,
faith [I wil doe vengeance in furie, and in indignation amog al the nations, that haue not heard] which
doe not with heart heare and beleue. Likewife faith
the Prophet Abacuc [Behold he that is incredulous,
his foule fhal not be right in him felf, but the iuft fhal
liue in his faith.] Which laft wordes, S. Paul al-
ledging, expoudeth two waies in three of his Epiftles.
For to the Romanes, and Galatians, he proueth by
thefe Wordes, that not workes, how good foeuer
they feme, done by Iew, or Gentil, without faith,
can iuftifie; but that faith is neceffarie, els there
can not be fpiritual life, and that therfore [by faith
the iuft liueth] becaufe without faith, euery one is
fpiritually dead; and by faith, fuch as the Prophets
and Apoftles teach to be requifite, the iuft man liueth. And writing to the Hebrewes, to comforth
them in their afflictions, he exhorteth them to perfeuer conftant, congratulating with them, their great
progreffe in Chriftian Religion, [for you both had
compaffiion (faith he) on them that were in bondes,
and

Ifa 7.
v. 9.

If. 53.
v. 1.
Mat. 13.
v. 15.

Mich. 5.
v. 14.

Abac. 2.
v. 4.

Rom. 1.
v. 17.
Gal. 3.
v. 11.

Heb. 10.
v 34. 35.
36.

Ifaias.

Micheas.

Abacuc

S. Paul. ex-
poundeth the
Prophets wor-
des in two fen-
fes.

and the spoile of your owne goodes, you tooke with
ioy, knowing that you haue , a better, and a permanent substance : doe not therfore leese your confidence which hath a great remuneration; for patience is necessarie for you, thar doing the wil of God,
you may receiue the promise . For yet a litle, and
a verie litle while, he that is to come, wil come, and
wil not slack .] Then concluding, saith [and my iust
liueth of faith .] Thus the great Apostle in the former two places alledgeth the Prophets doctrine touching the necessitie of faith, as it is the substance or
ground of thinges hoped for, and in this last place,
as it is the argumēt (or credible assurance) of thinges
not appearing .

v. 37.

The same ne-
cessitie of faith
proued by the
new Testam .

5   But the testimonies of the new Testament doe
also abound, shewing the necessitie of faith, as wel
for obtaining particular benefites, by way of extraordinarie miracles; as for iustification, and eternal
saluation . According to which distinction, we shal
first recite examples of such faith, as at least had the

First concer-
ning particular
benefites .

former effect, though most commonly, when our B.
Sauiour cured by miracle, corporal infirmities, he
also by the same diuine power, remitted the sinnes
of the parties cured ; & so their soules were iustified :
And if they perseuered in iustice, were also eternally saued . Touching which last effect he expresly admonished one, that had beene lame thirtie eight

Examples of
faith required
in miracles .

yeares, saying vnto him : [Behold thou art made
whole, sinne no more, lest some worse thing chance
to thee] but for the present miraculous curing, faith
of the patient was specially required . So when he
heard a leper say vnto him : [Lord if thou wilt, thou
canst make mee cleane (wherby the man professed
his faith of Christes power) he streching forth his
hand touched him, saying : I wil : (and withal added
his operatiue word, saying) Be thou cleane. And

Ioan. 5.
v. 14.

Math: 8.
v. 2. 3.
Luc. 5.
v. 12.
13 .

forthwith

forthwith his leprofie was made cleane .] Likewife
our Sauiour much commending the Centurions faith,
faid vnto him [As thou haft beleued, be it done to
thee .] On the other fide , he gently rebuked the
weake faith of his Difciples, diftreffed in a tempeft
on the fea faying, [Why are ye fearful, o ye of litle
faith?] Againe, he both remitted the finnes, & cured
the body, of one ficke of the Palfey, in regard , not
only of the ficke mans owne faith, but alfo of others
that brought him in his bed . For [feing their faith
(fo declared by fact,) he faid to the ficke of the palfey,
haue a good hart fonne , thy finnes are forgeuen
thee] And to anfwer calumniators, that iudged him
to blafpheme; our Sauiour faid, [that you may know
that the Sonne of man hath power on earth to forgeue finnes, (then faid he to the ficke of the palfey)
Arife, take vp thy bed, & goe into thy houfe .] The
like comforth and helpe he gaue to the woman trubled with an iffue of bloud, that with great faith touched the hemme of his garmenr faying to her ; [Haue
a good hart daughter, thy faith hath made thee fafe.]
Of the Archifinagogue, whofe daughter he raifed
from death, he required no more for this purpofe, but
that he fhould beleue he could do it, and put away all
feare and doubt, faying to him ; [Feare not, only beleue .] And to two blinde men he faid, [Doe you beleue that I can doe this vnto you? According to your
faith be it done to you .] The fame to an other that
fought help to his fonne, our Lord faid, [If thou
canft beleue, al thinges are poffible to him that beleueth .] To the woman of Chanaan, more inftantly
perfeuering in her fuite for her danghter, and not
ceafing for anie repulfe, he faid, [O womā great is thy
faith, be it done to thee as thou wilt] . To that leper,
more gratful then his neene felowes, who returned
and gaue thankes, he denounced a better fentence

D   then

Mat . 8 .
v . 13 .

v . 26 .
Luc . 8 .
v . 25 .
Mat . 9 .
v . 2 .

v . 6 .
Mat . 2 .
v . 10 .
Luc . 5 .
v . 20 .

Math . 9 .
v . 22 .
Luc . 8 .
v . 48 .
Mar . 5 .
v . 36 .
Mat . 9 .
v . 28 . 29 .
Mar . 9 .
v . 23 .

Mat . 15 .
v . 28 .

then the others deferued, [Thy faith hath made thee *Luc.* 17.
fafe.] Alfo to an other reftoared to fight, he faid, *v.* 19.
[Thy faith hath made thee whole.] So alfo S. Paul *Ch.* 18.
being requefted to cure a lame man, [feing that he had *v.* 42.
faith for to be faued, he faid with a loude voice: *Act.* 14.
Stand vpright on thy feete. And he leaped vp and *v.* 8. 9.
walked.] In thefe and the like benefites, faith was
only, or cheifly required.

True faith is e-
fpecially re-
quired in the
vifible head of
the Church.

6. And that true and intire faith, is moft neceffarie
to the fupreme Iudge in al doubtes of faith and Religion, our Sauiour, in his verie laft document before
his Paffion teacheth by his fact and word, when he
declared that [he had praied his heauely Father, that *Luc.* 22.
Peters faith fhould not faile, and that he, (& con- *v.* 32.
fequently his fucceffors) fhould confirme his brethren,] wherof we fhal fay more in the proper Arti- *Art.* 36.
cle pertaining to S. Peters Succeffor, in the Apoftolique Sea.

Faith neceffa-
rie to iuftifica-
tion.

7 Here we fhal adde more textes of holie Scripture
which proue the neceffitie of true Chriftian faith to
Iuftification. To this end S. Iohn Baptift was fent,
to geue teftimonie of Chrift, [that al might beleue in *Ioan.* 1.
him] becaufe he geueth power to be made the fonnes *v.* 7. 12.
of God, (not to al, but) to thofe that beleue in his
name.] Our Lord alfo him felf beginning to preach,
faid [The kingdome of God is at hand: be penitent, *Mar.* 1.
and beleue the Gofpel.] And when the pharefees car- *v.* 15.
ped him for permitting the deuout penitent Marie
Magdalen to touch him, and for faying, thy finnes
are forgeuen thee,] he finally faid to her, [thy faith *Luc.* 7.
hath made thee fafe,] that al might know faith to *v.* 48.
be neceffarie to faluation: ftil inculcating the fame
doctrine, [that euerie one that beleueth in him; pe- *Io.* 3. *v.*
rifh not, but may, (doing that which by his grace 16.
lieth in the) haue life euerlafting.] Cotrariwife, [he *v.* 18.
that doth not beleue, is alreadie iudged. For he that *v.* 36.
is and

is (& fo perfifteth) incredulous to the Sône (of God) fhal not fee life, but the wrath of God remaineth v - pon him .] Forthis caufe moft efpecially, our Lord wrought fo manie great *Miracles* (though he wrought them alfo to the particular benefite of ma - nie , that the faithful might receiue, both temporal & fpiritual good . For fo he turned water inro wine , wherby not only the want of wine was fupplied, but alfo [he manifefted his glorie, and his Difciples bele - ued in him .] He cured a Lordes fonne by his only word, [& the man beleued, & his whole houfe.] To an other that was borne blind, he gaue fight, who for fpeaking wel of CHRIST , was caftforth of the Sinagogue by the Pharifies . But therupon being fur - ther inftructed, more exprefly [beleued in the Sonne of God and falling downe, adored him,] our Saui - our ftil admonifhing the fame wilful blind Pharifies. [If I doe not the workes of my Father, beleue me not ; but if I doe, and if you wil not beleue me, beleue the workes .] Againe, though our Lord wept for Laza - rus his death, yet he was glad therof [for his Dif - ciples fake that they might beleue] when they fhould fee him raifed from death . And therfore he alfo ad - ded praier, with thankes to his heauély Father [And that I did (faith he) for the people that ftand about, that they may beleue that thou haft fent me .] For this purpofe finally he appeared often after his owne Refurrection, fo checking fome for not beleuing fo - ner, that he not only wel accepted of them that faw him and beleued, but alfo more efpecially pronoun - ced them [bleffed that haue not feene and haue be - leued.] And here the holy Euangelift teftifieth , that [our Lord Iefus alfo did manie fignes in the fight of his Difciples , which are not written in this booke] And that [many other thinges there are which Iefus did. And thefe are written (faith the fame Euange -

Together with temporal be - nefites Chrift ioyned fpiritu - al good.

To this end al - fo that al men might beleue, Chrift did more miracles, and manie o - ther thinges that are not

Ioan . 2 .
v . II .
Io . 4 .
v . 53 .

Io . 9 . v .
35 . 38 .

Io . 10 . v .
37 . 38 .

Io . 11 .
v . 15 .

v . 42 .

Luc . 24 .
v . 25 .

Io . 20 .
v . 29 .
v . 30 .

Ch . 21 .
v . 25 .

lift

lift,) that you may beleue that Iesus is Chrift the   *Ch.* 20 .
Sonne of God, and that beleuing, you may haue life   *v.* 31 .
in his name. Al conformable to our B. Sauioures
perpetual doctrine, and laft inftruction before he afcended into heauen : when he againe [exprobrated   *Mar.* 16.
his Difciples (former) incredulitie & hardnes of hart,   *v.* 14. 15.
becaufe they did not beleue them that had fcene him
rifen againe .] And fo concludeth, geuing commiffi-
ö to his Apoftles to preach the Gofpel in al the world.
And generally demonftrating to al men, [He that be-   *v.* 16.
leueth, and is baptifed, fhal be faued, : but he that
beleueth not, fhal be condemned .] Loe, both beleefe and Sacrament are required to faluation : but
want of faith (for then al Sacraments & other workes
are vnprofitable) is fufficient caufe of damnation.

Which cleare fenfe fo diftinctly expreffed in the facred
text, iuftifieth the practife of the Church ; which cö-
tinually before Baptifme (confequently before al o-
ther Sacraments) requireth faith, either actual, as in
al that haue vfe of reafon, or els the confeffion of o-
thers for them, as in Infantes. So after S. Peters   *Mat.* 19.
firft fermon, [they that receiued his word, were bap-   *v.* 14.
tized] After thefe, others in like fort. And when   *Act.* 2.
certaine had heard and [beleued Philip (the Deacou)   *v.* 41. *Ch.*
euangelizing of the kingdome of God, and of the   4. *v.* 4.
name of Iefus Chrift, they were baptized men & we-   *Act.* 8.
mon.] The felf fame difpofition and preparation,   *v.* 12.
the fame holie Deacon required in the Eunuch, the
treafurer of the Queene of the Ethiopians, requefting to be baptized. Vnto whom he faid, [If thou
beleueft with al thy heart, thou maift be baptifed.]
And fo it was done. S. Peter likewife taught Cor-   *Act.* 8.
nelius, the Centurion, the fame thing, that by the te-   *v.* 37.
ftimonie of all the Prophets, [al receiue remiffion of   *Act.* 10.
finnes, by Iefus Chrift his name which beleue in him.]   *v.* 43.
So the Gailor, and his familie, at Philippi, were
taught

Act. 16.
v. 31. 33.

taught by S. Paul and Silas, firſt to beleue in our Lord Ieſus, & then were baptized incontinent.]

8 I would be breefer, but I may not omitte to re-cit ſomthing of S. Paules Epiſtles, & the reſidue of the ew Teſtament, that al may ſee, how abundantly holy criptures teach the abſolute neceſſitie of faith, & ho v ſome harder places are illuſtrated and expoun-ded b, others. Al indeede confirming ech other. S. Paul eſpecially inſiſteth vpon this point, highly prai-ſing the Romanes, & geuing thankes to God in their

Rom. 1.
v. 8.
v. 16.

behalf; [becauſe (ſaith he) your faith is renowmed in the whole world.] And to confirme them therin, affirmeth, that [the Goſpel is the power of God vn-to ſaluation, to euery one that beleueth ; to the Iew, and to the Greeke. For the iuſtice of God is reuea-

v. 17.

led, by faith, into faith, as it is writen; And the iuſt liueth by faith.] For faith in general, produceth faith

Io. 4.
v. 14.
Rom. 3.
v. 22.
v. 27.

in particular Articles, by his grace, as [a fountaine of water ſpringing vp vnto life euerlaſting.] And [the iuſtice of God, by faith of Ieſus Chriſt, vnto al, and vpon al, that beleue in him.] without which noe workes auaile to iuſtification. For al ſuch [boaſting is excluded, not by the law of deedes, but by the law

v. 28.

of faith. For we account a man (ſaith the Apoſtle) to be iuſtified by faith, without the workes of the

Gal. 2.
v. 16 21.
Gal. 5.
v. 6.
Gal. 6.
v. 15.

Law] that is, without Circumciſió, or other workes of the Law of Moyſes, or of nature, or what workes ſoeuer without faith. [For in Chriſt Ieſus neither Circumciſion auaileth ought, nor prepuce, but a new creature] So if Abraham (or any other) did workes which were morally good, before he beleued, he was not therby iuſtified : but [Abraham beleued

Rom. 4.
v 3. *Gal.*
3 *v.* 6.
Iac. 2.
v. 22.

God and it was reputed him to iuſtice.] So that by faith preceding his workes he had life : for faith did worke with his workes : and [by the workes (fo-lowing) the faith was conſummate.] Therfore [the

S. Paul teach-eth very often, that faith is ne-ceſſarie : but neuer, that on-lie faith doth iuſtifie.

Faith without precedét wor-kes, but not without ſubſe-quent workes iuſtifieth. And ſo not faith on-ly. *Iac* 2. *v.* 24.

Gentiles

Gentiles which pursued not after iustice, haue (b, Ro.9.
Chriſtes grace) apprehended iustice ; but the iu- *v.* 30.
ſtice that is of faith . But Iſrael in purſuing the L w 31. 32.
of iuſtice, is not come to the Law of iuſtice . Why o?
Becauſe not of faith, but as it were of worke] to
wit, without faith in Chriſt . [Becauſe of incr ɖuli- Rom.11.
tie, they (the Iewes) were broken from the oliue *v.* 20.
tree (that is, from the Churh) but thou by fai ɪ doſt

Special imagi-
nation of anie
man, that him
ſelfe ſhal be ſa-
ued, is not
faith, but a
vanie phanta-
ſie .

ſtand] not any mans priuate framed phantaſie, that
him ſelf is iuſt, or ſhal infallibly be ſaued, but [by Rom. 16.
obedience of faith, knowne in al Gentiles .] Nor by *v.* 26.
faith alone, for the ſame Apoſtle ſaith, [Now there 1.Cor.13.
remaine Faith, Hope, Charitie, theſe three] al neceſ- *v.* 13.
ſarie to iuſtification and ſaluation . Againe to ſhew
the inualiditie of Moyſes Law, he teacheth that [the Gal. 3.
Law was our Pedagogue in Chriſt, that we may be *v.* 24.
iuſtified by faith : But when the faith came, now
we are not vnder a pedagogue, not the Children Gal. 4.
of the bond-woman (Agar, ſignifying the old Te- *v.* 24. 31.
ſtament) but of the free-woman] Sara, ſignifying
the new Teſtament.

Faith is alſo
neceſſary to
perſeuerance
in iuſtice .

9   And this faith being receiued, is noe leſſe neceſſarie to be kept, as the ſame Apoſtle often admoniſheth the Coloſſians, and al the faithful, that [they Coloſ. 1.
may be preſēted, holie, & immaculate & blameles be- *v.* 22. 23.
fore Chriſt, if yet ye continue (ſaith he) in the faith,
grounded, & ſtable, & vnmouable frō the hope of the
Goſpel.] And in ā other Epiſtle, aduertiſing that [we 1.Theſ.
be made pertakers of Chriſt, yet ſo, if we kepe the be- 3.*v.*3.
ginning of this ſubſtance firme vnto the end] ex- 5. 10.
horteth to procede to perfection, [not againe lay- 2.Theſ.
ing the fundaion of penance from dead workes, 1.*v.*3.
(for ſuch were the verie beſt workes before faith) & 11. Ch.
of faith towards God : but to approch with a true 2.*v.*12.
hart in fulneſſe of faith, ſeeke a Countrie, not terre- 1.Tim. 2.
ſtrial, but a heauenly. *v.*15. Ch.

And 4.*v.*6.

10 And wheras the other foure Apostles, which write Epistles, doe more especially teach the necessitie of good workes, as likewise S. Paul verie abundantly, yet they first require faith, euen as S. Paul. and al the Euangelists doe. And therfore S. Iames encoraging vs [to esteme it al ioy, when we shal fal into diuers tentations] or persecutions : yeldeth this reason, [knowing (saith he) that the probation of your faith, worketh patience :] where he presupposeth faith most necessarie, and the probation therof, passing profitable. Yea he proueth the necessitie of good workes, that faith may be shewed ; that it [may not be idle (saith he) but consummate ; that it may be liuing, not dead.] S. Peter also teacheth both the necessitie and profit of faith, [to you that beleue, is honor ; but to them that beleue not, the stone, which the builders reiected, is made into the head of the corner, and a stone of offence, and a rocke of scandal, to them that stumble at the word, neither doe beleue.] Againe he saith, [the time is, that iudgment begin at the house of God. And if first of vs (saith he) what shal be the end of them that beleue not the Gospel of God :] that is to say ; If best Christians must passe through manie tribulations, here called iudgment, then such as beleue not at al, shal be iudged and punished without end. He againe warneth al the faithful, not to folow priuate interpretation of Scripture, for [there shal be lying Maisters, which shal bring in sectes of perdition.] The verie same S. Iude aduiseth al, [to contend for the faith once deliuered,] adding, that euen then in his time, [there were certaine men secretly entred in, which (saith he) were long agoe prescribed into this indgement, impious, transferring the grace of our God, into riotousnes, and denying the onelie Dominator, and our Lord Iesus Christ.] For that

in ef

2. *Tim*. 1.
v. 13. 14.
Heb 3. *v*.
14. *Ch*.
6. *v*. 1.
12. *Ch*.
10. *v*. 21.
Ch. 11.
v. 14. 16.
Iac. 1. *v*. 4
2. 3.
Ch. 2.
v. 18. 20.
22. 26.
1. *Pet*. 2.
v. 7. 8.

Ch. 4.
v. 17.

2. *Pet*. 1.
v. 20.
Ch. 2. *v*.
1. *Iud*. *v*.
3. 4.

in effect the denying of anie point of faith, is denying Chrift, who is truth it felf.

11   To conclude, therfore this firft Article with S. Iohn : He as wel in his Epiftles, as in the Apocalypfe,

S. Iohn both in his Epiftles and Apocalipfe teftifieth the fame doctrine.

crieth vnto vs, that [this is Gods commandement, that we beleue in the name of his Sonne Iefus Chrift, and loue one an other.] Writing to the feauen Churches, and in them, to the whole Church militat, praifeth them which admitte not the doctrine of heretikes, but [tried them, which fay them felues to be Apoftles and are not, and found them liars .] And efpecially fuch, as [dwelling where the feate of Satan is, hold Chriftes name, and denie not his faith] but [fuch as had the name that they liued, and were dead, he threatned to punifh feuerely.] And [the luke-warme, the Holy Spirit vomiteth out of his mouth.] Elswhere he addeth, that [in trial and tribulatiós, is the patience of Sainctes, which kepe the commandementes of God, and the faith of Iefus.] For [he that fhal ouercome, fhal poffeffe al glorious thinges, and I wil be his God (faith God almightie) and he fhal be my Sonne. But to the fearful, and incredulous, their part fhal be in the poole, burning with fire & brimftone, which is the fecond death.]

1. Io. 5.
v. 10.

Ch. 3.
v. 23.

Apoc. 2.
v. 2. 13.

Apoc. 3.
v. 1. 16.
Ch. 14.
v. 12.

Chap. 21.
v. 7. 8.

An aduertifment, with a requeft to our aduerfaries.

12   I doubt not but fome fmal part of thefe holie Scriptures, might haue fuffifed to proue, and manifeftly to fhew, not only the abfolute neceffitie of the true Chriftian faith, but alfo that it is firft of al required ; as without which, noe workes doe iuftify, nor bring anie to faluation. But I haue collected thus much (omitting alfo much) to geue more abundant fatisfactió, touching this firft ground of al Religion : becaufe our aduerfaries, often in their writinges, & much more in pulpittes, and frequent difcourfes, vntruly charge Catholiques, to build their Religion vpon their owne good workes, and to afcribe litle

to faith

to faith : wheras indeede, we doe affuredly beléue, and plainely profeffe, that as faith is dead without good workes , fo al workes are dead without true faith. Wherfore we pray al Proteftantes and Puritanes, in this point efpecially, to ioyne right handes with vs, that true faith is neceffarie to faluation, and that there is but one true Religion, for the reclaming of al careles mifcreantes, & fenfles wordlinges, who frame to them felues a new paradoxical phanfie , that men may be faued in any Religion : which you know is a moft groffe error ; and that they which are indifferent to any Religion, haue in deede noe Religion , and fo walking in the brode high way of perdition, draw ouer nere to defperate Atheifme .

Mans witte , or reach of natural reafon , can not attaine Faith . Neither is mans teftimonie fufficient to affure it , but Gods word only .

ARTICLE. 2.

Heb. 1 1. v . 1 .

BY the later part of the defcription of Faith , where the Apoftle faith . It [is the Argument of thinges not appearing :] he teacheth, that it is not a fenfible demonftration, but a credible affertion, neither of thinges euident, but of thinges not appearing to our fenfes, nor to natural reafon , or vnderftanding, and fo is aboue nature : wheruppon al matters of faith are called fupernatural, yet not contrary to nature, or reafon . For as Art doth perfect nature, and not deftroy it : fo diuine Grace , excelling both nature and art, by faith which furmounteth the vfe of fenfe, and difcourfe of reafon, fupplieth their imperfections ; becaufe they are defectiue, and fo ntimes doe erre . For example . It feemeth to our eyes, that the Moone is as great as the Sunne, and greater then anie other planet, or Starre ,

E   but

Matters of faith are not naturally demoftrable , but by Gods word made credible .

Faith is not cótrarie to nature : but aboue nature .

As reafon is aboue fenfe , fo faitth is aboue reafon ,

but reason considering the difference of their distāce frō the earth , iudgeth otherwise. We cā not bynatural reasō conceiue, that mans bodie dead & turned into dust , or other matter, shal rise againe to life : but faith teacheth vs, that it shal rise, by the omnipotent power of God ,[to whom al thinges are possible .] *Math . I*, And therfore pointes of faith, are not alwaies proued *v . 26 .* and demonstrated , in such sort as may conuince the repugnant vnderstanding to yeld assent therto , but are proposed as reuealed by God almightie, as being in him possible, in them selues conuenient, & by his reuealing who is truth it self, made credible.

And the light of glorie is a-boue faith .

2 . So the Royal Prophet testifieth, speaking vnto God in the person of al his faithful seruantes . [Thy testimonies are made credible exceedingly .] *Psal . 92.* Yea al pointes of faith , are so merely and only cre- *v . 5 .* dible, and not demonstrable, that when they become cleare , and euident to sense or natural reason, they are not then properly matter of faith, but of know-ledge . And this is the reason why our B . Sauiour , knowing perfectly from the first instant of his incarnation, al thinges past, present, & to come , had not this vertue of faith, but in place therof, had know-ledge of al diuine misteries, which to vs are pointes of faith . Likewise Angels and other Sainctes, haue not faith, because they now euidently know, by light of glorie , the thinges which they beleued before by light of faith, as S, Paul instructeth vs saying . [When that shal come that is perfect, that shal be *I . Cor . 13.* made voide that is in part . We see now by a glasse *v . 10.12 ,* in a darke sorte, but then face to face. In an other place he also saith , that [we walke by faith, and *2 . Cor . 5.* not by sight .] *v . 7 .*

Al pointes of faith are made credible by Gods propo-sing them.

Christ had not faith but in Place therof konwledge.

Neither An-gels and other Sainctes in heauen, haue faith but knowledge.

3 The reason wherof, the wise man yeldeth say-ing That, (whiles we are in this life) [The bodie *Sap . 9.* that is corrupted, burdeneth the soule , & the earth- *v . 15 .* ly

ly habitation, preſſeth downe the vnderſtanding that thinketh many thinges. And we doe hardly con-iecture the thinges that are in the earth; & the thinges that are in ſight, we finde with laboure : But the thinges that are in the heauens, who ſhal ſearch out? And thy ſenſe (ſaith he turning his ſpeach to God) who ſhal know, vnleſſe thou geue wiſdome, and ſend thy holy Spirit frõ on high? And ſo the pathes of them that are on the eatth, may be corrected, and men learne the thinges that pleaſe thee.] By which ſacred doctrine, we are inſtructed, that in this life, we can neither know diuine myſteries by diſcourſe of reaſon, but only by faith ; neither can we beleeue them, vntil our vnderſtanding be eleuated by Gods grace, aboue natural capacitie. And therfore faith can not be aſcribed to mans natural witte, nor hu-mane reaſon, but to Gods illumination, infuſing the Theological vertue of faith into the ſoule. Neither doth God ordinarily chooſe, the wiſe of this world, but the plaine and ſimple without guile. Cain doubt-les was not inferiour to Abel in humaue witte, but being couetous of temporal riches, kept his better fruites to his owne vſe, offering the worſe to God ; and circumuenting his brother, drew him forth into the fielde, and there ſlew him. And afterwardes [go-ing forth from the face of our Lord] albeit [he dwelt as a fugitiue on the earth] yet he ſo proſpered in the world, that [he built a Citie, and called it by the name of his ſonne Enoch.]- Thoſe of his race are no-ted alſo to be worldly wiſe. [Iabel, was the inuen-tor of Tentes . Iubal, of ſinging (or playing) on harp & Organes. Tubalcain of working in braſſe and I-ron] But [Enos the ſonne of Seth, began to inuo-cate the name of our Lord] in publique and ſolemne maner, aſſembling many together, as is moſt proba-ble. For ſome ſuch viſible diſtiction there was be-twene

ħ.

17.

18.

Gen. 4.
v. 8.

v. 16.

v. 17.

v. 20.
21. 22.

26.

Man can not attaine faith by natural witte.

Faith is the gift of God.

It is rather ge-uen to the ſin-cere of hart, then to the worldlie wiſe,

Exampleſſe therof in the Scriptures.

twene those which were called [The sónes of God,& **Gen . 6.**
others called the sónes, or daughters of men .] Nem- **v . 2.**
rod and his complices, had witte enough, like world- **Gen . 11.**
ly politiques, to deuise and conspire, to build the **v .4.**
Towre of Babel : but Heber, and his familie, beleuing gods promise, that [he would no more destroy al **Gen . 9.**
flesh by waters] was free fró their crime & punish- **v . 11.**
ment . Not the lerned Egiptiás, the sutle Assiriás, the
wise Grecians, the puisát Romás; no not the renowmed Philosophers, Pithagoras, Socrates, Plato, A-
ristotle, : but [Abraham, Isaac, Iacob,] and their **Gen . 12.**
particular progenie, especially the children of the **v .22. 28.**
same Iacob, were illuminated with true faith, & confirmed therin. This is it, wherof S . Paul admonished
the Corinthians, according to the Prophets doctrine :

Testimonies of holy Scriptures.

[For it is writen (saith he) I wil destroy the wis- **1 . Cor . 1.**
dome of the wise, and the prudence of the prudent I **v . 19.**
wil reiect . Where is the wise ? Where is the Scribe ? **Isa . 33.**
Where is the Disputer of this world? Hath not God **v .18.**
made the wisdome of this world foolish ?] For the
same cause he also auoucheth, that his speach & [prea- **1 . Cor . 2.**
ching was not in the persuasible wordes of humane **v .4.**
wisdome, but in shewing of spirit and power .] And
why? [that your faith (saith he) might not be in **v . 5.**
the wisdome of men, but in the power of God.]

Gods grace being the principal meanes of beleeuing : the lawful preaching, and diligent hearing of Gods word, is the secondarie meanes.

4   It is true also, that mans industrie is required.
For [faith is by hearing.] Therfore men must im- **Rom . 10.**
ploy their diligence, lending their eares to heare . **v . 17.**
And for this purpose, God prouided that there were
euer some that did preach his word [diuersly, and di- **Heb . 1.**
uers waies in times past, God speaking to the Fathers **v . 1.**
in the Prophets : last of al in these daies , haith spoken to vs in his Sonne .] And his Sonne, our Lord and
Sauiour, stil speaketh by his Apostles, and other preachers, to whom he said . [As my Father hath sent me ; **Ioan . 20.**
I also doe send you . **v . 21.**

Yet

5 . Yet here we muft adde one other neceffarie do- Faith is groun-
cur ent, that as only Gods grace, doth difpofe the ded in Gods
fouls of men to heare willingly, and illuminateth the word only, not
vnde ftanding to conceiue that which is propofed : in anie mans
fo on Gods word doth affure vs of the truth, in al wordes.
pointe of faith. Becaufe al men (fpeaking of hu - Euerie man
mane ertitude) may in fpiritual thinges be deceiued, may be decei-
or being malicioufly difpofed, may decceiue . But god ued or may de-
who neither can be deceiued, nor can deceiue; doth ceiue, but not
by his word infallibly awarant our faith, more affu- God.
redly then we doe, or can know any thirg, by our
experimental fenfes, or natural reafon, or humane Proued by tef-
reporte. In confideration wherof, S . Paul faith ; timonies of ho-
Rom . 3 . [God is true, and euery man is a liar] Yea in confi- ly Scriptures.
v . 4 . deration of the general infufficiency, of man, our Saniour Chrift, God and man, who is truth it felf, and And by our
can not lie, yet to geue men more fatisfaction, cha- Sauiours pro-
lenged no more credit (as he is man) but as his doc- cedinges.
Ioan . 12 . trine is warranted by God . [For of my felf (faith he)
v . 49 . I haue not fpoken, but my Father that fent me , he
gaue me commandement what I fhould fay, and what
I fhould fpeake .] For God the Father, together with
the Holie Ghoft, gaue him teftimonie fenfibly, in the
fight and hearing of men, when he was baptized by
Mat . 3 . S . Iohn Baptift: where S . Iohn [faw the Spirit of
v . 16. 17 . God defcending as a doue, and comming vpon him .
And behold a voice from heauen faying: This is
my beloued Sonne in whom I am wel pleafed .] A-
gaine in his Transfiguration. [A bright cloude o-
Mat . 17 . ueifhadowed them, and loe a voice out of the cloude
v . 5 . faying, This is my welbeloued Sonne, in whom I
am wel pleafed, heare him .] By which warrant, our
Sauiour conformably, fending his Apoftles, and o-
ther Difciples, faid to them in like cleare wordes,
Luc . 16 . [He that heareth vou , heareth me .] So therfore,
v . 16 . Chrift as man, fpake no other thing, but as God the

E 3 B . Trininite

B. Trinitie gaue him commaundement . And so the
Prophets, Apostles, and al true preachers, [draw   *Is* . 12 .
waters in ioy, out of the Sauiours fountaines . So   *v* . 5.
[the holie men of God , spake inspired by the holie   2. *Pet* . 1 .
Ghost] Yea Balam, (though his intention was per-   *v* . 21.
uerse , desiring to haue pleasured Balac, was forced
to speake true and good thinges of the Israelites,
and for his excuse to Balac, vttered also this truth
that [God is not as man, that he may lie , nor as the   *Nu* . 23 .
sonne of man, that he may be chauged .] Dauid re-   *v* . 19.
citeth Gods speach saying . [The wordes that pro-   *Ps* . 88 .
cede from my mouth, I wil not make frustrate. Once   *v* . 35 .
I haue sworne in my holie, I wil not lie to Dauid .
His seede shal continue for euer .] Our Sauionr saith.
[The wordes that I haue spoken vnto you, be spi-   *Io* . 6. *v* .
rit and life . Heauen and earth shal passe, but my   43.
wordes shal not passe.]   *Mat* . 24 .
6   Whether therfore God speake by his Sonne, by   *v* . 35 .
his Prophets, by his Apostles, or by other men rightly sent, his worde is true, certaine, and infallible, &
so the people of Israel securely [beleued our Lord ,   *Exo* . 14 .
and Moyses his seruant .] So the Thessalonians, and   *v* . 31 .
other good Christians, [receiued the word of the A-   1 . *Thes* . 2 .
postles, not as the word of men, but (as it is indeede)   *v* . 12 .
the word of God.] Al which shew this fundamen-
tal doctrine , that faith is grounded in the word of
God . Now the next point is to know, which is the
word of God.

Gods word is partlie writen in the holie Bible , part-
ly knowne and kept by Tradition .

A R T I C L E   3.

Protestantes
not only denie
many traditiōs :
but also some
partes of the

HEre our Aduersaries dissent from vs : not
only denying Traditions to be the word of
God, but also refusing the Bookes of Tobie,
Iudith

Iudith, Wisdome, Ecclesiasticus, The first and second of Machabies, and partes of Hester, and Daniel. Some also denie the Prophesie of Baruch, with Ieremies Epistle. And Lutheranes resist diuers Epistles of the new Testament ; al which, the Catholique Romane Church holdeth as Canonical Scriptures, no lesse then the others, which both we and they receiue for the vndoubted word of God. For proofe of the Authentical auctoritie of these partes called into controuersie, I remitte you to the Catholique Edition of the English Bible, & to the Auctors there cited.

Bible, which Catholiques hold to be authentical.

2 But the Controuersie of Traditions, may not be omitted in this place, because not only some other pointes of Christian Faith, namely that our vsual Crede, is authentical doctrine, but also the assurance which we haue of the whole sacred bible, dependeth especially vpon Tradition. For except we admitte the testimonie of our Ancesters, & predecessors, who say, that they receiued this booke, of their elders, as the writen word of God, and that it hath bene so deliuered and receiued, from one age, to an other, from the times when the seueral partes therof were writen, we should not haue more certaintie of anie part of the holie Bible, then of the Gospels, which are said to be writen by S. Peter, S. Thomas, S. Bartlemew, and Nicodemus. But by Tradition and iudgment of the Church, we assuredly know, what Bookes are the writen word of God : which otherwise the Scripture it self decideth not. Neither doe we therfore say, that the Church maketh any booke to be the word of God, but that the Church declareth it so to be. And this is noe more inconuenient, then that Christ him self, was declared by S. Iohn Baptist, and by the Apostles, to be our Redemer. For euen as Christ did not depend vpon S. Iohn, nor vpon the Apostles, but they wholly depended

Which is no more inconuenient then that Christ was made knowen by S. Iohn Baptist and the Apostles.

pended

pended vpon him; yet he tooke teſtimonie of them, and they declared him to be the Meſſias ſent of God: ſo the holie Scriprures in them ſelues, depend not vpon the Church, yet are made knowen to vs, to be the written word of God, by the teſtimonie of the Church. And that the Church did ſo teſtifie, we know by Tradition. Yea Proteſtantes alſo, vpon the ſame ſpecial ground, accept of the farre greater part of the holie Bible. And it were verie abſurde, that leauing the common ſpirit of the Church, the priuate ſpirites of particular men ſhould Iudge, which bookes are the word of God, and which are not: for ſo the contention were endles, as appeareth by Luthers reiecting of S. Iames his Epiſtle, and ſome other partes of the new Teſtament; which Caluin coming after him, and generally Engilſh Proteſtantes, acknowledge to be the true word of God. By which, and other like examples, almen may ſee, how neceſſary the auctorite of Eccleſiaſtical Tradition is, for deciſion of this principal point, to know which Bookes are diuine Scriptures.

Io. 1. v. 7. 32. 34
Luc. 24. v. 48.
Act. 1. v 8. 21. 22.

3   It is moreouer to be obſerued, that as the wil & word of God, was a longe time knowen to the faithful people by only preaching and Tradition, without writing: ſo after that God gaue alſo a written Law, Traditions did not ceaſe, but remained ſtil in force, retayning their former auctoritie. For al was not written, as we ſhal here ſhew, by teſtimonie of the written word. Firſt then it is cleare, the ſpace of aboue two thouſand, four hundred yeares, from the creation of this world, and beginning of the Church, there was noe Canonical Scripture at al: til Moyſes writte the fiue firſt Bookes, called Pentatheucon; & as it is verie probable, tranſlated the Booke of Iob, into Hebrew, written not longe before in the Arabike tougue. And in the laſt propheſie of the old

*Traditions did not ceaſe when Gods law begane to be written.
There was no Scripture for the ſpace of 2400. years. And 1000. yeares more, before the laſt part of the old Teſtament was written.*

Teſtiment

Teſtament which is Malachias, (for I wil not geue inſtance of other Bookes called into controuerſie) was written about the yeare of the world, three thou ſand, and fiue hundred : to witte, after the relaxa- tiō of Gods people, from their captiuitie in Babilon. In ſo much, that if the meanes of knowing true Re- ligion, be limited within the precinctes of holy Scrip- tures, it was paſſing longe without this meanes, and yet longer before it was complete.

4 Likewiſe there paſſed ſome yeares, after the be- ginning of the Church of Chriſt, by preaching, and propagation of the Goſpel in diuers nations, before anie part of the new Teſtament was written. For S. Mathew writte the firſt part, about the eight yeare after our Sauiours Aſcenſion : And the laſt part was written by S. Iohn the Euangeliſt, nere three ſcore yeares after the firſt. This manifeſt truth conuinceth you of errour that ſay : Al doubtes in Religion, muſt be immediatly tried, and finally decided, by onely Scriptures. For needes you muſt firſt confeſſe, that before the holy Scriptures were written, there was ſome other ſufficiét meanes of trial, & deciſiō of doubt- ful caſes. Secondly, you muſt tel vs, when that for- mer meanes ſeaſed, and this other of only Scriptures came in place. Whether ſo ſone as anie holie Scrip- tures were extant, or not vntil ſome great part, half, or more, or al, were deliuered to the Church. If you ſay that before al was written, the reſt ſuffiſed for this purpoſe : then that which was written after, was needles : ſo the later Prophets in the old Teſtament, and S. Iohns Goſpel, with the Apocalipſe, are ſuper- fluous, or not neceſſary. If you ſay, that holie Scrip- tures alone, did not ſuffice til al were written, then you muſt graunt, that al the time, betwene the firſt, and laſt writing of holie Scriptures, (which was a- boue a thouſand yeares in the old Teſtament, and a-

Neither was the new Teſta- ment written preſently after Chriſtes Aſ- cention.

Before there were Scrip- tures, doubtes were decided by the Church.

F   bout

bout threescore yeares in the new Testament) some
other meanes was also necessarie together, with so
much of them as was then written, to declare & determine questions rising in the Church of God.

Some Scrip-
tures are now
wanting which
were sometime
extant.

5   But after that al were written & published which
now we haue, you wil say: They are the only trial
of Christian truthes, and are sufficient without help
of Traditions, or of interpretations, either of ancient Fathers, or the Church present. But that you
may also see your weaknes in this euasion, we demand
of you, what supplie you haue of such Scriptures as
were once written, and are longe since perished.
For there were some other partes of holie Scripture,
which are not now in our Bible, as appeareth in the
third Booke of Kinges, where it is written, that [Sa-
lomon spake three thousand Parables, and his songes
were a thousãd & fiue. And he disputed of trees, frõ
the Cedar that is in Libanus, vnto the Hissope which
cometh out of the wal : And he discoursed of beastes,
and foules, and creeping wormes, and fishes.] And
by S. Paules Epistle to the Colossians, where he signifieth, that he [writte an Epistle to the Laodicians]
which is not now extant.

3. *Reg.* 4.
v. 32.

Coloss. 4.
v. 16.

6   More particularly we require you to proue this
assertion of youres by expresse holie Scripture, That
al necessarie pointes of Christian Faith and Religion,
may be immediatly proued by onlie Scriptures. And
that none other auctoritie is to be admitted. Let vs
see therfore by what holie Scriptures, you mantaine

The Scriptures
which Protes-
tantes alleage
for their opini-
on doe not
proue it.

The first place.

this your position. I wil recite some textes for you,
the verie fittest you haue, as I dare boldly presume.
I know you vse for this purpose, to alledg the word
of God written by Moyses in the fourth Chapter of
Deuterenomie saying [you shal not adde to the word
that I speake to you, neither shal you take away from
it : kepe the commaundement of the Lord your God
which

Deut. 4.
v. 2.

which I commaund you.] The moſt plaine and literal ſenſe of this precept is, that we muſt not by addition, nor by ſubtraction, alter or change Gods
word or commaundement, neither muſt we cal that
Gods word or commaundement, which is not his
word nor commaundement. But deduction of one
truth from an other, is not here, nor elſwhere forbid.
And whatſoeuer is deduced of the holie Scripture by
the Church inſpired and aſſiſted by the holie Ghoſt, is
Gods word, in that it is the word of the holie Ghoſt.

7   An other like place is, in the twelft Chapter of *The ſecond*
Ch. 12.   the ſame booke [what I commaund thee, that only *place.*
v. 32.   doe to our Lord : neither adde anie thing, nor diminiſh .] This is an admonition concerning Hóſtes to
be offered in Sacrifices : commaunding, that al thoſe
thinges ſhould be offered, which are preſcribed by
the Law, & prohibiting other kindes of thinges.
Neither was the ordinance of King Dauid, contrarie
to theſe precepts, that [there was equal portió of him
that went down, into battle & of him that abode at
1. *Reg.*   the baggage : for this was done from that day, & euer
30. *v.*   after, it was decreed and ordeined as a Law in Iſra-
24. 25.   el.] Neither was the inſtitution of a new Feaſt, in
Ioan. 10.   the Dedication of an Altar, contrarie to Gods Law,
v. 22.   but was verie agreable therto, which Feaſt chriſt ho-
23.   noured and kept, as is cleare in the Goſpel, wheras
Mat. 15.   otherwiſe our Sauiour ſharply reprehended and con-
v. 3. 4.   demned the friuolous Traditions obſerued by the
9.   Iewes, & pretéded by them as Traditions of the Ancientes : and he likewiſe condemned the commandementes of men, which were contrarie to Gods com-
maundementes.

Ioan. 5.   8   Alſo our Sauiour willed the Iewes, to [ſearch *The third*
v. 59.   the Scriptures (that is, not only to reade ſuperficial- *placce.*
ly, but aſo to ſearch the ſenſe depely.) for (ſaith he)
you thinkin them to haue life euerlaſting, and the

F   2   ſame

fame are they that geue teſtimonie of me] but he
doth not ſay, the ſame only, for beſides the Scriptures, he alledged alſo the teſtimonie of S. Iohn Baptiſt, likewiſe his owne workes, and the voice of his
Father, none of al which was as yet written. And
afterwardes he ſent his Apoſtles to be [witneſſes of
him in Ieruſalem, and in al Iewrie, and Samaria, &
euen to the vtmoſt of the earth.

v. 33. 36. 37.

Luc. 24. *v. 48.*

Act. 1.

The fourth place.

9   S. Paul alſo willeth his ſcholer S. Timothie,
to learne true doctrine in the holie Scriptures [becauſe (ſaith he) from thine infancy, thou haſt knowen the holie Scriptures, which can inſtruct thee to
ſaluation, by the faith, that is in Chriſt Ieſus.]
Then further ſhewing the vtilitie, and vſe therof, he
ſaith [All (or euery) Scripture, inſpired of God, is
profitable to teach, to argue, to correct, to inſtruct
in iuſtice, that the man of God may be perfect, inſtructed to euery good worke.] In al which paſſage,
it is cleare, that holie Scriptures are propoſed, not
as the onely, but as one ſpecial meanes, to learne
Faith, and other vertues, wherby to be perfect & inſtructed to euery good worke. But in no wiſe doth
the Apoſtle detract from his other inſtructions, which
he gaue immediatly before ſaying, [continue thou
in thoſe thinges which thou haſt learned, & are committed to thee, knowing of whom thou haſt learned.

v. 8. 2. *Tim.* 3. *v.* 15.

v. 16. 17.

v. 14.

The fift place,

10   Finally S. Iohn in the end of the Apocalypſe,
geueth this threatning charge, [I teſtifie to euery
one, hearing the wordes of the Propheſie of this
booke; If anie man ſhal adde to theſe thinges, God
ſhal adde vpon him the plagues writen in this booke.
And if anie man ſhal diminiſh of the wordes of the
Booke of this Propheſie: God ſhal take away his part
out of the Booke of life, and out of the holie Citie,
and of theſe thinges that be written in this Booke.]

Apoc. 22. *v.* 18. 19.

F   2   which

Which curse falleth vpon thofe, whofoeuer by ad-
d. g, or diminifhing, corrupteth this prophefie. And
no doubt, the fame plague and punifhment pertaineth
alfc to whofoeuer corrupteth anie part of holy Scripture : but maketh nothing at al againft true expofiti-
ons, nor againft Traditions, agreable to holie Scriptures nor againft writing more holie Scriptures after this Booke. For the fame S. Iohn him felf, writte
his Gofpel, after this Prophefie of the Apocalypfe :
& concludeth the fame Gofpel thus. [But there are
manie other thinges alfo that Iefus did, which if they
were written, in particular, neither the world it felf
I thinke, were able to containe thofe Bookes, that
fhould be written.] Thus much concerning thofe
holie Srriptures, which Proteftantes commonly produce againft the authoritie, & vfe of Traditions.

11 Now let vs further fee fome examples, and other
teftimonies of the written word of God for Traditions, which the Church calleth the vnwritten word.
Gen. 1. It is cleare in the beginning of Genefis, that God hauing created the world, according to Moyfes his re-
Ch. 2. lation, in fix daies, [he refted the feauenth day, from
v. 2. 3. al worke that he had done, and he bleffed the feuenth
day and fanctified it.] Wherupon Gods people obferued the feuenth day, refting from feruile worke,
wherof it was called the Sabbath, which in Englifh,
fignifieth Reft; and the fame continued by Tradition, for there were as yet no Scriptures (as is alreadie noted, til the written Law was geuen. And in
the written Law it was continued and confirmed by
Exo. 20. fpecial forme of wordes, as a thing wel knowen, &
v. 8. 9. fo is confirmed by thefe termes to the people. [Re-
10. 11. member that thou fanctifie the Sabbath day. (In Deu-
Deut. 5. tronomie) Obferue the day of the Sabbath.] Alfo
v. 12. the maner of keping it holy, is largely defcribed, &
13. 14. the reafon of it alleaged, from the firft inftitution.
15. F 3 And

The neceffitie
of Traditions
proued by ex-
preffe Scrip-
tures. And firft
by examples.

The Sabbath
day inftituted.

And scarce anie other Precept, is so oft inculcated in
al the old Testament, as this of keping the Sabbath,
that is, the seuenth day of the weeke, holie, and
vacant from worke. Neuerthelesse this seuenth and
Sabbath day, is now a worke day, as the other fiue
daies of the weeke ordinarilie are. And both the
old Traditions of Patriarkes, and the old precept of
Moyses Law, are abrogated, without any expresse
holie Scripture, for the omission therof. Yet are al
Christians wel warranted herein, by Apostolical Tradition, to worke on Saturday, which is the Sabbath
day.

Sunday called our Lords day, kept holie day, by Ayostolical Tradition.

12   And by the very same Tradition, the Sunday,
called the Dominical and our Lordes day, is made holie Day. Because on this day (called by al the Euangelistes, the First of the Sabbath) our Lord rose frō
death. And it began first to be kept holie day in the
Apostles time. For S. Paul calleth it, [the first of the
Sabbath] in which Christians assembled together.
And so doth S. Luke cal it [the first of the Sabbath]
when they were assembled to breake bread (that is to
minister the blessed Sacrament.) And shortly after,
being alreadie a holy day, it was called, our Lordes
day. But the Iewes kepe the seuenth and Sabbath
day stil, as is to be seene at Rome, Venice, Amsterdam, Frankford, and wheresoeuer they dwel. And
Protestantes receiue & obserue in their maner, both
these Tradations, aswel in working on Saturday,
which is the Sabbath and seuenth day, as in abstay-
ning from worke on Sunday, which is not the last
but the first day of the weeke, now called our Lordes
day. And that there was a day so called, before al the
Apostles were parted from this world, appeareth by
S. Iohn, making mention therof in the beginning of
the Apocalypse, but no expresse mention is there, nor
elswhere in al the holie Scriptures, that Saturday is
now

*Mat. 28.
v. 1. Mar.
16. v. 2.
Luc. 24.
v. 1.
Ioan. 20.
v. 1.
1. Cor. 16.
v. 2. Act.
20. v. 7.*

*Apoc. 1.
v. 10.*

now a day of worke, nor that Sunday was made the holy day, both which we know and obserue by Apostolical Tradition.

13 A third example we haue, in the obseruation ofthinges reputed [Cleane, and vncleane .] God commanded Noe to receiue into the Arke [of al beaftes that are cleane, feuen and feuen, male and female, but of the beaftes that are vncleane, two and two, male and female] either by Traditió, as it might be reuealed to his Ancefters, or els by particular inftructions, Noe knew this difference of cleane & vncleane beaftes, and from Noe to Moyfes, the fame was knowen by Tradition. Afterwardes by the writen Law, it was largely expreffed ; Efpecially in the Booke of Leuiticus, with many other Ceremonial Precepts, which were of vigour and force til our Lordes Paffion and death. And fome of them were continued after his Afcenfion and coming ofrhe Holie Ghoft, the fpace offome yeares, and that by expreffe Decree of the Apoftles gathered in a folemne Councel : where they definitiuely determined, that Chriftians fhould kepe a certaine Ceremonial precept of the old Law, in thefe wordes. [It hath femed good to the Holie Ghoft, & to vs, to lay no further burden vpon you, then thefe neceffarie thinges, that you abftaine from thinges immolated to Idoles, and bloud, and that which is ftrangled, and fornication.] This prohibition of eating bloud and ftrangled meates, (as puddinges, and rapets,) which were alfo forbid long before the written Law, in the daies of Noe, and renewed by the Apoftles, as neceffarie vnder the fame tenure of wordes, with Idolatrie and fornication (which two, alwaies were, and are, greuous finnes,) is fince fo euacuated, that now thefe meates are lawfullie eaten in due times, as other thinges are : And that by cuftome and Tradition of the
Church

Gen. 7. v. 2. 3.

Leuit. 11. v. 2. &c.

Act. 15. v. 28.

v. 29.

Gen. 9, v. 4.

What thinges were reputed cleane and vncleane, was knowne by tradition.

Aftinence fró eating bloud of beaftes fome-time commanded, is now abrogated by Tradition.

Church, els we fhould be bound to abftaine from them ftil.

14   A fourth example is, concerning the time, when the Sacrament of Circumcifion, ceafed to be lawful : which was firft inftituted in the time of Abrahã, continued, & confirmed by the written Law : [Not that it is of Moyfes (faith our Sauiour) but of the Fathers] whereof S. Stephen making mention, in his Apologetical Sermon, calleth it [the Teftament of Circumcifion, which God gaue to Abraham.] For although Chriftians, whether they were borne Iewes, or Gentiles, were not bound to obferue it, as we fee by the Apoftolical Decree euen now recited; yet it remained lawful if any would vfe it. And fo S. Paul knowing, and mantaining it, not to be neceffarie, nor in fome perfons cafes and conneuient, auoucheth that [Titus, wheras he was a Gentile, was not compelled to be Circumcifed,] neuertheleffe [he Circumcifed Timothee becaufe of the Iewes that were in thofe places; for they al knew, that his father was a Gentile ;] and returning after this to Ierufalem, where it was reported that [he taught thofe Iewes, that were among the Gentiles, to depart from Moyfes, faying, that they ought not to circumcife their children, nor walke according to the cnftome .] To purge him feif of this fufpition, and [that al fhould know, that the thinges which they heard of him were falfe, & that him felf alfo walked keping the Law: he taking certaine men vnto him that had a *Uow*, was purified with them (according to the LAW of the Nazarites) and entred into the Temple ; fhewing the accomplifhment of the daies of the Purification, vntil an Oblation was offered (particular Sacrifice of Holocauft, and finne, and a pacifique Hoft) for euerie one of them.] Thus did S. Paul teach, both by practife and word, that circumcifion, and
other

Gen. 17.
v. 10.
Leuit. 12
v. 3.
Ioan. 7.
v. 22.
Mat. 7.
v. 8.

Gal. 2.
v. 11.
Act. 16.
v. 3.

Act. 21.
v. 21.

v. 22. 26.

Num. 6.
v. 13.
v. 14.

Circumcifion firft obferued, and afterward omitted by Tradition.

The vow of Nazaretus, made and accomplifhed by S. Paul, is now changed.

other pointes of the old Law, were neither hurtful if they were obferued, nor of them felues neceffarie to be obferued. [As God hath called euerie one *1. Cor.* (faith he) fo let him walke, and as in al Churches *7. v. 18.* I teach. Is anie man called being circumcifed? Let him not procure prepuce. Is anie man called in prepuce? let him not be circumcifed] But when, and by what auctoritie this indifferency ceafed, and that circumcifion, and other obferuances of the old Law became to be vtterly vnlawful and damnable, as now they are, and haue bene many hundred yeares, is not expreffed in anie part of holy Scriptures. Al that we know herein, is by only Tradition, practife and iudgment of the Church. Many other examples occurre in the Law of Moyfes, as the precept of mariages *Nu. 36.* within the fame Tribes, written in the Booke of Nu- *v. 7.* meri. Yet Leuites maried with the Tribe of Iuda, as *Luc. 1.* appeareth in S. Lukes Gofpel. The Ceremonies *v. 36.* recited by S. Paul in the ninth Chapter of his Epi- *Heb. 9.* ftle to the Hebrewes, are not al expreffed by Moyfes *v. 19.* in the written Law. *20. 21.* *22.*

15   There be alfo diuers other examples in Chrifti-an doctrine, yea euen in thofe thinges, which our aduerfaries acknowledg to be matters of faith, and important pointes of Religion, which are not expreffed in the holie Scripture. Baptifme, and the Eucharift, are nowhere called Sacramentes, in al the holie Bible. Neither the Rites or maner of adminiftrating them. In what maner thofe three thoufand were *Act. 2.* baptized, whom S. Peter conuerted in his firft fer- *v. 41.* mon, is not fet downe. It is particularly related, that Philip the Deacon, and the Eunuch, (a certain Queenes thre furer;) went out of the Chariot, into *Act. 8.* the water, and there Philip baptized the Eunuch. *v. 38.* Chrift our Lord commanded his Apoftles to baptize, but the Rites how it is to be done, are no where ex-

G   preffed

The Iewes being bound by their Law, not to mixe their Tribes by mariage, yet the Tribe of Leui was exempted by Tradition.

They obferued fome Ceremonies not writé.

Other examples in the new Teftament. Baptifme & Eucarift Sacramentes.

Rites in adminiftration of them.

preſſed in holie Scripture. Our Lord inſtituted the *Mat . 26.*
B. Sacrament of his Bodie and Bloud, and admini- *Mar . 14.*
ſtred the ſame late in the euening after ſupper, wher- *Luc . 22.*
in he and his Apoſtles had eaten the Paſchal Lambe ; *1 . Cor .11.*
And bade his Apoſtles [Doe this &c .] The Chri- *v . 20. 21.*
ſtians at Corinth, coming together to eat our Lordes
Supper, [euerie one tooke his owne ſupper before]
which was then lawful, ſo they had done it at home
in their houſes, but the Apoſtle reprehended the richer ſorte, for eating in the Church, with confuſion
of the poore; concluding his admonition, that [when
he ſhould come] to Corinth, [he would diſpoſe]
ſome thinges, which he did not then write .

Other ſacred actions ac-knowledged by Proteſtantes. Confirmation, Confeſſion, Ordination, Mariage, with their ſet forme.

16   Moreouer Engliſh Proteſtantes , acknowlege
Confirmation after Baptiſme, Confeſſion of ſinnes
in general, when people aſſemble together to common praier; And in particular, for the ſicke . Alſo
the ordeyning of men to eſpecial ſpiritual functions,
& the publique celebrating of mariages, with the ſet
formes of adminiſtrating al the ſame, to be holie religious actiós, not wholly expreſſed in the writé word
of God, but partly gathered of the wordes of holie
Scriptures, and the reſt they pretend to be agreable
therto . By which maner of proofe, ſo approued by
them, we prooue the ſame foure ſacred actions , being rightly adminiſtred : and alſo Extreme Vnction,
(wherof they haue no reſemblance at al) to be indeede perfect Sacraments, ſome of them greater then
Baptiſme ; and al as properly, and certainly Sacramentes, as it is . Wheras alſo Proteſtantes haue a
formal ſeruice for burials, and kepe certaine Feaſtes
not only of our Lord, but alſo of S . Michael, & of
Chriſts Apoſtles, with ſome faſtes; & read in their
publique ſeruice, the Crede of S . Athanaſius, &
Canticle of S . Ambroſe & S . Auguſtine : we do by
as good warrant of holie Scriptures, prooue praier
for

A ſet forme of Funerals, Feaſtes, Faſtes, Canticles, Quicunque vult, Te Deum.

for foules departed : Praier to our B. Ladie, and o-
ther Sainctes : Al Faftes and abftinence decreed by
the Church : The reading of Sainctes liues, & other
writinges of holie Fathers, and Praiers of Angels,
and other Sainctes in glorie, to be verie profitable
and neceflarie for fupplie of our weaknes, daylie infirmities, and defectes.

15 Now becaufe we vndertake, by holie Scriptures
to proue al Chriftian Doctrine, more clearly, and
certainly, then our aduerfaries can proue their owne
doctrine & practife, which indeede neither they, nor
we can doe in fome pointes immediatly, but muft recurre vnto approued Traditions : As wel for their
helpe herein, as our owne, (for we al profeffe to relie principally vpon holie Scripture) it remaineth,
for complement of this Article, that we fet before
your eyes, certaine cleare places, which exprefjie remitte vs for further inftruction, to the teftimonies, *Holie Scrip-*
cuftomes, and Traditions, of former times, & of our *tures doe ex-*
Predeceffors, who teftifie the iugemēt of the Church *prefjy remitte*
in their times. The Royal Prophet, reciting fome *vs to Traditi-*
times in his Pfalmes, Gods workes written in for- *ons.*
mer Hiftories, addeth alfo fome thinges, which he *For knowlege*
knew by Tradition. So he fignifieth in his Preface of *of the facred*
an Hiftorical Pfalme faying. [How great thinges *Hiftorie.*
Pf. 77. haue we heard, and haue knowne them, and our Fa-
v.3.4. thers haue tould vs; they were not hidde from their
5.6. children, in an other generation; telling the praifes
v.47. of our Lord, and his powers, and his meruelous workes which he hath done.] And fo him felf telleth
there fome thinges, which were not written before :
But ftil exhorting the people, afwel to heare, as to
reade, [how great thinges our Lord commanded our
Fathers, to make the fame knowen to their children,
that an other generation may know : the children
that fhal be borne, fhal rife vp, and fhal tel their children

dren.

For precepts of maners.

18 Concerning Precepts of good life, King Salomon admonisheth thus [Transgresse not the anci- *Prou.* 2. ent bondes which thy Fathers haue put.] Yea, *v.* 28. [Thus saith our Lord, stand ye vpon the waies, & see, *Iere* 6. and aske of the old pathes which is the good way, *v.* 16. and walke ye in it, and you shal finde refreshing for your soules.

Diuers Diuine Mysteries re-uealed to the Apostles.

19 Our Sauiour aduertiseth his Disciples. that he omitted to teach them manie thinges necessarie to be knowne, which they should learne of the Holie Ghost. [Yet manie thinges (saith he) I haue to say *Ioan.* 16: to you, but you cannot beare them now : But when *v.* 12. 13. the Spirit of truth cometh, he shal teach you al truth] *Ch.* 21.

Which are not al written.

S. Paul, as wel in his preaching, as writing, often *v.* 25. inculcated, the point of Apostolical Precepts and Decrees [He walked through Syria, and Cilicia, con- *Act.* 15. firming the Churches : commanding them to kepe *v.* 41. *Ch.* the Precepts of the Apostles and the Ancients.] 16.*v.* 4. Also of Precepts not written, commending the Romanes, [Thankes be to God (saith he) that wheras *Rom.* 6. you were the seruants of sinne, but haue obeyed from *v.* 17. the hart vnto that forme of Doctrine, into the which you haue bene deliuered.] which was a particular instruction in Religion, agreed vpon and obserued by the Apostles in catechizing the people, called the

The Rule of Faith, a cer-taine forme of Christian doc-trine.

[Rule of Faith] where he further admonished them, *Rom.* 12. hauing diuers giftes of Grace, to kepe vnitie, name- *v.* 6. ly those that had the gift of Prophecie, that is of interpreting, to vse it [according to the Rule of faith] And to the verie same he remitted the Philippians, *Philip.* 3. exhorting them [to continue in the same Rule, wher *v.* 16. 17. unto they were come.] And lest they might be seduced by false Prophets, he once more vrged them, [Be folowers of me Brethren, and obserue them that walke so, as you haue our forme,] as wel in life, as in doctrine

doctrine. The Corinthians, as his owne proper spi-
rituial children, he besought to be folowers of him
sel g, [and therfore (faith he) haue I sent to you Timothee, who is my dearest Sonne, and faithful in our
Lord ; who wil put you in mind of my waies, that are
in Christ Iesus, as euerie where in euery Church I
teach] Againe praying them [Be ye followers of
me, as also of Christ,] praysing them, for that in al
thinges , they were mindful of him, and as he had deliuered vnto them, they kept his Preceptes :] decideth the controuersie by many reasons . Finally by
this [But if anie man seme to be contentious, we
haue noe such custome, nor the Churches of God .]
And after his reprehension of abuses ; some thinges
he ordeyneth , & for some thinges, he remitteth them
to that which he would ordaine saying, [For the
rest, I wil dispose when I come .] To the Galatians
he declareth, that [he had bene more abundantly an
emulator of the Traditions of his Fathers,] not of
friuolous or wicked Traditions, which our Sauiour
condemned in the Scribes and Pharises, when they
calumniated his Disciples : for S. Paul neuer folowed such Traditions, as were contrary to Gods commandement,] but of the Traditions (faith he) of
my Fathers] agreable to that he said [according to
the most sure sect of our Religion, which they cal heresie, I liued a Pharisee.] Such religious Traditions of the old Testament, S. Paul obserued in Iudaisme. And being conuerted to Christ, and made
an Apostle, though he learned the Gospel immediatly of Christ him selfe, and not of the other Apostles yet he conferred with them [lest perhaps, he
should runne, or had runne in vaine ,] and kept and
taught the same forme and rule of faith as they did ,
both he an ! they teaching much more, & often more
effectually by wordes present, then by writing ab-

Marginal references (left):
1.Cor.4. v.17.
1.Cor. 11. v. 1.2.
v.16.
v.34. Gal. 1. v.14.
Act. 24. v.14. Ch. 26. v.5.
Gal. 2. v.2.

Marginal notes (right):
Custome of Churches is a special rule.

S. Paul found it necessarie for him self to conferre with other Apostles by word of mouth.

sent

fent. And therfore thanking God, and reioycing for the converfion of the Theffalonians, he writ th thus vnto them. [For what thankfgeuing can we render vnto God for you in al ioy wherwith w re-ioyce for you before our God? night and day more abundantly praying, that we may fee your fac, and may accomplifh thofe thinges that wante i your faith.] In the meane time defired and befougut them [as they had receiued, how to walke, and did walke, fo to abund more. For you know what precepts I haue geuen to you by our Lord Iefus.] Yet more expreffly he exacteth, the obferuation of fuch Tradi-tions, as he had deliuered them, writing againe to the fame people thus: [Therfore brethren, ftand, and hold the Traditions which you haue learned, whether it be by word, or by our Epiftle.] And in reguard that fome falfe brethren, walking inordinat-ly, endeuored to feduce others [We denounce vnto you brethren (faith he) in the name of our Lord Ie-fus Chrift, that you withdraw your felues, from eue-rie brother walking inordinatly, and not accouding to the Tradition which they haue receiued of vs.] The felf fame in other termes, no leffe fignificant the Tradition, he commendeth to S. Timothie faying, O Timothie, kepe the *Depofitum*, auoyding the pro-phane noueltics of voyces, and oppofitions of falfly ealled knowlege. Haue the forme of found wordes, which thou haft heard of me, in faith, and in the loue in Chrift Iefus. Kepe the good *Depofitum*, by the Holie Ghoft which dwelleth in vs. So al Prophets, al Apoftles, innumerable [holie men of God, fpake infpired with the Holie Ghoft.] Marie of them al-fo write, infpired with the fame Holie Ghoft. Some did both. And S. Iohn was fome time comanded by the Holie Ghoft faying: [That which thou feeft, write in a Booke.] And an other time, [Signe the thinges

Margin notes

Preceptes writ-ten, and not written, were to be obferued.

Tradition is called Depofi-tum.

And, good de-pofitum.

Gods word is partly written, partly not writ-ten.

Margin references

1. Thef. 3. *v.* 9. 10.

Ch. 4. *v.* 1. 2.

2. Thef. 2. *v.* 15.

Ch. 3. *v.* 6.

1. Tim. 6. *v.* 20.

2. Tim. 1. *v.* 13. 14.

2. Pet. 1. *v.* 21.

Apoc. 1. *v.* 11.

thinges which the feuen Thunders haue fpoken , &
write them not.

Some holie Scriptures are hard: and require au-
thentical Interpretation.

ARTICLE. 4.

TO fearch the particular caufes, why God
would haue fome holie Scriptures to be more
obfcure, we do not prefume, but leaue the
fame with manie other hidden Myfteries to his diuine wifdome, contenting our felues with that general reafon, which we finde more clearely reuealed.
Mat. 11.
v. 25.
26.
Our B. Sauiour rendered thankes to his heauenly
Father, for that [he hath hid fome thinges from the
wi'e and prudent, and hath reuealed them to litle
ones: yea Father (faith he) for fo hath it wel pleafed thee]: Hereby inftructing vs to feeke no further
why this is done, but to know in general, that higheft pointes of faith & religion, are hid from proud
fpirits which thinke the felues to be moft wife & prudent, and are made knowen (fo mnch as is requifite)
to the humble which acknowledge their owne in-
Mat. 18.
v. 3.
fufficiencie, & fo become fuch [litle ones] as our Sauiour requireth, though otherwif they be learned.
For fo the holie, ancient, and moft learned Fathers,
and Doctors of the Church, found many places of
holie Scriptures ouer hard for them to interprete.
And that nothing is more certaine, then that the
right, and affured true fenfe of fome places is vncertaine, til the Church which hath the fpirit of truth
declareth it.

2   Their hardnes is proued two waies: by experience, if anie wil diligently confider the letter as it
is written, and by teftimonie of holie Scripture it felf.
Gen. 1.
v. 2.
For example. The verie firft wordes of Genefis: [In
the beginning God created heauen and earth] conteine

Though we
know not the
particular
caufe, yet we
fee fome Scrip-
tures are hard.

Not only fer-
ning, but alfo
humilitie of
fpirite, is re-
quired to vn-
derftand high
Myfteries, and
the true fenfe
of holy Scrip-
tures.

Experience
teacheth that
fome Scrip-
tures are hard.

Examples, of
the general

teine a doctrine veric necessarie for vs to know ; that
heauen and earth, had a beginning when they were
created of nothing, before which time, there was no
creature at al, there was no time at al, a thing aboue
mans natural capacitie to conceiue : Aristotle could
not conceiue it, and so erred, teaching that the world
is eternal, aswel in respect ofthat is past, as of that
which is to come . And this consisteth in the depth of
the Mysterie, reuealed by God, recorded by Moyses,
and beleued by faith . Here is also an higher Mysterie
insinuated, of the B . Trinitie, three diuine persons .
The word, *Created*, appropriated to God the Father:
Beginning, to God the Sonne : and the *Spirit of God*,
to the Holie Ghost, al one God . An other difficultie
followeth by and by in the letter, how we shal vnderstand, in what subiect or substance, was the *Light*,
which was created the first day, vntil the fourth day,
in which the *Sunne, and Moone, and al the Starres*,
were created ? If we say with some interpreters, that
the accident remained without subiect, the thing is
hard, yet may be true in this thing, and in some other
Mysterie, is most true, by the omnipotency of God.
If we say with other Expositors, that the Sunne, with
the other Planets and Starres, and consequently al the
first kindes of creatures, were created in one moment,
or instant, then the text is hard to be vnderstoode,
which relateth the creation of distinct thinges, as in
six distinct daies . It is likewise a great question,
how there be [waters aboue the firmament .] But
let vs passe ouer the rest of this first Chapter, wherin are diuers other difficulties . It is also hard to resolue, where the terrestrial *Paradise* is . It wil be hard
for a Protestant to shew by expresse Scripture, that
the Serpent that tempted and seduced Eue, was the
diuel For in al that passage, the diuel is not expresly
named . The diuel hath no corporal members, no
brest

The B. Trini-
tie insinuated.

How there was
light before
the fourth day.

Other dificul-
ties in the text.

Iob. 38.
v. 4. 5.

Heb. 11.
v. 3.

Ch. 1. *v*. 3.
v. 14.

v. 7.

Gen. 2.
v. 8.
Gen. 3. *v*.
1. 4. 13.
14. 15.

breſt to goe vpon, no ſenſible head to be bruiſed, neither doth the diuel eate earth, accoding as the letter ſoundeth. The firſt place of the whole Bible, that explaneth this Hiſtorie of the diuel, is in the Booke of wiſdome, which Proteſtantes denie to be Canonical Scripture : where it is ſaid [God creaƚed man incorruptible, and to the Image of his owne likenes he made him, but by the enuie of the diuil, death entred into the world.] Before this Booke of wiſdom was written, this moſt certaine truth was knowne, only by Tradition, that by the Serpent, is vnderſtoode the diuel, and ſeing there is nothing in holy Scripture but that is of importance : we wil not omitte an other difficultie in the next Chapter, what ſtripling yong man was he whom Lamech ſlew, together with old Cain.

3 But to our Aduerſaries, thoſe eſpcially may ſeme hard places, by which we proue thinges that they deny : As that Enoch and Elias are yet liuing in their bodies, which we proue by Moyſes ſaying that [Enoch walked with God, and was ſene nomore, becauſe God tooke him] affirming of the other neene firſt Patriarches, that they dyed. S. Paul ſaith, [Enoch was tranſlated that he ſhould not ſee death : And he was not found, becauſe God tranſlated him.] Other Scriptures ſay the like of Elias, that [he aſcended by a whirlewinde in a fyrie Chariot, into heauen.] And [Behold I wil, ſend you Elias the Prophet, before the day of our Lord come, great and dredful.] Of this ſort, there be innumerable places, which would leade vs into long digreſſions, and therfore I returne to my preſent purpoſe.

4 It is not eaſie to explicate that, which was ſaid to Noe [Man his daies, ſhal be an hundred & twentie yeares.] There be diuers difficulties alſo concerning [the Giantes which were vpon the earth in thoſe

H

Marginal notes (left):
Sap. 2.
v. 23.
24.
An. mū-
di. 3800.

Gen. 4.
v. 23.

Gen. 5.
v. 24.

Heb. 11.
v. 5.

4. Reg.
2. v. 11.
Mal. 4.
v. 5.

Gen. 6.
v. 3.
v. 4. 15.

Marginal notes (right):
Al thoſe places, may wel ſeeme hard to Proteſtantes, which ſeeme to affirme that which they deny.

Other difficulties of matters, not now in controuerſie.

those daies .] And concerning the Arke , and the bignes therof . In the Genealogie of the Patriarches, after the floud . For Moyſes ſaith., [Arpharad be- *Gen . I F*gate Sale .] And S . Luke ſaith : Sale was the Sonne *v . 12.* of Cainan , and [Cainan was of Arphaxad.] The *Luc . 3.* names of Eſaus wiues, are different in the 26 . Chap- *v . 36.* ter of Geneſis : and in the 28 . and 36. only we are *Gen .26.* certaine , that al is true, but how it is true, we are *v . 34. Ch.* not certaine . Iacobs Propheſie, in moſt partes of it, 28 . *v . 9.* is hard to be vnderſtoode . It is certaine alſo that *Ch . 36. v.* [the hart of Pharao, was indurate] but it is hard 2 . 3 . to explicate the textes where our Lord ſaid , [I *Gen .49.* wil indurate his hart .] For it is a blaſphemous here- *Exod. 4. v.* ſie to ſay, that God is the auctor of ſinne, or ma- 21 . *Ch. 7.* keth man to ſinne . Yet it is cleare, that obduration *v . 3. 13.* of hart, is a verie great ſinne . Likewiſe how the Ta- 22 . *Ch. 8.* bernacle, & thinges pertayning therto, reſēbled the *v . 19. 32.* Church of Chriſt wherof they were figures : How the *Item . Ch .* external Sacrifices , with other Ceremonies of the old 8. *v . 15.* law, (beſides other ſpiritual profites) did ſignify & 32 . *Ch. 9.* reſemble greater Myſteries in the Law of Grace, as *v. 7. 35.* the Apoſtle teſtifieth that they did ; is not eaſie to be *Ch. 13. v.* declared in particular . The numbers of perſons, and 15. *Ex. 25.* manſions, deſcribed in the Booke of Numeri, are, be- *v . 8. 9.* ſides the difficulties, in the literal ſenſe, verie miſti- 10 . *&c.* cal and profound . The Propheſies alſo concerning *Leuit . 1. v.* Chriſt, are verie hidden to the iudgment of men, e- 2 . 2 . *&c.* ſpecially in the Bookes of Moyſes, and yet our Saui- *1 · Cor . 10.* our ſaith expreſly, that [Moyſes had written of him] *Coloſ . 1. v.* And [interpreted from Moyſes and al the prophets, 17 . *Heb. 8.* the thinges concerning him ſelf] . Otherwiſe who *v . 5. Ch.* would haue thought, there had bene ſo much in the 10 . *v . 8.* Bookes of Moyſes, of Chriſt, as there is ? Yea who *Num . 1.* would not haue thought, that the promiſe of which *Ch . 2. Ch.* Moyſes ſpeaketh, ſaving to the people, when they 3 . *v. 39.* deſired a Succeſſor after him [A Prophet of thy Na- *Ioan . 5. v.* tion 46 . *Luc.*

24. v.
27. 44.
Deut .18.
v. 15.

Nation, and of thy brethren, like vnto me, wil our Lord thy God raiſe vp to thee, him thou ſhalt heare] had bene ment, only of Ioſue, or at furtheſt, of Io- ſue, and other like Succeſſors after him? as indeede it is the firſt and immediate literal ſenſe ; but it is moſt principally ſpoken, of our B . Redemer and Sauiour, as both him ſelf inſinuateth in the wordes now re-

Act. 3.
v. 22.

cited : and S . Peter moſt clearly expoundeth it ſay- ing: [Moyſes indeede ſaid, that a Prophet ſhal the Lord your God raiſe vp to you, of your brethren, as my ſelf, him you ſhal heare, according to al thinges whatſoeuer he ſhal ſpeake to you.] Theſe few par- ticular examples, only of the Bookes of Moyſes , o- mitting many others, may ſuffice to ſhew the hardnes of ſome holy Scriptures, which neede to be explica- ted by other places more cleare .

5 If we ſhal ſpeake more generally, then muſt we ſay, that no Booke in the whole Bible , ſcarce anie Chapters, are without ſpecial difficulties , euen the Legal and Hiſtorical Bookes, which are ordinarilie more eaſie, then the others, yet haue ſome intricate hardnes to be reconciled, in ſeming contradictions : Namely the Bookes of Kinges, and Paralipopenon.

See An-
not.
1. Par.
1.

For the better ſoluing of doubtes occurring therir, we haue obſerued tenne general rules, which may helpe, but not fully ſuffice for this purpoſe .

6 The Sapiential Bookes, aſwel of the old, as new Teſtament, require illuminating wiſdome, to al that ſhal read them : much more to ſuch as ſhal expound them. Among the reſt, the Canticle of Canticles , and S . Paules Epiſtle to the Romanes, ſeme to be moſt profound . But the prophetical Bookes for the

Pſal. 1.
2. 3. 4.
&c.
67. 118.

greateſt part, eſpecially ſome Pſalmes, the Lamēta- ons of Ieremie, the three firſt Chapters, & neene laſt of Ezechiel: almoſt al the Apocalipſe, ſeme in this point, of deepe miſtical ſenſe, to excede the reſt :

It is no ſmal di- ficultie to re- concile places , which may ſeme contrary.

The Sapiential & Prophetical Bookes, eſpe- cially ſom par- tes of them do manifeſtly ap- peare to be hard.

H 2   The

The proofe wherof, I remitte to the teftimonie of al that haue made, or wil make, trial by experience.

Some Scrip-
tures doe ex-
prefly witnefle
that fom other
Scriptures are
hard.
7   Neuertheleffe, take alfo here furer teftimonies of the holie Scripture it felf. King Salomõ exhorting al to wifdom (wherin is cõprifed the whole frame of al vertuous, and religious perfection) fheweth that parables are profitable for the atteining of wifdome, but not without interpretation, & therfore faith : [He that wil learne wifdome, fhal vnderftand a Para- ble ; and interpretation, the wordes of the wife, *and their darke fayinges .*] for fo he calleth al Parables, darke fayinges, to witte, his whole Booke of Pro- uerbes and Parables : which kindes of fpeach, is alfo inferted in manie other partes of holie Scripture, e- fpecially by our Sauiour him felf in his Gofpel, pro- feffing that he fpake fo of purpofe, [Becaufe (faith he to his Difciples) to you it is geuen to know the Mifteries of the kingdome of heauen (according vn- to that which Salomon addeth in the fame place, [The wife man hearing, wil be wifer) but to them (that were euil difpofed) it is not geuen ; therfore in Parables I fpeake to them, becaufe, feeing, they fee not, and hearing, they heare not, neither do thcy vnderftand] Some Parables our Sauiour expounded, leauing the reft to his Apoftles interpretation, as to men of vnderftanding, to take inftruction therby, & to teach others. And when fomtimes they vnder- ftood him not, he fatherly rebuked them faying, [Are you alfo as yet without vnderftanding ?] As if he fhould fay. It is leffe to be merueled at, if the peo- ple vnderftand not. Nay it were to meruel at, if a- nie man by his owne witte, could vnderftand Para- bles or Prophecies. And therfore the Queenes trea- furer of Ethiopia, being demanded whether he vn- derftoode Ifaias Prophefie, which he diligently read, anfweared, [And how can I, vnleffe fome man fhew me ?]

Parables are
darke fayinges.

Ordinarily mé,
otherwife pru-
dent & iudici-
ous, doe not
vnderftand
Scriptures

Prou. 1.
v. 6.
Ch . 10.
v. 1.

Mat. 13.
v. 11.

Pro. 1. *v.*
5. 13. *Ifa.*
6. *v.* 9.

Math. 15.
v. 16.

Act. 8.
v. 31.

me?] This same Prophet Isaias semed to writ more without an Interpreter.
painely then most other Prophets did : yet he saith,

Isa. 29. [I s Prophesie was to the people, as a sealed Booke.]
v. 11. or Is was to them, as [to men that can not read.
v. 12. And the vision of al (saith he) shal be vnto you, as
the v ordes of a Booke sealed, which when they shal
geue o him that knoweth letters, they shal say, read
this : nd he shal answear, I can not, for it is sealed.
And the booke shal be geuen to one that knoweth not
letters, and it shal be said to him, read, & he shal answeare, I know not letters.] Scribes and Pharisies
could read Isaias & other Prophets, but to them, the
Bookes were sealed that the sense was not vnderstood
by them, so that they could not finde Christ therein.
The vulgar people could not read, much lesse vnderstand without Interpreters, wherby neither the learned nor vnlearned, reape profit, by the holie Scriptures, vntil the key of vnderstanding, which is the
holy Spirit of truth, promised and sent to the Apostles, doth open this holie Booke.

8   The Apostles are they, who first had Commission The Apostles &
Mat. 28. [to teach al Nations :] And their Successors haue stil their successors
v. 29. the same Commission. For our Sauiour prouided, are the proper,
Ioan. 14. whe he promised [to send the Holie Ghost to be with Interpreters of
v. 16. them for euer.] And also signified, that him self, the holie
Mat. 28. by the same Holie Ghost, wil be with them [euen al Scriptures.
v. 20. daies, to the end of the world.] In like sort the Prophet Ezechiel, preached and writte, and was not vnderstoode, for his Prohhesie semed to be as harde as
Ezech. Parables : Wherupon he said; [O Lord God, they Some prophe-
20. *v.* say of me; doth not this man speake by Parables?] cies as hard, as
49. Daniel testifieth that to him it was said; [shutte vp Parables.
Dan. 12. the wordes and seale the Booke, euen to the time ap- Yea Prophe-
v. 4, 9. pointed; verie manie shal passe ouer, and there shal cies are pur-
13. be manifest knowlege :] So hard are most Prophesies posly shut vp,
to be vnderstoode, til they be fulfilled : Euen our til the time of
performing
them.

H   3   Sauiours

Sauiours prediction of his owne death, which he signified to his Apostles, that [al thinges should be consummate which were written by the Prophets of the
Sonne of man. For he shal be deliuered to the Gentiles, and shal be mocked, and scourged, and spit e v-
pon, and after they haue scourged him, they will kil
him, and the third day he shal rise againe. Yet they
vnderstoode none of these thinges, and this word was
hid from them.] But after his Resurrection, he not
only put them in mind what he had said before: but
also then [He opened their vnderstanding, that they
might vnderstand the Scriptures.] Finally, that
some other holie Scriptures besides Prophesies, and
Parables, doe also conteine thinges hard to be vnderstoode: S. Peter witnessith, that [in the Epistles
of S. paul are certaine thinges hard to be vnderstood,
which the vnlearned and vnstable, depraue, as also
the rest of the Scriptures, to their owne perdition.]
What then doe we say, that holie Scriptures are insufficient? No, God forbid; for they are most sufficient, & do coteine, either expresly, or implicitly, al
doctrine necessarie to saluation, yea incomparablie
and by infinite degrees, more sufficiently, then anie
other written worke or Booke conteyneth, what
Art or Science soeuer. This stil we say, and withal,
that it requireth interpretation, and somtimes the liuing voice of an authentical Interpreter.

Luc. 18.
v. 31. 32.
33. 34.

Luc. 24.
v. 45.

S. Peters ex-
presse testimo-
nie of this mat-
ter.

2. Pet. 3.
v. 16.

Act. 8.
v. 31.

True miracles are an assured proofe of Faith: or
other truth, for which they are done.

ARTICLE. 5.

Hitherto we haue proued by holie Scriptures,
that Faith is necessarie to saluation, that it
is the special gift of God, and is grounded
in his

Article 1.
2.
3.

4.

in his word: either written, or deliuered without writing: and that the written word somtimes requireth interpretation. Now we are to speake of an other ground of faith more extraordinarie, which is of miracles. For God Creator and Lord of al, so disposeth of his workes, that some succede according to natural causes, and efficacie which he geueth to creatures; some according to supernatural grace, which he also geueth of more abundant fauour. And of this greater sort, some are by his goodnes made ordinarie, and so are become more familiar to his seruantes, as the benefites of holie Sacrifice and Sacraments, and other daylie spiritual giftes: some are extraordinarie, and therfore seme more meruelous, as miracles, which are workes also done aboue the ordinarie course, & natural power of al creatures, such as neuer were, neither can be wrought, but by God only, geuing supernatural force & efficacie, as pleaseth his diuine goodnes. And therfore true miracles, are an infallible ground of assured truth, of whatsoeuer is confirmed by them, Because God, who is truth it self, and can not lye, beareth witnes by his fact that the thing is true which is so proued.

Psal. 71. *v.* 18.

Miracles are an infallible proofe of truth.

2. This maner of proofe we find in holie Scriptures, to haue bene practised by diuine ordinace in diuers cases: and in two more general. First when it pleased God according to his eternal wil and decree, to change the external forme of his Law, as he did by Moyses; and againe by our B. Sauiour Christ: He gaue his messengers power to worke miracles, in proofe and confirmation of their seueral missions, agreable to their different functions. Secondly in case, when a nie are sent to preach and plant Faith & Religion in anie Countrie, or among anie people, where it was not before, as now in the East, and West Indies, and other remote partes: God geueth power to his preachers.

Miracles are most necessary, when the external forme of Religion is changed: and where it is to be newly planted.

chers.

chers to worke miracles, for the better conuerfion of fuch Infidels to Chriftianitie. More particular cafes are, when it pleafeth God alfo in Chriftian Coútries, to fhew his grace of miraculous power, either for proofe of fome fpecial truth perteyning to faith, or of other thing in controuerfie; or for the greater confolation of his feruantes, or confufion of aduerfaries. But where Religion is once planted, wel watered, and hath taken firme roote, miracles are more rare, and not neceffarie for trial of truth in religious caufes, becaufe al doubtes of that kinde, may be in fuch places fufficiently folued, and decided by manie other meanes, and amongft the reft, by diligent furueying of ancient miracles, if any haue bene wrought in confirmation of fuch pointes as are now called into queftion; or at leaft by that Church which was approued and eftablifhed by miracles, that is to fay, by Gods owne worke, which in it felf is al one with his diuine word; but to men, his miraculous worke may geue more credibilitie, by how much it is to vs more manifeft.

3   Wherfore to come to our prefent purpofe, concerning the two more general cafes, wherin miracles are moft neceffarie, when the outward forme of Religion is changed amongft the faithful, & when preachers are fent to conuert Infidels: we fhal begin with

Moyfes was confirmed by a miracle that God did fpeak to him.

Moyfes his miffion, who being fent to deliuer Gods people from Egipt, was firft himfelf confirmed by miracle, before he was imployed in that great Embaffage. For when as yet he fed the fheepe of Iethro his fatherinlaw, [Our Lord appeared to him in a flame of fire, out of the middeft of a bufh: and he faw that the bufh was on fire and was not burnt:] Wherat he admiring and going nearer to fee the bufh, God bade him not to approach, but tould him his wil faying, [I am the God of thy father, the God of Abraham, the God

Exod. 3.
v. 2. 3.

6.

the God of Isaac, and the God of Iacob . I haue seene
the affliction of my people in Egypt, and I haue heard
their crie, and I am descended to deliuer them out of
the handes of the Egiptians : but come and I wil send
thee to Pharao, that thou maist bring forth my people the children of Israel out of Egipt .] And after
Gods declaration of his diuine name, and of his pur-
Cb. 4.   pose in this behalfe, as in the sacred text [Moyses an-
v. 1.   swering said : they wil not beleue me, nor heare my
voice, but they wil say ; Our Lord hath not appeared to thee .] Wherupon our Lord shewed to him   And receiued
two other miracles, turning a rodde into a serpent :   power to work
and making leprosie in his hand, and gaue him po-   miracles, for
wer to worke the same before the people, & if neede   proofe of this
required, a third in confirmation that our Lord had   mission .
appeared to him, & that he was indeede sent of God .
Neither did God admitte other excuses of difficulties
v. 11. 12.   or impedimentes, but said : [Goe on, I wil be in thy
v. 16.   mouth, and I wil teach thee what thou shalt speake.
This rodde also (wherby God had already wrought a
miracle) take in thy hand, wherwith thou shalt doe
v. 21.   the signes .] And further our Lord said : [See that
thou doe al the wonders which I haue put in thy hand
before Pharao .] This so strange and mightie power
to worke miracles, God gaue to Moyses, in place, as
it were, of Letters of credit, & of a seale to his Commission, aswel to the Children of Israel, as to the king
and people of Egipt . Which, when he performed in
Ch. 7.   signes both great and euident : the Magicians vsing   Magicians do-
v. 11.   al their skil of inchantments by the diuels power,   ing some pro-
22. *Ch.*   wrought some false prodigious signes, but failing in   digious thing-
8. *v.* 7.   the third attempt, confessed plainly, & [said to Pha-   es, could not
v. 18.   rao, *Digitus Dei est hic* . This is the finger of God .]   racles.
19.   And after tenne great plagues miraculously inflicted
vpon the Egyptians for their obduration and cruel-
Ch. 11.   tie, wherof the last was [the death of al the first borne
v. 5. 7.   I   of men

ofmen & beaftes in the Egiptians; the Ifraelites (be- **Ch . 12.**
ing ftil free fró al) then paffed by dry ground through **v . 29.**
the red fea; where King Pharao and al his armie fo- **Ch . 14.**
lowing them, were drowned. Wherupon the peo - **v . 21 . 22 :**
ple of Ifrael more firmly [beleued our Lord & Moy- **28 . 31.**
fes his feruant .] And fo he and they fang a folemne **Ch . 15.**
Canticle of praife and thankefgeuing to our Lord.
And this was the firft part of Moyfes his Commiffion,
wherin miracles were neceffarily required, and as effectually performed .

His cheefe of-   4   The other part of this great Commiffion, was to
fice being to re-   be the [Mediator betwene God and his people] in
ceiue and deli-   that which God then intended to doe vnto them :   **Deut . 5.**
uer Gods writ-   which was to geue them a written Law. And this   **v . 5 .**
ten Law, the   was fo great an office, and withal fo new & ftrange,
fame was alfo   that it no leffe required côfirmation by miracles , but
confirmed by   rather more then the former of their deliuerie from
miracles .   Egipt. For here they receiued Gods Commandementes written in two Tables, with a multitude of o-
ther Precepts, Ceremonial, & Iudicial, the one forte
perteyning to the explication and particular inftruction, how to put in practife thofe moral Precepts of
the firft Table, côteyning their duties towardes God :
the other, for better performing the precepts of the
fecond Table, concerning their duties ech one to -
wardes others . And therfore to this purpofe, that
more refpect might be in the people towardes God
the geuer of this Law, and towardes Moyfes by whô
they receiued it, and that the people might be ftirred   **Exo. 19.**
vp to mature confideration, who were to geue their   **v . 5 . 6 . 8.**
confent and promife to kepe the fame Law, as God
in this mutual Couenant, promifed his protection, affiftance, and remuneration : extraordinarie teftimonie was requifite of Gods part, which he exhibited
by great and vnwonted miracles . For after their pre-   **Exo. 19.**
fcribed preparation, when [the third day was come ,   **v . 15 . 16.**
and

and the morning appeared, behold thunders began to be heard, and lightninges to flash, & a verie thick cloude to couer the mount, and the noise of the trumpet sounded excedingly : and the people that was in the campe feared. And al the mount Sinai smoked, for our Lord was descended vpon it in fyre, and the smoke arose frō it as out of a furnace, & al the mount was terrible. And the sound of the Trumpet grew lowder by litle & litle ; & was drawen out a length.]

Exo. 20.
v. 1. *&c.*
v. 18. 19.

In this meruelous maner, our Lord beginning to deliuer his Law, [the people strooken with feare, said to Moyses; Speake thou to vs, and we wil heare. Let not our Lord speake to vs; why shal we dye, and this exceding great fyre deuoure vs ? For if we heare the voice of the Lord our God anie more, we shal

Deut. 5.
v. 25.

dye. Approch thou rather and heare al thinges that the Lord our God shal say to thee, & thou shalt speak to vs, and we hearing wil doe them.

5 When also Moyses had receiued the whole Law, & declared the same to the people, it was yet watered (as a new graffed plant) with more miracles, as occasion required in confirmation therof, and namely in

It was yet more confirmed by other miracles, in punishing the transgressors.

Leuit. 10.
v. 1. 2.

punishment of transgressors. For [Nadab and Abiu, Preistes, the Sonnes of Aaron, offering strange fyre, which was not cōmanded,] other [fyre coming forth

Nu. 16.
v. 1. *&c.*

from our Lord deuoured thē, and they died.] Againe, Core, Dathan, and Abiron, with two hundred fiftie complices, rising againft Moyses and Aaron, pretēding that [al the people being holie] they should not be lift vp aboue the rest, Moyses said to them. In

v. 5.

the morning our Lord wil mak' it knowne who perteine to him, and the holie he wil ioyne to him self.] And to the people (after other admonition) he said :

v. 28.

[In this you shal know that our Lord hath sent me to doe al thinges that you see, and that I haue not

29.

forged them of mine owne mind. If they dye the ac-

cuftomed

cuſtomed death of men, and if the plague wherwith others alſo are wont to be viſited, doe viſit them, our Lord did not ſend me : But if our Lord doe a new thing, that the earth opening her mouth, ſwalow them downe, and al thinges that perteine to them, and they deſcend quick into hel : you ſhal know that they haue blaſphemed our Lord. Immediatly therfore as he ceaſed to ſpeake, the earth brake in ſunder vnder their feete, and opening her mouth, deuoured them, with their Tabernacles and al their ſubſtance : and they went downe into hel quick, couered with the ground, and periſhed out of the middeſt of the multitude.] Neither only the principal rebels thus ſodenly periſhed : But [a fyre alſo coming forth from our Lord, ſlew the two hundred fiftie men that offered the Incenſe.] Nay yet more tranſgreſſing, were likewiſe puniſhed, and the ſame alſo miraculouſly. For [al the multitude murmured the day folowing againſt Moyſes and Aaron ſaying : you haue killed the people of our Lord. And when there roſe a ſedition, and the tumult grew furder, Moyſes and Aaron fleeing to the Tabernacle of the Couenant, our Lord ſaid to them : depart from the middeſt of this multitude, euen now wil I deſtroy them. And the burning fyre did waſt the multitude : and there were ſtrooken fonrtene thouſand and ſeauen hundred men, beſide them that had periſhed in the ſedition of Core.] Wherto we may adde a more comfortable, but no leſſe potent miracle, in Aarons Rodde, floriſhing & bringing forth frute.

30.

31.

32.
33.

v.35.

v.41.

v.42.

v.45.

v.47.49.

Num. 17.
v. 8.

Other miracles in beſtowing benefites.

6   Marie other miracles were alſo done in the ſame time of Moyſes, both for the peoples confirmation in faith, and feare of God ; and for their particular benefites. As [when bitter waters were made ſweete ; and waters drawne out of rockes. The continual prouiſion of Manna for their ſuſtenance, al the fourtie yeares

Exo. 15. *v.* 25. *Ch.* 17. *v* 5. *Nu.* 20. *v.* 11.

Exo. 16. yeares in the defert. Flefh alfo was geuen them to
v. 15. *et* their fil. When Moyfes praying held vp his handes,
v. 12. the people of Ifrael preuailed in batel, but if he let
Nu. 11. then downe a litle, then Amelec (their enemie) o-
v. 18. uercame. The euil purpofe of Balac and Balam to
Exo. 17. haue curfed them, was turned into blefling.]

v. 11. 7 Againe a new great miracle was wrought by Io-
Nu. 23. fue in the Riuer of Iordan [the vpper part ftanding
v. 8. 11. and fwelling vp like to a mountaine, the lower part
Iofue. 3. defcending into the fea, that the Preiftes, with the
v. 16. 17. Arke, ftoode vpon the drie ground in the middeft of
Iordan, whiles al the people paffed ouer through the
Iof. 12. drie chanel.] Likewife the victories atchiued by Io-
v. 24. fue againft mánie Kinges; and conqueft of the promifed land, were al ful of miracles.

Iudic. 6. 8 Some alfo in the times of the Iudges, and of the
v. 21. 36. Kinges, which are recorded in thofe Hiftories : Efpe-
39. cially where more neede recuiled, in the tenne Tribes called the Kingdome of Ifrael ; where they made
a notorious wicked fchifme, & manie fel into Idolatrie and infidelitie. For whofe reduction to true
faith and vnitie in Religion, God fent them Prophets,
which both by preaching and miracles, reclamed &
confirmed manie. Elias the zelous Prophet among
3. Reg. other his heroical Actes, him felf alone chalenged
18. v. 23. four hundred and fiftie Prophets of Baal, to trie by
miracle, who is true God , [they laying an oxe vpó
wood for Sacrifice without fyre, and he an other, he
bade them inuocate the names of their goddes, and
v. 24. I wil inuocate (faith he) the name of my Lord, and
the God that fhal heare by fire, let the fame be God.]
which thing they attempting and not performing,
[he dreffed his oxe, and (that the worke of God
might be more confpicuous) powred much water in
a gutter which he made rownd about the Altar, and
v. 36. praied faying : Lord God of Abraham, and Ifaac, &

*Iofue his auc-
thoritie & ac-
tions were alfo
confirmed by
miracles.*

*Diuers mira-
cles were like-
wife wrought,
in the times of
the Iudges, &
Kinges.*

*Elias proued
by a miracle
that our Lord
is the only
true God.*

I 3   Ifrael

Ifrael, fhew this day that thou art the God of Ifrael, and I thy feruant, and that according to thy commandement I haue done al thefe thinges. Heare me *v*. 37. Lord, heare me, that this people may learne, that 38. thou art our Lord God, & thou haft connerted heir hart. And the fyre of our Lord fel, and deuoured the holocauft, and the wood, and the ftones, lick al fo the duft, and the water that was in the war r gutter. Which when al the people had feene, they fel on 39. their face and faid : Our Lord he is God, our Lord he is God.] Why could not the diuel that procured fyre to confume Iobs feauen thoufand fheepe; *Iob*. 1. *v*. bring fire alfo to faue the credit of his owne prophets, 3 . 16. but that God permitted the one for manifeftation of Iobs patience, and not the other when it fhould haue hindered the manifeftation of truth, and had bene a witnes of falfhood, Other miracles done by this Prophet : his hindering of raine three yeares, then 3 . *Reg* 17. procuring it ; His fuftenance brought vnto him by ra- *v*. 1. *Ch*. uens ; His multiplying of a poore widowes meale, & 18. *v*. 41. oyle ; The raifing of her fone from death ; His fafting *Ch*. 17. from al meate and drinke, fourtie daies and nightes *v*. 6. together ; His procuring fyre, which burnt two cap- 14. 19. taines, and their hundred men ; His deuiding of the *Ch*. 19. riuer of Iordan, and paffing through it in the drie cha- *v*. 8. nel ; And his owne taking away in a fyrie chariot. 4 . *Reg*. 1. And manie other miracles done by Elizeus, & diuers *v*. 10. other Prophets and holie men. Alfo the childrens de- *Ch*. 2. liuerie from fyre in Babilon ; doe al fhew the affured *v*. 8. *v*. 11. truth of thofe thinges for which they were wrought. *Ch*. 2. *v*. And thefe may fuffice touching the old Teftament, 14. &*c*. and the Law which was geuen by Moyfes. It refteth *Dan*. 3. *v*. now to declare the fame neceffitie & vfe of miracles 17. 23. in the Law of Grace. 24. 91.

9   How much Chrift our Sauiour, the verie Sonne *Heb*. 1. 2. of God, excelleth Moyfes, and al other Prophets of & 10.

God permitted the diuel to trie Iobs patience ; but not to delude in trial of truth.

Manie miracles wrought by Elias, Elifeus, and others.

Our Sauiour Chrift wrought innumerable

God

God; S. Paul teacheth largelie in his Epiſtle to the
Hebréwes, as alſo manie other holie Scriptures. Yet
[did not Chriſt (the creator of the world) glorifie
him ſelf (as the ſame Apoſtle witneſſith) but his Father that ſpake to him.] For ſo likewiſe him ſelfe
had ſaid in his Goſpel, [If I doe glorify my ſelf, my
glorie is nothing. It is my Father that glorifieth me]
Therfore as Moyſes coming to deliuer the Iſraelites
from the ſeruitude of Egipt, and to geue them a written Law, proued his Commiſſion by ſundrie miracles:
ſo Chriſt our Lord coming to deliuer al that wil obey
him, from ſeruitude of ſinne, and to geue vs his Law
of Grace, beſides his owne teſtimonie (which is alſo
moſt true) vſeth other proofes, as the teſtimonie of
his Father; of S. Iohn Baptiſt; of Moyſes & al the
Prophets. But amongſt al, moſt vrgeth the incredulous with his miracles. [I haue a greater teſtimonie (ſaith he) then Iohn. For the workes which the
Father hath geuen me to perfect; the verie workes
them ſelues which I doe, geue teſtimonie of me, that
the Father hath ſent me.] Againe he inculcateth the
ſame at other times ſaying: [I ſpeake to you, and
you beleue not: the workes that I doe in the name
of my Father, they giue teſtimonie of me. If I doe
not the workes of my Father, beleue me not: But if I
doe, and if you wil not beleue me, beleue the workes,
that you may know and beleue, that the Father is in
me, and I in the Father.] Thus doth our Sauiour
often ſignify, that he wrought his miracles principally for this cauſe, that they might beleue in him.
Which S. Paul much vrgeth to the Iewes, that [they
ſhould not eſcape ſeuere puniſhment, if they neglected ſo great ſaluation, declared, not by Angels (as
was the old Law) but by our Lord the only Sonne
of God, God withal teſtifying by ſignes and wonders, and diuers miracles, and diſtributious of the
Holie

Side notes (left margin):

Heb. 5. v. 5.

Ioan. 8. v. 54.

Act. 5. v. 31. 32. Io. 8. v. 14. 18.

Ioan. 5. v. 33.
Luc. 24. v. 27.
Ioan. 5. v. 36.
v. 46. 47.

Io. 10. v. 25. 37. 38.
Io. 14. v. 11.

Heb. 2. v. 4.

Side notes (right margin):

miracles, to prouc his miſ-ſion. And moſt eſpecially vr-ged them a-mongſt other proofes.

See Mat. 3.
v. 17. Ch.
11. v. 21.
Ch. 17. v.
5. Ch. 21.
v. 26.
Mar. 1.
v. 7.
Ch. 11. v.
31. Luc. 4.
v. 18. Ch.
20. v. 5.
Ioan. 1. v.
32. Ch. 12.
v. 28.

By miracles he also proued his doctrine; namely his power to forgeue sinne.

Holie Ghoft, according to his wil,] And particularly that he came to deliuer men from finne, he sheweth in these expresse wordes [that you may know that the Sonne of man, hath power in earth to forgeue sinnes (then he said to the sicke of the palfey) arise, take vp thy bed, and goe into thy house.] And after diuers other miracles recited, the Euangelist thus conioyneth them with his preaching [He went about al the Cities and Townes, teaching in their Synagogues, and preaching the Gospel of the kingdome, and curing euerie disease, and euerie infirmitie.] Also to satisfie S. Iohnes Disciples (for S. Iohn him self doubted not) our Sauiour said to them, [Goe and report to Iohn what you haue heard and seene; the blind see; the lame walke; the lepers are made cleane; the deafe heare; the dead rife againe: to the poore the Gospel is preached.] Against calumniators he auoucheth [If I in the Spirit (or finger) of God, doe caft out diuels, then furely is the Kingdome of God come vpon you.] He sheweth more ouer, that by the special prouidence of God [a certaine man was borne blind; saying [that it was neither for his finne, nor his parents finne, but that the workes of God may be manifested in him.] The self fame he teacheth of Lazarus his sicknes and death; [this sicknes is not to death, but for the glorie of God; that the Sonne of God may be glorified by it.] Lastly the verie night of his Passion, speaking to his eleuen Apostles of the Iewes obstinacie, he saith : [If I had not done among them workes that none other man hath done; they should not haue fin: but now both th y haue seene (my workes) and they doe hate both me, and my Father.] After his Refurrection, S. Iohn teftifieth generally to the whole world, to what end these signes are written, [that you may beleue (faith he) that Iesus is Chrift, the

Mat. 9. v. 6. Mar. 2. v. 10.

Mar. 2. v. 35.

Mat. 11. v. 4. 5. Luc. 7. v. 22. 23.

Mat. 12. v. 28. Luc. 11. v. 20.

Ioan. 9. v. 3.

Ioan. 11. v. 4. 15.

Ioan. 15. v. 24.

Ioan. 20. v. 31.

Sonne

Sonne of God; and that beleuing you may haue life in his name.] And thus much touching the necessitie of miracles, when the outward forme of Religion is changed, as it firſt was by Moyſes, and againe by our B. Sauiour Chriſt.

10 Now concerning the ſecond general caſe wherin miracles are required; when Chriſtian Religion is propagated, by preaching to ſuch people as haue not receiued it : holie Scriptures doe teſtifie, that God euer geueth this power to his preachers, when he ſendeth them for this purpoſe, to proue therby their miſſion, and that their hearts may beleue their doctrine. So our B. Sauiour ſending his Apoſtles to preach his Goſpel in other places where him ſelf had

*Mat.*10. not yet bene, [gaue them power ouer vncleane ſpi-
v. 1.7. rites, that they ſhould caſt them out, & ſhould cure
8 .*Mar.* al maner of diſeaſe, & al maner of infirmitie. Preach
3 .*v.*15. (ſaith he,) that the kingdome of heauen is at hand.
Ch.6. Cure the ſick, raiſe the dead, clenſe the lepers, caſte
*v.*7.13. out diuels.] After this [our Lord deſigned alſo o-
Luc. 9. ther ſeauentie two Diſciples, and he ſent them two &
v. 1.2. two before his face, into euerie Citie and place, whe-
*Luc.*10. ther him ſelfe would come. And he ſaid vnto them,
v. 1.9. cure the ſick, &c. And they returned with ioy ſay-
17. ing. Lord, the deuils alſo are ſubiect vnto vs in thy
*Ioan.*12. name.] When our Lord alſo [praied that his Fa-
*v.*28. thers name might be glorified ; a voice came from hea
uen ; Both I haue glorified it, and againe I wil glori
*v.*30. fie it : Our Lord ſaid to the people that heard it ; This
32. 33. voice came not for me but for your ſake ;] Signifi-
ing, that after he ſhould be exalted by death on the
Croſſe, this miraculous voice ſhould haue more effect, becauſe Gods name ſhould then be more glo-
rified, by the conuerſion of al Nations. And therfore after his Reſurrection, our Lord ſent his Apoſtles
*Mat.*10. [not only to the Iewes as before,] but [to preach
*v.*5.6. Penance
K

Neither Luther, nor Caluin, changing the forme of Religion : haue wrought aniē miracles.

Miracles are likewiſe neceſſarie where Chriſtian faith is firſt preached.

penance, and remiſſion of ſinnes vnto al Nations; beginning in Ieruſalem, and ſo into al Iewrie, and Samaria, and euen to the vtmoſt of the earth. And they *Luc. 24.*
(after his Aſcenſion, and coming of the holie Ghoſt) *v. 47.*
going forth, preached euerie where ; our Lord wor- *Mar. 16.*
king withal, and confirming the word, with ſignes *v. 20.*
folowing] ſaith S. Mark.

First the A-
poſtles with o-
ther faithful,
were ſtrength-
ned by the Ho-
lie Ghoſt co-
ming vpon the
in viſible
ſignes.

11   Yet firſt of al our Lord by viſible miracles, con-
firmed aſwel his Apoſtles, as the whole multitude *Act. 1.*
of perſons perſeuering with one mind in praier (al- *v. 14. 15.*
moſt an hundred and twentie) according as he had *Luc. 24.*
promiſed, and they now expected [with power from *v. 49. Act.*
high] the vertue of the holie Ghoſt. For [when the *1. v. 8.*
daies of Pentecoſt were accompliſhed, they were al *Act. 2.*
together in one place; and ſodanly there was made *v. 12.*
a ſound from heauen, as of a vehement wind coming,
and it filled the whole houſe where they were ſitting.
And there appeared to them parted tongues, as it *v. 3.*
were of fire, and it ſate on euerie one of them, and *4.*
they were al repleniſhed with the Holie Ghoſt, and
they began to ſpeake with diuers tongues, according
as the Holie Ghoſt gaue them to ſpeake, *Magnalia* *v. 11.*
Dei, the great workes of God.] Here the Church of
Chriſt, then ſo ſmal a flock of an hundred and twentie perſons, aſwel by this viſible miracle, as by S. Pe- *v. 14.*
ters ſermon, but principally by the inuiſible power
of the Holie Ghoſt, inſtantly ſo increaſed, that [there *v. 41.*
were added that day, about three thouſand ſoules.]
Thus [after the grane of wheat] our Lord Ieſus Chriſt *Ioan. 12.*
died] on the Croſſe; [The grane of muſtard ſeede] *v. 24.*
his Kingdome the Church, roſe into a tree, our Lord *Mat. 13.*
confirming the word (as is ſaid) with ſignes folow- *v. 32.*
ing. For ſo S. Luke teſtifieth, not only in general, *Act. 2.*
that [manie wonders and ſignes were done by the *v. 43.*
Apoſtles in Ieruſalem,] but alſo reciteth manie in
particular, almoſt in euerie Chapter throughout his
                                            whole

whole Booke of the Actes of the Apoſtles, which is a breife Hiſtorie of the beginning of the Chriſtian Church.

12 But omitting here other pointes, we ſhal as breifly as may be, only touch the miracles, as the particular motiues, by which multitudes beleued in Chriſt. [Peter and Iohn went vp into the Temple at the Ninth hour of praier, and a certaine man that was Lame from his mothers wombe was caried and laid at the gate of the Temple to aske almes. S. Peter in ſtead of geuing money which he had not, bade him [In the name of Ieſus Chriſt of Nazareth, ariſe and walke ; And taking his right hand, he lifted him vp, and forthwith his feete and ſoles were made ſtronge ; And ſpringing, he ſtoode and walked, and went in with them into the Temple, walking and leaping & praiſing God.] S. Peter alſo preached, that this was done in the name of Chriſt. Manie beleued, & the number of beleuers, was made fiue thouſand.]

13 The high Preiſt, with the Ancients and Scribes, threatning the Apoſtles : and they with other faithful, [praying for côſtant fortitude, & that God would extend his hand to cures, and ſignes, and wonders, to be done by the name of his holie Sonne Ieſus; The place was moued wherin they were gathered; & they were al repleniſhed with the Holie Ghoſt. And they ſpake the word of God with confidence.] In which good progreſſe, whiles the Church did grow in number, and vertue, vice alſo crept in, as chaffe groweth with good corne. A coople pretending perfection [Ananias with Saphira his wife, defrauded the communitie, and for their lying to the Holie Ghoſt, were ſtroken dead with S. Peters wordes of reprehenſió. And here againe, the ſacred Hiſtoriographer ſaith : [By the handes of the Apoſtles, were manie ſigues and wonders done among the people] adding

Act. 3.
v. 1.

v. 6.
7.
8.

12.
Ch. 4.
v. 4.
v. 5. *ad*
21.
23.
29. 30.
31.

Ch. 5. *v.*
1. 2. 3.
5. 10.
v. 12.
14.

Sundrie miracles are recorded, by which manie were conuerted to Chriſt.

Al the Apoſtles with others, prayed for miracles, & obtained their requeſt.

alſo

also the effect [And the multitude of men and women that beleued in our Lord, was more increased.

In particular S.
Luke reciteth
many miracles
wrought by S.
Peter.

14   In particular, he especially reciteth S. Peters
miracles, togetherwith the great faith of the people,
who for their wôderful estimatiô of his eminêt power, & vertue, did bring forth the sicke into the streets,
& laid them in beddes and couches, that when Peter   *v.* 15.
came, his shadow at the least, might ouershadow any
of them, and they al might be deliuered from their
infirmities. And there ranne together vnto Ierusa-   *v.* 16.
lem, the multitude also of the Cities adioyning, bringing sicke persons, and such as were vexed of vncleane spirits; who were al cured.] The enemies stil   17. 18.
raging, put the Apostles in the common prison [But   19.
an Angel of our Lord by night, opening the gates of   20.
the prison, and leading them forth said: Goe, and   21.
standing speake in the Temple to the people, al the
wordes of this life, who hauing heard this, early in
the morning, entred into the Temple and taught,
& after manie threatninges, that they should preach
nomore in the name of Iesus: Peter answearing and   *v.* 28. 29.
the Apostles, said; God must be obeyed rather then
men.

15   Omitting here the Historie of the institution of   *Act.* 6. 7.
seauen Deacons, the Martyrdome of S. Stephen;   8.
the preaching also of S. Philip, with singular good
fruit, with special mention of sundrie miracles: we
In the meane
time S. Paul
was miracu-
loufly conuer-
ted.
come to the miraculous conuersion of Saul afterward   *Act.* 9.
called Paul, and made an extraordinarie Apostle, who   *v.* 1.
as yet breathing forth threatninges, and slaughter,
against the Disciples of our Lord, as he drawing to
Damascus, [sodenly a light from heauen shined roûd   3.
about him, & falling on the ground, he heard a voice   4.
saying to him: Saul, Saul, why persecutest thou me?-   5.
who said. Who art thou Lord? And he; I am Iesus
whom thou dost persecute. It is hard for thee to
                                                    kick

kick againſt the pricke.] This was S. Paules mi-
1 culous conuerſion as you know. The frute wherof,
a Chriſtendome reapeth, and reioyceth therin. Of
m. acles alſo wrought by him, we ſhal ſe more by and
by

16   For thus much being ſaid by the way of S.
Pau, s conuerſion; the sacred Hiſtorie reporteth
more of S. Peter, who as yet conuerſing among the
Iewe-, conuerting and confirming al that he could:
ſo [came to the Sainĉts (that is to the faithful) that
dwelled at Lidda; and he found there a certeine mã
named Æneas lying in his bed, from eight yeares before, who had the palſey. And Peter ſaid vnto him,
Æneas, our Lord Ieſus Chriſt heale thee; ariſe &
make thy bed. And incontinēt he aroſe. And al that
dwelt at Lidda and Sarona ſaw him, and conuerted
to our Lord.] Againe in Ioppe, a certaine woman
named Tabitha, ful of good workes and almes deedes
died. And Peter being requeſted by the Diſciples,
came thither, and falling on his knees praied; and
turning to the bodie he ſaid; Tabitha ariſe. And ſhe
opened her eyes, and ſeing Peter, ſhe ſate vp, and
geuing her his hand, he lifted her vp. And when he
had called the Sainĉtes, and the widowes, preſented
her aliue; and it was made knowne throughout al
Ioppe: and manie beleucd in our Lord.

17   The propagation of the Church to the Gentiles, began alſo by miraculous viſions, and S. Peters Miniſtery. For Cornelius a Gentile, was warned in a viſiõ by an Angel, to ſend into Ioppe for S.
Peter; & S. Peter by warrant of an other comfortable viſion, repairing to him, and preaching Chriſt vnto him, and other Gentiles, [as he was yet ſpeaking,
the Holie Ghoſt fel vpon al that heard the word; &
the faithful of the Iewes that accompanied Peter,
were aſtonied, for that the grace of the Holie Ghoſt,
was powred

Ch .9.
v.32.
33.
34.
35.

v.40.

41.

42.

Ch. 10.
v.1.&c.

v.44.
45.
46.

Manie other
miracles
wrought by S.
Peter.

Conuerſion of
Gentiles be-
gan by mira-
culous viſions.

K 3

red out vpon the Gentiles alſo. For they heard
them ſpeaking with tongues, and magnifying Go( ]
Wherupon they were al baptized. And by relati(g   *Ch*.11.
theſe two viſions, with the effect therof, by com ng   *v*.5.
of the Holie Ghoſt vpon theſe Gentiles, as vpor the
Iewes in the beginning; S. Peter gaue ful ſatisſ(cti-   *v*.15,
on to thoſe Chriſtian Iewes in Ieruſalem, whic(be-   *v*3.
fore diſliked his dealing with the Gentils; [an(they   *v*.18.
glorified God ſaying, God then to the Genti(s alſo
hath geuen repentance vnto life.

18 An other miracle perteyning to S. Peter, but not   *Ch*.12.
wrought by him, but vpon him, by the praiers of the
Church, for the cōmon good, is this. For whē King
Herode had killed S. Iames the greater; & [apprehended and impriſoned S. Peter (within the feaſt of   *v*.2.3.
Paſch) meaning after the feaſt to bring him forth to   4.
the people : Praier was made of the Church,   5.
without intermiſſion vnto God for him. And the   6.
ſame night he ſhould haue bene brought forth, Peter ſleping betwene two ſouldiers, bound with two
chaines, & the kepers before the doare keping the
priſon, an Angel of our Lord (miraculouſly) deliue-   7.
red him out of Herodes hand, and from al the ex-   11.
pectation of the people of the Iewes.] But Herod   19.
not long after in Cæſarea, puffed vp with ſuch pride
that he refuſed not to be honored as god, [was forth-   22.
with ſtrooken by Gods Angel, and being conſumed   23.
of wormes, gaue vp the Ghoſt.] And this miracle
alſo, had great effect.

19   For after this perſecuters death, S. Luke ad-   24.
deth, that [the word of our Lord increaſed and multiplied] ſtil inſerting among other thinges of his
Hiſtorie, more miracles with their effectes eſpecially wrought by S. Paule, who with Barnabas, be-   *Ch*.13.
ing [ſent of the Holie Ghoſt, ſailed into Cipres.
And when they had walked throughout the whole I-   *v*.4.
land

6.
land as farre as Paphos, they fonnd a Magician, a falſe Prophet, a Iew, with the Proconſul Sergius Paulus, a wiſe man. This Proconſul, deſiring to heare

7.
the word of God, and the Magician ſeking to auert

8.
him from the faith: S. Paul with a ſharp reprehen-ſion, denoũced vnto him that he ſhould be blind, not

9.
ſeing the Sunne vntil a time. And forthwith there fel dimnes and darknes vpon him, and going about,

11.
he ſought ſome bodie that would geue him his hand.

12.
Then the Proconſul, when he had ſeene what was done, beleued, merueling at the doctrine of our Lord.

Cb. 14.
At Lyſtra was [a man impotent of his feete, lame

v. 7.
from his mothers wombe, that neuer had walked;

8.
vpon whom S. Paul loking, and ſeing that he had

9.
faith to be ſaued (or healed) he ſaid with a loude voice, ſtand vpright on thy feete; And he leaped &

10
walked. Wherupon the heathen people, & the preiſt of Inpiter, would nedes haue offered ſacrifice to Paul,

11.
and Barnabas, as to Gods.] Contrariwiſe ſome ob-

12.
ſtinate [Iewes ſtoned S. Paul almoſt to death:] But

18. 19.
the Diſciples being ædified by the miracle, reſcued

Cb. 15.
him from that furie. After this at Ieruſalem, the mul-

v. 12.
titude gladly heard Barnabas and Paul, telling what great ſignes and wonders God had done among the Gentiles by them,

Cb. 16.
20 By a viſion ſhewed to S. Paul, they were wil-

v. 9.
led to goe into Macedonia, which they did, [being aſſured that God had called them, to euangelize vn-

10.
to that people.] Amongſt other fruit, S. Paul ex-

17.
pelled a pythonical ſpirit out of a yong woman, not

18.
ſuffering her to geue teſtimonie, that [they were the

19.
ſeruantes of the high God, which preach the way of ſaluatiou] wherof roſe a tumult and perſecution,

22.
S. [Paul and Silas were beaten with roddes, caſt in-

23.
to priſon, and put into the ſtockes; who praying, &

24.
prayſing God at midnight, ſodainly there was made

an

Relation of Gods workes, doth much edi-fie good peo-ple.

an earth-quake, so that the fundation of the prison 26.
was shaken, and forthwith al the doares of the prison were opened, and the bandes of al were loosed,]
the Gailor was conuerted, and [baprized, with al his 33.
house incontinent.] the Magistrate sending serge- 35.
antes to deliuer them, they expostulated the contu- 39.
melious iniurie done to them, & did not part til [the
Magistrates came and besought them, and brought
them forth of the Citie .] In Athens also S. Paules
preaching of Christ, had wonderful effect in the cō-
uersiō of renowmed S. Dionise, & other most learned
Philosophers, who at first scornfully called him, [a

Temporal in- *Word sower,* and preacher of new goddes.] By war-
terest is the rant of an other vision, S. Paul staieth at Corinth, a *Ch.17.v.*
most common yeare and fixe monethes, teaching among them the 16.17.18.
cause of perse- word of God. At Ephesus, by S. Paules impositi- 19.33.
cution. on of handes vpon twelue men newly baptized, the
Holie Ghost came vpon them, and they spake with
Confirmation tongues, and prophecied. [There were also brought *Ch.18.v.*
of the Bapti- from (S. Paul) his bodie, napkins or handcarchefes 9.11.
zed by imposi- vpon the sicke, and the diseases departed from them, *Ch.19.v.*
tion of the A- & the wicked spirits went out .] Whiles he preached 6.7.12.
postles handes. long in the night, a yong man oppressed with heauie *Ch.20.*
sleepe, sitting in a window, fel downe from the third *v.9.*
loft, and was taken vp dead; to whom, when Paul *v.10.*
was gone downe, he lay vpon him, and embracing
him he said: Be not troubled, for his soule is in him.
And (after the sermon was ended) they brought him *v.12.*
Gods singular- aliue, & were not a litle comforted .
prouidence in 21   It may seme to some perhaps, that thus ma-
ordening that nie, and so excellent miracles alreadie recited, may
S. Paul the abundantly suffice, to shew, both a necessitie in some
Doctor of the cases, & special fruite of these extraordinarie workes
Gentiles, of God : yet may we not for al that sleightly passe
should preach ouer Gods singular prouidence of his extraordinarie
in Rome the Apostle (so particularly ordained for the Gentiles)
head Citie of
the Gentiles.   his going

his going to Rome the head Citie of the Gentiles. In relating of which miſtical Hiſtorie, the Euangeliſt S. Luke exactly recordeth both diuers Diuine viſions, and other great miracles, with their admirable ef‐fectes. For not only S. Paul him ſelf being at Ephe‐ſus, vttered this ordinance of God by way of Prophe‐

Ch. 19. cie ſaying: [after I ſhal haue bene at Ieruſalem, I

v. 21. muſt ſee Rome alſo] But likewiſe being at Ceſarea,

Ch. 21. [a Prophet coming frō Iewrie named Agabus, tooke

v. 10. 11. Paules girdle, and binding his owne handes & feete, he ſaid: Thus ſaith the Holie Ghoſt; The man whoſe girdle this is, ſo ſhal the Iewes bind in Ieruſalem; and ſhal deliuer him into the handes of the Gentiles] to witte, into the handes of the Romanes, to whom

v. 12. Ieruſalem was then ſubiect; Wherunto did merue‐

13. 14. loufly cooperate his owne ſetled purpoſe, to goe ne‐

17. uertheleſſe to Ieruſalem, his frendes moſt vehement‐ly diſſwading him from it. And being come to Ieru‐

v. 30. ſalem, his enemies there [laying handes vpon him,

31. drew him forth of the Temple. But as they ſought to kil him, it was tould the Tribune of the band, that

32. al Ieruſalem is in confuſion. Who forthwith, taking

33. ſouldiers and Centurions, ranne downe to them;

34. wherupon the Iewes ceaſed from ſtriking him.] And the Tribune to appeaze them, apprehended him, and commanded him to be bond with two chaines, and to be led into the Caſtel, whither the multitude of the

36. people folowed crying, away with him.] Yet co‐

Ch. 22. ming to the ſtares, [he was permitted to ſpeake.]

v. 1. &c. And ſo he tould them particularly of his conuerſion.

v. 19. And laſtly of [a voice in a viſion, ſaying vnto him; Make haſt and depart quikly out of Ieruſalem;] A‐

22. gaine ſaying; [Goe, for into the Gentiles a farre,

23. wil I ſend thee.] Then they cryed againe: [Away with ſuch an one from the earth, for it is not meete

Ch. 23. he ſhould liue. In the open court, before Iewes and

v. 7. L Gentiles

S. Paul him ſelfe ſaw it by the ſpirit of prophecie.

An other Pro‐phet foretold the ſame.

Gentiles, there arofe fuch diffenfion betwene the Pharifies and Saducees, the whole multitude being deuided, that the Tribune fearing left Paul fhould be torn' 10.
in peeces by them, commanded the fouldiers, to take
him out of the middeft of them, and to bring him a-
gaine into the caftle,] where the night folowing, our 11.
Lord ftanding by him faid; [Be conftant, for as thou

God côfirmed haft teftified of me in Ierufalem, fo muft thou teftify 12.
the fame by an at Rome alfo. The next day, more then fourtie Iewes 13.
other vifion. confpiring, vowed, that they would neither eate nor
drinke, til they killed Paul ;] But God def.ated 16.
their wicked purpofe ; For this confpiracie was dif- 23.
couered, and the Tribune fent away Paul at the third
hour of the night, with a ftrong conuey towardes 24.
Cæfarea.

22   Wherupon the Iewes (ftil perfifting in their *Ch . 24.*
malice) went thither, and afrefh accufed him before *v . 5.*
Felix the Prefident, but could not conuince him of
anie crime. Neuertheleffe the Prefident temporifing 22.
differred them, and kept him prifoner two yeares,
and fo left him to a new Prefident, Portius Feftus; 27.
Before whom they accufed him againe; but prouing
nothing, [Feftus willing to pleafure the Iewes, faid *Ch . 25.*
to Paul ; Wilt thou goe vp to Ierufalem, and there *v . 7. 8.*
be iudged of thefe thinges before me ? And Paul faid, 9.
At Cæfars Iudgment feate doe I ftand, where I ought *v* 10.
to be Iudged. The Iewes I haue not hurt, as thou
verie wel knoweft. For if I haue hurt them, or done
anie thing worthie of death, I refufe not to die; But 11.
if none of thefe thinges be, wherof thefe accufe me,
noe man can geue me to them, I appeale to Cæfar.

S. Paul com- Then Feftus hauing conferred with the Counfel, an-
pelled by the fweared; Haft thou appealed to Cefar ? To Cæfar fhalt 23.
Iewes importu- thou goe :] Yet being brought before King Agrip- *Ch . 26.*
nitie againft pa, he fo fullie fatisfied them al, that this King faid *v . 2. 32.*
him, appealed to the Prefident [this man might be releafed, if he
to Cæfar.
had no

Ch. 27. had not appealed to Cæfar.] Being therfore fent
v. 1.2. towardes Rome, arriuing at diuers places, [and fai-
6. ling flowly, winter alfo growing on]manie great dif-
9.14. ficulties and dangers happened in this Iourney : Somtime tempeftious windes driue them from their pur-
15.16. pofe. And [as the winde carried them, fo were they
17.18. mightily toffed, in peril of Ilandes and quick fandes,
19.20. forced to caft forth their loading, euen the taklinges
of the fhip. And neither Sunne nor ftarres appearing for manie daies, and no fmale ftorme being toward : al hope was taken away of our fauing (faith
v. 10. S. Luke) In this diftreffe [S. Paul (notwithftan-
21. ding they had not folowed his former counfel) exhorted al to be of good cheare, for there fhal be no
22. loffe (faid he) of anie foule among you, but of the
23. fhip. For an Angel of the God whofe I am, & whom
24. I ferue, ftoode by me this night faying : feare not
25. Paul, thou muft appeare before Cæfar, and behold,
God hath geuen thee al that faile with thee. For the
which caufe be of good cheare ye men; For I beleue
God that it fhal fo be as it hath bene faid to me. And
we muft come to a certaine Iland.] Againe affuring
26. them [that there fhal not an haire of the head pe-
v. 34. rifh of anie of you.] Then failing towardes a fhore,
37.40. [falling into a place betwene two feas, they graue-
41. led the fhip; the forepart fticking faft, the hinder
part was broken, by the violence of the fea.] The
43. fouldiers gaue counfel to kil the prifoners, left anie
fwimming out, might runne away. Bnt [the Captaine willing to faue Paul, forbade it to be done.
And he commanded them that could fwimme, to caft
out them felues firft, and efcape, and goe forth to
land. And the reft, fome they caried on bordes, &
44. fome vpon thofe thinges that were of the broken
fhip. And fo it came to paffe, that al the foules e-
fcaped to land, being in al, two hundred, feauentie
sixe

S. Paul and o-
thers with him,
miraculoufly
deliuered in
long & dange-
rous tempeftes
on the fea.

An other vifió.

More dangers,
but ftil God
protecteth the
for S. Paules
fake.

fixe .] And the Iland was called Mitilene, otherwife
Melita, or Malta, where yet happened more miracles,

Other mira-
cles wrought
by S. Paul in
Malta .

23 For [whiles they made a fire, S . Paul laying fome　*Ch* . 28 .
ftickes on the fire, a Viper iffuing out of the heate ,　*v* . 3 .
inuaded his hand, and he fhaking of the beaft, into
the fire, fuffered no harme;] Whereupon the people firft fuppofed him to be a murderer; but expecting a while and feing no harme, changed in conceipt, faid he was a God . It chanced alfo, that a no-　*v* . 6 .
ble man lay there vexed with feuers, and the bloudie　*v* . 8 .
flixe; vnto whom Paul entered; & when he had praied and impofed handes on him , he healed him: which　9 .
being done, al in the Iland alfo that had infirmities,　11 .
came, and were cured . Then after three monethes　12 .
abode, winter being ended, taking fhip againe, they
came by Syracufa, Rhegium. & Puteoli (neare to Na-　13 .
ples in Italie ,) where finding Chriftians, and ftay-　14 .
ing with them feauen daies, the report of their a-　15 .
riual rūning before them to Rome, other Chriftians
came thence to meete them, vnto Apii forum, & to
the place called the three Tauerns . And finally [co-

S . Paul finding
Chriftians in
Rome, prea-
ched to them,
and to others
both Iewes and
Gentiles .

ming to Rome, Paul was permitted to remaine to　16 .
him felf with a fouldier that kept him] which opportunitie fo prouided of God, he fructfully vfing,
declared to the Iewes the caufe of his coming . And
on a day by them appointed , to heare his iudgment,　*v* . 22 .
he preached to them the Kingdome of God, by Ie-　23 .
fus Chrift, according to the Law of Moyfes, and prediction of the Prophets, from morning vntil euening .] And certaine beleued, certaine beleued not .　28 .
But to the Gentiles being willing to heare, he preached ful two yeares in his hyred lodging, to al that　30 .
came; teaching the thinges that concerne our Lord　31 .
Iefus Chrift with al confidence without prohibition .

Thꝭ

24 This special note of S. Paule coming to Rome, together with his, & S. Peters, & others miracles, I could not omitte in this place; becauſe here it is

euident by expreſſe holie Scripture (beſides other places, and diuers other aſſured proofes) that the Romanes at firſt receiued and profeſſed the true ſincere Chriſtian faith and Religion, which can neuer be ſhewed that they loſt, or changed at anie time ſince. And this narration of S. Luke, may alſo ſerue, as a ſtrong bulwork of defence, againſt impugners of other true miracles done afterwardes, aſwel by the ſame two cheife Apoſtles, who liued and laboured in the ſame harueſt, about fourtene yeares more after S. Paules coming to Rome; wherwith this Hiſtorie ceaceth, as by al the other Apoſtles then diſperſed, and working in al partes of the earth, though their particular actes be not written in the holie Scriptures; and by al other Apoſtolical men and Sainctes of God, both then and euer ſince, euen at this preſent time, moſt neceſſarily and frequently, the countries where people are firſt conuerted to Chriſt. And ſomtime alſo in Chriſtian Countries as it pleaſeth God, miracles are ſtil wrought and made manifeſt to innumerable eye witneſſes: And ſo authentically teſtified, that it is mere obſtinate wilfulnes to denie or diſcredit them, or the like heretofore written in the ſeueral liues of Sainctes; ſeing theſe ſo authentically recorded in the holie Scripture, are euen as ſtrange to ſenſual men, as anie others which they reiect, or deride. Wheras alſo Gods prouidence and promiſe, was not only for the Apoſtles time, but alſo for al times ſo much as is neceſſarie in euerie Countrie, this grace of miracles haith bene, and ſtil is geuen. In ſo much, that it hath alwaies bene moſt truly ſaid of ſome of the Church, that [by word and deedes [in vertue of ſignes and wonders, in the ver-

L 3   tue of

tue of the Holie Ghoſt, they haue preached, plan- *Mar*. 10.
ted, and wattered] the faith of Chriſtes Goſpel [our *v*. 20.
Lord woorking withal, and confirming the word
with ſignes that folowed.]

God is one, and there can not be anie other God.

ARTICLE 6.

Henceforth we are to ſpeake of ſpecial Ar-ticles in parti-cular.

HAning alreadie ſhewed in general, the prin-ciples of Chriſtian Doctrine : that faith is neceſſaric to ſaluation ; that it is the gift of God ; grounded in his word ; either written in Ca-nonical Scripture ; or deliuered by Tradition, agrea-ble to the written word ; and in ſome caſes confirmed by his miraculous workes : Now we are to declare in particular, the more eſpecial pointes of Faith ; that God is one in ſubſtance ; three in perſons ; that he is omnipotent ; knoweth al thinges ; is goodnes it ſelf, with other attributes. Then the creatió of al thinges, namely of Angels, & men ; the Redemption of Man ; by Chriſt ; God and man ; Mans ſanctification ; in the Catholique Church ; and the laſt Iudgment, ac-cording to euerie ones final deſertes, to eternal glo-rie or paine.

Al Chriſtians, Iewes, & Tur-kes, acknow-lege one God. Other Nations ſerue manie falſe Goddes.

2 Concerning therfore the firſt point, al Chriſtians, yea alſo Iewes & Turkes, doe acknowlege, that there is one only God, the Creator, Conſeruer, and Lord of al thinges. But moſt Heathen Nations doe think there be manie Gods, and doe ſeuerally ſerue diuers Idoles for God : Though God alſo among them, as S. Paul teacheth [haith not left him ſelf without te- *Act*. 14.
ſtimonie, being beneficial from heauen, geuing raines *v*. 16.
and fruitful ſeaſons, filling our hartes with foode & gladnes.] And euer from the creation of the world [his inuiſible thinges, his eternal power, and Diui- *Rom*. I.
nitie *v*. 20.

nitie, are feene, being vnderftoode by thofe things
that are made .] Which natural knowledge, either
of Iewes, Turkes, Heritikes, or other Infidels, ma- And are inex-
cufable.
Rom . 1. keth them [inexcufable, not glorifying God as they
v . 20. know him] but doth not auaile them to iuftification
21 . without true faith . For it is only the true Catholique faith , wherby we beleue , not only that there
is but one God , but alfo that al other things whatfoeuer he reuealeth by his word , are likewife moft
affuredly true , euen for his only auctoritie, abftrac-
ting from al other reafons and perfwafions , which
may moue vs therunto . For this only is the true faith,
the fame which is in the whole Church; wheras o-
therwife it were but our owne priuate conceipt, o-
pinion, or perfwafion .

3   Albeit therfore, we nothing at al doubt in this
point : yet if not for more confirmation, at leaft for
more actual exercife of our faith, I fhal recite fome Our faith in
one God, is
proued by holy
Scriptures.
And firft by the
bookes of the
Law.
holie Scriptures, which exprefly teftify and admo -
nifh vs, that there is but one only God . So doth
Gen . 1. Moyfes inftruct vs, writing that [God (our Lord
v . 1. 6. God) created heauen and earth, the firmament, the
Pf. 145. waters, and al things that are in them] vifible &
v . 6. inuifible , euen the Idoles , the falfe gods, whether
Deut . they be diuels, or men, or other things, are accor-
10. *v*. ding to their natures, the creatures of God . Him
17 . Melchizedech calleth [God the higheft, which cre-
Gen . 14. ated heauen and earth .] Of him Abraham faith [I
v . 19. lift vp my hand to my Lord God moft high, poffeffor
22. of heauen and earth.] God him felf faith [*I am*
Exo . 3. *which am* . Thus fhalt thou fay to the children of If-
v . 14. rael; He which is, hath fent me to you] wheras al
creatures, are thofe fpecial things which they are
made to be : fome are Angels, fome are men, fome
are ftarres, fome are elements, and fo of the reft ;
but [God is he which is] al in al, Immenfe, without

out limite. This is that name which God reuealed
to Moyſes when he ſaid [I am the Lord, that ap- *Exod.6.*
peared to Abraham, to Iſaac, and to Iacob, as God *v.3.*

The name of
God conſiſting
of four letters
(which the
Iewes doe not
pronounce)
ſignifieth :
He which is.

almightie, & my name A D O N A I : I did not ſhew
them.] When he gaue his Commandements, he
began thus. [I am the Lord thy God : Thou ſhalt *Exo.20.*
not haue ſtrange Gods before me ;] which in the re- *v.1.2.*
petition of the Law, is more clearly expreſſed [Our *Deut.4.*
Lord he is God, and there is none other beſides him.] *v.35.*
Againe thus [Heare Iſrael; the Lord our God, is one *Deut.32.*
Lord.] And in the ſummarie concluſion of the ſame *v.39.*
Law, it is thus explicated. [See ye that I am onlie *Ioſ.2.*
and there is none other God beſides me.] *v.11.*

By the Hiſtoir-
cal bookes.

4 Rahab in Iericho, indued with true faith, pro- *Heb.11.*
feſſed one God before the diſcouerers, whom Ioſue *v.31.*
ſent ſaying to them. [The Lord your God, he is God *Ioſ.22. v.*
in heauen aboue, and in the earth beneth.] The *22.34.*
Tribes of Iſrael which dwelt in Galaad [called their
Altar which they built by the bankes of Iordan ; their
[teſtimonie, that our Lord he is God ; the moſt mightie God our Lord.] King Salomon in the conclu- *3.Reg.8.*
ſion of his deuout praier, in the firſt Dedication of *v.59.60.*
the Temple [beſought God to direct him and al his
people Iſrael, day by day ; that al the peoples of the
earth may know, that our Lord he is God, and there
is none other beſides him.] The Prophet Elias with *3.Reg.18.*
great zeale, expoſtulated with the People of Iſra- *v.21.*
el, that would ſeme to temporize betwene God and
Baal, rather wiſhing them to ſerue Baal only, (becauſe there can be no more Gods but one) then to
ſerue both him and God ſaying : [how long ſhalt you
on two ſides? if our Lord be God, folow him, but
if Baal, folow him.] Holie Tobias in captiuitie, *Tob.13.*
exhorteth his brethrē, to geue thankes to our Lord, *v.3.4.*
and in the ſight of the Gentiles, to praiſe him [becauſe he hath therfore diſperſed you among the Gentiles

tiles, which know not him, that you may declare his meruelous workes, and make them know, that there is none other God omnipotent befides him .] A-

Iudith . 5 .
v. 9.
chior an Ammonite, boldly reported to Holofernes, that the [Israelites, (hauing long before departed frō Mesopotamia where was multitude of Gods) worshiped one God of heauen .]

Pſal. 13. 5
v. 1.
Pſal. 17.
v. 32.
Pſal. 83.
v. 10.
Pſ. 89 .
v. 2. Pſ.
95. v. 5.
148. v.
13. 150.
v. 6.
Iſa. 40.
v. 12.

v. 13 .)
14.

18.

19.
25.
26.

The Royal Prophet eſtemeth it the greateſt igno- rance that may be, to ſay [there is no God] and no leſſe wickednes, to acknowledg anie other God but one . [For who (ſaith he) is God, but our Lord? or who is God, but our God ?] And therfore to God he ſaith [Thou only art God, from euerlaſting euen to euerlaſting thou art God ; becauſe al the gods of the Gentiles are diuels, our Lordes name alone is ex- alted. Let euerie ſpirit praiſe our Lord.] The ſame doe al other Prophets verie often vrge againſt Ido- laters. Let one or two ſentences ſerue for example of manie. Iſaias thus writeth of the incomparable Maieſtie of God . [who hath meaſured the waters with his fiſt, and pondered the heauens with a ſpāne? Who hath poyſed with three fingers, the huge great- nes of the earth, & weyed the mountaines in weight, and the litle hilles in balance? Who hath holpen the ſpirit of our Lord, or who hath bene his coun - ſeler and ſhewed to him? With whom hath he ta- ken counſel, and who hath inſtructed him, and taught him the path of Iuſtice, and taught him knowlege, and ſhewed him the way of prudence? To whom then haue you made God like? Or what Image wil you ſet to him? Hath the artificer caſt a ſculp- tile? or hath the gold-ſmith figured it with gold, or the ſiluer-ſmith with plates of ſiluer? And to whom haue you likened me, & made me equal, ſaith the ho- lie one? Lift vp your eyes on high and ſee, who haith created theſe thinges? He that bringeth out

By the Pro- phetes.

M   the

the hoſt of them in number; and calleth them al by
name . Thus ſaith our Lord the King of Iſrael; and   *Iſa* . 44 .
the Redemer therof; the Lord of Hoſtes : I am the   *v* . 6.
firſt, and I the laſt, and beſides me there is no God.   *Ch* . 45 .
I the Lord, and there is none els; I the Lord, & there   *v* . 5 . 26 .
is none other.] Ieremie in his Epiſtle to the Iewes   *Baruc* . 6 .
in the time of captiuitie, forewarning them to auoid   *v* . 2 . 3 . 4 .
Idolatrie, by manie and great abſurdities, in forging   7 . *&c.*
and adoring falſe gods : ſheweth how fooliſh and   *Ioel* . 2 .
ſenſeleſſe they are, that ſerue Idoles or anie Images   *v* . 17 .
for gods .

6   Moreouer beſides the zealous confeſſions, and
diligent inſtructions of Gods true ſeruantes, alſo his
profeſſed enemies, and notorious perſecutors of his

By the confeſ-
ſion of ſome
Ethniques .

faithful people, haue ſomtimes, either after chaſtiſ-
ment, or being conuinced by the ſenſible euidence
of Gods miraculous workes, acknowleged him to be
the only true omnipotent God, ſubiecting them
ſelues, & commanding al vnder their obeyſance, to
feare and ſerue him, as the only eternal God . So
King Nabuchodonoſor, after that he had bene ſeauen yeares ſo frantick, that he imagined him ſelf to
be a brutiſh beaſt, and in al reſpectes liued as a beaſt,
among beaſtes, naked, going on his handes and feete
as a four footed beaſt, gnawing the graſſe with his
teeth, and eating it as an oxe, or a horſe : being a-
gaine reſtored to vſe of reaſon, and to his former ſtate
of a King, he openly confeſſed God moſt iuſt ouer
al ſaying : [Now therfore I Nabuchodonoſor, praiſe   *Dan* . 4 .
and magnifie, and glorifie the King of Heauen; be-   *v* . 34 .
cauſe al his workes are true, and his waies iugements;
and them that walke in pride, he can humble.] So
alſo King Darius, after he had condeſcended (wicked coũſelers importunely vrging him) to caſt Daniel
into the Lyons denne, and that Daniel by Gods power was conſerued without hurt, and deliuered from
                                                    the

Dan. 6.
v. 25.
26.

the crueltie of his enemies. Thē did this King [write to al peoples, Tribes, and tongues dwelling in the whole earth. Peace be multiplied vnto you. By me a Decree is made, that in al mine Empyre, and Kingdome, they dread and feare the God of Daniel; for he is the liuing, and eternal God for euer; and his Kingdome fhal not be diffipated; and his power e-

27.

uen for euer. He is the deliuerer, and Sauiour, doing fignes and meruels in heauen, and in earth, who hath deliuered Daniel out of the Lake of the Lyons.]

7 In the new Teftament, and time of grace, which perteyneth to al Nations in the world, this doctrine of one God is moft neceffarie, to extirpate the general error of manie gods. And therfore the Apoftles, before al other pointes, moft diligently preached this, and taught it by word, rather then by writing. For preaching, not writing, is the more ordinarie meanes to couert Infidels. And this Article being once fetled in the hartes of the faithful, the Euangeliftes and other Apoftles, had leffe occafion to write thereof, then of other pointes of faith and maners, wherin Chriftians oftener fayled. Yet it is not only prefuppofed, but alfo exprefly recorded by them in fome places. By this doctrine, our B. Sauiour confuted and confounded the diuel; citing and confirming by fact and word, the Law where it is wri-

The fame faith is confirmed in the new Teftament.

Deu. 6.
v. 13.
Mat. 4.
v. 10.
Mar. 12.
v. 29.
32.

ten [The Lord thy God fhalt thou adore, and him only fhalt thou ferue.] The like our Lord anfweared to a Scribe which alfo tempted him, feking a quarel againft his doctrine, repeating vnto him thefe wordes of the Law [Heare Ifrael, the Lord thy God is one God.] Which the quareling Scribe hearing, could not but confeffe it to be true, that there is one God, and there is none other befides him.

By our Sauiours anfwers.

Act. 17.
v. 23.

8 S. Paul amongft the learned Gentiles at Athens, tooke

By S. Paul, and other Apoftles.

M 2

tooke fitte occafion of their owne iudgment, to difproue the multitude of gods whom they ferued. For
that by their fact in dedicating an Altar to the vnknowne God; they fhewed the imbecilitie of al
their fuppofed knowne gods; & that befides al them,
there is fome other moft worthy to be ferued with an
Altar, and confequently with Sacrifice, which is the
proper homage due to fupreme Dominion. Wherupon he preached to them, him whom they imagi-
ned, but knew not, to witte, [the God that made the   *v*. 24.
world, and al thinges that are in it, he being Lord   25.
of heauen and earth &c. geueth life vnto al, and
breathing, and al thinges.] After this, writing to
the Corinthians (whom in the meane time he had
conuerted to Chrift) to fhew that it is vnlawful wittingly to eate meates that were offered to Idoles:
he teacheth that [an Idol is nothing in the world,   1. *Cor*. 8.
(that is, haith no maner of diuine power in it as   *v*. 4.
Idolators imagine) & that there is no God but one.]
Againe vpon an other occafion, commending vnitie
amongft Chriftians, he proueth the neceffitie therof
by this knowne and confeffed principle ; becaufe
[there is one Lord, one faith, one baptifme; one   *Ephef*. 4.
God and Father of al, which is ouer al, and by al,   *v*. 5. 6.
and in al vs.] The fame Apoftle alfo, by way of   1. *Tim*. 1.
thankefgeuing & praifes to God, calleth him [the   *v*. 17.
King of the worldes, immortal, inuifible, *only God*.
Who onely (of himfelf) hath Immortalitie, and in-   1. *Tim*. 6.
habiteth light not acceffible, whom no mã hath fene,   *v*. 16.
yea neither can fee : to whom be honour and em-
pire euerlafting. Amen.] This is the God that faid
to S. Iohn [I am Alpha & Omega, the beginning &   *Apoc*. 1.
the end, the firft and the laft.] This is the only God,   *v*. 8.
whom heritiques and diuels can not denie, as S,   *Ch*. 21.
Iames noteth, arguing the Solifideans [Thou b le-   *v*. 6. *Ch*.
ueft (faith he to his aduerfarie) that there is one God;   22. *v*. 13.
thou

Confeffed by
the diuels.

Iac.2. thou doſt wel; the diuels alſo beleue and tremble]
v.19. So vndoubted a truth it is, that Iewes, Turkes, He-
rit'ques, and diuels confeſſe it, and in their maner, verie vnproperly, beleue it.

9 Al which notwithſtanding, if it were tollerable
to find vpon the bare letter, without conference of
place, contentious ſpirits that would proue pluralitie o Gods, may finde holie Scriptures which found
for their purpoſe, geuing the name of God, to creatures. For [God himſelf (our Lord God) ſaid to
Exo.7. Moyſes; Behold I haue appointed thee the God of
v.1. Pharao, & Aaron thy brother ſhal be thy Prophet.]
Alſo in the Iudicial precepts of Moyſes Law it is written. If a ſeruant that may be made free, wil of his
Exo.21. owne accord, remaine bound [his Lord ſhal preſent
v.6. him to the gods] that is to ciuil, & temporal Iudges,
that they may in a certaine pre ſcribed maner, ratifie
the couenant, and he ſhal be his bond-man for euer.
Ch.22. Likewiſe for trial of ſome kind of theft [the maiſter
v.8. of the houſe (who had the cuſtody of the thing that
is ſtollen) ſhal be brought to the gods (meaning
to the Iudges) and he ſhal ſweare that he did not extend his hand vpon his neighboures good.] Another Precept prouiding that due reuerence be obſerued to Iudges and Princes : is expreſſed in theſe wor-
Ibidem. des. [Thou ſhalt not detract from the gods : and the
v.28. Prince of thy people, thou ſhalt not curſe] which S.
Act.23. Paul applieth to the high Preiſt. The Royal Prophet
v.5. in his pſalēs ſaith :[The God of gods our Lord hath
Pſ.49. ſpokē. God ſtoode in the aſſemblie of gods, & in the
v.2. middeſt he iudgeth goddes.] Which can not be vn-
pſ.81. derſtoode only of falſe goddes, though he is alſo God
v.1. and iudge of them, but of men in eminent auctoritie,
who repreſent God, amongſt whom God ſitteth, &
whom God wil iudge. For God him ſelf ſaith to them
in the ſame pſalme. [I ſaid ; you are goddes, & the

Some men are
called goddes

Moyſes called
God.

Iudges, Prin-
ces, & Preiſtes,
called goddes.

M 3   ſonnes

fonnes of the higheft :] By al which places a wran-   *v. 6.*
gler may contend, that there be manie goddes.

This obiection
is anfwered,
by conference
of other textes.

10   But the true fenfe of them al, may be gathered
by the laft cited, which our Sauiour alledgeth ; taking an Apologie or defence of his owne fpeech.
For hauing faid ; [I and the Father are one (*v um :*   *Ioan. 5.*
one thing, one in diuine fubftance :) the Iewes looke   *v. 18.*
vp ftones,to ftone him] as a blafphemer, [becaue (fay   *Io. 10. v.*
they) thou being a man, makeft thy felf God.]   *30. 31.*
Wherupon our Lord , not further explicating the high   *33. &c.*
mifterie of his true Godhead, to fo vnworthie audience, but equiuocating In this cafe, anfweared them,

Men in eminét
auctoritie do
not only parti-
cipate of Gods
power, but alfo
of his name .

[Is it not written in your Law, that ; *I faid, you are*
Goddes ? If he called them Goddes to whom the word
of God was made, and the Scripture can not be bro-   *Pf. 81.*
ken : whom the father haith fanctified and fent into   *v. 6.*
the world, fay you ; that thou blafphemeft, becaufe
I faid, I am the Sonne of God.] By which anfwear,
our Sauiour infinuateth, that albeit God, fignifiyng   *Sap. 14.*
the Diuine nature and abfolute Effenfe, is the incó-   *v. 21.*
municable name that can not be geuen to anie creature : yet if he were not God, he might without
blafphemie be called the Sonne of God; or God, as
fome men by participatió are called goddes, to whó
Goddes word is committed to teach others , and to
whó Goddes auctoritie is geuen to gouerne & iudge
others. [But fuch Goddes fhal die as men (faith the   *Pf. 81.*
pfalmift) and (if they peruert Goddes word or wil)   *v. 7.*
fhal fal as one of the Princes.] S. Paul alfo expoundeth al fuch fpeaches faying : [although there be ,   *1. Cor. 8*
that are called goddes, either in heauen or in earth ,   *v. 5. 6.*
(for there are manie Goddes, and manie Lordes)
yet to vs there is one God the Father , of whom al
thinges, and we vnto him : and one Lord Iefus Chrift,
by whom al thinges, and we by him .] So thefe holie Scriptures proue not pluralitie of Goddes, againft
other

other holie Scriptures, which clearly fhew, that there is but one God, and that befides him, there is none other God, but fhew the excellent offices of Goddes Lieutenants in earth, with participation of his aucto-ritie, and alfo of his name . And al holie Scriptures are moft true, & being rightly explaned, haue a true fenfe, and [are profitable (as the fame Apoftle auoucheth) to teach, to argue, to correct, and to inftruct in iu-ftice, that the man of God may be perfect, inftructed to euerie good worke .

2. Tim.
3. v. 16.
17.

The Scriptures aboue cited, doe indede proue the ex-cellencie of Gods cheefe Minifters.

In God is Trinity of Perfons, the Father, and the Sonne, and the Holie Ghoft.

ARTICLE. 7.

IN the old Teftament, the children of Ifrael were commanded [to eate al the Pafchal Lambe ; the head with the feete and entrals they muft deuour. Neither muft there remaiue anie thing therof vntil morning. If anie thing were left (not eaten) it muft be burnt with fire.] In the new Teftament Chrift our Sauiour commanded his Apoftles [to teach al na-tions, baptizing them in the name of the Father, & of the Sonne, and of the Holie Ghoft .] Where it is fuppofed that they muft teach, and the people muft learne the high mifterie, of three diuine perfons in one fubftace, which hath this fenfe, that in al points of Chriftian doctrine, which our natural reafon can not comprehend, we muft by the fire of Goddes grace inflaming our hartes f captiuate our vnderftanding vnto the obedience of Chrift, who fo reuealing, we muft beleue, that there is one Perfon of the Father, an other of the Sonne, & an other of the Holie Ghoft : that euerie perfon is God, and yet but one God.

Exod. 12.
v. 10.

Mat. 28.
v. 19.

2. Cor.
10. v. 5.

The Myfterie of the B. Tri-nitie, muft be beleued, but can not be ful-ly vnderftood in this life.

2 And the fame may, though not demonftratiuely

tiuely or plainly, yet notwithstanding (as the Church
speaketh) credibly, in some sorte, be declared .

A breefe de-
claration of
three Duine
persons in one
substance.

For God being one , by vnderstanding him selfe
begetteth him self, and is begotten; who in respect
he begetteth, is God the Father, in repspect he is begotten is God the Sonne. Likewise this one God
as being both Father and Sonne, loueth him self, and
in respect he loueth, he produceth him self, in respect
he is loued him self is produced ; and so from the Father and from the Sonne, procedeth an other person
God the Holie Ghost. Thus we beleue and confesse
three diuine Persons, and one God. Againe in respect of producing and not proceding, the Father fró
whom, both the Sonne and the Holie Ghost, diuersly proceede, is called the first Person. The Sonne proceding from the Father by generation, and together
with the Father, producing the Holie Ghost, is called the second Person. And the Holie Ghost no way
producing, but only proceding, and that by produc-
tion, not by generation, is called the third Person.
Yet must we not imagine, that this order in the diuine Persons, of first, second, and third , importeth
anie thing at al, firster, or later, greater or lesse; neither may we thinke, that euer God was not the Father, or was not the Sonne, or was not the Holie
Ghost. For as God in his substance wherin he is
one : euen so in his notional relations wherin he is
three, is euerie way, and in al respectes, eternal, immense, immutable, omnipotent, one & the self same
God, and al the diuine persons coeternal, of the same
equal immensitie, immutabilitie, omnipotencie, maiestie, & consubstantialitie .

It must be
humbly be-
leued, not ouer
curiously dis-
cussed.

3   Neuerthelesse for so much as in none other Article of our belife, can be more greeuous errour, if
anie wilfully persist in false opinion, nor more difficultie, how to thinke, and how to speake, then in
                                                    this

this higheſt pointe of the B. Trinitie, it behoueth vs in ſtead of ſutle diſcuſſing that which we know excedeth our capacitie, rather to relie vpon the Churches faith, then vpon our owne, or anie other priuate conceipt, and withal vpon holie Scriptures, as the ſame [piller of truth] vnderſtandeth & expoũdeth them. For ſo albeit the word *Trinitie*, is not extant in al the holie Bible, neither the word *Perſon*, in this ſenſe, to ſignifie diſtinction of diuine perſons: yet the miſterie it ſelf is ſufficiently proued to ſatisfie an humble Chriſtian, but not ſo plainly as wil conuince an obſtinate Iew, a wilful pagane, or a wrangling Heritique, interpreting Goddes word by his owne priuate ſpirit.

1. *Tim.* **3.** *v*.15.

4   To begin therfore with the old Teſtament, this holie Miſterie is proued by the hebrew text of the verie firſt wordes of holie Scripture [In the beginning God created heauen and earth:] and in the next verſe: [the Spirit of God moued ouer the waters.] The word God, in hebrew *Elohim*, is of the plural number (wherof the ſingular is *Eloha*,) and ſo ſignifieth pluralitie, and muſt needes be vnderſtoode of perſons, becauſe God is only one in ſubſtance, the verbe *bara*, in engliſh *created*, is of the ſingular number, and by vſe of holie Scriptures is appropriated to the Father, of whom are al thinges, Likewiſe the word beginning, is appropriated to the Sonne, becauſe in him were created al thinges in heauen and in earth, viſible and inuiſible. [He the beginning, the firſt borne.] And the wordes *Spirit of God*, are appropriated to the Holie Ghoſt. As where the Prophet Daniel ſaith. [Thou ſhalt ſend forth thy Spirit, and they ſhal be created.] So we haue in the word *Elohim*, pluralitie, in other wordes, particular mention of the three diuine perſons miſtically inſinuated. Againe pluralitie of perſons is ſignified, when God ſaid,

Gen. 1. *v*.1.2. *Iob.* 12. *v*.4.*Ch.* 36.*v*.2. *Dan* 2. 28. *Hab.* 1. *v*.11. *Ch.*3. *v*.3. 1.*Cor.* 8. *v*.6. *Coloſ.* 1. *v*.16. 18. *Io.* 8.*v*.25. *Pſ.* 103. *v*.30.

Pluralitie of Goddes ſignified by holy Scripture muſt needes be vnderſtood of perſons.

N   Let vs

[Let vs make man to our owne image & likenes] the
wordes *vs* & *our* importing more persós, but *image* &
liknes one in substáce. The same doctrine is gathered
in other places. God appearing to Abraham in forme
of three men [Abraham saw three and adored] as
appeareth by his wordes, but one. For so he spake
as to one [Lord if I haue found grace in thy sight
goe not past thy seruant :] and forthwith as to moe,
[wash ye your feete, and rest ye, for therfore are ye
come aside to your seruant.] So also Moyses writeth
in the same place, both as of moe, and as of one saying : [When they had eaten, they said] a litle after
[he said, Our Lord said ; and our Lord departed, after that he had ceased to speake vnto Abraham.]

Gen . 1.
v . 26.

Gen . 18.
v . 1 . 2 . 3.
4. 5.

v . 9.
13 . 17 . 33.

Gen . 19.
v . 1 . 24.

**Sometimes
but two Persós
signified.**

Two Persons also of the B . Trinitie seme to be signified, aswel by the two Angels coming to Lot, in
the shape of two men, as by Moyses wordes writing,
that [our Lord rained brimstone and fire from our
Lord.] But three persons are more distinctly vnderstoode by the ordinarie solemne blessing prescribed
in these wordes [Our Lord blesse thee, & kepe thee :
our Lord shew his face to thee, and haue mercie vpon

Num . 6.
v . 24 . 25.
26.

**Three effectes
appropriated
to the three
Diuine persós.**

thee : our Lord turne his countenance vnto thee, &
geue thee peace.] Where our Lord thrice recited,
with the special desired effectes, may verie aptly be
appropriated, the first to the Father, the second to the
Sonne, and the third to the Holie Ghost. And by like
special termes, Iob semeth to distinguish the same
diuine persons, attributing to the Father *strength* &
power, to the Sonne, *wisdome*, & *spirit* to the Holie
Ghost saying thus of God : [In his strength sodenly
the seas are gathered together ; and with his wisdom
he stroake the prowde man ; his Spirit haith adorned the heauen .

Iob . 26.
v . 12.
13.

5   The Royal Prophet foresheweth the Church of
Christ praying for Goddes *mercie, blessing, & illumi-*
nation, three graces appropriated to the three diuine

persons; And concluding the pfalme, thrice inuocateth God the Bleffed Trinitie thus [God; our God
bleffe vs; God bleffe vs.] In an other pfalme he inuiteth al Chriftians to render praife to the B. Trinitie, for the Incarnation of the Sonne of God faying:
[Sing ye to our Lord a new fong; fing to our Lord
the whole earth; fing ye to our Lord, and bleffe his
name.] In like maner profecuting the fame inuitation faith : [Bring to our Lord ye Families of *Gen*-
tiles; bring ye to our Lord glorie, and honor; bring
to our Lord glorie vnto his name.] In both places,
our Lord is thrice named, to fignifie that eueri perfon of the B, Trinitie, is our Lord, but concludeth
in one name : becaufe there are not three Lordes but
one Lord. At an other time he confeffeth the fame
ineftimable benefite of the incarnatiõ, to be the work
of the whole Trinitie, faying : [The right hand of
our Lord hath wrought ftrength; the right hand of
our Lord hath exalted me; the right hand of our
Lord haith wrought ftrength] yet not three right
handes, but one right hand. The Prophet Ifaias faw
and heard in a vifion, that [the Angelical Seraphimes
cried one to an other and faid, Holie, Holie, Holie,
the Lord God of Hoftes] reciting thrice Holie, to
the three dinine perfons, al one God of Hoftes.

6 In fome places, diftinct mention is made of
fome one diuine perfon, and not of the other. As
in Daniels prophecie, the Father alone femeth to be
defcribed thus. [Thrones were fet, and the ancient
of daies fate; his vefture white as fnow, & the haires
of his head, as cleane wolle, his Throne flames of
fire.] He is called ancient of daies, not only becaufe
he is eternal, for fo are alfo the Sonne and the Holie
Ghoſt; but rather becaufe in order of diftinguifhing
the perfons, he is firft, from whom the other two perfons procede, and he from none. In an other part of
the

Pf. 66.
v.1.8.
Pf. 95.
v.1.2.

v.7.
8.

*Pf.*117.
v.16.

Ifa.6.
v.3.

Dan.7.
v.9.

God thrice in-
uocated in one
breefe prayer,

Not three
Lordes but
one Lord.

Al workes of
God in crea-
tures, are the
workes of al
the B. Trini-
tie.

Somtimes mẽ-
tion is made
of one Diuine
perfon, only of
God the Fa-
ther.

Of God the
Sonne.

the fame prophecie, the Prophet praying, fometh to
direct his praier to the Sonne, faying : [Now ther-   *Dan .9 .*
fore heare, o our God, the petition of thy feruant,   *v . 17 .*
and his praiers, and fhew thy face vpon thy fanctu-
arie which is defert, for thine owne fake] that is, for
thine owne merites, which can only be vnderftoode
of that diuine perfon, which is incarnate, who by his
humanitie merited for the Church . And fo muft that
neceffarily be vnderftoode only of the Sonne of God
which is written by Habacuc the Prophet in his Canticle [God wil come from the South, and the holie   *Hab . 3 .*
one from the mount Pharan ;] a cleare prediction of   *v . 3 .*
Chrifts Natiuitie, who was borne in Bechelem, fitu-
ated fouthward frō Ierufalem . As alfo it is the fpeach
of God the Sonne, written by the Prophet Zacharie
faying : [They fhal looke toward me whom they   *Zach. 12 .*
pearced] verified when fome Iewes were conuerted   *v . 10 .*
after they had crucified the Sonne of God . Of the

Of God the
Holie Ghoft.

Holie Ghoft, Nehemias maketh mention as is verie
commonly vnderftoode, where amongft other benefites beftowed vpon the children of Ifrael, he recoū-
teth diuine infpirations, faying to God : [Thou ga-   *2 . Efd . 9 .*
ueft them thy good Spirit, which fhould teach them.]   *v . 20 .*
By Ezechiel, God fpeaketh thus [I wil put my Spi-   *Ezech . 36 .*
rit in the middeft of you .] And the Prophet Za-   *v . 26 . 27 .*
charie fpeaking of finners which refift the Holie Ghoft   *Zach . 7 .*
faith : [They made their hart as the Adamaut, left   *v . 12 .*
they fhould heare the Law, and the wordes which
the Lord fent in his Spirit by the handes of his for
mer Prophets .] In which and the like places, the
Spirit of God, is diftinguifhed from God, as one perfon from an other .

This higheft
Myfterie is,
more exprefly
reuealed in the
newTeftamēt.

7   In the new Teftament this mifterie of three di -
uine perfons in one fubftance, is more exprefly reuealed . As when our Sauiour was baptized, al the three   *Mat . 3 .*
perfons feuerally appeared, the *Father,* by a voice   *v . 16 . 17 .*
from

from heauen, teftifying that this is his Sonne which there appeared in humanitie affumpted; and God the *Holie Ghoft* appeared defcending as a doue. Againe the Father appeared by the like voice in our Sauiours Transfiguration teftifying the fame, that this is his Sonne in whom he is wel pleafed; the Holie Ghoft was reprefented in the bright cloude.] Moreouer the Holie Ghoft, as proceding from the Father, and from the Sóne, is fignified by our Sauiour in one place faying: [The Paraclite the Holie Ghoft, whom the Father wil fend in my name] In an other place [When the Paraclite cometh whom I wil fend you from the Father] and as he addeth there [which procedeth from the Father] fo repeating afterwardes [I wil fend him to you] he addeth alfo [he fhal *receiue of mine,* and fhal fhew to you.] But the moft principal proofe is by the forme of Chrftian baptifme prefcribed by our Sauiour to his Apoftles in thefe wordes [Going teach al Nations, baptizing them in the name of the Father, and of the Sonne, and of the Holie Ghoft] expref-fing the three perfons, not in the names, but fingu-larly, in the name, becaufe al three are one God. The next principal proofe is, by the wordes of S. Iohn the Apoftle faying : [There be three which geue te-ftimonie in heauen, the Father, the Word, and the Holie Ghoft] by the Word, fignifying the Sonne, the eternal word of the Father [the word which is made flefh.]

8   That the Sonne is God equal and confubftantial with the Father and the Holie Ghoft, and that the Holie Ghoft is alfo God, equal and confubftantial with the Father and the Sonne; is further proued by manie holie Scriptures, where the Incarnation of Chrift, the Remiffion of finnes, fanctificatió of foules, and other workes proper to God, are afcribed to the Soone, or to the Holie Ghoft; and particularly S.

Al three perfós are equal, and confubftantial.

Margin references:
Mat. 17. *v.* 5.
Ioa. 14. *v.* 26. *Ch.* 15. *v.* 26. *Ch.* 16. *v.* 7. 14.
Mat. 28. *v.* 19.
1. *Ioa.* 5. *v.* 7. *Ioan.* 1. *v.* 14.
Mat. 1. *v.* 20. *Luc.* 1. *v.* 35. *Io.* 20. *v.* 22. *Act.* 28. *v.* 25.

Paul

Paul calleth the Holie Ghost [one Spirit, one Lord, *Rom.* 15.
one God, one and the fame Spirit.]   *v.* 16.

Heretical ob-
iections. 9   Neuerthelefle, as the Iewes reiect al the proofes *1. Cor.* 12.
which Chriftians make out of the old Teftament, & *v.* 4. 5.
fcorne to heare anie thing of the new : So Arrius, Eu- 6. 11.
nomius, Macedonius, & their folowers, not only find
euafions againft al that can be alledged of holie Scrip
tures, but alfo pretend and vrge other apparent texts
to proue inequalitie in thefe three Perfons, and fo
contend that either there are three Goddes, greater
and lefle : or els that neither the Sonne, nor the Holie Ghoft, is God. Againft the Sonne of God, they
alledge his owne wordes [the Father is greater then *Io.* 14.
I.] Againft the Holie Ghoft, the wordes of S. Paul *v.* 28.
[the Spirit him felf requefteth for vs, with gronings *Rom.* 8. *v*
vnfpeakable. And he that fearcheth the hartes, know 26. 27.
eth what the Spirit defireth.] wherupon they inferre,
Seing the Father is greater, the Sonne is not equal;
and feing the holie Ghoft requefteth, and defireth,
he can not be God; for God neither wanteth anie
thing, nor defireth, but hath al thinges.

Anfwerrs. 10   Holie Church anfweareth to the firft, that our
Sauiour Chrift according to his manhood, is inferi-
or to his Father : according to his Godhead, he is
equal with the Father. To the fecond, that the Holie Ghoft is faid to defire and requeft, in that he maketh the faithful to defire and requeft good thinges.
For whe they pray or fpeake that which is to Goddes
glorie, it is [the Holie Ghoft that fpeaketh in them] *Mat.* 10.
by teaching and infpiring them [what to pray, & *v.* 20
what to fpeake] as the Euangeliftes report our Sa- *Mat.* 13.
uiours doctrine, appropriating the confeffion of truth *v.* 11.
and other good workes, to the gratious gift of the *Luc.* 12.
Holie Ghoft : Who with the Father, and the Sonne, *v.* 12.
is one God.

A general anf-
wer to al wrag-
lers. 11   But when anie are contentious, oppofing Scrip- *Rom.* 12.
ture *v.* 6.

ture againſt Scripture, admitting no ſenſe therof but
their owne; then muſt we hold faſt the Rule of faith

2. Tim. and forme of ſound Doctrine, kepe the good *Depo-*
1.v.13. *ſitum,* beleue and confeſſe that faith wherein al nati-
14. ons are baptized [In the name of the Father, and of
the Sonne, and of the Holie Ghoſt, one God; for

*Rom.*11. of him, and by him, and in him, are al thinges . To
v. 36. him be glorie for euer. Amen.]

God is Omnipotent.

ARTICLE 8.

THe natures of al creatures, are beſt knowne
by their definitions, conſiſting of their eſſential partes , or by their deſcriptions, which
conſiſt of ſome eſſential part, if anie be knowne, &
ſuch particnlar proprieties, or other accidents, fewer, or more, as agree to them only, and to none o-
ther thing. And ſo names are geuen them anſwea-
rable to their natures; wherby one man vnderſtandeth an other, ſpeaking of the ſame thinges. But the
nature of the Creator being infinite, can not be defined, nor by anie deſcription, fully declared; nor
comprehended by anie creature. For neither can his
proprieties be ſufficiently conceiued, nor anie name
accommodated to him, wherby like knowlege may
be atteyned of him, as of his creatures, by reaſon of
the infinite difference betwene him and them. Only we know obſcurely, certaine proprieties, and ſpecial names aſcribed vnto him, by which we conceiue
that one thing there is which created al other thinges,
of whom al haue their being, and on whom they al
depend.

2 Such proprieties, as we in ſome ſorte conceiue,
are gathered out of the conſideration, of his incomparable

God being in-
finite, can not
be defined, nor
fully deſcribed.

Certaine pro-
prieties of
God, are

parable excellencies, aboue al creatures. For wheras al creatures (that is to fay, al thinges but one)
had a beginning, he alone had no beginning, but is
eternal. Secondly al creatures haue their limited natures; he alone is immenfe, without anie limitation.
Thirdly al creatures in their proper nature, are or
fomtime were mutable; he only is altogether immutable. Fourthly al creatures haue fome power geuen
them more or leffe; he only hath al power, and that
of him felf. Fiftly certeine creatures haue fome know
lege diuerfly, more and leffe; he alone hath al knowlege. Sixtly al creatures by their creatió were good,
fome alfo by fpecial grace, were, and fome are good;
the Creator only is abfolutely, and of him felf good,
yea goodneffe it felf. According to thefe, and the
like moft excellent proprieties: fpecial names are geuen to this only Creator of al. Of which, the moft
proper name is that which him felf fhewed to Moyfes [HE WHICH IS.] For fo he called
him felf faying: [I am which am] and commanded
Moyfes to tel the children of Ifrael that [*He which
is* had fent him to them:] who is alfo called *Ens ab-
folutum*, or *Ens entium*. The abfolute being; or the
being of al thinges. But his moft vfual name is *God*,
which in many tongues, and namely in ours, appeareth to be deriued oƒ *Good*; becaufe he is *al Good*, &
that of himfelfe; and therfore is goodneffe it felf:
[For there is none other (abfolutely) good but only God.] Manie other names are alfo expreffed in
holie Scriptures, wherof learned holie men haue
written whole workes, intituled, *de Diuinis nomini-
bus*; of Goddes names. To the which I remitte the
learned in facred tongues.

3   For our prefent purpofe, it fhal be more fitte to
declare by holie Scriptures, the aboue mentioned
proprieties; firft of al noting, left anie miftake, that
the

the fame and al other attributes afcribed to God, as his Iuftice, Truth, Mercie, Benignitie, Longanimitie, and (which conteyneth al) his Charitie, are not in God as qualities, and other accidents are adhering to, and exifting in fubftantiue creatures. For God admitteth no maner of mixture, nor acceffarie thing, nothing in himfelf, but him felf; for al that is in him,

1. *Io.* 4. is his owne fubftance. [God is Charitie] as S. Iohn
v. 8. 16. teacheth vs; and fo God is omnipotencie it felf, wifdome it felf, Goodnes it felf, Truth it felf, and the reft. Concerning therfore the omnipotencie of God, which is peculiarly afcribed vnto him, in al the three Credes, of the Apoftles, of Nicene Councel, & of S. Athanafius, verie often in holie Scriptures, and is fo familiar with al Chriftians, to geue to God the title almightie, that here one place may fupplie for an hū-dred. His felf reuealed this name to Abraham (whē moft men ferued manie falfe goddes) for diftincti-

Gen. 17. on fake faying : [I am the God almightie.] And
v. 1. this title is fo proper to him only, that albeit Moyfes
Exo. 7. was called the God of Pharao, and others alfo called
v. 1. goddes for participation of power : yet none is cal-
Pf. 81. led Almightie, but our Lord God only. And ther-
v. 1. *&c.* fore Moyfes with the children of Ifrael, in their Canticle of thankefgeuing, when they had paffed the
Exo. 15. red fea, fang this title to God [*Omnipotent*, is his
v. 3. name.]

4 Which fame thing, is manifeftly fhewed by his workes. As by creating al thinges of nothing, wheras no creature can create anie leaft thing of nothing. For *Ex nihilo nihil fit*, according to al natural power of creatures. And if God fhould communicate power of creating to a creature, as fome futtle Chriftian Philofophers fuppofe he may (though the negatiue femeth more reafonable) yet this alfo fheweth that God only is omnipotent, for that without his

O   gift

Onlie God is omnipotent.

Proued by manie teftimonies, and confeffed by al of anie confideration.

Proued by his workes.

gift, none hath, nor can haue, this imaginarie power. Likewife Goddes only omnipotencie appeareth, by his conferuing al thinges in their being; by
changing them into what he pleafeth, and by deftroying what he wil into nothing. Becaufe neither anie
creature can confift as it is, but by his power; nor
be turned into an other thing, but by him as the firft
efficient caufe, or be annihilated or brought to mere
nothing, but by Goddes power only. For al that nature can worke, is to depriue thinges of their formes,
and fo change them into other thinges, but to depriue them of al formes, to bring them to nothing,
yea or to that which is called, *Materia prima* (which
is next to nothing) is only in the power of God almightie. Againe, his omnipotencie is proued, by
reftoaring thinges deftroyed, to their former natural ftate, to be the felf fame fubftance, and to haue the
fame accidentes which they had before their deftruction, which is beft exemplified, in the Refurrection
of mankind after death. For God fo raifeth and re-
ftoareth the dead, that the felf fame perfon which formerly liued, and afterwardes died, is againe liuing.
Not as in natural and artificial workes, where fomtimes of the fame matter (as of earth, waxe, mettal,
or like fubftance) fomthing is framed, afterwardes
defaced or vnmade, and againe repaired, which may
feme to be the fame thing; but indeede is an o-
ther thing of the fame fpecial kind, not the fame indiuidual. But the fame foule of man, by Goddes
omnipotent power, in the refurrection, fhal receiue
& informe, the felf fame bodie, bones, flefh, bloud,
finewes, vaines, skinne, and al which it had before
death. Wherof more in the Article of the Refurrectió.
   5   Goddes power alfo reacheth ouer and befides al
thinges that are, or haue bene, or fhal be, euen to
thinges that neuer were, or euer fhal be : Becaufe
                                                        they

Iob. 19.
v. 27.
Art. 49.

Goddes power
is without li-
mite

they can be. And fo God can make innumerable worldes, innumerable thinges, of incogitable per-fection; becaufe his infinite power, is without limite,

Pf. 113.
v. 11.
bounden only by his diuine wil. [He hath done al thinges whatfoeuer he would : & difpofed al thinges

Sap. 8.
v. 1.
fweetly.] So beleued the three children captiues in Babilon, when they anfwered King Nabuchodono-

Dan. 3.
v. 17.
18.
for faying [Behold our Lord whom we worfhip, can faue vs from the fornace of burning fire, and out of thy handes, o King, deliuer vs. But if he wil not, be it known to thee o King, that we worfhip not thy gods]

Luc. 1.
v. 37.
So the Archangel Gabriel auouched [There fhal not be impoffible with God anie word.] So our bleffed

Mat. 19.
v. 24.
26.
Sauiour teacheth, that [for a camel to paffe through the eye of a needle, with men is impoffible : but with God, al thinges are poffible.]

6   By this attribute of Goddes omnipotent power, fo prouidently fet downe, in the beginning of our Crede ; fo clearly confirmed by holie Scriptures ; & fo vniuerfally confeffed by al Chriftians : we are firm-ly ftrengthned in faith to beleue whatfoeuer foloweth in al Chriftian doctrine, how hard foeuer it otherwife feme, or impoffible by nature , and by the power of al creatures . By the fame alfo we are no leffe enco-raged and confirmed in the next Theological vertue of Hope, to pray with al confidence , and humblie to craue with affurance on Goddes part, that we fhal ob-teine in due time, al neceffarie good thinges , which we fhal aske of his bountie, who is *al good*, and *al-mightie*.

The beleefe of Gods omnipo-tencie ftrégth-neth our faith in al other pointes of Re-ligion.

It alfo ftrétgh-neth our Hope.

God

God knoweth al thinges.

ARTICLE 9.

Only God,
who is wisdom
it self increa-
ted, knoweth
al thinges.

WHosoeuer can make, or frame anie thing, *Pf. 93. v.*
necessarilie hath a competent knowlege *9.10. Pf.*
of the same thing: much more assuredly *135. v. 5 :*
God the principal maker of al thinges, doth perfectly *Pf. 138.*
know, not only al thinges, which are, and haue bene, *v. 1. 2.*
and shal be, but also which can be, though actually, *Prou. 3.*
they neuer were nor shal be. This diuine wisdome, *v. 19.*
Omniscience, and vniuersal knowlege, is an other
attribute of God, and so is God him self called the
increated wisdome; so farre excelling al created wisdome, whether it be natural and humane, or the spiritual gift of the Holie Ghost, as the Creator surpas-
seth his creatures. For al the wisdom and knowlege
which either Angels or men haue, or can haue, is the
gift of God, and the perfectest that is in them, is, as it
were a sparcle, and (as holie Scripture calleth it [a va- *Sap. 7. v.*
pour of the power of God, and a certain cincere ema- *29.*
nation, of the glorie of God omnipotent] and so is a
participation of widome increated, limited within
larger or straiter bondes, that no mere creature can
know al thinges.

Examples of
Salomon and
other.

2 [It is the glorie of God, to conceale the word] *Prou. 25.*
(saith Salomon) signifying that al misteries are not *v. 2.*
reualed. [There is a man (saith he meaning him *Eccle. 8.*
self) that daies and nightes taketh no sleepe with his *v. 16. 17:*
eyes. And I vnderstood, that man can find no rea-
son of al those workes of God, which are done vnder
the sonne : and the more he shal labour to seeke, so
much the lesse he can finde ; yea, if the wise man shal
say, that he knoweth, he is not able to finde] that is
if the wise supposeth that he knoweth al thinges, or
anie

anie thing perfectly; euen therby it appeareth, that he knoweth not his owne imperfection. King Dauid his Father, most humblie acknowledged, that God had reuealed to him some Misteries vnknowne to others saying: [Hidden thinges of thy wisdome, thou hast made manifest to me] not al hidden thinges but some. Neither could he perfectly know them, but in part as in a glasse. [For in part we knowe, (saith S. Paul) & in part we prophecie.] The Prophet Elizeus knew and foretolde to the Sunamite woman, who had bene long barren, that she should haue a sonne, but knew not when the same afterwardes dyed, til the mother was come to him for comforth, & lay lamenting at his feete; for then he said [Her soule is in anguish, and our Lord hath hid it from me, and hath not told me.] So al the Prophets knew more or lesse, as God reuealed to them.

Ps. 50. v, 8.

1. Cor. 13. v. 9. 12.

4. Reg. 4. v. 16.

v. 27.

Prophetes that knew manie Mysteries, but not al.

3 He only knoweth al, who made al, disposeth al, and gouerneth al. As we may partly know by his workes, if we consider but the workes of nature, how admirable they are: for we easilie conceiue, that the auctor of nature, excedeth al our admiration. If we then compare manie thinges together, to see how diuersly they represent the wisdome of him that made them al, their manifold differences, with mutual correspondences and inexplicable powers, proprieties, and al their qualities, shew that there is none end of Goddes knowlege, trulie called *Omniscience*. Or if we wil also reflect into our selues (for Angels are tooto excellent, and are placed aboue the celestial Spheres to vs inuisible) euen mans person consisting of spirit the inuisible soule, and earthlie bodie; we find a litle world, a smal momentarie parcel of the great world, framed by the infinite wisdom of God, made of nothing, by omnipotent power, ordeyned to eternal glorie, and euerlasting felicitie, by his ab-

Gods infinite knowlege appeareth by his workes.

Example in our selues.

O 3   solute

solute goodnes. And here I omitte the highest consideration of the workes of grace, as more properly
perteyning to the next attribute of Goddes goodnes,
to be explicated in the next Article.

Proued by tes-
timonie of ho-
lie Scriptures.

4   In the meane season, let vs recite some few textes
of manie in holie Scripture, which testifie Goddes
infinite wisdom, & vniuersal knowlege of al thinges;
especially exemplifying in thinges hidden from the
natural knowlege of man; in thinges known to him
before they come; and in thinges conditional which
might be, & are not in them selues, yet are in Goddes
knowlege. Of the first sort of thinges vnknowne to
man, God him self geueth instance in the number of
starres, when he blessed Abraham, and promised him
the like innumerable progenie saying : [Looke vp   *Gen*. 15.
to heauen and number the starres if thou canst. And   *v*. 5.
said to him : so shal thy seede be.] This place importeth, and experience must needes confesse, that
aswel the starres in the firmament, as the issue of A-
braham, can not be numbred: much lesse may we i-
magin that anie man can know either of both in al respects. But of Gods perfect knowlege of both these
thinges proposed, the Royal Prophet testifieth, that
[he numbreth the multitude of starres : and geueth   *Ps*. 146.
names to them al.] which sheweth, that he both ex-   *v*. 4.
actly knoweth the number of al the starres, and so
perfectly their nature, that he geueth to euerie one
a proper name according to their singular differences
and proprieties. As for the innumerable issue of A-
braham, is not only most perfectly knowne to God
euerie way: but further it pleased him to be called peculiarly [the God of Abraham. And of the seede of   *Ps*. 46.
Abraham he hath bene mindful for euer, of his Te-   *v*. 10.
stament, of his word which he commanded vnto a   *Ps*. 104.
thousad generations, which he disposed to Abraham]   *vi*. 6. 8.
with most great, meruelous, and continual benefices.   9.

                              [Becaufe

*v.*42.

[Becaufe he was mindful of his holie word, which he had vttered to Abrahã his feruãt.] But what fhal anie thinke Goddes knowlege to be of al the Iffue of

Pf. 32.
*v.*13.
14.
15.

Adam? [Our Lord hath loked from heauen, he hath feene al the children of men. From the prepared ha - bitation, he hath loked vpon al that inhabit the earth. Who made their hartes feuerally, who vnderftandeth

Pf. 43.
*v.*22.

al their workes. For he knoweth the fecrets of the hart. Our Lord knoweth the cogitations of mē, that

Pf. 93.
v. 11.

they be vaine. The hart of a wicked man is peruerfe, and (naturally to other men) vnfearchable, who fhal konw it? I the Lord that fearch the hart, and proue

*Iere.*17.
*v.*9.10.

the reynes. Great is God in counfel, and incompre - henfible in cogitation, whofe eyes are open vpon al the waies of the children of Adam. Thus faith our

*Iere.*32.
v. 19.
*Ezech.*11.
v. 5.
*Prou.*15.
*v.*3.
*Gen.*1.2.
3. *&c.*
4. *Reg.*
6.*v.* 9.
12. 17.
*Ezech.*8.
*v.*10.11.

Lord; So haue you fpoken, o houfe of Ifrael, and the cogitations of your hart I know.] God alfo maketh fome men, his feruantes, to fee and know hidden thinges; fo Moyfes faw thinges paft, the creation of the world, and other thinges fucceding til his time, much more perfectly then anie could haue related. [Elizeus the Prophet faw and reuealed to the King of Ifrael, the King of Siria his fecret plottes & purpo- fes : Yea the Prophets feruant faw, a fpiritual armie of inuifible Angels, as if they had bene vifible, and the mountaine ful of horfes & of firie chariots rounde about Elizeus.] The Prophet [Ezechiel in a vifion faw abominable and fecret Idolatries committed by feuentie men, of the ancients of the houfe of Ifrael] Such examples abound in the holie Scriptures. Pa- ganes alfo confeffe infinite knowlege to be in God.

God imparteth knowlege of fome fecret thinges to fom perfons.

*Efth.*16.
*v.*1.4.

[King Artaxerxes, by publique Edict, admonifhed al his Dukes, Princes, and Peoples of his hundred twen - tie feauen Prouinces, which obeyed his commande - ment, that they fhould feare the fetence of God who feeth al chinges.] Much more doe the faithful know

that

that [Great is our Lord, and great is his ſtrength, & of his wiſdome there is no number .]

Pſ. 146. *v.* 5.

Al times are preſent to God.

5   Neither is Gods wiſdome limited in reſpect of time. For he being eternal, the thinges that with men are to come, are with him preſent. As alſo the thinges which to vs are paſt, are to God preſent and permanent. For with him, there is no time nor mutation, but al eternitie. Only in this tranſitorie world [there is a time for al buſines (ſaith the wiſe King) and opportunitie & much affliction to man, becauſe he is ignorant of thinges paſt, and thinges to come he can know by no meſſenger] In ſo much that amongſt other prooſes, it is an eſpecial ſigne of a true prophet, to foreſhew hidden thinges to come. And therupon the Prophet Iſaias, prouoked the falſe prophets, and their falſe goddes ſaying : [Let them come and tel vs, what thinges ſoeuer are to come; tel the former thinges what they haue bene, and we wil ſet our hart, and ſhal know the later endes of them, & tel vs the thinges that are to come. Shew what thinges are to come herafter, and we ſhal know that you are goddes. The ſame kind of prooſe God him ſelf propoſeth, to ſhew the vanitie of falſe goddes ſaying : [Who is like to me; let him cal and declare, and let him expound me the order ſince I appointed the ancient people; the thinges to come, and that ſhal be hereafter, let them ſhew vnto them.] Wel did the Prophet Ezechiel conſider that only God knoweth what his diuine goodnes wil bring to paſſe. When not able to anſwer the thing that God demanded of him [whether the drie bones which he ſaw, ſhould liue ? he ſaid : Lord God thou knoweſt] Wherupon God made him to know that they ſhould liue, ſhewing the ſame to him in viſion.

Eccle. 8. *v.* 6. 7.

Iſ. 41. *v.* 22.

v. 23. *Iſ.* 44. *v.* 7.

Ezech. 37. *v.* 4.

God gaue to diuers Patriarches fore-

6   And ſo from the beginning of this world, **God hath beſtowed the Spirit of prophecie, vpon ſome**
particular

particular perſons, for the benefite of the whole knowlege of thinges to come. Church, imparting therby the knowlege of ſundrie miſteries. Adam ſpake manie times in figure of thinges to come, which are ſince performed. [Enoch prophecied (as S. Iude witneſſith) of the general Iudgment] which is yet to come. To Noe the preacher of Iuſtice, God reuealed the diluge, commanding & inſtructing him to make the Arck, more repleniſhed And inſpired manie Prophets. with ſacred miſteries, then with mortal creatures. After the floud, Noe amongſt other Prophecies in forme of thankeſgeuing. ſaid; [Bleſſed be the Lord God of Sem : Chanaan be his ſeruant] which being a Prophecie, was fulfilled according to the letter, when the children of Iſrael, of the progenie of Sem, conquered the land of Chanaan, & particularly moſt of the Chananites being ſlaine with the ſword, [the Gabaonites (a people of the ſame generatiõ of Chanaan) were glad to ſaue their liues, with condition that they and al their poſteritie, ſhould ſerue in the miniſterie of the people (of Iſrael) and of the Altar of our Lord, hewing wood, and carrying water.] To Abraham likewiſe God reuealed the deſtruction of Sodome, with the other Cities neare adioyned. [Can I (ſaid our Lord) conceale from Abraham, the thinges which I wil doe.] Manie farre greater miſteries, did God alſo reueale to Abraham, Iſaac, Iacob. and other Patriarches, and Prophets, wherof we ſhal ſpeake in other places more proper. Ioſeph alſo receiued the gift of Prophecie, to ſee in ſleepe, thinges to come, and to interprete other mens dreames. For that thoſe dreames were reuelations from God, is gathered by Ioſephes wordes ſaying to Pharao : [God hath ſhewed to Pharao the thinges which he wil doe.] So Daniel ſaw Goddes wil, and interpreted King Nabuchodonoſors dreames, read & interpreted obſcure wordes written in the ſight of King Baltaſſer

Gen. 2. *v.* 19. 23. *Iude.v.* 14. 15. *Gen.* 6. *v.* 5. 6.

Gen. 9. *v.* 26.

Ioſu. 9. *v.* 27.

Gen. 18. *v.* 17. 20.

Gen. 41. *v.* 25.
Dan. 2.
Dan. 4.
v. 5.

† *Iob.* 24. *v.* 1. *Ch.* 28. *v.* 39. *Iſa.* 44. *v.* 28. *Ch.* 45. *v.* 1. 2. *Par.* 36. *v.* 22. 1. *Eſd.* 1. *v.* 1. 2. *Eſth.* 11. *v.* 3. *Sap.* 4. *v.* 7. 11.

P

Ch. 19. v.
17. Dan.
13. v. 42.
Ofee. 2. v.
10. Amos.
3. v. 6.
Mich 3. v.
6. Nahum.
3. v. 5.
Mat. 10.
v. 26. Ch.
11. v. 25.
27. Act. 2.
v. 23. Rom.
8. v. 30.
Ch. 9. v. 11.
&c. Ch. 11.
v. 33.
Ephef. 1. v.
5. Heb. 4.
v. 13.
Apoc. 1. v.
1. 2. &c.

† God alfo fe-
eth what
fhould be con-
ditionally,
though the ef-
fect folow not.

Baltaſſer; by an inuiſible writer. Al which, and
† manie the like, doe declare, that as no man knoweth more of ſupernatural thinges then God reuealeth : ſo God doth abſolutly know al thinges, aſwel
to come, as alreadie paſt, being al to him preſent.

7 And that God alſo knoweth al thinges that can
be, or conditionally ſhould be; in certaine ſuppoſed
caſes which indeede ſhal not be; two or three places
may ſufficiently ſhew. Holie Dauid being in diſtreſſe   1. Reg. 23.
and iuſt ſuſpition, how the people of Ceila (where   v. 9. 10.
he was entered) would deale with him, † conſulted   11. 12.
our Lord, by way of the high Preiſt, applying the E-
phod, whether the men of Ceila, would deliuer him
into the handes of Saul? [And our Lord ſaid; they
wil deliuer thee.] Which anſwear was to be vnderſtoode conditionally, if he taried there. But parting
from thence he was not deliuered to Saul. King Io-   4. Reg. 13.
as being willed by Elizeus the Prophet, to ſtrike the   v. 18. 19.
earth with a iauelin [ſtroake it three times, and then
ſtoode ſtil : the Prophet was angrie with him & ſaid :
If thou had ſtriken fiue, or ſixe, or ſeauen times, thou
hadſt ſtriken Siria euen to deſtuction; but now three
times thou ſhalt ſtrike it] The Prophet Ieremie ſaid   Iere. 48.
to King Sedecias [Thus ſaith the Lord of hoſtes,   v. 17.
the God of Iſrael: If going forth, thou wilt goe out
to the Princes of the King of Babilon, thy ſoule ſhal
liue, and this Citie ſhal not be burnt with fire, and
thou ſhalt be ſaife, and thy houſe : But if thou wilt   v. 18.
not goe out to the Princes of the King of Babilon,
this Citie ſhal be deliuered into the handes of the
Chaldees, and they ſhal burne it with fire, and thou
ſhalt not eſcape out of their handes.] The ſame Prophet vttered the like conditional Prophecie, to the
people which deſired to flee into Egipt from the danger of the Chaldees ſaying : [Thus ſaith our Lord   Iere. 42.
the God   v. 9. 10.

the God of Iſrael; If reſting you wil abide in this
land, I wil build you, and not deſtroy you; I wil plant
you and not pluck you vp; for now I am pacified v-
pon the euil that I haue done to you. But if you ſhal
ſay; we wil not dwel in this land, neither wil we
heare the voice of the Lord our God; ſaying No,
not ſo, but we wil goe forward to the land of Egipt:
If you ſhal ſet your face to goe into Egipt, and ſhal
enter to inhabite there, the ſword which you feare,
ſhal there take you in the land of Egypt : and the
famine for which you are careful, ſhal cleue to you
in Egipt, and there you ſhal dye.] S. Paul in like
ſort affirmed conditionally, when certaine ſhipmen
ment for feare of drowning, to flee out of the ſhip,
[vnleſſe theſe tarrie in the ſhip, you can not be
ſaued.]

8 In al which and the like, the aſſertion is as certainly true, and ſo kowne to God, which happeneth
not, the condition failing, as is the contrarie, which
together with the condition, being performed, cometh actually to paſſe : wherby we learne, and may
clearly ſee that Gods preſcience, and our inſcience
of al thinges, alſo to come, and poſſible to come,
and howſoeuer, doth no way, nor in anie caſe, neceſſitate the thing that is to come, or not to come; but it
remaineth free, & in it ſelf indifferent, depending vpõ
the proper cauſes, natural, or ſupernatural : As harueſt vpon ſowing, with other husbandrie; Saluation, vpon faith and good workes, with perſeuerance
therin to the end : is in it ſelf, and to vs vncertaine,
notwithſtanding Gods moſt certaine foreknowlege
of the verie effect, which ſhal be. For ſtil he ſeeth
al together the end and the meanes wherby euerie
thing cometh to anie end : wherof we may for explication ſake propoſe example in our owne knowlege; when we ſee a thing preſent we are certaine

v.13.

14.

15.

16.

Act.27.
v.31.

Gods fore
knowlege doth
not neceſſitate
anie thing that
is voluntarie or
contingent.

Example in
mans know-
lege.

that

that so it is, and that the contrarie cannot be true:
yet it is not our sight, nor knowledge, that maketh
it true which we see, but the truth of the thing dependeth vpon the proper cause thereof. And if we
could as certainly know future thinges, yet that know
lege should not make the thinges necessarie, but
they are as their proper causes make them, according to their owne nature, either necessarie, or voluntarie, or contingent.

God is absolute goodnesse: & al his actions are good.

ARTICLE. 10.

Gods goodnes
appeareth in
his creating al
thinges good.

Gods infinite goodnes, which is a other diuine
attribute, appeareth manie wayes: & is made
manifest by al his workes, if they be rightly considered. For al creatures in their nature, and
essense are good. Euen diuels, and wicked men.
There is nothing euil but sinne, and that indede is
no creature, nor anie way the worke of God. For
it is onlie a deforming priuation, or want of that
rectitude, which ought to be in euerie action, de-
prauing the same, & making it faultie, against reason which requireth that al thinges should be done
rightly. So that sinne is an enimie to nature, the
corrupter of creatures, odible to reason, contrarie
to al that is right, iust, and good. And therefore

By punishing
sinne.

by punishing sinne, Goddes goodnes is particularly
declared; making it manifest, that his goodnes loueth al creatures (in that they are his creatures) &
hatteh that euil which defaceth & deformeth them.
Wherfore as we haue alreadie seene in the former

In ordaining
thinges to
good endes.

Articles, that Goddes omnipotent power is shewed
in creating al thinges, and his diuine wisdome shy-
neth in disposing al: so his goodnes is no lesse reuealed in

Art. 8. 9.

ordaining al the fame to particular good endes, and most especially in defigning Angels and Men to ferue him in a higher degrie, and fo to be made partici-pant of his owne eternal glorie : A benefite fo much furmoûting their creation, as grace excelleth nature, and more fingularly abunding towardes men, then Angels, in that al mankind finning, yet his good-neffe recalleth them by new grace, to repentance, through the infinite merits of Chrift our Redemer, reparing the loffes of al thofe which refift not, but accept therof; with increafe of more grace, & glo-rie then other wife anie could haue merited.

2   This immenfe and vnfpeakable goodneffe of God is moft cleare to al men of right vnderftanding, and is teftified euerie where in the holie Scriptures. Moft frequently in the Pfalmes, al the faithful fer-uantes of God confeffing their owne pronnes to euil, and weakneffe to doe good, befeke his moft boun-tiful goodneffe to powre vpon them abundance of grace with remiffion of finnes that they may rightly ferue him, and duly render al poffible thankes and prayfes to his holie name. So the Royal Pfalmift mindful of his daylie neceffities prayeth thus [Attēd o Lord to the voice of my prayer, my King, and my God. Becaufe I wil pray to thee Lord in the morning, thou wilt heare my voice. In the morning I wil ftand by thee: I wil fing to our Lord, who geueth me good thinges, and I wil fing to the name of our Lord moft high. Haue mercie on me o God, according to thy great mercy, and according to the multitude of thy commiferations, take away mine i-niquitie. I wil expect thy name, becaufe it is good in the fight of thy Sainctes. I wil confeffe to thy name, becaufe it is good. Once hath God fpoken; thefe two thinges haue I heard, that power is gods, and mercie o Lord is to thee.] Somtimes in extafes

Pf. 5.
v. 3. 4.

Pf. 12.
v. 6.
Pf. 50.
v. 3.

Pf. 51.
v. 11.
Pf. 53.
v. 8.

Gods goodnes is abundantly teftified in ho-lie Scriptures.

P 3   or trance

or trance, admiring Goddes vnſpeakable goodnes, *Pſ. 61. v.*
he crieth out [How good is God to Iſrael, to them   6. 12. 17.
that are of right hart .] And ſeing how litle able mã *Pſ. 72. v.*
is to render due thankes, and praiſes to God : al muſt   1.
ioyne in voice and lubily, yea al creatures are inui -
ted to yeld praiſes, teſtifying that [Our Lord is pitiful, and merciful, long ſuffering , and verie merciful. Bleſſe our Lord, al ye his Angels : Bleſſe our Lord *Pſ. 102. v.*
al ye his hoaſtes; Bleſſe our Lord al ye his workes ,   8. 20. 21.
in euerie place of his Dominion, my ſoule bleſſe thou   22. *Pſ. 105.*
our Lord. Confeſſe ye (with thankes and praiſe)   *v. 1. Pſal.*
to our Lord, becauſe he is good : becauſe his mer-   106. *v. 1.*
cie is for euer . O Lord thou art good, and in thy   *Pſ. 117. v.*
goodnes, teach me thy iuſtifications . Praiſe ye our   1. *&c.*
Lord, becauſe our Lord is good : ſing to his name,   *Pſ. 118.*
becauſe he is ſweete . Our Lord is ſweete to al : &   *Pſ. 134.*
his commiſerations are ouer al his workes .] The   *v. 1. 3.*
ſeauen laſt pſalmes are wholly compoſed of Goddes   *Pſ. 135. v.*
praiſes, for his infinite goodnes, excellencie, mer-   1. *&c.*
cie, benignitie . [Let al thy workes o Lord, con-   *Pſ. 144. v*
feſſe to thee : and let thy Sainctes bleſſe thee] with   *v 10. Pſ.*
hart, lubilie, voice, inſtrument . [Let euerie ſpirit   150. *v. vlt.*
praiſe our Lord .] God hath made al thinges good,
and therfore al muſt praiſe him, for his abſolute goodnes, wherof he hath made them participant. [For   *Gen. 1. v.*
God ſaw al thinges that he had made, and they were   31.
verie good :] only ſinners perſiſting in ſinne, are
excluded from praiſing God. To ſuch God ſaith :
[Why doſt thou declare my iuſtices, and takeſt my   *Pſ. 49.*
Teſtament in thy mouth ?]   *v. 10.*

2   And for this cauſe God often expoſtulated with
ſinners for degenerating from that goodnes wher -
with he endued them. ſaving to his peculiar people :
[I planted thee an elect vineyard, al true ſeede .]   *Iere. 2.*
That God alſo puniſheth offenders, it is for their a-   *v. 21.*
mendement, But [manie wil not receiue diſcipline.]   *v. 30.*
                                Therfore

Al creatures
are good, & al
conſidered to-
gether are ve-
rie good.

God would
haue al ſinners
to be conuer-
ted and ſaued.

Therfore God difclaming from being the caufe, or
auctor of their finne and ruine, againe expoftulateth

Ezech.18. faying: [Why is the death of a finner my wil, faith

v.23. our Lord God, & not that he conuert from his waies

Ch.22.*v*. and liue?. &c Behold I haue wrong my handes v-

13. pon thy couetoufnes which thou haft done, and v-
pon the bloud which hath bene fhed in the middeft
of thee. Say to them, liue I, faith our Lord God :
I wil not the death of the impious, but that the impious conuert from his way and liue.] And fo cri-

Ch. 33. eth vnto them [Conuert, conuert ye from your moft

v.11. euil waies. And why wil you dye, o houfe of Ifra-

Ofee. 13. el? Perdition is thine, o Ifrael : only in me is thy

v.9. helpe.]

4 Our B. Sauiour confirmeth al this goodnes, as
perteyning, not to the Iewes only, but to al mankind, Chrift and his Apoftles con- firme the fame.

Mat.5. for that God is Creator of al. [Our Father in hea-

v. 45. uen (faith he) maketh the Sûne to rife vpon the good
and the badde; and rayneth vpon the iuft and the vn-

Ch.18. iuft. Reioyceth with his Angels vpon euerie lofte

v.14. fheepe that is found againe. Euen fo it is not the

Luc. 15. wil of your Father which is in heauen that one perifh

v. 10. of thefe litle ones.] Likewife S. Paul vrgeth al

Rom. 12. finners faying : [Be reformed in the newnes of your

v. 2. mind, that you may proue, what the good, and accep-

1.*Tim*. 2. table, and perfect wil of God is. God wil (or of his

v. 4. part would) haue al men to be faued, and to come

2.*Pet*.3. to the knowlege of the truth. Our Lord flackeneth

v.9. not his promife, as fome doe efteme it, but he doth
paciently for you, not willing that anie perifh, but
that al returne to penance.] To conclude this point
that goddes goodnes is abfolute, and infinite, and
al his actions good : The two great Apoftles, S.
Peter, and S. Paul, fhew, that euen his delayes, o-

2.*Pet*.3. miffions, and expectations are good. [The longa-

v. 15. nimitie of our Lord, doe you accompt faluation]
faith

faith S. Peter, which S. Paul had also written before [Dost thou contemne the riches of his goodnes, and pacience, and Longanimitie, not knowing
that the Benignitie of God, bringeth thee to penance?] Therfore willeth al, to [be reformed in
newnes of mind, that you may proue, what the good
and acceptable, and perfect wil of God is. *For I say*
by the grace that is geuen to al that are among you, not
to be more wise, then behoueth to be wise: but to be
wise vnto sobrietie.

Rom. 2. v.
4. Ch. 12.
v. 2.
v. 3.

No place of holie Scripture is contrarie to anie other place. Therfore such as may seme contrarie must be explicated, & so reconciled.

5 As for certeine places of holie Scriptures, which
may seme to contentious people ; perhaps also vnto
weake mindes, or scrupulous persons, to sound, as
if God were rigide, rigorous, or desireous to punish; they are in true sense, conformable to other
Scriptures (for al are most true) importing no action of God concurring, nor cooperating to sinne,
but his permission only: And that for the good of
the same sinners if they wil: As also (and that alwaies infallibly) for the good of al that loue him, &
rightly loue their owne soules. As where it is written, that God said to Moyses. [I wil indurate Pharao his hart] And to Pharao him self (by the mouth
of Moyses) God saith : [Therfore haue I set thee,
that in thee I may shew my might, and my name
may be told in al the earth:] which S. Paul thus
citeth: To this verie purpose haue I raised thee, that
in thee I may shew my power: and that my name
may be renowmed in the whole earth.] It is written by the Prophet Samuel, that [Ophni and Phinees, the sonnes of Heli the high Preist, heard not
the voice of their Father, because our Lord would
kil them.] King Dauid being egregiously calum-
ated, by wicked Simei, said: [Our Lord hath commanded him to curse Dauid; and who is he that dare
say; why hath he so done? Let him alone, that he

Places allea-ged by Aduer-saries.

Exo. 4. v.
21. Ch. 7.
v. 3. Ch.
9. v. 12.
16. Ch. 11.
v. 37.
Rom. 9.
v. 17.
1. Reg. 2.
v. 25.

2. Reg. 16.
v. 10. 11.

may

may curſe according to the Precept of our Lord .] *Iudic* . 9 .
Concerning Dauids ſinne, in nũbring of the people : *v* . 23 .
it is writē [The furie of our Lord added to be angrie 3 . *Reg* . 12 .
againſt Iſrael and Iuda.] Micheas a Prophet, ſaid *v* . 15 . *Ch* .
to King Achab : [Behould our Lord hath geuen the 22 . *v* . 20 .
ſpirit of lying in the mouth of al thy prophets.] The 2 . *Par* . 25 .
Royal Prophet ſaith [God turned the hartes of the *v* . 20 . *Ch* .
Egiptians, that they hated his people, and to work 35 . *v* . 22 .
guile towardes his ſeruantes .] The Prophet Iſaias *Iudith* . 9 .
praying for the people, ſaith to God [Why haſt thou *v* . 13 . *Iob* .
made vs ſrre, o Lord, from thy waies, haſt thou hard- 1 . *v* . 12 .
ned our hartes that we feared not thee ?] S . Paul in *Ch* . 2 . *v* . 6 .
his profoũd diſcourſe of gods election, exemplifying *Pſ* . 103 . *v* .
in Iacob, & Eſau, ſaith : that [whē they were not yet 27 . *Iere* .
borne, nor had done anie good or euil, that the pur- 35 . *v* . 23 .
poſe of God, according to election , might ſtand, *Amos* . 4 .
not of workes, but of the caller, it was ſaid to Rebec- *v* . 4 . *Mat* .
ca their mother, that the elder ſhal ſerue the yonger : 4 . *v* . 12 .
as it is written ; Iacob I loued, but Eſau I hated .] *Luc* . 2 . *v* .
Theſe eſpecial places, and * ſome others, make at 34 . *Mat* . 6 .
firſt ſight, apparant ſhew, for Zuinglius, Caluin, and *v* . 12 . *Io* .
Beza, teaching that God maketh men tranſgreſſors : 12 . *v* . 39 .
that he moueth them, driueth them on, and enforcēth *Act* . 2 . *v* .
them to doe that which is ſinne (as them ſelues ſpeak) 23 . *Rom* . 1 .
which is indeede to commit ſinne, and by neceſſarie *v* . 24 . *Ch* .
conſequence, they teach, that God ſhould be cauſe 3 . *v* . 5 . *Ch* .
and auctor of ſinne. 11 . *v* . 8 .

6 † But becauſe moſt Engliſh Proteſtants, either de- 2 . *Theſ* . 2 .
nie this ſequele, endeuoring to excuſe their forraine *v* . 11 . *Apoc* .
Maiſters, or els diſclame from their doctrine : it ſhal 17 . *v* . 17 .
not be needful further to explicate the places which
they alleage for their purpoſe, then is alreadie done † A breefe
in the Catholique Edition of the Engliſh Bible, e- anſwer concer-
ſpecially vpon the ſeuenth Chapter of Exodus : and ning the places
the ninth of S . Paules Epiſtle to the Romanes : Con- alleaged,
ſidering withal, that the wordes of Zuinglius, Cal- which is more
uin , largely expli-
cated in the

Left margin references:

2 . *Reg* .
24 . *v* . 1 .
3 . *Reg* .
22 . *v* .
23 .
Pſ . 104 .
v . 25 .
Iſa . 63 .
v . 17 .

Rom . 9 .
v . 11 .
12 . 13 .

Mal . 4 .
v . 2 . 3 .

Iudic . 9 .

uin, and Beza saying, that God * maketh men transgressors, moueth them, driueth them on, enforceth
them to doe that which is sinne : are no where to
be found in the holie Scriptures. Remember also that
both God and men, are some times said to doe those
thinges, which they only permitte . And consider
likewise aswel the places here cited , which testifie
Goddes inexplicable goodnes ; as also other holy
Scriptures, which in expresse termes, not only exclude
al sinne and iniquitie from God : but also testifie, that
his diuine wil is, that no sinne should be commit -
ted. For it is not only said by Moyses, that [the
workes of God are perfect, and al his waies iudge-   *Deut.* 32.
mentes ; God is faithful, and without anie iniquitie,   *v .* 4.
iust & right] but also it is said by Dauid speaking to
God, [thou art not a God that wilt iniquitie .] S.   *Ps.* 5. *v.* 5.
Paul doth not only confute the imagination of such
as should thinke God were vniust or partial, in that
he calleth some to his mercie, and leaueth others in
their sinne, being al equally in the masse of damnation, lest anie should so misunderstand his discourse,
he addeth, demanding of him self [what then, is there   *Rom.* 9.
iniquitie with God ?] and therto answeareth reso-   *v .* 14.
lutly [God forbid] but he also teacheth, that God
of his part, if men wil them selues [wil haue al men   1. *Tim.* 2.
to be saued .] And S . Iames not only presupposeth   *v.* 4.
that God is no way the cause, nor hath a wil that
anie be ouercome in tentation ; but also teacheth ,   *Iaco.* 1.
that no man is tempted of God [for God is not a   *v.* 13. 14.
tempter of euils ; and he tempteth no man . But euerie man is tempted of his owne concupiscence, abstracted and allured .] Our Sauiour saith, that [the   *Mat.* 13.
enemie which ouersoweth cockle vpó the good seed ,   *v.* 25. 39.
is the diuel .]

7   In that God suffereth sinne to be committed, he
is also good, because he draweth good of it, turneth
                                                    it to

turneth it to good. Holie Ioseph the Patriarch with this consideration, comforted his brethren, when it repented them, that they had betrayed, & sold him.

Gen. 45. v. 5.

[Let it not seme to you a hard case (saith he) that you did sel me into these Countries; For God sent me before you into Egipt, for your preseruation.]

Gen. 50. v. 19. 20.

Againe after their Fathers death, [he said vnto them: Feare not: Can we resist the wil of God? You thought euil against me, but God turned that into good, that he might exalt me, as presently you see, and might saue manie peoples.] This expresse distinction, that they thought euil, and God turned their fact to good, sheweth, that sinne is wholly of the sinner, and that God hath no part therin, but turneth it to good. And so out of euerie euil, draweth good, by his omnipotent *Power*, infinite *Wisdome*, and absolute *Goodnes*.

8   Which three diuine attributes, I haue rather explicated in this place, then the others, because they are more often mentioned in Christian Doctrine, & are commonly appropriated to the three diuine persons: Power, to the Father, Wisdome, to the Sonne, and Goodnes, to the Holie Ghost. Albeit, aswel these three, as al the rest; Goddes Eternitie, Immensitie, Immutabilitie, Iustice, Truth, Mercie, and al vertues in God; being, not qualities, nor accidents, but Goddes proper substance (as was noted before)

Article. 8. nu. 2.

doe equallie agree to the whole B. Trinitie, and to euerie person therof. Now we are to speake of his creatures, and of the meanes, wherby man may be saued, and eternally glorified.

Though diuers diuine Attributes be appropriated to the three diuine persons; yet al doe agree to euerie one.

Angels

Angels the first creatures which God made, are, the most part in eternal glorie. Manie also are damned diuels.

ARTICLE. II.

Angels excel
al other crea-
tures in natu-
ral giftes.

A L the workes of God are admirable ; but a boue al others, Angels doe excel in natural giftes, and none but Angels and men, recei ued supernatural grace : by right vse wherof, they were al ordeined to enioy eternal glorie.. It farre exceedeth mannes natural capacitie, perfectlie to know the nature of Angels, being pure spiritual sub-stances, voide of al corporal mixture, and imperceptible to our external senses. The nearest in likenes to them, are mennes soules, in that they also, are spiritual substances, endued with reason, and free wil, immortal, and capable of eternal felicitie, or miserie, as Angels first were.. But this is one great difference, (besides others) that soules haue a natural disposition, inclination, and desire, to their proper bodies, wherof they are the essential formes. In so much, that neither the soule nor the bodie, seperated the one from the other, is perfect in their specifical nature, neither of them is a man, being seperated, but being actually vnited as matter and forme, doe constitute a reasonable or rational person; wheras Angels are naturally perfect, without al composition, for they are not, neither can be, the formes of anie bodie.

Heathen Phi-
losophers haue
diuers errors
concerning
Angels.

2   Of these excellent Spirits, certaine Philosophers conceauing some thing, cal them *Intelligentias sepe-ratas*. Intelligences seperated from bodies, at least from earthly bodies. For most heathen Philosophers by occasion of apparitions in visible shape, and so-

denly

denly vanifhing out of fight, erronioufly fuppofed
that they had aerial bodics. Such Philofophers, had
alfo other groffe errors, that Angels are coeternal
with God, yea that they are goddes, fome greater,
and fome leffe . Plato calleth them *Demones*, not diftinguifhing betwene holie and wicked Angels; teaching to offer Sacrifice to them, which no good Angels, but only diuels, accepted .

3   Of this heathnifh doctrine, it femeth, Simon Ma-
gus, and others drew their herefie, that Angels are
our Mediators, not Chrift ; of which, both heathnifh
and heretical doctrine, S . Paul warneth Chriftians

An old herifie ;
that Angels
fhould be me-
diators, & litle
goddes.

Colof. 2 .
*v.*18.19. to beware, faying : [let no man feduce you, willing
(or felf willed) in the humilitie & religion of Angels, not holding the head] Chrift our only Medi-
diator and Redemer . For thofe heritikes contemning Chrift, kept conuenticles, in the name of fpirits,
and Idoles ; and taught the Coleffians, to keepe the
old Law, and to honour Angels, as the geuers of the
fame, and as leffe goddes, prefcribing facrifices to
be offered vnto them, calling fuch feruice, humilitie,
that they might bring them to the great God. So

Gal. 3 .
v. 19. they mixed falfhood with truth . For the old Law
was indeede the Law of God, and was deliuered by

Heb. 2 .
v. 2. Angels to Moyfes, and by Moyfes, to the people; &
fo not only Angels, but alfo Moyfes, was in a true
fenfe, called, the Arbiter, & Mediator, betwixt God,

Deut. 5 . and the people . But after that Chrift our Lord was
v. 5 . crucified, dead, rifen from death, and afcended into
heauen; the old Law ceafed, and, the new Law came
in place . And of the new Law, Chrift is the Media-

*Colof.*1 . tor, being our only Redemer. And therfore the A-
*v.*15.16. poftle taught thefe deceiued Coleffians, that Chrift
is God, the creator of Angels; the head of the Church,
and that by him, we muft goe to God. And in other
places alfo proueth, that Chrift fo farre excelleth

Angels

Angels, as the verie Sonne of God, is greater, then his best and most holie seruantes. And it is Goddes expresse commandement [Let al the Angels of God adore him.]

Ps. 96.
v. 8.
Heb. I. *v.*
5. 6.

Angels, and time it self and al creatures had a begin-ing.

4   The same true faith teacheth vs, that God only, is from al eternitie, without beginning; that al other thinges, namely Angels, were created by God, in time, or together with time (which is also a creature) & had a beginning. But whether long or short time before man, and the rest of this world, the holie Scriptures doe not expresse, neither hath the Church hitherto declared; neither wil we here discusse it further. Moyses w iteth in general thus [In the beginning God created heauen and earth] then in particular describeth, that he made light & other seueral thinges; Lastly man, not there naming Angels: Of whom neuerthelesse, both he, and other sacred writers, doe verie often make mention, as of principal creatures of God. And that they are innumerable, may be gathered in diuers passages of holie Scriptures. When Iacob returning from Mesopotamia, saw the Angels which mette him; he called them [the Campes of God] because they were manie; & doubtles they were a verie smal part of the whol hoast of heaue. The Royal Psalmist calleth them the [Chariot of God] insinuating their inexplicable multitude, by the greatest vsual number of thousandes, saying : [The Chariot of God, is tenne thousand fold, thousandes of them that reioyce.] Which the Prophet Daniel also describeth by the vniuersal numbers of tenne, and hundred, and thousand, multiplied thus, [Thousandes of thousandes, ministred to him, and tenne thousand, hundred thousand, assisted him.] geuing vs to vnderstand, that their number excedeth our capacitie. Wherto agreeth that of S. Iohn in the Apocailps: [I heard the voice of manie Angels, round

Gen. I *v.* I.

v. 3. 27.

Angels are innumerable.

Gen. 32.
v. 2.
Ps. 67.
v. 18.

Dan. 7.
v. 10.

Apoc. 5.
v. 11.

round about the Throne, and of the liuing creatures, and of the Seniors : & the number of them was thou-fandes of thoufandes.] Likewife that difcourfe of one of Iobes frendes faying [Power, and terrror is with God, that maketh coucord in his high ones.] And [Is there anie number of his fouldiers ?] meaning that they paffe al nūbers which we can expreffe. Yea as Diuines doe probably thinke, they exceede the number of al corporal indiuidual liuing creatures.

Iob. 25.
v. 2. 3.

5   But this is more certaine, and proued by holie Scriptures, that they are diftinguifhed into certaine *Hierarchies* or facred fubordinations, & into fpecial orders, according to thefe nine particular Titles, afcribed vnto them [Angels, Archangels, Powers, Poteftates, Principalities, Dominations; Thrones, Cherubims, and Seraphimes.] The name Angel being common to al, is appropriated to the loweft Order, becaufe ordinarily thofe are fent, as meffengers in particular affaires, and to particular perfons. Of which fort holie Dauid faith [God maketh fpirites his Angels] that is, his meffengers. As to Abraham the Pathiarch; to Lot a iuft man, to Agar in her affliction; to holie Tobie and others. Thefe fecond Order called Archangels are fent in greater affaires, perteyning to the whole Church, and concerning more principal myfteries: As S. Gabriel (who was fent to the B. Virgin Marie to declare Gods wil, that the Sonne of God fhould be incarnate, the Redemer of mankinde) is vniuerfally faid to be an Archangel. S. Michael is exprefly called an Archangel, by S. Iude the Apoftle. And S. Paul faith that our Lord wil come to iudgemēt in the voice of an Archangel. The third Order is called *Virtutes*, Powers; of which the fame S. Paul maketh mention together with Angels, and Principalities, in his Epiftle to the Romanes; and the Ephefians. And in his

Pf. 103.
v. 4.
Gen. 16.
v. 7. Ch
19. v. 1.
Ch. 22.
v. 11.
Tob. 3.
v. 25.
Luc. 1.
v. 26.
Iud. v. 9.
1. Thef.
4. v. 16.
Rom. 8.
v. 38.
Eph. 1.
v. 21.

Angels are diftinguifhed into three Hierarchies: & nine Orders.

Angels.
1. Archangels.
Powers.

Poteftates.
2. Principalities.
Dominatiōs.

Thrones.
3. Cherubims.
Seraphims.

his Epſtle to the Coloſſians nameth other foure orders, for example, to ſhew that al were created by Chriſt [whether Thrones; or Dominations; or Principalities; or Poteſtatęs. Of Cherubimes, is oftner mẽntioned in the bookes of Moyſes. And of the Seraphimes, is only mention in the Prophecie cf Iſaias, which make in al nine Orders.

Coloſ. 1. v. 16.
Ex. 25.
v. 18. Nu; 7. v. 89.
Gen. 3. v. 34. 3. Reg. 6. v. 23.
Iſ. 6. v. 1; 6.

The greater part of Angels being eſtabliſhed in eternal glorie; cõtinually praiſe God.

6   An other principal point for vs to obſerue is, that al Angels being at their creation indued with grace, moſt of them vſing it rightly, were confirmed therein, and eſtabliſhed in eternal glorie. Others, and thoſe alſo manie, proudly auerting them ſelues from God, their Creator, and Lord, are damned to euerlaſting torments. For as they haue receiued diuerſly according to their workes; ſo ſhal men alſo finally be iudged, and either rewarded, or puniſhed eternally. The B. Angels, haue the fruition of God, and perpetually praiſe him. As the holy pſalmiſt ſignifieth, who finding him ſelf, and al mortal men vnable to render due thankes to God for his benefites; imitateth theſe glorious Citizens of heauen, to aſſiſt men herein, ſaying: [Bleſſe our Lord al ye his Angels; mightie in power, doing his word. Bleſſe our Lord al ye his hoaſtes : you his miniſters, that doe his wil. Praiſe ye our Lord from the heauens : praiſe ye him in the high places. Praiſe ye him al his Angels : praiſe ye him al his hoaſtes.

Pſ. 102. v. 20. 21.
Pſ. 148. v. 1. 2.

Apoſtata Angels wicked diuels, cõtinually blaſpheme God, and are eternally damned.

7   Contrariwiſe, the wicked ſpirits [not ſtanding in the truth, but ſtriuing [to aſcend, and to be like the Higheſt] being caſt into hel, doe continually curſe, and blaſpheme God, in their tormentes, which they ſuffer. For as it is written in the book of Iob that [God in his Angels found wickednes :] So S. Peter teacheth that [God ſpared not Angels ſinning, but with the ropes of hel being drawne downe into hel, deliuered them to be tormented, that they ſhould be

Io. 8. v. 44.
Iſ. 14. v. 12.
Iob. 4. v. 18.
2. Pet. 2. v. 4.

                                                    reſerued

Iud.v.6. referued vnto Iudgment.] S . Iude alfo repeating the fame fal and punifhment of the diuel, & his complices, faith, that [the Angels which kept not their Principalitie, but forfooke their owne habitation, God hath referued vnder darknes in eternal bondes, vnto the iudgement of the great day] that is , the general day of Iudgement; fignifying , that then alfo they fhal eternally remaine in the fame [execrable iudgement againft them] as S . Peter fpeaketh : Yea with increafe of torment, as thofe diuels feared who our Sauiour caft out of men, and permitted to goe into hogges, when they cryed faying to him [art thou come hither to torment vs before the time ?]

2. Pet.
2. v. 11.

Mat. 8.
v. 29.

Diuels (at leaft fome of them) fhal fuffer greater torments then as yet they doe.

Holie Angels by their minifterie and praiers, protect & help men. Diuels feeke theire ruine.

ARTICLE. 12.

SO doth our heauenly Fathers prouidence, gouuerne the vniuerfal world, that therin appeareth a moft admirable correfpondence, by continual imparting, and receiuing of benefites amongft his creatures ; al proceding from his incomprehenfible goodnes, the Auctor, and firft caufe of al that is good. The lower elemental bodies, afwel of men, as of other thinges, receiue and enioy, more or leffe, natural vigour, ftrength, and perfection, by the influence of the celeftial planets, and other ftarres, which is found to be true, by diligent obferuations of learned men ; is approued by experience, and credited by al perfons of better vnderftading. The fame diuine prouidence, hath alfo ordeined, that mennes foules may receiue fpiritual good by the mediation of celeftial fpirites ; and by their minifterie, protection, & praiers, profper more in their daily affaires, corporal, &

The inferiour world participateth of the influence of the planetes, and other ftarres.

So may the foules of mén receiue benefite by the glorios fpirites in heauen.

R   fpi-

spiritual: Namely by the helpe and affiftance of B.
Angels. A point of doctrine wel knowne to the ancient holie Patriarches, Prophets, Apoftles, and other
feruantes of God; confirmed by frequent examples;
beleued by al Catholiques, and clearly proued by
holie Scrptures, as wel of the old, as new Teftament.

2   For albeit certaine workes, as the creation of al
thinges, the Incarnation of Chrift, the infufion of
grace, Inftitution of Sacraments, and fome others,
are immediatly performed by God him felfe; Yet
moft other Benefites, both natural, and fupernatural,
procede from God, by fecundarie caufes. And a-
mongft the reft, it pleafeth his diuine goodnes, to
impart manie thinges, to men by the adminiftratiõ of
Angels. Al the apparitions made vnto Adam, Noe,
Abraham, and others, in the name of God; were
accomplifhed in the perfons of Angels fent by him,
and fpeaking as if God him felf had fpoken, and conuerfed with men. Which is certeinly proued by the
anfwear made from God to Moyfes, when he fo fer-
uently defired to fee God. Thou canft not fee my
face, for man fhal not fee me and liue.] Wheras
therfore it is recorded, that God brought Eue, and
other creatures vnto Adam, fpake to him. and alfo
to Eue, to Cain, (and verie like alfo, to Abel, Seth,
Enos, Enoch, though it be not expreffed) and afterwardes, to Noe, Abraham, Ifaac, Iacob, Moyfes,
and other Patriarches, and Prophets: al the fame
was done by Angels. So doubtles an Angel by Gods
ordinance fhutte the dore of the Arck on the out
fide] when Noe with his familie, and other liuing
creatures, were entred in. An Angel (reprefenting
God) rained fire and brimftone, vpon Sodom: and
Gomorha, & the like.

3   But to fatisfie al doubtes, we wil recite fome fpecial

God imparteth manie bene-fites by the mi-nifterie of An-gels.

Holie Scrip-tures expeffly

Exo . 33.
v . 20.
Iudic . 13.
v . 22.
Gen . 2.
v . 16. 19.
Gen . 3.
v . 13.
Gen . 4.
v . 6.
Gen . 7.
v . 16.
Gen . 19.
v . 24.

cial Scriptures, which make expresse mentió of apparitions, protections, ministeries, and praiers of Angels. When Adam had transgressed, and was cast
Gen. 3. out of Paradise [God placed there Cherubimes with
v. 24. a flaming and burning sword, to kepe the way of the
Gen. 19. tree of life] lest anie man should eate therof. [Two
v. 1. 13. Angels came to Sodome, and said to Lot; we wil
destroy this place, for their crie is waxen lowde before our Lord, who hath sent vs to destroy them.]
Gen. 16. [An Angel of our Lord, finding Agar in the wilder-
v. 7.9. nes, bade her returne to her mistresse] Againe afterwardes called to her from heauen saying [what dost
Gen. 21. thou Agar ? Feare not, for God hath heard the voice
v. 17. 18. of the boy: Arise, take vp the boy, & hold his hand,
for into a great Nation wil I make him .] So the Angel promised ; which he could not otherwise say, nor
performe, but as the minister of God. When Abra-
Gen. 22. ham was readie to kil & sacrifice his Sonne Isaac [an
v. 11. 12. Angel of our Lord from heauen cried saying; Abraham, Abraham; Stretch not forth thy hand vpon the
boy, neither doe thou anie thing to him] and by &
by, added, as if God him self had spoken saying ;
v. 16. [By mine owne self haue I sworne, saith our Lord:
because thou hast done this thing, and hast not spa-
v. 17 red thine only begotten sonne for my sake : I wil
blesse thee, and I wil multiplie thy seede, as the starres
of heauen.] After this , Abraham sending his seruant into Mesopotamia, & assuring him of good suc-
Gen. 24. cesse, said, [Our Lord God of heauen, shal send his
v. 7. 40. Angel before thee, and with thee, and wil direct thy
way, and thou shalt take a wife for my sonne, of
mine owne kinred, and of my Fathers house .] Iacob
Gen. 28. in vision saw Angels ascending, and descending by
v. 12. a ladder, that reached fró the earth to heauen.] And
when he had serued his vncle Laban twentie yeares,
and was to returne to his Countrie [an Angel of
God

God appearing to him in sleepe said: I am the God
of Bethel, where thou didest annoint the stone, &
didest vow the vow vnto me.] And [in the way
Angels mette him, whom (because they were many)
he called *Mahanaim*, that is Campes.] And he praied that his nephewes, the sonnes of Ioseph, might
be blessed of one peculiar Angel, as him self was by
him protected, saying: [the Angel that deliuereth
me from al euils; blesse these children.] It was an
Angel that guided the Israelites, parting from Egipt,
and remaining in the desert, by a piller of a cloude
in the day, and in the night, by a piller of fire. For so
Moyses expresly signifieth saying : [the Angel of
God that went before the campe, remouing him self,
went behind them.] That the Law was deliuered by
Angels, S. Paul affirmeth saying : [It was ordeined
by Angels, in the hand of a mediator.]

Gen. 31.
v, 11.13.
Gen. 32.
v. 1.2.

Gen. 48.
v. 18.

Exo. 13.
v. 21.
Exo. 14.
v. 19.
Gal. 3.
v. 19.

The ministerie
of Angels con-
tinued also af-
ter the law was
receiued.

4   Likewise, after that the Law was geuen, God
promised stil the protection of an Angel, with admonition to the people, to respect and obey him.
[Behold (saith God) I wil send mine Angel, which
shal go before thee & kepe thee in thy Iourney, &
bring thee into the place that I haue prepared; obserue him, & heare his voice; neither do thou think him
one to be cótemned, for he wil not forgeue whé thou
hast sinned, & my name is in him. But if thou wilt heare
his voice, and doe al that I speake ; i wil be enemie
to thine enemies, & wil afflict them that afflict thee.
&c] An Angel also appeared to Iosue in shape of
a warrier, who auouched him self to be [a Prince of
the hoast of our Lord.] After Iosue his death, an
Angel appearing to the people assembled together,
when they were afflicted, admonished them of their
sinnes. Wherupon they repented, and were deliuered from their enemies. In like sorte, falling often
to sinne, and in affliction repenting : God raised vp
Iuuge

Exo. 23
v. 20.
v. 21.

v. 22.

Ies. 5.
v. 14.

Iudic.:
v. 14.

Iudges, and warriers, which deliuered them from in-

Iudic .6. uations. Amongſt which, Gedeon was ſent by an An-
v. 11.12. gel, confirming his miſſion to be from God, by two
14. miracles [in a fleece of wolle, which was moiſt with
v. 37. dew, when the ground where it lay, was drie; and
v. 39. againe was drie, when the ground was wette with
40. dew.] To the Mother of Samſon [an Angel of our
Iudic .13. Lord appeared and ſaid; thou art barren and without
v. 3. 4. children, but thou ſhalt conceiue and beare a ſonne]
7. warned her to abſteine from wine, ſicer, and vncleane
thinges, becauſe the child ſhould be a nazarite al his
v. 13. life.] Appearing alſo to Manue her husband, con-
4. *Reg.* firmed the ſame. When [Elizeus was beſet in the Ci-
6. *v.* 16. tie of Dothan, with troupes of men: he not only ſaw,
17. but alſo obteined by praier, that his ſeruant likewiſe
did ſee the mountaine ful of horſes, and of firie chariots round about] which were Angels; by whoſe
4. *Reg.* protection, he was deliuered. Being alſo in Samaria
7. *v.* 6. when it was beſieged, and in extreme diſtreſſe: he
ſaw and propheſied, the fleeing away of their ene-
v. 7. mies, which was wrought by [Angels terrifying the
Aſſirian Campe, by a ſound of chariots, and horſes, and of a verie great armie; wherupon they fled
in the darck, and left their tentes, and their horſes,
and aſſes in the campe, deſireous to ſaue their liues
only.] When Ieruſalem was diſtreſſed by Sennache-
rib, King of the Aſſirians, after that the Prophet I-
4. *Reg.* ſaias, and King Ezechias had praied, [an Angel of our
19. *v.* Lord came, and ſtroke, in the campe of the Aſſirians,
35. an hundred eightie fiue thouſand.] What profit, &
2 *Par.* protection, Tobias, and his Soñe, and daughter in
32. *v.* law, receiued by the miniſterie of S. Raphael, the
2. *Iſa.* Angel of our Lord, is written at large in the book of
33. *v.* 3. Tobias, from the third Chapter, to the twelft. Ho-
Iſ. 37. lie Iudith alſo, was protected and guided, by an An-
v. 36. gel of our Lord, in her heroical, and admirable ex-

R 3 ploite

ploite, for the faiftie of her countrie . As I cite not
thefe bookes for want of others : fo I would not here
omitte them, being alfo Canonical . It femeth by the
doctrine of holie Iob, that Angels are the mouers of
the celeftial Spheres, where he faith : that [vnder God
they ftoupe, that carie the world .]

5   The Royal Pfalmift clearly faith : [The Angel of
our Lord fhal put in him felf about them that feare
(our Lord) and fhal deliuer them . Becaufe he hath
geuen his Angels charge of thee, that they kepe thee
in al thy waies .] In refpect of Angels prefence,
Salomon aduifeth al men, to gouerne wel their fpeach
faying : [Geue not thy mouth to make thy flefh to
finne ; neither fay thou before the Angel ; there is no
prouidence .] Ieremie the Prophet, in his Epiftle
to the Iewes, reciteth Goddes admonition faying :
[Mine Angel is with you : and my felf wil aske account of your foules .] Daniel recordeth, that [the
Angel of our Lord defcended with Azarias and his
felowes into the furnace, and he fhooke the flame of
the fire out of the furnace, and made the middeft of
the furnace, as a wind of dew blowing, and the fire
touched the not at al, nor pained them, nor did them
anie greuance] which was fo cleare, that King Na-
buchodonofer, hauing put three men into the furnace [faw alfo a fourth perfon walking with them]
and confeffed, that [God whom they ferued, had fent
his Angel, and deliuered his feruants that beleued in
him .] Daniel him felf being caft into the Lions dene,
and there protected, faith [My God hath fent his
Angel, and hath fhut vp the mouthes of the Lions, &
they haue not hurt me .] An Angel alfo caried Habacuc, from Iurie, into Babilon, with meate for Daniel, when he was at an other time, fixe daies in the
denne of feauen hungrie Lions . And as the Prophet
Zacharie writeth [an Angel faid (and praied) in
thefe

*It is probable
that the celef-
tial fpheres are
moued by An-
gels .*

*Minifterie of
Angels is often
teftified by the
Propehts .*

Tob. 3 . v.
25 . ad . cap .
12 . v . 21 .
21 . Iudith .
13 . v . 20 .
Iob . 9 . v .

13 .
Pf . 33 . v .
8 . *Pf* . 90 .
v . 11 .

Eccle . 5 .
v . 5 .
Baruc . 6 .
v . 6 .

Dan . 3 .
v . 49 . 50 .

v . 92 .
v . 95 .

Dan . 6 .
v . 22 .
Dan . 14 .
v . 20 . 31 .
Zach . 1 .
v . 11 . 12 .

Zach . 3 .
v . 7 .

thefe wordes . O Lord of hoaftes, how long wilt thou not haue mercie on Ierufalem, and on the Cities of Iuda, with which thou haft bene angrie .] God alfo promifed, that Angels fhal affift the Prelates of the Church faying to them [I wil geue thee walkers of them that now affift here] .

Angels affift the Prelates of the Church .

6 That Angels haue protection of Countries, appeareth by the relation of the fame Prophet Daniel , whofe Angel faid to him, that whiles he praied for the deliuerie of the Iewes [the Prince (faith he) of the Kingdome of the Perfians , refifted me one and twentie daies . And behold Michael, one of the cheife princes, came to aide me :] And being ftrengthned and going forth, there appeared the Prince of the Greekes coming . (And Gabriel the Angel faid) [But yet I wil tel thee, that which is expreffed in the Scripture of truth : and none is my helper in al thefe, but Michael your Prince .] And againe, forefhewing to Daniel the perfecutions of Antiochus, and of Antichrift, fignifyeth plainly, that S . Michael is the fpecial protector of the Church, faying : [But in that time fhal rife vp Michael the great Prince, who ftandeth for the children of thy people.] In part fulfilled, when Iudas Machabeus, with a fmal armie vifiblie encoraged, and inuifiblie affifted by the Angel that appeared, going before them as [an horfeman in white cloathing, with armor of gold, fhaking a fpeare] fo ouerthrew Lyfias with his armie of fourfcore thoufand footemen, and a great band of horfmen, that Lyfas was forced to feeke peace : and Antiochus conftrained to graunt it, by his feueral letters prefently fent, both to Lyfias and to the Iewes them felues ; with pretence of great good wil towardes them .

Angels protectors of countries and kingdomes : And doe pray for them .

S . Michael the protector of the Church in the old Teftament : and alfo of the Chriftiã Church.

Dan . 10.
v . 13 .

v . 19 .
20 .
21 .

Dan . 12 .
v . 1 .

2 . *Mac* .
11. *v* . 6 .
8 .

v . 22 .
27 .

7 In the new Teftament alfo it is cleare, that God vfeth the minifterie of Angels, and that we receiue

God ftil vfeth the minifterie of Angels,

manie

in this time of grace.

manie gracious benefites, by the same ministerie, & mediation of the holie Angels. The Archangel [Gabriel, was sent from God (to declare his Diuine wil) to the most B. Virgin] and taking her submissiue consent therto, the Sonne of God was incarnate and made Man, our Redemer. [An Angel signified to Ioseph her spouse, that she had conceiued, not of man but of the Holie Ghost.] An Angel declared the ioyful birth of our B. Sauiour, to Shepheardes : and a multitude of Angels, praised God for the same saying : [Glorie in the highest to God : and in earth peace to men of good wil.] An Angel admonished Ioseph, to flee with the Childe, and his Mother into Egipt. An Angel recalled them from thence. Angels ministred to our Sauiour in the desert. Our Sauiour threatneth the scandalizers of litle ones, subnecting this reason, why such should feare reuenge, [Because their Angels in heauen, alwaies see the face of his Father] which importeth that Angels are Guardians, and protectors of men. He also affirmeth, that [there shal be ioy before the Angels of God, vpon one sinner that doth penance] which could not be, except they knew when sinners repent. [The soule of poore Lazarus was caried by Angels into Abrahams bosome.] The Pond of Probatica [the water being stirred by an Angel] had vertue to heale anie corporal infirmitie. [Our B. Sauiour vouchsaifed to receiue comforth of an Angel, when he was in agonie.] The night of his Passion [Angels declared his Resurrection.] Angels appearing at his Ascension, [warned vs to expect his coming] to iudge. An Angel deliuered the Apostles out of prison, when they were imprisoned : And particularly S. Peter, when Herode ment to haue slaine him. And when he repaired to his faithful frendes, they hearing suddenly of his being at the doare, thought it had bene [his *Angel*

Luc. 1.
v. 26. 28.

Mat. 1.
v. 20.

Luc. 2. *v.*
10. 14.

Mat. 2. *v.*
13. 19.

Mat. 4.
v. 11.

Mat. 18.
v. 10.

Luc. 15.
v. 10.

Luc. 16.
v. 22.
Ioan. 5.
v. 5.
Luc. 22.
v. 43.
Mat. 28.
v. 5. *Io.*
20. *v.* 12.
13.
Act. 1. *v.*
10. *Act.* 5.
v. 19. *Act.*
12. *v.* 7. 15.

Euerie one hath a proper Angel Guardian.

Angel] fo firmly they beleued, that he had an Angel his proper Guardian. An Angel fignified to Cornelius, that his praiers & almes deedes, were afcended into heauen. *An* Angel told S. Paul [that he muft appeare before Cæfar (at Rome) and that [God had geuen him the liues of al thofe that failed with him.] S. Paul teacheth that [it is meete for women to be couered, in refpect of Angels] which are prefent in the Church. He affirmeth that [Angels are miniftring Spirites, fent to minifter for them that fhal receiue the inheritance of faluation.] *An* Angel [reuealed to S. Iohn, the high and hard mifteries] writen by him in the Apocalyps. Finally, in the end of this world, an Archangel fhal cal al men to Iudgement, founding his Trumpet. And then Angels as [the reapers (of Goddes corne) fhal gather the good (as his wheate) into the barne (the glorious kingdome of heauen) And fhal caft the wicked into the furnace of fire.] In the meane time, Angels, and other Sainctes in heauen, [do prefent before the Lambe (Chrift) the odoures (that is the praiers) of the faithful in earth.]

8   Contrariwife, diuels, of mere malice and enuie, tempt men, and feeke their ruine, to bring them by offending God, to be bond-flaues to finne [For wherwith a man is ouercome, of that he is the flaue alfo] faith S. Peter. And our Lord faid to certaine reprobate Iewes [you are of your father the diuel, & the defires of your father you wil doe. He was a man-killer from the beginning] that is, a deftroier of fpiritual life in man, when he ouercame our firft Parents, tempting them to breake Goddes commandement. So alfo [the diuel put into the hart of Iudas Ifcariote, to betray Chrift.] This inueterate aduerfarie the diuel [as a roaring Lyon, goeth about, feeking whom he may deuoure.] It is moft true & confeffed

Act. 10.
v. 4.

Act. 27.
v. 23.24.

1. *Cor.* 11.
v. 10.

Heb. 1.
v. 14.

Apoc. 1.
v. 1. *&c.*

Mat. 13.
v. 30.39.
40.44.

1. *Thef.* 4.
v. 16.

Apoc. 5.
v. 8.

2. *Pet.* 2.
v. 19.

Ioan. 8.
v. 44.

Gen. 3.
v. 4.6.

Ioan. 13.
v. 2.

1. *Pet.* 5.
v. 8.

Diuels doe tempt men by fuggefting euil motions.

S

fessed by al, that diuels can, and doe, suggest, by secret internal motions, to mennes hartes, al kindes of sinne. And it is no lesse certaine, both in reason, & Catholique faith (though the diuel haue bewitched some not to beleue it) that holie Angels, can, & doe, suggest good motions, to the secret mindes of men : not by corporal tongues, eares, nor eyes (for this is as friuolous an imagination in respect of diuels, as of holie Angels) but by other meanes to vs insensible, or at least inexplicable. And it is tooto absurd, to denie that power and habilite, to be in the B. Angels ; which can not be denied to be in wicked diuels. And how like in this respect, glorious soules are to holie Angels, is to be shewed in the Articles of praying to Sainctes.

It is verie absurd to denie, that good Angels can suggest good motions.

Parte 4.
Article 44
45.

Man at first received Original Iustice, which he lost by transgressing Goddes Commandement, and infected al his Progenie, with Original sinne.

A R T I C L E . 13 .

Man made to the image and liknes of God.

AFter Angels, Man is the most principal creature, whose bodie being formed of the slime of the earth, his soule was created immediatly by God; not produced of anie thing preexisting. For as holie Scripture saith : [Our Lord breathed into his face the spirit of life, and man became a liuing soule.] Not as the soule or life of beastes, and plantes, but a liuing soule for euer immortal ; indued with vnderstanding, and free wil ; a rational creature [made to the Image and likenes of God] capable of the vision of God, which is eternal glorie. His Bodie perfected with health, strength, beawtie, agilitie, and other excellent qualities, with admirable

Gen. 2.
v. 7.

rable diſpoſition of partes, and members apt for al humane functions. His ſoule was adorned further, not only with al natural knowlege, but alſo with ſupernatural grace. And ſo man was placed in the Paradiſe of pleaſures, and had Dominion ouer al the earthly and corporal creatures of this lower world. in diuers reſpectes participant of the natures of al other creatures. And therfore is aptly called *Michrocoſmos: A litle world* within him ſelf. Al which is teſtified, and proued by holie Scriptures.

A litle world.

2   When God had made heauen and earth, & other particular creatures, behooful for mannes vſe : then he ſaid [Let vs make man to our Image & likenes; and let him haue dominion ouer the fiſhes of the ſea, and the ſoules of the aire, and the beaſtes, and the whole earth, and al creeping creature, that moueth vpon the earth.] Such was then mannes natural knowlege, that when [our Lord brought vnto him al beaſtes of the earth, and ſoules of the aire, that he might ſee what to cal them, he called them al by their names; for as Adam called anie liuing creature, the ſame is his name] that is, the ſame is the Etimologie or breefe deſcription of their ſeueral natures . And when [God had caſt a dead ſleepe vpon Adam, & had taken one of his ribbes, and built (or framed) the ſame into a woman, and brought her to Adam] he ſaid [this now is bone of my bones, and fleſh of my fleſh . ſhe ſhal be called woman, becauſe ſhe was taken out of man] : As the original tongue ſignifieth which in latin is interpreted *virago*, that is, *virum agere*, or *virum repreſentare*, to act or repreſent a man. Much greater, were his ſpiritual graces, original iuſtice, pure innocencie, from al fault and ſinne; habits of al vertues, theological and moral, in that perfect rectitude of mind, that his reaſon and wil were readily ſubiect to Gods wil; the inferiour powers of his ſoul ſubiect to reaſon; and alſo al elemental

Gen . 1 .
v . 26 .

Gen . 2 .
v . 19 .
20 .

v . 21 .
v . 22 .

v . 23 .

Mans excellēt knowlege in his ſtate of innocencie.

He was more excellent in ſupernatural grace.

tal liuing creatures; euen the terrible Lions, the cruel Tigers, the great Elephantes, wildeſt birdes, moſt hidden and huge fiſhes, were obedient to his commãdement.

God gaue man a particular precept, for excerciſe of obedience. And ſo to merite more grace.

3　In this ſo happie ſtate, whiles man knew and enioyed much good, and neither knew nor felt anie euil; God who is goodnes it ſelf, for mannes more good, for his exerciſe in vertue, that he might merit and receiue more grace, & perſeuering therin ſhould neuer haue died, but haue bene tranſlated to eternal glorie : gaue him a particular precept, not to eate of the frute of a cettaine tree (vpon this occaſion afterwardes called the tree of knowledge of good and euil) with charge and fore-warning, that if he ſhould tranſgreſſe this commandement [what day ſoeuer he ſhould eate of it, he ſhould dye the death.]　*Gen.* 2.　*v.* 17.

The diuel deceiued Eue, by ſutletie, and three egregious lies.

4　But the ſerpent (the diuel in forme of a ſerpent) malicious againſt God, and enuious of mannes good, ſuttly aſſaulting the woman, ſaid vnto her : [why hath God commanded you that you ſhould not eate of euerie tree in paradiſe ?] added alſo to his ſutle and calumnious demand, three moſt pernicious lies : that by eating of this frute, they ſhould not incurre death; that they ſhould become as goddes; & that God therfore forbade them to eate therof, leſt they ſhould be as goddes. Which ſhe hearing, and not ſuſpecting the diuels craft, nor malice, and ſeing withal the tree, and frute to be good [faire to the eyes,　*Gen.* 3.　*v.* 1.　*v.* 4.　*v.* 5.　*v.* 16.

She allured Adam & ſo they, and al mankind, loſt original iuſtice; incurred ſinne & death.

and delectable to behold, toke of the frute theerof, and did eate, and gaue to her husband, who did eate. And by and by, they were aſhamed, perceiuing their owne nakednes which before had no deformitie. But by their diſobedience to God, al was changed, innocencie, with al vertues, loſt; nature corrupted; and they made ſlaues to the diuel, ſubiect to ſinne and death, with other loſſes perteyning to al　*v.* 7.
　　　　　　　　　　　　　　　　　　　　　　　　　　　mankind

mankind.

5   Al which holie Dauid amongst other Prophets & godlie persons, considering, and admiring the goodnes of god, who after so great benefites bestowed vpon man, and his ingratitude in so transgressing; yet recalled him to repentance, and promised a Redemer to deliuer him from thraldome; crieth thus vnto God

Pʃ. 8.
*v.*2.
our so merciful Sauiour [O Lord our Lord, how meruelous is thy name in the whole earth ?] Meruelous in verie deede in al thinges, aswel in heauen, as in earth : but to mankind, aboue al, most bountiful, in first and last benefites, who deseruing nothing, recciuing much good, and rendring euil; is not for al that vtterly reiected, as he iustly deserued, but eftsons

*v.*5.
recalled to new grace, and to eternal glorie [what is man (saith the same Royal Psalmist to our Lord God) that thou art mindful of him; or the sonne of man that thou visitest him] then describing his first

*v.*6.
dignitie and happie state, addeth [thou hast minished him a litle lesse then Angels : with glorie and honour thou hast crowned him, and hast apointed him

v. 7.
v. 8.
ouer the work of thy handes. Thou hast subiected al thinges vnder his feete : al sheepe and oxen ; more-

*v.*9.
ouer also the beastes of the feelde . The birdes of the aire, and fishes of the sea, that walke the pathes of the sea.] In fine, because Goddes loue lasteth to the end, redeming and sauing his seruants perseuering

*v.*10.
in grace, concludeth the psalme as he beganne [O Lord our Lord, how meruelous is thy name in the whole earth ?]

*Pʃ.*13.
*v.*1.
6   The same Prophet in an other psalme affirmeth, that al are become abominable, there is not one that doth good, no not one. And so bewailing mannes doleful state after sinne, saith in the name of al mankind. [The sorowes of death haue compassed me : & tormentes of iniquitie haue troubled me . The so-

Gods wonderful mercie in redeming man, and recalling him to repentance.

That al mankind was infected with sinne by Adams fal, is proued by Holie Scriptures.

S 3   rowes

rowes of hel haue compaſſed me ; the ſnares of death haue preuēted me .] And exhorting penitents to ſinne nomore ; putteth vs in mind, that lack of conſidera- tion, bronght our firſt parents to ſinne, who hauing reaſon and vnderſtandiug, did not vſe it in time of tentation [Man (ſaith he) when he was in honour, did not (actually) vnderſtand (was ſo negligent, & ſo allured with vaine and falſe imagination, as ifhe had bene without vnderſtanding) he was compared to beaſtes without vnderſtanding, and became like to them.] Signifying that not actual vnderſtanding and conſidering, when preſent vſe therof is required, maketh a man like to beaſtes, which indeede haue no vnderſtanding .

Pſ. 17. *v.* 5.6.

Pſ. 48. *v.* 13. 21,

Not God, but man him ſelf, by the diuels tentation was the cauſe of ſinne, & death.

7　Now that this great alteration of mannes ſtate, & cauſe therof, proceded from him ſelf, (yelding to ten- tation) and not of God: Salomon breefly teacheth after a large diſcourſe of mannes preſent infirmitie , in theſe few wordes [onlie this (ſaith he) I haue found, that God made man right, and he hath entan- gled him ſelf with infinite queſtions .] Of al queſti- ons, that firſt was moſt hurtful to mākind, which was propounded by the diuel [why God commanded ab- ſtinence from one tree ?] wherwith our firſt parents ought not to haue entangled them ſelues. for that true obedience performeth whatſoeuer is comman- ded, without asking, or anſwearing, but leauing to God the reaſon, why he hath ſo commanded. Con- formablie to Salomon, the Auctors of the bookes of Wiſdome and Eccleſiaſticus, ſpeake of the alterati- on of mannes ſtate, and of the cauſe therof procedirg from him ſelf, by yelding to tentation, and not from God [For God created man iacorruptible (ſaith the ſacred text) and to the Image of his owne likenes he made him .. But by the enuie of the diuel, death en- tred into the world] In the former verſe ſhewing,

Eccle. 7. *v.* 30.

Sap. 2. 23. 24.

that God

that God made man according to his owne Image,
without corruptiõ, that he might haue escaped death,
if he had refrained from sinne : in the next verse he
ascribeth the cause of death to the diuel, as first auctor of mãnes sinne, by which death entred vpon man,
who leauing Goddes commandement, folowed the
perswasion of the craftie enuious serpent. And so
this diuine writer addeth in the last verse ; [that they
folow him (the diuel) that are of his part] that is,
those that embrace the diuels suggestion, and ioyne
partie with him, are the folowers and the seruants of
the diuel. Which same doctrine, the other holie writer explicateth somwhat more largelie saying : [God
from the beginning made man; and left him in the
hand of his owne counsel . He added his commandements and precepts. If thou wilt kepe the commandement, and kepe acceptable fidelitie ; for e-
uer they shal preserue thee . He hath set before thee
water and fire, to which thou wilt, stretch forth thine
hand . Before man there is life and death, good and
euil, what pleaseth him, shal be geuen him .] And
the reason why God left man in his free choice, is
here ascribed to his diuine wisdome, power, & goodnes [because the wisdome of God is much, and he
is strong in might, seing al men without intermission .
The eyes of our Lord are towardes them that feare
him, and he knoweth al the worke of man . He hath
commanded no man to doe impiously, and he hath
geuen no man space to sinne . For he desireth not a
multitude of faithles and vnprofitable children .] A-
gaine the same is inculcated for better impression ther
of in our mindes . [God created man of the earth,
and after his owne Image he made him . And againe
he turned him into it, and conformable to him self,
cloathed him with strength .] For man at first receiued original iustice, and strength of grace, wherby
he might

v . 25 .

*Eccle.*15.
v . 14 .
15. 16.

17.

18.

v. 19 .

20.

21.

22.

*Eccle.*17.
v 1. 2.

Gods wisdom
requireth mã s
cooperation to
merite

His power
draweth good
of euil. His
Goodnes ha-
teth sinne .

he might if he would, haue refifted al tentations . He
receiued alfo other power and dominion in the earth
as foloweth in the text . [God gaue him a number of ~~v~~ . 3 .
daies, and time; & gaue him power of thofe thinges
that are vpon the earth . He put his feare ouer al flefh ~~v~~ . 4 .
and he had dominion of beaftes, and foules . He cre- 5 .
ated of him an helper like to him felf; he gaue them
counfel, and tongue, and eyes, and eares, and hart
to deuife : and he filled them with the difcipline of
vnderftanding . He created in them the knowlege of 6 .
the fpirit, he filled their hart with vnderftanding, &
euil and good he fhewed them . He fet his eye v- 7 .
pon their hartes, to fhew them the great thinges of
his workes; that they might praife the name of
fanctification ; and glorie in his meruelous workes, 8 .
that they might declare the glorious thinges of his
workes . He added difcipline vnto them, (geuing 9 .
them a precept for exercife of their obedience, ther -
by to merit reward) and made them inherite the Law
of life . He made an euerlafting Teftamēt with them; 10 .
and he fhewed them Iuftice, and his iudgementes .]
Thus writeth the wife man concerning the firft ftate
and fal of mankind . In al his booke teaching, and
exhorting al men, to ferue God, and to contemne
this world . [Who is proued therin (faith he) and *Eccl* . 31 .
perfect ; fhal haue eternal glorie .] In fumme he de- ~~v~~ . 10 .
fineth who it is that fhal be fo happie ; to witte ,
[he that could tranfgreffe, and hath not tranfgreffed; & doe euils, and hath not done .]

The merite &
glorie of the
iuft is by reafō
of their free
choice, not to
doe euil when
they could doe
it.

8　Wherin we may eafilie confider, not only the
wifdome, power, and goodnes of God; but alfo the
euerlafting ioy of the B. Sainctes to be herein declared, that thofe doe merit and receiue eternal glorie,
which could tranfgreffe and did not, wheras if God
had made man fo, that he could not tranfgreffe ; there
had not bene this iuft caufe of merite, nor of reward .

　　　　　　　　　　　　　　　　　　　　　Yea

Yea albeit man by the abuse of this power, fel from God, and from his firſt happie ſtate : yet God turneth this euil, both to his owne more glorie, & to the greater good of al thoſe, that wil receiue and rightly vſe his new grace, then if Adam had not fallen.

9   For his ſinne had (as is reueled in holie Scripture) two farre different effeces, the one proper and connatural to his offence, which was the infection of al his progenie, borne (by natural generation) with original ſinne ; the other effect, was alſo by occaſion of this infection of al mankind ; but properly of the inexplicable goodnes of God, ordeining for remedie of this vniuerſal euil, the incarnation of our B. Sauiour Chriſt ; by whoſe ſuperabundāt grace, his faithful children are clenſed from al ſinnes, original, and actual ; and made participant of greater grace, and conſequently of greater glorie, then otherwiſe they ſhould haue bene. Both which effectes, S. Paul teacheth : Eſpecially in his Epiſtle to the Romanes. Of the former writing thus. [As by one man ſinne entred into this world, and by ſinne death : ſo vnto al men death did paſſe, in which al ſinned.] Which he confirmeth anſwearing to an obiection, that it might ſeme, there was no ſuch general ſinne in al men, ſeing before the Law, it did not ſo appeare in al ; therfore he ſaith, [that alſo in that former time, euen vnto the Law, ſinne was in the world ; but ſinne was not imputed (or did not appeare) when the Law was not. But death (which is the effect of ſinne) reigned from Adam vnto Moyſes ; euen on them alſo, that ſinned not, after the ſimilitude of the preuarication of Adam] to witte on thoſe more iuſt perſons alſo, that did not actually tranſgreſſe as Adam had done, yet they died, becauſe they were originallie ſinners. And ſo the Apoſtle concludeth this firſt point with an appendix that [Adam is a figure of him

T   to come

Adams ſinne had two effectes. One euil of the nature of ſinne. The other good, by the goodnes of God.

The firſt effect: infection of al man with ſinne.

Rom. 5.
v. 12.

v. 13.

v. 14.

to come] fignifying that as by the finne of Adam we
al dye ; fo by the grace of Chrift, al his children liue .

The other ef-
fect; abun-
dance of grace
by Chrift.

10   Touching the other effect, he addeth the great
difference, faying : [But not as the offence, fo alfo   *v .* 15.
the gift . For if by the offence of one, manie dyed :
much more the grace of God, & the gift in the grace
of one man Iefus Chrift, hath abounded vpon manie .
[And not as by one finne, fo alfo the gift; for iudg-   16.
ment indeede is of one to condemnation : but grace
is of manie offences to iuftification . For if in the of-   17.
fence of one, death reigned by one : much more they
that receiue the abundance of grace, and of the do-
nation, and of Iuftice; fhal reigne in life, by one Iefus Chrift . Therfore as by the offence of one vnto al   18.
men, to condemnation : fo alfo by the iuftice of one,
vnto al men to iuftification of life . For as by the dif-   19.
obedience of one man, manie were made finners : fo
alfo by the obedience of one, manie fhal be made
iuft .] Thus S . Paul in that place . By which doctrine of the Apoftle, is verified that which the Church
fo folemnly fingeth in the feftiuitie of our Redemption : *O certe neceffarium Adæ peccatum, quod Chrifti*
morte deletum eft ! O fælix culpa, quæ talem et tantum
meruit habere Redemptorem . Wherto agree manie o-
ther paffages in the reft of S. Paul his doctrine . And
the fame is breefly comprifed, in that which S . Iohn   *Ioan .* I .
Baptift denounced of Our Sauiour, faying : [Behold   *v .* 29.
the Lambe of God; behold him that taketh away
the finne of the world .] That is, Principally Chrift
came to take away that general finne, which being
actual in Adam, is original in the whole world; and
therof called *The finne of the world* . And the fame is
the general doctrine of S . Iohn the Apoftle and E-   1 . *Ioan .* I .
uangelift, faying : [If we walke in the light, as God   *v .* 7.
alfo is in the light; we haue focietie one toward an
other, and the bloud of Iefus Chrift his Sonne, cleanseth vs

feth vs from al finne] firft trom Original, then alfo
from actual.

Mannes vnderftanding & Freewil, are weakned by
finne, but not wholly loft.

ARTICLE. 14.

Luc. 10.
v. 30.
&c.

A Certaine man (faith our Sauiour in a Parable) went downe from Ierufalem into Iericho , and fel among theues, who fpoyled
him, and geuing him woundes, went away, leauing
him half dead.] Of no particular man, can this parable be fo properly expounded, as of al mankind in
general, conteined in Adam our firft Parent : who
being indued with al neceffarie giftes, natural, and
fupernatural, going from Goddes commandement,
yelded to falfe imagination of bettering his ftate, as
it were defcending frō Ierufalem, the vifion of peace,
to Iericho, fignifying the moone (which is vncon-
ftant, and mutable) fel among theues, the diuels,
who fpoiled and wounded him, & left him half dead.
For fo Adam by finning, and al men in him, were
fpoiled of original Iuftice, and fupernatural grace,
and wounded in natural powers of vnderftanding,
and freewil : not wholly depriued of al, but fpoiled
of the beft part, and wounded in the reft : fpiritually
dead, and fubiect, both to temporal & eternal death :
yet not actually dead in bodie, nor defperatly in foule,
but *femiuiuo relicto* , *left half dead, & half aliue,* though
left without helpe by the Preift, and Leuite, the Sa-
rifices, and other minifteries of the old Law ; yet releued by the merciful Samaritan, our Sauiour Chrift,
by him brought into the Inne the Catholike Church;
wherein al fpiritual woundes are curable, and loffes re-
couerable, by Goddes grace ftrengthning, and inha-

Al mankind
was fpoiled of
grace, & woū-
ded in natural
faculties by A-
dams fal.

T 2   bling

bring man to cooperate therwith, by faith and good workes. For as it is impoſſible for anie man, without grace, either to doe, or to think anie good thing: ſo by grace, mannes vnderſtanding is illuminated, & his wil is inclined, to beleue, and to kepe Goddes Law . And as for the power of vnderſtanding , no man is altogether ſo ſottiſh, but he ſuppoſeth & confeſſeth, that he hath the ſame in his ſoule, els he were a mere brute beaſt, not a man, if he had no reaſon, nor vnderſtanding at al, actually, or potentially, as we ſpeake in ſcooles . But touching the other connatural power of freewil : ſome men haue ſo litle reaſon left, that they denie it to be in man, ſince the ſinne & fal of Adam . So phantaſtical were the Maniches, an old infamous ſect of heretikes. And ſo ſenſles was Luther, the father of al Proteſtantes, that he could not brooke, the verie name and word *Liberum arbitrium*, but changed it into the contrarie terme *ſeruum arbitrium*. And ſo being moued to write againſt Freewil, intitled his brutiſh worke; *De ſeruo arbitrio*, of ſeruile, or ſlauiſh wil . For ſo much therfore, as moſt Proteſtants hold with Luther in this doctrine : I ſhal here recite ſuch holie Scriptures, as moſt plainlie ſhew, that euerie man, whether he be iuſt, or wicked, if he haue the vſe of reaſon, hath alſo fredom of wil to conſent, or not to conſet, to thoſe thinges, thoughtes, wordes, and deedes, which his vnderſtanding cenceiueth. For euen as the conceipt, is the proper act of the vnderſtanding : ſo is conſent the proper act of the wil .

2 To begin therfore with the ſtate of wicked men, more enormous ſinners, wherof there may ſeme to be more doubt : it is cleare , that Cain hauing conceiued malice and enuie againſt his brother Abel; when he was exceding angrie, and his countenance abated ; [Our Lord ſaid vnto him ; why art thou angrie ? & why

2 . *Cor*. 3. *v*. 5. *Phil*. 4. *v*. 13.

Gen. 4. *v*. 5. 6. 7

Proteſtantes acknowlege that man was not wholly depriued of vnderſtading. Yet Manichees and Proteſtãts denie freewil to remaine in man .

That freewil remaineth in ſinners is proued by holie Scriptures .

why is thy countenance fallen? If thou doſt wel, ſhal thou not receiue againe? but if thou doeſt il, ſhal not thy ſin forthwith be preſent at the dore? But the luſt therof ſhal be vnder thee, and thou ſhalt haue dominion ouer it.] Which laſt wordes, doe ſo inuinciblie proue freewil to remaine in a wicked ſinner (the luſt of ſinne being vnder him, and he hauing dominion ouer it) that our aduerſaries to auoide the force of ſo manifeſt conuiction, haue corrupted the holie text in their Engliſh tranſlations, making it to ſay thus. *Vnto* thee his deſire ſhal be ſubiect: and thou ſhalt rule ouer him. Abſurdly referring that to Abel (who is not at al named in Goddes expoſtulation with Cain) which is directlie ſpoken of the luſt or concupiſcence of ſinne. As if God had ſaid, that the deſire of Abel, ſhould be ſubiect to Cain; and Cain, ſhould haue dominon ouer him. An other example is in the caſe of Pharao being indurate in hart. In whom yet remained freewil, as plainly appeareth by Goddes admonition, which Moyſes declared vnto him ſaying: [This ſaith our Lord: Diſmiſſe my people to ſacrifice vnto me. And if thou wilt not diſmiſſe them, behold I wil ſend in vpon thee, and vpon thy ſeruantes, and vpon thy people, and vpon thy houſes, al kind of ſlees] which conditional threatning of puniſhment, if pharao would not diſmiſſe the Iſraelites: ſheweth that it was in his choiſe, whether he would diſmiſſe them or no. Neither could God haue iuſtly puniſhed him, if it had not bene in his choiſe & power.

Euliſh Bibles. *An.* 1579. 1602

Exo. 8. *v.* 20. 21.

3 Goddes couenãts alſo made with his people, doe proue the ſame libertie of wil, to be in al men. For vnleſſe men haue ſee wil, to breake, or not to breake Goddes precepts, the couenant were in vaine, and the precepts ſhould not haue bene geuē in ſuch forme of wordes as they are, with expreſſe termes of con - ditions

That men haue freewil is proued by the couenantes made betwene God and his people.

ditions, to be rewarded or punished, accordidg as
they would kepe, or not kepe, Goddes commandement. As when Moyſes praied God to remaine, &
goe with the people, and [take away their ſinnes &   *Exo.*34.
iniquities, and poſſeſſe them: our Lord anſweared;   *v.*9.
I wil make a couenant in the ſight of al] which be-   *v.*10.
ing made by the peoples good liking, and free conſ-
ſent, that none afterwardes ſhould plead ignorance,
or pretend obliuion for excuſe: Moyſes repeateth
it vnto them, and left it written in theſe wordes.
[Thou haſt choſen our Lord this day to be thy God   *Deut.*26.
and to walk in his waies, and kepe his ceremonies,   *v.*17.
and precepts, and iudgements. And our Lord hath   *v.*18.
choſen thee this day, that thou ſhould be his peculi-   *v.*19.
ar people: and he wil make thee higher, then al nations which he created, that thou maiſt be a holie people of our Lord thy God:] But euer with this condition [If after thou haſt heard theſe iudgements,   *Deut.*7.
thou kepe and doe them: the Lord alſo thy God wil   *v.*12.
kepe the couenant vnto thee, and the mercie which   *Deut.*11.
he ſware to thy Fathers.] And for that there can   *v.*16.
be no doubt on Goddes part: that the people ſhould
not fail; Moyſes againe and againe warneth them ſaying [Beware leſt perhaps your hart be deceiued, &
you depart frō our Lord, and ſerue ſtrange goddes,
and adore them.] Yea if they fal, they haue ſtil,
through grace which God wil geue them, power to
returne if they wil, and then God wil agane reioyce
vpon them [Yet ſo (ſaith he) if thou heare the voice   *Deut.*30.
of our Lord thy God, and kepe his precepts. Con-   *v.*9.10.
ſider that I haue ſet before thee this day, life & good;   *v.*15.
and contrariwiſe, death and euil.]   * I cal for wi-   * *v.*19.
tneſſes this day heauen and earth, that I haue propoſed to you, life and death; bleſſing and curſing:
Chooſe therfore life, that both thou maiſt liue, & thy
ſeede.] Ioſue in the verie ſame maner, a litle before   *Ioſue.*24.
his   *v.*14.

his death, so iterateth these admonitions, as he mult
needes suppose, that it is in mannes freewil, to break,
or not break, Goddes cōmandements saying : [Now
therfore feare our Lord, and serue him with a perfect
and verie true hart : and take away the goddes which
your fathers serued in Mesopotamia, and in Egipt,
v.15. and serue our Lord. But if it like you not to serue
our Lord, choice is geuen you; choose this day that
v.16. which pleaseth you &c. And the people answeared
and said : God forbid we should leaue our Lord, &
serue strange goddes.] Wherupon Iosue, to ratifie the couenant, concludeth it, saying to the people :
v.22. [you are witnesses, that your selues haue chosen vnto
you, our Lord for to serue him. And they answeared
v.23. witnesses. Now therfore (quoth he) take away
v.24. strange goddes out of the middest of you, & incline
v.25. your hartes to our Lord the God of Israel· And the
people said to Iosue, we wil serue our Lord God, &
wil be obedient to his precepts. Iosue therfore that
day made a couenant, and proposed to the people
precepts & Iudgements in Sichem.] After al which
good purposes, and solemne promises, this people fel
often from God, and were punished : repenting also
were releued; as is recorded in the Histories folowing, of the Iudges & Kinges.

4   In which meane time, manie Prophets, with great
zeale and diligence admonished sinners, as hauing power of the wil, to sinne, or not to sinne. Dauid cri-
Ps.31. ed [Doe not become as horse and mule, which haue
v.9. no vnderstāding.] Arguing, that seing they haue vnderstanding, wherby they excel horse and mule, and
al brute beastes; it behoueth them not to become
in life and maners, like to brute beastes, but doing
that which reason directeth, shew them selues by
right vse of their wil, that they therin also excel
beastes. And because wilful obstinacie doth obscure

Proued by the
admonition of
Prophetes, &
other godlie
men.

the

the vnderstanding; he imputeth affected ignorance to
the wil saying of such a one [he would not vnder- *Pf*. 35.
stand tliat he might doe wel .] And for that no man *v*. 4.
can without special grace, doe that is right, as the
Prophet Iereremie affirmeth saying : [I know Lord, *Iere*. 10.
that mannes way is not his owne, neither is it in a *v*. 23.
man, to walke, and to direct his steppes:] So much
the more man is bond, not to resist grace, being often offered by God ; which holie Dauid calleth making of the way, wherof he saith : [Make way to him *Pf*. 67.
who mounteth vpon the west] that is, resist not, *v*. 5.
but ioyfully with consent of wil, receiue the inspirations of God. Which sense is confirmed by that
the same Royal Prophet, shewing the cause why some
perish, to be their refusing to approach to God, &
fleeing from him [For behold (saith he) they that *Pf*. 72.
make them selues farre from thee, shal perish .] Ther- *v*. 27.
fore also God him self saith [Heare, o my people, *Pf*. 80.
and I wil contest thee (most seriously admonish thee) *v*. 9
Israel, if thou wilt heare me.] Againe the same prophet crieth vnto the Israelites [To day if you wil *Pf*. 94.
heare his voice, harden not your hartes.] Of the *v*. 8.
same wilful resistance, wisdome admonisheth, and *Heb*. 3.
threatneth ruine for this contempt [Because I called *v*. 8.
(saith wisdome) and you refused ; I streatched out *Prou*. 1.
my hand, and there was none that reguarded ; You *v*. 24.
haue despised al my counsel, and haue neglected my 25. 26.
reprehension : I also wil laugh in your destruction, 29. 30.
and wil scorne, when that shal come to you, which
you feared. For they haue hated discipline, and not
receiued the feare of our Lord, nor consented to my
counsel.] Likewise on the other side, wisdome pro- *Prou*. 2.
miseth al good thinges to those that wil heare & con- *v*. 1.
sent to good inspirations. [My sonne, if thou wilt
receiue my wordes, and wilt repose my commandements with thee, that thine eare may heare wisdome,
incline

Ieremies wor-
des doe not dis-
proue freewil,
but testifie
the weaknes
therof without
Gods grace.

incline thine harte to know prudence .] Againe ,
[If wifdome fhal enter into thine harte, and knowlege pleafe thy foule : counfel fhal kepe thee, & prudence fhal preferue thee.] Yea the whole tenure of
al the Sapiential bookes is, to teach and perfwade
man, to vfe rightly the two powers of his foule, vnderftanding, and free wil , by moft wholfome and
diuine precepts, which may illuminate the vnderftanding, to fee that is right and iuft, and inflame the
wil, and internal affection, to defire, loue, choofe, &
preferre, the right path of Goddes Law, before whatfoeuer otherwife feemeth pleafant, or profitable .

5   Neuertheleffe, let vs adde fome few fentences of
other Prophets, to the fame purpofe . Ifaias, as in the
behalf of God, promifeth the people, both remiffion
of finnes, and relaxation from captiuitie, with this
perpetual condition, if they be willing , and wil heare
him : then [If your finnes (faith he) fhal be as fcarlet, they fhal be made white as fnow; and if they be
red as vermileon, they fhal be white as wool : If you
be willing, & wil heare me, you fhal eate of the good
thinges of the earth . But if you wil not, and wil prouoke me to wrath : the fword fhal deuoure you, becaufe the mouth of our Lord hath fpoken .] Towards
the end of his prophecie, forefhewing the reprobation of the Iewes ; he fignifyeth the caufe therof to
be, their wilful refufing, to heare God calling them ;
and wilful choife of thinges which God would not.
[You fhal al fal by flaughter (faith he) becaufe I called, and you haue not anfweared ; I fpake, & you
haue not heard; and you did euil in mine eyes ; and
you haue chofen the thinges that I would not.] The
Prophet Ieremie in the verie fame phrafe faith [If
thou wilt returne, o Ifrael faith our Lord, returne
to me : if thou wilt take away the ftumbling blocks
from my face, thou fhalt not be moued . Becaufe you
haue

v. 10.

Ifa. 1.
v. 18.
v. 19.
v. 20.

If. 65.
v. 12.

Iere. 4.
v. 1.

Iere. 7.
v. 13.

More teftimo-
nies of the
Prophets,

V

haue done al thefe workes, faith our Lord, and I haue 14.
fpoken to you early rifing, & fpeaking, and you haue
not heard, and I haue called you, and you haue not
anfweared: I wil doe to this houfe (the Temple) as
I did to Silo. And they heard not, nor inclined their　v.24.
eare, but haue gone in their pleafures, and in the per-　Iere.21.
uerfitie of their wicked hart.] In an other place, he　v.8.
reciteth and vrgeth the Law, where our Lord faith.　Iere.22.
[Behold I geue before you the way of life, and the　v.4.5.
way of death.] Not God, but them felues, hardned　Ch.26. v.
their owne neckes, as is written by Efdras [And　3.4.
they would not heare, and they remembred not thy　2. Efd. 9.
meruelous workes which thou haft done to them.　v.16.17.
And they hardned their neckes, and gaue their head
to returne to their feruitude, as it were by contention.] So al the Prophets in their admonitions, and
comminations, ftil afcribe the calamities, inuafions
of enemies, and the captiuities of Goddes people, to
their wilful reuolting from God. As hauing freewil
and power, through Goddes grace, which is neuer
wanting to doe wel, and alfo power to doe euil notwithftanding Goddes grace which forceth not with
neceffitie, but draweth fweetlie, as God him felf fpeaketh by Ofee his Prophet faying: [In the cordes of　Ofee.11.
Adã I wil draw them, in the bandes of Charitie. And　v.4.
I wil be to them as lifting vp the yoke vpon their
cheekes, and I declined to him that he might eate.]
6　This is the fweete yoke of Chrift, by which Gods　Mat.11.
grace, and mannes freewil, draw together. And this　v.30.
is the light burden of Goddes commandements, &
fweete meanes to obteine remiffion of finnes. For
what can be fweeter, lighter, or more reafonable,
then the condition propofed by our B. Sauiour [If　Mat.6.
you wil forgeue men their offences: your heauenly　v.14.15.
Father wil forgeue you alfo your offences. But if
you wil not forgeue: neither wil your heauenly Father

freewil with Gods grace can merite: and can doe il, notwithftand-ing Gods grace offered.

The fame doc-trine is confir-med by tefti-monies of the new Teftamét.

ther forgeue you your offences .] Shewing that it
is in our wil, to forgeue, or to defire reuenge. And

Mat. 23. to Ierufalem he faid : [How often would I gather
v. 37. together thy children, and thou wouldeft not ?]
Plainly fignifying, that their wil refifted his wil. Yea
though [the houfhoulder bade his feruant goe forth

Luc. 14. into the waies, and compel them, whom he fhould
v. 23. find to enter, that his houfe might be filled] it was
not properly by compulfion, but by earneft and frend-

Luc. 24. ly inuitation to his feaft. As when [the two Difci-
v. 29. ples going to Emaus forced (or conftrained) our Sa
uiour, to tarie there with them .] S. Iohn faith :

Ioan. 1. [As manie as receiued Chrift : he gaue them power
v. 12. to be made the Sonnes of God.] S. Peter faid to

Act. 5. Ananias that [it was in his power] to haue offered,
v. 4. or not offered his goodes to be in common, fignifying that his finne proceded merely from his freewil.

7 In al good workes it is moft certaine, that Goddes
grace, is the firft and principal caufe, and freewil the
fecundarie caufe, according to that which S. Paul

1. *Cor.* 15. faith of him felf [By the grace of God, I am that
v. 10. which I am, and his grace in me hath not bene void,
but I haue labored more abundantly then al they : yet
not I, but the grace of God with me :] Neither the
Grace of God alone, but the grace of God with me.
Both together doe effectually inhable men, to make
them felues veffels of faluation, as the fame Apo-

2. *Tim.* 2. ftle likewife writeth to Timothie [if anie man ther-
v. 21. fore fhal cleanfe him felf from the veffels of contumelie : he fhal be a veffel vnto honour, fanctified and
profitable to our Lord ; prepared to euerie good

Phile. *v.* worke] Becaufe he would that Philemon fhould haue
14. occafion to merite, by geuing his free confent to a
good worke, he faith to him [Without thy counfel I would doe nothing (touching Onefimus) that

V 2   thy

Side notes:

God doth not
otherwife com-
pel, but by
good motions :
as a frend effec-
tually perfwa-
deth by ear-
neft inuitation.

In al good
workes Gods
grace being
the principal
caufe : Yet
freewil is the
fecundarie
caufe of me-
rite.

thy good might be, not as it were of neceſſitie but
voluntarie.] He exhorteth the Hebrewes to [folow peace and holines; looking diligently left anie
man be wanting to the grace of God .] S Iames willeth al to [be ſubiect to God, and to refiſt the diuel, and he wil flee from you; approach to God &
he wil approache to you. Cleanſe your handes
you ſinners, and purifie your hartes .] S . Iohn ſaith
[Euerie one that hath hope to ſee God; ſanctifieth
him ſelf] euen [Iezabel (or the moſt wicked) hath
time geuen her, that ſhe might doe penance, & ſhe
wil not repent . To al without exception God ſaith.
[Behold I ſtand at the doare and knock : If anie man
ſhal heare my voice, and open the gate, I wil enter
into him; and I wil ſupp with him, and he with me .]
Thus much, yea anie one of theſe ſo cleare textes of
holie Scripture, may ſuffice al men that haue anie conſideration, to ſhew, that as they haue reaſon, they
baue alſo freewil, to open, or not to open the doare
of their hart, when God knocketh by good inſpirations.

Heb. 12.
v. 15.

Iac. 4. *v.*
7. 8.

1. *Ioan* .3.
v. 3.
Apoc. 2.
v. 21.
Apoc. 3.
v. 20.

God offereth
grace to al,
ſomtimes
knocking at
the doore of
their hartes.

After the fal of man, God promiſed a Redemer :
who was alſo foreſhewed by manie figures,
and by al the Prophets.

ARTICLE · 15.

God of his
mere mercie
decreed to
ſend a Rede-
mer of man-
kind.

When man had forſaken God by yelding
to the ſuggeſtion of the diuel, who by fal-
ſed and ſubtiltie, ſeduced our mother Eue ;
and by her alurement ouerthrew Adam : yet God
forſooke not man, but by new grace, recalled him to
repentance, and for his Redemption , promiſed a ranſome, in rigour of iuſtice ſuperabundant . For wheras no men nor Angels, nor anie other creatures were
able

1. *Tim.* 2.
v. 14.

able, in this cafe, to fatisfie Goddes iuftice : God him felf ordeined to fend his onlie Sonne, to be made man, and by dying temporally for al mankind, to pay mannes debt of eternal death, and fo to reconcile man to his eternal Father, that al, which wil cooperate with his grace, may be reduced to eternal life; conquering death, finne, hel, and the diuel. Al which we fhal, God willing, clearly fhew by holie Scriptures, in the Articles folowing.

2 Firft therfore that God decreed to fend a Redemer of mankind, is proued by his promife made to certaine Patriarches; alfo by fundrie figures, and by al the Prophets of the old Teftament. But firft of al, this veritie is manifeft by that which God denounced to the old ferpent the diuel (when he called our firft parentes to account for their finne which they committed, being deceiued by the diuel) faying : [I wil put enmities betwene thee and the woman; & thy feede, and her feede : She fhal brufe thy head in peeces.] Signifying that notwithftanding the diuel had preuailed by deceiuing Eue, yet he fhould not ftil triumph for that victorie, but enmities now vnhappilie begunne, fhould continue betwene them; and betwene his complices, and her progenie : and that fhe fhould ouerthrow him, with al his power, & fo man fhould be fet free from his thraldome, by the feede of the woman, that is by a Redemer of mankind. This Redemer, God more exprefly promifed to Abraham, that he fhoud be borne of his feede faying to him : [In thee fhal al the kindredes of the earth be bleffed.] God alfo reuealing to him his determination to deftroy Sodom, geueth this reafon of that familar dealing, for that [in him are to be bleffed al the nations of the earth.] Againe to him after his prompt obedience (being readie to haue facrificed his fonne Ifaac) God faid : [In thy feede,

Gen. 3. *v*. 15.

Gen. 12. *v*. 3.

Gen. 18. *v*. 18. *Gen*. 22. *v*. 18.

God promifed this Redemer to diuers Patriarches.

Firft denounced to the diuel, that the fede of a woman fhould ouercome him.

Pormifed it exprefly to Abraham.

fhal
V 3

shal be bleſſed, al the Nations of the earth; becauſe thou haſt obeyed my voice .] .God renued and con-firmed the ſame promiſe to Iſaac ſaying : [In thy ſeede ſhal be bleſſed al the Nations of the earth .] Likewiſe the verie ſame to Iacob [In thee, and thy ſeede, al the Tribes of the earth ſhal be bleſſed .] The ſame promiſe was alſo iterated and confirmed to King Dauid, as him ſelf witneſſeth ſaying : [Our Lord hath ſworne truth to Dauid, and he wil not diſapoint it : of the frute of thy wombe, I wil ſet vpon thy ſeate.] Theſe ſpecial promiſes, are accounted verie authentical by the Iewes, wherupon they alſo expect a Redemer, of the ſeede of Abraham , Iſaac, and Iacob : and the ſame to be the ſonne of Dauid, but groſly erred, and ſtil erre, in not receiuing him being now come, as in the next Article is to be pro-ued aginſt them .

3　He was alſo prefigured by diuers perſons , and other thinges, according to his manifold power and qualities; which can not be ſufficiently ſignified by few, no nor by many ſimilitudes, which as they are like in ſome reſpectes, ſo they are al vnlike in manie other pointes . And therfore we muſt alwaies eſteme the thing prefigured, farre to excel the figure ; euen as a bodie is more perfect, then the ſhadow therof. So Abel being vniuſtly murthered by his brother Cain, was a figure of our Redemer, who was perſecuted, condemned as worthie to die, and deliuered by his owne nation the Iewes, to be crucified : though ac-tually they did not kil him, as Cain did kil Abel, for they denie to haue ſo done; and ſo Cain being de-manded where his brother Abel was , anſweared, [I know not] yea expoſtulating with God; deman-ded againe ſaying : [Am I my brothers keeper ?] Noe in that he was iuſt and perfect according to the perfection of this life, was an other figure of our Sa-uiour

Margin notes:

To Iſaac.

To Iacob.

To Dauid.

Our Redemer was prefigured by diuers per-ſons, & thing-es.

By Abel.

By Noe.

Gen .26 . v . 4.
Gen .28 . v . 14.
Pſ .131 . v . 11.

Coloſ. 2 v .17 .
Gen .4. v . 8.

v . 9 .

Gen. 6, v . 9.

uiour, who is abfolutely perfect, of whofe fulnes of grace, al other iuſt receiue. Alſo in that Noe prepared the Arck, in which, and no where els, was ſaiſtie from the floud : So our Sauiour hath prepared his Church, out of which is no ſaluation . Melchizedec was a notable figure of our Redemer; both a King and a Preiſt. Abraham the Father of manie Nations ; Iſaac, ouercoming his aduerſaries with patience; Iacob clothed with Eſaus Garments, & kiddes skinnes, were figures of Chriſt , redeming al Nations by his Paſſion, in his aſſumpted humanitie : Ioſeph being enuied, betraied, and ſold by his brethren ; But aduanced, & called the Sauiour of the world ; preſigu.red him who by his humiliatió , ouercame al iniuries, and ſaueth his people from ſpiritual famine . So Moyſes, Ioſue, Samuel Dauid, Salomon, and other Prophets, Iudges, and Kinges, were in diuers reſpectes, figures of the ſingular Prophet, Iudge of the world, and King of kinges; the promiſed Meſſias; who was alſo preſigured by the Paſchal Lambe ; by Manna from heauen ; by the Arck of the Teſtament ; braſen Serpent, and manie other thinges . Breeſly the whole Law of Moyſes, yea and the former ſtate of Goddes people, from the beginning of the world, did obſcurely conteine & ſignifie Chriſt, and his Church, hidden in the old Teſtament, and reuealed in the new .

4 Prophecies are yet more abundant, and more direct teſtimonies of the ſame coming of our Redemer, not only in the bookes properly called prophetical , but alſo in the other partes of the old Teſtament . But becauſe we ſhal haue occaſion to produce more in diuers miſteries of Chriſtian Religion; here it may ſuffice to recite a few. Iacob bleſſiing his ſonnes, prophecied much of Chriſt our Sauiour. Amongſt the reſt, ſpeaking of Iudas , of whom Chriſt ſhould be

borne

Marginal notes (left):
Gen . 7.
v . 23 .
Gen. 14.
v. 18 .
Gen . 17 .
v . 5 .
Gen. 26 .
v . 28 .
Gen .27 .
v . 15 .
Gen. 37 .
v .4 .
Gen .38 .
v . 1. &c.
Gen . 41 .
v . 45 .
Exo . 3 .
Nu . 13 .
Iudic . 17.
Exo . 12 .
16. et 25 .
1 . Cor.
10 . v.
11 .

Marginal notes (right):
By Melchiſedech
By Abraham, Iſaac & Iocob.
By Ioſeph.
By Moyſes, Ioſue, Sampſó, Samuel, Dauid, Salomon.
By the Paſchal Lambe : Manna, the Arke : Braſen ſerpent,
Al the Prophets foretould of our Redemer.
Iacob prophecied of him.

borne, faith thus : [The Scepter fhal not be taken *Gen. 49.*
from Iudas; and a Duke out of his thigh, til he doe *v . 10.*
come that is to be fent ; and the fame fhal be the expectation of the Gentiles .] That which was literal-

In the figures were incliuded prophecies.

ly faid of the Pafchal Lambe [You fhal not break *Exo . 12.*
a bone of him] was propheticallie foretold of *v . 40.*
Chrift, & fulfilled, whē the fouldiers breaking the legs
of the other two, crucified with him ; broke no bone
of him, but pearced his fide with a fpeare, fulfilling
alfo an other prophecie which faid [they fhal looke *Zach . 12.*
on him whō they pearced.] The facrificing of Goates, *v . 10.*
oxen, & other thinges, and the killing of hoaftes for *Leuit . 9.*
finne, with the carrying of their bodies without the *v . 3 . et 15.*
Campe ; did prefigure and prophecie the crncifying *16 . v . 27.*

Prophecied by Balaam.

of Chrift without the gate . It is a cleare prophecie *Heb . 9. 10.*
which Balaam vttered (though him felf was wicked) *et . 13.*
faying : [I fhal fee him, but not now; I fhal behold
him, but not nere . A ftarre fhal rife out of Iacob, *Num . 24.*
and a rodde fhal arife from Ifrael; and fhal ftrike the *v . 17.*
Dukes of Moab, and fhal waft the children of Seth .] *Deut . 18.*

By Moyfes more directly.

Moyfes faith exprefly : [A Prophet of thy Nation, *v . 15. 18.*
and of thy brethren, like vnto me, wil our Lord thy *Ch . 33.*
God, raife vp to thee, him thou fhalt heare.] Of *v . 2.*
the fame Prophet he faith : [Our Lord came from
Sinai, and from Seir, is he rifen to vs . He hath ap- *Num . 13.*
peared frō mount Pharaan, and with him thoufandes *v . 17.*
of Sainctes : in his right hand a firie Law .] Iofue, *Iof . 3 . &c*
in name and office, was a figure forefhewing our Sa- *Indic . 2.*
uiour Iefus Chrift, who bringeth his people from the *v . 16 Ch .*
defert of this world, into the land of promife, the *3 . v . 9.*
Kingdome of Heauen . Al the valiant Iudges were *&c.*

Iofue and al the Iudges were prophe-tical figures of our Redemer.

prophetical figures of our Sauiour, in that they deliuered & faued the Ifraelites from their ene mies . And
namely Samfon a profeffed Nazarite, killing his aduerfaries by his owne death . Holie Anne, the Mother of Samuel, in her Canticle of thankefgeuing,
pro

1. *Reg.*
2. *v.*10.
prophecied of Chrift our Redemer faying : [Our Lord fhal iudge the endes of the earth, and fhal geue empire to his King, & fhal exalt the horne of his Chrift.] In al the hiftorical bookes, are not only inferted diuersprophecies of Chrift, but alfo the Hiftories them felues are prophetical, forefhewing Chrift, and mifteries of the new Teftament. So likewife the Sapiential bookes, conteine fome prophecies of Chrift, the eternal increated wifdome, the Sonne of God, [who by wifdome founded the earth, eftablifhed the heauens by prudence] who taking flefh of man [built an houfe, cut out feauen pillers] teacheth to contemne al tranfitorie thinges of this world, and to feke the kingdom of heauen, which our Sauiour teacheth; Efpecially the Canticle of canticles, is a moft diuine Bridal fonge, fhewing the eternal mariage of Chrift and his Church. As for the whole diuine Palter of Dauid, verie manie pfalmes, are properly of Chrift our Redemer, Sauiour, Iudge, and remunerator; the reft are ful of other mifteries, incomparably more perteyning to the new Teftament, then to the old.

Pron. 3.
v. 19.
Ch. 9.
v. 1.
Eccle. 1.
v. 1. 2.
&c.
Cant. 1.
v. 1. 2.
3. *&c.*
Pf. 2. 8.
13. 16.
20. 21.
33. 34.
39. 40.
&c.

5 And albeit the other Prophets doe treate of particular thinges belonging to the Iewes, and their ftate in the old law, fomtimes alfo of other nations, yet moft efpecially they forefhew what fhould come to paffe, afwel touching the Gentiles of al nations, as the Iewes, by Chrift the promifed, and expected Redemer. 4 Al that they fay of Chrift, if it fhould be gathered into a compendium would make a competent volume by it felf. And therfore we wil only here take out as it were of euerie one fome one fpecial Prophecie of Chrift, for breuitie fake, becaufe our Sauiour him felf teftificth that al the *Prophets* fpake of him. Firft then out of Ifaias who is by fome called the Euangelical Prophet, becaufe his booke in fome places femeth rather to be a Gofpel then

Luc 24.
v. 27.
44.
Act. 3.
v. 18.
24. *Ch.*
30.

Anna prophecied of him.

The Sacred Hiftories are prophetical. Alfo the Sapiential Bookes.

Efpecially the Canticle of Canticles.

Manie Pfalmes defcribe our Sauiours Incarnation, Paffion, Refurrection &c.
Al the Prophets forefhew our Redemer. See the inner Margen. And if anie defire to haue more teftimonies of the Prophetes may fee.

4 *Ifa.* 8. *v.*
13. *&c.*
Ch. 9. *v.*
1. 6. *Ch.*
10. 23. *Ch.*

W   a pro

11.v.2. a Prophecie, let this sentence stand for manie, where *v.43. Isa.*
*Ch.*12.*v.* he saith [Behold a Virgin shal conceiue, & beare 7.*v.*14.
6.*Ch.*16. a sonne: & his name shal be called Emanuel] which
*v.*1.*Ch.* signifieth [God with vs.] The like sentence hath
19.*v.*1. I.remie saying [Our Lord hath created a new thing *Iere.*31.
*Ch.*32.*v.* vpon the earth: A woman shal compasse a Man,] *v.*22.
1.*Ch.*40. most mature in vertue, & iudgement, though an In-
*v.*3.9.*Ch.* fant. The Prophet Baruch, after the acknowlege- *Baruc.*3.
42.*v.*1.2. ment of Gods benefites, in the old Testament, saith *v.*38.
3.*Ch.*45. [After these thinges, he was sene vpon the earth, &
*v.*8.*Ch.* was conuersant with men.] So Prophets often
46.*v.*10. speake of thinges to come, as if they were alreadie
11.*Ch.*50. come. Ezechiel denounceth that our Lord saith
*v.*4.*Ch.* [Behold I my self wil seeke my sheepe, and wil visite *Ezech.*34.
61.*v.*1. them: And I wil raise vp ouer them one Pastor, who *v.*11.23.
*Ch.*64.*v.* shal feede them, my seruant Dauid] to witte Christ
1.*Ch.*65. the Beloued, for this Prophecie mas vttered aboue
*v.*1.*Ch.* foure hundred yeares after king Dauids reigne. Da-
66.*v.*5. niel describeth the time when our Redemer should
*Iere.*11.*v.* come as the Angel had declared to him, saying
18.*Ch.*23. [Seuentie weekes are abridged vpon thy people, & *Dan.*9.
*v.*5.*Ch.* vpon thy holie citie, that preuarication may be con- *v.*24.
33.*v.*14. summate, and sinne take an end, and iniquitie be a-
*Ezech.*34. bolished, and euerlasting iustice be brought, and the
*v.*26.*Ch.* vision be accomplished, and prophecie, & the Ho-
37.*v.*25. lie one of holies be annointed.] Ofee reporteth *Ofee.*13.
*Ch.*41.*v.* Gods promise saying, [out of the handes of death *v.*14.
19.*Ch.*43. I wil deliuer them, from death I wil redeme them, I
*v.*2.5. wil be thy death o death, thy bitte wil I be o hel.]
*Ch.*44.*v.* Ioel biddeth the children of Sion [reioyce and be *Ioel.*2.
2.*Dan.*7. ioyful in the Lord your God, becaufe he hath ge- *v.*23.
*v.*13.*Ch.* uen you a Doctor of iustice.] Amos warneth the *Amos.*4.
9.*v.*26. Iewes [to be prepared to mete their God. Becaufe *v.*12.13.
27.*Ofee.*1. he that formeth the mountaines, & createh the winde,
*v.*11.*Ch.* declareth his word to man: our Lord the God of
11.*v.*2.9. hoastes is his name.] Abdias saith that [in mount *Abd.v.*17.
Sion

Sion fhal be faluation, and it fhal be holie : and the

Ion . 1 . *v*.
15. *Mich*. 2.

house of Iacob fhal poffeffe thofe that had poffeffed

v. 12. 13.

them.] Ionas not only in word but alfo in act, or

Ionas. 2.
v. 1.

rather in paffion, prophecied our Redemer in that he

Ch . 4 . *v* .

[was in the bellie of the fifh three daies and three

13 . *Ch* . 7.

nights.] Micheas fheweth the place of our Sauiours

v . 20 .

Mich . 5 .
v . 2 .

natiuitie, faying [Thou Bethlehem-Ephrata, art a

Habacuc. 2 ;
v. 3. *Zach* .

litle one, in the thoufandes of Iuda, out of thee fhal
come forth vnto me, he that fhal be the dominator

4. *v*. 2. *Ch*.
12 . *v* . 10 .

in Ifrael : and his coming forth from the begining,

Mal . 4 . *v* .

from the daies of eternitie.] Nahum forefheweth

1 . 2 .

Nah . 1 .
v . 15 .

the deftruction of Idolatrie, by our Sauiour faying;

2 . *Mach* .

[Behold vpon the mountaines, the feete of him that

14 . *v* . 41 .

Euangelizeth, and preacheth peace : celebrate o Iuda thy feftiuitie, and render thy vowes; becaufe
Belial fhal no more adde to paffe through thee,

Hab . 3 .
v . 2 . 3 .
&c .

he is wholly perifhed.] Habacuc in his Canticle defcribeth Chrifts Incarnation, Natiuitie, Doctrine,
Miracles, Paffion, and Refurrection, & other myfteries [God (faith he) wil come from the South;

Sopho . 3 .
v . 8 . 9 .

and the holie one from mount Pharon.] Sophonias telling the Iewes of their reprobation for their
wickednes, prophecieth the vocation of the Gentils
by Chrift faying : [Wherfore expect me faith our
Lord in the day of my refurrection, til hearafter,
becaufe my iudgment to affemble the Gentiles, and
to gather kingdomes, & to powre vpon them myne
indignation, al the wrath of my furie. Becaufe then
wil I reftore to the peoples a chofen lippe, that al
may inuocate in the name of the Lord, and may ferue
him with one fhoulder] that is with Chriftian fortitude. Aggæus perfwading the people to profecute

Aggæ.
2. *v*. 8.

the building againe of the Temple, after their relaxation from captiuitie, encorageth them with hope of
their much defired, and long expected Meffias faying:
[The defired of al Nations fhal come, and I wil fil

W 2   this

this houfe with glorie, faith the Lord of hoaftes.]
Zacharias admonifheth the high Preift(called Iefus)　*Zach.* 3.
of his negligence, in not vrging forwardes to build　*v.* 8.
againe the Temple faying : [Thus faith the Lord of
hoaftes. Heare o Iefus thou grand Preift, thou and
thy frendes that dwel before thee; becaufe they are
portending men. For behold I wil bring my feruant
the Orient (Chrift in his manhood) the Orient of al
grace and faluation, who from on high vifiteth vs.]
And fo the fame Prophet defcribeth [the rifing king-　*Ch.* 6.
dome] and Preiftly power of Chrift in his Church.　*v.* 12.
[Thus faith the Lord of hoaftes. Behold a man Orient is his name ; and vnder him fhal fpring vp and fhal
build a Temple to our Lord. And he fhal build a Tem-　*v.* 13.
ple to our Lord; and fhal bear glorie, and fhal fitte
and rule vpon his Throne, and he fhal be a Preift vpon
his Throne, and the counfel of peace fhal be betwene
them two.] In al which power, he forefheweth that
the fame Redemer is alfo moft meeke faying : [Re-　*Ch.* 9 *v.* 9.
ioice greatly, o daughter of Sion, make iubilation
o daughter of Ierufalem; behold thy King wil come
to thee, the iuft and Sauiour him felf, poore and riding vpon an affe, and vpon a colt the fole of an affe.]
Malachie, the laft that writte prophecie in the old
Teftament, ioyning together, the precurfor, and the
Maifter, firft telleth of S. Iohn Baptift (who was
more then a prophet, in that he did not only foretel
of our Redemer to come, but alfo with voice & finger fhewed him prefent) and then immediatly addeth of our Meffias, relating what God faid of them
both [Behold I fend mine Angel (meffenger & pre-　*Mal.* 3.
curfor) and he fhal prepare the way before my face,　*v.* 1.
and forthwith fhal come to his Temple the Dominator, whom you feeke, and the Angel of the Teftament
whom you defire (He that reconcileth man to God,
making couenant of peace) Behold he cometh faith　*Luc.* 24.
the　*v.* 27.

the Lord of hoaſtes.] And this may ſuffice for declaration that [God by the mouth of al the Prophets] foreſhewed that he would ſend a Redemer of mankind into the world.

*Our Lord Ieſus of Nazareth, is Chriſt our
Redemer.*

ARTICLE. 16.

Hauing now declared by holie Scriptures of the old Teſtament, that God decreed & promiſed a Redemer of mankind, as alſo both Iewes and Turkes acknowlege : we are conſequentlie to proue, which they denie, that this diuine promiſe, is longe ſince performed, in I E S V S of Nazareth, the Sonne of the moſt Bleſſed Virgin Marie. Which moſt important point of Religion, & groūd of al Chriſtianitie, is principallie teſtified by the New Teſtament. But for ſomuch as the Iewes vtterly reiect it, as they did the Auctor therof, perſecuting him to death; and albeit the Turkes acknowlege him to be an excellent Prophet, ſent, and approued of God : yet for ſomuch as they preferre their falſe prophet Mahomet aboue him, and eſteme their Alcheron before al holie Scriptures, we muſt in this, and in moſt other diuine miſteries againſt theſe aduerſaries, neceſſarily recurre to Traditions; to confeſſed Hiſtories ; to Miracles, and other proofes of the Catholique euer viſible Church. By which meanes, the whole ſacred Bible, aſwel the old, as the New Teſtament, being firſt proued to be the aſſured true writtē word of God, at leaſt, being vndoubtedly accepted by al Chriſtians, (for whom this ſmal work is ſpecially intended :) we ſhal here againſt theſe, and al other aduerſaries, breefelie ſhew by a competent

W 3

number

number of correspondent places of both Testaments, that (as al Christians professe) the promised Redemer is indeede come into the world, the verie same in whom we beleue, and by whom we hope to be saued .

This truth is proued by consideration of the time of coming .

2   First therfore concerning the time of his coming, the prophecies of Iacob and of Daniel, doe clearly agree with the Euangelists narration . For wheras Iacob said [The scepter shal not be taken from Iudas, and a Duke out of his thigh, til he doe come that is to be sent .] And wheras Daniel wrote the Angels declaratiō that [seuentie weekes (that is to say , seuentie times seuen yeares, counting as al vnderstand it, yeares for daies) are abridged, that preuarication may be consummate &c. and the holie one of holies may be annointed] Agreable to both it came to passe, when Herod (Ascalonita) a stranger, his father an Idumean, his mother an Arabicke, was made king of Iudea, and so al Royal title of King or Duke whollie taken from the Iewes . And when these seuentie weekes mentioned by Daniel, were neare expired; euen then we see it came to passe, as S . Mathew writeth, that [IESVS was borne in Bethelhem of Iuda, in the daies of Herod the king .] And not only borne, but also confidently proclamed by the [Sages, and feared by king Herod, to be the true king of the Iewes .] S . Luke also writeth, that [S . Iohn Baptist was conceiued, and borne in the daies of the same Herode king of Iurie . and our Sauiour sixe monethes after .] Moreouer addeth, that [In the fiftenth yeare of the Empyre of Tiberius Cæsar (king Herod being dead) and the kingdome of Iurie more alienated from Royal state, for it was thē diuided into Tetrarchies, of four gouerners : Pilate, an other Herod, Philip, and Lysanias . [S . Iohn was sent to preach and baptize] which concurring with the seuentie

*Gen.*49, *v.*10.

*Dan.*9, *v.*24.

*Mat.*2, *v.*1. *v.*2.3. *Luc.*1, *v.*

5.16. *Cb.* 2.*v.*6.7. *Cb.*3.*v.*1,

uentie

uentie weekes nere about complete, al men so assuredly then expected the promised Messias, that [they
sent from Ierusalem Preistes and Leuits to him, to
aske him, not only if he were Elias, but also if he
were the Prophet] that is the especial Prophet Messias shewing them selues most willing and readie so
to accept, if he would haue agreed therunto : yea
this circumstance of time, with other thinges agreable, was so pregnant a proofe of the Messias, that the
former Herode wanted not sicophantes which held
opinion, that he was the Messias ; wherof arose the
sect called Herodians ; those that ioyned with the
pharisies to haue entrapped our B. Sauiour in his
speaches. Al which manifestlie detecteth, the wonderful blind follie of the Iewes, expecting their Messias as yet to come they know not when, after their
long depriuation of king or Duke, more then three
other such seuentie weekes, as were declared to the
Prophet Daniel.

Ioan. 1.
v. 19. 21.
Deut. 18.
v. 15.

Mat.
22. *v.* 15.
16. *Mar.*
2. *v.* 6.
Luc. 20.
v. 20.

3   To this purpose we may also obserue, the like
concordance of Genealogies, in both Testaments.
Moyses after his narration of the worldes beginning,
and mannes fal, as one wel vnderstanding, and right-
lie considering, of Goddes ordinance to restore man ;
amongst other passages of his Historie, inserteth the
Genealogies of certaine first Patriarches, from Adam
to Noe; and againe from Noe, to Abraham; and
from Abraham, by his Sonne Isaac, and Nephew Iacob; to Iacobs twelue sonnes, who were, the heades
of the twelue Tribes, the selected peculiar people of
God, to whom, and of whom, he promised that a
Redemer should come. Likewise he recordeth the
particular birth of Phares, and Zara, sonnes of Iuda,
one of Iacobs sonnes : the lineal progenie of which
Phares, is afterwardes set downe in the Historie of
Ruth, til it come to King Dauid. As in like sorte
for

The summe is
proued by the
exact noting of
the Genealo-
gies of Patriar-
ches to Dauid,
& so forwards.

Gen. 5. *
Ch. 10. *
Ch. 21.
v. 2. *Ch.*
25. *v.*
25. *Ch.*
38. *v.*
29.
Ruth. 4.
v. 18.
&c.

for an other miſtical purpoſe, the Genealogie of Le- *Exo.6.*
ui (an other of Iacobs ſonnes) is expreſſed ſo far, as *v.20.*
to Aaron, & Moyſes & to Aarons ſón Eleazar, & Ele- 23.25.
azars ſonne Phinees. Which two Genealogies, are 1. *Paral.*2,
moſt eſpecially among manie others, repeated, & pro- 3.4.6.
ſecuted in Paralipomenon, and ſo forwardes partly
by the written holie Scriptures, the reſt by Tradition, euen to Ieſus Chriſt, the omnipotent King, and
eternal Preiſt. Al which diligence was doubtles imployed by the prouidence of God, to the verie ſame
end and purpoſe, to which the Euangeliſts doe vſe it :
to ſhew that our Lord Ieſus, the Sonne of the B. Virgin Marie, is that ſonne of Dauid, and of Abraham,
which was ſo ſingularly promiſed to them, that Sóne
in whom al Nations ſhould be bleſſed. And therfore
S. Mathew not only reciteth the generations from
Abraham, to King Dauid, and ſo to Ioſeph, the ſpouſe *Math.1.*
of the B. Virgin Marie, of the ſame houſe and fami- *v.1.&c.*
lie of Dauid, and ſo by his pedegree ſheweth alſo the *v.16.*
pedegree of the B. Virgin his Spouſe, of whom was
borne Ieſus; but alſo therupon inferreth this neceſſarie conſequence, that [this Ieſus is he who is called
Chriſt] In Greke, *ho Chriſtos;* In Hebrew, *Meſſias,*
In Latin, *Vnctus,* or rather, *Ille ſingulariter vnctus,*
In Engliſh, *The annointed.* As elſwhere may be more *Art.*20.
fullie explained, as alſo the B. name Ieſus.

His ſingular
maner of gene-
ration of a Vir-
gin, not by
man, but by
the Holie
Ghoſt, ſhew-
eth him to be
the Meſſias.

4 Further touching his Genealogie, S. Luke alſo
though in other maner, aſcending by his legal pa- *Luc.*3,
rentage, from Ioſeph to Dauid and Abraham, and ſo *v.23.*
vpwardes to [Adam, who was of God] declareth
him to be come into the world, whoſe generation,
reduceth vs againe to God. Wherfore both the ſame
Euangeliſtes, exactly declare withal, that his genera- *Mat.1.v.*
tion being of man, yet was not by man, after the or- 18. 20. 23.
dinarie natural maner of al others from Adam & Eue : *Luc.1.v,*
but that he was ſupernaturally both conceiued and 24.26,
borne

borne of a Virgin by the Holie Ghoſt] agreable to
the Prophecie of Iſaias ſaying : [A Virgin ſhal conceiue and beare a Sonne, and his name ſhal be called
Emanuel, that is, God with vs.] Againe he ſaith :
[A litle child is borne to vs, & a Sône is geuen to vs.]

Iſa.7.
v.14.
Ch.9.
v.6.

5   The verie ſame agrement is alſo in al other
pointes of this Miſterie betwixt the Prophets, & E-
uangeliſts. Concerning the place, the Prophet Micheas ſaid : [This Duke or Dominator, which ſhould
gouerne Iſrael, ſhould come out of *Bethlehem.*] His
name IESVS, was prefigured, by the changing of
Oſee, into Ioſue, or Ieſus, which in the original tôgue
is the ſame, & was propnecied in the Canticles wher
the Spouſe ſaith : [Oile powred out, is thy name]
ſignifying his ſuperabundant mercie, in ſpending him
ſelf, to ſaue others. His adoration by the Sages ,
(commonly called the three Kinges) was foretold
in the booke of Numeri, by ſtrang inſtinct, againſt
the mind of him that vttered it, which was Balaam
ſaying : [A Starre ſhal riſe from Iacob] More plainlie by King Dauid, and by Iſaias the Prophet [The
Dromedaries of Madian & Epha, al of Saba ſhal com,
bringing gold and Frankencenſe, and ſhewing forth
praiſe to our Lord.] His preſentation in the Temple was prophecied by Malachias ſaying to the Iewes,
[Forthwith (after the birth of his precurſor) ſhal
come to his Temple the Dominator whom you ſeeke,
and the Angel of the Teſtament, whom you deſire.]
His fleeing into Egipt was prophecied by Iſaias ſaying : [Our Lord wil aſcend vpon a ſwift cloude, &
wil enter into Egipt.] The ſlaughter of the Innocent children Martyrs, in and neare Bethlehem, was
prophecied by Ieremie ſaying : [A voice of lamentation is heard on high, of the mourning and weping
of Rachel weping for her children , and refuſing to
be comforted for them, becauſe they are not.] Alſo our

Mich.5.
v.2.

Nu.13.
v.17.

Can.1.
v.3.

Nu.24.
v.17.

Iſa.60.
v.6.
Pſ.71.
v.10.

Mal.3.
v.1.

Iſa.19.
v.1.

Iere.31.
v.15.

It is further
proued by the
place of his
Natiuitie.

By his Name :

His Adoration.

His preſenta-
tion.

His flying into
Aegipt.

The murther
of the Inno-
centes.

X

His returne fró Aegipt.

fo our Sauiours returning from Egipt after the death of King Herode, was prophecied by Ofee, comprifing his prophecie in his recital of a former benefite of al Ifraels deliuerie from Egipt faying of them both (the one being a figure of the other) [Out of Egipt I called my Sonne.] His dwelling thenceforth in

Ofee. 11. *v.1.*

His dweling in Nazareth.

Nazareth, wherof he was called, *Iefus Nazerenus*; was prophecied by the vniforme defcriptions of al the Prophets, that he fhould be [a Nazarite] which fignifieth *a keeper*, *a yong fpring* and *a floure*, moft eminently verified in our Sauiour, the faithful fure keeper of his Citie the Church, and of al that relie on him : the frutful yong fpring, whence al grace procedeth, and floure of glorie, wherto al the godlie tend. He that geueth grace and glorie. He that farre paffeth al other profeffed Religious Nazarites in excellent puritie, and holines of life. Of other particulars in the refidue of our Sauiours actes and paffions, we fhal haue more occafion to fpeake, in the Mifteries folowing.

Pf. 126. *v.1. Pf.* 145. *v.7.* 9. Pf. 83. *v.12.*

Cant. 2. *v.1.* Num. 6. *v.2. &c.*

Though fome of thefe proofes may feme not to conuince: Yet al together doe confirme the faithful in beleefe of this truth.

6 Thefe now reherfed, perteyning to his firft entrance into this world, may ferue for proofe, that the Euangeliftes reportes are al conformable to the prophecies, figures, and promifes of the old Teftament. If perhaps fome textes be more obfcure, or not fo manifeft as may conuince the contradicting fpirites of Iewes, or others ; yet manie other fentences are more cleare, and may fuffice, afwel to explaine the reft ; as to fatisfie the wel difpofed mindes, of al that fincerly loue and feeke the truth.

Faith helpeth the vndrftanding in thinges which to Infidels feme verie hard.

7 For howfoeuer we are able, or not able, to vnderftand diuine mifteries : we Chriftians muft hold faft our faith, which [is the fubftance and ground, of al fpirituial hopes (not of thinges feene by corporal eyes, or perceiued by outward fenfe, but) of thinges not appearing.] We muft hold faft our faith which exacteth

Heb. 11. *v.1.*

exacteth not senſible demonſtrations, but is content with conuenient Argumentes, proofes, and declarations, of credible documentes : we muſt hold faſt our faith which telleth vs, that the new Teſtament is the aſſured true word of God. Then ſhal we be infalliblie warranted, that al pointes of doctrine, and maners, particular, and general, expreſſed, and neceſſarilie implyied therein, are moſt true, and moſt certaine.

8   Namelie touching this preſent particular, we ſhal hold faſt our faith, that as S. Paul affirmeth [IESVS of Nazareth, who was crucified, whom he had perſecuted, is Chriſt] the Meſſias, the annointed of God, the Redemer of man. And as S. Peter teacheth, that [to this Ieſus, al the prophets geue teſtimonie] to be the Sauiour [by whoſe name, al receue remiſſion of ſinnes, which beleue in him.] For neither is there (ſaith he at an other time) anie other name vnder heauen geuē to men, wherin we muſt be ſaued] then may we ſecurely beleue, as S. Paul againe preached at Antioch, to the Iewes and Gentiles, that [of the ſeede of Dauid , God according to his promiſe , hath brought forth to Iſrael, a Sauiour Ieſus . whom God raiſed from death the third day ; whoſe bodie ſaw no corruption, according as Dauid had written in the pſalmes, thou ſhalt not geue thy holie one to ſee corruption] And as the ſame Apoſtle [with vehemency conuinced the Iewes, openly ſhewing by the Scriptures, that Ieſus is Chriſt :] we wil therfore, omitting other teſtimonies, conclude with S. Iohn, that he erreth damnablie, and is a pernicious [liar , that denieth Ieſus to be Chriſt : In this (ſaith he againe) is the Spirit of God knowne. Euerie ſpirit , that confeſſeth Ieſus Chriſt to haue come in fleſh, is of God ; and euerie ſpirit that diſſolueth Ieſus (ſeperating Ieſus from Chriſt, or from being God, or from

Act. 9. *v.* 22.

Act. 10. *v.* 43. *Act.* 4. *v.* 12.

Act. 13. *v.* 23. 30. 37. *Rom.* 1. *v.* 3.

Pſ. 15. *v.* 10.

Act. 18. *v.* 28.

1. *Io.* 2. *v.* 22. 1. *Io.* 4. *v.* 2. 3.

That our Lord Ieſus, is Meſſias, is clearly auouched by holie Scriptures and beleued by Chriſtians.

X 2   being

being man) is not of God.] This was then a note,
& one fpecial marke, to difcerne the fpirites of truth,
and of herefie, as it is ftil the principal difference betwene Chriftians, & Iewes .

Ch . 5 . v . 1

*Our Lord Iefus Chrift, is God, the fecoud perfon
of the Bleffed Trinitie .*

A R T I C L E . 17 .

Diuers old he-
refies touching
Chrift.

BEfides the Iewes infidelitie , denying that
Chrift our Redemer is come into the world:
there be other impieties no leffe damnable of
old Heretikes, diffoluing Iefus Chrift (as the Apoftle fpeaketh in the place before alleaged) that is
lofing a fuder things vnited in our Sauionr , as are his
deitie, humanitie, foule , & Bodie, al fubfifting in his
diuine Perfon, the true natural Sonne of God , the
fecond Perfon of the B . Trinitie : Contrarie to
which Catholique faith and doctrine , Cerinthius ,
Ebion, and their folowers, denied Chrift to be God :
the Manichies denied him to be man, imagining that
he tooke not a real humane foule, and bodie ,
but phantaftical . Neftorius denied, that humane nature, is affumpted into the diuine perfon, by Hipofta-
tical, or Perfonal vnitie, but as by way of an inftrument, and fo denied Chrift to be the verie Sonne of
God , but his inftrument. Fotinus denied Chrift to
be God, by nature, but by grace, and adoption, only by more abundant grace, then other Sainctes . Fu-
tiches, Appolinaris, and others, coyned an other herefie, that there be two perfons in Chrift . Arrius denied the Sonne of God, to be equal and confubftantial to the Father . Al which, and the like heretikes,
our holie mother the Catholique Church, hath iuftly
condemned : And manie ancient Fathers, and learned D

*I . Io . 4.
v . 3 .*

ned doctors, haue confuted their erroures by thefe e-
fpecial facred Scriptures, which here we fhal recite,
vnderftanding and expounding them, not by priuate,
but by the common fpirit, of the fame vniuerfal
Church.

2 To this purpofe it is efpecially requifite to proue
two principal pointes of faith, in which diuers other
particulars are comprifed, and therby al the ahoue
mentioned herefies are refuted. The firft is, that Iefus Chrift is verie God. The other, that he is alfo
perfectly and truly man. And albeit moft places that
proue the one, doe alfo proue the other : yet for more
explication of both, we fhal diftribute them into two
Articles. Gods firft promifes, to fend one of womãs
feede, that fhonld [brufe the ferpents head] and that
[in the feede of Abraham, (and of other Patriarches)
al Nations fhould be bleffed] doe fhew, that he muft
nedes be a man, being the Iffue of man, and alfo muft
be God, becaufe only man could not performe thofe
promifes which were to be accóplifhed. More clearly the Royal Prophet in plaine termes, fpeaking in
fpirit to the Meffias, calleth him God faying : [Thy
feat o God for euer & euer : a rodde of direction, the
rodde of thy Kingdom.] And fpeaking to the
Church his Spoufe faith [The King wil couet thy
bewtie, becaufe he is the Lord thy God, and they
fhal adore him] Which wordes S. Paul applieth to
our Sauiour Chrift, prouing therby his excellencie a-
boue the Angels, fo farre alfo preferring him before
al Patriarches, Prophets, and Angels, as the Sonne
of God excelleth his creatures. Againe the Pfalmift
faith of Chrift [He haith chofen his inheritance in vs,
the bewtie of Iacob which he loued. God is afcended in Iubilation, and our Lord in the voice of Trumpet.] In commendation of the Church, firmly founded by Chrift, he faith [The Higheft him felf founded her]

2. Pet.
3. v. 20.

Gen. 3.
v. 15.
Ch. 12.
v. 3.
Ch. 26.
v. 4.
Ch. 28.
v. 14.
Pf. 44.
v. 7. 12.

Heb. 1.
v. 8.

v. 2. 5.
Pf. 46.
v. 5. 6.

Pf. 86.
v. 5.

ded her .] If Chrift were not God, he could not trulie be called the higheft . Inuiting al to praife Chrift,
he faith [Exalt ye the Lord our God : and adore *Pf.* 90 :
his foote- ftoole becaufe it is holie .] Of the fame *v . 5 .*
Chrift our Redemer, and of God the Father, with
diftinction of diuine perfons, which are one God, he
faith [Our Lord faid to my Lord : fitte on my right *Pf.* 109 .
hand, til I make thine enemies the foote-ftoole of *v . 1 .*
thy feete.] Of which fpeach, when our Sauiour propofed a queftion to the Pharifies, demanding; How
he is both Lord, and fonne of Dauid ? they could *Mat . 22 .*
not, or els would not anfweare; becaufe they would *v . 43 . 44 :*
neither confeffe him to be Chrift, nor Chrift to be
God . Of both which he conuinced them, and put
them to filence . What can be more manifeft, then
that which the fame Pfalmift, in the perfon of the
Church of Chrift, faith vnto him : [Thou art my *Pf.* 117 :
God, and I wil confeffe to thee : thou art my God, *v . 28 .*
and I wil exalt thee . I wil confeffe to thee, becaufe
thou haft heard me : and art become my faluation]
Euen he whom the Iewes reiected [the ftone which *v . 22 .*
the builders reiected, the fame is made into the head
of the corner.] The fame is our Sauiour, the fame
is God [Bleffed is he, whofe helper is the God of *Pf.* 145 .
Iacob . Our Lord wil reigne for euer ; thy God o Si- *v . 5 . 10 :*
By the booke   on in generation and generation .] To this fecond
of wifdome .   Perfon of the B . Trinitie, by the title of wifdome,
his proper attribute ; the Auctor of the Booke of wifdome , afcribeth the Redemption of Adam our firft
parent faying [Wifdome kept him that was firft made *Sap . 10 :*
of God, father of the world, when he was created a- *v . 1 :*
lone, and fhe brought him (Adam) out of his finne .]
By other Pro-   The Prophet Ifaias defcribeth our Redemer, to be [a
phets .   child borne, and a Sonne geuen to vs] with diuers
excellent names, or rather one name framed of manie titles, al aboue the dignitie of al creatures . A -
mongft

Iſ. 9.
v. 6.
mongſt the reſt, expreſly called him God [A litle Child (ſaith he) is borne to vs, a ſonne is geuen to vs : and principalitie is made vpon his ſhoulder, and his name ſhal be called, Meruelous, Counſeler, God, ſtrong, Father of the world to come, Prince of peace .] In an other place he geueth vs to know, that albeit our Redemer be a Sonne, yet he is of inexplicable generation . Wherfore he ſaith, or rather

Iſa. 53.
v. 8.
negatiuely demandeth [Who ſhal declare his generation ?] Signifying that none ſhal, yea that none can declare it. Eſpecially his eternal generation of God the Father. No nor perfecʈlie explicate his temporal generation, of his Virgin Mother, without Father in earth : and that he ſpeaketh of one only perſon, who both is of eternal, and ineffable generation, and who alſo by his Paſſion, ſhould Redeeme mankind; is manifeſt by his next wordes ad-

Aƈ. 8.
v. 35.
ioyned ſaying [Becauſe he is cut out of the land of the liuing (which the ſeauentie interpreters tranſlate; From the earth ſhal his life be taken) for the wickednes of my people, haue I ſtriken him.] From this Scripture, S. Philip the Deacon beginning to inſtruct the Enuch of Ethiopia [Euangelized vnto him Ieſus.] Ieremie prophecying the Iewes relaxation frõ

Iere. 30.
v. 18.19.
20. 21.
their captiuitie in Babilon ; and withal of the Redemptió of man from the captiuitie of ſinne by Chriſt ; ſheweth the reſtauration of the Citie, and Temple of Ieruſalem; and of the proſperous fundation of the Church of Chriſt; then addeth, that [the Duke and Prince (Chriſt the founder therof) ſhal be of him ſelf] that is of Iacob, and of their owne kindred;

v. 18.
v. 21.
and alſo ſhal be neuertheleſſe nere to God. [For thus ſaith our Lord : Behold I wil conuert the conuerſion of the Tabernacles of Iacob &c. And his Duke ſhal be of him ſelf, & the Prince ſhal be brought forth from the middeſt of him] which is neceſſari-

ly

ly vnderstoode of Chriscs humanitie. And touching
his Diuinitie, God the Father saith in the next wordes
[And I wil bring him nere, and he shal come to me]
which our Sauiour explaneth saying [that he is in the
Father, and the Father in him.] The Prophet Baruch
declaring that al mānes true wisdome, procedeth from
wisdom increated; affirmeth the same to be God say -
ing [This is our God; and there shal none other be
estemed against him] And likewise teacheth, that the
same person is also man saying [After these thinges
he was seene vpon the earth; and was conuersant
with mē.] Micheas foreshewing, that Christ [should
come forth of Bethlehem] according to his humanitie, addeth [And his coming forth, is from the beginning, from the daies of eterritie] signifying his
Deitie. So other Prophets which we here omitte,
al doe teach against the Iewes, that Christ is God.

Ioan. 14.
v. 10. 11.

Baruc. 3.
v. 25.

Mich. 5.
v. 2.

Proued by textes of the new Tastamēt, as the Church vnderstandeth them.

3   As for the heretikes, albeit the same conuince
them, we haue yet more manifest testimonies in the
new Testament. We wil only recite the wordes, of
which together with the explanation of the Church,
euerie faithful Christian, may readily inferre, the Catholique conclusion. First, the Archangel Gabriel
in his diuine Message from God, to the B. Virgin,
declared both these pointes of faith; that she should
haue a sonne, the Sauiour of mankind, who should
therfore be called Iesus: And that the same her Sóne
is also God. And therfore (said the Angel) [that
which of thee shal be borne Holie; shal be called the
Sonne of God.] The same was shortlie after, te-
stifiied againe, in the seueral Prophecies of our B.
Ladie, of Zacharie, and of Simeon. Yet more plainly by others. Our Sauiour himself, to establish this
fundamental doctrine, demanded of his Apostles; first
what ordinarie men, the vulgar sort, thought him to
be, and diuers iudgeing diuersly, but not rightly :

Luc. 1. v.
35. 47.
v. 69. 76.

Luc. 2. v.
30. 31. 32.

Mat. 16.
v. 16.

secondly he asked what them selues his chosen Apostles thought therof. And Peter answearing said :
[Thou art Christ the Sonne of the liuing God] which
most solide answear, he not only approued, but also
highly commended : and presently promised , vpon
this confession, and vpon this confessor (as vpon the
principal point, and cheif visible pastor of Christian
faith) he would build his Church. For here is confessed, that [Iesus is Christ the expected Redeemer, &
that he the same, is also the very true & natural Sonne
of God.] The selfsame doctrine was againe confirmed in his Transfiguration, by the voice of God the
*Mat.*17. Father saying : [This is my welbeloued Sonne (which
*v.*5. sheweth him to be God the Sonne) in whom I am
wel pleased] which sheweth him to be the Redeemer,
by whom man is reconciled to God ; who only, and
none other was able to please God, and appease his
iust wrath against mankind . Thus much may wel
suffice against al miscreantes, that denie Christ Iesus to be God .

4 Yet for our more consolation against al aduersaries of Christ, we wil adde more . S. Iohn writing
his Gospel more amply then the other Euangelistes,
touching this point of Christes Deitie , to confute
certaine heritikes risen in his time , beginneth with
the eternal generation of the Sonne of God, who is
called the *Word* (that is, the mental conception of
God, vnderstanding him self. For as God so produceth him self, he is God the Father, and as he is so
produced, he is God the Sonne; therfore called the
eternal word.) And therfore the same Euangelist
*Ioan.*1. saith [In the beginning was the word, and the word
*v.*1.2. was with God, and the word was God. this was in
the beginning with God] signifying that this diuine
word, the Sonne of God, was in eternitie before a-
*v.*3. nie time, or anie creature was [Al thinges, euen

S. Iohn of pur-
pose writeth
much in proof
of Christs
Godhead, a-
gainst here-
tikes which de-
nied it.

Y   time

time it felf, Angels, and whatfoeuer created thing)
were made by him, & without him nothing was made]
And fo teftifying Chriftes Godhead, applyeth his narration to his purpofe faying [the word was made *v.* 14.
flefh] al one as if he fhould fay, God the Sonne was
made man [and dwelt in vs (a man among men) the 5.18.
only begotten of the Father, the only begotten,
which is in the bofome of the Father.] Wherunto
perteyneth alfo the teftimonie of the Precurfor S.
Iohn Babtift faying [This (Iefus) is the Sonne of *v.* 34.
God] which veritie moreouer the fame Iefus Chrift
God and man, vpon fundrie occafions, affirmed, and
confirmed. In his difcourfe made to Nicodemus, tea- *Ch.* 3. *v.* 5.
ching him, that Baptifme is neceffarie to faluation, 9. 10. 11.
which, whiles he vnderftoode not, our Lord telleth
him further, that he muft beleue it, as being taught,
and teftified by him that is come from heauen, and is
in heauen faying [No man hath afcended into hea- *v.* 13.
uen (and fo no man can by terreftrial meanes know
heauenly Mifteries) but he that defcended from heauen (knoweth and teacheth them) the Sonne of man
which is in heauen] geuing hereby to vnderftad, that
he him felf the fame perfon Iefus Chrift, is both in
earth, & in heauen, being the Son of man, & the Son
of God. To the Iewes that perfecuted him, he faid,
[My Father worketh vntil now, and I doe worke] *Ch.* 5. *v.*
which they vnderftoode to fignifie, that he faid [God 16.17.18.
was his Father, making him equal to God] Neither
did he forbear to vtter this truth for their malignitie,
but manteyned the fame faying [What thinges fo - *v.* 19.
euer my Father doth, thofe alfo the Sonne doth in *v.* 21.
like maner] Yea exemplifyeth in particular [As the
Father doth raife the dead & quikneth : fo the Sonne
alfo quickneth whom he wil.] And when they de -
manded of him, who art thou ? he anfweared [I am *Ch.* 8.
the beginning, who alfo fpeake to you] that is the *v.* 25.
efficient

efficient caufe of al creatures, euen I who alfo
v. 33. fpeake now to you. And they preferring Abraham
v. 58. before him, he anfweared faying [Amen, Amen I
fay to you, that before Abraham was made, I am.
v. 59. They tooke ftones therfore and caft at him.] In an
other conflict with this obftinate people, he faid in
Ch. 10. plaine termes [I and the Father are one] *vnum fu-*
v. 30. *mus,* we are one in fubftance, one and the fame God.
Neuerthelefle in refpect of his humanitie (for in that
refpect, he is our Mediator) he declared to his A-
poftles, comforting them for his departure, and that
they fhould be gladde that he went to the Father, &
Ch. 14. that he would intercede for them, [becaufe (faith he)
v. 27. the Father is greater then I] vpon which wordes,
28. the Arrianes ftand very peremptorily, not admitting the true fenfe, which is, that God is greater then
man, neceffarily deduced, by conference of fo many
other places, as fhew that Chrift is God : and that
there is but one God, and there Diuine perfons, coeternal, and confubftantial ; and yet as man, is inferior to God.

4 If anie defire yet more proofe, let him repaire to   The fame is
S. Paul, who fomtime impugned Chrift, as if he had   further proued
bene neither God nor good man : but being once   by S. Pauls
conuerted, he preached with great zele, & diligence,   doctrine.
Act. 9. that [this Iefus is the Sonne of God.] Writing
v. 20. to the Philippians, he auerreth, that [Chrift Iefus
Philip. 2. thought it no robberie, him felf to be equal to God.]
v. 6. And to the Coloffians affirmeth, that [in him were
Colof. 1. created al thinges in heauen and in earth, vifible and
v. 15. inuifible ; And that in him dwelleth al the fulnes of the
Godhead corporally.] In his Epiftle to Titus, prefuppofing it to be a knowne doctrine of faith, he ioy-
Ch. 2. neth, as in appofitiue termes belonging to the fame
v. 9. perfon, [our Sauour God. Chrift Iefus our Sauiour.]
Likewife to the Hebrewes he faith that wheras [God

in former

in former times, fpake to their fathers in the Prophets; *Tit*. I.
laft of al in thefe daies hath fpoken to vs in his Sonne, *v*. 3. 4.
whom he hath appointed heyre of al (according to *Ch*. 3.
his humanitie) by whom he made alfo the worldes] *v*. 4.
which muft needes be vnderftoode of his Deitie. *Heb*. I.
And confequently the Apoftle proueth his incom- *v*. I. 2.
parable excellencie, aboue Angels, Moyfes, Iofue, *Ch*. I. 2.
and al other Prophets, by the expreffe word of God 3. *et* 4.
1. Pet. I. the Father, faying to him [Thou art my Sonne, to *Pf*. 2. *v*. 7.
v. 17. 18. day haue I begotten thee.] And againe faying : [Let
1. Ioan. I. al the Angels of God adore him.] And fo let vs
v. I. 2. 3. acknowlege, and adore him, omitting more proofes
Ch. 5. *v*. I. of S. Peter, S. Iohn, and other holie Scripures.
6. 13.
Apoc. I. *v*.
4. 8. *Ch*.
21. *v*. 6.
Ch. 22. *v*.
13.

Our Lord Iefus Chrift, is trulie Man.

ARTICLE. 18.

Relying vpon
priuate fpirite,
is caufe of er-
rors, and here-
fies.

Becaufe manie of the facred textes, recited in
the former Article, which fhew that our Sauiour Chrift is God, doe alfo Proue that he is
Man; not repeating the fame, I wil alfo adde a
few more, which efpecially declare the fame truth
againft the Manichees, phantaftically imagining that
Chrift tooke a phantaftical, not a true and real foul
or bodie. And againft Eutiches, Diofcorus, and o-
ther old heritikes, denying that there be two natures (diuine, and humane) in Chrift, falfly fuppofing, that as there is but one perfon, fo there fhould
be but one nature, and confequently feing Chrift
is God, he fhould not be man. Thus heritikes difcuffing high Mifteries by their owne imaginations,
runne into manie abfurdities, for one being grann-
ted a thoufand doe folow. But whofoeuer wil auoid
al errors in faith, afwel concerning the B. Trinitie,
and this of the Incarnation of Chrift, as al others
which

which exceede the capacitie of our vnderstanding, muſt confidently relie vpon the Church, which hath

2. *Pet.* 1.
v. 20.

that [ſpirit of truth to interprete the holie Scriptures, by which the ſame were written †. And with this reſignation of our priuate opinions, and reſolution to folow the Churches interpretation, we may with more ſpiritual profit and comfort, ſearch the true ſenſe of ſuch places, as are comõly, or may be probablie alleaged, for confirmation of anie truth.

Exo. 12.
v. 6.

2   As to this preſent purpoſe, amongſt other more euident proofes, the figure of the Paſchal Lambe, being indeede a verie Lambe trulie and really ſacrificed by the Iewes; importeth that Chriſt therby prefigured, is in verie deede, that he appeared to be, a verie man, conſiſting of ſoule and bodie, and was reallie ſacrificed, and that to greater effect infinitly, then was that lambe, and al other figures. he being the Sonne of God, and in vnitie of the ſame Per-

Ioan. 1.
v. 29.

ſon, being [the Lambe of God, which taketh away the ſin of the world.] And breſly al the other old Sacrifices, bloudie, & vnbloudie, of Abel, Noe, Mel-

Leuit. 1.
v. 2.
Ch. 2.
v. 12.
14. †
Ch. 6.
v. 14.

chizedech, Abraham, Iſaac, Iſrael, and al Sacrifices preſcribed by Moyſes Law, in catle, birdes, frutes, and whatſoeuer, with their libaments, doe vndoubtedly ſhew, that Chriſt our Sauiour by them prefigured, is abſolutly a real, and not an imaginarie man, really ſacrificed, really accompliſhing, al that which they foreſignified.

Ch. 7.
v. 29.
Deut. 18.
v. 15.
Act. 3.
v. 22.

3   In like ſort al the Prophets doe plainly deſcribe a real man, as Moyſes ſaid to the people [A Prophet of thy Nation, and of thy brethren, like vnto me, wil our Lord God raiſe vp to thee] which S. Peter teacheth to be performed in Chriſt. King Dauid, amongſt manie particulai thinges done to our B. Sauiour in his Paſſion, ſheweth that his perſecuters

Chriſts true humanitie is proued, by the Paſchal Lãbe, and other thinges.

By manie Prophecies.

Y 3   would

would abuſe him ſo cruelly, and contemptibly, as if
he were [a worme, and not a man, a reproache of *Pſ. 21.*
men, and an outcaſt of the people] Neuertheleſſe, *v. 7. 17*²̣.
whiles [manie dogges compaſſed him, and the counſel of the malignant beſieged him] yet his wiſdom
ouer-reached and ouerthrew their counſel, as the
ſame Pſalmiſt alſo propheciedſaying [Man ſhal com *Pſ. 63*⁇
to a deepe hart] euen then fulfilled, when the wic- *v. 8.*
ked bragged moſt againſt him, when his moſt depe
wiſdome ſuffered him ſelf to be apprehended bound,
ledde away, beaten, derided, , ſpitte vpon, whipped,
and crucified in his humane fleſh and bodie. Al
which had bene no real ſuffering, no real ſatisfaction for ſinne, no real Redemption of mankind, no
real victorie, if he were not really a man. Nei-
ther were Chriſt our Lord trulie [raiſed vp to the *Iere. 33.*⁷
houſe of Iſrael (as God promiſed by his Prophet *v. 14. 15.*
Ieremie) and to the houſe of Iuda : the ſpring of
Iuſtice had not trulie budded forth vntó Dauid j if
he were not indeede, and really of the ſeede of Iſrael, Iuda, and Dauid, a verie man. Neither ſhould he *Mal. 1.*⁇
more perteine to them, then to others in kindred of *Ch. 22.*
bloud, if he were no man at al.

By his frequēt
title of the
Sonne of man.

4   It may therfore ſuffice, for confirmation of this
truth, againſt al heretical phanſies, that holie Scriptures euerie where cal Chriſt [the Sonne of Dauid, *Rom. 1.*⁷
the Sonne of Abraham] and that moſt frequently *v. 3.*
he calleth him ſelf [the Sonne of man.] S. Stephen *Heb. 2.*
alſo after Chriſtes Aſcention, in his owne laſt con- *v. 16.*
flict at the point of death, called him the Sonne of
man ſaying, that [he ſaw the heauens opened, and *Act. 7.*
the Sonne of man ſtanding on the right hand of God. *v. 56.*

By S. Paules
doctrine.

5   S. Paul expreſly teacheth, that God ſent his
Sonne, made of a Woman] and calleth Chriſt
as abſolutly a man, as he calleth Adam a man ſaying,
[By the offence of one (man Adam) manie dyed : *Gal. 4*⁇
much *v. 3.*

Rom . 5.
v . 15 .

Cor . 15 .
21 . 22.

much more the grace of God, and the gift in the grace of one man Iesus Christ, hath abunded vpon manie.] Againe he saith [By a man death : & by a man, the Resurrection of the dead. As in Adam al die; so also in Christ, shal al be made aliue . The first man of earth earthly, the second man from heauen heauenly] stil shewing, that Christ our Lord, in substance of humane nature, differeth not from Adam & other men : but in manie qualities, he infinitly excelleth al others, and in manie, is also like vnto other men ; as we shal declare in the next Articles.

Christ our Lord, from the instant of his Incarnation, had fulnes of grace, knowlege, & power .

ARTICLE 19.

Together with humane nature , Christ the Sonne of God , assumpted such qualities in soule and bodie , as were most requisite and withal agreable, both to his diuine person, and to the worke of our Redemption, for which he came into this world. For so his sacred soul at the verie first instant, was indued with al sortes of grace , al maner of knowlege, and al kind of power . Concerning grace, none can be greater then to be vnited in person to God, wherby this singular man Iesus Christ is God , in that his humane nature is vnited to diuine nature, in diuine person, in that very act and instant, when the word was made flesh. Also habitual grace, that superexcellent spiritual qualitie , which maketh the subiect grateful to God ; was eué then, & euer after, most eminétly in the same most holie soule, as more then al others participating diuine influence; by how much it is nearer ioyned in personal vnion, which none other is, nor euer shal be,

by how

Our Lord assumpted such qualities as were agreable to his perfection, and mans redemption.

by how mnch it is more noble, then anie other is, or can be ; and by how much the fpringing fountaine excelleth the pound therehence dinerfly replenifhed. So that he is the endles and indeficient Threfurie of al vertues, and of al other graces, and of al giftes for the affiftance and enriching of al.

He had al fpiritu al graces incomparably aboue al other men.

2　For wheras al vertues, which doe perfect and adorne foules, confift in two fpecial pointes, in declyning, and hating of finne, and in louing and doing iuftice : the Royal Pfalmift contemplating the perfection of al the fame in our Sauiour, faith vnto him in prophetical fpirit [Thou haft loued iuftice, and haft hated iniquitie : therfor God (from whom euerie good and perfect gift defcendeth) thy God (peculiarly thy God by perfonal vnion) hath annointed thee with the oile of gladnes, aboue thy felowes] aboue al other participantes, which are more or leffe indued with like diuine infpiration, but he farre aboue al, as alfo Ifaias denounceth faying [The Spirit of our Lord fhal reft vpon him : the Spirit of wifdome and vnderftanding, the Spirit of counfel and ftrength, the Spirit of knowlege and pietie, and the Spirit of the feare of our Lord fhal replenifh him.] And fo defcribing other ftreames of grace, in his Kingdome the Church, fheweth that al are deriued from him, faying to al the faithful [You fhal draw waters in ioy, from the Sauiours fountaines .] And accordingly the Euangeliftes write, that f he is ful of grace and veritie, ful of the Holie Ghoft, that God did not geue him the Spirit by meafure] fignifying that fome others are ful of grace, receiuing anfwearable meafure therof to their capacitie. But our Sauiour receiued fuperabundance tor al, wherupon S. Iohn Baptift faid [Of his fulnes, al we haue receiued] S. Paul faith, that [to euerie one of vs, is geuen grace according to the meafure of the gift of Chrift.

Pf. 44. *v.* 8.
Iac. 1. *v.* 16.

Ifa. 11. *v.* 2. 3.

Ifa. 12. *v.* 3.
Ioan. 1. *v.* 14.
Luc. 4. *v.* 1.

Ioa. 3. *v.* 3. 4.
Ioa. 1. *v.* 16.

In like

3 In like ſort euen from his incarnation, Chriſt Chriſt as man had al knowlege euen from his Incarnat.ō.
our Lord had al knowlege, not only by his perſonal
vnion, but alſo his glorious ſoule, by fruition of God
peꝛfeꝛly ſeing al things, that euer were, are, or ſhal
be. A figure hereof was [the wiſdome of Salomon, *3.Reg.*
which paſſed the wiſdome of al them in the eaſt, & *4.v.30.*
of the Egiptians. And he was wiſer then al men : *31.*
wiſer then Ethan the Ezralite, and Heman, & Chal-
col, and Dorda, the ſonnes of Mahol. And he was
renomed in al nations round about. And there came *v.34.*
from al people to heare the wiſdome of Salomon, &
from al the Kinges of the earth which heard his wiſdome. The Queene of Saba came and proued his *3.Reg.*
wiſdome : and ſeing and hearing him, ſhe had no *10.v.1.*
longer breath : And ſhe ſaid to him. The report is *v.5.6.*
true which I heard in my Countrie, concerning thy
wiſdome, and I did not beleue them that told me, til
my ſelf came, and ſaw with mine eyes and haue proued, that the halfhath not bene told me ; greter is thy *v.7.*
wiſdome, and thy workes, then the rumor which I
haue heard.] This and much more is recorded of
King Salomon ; and al is but a dark ſhadow of our
Sauiorus wiſdome. Him ſelf auoucheth plainly to
the proud Scribes and Phariſees, that [this Queene *Mat.12.*
ſhal riſe in the Iudgement, and ſhal coudemne them, *v.42.*
becauſe ſhe came from the endes of the world, to hear
the wiſdome of Salomon, & behold (ſaith he) more
then Salomon here.]

4 Moyſes, and manie other Prophets by inſpira- Proued by the Prophets.
tion, ſaw this wiſdome of Chriſt, and were therby
illuminated. For [he is the light that lightneth al o- *Ioan.1.*
ther lightes that come into this world.] Ieremie ſaw *v.9.*
this perfeꝛion of al grace, vertues, and knowlege, *Iere.31.*
to be in our B. Sauiour, whileſt he was yet in the B. *v.22.*
Virgins wombe, when he ſaid [Behold our Lord
hath created a new thing, a woman ſhal compaſſe a

Z   man

man] *circundabit virum ,* not only *hominem ,* which might be a child aſwel in ſenſe and vnderſtanding , as in bodilie ſtature, but *virum ,* a mature man, of virile iudgement, in the ſtate of an infant newly conceiued, not borne into the world . Wherto holie Simeon agreeth, ſinging in his Canticle, when he ioyfullie held the ſame infant in his armes, at his preſentation in the Temple , being the fourtith day from his birth, pronouncing him to be [the light to the reuelation of the Gentiles : and the glorie of the people of Iſrael .] *Luc.* 2 . *v.* 32 .

The firſt maniſ-
feſtation of his
wiſdome was at
the age of
twelue yeares .

5 His firſt manifeſt reuelation recorded in the holie Scriptures, was at the age of twelue yeares, when he was found in the Temple of Ieruſalem, ſitting in the middeſt of the Doctors hearing them, & asking them queſtions. Shewing ſo profoũd knowlege, that as the Euangeliſt writeth [al were aſtonied that heard him, vpon his wiſdome and anſweares .] What more he *Luc.* 2 . *v.* 42 . *v.* 46 . 47 .

From the age
of thirtie
yeares, he
ſhewed more
and more wiſ-
dom .

did, is not written; til he was about thirtie yeares old, when he came to S . Iohn Baptiſt, cauſing S . Iohn otherwiſe vnwilling , to baptize him [for ſo it becometh vs (ſaid he) to fulfil al iuſtice] to participate and performe al good worke, though to them not needeful, for edification to others . Thence he paſſed into the deſert, faſted fourtie daies and nightes, was tempted, and ouerthrew the tempter . Then called diſciples, preached the kingdome of heauen . Al with ſuch manifeſtation of knowlege, and wiſdome, that the Iewes ſtroken with admiration, ſaid ech to other wondring [How doth this man know letters wheras he hath not learned anie] For al the neighboures and Countrie knew that he had not gone to ſchole : That he had ſtil liued with his parentes, Ioſeph (whom they ſuppoſed to be his father) and Marie his Mother, and was ſubiect to them . And ſo accounting him the ſonne of a Carpenter, vnlearned and *Luc.* 3 . *v.* 23 . *Mat.* 3 . *v.* 15 . *Mat.* 4 . *v.* 1 . 2 . 3 *v.* 17 . *Ioan.* 7 . *v.* 15 .

Mar. 6. ned, and of the same trade of life. [How came this
v. 3. man (say they) by this wisdome and vertues, as are
Mat. 13. wrought by his handes ? Is not this the carpenters
v. 54. sonne ? (a carpenter as Sainct. Marke relateth)
55. 56. Is not his Mother called Marie ? (perhaps Ioseph
was now departed this life) and his brethren Iames
and Ioseph, and Simon, and Iude, and his sisters are
they not with vs (for such indeede were his cosins
by bloud) whence therfore haith he al these thinges ?
v. 57. And they were scandalized in him. But wisdome
Mat. 11. is iustified of her children.] Further he shewed his
v. 19. wisdome and inscrutable knowlege, by detecting
the secret cogitatiõs of his aduersaries, & answering
Mat. 9. therunto [Iesus seeing their thoughtes, said : wher- He knew the
v. 4. fore think you euil in your hartes ?] Againe, to secrete
proue his forgeuing of sinnes, to be no blasphemie thoughtes of
as they thought [he said to the sicke of the palsey, a- mens hartes.
v. 6. rise, take vp thy bedde, and goe into thy house.]
And when manie beleued in his name, seeing the
miracles which he did, yet he did not commit him
Ioan. 2. self vnto them [For he knew al (saith the Euange-
v. 24. list) and because it was not nedeful for him, that
25. anie should geue testimonie of man, for he knew
Mat. 16. what was in man.]
v. 8. 6 Of which his vniuersal knowlege, the Apostles He knew the
Luc. 9. hauing good experience, both in them selues and o- day of Iudge-
v. 47. thers [asked him when Ierusalem should be destroy- ment but
Mat. 24. ed, and when the general Iudgment should be ?] of would not re-
v. 36. both which he gaue them certaine signes, but the ucale it.
Mar. 13. very time and day, he would not tel them saying,
v. 31. [that no bodie knoweth it, neither the Angels in heauen, but the Father alone, nor the Sonne, but the Father] which last wordes, the Arrians alleage, for
their heresie, to proue that the Sonne of God is inferior and inequal to the Father. And other heretikes called Agnoites, vrge the same, against the v-
niuersal

uiuerſal knowlege of Chtiſt as he is man. But one
anſwear of the Catholique Church ſerueth to both
the errors, that our Sauiour, whoſe office is to reueale al thinges that are nedeful, and conuenient to
be knowne, hath not in commiſſion to reueale the
laſt day of general Iudgement, and ſo he knoweth it
not to tel it to others ; But that himſelf knoweth it
no man of vnderſtanding can doubt, ſeing he is the
Iudge of al, and therfore knoweth al thinges perteyning therto : Els he were not a competent Iudge, if
he knew not, aſwel the time, as al other pointes belonging to that office. Neither can that prophecie
of Zacharie be wel vnderſtoode of anie other day,
then the day of general Iudgement, where he ſaith :
[There ſhal be one day, *which is knowne to our Lord*, *Zach.* 14.
not day nor night, and in the time of the euening, *v.*7.
there ſhal be light] : Much leſſe as he is the Sonne
of God can he be ignoraut (as the Arrians ſaid) of
this or anie other thing, that either ſhal be or can
be. As for other obieċtions made by the ſame Ag- *Luc.* 2.
noites vpon the wordes of S. Luke [Ieſus proce- *Luc.* 2.
ded in wiſdome, and age, and grace, with God, and *v.*52.
men :] And that he merueled at the great faith of *Mat.* 8.
the Centurion, which (ſay they) importeth that he *v.*10.
was ignorant of the cauſe of the Centurions great
He proceeded faith; is as clearly anſweared. For thoſe wordes of
in experimen- S. Luke import only experimental knowlege, & in
tal knowlege. this our Sauiour proceded, hauing before habitual
He would ſeme knowlege of the ſame thinges. And wheras he mer-
to maruel ueled at the Centurions faich; he therby gaue al to
though he vnderſtand, that the Iewes faith was defeċtiue, and
knew the ſame this Gentiles faith admirable, and worthie to be ad-
thing before. mired, and imitated by the Iewes. And ſo by this,
and by other continual occaſions, he more and more
made knowne, that he euer from his Incarnation,
had al knowlege. And ſo S. Peter profeſſed ſaying,

Lord

Ioa.21. [Lord thou knoweſt al thinges : thou knoweſt that
v.17. I loue thee.] Neither did he learne anie thing of
men, nor of Angels, but is the abſolute Maiſter and
Doctor of al, as the Prophet Ioel calleth him : wil-
Ioel. 2. ling [the children of Sion to reioice in our Lord,
v.23. becauſe he hath geuen you a Doctor of Iuſtice .] So
Ioa. 13. alſo his Apoſtles rightly called him Maiſter, which
v.13. title him ſelf approued and ratified, ſaying to them
[You cal me Maiſter, and Lord, and you ſay wel, for
I am ſo] As alſo before this he had taught them
Mat.23. ſaying [One is your Maiſter Chriſt] Not that there
v.8.10. may not be other maiſters vnder him (for S. Paul
2. Tim. was appointed a maiſter of the Gentiles) but becauſe
1.v.11. Chriſt is the eminent and principal Maiſter of al : He
is only abſolute Maiſter, independent of others ; He
Ephſ. 1. [whom God hath ſet on his right hand in celeſtials,
v.20. aboue al Principalitie and Poteſtate, and Power, &
21. Domination, and euerie name that is named in this
world, or in the world to come .]

7 Finally Chriſtes incomparable power, which is
an other principal excellencie, is alſo proued by manie holie Scriptures. For firſt his holie name IE-
SVS, that is Sauiour, importeth his ſingular power,
that by him and by no other there is ſaluation, as
S. Peter auouched to Caiphas, and other rulers a-
Act. 4. mong the Iewes, ſaying : [Be it knowne to al you,
v.10. and to al the people of Iſrael, that in the name of
Ieſus Chriſt of Nazareth this man (who hath bene
lame from his mothers wombe) ſtandeth before you
v.12. whole. For neither (ſaith he) is there anie name
vnder heauen, geuen to men, wherein we muſt be ſa-
Phil. 2. ued.] And S. Paul teacheth that [in the name of Ie-
v.10. ſus euerie knee bowe, of the celeſtials, terreſtrials,
and infernals .]

8 Alſo the name CHRIST, that is the Annointed
ſheweth to vs his three ſingular offices ; that he is
the

Chriſts omni-
potent power
is ſignified by
the name
IESVS.

Alſo by the
name
CHRIST.

Z 3

the *Prophete*, of whom al the other Prophets did foretel: *the Preift* for euer according to the order of Melchifedech, and *the King* of kinges, whofe kingdom
fhal haue no end. Of him therfore al true Prophets,
Preiftes, and Kinges, haue both their title, & power of perfons annointed. This his power he exprefly fignified to his Apoftles as his Patentes of commiffion faying: [Al power is geuen to me in heauen,
and in earth: going therefore teach ye al nations.
As my Father fent me, I alfo doe fend you, whofe
finnes you fhal forgeue they are forgeuen them, &
whofe you fhal reteine, they are reteined] fignifying as wel that he had receiued power as man, from
God, as that his power extendeth it felf, to geue
and conferre power to other men, his Minifters:
wherof is more frequent mention then I fhal nede
here to recite.

Ioan. 1.
v. 22.
Pf. 109.
v. 4.

Luc. 1.
v. 33.
Mat. 28.
v. 18. 19.
Ioan. 20.
v. 22. 23.

He had alfo
temporal pow-
er.

And practifed
the fame in
correcting
faultes.

9   In way alfo of correction our Sauiour temporally punifhed offenders: as [when he found in the
Temple fome that fold oxen, and fheepe, & doues,
and the bankers fitting, he made as it were a whippe
of fmal cordes, and droue them al out of the Temple with their fheepe and oxen, and the money of the
bankers, he powred out, and ouerthrew the tables]
which was one of the firft thinges he did, in mani-
fefting him felf to be Chrift our Redeemer. Againe
in the fame kind, not long before his Paffion, on
Palme Sunday [when he was receiued with ioyful
acclamations into Ierufalem, he entred into the Temple of God, and caft out al that fold and bought in
the Temple, and the tables of the bankers, and the
chaires of them that fold pigions, he ouerthrew.] So
without limitation of thinges or perfons [God hath
geuen al thinges in his handes] as the Euangelift teftifieth, and as S. Paul alfo writeth [God hath fubdued al thinges vnder his feete, and hath made him

Ioan. 2.
v. 14. 15

Mat. 21.
v. 12.

Which power is
vniuerfal ouer
al perfons, and
al thinges.

Ioa. 3.
v. 35.
Ephef. 1.
v. 22.

head

head ouer al the Church , which is his bodie] not
of part, but of al the Church : Angels and men, Clergie and Laitie , Princes and Peoples : not only a
Maifter to teach, and to inftruct, but alfo a Lord
to command, and to correct [He onlie the Sauiour of
al men, efpecially of the faithful] to witte of the
faithful, as of members actually vnited to the head ,
and of al others liuing in this world, as of thofe that
haue it in their power, through his grace , which is
wanting to none, that they may be vnited if they wil,
and be faued . Which vniuerfal power, of Chtift, the
fame Apoftle againe auoucheth and proueth by Dauids Prophecie , that Chriftes dominion is ouer al .
[For in that (faith the Apoftle) God fubiected al
thinges vnto him, he left nothing not fubiect to
him .]

Ioa. 13.
v. 13.
1. *Tim*.
4. *v*. 10.

Pf. 8.
v. 7. 8.
Heb. 2.
v. 8.

*Chrift our Lord tooke alfo mans infirmities, not
opposite to perfection .*

ARTICLE. 20.

AS our Lord in humane nature, had euen fró
his incarnation, al qualities of perfection :
fo he alfo tooke al mannes infirmities not con
trarie therunto . fubiecting him felf to death and o-
ther penalties as the debtes of mannes finnes, for the
which he came to fatisfie . But to finne it felf, he was
in no wife fubiect. As al the Prophets and Apoftles
teach vs, he euer moft perfectly [loued Iuftice, and
hated iniquitie . He did no finne, neither was there
guile found in his mouth.] Wherfore him felf moft
worthilie chalenged his aduerfaries, to charge him
therwith if they could [Which of you (faith he) fhal
argue me of finne ?] Neither had he, nor could
haue anie inclination to finne (called *fomes peccati,*
foode

Pf. 44.
v. 8. *if*.
5?. *v*. 9.
1. *Pet*. 2.
v. 22.
Ioan. 8.
v. 46.

Chrift fubiec-
ted himfelf to
death and pe-
nalties of this
life , but not
to finne .

foode or norifhment of finne) being the holie one, *Mat*. 1 . *v*
côceiued by the Holie Ghoft, vnited in perfon to God 18 . *Luc* . 1
the Sonne, and hauing fruition of God in his euer *v* . 35 . *Io*
bleffed foule . He was euer fo whollie free from al 14 . *v* . 30
fpiritual defectes, that [the Prince of this world had *Io* . 8 . *v* . 12
not in him anie thing at al .] Neither could he be *Luc* . 1 .
ignorant of anie thing, who is [the light of the world *v* . 79 .
fent to illuminate al that fitte in darcknes . Neither

Nor to igno-rance.

in bodie was he fubiect to anie deformitie , mon-
ftruoufitie, or vnacuftomed natural difeafes, as lame-
nes, blindnes, deafnes, palfey, leprofie, or the like .

Nor to anie deformitie .

For of him is verified alfo, according to his corporal conftitution, that faying of the Pfalmift [Good- *Pf*. 44 .
lie of bewtie aboue the fonnes of men ; grace is pow- *v* . 3 .
red out in thy lippes .]

He tooke al o-ther infirmi-ties .

2 Other general infirmities common to al mankind,
for the finne of Adam; our celeftial Adam Chrift,
voluntarily admitted, and vndertooke in him felf.
He would be paffible and mortal ; that he might fuffer and dye for al men : he was wounded (faith I- *Ifa* . 53 .
faias the Prophet) for our iniquities; he was brokē *v* . 5 . 7 .
for our finnes . the difcipline of onr peace vpon him,
and with the waile of his ftripe, we are healed . And
he was offered, becaufe him felf would] Yea his Paffion exceded al others, wherupon he faith in the Lamentations [O al ye that paffe by the way, attend *Lamen* . 1 .
and fee, if there be forrow like vnto my forrow] Be- *v* . 12 .
caufe he fuffered for al, he would fuffer moft of al .
[Becaufe the children (faith S. Paul) haue commu- *Heb* . 2 .
nicated with flefh and bloud, him felf alfo (that is *v* . 14 .
Chrift) in like maner hath bene partaker of the fame]
hath alfo taken flefh like to the flefh of finners, paffible and of the fame kind that finners haue, which
in an other place, he calleth [the fimilitude of the *Rom*. 8 .
flefh of finne] For others hauing flefh of finne, he *v* . 3 .
had the like flefh, but without finne [that by death
he might

he might deſtroy him that had the Empyre of death]
that is to ſay the diuel . For ſeing he hath taken the
ſeede of man [he would in al thinges be like vnto his
brethren, that he might become a merciful and faithful *High Preiſt* before God, that he might repropi-
tiate the ſinnes, (or make a reconciliation for the
ſinnes) of the people .]

3   Neither did he only take this mortalitie, and paſ-
ſibilitie in fleſh that he might therby dye, but alſo
that he might therin ſuffer other penalties for our
ſinnes, and to make our ſuffering acceptable & fruictful [yet if we ſuffer with him, that we may alſo be
glorified with him .] For our benefite therfore, &
for our example, he would be hungrie after fourtie
daies faſt in the deſert . He would then alſo be tempted, to teach vs to reſiſt tentation . He would be wearied of his iourney and ſitte downe to reſt him by a
fountaine in the Countrie of Samaria . He would be
thirſtie on the Croſſe ; and innumerable the like .
[For in that wherin him ſelf ſuffered, and was proued,
he is able to helpe them that are tempted & proued .]

He ſuffered to make our ſuffe-ring accep-table .

Rom . 8 .
v . 17 .
2 . Tim .
2 . v . 12 .
Mat . 4 .
v . 2 .
Ioa . 4 .
v . 6 .
Ioa . 19 .
v . 28 .

4   Likewiſe in his ſoule, to witte, in the inferiour
ſenſitiue part or power therof, our Sauiour aſſumed
our infirmities . For albeit his B . Soul was euer glorious, ſeing God moſt perfectly of al the bleſſed, yet
the influence of his ſoule, which ſhould otherwiſe redound euen to the bodie, was by Goddes diſpoſition, for more merite, and our greater benefite, ſuſ-
pended, that not only our Sauiours bodie, but alſo
the ſenſitiue power of his bleſſed ſoule, was ſubiect in this life to ordinarie afflictions of other ſoules.
Hence it was that by the Prophet Dauid our Sauiour ſaid [My ſoul is repleniſhed with euils] with
great tribulations . For ſo was his ſoul afflicted in
the garden of Gethſemanie, the firſt night of his

He alſo ſuffe-red in the ſen-ſitiue power of his ſoule .

Pſ . 87 .
v . 4 .

A a   Paſſion

passion when [he began to waxe sorowful, & to be
sadde;] when he also said to his Disciples [My soul
is sorrowful euen vnto death] And as S . Mark relateth [began to feare, and to be heauie] which motions in Christ our Lord, were real afflictions, infirmities of humane nature, and called in him *Propassi-*
ons ; wheras the like in vs are real passions preuenting the order of reason, but in him folowing the order of reason, for that his reason so directed, & his
wil subiecting it self to Goddes wil, so ordeyned,
that the sensitiue power of his soule, should be subiect to feare, sadnes, and sorrow : but withal, stil
subiect to reason, and his wil submitted to Goddes
wil : As in the same Agonie he absolutly prayed [Father not as I wil, but as thou wilt, not my wil, but
thy wil be done .] Al which infirmities voluntarily
assumpted, with the vnspeakable dolours therby euen
as wilingly susteined, did not depriue his soule of glo
rie . For he was stil, aswel in the time of his Passion,
as al the rest of his temporal life, both *Comprehen-*
sor, & Viator, to witte, he was both in possession
of eternal glorie, and also in the way to eternal glo
rie : both in heauen, as him self said [the Sonne of
Man which is in heauen] and also traueling in the
way to heauen, as Ieremie the Prophet signifieth,
admiring therat, and demanding of him [Why wilt
thou be as a soiourner (or stranger) in the lande, &
as a wayfaring man, turning into lodge] or tending
towardes lodging place ?

Mat . 26.
v . 27. 38.
Mar . 14.
v . 33 .

Mat . 26.
v . 39 . 42.
Luc . 22 .
v . 42 .

Ioan . 3 .
v . 13.
Iere . 14 .
v . 8 .

Our Lord had
not passions,
but propassiós .

He was both
viator, & com-
prehensor.

The blessed Virgin Marie, is the Mother of God:
and most excellent of al created persons.

ARTICLE. 21.

BEfore we procede further to speake of particular thinges which our B. Saulour did, and suffered in this transitorie life : it resteth for cóplement of the third Article of the Apostles Crede, to declare brefely, a special point of the Christian doctrine, that the B. Virgin, Mother of Iesus, is therby also MOTHER of GOD. And consequently, by the same exaltation and pearles dignitie, is the most excellent of al created persons. I say of al persons created, because Christ our Sauiour, is a Diuine Person Increated. Concerning therfore the former point, that she is trulie the Mother of God, although it be not expresly said in the holie Scripture, that the B. Virgin is the Mother of God, as the heritike Nestorius obiected : yet is it necessarily deduced from holie Scriptures ; and the denial therof is condemned to be heritical, by the holie Ephesine Councel. Which yet we vrge not in this present trial, but according to our purpose, proue it by the confessed written word of God.

Mat. 1. 2   The Euangelist S. Mathew writeth, that [of this
v. 16. B. Virgin Marie, was borne IESVS, who is called
v. 23. CHRIST : who is also called EMANVEL, (which being interpreted, is) God with vs] Alleaging against the Iewes, that Isayas so prophecied, and so
Isa. 7. called the child her sonne. S. Luke writeth, that
v. 14. [S. Elizabeth, being replenished with the Holie Ghost, (admiring the B. Virgins humilitie) cried
Luc. 1. out with a lowde voice and said, [Whence is this to
v. 41. me, that the Mother of my Lord doth come to me.]
42. 43.   A a 2   It is

It perteineth to al Christians to beleue, that the B. Virgin Marie, is the Mother of God.

It is proued by necessarie consequence of holie Scriptures.

It is true, that Chriſt, not only as God, but alſo as man, is our Lord: yet here the title of Lord, importeth the greater cauſe of admiration, rather then the leſſer, and ſhe ſpeaking by the inſpiration of the Holie Ghoſt, rather meant our Lord God, then Lord as he is man. Which is alſo confirmed by her next wordes explicating ſuch an effect, as importeth diuine power in the Virgins Sonne ſaying [For behold as the voice of thy ſalutation ſounded in mine eares, the infant in my wombe did leape for ioy.] And therfore ſhe might wel cal her, the Mother of our *Lord God,* from whoſe Sonne, her owne ſonne receiued ſuch grace, as could not procede from anie other, then from God. S. Paul alſo teſtifieth, that God was borne of the Iſſue of Dauid, ſaying [Chriſt, who is aboue al thinges G O D, bleſſed for euer, was borne of the Iewes, according to the fleſh; & of the ſeede of Dauid] which was by his Mother the B. Virgin. And therfore ſhe, of whom God was borne, is as properly called the M O T H E R of G O D, as is ſaid, [God is borne of the Iewes.] Likewiſe S. Iohn ſaith expreſſy [Ieſus is the Sonne of God : This is the true God] which is alreadie declared by manie other ſacred textes. Vpon al which premiſſes, is neceſſarily inferred, that the B. Virgin, being the Mother of Ieſus, who is God : is the Mother of God; euen as certeinly and demonſtratiuely, as it is inferred that ſhe is the Mother of Chriſt. For neither had Ieſus his annointing, or offices, of Prophet, King, and Preiſt, wherof he is called Chriſt, from his Mother.

v . 44.

Rom . 9.
v . 5 . *Ch* . 1.
v . 3 .

1 . *Ioan* . 5 .
v . 5 . 20 .
Article 17 .

Proued by a cleare example and proper ſpeach of al men.

3   As likewiſe neither had he his ſoule from his Mother, nor anie other men haue their ſoules from their parents : and yet is not ſhe, nor anie other mother, called the Mother of the fleſh of her child, but of the child conſiſting of ſoule and bodie, and ſubſiſting

in

in humane perſon (ſpeaking of al other mothers and children) ſo our B. Ladie the Virgin , Mother of Ieſus her Sonne, conſiſting of diſtinct natures, diuine and humane; and his humanitie conſiſting of ſoule and bodie, and al the three natures, Deitie , Soule, & Bodie, ſubſiſting in diuine perſon ; moſt trulie & is moſt properly called the Mother of God . An other example, though it doth not proue our purpoſe, yet to illuſtrate this truth, is in a Queene, the wife of an abſolute King, bearing a Sonne, is trulie the mo-ther of a Prince. And. when this Prince her Sonne cometh to be King, ſhe is trulie the mother of the King. And it were too nice, too preciſe, yea, an vn-proper and falſe ſpeach, to ſay, ſhe is not mother of the kin g , but onlie of that man who is king, though he had not his kingdome by his mother . So the B, Virgin, bearing her Sonne Ieſus, who is Chriſt, & who is alſo God : is no leſſe trulie the Mother of God , then ſhe is the Mother of Chriſt, and the Mo-ther of Ieſus . Becauſe God, the moſt B . Trinitie , vouchſaifed to make her the Mother of Ieſus, who is Chiſt & God .

An other ex-ample ; illurat-ing this point of faith .

4 In that therfore this moſt bleſſed Virgin is ſo exalted as none can be higher to be the Mother of God, it neceſſarily foloweth that ſhe excelleth al o-ther humane , and Angelical perſons, in grace and glorie : and after the moſt ſacred humanitie of Chriſt her ſonne, is moſt excellent of al other creatures . For further declaration wherof we haue abundance of figures, prophecies, teſtimonies , & other proffes in the holie Scriptures. Firſt of al that decree of God to ſend a redemer of mankind reueiled ſtraight after our fal, includeth this B . Virgin as principally cooperating with our B . Sauiour, in the combate a-gainſt the diuel . For wheras the diuel firſt aſſaulted our mother Eue , and then by her meanes ouercame

The B . Virgin mother of God is moſt excel-lent of al crea-tures, except only the hu-manitie of Chriſt.

Proued by Gods promiſe that the diuel ſhould be ouercome by the ſeede of a woman .

Gen . 3 .
v. 1 . 6 .

A a 3   our

our father Adam ; our merciful God in examining this *v* . 9 .
tranfgreffion, began with Adam, whofe finne, and
not Eues, infected and ouerthrew vs al. But vpon 12 .
his anfwere, alleaging Eues allurement, wherunto 13 .
he confented ; God alfo hearing her excufe, and accufation of the ferpent (the diuel) that had decei- 15 .
ued her ; premonifhing them, and in them vs al, that
this enmitie begunne betwene the ferpent and the
woman [fhonld continue betwene them, and betwene the ferpents feede (folowers or adherentes)
and the womans feede, and that fhe and her feede,
fhould brufe the ferpents head in peeces] Signifying, that as the diuel by the cooperation of a woman, ouercame man : fo by cooperation of a woman
he fhould be ouercome, his head brufed in peeces .
Neither can the Iewes denie, but that this prediction perteyneth to the Mother of Meffias, who indeede is the B . Virgin Mother of God .

The fame was
prefigured by
the name of
Eua .

5   To whom alfo perteyned, that Adam called the
name of his wife Eue [becaufe (faith the holie text) 20 .
fhe was the mother of al the liuing] for fo Eue fignifieth . And moft properly agreeth to the Mother
of God, truly called the mother of al the liuing ;
being Mother of life it felf, Iefus Chrift, God, and
Man : [who is the way, the veritie, and the life] *Ioan* . 14 .
wheras the other Eue was to be mother of vs al, as *v* . 6 .
we are mortal and continually dying . But was called mother of the liuing, in figure of her that moft
efpecially and moft nearly, fhould cooperate to the
incarnation of our Redemer Chrift, by whom al men
fhould recouer life .

Other figures
of the old Tef-
tament of the
moft bleffed
Virgin were
thefe .

6   As wil alfo more euidently appeare if we confider
the fpecial graces of certaine other renowmed holie
women, & compare them with the Mother of God .
For fo we fhal eafily fee, that they were indede,
fome in one refpect, fome in an other, fignificant
figures

figures, or shadowes forefhewing this fupereminent Virgin, who by manie degrees excelleth them al. Sara the wife of Abraham when by fpecial grace fhe had bene long barren, & nature was deficiēt; cōceiued & bare a fonne in her old age of nintie yeares. Rebecca the wife of Ifaac, and mother of Efau & Iacob, twinnes. Lia, and Rachel wiues of Iacob, mothers of the more principal heades, of the Tribes of Ifrael. Marie the fifter of Moyfes and Aaron, a virgin Prophetefle. Debora the wife of Lapidoth, a Prophetefle, that directed Barach the Iudge, or Capitane general of the Ifraelites armie. Iahel that killed Sifara their inuading enemie. Anna, the wife of Elcana, and mother of Samuel the Prophet, and fhe alfo a Prophetefle. Iudith a widow: And Efther, a Qreene, who vpon feueral occafions, and by diuers meanes, deliuered the whole people of Ifrael, from great diftrefles, and imminent dangers of ruine. Laftly, S. Anne, our B. Ladies owne mother; and S. Elizabeth, the mother of S. Iohn Baptift: and another holie Anne, a Prophetefle, the daughter of Phanuel, a religious old widow; were al indued with manifold graces, moft of them more by miracle, then by the ordinarie power of nature, became mothers of moft renowmed children; one of them a Virgin, and two widowes, and the reft wiues: by their manie noble vertues, and fundrie heroical actes, did wel fore-fignifie, but none of them, nor al together, if they had bene ioyned in one perfon, could match this fingular fpoufe of God, the Tabernacle of the Holie Ghoft, fome time a wife, and afterwardes a widow, but ftil a perpetual Virgin, and the chofen Mother of God: which is the greateft preeminence that could be geuen her.

7 An other verie great preeminent grace, was her fingular priuilege, to be both a Virgin, and a Mother

Marginal references (left):
Gen. 11. v. 29.
Ch. 17. v. 17.
Ch. 18. v. 11. Ch. 21. v. 2. Ch. 24. v. 67.
Ch. 25. v. 24. Ch. 39. v. 32. Ch. 30. v. 22.
Exo. 15. v. 20. Iudic. 4. v. 4. 17.
1. Reg. 1. v. 2. Ch. 2. v. 1. &c.
Iudith. 15. v. 10. Eft. 9. v. 1. *
Luc. 1. v. 5. Ch. 2. v. 36. 37.

Marginal notes (right):
Sara.
Rebecca.
Lia.
Rachel.
Marie.
Debora.
Iahel.
Anna.
Iudith.
Efther.

Anna, her own mother.
Elizabeth & another Anna, a Prophetefle.

Her fingular priuilege to be

both a perpe-
tual Virgin, &
a Mother, was
prefigured by
the bush bur-
ning, and not
confuming.

ther; which befides the examples of barren women,
by Goddes power made fruteful, was further fignified by other miraculous operations, verie aptly re-
fembling this particular mifterie. As when our Lord *Exo*. 3.
appeared to Moyfes in a flame of fire, out of the mid- *v*. 2.
deft of a bush : he faw that the bush was on fyre,
and was not burnt. which as a figure, did wel repre- *Luc*. 1.
fent the moft B. Virgin, who being ouerfhadowed *v*. 35.
with the flaming fire of the holy Ghoft, did conceiue
and beare a fonne, her moft pure Virginitie ftil con-

Aarons rodde. ferued. Alfo Aarons drie rodde, bringing forth *Num*. 17.
floures and frute, was a like figure of the fame im- *v*. 8.
maculate Virgin, made fertile aboue al courfe of na-

Gedeons
fleece.
ture. So likewife Gedeons wool fleece, at one time *Iudic*. 6.
found ful of dew, al the ground being drie about it; *v*. 38. 40.
an other time found drie, al the ground being wette,
prefigured the felf fame fertile Mother of God, ftil
remaning a pure and perpetual Virgin.

The fame pri-
uilege foretold
by the Pro-
phets:
Dauid,
Ifaias.
8   To al which and the like prophetical figures
rightly agree the predictions of prophets. For the
Royal Pfalmift faid, that Chrift by his incarnation
fhould [defcend as raine vpon a fleece, & as droppes *Pf*. 71.
of raine falling vpon the earth] Ifaias the prophet *v*. 6.
affirmed that [a rodde fhould come forth out of the *Ifa*. 11. *v*.
roote of Ieffe (who was otherwife called Ifai the 1. *Ruth*. 4.
father of Dauid) and that a floure fhould rife vp out *v*. 22.
of this rodde.] Which rodde none but Iewes denie,
to be the B. Virgin; & that the floure is the Meffias the fame Iewes willingly confeffe. And more
exprefly Ifaias faith : [A virgin fhal conceiue & beare *Ifa*. 7.

Ezechiel.
a fonne] whom alfo Ezechiel femeth to prophecie, *v*. 14.
though vnder the fhadow of the Temple, faying [the *Ezech*. 43.
earth fhined at his Maieftie, and the houfe was filled *v*. 2. 5.
with the glorie of our Lord.] For fo was the B.
Virgin more and more replenifhed with grace, by
conceiuing Chrift the fountaine of grace and glorie.

And

And concerning her perpetual Virginitie, the same Ezechiel saith more plainly (if by the east part of the Temple, we vnderstand, as al Christian writers doe, the Mother of Christ) that [this Gate shal be shutte, & it shal not be opened.]

Ezech.
44. v. 3.

9 Of her singular spiritual perfection, aboue al others, King Salomon haith manie goodly sentences in his Canticles, by which God him self testifieth al her vertues in general, saying [as the Lillie among the thornes : so my loue among the daughters. How bewtiful art thou o my loue, & how bewtiful art thou. How comlie my dearest in delightes?] and innumerable the like. Which albeit they are spoken also of the whole Church, the general spouse of God, and of euerie faithful soule his particular spouse : yet singularly perteine to the most excellent, and most eminent of al. Especially that praise which comprehendeth al sanctitie, together with al puritie : [Thou art al faire my loue, and there is not a spotte in thee.] More fiigures and prophecies might be recited, of the old Testament, but these may suffice.

Cant. 2.
v. 2. Ch.
4. v. 1.
Ch. 7.
v. 6.

Ch. 4.
v. 7.

Her singular perfection in al vertues.

10 Now let vs more particularly touch, the sacred historie of her most blessed life, wherof be manie worthie workes extant, and therfore I wil here only name the especial heades. Whether this chosen Vessel of God, being ordeyned before al worldes, and in the fulnes of time, prepared to be the Mother of God, was euer subiect to original sinne, or rather preuented by sanctifying grace, is a question disputable, which I wil not discusse. Only this we may say as certaine, that Christ her Sonne, is also her Sauiour, for so he is of al mankind, which he performed to her in such maner, as was most to his owne honour, as he was both God and Man; which should also be to her most merite, and most glorie. But that

It is most probable that our B. Ladie was preserued from original sinne.

That she was sainctified be-

B b

that she was sanctified before her birth, is a point of faith, beleued and defined by the Church, though it be not expressed in the holie Scriptures. As neither is there anie mention at al of her Parentes nor of the time nor place of her birth, nor education : which yet are knowne by Tradition. And to al persons of reasonable vnderstanding, & discourse, it is sufficiently credible, that the Mother of God had, not lesse, but greater Priuileges in her maner of sanctification, then anie other setuant of Christ : and namely greater prerogatiue therin, then the Prophet Ieremie, or her Sonnes Precursor S. Iohn Baptist,

both which were sanctified before they were borne, in their mothers wombe ; as holie Scriptures testifie. Of Ieremie thus [before I formed thee (saith God) in the wombe, I knew thee, and before thou camest forth of the matrice, I sanctified thee.] Of S. Iohn Baptist, the Angel said to Zacharie his father [He shal be replenished with the Holie Ghost, euen from his mothers wombe.] Much more the elected Mother of God was sanctified, and replenished with the Holie Ghost, either in the same instant, or presently after, that her B. soule informed her natural bodie. And so the Church celebrateth her immaculate coming into the world, with two solemne feastes ; the one of her Conception, or first sanctification ; the other of her holie Natiuitie. By which

Iere. 1. *v.* 5.

Luc. 1. *v.* 15.

sanctification she was so confirmed, and established in grace (as the piller of truth beleueth) that in al her life she neuer committed anie actual sinne at al, neither mortal, nor venial : but made continual progresse in al vertues.

1. *Tim.* 3. *v.* 15.

11 At the age of three yeares, as constant Tradition teacheth, she was presented by her parentes, to be instructed amongst virgins in the Temple : and there remained, til she was espoused to holie Ioseph
by Goddes

Mat. 1. *v.* 18.20.

by Goddes especial ordinance, for diuers great reasons; aswel in respect of our B. Sauiour, whom she
should conceiue and beare, lest he might haue bene 1.
reputed of illegitimate birth; and that some besides 2.
his Mother, might take a fatherly care of him in his
infancie; as in respect of the holie Virgin, lest she 3.
might haue bene defamed, or punished as a forni-
catrix; and that she might haue comfort and helpe 4.
of her spouse in al difficulties, fleeing into Egipt,
remayning there, destitute of other frendes, returning thence, and in other necessities. As also her 5.
mariage was requisite, in respect of others, that they
might haue the confident and irrefragable testimonie of Ioseph, that Christ was borne of a Virgin,
because in this case, his only Mothers assertion,
might seme suspected & insufficient.

12 That her Virginitie, was confirmed & consecrated to God by vow, is inuinciblie proued by her prudent replie to the Angel, demanding of him by what
meanes she must conceiue, as he had told her that
she should, not expressing the maner how. And therfore she said not; How can this be done, as doubting, but [how shal this be done?] and withal yelding her reason, why she inquired [because (saith
she) I know not man] which necessarily implieth
her vowed state of life neuer to know man. Els this
reason should haue had no ground, if she had bene
in state to haue knowne man afterwardes. But because she had by Goddes wil, & her spouses consent,
vowed perpetual Virginitie, the Angel made not answeare that she might know man, and so conceiue &
beare a Sonne; but he answeared [the Holie Ghost
shal come vpon thee, and the power of the most
high shal ouershadow thee. And therfore also that
which of thee shal be borne Holie, shal be called the
Sonne of God; because there shal not be anie thing

Sap. 4.
v. 3.

Deut.
22. *v.*
21.
Mat. 2.
v. 13.
14. 20.
Mat. 1.
v. 19.

Luc. 1.
v. 34.

Num.
30. *v.*
14.

Luc. 1.
v. 35.

v. 37.

She vowed
perpetual vir-
ginitie.

impos-

impoſſible with God.] By whoſe omnipotent power, perpetual virginitie could not hinder his wil, &
decree, to be borne of a Virgin.

As her dignitie exccelleth al others: ſo her fulnes of grace excel'ed, by which God made her worthie to be his Mother.

13 Wherfore being by the wil of God, both a wife,
and a vowed Virgin, and in al other reſpectes, made
a fitte Habitacle for the Sonne of God : the moſt B.
Trinitie addreſſed vnto her a Legate from heauen,
the Archangel Gabriel, who accordingly ſaluted her
[Haile ful of grace, our Lord is with thee : bleſſed *Luc*. I.
art thou among women .] Ful indeede, euen ſo ful, *v*. 28.
of grace, as made her moſt worthie before al other
women , that euer were, or ſhal be , to be Goddes
Mother. For it is a general and infallible rule, that to
what purpoſe, office, or function ſoeuer God calleth
anie perſon, he withal geueth anſwerable grace to
performe the ſame, if the partie ſo called, hinder it
not. So ſaith S. Paul of him ſelf and other Apoſtles,
[God hath made vs meete Miniſters of the new Te- 2. *Co*. 3.
ſtament.] Euen ſo ſhe being choſen to the higheſt *v*. 6.
dignitie that can be in anie degree of Motherhood ,
was repleniſhed with correſpondent grace to the pur-

Wherby ſhe ſtil proceded in al vertues .

poſed effect. By vertue wherof, her vertues ſtil increaſed. No ſooner did ſhe vnderſtand, that ſhe was
choſen to be the Mother of God, but ſhe profeſſed
her ſelf his-meaneſt ſeruant [Behold (ſaith ſhe) the *Luc*. I.
handmaide of our Lord] and with moſt prompt o- *v*. 38.
bedience to Goddes wil, addeth [Be it done to me
according to thy word.] No ſoner doth ſhe heare
of her old Coſin Elizabeths eſtate, being ſixe monethes gone with child, but [with ſpeede riſing vp, *v*. 39.
ſhe went into the hil Countrie] from Nazareth in
Gallilie, into Iuda, to viſit and ſerue her aged Coſin, abiding with her the other three monethes, with
much and mutual congratulation of each to other,
for ſo vnſpeakable workes of God performed in them
both . Where alſo at the very firſt ſalutation of the
Bleſſed

B. Virgin imparted to S. Elizabeth [the child (S. Iohn) in his mothers wombe, did leape] for ioy.

v. 41.

44.

42.

[Elizabeth alſo repleniſhed with the Holie Ghoſt, cried out with a lowde voice] with the ſame wordes vttered before by the Angel [Bleſſed art thou among al women] adding therto the ground & cauſe of al bleſſednes [and bleſſed (ſaith ſhe) is the fructe of thy wombe] which is Ieſus Chriſt. Againe, expreſſing her hartie ioy [And bleſſed is ſhe that beleued : becauſe thoſe thinges be accompliſhed, that were ſpoken to her by our Lord. Where we alſo may obſerue, that our B. Ladies beleefe & conſent cooperated to the accompliſhing of our B. Sauiours Incarnation. In this moſt holie Viſitation alſo, the B. Virgin Mother, vttered the Diuine Canticle, MAGNIFICAT, conteyning no fewer Miſteries then wordes.

45.

She was alſo an eſpecial Propheteſſe.

46.

14 After her returning from her Coſin, diuers afflictions hapened to the ſame moſt B. Virgin, for exerciſe of her prudence, patience, humilitie, and al her vertues. Iuſt Ioſeph her deare Spouſe, now perceiuing her to be with child, not yet knowing the Miſterie, which God had wrought in her, is ſo troubled, that to auoide perplexitie in this caſe to him as yet doubtful, he reſolued to depart from her. But the God of al comfort is at hand [An Angel of our Lord appeared vnto him in ſleepe ſaying : Ioſeph ſonne of Dauid, feare not to take Marie thy wife, for that which is borne in her, is of the Holie Ghoſt.] Againe, ſhortly after this, they vndertake no ſmal iourney, from Galilee into Iuda, to be enrolled there in Bethlehem, according to the Emperours Edict, in the place of their proper Lineage [being of the houſe & famil e of Dauid.] There our B. Sauiour is borne in pouertie [wrapped in clothes, and laid in a manger] for want of a cradle, But Angels ſing praiſes,

Diuers tribulations happened vnto her for increaſe of merite, mixed with comforthes, and continual ſpiritual ioyes.

Mat. 1.

v. 19.

v. 20.

Luc. 2.

v. 4.

v. 7.

B b 3   Glorie

Glorie in the Highest to God, and in earth peace to *v* . 14 .
men of good wil .] Shepherdes visit the Infant, glo- *v* . 15 . 20 .
rifie and praise God . Ere long, there came also from
farre Countries [Sages (or Kinges) ledde by a starre] *Mat* . 2 .
the first fruictes of Gentiles, with their riche & Mis- *v* . 1 . 2 .
tical offeringes [of Gold, Mirh, and Frankencense.] *v* . 11 .
In the meane season (so were afflictions stil mixed
with ioyes) [the child was circumcised the eight day] *Luc* . 2 .
from his birth, sheeding his fiirst precious bloud for *v* . 21 .
our sakes [and was called I E S V S] that is to say, S A-
V I O V R . The fourtith day also from his birth , he
was by his parentes [Presented in the Temple] & *v* . 22 .
the most immaculate Virgin Mother, although ex- *Exo* . 13 .
empted from the bonde of the Law, because she con- *v* . 2 .
ceiued not by seede of man, yet for humilitie and e-
dification [offered, as the Law (of others) required, *Leuit* . 12 .
a paire of Turtles, or two yong pigeons] where she *v* . 2 . 8 .
was admonished by old holie Simeon, of future great *Luc* . 2 .
tribulations : wherof some presently ensued , being *v* . 24 .
forced to flee into Egipt . Neither at their returne
frõ thence, could they dwel in anie part of Iuda [fea- *v* . 34 . 35 .
ring Archelaus] the Sonne and successor of that He-
rod which killed al the male infantes of two yeares
old and vnder, in and neare to Bethlehem, and therfore retired againe to Nazareth . In the residue also
of her cohabitation with her B . Sonne, we may consider, that enterchanges of sorowes and gladnes ,
continually occurred, though one only is recorded ,
from their returne out of Egipt, til the thirtith yeare
of our Sauiour his age . That one was, when she &
Ioseph vnwitting, left the child [Iesus of the age of *Luc* . 2 .
twelue yeares in Ierusalem, and not finding him (as *v* . 43 .
they thought they should) amongst their kinsfolke,
and acquaintance ; with great greife returned seeking,
and the third day (with ioy) found him in the Tem- *v* . 46 .
By our B . La-   ple, sitting amongst the Doctors .] Al which, as-
dies example   wel

wel written as not written, fhe ftil kept in minde, we are admo-
[conceruing them in her hart] as the Euangelift twice nifhed, to me-
recordeth vpon occafions of the Angels and fhep- ditate holie
herdes, firft reioycing at her Sonnes Natiuitie, and of Myfteries.
this abfence and conference of the childe Iefus with
the faid Doctors in the Temple : which may fuffice
to admonifh vs by fo deuout example, to confider &
meditate thefe and the reft. For of the reft of her
moft pious life, after the coming of the Holie Ghoft
vpon her with the Apoftles; and others and of her
death, happie and glorious affumption, nothing is
written in holie Scriptures, but verie much in authentical Hiftories, to which we remitte you.

15   And fo with the zealous deuout woman defcri- Eor her nere-
bed in the Gofpel, we may fay, as fhe did with hart nes in nature
and voice [Bleffed is the wombe that bare this Sonne to our B. Sa-
of God, and bleffed are the breaftes that gaue him uiour, and for
fucke : yea, and moft bleffed is fhe aboue al other her manie
women] and men, and Angels, next after her Sonne, moft eminnet
becaufe fhe aboue al the other [heard his word, and graces, al
kept it.] She the Mother of grace, the Mother of faithful generations accout
mercie, the Mother of life, the Mother of Chrift Ie- the glorious
fus, God and Man, who [on the Croffe, commending virgin mother,
her to the prouident care of S. Iohn the Euangelift moft bleffed.
peculiarly beloued, commended him alfo reciprocally
to her, and in him, al the faithful to her potent interceffion. She whom [al generations (that is al true
feruants of God worthilie) cal bleffed : becaufe (faith
fhe) he that is Mightie, hath done great thinges to
me, & holie is his name.   Amen.

Luc. 2. *v.*19. 51.
Luc. 11. *v.*27. 28.
*Mat.*12. *v.*50.
Ioa. 19. *v.*26. 27.
Luc. 2. *v.*49.

Chrift our

*Chrift our Sauiour, after thirtie yeares priuate
ltfe (when S . Iohn Baptift had firft begūne)
preached his Gofpel : confirming it diuers wayes .*

ARTICLE. 22.

S . Iohn Bap-
tift indued
with manie fpi-
ritual graces,
prepared the
way to our Sa-
uiours mani-
feftation.

WE may not wel otherwife begin, to recite the actes and fufferinges of our B .
Sauiour, then by touching firft breifly
the principal thinges which his precurfor S · Iohn
Baptift, did and fuffered; who prepared the way to
his manifeftation, and fo procede by way of an Epitome, according to the larger narrations of the E-
uangeliftes. When therfore S . Iohn was conceiued, more by miracle, then by courfe of nature, of
a mother both [long barren, and become old ; he
was replenifhed with the Holie Ghoft (and fanctified) in his mothers wombe] as the Gofpel exprefs-
ly teftifieth . And it is moft probable, that the fame
was done, when the B . Virgin hauing conceiued,
and then bearing our B . Sauiour in her wombe, vifited and faluted Elizabeth her Cofin his mother .
For [then the fame childe (as is before faid) did leape
for ioy, in Elizabethes wombe ; and fhe alfo was replenifhed with the Holie Ghoft.] Whether this vfe
of reafon was accelerated, that he could then vnderftand Chrift to be prefent ; is not certaine to vs, nor
neceffarie to be difcuffed . For it fufficeth that his
foule was fanctified , whether it actually vnderftood
or no, as infantes are fanctified in baptifme, and receiue faith in habire, but not in act, til they come
to the vfe of reafon . In his yong age being a child,
both very vertuous and wife, as may be clearly vn-
ftoode, by the fequele of his life, related by the E-
uangelifts.

*Luc. 1. v.
7. 15.*

v .41. 44.

He liued from
his childhode
in the defert an
auftere life.

uangeliſtes, he retired into the deſert, there, as the ſacred Hiſtorie expreſly reporteth, he liued ſo auſterly, that he had his garment (not manie, but one garment) of Camels haire, and a girdle of a skinne about his loynes : and his meate was Locuſtes, and wilde honie.] He came [neither eating bread, nor drinking wine] ſo abſtineous, that the caueling calumniators, neither liking of his hard life, nor of our Sauiours familiar conuerſation, ſaid [the one had a diuel, and the other was a gurmander, a drinker of wine, & a frend of publicans & ſinners.]

Mat. 3.
v. 4.
Luc. 1.
v. 80.
Luc. 7.
v. 33.
34.

2 At the age of neare thirtie yeares, coming by direction of the Holie Ghoſt, from the inner deſert, to the deſert of Iurie, neare to Iordan [he preached the Baptiſme of Penance vnto remiſſion of ſinnes, to doe penance, and to yeald fruictes worthie of penance] and baptiſed in water ſaying [there cometh a ſtronger then I, after me, whoſe lachet of his ſhooes, I am not worthie, ſtouping downe, to looſe. I baptiſe you in water, but he ſhal baptiſe you with the Holie Ghoſt.] Yet would our Sauiour, amongſt others, receiue the baptiſme of Iohn, who otherwiſe thought it not meete. And by voice of God from heauen ſaying [this is my welbeloued Sonne, in whom I am wel pleaſed] S. Iohns teſtimonie was confirmed; geuen by him, aſwel to the Legates of the Iewes, ſent of purpoſe; as to the people, and alſo to his owne Diſciples : he ſtil auouching, that not he, but Ieſus, is the Meſſias. For [his diſciples hauing emulation for him] when manie reſorted to our Sauiour, they came to him and ſaid [Rabbi, he that was with thee beyond Iordane, to whom thou dideſt geue teſtmonie, behold he baptiſeth, and al come to him. S. Iohn anſweared and ſaid : A man can not receiue anie thing, vnleſſe it be geuen him from heauen. your ſelues doe beare me witnes that I ſaid, **I am not Chriſt,**

Mat. 3.
v. 1.
Mar. 1.
v. 4.
Luc. 3.
v. 3.
Mat. 3.
v. 8.

v. 14.
17.
Ioa. 1.
v. 27.
30. 36.

Ioan. 3.
v. 26.

v. 27.
28.

He afterwardes preached penance, baptized, and gaue teſtimonie, that by Chriſt, is remiſſion of ſinne, and ſaluation.

C c   **but that**

but that I am fent before him . He that hath the 29 .
Bride (to witte the Church) is the Bride-grome :
but the frend of the Bride-grome, that ftandeth and
heareth reioyceth with ioy, for the voice of the bride-
grome : this my ioy therfore is filled . He muft in - 30 .
creafe, and I muft diminifh .] Thus did S . Iohn moft
faithfully difcharge, the high office of precurfor, cómitted vnto him from heauen, in no wife arrogating
more to him felf, then trulie belonged vnto him . And *Mat.* 11 .

Our Sauiour alfo gaue tefti-monie, and great commé-dation of S . Iohn .

fo our B . Sauiour mutually gaue him teftimonie with *v . 7 .*
fingular commendations and praifes, that [he was indeede a Prophet, and more then a Prophet] a moft *v . 8 . 9 . 10 .*
conftant witneffe of the truth [not cloathed in foft
garmentes] like to courtiers ; for [there hath not 11 .
rifen among the borne of women (Chrift borne of a
Virgin, excelleth al) a greater then Iohn the Baptift]
As an Angel in puritie, and office of his miffion, in
fpirit Elias . He failed not to tel the Pharifees, and. *Mat . 3 .*
Saduces, that they were vipers broode . He fpared *v . 7 .*
not to rebuke Herod the Tetrarch of Galilee, for in - *Mat . 14 .*
ceftuous, adulterie: keeping the wife of his brother *v . 3 . Mar .*
Philippe, an other Tetrarch of Iturea , and Tracho- *6 . v . 14 .*

† An Epitome of Chrifts Acti-ons from his Baptifme to his paffion: the fpace of three yeares .

nitis . For which his iuft admonitió, Herode incen- 18 . 27 .
fed alfo by the harlot whom he kept , picking an oc-
cafió by the friuelous pretence of a facrilegious oath,
beheaded S . Iohn .
† 3   In the meane feafon, whiles S . Iohn did preach, *Mar . 1 .*
and baptife , our B , Sauiour immediatly after his *v . 12 . 13 .*
owne Baptifme, going into the defert, fafted there *Mat . 4 .*
fourtie faies, and fourtie nightes ; in the end wher - *v . 1 . 2 . 3 .*
of, fuffering the diuel to tempt him, ouercame the

Which being almoft al in the wordes of the facred text, we here omitte to in-clude thẽ in the forme of

tempter . Then calling, or rather admitting fome
Difciples, and him felf with them being inuited to a *Ioan . 2 .*
mariage in Cana of Galilee ; wrought his firft pu- *v . 2 . 8 . 9 .*
lique miracle, by turning water into wine . A figure,
and an example of tranfubftantiating bread into his
owne bodie, and of wine into his bloud . [At the

feaſt of Paſch, going to Ieruſalem, and finding in the
Temple ſome that ſold oxen, and ſheepe, & doues, &
the bankers ſitting, he droue them al out with a whip
& the money of the bankers he powred out, and o-
uerthrew their tables.] And ſome expoſtulating,
by what auctoritie he did theſe thinges] requiring a
ſigne or miracle, he not vouchſaifing to doe anie o-
ther miracle at that time, (the effect indeede declaring his power) he obſcurly inſinuated his death and
Reſurrection : which ſome not vnderſtanding, calumniated his ſpeach. Neuertheleſſe [manie beleued
in his name, ſeing the ſignes which he did. Then
came Nicodemus, a Phareſee and Prince of the Iewes
to him by night, whom he inſtructed of the neceſſitie of Baptiſme, and in other pointes of faith.
And as he taught, he alſo practiſed, baptizing manie
by the miniſterie of his Diſciples ; S. Iohn, as yet
baptizing in the ſame Countrie of Iurie, in Enon,
beſide Salm.

4   But when S. Iohn was caſt into priſon by Herod,
and the Phariſees vnderſtoode that our Sauiour made
manie Diſciples, or had manie folowers, he left Iurie
and went againe into Galilee. * In which iourney,
paſſing through the Countrie of Samaria, he made a
large and diuine ſpeach, to a Samaritane woman,
which came to draw water at Iacobs fountaine where
he ſate. Henceforth, leauing Nazereth, he made his
ſpecial aboade in Capharnaum, a ſea-towne of Galilee, bordering vpon the Tribes of Zabulon & Nep-
thali. There he firſt healed a Lordes ſonne of an a-
gue by his word, abſent, not going to him as the noble man requeſted. Wherupon he, and his whole
houſe beleued. So he preached publikly in Galilee,
and became famous. Then he called Diſciples to remaine with him, as of his retinew and familie, which
hitherto had not left their former trades, and ſtates

C c 2   of life

Side notes left column:
Ioan . 2.
v. 13.
14. 15.
18.

19.
23.
Io. 3. *v.*
1. 3. 5.
22. 26.

Ioan . 4.
v. 2.

* Ioan. 4.
v. 3.
v. 4. *ad*
43.
Mat. 4.
v. 13.
Io. 4. *v.*
46. I*ſa.*
9. *v.* 1.
Ioan . 4.
v. 50.
53.
Mat. 4.
v. 13.
Mat. 4.
v. 18.
Mar. 1.
v. 16.

Side notes right column:
Our Sauiour
being baptized
of S. Iohn wét
into the deſert,
faſted fourtie
daies, & ſuffe-
red him ſelf to
be tempted.
In preſence of
manie turned
water into
wine.

More publique
ly he corrected
diſorders in the
Temple.

Then he prea-
ched much.

Wrought ma-
nie miracles &
became fa-
mons.

His diſcourſe
with Samari-
tanes.

His habitation
in Capharna-
um, & Actes
in ether partes
of Galilee.

of life . The firſt was Simon (whom he had alreadie *Luc* . 5.
purpoſed to cal *Peter*, as afterwardes he did) and *v* . 10.
Andrew his brother ; Iames and Iohn alſo brethren ;
al foure fiſhers · When he called the other Apoſtles, *Mat* . 9.
excepting S . Mathew, whom he called frõ the banke *v* . 9.
of money or cuſtome houſe , is not recorded in holie
Scripture . Neither as yet did he make anie of them
Apoſtles, til about a yeare after : But procedeth in *Mar* . I.
worke and doctrine. In the Sinagogue at Capharna- *v* . 25.
um, he expelled a diuel out of a man ; and taught the *Luc* . 4.
people as hauing power (working in their hartes) *v* . 35.
not as the Scribes, only filling their eares with vaine
ſound of wordes. Going into Peters houſe, he cu- *Mat* . 8.
red his mother in law of a feuer , by touching her. *v* . 14. 15.
hand, ſo preſently, that ſhe aroſe and miniſtred vnto him . In like maner he caſt out diuels, and cured
al diſeaſes, euen of al that came, or were commended vnto him . He refuſed two that offered to folow *Mat* . 8.
him ; and aduiſed an other to ſtay with him, that of- *v* . 19. 22
fered to goe burie his father, for reaſons to him ſelf *Ioan* . 2.
olny knowne : for he knew what was in euerie man. *v* . 25.
On the ſea he appeaſed a great tempeſt by his only *Mat* . 8.
word, commanding the windes and the ſea, and they *v* . 26. 28
obeyed him . He expelled moe diuels out of two men, *&c* .
in the Countrie of Geraſens, and permitting them to
enter into ſwine, the whole heard ranne with violẽce
headlong into the ſea, and ſo were drowned ; that
al might know the malice of diuels againſt men , if
Chriſts power they were permitted : And withal ſee Chriſtes domi-
ouer mens nion ouer al wicked ſpirits and power ouer mennes
temporal temporal poſſeſſions, for their ſpiritual good , though *v* . 34.
goods, for theſe worldly Geraſens did not make that fruict of
their ſpiritual it ; but contrariwiſe came and beſought our Sauiour
good. Chriſt, that he would paſſe from their quarters.

5 Taking therfore a boate and returning to Capharnaum, whiles he preached in a houſe, there came *Mat* . 9.
ſo manie *v* . 1.

Mar. 2. so manie together to heare the word, that there was
v. 1. no place, no not to enter in at the dore, and foure
men crying one ficke of the palfie in his bed, when
they could not enter by the dore for the multitude,
they vncouering the roofe did let downe the couche
wherin the fick man lay. And our Lord Iefus feing
their faith, faid to the fick of the palfey; Haue a good
hart fonne, thy finnes are forgeuen thee. Which whē
certaine Scribes and Pharifees there prefent heard,
they thought in their hartes, that he fpake blafphemie. But he feing their fecret thoughtes, detected
them faying: wherfore think you euil in your hartes?
And to make them know, that the Sonne of man
hath power in earth to forgeue finnes; he faid to the
fick man : arife, take vp thy bedde, and goe into thy
houfe. And forthwith ryfing before them, he tooke
vp his bedde and went into his houfe, magnifying

Chrift decla-
red his power
to remitte fin-
nes by a vifible
miracle.

Mat. 9. God. And al the multitude feing it, glorified God,
v. 8. that gaue fuch power to men. After this, he inftruc-
Mat. 9. ted S. Iohnes Difciples concerning fafting, which
v. 14. they and the Pharifees practifed, more then his Dif-
15. ciples, yelding them a reafon, why his Difciples as
Mar. 2. yet fafted not, but fhould doe afterwardes. He alfo
v. 18. raifed the Archifinagogues daughter from death, cu-
Luc. 5. red a woman of a bloudie fluxe; healed two blinde
v. 33. men; and difpoffeffed an other of a diuel which had
Mat. 9. made him blind, and dūme, and fo was reftored both
v. 23. to fight and fpeach. Al which, the Euangelifts relate
Mat. 9. of his actions, the firft yeare of his preaching, adding
v. 35. in general, that he went about al the Cities & townes,
teaching in their Synagogues, preaching the Gofpel
of the Kingdome of Heauen, and curing euerie dif-
eafe, & euerie infirmitie,

Though manie
of our Souiours
miracles be re-
corded, yet
not al in par-
ticular.

Chrifts Actes
in the fecond
yeare.

Ioan. 5. 6 At the Feaft of Pafch, in the beginning of the fe-
v. 8. cond yeare, coming to Ierufalem, he healed a man
by his only word, that had bene thirtie eight yeares

fick

Vertue of miracles is sometimes geuen to creatures, especially to such as belong to sacred vses. The Scribes & Pharisees were very supersticious in keping the Sabbath day, which is now abrogated by Christ.

sick, and was come to the pond of Probatica, to g... health, but others stil preuenting him, could not enter first into the water, after the motion therof by an Angel. Wherupó the Iewes picking a quarel, because it was the Sabbath day, persecuted our Sauiour, & the more, because in iustifying his fact, he insinuateth, that God is his Father. He also confuted the Pharisees, which blamed his Disciples, for brusing the eares of the corne on the Sabbath day, and told them plainly, that the Sonne of man, to witte him self, is Lord of the Sabbath also : foreshewing (which by his Resurrection is effected) that the Sabbath day should ceafe to be the holie day. And as for such necessarie workes, to draw a sheepe or other cattel out of a ditch ; much more to cure a man in bodie or soule, is good and lawful anie day. And on another Sabbath day, preaching in the Synagogue, where was a man with a withered hand, looking round about vpon them with anger, being sorowful for the blindnes of their hart, he said to the man that had the withered hand, arise and stand forth into the middest : Stretch forth thy hand. And he stretched his hande forth and it was restored to health, euen as the other. Wherupon the Pharisees replenished with madnes, commoned one with another, what they might doe to Iesus : And going forth, made consultation against him, not only amongst them selues but also with the Herodians, how they might destroy him.

7   But our Lord Iesus ascending into a mountaine, passed the whole night in praier, and when the day was come, he called his Disciples, and chose & made

Our Sauiour out of al his disciples made twelue Apostles.

twelue of them Apostles. Their names be these : The first Simon (to whom, saith S. Mark, he gaue the name Peter) and Andrew his brother : Iames of Zebedee, and Iohn his brother : Philippe, and Bartholomew : Thomas, and Mathew : Iames of Alpheus &

Io.5.v. 17.18. Mat.12. v.3.

8.

11.

Mar.3. v.5.Luc.6. v.8.10. Mat.12. v.12.

Mat.12. v.14.Mar. 3.v.6. Luc.6.v. 12.13. Mat.10. v.5.Mar. 6.v.7. Luc.9. v.1.

us, and Thaddeus : Simon Chananeus, and Iudas Iſcariot, who betraied him. Theſe twelue our Sauiour ſent to rhe Iewes only (the time being not yet come to cal the Gentiles) to preach, that the Kingdome of Heauen is at hand. Alſo to cure the ſick, raiſe the dead, clenſe the Leepers, and to caſt out diuels, al free-coſt, ſaying to them, gratis you haue receiued, gratis geue ye.

8 In the ſame mountaine before that his Apoſtles went with their great commiſſion, he made that diuine Sermon, called the Sermon of our Lord in the mount, conteining the perfect paterne of a Chiſtians life, as wel of the Clergie as Laitie, ſhewing that the Scribes and Phariſees iuſtice (which was then coũted moſt perfect) was vnſufficient : namely touching the precepts againſt Murder, Adulterie, Auarice, Swearing, Reuenging, Vſurie, & Hatred, of Enemies. Teaching likewiſe that the Phariſaical pretended iuſtice was alſo vnſufficient in other workes of iuſtice concerning Almes, Prayer, Faſting, and care of temporal neceſſaries : warning to beware of raſhly iudgeing other mens intentions, and ſmale imperfections. Neuertheles to take notorious wicked perſons (whom he called dogges, and ſwine) for ſuch as they plainly appeare.

9 Finally he exorteth to frequent & feruent prayer, for Gods grace; to doe to al as we would they ſhould doe to vs : laboring to enter in by the narrow gate, and ſtraite way that leadeth to life. Becauſe only hearing and ſaying wel, without doing the wil of God, ſufficeth not to ſaluation. which Sermon S. Mathew compriſeth in the fifth ſixth and ſeuenth chapters of his Goſpel. S. Marke & S. Luke touch ſome pointes of it more breifly. After theſe ſo ful inſtructions the Apoſtles proceeded in there miſſion.

10 Our Lord ſo proſecuting his workes, & multitudes

Mat. 5.
v.1.2.
&c.
Luc. 6.
v.20.
21.
Mar. 4.
v.21.24.
Mat. 6.
v.1.2.
&c.
Mat. 7.
v.1. 2.
&c.

v.7.8.
&c.

Our Lords Sermon in the mount conteyneth a perfect forme of good life.

Not only faith but alſo other good workes not in outward ſhew, but ſincere from the hart, are neceſſarie to ſaluation.

Chriſts moſt excellent

titudes fo reforted vnto him, that they could not haue leafure to eate, infomuch that fome of his kinf-folke thought he was become madde. But the Scribes more malicioufly faid: that in Beelzebub prince of diuels, he caft out diuels. In particular fo foone as he was defcended from the monntaine he clenfed a Leper that profeffed belefe in his onlie word, and touch, faying: Be thou cleane; and he was cleane. With like expedition, yea abfent from the ficke par-tie, he healed a centurions feruant of the palfie: And raifed a widowes fonne of Naim, only faying, yong man, I fay to thee, arife. And he that was dead, fate vp and began to fpeake; and he gaue him to his mother. S. Iohn in prifon, feing his Difciples not yet fatisfied, that our Lord Iefus is Chrift, fent two of them vnto him; and they fee, and heare, that he made the blind to fee, the lame to walke, the le-pers cleane, the deafe to heare, the dead rife againe. And when they were departed, our Sauiour highly praifed S. Iohn as is before related. Then a Pharifee inuiting Chrift to dinner, the renowmed penitent Marie Magdalene, watered his feete with teares, wi-ped them with the haires of her head, kiffed them of-ten, and annointed them with ointment. which the Pharifee difliking, defpifed her. But our Sauiour preferred her much before him: And inuited al to true repentance, with promife to remitte their finnes faying: Come ye to me al that labour and are bur-dened, and I wil refrefh you. take vp my yoke vpó you, and learne of me, becaufe I am meeke and hú-ble of hart, and you fhil find reft to your foules: For my yoke is fweete, and my burden light. Nei-ther did he only releue their foules, but alfo their bo-dies from ficknes and vexations of diuels, as hath bene faid, and yet more folow. For euen in the prefence of calum

Sidenotes (left):
zeale was cou-ted madnes by worldlie men.

The renow-med penitence ofS. Marie Magdalene.

Sidenotes (right):
Mar. 3.
v. 20. 21.

Mat. 8.
v. 3.
Mar. 1.
Luc. 5.
Mat. 8. *v.*
13. *Luc.* 7.
v. 14. 15.
&c.

Mat. 11.
v. 2. 4. 5.

v. 7. *&c.*

Parag. 2.

Luc. 7.
v. 36. *&c.*

Mat. 11.
v. 28. 29.

Mat. 12.
v. 28.

of calumniators, he caft out a diuel which made a man

Luc. 8. blind and dumme, that he forthwith fpake, & faw.

v. 2. And taught exprefly, that the hearing and keping of
Goddes word, farre excelled kinred of mother, brothers, and fifters; and that thofe kindsfolke were

Pf. 77. more bleffed for doing the fame, then for their ner-

v. 2. *If.* nes to him in bloud. † But in regard of manie vnto -

6. *v.* 9. ward and reprobate hearers, he fpake manie thinges

Mat. 13. in parables, as the Prophets had foretold, comparing

v. 4. 24. the Kingdome of heauen, that is the militant Church

31. and the meanes of ateyning erernal faluation, vn-

33. to vifible knowne thinges. So he propofed a parable
of one that fowed feede, which fel on fundrie fortes
of ground; of one that fowed good feede, and of his

44. enemie fowing cocle vpon it : others, of muftarde

47. feede, of leauen, of threafure hid in the feild, of the

Mat. 13. precious ftone, and of the nette. Returning to Na-

v. 54. zareth, he preached in the Sinagogue, and did fome

55. miracles; but few beleuing, not efteming him, as
knowing his parents and priuate education; there he
blamed their incredulitie, and parted from thence.
Hearing then that Herode had beheaded S. Iohn,
to geue example of conuenient mourning for the departed, and to fhew horror of fo execrable murther,
he retired by boate with his Apoftles, into a defert,

Mat. 14. place of Tiberias.

v. 16. 11 Whither notwithftanding great multitudes fo-

Mar. 6. lowed him on foote out of the Cities, who, befides

v. 37. fpiritual foode, he fed alfo corporally; fiue thoufand

Luc. 9. men, befides women and children, with only fiue bar-

v. 13. lie loaues, and two fifhes; who hauing eaten fo much

Io. 6. *v.* as they would, the twelue Apoftles filled twelue ba-

5. 6. *&c.* fkets of the fragments that remained. The night fo-

Mat. 14. lowing, he fpent in praier in the mountaine, whileft

v. 29. his Difciples were toffed on the fea, fayling with a
contrarie winde til the fourth watch of the night.

Our B. Ladie
more happie
for hearing &
keping Gods
word, then for
nerenes in
bloud to Chrift
our Lord.

† The Church
is compared to
diuers thinges.

S. Iohn Bap-
tifts martyrdō
in the fecond
yeare of our
Sauiours
preaching.

Aftes of the
third yeare.
Our Sauiour
fedde fiue
thoufand men,
with fiue
loaues.

He walked on the water: and gaue S. Peter power to walke on the water.

For then he came to them walking on the water, & gaue Peter also power, to walk vpon the waters. Much people againe flocking to him at Capharna-um, some required of him a further signe, alleaging that their fathers did eate *Manna*, in the desert (a bread from heaueñ.) Wherupon our Sauiour said to them : Moyses gaue you not the bread from hea-uen, but my Father geueth you the true bread from heauen. And auouched to them that he would geue, (not the figuratiue, but) the true bread, his owne flesh to eat, which farre excelleth Manna. And the more they replied, and murmured, the more he affirmed, and confirmed his speach saying : My flesh is meate indeede, and my bloud is drinke indeede. With the like assertions in plaine termes, without parable; which discourse hapened about Pasch, in the beginning of the third yeare of his preaching.

Io. 6. v. 30.

32.

51

55.

Manna being a figure of the B. Sacrament, Christ promi-sed to geue the thing presigu-red farre more excellent then Manna.

Christ repro-ued friuolous traditions which were contrarie to the Law.

12 Then came to him from Ierusalem, Scribes and Pharisees, saying : Why doe thy Disciples trans-gresse the traditions of the Ancientes ? For they doe not wash their handes when they eate braed. To which cauil our Sauiour answeared; not by reiec-ting lawful Traditiõs, but by shewing this which they alleaged, to be a friuolous tradition ; and withal con-uinced them of transgressing Goddes commande-ment for their owne tradition, and temporal lucre.

Mat. 15. v. 1. 2. 3.

Did manie mi-racles, & con-tinued his di-uine doctrine.

Which manifest difference, betwene Authentical, & Pharisaical Traditions, is declared before. Art. 3. Breifly we here recite his actions only, and so re-mitte you to the sacred text. In this third yeare he healed the daughter of the Cananite, womã most ear-nestly crauing the same. Cured a man deafe & dũme, vsing ceremonial Rites of *spitle*, putting his fingers into the mannes eares, touching his tongue, loking vp vnto heauen, groning, and saying *Epheta*. Fedde foure thousand men, besides manie cures in the de-sert

Mat. 15. v. 21. 28.

Mar. 7. v. 32. 33.

Mat. 15. v. 29. 30. 32. &c.

sert mountaine neare to the sea of Galilee, with seauen loues, and a few litle fishes, after three daies a-
boade there, al other victuales being spent; & there

Mat . 16. remained seauen baskets ful of fragmentes. Denied
v. 4. to geue anie other signe to the temptimg Pharisees,
and Saduces, but the signe of Ionas the Prophet,
who was three daies and nightes in the whales be-

6 .12. lie. But willed his Disciples, to beware of their lea-
Mar. 8. uen, that is their corrupt doctrine. Healed an other
v. 23. blind man in Bethsaida, by spittle, and imposition of
25. handes, and that by degrees, making him first to see
Mat . 16. a litle, and then perfectly. Demanding of his A-
v. 13. postles first, what other men said of the Sonne of Man,
15. 16. him self; then what they his Apostles said of him;
&c. and Simon Peter answearing: thou art Christ, the
Sonne of the liuing God; he said: Blessed art thou
Simon Bariona. And I say to thee, thou art Peter,

Mat . 16. and vpon this Rock, I wil build my Church. He
v. 21. told them also that he should be slaine in Ierusalem,
24. 25. and rise againe the third day: and admonished them
Mat . 17. that al must be readie, in preparation of mind, and
v. 2. resignation of them selues to suffer, and to dye if
Mar. 9. neede shal require for him, then, for theirs, & al o-
v. 24. thers encoragement, to suffer with patience, in hope
Luc. 9. of glorious reward. He was transfigured in mount
v. 28. Thabor, called by S. Peter, the holie mount; but
2 .*Pet .* 1. would not haue it knowne til after his death & Re-
v. 18. surrection. In the meane time, he prosecuted his ac-
Mat . 17. customed workes, cast out a diuel which his Disciples
v. 21. could not doe, for which were required Praier and
27. Fasting. Paied Tribute for him self, and for Peter
Mat . 18. though they were free. Taught Humilitie against
v. 1. 6. ambition: Threatned the scandalizers of litle ones,
10. admonishing that their Angels guard them. That
21. 34. it is necessarie to forgeue each other from the hatt.

13   At the Feast of Scenopegia, or Tabernacles (in

the

He declared S.
Peter to be a
Rocke, pro-
mising theron
to build his
Church.

The time of
his passion

the seuenth Moneth) he leauing Galilee, went into *Io . 7 . v . 2.*
Iewrie toward his Passion. In this Iourney, the Sa- 10 .
maritanes, not affording him lodging, yet he taught *Luc . 9 . v.*
mildnes to be vsed towardes them. In the way, he 53 .
healed tenne lepers, of which, one only shewed him *Luc · 17 .*
self gratful, and the same was a Samaritane. Coming *v . 11 . 15.*
to Ierusalem, he taught openly in the Temple : And *Ioan .7.*
great dispute arose amongst the people, some defen- *v . 14.*
ding, others impugning him . He absolued a wo- *Ioan . 8. v.*
man taken in adulterie, not fauoring sinne, but ioy- *4 . 11 .*
ning mercie with iustice. After much diuine doctrine, *31 . 40.*
some endeuoring to kil him, he hid him self, & went *59 .*
out of the Temple . Presently after he gaue sight to *Ioa . 9 . v.*
a man that was borne blind, by annointing his eyes *1 . 6 . 7.*
with clay and spitle, and by the mannes washing in *40 . 41.*
Siloe : and charged the Pharisees with wilful blind- *Ioa . 10. v.*
nes . Continuing his speach to them, taught the *1 . 2 . &c.*
true office of good Pastors, and dutie of good sheepe.
Then he sent also seauentie two Disciples, to preach
saying : the haruest trulie is much, but the workmen *Luc . 10.*
few. And they returned with ioy, shewing that the *v . 1 . 17.*
diuels were subiect vnto them in his name . By a pa- *Luc . 10.*
rable of a wounded man releued by a Samaritane, *v . 30.*
he taught that al men are neighboures, and to be 38 .
holpen in their necessities. Martha enterteyning him, 42 .
he preferred Maries contemplatiue life, before her ac-
tiue : And taught the force of praier : Reprehended *Luc . 11.*
the preposterous cleanes of the Pharisees, denoun- *v . 1 . 2 . 38*
cing woe to them, & to the Scribes, for manie faultes . *Luc . 12. v.*
He taught his Disciples, not to feare the killers of the *4 · 15 · 35 ·*
bodie : To cast away care of riches : And watche as 36 .
faithful seruantes, the coming of our Maister. By *Luc . 13.*
occasion of Pilates crueltie, killing certeine in Gali- *v . 1 . 4.*
lee, and of the fal of the Towre of Siloe : he admo- *5 . 6 . 7.*
nished al to haue repentance, lest they also perished
sudenly : Declared Goddes patience by the Parable

of a

of a fructles figge tree, suffered to stand one yeare

v.10.11. more. Healed a woman that had bene crooked eigh-
12. 14.15. tene yeares, iustifying the doing therof on the Sab-
32. bath against a calumniator, & cōtemned the threates
Luc.14.*v*. that Herode would kil him. Againe on the Sabbath
2. 26. day, he healed one sicke of the dropsie. And againe
taught al the faithful, to renounce al they had euen
Io. 10. *v*. their life, to folow him. In the feast of Dedication,
22. some attempting againe to apprehend him, he went
Luc.15.*v*. forth of the Temple, and passed ouer Iordan. Against
3. 8. 11. the Scribes and Pharisees, he iustified the admission
of publicans and sinners, by the parables of a lost
sheepe, the lost groate, and of the prodigal sonne.
Luc. 16 *v*. Aduised to doe almes and good deedes, for gayning
1. euerlasting life, hy the parable of a prudent, though
Mat.19.*v*. vniust balife. To the tempting Pharisees, seeking to
3.*Mar*.10. draw somthing from his Doctrine against Moyses,
v. 2. *Luc*. he answeared, that Mariage is indissoluble. And
16. *v*. 18. thereupon commended single life, for the better
Mat.19.*v*. atteyning of heauen. Against vnmerciful rich men,
10.12. he proposed an example, of a rich glutton, and poore
Luc. 16. Lazarus. Foretelling that scandals wilbe, pronoun-
v. 19. *Luc*. ced woe to the scandalizers. Shewed the force of
17.*v*.1.2. Faith, euen to remoue trees with a word, and moun-
Luc.17.*v*. taines if neede be. Taught humilitie by example of
6.*Mar*.17. a publicane, and a Pharisee, praying with diuers di-
v. 29. spositions of mindes and opinions of them selues.
Luc.18.*v*. He receiued and blessed litle children. And exhor-
10. *Mat*. ted a rich yong man, to forsake al, and become per-
19. *v*. 14. fect. By a parable of a housholder, hyring work-
Mat. 20. men into his vine-yerd, he shewed, that God neuer
v.1.7. 8. ceaseth, from the beginning of the world, vnto the
end therof, to cal men into his Church, to worke
there, and to haue eternal life for their wages.

Ioa. 11. *v*. 14 In Bethania (not ful two miles from Ierusalem)
1. 39. 44. he raised Lazarus from death, when he had bene
47. 51.

Proposed E-
uangelical
counsels with
out precept.

The raising of
Lazarus from

D d 3 four

death, with al
other actions
and doctrine,
so vexed the
malignant that
they ceased n t
til they had
procured our
Sauiours death
vpon the
Crosse.

four daies buried. Wherupon the cheif Preistes &
Pharisees gathered a Councel against him : and Caiphas being high Preist, prophecied, that Iesus should
die for the Nation. Our Sauiour also him self more *Mat.* 20.
plainly foretold to his Apostles, that he should very v. 18. 19.
shortly be deliuered to the cheif Preistes, & Scribes,
and by them to the Gentiles, and be mocked, scourged, and crucified. And the third day should rise a- *Luc.* 18.
gaine. After this, going to Iericho, he healed a v. 42.
blind man, before he entered into the towne. In the
towne he lodged with Zacheus a publicane : and a- *Luc.* 19.
gainst murmurers, iustified his fact. Going out of v. 1. 10.
the towne, healed other two blind men. Being returned to Bethania, and sitting at supper in the houie *Mat.* 20.
of Simon the Leper : Marie Magdalene powred v. 29.
a boxe ful of precious ointment vpon our Sauiours *Mat.* 26.
head, wherat some murmured, counting it wast: pre- v. 6. 7. 12.
tending that it might hane bene sold, and geuen to
the poore; but our Lord commended her act, as a *Mar.* 14.
good work, and done in good season, annointing v. 3. 8.
his bodie, for his future burial, the which he knew
to be neare at hand.

Christ entred
into Ierusalem
with great so-
lemnitie, a
litle before his
death.

15   In the meane time, he conuersed as publikly *Mat.* 21.
as before, yea with more solemnitie then hitherto, v. 7. 8. 9.
he came ryding on an Asse into Ierusalem, his Dis- *Mar.* 11.
ciples spreading their garmentes, and the people v. 1. 7. 10.
with Palmes in their handes, going forth to mete *Luc.* 19.
him; strowing bowes in the way saying : Osanna, v. 35.
Blessed is he that cometh in the name of our Lord. *Io.* 12.
Blessed is the Kingome of our father Dauid, Osan- v. 13.
na in the highest, the King of Israel. When he was
Gloriously entred, the whole Citie was moued.

He not only
continued his
doctrine, but
also practised
his power in
correcting a-
buses.

And coming into the Temple, he cast out al that *Mat.* 21.
bought and sold in the Temple, and ouerthrew the v. 12.
tables of the bankers, and chaires of them that sold *Luc.* 19.
pigeons, as he had three yeares before corrected the v. 45.
                                                     same

same abufe. He alfo healed al the blind and lame. Gentiles fought alfo to fee him. He curfing a figge tree, it prefenthe withered. To his enemies he auouched, his power to be of God. Forefhewed by parables, their reprobation, and vocation of the Gentiles. As of the hufbandman that killed both the feruants, and the fonne of the Landlord. Of the king that inuited gheftes, to the mariage feaft of his fonne. He defeated their malice, anfwearing the queftion of paying tribute to Cæfar. Stopped alfo their mouthes, by anfwearing the Sadduces queftion, concerning the Refurrection. And the Pharifees, touching the greateft Commandement. And by demanding of them, how Chrift is both the fonne, and the Lord of Dauid? He taught his Difciples and the multitudes, to doe as they teach which fitte in Moyfes chaire, but not as they doe. He preferred a poore widowes offering of two mites, before the offering of the rich. He foretold to fome of his Difciples, the deftruction of the Temple, and of Ierufalem. And by that occafion, of the coming of Antichrift in the end of the world; and of his deftruction, and confummation of the world. And by parables of tenne virgins, & of talentes deliuered to feruantes, fhewed how it fhal be with the faithful at the day of Iudgement; but without parables, that they which doe not good workes, fhal be damned. Iudas bargained with the high Preiftes, to betray our B. Sauiour.

Mat. 21.
v.20. Luc.
20. v.2.3.
9.18.19.
Mat. 21.
v.23.33.

Mat. 22.
v.21.30.
41.
Mat. 23.
v.3.

Mar. 12.
v.42.

Mat 24. v.
4. &c.

Mat. 25.
v.3.14.
31.

16　And our Sauiour eating the Pafchal Lambe with his twelue Apoftles, wafhed their feete, inftituted the B. Sacrifice, and Sacrament, of his Bodie and Bloud in formes of bread & wine; made them Preiftes to confecrate and offer the fame. Iudas went forth; and our B. Sauiour, made a long Sermon to the reft. and his Praier to God for them, and for al the electe.

Mat. 26.
v.14.
Mat. 26.
Mar. 14.
Luc. 22.
1. Cor. 11.
Ioa. 14.15.
16.17.

Our Lord inftituted his euerlafting teftament in the Sacrifice & Sacrament of his owne bodie & bloud: concluding with exhortation & prayer.

Chrift

Chriſt our Lord ſuffered moſt greuons tormentes :
Death on the Croſſe : and was buried .

ARTICLE . 23 .

That God
would be
made man, &
dye on the
Croſſe for
man, was to
the Iewes a
ſcandal : and
ſemeth to the
Gentils foo-
liſhnes .

AL Chriſtians know, that Chriſt our Sauiour,
beſides his manifold laboures, ſuffered great
perſecutions ; & finally death on the Croſſe .
But manie either doe not know , or doe not dulie
conſider, the cauſe why God would not only be made
man , but alſo dye on a Croſſe for man : which miſterie, is ſo ſtrange to mannes conceipte, that [to
the Iewes (expecting a Redemer worldlie potent)
it was a ſcandal : to the Gentiles (ſeking humane
wiſdome) it ſemed fooliſhnes .] Neuertheles [God
haith choſen the fooliſh thinges of the world, to cō-
found the (worldlie) wiſe : and the weake thinges
of the world hath God choſen, that he may confound
the ſtrong] For this is the true wiſdome, and mightie power of God, as S . Paul teacheth [Becauſe
(ſaith he) in the wiſdome of God , the world did
not by wiſdome (by conſideratiō of Goddes workes)
know God : it pleaſed God by the fooliſhnes (as it
ſemeth to worldlie men) of preaching Chriſt crucified, to ſaue them that beleue in him] Becauſe the
world would not, by conſideration of Goddes ſo
admirable workes (as the heauens, the earth, Angels,
Men, Planets, Starres, Elements, and al other creatures) know and rightly ſerue the Creator : it pleaſed the ſame Creator of al [to exananite him ſelf]
to become man, yea, a very poore man; to vndertake great trauailes, to ſuffer moſt ſpitful reproa-
ches, and moſt cruel tormentes, to be nailed vpon a
Croſſe , and ſo to dye : therby to ſaue al mankind,
if them ſelues wil, that is, effectuallly to ſaue al them
that

1. Cor . 1
v. 23 .

27.

21.

that beleue in such a one, and withal dulie serue him
Mat. 16. [by taking vp each one their owne Crosse and fo-
v. 24. lowing him.]

2   Seing therfore this is the only meanes ordeyned
for mánes Redemption & saluation, then the which,
no other point of faith, can seme more strange ; our
Lord God hath neuer ceased, since the fal of man, to
make this misterie knowne, by signes, preachinges,
examples, and in the appointed time, by real performance therof in his humane nature, to the ful accomplishing of al that was thus decreed to be done, and
suffered by Christ our Redemer. To this purpose,
God gaue notice to Adam and to Eue, with grace of
repentance for their transgression, that they, and al
mákind, not herein excepting that seede which should
bruse the serpentes head ; must both dye, and also suffer, other penalties of mortal flesh, exemplifying in
Gen. 3. these, that [Adam with much toyling, should la-
v. 16. bour the earth, and in the sweat of his face, should
17. 18. eat bread, til he returned againe to earth : and that
Eues trauailes should be multiplyed in children bearing] and the like. A more proper example of our
Sauiours death, was in iust Abel, the very first that
died of mankind. For as he being innocent, and his
Gen. 4. workes good, was slaine by his natural brother Cain,
v. 4. 8. not for anie other reason, but because [Cain his
1. *Io.* 3. workes were wicked, and his brothers iust] so the
v. 12. iust one Christ, God and man, was persecuted to
death, by the Iewes his brethren in flesh [because
his life and doctrine, was contrarie to their workes.]
An other figure of our Sauiours death was shewed in
Sap. 2. [Isaac, the beloued sone of Abraham] together with
v. 12. [the ramme that was sacrificed in his place.] For so
Gen. 22. Christ our Redemer offered him self in Sacrifice, dy-
v. 2. 10. ing on the Crosse, not in his diuinitie, being im-
13. passible ; represented by Isaac remaining aliue, but

Side notes:
God did mani wayes fore-shew this Mysterie.

It was prefigu-red by Adams and Eues pe-nalties and death.

By the death of Abel.

By Isaac & the Ramme.

E e   in his

in his Humanitie, fignified by the ramme, that was
flaine in the Sacrifice . Iofeph the fóne of Iacob, befides other refpectes, in that he was for his innocent
life hated, fold for money, & betraied by his brethré,
prefigured our B .Sauiour, hated by the Iewes, betraied and fold by Iudas, for thirtie filuer peeces . The
which is more plainly prophecied hy Zacharie, who
foretelleth of Chrift, fpeaking thus [They weygh-
ed my hyre(or price) thirtie peeces of filuer : caft
it forth to the ftatuarie ; a goodlie price that I was
priced at by them .] The Pafchal Lambe, very particularly, and al bloudie Sacrifices generally, were
figures of the Lambe of God, facrificed vpon the
Altar of the Croffe, though alfo in manie refpectes,
they did withal fignifie the felfe fame Sacrifice offered daily in vnbloudy maner, in the Catholique Chuch
of Chrift . Holie Iob, in his great afflictions (a paterne of patience) was fo expreffe a fignre of our Sauiours fufferinges, that not only al the worldlie and
bodilie calamities, which fel vpon him, were more
eminent in Chrift, but alfo fome thinges were affirmed of Iob, which are only verified in our Lord . As
his fpeach, that if [his finnes and calamities were
wayed in a balance, according to the number of the
fand of the fea ; his calamitie would appeare heauier]
which can not be otherwife expounded but by vnderftanding it of Chrift, who had no finne at al . And
fo betwene much, and nothing, is an infinite comparifon . Wheras Iob alfo faith, that [his aduerfaries were not affraied to fpitte in his face] he doth
not fay that they fo did to him, but the Euangeliftes
write, that the rabble of cruel tormenters, did fpite-
fully fpitte, in our B . Sauiours face . [Iob was ftriken by Sathan, with a verie fore boile, from the fole
of the foote, euen to the toppe of his head .] Our
Lord and Sauiour, was tyed to a piller, and beaten
with

By Iofeph .

By the Pafcal
Lambe and o-
ther facrifices .

By Iobs fuffe-
ring .

Gen . 37 .
v . 4. 27 .
28 .

Zach . 11 .
v . 12 . 13 .

Exo . 12 .
v . 3 . 6. 18 .

Exo . 24.
v . 8.

Leuit . 1 .
v . 3 .
Nu . 19 .

Iob . 6.
v . 2. 3 .

Iob . 30.
v . 10 .
Mat . 26.
v . 67.
Iob . 2 .
v . 7.
Mat . 27. *v* .
30. 39. 40.

with whippes, from the feete, to the head, crowned
with thornes, & his handes and feete striken through
with nailes, were made fast to the Crosse; and then
was also reproached by the Synagogue of the wicked,
much more then Iob was by his wife. Strong Sam- By Samson.
son, was an other figure of our Sauiour, especially
in his death, making greater slaughter of his enemies,
therby, then by his life.

Iob.2.
v.9.
Iudic.16.
v.30.

3   Moreouer al the Prophets, were not only, by It was often
their great and manie tribulations, some also by their foretold by the
deathes, figures of our Sauiours afflictions & death Prophets.
but also prophecied expresly, that he should both
suffer manie tormentes and despites, and finally dye
for mannes Redemption. The Royal Prophet Dauid in sundrie persecutions, resembled greater which
happened to Christ our Sauiour. As when fleeing frō
Absalon, he cryed to God [why are they multiplied
that trouble me? manie rise vp against me. O Lord
my God, I haue hoped in thee : saue me from al that
persecute me] and often the like in other distresses.
He prophecieth also of Christes Passion, expressiing
diuers particular partes, euen as the Euangelists haue
written them, since they were accomplished. As be
those wordes of his [God my God haue respect to
me, why hast thou forsaken me ?] signifying, that
by the wil and power of God, the glorie of Christes
soule should not redound to his release of paines on
the Crosse, but that he should suffer as if his soul had
not bene glorious, or not vnited to his Diuinitie,
yea more then anie other seruantes of God. Wher-
vpon he saith [In thee our fathers haue hoped : they
hoped, and thou didest deliuer them ; they cried to
thee, and were saued (were temporalie deliuered or
redemed) they hoped in thee, and were not confounded] (not denied particular consolation) [But I am
a worme and no man, a reproach of men, and an out-

Psf.3.
v.2.Psf.
7.v.2.

Psf.21.
v.1.
Mat.27.
v.46.
Mar.15.
v.34.

Psf.21.
v.5.6.

v.7.

E e 2   cast

caſt of the people. Al that ſee me, haue ſcorned me, *v.* 8. 9. *et*
they haue ſpoken with the lippes, and wagged the *Sap.* 2.
head ſaying [He hoped in the Lord, let him deliuer *v.* 12.
him; let him ſaue him, if he wil haue him.] Further
he addeth [Manie dogges haue compaſſed me, the *Mat.* 27.
counſel of the malignant, hath beſeged me.] Spea- *v.* 39.
king of the reproches, he ſaith [They haue deuided
my garmentes amongſt them : and vpon my veſture,
they haue caſt lot.] Likewiſe of Iudas the traitor *Io.* 19. *v.*
he ſaith [The man alſo of my peace (one of his par- 24.
ticular familie) in whom I truſted, who did eate my *Pſ.* 40. *v.*
breades, hath greatly troden me vnder foote. Let 10. *Io.* 13.
their habitation be made deſert : & in their Taber- *v.* 18. *Act*
nacles, let there be none to dwel] fulfilled in Iu- 1. *v.* 16.
das, and thoſe that plotted the treaſon, and barganed
with him. Of Iudas his deſperate ſodaine deſtruction, and of ſupplying the place and office of his A-
poſtleſhip, the ſame Prophet ſaith [Let his daies *Pſ.* 68. *v.*
be made few (fulfilled in that he hanged him ſelfe 26. *Act.* 1.
the ſame day) and let an other take his Biſhoprick] *v.* 19.
performed in S. Mathias. Againe the Royal Pro-
phet, as in Chriſtes ſpeach ſaith [They gaue me gale *Pſ.* 108. *v.*
for my meate, and in my thirſt, they gaue me vine- 8. *Act.* 1.
gre to drinke] fulfilled when gale and vinegre were *v.* 1.
geuen to him on the Croſſe. And preſently was ful- *Pſ.* 68. *v.*
filled that which the ſame Prophet foretold, that our 22. *Mat.*
B. Sauiour ſhould finally ſay in the inſtãt of his death 27. *v.* 48.
[Father into thy handes I commend my ſpirit.] The *Ioa.* 19. *v.*
Spouſe alſo in the Canticles, meditating our B. Sa- 29.
uiours Paſſion and death, compriſeth much in few *Pſ.* 30. *v.*
wordes ſaying [A bundel of Mirhe my beloued is to 6. *Luc.* 23.
me, he ſhal abide betwene my breſtes] as if ſhe *v.* 46.
ſhould ſay I neede not ſay more by wordes, but I *Cant.* 1.
wil euer meditate of his Paſſin in my hart. As *v.* 13.
breifly the Prophet Iſaias deſcribeth our Sauicurs
ſtate in the time of his death [as one deſpiſed, and *Iſ.* 53. *v.*
most 3. 12.

moſt abiect of men : a man of ſorowes, and knowing infirmitie. He hath deliuered his ſoul vnto death:
and was reputed with the wicked .] And by the ſame
Prophet our Lord him ſelf ſpeaketh thus [I haue troden the preſſe alone, and of the Gentiles, there is not
a man with me .] By Ieremie thus [I as a mild lambe
that is caried to a victime] Conformably therto ſaith
the ſame Prophet Ieremie [He ſhal geue the cheeke
to them that ſtrike him] as the Euangeliſtes record,
that al was fulfilled. Daniel alſo telleth the time ,
[from the going forth of the world (fiom the time
that the promiſe ſhal be performed that Ieruſalem
be built againe after the captiuitie) vnto Chriſt the
Prince, there ſhal be ſeauen weekes, and ſixtie two
weekes. And after ſixtie two weekes, Chriſt ſhal be
ſlaine. And Zacharie inſinuated, that he ſhould be
nailed on the Croſſe [for it ſhal be ſaid to him :
what are theſe woundes in the middeſt of thy handes ?
And he ſhal ſay; with theſe was I wouded in the houſe
of them that loued me foretelling withal , that his
dearcſt trendes, al his Diſciples, ſhould flee for feare,
in the inſtant of his apprehenſion [Strike the Paſtor ,
and the ſheepe ſhal be diſperſed .]

4   After al theſe , and other Prophets, Chriſt him
ſelf amiddeſt his workes and doctrine, premoniſhing
his Apoſtles, foretould them that [he muſt goe to Ieruſalem and ſuffer manie thinges, of the Ancients &
Scribes, and cheife Prieſtes, and be killed , and the
third day riſe againe. And as they had done to Iohn
Baptiſt : ſo alſo the Sonne of man ſhal ſuffer of them]
Againe almoſt a yeare after he foretold them the ſame
thing [Behold (ſaith he) we goe vp to Ieruſalem, &
the Son of man ſhal be deliuered to the cheife Prieſtes
and to the Scribes, and they ſhal condemne him to
death, and ſhal deliuer him to the Gentils to be moc -
ked, & ſcourged and crucified .] He alſo inſinuated
to this

If. 63.
v.3.
Lam. 3.
v. 30.
Mat.26.
v.67.

Dan. 9.
v.25.

Zach.13.
v.6.

v.7.
Mat.26.
v.31.

Mat.16.
v.21.
Ch. 17
v.12.
Ch. 20.
v.18.19.
Mar. 8.
v.31.
Ch. 10.
v.33.
34.Luc.
9.v.22.

Chriſt him ſelf
did foreſhew
his death on
the Croſſe.

E e 3

to his enemies, which fought to kil him, that indede *Ch*.18.
they should haue their wil therin, but not so soone *v*.31.
as they desired [My time (saith he) is not yet come: *Io.*7.*v*,6.
but your time is always readie my time is not yet 8.
accomplished.] Againe he said to them plainly [I *Io.*10.*v.*
yeld my life ,,for my sheepe. No man taketh it a- 15.18.
way from me: but I yeld it of my selfe.] The same al- *Mat.*21.
so by a parable of husbandmē, that killed both the ser- *v*.35. 36.
uants, and sonne of their Lord. By al which it is
manifest that the death of our Redemer was ordained by God, and reuealed to the Patriarches & Prophets;l & by them, as also by him self, foretold to o-
thers, euen as it is come to passe, and largely written
by the Euangelists, which may suffice against the
Iewes, and Pagane Infidels.

The Crosse
wheron Christ
died, is therby
made holie &
honorable.

5   But against some other Infidels which bearing
the name of Christians [are enemies of the Crosse *Phil*. 3
of Christ] disdaining & condemning the holie signe *v*.18.
therof as if the kind of death which our B. Sauiour
susteined, had added nothing at al worthie of special
consideration, and grateful memorie: it resteth to be
declared, that not by chance; nor by the only malice of the Iewes, but by diuine ordinance, for important reasons, the Crosse was chosen rather then
anie other maner of death, because it was most pain- *Deut*.21.
ful, most reproachful, and most odious. For [the law *v*.23.
denouncing him accursed of God that hangeth on a *Gal*. 3. *v*.
tree] our Sauiour [would be made a curse, to deliuer 13. *Colos.*
vs] from other curses of the law [wyping out the 2. *v* 14.
hand writing that was against vs, fastening it to the
Crosse] And that with this diuine promise, that it
should become most honorable & cōfortable to ture
Christiās, terrible to the diuel, & forcible against al *Phil*.2. *v*.
spiritual enemies. For as S. Paul expresly teacheth 8. 9.10.
that because Christ our Lord humbled him self made
obediēt vnto death: euē the death on the Crosse: For
this thing God also hath exalted him, and hath ge-

uen him a name which is a boue al names; that in
the name of *Iefus* euerie knee bow of the celeftials,
terreftrials, and infernals] wherfore as the name of
Iefus Chrift is the more exalted becaufe he dyed on
the Croffe: fo the Croffe it felf wheron he dyed is
fingularly eftemed amongft fpecial Reliques, as an inftrument of his more glorie, & of our Redemption.

6   And alfo the figne therof worthily kept, and v-
fed in memorie of his fo glorious and triumphant
victorie, and of the ineftimable benefite, which we
receiue by this occafion; as alfo to the greater confufion of the diuel who was therby ouerthrowne;
the wifdom and power of God fo placing the faluation of mankinde in the wood of the Croffe, that
from whence death did rife, thence alfo life might
rife againe: and he that did ouercome in wood, in
wood alfo might be ouercome through Chrift our
Lord dying theron. Which moft ancient and vniuerfal doctrine of the Church, is grounded in the holie Scriptures. Iacob the holie Patriarch formed a
Croffe by laying his handes vpon the heades of Io-
feps two fonnes, the one arme croffing the other.
For when Iofeph had fet his elder fonne to the right
hand of Iacob, and his yonger fonne to the left hand;
[Iacob chaunging handes, put his right hand vpó the
yonger, and his left hand vpon the elder] and that
wittingly, contrarie to Iofephs minde, becaufe his
bleffing geuen to thofe children was myftical, fignifying not only that the yonger of thofe brethren
fhould be preferred before the elder, but alfo that
in time of grace and new teftament, the Gentils being yonger people of God, fhould excel the Iewes;
which fhould be effected by our Sauiour Chrift dying vpon a Croffe. Otherwife if Iacob would not
haue reprefented the Croffe, he might either haue
laide his right hand firft vpon one, and then on the
other

Marginal notes:

Alfo the figne of the Croffe is profitabe to the faithful, & terrible to the diuel.

Gods wifdom ordayned like inftruments of our fpiritual good, as had bene occafion of our fal.

The Croffe was prefigured in the old Teftament.

other, or els haue caufed them to change places.
It is true that the miftical fenfe doth not alwaies demonftratiuely proue that thing which is otherwife
doubtful : yet it doth wel illuftrate, and make that
more credible which is more obfcure in Chriftan Religion. And that the croffing of Iacobs armes fo wittingly done, was myftical, is confeffed by al Diuines,
and al Cotholiques generally vnderftand it to be a
myfterie of the Croffe of Chrift. [The peece of   *Exo* 15.
wood alfo which Moyfes by Gods commandement   *v.* 25.
caft into the bitter waters, werby they were made
fweete] doubtles was myftical & doth aptly refemble
the daylie benefites which we receiue by the holie
vfe of the Croffe, in Sacraments and other bleffinges.
Likewife when [Moyfes lifted vp his handes praying]   *Exo.* 17.
for the armie which fought againft Amelech: and   *v.* 11.12.
[Aaron ftreching forth his hand when he bleffed the   *Lexit.* 9.
people] wel prefigured the facred handes of Chrift,   *v.* 22.
lift vp and ftreched out on the Croffe. And as the
rocke in the defert yelding plentie of water, fignified Chrift geuing abundance of grace; fo [the   *Nu.* 20.
rodde wherwith it was ftroken] reprefented the   *v.* 11.
Croffe made of two peeces of wood. As for the   *Nu.* 21. *v.*
brafen ferpent, which hath no more refemblance in   9. *Io.* 3. *v.*
it felf then the other thinges had: yet is propofed   14. *Ch.* 12.
for an example, and fimilitude by our Sauiour, that   *v.* 32.
[as Moyfes exalted the ferpent in the defert, fo muft
the fonne of man be exalted] to witte on the
Croffe.

The vertue &
vfe of the
Croffe, was
prophecied be-
fore Chrift.

7   By the Prophet Dauid Chrift fo plainly fignifieth his death on the Croffe faying: [they haue dig-   *Pfal.* 21
ged my handes, and my feete] that the obftinate   *v.* 18.
Iewes finding no better euation from fo cleare a prophecie, haue fhamefully corrupted the facred text.
By the Prophet Ifaias our Lord faith: [I wil put a   *Ifa.* 66.
figne in them, that in the day of Iudgement fhal fee   *v.* 19.
                                                                            his

his glorie.] No doubt this figne is fome general marke of diftinction betwene his children and his e-nemies, and may more then probably be vndreftood to be the figne of the Croffe. But in Ezechiel a par-ticular figne is appointed wherwith al muft be figned that fruictfully mourne for their finnes [Paffe (faith our Lord to his Scribe) through the middeft of the Citie, in the middeft of Ierufalem, and figne *Thau* vpon the forheades of the men that mourne and la-ment al the abominations that are done in the mid-deft therof.] *Marke them with Thau*, that is with the Hebrew letter, which is formed like to a Croffe,& fignifieth a figne or marke, which is alfo refembled by the greeke letter *Tau*, and the latin T. And fo [thofe in whofe forheades this figne was found, were faued from the deftruction] wherin [al others old & yong perifhed that were not fo figned.]

8   Neither can anie man tel, nor reafonably ima-gin, what other figne it fhould be, but the figne of the Croffe, which fhal appeare in the cloudes, in fight of the whole world, when our Sauiour fhal come in Maieftie to iudge the world, wherof him felf hath foretold faying [The powers of heauen fhal be moued: And then they fhal fee the Sonne of man coming in the cloudes with much power and glorie. And then fhal appeare *The figne of the Sonne of man* in the heauen] which figne doubtleffe, wil no leffe confound al other enemies of the Croffe, then the cruel and fpiteful Iewes, that would needes haue Chrift to be crucified vpon the Croffe, preten-ding that [it was not lawful for them to kil anie man] meaning to crucifie anie man. For fo it is plaine by S. Iohns wordes faying [that the word of Iefus might be fulfilled which he faid, fignifying what death he fhould dye.] Thus holie Scriptures witneffe that Chrift our Redemer muft fuffer death, & that on the

Ezech.9.
v.4.

v.5.6,

Mat.24.
v.29.
30.
Mar.13.
v.26.

Ioa.18.
v.31.
32.
Luc.24.
v.25.
26.

Croſſe [and ſo to enter into his glorie.]

Chriſts glorie
began to be
ſpred, imme-
diatly after his
death.

9 For no ſoner had our B. Sauiour yelded vp his
moſt holie ſoule, but his glorie began to appeare.
The Sunne, whiles he was dying on the Croſſe, had
loſt his light. And [from the Sixt Hour, there was *Mat. 27.*
darknes made vpon the whole earth, vntil the Ninth *v. 45. 50*
Hour] but then [he putting forth a mightie voice, *Mar. 15.*
and ſo geuing vp the Ghoſt] immediatly [the veile *v. 37. Luc.*
of the Temple was rent in two peeces, from the toppe, 23. *v.* 45.
euē to the bottome, the earth did quake, & the rockes 46.
were torne] yea and the ſtonie hartes of the people
were mollified [the Centurion (who had charge to *Io.* 19. *v*
ſee the wicked ſentence executed) ſeing that toge- 30. 38. 39.
ther with the mightie voice, he had yelded vp the
Ghoſt] and the reſt which was done, glorified God
ſaying [Indeede this man was the Sonne of God :
this man was iuſt.] And [al the multitude of them
that were preſent together at that ſight, and ſaw the
thinges that were done, returned, knocking their
breaſtes.] The deuout [women bought ſpices, and *Luc.* 23. *v.*
prepared coſtlie ointmentes for his burial. Ioſeph, 45. 46.
a Senator of Arimathea, a ſecret Diſciple, went in *Io.* 19. *v.*
boldlie to Pilate, obteyned the Bodie of our Sauiour ; 30. 38. 39.
and Nicodemus, a Prince of the Iewes (hitherto
alſo a ſecret Diſciple) bringing a mixture of Mirh
and Aloes, about an hundred poundes (together with
Ioſeph) taking the ſacred Bodie, wrapping it in Sin-
don, bound it in linnen clothes, with the ſpices :
And ſo laid it in a new monument, hewed in a rock
of ſtone, wherin neuer yet anie man had bene laid.]
So would our B. Sauiour ſhew example in him ſelf
[by his glorious Sepulchre] long before propheci- *Pſ.* 15. *v.*
ed by Iſaias, how the glorie of the iuſt, beginneth 10.
from their death, where the glorie of the wicked *Iſ.* 11.
endeth. *v.* 10.

The

The glorious foule of our B . Sauiour , parting from his bodie , defcended into hel .

ARTICLE. 24.

For better declaration of this Article, it muft first be vnderftoode, what the holie Apoftles meane by the word *Hel*, in this place. In the written hiftorie, of the creation of the vniuerfal world : mention is firft made only of heauen & earth, as the two general places, conteyning al creatures of the whole world. In which general fignification, the name Heauen, cóprehendeth, not only the Emperial higheft heauen, where holie Angels & other glorified Sainctes, fee God in eternal bliffe : but alfo other heauens or fpheres of *Primum mobile*, of the fixed Starres, and of the feauen Planets, yea and the ayre ; for birdes are called *Volatilia cæli*, Foules of the heauen, that is of the ayre : And confequently the element of fire (which is betwene the ayre and the Moone) is cóprehended in the fame general name of heauen. In like maner, the name of earth, conteyneth not only the land, but alfo the feas, & other matters, as is more diftinctly expreffed in thofe wordes [God called the drie land, earth ; & the gathering of waters, he called Seas .] But of Hel, there is no expreffe mention, before the Hiftorie of the Patriarch Iacob, where he faith : [I wil defcend vnto my fonne into hel.] And in the Hiftorie of the fchifmatical rebels, Chore, Dathan, and Abiron, with their complices, it is writen, that [they defcended quick into hel] yet in neither of thefe places is defcribed, what, nor where hel is, more then that the way to it, is defcending downwardes. And is moft generally faid, to be within the earth, and fo

What place is vnderftood by the word HEL in our Crede.

Gen . 1 .
v . 1 .
Ch . 2 .
v . 1 . 4 .
6 . 8 .

26 .

v . 10 .

Gen . 37 .
v . 35 .
Ch . 42 .
v . 38 .
Nu . 16 .
v . 30 .
33 .

is fur

is furtheſt diſtant from heauen : the whole orbe of
land and water being compaſſed with the ayre . Moſt
certaine it is by holie Scriptures, that hel is a diſtinct
place both from heauen , and earth . So Iob ſaith
[God is higher then heauen, deeper then hel, lon- *Iob* . 11 .
ger then the earth, and broader then the ſea] where *v* . 8 . 9 .
Heauen, Hel, Earth, and Sea, are recited as the four
general partes of the vniuerſal world . S . Paul reduceth them to three ; ſhewing that [to the name of
Ieſus, euerie knee muſt bow, of the *Celeſtials, Terre-* *Phil* . 2 .
ſtrials, and *Infernals*] that is to ſay , in Heauen, in *v* . 10 .
Earth, & in Hel . By which, and manie other holie
Scriptures , it is cleare, that there is a hel , and that
it is diſtinct in ſituation from heauen, & from the
face of the earth .

That there are
diuers helles, is
proued by ma-
nie ho lie
Scriptures .

2   And it is no leſſe certaine, that there be diſtinct
and different partes of hel ; which is inuincibly proued by manie places of holie Scriptures . Firſt by the
two places alreadie recited . For it can not be, that
Iacob ſaying, that [he would deſcend into hel]
where he ſuppoſed his Sonne Ioſeph to be, ſpake of
the ſame hel, or ſame part of hel, into which Moy -
ſes ſaith the rebels [deſcended downe quicke] the
one being the place of eternal damnation, & tormentes of the wicked : the other a place of reſt, &
aſſured expectation of iuſt ſoules, not aboue the earth,
but beneath, according to the proprietie of his ſpeach
ſaying [I wil deſcend vnto my ſonne into hel .] Likewiſe the renowmed old Martyr Eleazarus, ſaying
[he would rather be ſent into hel] then feyne con- *2 . Mac* . 6 .
formitie vnto wicked lawes, againſt the Lawe of God; *v* . 23 . 24 .
could not meane the hel of the damned . For euen 26 .
therfore, he yelded his bodie to temporal death, that
he might [eſcape the hande of the almightie] and
auoide damnation of his ſoule . Holie Iob alſo di- *Iob* . 17 .
ſtinguiſheth two helles : one wherin is reſt and re- *v* . 13 .
peſe

pose, where he faith [If I fhal expect, hel is my houfe, and in darknes I haue made my bed] an other hel, wherin is no reft nor hope, which he expreffeth by a negatiue interrogation, putting the cafe that al

v.16.　his thinges fhould [defcend into moft deepe hel : there at leaft (faith he) fhal I haue reft thinkeft thou] And this he calleth [*profundiffimum infernum,* the moft deepe hel :] of which hel no doubt he fpeaketh, where he defcribeth the wretched ftate of wicked men

Iob. 21.　that profper in this world, faying [They leade their
v. 13.　daies in wealth, and in a moment they goe downe to hel] Conformably to this diftinction of diuers helles,

Pf. 85.　the Royal Prophet faith to God [Thou haft deliue-
v. 13.　red my foule out of the lower hel] And fpeaking

Pf. 87.　of his enemies malicious endeuours, he faith : [they
v. 7.　haue (. fo much as lay in them) put me in the lower lake.] Salomon alfo fignifieth, that there be diuers

Prou. 15.　helles where he faith [The path of life aboue the
v. 24.　learned, that he may decline from the loweft hel.] Seing then the holie Scriptures teftifie diuers helles, or diuers partes of hel, much different in qualitie of tormentes, and of reft, and in fituation higher and lower : it muft needes be the higheft hel, into which we profeffe in our Crede, that Chrift our Sauiour defcended in his glorious foule, leauing his facred Bodie on the Croffe.

Chrift defcen-ded into the hel of reft, not of torment.

3　This doctrine is further confirmed by the eftate of the holie Patriarches, Prophets, & other iuft per-fons, departed this life in the old Teftament, whofe foules were free from hel of the damned; and yet could not enter into heauen before our Sauiour came in flefh and opened the way, which is proued by manie holie Scriptures. Firft in fignification hereof

That none of mankind en-tred into heaué before Chrift : was fignified by the keping of the gate of Paradife.

Gen. 3.　holie [Cherubims, and a flaming and turning fword,
v. 24.　were placed at the gate of paradife, to kepe the way of the tree of life.] In the law of Moyfes which was in moft

Prefigured in the high Preift.

in moſt thinges figuratiue, Aaron being high Preiſt
was forbid to enter at al times into the Sanctuarie,
that was within the veile before the Propiciatorie:
into which he could enter only [once in the yeare, *Leuit*. 16.
in the feaſt of general Expiation] and no other but *v*. 2. 17.
the high Preiſt at anie time. [The holie Ghoſt ſigni- 30.
fying this (ſaith S. Paul) that the way of the ho- *Heb*. 9. *v*.
So expounded lies, was not yet manifeſted, the former Tabernacle 8. 9.
by S. Paul. as yet ſtanding. Which (ſaith he) is a Parable (or
figure) of the time preſent.] An other like figure
By other fi- was in Moyſes, who [was not ſuffered to enter into *Deut*. 1. *v*.
gures. . the promiſed land of Chanaan] ſignifying that the 1. *Ch*. 34.
Law deliuered by him, could not bring anie to hea- *v*. 5.
uen, the true land of promiſe. [Behold (ſaid Moy- *Deut*. 3. *v*.
ſes in the Champian wildernes of Moab) I dye in 27. *Ch*. 4.
this ground, I ſhal not paſſe ouer Iordan, you ſhal *v*. 22.
paſſe, and poſſeſſe the goodlie land.] Againe the
ſame was prefigured by that al the children of Iſrael mourned vpon Aarons death, and likewiſe vpon
Moyſes, but not vpon Ioſue, becauſe they repreſented the old Law: and Ioſue bringing the people in-
to Chanaan, and ſetting them in poſſeſſion of it, ſig- *Deut*. 31.
nified our Sauiour Chriſt, who bringeth his ſeruantes *v*. 7.
and children into heauen, and geueth them poſſeſſion
of eternal inheritance. Of Aarons death, it is written thus [Al the multitude ſeeing that Aaron was *Nu*. 20.
dead, mourned vpon him thirtie daies, throughout al *v*. 30.
their families.] Of Moyſes the verie like wordes
are recorded, that [the children of Iſrael mourned *Deu*. 34.
him, in the champion Coûtrie of Moab, thirtie daies] *v*. 8.
But of Ioſue, it is only ſaid [After theſe thinges, *Ioſue*. 24.
(after the hiſtorie of his actes) Ioſue the ſonne of *v*. 29. 30.
Nun, the ſeruant of our Lord dyed, being an hun-
dred and tenne yeares old; and they bruied him in
the coaſtes of his poſſeſſion, in Thamnath-ſare which
is ſituated in the mountaine of Ephraim, on the north
part

part of mount Gaas] without anie word of mourning, which affuredlie was not without Mifterie.
Neither can it be without Mifterie, nor wel fignifie
anie other thing, then this wherof we here treate,
that fuch a one, as being innocent from wilful murder, hauing not voluntarily, but by chance medlie,
Nu. 35. killed anie man [was deliuered from the hande of
v. 11. 13. the reuenger, and by fentence brought into a Citie
22. 23. of refuge, (to which he had fledde) muft tarie there
vntil the High Preift that is annoynted with the ho-
25. 28. lie oyle doe dye. And after that the high Preift is
dead, then fhal he (that had without hatred and enmitie flaine a man) returne into his Countrie .] For
euen fo after the death of our High Preift Iefus Chrift,
the iuft and innocent foules being in faiftie from the
reuenger, in that part of hel called Abrahams bofom,
and *Limbus Patrum*, the Lake of the Fathers, were
deliuered from thence, and with him returned into
their Countrie which is Heauen.

4 Befides myftical figures, the Prophets did alfo
forefhew, that Chrift our Sauiour defcended into hel, The
prou...
and from thence deliuered the captiues, which were Prophets.
reteined there vntil he came. For what can be more
plaine proofe that our B. Sauiour was fometime there,
then that which him felf faith by his Prophet Dauid
Pf. 15. directing his fpeach to God [My flefh fhal reft in
v. 9. 10. hope: Becaufe thou wilt not leaue my foule in hel.]
If there were no other place to proue this point of
our faith, this alone is fufficient. But for fuperabundance let vs fee more. The fame Royal Prophet in
an other Pfalme faith litterally of himfelf, or in the
perfon of anie iuft foule after great affliction, but
Pf. 87. prophetically of Chrift [I am become as a man with-
v. 5. 6. out helpe: free among the dead.] For fo was our
B. Sauiour *free* among the dead, that were *in cap-*
tiuitie, yea fo potent and glorious, that he made the
place

place of former captiuitie, a place of Ioy, performing there, that which he moſt graciouſly promi-
ſed to the penitent theeſe on the Croſſe ſaying [A- *Luc.* 23.
men I ſay to thee, this day thou ſhalt be with me *v.* 43.
in Paradiſe.] The wordes alſo of God the Father to
Chriſt our Sauiour, written by Iſaias [I haue geué *Iſ.* 42.
thee for a Couenant of the people, for a light of the *v.* 6.7.
Gentiles, that thou mighteſt open the eyes of the
blinde, and bring forth the priſoner out of priſon,
and them that ſitte in darcknes, out of the priſon
houſe] which Prophecie, beſides the moral ſence of
lightning thoſe that are in errour or ignorant, and
deliuering ſinners from captiuitie of ſinne, doth al-
legorically ſignifie the light and libertie which our
Sauiour brought to the Sainctes in Limbo, by his
deſcending into that hel, where they were in darcknes and in priſon, til he came and releued them. In
both which ſenſes the Prophet *Oſee* ſemeth to deſcribe the victorie of Chriſt ouer death and hel ſaying: [I wil be thy death o death: thy bitte wil I be *Oſee.* 13.
o hel.] And Zacharias more plainly ſpeaketh thus *v.* 14.
to Chriſt our Redemer [Thou alſo in the bloud of *Zach.* 9,
thy Teſtament, haſt let forth thy priſoners out of the *v.* 11.
lake, wherin is no water] And congratulating with
the ſame priſoners for this deliuerie ſaith to them
[Conuert to the munition ye priſoners of hope, to 12.
day alſo declaring I wil render thee duble.] So it
was a duble benefite to be deliuered from priſon, and
to be made partakers of glorie.

The ſame doc-
trine is confir-
med by the
new Teſtamét.

5   In the new Teſtament this Myſterie is more reueled. The Euangeliſt writeth that when our Sauiour was Baptized [the heauens were opened] ſigni- *Mat.* 3.
fying that heauen was ſhut in the old law, til Chriſt *v.* 16.
opened the way by his paſſion, and that none could
enter therin before him. In the meane ſeaſon he

The firſt con-
firmation.

preached and ſent his Diſciples to preach [that the *Mat.* 4,
                                    kingdome *v.* 17,

Ch. 10.
v. 7.

Luc. 8.
v. 55.
Luc. 7.
v. 55.
Ioan. 11.
v. 44.
Luc. 16.
v. 23.
25.

26.

Ephes. 4.
v. 9.

v. 10.

Heb. 10.
v. 20.

Heb. 11.
v. 39.

kingdome of heauen is at hand] which euidently The second.
sheweth, that as yet, whiles Christ was mortal in
earth, there was no entrance into heauen, but shortly should be entrance thither. The soules also of The 3.
those persons, whom our Sauiour raised from death,
in the meane time til they returned to their bodies,
were neither in heauen (for then it had bene no benefite, but a great damage for them to come againe
into this wotld) neither in hel of the damned (for
from thence there is no redemption) nor returning.
And therfore they were in some other place. The 4.
soules of poore Lazarus the begger, and of the rich
glutton, were in [places farre distant] yet both in
lower partes, both in hel, but the one [in Abrahams bosome] the other [in hel of tormentes] For
it foloweth in the text, that Abraham said to the dā-
ned glutton, that [Lazarus is comforted, and thou
art tormented. And besides this, betwene vs & you,
there is fixed a great Chaos, that none can passe frō
hence to you, neither from thence hither.] Againe 5.
concerning Christ him self S. Paul expresly saith that
[he descended into the inferiour partes of the earth]
which no caueler can possibly interprete of his graue.
For besides that his graue was hewed in a rocke v-
pon the face of the earth, not in the inferiour, or
lower partes of the earth, the Apostle in the next
wordes saying [He that descended, the same is also
he that ascended aboue al the heauens] speaketh of
places quite opposite, the one farre aboue the other
beneath the earth. He teacheth also in an other E- 6.
pistle, that [Christ *Dedicated* a new way into the Ho-
lies] that is into Heauen. By which word *Dedica-*
ted, he sheweth that he was Auctonr, beginner, and
the first that entred of al mankind. And he saith al- 7.
so, that the Ancient Sainctes of the old Testament,
[being approued by faith receiued not the promise]

G g   til others

til others of the New Teſtament, ſhould receiue it
with them.

*Our Sauiour Ieſus Chriſt, roſe from Death the
third day.*

A R T I C L E. 2 5.

Our B. Saui-
our moſt of al
men humbled
himſelf; and
therfore is
moſt exalted.

Eing moſt true (for truth it ſelf ſpæke it) that
[he which humbleth him ſelf, ſhal be exalted] *Luc* · 18.
the ſame is cheiſly verified in him that ſaith *v* · 14.
it, our Lord Ieſus Chriſt. Of whom we haue ſeene
in the precedent Articles, that he humbled him ſelf
much more, then anie other euer did, or could doe.
Which is moſt euident, if we conſider his Perſon,
and humiliation, comparing them with other greateſt perſons of the whole world and their humbleſt
actions : If we may cal it comparing, when we frame
a mutual conceipt in our mind thinges of infinitly differing, becauſe properly ſpeaking, there is no côpari-
ſô betwen the Creator, & creatures. For Kinges, Em-
peroures, and Popes, yea Angels, Archangels, Che-
rubines, & Serapimes, with al other glorious Sainctes :
Alſo the moſt Bleſſed Mother of God, are creatures:
Chriſt our Lord, is God the Creator. Who deſcending from the Throne of God, exinaniting him ſelf,
tooke mannes nature, and therin [humbled him ſelf *Phil* · 2.
made obedient vnto death, euen death of the Croſſe] *v*. 8.
which was moſt contemptible. And albeit ſome men
wilingly, for Goddes cauſe, ſuſteyned the ſame kind of
death, as S Peter, S. Andrew, and others, yet they
hauing bene ſomtimes ſinners, had deſerued to ſuffer paines for their owne ſinnes ; but our B. Sauiour
neuer was, neither could be, a ſinner, and ſo infinitly excelled al others in humbling him ſelf. And *v*. 9.

for

for this verie caufe, is exalted infinitly, aboue al others.

2   Which his exaltation immediatly began, when he came to the laft point, and ful confummation of his noft profound humilitie, which was, when his moft facred bodie hang bloudleffe, and fouleleffe, on the Croffe : his moft precious bloud lay al poured out in fundrie places, in Pilates palace, in the high waies, troden vnder feete, but moft part therof on the Croffe, and ground where it ftoode, & his foule defcended into the lower partes of the earth, the prifon of captiues, a part of hel. Loe this was the ful periode of perfecteft humilitie that euer was, or fhal be. Now therfore inftantly his exaltation began. For inftantly his glorious foule (whofe motion from place to place, is by inftantanial action of the mind) was in Limbo with the holie Fathers, Patriarches, Prophets, and other Sainctes of the old Teftament, lightning the place, and al that were therin, by his diuine light, with inexplicable claritie, brightnes, ioy, bliffe, and fruiton of eternal glorie. And al this alfo according to the fenfitiue power of his foule, which hitherto was paffible : the fuperior power being alwaies glorious. Exaltation alfo of his fame and reputation, began by and by after (as is alreadie noted) when the Centurion and manie others, frely and publikly, faid of him, this was a iuft man, the Sonne of God. And very fhortly began the exaltation of his facred Bodie (as we haue alfo faid alreadie) when Iofeph and Nicodemus, with other deuout refpectable perfons, tooke it downe frō the Croffe, and with coftly fpices, and fineft linnen, buried it moft folemnly, in a new moft honourable Tombe. Thus his Exaltation began, and proceded that firft euening after his victorious death. Al the next day being the Sabbath day, and the greateft of

Art. 20.
parag. 4.
Art. 23.
parag. 8.

al the

al the yeare by reason it was within the Feaſt of Paſch,
& Azims, he became more & more renowmed by pu-
blick diſcourſes, which were made of his admirable
vertues, as of [an excellent Prophet, mightie in
worke and word, before God and al the people ;
and how their cheif Preiſtes and Princes, had deliuered him into condemnation of death and crucified
him] a thing ſo famous, that none, no not ſtrangers in
Ieruſalem, could be ignorant therof, as plainly appeareth by the report of the two Diſciples going to
Emaus the third day.

Luc. 24.
v. 18. 19.
20.

Much more his
glorie appea-
red in Limbus.

3   But what congratulations were among the holie Patriarches, Prophets, Martyrs, and bleſſed confeſſors, in Limbus for their fruition of Chriſt our
Lord his preſence, and of their long expected glorie;
is to be meditated in hart, for with wordes it can

The third day
his bodie alſo
became glori-
ous.

not be vttered. Much more the third day his glorious exaltation proceded. For then his ſoule returning into his bodie, made the ſame alſo glorious, &
ſo he roſe from death. which Myſterie was fore-

Which was
prefigured in
the old Teſta-
ment.

ſhewed aſwel by figures, and prophecies of the old
Teſtament, as by our B. Sauiours owne prediction,
whiles he was mortal. Amongſt other figures, the
ſudden [aduancement of Ioſeph] the Patriarch, after his manie afflictions, did wel reſemble our Sauiours ſpedie riſing from death after his ſo great hu-
miliation. The ſpace of three daies was alſo inſinuated by [the carying of the Arke of the couenant of
our Lord, three dayes before the people of Iſrael, prouiding a place for the campe.] So him ſelf ſaid [It is
expedient for you that I goe, for I goe to prepare
you a place. And if I goe and prepare you a place, I
come againe and wil take you to my ſelf : that where
I am you alſo may be.]

Gen. 41.
v. 43.

Nu. 10. *v.*
33.
Io. 16. *v.*
7. *Ch.* 14.
v. 23.

Foretold by
the Prophets.

4   The Royal Pſalmiſt verie often prophecieth of
our Sauiours Reſurrection : as implicitely ſignified
in his

iu his owne deprefment, and deliuerie with more ad-

Pſ.3. uancement [I haue flept (faith he) and bene at reft;

v.6. and haue rifen vp ; becaufe our Lord hath taken me]

Pſ.15. More plainly in an other Pſalme [My flefh fhal reft

v.9. in hope, becaufe thou wilt not leaue my foule in hel

(which neceſſarilie prefuppofeth, that his foule fhould

10. defcend into hel) neither wilt thou geue thy holie

one, to fee corruption.] Chriftes natural Bodie, be-

ing naturally corruptible, efpecially being dead, was

Aĉt.2. by diuine power, preferued from corruption. Wher-

v.31. by S.Peter conuinced the Iewes, that Chrift is rifen

Aĉt.13. from death, and that this prophecie is verified in

v.35. our Sauiours bodie, and could not be verified in Da-

36. uid. And fo concludeth no leffe againft the heri-

tikes, of this time denying Chriftes defcending into

hel, then againft the Iewes denying his Refurrecti-

on in thefe plaine wordes [that Dauid forefeeing,

fpake of the Refurrection of Chrift : For neither was

he left in hel, neither did his flefh fee corruption.]

The fame is proued by the title of an other Pfalme,

which is alfo Canonical Scripture, where it is faid

Pſ.21. [*vnto the end, for the morning enterprife*] The Pfalme

v.1. is whollie of Chrift, and the greateft part, is of his

Paffion and death, And the title infinuateth the ef-

fect of his death, which is mannes Redemption:

Rom.4. made knowne by his Refurrection [who was deli-

v.25. uered vp for our finnes, and rofe againe for our iuf-

tification] Likewife an other title fheweth that this

Pſ.23. effect of Chrifts Refurrection fhould happen [in the

v.1. firft of the Sabbath] the firft day of the weeke; which

is our Lords day the Sunday. Againe holie Dauid as

it were in his owne perfon, but prophetically in

Pſ.34. Chrifts name faith [Lord when wilt thou regard?

v.17. reftore thou my foule (or life) from their maligni-

22. tie, mine only one (my bodie) frō the Lions. Thou

Pſ.40. haft fene o Lord, kepe not filence. Lord depart not

v.9. from

from me . They (mine enemies) haue determined an vniuſt word againſt me . Shal not he that ſlepeth adde to riſe againe ? Let not the tempeſt of water drowne me, nor the depth ſwallow me ; neither let the pitte ſhutte his mouth vpon me : Thy ſaluation o God hath receiued me] Elſwhere, changing his forme of ſpeach, he ſaith directly of Chriſt [Our Lord hath reigned, he hath put on bewtie, our Lord hath put on ſtrength, and hath girded him ſelf] He that tooke vpon him our infirmities and as a Lambe ſuffered him ſelf to be ledde vnto tormentes ; after his death, tooke vpon him armour, and girdle of warfare , to reigne in his Kingdome [His right hand hath wrought ſaluation to him ſelf . Our Lord ſaid to my Lord, ſitte on my right hand, til I make thine enemies the footſtoole of thy feete . Ariſe Lord into thy reſt ; thou, and the Arck of thy ſanctification . Our Lord hath ſworne truth to Dauid, and he wil not diſapoint it (ſaying) of the fruict of thy wombe, I wil ſet vpon thy ſeate .] Againe as if Chriſt ſpake, he relateth him praying to his Father thus [Bring forth my ſoule out of priſon, to confeſſe vnto thy name : the iuſt expect me vntil thou reward me .] Generally al the Prophets, fore-ſhewing Chriſtes Paſſion, and his death, adde therto his ſpeedie Reſurrection . But Oſee more particularly ſaith [He wil reuiue vs after two dayes ; in the third day, he wil raiſe vs vp, and we ſhal liue in his ſight .] And Ionas prophecied the ſame by fact, being [in the belie of the fiſh three dayes, and three nightes] which our Sauiour him ſelf ſaith was ſo ſufficient a ſigne, that the wicked & adulterous generation , ſhould haue none other . [For (ſaith he) as Ionas was in the whales belie three dayes and three nightes : ſo ſhal the Sonne of man be in the hart of the earth, three daies, & three nightes .]

Pſ. 68 . v. 16 . 30 .

Pſ. 92 . v . 1 .

Pſ. 97 . v . 1 . *Pſ*. 109 . v . 1 . *Pſ*. 131 . v . 8 . 11 . *Act* . 2 . v . 30 . *Pſ*. 141 . v . 8

Oſee . 6 . v . 3 .

Ions . 2 . v . 1 . 11 .

Mat . 12 . v . 39 . 40 .

Chriſts owne predictions of

5 He had before this, told the ſame incredulous

wran

wrangling people, when they demanded a figne : that his Refurrecti-
they fhould kil him, and that he would raife him felf on .

Ioan . 2 . againe, but he fpake it in a parable faying : [diffolue
v . 19 . this temple, and in three daies I wil raife it] which
21 . they did not, or rather would not, vnderftand . For
he fpake of the temple of his bodie . But to his difciples he faid without parable in proper and plaine
Mat . 16 . termes : that [he muft goe to Ierufalem , and fuffer
v . 21 . manie thinges of the Ancients, and Scribes, & cheife
Preifts , and be killed, and the third day rife againe]
Nere about a yeare after he told the fame being then
Mat . 20 . nere at hand, faying : [Behold we goe vp to Ierufa-
v . 18 . lem, and the Sonne of man fhal be deliuered to the
Mar . 8 . cheife Preifts , and to the Scribes, and they fhal con-
v . 34 . demne him to death : and fhal deliuer him to the Gen-
Ch . 10 . tiles to be mocked, and fcourged, and crucified : and
v . 34 . the thitd day he fhal rife againe .] Al which predic-
Luc . 9 . tions duly examined, and confidered, may abundant-
v . 22 . ly fuffice to proue againft the Iewes , that Meffias
Ch . 18 . fhould both dye on the Croffe, and rife againe from
v . 33 . death, to immortalitie, euen as al the Euangeliftes,
and fome other Apoftles haue written that Chrift our
Lord did . And now it were bootles to alleage
more of the new Teftament againft them becaufe they
vtterly reiect it . And we fhal haue more oportune
place in the next Article, to recite fundrie apparitions together with other fpecial actes of our B . Sauiour, betwene his Refurrection and Afcenfion .

6 In the meane while, it refteth to refolue a fmale How our Sauiour was three
dayes & three
nightes in the
hart of the
earth .
doubt : How our B . Sauiour was three dayes & three
nightes in the hart of the earth, as S . Mathew writeth that him felf faid he fhould be : feing the fame
& other Euangeliftes affirme , that he yelded vp his
Ghoft at the Ninth Hour, which is three houres after midday, was buried that euening , and after one
whole day more, rofe from death the next morning
very

very early . So that it semeth there was no more time betwene his death and Resurrection , but one whole day, & smale partes of other two dayes, with only two whole nightes (which we cal, Friday night, and Saturday night, & no part at al of a third night . This difficultie may be explicated two wayes ; First by vnderstanding the wordes three dayes, and three nightes to signifie three natural dayes of twentie four houres the day and night, as in the beginning of Genesis it is said [Euening and morning made one day] And so by the figure Sinecdoche, in vsual maner of speach, there were three dayes, to witte, part of Friday, al Saturday, and part of Sunday. Secondly vnderstanding artificial dayes which are only whiles the Sunne is in our Horison ; and the time of darknes without the Sunne, is called night, which may seme more agreable to our Sauiours distinct speach. of three dayes and three nightes . Then we answere, that the space of time on Friday betwene our Sauiours death, and the night folowing, by Sinecdoche, was the first day of the three dayes : the first half of night folowing belonging to Friday, was the first night of the three nightes ; the other half from midnight forward, belonging to Saturday, was the former part of the second night, to which succeded the second artificial day ; & the former part of night, which was til midnight, perteyning also to Saturday, did make the second night complete ; then fro midnight forwardes perteyning to Sunday , was therfore the third night, counting part for the whole. And the morning which then folowed , though it was a very smale part, yet was it the beginning of the third artificial day . And so our B . Sauiour was three dayes , & three nightes, that is, some part of euerie one of three dayes and of three nightes , in the hart of the earth. More clearly verified of his
soule

Gen. I . *v.* 5 . 8 . 13 .

The first explication.

The second explication more conformable to the text.

foule in Limbo; then of his bodie in the graue; for that his bodie was neither so soone in the graue, neither was the graue in the hart of the earth.

Chriſt our Lord appeared often after his Reſurrec-
tion; and ordeyned diuers thinges perteyning
to his Church.

ARTICLE. 26.

AS in other pointes of faith our Sauiour confirmed his doctrine, not only by preaching, but alſo by viſible factes, eſpecially miraculous workes: ſo in this ſpecial Article of his Reſurrection from death, it pleaſed his diuine wiſdome, not only by teſtimonies of holie Scriptures, & his owne predictions; but alſo by viſibly appearing aliue, after his death and burial, and by other ſenſible Actes, to proue and confirme, that he is trulie riſen againe, with the ſelf ſame natural bodie, which he had before; but changed in ſome qualities, being now made glorious, and immortal. Yet would he not appeare to al men in publique, as he conuerſed when he was paſſible and mortal. For that was neither conuenient for his glorious ſtate, nor neceſſarie; no, nor ſo profitable to the faithful: whoſe merite is greater [beleuing without ſeing] then when they are perſwaded therto by viſible meanes. And for inducing al to beleue Chriſtes Reſurrection, it is ſufficient, that after he was publiquely killed by the Iewes, [God raiſed him vp (as S. Peter teacheth) the third day, and gaue him to be made manifeſt, not to al the people, but to witneſſes preordeined of God: to vs who did eate and drink with him after he roſe againe from death.] But beſides this cauſe of propagating the beleefe of this Article

Ioa. 20. *v.* 29.

Act. 10. *v.* 39. 40. 41.

Our Lord proued his Reſurrection by ſundrie apparitions.

He apeared alſo for ſpecial affaires.

And for more conſolation of ſuch as beleued alreadie.

H h

by such witnesses : he appeared also for other affaires, of ordeining more Sacraments, and the Hierarchie of his Church : And thirdly for the more consolation of his Apostles, & some others .

1.
Our Sauiour first appeared to his mother after his Resurrection.

2 To which particular effect, he appeared no doubt : And that first of al, to his afflicted Mother, of al others most faithful, most hopeful, most dearly louing him, and most dearly beloued of him ; though there be not expresse mentió therof in the holie Scriptures, as a thing nedeles to be there written, being in it self, so conuenient, meete, and reasonable, that whosoeuer wil not so thinke without proofe of expresse Scripture, proueth him self ouer simple [without vnderstanding .] Wherfore presupposing that our Lord and Sauiour appeared first to his B. Mother, his next apparition (the first of those that are written by the Euangelistes, wherby anie was induced to beleue, and might be a sitt witnes to others) was the

Luc. 2.
v. 35.

Mat. 15.
v. 16.

Mar. 16.
v. 1. 9.

2.
To S. Marie Magdalene.

same morning of his Resurrection, to S. Marie Magdalen, who with other [deuout women , visiting the holie Sepulchre, were told by two Angels, that he was risen, and so were bidde to tel the Apostles , which they did] wherupon [S. Peter, and S. Iohn, rūning to the monument, & not finding him, departed thence] but she returning [stoode there alone weping : and our Lord appeared to her, seming to be the Gardener : but he calling her by her name , she knew him, and fel at his feete, yet was not permitted to touch him.]

Mat. 28.
v. 1. *Mar*.
16. *v*. 1.
Luc. 24.
v. 4.
Ioan. 20.
v. 3. 4. 10.

3.
To her againe with other two deuout womē.

Thirdly he appeared againe to her and the other holie women in the way, saying to them [Al haile. And they came neare , & tooke hold of his feete, and adored him.]

Io. 20. *v*.
11. 15. 16.
17.
Mat. 28.
v. 9.

4.
To S. Peter.

Fourthly he appeared to S. Peter : For in the euening, the two Disciples returning fron Emaus, testified that [our Lord is risen in dede, and hath appeared to Simon.] And S. Paul saith, that he was seene of Cephas

Luc. 24. *v*.
34. 1. *Cor*.
15. *v*. 5.

Cephas : and after that of the eleuen.] Fiftly he
appeared to S. Iames, for fo S. Paule addeth [Mor-
ouer he was feene of Iames; then of al the Apoftles]
fignifying that our Lord appeared particularly to S.
Peter and to S. Iames, before his apparition when
they were many together. Sixtly towardes euening
of the fame firft day [our Lord ioyned him felf in có-
panie of Cleophas and an other Difciple going to
Emaus. to whó he interpreted holie Scriptures concerning him felf. And going with them as to lodge,
was at laft knowne to them in breaking of breade,
and then he vanifhed out of their fight.] Seauenth-
ly yet [the fame euening, our Lord appered to his
Apoftles, being together (al but S. Thomas) the
doares being fhutte.] Eightly [the eighth day, he
appeared againe to his Apoftles, S. Thomas being
alfo prefent.] Ninthly he appeared to S. Peter, and
other Sixe at the fea of Tiberias. Tenthly he appeared againe to the eleuen Difciples in Galilee.] E-
leuenthly he was feene of more then fiue hundred brethren together, as S. Paul writeth, though he neither expreffeth the time nor the place. Twelthly our
Lord appeaing againe to his Difciples, brought
them forth into Bethania, and in fight of them, and
others, afcended into heauen. This is the fumme,
and order, fo neare as we can gather it out of the four
Euangeliftes, with a fuplement of S. Paul, of the apparitions of our Sauiour betwene his Refurrection,
and Afcention.

3 wherunto S. Paul adioyneth that laft of al [Chrift
our Lord was fene alfo of him felf] And that the fame
was a real apparition of our Sauiour in his humanitie, is euidently confirmed, by that the Apoftle alleageth it, euen as he doth the other apparitions,
to proue that Chrift is indede really rifen from death
to glorious immortalitie. And by the verie fame

H h 2   funda

Side notes (left margin):

v. 7.

Luc. 24.
v. 15.
18. *ad*
35.

Luc. 24.
v. 36.
Ioa. 20.
v. 19.
Io. 20.
v. 26.
Io. 21. *v.*
1. 4. 7.
Mat. 28.
v. 16.
17.
1. *Cor.*
15. *v.* 6.
Luc. 24.
v. 50.
51.

1. *Cor.*
15. *v.* 8.

Side notes (right margin):

5.
To S. Iames.

6.
To two difci-
ples going to
Emaus.

7.
To tenne of
his Apoftles.

8.
To al the eleué
Apoftles, the
eight day.

9.
To S. Peter &
other fixe.

10.
To the eleuen
in Galilee.

11.
To more then
fiue hudred.

12.
To the Apo-
ftles & others
at his Afcenfi-
on.

He appeared
alfo to S. Paul
really in bodie :
proued by fiue
arguments.

Firft proofe.

2. Proofe.

fundamental point of faith, he proueth alfo the general Refurrection of al mankind, at the laft day of
3. general Iudgement. And it is likewife proued to be a real apparition of Chrift in his bodie, by the wordes of Ananias faying to S. Paul [Brother Saul our Lord Iefus hath fent me, he that appeared to thee in the way : the God of our Fathers hath preordeined thee, that thou fhouldeft know his wil, and fee the iuft one, and heare a voice from his mouth (Marke alfo the reafon why he fhould fee and heare Chrift from his owne mouth) becaufe (faith Ananias) thou fhalt be his witnes to al men, of thofe thinges which
4. thou haft feene and heard .] Yet further the fame is confirmed by our B. Sauiours owne wordes to S. Paul faying [Rife vp, and ftand vpon thy feete ; for to this end haue I appeared vnto thee, that I may ordeine thee a minifter and witnes of thofe thinges, which thou haft feene, and of thofe thinges wherin I wil appeare to thee] which laft wordes import his extraordinarie Miffion like to the other Apoftles,
5. fent immediatly by our Sauiour him felf. According wherto, S. Paul writeth to the Galatians thus [Paul an Apoftle, not of men, neither by man ; but by Iefus Chrift, and God the Father, that raifed him from the dead] So we fee, that Chrift our Lord, appeared in earth after his Afcenfion. And that he cã difpofe of his moft facred bodie, as it pleafeth him.

Act. 9. v. 17. Ch. 22. v. 15. 16.

Act. 26. v. 16.

Gal. 1. v. 1.

Chrift ordained diuers thinges in the fourtie dayes after his Refurrection.

4 ’Here alfo we are to confider of S. Iohns aduertifement ; that [there are manie other thinges which Iefus did, that are not written] in the holie Scriptures. And touching his Actes in this time, wherof we now fpeake, S. Luke faith that [he fhewed him felf aliue to his Apoftles after his paffion, in manie arguments, for fourtie dayes appearing to them, & fpeaking of the kingdome of God] which neceffarily importeth

Io. 21. v. 25.

Act. 1. v. 3.

ly importeth that he did more then is expressed in
the twelue Apparitions aboue recited : wherof more
then halfe were performed the first day of the fourtie .
And the former six of them, were particular and priuate to verie few persons : the last two were publique
to manie ; so that only foure of these Apparitions perteyne properly to the Collge of the Apostles . In the
first of which foure, by coming vnto them, the doares
being shut , he declared his bodie to be glorious,
which could penetrate and passe through an other
solide bodie : and also to be his true bodie consisting

Luc. 24.
v. 39.

of flesh and bones, which a spirite hath not . There
he gaue them power to forgeue, & to reteine sinnes :
instituting the holie Sacrament of Penance : And

Ioan. 20.
v. 22.
23 .

that with a solemne Ceremonie . For [he breathed
vpon them and said: Receiue ye the Holie Ghost :
whose sinnes you shal forgeue, they are forgeuen the:
and whose you shall reteine, they are reteined .] In

Ioa. 20.
v. 26 .
28 .

the next apparition, [our Sauiour coming in like maner to the Apostles, the doares being shutte, said to
Thomas, (who was absent before, and would not beleeue) put in thy finger hither, and see my handes ; &
bring hither thy hand, and put it into my side; and
be not incredulous, but faithful] whervpon S . Tho-

v. 28 .

mas then said [My Lord, and my God] Whether
he did touch our B . Sauiour , or no, the Euangelist
doth not tel, but it semeth more probable, that he
beleued vpon sight without touching ; for our Saui-

29 .

our said to him [Becaufe thou hast seene me Thomas, thou hast beleued] He saw the outward apparance, and so beleued, not only that it was his Maister and Lord; but also God, that so appeared and
spake vnto him. And so had part of that blessing,
which our Lord vpon this occasion announced to al

29 .

saying [Blessed are they that haue not seene, & haue
beleued .] In the third apparition to the Apostles,

H h 3   for so

Side notes (right margin):

Some of his
apparitions
were priuate to
few .
Some more
publique to
manie.

Some were
proper to the
College of the
Apostles .

Our Lord gaue
his Apostles
power to re-
mitte sinnes.

He remoued al
doubt and
scruple touch-
ing his Resur-
rection .

(for so S. Iohn calleth it, though they were not al *Io*.21.*v*.1.
prefent, but so manie, and such as represented their 4.7.10.

He constituted S. Peter the visible head of the whole militant Church.

College) our Sauiour constituted his Apostle Simon
Peter, his general Vicar in earth, with commandement and Commission [to feede both his Lambes, & *v*. 17.
his sheepe] which are al Christes flocke, Cleargie,
and Laitie. And withal signified vnto him [by what 18. 19.
death he should glorifie God]But would not reueale
the like touching S. Iohn; bidding them be content 22.

He gaue his Apostles comission to preach his Gospel in al the earth.

not to know it. In the fourth of those apparitions *Mat*. 28.
that seeme more proper to the Apostles, which was *v*. 17.
in Galilee; our Sauiour gaue to them al a most ample *Mar*. 16.
Commission, to preach in the whole earth, and [to *v*. 14.
teach al Nations, baptizing them and teaching them *Mat*. 28.
to obserue al thinges, whatsoeuer he had comman- *v*. 20.
ded them, with promise also to be perpetually with
them (by assistance of his Spirit) al dayes, euen to
the consummation of the world.] And either in the
same place, or rather when they were returned to Ie- *Luc*. 24.
rusalem, he gaue them a special commandement, to *v*. 49.
tarie together in that Citie, til they should be endu- *Act*. 1.
ed with power from high, saying [you shal receine *v*. 8.
vertue of the Holie Ghost coming vpon you, & you
shal be witnesses vnto me in Ierusalem, and in al Iurie, and Samaria, and euen to the vtmost of the earth]
These particular actions of our Blessed Sauiour, are
easily, and clearly gathered out of the sacred text.

Some Sacraments were instituted in those fourtie dayes.

5   By other sacred textes, it is also certeine, though
not so euident, that Christ likewise instituted other
Sacramentes, and made other ordinances, whiles
he was on earth, after his Resurrection, as is knowne,
and continually preached in his Church, warranted

And other ordinances made.

by diuers holie Scriptures, and namely by the places euen now recited, where S. Luke writeth, that
[for fourtie daies remaining in earth he appeared to *Act*.1.*v*.3.
his Apostles, & spake of the Kingdome of God] that
is of

Mat. 28.
v. 20.

is of thinges perteyning to the Church which is his Kingdome : wherof S. Mathew testifieth, that Christians [must be taught to obserue al thinges whatsoeuer Christ commanded to his Apostles to teach them] yet expresseth not what those thinges are. And where S. Iohn in the last conclusion of his Gospel, which was last written of al the new Testament, saith expresly [that al thinges are not written.] Diuers other places doe further testifie, the practise and vse of other Sacrmentes, which necessarily presuppose their institution by Christ : because none other euer had, nor anie Apostle, or anie their successors euer presumed, to haue auctoritie or power to institute anie Sacrament. Where els our Sauiour was, or whom els he admitted *to* his presece, albeit the holie Scriptures doe not expresse : yet not without cause it is supposed, that those holie soules whom he lightned in *Limbus*, remained with him, and so ascended with him into heauen. For that they were deliuered from Limbus, is proued by the apparitions testified by S. Mathew, that [their bodies also (for some time) rose out of their graues (which could not be without their soules) and after Christes Resurrection, came into the holie Citie, & appeared to manie.]

Joa. 21.
v. 25.
ultimo.

Mat. 27.
v. 52.
53.

None can institute anie Sacrament but Christ onlie.

Christ our Lord ascended into heauen : sitteth on the right hand of God.

ARTICLE. 27.

AN other great degree of our B. Sauiours exaltation, is his Ascension into heauen. A point of like necessitie to be proued against the Iewes, as his Resurrection. And therfore we wil first proue it by Auctoritie of the old Testamet, which they acknowlege to conteine both figures, and prophecies

Christs Ascension is proued by figures of the old Testament.

phecies of Meſſias . And for more conſolation of Chriſtians , declare the ſame by the New Teſtament alſo . Enochs tranſlation , and Elias aſſumption be - ing, as the Iewes Rabbins confeſſe, not only ſtrange and miraculous workes of God, but alſo Propheti- cal ſignes of ſome thinges to be done by Meſſias; doe moſt directly repreſent , our Sauiours admirable Aſ- cenſion into Heaueu : with conformable reſemblance of the figures or ſignes to the thing ſignified . For they being yet mortal , were remoued from the com- mon conuerſation of other mortal men , by the mi- niſterie of Angels : the one tranſported; the other taken vp in a fyrie chariot into the ayre : and muſt re- turne to preach, and giue teſtimonie of truth againſt Antichriſt, and finally by glorious Martyrdome , pay the debt of death . But Chriſt our Redemer hauing by his proper death payed abundant ranſome for al mankind, can not dye anie more, is now immortal, by his owne proper power , is aſcended aboue al the heauens, ſitteth on the right hand of God. So the thing prefigured, incomparably excelleth the fi- gure . Likewiſe Ioſue (otherwiſe Ieſus) both in name and office, ſauing the Iſraelites from their enemies, and bringing them out of the deſert through Iordane into the promiſed land : clearly prefigured Chriſt our Sauiour, who brought al the Sainctes of the old Te- ſtament out of Limbus , and continually bringeth Sainctes of the New Teſtament , from this vale of affliction, through Baptiſme, and other Sacramentes, into heauen the true land of promiſe, of eternal reſt and ioy; whither he firſt of al aſcending , opened the gate, and made way for others, which by Moy- ſes & his Law, could not be done.

Gen . 5 . v . 24.
4 . Reg . 2 . v . 11 :

Mal . 4 . v . 5 . Apoc . 11 . v . 3 .

Ioſ . 3 . v . 3 . 15 .

The ſame was foretold by the Prophets.

2 As the Royal Pſalmiſt ſaw in ſpirit, and prophe- cied by way of inuiting the glorious Angels to con- gratulate the aſſotiation of humane nature with An- g elical

*Pſ.*23. gelical [Lift vp your gates ye Princes (ſaith he)
v. 7. and be ye lifted vp, o eternal gates, and the King
of gloric ſhal enter in . Who is the King of glorie
(ſaid the holie Angels?) Our Lord ſtrong & mightie (ſaith the Prophet) our Lord mightie in battle .

8. Lift vp your gates ye Princes (ſaith he againe) and
be lifted vp o erernal gates : and the King of glorie
ſhal enter in . Yet the bleſſed Angels admiring de-

9. mand againe [who is this King of glorie ?] The prophet anſweareth [The Lord of powers (that is the
Lord of al powers aſwel Angelical as humane) he
is the King of glorie.] In humane nature aſſump-

*Pſ.*8. ted, Chriſt is [diminiſhed leſſe then Angels] In Di-
v. 5. uine nature, Creator and Lord of Angels. And not
only by Hypoſtatical vnion, but alſo by merit of his

*Pſ.*8.*v.* Paſſion, and ſtate of Kingdome [He is crowned with
6.7.8. glorie and honor; appointed ouer al creatures, al
Pſ. 46. thinges ſubiected vnder his feete. God (Chriſt God
*v.*6.7. and Man) is aſcended in Iubilation : and our Lord
8. in voice of Trumpet . Sing ye to our God, ſing ye;
ſing ye to our King, ſing ye. Becauſe God is King
of al the earth, ſing ye wiſly.] In an other pſalme,
the ſame Prophet directing his ſpeach to Chriſt him

Pſ. 67. ſelf ſaith [Thou art aſcended on high : thou haſt ta-
v. 19. ken captiuitie, thou haſt receiued giftes in men]
Fulfilled, when our Lord aſcending with triumph,
caried with him, thoſe which were captiues, vntil he
ſpoyling the enemie, ſet them free, and receiued them

Pſ. 2. with al other elect of mankind, as a gift of God, a
v. 8. reward of his victorie; making them then, and con-
*Epheſ.*2. tinually others [to ſitte with him in the celeſtials]
v. 6. and ſo [gaue giftes to men] as S. Paul interpreteth
Ch. 4. the ſame prophecie. In this alſo is fulfilled an other
v. 8. teſtimonie of Dauid ſaying [The Lord ſaid to my
*Pſ.*109. Lord; ſitte on my right hand] And the queſtion is
v. 1. hereby ſolued, which the phariſes could not anſwear.

I i   How

How Chriſt is both the Sonne and Lord of Dauid. *Mat. 22.*
[For (ſaith S. Peter) God hath made this Ieſus, *v . 43 .*
whō the Iewes haue crucified, both Lord, & Chriſt.] *Act . 2. v ,*
Now the Church beholdeth king [Salomon in the *35. 36.*
Diademe wherwith his mother hath crowned him, *Cant . 3,*
(or wherwith his bodie which he tooke of his mo- *v . 11 .*
ther, is crowned) in the day of his deſpouſing, and
in the day of the ioy of his hart .] To the ſame purpoſe, the Prophet Iſaias foretold, that whē our Lord,
after his bloudie conqueſt, ſhould riſe from dearh,
and aſcend in triumph ; the Angels with admiration
ſhould ſay [who is this that cometh from Edom with *Iſa . 63 ,*
dyed garmentes, from Boſra ? this bewtiful one in *v . 1 ,*
his Robe, going in the multitude of his ſtrength ?]
To which demand, our almightie Conquerour, anſweareth [I that ſpeake iuſtice, and am a defender
to ſaue] ſhewing that by very iuſtice, not by violent
inuaſion, but by rigorous ſatisfaction for al mennes
ſinnes, he had ouercome the enemie of mankind, recouered the pray, poſſeſſed his owne Kingdome, &
deſerued crowne . Of this alſo the Prophet Micheas ſpeaketh , who foretelling the progreſſe of the
Church, aſcribeth it to Chriſtes merites , by which *Mich . 2 ,*
he opened heauen gates : [For he ſhal aſcend (ſaith *v . 13 .*
this Prophet) opening the way before them : they
ſhal deuide, and paſſe through the gate, and ſhal enter by it, and their King ſhal paſſe before them : and
our Lord in the head of them .]

Our Sauiour did foreſhew that he would aſcend .

3 Moſt agreable to theſe and other Prophets, our
Lord him ſelf foretold, that not only after his Paſſion he would riſe from death, but alſo that he would
aſcend into heauen . [To Nicodemus he ſaid, that
no man hath aſcended into heauen (a plaine text, that *Io . 3 . v . 13 ,*
before Chriſt, no man had aſcended into heaeuen)
but he that deſcended from heauen, the Sonne of man
(by takiing humane nature; for then his only ſoule
entred

entred into heauen, being alwaies glorious, & therfore he addeth) which is in heauen.] But concerning his Bodie being then mortal, he said to his A-
postles the very night before his death [I goe to prepare you a place. And if I goe and prepare you a
place; I come againe, and wil take you to my self,
that where I am, you also may be. I told you not
these thinges from the beginning, hecause I was with
you. And now I goe to him that sent me. I tel you
the truth, it is expedient for you that I goe : for if I
goe not, the Paraclete shal not come to you; but if
I goe, I wil send him to you.] Againe, after his
Resurrection, he said to Marie Magdalen [Goe to my
brethren, and say vnto them, I ascend to my Father,
and your Father; my God, and your God.] And in
the fourtith day, from his Resurrection, when in
sundrie Apparitions, conuersing with his Apostles, &
others, he had disposed whatsoeuer was requisite for
the time : lastly, [lifting vp his handes, he blessed thē.
And whiles he blessed them, he departed from them,
and a cloude receiued him out of their sight.] Thus
were they made eye witnesses, of our Sauiours admirable Ascension into the cloudes : but with eyes of
faith, they saw him also [mounted vpon the Heauen
of heauens.] And so [adoring, went back into Ierusalem with great ioy.]

4 For albeit his visible presence is taken from the
faithful, yet the merit of faith is hereby the greater
[beleuing and not seing] And for so much as humane flesh is in him alreadie ascended into heauen,
Christian hope of others ascending, at the general
Resurrection, is so strengthned, as the Apostle doub-
ed not to say ; that [God hath made vs to sitte with
him in the cælestials.] Charitie Likewise is hereby
inkindled in Christian hartes [to loue, and to seeke
the thinges that are aboue, where Christ is sitting

*Io.*14.
*v.*2. 3.

Io. 16.
v. 5. 7.
10.

*Io.*20.
v. 17.

*Luc.*24.
*v.*50.
51.
*Act.*1.
*v.*9.
*Mar.*16.
v. 19.
Ps. 67.
v. 34.
Luc. 24.
v. 52.
*Io.*20.
v. 29.

*Ephes.*2.
v. 6.
*Colos.*3.
v. 1. 2.

Declareth rea-
sons why it was
expedient.

Merite of faith
is greater by
Chrifts Ascen-
fion.

Hope is also in-
creafed.

And Charitie
more inflamed.

I i 2   on the

on the right hand of God : to minde and affect the
thinges that are aboue, not the thinges that are on
the earth.] In regard therfore of such spiritual benefites receiued by Chrifts Afcenfió, the Apoftles were
replenished with great ioy, & moft diligently taught
how neceffarie and profitable it was for mans eternal aduancement; & fo ordained of God, that Chrift
hauing payed mans ranfome, and being rifen from
death fhould not remaine vifibly in earth, but that
[heauen (faith S. Peter) muft receiue him, vntil the
times of the reftitutió of al thinges, which God fpake
by the mouth of his holie Prophets fró the beginning
of the world] And that this is for our behoofe he confirmeth in his Epiftle [Iefus Chrift (faith he) is on
the right hand of God, fwallowing death, that we
might be made heires of life euerlafting, being gone
into heauen: Angels, and Potentates, and Powers
fubiected to him.] S. Paul in like maner exhorting
the Romane Chriftians, to confidence of Chrifts affiftance in perfecution, for the faith proueth the affurance of helpe, and protection [againft al accufers,
al condemners, al perfecuters, becaufe the fame Chrift
Iefus, is the defender of his elect; that dyed, yea
that is rifen alfo againe; who is on the right hand
of God, who alfo maketh interceffion for vs.] Inftructing alfo the Ephefians touching Goddes goodnes, and power, to bring them into the excellent
inheritance of heauen propofeth to them an example
of his mightie power, in the fupereminent exalting
of our Sauiour Chrift [which he wrought, in raifing
him vp from death, and fetting him on the right hand
in celeftials, aboue al Principalitie, and Poteftate, &
Power, and Dominetion, and euerie name that is named, not only in this world, but alfo in that to come.]
Which his Exaltation aboue al creatures, being moft
due for his merites, was alfo conuenient for other

Act. 3.
v. 21.

1.*Pet.* 3.
v. 22.

Rom. 8: *v.*
33. 34.

Chrift as man
is the principal
Interceffor for
men.

Ephef. 1.
v. 20. 21.

mennes

mēnes faluation, as the fame Apoftle teacheth the Hebrewes, [for it was femely (faith he) that we fhould haue fuch a high Preift, holie, innocent, impolluted, feperated from finners, and made higher then the heauens.]

Heb. 7.
v. 26.

*Chrift our Lord wil come in Maieftie, and iudge
the world.*

ARTICLE. 28.

OF Chrift our Lord his former coming into this world, in al humiltie, to Redeme mankind: we haue according to our imbecilitie, fo declared the Chriftian doctrine, as we truft may fuffice and fatisfie the wel difpofed that require proofe, or confirmation therof, by holie Scriptures alone. Now we are in like maner to fpeake of his fecond coming, which wil be in great Maieftie, to iudge the world, rendering to euerie one according to their wel or euil deferuing, reward, or punifhment euerlafting. For although it be alfo certaine by our Catholique faith, that euerie foule parting from the bodie, immediatly receiueth an immutable fentence of eternal faluation, or damnation; yet muft there be a general iudgement of al together, agreable to the former particulars: that al may clearly fee, the iuftice therof, the fecrets of hartes being then to be reueled: & prefently withal, fhal the fame fentences be put in execution, afwel in the bodies, as in the foules; which vntil the day of general Refurrection, are not felt in the dead bodies, but in the foules only.

Eccle. 11.
v. 3.
Mat. 10.
v. 26.

As our Sauiour came firft in humilitie: fo he wil come in Maieftie.

2   Of both which diuine Tribunals, holie Scriptures afford abnudāt proofes, partly by examples of Goddes procedinges both towardes the godlie, and the wicked the

The particular Iudgement is proued by manie holie Scriptures.

ked; the penitent and impenitent; and moſt clearly by expreſſe Prophecies and teſtimonies, that Chriſt
our Redemer, is the appointed Iudge of the whole
world, Angels and men. The firſt example of man-
kind(which moſt properly perteineth to vs) was in *Gen.* 4.
Abel, the firſt man that dyed, whoſe cauſe God iu- *v.* 9. 10.
ſtifying, after his death, ſhewed his ſtate to be happie and bleſſed. And ſo he is the firſt in the Catalogue *Heb.* 11.
of Sainctes recited by S. Paul. And contrariwiſe, *v.* 4.
Caine for murdering of him, was curſed vpon earth.
An other example of particular iudgement, is pro- *Gen* 4.
poſed in holie Enoch yet liuing in bodie, who after *v.* 11.
three hundred ſixtie fiue yeares, was taken by God, *Gen.* 5.
to ſome place of reſt and ioy, from the troubles of *v.* 24.
this world. The cauſe of which particular priuilege,
(beſides Goddes prouidence, reſeruing him for the
Churches ſeruice in time of Antichriſt) S. Paul ſignifieth ſaying [for before his tranſlation, he had te- *Heb.* 11.
ſtimonie that he had pleaſed God.] Somtimes alſo *v.* 5.
God exerciſeth iudgement vpon ſinners by death.
As when [he cleane deſtroyed al liuing ſubſtance *Gen.* 7. *v*
that was vpon the earth, from man, euen to beaſt, 22. 29.
but only Noe, and thoſe that were with him in the
Arke.] And when [he rained vpon Sodome and Go- *Gen.* 19. *v.*
morha brimſtone and fyre; deliuering iuſt Lot from 23. 24.
that deſtruction.] So likrwiſe [Pharao, and his ar- *Exo.* 14. *v.*
mie, were ſo ouerwhelmed in the red ſea, that not 28. 29.
ſo much as one of them remained] but the children
of Iſrael marched through the middeſt of the drie ſea,
& the waters were vnto them, as in ſteade of a wal,
on the right hand, and on the left. Holie Iob teſti- *Iob.* 27.
fieth, the iuſt iudgement of the wicked ſaying [the *v.* 21.
burning wind ſhal take him vp, and carie him away,
and a whirle winde ſhal put him violently, out of
his place.] Breifly that God geueth particular ſentence at the death of euerie one, is cleare in the examples

Luc. 16.
v. 22.
Mat. 17.
v. 12.

amples of [poore *Lazarus* and the rich glutton] of S. [Iohn Baptift] the precurfor of our Sauiour and [of Iudas the traitor] and of manie others whofe faluation or damnation is expreffed in the holie Scriptures.

Act. 1.
v. 18.
Nu. 16.
v. 32.
Heb. 11. *

3 And that neuertheleffe there fhal be a general Iudgement of al, is likewife teftified in manie places : & withal that Chrift our Sauiour is the Iudge. So the Royal Prophet, in the fecond Pfalme, defcribing Chriftes kingdome, concludeth with their happines, that fhal be found his true feruantes, in that day of

The general Iudgement is often prophecied in the Pfalmes.

Pf. 2.
v. 13.
Pf. 49.
v. 3. 4.
6.

wrath faying [When his wrath fhal burne in fhort time; bleffed are al that truft in him] More clearly in diuers other pfalmes [God wil come (faith he) manifeftly, our God, and he wil not kepe filence. Fyre fhal burne forth in his fight; and round about him a mightie tempeft. He fhal cal the heauen from aboue, and the earth to difcerne his people. And the Heauens fhal fhew forth his iuftice, becaufe God is iudge. Behold he wil geue to his voice, the

Pf. 67.
v. 35.

voice of ftrength; geue you glorie to God vpon Ifrael; his magnificence & his power in the cloudes.] Chrift him felf by the penne of the fame Prophet,

Pf. 74.
v. 3. 4.

faith [When I fhal take time, I wil indge iuftices. The earth is melted, and al that dwel in it. I haue confirmed the pillers therof.] Againe the Prophet

Pf. 75.
v. 8. 9.
10.

faith to Chrift [Thou art terrible, and who fhal refift thee? From that time thy wrath. From heauen thou haft made thy iudgement heard. The earth trembled, and was quiet (filent for feare) when God arofe vnto Iudgemét, that he might faue al the meke of the earth.] And becaufe our Sauiour practifeth mercie, efpecially in this life, and in the day of Iudgement, wil doe ftrict iuftice : the pfalmift calleth him

Pf. 93.
v. 1.

God of reuenge faying [Our Lord God of reuenges, the God of reuenges, hath done freely (not
fearing

fearing, nor respecting anie person) wil iudge freely and iustly. As therfore the wicked feare iudgement, so the iust (when their conscience is cleare) desire it. Wherupon the holie Prophet prayeth in iust zeale, saying: [Be exalted thou which iudgest *v.* 2 .3. the earth; render retribution to the proud. How long shal sinners o Lord; how long shal sinners glorie? Let the heauens be glad, and the earth re- *Psf.* 95. *v.* ioyce, the sea be moued, and the fulnes therof. the 11.12.13. fieldes shal be glad, and al thinges that are in them. then shal the trees of the woodes reioyce before the face of our Lord, becaufe he cometh: becaufe he cometh to iudge the earth. He wil iudge the round *Psf.* 96. *v.* world in equitie: and peoples in his truth. Cloud & 2.3.4. mist round about him; iustice and iudgment the cor- 5.6. rection of his feate. Fyre shal goe before him, and shal enflame his enemies round about. His lightnes shined, (that is shal most assuredly shine) to the round world: the earth faw, and was moued. the mountaines melted as waxe, before the face of our Lord: before the face of our Lord al the earth, the heauens haue shewed forth his iustice, and al peoples haue sene his glorie.] So certainly shal al these thinges come to passe that the Prophet speaketh as if they were past alreadie [The riuers (such as haue wattered *Psf.* 97. *v.* true faith with good workes) shal clappe with hand: 8. 9. the mountaines (those that seeke heauenly thinges not earthly) together shal reioyce at the sight of our Lord, becaufe he cometh to iudge the earth: He wil iudge the round earth in iustice, and the peoples in *Psf.* 128. equitie. Our iust Lord wil cutte the neckes of sin- *v.* 4. ners] al that to the end persist in sinne.

The same great day is forefhewed by other Prophets.
4 Other Prophets also forewarne vs of the same great day, most terrible to the wicked, and most ioyful to the blessed [Behold (faith Isaias) the day of *Isa.* 13. our Lord shal come cruel and ful of indignation, & *v.* 9.
of wrath

of wrath, and furie, to bring the land to a wildernes,
and to deſtroy the ſinner therof, out of it] which pro
phecie was verified, in the deſtruction of Babilon,
as in the figure; but more exactly ſhal be fulfilled in
al the wicked at the day of Iudgement, as is more
cleare by the wordes folowing, fore-ſhewing the

v. 10. ſignes that ſhal come before the laſt day [Becauſe
(ſaith he) the ſtarres of heauen and their brightnes,
ſhal not diſplay their light; the ſunne is darkned in
his ryſing, and the moone ſhal not ſhine in her light.

11. And I wil viſit ouer the euils of the world (ſaith our
Lord by his Prophet) and againſt the impious their
iniquitie: and I wil make the pride of infidels to ceaſe
and wil humble the arogancie of the ſtrong.] Al
which was fulfilled in Babilon, in ſmal part, in compariſon of that which ſhal be perfectly performed in
the whole world, when Chriſt ſhal iudge al. In like
maner the ſame Prophet ſpeaketh againe, both of
the ruine of Babilon, and of the end of this tranſi-

Iſ. 30. torie and ſinful world. [Behold (ſaith he) the name
v. 37. of our Lord cometh from farre, his burning furie, and
Ch. 34. heauie to beare: his lippes are filled with indigna-
v. 1.4. tion, and his tongue is a deuouring fyre. Come nere
Ch. 66. ye Gentiles and heare, and ye peoples attend; let the
v. 14. earth heare, and the fulnes therof; the round world
and euerie ſpring therof. The heauens ſhal be ſoli-
ded together as a booke, and al their hoaſt ſhal fal
away, as the leafe falleth from the vine, and from the
figge tree.] In his laſt Chapter in plainer termes,
he ſaith [The hand of our Lord ſhal be knowne to
his ſeruantes, and he ſhal be wrath with his ene-

15. mies. Becauſe loe our Lord wil come in fyre, & his
Chariots as a whirle wind; to render his furie in in-

16. dignation, and his rebuking in flame of fyre. Becauſe
our Lord ſhal iudge in fyre, and in his ſword to al
fleſh; and the flame of our Lord ſhal be multiplied.

K k   I come

I come that I may gather together (their workes, & *v.8.*
their cogitations) with al Natiós, & tongues & they
shal come, & shal see my glorie.] Ieremie also pro- *Iere.50.v.*
phecied the vtter destruction of Babilon, mistically *15.16.&c.*
signifying the like miserable end, yea farre greater
miserie of the citie of the diuel, which is the vniuersal congregatió of the wicked, opposite to the Citie
of God ; concluding in the very same maner concerning Babilon, as S. Iohn concludeth concerning the
vniuersal companie of the reprobate, saying to the Le- *Ch.51.v.*
uite that should read his Prophecie to the people *63.64.*
[When thou shalt haue finished reading this book
(saith he) thou shalt tye a stone to it, & shal throw
it into the midest of Euphrates : and thou shalt say
So shal Babilon be drowned, and she shal not rise vp
from the face of the affliction, that I wil bring vpon
her; and she shal be dissolued.] Thus the Prophet.
And the like wordes S. Iohn writeth of an Angel
[Fallen, fallen is the great Babilon (so he calleth the *Apoc.14.*
diuels citie) which of the wine of the wrath of her *v.8.*
fornication, made al Nations to drinke.] The like
fact also, that [a stronge Angel, tooke vp as it were *Apoc.18.*
a great milstone, and threw it into the sea saying : *v.21.*
with this violence, shal Babilon the great citie be
throwne, and shal now be found nomore.] The Pro- *Ioel.2.v.*
phet Ioel foretelleth certaine terrible singes, which *30.31.*
God wil send before the day of Iudgement saying
[I wil geue wonders in heauen, and in earth ; bloud,
and fyre, and vapour of smoke. The Sunne shal be
turned into darknes, and the Moone into bloud, before the great & horrible day of the Lord doth come.]
Againe of the Iudgment it self, and of the place,
God almightie saith [I wil gather together al Na- *Ioel.3.*
tions, and wil leade them into the valley of Iosaphat, *v.2.*
and I wil plead with them there, vpon my people,
and vpon mine inheritance Israel, whom they haue
dispersed

**The concor-
dance of Iere-
mie, and S.
Iohn, Prophe-
cying by word,
& by fact, the
destruction of
the wicked.**

diſperſed in the Nations, and haue deuided my land]
by making ſchiſmes in his Church. Habacuc foreſeing the cruel perſecution of the faithful by Antichriſt
as one that reſolueth to ſuffer al afflictions with patience, to gaine euerlaſting peace in the day of Iudgement, ſaith [I heard, and my bellie was troubled;
at the voice, my lippes trembled] to which natural
infirmities, al men are ſubiect; but by ſpiritual fortitude, euerie one muſt ſay with the Prophet as foloweth [Let rottennes enter in my bones, and ſwarme
vnder me; that I may reſt in the day of tribulation,
that I may aſcend to our girded people] He calleth
that laſt day, the day of tribulation, becauſe none o-
ther is comparable to it; and the elect Sainctes, he
calleth the girded people, becauſe they feight man-
fullie in [this life, which is a warfare vpon earth.]
Sophonias prophecying the deſtruction of Ieruſalem,
hath theſe wordes more perfectly to be fulfilled in
the whole troupe of the wicked, then they were in
the deſolation of that one Citie [their ſiluer (ſaith
he) and their gold, ſhal not be able to deliuer them
in the day of the wrath of our Lord; in the fyre of
his ieloulie, ſhal al the earth be deuoured, becauſe
he wil make conſummation with ſpeede to al that
inhabite the earth.] In like ſort prophecyeth Zacharias of the deſtruction of Ieruſalem, and ioyntly, &
that more eſpecially, of the final ruine of al the wicked ſaying : [Our Lord my God ſhal come, and al
the Sainctes with him. And it ſhal be in that day,
there ſhal be no light, but cold and froſt. And there
ſhal be one day which is knowne to our Lord, not
day nor night; and in the time of the euening, there
ſhal be light] ſignifying, that after that day, there
be no more dayes and nightes, but petpetual night
to the damned, and perpetual day to the bleſſed.
Moſt planly ſaith Malachias [Behould the day ſhal

Hab. 3.
v. 16.

Ibidem.

Iob. 7.
v. 1.

Soph. 1.
v. 18.

Zach. 14.
v. 5. 6.
7.

Mal. 4.
v. 1.

come

come kinled as a furnace, and al the proud, & al that doe impietie, shal be stuble, and the day coming shal inflame them, saith the Lord of hosts, which shal not leaue them roote, and spring.] For during this life there stil remaineth the roote of Goddes grace, wherby sinners may repent, if they wil, and bring forth fruicte worthie of penance. but after death the doare of grace; and consequently of repentance is shutte for euer.

During this life al sinners may repent, but they that dye in mortal sinne are eternally impenitent.

5 In the new Testamēt we are ofté & more clearly forwarned to expect & be readie for Christ our Redemer his coming to iudge : not only at the death of euerie one, but also at the end of this world in his general Iudgement. Our Sauiour him self presupposing that the Iewes knew, or ought to know, this necessarie point of beleife, told such as beleued not in him at his first coming, how hard it wil be with them, when he shal come to iudge, saying : [to the cities of Corozaim, Bethsaida, and Capharnaum] that [it shal be more tollerable to Tyre and Sidon, and to the land of Sodom, in the day of Iudgement, then for you.] That also [the men of Niniuie, and the Queene of Saba, shal condemne the Iewes] that liued in his time. Contrariwise, to those that contemning the world, folow him, he said : that [you which haue folowed me in the regeneration when the Sonne of man shal sitte in the seate of his Maiestie; you also shal sitte vpon twelue seates, iudgeing the twelue Tribes of Israel.] Discoursing also with the quareling Iewes, he auoucheth his auctoritie of the vniuersal Iudge, saying [the Father hath geuen al iudgement to the Sonne, that al may honour the Sonne, as they doe honour the Father. And he hath geuen him power to doe iudgement, because he is the Sonne of man.] An other time his Disciples demanding, what signes shal be of his coming to iudge, and of the consummation

Our Lord hath foretold that the Iudgement wil be strict & terrible.

He told to his Apostles fiue signes, which

Heb.6. v.2.

Mat.11. v.22.24.

Mat.12. v.41.42.

Mat.19. v.28.

Io.5.v. 22.23. 27.

mation

mation of the world, he told them these fiue . First shal come before the day of Iudgement. that [manie false prophets (or preachers) shal come, and shal seduce manie] and procure warres & persecution against the faithful [but the end is not yet .] 1.

Secondly, that notwithstanding persecution [his Gospel shal be preached in the whole world, for a testimonie to al Nations : & then shal come the consummation] yet not immediatly, but shortly after . Thirdly (not long before the end of the world) there shal be great decay of faith and Religion , and publique practise of abominable heresies, which our Sauiour calleth [*Abomination of desolation* .] S . Paul calleth it [*Apostacie,* or *Reuolt*] to be made by Antichrist, and extreme persecution, greater then euer before or after .] Fourthly [for the elect, the daies of this greatest 4. persecution shal be shortned] Antichrist being sodenly destroyed, when he shal haue reigned fourtie two monethes, that is, three yeares and a half . Fifthly that [after the tribulation of those daies , the 5. Sunne shal be darkned, the Moone shal not geue her light ; the Starres shal fal from heauen, and the powers of heauen shal be moued .] Besides these, S . Two other signes. Iohn hath prophecied a Sixt signe, that [two witnesses (which by conference of other holie Scriptures, are proued to be Enoch and Elias) shal come in the time of Antichrist ; and shal prophecie, a thousand, two hundred, sixtie daies (which is almost three yeares, and a half) cloathed with sack-cloath ; shal be slaine by the beast] Antichrist [and after three daies and a half, they shal rise from death, and ascend into heauen .] Manie holie Scriptures testifie 7. also, an other signe to come neare to the end of the world ; that the whole Nation of [the Iewes , shal be conuerted to Christ .] Shortly after these signes, shal come the last day , very sodenly, when men doe not think of it .

Margin references:
Mat. 24. u . 3 . 4 .
6.
14.
15.
2. Thes. 2 . v . 3 .
Mat. 24 . v . 21 .
22.
Apoc . 13 . v . 5 .
Mat. 24 . v . 29 .
Apoc . 11 . v . 3 .
7.
11 . 12 .
Deut . 4 . v . 30 .
Is . 50 . v . 20 .
Ezech . 16 . v . 15 .

K k 3   Our

6   Our Sauiour alſo deſcribeth in general, the forme of the Iudgement . that [the ſigne of the Sonne of Man (doubtles the Glorious Croſſe) ſhal appeare in the cloudes before him, coming in much power, & Maieſtie] the Angels inſtantly bringing al men in their reuiued bodies, and ſetting the bleſſed on his right hand, and the wicked on his left hand ; he wil ſay to al on his right hand : Come ye bleſſed of my Father, poſſeſſe you the kingdome prepared for you from the fundation of the world] reciting the rea- ſo of his ſentence to be the performing of the workes of mercie and to them at the left hand, he wil ſay, [get ye away from me ye curſed into fyre euerlaſting, which was prepared for the diuel and his Angels] becauſe ye haue not done workes of mercie [& theſe ſhal goe into puniſhment euerlaſting ; and the iuſt, into life euerlaſting .] Againe our Lord in the laſt night of his Paſſion, ſaid to Caiphas and other per- ſecuters [Hereafter ye ſhal ſee the Sonne of man, ſit- ting on the right hand of the power of God, & co- ming in the cloudes of heauen .]

Am . 4 . *v* . 12 . *Mich* . 4 . *v* . 6 . *Mal* . 4 . *v* . 6. *Rom* . 11. *v* . 26. *Mat* . 42. *v* . 30. 31 . *Mat* . 25 . *v* . 33 . 34 . 35 . 41 . 46 . *Mat* . 26 . *v* . 64 .

7   Immediatly as our Lord was aſcended into hea- uen; two Angels appearing in white garmentes, te- ſtified to the beholders, that [he ſhal ſo come, as they haue ſeene him going into heauen .] S . Paul preaching to the Athenians, declared, that [God de- noūceth vnto men, that al euerie where, ought to doe penance ; for that he hath appointed a day, wherin he wil iudge the world in equitie, by a man whom he hath appointed] plainly teaching, that our Sauiour Chriſt as man, is conſtituted Iudge of al ; quick, & dead ; good, and euil . [For whether we liue (ſaith S . Paul) we liue to our Lord ; or whether we dye, we dye to our Lord : therfore whether we liue or dye, we are our Lordes . For to this end, Chriſt died and roſe againe, that he may haue dominion, both

Act . 1 . *v* . 11 . *Act* . 17 . *v* . 30. 31 . 2 . *Tim.* 4 . *v* · 1 . *Rom* . 14 . *v* . 8. 9 . 10 . 12 .

of the

1 . *Thef.* of the dead, and of the liuing . For we fhal al ftand
4 . *v* . 16. before the Iudgement feat of Chrift :] Therfore e-
1 . *Thef.* uerie one of vs, for him felf, fhal render account to
5 . *v* . 2. God . For our Lord him felf, in commandement, &
3 . in the voice of an Archangel. and in the Trumpet of
2 . *Thef.* God, wil defcend from heauen . The day of our Lord
1 . *v* . 10. fhal come, as a theefe in the night. For when they
fhal fay, peace and fecuritie , then fhal fudaine deftruction come vpon them, as the paines to her that
is with child, and they fhal not efcape : when he fhal
come to be glorified in his Sainctes, and to be made
meruelous in al them that haue beleued .]

8   S . Peter alfo forefeing in fpirit of prophecie, that
certaine heritikes, in the latter daies wil denie the Refurrectió, & general indgemét ; warneth al to be mindful, what the Prophets, Chrift him felf, & his Apoftles
2 . *Pet.* haue taught [knowing this firft (faith he) that in
3 . *v* . 2. the laft daies fhal come mockers in deceipt , wal-
3 . king according to their owne concupifcenfes faying :
Where is his promife , or his coming ? For fince the
time that the Fathers flept, al thinges doe fo perfeuer
from the beginning of creature] To which vaine Argument the Apoftle anfweareth, charging them with
v .6. wilful ignorance : fhewing that [as the world was
7 . once ouerflowed with water ; fo it fhal be deftroied
8 . by fyre] at the day of Iudgement [that with our Lord
a thoufand yeares, are as one day . our Lord flac-
9 . keth not his promife, as fome doe efteme it , but
doth patiently, not willing that anie perifh, but that
10 . al returne to penance . And the day of our Lord fhal
come as a theefe , in the which, the heauens fhal
paffe with gerat violence : but the Elementes fhal
be refolued with heate ; and the earth, and the workes which are in it, fhal be burned .] Likewife
S , Iohn exhorteth to abide in the doctrine, which
is alreadie deliuered, and receiued ; and not to harken to

There wil
come Here-
tikes that wil
denie the Re-
furrection and
Iudgement .

ken to new maisters [Now litle children (faith he)
abide in Chrift, that when he fhal appeare, you may
haue confidence & not be confounded of him in his
coming .]

1. Io .3.
v . 28.

Diuels fhal al-
fo be iudged .

9 S . Iude teacheth alfo exprefly , that Angels are
fubiect to this general Iudgement; & that fuch as did
reuolt from God, fhal then haue a further fentence
befides that is geuen- alreadie faying [The Angels
which kept not their principalitie, but forfooke their
owne habitation , he hath referued vnder darknes in
eternal bondes, vnto the Iudgement of the great
day .]

Mat. 8 .v.
29 . 1.*Cor*.
6. v. 3.
Iud. v. 6.

Chrifts exalta-
tion fhal be
complete al
the day of
Iudgement .

10 That day fhal our B. Sauiours exaltation, be
fully complete . Then wil he alfo make complete, the
glorie of al his Sainctes , making them a kingdome
euerlafting . [Behold he cometh (faith S . Iohn)
with the cloudes, and euerie eye fhal fee him, & they
that pricked him (crucifying him)& al the tribes of the
earth (that are his enemies) fhal bewaile them felues
vpon him . The kinges of the earth, and Princes, &
Tribunes, and the rich, and the ftrong, hidde them
felues (in vaine fo endeuoring) becaufe the great
day of their wrath is come . And fo fhal it be pro-
clamed by Angelical [Trumpet, and loude voices,
that (not only the Empereal heaue but alfo) the king-
dome (of this world) is made our Lordes, and his
Chriftes , and he fhal reigne for euer , and euer.
Amen .

Apoc . 1 .
v . 7.

Apoc . 6 .
v . 15 . 17.

Apoc . 11 .
v . 15 .

God the Holie Ghoft (with the Father & the Sonne)
infpireth & fanctifieth the Church, & al true mem-
bers thereof.

ARTICLE. 29.

The fignificati-
on of the word
Holie Ghoft.

S O much more neceffarie it is to declare this Ar-
ticle, of our beleefe in the Holie Ghoft : becaufe
manie

manie hauing in some competent sort, learned the former Misteries, concerning the creation of the world, & Redemptió of man; yet haue so smal knowlege of this, which more particularly perteyneth to sanctification; that if they be demanded, as certaine

Act. 19.
v. 2.

Ephesians were, by S. Paul [whether they haue receiued the Holie Ghost] perhaps they wil answear as those did [Nay; neither haue we heard, whether there be a Holie Ghost] wheras al Christians, are bound to know, that the Holie Ghost, is the third Person of the B. Trinitie. From whom, equal with the Father & the Sonne, the Church, and the members rherof, receiue al godlie inspirations sanctifications, and other spiritual giftes. For albeit the name Holie Ghost, or Holie Spirit, generallie taken, may signify glorious Angels, or blessed soules, for they are holie spirits: yet being expressed without limitation of Angel or man, when it is absolutly said,

Ioan. 4.
v. 24.

[the Holie Ghost] or [the Holie Spirit] it properly and only signifieth the most eminent holie Spirit, God the Creator of al other spirits. And so it is common to al three persons of the B. Trinitie. But for distinction of the same diuine Persons, this name *Holie Ghost*, in a strict sense, is appropriated to the third Person only; which proceding from rhe Father, and from the Sonne; is personally and really distinct from them both, being al in nature one God, in persons three, al equal, coeternal, and consubstantial, as is before declared in the Article of the

Art 7.
parag. 8.

B. Trinitie. Wherfore hauing considered the former workes of God, which (as likewise al others done in his creatures) being common to the whole B. Trinitie, are by vse of holie Scriptures, appropriated to the Father, and to the Sonne: now we are in like maner (by his grace of whom we speake) to shew other diuine workes appropriated to the Ho-

It is appropriated to the third Person of the B. Trinitie.

L l
lie Ghost

lie Ghoſt. How through his gracious inſpirations, Goddes ſeruantes haue euer bene, and ſhal be illuminated in knowlege of truth, and ſanctified with holines of life.

Al knowlege
natural and ſu-
pernatural, is
Gods gift.

2   Of innumerable examples, a few may ſuffice, aſwel concerning knowlege of natural thinges, as of ſupernatural. Adam not only in the ſtate of innocé, cie, knew the natures of beaſtes [geuing them names agreable therto] and that the firſt [woman was taken out of man] but alſo after his fal by new inſpiration he [called the ſame woman Eua] miſtically ſignifying, that a woman (the B. Virgin Mother of God) ſhonld be the Mother of al the liuing. For ſhe is the ſingular woman [that hath bruſed the ſerpentes head] not Eue, who was the mother of al that dye, and a ſpecial occaſion of death. [Enos (by like inſtinct of the Holie Ghoſt) inuocated the name of cur Lord.] Abraham knew that the Egiptiaus would take his wife, and by what meanes, both his owne life, and her chaſtitie, ſhould be preſerued. His ſeruant Eliezer foreſaw what the maide would anſwear that ſhould be wiſe to Iſaac. Rebecca the ſame woman, directed her ſonne Iacob how to obteine his Fathers bleſſing, and inheritance. Ioſeph had ſignificant dreames; and interpreted the dreames of the two Eunuches, and of Pharao. Iacob prophecied of al his ſonnes. Iob was learned and holie. Moyſes writ the Hiſtorie of thinges paſt, aboue two thouſande yeares before he was borne. It ſhal not neede to ſpeake of his ſingular knowlege of greateſt Miſteries, compriſing manie in two Canticles. Al theſe & manie moe receiued both knowlege and ſanctitie of the Holie Ghoſt, not by natural witte, nor by only humane induſtrie. But as the Royal Pſalmiſt ſingeth [The voice of our Lord] God the Sonne, being the word of God the Father [the voice of our Lord] proceding

Gen. 2. v.
20 . 23 .
Gen. 3.
v . 20.

Gen . 4.
v . 26.

Gen . 12.
v . 12. 13 .
Gen . 24.
v . 14. 18.
Gen . 27 .
v . 8 .
Ch . 39.
v . 8 .
Ch . 4. v. 8.
Ch . 41.
v . 16.
Ch . 49 . *
Exo . 15 .
Deut . 32 .

Pſ . 28 . v .
3 . 4. 5 .

proceding from them both, which is the Holie Ghost
[vpon waters] the God of Maiestie hath thundred;
v.7. 8 . our Lord vpon manie waters : the voice of our Lord
in power, in magnificence, breaking Ceders ; the
voice of our Lord deuiding flame of fyre, shaking
9 . the desert preparing hartes (swift dear) In his Temple al shal say glorie .] Againe the same Psalmist
acknowleging that he receiued the spirit of Prophecie by the inspiration of the Holie Ghost, saith
Ps.44. [My hart hath vttered a good word : my tongne is
v.2. the penne of a Scribe that writeth swiftly.]
3 Concerning also sanctification, the samt Prophet describeth the Church, being euriched with the
Ps.67. giftes of the Holie Ghost ; to be as [a fatte moun-
v.16.17. taine . a mountaine crudded as cheese] vnited in
her godlie members [wherin it hath pleased God to
dwel euen to the end .] For which meruelous workes of the Holie Ghost, making men new in spirit,
Ps. 97 . al are inuited to [sing to our Lord a new song ; be-
v.1.*&c*. cause he hath done meruelous thinges .] Confor-
Sap.1. mablie hereto saith the wise man [The Spirit of our
v. 7. Lord hath replenished the whole world : and that
which conteyneth al thinges, haith the knowlege of
voice .] Of the voice of the Holie Ghost, speaking
of the Church, the Prophets make frequent mentio.
Is.6. [Manie peoples (saith Isaias) shal goe and shal say,
v.8 . Come, and let vs goe vp to the mountaine of our Lord
and to the house of the God of Iacob : and he wil
teach vs his wayes, and we shal walke in his pathes.
Act.28. I heard the voice of our Lord (the Holie Ghost saith
v.25. S. Paul) saying, whom shal I send ; and who shal
Is. 34. goe for vs ? Search ye diligently in the booke of our
v. 16. Lord, and read : because that which procedeth out
of my mouth, he hath commanded, and his Spirit ;
the same hath gathered them. Come ye to me and
Is.48.*v*. heare this : I haue not spoken in secret from the be-
16. 17. ginning

Iustification &
sanctification,
are greater
giftes of God:
and are appro-
priated to the
Holie Ghost.

L l 2

ginning, from the time before it was done. I was there, and now the Lord God hath sent me. & his Spirit. I the Lord thy God, that teach thee profitable thinges, that gouerne thee in the way that thou walkest.] It would be endles to recite al that perteine to this purpose in the Prophets : and is nedeles in so certaine a doctrine. Let the wordes of Ioel serue for the rest speaking of the coming of the Holie Ghost to the Apostles : [It shal be after this, I wil poure out my Spirit vpó al flesh : & your sónes & your daugh ters shal prophecie, your Ancients shal dreame dreames, and your yong men shal see visions : yea and vpon my seruants, and handmaides, I wil poure out my Spirit.] The same did Amos Prophecie in fewer wordes, the Holie Ghost saying by him [I raised vp of your sonnes to be Prophets, and of your yong men Nazarites. Is it not so, o children of Israel saith our Lord. Signifying, that as in the old Testament there were Prophets that taught the truth, and Nazarites that professed a special state of life, absteyning from wine, and al delicious drinkes : so in the New Testament, there should be both true Pastors to teach al truth, and votarie religious persons, which embrace, and obserue Euangelical counsels, by inspiration and operation of the Holie Ghost.

Ioel. 2. *v*. 28. 29.

Amos. 2. *v*. 11.

Ioan. 14. *v*. 26. *Mat*. 19. *v*. 12. 21.

Sanctifying grace is more abundant in the new Testament.

4   For this is that mightie power and vertue, which Christ our Sauiour said his Father had promised to send : for which [he cómanded his Disciples, to tarie & expect in Ierusalem, til they should be endued therwith] which strength being geuen them, they were not the affraid [to goe as sheepe & lambes in the middest of wolues. without solicitude how to answear persecutors, always confident in that our Sauiour hath taught, that it is not the weake and fraile man, that speaketh but the Holie Ghost [the Spirit of the heauély Father that speaketh in thé] This is that

Luc. 24. *v*. 49.

Mat. 10. *v*. 16. 20. *Mar*. 13. *v*. 11. *Luc*. 21. *v*. 15.

[power of

Luc. 1.
v. 35.

wer of the moſt high, which came vpon the B. Virgin, ouerſhadowed her] and wrought the moſt B.
Incarnation of the Sonne of God. This is the power
of al powers, that worketh in nature, aboue the

Mat. 12.
v. 28.
Luc. 11.
v. 20.
Act. 2.
v. 1. 4.

courſe and power of al creatures. In this power [our
Sauiour him ſelf as man, caſt diuels out of men.] With
this Holie Spirit, al the faithful which were together
in Ieruſalem were repleniſhed] both with confirmation, and augmentation of ſanctitie; and alſo with
miraculous power [to ſpeake with diuers tongues,
according as the ſame Holie Ghoſt, gaue them to
ſpeake.] S. Paul likewiſe (being conuerted) receiued the ſame effectes of graces, both ſanctſying, &
enabling him to work miracles. Wherupon he ſaith

1. Theſ.
1. v. 5.

[Our Goſpel hath bene to you, not only in worde,
but in power alſo, and the Holie Ghoſt] though iuſtifying grace, and ſanctitie, be the principal, and
moſt neceſſary gift, and therfore the ſame Apoſtle

1. Theſ.
4. v. 7.

ſaith [God hath not called vs into vncleannes, but
into ſanctification] becauſe ſinne may conſiſt, with
other power of auctoritie, prophecying, working
miracles, and the like; but not with ſanctification.
Therfore (ſaith he) he that deſpiſeth theſe thinges,
deſpiſeth not man but God : who alſo haith geuen
his Holie Spirit in vs.

Two kindes of
grace thone
called only
*gratia gra-
tis data* :
thother alſo
*gratum fa-
ciens.*

5   And becauſe Gods goodnes often offereth his
grace to euerie one, the Apoſtle admoniſheth al, to
accept and cooperate therwith, without reſiſtance

Mans coopera-
tion is requi-
red with Gods
grace.

1. Theſ.
5. v. 19.
20.
1. Cor.
12. v. 4.
5. 6.
11.

[the Spirit (ſaith he) extinguiſh not : Prophecies
deſpiſe not. there are diuiſions (or varieties) of graces, but one Spirit. there are diuiſions of miniſtra-
tions : but one Lord. there are diuiſions of operations, but one God, which worketh al in al. And
al theſe thinges worketh one and the ſame Spirit,
diuiding to euerie one according as he wil. that
which euerie one hath receiued, in that muſt he la-

boure.] So muſt the whole bodie of the Church and euerie member [Kepe the good depoſitum by the Holie Ghoſt, which dwelleth in vs.] S. Peter ſpeaking of the aſſured truth which is in the whole Church grounded his aſſertion in this, that God by inſpiration hath reueaded the ſame truth to ſome ſpecial ſeruants of his, to inſtruct the reſt, ſaying: [the holy men of God ſpake inſpired with the Holie Ghoſt.] And S. Iohn ſpeaking of euerie particular faithful ſoule, grounded in true faith which he hath not of him ſelf, but by the gift of the Holie Ghoſt ſaith [It is the Spirit, which teſtifieth that Chriſt is the truth.]

2. Tim. 1, v. 14.

2. Pet. 1, v. 21.

1. Io. 5, v. 6.

The vniuerſal Church conſiſteth of holie Angels, & other glorious Sainctes, with the faithful in earth: of al which Chriſt as Man, is the Head.

ARTICLE. 30.

OF al the workes, and creatures of God, his Church is moſt principal; cõprehending two partes. the one triumphãt in heauē, cõſiſting of glorious Angels, and other Sainctes, which haue vanquiſhed the world, the fleſh, and the diuel. the other part being yet in warfare againſt the ſame enemies, is therfore called Militant. Of both theſe partes; & alſo of other men, ſo long as they liue in this world, Chriſt as Man is the immediate Head vnder God. For better explication wherof we may obſerue fiue diſtinct ſortes of members, diuerſly vnited to Chriſt our head, and in him, each to others. The firſt and moſt excellent ſort, are thoſe who are vnited to our B. Sauiour in eternal glorie. The ſecond, which being yet mortal, are vnited to him by the perfect vertue of Charitie, and iuſtifying grace. The third, which are vnited by true faith, but without good workes. The fourth, which are in poſſi, bilitie

Chriſt is Head of the vniuerſal Church: and of al men liuing in this world, but not of the damned.

Io. 10. 16.

bilitie, and fhal be vnited : but are not for the prefent actually. The fifth, which are alfo in poffibilitie to be vnited, fo long as they are in this tranfitorie life : but wil neuer be actually vnited. For Chrift our Lord is alfo their head and Sauiour, hauing redemed them meritorioufly, though not effectually, as S. Paul diftinctly teacheth faying [Our Lord is the Sauiour of al men, efpeciially of the faithful.] And S. Iohn faith : [Chrift is the propitiation for our finnes, and not for ours only, but alfo for the whole worldes .] But after the death of the reprobate, Chrift is their Iudge, hauing redemed them among the reft of al mankind, but is not their head anie longer, becaufe they are vtterly cut of, and are out of al poffibilitie to be vnited. Yet for fo much, as the two laft fortes are not actually vnited to Chrift nor actual members of his miftical bodie the Church; we are not to fpeake more of them in this prefent Article. Only we are to fhew, that the triumphant part (conteyning al the glorious Sainctes) & the militant, contening both the iuft (afwel in Purgatorie, as in earth) and other faithful though not iuft ; doe make one vniuerfal bodie with Chrft our Lord head therof.

I. *Tim.* 4. *v.* 10 .
I . *Io.* 2.
v. 2 .

Yet is Iudge both of the bleffed, and damned .

2 Which may be declared by manie holie Scriptures; namely by the vifion of the Patriarch Iacob, who [faw in his fleepe, a ladder ftanding vpon the earth, and the top therof touching heauen ; the Angels alfo of God, afcending and defcending by it, and our Lord leyning vpon the ladder. And when he was awaked out of fleepe, he faid : Indeede our Lord is in this place and I knew not. And trembling he faid : how terrible is this place · this is none other but the houfe of God, and the gate of heauen] wherby is euidét, that the militant part of Goddes Church on earth, and the triumphant in heauen, is one houfe,

Gen. 28 .
v. 12 . 13 .

That Chriift is Head of the whole Church, triumphant and militant, is proued by holie Scriptures.

conteyning

conteyning mortal and immortal perfons, our Lord
as head and Maifter of both, reigning in both, as appeareth by his leyning on the ladder, which touched
both heauen and earth. Al which the wife man (re-
fiting this vifion) calleth the King dome of God faying : that [wifdome conducted iuft Iacob , fleeing
his brothers (Efaus) wrath, by the right wayes ; &
fhewed him the Kingdome of God.] Alfo the fpecial numbring of Goddes people , afwel in the defert,
expecting to poffeffe the promifed land of Chanaan,
as returning from the captiuitie of Babylon , vnto the
fame land eftfones promifed, & after feauentie yeares
reftored, doth reprefente the two eftates of one and
the fame Church, firft militant, and finally, triumphant , in the meane time fome bleffed members refting in poffeffion of eternal glorie ; others laboring
in hope to enioy the fame heauenly kingdome.

Sap . 10.
v . 10.
Nu . 1. v.
2. ad 46.
Ch . 3. v.
14. Ch. 26.
v . 51. Ch
33 . v . 1.
&c.
1 . Efd . 2.
v . 1 . ad 66.

Confirmed by
other figures &
prophecies .

3   Manie like figures doe refemble this one Myftical
bodie, the citie of God ; which is verie largely defcribed in a vifion to Ezechiel the Prophet, & written
by him in his nine laft chapters alluding to the reftauration of Ierufalem, after the captiuitie of Babilo.
but fo defcribing a Temple to be reedifyed, as farre
eccelleth, not only that which was built by Zorobabel vpon the old ruines, but alfo Salomons firft Temple, and that alfo which was enlarged, adorned, &
enriched, by Herod Afcalonites ; but muft therfore
needes be vnderftoode of the whole Church of God,
partly in the old Teftament, more amplie in the new,
but moft fullie and complete, in the ftate of glorie.
And therfore the whole defcription feuerally perteyning to diuers partes , fheweth that al is one perfect bodie . For where the Prophet faith : that [the
Spirit of God brought him into the land of Ifrael]
he fignifieth that he being then perfonally prefent in
Chaldea nere to Babilon , his vifion imported what
fhould

Ezech . 40.
41. &c.

Ch . 40.
v . 1.

should be done in the land of Israel. Where he ad-

v.2. deth [and left me ypon a mountaine] he vnderstandeth Mount Syon wheron the Temple stoode, but
saying [exceding high] hath an higher sense then cā
be verified of Mount Sion, not being so extraordi-

v.22. 26. narie in height. Where the [ascent to the gates of
31.32.34. the vtter wal, had seauen steppes, and the ascent to
49. the gates of the inner wal had eight] it wel signifieth the greater perfection required in the New
Testament, then in the old. And the inner court into which those gates gaue entrance, represented the
court of heauen. Likewise in the whole description,
and in the conclusion knitting vp al, and saying:
[these are the names of the Tribes. these shal be the

Ch.48.v. first fruictes of the Sanctuarie, of the Preistes. these
1. 10. 16. are the measures of the citie. this is the land which
29. you shal diuide by lotte, to the Tribes of Israel.] It
is euident that the old Testament had these thinges
as figures of the new; and the Mysteries in the new
Testament are representations of greater thinges in
heauen. As namely Christ him self the Head of this
vniuersal Church, was in the old Testament only in
figure, prefigured by diuers persons, Sacrifices, Sacramentes, and other thinges. In the new Testament
he came really in bodie, but mortal in infirmities,
his glorie hidden, stil remaineth in the B. Sacrament,
but inuisible. In heauen he the self same is in glorie,
and most visible: filling al with his Maiestie. As yet
vntil the end of this world there shal be manie *via-*
tores wayfaring holie persons, seruants of God in this
time of warfare. In the end al members of the
Church shal be *comprehensores* participating glorie:

1.Cor.13. which [now doe see as in a glasse, & shal then see face
v.12. to face] then shal there not be these two names of
militant and triumphant Church, for al shal be triumphant: not two names of one Citie as now there are,

M m but

The old Testa-
ment prefigu-
red the new:
and the new
resembleth the
state of glorie.

but one . For [the name of the Citie (faith this ho-   *Ch . 48.*
lie Prophet) from that day: *Dominus ibi*, *our Lord*   *v . 35.*
there .] Signifying that to be the perfect complet Citie of God , where our Lord is vifible, and glorious
lightning al .

The trium-
phant and the
militant
Church is one
intire bodie
vnder one
head: Chrift .

4   Which S . Iohn in a like vifion, declareth fay-   *Apoc. 22.*
ing: [Night fhal be nomore, & they fhal not neede   *v . 5.*
the light of lampe, nor the light of the funne: becaufe our Lord God doth illuminate them: and they
fhal reigne for euer and euer .] Generally al thofe
places of holie Scripture which fhew that our Sauiour Chrift, is Head of al the Church militant & triumphant; doe proue withal that both thefe eftates of
the Church are but one bodie [one flocke, as hauing   *Ioan.* 10.
one head, one Paftor] the lambe that fhal ouercome   *v . 16.*
al fierce enemies that fight againft him: becaufe [he is   *Apoc.* 17.
the Lord of Lordes, and King of Kinges] and they   *v . 14.*
(fhal alfo ouercome al enemies) that are with him
called elect, and faithful .] For which victorie [God   *Ch . 19.*
hath alfo fette the fame Iefus Chrift] our Sauiour   *v . 16.*
[aboue al Power, and Domination, both in this   *Ephef . 1.*
world and in heauen: and hath made him Head (not   *v . 23.*
ouer part, but) ouer al the Church which is his bodie,
(not bodies) the fulnes of him which is filled al, in
in al] being made the ful and perfect head by his dominion ouer the whole bodie.

The militant Church conteyneth two general mem-
bers : the Cleargie, and Laitie ; vnder one vifible
head.

ARTICLE. 31.

The vniuerfal
Church is the
moft complete,
and moft ex-
cellent Armie .

B Y how much an Armie is more or leffe fur-
nifhed with neceffarie men, money, and munition; better or worfe fette in batle ary; fo is
it in

it in it self stronger or weaker, more or lesse pleasant to behold; and to the enemie more or lesse terrible. The whole Church of God is an Armie most complete, most puisant, most glorious, and most terrible to the contrarie confused conuenticles of the diuel. Of this whole perfect Armie, we haue begunne to sheake in the precedent Article; shewing that during the course of this world, it conteyneth two patres Triumphant & Militāt, yet is al one bodie, and hath one head. To the more principal part which is the celestial Ierarchie, and heauenlie Armie; Salomon, or rather Christ him self by the name of Salomon, saith [Thou art al faire o my loue, and there is not a spot in thee.] In the end also the same shal be said of the whole bodie, when [Christ shal present to him self (as S. Paul teacheth) a glorious Church, not hauing spot, or wrinckle, or anie such thing, but shal be holie and vnspotted.] Now that this glorious Armie is most beautiful, most strong, and most terrible to al damned reprobates, may be more conueniently auouched, then with needles proofes further demonstrated.

2 But that the other part also is the most holie, most fayre, most strong, and euerie way the most excellent Armie, that can be in earth; and absolutly inuincible, we shal in seueral chapters folowing declare, by holie Scriptures. And first ingeneral, as Christ hath said to his Triumphant spouse [thou art al fayre o my loue, and there is not a spot in thee] so he said to the part as yet militant: [thou art fayre o my loue, sweete and comlie, as Ierusalem, terrible as the armie of a campe sett in aray.] For albeit this militant Church be not al fayre, and vnspotted, as the triumphant is: yet it is truly called [*fayre*] by remission of sinnes [*the beloued*] of Christ our Redemer: [*sweete*] by infused vertues, Faith, Hope, Charitie

Cant.4. v.7. Ephes.5. v.27.

Cant.4. v.7. Cant.6. v.3.

The triumphāt Church is al fayre without spotte.

The militant Church is fayre, but not al fayre, yet the fayrest of al Congregations in earth.

ritie

ritie, Religion, with al moral vertues, and giftes;
[*comely*] compofed of requifite wel ioyned members,
perfons of al fortes and degrees, adorned with varieties of fpiritual furniture: [*as Ierufalem*] ftrongly v-
nited & walled [*terrible*] to al enemies [*as the armie of
a campe fette in aray*] fenfed within and without, with
internal vertues, and external behauiour, [armed
with two fwordes [fpiritual and temporal ; [brother   *Luc. 22.*
holpen of brother] a moft ftrong citie] two campes in   *v. 38.*
one ; the Cleargie and Laitie, as two armes, & two   *Prou. 18.*
fhoulders, but one bodie vnder one head.   *v. 19.*

The Cleargie
and Laitie as
two armes, &
two fhoulders
of one dodie,
vnder one
head..

3   Which diftinction, of fpiritual and temporal ftates, with their diftinct functions, and powers, is fo
neceffarie for vniforme gouernment in al cities,
kingdomes, and common welthes, (by reafon that
men confift of foules and bodies) that alfo heathen

Proued by the
law of nature,
and of al nati-
ons.

Infidels by inftinct of nature, and law of al nations,
haue thefe offices of Preiftes, and ciuil Magiftrates.
So holie Scriptures reporte, that in Egipt were preiftes   *Gen. 41.*
[Putiphar the preift of Heliopolis.] of fuch eftima-   *v. 45.*
tion, that his daughter was thought a meete wife for
Iofeph, being made gouernour of the land, next vn-
der the king. There alfo [the Preiftes were not on-   *Gen. 47.*
ly endued with landes, but alfo had a lowance in the   *v. 21. 22.*
time of famine and fcarcitie of corne, out of the com-
mon barnes, and were not driuen to fel their poffeffions, as the people did ; fo that in the whole land of
Egipt the fift part of al fruictes was payed to the king,   *26.*
fauing the land of the Preiftes, which was free frõ this
condition.] And by this meanes the preiftes not needing to trauel corporally for their liuing, had leafure
to ftudie, & became great Mathematicians ; & manie
of them with al, were Magicians: as they were alfo
Idolaters, feruing falfe gods. In like maner al coun-   *Exo. 2.*

Where is no
Preift, or no
Sacrifice, is no
Religion.

tries had preiftes conformable to their Goddes, and   *v. 16.*
pretenfed religions. For where is no preift, no facrifice

crifice : there is no religion, no God.

4 But especially among the faithful from the beginning were alwayes true Preistes. The first borne
and head of euerie familie was a Preist ; vntil God
chaunged that course, geuing a written law to his
peculiar people, the children of Israel, by the hand
of Moyses : as appeareth by the same law where God
commanded Moyses saying : [Take the summe of the
whole assemblie of the children of Israel by their
kindreds, and houses, and the names of euerie one
whatsoeuer, of the male sexe] yet with exception
saying [Number not the tribe of Leui ; neither shalt
thou put the summe of the with the children of Israel :
but appointe them ouer the tabernacle of testimonie,
and al the vessel therof ; and whatsoeuer perteyneth
to the ceremonies. they shal carie the tabernacle,
and al the furniture therof : and they shal be in the
ministerie, and shal pitch round about the tabernacle. When you are to goe forward, the Leuittes
shal take downe the tabernacle : when you are to
campe, they shal sette it vp : what stranger soeuer
(of anie other tribe) cometh to it he shal be slaine.
And the children of Israel (the other tweule tribes)
shal campe euerie man by his troupes, and band,
and hoste. Moreouer the Leuites shal pitch their
tentes round about the tabernacle, left there come
indignation vpon the multitudes of the children of
Israel, and they shal watch in the custodies of the
tabernacle of testimonie.] Thus the offices of the Leuites were designed in general. And after the setting
of them and al the rest of this campe in aray, the Leuites euer in the midest of the whole armie, & subor-
dinated to Aaron ; God particularly signifieth the
disanulling of Preistes, and cleargie men in al other
tribes, which hitherto were the first borne, saying ex-
pressly [I haue taken the Leuites from the children of

M m 3   Israel

Marginal scripture references (left):
Exo. 3.
v. 1.
Nu. 1.
v. 2.
v. 49.
50.
51.
2. Reg.
6. v 6. 7.
Nu. 1.
v. 52.
53.
Nu. 2.
v. 4. 10.
17. 18.
25.
Nu. 3.
v. 9. 11.
41. 45.

Marginal notes (right):
In Goddes Church before the written law, the first borne of al families were Preistes.

Thenceforth onlie the tribe of Leui were cleargie men.

And in that tribe, onlie the familie of Aaron was capable of preisthood.

Israel , for euerie firſt borne ; and the Leuites ſhal be mine . More particularly concerning preiſtes the *Nu*. 8. *v.* higheſt order of al the Leuites, our Lord ſaid to Moy- 16. 18. ſes [Take vnto thee Aaron thy brother with his ſon- *Exo*.28. nes , from among the children of Iſrael, that they may *v*. 1. doe the function of Preiſthoode vnto me .] Againe to ſignifie that not only vocation, but alſo ordina- tion , and diuers conſecrations , for diuers orders, were to be made [our Lord commaunded Moyſes *Leuit*.8. to take Aaron and his foure ſonnes, and by preſcripte *v*. 2. *&c.* different maners of annointing, & with diuerſitie of Ceremonies, to conſecrate Aaron High Preiſt , and his ſonnes preiſtes . The other Leueites were alſo orday- *Nu*. 8. *v.* ned by a preſcript forme, and ceremonial rite, & then 6. 7. *&c.* imployed to their ſeueral offices in the tabernacle of couenante .

Al the other tribes were ſubiect to the Cleargie in ſpi- ritual cauſes .

5 Al other tribes were the Laitie , or people of 15. the ſelf ſame faith and religion , with the Preiſtes & other Leuites , but remaining in their temporal ſtate, were alſo diſpoſed in the campe of Gods Church, ſome in auctoritie, others in ſubiectió, manie in both, in reſpect that they were ſubordinate ſuperiors to ſome, and ſubiectes to others. And for moſt part one was ſupreme of temporal perſons, and cauſes, but in ſpiritual cauſes theſe were al ſubiect to ſpiritual ſu- periors. So was Ioſue by Gods ordinance made ſuc- ceſſor to Moyſes, not in al his auctoritie, (for Moy- ſes had both ſpiritual and temporal) but as the ſacred text declareth [in part of his glorie] which was in *Nu*.27.*v.* temporal gouernment : for Eleazer was high preiſt, 18.19.20, and to him was Ioſue directly ſubiect in al ſpiritual

And in tempo- ral cauſes alſo when theron depended ſpi- ritual good.

cauſes : and in ſome ſort in temporal affaires. For [when anie thing was to be done, Eleazar the preiſt *v*. 21. ſhal conſult the Lord (ſaith our Lord him ſelf) At his word ſhal he goe out, and goe in (that is vnder- take or not vndertake anie common important en- terpriſe

terprise) al the children of Israel with him, and the rest of the multitude.] So were both Iudges, and Kinges, being successors to Iosue, not only subiect in spiritual causes to the High Preistes, but also were to consult God by them, & to take direction of them in temporal doubtes, and difficulties. So king [Dauid willed Abiather the Preist to apply the Ephod] for that was the maner of consulting God (and according to Gods answer receiued) by that meanes [Dauid parted from the citie of Ceila] where otherwise Saul would haue supprised him. So Amarias the high Preist ruled in those thinges, which perteyned to God (in spiritual thinges) and Zabadias a prince of the house of Iuda, was ouer those workes which perteyned to the kinges office. So our Sauiour him self distinguished Cleargie and Laitie, bidding vs repare to the Church for the correction of such as are obstinate in error: And to render to Cæsar the thinges that are Cæsars: and the thinges that are Gods to God.

1.Reg.
23.v.9.
10.11.
Exo.28.
v.30.
Leuit.8.
v.8.
2.Par.
19.v.11.
Mat.18.
v.17.
Mat.
22.
v.21.

Our Sauiour commanded to repaire to the Church for correction of obstinate offenders.

6 And being to establish a new Law, he planted a new Cleargie; neither of the only first borne as in the law of nature; nor of one tribe or kindred only as in the law of Moyses; but of al tribes, and al nations, whether first or later borne, by due vocation and ordination, to be consecrated preistes, according to the order of Melchisedech; with other inferior Cleargie men of greater and lesse distinct orders: with spiritual power both of oder and Iurisdiction. So onr B. Sauionr, our eternal high Preist, ordayned first his Apostles, and after them other seuentie two disciples. *So his Apostles ordayned Deacons, also more Bishopes, and Preistes. So S. Paul affirmed of him self saying: [I am appointed a preacher, and an Apostle: doctor of the Gentiles] He ordayned S. Timothee, S. Titus and others. And al by right vocation

Christ in the law of grace ordained a new Cleargie, by vocation & ordination.

* Mat.10.
v.1.2.
Luc.10.
v.1.2.
Act.6.
v.6.
Act.13.
v.3.

cation, and ordination, euerie high preift (and the
fame rule is of al the Cleargie) being taken from a-
mong men (taken from the people or Laitie) is appointed for men in thofe thinges that perteine to
God. Neither doth anie man take the honour (of
fuch function) tó him lelf, but he that is called of
God as Aaron.]

I. Tim.*2.*
v.*3*.*Ch.*
3.*v*.*2*.
Heb.*5*.
v.*1*.*4*.

Secular power
and fubordina-
tió of Princes,
and other Ma-
giftrates, is by
dinine ordi-
nance.

7   Secular power likewife is of Gods ordinance
[For there is no power but of God.] And therfore
whatfoeuer commandment, or coaction is not of God,
is not of his ordinance, but by his permiffion only.
So that by Gods ordinance al fubiectes are bound to
obey al fuperiors fpiritual and temporal in thinges
good or not euil [Let euerie foule be fubiect (faith
S. paul) to higher powers] willeth his difciple Titus [to admonifh the people to be fubiect to Princes
and Poteftates; to obey at a word, and to be readie to euerie good worke.] To the Hebrewes he
writeh alfo thus: [obey your Prelates, and be fubiect to them: for they watch as being to render account for your foules.] S. Peter as often in his actions, fo alfo in his writing by his fpiritual auctoritie,
admonifheth al to obey temporal auctoritie, faying:
[Be fubiect to euerie humane creature for God: whether it be to king as excelling; or to rulers as fent by
him, to the reuenge of malefactors, but to the praife
of the good.] By al which we fee the admirable
beautie, ftrength, and excellencie of Gods Church,
aboue al other companies, or common welthes, beft
fette in aray; [for there is no other nation, no other
people fo renowned that hath thefe ordinances (thefe
fpiritual & temporal iudgements, ceremonies, holie
rites, and orders) as God hath fette in his people
his fpoufe the Church.]

Rom.*13*.
v.*1.*

Ibid.   ,

Tit.*3*.*v*.*1.*
Heb.*13*.
v.*17*.

1. *Pet*.*2.*
v.*13*.*14*.

Deut.*4.*
v.*7*.*8*.

As wel

As wel the Cleargie as Laitie conteine particular
bodies (communities and corporations) with se-
ueral heades : al subordinate in one whole bo-
die, to one supreme visible head.

ARTICLE. 32.

I T doth not a litle both beautifie and strengthen
the militant Church, that there be in it diuers
particular bodies to witte : the Pastoral Cleargie
distinguished into Archbishopriques, Bishopriques,
diuers Religious orders ; and other spiritual communities : also distinct temporal Kingdomes, Dominions, free Cities, and other Christian Commonweal-
thes, with innumerable Corporations ; al spiritually
vnited in one mistical bodie . For as varietie doth
much adorne : so doth vnion fortifie the whole communitie. Wheras otherwise if anie either particular
[house, or vniuersal kingdome, be diuided in it self,
it must needes come to ruine and desolation .] But
by how manie moe members and partes it hath wel
combined euerie part assisting and defending others :
so much the more firmly the whole is conserued .
We shal therfore first declare that the Church of God,
euer had, and perpetually is to haue, great diuersitie
of states, professions, and functions : and then shew,
that by the same diuine prouidence, they are al perfectly vnited. Concerning the former point euen frō
the beginning of the world, as men increased & multiplied, they professed diuers trades of life, and excercised sundrie offices . First Adam (as common tradition telleth vs) did digge, and Eue did spinne,
certaine it is, that they did trauel in laboures . Abel
was a shepheard, and Cain a husbandman. Iabel
was the father of them that dwel in tentes, & hear-

Mat. 12.
v. 25.
Mar. 3.
v. 24.
25.
Luc. 11.
v. 17.

Gen. 3.
v. 17.
Gen. 4.
v. 2. 20.

Varietie of
members wel
vnited, doth
both beautifie
and strengthen
the bodie .

desmen

defmen. Iubal father of them that fang on harpe & 21.22.
orgaines. Tubalcaine was a fmith, working in braffe 26.
and Iron. Enos is renowmed for his fpecial deuotion
in the feruice of God. So are Seth, Enoch, Noe, & *Gen. 6.*
others. who were therfore called the fonnes of God. *v. 2.*
At which time and fo forwardes vntil the law of Moyfes, the firft borne and heades of families were
Preiftes.

Subordination in fpiritual caufes, where was no fubordination in temporal dominion.

2 And amongft Preiftes there was fubordination
of fuperiors, and inferiors. For Melchifedech did *Gen. 14.*
bleffe Abraham, who was alfo a Preift and tooke ty- *v. 19. 20.*
thes of him, both which preeminences fhew fpiritu-
al fuperioritie, and fubiection; though in temporal-
ties neither of them was fubiect to the other. Iob *Iob. 1. v. 5.*
was a Preift for he offered facrifices for his children,
and was alfo a King or abfolute Lord. Moyfes being conftituted fupreme gouernour fpiritual and temporal of Gods peculiar people, with fpiritual auctoritie alfo ouer the king of Egipt, had his brother Aaró
fubordinate to him, as a prophet, to fpeake as he
fhould direct him [I haue appointed thee (faid our *Exo. 7. v.*
Lord to Moyfes) the God of Pharao : and Aaron thy *1 . 2.*
brother fhal be thy prophet : Thou fhalt fpeake to
him al thinges that I command thee, and he fhal
fpeake to Pharao, that he difmiffe the children of Ifrael out of his land.] In temporal affayres Iofue of *Exo. 17.*
the tribe of Ephraim, was his fubftitute, & appointed *v. 9. 10.*
by him general captaine, to fight againft Amelec.
Hur of the tribe of Iuda was an other affiftant in
publique occafions. As appeareth by that which
Moyfes faid to the people when he went into the
mountaine : [Expect here (faich he) til we returne *Exo. 24.*
to you : you haue Aaron, and Hur with you : If anie *v. 14.*
queftion fhal rife you fhal referre it to them.] Be- *Exo. 18.*

Magiftrates not fubiect to one an other, were al fubiect

fides thefe Moyfes ordained Tribunes, and vnder *v. 21. 25.*
them Centurions; Quinquagenerians, & Decurians.
al which

Al which were superiors of certaine companies and to one cheife particular bodies. Againe of euerie tribe one was head: made the Prince, and so were accepted and called

Nu.1. [the most noble princes of the multitude by their
v.4.16. tribes and kindereds, and the heades of the host of Israel] the temporal state consisting of twelue Tribes: al which had their distinct portions of landes

Nu. 36. alotted them, & were bond by the law [not to make
v. 7. 8. mariages, but each Tribe within it self, that so their inheritances might not be mingled; & that the Tribes might remaine, as they were seperated by our Lord.

3   The spiritual Tribe of Leui, conteined four distinct communities. The first of Preistes, and three

Nu.3. degrees of other Leuites. For the Patriarch Leui,
v.17. hauing three Sonnes, Gerson, Caath, and Merari, of Ceathes Progenie, Aaron was assumed & made High Preist, and in him, and his ofspring, was established the whole order of Leuitical Preisthood. The rest of Ceaths issue, were made the first degree of Le-

Nu.3. uites after the Preistes called [Caathites; whose offi-
v.31. ces were to guard the Sanctuarie, and to carie the Ark
Ch.4. and Table wheron it stoode. Also the Candlestick
v. 16. the Altares, and al the vessels of the Sanctuarie; to prepare and kepe the oyle for lampes, incense, and holie oyle of vnction, the veile, and al other imple-

Nu.3. mentes.] The second degree were [the Gersonites,
v. 26. the sonnes of Gerson, whose charge was, to guard &
Ch.4.v. carie the Tabernacle, the couer therof, the han-
26. ginge curtaines, cordes, al the furniture therof, and

Nu.3.v. vessels perteyning to the Altar.] The third and in-
36. Ch. feriour degree, were Merarites, the Sonnes of Me-
4.v.31. rari, whose office was to kepe and carie the bordes, barres, pillers, with their feete, pinnes, and cordes belonging therto.] Euerie degree had their seueral

Ios. 21. Superiour. And when the Temple was built, & vse
v. 34.   N n 2   of the

Foure distinct communities in the Tribe of Leui, with particular superiors.

1.
Preistes.

2.
Caathites.

3.
Gersonites.

4.
Merarites.

of the Tabernacle ceased, these orders were disposed [to serue in and about the Temple; some Musitians, some thresurers, others porters] al serued the
Preistes : For so [our Lord said to Aaron . Thy bre-
thiren of the Tribe of Leui, and the Scepter of thy
Father, take with thee, and let them be readie at
hand, and minister to thee : but thou and thy Sonnes,
shal minister in the Tabernacle of testimonie, & the
Leuites shal watch vpon thy Precepts, and vpon al
the workes of the Tabernacle . I haue geuen you your
brethren, the Leuites out of the middest of the children of Israel, and haue deliuered them a gift to the
Lord, to serue in the ministeries of his Tabernacle .
And thou and thy Sonnes, loke to your Preisthood;
and al thinges that perteine to the seruice of the Altar, and that are within the veile, shal be executed
by the preistes . If anie stranger approach, he shal be
slaine .] Wel resembling in diuers respectes, the ministerie of Christian Preistes, with Deacons, Subdeacons, and inferiour orders, seruing them in the holy
Sacrifice of the Altar.

The superior of the Preistes, was cheife superior of al.

Ch .3 . v . 36. Ch . 4. v . 31. 1 . Par .23. v . 26. Ch . 25 . v . 26. Nu. 18 . v. 2 . 3. 6.

4   There were also in the old Testament, certaine
Religious orders, obseruing special rules of life, binding them selues therto by voluntary vowes [the
Nazarites, Recabites] and others . Likewise many
holie Prophets were raised vp by God, and sent to
admonish al sortes (Preistes and people) of diuers
Tribes besides the Leuites . Moreouer [our Lord ordeined seauentie Ancientes of Israel, for Counselers,
and Rulers, to ease the burden of the cheif Superiour, imparting to them of the spirit wherwith Moyses was indued, and they prophecied from thence forward] and assisted in the gouernment . After Moyses
and Iosue, there were manie changes, and also ir-
terruptions of temporal cheif gouerners . And at
sundrie times, God raised vp certaine men of diuers

Religious orders in the old Testament. Also special

Prophets were sent extraordinarily.

Likewise God ordained temporal Magistrates ordinarie.

Sometimes extraordinarie.

Iudic .13. v . 5. Nu. 6.v . 2. Iere .35. v . 2. 4 . Reg . 1. v .7 . Ch. 2 .v .7. Ch.6.v .1. 1 .Mac.2. v . 12. 2 . Mac. 14. v .6. Nu .11.v. 16 . 17.

Tribes *25.*

Iudic. 2 . *v* .
16 . 1 . *Reg* .
8 . *v* . 5 .
3 . *Reg* . 12 .
v. 16. 19.
4 . *Reg* . 17 .
v . 6 . 2 .
Par . 11 . *v* .
13 . 1 . *Reg* .
25 . *v* . 11 .
1 . *Eſd* . 1 .
2 . *Eſd* . 1 .

Tribes, by the title of Iudges, to deliuer and defend the people from inuaſions of enemies. After which, they had Kinges, Saul, Dauid, and Salomon, reigning ouer al Iſrael. Then tenne Tribes reuolting, made them ſelues by Goddes permiſſion, a ſeueral King, & were a diſtinct kingdome til they were caried captiue into Aſſiria. The other two Tribes (and the Tribe of Leui) remaining ſubiect to K. Dauids ſucceſſors, til they alſo were caried captiues into Babilon : From which time they neuer recouered the Royal ſtate of a Kingdome ; though after ſeauentie yeares captiuitie, the Medes & Perſians conquering Babilon, releaſed the Iewes, permitting them to returne, and repaire their Temple, and Citie of Ieruſalem . But againe after this, they were brought vnder the Grecians, and by them, extremly perſecuted. Laſt of al, they were ſubdued by the Romanes, & ſuffered to vſe more priuileges, eſpecially in Religion, yet ſtil ſubiect in ciuil cauſes. But the ſtate of Preiſtes and Leuites, was ſtil conſerued : Namely the ſucceſſion of High Preiſts, was continued en ento Caiphas. Who

Ioa. 11 . *v* .
50. 51.

(though with wicked meaning) truly iudged it [expedient, that one man ſhould dye for the people, and the whole Nation periſh not.] Thus did the Church of the old Teſtament conteine manie particular ſocieties, with their ſeueral heades, both in the ſpiritual, & temporal ſtates remaining al one intyre bodie, with one ſpiritual ſupreme head.

5   Much more the Church of Chriſt conſiſting of al nations, is adorned and fortified with varieties, in both ſtates. the temporal conteyning manie Kingdomes, Dukedomes, Dominions, free Cities, and other abſolute common wealthes, ſome gouerned in forme of Monarchie, ſome by Ariſtochracie: ſome by Diuiochacie, others more or leſſe mixt. And in theſe are innumerable corporations, euerie one hauing a   N n 3   proper head

Temporal gouernment ſometime changed.

And interrupted.

Succeſſion of High Preiſtes ſtil conſerued and continued.

In the Church of Chriſt, are diſtinct temporal Dominies; al ſubiect to one ſpiritual head.

per head fubordinate to fuperiors, yet not one tem-poral head as King or Emperour of al. But al fub-iect to one fpiritual fupreme head; els al could not be one perfect bodie. In this whole Militant Church of Chrift, are alfo conteyned manie particular Chur-ches with perfect fubordination to one fupreme vi-fible head: vnder whom are others alfo in fubordi-nation, making a formale Ecclefiaftical Ierarchie of Preiftes, Bifhopes, Archbifhopes, Primates, Patriarches, and one fupreme vifible Paftor of al. To the Cleargie alfo perteyne al Religious orders who though they haue not ordinarie Iurifdiction, or charge of foules, yet by fpiritual laboures, prayers, preaching and manie other good workes, nourifh, ftrengthen, and beautifie the whole Church. Like-wife Vniuerfities, Colleges, Seminaries, and other houfes of ftudentes in liberal Artes: efpecially pro-feffing the facred, and honorable faculties of Diui-nitie, Canon, Ciuil, and municipial Lawes, and of Phifike, with the like vnited companies, are al mem-bers, ornamentes, and fortifications of one and the fame Catholique militant Church, wherof both the Prophets and Apoftles haue written. Holie Dauid calleth this Church [a Queene ftanding on the right hand (in profperous ftate) in golden rayment, com-paffed with varietie. Set your hartes on her ftrength (faith the fame Prophet to al her children) & dif-tribute ye her houfes] obferue wel how manie par-ticular Churches were fpidily founded in the world by the Apoftles, and other Apoftolical men [In Churches bleffe ye God our Lord. Let Ifrael (the Church of Chrift) now fay, that our Lord is good: that his mercie is for euer. Let the houfe of Aaron (the cleargie) let them which feare our Lord (al fortes of faithful perfons) now fay that his mercie is for euer.] In an other Pfalme thus: [Seates fate there

Pf. 44. *v.* 11.

Pf. 47. *v.* 14.

Pf. 67. *v.* 27.

Pf. 117. *v.* 2.3.4.

Pf. 121. *v.* 5.

There are alfo manie particu-lar communi-ties of the Cleargie with feueral heades, but al fubiect to the Su-preme vifible head of the mi-litant Church.

Proued by ho-lie Scriptures.

there in Iudgementes (in Ierufalē) & Seates vpon the house of Dauid] in the Church of the new Teſtament.

If. 1.
v. 26.

So God promiſed by Iſaias, faying : [I wil reſtoare thy Iudges, as they haue bene before, and thy coun-ſellers as of old. After theſe thinges thou ſhalt be called the Iuſt, a faithful Citie.] Al fully performed in the Church of Chriſt : into which are entered, & ſtil doe enter, al nations. So our Lord ſending his

Act. 2.
v. 9. 41.
47.

holie Spirit [encreaſed the faithful dayly together] al in one Church ; yea manie Churches in one. S.

Manie particu-lar Churches are al one Church.

Ro. 16.
v. 3.
Phil. v.
2.
Apoc. 1.
v. 4.

Paul [rendered thankes to Priſca and Aquila, in the behalfe of al the Churches of the Gentiles] and [ſa-luted their domeſtical Church.] He ſhal ſalute alſo an other [domeſtical Church, in the houſe of Phile-mon] & writte ſeueral Epiſtles to particular Chur-ches. S. Iohn likewiſe writte his Apocalipſe [to ſeauen Churches] in the prouince of Aſia. Manie Churches, manie Nations, manie Dominions, manie Corporations, of the faithful, which, as they doe ex-cellently adorne the whole Church with varietie : ſo doe they alſo ſtrongly fortifie it, being perfectly v-nited : wherby they al make but one Church ; which is the ſecond point propoſed in the beginning of this Article. And ſo we ſhal now further declare it with other markes, by which the true Church is knowne from al other congregations.

The true Church of Chriſt is knowne by ſpecial markes : the firſt of which is Vnitie.

ARTICLE. 33.

AL Chriſtians acknowlegeing that there is a Church, not only in heauen, but alſo in earth : it is neuertheleſſe the maine queſti-on called into controuerſie at this time, which is the

It is a princi-pal controuer-ſie at this time to know the true Church.

true

true Church of Chrift ? Some fuppofing one congregation, to be the faithful children of God, fome
an other, according to their contrarie doctrines in
pointes of faith; fome thinking there may be manie
without fubordination of one Superiour of al, yea
different in opinions, touching matters of belefe;
fome alfo imagining, that the true Church haith fomtimes failed, and bene no where vifible to the world;

It may be
knowen by
certaine
markes.

and that it may fo decay hearafter : Yet al agree in
general, that it may be knowne by fpecial markes &
notes, but what thofe are, is the verie iffue of controuerfie betwene Romane Cotholiques, and other
pretenfed Religions . For al proteftantes and others,
proceded, or parted from them, doe commonly af-
figne thefe two : the true preaching of Goddes word,
& the right adminiftration of his Sacramentes, which
indede agree to the true Chnrch, and to none other

The markes
affigned by
Proteftantes,
are as hard to
be knowne as
the thing
which is
fought.

congregation; but are not the proper markes therof wherby to know it . Becaufe markes or notes
wherby to know anie thing, muft be more cleare,
then that thing which we defire to know : otherwife, as the prouerbe faith, it were to teach *igno-
tum per ignotius*, a thing vnknowne, by that which
is leffe knowne, or as litle knowne. Wheras thefe
two which they cal the proper markes are as hard to
be knowne as is the Church it felf, or rather harder :
and are chalenged by al Sectaries, euerie forte arrogating to them felues that they only haue the fpirit of truth, preach the true word of God; rightly
adminifter his Sacramentes: and are the true Church;
and that al others are in error, and no members of
the true Church. Wherefore we muft of neceffitie
trye this caufe by other euidences; and what better
trial can anie reafonable perfons require, then the
verie wordes fet downe by the holie Apoftles, in their
Creede, which al Chriftians euerie where profeffe;

Rom. 12.
v. 6.

I beleue

I beleue the Holie Catholique Church. In that they say Church, not Churches, they plainly signify, that al particular Churches are vnited, and make one only complete Church : one intyre bodie, consisting of manie members, with vniforme consent in the same faith and Religion. And so *Vnitie*, is the first marke and note of the true Church . The second is *Sanctitie*, the Apostles saying, it is Holie . In the word Catholique, we haue the third marke which is *Vniuersalitie* . And in that the Apostles, who taught this Crede, were the first planters of this Church of Christ it is trulie called Apostolical, not only by the holie Councel of Nice, but also English protestantes admitte the same Nicene Crede, in their publique seruice. And so we haue the fourth marke, which is *Antiquitie* of the true Church, euen from Christ and his Apostles. And in this fourth, marke is necessarily included Succession of lawful Pastors rightly called & admitted into Ecclesiastical function . To take away also two common euasions of protestantes, pretending, that the true holie Catholique Apostolical Church, hath bene interrupted for a long time, and is now by them restoared, or at least (say they) it was somtimes inuisible, but not wholly corrupted, and vtterly decayed : We contrariwyse wil shew, by manie euident holie Scriptures, that the true Church is both perpetual; without interruption; and also perpetually visible, & *neuer inuisible* .

2   First then concerning *Vnitie*, which is the first marke, and consisteth in consent of al true members confessing the same faith, in subordination to one visible head : it was prefigured by the procreation of al mankind. For God creating only one man, & out of his side taking a ribbe ; built or framed the same into the first woman; of which two, al the rest

O o   are

Gen . 2 .
v . 22 .

The Apostles Creede acknowleged by al Christians, expresseth certaine markes of the true Church.
Vnitie.
Sanctitie.
Vniuersalitie.

The fourth marke is Antiquitie -

Other two markes are, Perpetuitie, & visibilitie .

Vnitie of the Chuurch was prefigured by the creation of Man.

By the Arke o Noe.

are propagated ; and ſo originally al from one. An other figure of the Churches vnitie was expreſſed in the Arke of Noe, which was but one, by which he & his familie with a few other earthly creatures were conſerued aliue, al the reſt being drowned in the diluge : which whole machine being great, had but one dore for entrance, and one window to lighten al, & it was in the toppe of the Arke finiſhed in on cubite : from whence the midle and loweſt rowmes

Gen. 6. v.
14. 16.

By the Arke of teſtimonie.

Tabernacle, & Temple.

receiued light, through the floores. The ſame was likewiſe fore-ſignified by the Arke of teſtimonie made of durable wood ſetim . Alſo by the tabernacle with manie appurtenances. And by the Temple. Euerie of which ſignified the Church in diuers particular proprieties, & namely in vnitie .

Exo. 25.
v. 10.
Exo. 26.
v. 1.
3. Reg. 6.
v. 1.

Proued by diuers Prophets .

3   As is more cleare in the Prophets. The Royal Pſalmiſt ſpeaking of the Church ſaith : [God in his holie place ; God that maketh men to inhabite of one maner in a houſe . A mountaine crudded as cheeſe] faſt combined into one . [Behold (ſaith he in an other pſalme) how good, and how ioyful a thing it is, for brethren to dwel in one .] Chriſt him ſelf, by the pen of Salomon ſaith : [My ſiſter Spouſe, is a garden encloſed, a garden (indeede) encloſed, a Fountaine ſealed vp . My doue is one, my perfect one , ſhe is the only to her mother] As the old Sinagogue was one conſiſting in maner of one nation : ſo is the Church of Chriſt but one, though it comprehendeth innumerable Nations . Iſaias in his Canticle of praiſe to God for the good change of the Iewes Sinagogue, into the Chriſtian Church, ſaith [In that day ſhal this ſong be ſung in the land of Iuda. Sion, the Citie of our ſtrength, a Sauiour : therin ſhal be put a wal, and a bulwarke . Open ye the gates, and let the iuſt Nation enter in, that kepeth truth ; the old errour is gone, thou wilt kepe peace] ſignifying that manie peoples

Pſ. 67. v.
6. 7. 17.
Pſ. 132.
v. 1.
Cant. 4. v.
12.
Can. 6. v.
8.
Iſ. 26. v.
1. 2. 3.

entring

entring into the Catholique Church of Chrift, who is of the Tribe of Iuda, fhal in truth & peace, preferre Sió the head Church, before al others, al being vnited therunto. This vnion was likewife forefhewed to E-

Ezech. zechiel by the hólie Spirit, faying to him [Thou
37. v. Sonne of man, take thee one peece of wood, and
16. 17. write vpon it. Of Iuda, and of the children of If-rael his felowes. And take an other peece of wood and write vpon it. Of Iofeph the wood of Ephra-im, and of al the houfe of Ifrael, and his felowes. And ioyne them one to the other for thee, into one peece of wood, and they fhal be into an vnion in thine hand. To the fame effect was reuealed to So-

Soph .3. phonias by our Lord faying [then(in the new Te-
v .9. ftament) wil I reftoare to the peoples a chofen lippe, that al may inuocate in the name of our Lord, & may ferue him with one fhoulder.] Manie peoples pro-feffing with their lippes one faith, and with ioyned forces as with one fhoulder, defend and manteine the fame.

Ioa .19. 4 Our Sauiours [coate wrought throughout with-
v. 23. out feame] was doubtles a miftical figure of his indi-uifible Church : yet his owne diuine doctrine, is more
Ioa. 10. manifeft, affirming, that [there fhal be one fold, &
v .16. one Paftor] And that in his Church, is manifeftati-on of truth ; out of it, al obfcuritie, vncerteintie, &
Mar .4. falfhood. [To you(that are within the fold) it is
v .11. geuen to know the mifterie of the Kingdome of God,
Act . 2. but to them that are without, al thinges are done in
v .47. parables] they may fee, and read, and heare, & not
Rom .12. vnderftand, til they enter into this one fold of al Chrift
v .5. his flock. When the Apoftles preached * [thofe that
1. Cor. beleued, were al gathered together that fhould be
10 .v. faued.] And [we being manie (faith S. Paul)are
17. Ch . one bodie in Chrift, and each one, an others mem-
12 .v. bers. Being manie, we are one bread ; one bodie,

E 2.

Signified by our Sauiours Coate.

Manifeftly taught by our Sauiour, & his Apoftles.

al that

al that participate of one bread . As the (natural) bodie is one, and hath manie members, and al the mé-
bers of the bodie, wheras they be manie, yet are one
bodie : fo alfo Chrift his miftical Bodie, is manie in
one . [And if al were one member, where were the *v. 19. 20.*
bodie ? But now there are manie members indeede,
yet one bodie : one Lord, one Faith, one Baptifme.] *Ephef. 4,*
Al which and the like, fhew, that the true Church is *v. 5.*
al one bodie, confifting in vnitie and confent in al
pointes of faith, and communitie of Sacramentes, &
other holie Rites, with the mutual felowfhippe of al

Vnitie confi-
fteth in profef-
fing of one
faith: and in
regiment vn-
der one head.

particular Churches, ioyned in perfect vnion, afwel
in doctrine of beleefe, as in regiment of one fupreme
head . Becaufe the Militant Church in earth, is a true
& perfect Monarchie as we fhal further declare by
holie Scriptures . And firft that it was fo in the old
Teftament, wherby is more clearly demonftrated that
fo it is in the new .

In the old Teftament there was euer on fupreme vi-
fible head of the Church .

ARTICLE. 34.

Moyfes before
he writte the
law, defcribed
the beginning
and progreffe
of mankind.

Moyfes being to write the law which he *Gen . 1. v.*
receiued of God, firft of al fheweth the be- *1. 2. &c.*
ginning of al creatures, and more particu- *26.*
lar of man, in what happie ftate he was in paradife ; *Ch. 2. v. 7.*
how he fel from it: how he and part of his progenie *21. 22. 25.*
through Gods fpecial grace which is offered to al , *Ch . 3. v. 1.*
were made his peculiar people ; though others wil- *6. 7. 15.*
fully running their owne wayes, fel further into wickednes and into innumerable groffe errors .

In the genea-
logies of the
Patriarches e-
fpecially fetteth
forth the fuc-
ceffion of the

2   In which hiftorie this facred Hiftoriographer moft
efpecially recordeth the thinges perteyning to Gods
felected people, and therin verie exactly reciteth the
generations of Adam the firft man, by his right line
                                                         to

to Noe, and ſo to Abraham, Iſaac, and Iacob, otherwiſe called Iſrael, of whom the ſame choſen people
were called the children of Iſrael: ſhewing hereby
the continual ſucceſſion of one ſuperior, from generation to generation. For there can be no other reaſon wel imagined, but becauſe theſe only were the
ſupreme heades, and rulers of the Church, why Moyſes profeſſing to write [the generation of Adam]
ſhould therin omitte both Cain, and Abel his firſt ſonnes, and al other ſonnes (for he begate alſo other
ſonnes and daughters) and only name Seth. Againe
omitting al other ſonnes of Seth, he nameth Enos a-
lone. Likewiſe in al the reſt til he come to Noe. Yet
expreſly noteth withal, that euerie one of them [begate other ſonnes and daughters.] In the ſame maner he proſecuteth the lineal ſucceſſion of Noe, by the
generations of his Sonne Sem to Abraham : and ſo to
Iſaac and Iacob : geuing vs by the way to vnderſtand
(which alſo confirmeth our purpoſe) that wheras
Abraham had an elder Sonne called Iſmael, whom
God [made alſo into a great Nation] yet [Goddes
ſpecial promiſe and couenant, was eſtabliſhed with
Iſaac.] And Iſaac hauing two Sonnes called Eſau, &
Iacob, the yonger which was Iacob, was preferred,
and made ſucceſſor to his father, as is often teſtified in
holie Scriptures [The elder ſhal ſerue the yonger.
Was not Eſau brother to Iacob ſaith our Lord ? &
I loued Iacob and hated Eſau,] Diuers other Genealogies, are alſo recited by Moyſes, but without
continuance, as of Cain before the flood. Afterward
of al Noes ſonnes ; vntil the diuiſion of tongues and
Nations. Thence forward, cn'v of Sem lineally by
[Arphaxad, Sale, Heber, Phaleg, Ragau, Serug, Nachor, Thare, Abraham] with breife mention, that
euerie one of them [begate other Sonnes and daughters] And namely of Abrahames brethren Nachor,

and

Gen. 5.
v. 1.
4.

v. 7. 10.
13. 16.
19. 22.
26. 30.
Gen. 11.
v. 10.

Gen. 17.
v. 20.
21.

Gen. 25.
v. 23.
Mal. 1.
v. 2.
Rom. 9.
v. 13.
Gen. 4.
v. 17.
Ch. 10.
v. 1. 2.
&c. Ch.
11. v. 10.

cheiſe Superi-
or.

Other genea-
logies are onlie
recited to a
few generati-
ons: but the
right line of
the Patri-
arches is de-
clared from A-
dam, to Iacob,
and his twelue
ſonnes.

and Aaron. Likewife the Genealogies of Nachor. *Gen*.25.*v*.
Alfo of Abrahames yonger fonnes by his lafte wife 1.3.12.
Cethura, and of Ifmael; and of Efau the elder Sonne
of Ifaac; are recorded to a few generations. But
Iacobs progenie, is continually declared, and exactly numbred by al his twelue fonnes, and their thir- *Nu*.1.*v*.2.
tene Tribes after their deliuerie from the Egiptians *Nu*.3.*v*.
dominion. But before this, whiles they were in E- 15.
gipt, the Princes of the three firft Families, Ruben, *Nu*.26.*v*.
Simeon, and Leui, are recited fo farre as Aaron and 2.17.
Moyfes, and no further, it fufficing for that prefent *Exo*.6.*v*.
purpofe to fhew the Pedegree of thefe two, by whom 14.15.16.
the whole Nation was to be brought out of the land 26.
of Egipt, God then putting the fupreme gonernmét
of them al into Moyfes his handes, and appointing
Aaron his chéif affiftant: vntil which time, the firft
borne, and al heades of Families, were their Preiftes,
and the cheife Prince, was alfo the cheife Preift.

In the written 3 Now therfore when it pheafed God to geue his
law Aaron was Church a written Law, with manie new facred Rites
ordained high and ordinances: & principally to change the r Preift-
Preift, with a hood [For the Preifthood being tranflated, it is ne- *Heb*.7.*v*.
perpetual fuc-
ceſſion. ceffarie (faith S. Paul) that a tranflation of the Law 12.
be alfo made] his diuine goodnes firft conftituted
Moyfes an extraordinarie both Prince and Preift,
making him [the God of Pharao, and Aaron his Pro- *Ex*.7.*v*.1.
phet] And fo proceding amongft other his diuine
ordinances [our Lord commanded Moyfes, to con- *Leuit*.8.*v*.
fecrate Aaron] the ordinarie [High Preift, and al 2.4.6.
his fonnes Preiftes] which Moyfes performed ac- 13. *&c*.
cordingly [in fight and hearing of the multitude, gathered before the dore of the Tabernacle.] To this
Inftitution were alfo added particular precepts declaring their offices, and the emineut power, and fupreme auctoritie of the High Preift in fpiritual caufes, with due correfpondence betwene him, & the
temporal

temporal cheife head . His fiſt preeminence & pri-

Exo. 28. uilege, was to teach the truth ; which is ſignified by

v. 15. his Preiſtly ornamentes called [Ephod, which he bare

22. 27. on his ſhoulders : and Rationale of Iudgement faſte-

ned on his breaſt, linked together with goldē chaines,

hookes, and ringes aboue , and with hyacynth lace

beneath , adorned with twelue moſt precious ſtones,

and the names of the twelue Tribes engrauen ther-

in.] Theſe did the High Preiſt carie with his other

veſtures, whenſoeuer he entred into the Sanctuarie.

And [in the Rationale.of Iudgement were written,

v. 30. *Doctrine & Veritie.*] And ſo by Goddes ſpecial aſ-

Leuit. 8. ſiſtance, he declared the veritie of doctrine in doubt-

v. 8. ful caſes . And therupon God expreſſly commanded

1. *Reg.* his people in great difficulties, to repaire for final

23 . *v.* 9. direction, to his high and moſt authentical Iudge,

Deut. 17. ſaying [If thou perceiue that the Iudgement with

v. 8. thee is hard and doubtful betwene bloud & bloud,

cauſe and cauſe, leproſie, and not leproſie ; and thou

ſee that the wordes of the Iudges within thy gates,

doe varie : ariſe and goe vp to the place which the

Lord thy God ſhal chooſe . And thou ſhalt come to

9. the Preiſtes of the Leuitical ſtocke, and to the Iudge

that ſhal be at that time ; and thou ſhalt aske of

them, who ſhal ſhew thee the truth of Iudgement :

and thou ſhal doe whatſoeuer they that are Preiſtes

10. of the place (which our Lord ſhal chooſe) ſhal ſay

and teach thee, according to his Law, and thou ſhalt

11. folow their ſentence ; neither ſhalt thou decline to

12. the right hand, nor to the left hand. But he that

ſhal be proude refuſing to obey the commandement

of the Preiſt , which at that time miniſtreth to the

Lord thy God, by the decree of the Iudge, that mā

ſhal dye, and thou ſhalt take away the euil out of Iſ-

rael. And the whole people hearing, ſhal feare,

13. that none afrerward ſwel in pride.] Theſe plaïne

wordes

wordes of the diuine Law, doe not only shew Gods ordinance of one preist to be cheife Iudge, aud President in the consistorie of Preistes, but also that others were then bonde vnder paine of death, to obey his sentence. In consideration of which Preistly power ; the Prophet Malachie so much the more blamed Preistes of his time for their faultes, which were aggrauated by reason of their function ; and therfore put them in mind therof saying [The lippes of the Preist shal kepe knowlege ; and others shal require the Law of his mouth, because he is the Angel of the Lord of Hostes] the messenger of God almightie.

Mal. 2. v. 7.

Rebellion rising against this ordinance, was suppressed, and Aarons Supremacie confirmed by diuers miracles.

4　By occasion also of this supreme auctoritie geuen to Aaron, and other High Preistes, certaine Leuites, with some of Rubens Tribe, disdaining the same, reuolted, and rebelled against Moyses, and Aaron : which enormious schisme God presently punished, with the miraculous destruction of manie. And by an other manifest miracle, declared Aarons auctoritie ouer al the Preistes of the other Tribes. [Take (said our Lord to Moyses) a rodde of euerie one of al the Princes of their Tribes, twelue roddes, and the name of euerie one thou shalt write vpon his rodde. And the name of Aaron shal be in the Tribe of Leui. one rodde shal conteyne al the Leuites families : and thou shal lay them in the Tabernacle of couenant before the testimonie where I wil speake to thee. Whosoeuer I shal choose, his rodde shal blosome. which when Moyses had laid before our Lord in the tabernacle of testimonie ; returning the day folowing he found Aarons rodde in the house of Leui budded, and the buddes therof swelling, the blossoms were shot forth: which spreading the leaues were fashioned into almondes. Moyses therfore brought forth al the roddes from the sight of our Lord, to al the

Nu. 16. v. 1. 3. 31. 39.

Nu. 17. v. 2.

3. &c.

the children of Israel, and they saw and euerie one
receiued their owne roddes. And our Lord said to
Moyses: Carie backe Aarons rodde into the tabernacle of testimonie, that it may be kept there for a
signe of the rebellious children of Israel, and let
their complaintes cease from me, lest they dye. And
Moyses did as our Lord had commanded] thus was
Aaron established high Preist. To him succeded his
sonne Eleazar. and so others for the most part of the
same line, and some of his brother Ithamars progenie, but al of Aarons familie: As is gathered by the
historie of Paralipomenon, vnto the captiuitie in Babilon, and by the testimonie of Nehemias, nere two
hundred yeares after, and euen to Annas, and Caiphas named in the Gospel. their auctoritie was directly, and principally in spiritual causes, of faith &
maners. And in temporal affayres so farre only as
perteyned to the spiritual. Which appeareth in the
substitution of Iosue, to succede Moyses in temporal gouernment. Where our Lord said thus to Moyses. [Take Iosue the sone of Nun, a man in whom
is the Spirit, and put thy hand vpon him. who shal
stand before Eleazar the Preist, and al the multitude:
and thou shalt geue him precepts in the sight of al,
and part of thy glorie; that al the Synagogue of the
children of Israel may heare him. For him if anie
thing be to be done, Eleazar the Preist shal consult
the Lord. At his word shal he goe out, and shal goe
in, and al the children of Israel with him: & the rest
of the multitude.

5 By this auctoritie *Ioiada the high Preist* calling
to him Centurions, & souldiars, with other Preistes,
and Leuites, restored Ioas the right King to his scepter, and kingdome of Iuda, and causing the vsur-
ping Queene Athalia to be slaine. By the same spiritual auctoritie, Azarias the High Preist, with four-

Margin left:
Nu.20.
v.25.
26.
1.Par.
6.v.3.
ad 14.
v.53.
2.Esd.
12.v.
10.
Ioa.11.
v.49.
Ioa.18.
v.13.
Nu.27.
v.18.
19.
20.
21.

4.Reg.
11.v.4.
12.15.
16.
2.Par.
33.v.1.
5.7.11.

Margin right:
Eleazar succe-
ding to Aaron,
was superior to
Iosue: not on-
ly in spiritual
causes, but also
in temporal, in
special cases.

The supreme
auctoritie of
high Preist, is
further proued
by practise.

score

score other Preiftes, repreffed king Ozias, hauing taken the Cenfer into his hand to offer incenfe to our Lord, faying vnto him [It is not thy office O- zias, to burne incenfe to our Lord, but of the Preiftes, that is of the children of Aaron, which are confecra- ted to his kind of minifterie : goe out of the Sanc- tuarie, contemne not, becaufe this thing fhal not be reputed to thee for glorie of our Lord God . And Ozias being angrie, and holding in his hand the Cen- fer to burne incenfe , threatned the Preiftes, & forth- with there rofe a leprofie in his forhead before the Preiftes in the houfe of our Lord by the Altar of in- cenfe. And when Azarias the High Preift had be- held him, and al the reft of the Preiftes, they faw the leprofie in his forhead, and in haft they thruft him out : yea and him felf being fore affraid, made haft to goe out, becaufe he felt by and by the plage of our Lord : Ozias therfore the king, was a leper vntil the day of his death, and he dwelt in a houfe apart ful of the leprofie for the which he had bene caft out of the houfe of our Lord .] So it pleafed God againe by miracle, to manifeft the High Preiftes 'auctoritie ouer kinges in caufe of Religion , as before his di- uine goodnes had declared Aarons fupremacie , a- gainft the fchifmatical rebels .

14. 15.

4. *Reg.* 15.
v. 5.
2. *Par.* 26.
v. 17. 18.

19. *&c.*

Acknowleged by good kinges .

6   But ordinarily there was very good correfpon- dence betwene the kinges, and High Preiftes, with mutual refpect of each to others. So king Iofaphat [commanding the Iudges of his Cities, to deale vp rightly, as exercifing iudgment, not of man, but of God] appointing alfo Leuites, and Preiftes, & Prin- ces of Families, to iudge caufes in Ierufalem ; ex- prefly diftinguifhed, the fpiritual and temporal offi- ces and officers faying [Azarias the Preift and your Bifhop, fhal be cheife in thefe thinges which perteine to God . Moreouer Zabadias the fonne of Ifmahel who

2. *Par.* 19.
v. 6. 8. 16.

who is the Prince in the houſe of Iuda, ſhal be o-
uer thoſe workes which perteine to the kinges office] plainly acknowlegeing, that ſpititual iudgementes (which he calleth thinges perteining toGod)
perteine not to the kinges office : but are of an o-
ther Iuriſdiction ; yet did kinges, and other temporal Dukes and Iudges, iuſtly, and laudably cooperate,
in putting ſpiritual precepts, and diuine ordinances in execution . So did Ioſue, Dauid, Salomon,
Ioſaphat, Ezechias, Ioſias, Zorobabel, and the ſame
did al good temporal Princes, together with the high
Preiſtes . And al other good Preiſtes and people,
duly obeyed them both.

Ioſ. 3. v.
8. 1.
Par. 16.
17-23.
24. 3.
Reg. 2.
2. Par.
19.
2. Par.
29.
4. Reg.
22.
1. Eſd.
2.3. 4.
&c.
Iere. 33.
v. 24.

7 And contrariwiſe, the euil diſpoſed impugned
them both when they could, and when force failed
the wicked, yet by murmurations, detractions, calumniations, curſinges, and other euil ſpeaches, they
maligned the two moſt renowmed families of Aaron,
and Dauid. Which God him ſelf, to whom nothing
can be hidde, reueled to his Prophet Ieremie ſaying,
[Haſt thou not ſeene what this people hath ſpoken
ſaying. The two kindreds which the Lord hath choſen, are caſt of, and they haue deſpiſed my people,
becauſe it is nomore a Nation before them.] So
did enuious detractors wiſh and ſpeake euil of theſe
two houſes, of Aaron and Dauid, which God had
eſpecially choſen, and ſtil protected. But al Prophets, being moſt holie men, yelded al honour and
euer had moſt due reguard, to ſerue both theſe eminent States. For example. The Prophet Aggeus
by Goddes inſpiration, directed his prophecie ioint-
lie to them both ; beginning thus [The word of our
Lord was made in the hand of Aggeus the Prophet
to Zorobabel, the ſonne of Salathiel, Duke of Iuda,
and to Ieſus, the ſonne of Ioſedec the Grand Preiſt]
who willingly heard his admonition, and vnder-

Agg. 1.
v. 1.

12.

Wicked men
eſpecially im-
pugned, both
Paſtoral, and
Royal ſuperio-
ritie.

But God pro-
tected them
both.

tooke

tooke the holie worke, to build againe the destroied
Temple of God, wherto he exhorted them.

Christ our Sauiour ordeined S. Peter cheefe of the
Apostles : and visible Head of the Militant
Church.

ARTICTE. 35.

It is no deroga-
tion to Christ,
to haue a Vi-
car general in
earth.

It is necessarie
for diuers
pregnant rea-
sons.

1.

2.

3.

4.

SAinct Paules doctrine, that [God hath made
Christ Head ouer al the Church] may sufficiently satisfie anie doubtful person, that it
doth nothing derogate from Christ, to haue a Vicarial head of his Church Militant. For seeing it
derogateth not from Diuine Maiestie, to haue made
Christ as Man, the head of al the Church, both Triumphant, and Militant : Neither doth it derogate
from Christ to haue a Vicar in earth. Moreouer,
Christ [so louing the Church, that he deliuered him
self for it] doth not lesse fortifie and furnish the same
with al thinges necessarie, then was the Church of
the old Testament. Seing therfore the Iewes Synagogue, had by Goddes special prouidence, a visible
supreme spiritual gouernour (as is shewed by the
holie Scriptures) it must needes be verie absurd to
say, that the Spouse of Christ hath not this so requisite strength and ornament of one supreme visible Pastor. It is also cleare, that the Gospel can not be
authentically preached in al Nations, except there
be one cheife Prelate of al, to whom the charge of
al perteyneth : because none can preach, vnlesse they
be sent. Againe to say, that the particular Churches
extant in this world, are not one intire Church, cō-
sisting of manie and diuers members, is directly a-
gainst S. Paules doctrine, and other holie Scriptures
before recited. Finally, to say that al these members

Ephes.1,v.
22.

Ephes.5.v.
25.29.

Art. 34.

Rom. 12.
v.5.
1.Cor.12.

v.12.
Ro.10.
v.15.
Apoc.12.
v.3.Ch.
17.v.3.
7.v.9.

bers doe make one vifible bodie; yet haue not one fupreme vifible head, but manie : is to account the Church a monftruous bodie, with manie heades.

2 But to conuince thefe abfurdities, with irrefraga- ble auctoritie of holie Scriptures : we fhal fhew fo breifly as fo important a caufe wil permitte, that Chrift our Lord, did actually conftitute his Apoftle S. Peter, the cheif of al the Apoftles, & fupreme vi- fible Paftor of the whole Militant Church in earth. For more difcuffion wherof, we may obferue, that his diuine wifdome, firft fignifyed his purpofe herein by wordes and factes; then promifed the fame thing; afterwardes actually performed it. And laftly that S. Peter practifed, and the other Apoftles acknow- leged, the fame fupremacie.

3 Firft therfore, when S. Andrew hauing already bene with our Sauiour, brought his brother Simon

Ioan.1.
v.42.

to fee him [Iefus looking vpon him faid; thou art Simon the fonne of Iona : thou fhalt be called Ce- phas, which is interpreted Peter. So the Hebrew or Syriake word *Cephas*, is in Greeke *Petros* or *Pe- tre*, in Latin *Petra*, in Englifh, a *Rock* ; which be- ing applied for a mannes name, the termination is altered, and fo in the Latin is called *Petrus*, & in Englifh (fo neare as our language wel ferueth) *Pe- ter*. But tranflating our Sauiours fpeach, into pro- per Englifh wordes, he faid : Thou art Simon, thou fhalt be called a Rocke. By which maner of impo- fing new names in holie Scripture, is euer fignified fome important Mifterie implied in the Etymologie or original fignification, of the fame word impofed for a proper name. As when God changed the name

Gen.17.
v.5.
Gen.32.
v.28.

[*Abram* into *Abraham*] he fignifyed therby, that the fame Patriarch fhould be the Father of manie Nati- ons. [Iacob] which fignifieth fupplanter, was chan- ged into [Ifrael] fignifying one that feeth, or con-

P p 3

templatteh

That S. Peter was cheife of the Apoftles & head of the whole militant Church, is proued by Chrifts pur- pofe, promife, and factes, and by S. Peters, and other A- poftles prac- tife.

The firft proof. Chrift foretold that Simon fhould be cal- led Peter, which fignifi- eth a Rocke.

templateth God. *Ofee* the fonne of Nun, was chan- | Ch . 35 : ❦,
ged into [*Iofue*] or *Iefus*, to fignifie, that in figure of | 10 .
our B. Sauiour, he fhould faue the children of Ifra-
el from their enemies, bring them into the promifed land of Chanaan. And our Lord and Redemer
[was named *Iefus* , fignifying Sauiour, before he was | *Luc.* 1. *v.*
conceiued, becaufe he fhould faue his people from | 31 . *Mat.*
their finnes] So this new name Rocke, or Peter, fore- | 1 . *v.* 21.
told by our Sauiour; did vndoubtedly forefhew, that | *Luc.* 2. *v.*
he fhould be imployed as a Rocke in fome fpecial | 21 .
worke of God. Whom the fequele did fhortly after declare to be the Rocke wherupon Chrift would
build his Church. Which meruelous wel accordeth | *Mat.* 7. *v.*
with the conclufion of his diuine fermon in the moūt, | 24 .
teaching that a wife man buildeth his houfe vpon
a Rocke.

The fecond
proofe.
Chrift prea-
ched in S. Pe-
térs fhippe, &
bade him
launch into
the fea.

4 Not long after our Sauiours prediction, of changing Simons name into Peter, he forefhewed alfo by
a fact his purpofe to make the fame Peter chcife of
his Apoftles . For when [by the lake of Genefareth, | *Luc.* 5. *v.*
the multitudes preffed vpon him to heare the word | 1 . 2 . 3 .
of God, he feing two fhippes on the fhoare, went
into one of them which was Simons, and there fitting, taught the multitudes out of the fhippe] And
after his fermon [he faid to Simon, Launch forth in- | 4 .
to the deepe, and let loofe your nettes to make a
draught. And Simon anfwearing, faid vnto him.
Maifter, labouring al the night, we haue taken nothing ; but in thy word, I wil let loofe the nette.
And when they had done this, they inclofed a very
great multitude of fifhes, and their nette was broken.
And they bekned to their felowes that were in the o-
ther fhippe, that they fhould come and help them.
And they came and filled both fhippes, fo that they
did finke. Which when Simon Peter did fee, he
fel downe at Iefus knees faying. Goe forth from
me

me becaufe I am a finful man o Lord. For he was
wholly aftonifhed, and al that were with him, at the
draught of fifhes which they had taken. In like maner alfo Iames and Iohn the fonnes of Zebedie, who
were Simons felowes. And Iefus faid to Simon, feare
not; from this time now, thou fhalt be taking men.]
Is it not cleare in this narration of S. Luke, that there
being two fhippes, our Sauiour (al whofe actions are
our inftructions) made choice to preach in that which
was Simons, making vfe alfo of the other, to helpe
Simon in the great draught of fifhes, that he bade
Simon only, launch into the deepe? That Simon only falling on his knees, exprefly acknowledged our
Lordes great worke, and his owne vnworthines?
That al being aftonifhed, our Lord fpake only ro
Simon, bidding him not feare? Foretelling him only before the reft, that he fhould become a fifher of
men? wheras Iames, and Iohn, and the other Apoftles, fhould become alfo fifhers of men? Is it not
here manifeft that our Lord in this fact, forefhewed
a future preeminence, and primacie of Simon, aboue
the reft.?

5 Let vs further fee how the fame proceded to effect. Immediatly after our Sauiour had fhewed thefe
apparant figures of his intention, calling difciples to
remaine with him, as of his proper familie (which
hitherto none did) albeit Simon was yonger brother
to Andrew, and by him firft brought to fee Chrift;
yet is firft named by al the Euangeliftes, as wel in
their firft calling to be Difciples, as when the twelue
were made Apoftles, and where foeuer their names
are recited he is continually firft named. And which
maketh the thing moft affured, S. Mathew addeth
it as his proper title faying: [the names of the twelue
Apoftles be thefe: the firft Simon, who is called Peter, and Andrew his brother] and then reciteth the
reft

Io. 1. *v.*
40. *Mat.*
4. *v.* 18.
Mar. 1.
v. 16.
Luc. 5.
v. 2.
Mat. 10.
v 2. 3.
&c.
Mar. 3.
v. 16.

The third
proofe.
The title
FIRST, is af-
cribed to S.
Peter, and he
is alwayes firft
named.

rest diuersly from the other Euangelistes: For S.
Marke nameth Iames in the Secondplace; S. Luke
in his Gospel, and in the Actes of the Apostles obserueth not the same order, but al put Simon Peter
in the head of their Catologue.

Luc . 6 .v 14. Act . 1 . v 13 .

The fourth
proofe.
Christ actually
gaue him the
name PETER.

6   Now concerning his new name, which our Sauiour foretolde when he first saw him, he actually
gaue it him, at the veric first time when he ordayned
this renowmed College of twelue Apostles, as al the
three Euangelists (which report their names together) doe testifie. S. Mathew saying : the first Simon,
who is called Peter. S. Marke more expresly signifying it to be done at that time, saith : [He (to
witte Christ) made, that twelue should be with him :
and he gaue to Simon the name Peter.] S. Luke
saith: He chose twelue whom he made Apostles : Simon whom he surnamed Peter. S. Iohn also in his
Gospel sufficiently sheweth the preeminence of S.
Peter, describing S. Andrew by the title of S. Peters brother saying : Andrew the brother of Simon
Peter. And so doth S. Luke.

Mat. 10. v . 2 . Mar. 3 . v . 14. 16. Luc . 6 . v . 14. Io . 6 . v . 3 . Luc . 6 · v . 14.

Christ gaue
him power to
walke on the
waters.

7   Neither may we here omitte the miraculous
walking of S. Peter vpon the waters, graunted to
him only, and sure not without mysterie. For when
he with others sayling in a boate, saw our Sauiour
walke on the Sea, and thinking it to be a ghost, for
feare cryed out. He saying to them : [Haue confi-
dece, it is I, feare not : Peter said; Lord if it be thou,
bid me come to thee, vpon the waters. And he said
come : then Peter descending out of the boate, walked vpon the water to come to Iesus.] As therfore
Christ by his walking vpon the sea, as wel as vpon
the land, shewed his power ouer the whole world:
so it pleased him by this fact, to signifie that Peters
Iurisdiction should be extended ouer al, by sea and
land. That also which immediatly foloweth in the

Mat . 14. v . 26. 27 .

next

v . 30.
31.

next wordes of S. Peters feare, feing the winde rough, and of his afking and receiuing helpe from Chrift, teacheth vs that notwithftanding the infir_mities of gouerners, Chrift our Sauiour holdeth them vp, and by them conferueth his Church. We know right wel that Proteftantes denie and contemne thefe proofes, and it is eafie to denie, when they can not otherwife refute Catholique doctrine; but we vrge them to tel vs directly what other true fenfe thefe fpeaches, and factes can haue? Nedes they muft grant, that al thefe thinges were done for fpecial purpofes, and written by the Euangeliftes, for con_firmation of Chriftian doctrine. And therefore we ioyne iffue with them, that this is the true fenfe which al Catholique writers auouch, rather then anie other which they can alleage to the contrarie.

6.
Chrift promi_fed to build his Church vpon Peter, as vpon a Rocke.

8 But now we come to more knowen places, yet not more frequent, then conuincing proofes in this pre_fent point of S. Peters Supremacie. The time ap_proaching that our Sauiour would paffe out of this world, for inftruction of his Apoftles concerning the forme of gouernment which he would ordeine, and leaue with them, for the ftabilitie of his Church, he demanded of them, afwel the peoples opinions, as their owne iudgements, whom they fuppofed

Mat. 16.
v . 13.

him felf to be, faying: [Whom fay men that the Sône of man is?] they reporting the diuers brutes of the people, according to their imaginations; he reply_

15.

ing, demanded of his twelue Apoftles [But whom doe you fay that I am? Simon Peter anfwered and

16.

faid; Thou art Chrift the Sonne of the liuing God.] Which point of faith is the ground of al Chriftian Religion: that Iefus, the Sonne of the B. Virgin, (therof called the Sonne of Man) is the promifed Meffias, & alfo the very natural onlie begoten Sonne of God. This confeffion being made by S. Peter in

behalf

behalf of them al (for al being demanded, he alone
anfwered) Chrift, not further requiring euerie ones
particular anfwere, but proceding to his purpofe,
approued and commended Peters anfwer, faying:
[Bleffed art thou Simon Bar-iona becaufe flefh and   *v*. 17.
bloud hath not reuealed it to thee; but my Father
which is in heauen. And I fay to thee: That thou art   18.
Cephas, & vpon this Cephas, wil I build my Church.]
So is the Siriake, or Hebrew text. In Greeke and
Latin, in thefe termes [Thou art Peter, and vpon
this Peter] In Englifh, tranflating the wordes into
their proper fighification, we muft fay thus [Thou
art a Rocke, and vpon this Rocke wil I build my
Church.] In al languages, the demoftratiue pro-
none *this*, hath neceffarie relation to the word going before, and can not be referred in right con-
ftruction, to anie other thing, as Proteftantes doe
wraft it, and abfurdly referre it to Chrift him felf, or
to the faith of Peter, not to his perfon. For if our
Sauiour had fo meant, as they wil feme to imagine:
then he would haue faid, vpon a Rocke, not vpon
this Rocke. But he did not fay fo, and therfore it is
cleare that he did not meane as they fay, but he ab-
folutly meant as he fpake to his Apoftle: Vpon that
which thou art, wil I build my Church, for none can
denie his wordes [thou art a Rocke, and vpon this
Rocke wil I build my Church] And fo in the next
wordes, declareth the ftabilitie of his Church being
built vpon a Rocke: faying that [the gates of hel,   18.
(that is al the forces coming from hel) fhal not preuaile againft it.]

7.
He promifed
him alfo to
geue him the
keyes of the
kingdome of
heauen

9   To the very fame purpofe he alfo addeth; fpeaking ftil to the fame Apoftle:[And I wil geue to thee   *Mat*. 16.
the keyes of the kingdome of heauen.] Euerie one   *v*. 19.
knoweth that the geuing of keyes, is geuing of power,
& auctoritie, to let in, or kepe out of that place, wher
                                                        to the

to the keyes perteyne. And our Sauiour geuing to
S. Peter the keyes of the kingdome of heauen, explicateth his meaning. yet further, that S. Peters
sentences, and iudgementes in earth shal haue effect,
not only in earth, but also in heauen, saying: [what-
soeuer thou shalt binde vpon earth it shal be bounde
also in the heauens: and whatsoeuer thou shalt
loose in earth, it shalbe loosed also in the heauens,
wherin is necessarily vnderstoode S. Peters Primacie aboue the other Apostles: who also receiued
spiritual power to bind and loose in earth which accordingly is bond & loosed in heauen. For in case a-
nie other should attempt to binde or loose contrarie
to S Peter, then must his sentence preuaile, and that
which anie other attempteth contrarie to him, is not
of force, because otherwise (which is absurde, and
impossible) Goddes word should be contrary to it
self, and in some place, should not be verified, if
the other Apostles binding and loosing, were not
subordinate, and subiect to S. Peter. But being so
vnderstoode, the seming contradiction is reconciled,
and the holie Scripture, in both places, is most true.

10   After this declaration of our Sauiour, in presence of al his Apostles, that he would build his
Church vpon S. Peter, whom for this purpose he had
made a Rocke: He shewed likewise by an other
acte, the same thing, that S. Peter should be head
of the Apostolical College and familie next and immediatly vnder him self. For condescending to pay
the Tribute of a Didrachme, exacted for the heades of
Families; he sent S. Peter where to haue a Statere,
being in valew two Didrachmes, and so to pay it
for them both. [Goe thy waies to the sea (said
our Sauiour to Peter) and cast a hooke; and that
fishe which shal first come vp, take; and when thou
hast opened his mouth, thou shalt finde a Statere,

Mat. 18.
v. 18.

Mat. 17.
v. 25.

27.

8.
He payed tri-
bute for S. Pe-
ter as for the
head of a fami-
lie.

Qq 2   take

take that and geue it them for me and thee] Why
our Sauour would haue this Tribute of house-hol-
ders, to be paide for Peter alone, and not for anie
other of the Apostles, there can not possibly be anie
other reason imagined, but because he was indeede
the head of that Familie, as Christes principal Vicar, & by him so to be constituted.

9-
The Apostles
vnderstoode by
this fact, that
S. Peter was
designed to be
the head of
them al.

11   If this text were not cleare enough, yet it is
made more manifest, by the Apostles present dispute about Superioritie, writen by S. Mathew in
the next wordes. And that it hapened presently, S.
Marke testificth saying, that our Sauour, when they
were come to Capharnaum, asked them [What did
you treate of in the way ? But they held their peace,
for in the way, they had disputed among themselues, which of them should be the greater ?] And
therfore to cure this infirmitie [he called the twelue
& said vnto them : If anie man wil be first, he shal
be last of al, and the minister of al. For he that is
the lesser among you al, he is greater] So teaching
humilitie, and withal auouching Superioritie. For
they al easilie vnderstoode, superioritie to be necessarie. And to obteine higher places, Iames and Iohn
had suborned their mother to intercede for them.
Wherupon she [adoring, requested, that these her
two sonnes might sitte, one at his right hand, and
one at his left hand in his kingdome] But our Lord
againe answearing them said : [You know not what
you desire] admonishing and exhorting them, to
thinke of suffering with him, and not of ruling and
ouerruling as Gentiles doe. And lastly said to them
al, the night before his deeth [He that is the greater
among you, let him become as the yonger, and he
that is the leader, as the waiter] stil confirming his
former wordes, and factes, that there must be a greater, and a leader amongst them; not S. Iames nor S.

                                                        Iohn

Mat. 18.
v. 1.2.&c.
Mar. 9. *v.*
33. 34.

35. 36.

Mat. 20.
v. 20. 21.
22.

Luc. 22.
v. 26.

Iohn, nor anie that fought the firft place, but he that was called, muft vndertake that office.

12 Accordingly S. Peter for moft part fpake in the name and behalf of al. And others ordinarily fpake of him as of the leader and cheife. When our Sauiour tooke only three to be prefent at his transfiguration, S. Peter, S. Iames, and S. Iohn, they were al rauifhed with ioy, feing a Glimfe of Chriftes glorie, [for his face did fhine as the Sunne, and his garmentes became white as fnow, gliftering exceedingly] only S. Peter was bolde to propofe that which they al thought [But Peter (faith S. Luke) and they that were with him, were heauie with fleepe. And awaking, they faw his Maieftie] Moyfes alfo and Elias appearing in Maieftie : Then [Peter faid, Lord it is good for vs to be here. If thou wilt, let vs make here three Tabernacles ; one for thee, one for Moyfes, and one for Elias .] At an other time, our Lord going forth into a defert place to pray [Simon Peter and they that were with him (faith S. Marke) fought him out.] Our Sauiour being preffed in the multitude, and demanding who had touched him [Peter (faith S. Luke) and they that were with him faid. Maifter the multitudes throng thee &c.] When manie went backe at Capharnaum, not vnderftanding his diuine difcourfe concerning Manna, & the B. Sacrament of his Bodie ; and he faying to the twelue [wil you alfo depart ? Simon Peter anfwering (for al) faid : Lord to whom fhal we goe ? Thou haft the wordes of eternal life .] When our Lord fhewed the fruict of contemning the world, and folowing him : Peter anfwering faid to him : Behold we (meaning him felf & the other Apoftles) haue left al thinges and haue folowed thee ; what therfore fhal we haue ?] When our Sauiour by a parable fhewed the neceffitie of diligent watching,

Mat. 17.
v. 2. 4.
Mar. 9.
v. 3. 5.
Luc. 9.
v. 29.
30. 31.
32.

Mar. 1.
v. 36.

Luc. 8.
v. 45.

Ioan. 6.
v. 68.

Mat. 19.
v. 27.

10.
S. Peter ordinarily fpake in the name of them al. And was reputed the cheife by the Euangelifts.

Q q 3 Peter

[Peter ſaid to him : Lord doſt thou ſpeake this parable to vs, or to al ?] And when he had curſed a figtree, and incontinent it withered, al the Diſciples merueled : but only [Peter (as the mouth of al) ſaid to him : Rabbi, behold the fig tree that thou didſt curſe, is withered .] Al which his ordinarie anſwearing, demanding, & ſpeaking as a publique perſon ; the Euangeliſtes relations alſo in that ſpecial maner ſaying : [Peter, & they that were with him] doe plainly ſhew that he was the cheife & head of the reſt .

Luc . 12. v. 41 . Mat . 21. v . 20. Mar . 11. v . 21 .

11.
Our Lord waſhing his Apoſtles feete, beganne with S. Peter.

13   To theſe euident proofes we muſt yet adioyne other factes, and ſpeaches of our Sauiour, confirming this doctrine of S . Peters Primacie . It pleaſed our Lord after the ſupper of the old Teſtament, before he inſtituted the new Sacrifice, to waſh al his Apoſtles feete . And that he began with S. Peter as the cheife, who firſt replying and refuſing, as ſeming to him vnmeete, but vpon Chriſts wordes ſubmitting him ſelf to his wil, is cleare by S. Iohns narration : telling that our ſauiour [roſe from ſupper, laide a ſide his vpper garment, tooke water in a baſon, girded him ſelf with a towel, and ſo came to Simon Peter ; and Peter ſaid to him : Lord doeſt thou waſh my feete . Ieſus ſaid to him : that which I doe thou knoweſt not now : hereafter thou ſhalt know.] yet [Peter ſaid to him : thou ſhalt neuer waſh my feete . But our Lord Ieſus anſwered ; If I waſh thee not, thou ſhalt not haue part with me.] then Peter ſubmitted him ſelf, and ſo without more reply al the reſt .

Io . 13 . v. 4 . 5 . 6 . 7 . &c .

12.
Praying for them, prayed ſingularly for S. Peter.

14   Againe the ſame night our Sauiour declared in plaine wordes an other important difference, and ſingular priuelege of S . Peter aboue them al, geuen to him as the head, for the confirmation of his brethren . Our Lord ſaid (in preſence of al, but directing his ſpeach to Peter only) [Simon, Simon behold

Luc . 22. v. 31 . 32.

hold Sathan hath required for to haue you for to fifte
as wheat : but I haue prayed for thee, that thy faith
faile not; and thou once conuerted, confirme thy brethren.] The diuel defired to fift and trie them al,
as this text maketh manifeft ; our Lord praied alfo
[for his other Apoftles, and for al that fhould beleue
by their word] as S. Iohn teftifieth, yet more efpecially [he praied for Peter, that his faith fhould neuer
faile] by which prerogatiue of the head, the whole
bodie is confirmed, and vpholden in vnitie and veritie, free from fchifme and herefie, againft al the affaultes of the diuel; and fo al are ftrengthned that
hold the faith and vnion of Peter. Thus much before Chriftes death.

Io. 17.
v. 11. 19.
20.

15   After his Refurection, the holie Angel that declared to S. Marie Magdalene, and the other deuout
women, that our Lord was rifen from death, willed them to goe and tel the Difciples, and Peter, only
naming Peter for his prerogatiue, and eminent place
aboue the reft, for els it might haue fufficed, to haue
comprehended him in the general name of Difciples,
if he had bene but equal with them.

Mat. 16.
v. 7.

13.
The Angel wil-
led the holie
women to tel
S. Peter by
name, that
Chrift was ri-
fen.

16   Neither otherwife neded S. Iohn, coming firft
to the monument to haue ftaied, that S. Peter might
enter firft, but for that he refpected S. Peter as his defigned Superior. There may be (we doubt not) fome
other Myfterie alfo vnderftood by this Act. for holie Sriptures are fertile of manie fenfes. But amongft
others the verie letter declareth Maioritie in S. Peter, aboue S. Iohn.

Io. 20.
v. 5. 8.

14.
S. Iohn refpec-
ted S. Peter as
his Superior.

17   And that our Sauiour appeared to S. Peter, before his apparition to them al together, is teftified
by the two Difciples, to whom he appeared the fame
firft day in the way to Emaus. For they returning
prefently to al the Apoftles at Ierufalem, affirmed exprefly, that [our Lord is rifen in deede, and hath appeared

Luc. 24.
v. 34.

15.
Chrift appea-
red to him firft
of al the A-
poftles.

peared to Simon.] And so S. Paul saith [He was seene
of Cephas, and after that, of the eleuen .] Al which
are signes sufficient of his Preeminence .

1. *Cor* . 15.
v. 5.

16.
Christ consti-
tuted S. Peter
the Pastor of
the whole
Church, of al
lambes ; and
al sheepe.

18 But his ful establishment in the Ecclesiastical Primacie , is most plainly described by the Euangelist
S. Iohn, in the third publique Apparition of our Sauiour to his Disciples, by the sea of Tiberias . Where
S . Peter vnderstanding that it was our Sauiour
which spake to him from the shore, walked to him
vpon the water, without anie further commadement,
as before he had done vpon our Lords word . Wheras
the other Disciples came in the boate, drawing the
nette of fishes. After which narration of our Lords
so appearing on the shore: of S . Peters going on
the water; of the taking of a great, & certaine number of fishes, without breach of the nette : of their dy-
ning together : and of the assurance which euerie one
of them had that it was our Lord, which so manifested
him self : Together with this so cleare an historie : he
proceeded to the principal point saying [Therefore
when they had dyned ; Iesus said to Simon Peter : Simon of Iohn louest thou me more then these ? He
said to him : yea Lord thou knowest that I loue thee .
He saith to him : Feede my lambes. Iesus saith to him
againe : Simon of Iohn louest thou me? he saith
to him : yea Lord thou knowest that I loue thee .
He said to him, Feede my lambes . Iesus said to him
the third time : Simon of Iohn louest thou me ? Peter
was strooken sad, because he said vnto him the third
time; louest thou me? And he said to him: Lord thou
knowest al thinges: thou knowest that I loue thee .
Iesus said to him: Feede my sheepe] Thus the sacred
text. Can anie man require more plaine wordes ?
more solemnitie? more ful auctoritie ? more am-
aple iurisdiction ? Wherfore did not equal loue suffice,
but more loue was necessarie in S . Peter then in
the

Io. 21.
v. 1. *&c.*

4. 5. 6.
&c.

Io. 21. *v.*
15.

Ib.

17.

**Christ requi-
red more loue
of S. Peter thē
of the rest.**

the other Apostles; but becaufe his charge of foules was greater then theirs ? Why was he demanded thrice the fame thing, but that by fo folemne an inftitution, he and al the world might know his greater obligation to feede our Sauiours flocke ? What needed the thre-fold admonition to feede, but that before al other good workes of almes deedes, praying, fafting, and other vertues, Charitie in feeding foules, with true faith, wholfome Lawes, and iuft regiment, excelleth in the fupreme paftor ? Finally who can be excepted, or exempted from S. Peters iurifdiction, when al Chriftes flocke, yong and old, Laitie, and Cleargie, [Lambes and fheepe] are by Chrift committed to S. Peters charge? Whofoeuer wil be counted a fheeepe or Lambe of Chrift, is vnder the charge of S. Peter; if not vnder him, then is he none of Chriftes folde, nor flocke.

49   It refteth breefly to fee fome practice of this fupreme office in holie Scriptures. Prefently after our Lordes Afcenfion, the eleuen Apostles, with our B. Ladie and other faithful perfons (in al nere an hundred and twentie) remaining together in praier, S.

Act.1.
v.13.14.
15.16.
&c.
Pf. 40.
v. 10.
Pf. 108.
v.8.
Act.1.v.
25. 26.

[Peter ryfing vp, in the middeft of the brethren faid: you men brethre, the Scripture muft be fulfilled which the Holie Ghoft fpake before by the mouth of Dauid concerning Iudas ; who was numbred among vs, and obteyned the lotte of this minifterie] And fo S. Peter beginning to execute his Vicarfhippe, gaue inftruction and order, by which S. Matthias was elected Apoftle in place from which Iudas was fallen, to make vp againe the number of twelue Apoftles.

20   When the Holie Ghoft was come, and had replenifhed the faithful with giftes of tongues, and

Act. 2.
v. 2.3.
&c. 12.
13. 14.

other graces, wherat al were aftonied, & fome fcorners deriding faid [thefe are ful of new wine: S.

17.
S. Peter praectifed his Primacie in the election of S. Matthias.

18.
S. Peter firft preached after the coming of the Holie Ghoft.

R r   Peter

[Peter ſtāding with the other eleuē Apoſtles (as heads in al their names) lifted vp his voice, and ſpake to them : Ye men Iewes and al you that dwel in Ieruſalem, be this knowne to you, and with your eares receiue my wordes] my wordes (ſaith he) For albeit he alone ſpake , yet he iuſtly chalenged audience and due regard to his ſpeach being Superiour, and ſpeaking with auctoritie, as alſo the effect by and by ſhewed . For he declaring that it was not drūkennes, as the deriders at firſt ſuppoſed, [but the Holie Ghoſt that gaue them knowlege and vtterance, with al tongues, to ſpeake the great workes of God] He proued [by the Prophets Ioel and Dauid, that *v. 16. 25.* Ieſus, whom the cruel Iewes had crucified, was riſen from death, aſcended into heauen, had ſent the Holie Ghoſt] powring out abundance of grace . [And the people hearing theſe thinges, were com- *37.38.* punct in hart] and by S . Peters further inſtruction, the reſt of the Apoſtles aſſenting and aſſiſting [three *41.* thouſand perſons were baptized the ſame day .]

19 .
S . Peter
wrought the
firſt miracle, &
anſweared the
Aduerſaries .

21   Together with preaching , S . Peter alſo firſt of al the Apoſtles, confirmed the faithful, and con- *Act. 3. v.* uerted infidels by working miracles . [S . Peter , *1 . 2 . 3 .* and S . Iohn, going into the Temple, there was in the porch a poore man lame from his mothers wombe, who aſking almes of them, S . Peter with S . Iohn *4.* looking vpon him ſaid : looke vpon vs] he ſo doing , & hoping to receiue ſome thing of them, S . [Peter ſaid, Siluer and Gold I haue not : but that which I haue, the ſame I geue to thee : In the name of Ieſus Chriſt of Nazereth, ariſe and walke . And taking his right hand, he lifted him vp ; and forthwith his feete & ſoles were made ſtrong . And ſpringing, he ſtoode and walked, and went with them into the Temple , walking and leaping, and praiſing God] wherupon al the people being [aſtonied, agaſt] and wonde- *12.* ring

ing : S. Peter declared, that [not in their owne
power, but in the power of Iesus, whom they had
killed, & in the faith of his name, this mã was strégth-
ned, and receiued perfect health in the sight of them
Act. 4. al] Manie of the hearers [beleued and the number
v. 1. 3. of the faithful was made fiue thousand] But [the Ma-
4. gistrates of the Temple, and the Sadduces, put these
two Apostles into ward al that night. And on the
5. morow, Annas, Caiphas, with other Princes, Ancientes, and Scribes, and as manie as were of the Preistes
stock, gathering into Ierusalem, causing the two A-
postles to be brought before them : asked, in what
power, or in what name, haue you done this ?]
6. Then S. [Peter said to them. Ye Princes of the
people and Ancientes, if we this day be examined for
a good deede, vpon an impotent man ; in what he
hath bene made whole : Be it knowne to al you,
and to al the people of Israel, that in the name of
Iesus Christ of Nazareth whom you did crucifie,
whom God hath raised from the dead ; in this same
this man standeth before you whole.]

22   In matter also of Iudgement and correction of

20.
He punished
the sacrilege of
Ananias, and
Saphira.

Act. 5. delinquentes among the faithful : S. Peter, as Head
v. 3. and Iudge, condemned and punished, the sacrilegious crime of Ananias and Saphira his wife. who by
diuine inspiration, knowing their secret fault, publiquely reproued them both seuerally. First the husband [For lying to the Holie Ghost, and defrau-
5. ding] the communitie [which he hearing, fel downe
& gaue vp the Ghost. And about three houres after, the wife not knowing what was chanced to her
7. husband, came in. And S. Peter said vnto her ;
tel me woman, whether did you sel the land for so
much ? And she said, yea for so much. Then said S.
Peter to her ; Why haue you agreed together, to
9. tempt the Spirit of our Lord ? Behold the feete of

them

them that haue buried thy husband, are at the doare, and they shal beare thee forth. And forthwith she fel before his feete and gaue vp the ghost. And the yong men going in, found her dead, and caried her forth, and buried her by her husband.] Other actes of Apostolical power and iurisdiction, were likewise first exercised by S. Peter. As [the imposition of handes vpon the baptized, wherby they receiued the Holie Ghost. The reprouing of Simon the Magitian, for offering to buy that spiritual power with money. Not that S. Peter only did these functions, but in that he first put them in executió, his primacie plainly appeareth.

margin: 10.

Act. 8. v. 14.17.

20.

23 And so doth not only his first working of miracles before the other Apostles, but also his greater and most frequent miracles of al the twelue Apostles, shew the same. S. Luke writeth, that al the Apostles praied for this special grace, to worke cures and signes in the holie name of Iesus : And when they had praied, the place was moued wherin they were gathered, and they were al replenished with the Holie Ghost, and they spake the word of God with confidence. In general also he saith, that by the handes of the Apostles, were manie signes and wonders done among the people : but of S. Peters miracles, he maketh more particular mention, then of al the rest. [The faithful people did bring forth the sicke into the streetes (saith he) and laid them in beddes, and couches, that when Peter came, his shadow at the least might ouershadow anie of them, and they al might be deliuered from their infirmities. And there ranne together vnto Ierusalem, the multitude also of the Cities adioyning, bringing sick persons, and such as were vexed of vncleane spirits, who were al cured.] Doubtles the other Apostles did also cure manie, yet only S. Peter is here named.

And

left margin:

21.
He wrought more frequent miracles then anie other of the eleuen Apostles, & the faithful respected him as the cheife.

right margin:

Act. 4. v 30.31.

Act. 5. v 12.

v. 15.

16.

29. And in their anſweares to the perſecuters, commanding them to ceaſe from preaching Chriſt. [But Peter anſwearing and the Apoſtles, ſaid : God muſt be obeyed rather then men,] Al anſweared by the mouth of S. Peter . Shortly after the Martyrdome of S . Stephen, & conuerſion of S . Paul, the Church being growne ouer al Iewrie, Galilee, and Samaria;

Act. 9. S. Peter viſiting al, wrought ſundrie miracles . [At

ʋ. 32. Lidda, he healed a man named Eneas, who had laid

33. 34. eight yeares in beddeſicke of the palſey.] At Iop-

40. 41. pa [he raiſed a godly woman named Tabitha from death.]

24 Moreouer S . Peter receiued the firſt Gentiles

Act. 10. into the Church of Chriſt, and that by warrant [of a

ʋ. 11. viſion from heauen ſhewed to him ſelf, with a commandement to admitte al nations.] wherto alſo agreed an other viſion made to Cornelius a Gentile.

ʋ. 5. 6. with expreſſe direction [to ſend into Ioppe, to Si-

28. 32. mon ſurnamed Peter, and of him to heare the word

38. of God] And finally S . [Peter inſtructing the ſame

24. 28. Cornelius, with al his familie, kindred, and ſpecial frendes, called for this purpoſe; commanded them to be baptiſed.] Before which fact of S . Peter, though

Act. 11. [ſome that had bene diſperſed (when S . Stephen

ʋ. 19. was ſtoned to death) walked vnto Phenice, Cypres, and Antioch : yet they ſpake the word to none but to the Iewes only] that were in thoſe places . But after that S . Peter had thus begune and returning to Ieruſalem, auouched and iuſtified the ſame, by warrant of the viſions, againſt other Chriſtian Iewes,

20. 21. which reprehended him for it . Then [others alſo ſpake to the Greekes in Antioch, preaching our Lord Ieſus . And the hand of our Lord was with them, & a great number of beleuers was conuerted to our Lord.]

25 In manie caſes, and namely in queſtion of Supe-

22.
He receiued the firſt Gentiles into the Church.

23.
He was moſt e-

especially per-
secuted by the
enimies.

rioritie, the Iudgement of aduersaries is a great confirmation, who impugning the whole bodie, especially assault the head. So the incredulous Iewes opposing with al their might against the Church of
Christ, more egerly persecuting S. Peter, shewed
therby that they held him for the cheife of the A-
postles. As appeared by king Herodes proceding:
who [seing it pleased the Iewes, that he had killed
S. Iames (to doe them a great pleasure in that kinde)
apprehended Peter also (attempting nothing against
the other S. Iames, being then also in Ierusalem)
but because it was the feast of Azimes, he cast him
into prison meaning after the Pasch to bring him forth
to the people] In the meane time keping him with
an extraordinarie guard [of foure quaternions of
souldiars, bound also with two chaines, and when he
slept, he laid betwene two souldiers.] Neither were
they deceiued in holding him to be the greatest of
the Apostles, for the whole Church did know him
so to be; which they declared by their more instant
[praier without intermission for his deliuerie] which
effect God graunted [deliuering him by the ministerie of an Angel, out of Herodes hand, and from al
the expectation of the Iewes] for the longer gouernment of the Church : Which can not stand without
vnitie, nor vnitie be conserued without one supreme
head : No not by a general Councel, except it haue
one cheif Iudge.

Act. 12. ⚓
2. 3.
17.

4.
6.

5.
7. &c.
11.

24.
He was cheife
head of the A-
postolical
Councel.

26 Example wherof is extant, in the Apostolical
Councel holden at Ierusalem, which shal be our last
proofe in this plaee of S. Peters Supremacie aboue
al the other Apostles. For [when al the Apostles
were mette, and when great disputation was made,
al hauing spoken that they thought most true, producing their particular iudgementes, according to
their seueral opinions, for better discussing of the có-
                                        trouersie

Act. 15.
v. 47.

Ibidem

Act .10.

v. 20.

25.

30.

13 . 14.

22.

23.

trouersie : then [Peter rising vp (saith S. Luke) said to them (to witte to the whole Councel assembled) Men brethren, you know that of old daies, God among vs chose, that by my mouth, the Gentiles should heare the word of the Gospel, and beleue .] And so he decided the case, that [the Gentiles were not to be burdened with Circumcision, and other partes of the old Law, which yoke (said he) is not to be put vpon their neckes. To whose sentence al agreed. And S. Iames, as proper Bishop of that place, promulgated the same ; therto ad ioyning his owne conformable iudgement, as Catholique Bishoppes euer since vse to doe in holie Coūcels. S. Paul also , and S. Barnabas, with Barsabas and Silas, were sent for this purpose to Antioch. And al the other Apostles (whatsoeuer anie of them thought before (for the controuersie was great) vniformly after S . Peters sentence [beleued , obserued, & taught the same, subscribing [by their handes] to that which he, as their head, definitiuely declared.

Act. 8.

v. 17.

Ch. 12.

1 . *Cor*.

9. *v*. 5.

Gal. 1. *v*.

18.19.

Gal. 2.

v. 27.

27 We might yet adde more proofes, as that S. Peter first administred Confirmation, that for him, being in prison, the whole Church made perpetual prayer, as we touched euen now : also that S. Paul in defence of his fact, which some Corinthians disliked, alleaged the example of other Apostles, and namely of Cephas, pleading that thing to be lawful , which Cephas the Rocke of the Church did approue . His going to Ierusalem to see Peter, abiding with him fiftene dayes, and conferring pointes of Christian doctrine with him, lest otherwise he might haue erred , and the like which I wil omitte : not doubting but that anie Catholique diuine may cōfidently ioyne issue vpō one anie of these foure & twentie proofes, which soeuer a Protestant his aduersarie, shal thinke to be

Other textes of holie Scripture which also proue this truth : are here omitted, because these before alleaged , may abundātly suffice.

to be the weakeſt, to proue this point of Catholique doctrine, that S. Peter was cheife of the Apoſtles: & viſible head of the whole militant Church in earth. Much more doe al theſe together, moſt fully & ſuperabundantly demonſtrate the ſame.

Luc .22.*v.* 36.39.50. *Io* . 18. *v.* 10.11. *Act.* 8. *v* . 20.

Christ ordeyned a continual Succeſſion of S. Peters
Supremacie : to the end of this world.

ARTICLE. 36

**The like neceſ-
ſitie of one ſu-
preme head
which was in
the beginning
of the Church,
continueth to
the end of this
world.**

Reaſon may ſatisfy al reaſonable perſons, that our Sauiour eſtabliſhing his Church, or-deined one, and the ſame forme of gouern-ment to continue therin, aſwel after the Apoſtles time, as during the ſpace of their temporal liues. Seing therfore he conſtituted one cheife head to be his Vicar in earth, which was S. Peter (as is clearly ſhewed in the precedent Article) it conſequently fo-loweth, that ſtil there is, and muſt be, one like ſu-preme viſible head, his Succeſſor, and Chriſtes Vi-car, from time to time, becauſe the ſame neceſſitie remaineth of one head, conformable to the bodie; which otherwiſe would be both monſtruous with manie heades, and ſubiect to ruine by diuiſion with-in it ſelf. And therfore our Lordes prouident care (that no ſuch incouenience fal vpon his Church) doth indeede continue without intermiſſion, to the very end of this world. For ſo he expreſly promiſed by theſe moſt louing wordes [Behold (ſaid he to his Apoſtles, before his Aſcenſion) I am with you al daies, euen to the conſummation of the world.] which promiſe we ſee, is not limited to any ſhorter time, but amply extended, euen vntil this world ſhal be conſummated. And ſo perteyned not only to the Apoſtles, but alſo to their true ſucceſſors. For nei-ther

Mat. 12. *v*. 25. *Mar* .3.*v.* 21. *Luc* . 11. *v.* 17. *Mat.* 28. *v* . 20.

ther could they, nor anie of them, alwaies tarie in this Militant Church, nor Chriſtes care ceaſe, nor his promiſe be fruſtrate at anie time.

2   How then is this performed ? The Royal Pſalmiſt in ſpirit of Prophecie, foreſeing the Succeſſion of Paſtors, which ſhould continually feede & gouern the Church of Chriſt, ſpeaketh thus vnto her [For thy fathers, there are borne ſonnes to thee : thou ſhalt make them Princes ouer al the earth .] The Apoſtles were the fathers ſent by Chriſt, which begate the Chriſtian Church : by preaching the Goſpel, conuerted manie Nations; by Baptiſme, manie ſonnes were borne to the Church ; by Apoſtolical miniſterie, manie particular Churches were founded , al members of one vniuerſal militant Church . Of theſe her owne ſonnes, the ſame Church ordeineth Biſhopes, and other Paſtors; ſo making them ſpiritual Princes ouer al the earth . And that in the ſame Monarchical forme of Eccleſiaſtical Hierarchie, and ſacred ſubordination, as at firſt our Sauiour ordeined : ſo doth he conſerue and continue it [For Ieſus Chriſt (ſaith S . Paul to the Chriſtian Hebrewes) yeſterday , & to day, the ſame alſo for euer .] And therfore his fact in ordeining one Apoſtle Superiour of the reſt, ſufficiently inſtructeth vs, that he hath therwithal inſtituted one Apoſtolical Biſhope, ſucceſſour of the ſae cheif Apoſtle , the ordinarie Superiour of al other Biſhopes, though there were none other proofe beſides in holie Scripture. Neuertheleſſe the ſame Chriſtian doctrine, is further confirmed, by diuers of thoſe ſacred textes, by which S . Peters Supremacie is alreadie declared , and alſo by ſome others . And by no place at al in holie Scriptures, can the contrarie euer be proued, nor with anie reaſon auouched .

3   Among other, proofes, this truth is eaſily vnderſtoode by the figure therof. For in the old Te
ſtament

Pſ. 44.
v. 17.

Heb. 13.
c. 8.

How ſonnes
are borne by
the Church &
made fathers

The perpetual
ſucceſſion of
one ſupreme
head in the

S s

Church of
Christ, is proued by example of the
old Testament.

stament, there was euer one visible head of Gods
Church : one cheif Patriarch in the Law of nature.
In the written Law, for his time, Moyses extraordinarie, but most part of the same time, Aaron was
the ordinarie high Preist. Him succeded Eleazer his
sonne; after him, his sonne Phinees, and so other
High Preistes in continual succession. Much more
assured is the succession of cheise Pastors in the new
Testament [They shal be mindful of Gods glorie
and name in al generation and generation. Vpon
thy wales (saith God to Ierusalem, the Church in
al Nations). I haue appointed watchmen al the day
and al the night; for euer they shal not hold their
peace : you that remember our Lord, hold not your
peace.] These and other Prophets, foreshewing
that there shal euer be Pastors in the Church, presuppose their subordination in vnitie, vnder one
head. Which Ezechiel expresly affirmeth of Christ,
by the name of Dauid [My seruant Dauid (saith
our Lord) shal be King ouer them, & there shal be
ONE PASTOR of them al] which vndoubtedly is
Christ, sometime visible in earth, & stil inuisibly teaching by his visible Vicar, one knowne supreme Pastor, who is also necessarie by this Prophets doctrine, for the vniting of al Nations in the Church

It is necessarie
for the sending
of preachers
into heathen
countries.

of Christ. Because none can be authentically sent,
to preach vnto infidels, but by the Supreme Pastor
of Christes flocke. For one flocke necessarily requireth one Pastor : and a visible bodie, a visible head.
Yea such a head, as doth and must mutually cooperate with other members, and be assisted by them,
as hauing neede of their helpe (which Christ our
principal head needeth not) For of such a head S.

S. Paul speaketh of such a
head as hath
neede of feete,
and other

Paul speaketh : exhorting al estates of the Church,
each sort to doe their functions with peace and concord : shewing that none is able to execute al requisite

Gen. 5. v.
1. 3. 6.
&c.
Gen. 10. v.
1. 22.
1. Par. 1.
v. 1. 2. 3.
4.
Exo. 6. v.
1. 28.
Exo. 29. v.
30. Leuit.
8. v. 2. 12.
Nu. 20. v.
25.
Ps. 44. v.
18. Is. 62.
v. 6.
Ezech. 37.
v. 24.

Rom. 10.
v. 15.

site

fite offices; but al haue neede of others helpe. For example. Amongſt other members of a natural bodie, reſembling the diuers members of the Church,

1. *Cor.* 12. *v.* 20.

[the head (ſaith he) can not ſay to the feete, you are not neceſſarie for me] which ſpeach can not be rightly applied to our Sauiour Chriſt, becauſe he can truly ſay to the feete, and to al other members of his Church, you are not neceſſarie for me. For although he of his good pleaſure, vſeth the miniſterie of his ſeruantes, yet he needeth them not, for he can doe what him pleaſeth without them. And [when

Luc. 17. *v.* 10.
Iob. 22. *v.* 3.

they haue done al thinges that were commanded them; they muſt ſay we are vnprofitable ſeruantes] becauſe to Chriſt, [they bring no profit] to him they are not neceſſarie. Two thinges therfore by this Apoſtolical doctrine we learne, very conformable to the Prophet euen now alleaged; that the Miſtical bodie of Chriſt, hath one viſible head; & that it hath ſuch a head, as nedeth other members, and namely feete,

Iſ. 52. *v.* 7.
Rom. 10. *v.* 15.

which are Preachers of Goddes word, called [the beautiful feete of them that Euangelize peace, that Euangelize good thinges.

4 This miniſterial head therfore, is the Paſtor of Paſtors in earth, the ſupreme viſible head, aboue al other members. more eſpecially priuileged, for the confirmation of his brethren; becauſe he is the inuincible Rocke, wheron is continually building, and daily adding, of moe faithful ſoules. [Vpon this Rocke (ſaid our Sauiour, hauing deſigned his Apoſtle S. Peter for this purpoſe) wil I build my Church.] It is cleare alſo, that our Lord after his Reſurrection conſtituted his former deſigned Deputie with charge to feede both Lambes and Sheepe. But this his fact was but the beginning of his promiſed worke, for this worke is, and ſtil wil be in hand, til the end of this world. And therfore this miniſterial viſible Rocke, is ſtil in the world. Els could not

Mat. 16. *v.* 18.
Io. 21. *v.* 16. 17.

This miniſterial head hath his eminent auctoritie for the confirmation of the whole bodie.

visible persons be adioyned to an inuisible or imperceptible fundation, which perpetual Apostolical office, and continual building, S. Paul describing, teacheth, that [Christ gaue, some Apostles, & some Prophets, and other some Euangelists, & other some Pastors and Doctors, to the consummation of the Sainctes (or faithful) vnto the work of the ministerie : vnto the building of the (Church the mistical) body of Christ, vntil we meete al into the vnitie of faith, and knowlege of the Sonne of God.] Wherby it is euident, that Apostolical auctoritie and function, remaineth in the Church, euen to the ende of this world.

Ephes.4.v. 11.12.

13.

Christs prayer that S. Peters faith should neuer faile, hath special effect in S. Peters successors.

5   And that the same resideth in S. Peters successor, is likewise euident, besides al former proofes, by our Sauiours declaration to S. Peter, that wheras [Satan had required to sift and trie them al: he had specially prayed that Peters faith should not faile.] Which different prouidence towardes him, more then towardes the others, perteined (as the euent haith shewed) to their successors, rather then to them selues. For none of them in their owne persons, euer failed in their faith, after they once beleued Christes Resurrection. But in their successors the difference is most cleare. For the successors of al the other Apostles, some soner, some later, al now manie hundred yeres since, haue failed in faith, and their particular Prouinces, are fallen from the vnion of one head, and into other errors. manie also into Turcisme, and Paganisme. Only the successors of S. Peter, remaine in the same faith and Religion, without change ; through the efficacie of Christes praier, and singular prouidence, that Peters faith shal neuer faile, nor the gates of hel preuaile, against the *Church builded vpon this Rocke.*

Luc. 22. v.31. 32.

6   Now to dispute who is S. Peters successor, is
no lesse

no leſſe ſtrange, then to make doubt of al the ſucceſſions, aſwel Eccleſiaſtical as temporal in the whole world. For there is no greater certentie, that Romulus, Numa, Cæſar, Cicero, and Nero, were ſomtimes in Rome. nor that our Engliſh Nation came from Germanie, and poſſeſſed the greateſt part of this land, which before perteined to the Ancient Britans, whom we cal Walſhmen ; nor that we the ſame Engliſh Nation, were conuerted from Paganiſme to Chriſtianitie by S. Auguſtine, and other Religious men, ſent for this purpoſe by S. Gregorie called the great, then Pope and Biſhope of Rome; nor that William Duke of Normandie, did conquere England, and became King therof; nor that King Henrie the ſeauenth, ouercame King Richard the third, and afterwardes reigned King of England. Neither is there more certaintie of the beginninges, and ſucceſſions of anie other Kinges, or Biſhopes of Chriſtian Countries : then there is of S. Peters reſiding ſomtimes, and finally dying, in Rome. A thing teſtified, not only by al Eccleſiaſtical Hiſtories, innumerable Fathers, both Greeke, and Latin : but alſo knowne from age to age, withont interruption, by the perpetual monuments of places in that Citie where he reſorted, exerciſed ſacred functions, where he was impriſoned, where he died by Martyrdome on a Croſſe. By the memories of his Sepulchre, & Reliques; together with S. Paules, who died there the ſame day. By the Recordes alſo of the Martyrdomes of other thirtie two Biſhopes his next ſucceſſors, al Martyrs for the ſame faith. Of S. Silueſter alſo a holie Confeſſor, and ſo of their continual ſucceſſors euen to this preſent Biſhope, and Pope, Paule the fifth. Beſides which vndoubtful witneſſes, to require further proofe of S. Peters being in Rome by holie Scriptures, is both ridiculous (as

The Proteſtáts paradox that S. Peter was neuer at Rome, is noe leſſe abſurde then to ſay: that William Duke of Normandie, did not conquere England. And the like.

　　　　　　　　　though

though neither point of faith, nor matter of fact, can be certaine, except it be expressed in holie Scriptures) and also superfluous, because it is abundantly proued otherwise. And therfore may we boldly say, that the denial of it, is obstinate follie, grounded in malice, of those that hate the same holie seate. A Paradox feaned by Iohn Caluin; broached, and bruted by him, & the like, for lacke of other meanes, for to holde vp their badde cause, and new doctrines.

We require of our Aduersarie to proue by holie Scripture, that S. Peter was neuer at Rome. We also proue by S. Peters Epistle, that he writte the same in Rome.

7 Wheras therfore our Aduersaries exact proofe of this point by the holie Scripture; we answeare. First, that we being so long and vndoubted possessors of the affirmatiue assertion, that S. Peter was at Rome, and died there; we iustly pleade prescription, and put our aduersaries to proue the contrarie by holie Scripture. Secondly, we auouch, that S. Peter writte his first Epistle extant in the New Testament, then resident in the Citie of Rome, which he mistically called Babylon saying : [The Church saluteth you that is in Babilon coelect.] This we say and hold, with manie Ancient, learned, & holie Fathers and Doctors, for more then probable. But whether this place proue it or no; we hold & beleue amongst other pointes of faith, that there is, and euer shal be, to the end of this world, an Apostolical seate in the Militant Church of Christ, according to S. Paules doctrine to the Ephesians.

1 . Pet. 5. v . 13.

Ephes. 4. v .11. 13.

No other Church doth, nor can, at this time chalenge continual succession from anie of the Apostles but onlie the Romane.

And by euident reason we deduce, that the Bishopes seate of Rome, is the Apostolical seate, and that none other seate, can rightly pretend, so to be at this day, but only that of Rome. And this may suffice for our purpose, touching the first marke of the true Church, which is vnitie and consent, consisting in belefe of the same faith and Religion of al faithful Christians, and in confession therof in vnion with

one

one supreme spiritual Pastor, and head of the whole
Church in earth : aud so I conclude the same . And
none other is the true Church of Christ which hath
this mark of vnitie and consent .

The true Church of Christ is Holie.

A R T I C L E. 37.

A N other marke of the true Church is Sanctitie, according to the Apostles Crede :
where we acknowlege the Church to be Ho-
lie . Our Sauiour also gaue this note to discerne true
Mat. 7. and false Prophets [by their fruictes . A good tree
v. 17. yeldeth good fruicte (saith he) & the euil tree yel-
18. deth euil fruictes . A good tree cannot yelde euil
fructes : neither an euil tree yelde good fruictes . ther-
20. fore by their fruictes you shal know them . For euerie tree is knowne by his fruicte .] Where therfore
we see holie and wholsome doctrine to be taught
yelding good fruictes , as frequent prayer, much fasting, manie good workes ; often repairing to holie
Sacramentes , special care to kepe Gods commandements, obseruation of Euangelical counsels , with
continual endeuoures to proceede in vertues, to the
honour of God, and edification of al men , there may
we wel thinke to be the true Christian Church .
Contrariwise , we may assuredly know that congregation to be a Sinagogue of Satan, which teacheth
and practiseth litle prayer, few, or inordinarie fastes,
but only when euerie one wil; which holdeth opinion, that no good workes merite anie reward, that
no Sacrament remitteh sinne, nor conferreth grace ;
that the commandements are vnpossible to be kept ;
al vowes of perpetual chastitie, and of other state of
Religious life, to be vnlawful, wherof foloweth both
leffe

As a tree is
knowne by the
fruicte, so the
true Church
by the effect of
her doctrine,
tending to pie-
tie and holi-
nes.

And those
which geue
way to loosnes
of life , can not
be the true
Church .

lesse care to keepe Gods precepts, or to doe other
good workes wherunto al men are bound : and also *Mat.* 25.
the breach and contempt of Sacred vowes ; which S. *v.* 42.
Paul calleth [Breach of faith & damnable.] Neither 1. *Tim.* 5.
is the Church only knowne and discerned especially *v.* 12.
in these dayes from the false pretended, and reformed
companies, by the note of holines, but by the same is
also most excellently adorned, and renowmed, that
albeit manie of her members are sinners, yet she
loseth not the denomination, but stil is Holie, by rea
son of her holie faith, holie doctrine, holie Sacrifice,
Sacramentes, with other Rites, and holie functions.
And in respect also of manie true holie seruants of
God, euer existing in the Church, out of which there
can not be anie holie person, nor true sanctitie at al
[no more then a branch can bring forth fruicte vn - *Io.* 15. *v.*
lesse it be in the vine] or a seperated member liue 4.
that is not in the bodie.

The true ser-
uants of God
were knowne
by their holie
conuersation.
2   Of which double priuilege as wel to be knowne
by her holines, as to be singularly adorned therwith,
let vs see more particular testimonies of holie Scriptures. By the holie conuersation of Abraham, and *Gen.* 20. *v.*
Sara, with their familie [Abimelech King of Gera- 14.
re, saw that they were the people and seruants of
God.] And wheras before he thought to make them
his subiectes ; seing them to be protected of God,
presented Abraham with honorable giftes, granting
him al freedome and priuilege : [the land is before 15.
you (said he) dwel wheresoeuer it shal please thee .]
Isaac also gained peace and estimation with the Phi- *Gen.* 26. *v.*
listines, who first expelled him from them ; but af- 16. 26. 27.
terward made leauge with him, yelding this reason 28.
of their better affection towardes him [we saw
(said they) that the Lord is with thee] when God
had multiplied the children of Israel brought them
out of Egipt, and made with them an expresse coue-
                                                          nant

nant, that he would be their only God, and they ſhould be his peculiar people. He promiſed them two eſpecial priuilegies; Preiſtly function, wherby they might rightly ſerue him; and ſanctitie, that he

Ex. 19. *v.* 6. might iuſtly reward their ſeruice ſaying : [You ſhal be vnto me a Preiſtly Kingdome ; and a holie Nation.] So he gaue them accordingly ſpiritual func-

Ex. 20. *v.* 21. tions, [holie Rites, and holie precepts] cauſed them to make a [holie Tabernacle, with the Arke of Teſtament, Propitiatorie, Altars, holie Veſtiments; al implementes and ornamentes] therunto requiſite.

Ex. 39. *v.* 29. Finally in the principal ornament of the High Preiſt [the Plate of ſacred veneration, God commanded to be engrauen ; The holie of our Lord.] Verie often inculcated his general [Precept to al the aſ-

Leuit. 11. *v.* 44. 46. ſembly of the children of Iſrael : Be ye holie, becauſe I the Lord your God am holie. Sanctifie your

Leuit. 19. *v.* 2. ſelues, and be holie, becauſe I am the Lord your God: kepe my precepts and doe them; I the Lord that

Ch. 20. *v.* 7. 8. 16. ſanctify you. You ſhal be holie vnto me, becauſe I the Lord am holie. And I haue ſeperated you frō other peoples that you ſhould be mine. This is your wiſdome and vnderſtanding before al Peoples. Nei-

Deut. 4. *v.* 6. 7. 8. 9. ther is there other Nation ſo great, ſo renowmed, that hath the Ceremonies , and iuſt iudgements, & the whole Law, which I wil ſet forth this day before your eyes : Keepe thy ſelf therfore, & thy ſoule

Deut. 7. *v.* 23. 5. 6. *Ch.* 14. *v.* 2. carefully. Thou ſhalt not make league with Idolaters, thou ſhalt not make mariages with them. Ouerthrow their Altares, and breake their ſtatues, and cutte downe their groues, and burne the ſculptiles: becauſe thou art a holie people to the Lord thy God. The Lord thy God hath choſen thee to be his peculiar people of al peoples that are vpon the earth.

Deut. 26. *v.* 18. 19. Our Lord hath ſpoken to thee, that thou ſhouldeſt kepe al his commandements, and he make thee high-

T t er then

The peculiar people of God were called a holie nation.

The law is holie, and requireth holines.

er then al Nations which he created, to his praise
and name, and glorie, that thou maist be a holie
people of our Lord thy God, as he hath spoken.

The same title
of holines is a-
scribed to
Gods peculiar
people, by the
Prophets.

3   As the Law, so likewise the Prophets, amongst
other excellent properties, ascribe holines to the
Church. King Dauid distinguisheth her by this title from al other congregations. For albeit God
worketh meruelous thinges in the whole world; yet
nowhere els doth he bestow sanctitie. [God in his   *Pſ. 67. v.*
holie place. God that maketh men to inhabite of *67.*
one maner in a house. Holines becometh thy house
o Lord. Exalt ye the Lord our God; and adore ye *Pſ. 92. v.*
in his holie mount; because the Lord our God is *5.*
holie. Iewrie was made his sanctificatiɔn, Israel his *Pſ. 98. v.*
Dominion] signifying that the Israelites were the pe- *8. Pſ. 113.*
culiar people whom God sanctified, and in whom he *v. 2.*
especially dwelled and reigned [Because our Lord *Pſ. 131. v.*
hath chosen Sion: he hath chosen it for an habita- *13. 14. 15.*
tion to him self. this is my rest for euer and euer *16.*
(saith our Lord) here wil I dwel, because I haue
chosen it. Blessing, I wil blesse her widow, her
poore I wil fil with breades. Her Preistes I wil cloth
with saluation : and her Sainctes shal reioyce, with
ioyfulnes.] This Spouse of Christ is described in the
Canticles [ascending by the desert as a litle rodde *Can. 3. v.*
of smoke of the aromatical spices of Mirh and Fran- *6.*
kencense, and of al pouder of the Apoticarie] that
is, ful of al holie vertues and good workes [Eue- *Iſ. 4. v. 3.*
rie one that shal be left in Sion, and shal remaine in
See Iſa. 4.
v. 3. Ch.
11. v. 9.
Ch. 27. v.
13. Ch. 48.
v. 2. Ch.
56. v. 7.
Ch. 62. v. 12. Ierusalem (saith Isaias) shal be called holie, euerie
one that is written in life in Ierusalem] General-
ly the Prophets vtter their discourses of the Church
by these termes [The holie Mount, The holie Citie The holie People : Israel is holie to our Lord,
The holie Citie Ierusalem; Mount Sion shal be holie
and the like.

According

†4 Accordingly in the new Teſtamēt, Holines is more *Ch.* 63.
required, and more abundantly geuen [that with- *v.* 18. *Ch.*
out feare (ſaid iuſt Zacharie) being deliuered from 64. *v.* 11.
the hand of our enemies, we may ſerue our Lord in *Iere.* 2. *v.*
holines & Iuſtice before him al our daies.] So his 3. *Ch.* 31.
bleſſed Sonne Iohn the Baptiſt, by life and doctrine , *v.* 23.
preached holines, teaching [ſinners to doe penance] *Ezech.* 20.
penitents [to bring forth worthie fruictes therof.] *v.* 40.
Our Sauiour confirmed the ſame in al his actions, & *Dan.* 3. *v.*
in his ſermons, affirming that [his ſeruants & frendes 28. *Ch.* 9.
are knowne by keping his Precepts.] S. Paule có- *v.* 11. *Ch.*
mendeth the Romanes, not only for their holie faith, 12. *v.* 7.
as being [renowmed in the whole world] but alſo *Ioel.* 2.
for [their obedience which was publiſhed in euerie *v.* 1.
place] encoraging them to procede, and [exhibite
their bodies to ſerue Iuſtice vnto ſanctification, a † Confirmed
liuing hoſt, holie pleaſing God ; not cóformed to this in the new te-
world, but reformed in the newnes of their minde] ſtament.
Admoniſheth the Corinthians [to purge the old leuen, and become new paſt, to feaſt in the Azimes
of ſinceritie.] Likewiſe the Galatians [that if they
liue in the ſpirit ; they alſo muſt walke in ſpirit, & doing good, not to faile, that ſo in time they may reape
good not failing. For in Ieſus Chriſt , neither Circumciſion auaileth, nor prepuce , but a new creature.] He teacheth the Epheſians , that [God hath
choſen vs in Chriſt, that we ſhould be holie & immaculate in his ſight] beſeeching [al to walk worthie
of the vocation in which they are called.] Not a
ſmale part of al his Epiſtles, is exhortatiue to holines of life : and the other Apoſtles, writte much
more of the neceſſitie of good workes, preſuppoſing
true faith. Both which are in the Church, and in
none other congregation, wherof we ſhal ſpeake
more in due place, hauing here only touched that
point as by the way, to ſhew, that notwithſtanding

Luc. 1.
v. 74.

Mat. 3.
v. 8.
Io. 15.
v. 14.

Rom. 1.
v. 5.
Ch. 16.
v. 19.
Rom. 6.
v. 19.
Ro. 12.
v. 1. 2.
1. *Cor.*
5. *v.* 8.
Gal. 5.
v. 25.
Ch. 6.
v. 9. 15.
Ephes. 1.
v. 4.
Ephes. 4.
v. 1.

Art. 45

great

great and daily finners amongft the faithful; yet the Church is trulie called holie.

Gods true feruants haue bene called by diuers names for diftinction fake.

5　But now efpecially we fpeake of holines as it is a notorious marke amongft other titles wherby the true Church is knowne. For as when [God hauing formed al beaftes of the earth, and foules of the aire, brought them to Adam, that he might fee what to cal them, and al that Adam called anie creature, the fame is his name] and by fuch names, each kind is knowne from others : euen fo the faithful feruants of God, haue alwaies bene diftinguifhed and known by certaine names and titles, from other that ferue falfe Goddes , or folow falfe religions. And therfore it wil not be vngrateful I fuppofe, nor vnprofitable, but rather neceffarie, for al fuch as be in doubt, which is the true Church, to confider by what ordinarie names the true feruantes of God haue bene vfually called and diftinguifhed from other peoples of falfe and of no religion. For by this very meanes if there were no other way of trial (as indede there be manie) al may be fufficiently fatisfied that fincerely fearch the truth, with refolute mind to embrace it when it is declared vnto them.

Gen. 2. *v.* 19.

6　Wherefore to repeate this point from the beginning; fhortly after that Cain made feperation from his parents, and brethren , and as the holie Scripture relateth it [went forth from the face of our Lord] Gods true feruants, not only for their more comforth, but alfo for diftinction fake, were called [*the fonnes of God*] And the other which were gone out, were called the fonnes of men. Thefe two fortes were fo diftinct companies, and perteyned to oppofite cities, of God, and of this wicked world, that it was a greuous fault in [the fonnes of God to take wiues of the daughters of men .] Of which vntowardly mariages, came the wicked generations of

Gen. 4. *v.* 16.

1.
The fonnes of God.

Gen. 6. *v.* 2. 4.

monftruous

monstruous great people called Giants.

7 For thefe & other finnes, the world being drowned, eight perfons only referued aliue, of whom mãkind being againe multiplied : the diuel yet eftfones feduced whom he could. And by falfe and violent dealing of fome, the moft part confpiring or yelding to build an high Towre vnder pretence to auoide the danger of the like floud : the Patriarch Heber with his familie was free from that prefumptuous attempt, which God fo confounded, by diuifion of their tongues, that they could no further build. And only Heber, and the reft that were innocent, kept their ancient tongue : which thence-forward, was called, for diftinctiõ fake, the Hebrew tongue. And thofe true feruantes of God, began to be called the *Hebrewes*, efpecially thofe that fucceded him in true Religion, and were of the line of his fonne Phaleg.

For of his other fonne Iectan, came thirtene Nations, of fo manie diuers tongues, as appeareth in the Genealogies of Sem. And fo [Abraham was furnamed the *Hebrew*, when he dwelt in Mambre, nere to Sodom] and fo were al of his progenie by Ifaac and Iacob, called *Hebrewes*. The Egiptians called Iofeph an Hebrew; and him felf called his Countrie where his Father and brethren dwelt, the land of the Hebrewes, which was a part of Chanaan, but this name belonged to the people, not to the Countrie. And which efpecially fheweth our purpofe, God was called, the Lord God of the Hebrewes.

8 But befides this name (which continued til Chrift his time) for more particular diftinction from other Nations, which were alfo defcended from Heber, and Abraham; the peculiar people of God, were called the * *Children of Ifrael*. Efpecially after their parting out of Egipt. Which fufficed til by the diuifion of their kingdome, the greater part violently vfur-

Gen. 11.*
v. 7.

Gen. 10.
v. 25.
26.
Gen. 14.
v. 13.
Gen. 39.
v. 14.
17. *Gen*.
40. *v*.
15. *Ch*.
41. *v*.
12. *Ch*.
43. *v*.
32. *Ex*.
3. *v*. 18.
Ch. 5.
v. 3. *Ch*.
7. *v*. 16
* *Gen*. 36.

2.
The Hebrews.

3.
The Children of Ifrael.

T t 3   ped

ped the name of Ifrael, calling them felues, the kingdome of Ifrael ; and the other was called the kingdome of Iuda ; wherwithal happened the enormous
fchifme firft made by Ieroboam, continued by others
til their captiuitie, and laftly renewed with erection
of a fchifmatical Temple in Garizim, in the Countrie of Samaria .

v. 31. *Ex.*
1. v. 1. 7.
9. 13. *Ch.*
3. v. 10.
Ch. 4. v.
22. *Ch.* 7.
v. 4. *Leuit.*

4.
The Iewes .

†9   By. which occafion, a further diftinction being
neceffarie, the true Ifraelites were called the *Iewes*, *&c.*
and the fchifmatikes, Samaritanes . Betwene whom
grew fo great difference, that each part refrained cō-
uerfation with the other . Albeit the Samaritanes
were in errour [adoring they knew not what , and
faluation was of the Iewes .] Thefe were the foure
general furnames appropriated to the faithful of the
old Teftament wherby the true Church was knowne
and difcerned from Infidels , Paganes , Heritikes , &
Schifmatikes .

1. v. 2.
† 2. *Efd.* 4.
v. 1. 2. *Ch.*
6. v. 2. 3.
4. *Mat.* 10.
v. 5. *Io.* 4.
v. 9. 22.
Apoc. 2. v.
9. *Ch.* 3.
v. 9.

10   Likewife the faithful of the new Teftament,
in fhorter time, euen in the primitiue Church of
Chrift, receiued proper titles, by which, the true
Church in al fucceding ages, hath bene, and is, cler-
ly knowne, from al Infidels, Heathnifh peoples,
Iewes, Turkes, Heritikes and Schifmatikes . Firft
whiles Chrift him felf in his owne perfon, preached
his holie Gofpel, thofe that beleued his doctrine,
were called his *Difciples*, not only thofe which in
fpecial maner were fent to preach : but alfo others,
as Nicodemus, Iofeph, ; yea alfo deuout women had
the general name of Difciples .

5.
Difciples .

Io. 3. v. 2.
Io. 19. v.
38.
Act. 9. v.
36.

11   But after the coming of the Holie Ghoft, thofe
that beleued in Chrift, and by holie baptifme were
incorporated into his miftical bodie, the holie Church, were intitled by the name of Sainctes : & therby knowne and diftinguifhed from the Iewes that
remained obftinate againft our Sauiour. By this name

6.
The Sainctes .
The Holie.

Ananias

Ananias a Diſciple at Damaſcus, côfidently called his
brethren of the ſame faith in Chriſt ; when he was
warned by a viſion from God, to repair to Saul newly conuerted . For hereupon he anſwered [Lord I haue
heard by manie of this man, how much euil he hath
done to thy *Sainctes* in Ieruſalem .] S . Luke calleth them by the ſame name, relating that S . Peter making a viſitation [came (ſaith he) to the
Sainctes that dwelt at Lidda .] Adding that S .
Peter being at Ioppe, called the Sainctes to receiue comforth of the reuiuing of a holie woman
from death . S . Paul acknowleging his owne former falſe zeale : ſaith he had ſhut vp manie of the
Sainctes in priſon . Seuerally in al his Epiſtles ſa-
luting thoſe to whom he writte , he calleth them
the Sainctes . Alſo vpon other occaſions he ſo v-
ſeth moſt frequently the ſame terme, requeſting the
Romanes to aſſiſt the neceſſitie of the Sainctes , telling them that he is going to Ieruſalem to miniſter
relife to the Sainctes [to the poore Sainctes that are
in Ieruſalem .] Beſecheth their praiers that he may
be deliuered from the Infidels in Iewrie, and that
the oblation of his ſeruice, may become acceptable
to the Sainctes . Saluteth al the Sainctes there . To
the Corinthians he auoucheth, that he taught peace
in al the Churches of the Sainctes . Commendeth
to them to make collections for the Sainctes . He
comforteth the Epheſians, & in them al the faithful, that they are Citizens of the Sainctes , and the
domeſtical of God . Without arrogancie ſaith of
himſelf . To me the leaſt of al the Sainctes, is geuen
this grace, a mong the Gentiles, to Euangelize . He
willeth them to pray inſtantly for al the Saincts . Salute (ſaith he to the Philippians) euerie Sainct . Al
the Sainctes ſalute you . I wil omitte other places
for this purpoſe . The other Apoſtles likewiſe
acknowlege

Act. 9 .
v. 13.

Act. 9 .
v. 33 .

41.

Act. 26.
v. 10.

Rom. 8.
v. 28.
Ch. 12.
v. 13.
Ch. 15.
v. 25.
26. 31.
Ch. 16.
v. 15.
1. *Cor.*
14. *v.*
33. *Ch.*
16 .*v.* 1.
Epheſ.
2. *v.* 19.
Ch. 3. *v.*
8. *Ch.* 6.
v. 18.
Phil. 4.
v. 21.
22.
Iac. 2,
v. 26.

wife acknowlege and vfe this title of holines as pro- | 1. *Pet.* 1.
per to the Church, and to her children in general. | *v.* 15. *Iud.*
S. Iohn, according as was reueled vnto him, decla- | *v.* 3 *Apoc.*
reth the communication that is betwene the Sainctes | 5. *v.* 8.
in heauen, and the Sainctes in earth faying [The four | *Ch.* 8. *v.* 3.
liuing creatures, & the twentie four Seniors (Sainctes | 4. *Ch.* 13
in heauen) fel before the Lambe, hauing harpes & | *v.* 7. 10.
golden vials, ful of odoures which are the praiers of | *Ch.* 14. *v.*
Sainctes, that is, of the faithful in earth. For he cal- | 12. *Ch.* 19.
leth them Sainctes againft whom Antichrift fhal make | *v.* 8. *Ch*
battle [whofe patience and faith fhal be tried] whofe | 20. *v.* 9.
conftancie in vertues, fignified by [filke, wherwith
the Church is clothed, & the iuftifications of Sainctes].
So proper it is to the Church of Chrift to be holie,
and to be trulie called [the Campe of Sainctes]
that moft Sectaries, efpecially of this time, rarely
or neuer in their fermons, or writinges, vouchfaife
her this title. For they wel know it agreeth not fitly to their congregation, but rather putteth Chriftian people in mind of our holie Mother, againft which
they make oppofition. But the holie Apoftles infpired by the Holie Ghoft, taught vs to cal her holie
in our daily Crede.

<p style="margin-left:2em">

7.
Chriftians.

12 An other moft renowmed title of the Church,
and of her children, is the name *Chriftian*, firft af-
fcribed to the faithful [Difciples of Chrift at Anti- | *Act.* 11.
och] when by S. Paules, and S. Barnabies prea- | *v.* 26.
ching, there was a great multitude conuerted. Of
which moft honorable name, there is but only twice
more anie mention in holie Scriptures. Once by
King Agrippa faying to S. Paul [A litle thou per- | *Act.* 26.
fwadeft me to become a Chriftian.] And once S. | *v.* 28.
Peter expreffeth this name in his firft Epiftle, admo-
nifhing al to looke to their behauiour, that [none | 1. *Pet.* 4.
fuffer as a malefactor ; but if as a Chriftian, let him | *v.* 15. 16.
not be afhamed, and let him glorifie God in this
name

name.] By this are the faithful rightly diftinguished from Iewes, Turkes, and Paganes, but not fo plainly from heritikes, who being once chriftened, kepe the name in fome fort of Chriftians. Neither did the holie Apoftles put this name Chriftian in their Crede, but after the title holie, added *Catholique*, by which we are to know true & falfe Chriftians .

Simb.
Apoftol.
Luc. 10.
v. 16.

8.
Catholiques.

The true Church of Chrift is Catholique .

ARTICLE. 38.

Amongft al Markes of the Church, the name Catholique, hath fo preuailed, that falfe pretending congregations, could neuer by anie fleight get this title; wherof finding them felues vtterly deftitute, partly they ftriue to difpoffeffe the true Church therof, by impofing vpon her other names framed for their prefent purpofe. As the Arrians called the defenders of Chriftes Confubftantialitie with God the Father; *Homoufians* : and the fectaries of this time., cal thofe which hold the fame faith with the Pope, the Bifhope of Rome, Papifts; partly they endeuour to extinguifh the name Catholque, as Lutheran Cathechifmes haue thruft it out of the Apoftles Crede, putting in Chriftian for it: and fome Englifh Bibles haue left out the word Catholique in the title of S. Iames, and S. Iudes Epiftles; fome others haue the word General in place of it, fearing and abhorring the very found of it, becaufe in the proper fignification which is *Vniuerfal*, it doth confound them : though in the titles of thefe Epiftles, it fignifieth, that wheras other Epiftles , namely of S. Paul, were directed to particular Churches or perfons for the benefite of al : thefe were immediatly written to the wholeChurch. So in this

Sectaries practife two wayes to depriue the true Church of the name Catholique .

By nicknaming Catholiques by other names .

And by putting the name Catholique out of the Crede.

point

point, as likewife in fome others, our Aduerfaries
are like to the woman whofe child being dead, contended for an others liuing childe , and when fhe
could not obteine it , cried to haue the liuing child
deftroied [-be it neither mine nor thine (faid the falfe
pretending mother) but let it be deuided] No (faid
wife Salomon) geue the liuing child to the true mother] let it not be killed . So our B . Sauiour greater then Salomon, proteƈor of his Church, wil not
haue the title Catholique, thruft out of our Crede,
not mangled nor extinguifhed, but to remaine intyre to our true and holie mother the Catholique
Church .

3 . Reg . 3 .
v . 26 .
27 .

That the
Church is vni-
uerfal, is
proued by ma-
nie holie
Scriptures .

2   By which efpecial marke amongft al others, the
true Chriftian Church is knowne from al heretical
conuenticles . For albeit in the whole Bible, the
Church is not exprefly called Catholique ; yet the
thing it felf that is fpredde in manie Nations , and
fhal be propagated into the vniuerfal terreftrial world
is abundantly proued by the holie Scriptures, wherof we fhal here recite fome ftore . Noe prophecying of his fonnes faid [Curfed be Chanaan, a feruant of feruants fhal he be vnto his brethren. Bleffed be the Lord God of Sem, Chanaan be his feruant.
God enlarge Iapheth, and dwel he in the Tabernacles of Sem, and Chanaan be his fernant .] Fulfilled as in the figure, when the children of Ifrael, of
Sems race , fubdued the land of Chanaan : Iaphets
progenie in the meane times, inhabiting the vtmoft
coaftes of the earth, afwel in the continent, as the
Ilandes . But in the miftical fenfe principally intended, this prophecy is more fully performed in this
time of the New Teftament, when Infidels , fignified by Chanaan, are fubieƈted to Chriftians, confifting
at firft both of Iewes and Gentiles , and the Iewes
fhortly after, for the moft part, failing in faith, &

Gen . 9 . v.
25 . 26 . 27.

                                        impugning

impugning Chriſt; the Gentiles not only ſucceded
in place of the Iewes, but alſo the Church by them
is dilated into al partes, euen to the endes of the
earth. And al Heritikes, and falſe ſectes of religion from time to time, are conuinced, and by auctoritie of the Catholique Church, ſubdued and corrected. The ſame dilatation of the Church, was pro-

Gen. 15. miſed by God to Abraham, that [his ſeede ſhould be
v. 5. *Ch.* innumerable, as the Starres of the firmament & ſandes
17. *v.* 5. of the ſea] and in confirmation therof, was called
Rom. 4. [the Father of manie Nations] not only verified in
v. 11. his natural progenies, but much more in his ſpiritual children, for ſo S. Paul expoundeth this promiſe, and calleth[Abraham the Father of al that beleue] in Chriſt. Alſo of faithful Gentiles, called
Gen. 22. prepuce, that are not circumciſed [Becauſe in his
v. 18. ſeede ſhould be bleſſed al the Nations of the earth.]
Ch. 26. Renewed alſo and confirmed to Iſaac, and to Iacob.
v. 4. *Ch.* Though the Iewes Church neuer failed [God being
28. *v.* propitious to the land of his people] yet in compa-
14. riſon of greater multitudes in the Gentiles borne to
Deut. Chriſt, holie Anna prophecied that [the barren wo-
32. *v.* man ſhould beare very manie, and ſhe that had ma-
43. nie children, was weakened; and our Lord (Chriſt)
1. *Reg.* ſhal iudge the endes of the earth.] The Royal Pro-
2. *v.* 9. phet ſignifieth alſo the vocation of manie Gentiles, in
10. place of the Iewes ſaying in the name of Chriſt vn-
2. *Reg.* to God [Thou wilt kepe me to be the head of the
22. *v.* Gentiles, the people which I know not, wil ſerue
44. 45. me, the children aliens wil reſiſt me (for ſome time:
Pſ. 17. neuertheleſſe) with the hearing of the eare, they wil
v. 44. obey me.] God alſo by the penne of the ſame pſal-
45. 50. miſt, ſaith to our Sauiour Chriſt [I wil geue thee
Pſ. 2. the Gentiles for thine inheritance, and thy peſſeſſion
v. 8. the endes of the earth.]

3 During the old Teſtament, the Church was al-
V v 2   moſt

That the
Church is

more propaga-
ted in the new
Testament thē
it was in the
old, is proued
by the
Psalmes.

most included in one Nation [God is knowne (said
this Royal Prophet) in Iewrie, in Israel his name is
great, his place is made in peace, and his habitation
in Sion] But since our Redemer paid the ransome
of mankind [When God arose vnto Iudgement, that
he might saue al the meeke of the earth.] Now is
his Kingdome most amply enlarged, as the same Prophet clearly testifieth, in these & the like diuine speaches through his whole Psalmodie saying [With
thee (o God) is my praise in the great Church.
Al the endes of the earth shal remember, and be
conuerted to our Lord. Al the families of the Gentiles shal adore in his sight. Because the Kingdom
is our Lordes, and he shal haue dominion ouer the
Gentiles. Our Lord vpon manie waters. Therfore
shal peoples confesse to thee. Our Lord a greate
King ouer al the earth. Al flesh shal come to thee.
Ye Gentiles blesse our Lord. In al Nations thy-
saluation. Let al Peoples o God confesse to thee.
I wil conuert into the depth of the sea. Ye Kingdomes of the earth sing to God: sing to our Lord.
He shal rule from sea vnto sea: and from the riuer
euen to the endes of the rownd world. The kinges
of Tharsis, and the Ilandes, shal offer presentes:
the kinges of Arabia, and of Saba, shal bring gifts.
Al kinges of the earth shal adore him: al Nations
shal serue him. Al Nations whatsoeuer thou hast
made, shal come and shal adore before thee o Lord:
and they shal glorify thy name. The fundations (of
this Church) in the holie mountaines; our Lord loueth the gates of Sion, aboue al the Tabernacles of
Iacob. Glorious thinges are said of thee, o Citie
of God. Our Lord hath reigned. he hath established the round world which shal not be meued.
Shew forth his glorie among the Gentiles: his meruelous workes in al peoples. Say ye among the Gentiles

Pf 75.
v. 2.3.

10.

Pf. 21. *v.*
26.28.29.
Pf. 28. *v.*
3. *Pf.* 34.
v. 18. *Pf.*
39. *v.* 10.
11. *Pf.* 44.
v. 18. *Pf.*
64. *v.* 3.
Pf. 65. *v.*
8. *Pf.* 66.
v. 3. *Pf.*
67. *v.* 23.
33. *Pf.* 71.
v. 8.10.
11. *Pf.* 85.
v. 9. *Pf.*
86. *v.* 1.
2.3.4. *Pf.*
88. *v.* 3.
31. *&c.*
Pf. 92. *v.*
1.2.3. *Pf.*
95. *v.* 2.
10. *Pf.*
101. *v.* 16.
Pf 116. *v.*
1. *Pf.* 137.
v. 4.

tiles, that our Lord hath reigned . The Gentiles
ſhal feare thy name o Lord : and al the kinges of
the earth thy glorie. Praiſe ye our Lord al ye Gentiles : praiſe him al ye peoples . Let al the kinges of
the earth, o Lord, confeſſe to thee.] What better proofe, then theſe ſo often repeated vniuerſal
termes, can anie man require, for the vniuerſalitie of
the true Chriſtian Church, aſwel in reſpect of al places, as perſons, Princes, and peoples of al degrees.
Eſpecially if we conſider the diuers maners of Propheticall vtterance, ſometimes by plaine affirmation,
other times by way of praying God it may be ; praiſing God that it is ſo ; congratulating with the faithful, in inuiting them to be grateful in wordes , and
deedes, euery way foreſhewing , that ſo it wil come
to paſſe .

4   Wil ye ſee alſo like predictions of other Pro-The ſame by
phets? Iſaias in a Canticle of thankes to God, for be-other Pro-
nefites beſtowed on al mankind by Chriſt , inuitethphets.
the faithful to make known among al people, Goddes
Iſ. 12. ſo gratious cogitations [Sing ye to our Lord, be-
v. 4. 5. cauſe he hath done magnifically : ſhew this forth in
al the earth.] In an other place, vnder the names
of Egiptians and Aſſirians , very great kingdomes,
Iſ. 19. he prophecieth the conuerſion of al Gentiles [In
v. 18. that day (ſaith he) there ſhal be fiue Cities (that
is manie Cities) in Egipt, ſpeaking the tongues of
Chanaan (which was then the Countrie of Goddes
peculiar people) and ſwearing (not by falſe Goddes
Ibid. but) by the Lord of hoſtes .] In that day ſhal Iſrael
v. 24. be a third to the Egiptian and Aſſirian (meaning
they ſhal agree in participating Goddes grace) a
Iſ. 25. bleſſing in the middeſt of the earth. The Lord of
v. 6. 7 . hoſtes wil make to al peoples in this mount, a feaſt of
fatte thinges, a feaſt of vintage of fatte thinges ful
Iſ. 27 . of marrow, of vintage purified from dregges. Iſra-
v. 6. el ſhal
V v   3

el shal florish and spring, and they shal fil the face
of the world with seede. Sing ye to the Lord a new *Is*. 42. *v*.
song : his praise is from the endes of the earth. Ye 10.
that goe downe to the sea, and you the fulnes therof.
Ye Ilandes, and inhabitantes of the same. Heare ye *Is*. 46. *v*.
Ilandes, and attend ye peoples from a farre. The 11.13.
Gentiles shal walke in thy light (saith this Prophet *Is*. 49. *v*. 1.
to the Christian Church) and kinges in the bright-
nes of thy rising. Lift vp thine eyes round about, & *Is*. 60. *v*. 4.
see; al these are gathered together : they are come
to thee : thy sonnes shal come from a farre, & thy
daughters shal rise from the side. Then shalt thou see
& abound, and thy hart shal meruel and be enlarged, 5.
when the multitude of the sea shal be conuerted to
thee; the strength of the Gentiles shal come to thee.
For the Ilandes expect me, and the shippes of the sea 9.
in the beginning, that I may bring thy sonnes from
a farre. They shal know their seede in the Gentiles, *Is*. 61. *v*. 9.
and their budde in the middest of peoples. Al that
shal see them shal know them, that these are the
seede which our Lord hath blessed. The Gentiles *Is*. 62. *v*. 2.
shal see thy IVST ONE, and al kinges thy noble
one ; and thou shalt be called by a new name, which
the mouth of our Lord shal name.] Conformably
to al this saith the Prophet Ieremie [In that time, *Iere*. 3. *v*.
Ierusalem shal be called the Throne of our Lord : 17.
and al Gentiles shal be gathered together to it in
the name of our Lord into Ierusalem] which is fulfilled in that al Nations some soner, others later, are
ioyned to the Church begunne in Ierusalem, when
most part of the Iewes impugning it, refused for to
heare. Yea euen such Nations as semed to be most *Iere*. 48. *v*.
reiected, as exprsly *Moab* and *Elam*, are named for 47. *Ch*. 49.
example : that al shal be conuerted in these laste *v*. 39.
daies of the New Testament. Ezechiel likewise foresheweth the conuersion of al Nations [elder and yon- *Ezech*. 16.
ger *v*. 61.

ger in place, and as daughters of the Iewes, but by an other couenant.] Ofee [admonifheth the kingdome of Iuda, not to difdainé to cal the Gentiles brethren, nor Samaria their fifter] in refpect that they fhould be conuerted to Chrift [in greater number] then the Iewes. Efpecially the Gentiles, vnto whom God wil fay [my people art thou .] God againe faith by his Prophet Ioel [I wil powre out my Spirit vpon al flefh .] Micheas faith [God fhal be magnified, euen to the endes of the earth .] Sophonias, that [al peoples fhal inuocate the name of our Lord with a chofen lippe, and ferue him with one fhoulder.] Zacharias, that [manie Peoples fhal come, and ftrong Nations, to feeke the Lord of hoftes in Ierufalem, and to befech the face of our Lord, and that our Lord fhal be King ouer al the earth .] Malachie relateth our Lordes premonition to the Iewes faying [From the rifing of the Sunne, euen to the going downe, great is my name among the Gentiles.] Al which moft affured prophecies, and others which we willingly omitte, doe neceffarily fhew, that the true Church cannot be conteined in one or few Countries, nor reftrained to few perfons at anie time, but is, and muft be, vniuerfal.

Ofe. 2.
v. 23.

Ioel. 2.
v. 28.

Mich. 4.
v. 4.
Soph. 3.
v. 9.
Zach. 8.
v. 22.
Ch. 14.
v. 9.

Mal. 1.
v. 11.

5   Yet here remaine principal proofes of this truth of the new Teftament ; which I wil touch fo breifly as wel may be. Our Sauiour vpon occafion of a Centurians great faith that was a Gentile, declared that [manie fhal come from the Eaft and weaft (and the North, and the South) and fhal fitte downe with Abraham, and Ifaac, and Iacob in the kingdome of heauen.] By fundrie parables he alfo teacheth that of a fmale beginning fhould grow a great bodie. For albeit when the feede of the Gofpel is fowen, three partes perifh, and only as it were the fourte part prospereth

Confirmed by Chrift and his Apoftles.

Mat. 8.
v. 11.
Luc. 13.
v. 29.
Mat. 13.
v. 4. 5.
7. *Luc.*
12. *v.* 32.

prospereth : yet that in respect of the whole world,
the Church is a litle flocke ; yet being compared
with anie other common-wealth of the whole world,
it clearly excelleth it, not only in value from the
beginning, but also in quantitie after that it was once
propagated by the holie Apostles. For [it is like
to a grane of mustard-seede, which is the least of al
seedes : but when it is growne it is greater then al
herbes, and is made a tree. It is also [like to a litle
leauen, which being put into a great quantitie, as it
were into three measures of meale, leueneth the
whole .] which we see verified of the Christian doctrine growne ouer al the world, more dilated then
Iudaifme (which was the true religion, but is long
since degenerate :) Larger also extended then Tur-
cifme, then anie forte of Paganifme, anie sect of herefie, Arianifme, Pelagianifme, Donatifme, Lolardifme
Lutheranifme, Caluinifme, or anie other whatsoeuer.

Mat. 13.
v. 32.

33.

No one Sect of
Heretikes, nor
other Infidels,
is equal in
greatnes to the
true Church.

6   For neither the Arrians which were somtime manie, could be spred in al Christian Prouinces, & are
long since decaied : nor the Turkes, who doe now possesse much, can compare with the Catholique Church
in number, or extension of Prouinces and peoples,
euen to the East and West Indies. And if they were
equal in largenes of place, or number of persons, yet
they faile also in vniuersalitie of time, beginning long
after Christianitie was planted in the world. But of
antiquitie with succession, we are to speake in the
next Article.

It is further
proued that
the Church is
vniuersal in re-
spect of al na-
tions.

7   Concerning Vniuersalitie of the Church, in respect of places and persons, our Lord further taught,
that [his Gospel should be preached in the whole
world for a testimonie to al Nations.] He also gaue
commandement so to preach it : ordeyning his A-
postles [to be witnesses vnto him in Ierusalem, and
in al Iurie, and Samaria, and euen to the vtmost of
the earth

Mat. 24.
v. 14.
Mar. 13.
v. 10.
Mat. 28.
v. 19.

Act. 1. the earth.] After Chriſtes Aſcenſion, S. Paul re-
v.8. ceiued the ſame Commiſſion as extraordinarily rai-
Luc. 24. ſed vp for the Gentiles. And to them, both he, &
v. 48. the former Apoſtles, and manie others, performed
Rom. 1. this function [By Chriſt (ſaith S. Paul to the Rom.)
v. 5. 8. we haue receiued grace, and Apoſtleſhip for obedience of the faith in al Nations] where he congratulateth with them by the way, that their faith (the Romanes faith) was renowmed in the whole world.
And to certify, that not in Ieruſalem only, nor in I-
lyricum, nor only in Antioch, in Corinth, or in Rome
but [certes into al the earth, hath the ſound of the
Apoſtles gone forth, and into the endes of the whole
Rom. 10. world their wordes.] In the ſame Epiſtle alſo he
v.18. ſheweth by the holie Scriptures, the priuilege of the
Pſ. 18. Church in the Gentiles aboue the old Sinagogue of
v.5. the Iewes [Chriſt Ieſus (ſaith he) hath bene miniſter
Rom. 15. of the circumciſion (that is of the Iewes) for the ve-
v.8. 9. ritie of God to confirme the promiſes of the Fathers. But the Gentiles to honour God for his mercie, as it is written : therfor wil I confeſſe to thee
10. in the Gentiles o Lord, and wil ſing to thy name :
11. Reioice ye Gentiles with his people. Praiſe our
Lord al ye Gentiles, and magnifie him al ye peoples.
12. there ſhal be the roote of Ieſſe : and he that ſhal
riſe vp to rule the Gentiles, in him the Gentiles ſhal
Rom.15. hope.] After which he concluding ſaith : [the mi-
v. 26. ſterie of the Goſpel, is opened by the Scriptures of
the Prophets, according to the Precept of the eternal
God, to the obedience of faith, knowne in al Gentiles.] Being at Rome, and finding manie Iewes
obſtinate ; he finally denounced vnto them, this miſterie of the Gentiles vocation, and great fruict of
Act. 28. preaching amongſt them ſaying : [Be it knowne ther-
v, 20. fore to you, that this ſaluation of God, is ſent to
the Gentiles : and they wil heare.] Yea the con-

W w   uerſion

uersion of this plenitude of Gentiles, was so hidden
a Misterie, that [it was notified to the Princes &
Potestates in celestials (that is to angelical powers)   *Ephes.* 3.
by the Chrurch] as the same Apostle writeth to the   *v.* 10.
Ephesians; and to the Colossians, with thankes to   *Colos.* 1.
God for their happines in receiuing the Gospel, sig-   *v.* 6. 23.
nifyeth that it is also [in the whole world, & fruc-
tifyeth, and groweth which is preached among al creatures that are vnder heauen.]

The true Church of Christ is Apostolique.

ARTICLE. 39.

Protestants &
we agree that
Antiquitie is a
true marke of
the Church.

Concerning the fourth principal Marke of
the true Christian Church, which is Antiquitie: the English Protestants agree with vs,
that the same is an assured note, acknowleging with
the Nicene Crede, which they recite in their publique
seruice, that the true Church is Apostolical, as being planted in the world by Christes Apostles. And
so they pretend, that themselues are of the same ancient Church and right successors therof, & charge
the Romane (commonly called Catholique) Church,
to be degenerate from the Apostles Church, about
some thousad yeares agoe ; wherby they would proue
their Church more Ancient then ours, by fiue or sixe
hundred yeares. For better discussing of which controuersie, being of singular importance ; we not only accept in very good part, that which they graunt,
but also that here proue it to be true by holie Scriptures, that Antiquitie is an infallible note of the true
Church. And withal, that the Christian Church, is
rightly called Apostolical. And then in a seueral Article shew, by this Marke of Apostolical Antiquitie,
that the commonly called Catholique (which they
now

now cal the Popifh Church) is the Apoftolique true Church of Chrift. And that their Proteftant church, nor anie other diffenting from the Romane, is not, neither can be, the true chriftian Church.

2   Touching therfore the former point, it is cleare there was a true Church in this world, before Cain began the firft malignant church, els it could not haue

Gen. 4. *v.* 16. bene faid, that [he went forth from the face of our Lord, and dwelt as a fugitiue on the earth] the true Church alfo continuing, not only to Noe, but alfo to Abraham, to Moyfes, and fo to Chrift. Wheras other broken companies rofe and changed, and multiplied into innumerable fectes of infidels, newer and newer, none in fpecial becoming ancient without notable mutation, no nor infidelitie in general, had anie fhew of fucceffion, like to true Religion; which ftil remained, where al Infidels were drowned in the diluge, and fome good time paffed before new rofe. In

Mat. 13. *v.* 25. the New Teftament our Sauiour teacheth plainly, that the good feede is firft fowne, and afterward cocle is ouerfowne by the enemie the diuel. As for Iudaifme, which fome may obiect to be more ancient then Chriftianitie, the contrarie is true. For al thofe holie Patriarches, and Prophets, and other godlie Iewes, beleued in Chrift, before he came in flefh, though when he came, manie obftinate Iewes oppofed againft him: and more afterwardes, til this day, fuch as S. Iohn writeth of to the Churches of Smir-

Apoc. 2. *v.* 9. *Ch.* 3. *v.* 9. *Io.* 5. *v.* 39. *Luc.* 24. *v.* 25. na and Philadelphia [which fay them felues to be Iewes, and are not, but are the Sinagogue of Satan] which Iewes, with their corrupted Iudaifme, are much yonger then the true Iewes, which confeffed Chrift to come in maner as he did, to whofe teftimonie our Sauiour remitted the incredulous, willing them to fearch the Scriptures; becaufe al the Prophets did write of him. So it is certaine that

W w 2   the

The true Church was before al Infidelitie.

Al Infidels were deftroyed in Noes floud.

Iudaifme which confeffeth Chrift, is more auncient then Iudaifme which denieth him.

the Catholique Church, and the Catholique religion, is not only [built vpon the fundation of the Apoftles] which may fatisfiie Chriftians; but alfo [of the
Prophets] which confoundeth the Iewes [Iefus
Chrift him felf being the higheft corner ftone . who
is the eternal Sonne of God.] As therfore antiquitie is a fure marke of the true Church and Religion :
fo is the rifing after of anie new contrarie opnion
an affured proofe of herefie in Chriftian countries,
Which note, whofoeuer wil auoide, muft needes appeale as the Proteftants doe, vnto the ancient faith
of the Apoftes, and pleade to be more ancient then
we . But how wel they can mantaine this plea, refteth to be tried.

Ephef. 2.
v. 20.

Deut. 13.
v. 1. 2. 3.

Apoftolical, or
miffiue power
remaineth ftil
in the Church.

3 In the meane time that the true Church is rightly called Apoftolical which they alfo acknowlege,
is further confirmed by al thofe holie Scriptures,
that teach the neceffitie ofvocation, and miffion of
Ecclefiaftical perfons, to preach chriftian doctrine ,
and to adminifter the holie Sacraments; with other
facred Rites. And by the verie fame alfo is clearly
proued, that proteftants doe not fuccede to the A-
poftles, as they pretend . For the true Church is not
only Apoftolical, becaufe the Apoftles did firft plant
it , which is one principal reafon as we haue alreadie
faid, and is allowed by Proteftantes : but alfo becaufe
al Ecclefiaftical power is deriued from Apoftolical
auctoritie, which ceafed not by the temporal death
ofthe Apoftles, but ftil refideth in the militat Church.
And becaufe the Cleargie ofthe true Church, more
peculiarly participateth of the name Apoftolical;
which fignifieth fent , ifthey were not fo fent they
were not Clerkes at al, nor Goddes fpiritual Meffengers .

True miffion
is either ordi-
narie, or ex-
traordinarie .

4 As neither in the old Law, could anie be a Preift
or a Prophet, except he were fent by Goddes ordinance

dinance. Wherupon God by his Prophet Ieremie, denounced them to be no Prophets, which pretended that office without Miffion faying [The Prophets

Iere. 14. *v.* 14.

prophecie falfly in my name: I fent them not, and I commanded them not, neither haue I fpoken vnto them. Lying vifion, and deceiptful diuination, guilfulnes, and the feduction of their owne hart, they prophecie vnto you.] This therfore, is an efpecial mark to be obferued in al preachers, whether they be fent or no. And fo God againe and againe warned his people not to heare them at al, that are not fent, for the very firft word which they fpeake faying

Iere. 23. *v.* 17. 21. 31.

[the Lord hath fpoken] is falfe, becaufe our Lord hath not fpoben to them [they take their tongues and fay, our Lord faith it] that is, they vniuftly take that auctoritie which is not *deliuered* vnto them. And therfore God alwaies made it manifeft, who were his true preachers, by one of thefe two meanes. Either by miracles, as when he fendeth extraordinarie, or by vifible ordination, when he fendeth or-

Exo. 3. *v.* 2. *Ch.* 4. *v.* 2. *Leuit.* 8. *v.* 2. *&c.*

dinarie Paftors. So Moyfes being extraordinarie, to proue his miffion, had power to worke miracles. Aaron being to be made ordinarie high Preift, was cōfecrated by Moyfes, and al his fonnes, confecrated Preiftes. Likewife other Prophets, and other Preiftes. Yea our Sauiour befides other proofes, & teftimonies, proued him felf to be Meffias by manie moft cleare miracles. And fent his Apoftles and other Difciples at firft with power to worke miracles:

Mat. 10. *v.* 1.

But eftablifhed their function, by the ordinarie courfe of Miffion [Hauing called his twelue Difciples (faith S. Mathew) he gaue them power ouer vncleane fpirites, that they fhould caft them out, and fhould cure al maner of difeafes, and al maner of infirmitie.]

v. 5. 6.

5 At which time he limited their miffion in refpect of place, and perfons; commanding them thus: { Into the way of the Gentiles; and into the cities of

Chrift at firft limited his Apoftles Iurifdiction to certaine places, &

persons.

the Samaritans enter ye not : but goe rather to the sheepe that are perished of the house of Israel.] And [after this (saith S. Luke) our Lord designed also other seaventie two, and sent them two and two into euerie Citie and place whether him self would come.] In which two Missions, appeareth the Paterne and order of sending, both the higher degree of Bishopes, and of the lower cleargie other Preistes. with special instruction, that albeit [the haruest be much, and the workmen few] yet must none passe their assigned limites, but [pray to our Lord to send

Lue. 10. v . 1 . 2 .

Afterwardes extended it into al the earth.

moe workmen into his haruest.] Afterwardes the Apostles iurisdiction, was extended into al the world. [Al power (saith our Sauiour to them) is geuen vnto me in heauen and in earth : going therfore, teach ye al Nations . (And as S. Marke relateth this commission) going into the whole world, preach the Gospel to al creatures . And they going forth, preached euerie-where, our Lord working with-al and confirming the word, with signes that followed.] In like sort S. Paul was extraordinarily sent to al Gentiles whosoeuer ; being made also an Apostle, [not of men, neither by men, but by Iesus Christ] touching his first calling ; yet tooke orders [by imposition of handes of other Apostles, by Goddes expresse commandement.] And further auouched his calling [by the signes of Apostleship done amongst the Corinthians] and in manie other places [In signes (saith he) & wonders, & mightie deedes.]

Mar.16. v . 15 . 20 .

Act . 9 . v . 1 . 15 . Gal .1.v.1. Act.13.v. 2 . 3 .

2 . Cor .12. v . 12 .

S . Mathias was ordained an Apostle by election.

6   By the ordinarie way S. Mathias was chosen, & ordained an Apostle, when S. Peter in the College of Apostles, and presence of the faithful people, declaring [that one of the other Disciples must be elected to supply the place from whence Iudas was fallen] two by Iudgement of voices were found fitte, and after [the publique praier, the lotte falling to Matthias

Act . 1. v . 15 . 21 .

Mathias, he was adioyned to the other eleuen A-
poftles] and the number of twelue made againe complete. Shortly after as the Church increafed, other
Bifhops, Preifts, Deacons, and al cleargie men were
ordained by Apoftolical auctoritie. The firft were
the feauen Deacons chofen by the faithful people
geuing teftimonie of their vertues, and fo they were
Act. 6. confecrated by the Apoftles impofition of handes:
v. 3. 6. which Deacons were not only the keepers, and di-
8. tributers of the Churches temporal goodes, which
Act. 7. was the occafion that thefe were then ordered; but
v. 1. 2. alfo their more principal functions were to preach,
&c. and to baptife, as apeareth in S. Steuen, S. Philippe
Act. 8. and the reft. Againe befides the twelue Apoftles,
v. 5. 26. by the expreffe commandement of the holie Ghoft.
37. S. Paul, and S. Barnabas, were adioyned aboue
Act. 13. their number, and made Apoftles. [Seperate me
v. 2. 3. Saul, and Barnabas (faid the holie Ghoft) vnto the
worke wherto I haue taken them] wherupon [the
other Apoftles fafting, and praying, and impofing
handes vpon them, difmiffed them.] They alfo prea-
Act. 14. ching and conuerting manie [ordained Preiftes in e-
v. 22. uerie Church with fafting, praying, and impofing of
handes.] Manie of them were alfo Bifhopes, for fo
S. Paul calleth them in his Sermom to the Cleargie,
made at Miletum, where he exhorted them to be
Act. 20. careful of their Paftoral charge faying: [Take hede
v. 28. to your felues and to the whole flocke wherin the holie Ghoft hath placed you Bifhopes, to rule the Church of God, which he purchafed with his owne bloud.]
Such alfo of the Bifhopes as firft conuerted anie citie,
or countrie to Chriftianitie, were in a fecundarie
degree called the Apoftles of the fame places. So
Phil. 2. was [Epaphroditus the Apoftle of the Philippians.]
v. 25. And [Epaphras the Apoftle of the Colloffians.]
Colof. 1. By which examples S. Gregorie the great, and S.
v. 7. Auguftine

Deacons were
ordained by
election, pofi-
tion of handes,
and miffion.

S. Paul, & S.
Barnabas ad-
ioyned to the
Apoftles, by
impofition of
handes, and
miffion.

Particular A-
poftles of thofe
nations which
they firft con-
uerted to
Chrift.

Auguſtine ſent by him, are called the proper Apoſtles
of our Engliſh nation. And ſo others of other nations. S. Timothee likewiſe and S. Titus, were Biſhopes, ordained by S. Paul, and they ordained o-
ther Biſhopes, Preiſts, and Deacons: As is cleare by
S. Paules Epiſtles inſtructing them, and in them al o-
ther Biſhopes, what qualities are required in al Cleargie men. Namely in the three greateſt orders of Biſhopes, Preiſts, and Deacons. To which the inferi-
or orders are preſuppoſed in euerie one that is to
aſcend to the higher. Wherof we ſhal ſay more in
the proper place. But of al conditions requiſite in
Cleargie men, due vocation and miſſion is moſt eſſential.

7   As the ſame Apoſtle manfeſtly teaceth in his E-
piſtles to the Romans, and Hebrewes: declaring how
much mens ſaluation dependeth vpon the lawful miſſion of paſtors by this deduction. For that [none can
inuocate God to ſaluation, vnles they beleue in God
whom they inuocate. And how ſhal they beleue in
him whom they neuer heard? And how ſhal they
heare without a Preacher? But how ſhal they preach
vnleſſe they be ſent?] Againe touching Miſſion,
he teacheth that [Euerie High Preiſt (& ſo euerie
Cleargie man) being taken from amongſt men (that
is, from the ſtate of lay-men wherin al are borne)
is appointed for men in thoſe thinges that perteine
to God. Neither doth anie man take the honour to
him ſelf, but he that is called of God as Aaron,]
Wherin is proued not only, that they ſinne moſt e-
normiouſly, that without due ordination exerciſe
ſpiritual functions: but alſo that al ſuch as take Eccleſiaſtical power to them ſelues, or take it of them
that cannot geue it, are in deede mere laimen, being
not ordained by power deſcending from Chriſts A-
poſtles. And ſo are no more Preiſtes, then thoſe
whom

Other Bi-
ſhopes, and
Preiſtes, were
alſo ordained
by the A-
poſtles, and
other Bi-
ſhopes.

1. *Tim.* 3.
v. 2. 8.
Tit. 1. *v.*
5. 6. 7.

Part 2.
Art.

Rom. 10.
v. 14. 15.

Heb. 5. *v.*
1. 4.

3. *Reg.* 12.
v. 31.

Ch. 13.   whom Ieroboam made of the abiectes of the people
v. 33.   which were not of the childeen of Leui.

The true Militant Church is perpetual, from the
beginning of the world to the ende.

A R T I C L E. 40.

Againſt theſe four principal Markes now declared, which are Vnitie, Sanctitie, Vniuerſali
tie, and Antiquitie : our Aduerſaries doe rather ſeeke euaſions, then make direct oppoſition. For
wheras they can not denie them to be very ſpecial
proprieties, of the true Church being ſo clearly proued by holie Scriptures : yet are they vnwilling to
trie by them which is the true Church ; foreſeing
that they agree whollie to the Romane, commonly
called Catholique Church ; & not ſo wel to their own
congregation, which they pretend to be the true Chri
ſtian Church. And therfore they flee ſo much as they
can from this kind of trial ; and when they are pref-
ſed therwith, they commonly anſwere ; that albeit
the true Church, is one, holie, Catholique, & Apoſtolique Church ; yet is it not (ſay they) alwaies extant in this world, but faileth ſome times ; or at the
leaſt is ſo hidden, that the world doth not ſee it nor
knoweth where or in whom it is. To theſe ſhiftes
did the Donatiſtes flee in Africk about twelue hundred yeares agoe : and al Proteſtantes vſe the ſame
plea now, in theſe partes of Europe, when they
are vrged to tel, where or in whom their pretended
Church was, before Luther broke from the Romane
Religion, wherin he liued til he was about fourtie
yeares old : was alſo a frier ; and fiftene yeares being a Preiſt, daily ſaid Maſſe. And ſo to our iuſt demand, they generally make this dooble doubtful an-

Though Pro-
teſtantes can
not denie the
former foure
Markes of the
Church, yet
they decline
from trial by
them.

X x   ſwear

ſwear, that either the true Church was for manie hundred yeares wholly decayed, which they ſay is poſſible; or els it was often times ſo ſmale, that it could
not be ſeene; except perhaps there were ſome few,
that knew one an other; though no man knoweth now
who they were, nor where they were hidden. But
that the reader may more fully ſee, how falſe theſe
imaginations are, we wil here ſhew by manie plaine
textes of holie Scripture, touching the former part of
their anſwear, that the true Church is perpetual: &
then concerning the later part, that it is alſo perpetually viſible.

2 Firſt therfore that the Church continued without
interruption from the beginning, til the written Law
was geuen, is manifeſt by the ſacred Hiſtorie, where
Moyſes moſt exactly declareth, the continual ſucceſſion of Patriarches, with the times of their birthes,
and termes of their liues. Wherby we ſee that each
of them ſaw their owne progenies multiplied by manie generations, al of them liuing manie yeares before they came to the ſupreme gouernment of the
whole Church. So farre was the Church from interruption that it conteined manie particular families,
as it were Dioſes and Pariſhes, ſubordinate to one
ſupreme head of al. For Adam the origine of mankind,
liued to ſee Mathuſale in the eight Generation; yea
and Lamech in the ninth. Mathuſale liued to ſee Sem
the Sonne of Noe nere an hundred yeares old. Sem
liued, til Iacob the Nephew of Abraham was borne.
So that theſe three Patriarches, Adam, Mathuſale, &
Sem, comprehend al the time from the beginning,
til the birth of Iacob, otherwiſe called Iſrael, father
of twelue ſonnes, which were the heades of the 12
Tribes. In al aboue two thouſand yeares. Al which
time, the ſame faith and Religion, continued in theſe
and the other Patriarkes, and in their proper families

not

Therefore we
alſo proue o-
ther two
Markes.

The perpetui-
tie of the
Church, is de-
clared by Moy-
ſes, from the
beginning of
the world til
his time.

Three Patriar-
kes compre-
hended in
their times, a-
boue two
thouſand yea-
res.

Gen. 5.
Gen. 10.
Gen. 5. *v.*
10. 26.

11.

notwithstanding the breaches which were made frō
them by collateral Generations of Chain, Cham, Ia-
phet, Lot, Ismael, Esau, and others whose progenies
fel into innumerable sectes of infidelitie. And the
same Church remained intire, more and more increasing, for al the cruel persecution of the Egiptians ; as

Exo. 1. Moyses recordeth saying : [The children of Israel
v .7. 8. increased, and as it were springing vp, did multi-
9. plie; and growing strong excedingly, filled the land.
In the meane time, there arose a new king ouer Egipt
that knew not Ioseph, and he said to his people.
Behold the people of the children of Israel, is much:
10. and stronger then we : Come let vs wisely oppresse
11. the same, lest perhappes it multiply. Therfore he
set ouer them maisters of the workes to afflict them
12. with burdens · And the more they did oppresse them;
so much the more they multiplied and increased . And
the king of Egipt said to the mid-wiues commanding
15 .16. them : when you shal be mid-wiues to the Hebrew
women, and the time of d liuerie is come, if it be a
man child, kil it ; If a woman, reserue her. He after this commanded al his people saying : whatsoe-
22. uer shal be borne of the male sex, cast it into the riuer . But God heard the crie of the children of Israel, and their groning, and remembred the couenant
Exo. 2. which he made with Abraham, Isaac, & Iacob .
v . 23. 3   In the desert, after their deliuerie out of Egipt ,
24. Balac, king of Moab, hired Balaam the sorcerer to
Nu . 22. curse them : But he contrariwise was forced, by
v . 2. Goddes ordinance, to speake good thinges of them,
Nu . 23. yea and God by him, blessed them, and deliuered them
v . 19. out of his hand : which he, in his excuse to Balac ,
20. Ios. confessed plainly saying : [God is not as man that he
24 . v. may lie, nor as the sonne of man, that he may be chan-
10. ged . But God (saith he) hath brought Israel out of
Egipt, whose strength is like to the Vnicorne] sig-

nifing

God also con-
serued his
Church al the
time of the
Iudges , and
Kinges .

nifying that God whose wil is immutable, hauing chosen them to be his people, & deliuered them from Egipt, wil conserue and protect them, til he haue performed his promise in them. The very same thing, Moyses assured them saying [Our Lord hath taken you, and brought you out of the iron fornace of Egipt, to haue you his people by inheritance.] And albeit he punish them for their sinnes, yet [he wil repay vegeance vpon their enemies ; & wil be propitious to the land of his people.] *Deut*. 4. *v*. 20. *Deut*. 32. *v*. 43.

The same Church also continued without interruption, in, & after the captiuitie in Babilon, til Christ.

4 Goddes promise also made concerning the sonne of Dauid saying : [I wil establish his kingdome, and he shal build a house to my name ; and I wil establish the throne of his kingdome for euer] is especially vnderstoode of Christ, & his Kingdome the Church. For otherwise Salomons kingdome was shortly diminished after his death, & afterwardes ouerthrown. Yet was the Church also of the old Testament conserued, though the temporal kingdome, with the Citie of Ierusalem, and the material Temple were destroyed. For manie Prophets, namely Ieremie, very often foretold the faithful peoples conseruation in captiuitie, and relaxation, with restauration of the Temple. And Esdras, and Nehemias, writte the Historie how the same was al accomplished. Neither did the Church perish by the furious persecution of Antiochus the Grecian king, and other persecuters and Apostataes ; but was made more illustrious by the most Heroical fortitude of the Machabees, and manie other constant Prestes, & people, euen to Christes time. Seing then the Church of God in the old Testament, was continual without interruption : it foloweth necessarily, that the Christian Church must needes be perpetual and inuincible, as hauing more grace, greater promises, and more excellent priuileges, which might suffice, though there were none other
2. Reg. 7.
v. 12. 13.

Iere. 4. *v.* 27. *Ch*. 5. *v*. 10. 18. *Ch*. 12. *v*. 14. *Ch*. 23. *v*. 3. *Ch*. 30. &. 11. *Ch*. 32. *v*. 37. *Ch*. 33. *v*. 17. 18. *Ezech*. 6. *v*. 8. *Ps*. 136. 1. *Esd*. 1 *v*. 5. *Ch*. 2. *v*. 1.

Not withstanding extreme persecution therof.

ther

CHRISTIAN DOCTRINE. *Art.* 39. 363
ther proofe.

5 Much more this truth is confirmed by other ir-refragable testimonies of the holie Prophets, and A-postles, and by Christ him self. Of manie we wil re-cite some competent number. The Royal Psalmist prophecying of our Sauiours victorie against his ra-

Pf.2.v. ging enemies faith: [he shal be king ouer Sion his
6.8. holie hil] that is the holie Church. And therin [re-cceiue the Gentiles for his inheritance.] If therefore the Church of Gentiles could faile Christ could loose his inheritance, which were absurde and impossi-ble. In respect also of the Church it self, especially of the more holie members therof, the same Prophet

Pf.11. speaketh thus to God [thou Lord wil preserue vs;
v.8. and kcepe vs from this generation for euer. Peoples
Pf.44. (not one people onlie but peoples) of manie nations
v.18. (which is the Christian Church) shal confesse to thee
Pf.45. for euer, and for euer and euer.] And that also in
v.4.5. persecution, though some fal, others shal be so much
6. the more constant [The violence of the riuer ma-keth the citie of God ioyful; God is in the midest therof, it shal not be moued :God wil helpe it in the

Pf.60. morning early. thou o God hast geuen inheritance
v.7. to those that feare thy name. Thou wilt adde dayes vpon the dayes of the king; his yeares euen vnto the

Pf.68. day of generation, and generation : Because God
v.36. wil saue Sion, and the cities of Iuda shal be built vp,
37. and the seede of his seruants shal possese it, and they
Pf.71. that loue his name shal dwel in it. there shal rise in
v.7. his dayes (in the dayes of Christ) iustice, and abun-dance of peace, vntil the moone be taken away.] Neither shal sinnes, which are more dangerous then

Pf.77. anie persecution, destroy the Church: for [God is
v.36. merciful, and wil be propitious to their sinnes, and
69. he wil not destroy them. He built his sanctuarie as of Vnicornes in the land, which he hath founded for

X x 3 euer

Much lesse is it possible that the Church of Christ in the new Testamēt should euer perish.

Proued by the Psalmes.

euer. We thy people (say true penitents in afflicti- *Pſ.* 78. *v.*
on) and the ſheepe of thy paſture, wil confeſſe to thee 13.
for euer. Vnto generation and generation we wil
ſhew forth thy praiſe.] In an other Pſalme God ſaith
of his Church ⌊ I haue ordeined a Teſtamēt with mine *Pſ.* 88. *v.*
elect : I haue ſworne to Dauid my ſeruant ; for euer wil 4. 5.
I prepare thy ſeede. And I wil build thy ſeate vnto
generation and generation. I wil kepe my mercie 29.
vnto him for euer ; and my Teſtament faithful vnto 30.
him. I wil put his ſeede for euer and euer ; & his 31.
throne as the daies of heauen. But if his children
ſhal forſake my Law, and wil not walke in my iudgementes. If they ſhal prophane my iuſtices and not 32.
kepe my commandementes : I wil viſit their iniqui- 33.
ties with a rodde, and their ſinnes with ſtripes. But 34.
my mercie I wil not take away from him : neither
wil I hurt in my truth. Neither wil I prophane my
Teſtament : and the wordes that procede from my
mouth, I wil not make fruſtrate. Once I haue ſworne
in my holie, I wil not lie to Dauid : his ſeede ſhal
continue for euer. And his throne as the ſunne in
my ſight, and as the Mone perfect for euer, and a
faithful witnes in heauen.] Al this in one paſſage,
of the permanent ſtabilitie of the Church ; notwithſtanding it may ſeme to the weake, in affliction, to 39.
be in danger of failing ; yet doth God ſtil reſpect mans 48.
infirmitie, his owne promiſe, and the reproach of the 50. 51.
enemies ; and ſo conſerueth it. As the ſame Prophet
very often inculcateth [Becauſe (ſaith he) our Lord *Pſ.* 93.
wil not reiect his people, and his inheritance he wil *v.* 14.
not forſake. The ſonnes of thy ſeruantes ſhal inha- *Pſ.* 101.
bite : and their ſeede ſhal be directed for euer. Of- *v.* 29.
ten haue they impugned me from my youth, let Iſra- *Pſ.* 128.
el now ſay, often haue they impugned me from my *v.* 1. 2.
youth : but they haue not preuailed againſt me. Be- *Pſ.* 131. *v.*
cauſe our Lord hath choſen Sion : he hath choſen it 13. 14.
for an 15. 16.

for an habitation to him felf. This is my reft (faith he) for euer and euer : here wil I dwel becaufe I haue chofen it. Bleffing, I wil bleffe her widow : her poore I wil fil with breades. Her Preiftes I wil cloath with faluation : and her Sainctes (al faithful good children) fhal reioyce with ioyfulnes.]

6   Thus therfore the beloued fpoufe of Chrift re-ioyceth in Canticle, for her perpetual coniunction

The fame is confirmed by other Prophets.

Cant. 2.
v. 16.
17.
If. 60.
v. 11.

with him faying : [My beloued to me, and I to him : who feedeth among the lillies til the day breake, & the fhadowes decline :] Ifaias faith to the Chriftian Church [Thy gates fhal be open continually : day & night they fhal not be fhutte. that the ftrength of the Gentiles may be brought to thee ; & their kinges may be brought .] Ieremie amongft his prophecies concerning the Iewes captiuitie, and relaxation, with continual conferuation of their Church vntil the co-ming of Chrift ; interpofeth often the perpetual fta-bilitie of the Chriftian Church. For example let one

Iere. 31.
v. 31.
32.

place ferue our prefent purpofe [Behold (faith he) the dayes fhal come faith our Lord, and I wil make a new couenant with the houfe of Ifrael, & the houfe of Iuda; not according to the couenant which I made with their fathers, in the day that I tooke their hand to bring them out of the land of Egipt, the couenant

33.

which they made voide. But this fhal be the coue-nant which I wil make with the houfe of Ifrael, after thofe dayes faith our Lord. I wil geue my law in their bookes, and in their hart I wil write it : and I

36.

wil be their God, and they fhal be my people. If the lawes (which are geuen to the Sunne, Moone, & Sea) fhal faile before me, faith our Lord, the feede of Ifrael fhal alfo faile thee, that it be not a nation

37.

before me for euer . Thus faith our Lord : If the hea-uens aboue fhal be able to be meafured, and the fun-dation of the earth beneath to be fearched out; I al-
                                                        fo wil

fo wil caft away al the feede of Ifrael, for al thinges
that they haue done, faith our Lord.] But the propofed fuppofitions being impoffible to be done, it is
alfo impoffible that God wil fuffer the feede of Iira-
el, the Chirftian Church, to faile. Ezechiel prophecying of Antichrift vnder the name of Gog, fheweth
that the whole Church fhal not be deftroyed by him,
much leffe by anie other meanes, but fhal preuaile a-
gainft him [I wil cal in, againft him (faith our Lord *Ezech.* 38.
God) in al my moutans, the fword; euerie mans fword *v.* 21. 22.
fhal be directed againft his brother. And I wil iudge
him with peftilence, and bloud, and vehement fhoure,
and mightie great ftones; fire and brimftone wil I
rayne vpon him, and vpon his armie, and vpon the
manie peoples that are with him. And I wil be magnified, and I wil be fanctified, and I wil be knowne, 23.
in the eyes of manie Nations: and they fhal know
that I am the Lord. Behould I vpon thee Gog, the *Ch.* 39. *v.*
Prince of the head of Mofoch and Thubal. And I wil 2. 3.
ftrike thy bow in thy left hand, and thine arowes I
wil caft downe out of thy right hand. Vpon the mou- 4.
taines of Ifrael fhalt thou fal, and al thy troupes, &
thy peoples that are with thee.] Daniel interpreting
Nabuchodonofers dreame, of the four great temporal Monarchies of the world; preferreth the Church
of Chrift farre aboue them al, as the only kingdome
that can neuer be deftroyed faying [In the daies of *Dan.* 2.
thofe kingdomes, the God of heauen wil raife vp *v.* 44.
a Kingdome that fhal not be diffipated for euer, and
his Kingdome fhal not be deliuered to an other people; and it fhal breake in peeces and fhal confume,
al thefe kingdomes, and it felf fhal ftand for euer.]
The fame four Monarchies being reprefented in a *Dan.* 7. *v.*
vifion, to the fame Daniel he faw laft of al, that God 2. 13. 14.
gaue to Chrift, as the fonne of man [power, and honour, and kingdome, and that al peoples, tribes, and
tongues

tongues fhal ferue him : His power, is an eternal
power that fhal not be taken away, and his King-
Dan . 11. dome fhal not be corrupted] no not in the perfe-
v . 32. cution of Antichrift, as is alreadie noted in Ezechiel; for then alfo [there fhal be a people that knoweth their God, and fhal obtaine , and fhal be faued .]
So by the other Prophets, God foretelleth, that he
Zach. 1. wil perpetually conferue his Church [I haue bene
v. 14. zelous for Ierufalem, and Sion with great zele . I
Zach. 2. wil be to it (faith our Lord) a wal of fireround a-
v. 5. bout. I wil be in glorie in the middeft therof. And
Mal. 2. you fhal know that I fent you this commandement,
v. 4. that my couenant might be with Leui, faith the Lord
of hoftes.]

7 Our Sauiour & his Apoftles, teach the very fame of-
tē admonifhing that the Church fhal be toffed as the
fea with great ftormes; but fhal neuer perifh. In
figne wherof, when the Difciples feared drowning,
Mat. 8. our Sauiour encoraging them faid [why are ye fear-
v. 24. ful, o ye of litle faith .] In this fpiritual Kingdom, the
26. Church [fhal be corne & chaffe, good & badde fifhes,
Mat. 3. euen to the confummation of the world .] In the
v. 12. world [the faithful fhal haue diftreffe, but haue con-
Mat. 13. fidence (faith our Sauiour) I haue ouercome the
v. 49. world. I wil geue you an other Paraclete, the Ho-
Ioan. 16. lie Ghoft, that he may abide with you for euer. I
v. 33. am with you (not for an hundred, or fiue hundred,
Io. 14. or for a thoufand yeares, not fomtimes with you, fom
v. 16. times forfake you, but) I am with you al daies, euen
Mat. to the end of the world.] It is [not built vpon fand,
28. *v.* but vpon a Rocke; hel gates fhal neuer preuaile a-
20. gainft it .] Euerie [counfel and worke that is of men
Mat. 7. (faid wife Gamaliel) wil be diffolued : but if it be
v. 24. of God, you are not able to diffolue it .] Manie haue
26. refifted and impugned, but al in vaine [Saul brea-
Mat. 16. thing forth threates and flaughter againft the Dif-
v. 18.

The perpetual
ftabilitie of the
Church, is yet
more exprefly
auouched by
our Sauiour, &
his Apoftles.

Y y   ciples

ciples of our Lord, assisted those that stoned S. Ste- *Act.* 5. *v.*
phen; gotte Letters of commission to persecute those 38.
that confessed Christ] but he being conuerted, innu- *Act.* 9. *v.*
merable others persecuted him, and the whole Church 1. 2.
three hundred yeares together, but could not ouer- 23.
throw it; stil it increased, and is continually [builded, *Act.* 13. *v.*
vntil we shal meete al in vnitie of faith, and know- 14. *&c.*
lege of the Sonne of God .]   If it were at al possi- *Ephes.* 4.
ble, that the Church could be for anie time extingui- *v.* 13.
shed, that should doubtles especially happen in the
persecution of Antichrist. But besides the Prophecies of Ezcehiel and Daniel aboue recited; it is yet
more cleare in the Apocalips of S. Iohn, that also
al that time of Antichristes reigne, it shal continue,
as is declared in these plaine wordes [there were *Apoc.* 12.
geuen to the woman two winges of a great Eagle, *v.* 14.
that she might flye into the desert, vnto her place
where she is norished, for a time, and times, and 15.
half a time, from the face of the serpent. And the
serpent cast water out of his mouth after the woman 16.
as it were a floud, that he might make her to be caried away with the floud . And the earth helping the
woman, opened her mouth, and swalowed vp the
floud which the Dragon cast out of his month.]
Where we see, that the Church shal flee, but not
perish; not the Church, but the furious floud of per- *Apoc.* 13.
secution, shal be swalowed vp. [Here is the patience *v.* 10.
and faith of Sainctes .] By the bloud of Martyrs,
the Church is norished, conserued, and strengthned.

The true Church euer hath bene , & wil be vifible .

ARTICLE. 41.

ALbeit the fame places of holie Scripture which fhew the Church to be perpetual, doe for the moft part, proue alfo that it is alwaies vifible : neuerthelesse, becaufe thefe two qualities are in them felues diftinct, and manie thinges are perpetual, which are not vifible, and manie things vifible, and not perpetual : and 'efpecially, becaufe our aduerfaries, fuppofing the Church may be perpetual, yet denie it to be alwaies vifible : we fhal here recite fome moe places of holie Scriptures which particularly proue this point of the Churches continual vifibilitie, euen from the beginning to the end of the world. As for the firft age before the general floud, it is fo cleare by the Catalogue of the Patriarches, with their manie families, and by the famous title of the fonnes of God, that no learned proteftant doth denie it.

*Gen . 5 . ***
Ch . 6 .
v . 2 .

2 The firft doubt which they make, is for the time betwene the death of Noe, and the parting of Abraham from Chaldea, into Chanaan, which time , by true calculation, was no more then the fpace of fourtie and eight yeares. And as certaine it is, that the Church of God was there alfo vifible, and wel known in the world, not only to the members therof, among them felues, but alfo to infidels which perfecuted them for profeffing one God, and refufing to ferue Idols. For Abraham who was neuer corrupted in faith nor religion, was twentie feauen yeares of age when Noe dyed. Moreouer at the time of Abrahams parting from his Countrie of Chaldea, where he had fuffered perfecution for his faith , there were

Gen . 11 .
v . 10 .
&c .
Ch . 12 .
v . 1 .

Some Proteftants acknowlege the Church to be perpetual, yet denie it to be alwayes vifible.

The firft obiection is, of the time betwene Noe , & Abraham.

Our anfwear. Sem , Heber , Abraham , and manie others were inuiolate in faith.

manie of his progenitors the faithful seruantes of God
yet liuing. Namely Sem (the first sonne of Noe)
and Arphaxad, Sale, Heber, Reu, Sarug, and Thare,
the father of Abraham. Melchizedech was then also
liuing in Chanaan, a Preist of God, and (as it is most
probable) a Chananite ; for that S. Paul saith [his
generation is not numbred among Abrahams chil- *Heb.* 7.
dren.] By al which it is manifest, that the Church *v.* 6.
was then also visible in these Patriarches, and their
families. From which time it increased stil in Abrahams familie, which was not smal : As it appeareth *Gen.* 14.
by his sudden arming of three hundred eightene men *v.* 14.
of his owne houshold, for an exploite when he re-
scued his Nephew Lot, with others out of their e-
nemies handes. Neither can it be doubted but al
these, besides women and children, beleued rightly
in one God, for that shortlie after, al the men of
his house aswel the home-bred, as the bought seruantes, and strangers, were circumcised together. 27.
After which time, the Church was more and more
conspicuous according to Goddes promise to Abra-
ham saying [I wil make thy seede, as the dust of the *Gen.* 13.
earth : if anie man be able to number the dust of *v.* 16.
the earth, thy seede also he shal be able to number.]
Which though S. Paul teacheth to be more perfectly performed in Christians, then in the Iewes ; more *Rom.* 9.
in the spiritual, then in the natural children of Abra- *v.* 7.
ham, yet it is also cleare, that manie of Abrahams issue, & their families, rightly beleued in God.

An other mere 3   An other obiection is made by Protestantes tou-
common ob-   ching the time when Elias lamented the decay of
iection is, of Goddes faithful children saying [With zele haue I *3. Reg.* 9.
the time of E- bene zelous for our Lord the God of hostes, because *v.* 10. 14
lias the Pro- the children of Israel haue forsaken thy ceuenant :
phet. thine altars they haue destroyed, and haue slaine thy
Prophets with the sword, and I alone am left, and
they

they feeke my life to take it away] *Ergo* (fay they)
the Church was then inuifible. But we deny their
confequence, for this Argument proueth nothing for
their purpofe, but fheweth their penurie of proofes.
And it either bewraieth their ignorance, or detecteth a malicious intention to deceiue the people with
fhew of wordes. For notwithftanding the perfecu- *Anfweared by the next wor-des, and other textes.*

Ch. 13. v.
11. 12. 15.
Ch. 22. v.
43. 2. Par.
14. v. 2.
Ch. 15. v.
8. Ch. 17.
v. 6. Ch.
19. v. 11.
3. Reg. 19.
v. 18. Ro.
11. v. 4.
4. Reg. 17.
v. 27. 28.
Tob. 1. v.
2. Ch. 2. v.
4. Ch. 3.
v. 7. Ch.
4. v. 21.

tion made by Achab and Iezabel in the kingdome of
Ifrael (the ten fchifmatical Tribes) the whole kingdome of Iuda remained intyre in Religion. where
king Afa then reigned; and after him king Iofophat
both good kinges, Amarias the High Preift gouerning in thinges which perteine to God. Yea alfo
in Ifrael the Church was vifible, though Elias being
then in mount Horeb, faw not who were conftant in
Religion. For God anfweared his lamentation, telling him that feauen thoufand were left, which had
not bowed their knees before Baal. And, when the
People of thofe tenne Tribes, were afterwardes caried captiues into Afiria, yet there remained fome faith
ful knowne feruantes of God, as [Tobias, Raguel,
Gabelus, and their families, with others that feared
God] Much more the Church continued vifible a-
mong thofe of the kingdome of Iuda in their captiuitie in Babilon al the time of their feauentie yeares
aboade there, befides manie remaining in the land of
Iuda : As is moft cleare in the Prophecies of Ieremie,
Baruch, Ezechiel, Daniel, Aggeus, Zacharias, Malachias, & bookes of Efdras.

1. Mac. 1.
v. 22. &c.
Ch. 2. v. 1.
17. 19. &c.

4 Neither could the crueltie of King Antiochus,
with other heathen Princes, and Captaines, nor the
Apoftafie of Manaffes, and other vfurpers of the high
Preifthood, ouerthrow the Church, or make it inuifible, but by thofe perfecutiós it became more known,
and famous in the world, through the conftancie &
valiant correge of manie Martyres, and other moft *Preoccupation of other obiec-tions.*

zelous

zealous obſeruers of Gods lawes. Namely by the · *Ch* . 14. *v.*
fortitude of Matthathias, and his two ſonnes, in whō · 41.
reſided the office of high Preiſts, by right and continual ſucceſſion, from whoſe time the Church ſtil continued viſible, and Chriſt ſo finding it, obſerued the
lawes therof, and approued cuſtomes.

Manifeſt ſa-
cred textes,
that the Chur-
ch euer was,
and ſhal be
viſible.

5   Now that the Chriſtian Church alwayes was &
muſt be viſible, is moſt aſſured by the more ſpecial
prouidence of God, as both the Prophets and Chriſt
him ſelf and his Apoſtles doe plainly teach. He put · *Pſ.* 18. *v.*
his Tabernacle in the ſunne (ſaith the Royal Prophet) · 6. 7.
and him ſelfe as a bridegrome, coming forth of his
bridechamber. That his tabernacle is his Church,
is manifeſt by al the proprieties of the figuratiue tabernacle, deſcribed by God, and framed by Moyſes · *Exo.* 26. *
direction, Bridegrome, and Bride, being perfect
correlatiues, cannot poſſibly be ſeperated, but if one
ceaſe to be bride, the other ſhould ceaſe to be the
bridegrome. By which termes S. Iohn Baptiſt alſo · *Io.* 3. *v.* 29.
ſheweth that [Chriſt is the bridegrome, becauſe he
hath the bride.] Nothing is more frequent with the · *Pſ.* 21. *v.*
ſame Pſalmiſt then ſuch termes, applied to the Chur- · 26. *Pſ.* 28.
ch, as neceſſarily import it to be alwayes viſible; · *v.* 2. *Pſ.*
calling it the great Church; inuiting al to adore our · 44. *v.* 13.
Lord in his holie court: [therfore ſhal peoples con- · *Pſ.* 47. *v.*
feſſe to thee for euer, and for euer and euer. As we · 9. *Pſ.* 67.
haue heard, ſo haue we ſeene in the citie of our Lord · *v.* 16. *Pſ.*
of hoſts, in the citie of our God. the mountaine of · 71. *v.* 16.
God a fatte mountaine. there ſhal be a firmament in · *Pſ.* 97. *v.*
the earth in the toppes of mountaines, the fruict ther- · 3. 4.
of ſhal be extolled farre aboue libanus. Al the endes
of the earth haue ſeene the ſaluation of our God.
Make ye iubilation to God, al the earth chaunt and
reioice, & ſing: I haue prepared a lampe to my Chriſt: · *Pſ.* 131. *v.*
vpon him ſhal my ſanctification flloriſh.] Likewiſe · 17. 18.
Salomon ſignifying, that wiſdome ſhal inuite al to
heare

heare her voice, prefuppofeth preachers in the vifible Church . [Doth not wifdome carie (faith he) &
prudence geue her voice, ftanding in the high and loftie toppes, ouer the way, in the middeft of the pathes ?
She hath fent her hand-maides to cal to the towre,
and the wales of the Citie. Her lampe fhal not be
extinguifhed in the night . The daughters haue feue
her, and declared her to be moft bleffed . What is
fhe that cometh forth as the morning rifing ? faire
as the moone, elect as the Sunne, terrible as the armie of a campe fet in aray ? What fhal thou fee in
the Sunamiteffe, but the companies of campes ?]
So likewife the other Prophets teftifie Goddes prouidence in conferuing his perpetual vifible Church.
[Vnleffe the Lord of hoftes had left vs feede (faith I-
faias) we had bene as Sodom, and we fhould be
like to Gomorha] which fentence S . Paul applieth
to the time when the Law, and forme of the Church
was changed by Chrift, fhewing that euen in that
cafe, there was feede, and vifible feede left . For al
the Apoftles, and manie other Difciples, ftil beleued the Law and the Prophets, though not actually that our Sauiour fhould rife, or was rifen fo fone
as indeede he was, being a matter of fact ; or if they
were defectiue, in fome other particular pointes, not
fully reueled : yet they beleued in general the omnipotencie, omnifcience, abfolute goodnes, and other attributes of God . So that thefe vifible reliqnes of the
Iewifh Nation, were neuer infidels : nor the Church
made inuifible nor vnknowne . According to that
the fame Prophet addeth in an other place, and the
fame Apoftle alleageth to this purpofe ; that the remnant fhal be conuerted, the remnant to the ftron-
geft God .] And of this remnant, the Chriftian
Church began, and moft vifibly increafed [In the
latter daies (faith he) the Mountaine (marke Chriftian

Prou. 8 .
v . 1 . 2 .
Cb . 9 .
v . 3 ,
Cb . 31 .
v . 18 .
Cant . 6 .
v . 8 . 9 .
Cb . 7 .
v . 1 .
Ifa . 1 .
v . 9 .
Rom . 9 .
v . 29 .
If . 10 .
v . 22 .
Rom . 9 .
v . 27 .

ſtian reader, that the Church is ſo often called a Moū- ‌*Iſa*.2.*v*.
taine) of the Houſe of our Lord ſhal be prepared in 2.*Ch*.54.
the toppe of mountaines, and it ſhal be eleuated a- *v*.9.
boue the litle hilles, and al Nations ſhal flow vnto
it .] Againe God ſaith [As in the daies of Noe, is
this thing to me, to whom I ſware, that I would nomore bring in the waters of Noe vpon the earth : ſo
haue I ſworne not to be angrie with thee, and not to
rebuke thee. For the mountaines (particular Chur- 10.
ches) ſhal be moued, and the litle hilles ſhal tremble; but my mercy ſhal not depart from thee, & the
couenant of my peace (made to the whole Church)
ſhal not be moued. Vpon thy wales Ieruſalem I haue *Ch*.62.*v*.
appointed watch-men; al the day and al the night, 6.
for euer they ſhal not hold their peace.] That we
may better obſerue the greater priuileges of the Chriſtian Church, aboue that of the old Teſtament : God
ſaith by diuers Prophets [I wil eſtabliſh vnto them, *Bar*.2.*v*.
an other Teſtament euerlaſting, that I be their God, 35.
and they ſhal be my people . I wil plant a bough of *Ezech*.17.
Cedar vpon a mountaine high and eminent. On the *v*.22.23.
high mountaines of Iſrael wil I plant it, and it ſhal
ſhoote forth into a budde, and ſhal yeld fruict, and it
ſhal be into a great Cedar : and al birdes, and eue- *Mat*.13.
rie foule ſhal dwel vnder the ſhadow of the boughes *v*.32.
therof, and ſhal there make their neſt. Thy hand ſhal *Mich*.5.
be exalted ouer thine enemies, and al thine enemies *v*.9.
ſhal periſh.] In a viſion [Zacharie ſaw a candle- *Zach*.4.*v*.
ſtick al of gold, and the lampe therof, vpon the head 2.*Ch*.6.
of it : and the ſeauen lightes therof vpon it.] Pro- *v*.13.
phecying of Cyriſt, he ſaith : that [he ſhal build a
Temple to our Lord; and ſhal beare glorie; & ſhal
ſitte & rule vpon his Throne.]

Our Sauiour
in diuers pa-
rables, and in
other more ex-
preſſe doc-
6   Al agreable to the Law and Prophtes, our Sauiour him ſelf deſcribeth his Church to be [the light *Mat*.5.*v*.
of the world : a Citie cituated vpon a mountaine : 15.16.
                                        a candle

candel not put vnder a bushel, but vpon a candelsticke
that it may shine to al that are in the house .] wheras some Protestants would rather expoūd these pro
perties , of the Apostles, or of the Doctors, and Pastors of the Church, or of the Cleargie; then of the
vniuersal Church; so much the more it proueth our
purpose . For seing some special partes, are so eminent, and visible, it is not imaginable that the whole
bodie should be hidden, or obscure . Againe our Sauiour necessarily supposed, that the Church is knowen and the gouerners therof, are both visible, and
accessible, when he prescribed , as a perpetual remedie against obstinate offéders , to informe the Church
Mat . 18. of their demeanour, saying : [If they wil not heare
v . 17 . two or three (priuate frendes) tel the Church] For
if the Church were not visible , or her Prelates vnknowen persons, this remedie should faile, & there
should be no meanes to correct the greatest pertur-
bers of common peace . Also foreseing that false
Ch . 24. prophets would say : [Loe here is Christ , or there :
v. 23 . (not in the publique knowen Church , but in secret
26 . corners of the world) Behold he is in the desert, goe
ye not out (saith our Sauiour) behold in the closets
(say heretikes) beleue it not saith our Lord.] At
the coming of the holie Ghost this Church was esta-
Act . 1 . blished in visible persons, and by visible signes, [the
v . 15 . multitude gathered in one house in Ierusalem, was al-
Ch . 2. most a hundred and twentie] the sensible signes were
v. 2.3. [a sound from heauen as of a vehement winde , ap-
4. 14 . pearing of parted and fyrie tongues] speaking vpon
47. *Ch .* the sudden diuers languages . By and by their num-
4. *v.* 4. ber increased to three thousand ; shortly after to fiue
Ch . 5. *v.* thousand ; and dayly more were added to the same
14. *Ch .* visible Church. [S . Peter being admonished by a
10. *v.* 11. vision, receiued Gentiles into the Church.] then [at
Ch . 11. Cypres, Cyrena, and Antioch, a great number was
v. 21.24 . Z z conuerted

conuerted to our Lord.] S. Barnabas being sent
from Ierusalem to Antioch [exhorted the faithful to
continue in our Lord : And a great multitude was
added] their preaching was open, ministration of Sacraments visible : Discipline visible ; heades and go-
uernoures visible, the prouision for their mantenance
visible; the persecution visible, their dispersio visible ;
S. Steuens, and S. Iames, their Martyrdomes visible ;
S. Peters imprisonment by Herod, as also his and o-
thers imprisoning by the Iewes, visible; the Churches prayer for S. Peters deliuerie, was knowen to
manie : the Apostles councel was visible : miracles
wrought visibly, the name of Christians publique;
the going out of heretikes visible : Simon the magician publiquely reproued, and punished for offering to buy spiritual power with money . the Nicolaites noted for heretikes . But of an inuisible
Church we haue not one word.

Act. 2. 3.
4. 5. &c.

Ch. 7.
Ch. 21.

Ch. 11. *v.*
26. *Ch.* 8.
v. 20.
Apoc. 2.
v. 6.

An other fri-
uolous euasion
of some Prote-
stants, conuin-
ceth their
principal late
Ministers to
haue liued in
damnable
state.

7 If anie wil say (as needes they must say, which
wil mantaine this paradox of an inuisible Church)
that Luther being a frier, and a Preist, and saying
Masse dailie fiftene yeares, was a secret protestant :
Likewise Ecolampadius, Carolostadius, Zuinglius,
Bucer, Cranmer, Caluin, and others, were secret
Protestantes, whiles they said Masses, and liued
in the Romane Church, and were members of their
inuisible Church : then must their Church consist
of manie heritikes mixed with true Christians ; for
that by the doctrine of these named, most of them
were heritikes, they so condemning one an other
of horrible heresies . Yea if anie of these, or other
sectaries, were true Christians knowing the truth as
their Aduocates pleade that they did; yet because
[they denied Christ before men ; he wil denie them
before the face of his Father in heauen.] If their
inuisible Church consisted then, and manie hundred

Mat. 10.
v. 33.

yeares

yeares before of such members : it was indeede of
repropate persons, dissemblers, fearful worldlinges,
lyers, and (as moderne Protestantes iudge) Idolaters, [whose part is in the pitte of hel, burning with
fyre and brimstone] for one of these two must necef-
sarily be graunted; that either none did beleue as
protestantes doe, and then by their doctrine, there
was merely no Church in the world, visible, nor in-
visible, but al were incredulous and Idolareis : or
els those which did beleue, (as these Doctors ima-
gin) and did not professe their faith before men,
were dissembling hipocrites, and so are damned to
moe stripes, and greater tormentes in hel, then if
they had bene infidels, and not knowne the truth
at al.

Apoc. 21.
v. 8.

Luc. 12.
v. 47.

*The Church can not erre in doctrine of faith, nor
of maners.*

ARTICLE. 42.

BEing now sufficiently proued, by the holie
Scriptures, that the true militant Church of
Chrift, is One, Holie, Catholique, Apoftolique, Perpetual, and Visible companie of Christians
confessing the same faith in vnion of one supreme visible head : By which proprieties, and special markes,
euerie one may easily perceiue, that neither the protestantes, nor anie other like pretending congregation; but only the commonly called Catholiques, are
the true Christian Church : it remaineth to be shewed, by the same diuine auctoritie, of holie Scriptures, that this perpetual visibe knowne Church,
hath neuer erred, nor can erre, in doctrine of faith,
nor of maners, declared by definitiue sentence in her
supreme Tribunal seat : that these two principal pointes being

Whosoeuer
knoweth the
true Church,
and that it can
not erre, may
by relying
therupon be
secure from er-
rour in Religi-
on.

res being made cleare, and that by the written word
of God, wherto alone, manie wil needes appeale :
al reasonable persons that doubt in anie part of true
Religion, may both know where to be resolued of
their doubtes, and securely rest vpon the resolution
so geuen : not as vpon only probable and comon o-
pinion, of manie good, wise, and learned men ; but
vpon most certaine diuine infallible Iudgement ; for
this singular priuilege ueuer to erre in publique Iudgement, cometh not to the Church by natural power,
nor power of auie mere creature ; but by the omnipotent power of God ; by diuine ordinance, & perpetual assistance of the Holie Ghost, the Spirit of truth
preseruing her from errour, wherinto euery priuate
man may fal, but not the vniuersal Church.

True Religion
was consetued
by the Patri-
arkes before
the written
law.

2 As we shal here make manifest, beginning with
the Church of the old Testament ; which albeit was
inferiour to the Christian Church in manie respects,
yet wanted not the meanes of infallible iudgement
in al doubtful cases. To this purpose, God proui- *Gen*.4. v
ded first in the Law of nature special Patriarches from 25.26.
Adam to Noe, end so to Abraham, Isaac, and Iacob, *Ch*. 5. *v*.
from whom descended the twelue Tribes. Then did 3. 9. 12,
God raise the extraordinarie Prophet Moyses ; su- *&c*,
preme head, Iudge, and gouernor of the visible
Church. By al which, the true faith and Religion
was continually conserued ; as is alreadie declared *Art*.34.
in diuers precedent Articles. 38.40,41.

An especial
Chaire of in-
fallible Iudge-
ment, was in-
stituted by the
written law.

3 In the writen law God expresly [commanded *Exo*. 25.
Moyses to make a special Tabernacle, or Sanctuarie] *v*. 8. 10.
with appurtinances. Namely to make [an Arke of 17.18.20
testimonie of the (durable) wood setim] signifying 22.
the Church : and ouer the Arke [to make a Propiciatorie (or Oracle) and two Cherubimes] which couered the Oracle with their winges. Thence (said
God to Moyses) wil I command, and wil speake to
thee

.thee ouer the propiciatorie, and from the middeſt of the two Cherubimes, which ſhal be vpon the Arke of teſtimonie, al thinges which I wil command the children of Iſrael by thee.] So it pleaſed God in ſuch maner to reueile his diuine wil to Moyſes, and by him to aſſure the people of the certantie therof.

Ch. 28. In like ſorte when God would ordaine Aaron his or-
v. 2. 4. dinarie high Preiſt, and in him a continual ſucceſſion
12. 23. of Preiſt-hood [he commanded Moyſes to make ſpe-
29. cial ſacred veſtiments and ornaments for Aaron:] a-
mongſt which are firſt named [the Rationale of
Iudgement, which he ſhould carie on the breſt, and
the Ephod on his ſhoulders: linked together aboue
with ringes, hookes, and chaines, of gold; and beneath with lace of hyacinth: both were adorned with
pretious ſtones, and in the Rationale were engrauen the names of the twelue tribes of Iſrael. And
[in the ſame Rationale of Iudgement, were alſo en-
Exo. 28. grauen the two wordes: DOCTRINE, and VERI-
v. 30. TIE, which ſhal be on Aarons breſt when he ſhal goe
Leuit. 8. befre the Lord; and he ſhal beare the Iudgement
v. 8. of the children of Iſrael on his breſt in the ſight of
the Lord alwayes] ſignifying that the high Preiſt obſeruing this preſcribed forme in conſulting God,
ſhould for the conſeruation of truth, and iuſtice, be
inſpired to know, and iudge equitie in al doubtful
cauſes. Conformably to this diuine ordinance is
Gods precept, expreſly commanding his people to
repaire to this high tribunal in difficult cauſes, and
vnder the paine of death, to accept the ſentence that
Deut. 17. ſhould there be geuen ſaying: [If thou perceiue that
v. 8. the iudgement with thee be hard, and doubtful,
betwene bloud, and bloud, cauſe, and cauſe, leproſie, and not leproſie: (in cauſes criminal, ciuil, and
religious) and thou ſee that the wordes of the Iudges
within the gates (of the inferior Iudges) doe varie:

ariſe

arise and goe vp to the place which the Lord thy God
shal choose. And thou shal come to the Preists of *v* . *9* .
the Leuitical stocke, and to the Iudge that shal be
at that time; and thou shalt aske of them: who shal 10.
shew thee the truth of the Iudgement. And thou shalt
doe whatsoeuer they that are presidents of the place
(which our Lord shal choose) shal say, and teach 11.
thee according to his law; and thou shalt follow
their sentence: neither shalt thou decline to the right
hand, nor to the left hand. But he that shal be proud,
refusing to obey the commandement of the Preist, 12.
which at that time ministreth to the Lord thy God,
by the decrie of the Iudge, that man shal dye; and
thou shalt take away the euil out of Israel. And the 13.
whole people hearing shal feare, that none afterwardes swel in pride.] By these holie Scriptures we
see that a supreme infallible tribunal, was instituted
in the old Law, for decision of al controuersies, and
doubtes, with assurance of true sentence, not by humane, but by diuine Iudgement: God him self speaking ouer the Propitiatorie, from the middest of the
two Cherubins, and promising that this consistorie
of Preistes shal shew the truth of iudgement.

The temporal
was bound to
take direction
of the high
Preist, in al
greater
affayers.

4   Generally also in the greater affaires of the tem- *9.*
poral Princes [the High Preist was to consult God, *Nu.* 27.
and at his direction and word, the Prince must goe *v.* 21.
out, or goe in] that is, vndertake, or not vndertake,
anie busines proposed [and al the children of Israel 1. *Reg.* 23.
with him.] So did [Abiathar the High Preist, con- *v.* 9. 10.
sult our Lord for Dauid, by applying the Ephod (& 11. 12
consequently also the Rationale) and by him Dauid receiued answeare] that Saul purposed to come
into the Citie of Ceila where Dauid then was: and
that the Citizens, would deliuer him into Saules
handes. And therfore Dauid with al his men, par-
ted from thence, and so auoided the danger. Vpon *Ch.* 30. *v.*
an other 7. 8. 9. &c.

an other occasion, he consulted againe by Abiathar in the same maner [applying the Ephod] and by diuine direction, pursued certaine theues his enemies, tooke them, and recouered the pray which they had taken. Neither was this priuilege lost at anie time, by the defectes or faultes of the Preistes, as not being geuen of God, for their sakes only, but for the stabilitie of the vniuersal Church. And therfore the Prophet Malachie, reprehending the Preistes for their

Mal. 1. *v.* 7. 8. couetousnes, and other sinnes, yet saith plainly [the lippes of the Preistes shal kepe kuowlege, & the Law they shal require of his mouth; because he is the Angel (that is to say) the messenger of the Lord of hostes.]

5   Our Sauiour also confirmeth the same warrant in the Scribes and Pharisies notwithstanding their personal vices, and actual transgressions of the Law, say-

Mat. 23. *v.* 1. 2. 3. ing to the multitudes, and to his Disciples [vpon the Chaire of Moyses haue sitten the Scribes, & the Pharisies; therfor whatsoeuer they shal say to you, obserne ye, and doe ye: but according to their workes doe ye not; for they say and doe not] Which is vnderstood, not of their priuate enormous doctrines,

4. 5. *&c.* and humane traditions of their owne inuentions, for *Ch.* 15. which our Sauiour by and by taxeth them, as also at *v.* 5. 6. other times, but of their doctrine, when they spake *&c.* difinitiuely in their Councels, and in the chaire of Moyses. For so euen wicked Caiphas pronounced true sentence in the councel of the cheife Preistes, &

Io. 11. *v.* the Pharisies [that it was expedient, one man should 47. 50. dye for the people, and the whole Nation perish not] Where the holie Euangelist obserueth, that neither anie other of that Councel, nor this man of him self,

49. 51. vttered this true sentence; but [being the high Preist of that yeare, he prophecyed, that IESVS should dye for the Nation.]

Our Sauiour testified the infallibilitie of Moyses Chaire.

Seing

God promised
an infallible
Iudgement
feate in the
new Teſta-
ment.

6 Seing therfore Moyſes Chaire was ſo eſtabliſhed
in true Iudgement; it neceſſarilie followeth, that
Chriſt our Lord, who came, not to breake the Law
but to fulfil it, hath moſt firmly placed, an other chaire
of infallible Iudgement in his Church, not with leſſe,
but with more auctoritie, and more aſſured ſtabilitie then was in the old law, which is now abrogated.
For ſo [God promiſed to geue a better Law, and a
better couenant.] And that particularly in this point
of the infallible ſtabilitie of his Church in al truth;
wherof are abundant teſtimonies both in the old and
new Teſtament. When King Dauid in his feruent
deuotion, determined to build a glorious Temple to
Goddes more honour, and feruice; it pleaſed God,
accepting his ſo good a purpoſe, in ſtead of the fact,
for Miſterie ſake, ſignifying the excellency of the
houſe which Chriſt the Sonne of God, and Sonne of
Dauid ſhould build; to promiſe the ſame ſhould be
an euerlaſting ſpiritual Kingdome [Thou ſhalt not
build me an Houſe to dwel in (ſaid our Lord to Dauid) but when thy daies ſhal be accompliſhed, and
thou ſhalt ſleepe with thy fathers; I wil raiſe vp thy
ſeede after thee, which ſhal come forth of thy womb,
and I wil eſtabliſh his kingdome: He ſhal build a
houſe to my name, and I wil eſtabliſh the Throne of
his kingdome for euer. And thy houſe ſhal be faithful and thy kingdome for euer before thy face; and
thy Throne ſhal be firme continually] verified in the
chaire wherin our Sauiour placed his Apoſtle S. Peter, and in his ſucceſſors, Chriſtes Vicars in the Sea
Apoſtolique. For none other Throne, but that Chair
only, is continued and conſerued ſince the Apoſtles
time.

Promiſes made
to King
Dauid, pertei-
ned eſpecially

7 Which great promiſe, the ſame Royal Prophet
wel foreſeing, not to be fulfilled in a temporal kingdome, but in the Church of Chriſt, reioycing ther-
in-

in, inuiteth the fame Church, to congratulate with

Pſ. 47.
v.12.13.
14.

him her happie ſtate [Let Mount Sion (ſaith he) be gladde, and the daughters of Iuda reioyce, becauſe of thy Iudgementes o Lord .] Againe to al the faith - ful he ſaith [Compaſſe ye Sion, and embrace her , tel ye in her towres. Set your hartes on her ſtrength] But becauſe this ſtrength is not of her ſelf, but of

Pſ. 117.
v.5.6.

God, ſhe confeſſeth [From tribulation I inuocated our Lord : and our Lord heard me in largenes. Our Lord is my helper : I wil not feare what man can

21.

doe to me. I wil confeſſe to thee becauſe thou haſt heard me, and art become my ſaluation .] With this

Pſ. 118.
v.43.

confidence ſhe ſtil praieth ſaying : [Lord take not away out of my mouth, the word of truth in anie wiſe .] And with the ſame confidence, doubteth not

Cant. 8.
v. 10.
11.

to ſay [I am a wal, and my breaſtes are as a towre, (or caſtle) ſince I was made before him, as one fin- ding peace. The peace-maker Chriſt, had a vine yard in that which hath peoples, he deliuered the ſame to kepers] his Paſtors, Prophets, Apoſtles, and their ſucceſſors. And aboue al other kepers, Chriſt him ſelf holdeth the principal care, and therfor ſaith :

22.

[My vine yard is before me] in his continual pro - tection . Wherfore it is wonderful blindnes to think as ſome doe, that the whole Church hath at anie time erred, or can erre ; and in the more learned, it muſt needes be extreme malice, ſo to charge the Spouſe of Chriſt; and ſo likewiſe to robbe Chriſt him ſelf of his inheritance, if there had bene none other viſible Church in the world, for manie hundred yeares, but ſuch a one, as they ſay, both taught, and committed abominable Idolatrie, quite contrarie to the doctrine of the holie Prophets.

8　For they ſay plainly, that in the Church of Chriſt,

Iſ. 2. v.
2.6.
18.20.

[al Idoles ſhal be vtterly deſtroyed] So ſaith Iſaias prophecying of the Church, that ſhould be gathered

A a a　　　　　of al the Chriſtian

of al Nations, and of the reiection of the Iewes. The same thing saith our Lord by his Prophet Micheas vnto the Gentiles that shal be conuerted [I wil make thy sculptiles to perish, and thy statues out of the middest of thee ; and thou shalt nomore adore the workes of thy handes.] Thus also writeth the Prophet Zacharias [It shal be in that day, saith the Lord of hostes, I wil destroy the names of Idoles out of the earth, and they shal be remembred nomore.] So clearly did the Prophets foreshew, that the Church of the new Testament, should be free from al Idolatrie, with which errour, our Aduersaries especially charge the visible Church before their time. From al other erroures also, it is most free, by the same diuine prouidence, as the Prophets yet further testifie [Behould, (saith Isaias) the king shal reigne in iustice, and the Princes shal rule in iudgement] foreshewing that Christ our King should performe al that was decreed by the Blessed Trinitie, concerning the Redemption, Iustification, and saluation of men : And that his Apostles and other Pastors, Prelates, & spiritual Princes of his Church, should rule, not in falshood and errour, but in iudgement, discerning and iudgeing what is right, good, and profitable, for the health of soules. Againe he saith [Looke vpon Sion, the Citie of our solemnitie ; thine eyes shal see Ierusalem, a rich habitation a Tabernacle that can not be transferred ; neither shal the nailes therof be taken away for euer, and al the cordes therof shal not be broken] Nailes in buildinges, & cordes in tentes and Tabernacles, ioyne and kepe the partes, in one total bodie : so doe holie Sacramentes, Rites & ordinances, hold together the members of the vniuersal Church, and shal neuer be taken away, nor broken. Because only (there, our Lord is magnifical. This is my couenant with them (saith our Lord) : my Spirit that

Mich. 5.
v. 12.

Zach. 13.
v. 2.

Is. 32.
v. 1.

Ch. 33.
v. 20.

21.
Ch. 59.
v. 21.

rit that is in thee; & my wordes that I haue put in thy
mouth, fhal not depart out of thy mouth, and out of
the mouth of thy feede, and out of the mouth of thy
feedes feede, faith our Lord, from this prefent, and
for euer.] Ezechiel concludeth his large and miftical defcription of the whole Church, afwel Militant
as Triumphant, with the infeperable coniunction of
Ezech. Chrift and her; in regard wherof he faith [The name
48. v. of the Citie from that day (fhal be called) *Our Lord*
35. *there.*] And where our Lord is, there is al truth,
and none errour, becaufe he is truth it felf.

    9 Al which our Lord hath accordingly auouched   Chrift built his
with his owne mouth, and publifhed by his Apoftles   Church vpon a
Mat.7. [A wife man (faith he) built his houfe vpon a Rock,   rocke: not vpō
v.24. and the raine fel, and the floudes came, & the windes   fand.
25. blew, and they beate againft that houfe. and it fel
not; for it was founded vpon a Rocke.] This was
his owne houfe his Church, which he the eternal wifdome promifed to build, vpon fuch a Rocke as him
felf had made, and ordained for this purpofe, & ther-
Ch. 16. upon exprefly auerred, that [the gates of hel (that is
v. 18. no forces of al the diuels of hel) fhould preuaile a-
gainft it] the reafon of which inuincible ftrength, is
his owne perpetual prefence in fpirit. For where his
Ch. 18. Apoftles, and their Succeffors [are gathered in his
v.20. name (in the vnitie of his Church) he is in the mid-
Ch.28. deft of them] and that [al daies, euen to the con-
v.20. fummation of the world.] For though neare the
end of the world, there fhal be fewer faithful, then
Luc.18. at other time, wherupon he faith : [the Sonne of
v.8. Man coming, fhal he find, trow you, faith in the
earth ?] fignifying then, faith fhal be moft fcarce,   Neither in An-
but not altogether wanting. For if there fhould be   tichrifts time
no faithful Chriftians at al vifible; how fhould An-   fhal the Chur-
tichrift perfecute fo furioufly, as then he fhal? An   ch faile.
example of which great Apoftafie and reuolt of ma-

nie but not of al, happened in Capharnaum, where
when our Sauiour preached of the high misterie of
his owne B. bodie and bloud to be geuen in the most
holie Sacrament, manie of his Disciples hearing him
say [My flesh is meat indeede, and my bloud is drink   *Io. 6. v.*
indeede] they said, this saying is hard, and who can   31. 51. 55.
heare it ? And manie went backe, and walked not   60.
with him. A litle before, there were fiue thousand   66. 68.
men, besides women and children, which might wel   10. 67. 7.
be so manie more, & now there remained but twelue,   71.
& one of those twelue (Iudas the traitor) was also
reuolted in hart, and the other eleuen were indeede
sincere. And S. Peter, in the name of the twelue,
answeared, that they ment not to depart : saying
[Lord, to whom shal we goe ? thou hast the wordes
of eternal life] therby professing, that whatsoeuer
our Sauiour said, the same he could and would performe : that his wordes are operatiue, effectually working that, which they signify, howsoeuer they see-
med hard to the incredulous carnal Capharnaites;   *Io.* 14.
Christes wordes dye not, nor faile not; but geue life,   *v. 6.*
& haue their effect.

This infallibili-
tie of the
Church is the
worke of the
Holie Ghost.
And therefore
the Churches
Iudgement is
not humane,
but diuine.

10   After this when our Sauiour was (according to
his visible presence) to part from the world, he promised an other comforter [I wil aske the Father, and   *Io.* 14. *v,*
he wil geue you an other Paraclete, that he may a-   16. 17.
bide with you for euer : the Spirit of truth : whom
the world can not receiue : because it seeth him not ;
neither knoweth him. but you shal knowe him because he shal abide with you, and shal be in you. He   26.
shal teach you al thinges : and suggest to you al
thinges whatsoeuer I shal say to you. when the Spi-   *Act.* 2. *v.*
rit of truth cometh (who came on whitsunday fo-   3.
lowing fistie dayes after his Sermon) he shal teach   *Io.* 16.
you al truth.] Ponder these wordes which exclude   *v.* 13.
al error, and al falshoode. For this so necessarie, &

important

mportant a benefite, our B. Sauiour in the conclusion of his diuine Sermon, prayed particularly for his
Apostles and their successors, saying: [Holie Father
keepe them in thy name whom thou hast geuen me:
that they may be one as also we. those whom thou
gauest me, haue I kept: and none of them perished
but the sonne of perdition: that the Scripture may be
fulfilled. I pray not that thou take thē away out of the
world.] Loe our Sauiour would not haue his Pastors
taken away out of the world, as Protestants imagine,
that a long time together there were no true Pastors,
[but that thou preserue them from euil] to witte
from error, which is a most pestilent infectious euil.
Against which he expresly prayed that they might be
continually protected, adding thus in his prayer.
[Sanctifie them in truth: thy word is truth. As thou
didst send me into the world, I also haue sent them
into the world, and for them I doe sanctifie my self
(offer my self in Sacrifice by death) that they also
may be sanctified in truth. yea lest anie thinke he
prayed only for the Apostles, or for some smale time,
marke what followeth. [And not for them only doe
I pray, but for them also that by their word shal beleue in me, that they al may be one. as thou (Father)
in me and I in thee, that they also in vs may be one,
that the world may beleue that thou hast sent me.]
See here the vnion of the Church without interruption is a motiue, and special reason for the world to
beleue in Christ, that he is sent from God.

11   His Pastors therfore being thus firmly established in perpetual succession, with warrant of true
doctrine, our Sauiour also ordained that al the flocke
should here and follow them, euen as himself. For
as he said [the sheepe heare their sheapheard and
follow him, because they know his voice, and my
sheepe know me.] so he saith to his Pastors [He

Ch. 17.
v. 11. 12.
15.

v. 17.
18. 19.
20. 21.
22. 23.

Io. 10.
v. 4. 14.

Al Christians
are bound to
relye vpon the
Iudgement of
the Church.

A a a 3   that

[He that heareth you, heareth me ; and he that deſpiceth you, deſpiceth me ; and he that deſpiceth me,
(whether it be in him ſelf, or in his Paſtors) deſpiceth him that ſent me .] And in an other place ſaith :
[He that wil not heare the Church, let him be to thee
as the heathen and the publicane .] In vigour of
this power geuen to the Apoſtles, with this warrant
to be directed by the Holie Ghoſt ; when a controuerſie was riſen, they gathered them ſelues into a publique Councel, and after mature diſcuſſion, decided
& decreed, what ſhould be done, with this ſolemne
Preface [*Viſum eſt Spiritui Sancto & nobis.* It hath
ſemed good to the Holie Ghoſt, and to vs] ſo con-
ioyning the Inuiſible, and viſible Iudges, as one
Iudge, that by the one, we may ſee the diuine auctoritie of General Councels : and by the other, be aſſured what is ſo defined ; and withal know whither to
repaire whē difficulties occurre , about the true ſenſe
of anie wordes or ſentence . Wherfore S . Iohn try-
eth by this Rule , who knoweth God and his truth,
and who doth not know him, ſaying [He that knoweth God, heareth vs : he that is not of God, heareth
vs not . In this we know the Spirit of truth, and the
ſpitit of errour] For to this end, as S . Paul alſo teacheth [Chriſt gaue ſome Apoſtles, ſome Prophets,
Euangeliſtes, Paſtors, and Doctors, that we be not
as children, waucring and caried about with euery
wind o f doctrine, in the wickednes of men, in craftines, to the circumuention of errour] And ſo exhorteth the Epheſians, whom he had conuerted from
Paganiſme, to Chriſtianitie, that they ſhould perſe-
uer in vnitie of the Church, and obedience of the Paſtors therof . But with the Corinthians, whom he
had alſo conuerted , and ſome of them were afterwardes ſeduced by falſe prophets ; he reaſoneth the
caſe, with expoſtulation, why they ſhould preferre
the

Luc. 10,
v. 16.

Mat. 18.
v. 17.

Act. 15.
v. 18,

1 . *Io.* 4.
v. 6.

2. *Cor.* the new maisters before him saying [I haue despou-
11. *v.* 2. sed you to one man, to present you a chast virgin
3. vnto Christ] and so presseth them not to harken to
suttle seducers, that teach otherwise then he had done.
Where it is to be wel obserued, that in euery Nation, when it was first conuerted to Christ, it was de-
spoused in puritie of Religion, wholly vndefiled, &
Ephes. 5. void of errour in al pointes [subiect to Christ] as
v. 24. the Apostle affirmeth againe of the whole Church, ad-
25. 29. ding that [Christ loueth (and consequently protec-
30. teth) his Church as his owne flesh and bodie, because
(saith he) we be members of his bodie.]

12   Finally this stabilitie of the Chutch is confirmed
by Chrifts cōtinual protection [For he walke thin the
Apoc. 1. middeft of the seuen candlestickes (which are manie
c. 13. 16. particular Churches) and houldeth seuen starres (the
20. *Ch.* Bishoppes called the Angels of the same Churches)
2, *v.* 1. in his right hand] as was shewed in a vision to S.
Iohn, with the interpretation that the candlestickes
are the Churches, and the starres the Angels that
guide, and gouerne the Churches. Wheras therfore
particular Churches are so visible, as so manie candlestickes, and so guided as by Angels, and holden vp
in Chrifts owne right hand, it is most certaine that
the vniuersal Church is both visible, and securely guided in truth. Againe S. Paul in few wordes compriseth the assured infallibilitie of the Church. de-
1. *Tim.* scribing it to be [the house of God; the Church of
3. *v.* 15. the liuing God : the piller and ground of truth]
wheras al the world is Gods, both heauen, and earth,
yet the Church is properly called his house. yea the
house of the liuing God, who is life, and geueth life,
and so can and wil euer preserue his house. the piller, and the ground of truth, pure from error, as wel
firm being deceiued, as from deceiuing. For that
is the vse of groudworke to beare the whole edifice
and

Christ neuer
ceaseth to pro-
tect his
Church, ther-
fore it can ne-
uer erre,

The Church is
truly called the
piller, and
ground of
truth.

and the vſe of a piller not alone to ſtand firme, but
to beare and vphould the flore, the wales, the roofe,
and couer, & whatſoeuer dependeth theron. And ſo
I wil adde no more proofes for this point, not doubting to conclude vpon euerie one of the ſacred textes
of diuine Scriptures here recited, as wel of the old,
as new Teſtament, much more vpon them al, that the
knowen perpetual viſible Church, commonly called
Holie Catholique, and Apoſtolique, neuer did erre,
nor can erre definitiuely deciding anie point of faith,
or of maners, by ſentence in tribunal ſeate.

In the whole Church, is communion of Sacrifice,
Sacramentes, Praiers, & other good workes.

ARTICLE. 43.

Al ſpiritual
good thinges
in the Church,
are profitable
to al the mem-
bers.

FOr our further inſtruction of the Churches excellencie, it pleaſed the Holie Ghoſt, by the
mouth of the Apoſtles, beſides the proprieties and priuilegies before recited, to ſignifie the ſpecial benefiite redounding to the members therof by
the Communion of Sainctes, that is communication and participation of ſpiritual fruict, which proceded principally from Chriſt the Head : ſecundari-
ly alſo, from one member to an other. For here the
word *Sainctes*, or *Holies*, ſignifieth not only holie perſons, as Chriſt him ſelf, al holie Angels, with other
Sainctes in heauen, & al the faithful in earth; but alſo
holie thinges, as Sacrifice, Sacramentes, with other
holie Rites, and al good workes which are made cómon to the vniuerſal Church, through the perfect v-
nion of the head, and members, and conſequently of
the felow members each to others. For firſt the con- Io. 15. v.
iunction of Chriſt with his faithful ſeruantes, is ſuch, 15.
that he not only calleth them his frendes, and which *Mat.* 25.
                              is more v. 50.

is more, his brethren, fifters, and his mother : but

Mat. 25.
v. 40.
45.
Act. 9.
v. 4.

alfo accounteth whatfoeuer is done, or left vndone, to
one of his leaft brethren, as done or not done to him
felf. Yea he calleth them him felf faying to Saul,
[why perfecuteft thou me] wheras he perfecuted him
not in his owne perfon, but in thofe that beleued in
him. The coniunction of the members among them

Ro. 12.
v. 5.
I. Cor.
12. *v.*
19.

felues is fuch, that [being manie, they are al one bodie in Chrift, and each one an others members. there
are manie members indeede, but one bodie.] By
meanes of which vnion, what good worke foeuer is
done, by Chrift is profitable to al the Church, & to
al the members wherto it is applied, according to the
meafure of his grace imperted to euerie one. For he
died for al, he redemed al, his ranfome is fufficient
for al; So bountiful is his mercy, fo abundant is the
price which he hath payed for al mankind, wherof al
that wil, may be participant, as S. Paul teacheth,

Heb. 5.
v. 9.

[Chrift being confummate, was made to al that obey
him, caufe of eternal faluation.] And by this communitie alfo of the members; one doth profitably pray
for an other yea and fuffer for others, as the fame A-

Col. 1.
v. 24.
2. *Cor.* 1.
v. 5.

poftle did for the Coloffians [accomplifhing thofe
thinges that wanted of the paffions of Chrift] that is
of Chriftes members; where againe his members are
called him felf, for the ftrict vnion of him and them,
for otherwife it is moft certaine, that nothing was
wanting of Chriftes paffions in him felf, for it was fu-
perabundant for al. But both his Paffion, and his
members paffions, and other good workes, are effectual only to thofe that are comembers of the Church,
or to make them members therof, or to become capable, & participant. which is clearly fhewed both
in the old & new Law.

2   For in Moyfes Law, none were to be admitted to
eate the Pafchal Lambe, nor were capable of the fpi-

ritual

In the old law
none could
eate of the
Pafchal lambe,

ritual grace which God imperted to them, that did rigdtly eate therof, except they were firft made members of the Church [This is the Religion of the Phafe (faid God to Moyfes) No aliene (or ftranger in Religion) fhal eate of it. Euerie bought feruant, fhal be circumcifed, and fo fhal eate of it; the ftranger, and hireling, fhal not eat therof. Al the affemblie of the children of Ifrael, fhal make it. And if anie of the foiournours be willing to dwel among you, and make the Phafe of the Lord; firft al the male that he hath, fhal be circumcifed, and then fhal he celebrate it according to the rite. And he fhal be as he that is borne in the land : but if there be anie man vncircũcifed, he fhal not eate therof. Al one Law fhal be to him that is borne in the land, and to the Profelite (a gentile conuerted) that foiourneth with you .] Euen fo in the Chriftian Church, none are capable of others fpiritual benefites, til they be baptized, and therby incorporated in this miftical bodie : otherwife this communion of Sainctes and participation of holie thinges, with faithful perfons, pertaineth not to them : Which is proued by manie holie Scriptures alreadie recited, fhewing that the true Church, is one whole bodie . namely by S. Paules doctrine faying to the Chriftian Corinthians [As the bodie (that is to fay, a mans natural bodie) is one, and hath manie members ; & al the members of the bodie, wheras they be manie, yet are one bodie : fo likewife Chrift (that is to fay, the miftical bodie of Chrift) hauing manie members, is one bodie] ordinarily called the Church, but in this place called Chrift, becaufe the Church being his bodie [is the fulnes of him] as the fame Apoftle writeth to the Ephefians . And in the place now alleaged, he teacheth, that al faithful members of the Church, and of Chrift [are one bodie, by the meanes of babtifme, in one Holie Ghoft

Exo. 12.
v. 43. 44.
45.

47. 48.

49.

I. *Cor.* 12.
v. 12. 13.

Ephef. I
v. 23.

13.

lie Ghoft] for (faith he) [in one Spirit, were we
al baptized into one bodie, whether Iewes or Gentiles, or bond men, or free .]

3   Of this vnion therfore, procedeth the communion of holie thinges, that the good worke of one
member, may profit an other. Which thing, holie
Iob wel knew and confidered, when he offered Holocauftes for euerie one of his Sonnes. And in reguard of this great benefite by communicating of
holie workes in the Church of God, the Royal Pfalmift faid [One thing haue I asked of our Lord, this
wil I feeke for : that I may dwel in the houfe of our
Lord, al the daies of my life. Bleffed are they that
dwel in thy houfe o Lord : for euer and euer, they
fhal praife thee] And expreffing the reafon of this
happines by remaining in the holie felowfhip of the
Church, he faith in his thankes for the fame to God
[I am partaker of al that feare thee : & that keepe thy
commandementes . [Againe congratulating this fingular benefite, in the whole Church, vnder the name
of Ierufalem, he faith [Ierufalem which is built as
a Citie, whofe participation is together in it felf.]
For this caufe of mutual communicating, and participating each with other in good workes ; our B.
Sauiour taught and commanded vs, to pray in common for our felues, together with al our felow members of the militant Church, calling vpon God for
his grace to al in this maner [Our Father (not only my
Father) geue vs : forgeue vs : let vs not be lead : deliuer
vs : which is the ordinarie forme of praying . Neuerthe
leffe, fingular praier for ones felf, or for fome one, is
alfo lawful and good in particular cafes. For fo S .
Paul requefted the praiers of the faithful for him felf,
which alfo proueth our prefent purpofe of mutual affiftance amomgft the members of Chrift [I befech
you brethren (faith he to Chriftian Romanes) by our

Iob . 1.
v . 5.

Pf . 26.
v . 4.
Pf . 83.
v . 5.

Pf . 118.
v . 63.

Mat . 6.
v . 9. 11.
12 . 13.

Rom . 15.
v . 30.

Vnion of the
members, is
the caufe of
mutual profi-
ting each o-
thers.

B b b   2   Lord

Lord Iesus Chrift, and by the Charitie of the Holie
Ghoft, that you help me in your praiers for me to
God.] So likewife he requefted the Corinthians to
[ioine with him in praier, and in thankefgeuing]   *2. Cor.* 1.
wherin he repofed fpecial confidence [to be deliue-   *v.* 11.
red from danger, and comforted in affliction, by their
helpe in praier, that by manie, (faith he) thankes
may be geuen in our behalf, for that gift which is in
vs] So did this great Apoftle efteme of the peoples
praiers and felowfhippe in the feruice of God. And
fo doth he teach al Chriftans, to efteme and be glad
each of others helpe [Seing Chrift, who onlie ne -   *Pf.* 15.
deth no mans helpe] hath fo ioyned vs to him felf,   *v.* 2.
that we may be holpen by him [al being called by   1. *Cor.* 1.
God, into the focietie of his Sonne Iefus Chrift our   *v.* 9. 1.
Lord] And feing al are fo difpofed in place, to affift each other, for he hath fet the members of his
Church with exceding great diftinction, of giftes,
orders, & offices [euerie one in the bodie, as he would   *Io.* 1. *v.* 3.
that there might be no fchifme in the bodie] but the   *Ch.* 12. *v.*
members together might be careful one for an other.   18. 24. 25.
[And if one member fuffer anie thing, al the members fuffer with it : or if one member doe glorie, al
the members reioyce with it.] This indeede is the
worthie fruict of the Gofpel, not that which liber -
tines talke of, making fchifmes, breaking from the
Churches communitie, & raifing daily more & more
new fectes, alwaies deuiding thofe that are ioyned,
neuer gathering Pagane Gentiles vnto Chriftianitie,
as the true Apoftles doe [bringing the Gentiles to
be coheires and concorporate, and comparticipant
of God his promife in Chrift Iefus, by the Gofpel,
bringing al liuing members of the militant Church,
to participate [with Mount Sion, the Citie of the   *Ephef.* 3. *v.*
liuing God; heauenly Ierufalem, and the affemblie   6. *Heb.* 12.
of manie thoufand Angels: and the Church of the firft   *v.* 22. 23.
borne   24.

borne, which are written in the heauens; & the Iudge
of al, God, and the spirites of the iust made perfect,
and the Mediator of the new Testament Iesus.

4 Such are the endeuours, and fructful labours of
the true Church, wherin is the communitie of Sinctes.
Wheras other congregations, false pretending Churches, neither performe nor commonly attempt anie
such thing : but quite contrarie imploy their trauailes
to draw Christians to their owne new deuised opinions, contend against vnitie, and communitie of the
whole bodie, and by pretence of reforming imagined errors, or of correcting other mens, either real,
or surmised faults, open the gappe to iunumerable
absurde heresies, (for there is but one only true religion) and into most detestable, beastly, yea and
diuelish crimes, wherunto the world is fallen since
Martin Luther with his folowers brake from that only knowen Church, which was then and manie hundred yeares before in the world : and so lost the
communion of Sainctes, and al holines. For at that
time of Luthers breach which is now an hundred
yeares since, al Christians publiquely porfessed the
same faith, acknowleged one visible head, serued
God in one vniuersal Church, at least outwardly by
confessing al one and the same communion of Sainctes.

The different
endeuours of
Catholique
Pastors, to v-
nite the disper-
sed, and of
Sectaries to
disperse the v-
nited.

An,
Dom.
1517.

*Soules in Purgatorie, doe participate of the Cõ-
munion of Sainctes, receiuing releife by the holie Sacrifice, and other Suffrages.*

ARTICLE. 44.

AS the glorified Sainctes in heauen, & the
faithful in earth, are members of the vniuersal Church : so likewise are the penitent
soules remayning for some time in purgatorie, which

Soules depar-
ted in state of
grace, are
members of
the Church.

parted from their bodies in state of grace, not hauing made sufficient satisfaction for their sinnes; &
they also pertaine to the Militant part of the Church
as being in the way, but not in possession of eternal glorie. And so being members of the same bodie, are releued by the holie Sacrifices, and other
suffrages offered for them by their felow members
in earth. As for the point of Catholique doctrine,
that manie soules be in state to neede such releife,
and consequentlie, that there is a place of temporal
punishment after this life called Purgatorie : it pertaineth to the third part of the Sacrament of Penance
which is satisfaction, and shal there by Goddes assistance, be further declared.

That there is a place of purgatorie, is proued in the second part. Article 31.35.

2   Here in the meane season it shal be breifly shewed by the holie Scriptures, that prayer for the dead
is both lawful and profitable. wherby the other
two pointes are also proued, that some soules departed from their bodies, haue nede, and also are capable of such spiritual helpe. For otherwise it were
in vaine to pray, or to doe other good workes for
them. That therfore it is not vaine but behoosul for
them, is first proued by these authentical examples.
Abraham the holie great Patriarch, when his wife
Sara was deade, performed an other office for her,
distinct from burial, called her obsequies. For so
Moyses relateth that [after Abraham was risen vp
from the funeral obsequies, he spake to the children
of Heth, concerning a place of burial] where it is
manifest that funeral obsequies was an other distinct
thing from the office of burying the bodie, and done
before he dealt for the place of sepulchre. It is also
manifest that Abraham did not then a new thing, but
obserued the accustomed rite, as appeareth by the
maner of Moyses narration of a thing knowen, and
vsually practised saying: [after that Abraham was
risen

Prayer for the dead is here proued by diuers holie Scriptures, to be lawful, and profitable.

Funeral Exequies is a distinct spiritual office from burial.

Gen . 23.
v . 3.

risen vp from the funeral obsequies &c.] So this text confirmeth the tradition of the Iewes, who to this day haue a solemne office, & prayer for the dead.

Gen. 50. *v.* 4.

Likewise when Iacob died in Egipt[his sonne Ioseph dealt not for his burial til the time of morning

Nu. 20. *v.* 30.

was expired.] In like maner [Al the people mourned vpon Aaron. Also for Moyses.] And though

Deut. 38.*v.* 8.

there be no mention of prayer (for that it semed not needful for anie of these) yet this mourning importeth a solemne religious office. And for King Saul and

Reg. 31. *v.* 13.

his three sonnes [the inhabitantes of Iabes Galaad, fasted seuen dayes. And King Dauid and his men,

2.*Reg.* 1.*v.* 12.

not only mourned, and wept, but also fasted vntil euening vpon them, and vpon the people of our Lord, and vpon the house of Israel, because they were fallen by the sword] which penal worke of fasting, perteineth to satisfaction for sinnes; and was done for the dead. Holie Tobias exhorted his sonne to

Tob. 4. *v.* 18.

geue almes for the dead saying [Set thy bread and thy wine, vpon the burial of a iust man] which worke of almes bestowed on the poore, could not otherwise profit the iust mans soule departed, but by way of satisfaction for his sinnes. Iesus the sonne of Sirach, amongst manie most godlie aduises, saith,

Eccle. 7. *v.* 38.

[From the dead, stay not grace.] When certaine sonldiers of the Iewes were slaine, and were found to haue committed especial sinne, in keping vnlawful

2.*Mac.* 12.*v.* 40.42. *Ios.*6.*v.* 18.43. 45.

spoiles; [the rest of the armie turning vnto praiers, besought God, that the same offence which was cómitted, might be forgotten.] And Iudas their general captaine, and High Preist, making a gathering, sent twelue thousand drachemes of siluer to Ierusalem, for Sacrifice to be offered for sinne, because he considered, that they which had taken their sleepe with godlines (that is, thinking that they died penitent) had very good grace laid vp for them] wherupon

Fasting, and Almes deedes for the dead.

upon the auctour concludeth, that [it is a holie &
healthful cogitation to pray for the dead, that they
may be looſed from ſinnes] which is the very pointe
we beleue, and hold againſt Proteſtantes . And it
is not ſo much as half a good anſwear, to denie theſe
three laſt cited auctorities, of Tobias, Eccleſiaſticus,
and Machabees, to be Canonical Scriptures ; ſeing **See Art . 3 .**
they are declared to be Canonical euen as ſufficiently
as diuers other partes of the holie Bible which Proteſtantes acknowlege . And ſeing alſo this preſent
pointe is proued by other places as you ſee , againſt
which they doe not pretend this euation . wherunto may be added manie places which ſhew that ſome
ſoules departed from this life, are neither in hel, nor
as yet in heauen . As the ſoules of thoſe which were
raiſed from death .

Prayer for the
dead is appro -
ued by S . Iohn
the Apoſtle .

3   But here one place ſhal ſuffice touching prayer
for the dead . S . Iohn in his Epiſtle diſtinguiſhing
two ſortes of ſinners, ſome ſinning to death, ſome not
to death, which muſt needes be vnderſtood of perſons departed from this world, for til their death it
can not be knowen who continue in ſinne to death ,
who not; he exhorteh, and encorregeth vs to pray
for him that ſinned before his death, and continued
not therin to death : but not for him that perſiſted
ſinning euen to death ſaying : [He that knoweth his **1 . Io . 5 .**
brother to ſinne a ſinne not to death, let him aſke, & **v . 16 .**
life ſhal be geuen him, ſinning not to death. there is
a ſinne to death : for that I ſay not that anie man
aſke] thus he. Agreeable wherto is the continual
practiſe of the Catholique Church ; praying for thoſe
ſinners that dye penitent, or geue ſignes of true ſorow at their death. As when they confeſſe their ſinnes before they dye ; and not praying for others that
perſiſt obſtinate in error of faith as heretickes doe ;
or dye deſperate killing them ſelues, or blaſpheming
                                               God

God ; or holie thinges and the like . For such are vncapable of this benefite. And therfore it were in
vaine to pray for them . And so this place proueth
that it is behoofull, and profitable, to pray for faith-
full soules departed from this life with true repentance : and good also to pray euen for the most wicked, and desperate, so long as they are in this life ;
but not after that they are dead in so miserable, &
wretched estate .

Noe infidels doe participate of the Communion of
Sainctes : neither is it lawful to communi-
cate with them in practise of Religion .

ARTICLE. 45.

IN this especially, the Arke of Noe was a figure
of the Church, that as the liuing creatures therin were saued from drowning , and al that staied
without were drowned in the floud : so spiritual saluation is only within the Church, and none without
can be eternally saued . For as then [al flesh was consumed that moued vpon the earth, of foule, of catle,
of beastes, and of al creepers that creepe vpon the
earth, al men, and al thinges wherin was breath of
life, dyed, but only Noe remained , and they that
were with him in the Arke] In [which few (saith
S . Peter) that is, eight soules, were saued, by water :] so now by faith and Baptisme, which is the gate
of other Sacramentes and entrance into the Church,
the worthie receiuers therof, are ingraffed in Christ
and made his members [Baptisme being (as the same
Apostle there saith) of the like forme vnto the water]
that caried Noe his shippe, with him, and al therin
from death [now saueth vs also from perishing with
the incredulous] that doe not beleue . An other fi-

Gen . 7 .
v . 21.
21 .
23 .
1 . Pet .
3 . v . 20.

21 .

No iustificatiõ,
nor saluation is
possible but in
the Church .

C c c   gure

gure was fhewed by the fact of Abraham, when [he *Gen.* 25.
gaue al his poffeffions to Ifaac his fonne, borne of *v.* 5.6.
Sara by Goddes promife ; and to the children of A-
gar and Cetura, he gaue giftes] that is to fay, moueable temporal goodes : fignifying that only the fpiritual children of the Church, are heires of the e-
uerlafting kingdome of heauen, and al the carnal
children, reprefenting al fortes of infidels, which are
Painimes, Iewes, Turkes, and Heritikes, haue none
other goodes, but the tranfitorie riches and pleafures
of this world, for reward of their beft deedes, and

for their euil [according to the meafure of the finne *Deut.* 25.
fhal the meafure of the ftripes be inflicted .] And *v.* 2.
as it is prophecied of the whole focietie of the damned [So much as fhe hath glorified her felf, & hath *Apoc.* 18.
bene in delicacies ; fo much geue her torments and *v.* 8.
mourning.] The fame exclufion from the Church,
is fignified by the fimilitude of [the blinde, and the 2 . *Reg.* 5.
lame, which were prohibited to enter into the *v.* 8.
Temple.] Al that want true faith, are fpiritually blind;
& not doing good workes, are alfo lame .

2   Goddes grace and mercie, is fufficient for al mankind, and is offered to al, but is receiued only in his
Church : As the Pfalmift profeffeth faying : [We *Pf.* 47.
haue receiued thy mercie o God; in the middeft of *v.* 10.
thy Temple] Neither are praiers or praifes grateful
to God, but only in his Church ; and therfore the
fame Pfalmift faith : [An Himne o God becommeth *Pf.* 64.
thee in Sion ; and a vow fhal be rendered to thee *v.* 2.
in Ierufalem. The God of Goddes fhal be feene in *Pf.* 83.
Sion. Becaufe better is one day in thy courtes (o *v.* 8.11.
God) aboue thoufandes . (elfwhere) I haue chofen 12.
to be an abiect in the houfe of my God, rather then
to dwel in the Tabernacles of finners . Becaufe God
loueth mercie and truth; our Lord wil geue grace &
glorie.] By which aduertifmentes we fee, that it is
in vaine

Moral good workes, done out of the Church, are only rewarded temporally .

Gods grace being fufficient for al, is only effectual to faluation, within the Church .

Proued by manie textes of the Pfalmes .

in vaine to flatter our selues with Goddes mercie, vnlesse we doe also receiue his truth, which is only in his Church; or to expect glorie in the next life, except we receiue grace in this : For [mercie & truth haue mette each other; iustice and peace haue kissed. Iurie was made his sanctification, Israel his dominion. Seauen times in the day, I haue said praise to thee for the Iudgementes of thy Iustice. Our feete were standing in thy courtes o Ierusalem. Ierusalem which is built as a citie; whose participation is together in it self. How shal we sing the songe of our Lord, in a strange land? Our Lord the God of Sion, declareth his word to Iacob : his iustices and Iudgementes to Israel. He hath not done in like maner to anie Nation : and his Iudgementes he hath not made manifest vnto them.] Nothing is more frequent in this and other Prophets, then the special graces, and spiritual benefites bestowed by God vpon his Church, & not vpon other kingdomes nor Nations.

Ps. 84.
v. 11.
Ps. 113.
v. 2. *Ps.*
118. *v.*
164. *Ps.*
121. *v.*
2. 3. *Ps.*
136. *v.*
4. *Ps.*
147. *v.*
8. 9.

3 Isaias hath recorded how God aduanced some temporally, and puni∫hed others for his Church sake. And prophecied namely of Cyrus, king of Medes & Persians, about two hundred yeares before he was borne, that he should ouercome the Assirians, possesse Babilon, and deliuer the Iewes from captiuitie saying : [thus saith our Lord to my Christ Cyrus, whose right hand I haue taken to subdue the Gentiles before his face, and to turne the backes of kinges and to open the doares before him, and the gates shal not be shutte.] And so it came to passe, that after seauentie yeares captiuitie, this Cyrus released them, and gaue them both leaue and assistance, to build againe their Temple in Ierusalem. But for al this, he not beleuing rightly in God, nor daily seruing him, was frustrate of spiritual benefite, as the Prophet also foreshewed sahing : [for my seruant

Is. 13.
45.

Is 45.
v. 1.

2. *Par.*
36. *v.*
22.

1. *Esd.* 1.
v. 1.

Proued by other Prophets.

Iacob

Iacob and Ifrael mine elect, I haue called thee by *&c.*
thy name : I haue refembled thee, and thou haft not *Ibid . v . 4.*
knowne me. (for this king ftil ferued falfe goddes,
and therfore God by his Prophet faid) I the Lord
and there is none els ; befides me, there is no God :
I girded thee , and thou haft not knowne me .] A- *5 .*
gaine the fame Prophet faith to the Chriftian Church *Ch . 60 .*
vnder the figure of Ierufalem [Arife, be illumina- *v . 1 , 2 .*
ted Ierufalem, becaufe thy light is come ; & the glorie of our Lord is rifen vpon thee . Becaufe loe darknes fhal couer the earth, and a mifte , the peoples ,
but vpon thee fhal our Lord arife, and his glorie
fhal be feene vpon thee .] Ezechiel moft fitly compareth the Church to a vine-tree which yeldeth much
fruict by her branches, remaining in the bodie ; but
none at al by anie feperated members, God thus fpeaking to him [Sonne of man, what fhal be made of *Ezech . 15 ;*
the wood of the vine, of al the trees of the woodes, *v . 2 . 3 .*
that are among the trees of the foreftes ? Shal there
be taken wood of it , that a worke may be made,
or fhal a pinne be made therof that anie veffel may
hang theró . Behold it is geuen to the fyre for foode ; *4 .*
the fyre hath confumed both partes therof, and the
middeft therof is brought into afhes ; why fhal it be
profitable for a worke ? .] Euen fo fruictles were
the Iewes refufing Chrift the true vine ; and fo fruict- *Ioan . 15 .*
les are al men remaining out of his Church : neither
rightly vnderftanding diuine Mifteries , nor reaping *v . 1 .*
fpiritual fruict of anie thing they doe .

The fame is confirmed by Chrift and his Apoftles .

4   Al which is yet more cleare in the new Tefta -
ment, our Sauiour often and plainly affirming , that
men can know nothing, nor doe anie thing without
him, nor out of his Church [Toyou (faith he to his *Mat . 13 .*
Difciples) it is geuen to know the Mifteries of the *v . 11 .*
Kingdome of heauen : but to them it is not gruen]
To them that are without, al thinges are done in *Mar . 4 .*
                           parables *v . 11 .*

Io . 15 .
v . 4 .

parables] so alluding to the Parable in Ezechiel [As the branch (saith he) can not beare fruict of it self, vnles it abide in the vine : so you neither vnles you abide in me. I am the vine, you the branches : he that abideth in me, and I in him, the same beareth much fruict : for without me you can doe nothing]

Mat . 12 .
v . 30 .

At other times he said [He that is not with me, is against me ; and he that gathereth not with me, scatereth .] Speaking of the schismatical Samaritanes,

Ioan . 4 .
v . 9 .

said plainly [Saluation is of the Iewes part] And in general of al the world [He that beleueth not (and

Mar . 16 .
v . 16 .

consequently is none of the Church) shal be condemned. [And therfore al that shal be saued, are first adioyned vnto the Church . they that receiued (and

Act . 2 .
v . 41 .
47 .

beleued) S . Peters word , were baptized] and so were added to the Church [And our Lord increased them that should be saued daily together .] Christ

1 . *Ioan* .
2 . *v* . 2 .

the Redemer of al, and the propitiation for al sinnes, euen of al the world] yet is properly [the head of the

Ephes . 5 .
v . 23 .

Church, the Sauiour of his bodie] which manifestly sheweth, that out of the Church there is no saluation. And the wordes of S . Iohn declare the same, say-

1 . *Io* . 1 .
v . 3 .

ing in the beginning of his Epistle [That which we haue seene, and haue heard, we declare vnto you, that you also may haue societie with vs, and our societie may be with the Father, and with his Sonne Iesus Christ] where we see, that whosoeuer wil haue societie with God, and Iesus Christ, must haue societie with the Apostles, and with that Church which is deriued by succession from the Apostles . Becaufe those that haue societie with the Apostles, & none other : they haue societie with Christ, and with God the B . Trinitie.

5   Now seing none out of the Church can participate of the communion of Sainctes, it foloweth by right sequele, that no true member of the Church can

That it is not lawful to yelde conformitie to the practise of

C c c   3   lawfully

heresie, or other infidelitie, by personal presence, at their seruice or sermons, is proued by manie holie Scriptures.

lawfully communicate with Paganes, Iewes, Turkes, Heretikes ; nor anie other Infidels, in practise of their Infidelitie, or pretended religion. As by personal presence at their seruice, or Sermons. which we shal further declare by the holie Scriptures. God expresly forbideth al Idolatrie, and seruice of false goddes, in his first commandement of the ten fundamental diuine precepts, saying to his people: [thou shalt not haue strange goddes before me. thou shalt not make to thee a sculptile, (or grauen thing) nor anie similitude that is in heauen aboue, and that is in earth beneath, neither of those thinges which are in the waters vnder the earth. thou shalt not adore them, nor serue them.] After this, further explicating this commandement, he also forbiddeth communication with Idolaters, either in anie practise therof, or in such occasions as may dangerously tempt them therunto saying: [Myne Angel shal goe before thee, and shal bring thee in vnto the Amorrhite, and Hetheite, and Pherezite, and Chananite, & Heueite, and Iebuzite, whom I wil destroy, thou shalt not adore their goddes, nor serue them. thou shalt not doe their workes, but shalt destroy them, and breake their statues. thou shalt not enter league with them, nor with their goddes. Beware thou neuer ioyne amitie with the inhabitants of that land, which may be thy ruine. Enter no trafficke with the men of those regions; lest when they haue fornicated with their goddes, and haue adored their Idols, some man cal thee to eate of the thinges immolated. Neither shalt thou take wife for thy sonnes of their daughters: lest after them selues haue fornicated they make thy sonnes also to fornicate with their goddes.] Further touching Mariages, not only to auoide Idolatrie, but also to shunne other execrable sinnes, our Lord commanded his people saying:

Ex. 20. *v*. 3. 4. 5.

Ch. 23. *v*. 23. 24.

32.

Ch. 34. *v*. 12. 15. 16.

According

Leuit.18.
v.3.

[According to the custome of the land of Egipt, wherin you haue dwelt, you shal not doe. and according to the maner of the countrie of Chanaan, into the which I wil bring you; you shal not doe,

Ch. 20.
v.26.

nor walke in their ordinances. I the Lord your God that haue seperated you from other peoples, that you shouldbe myne.] Vpon occasion of schisme raised by wicked men, our Lord by miracles, and by the ministerie of his Preistes, and Prophets, Moyses, and Aaron, declared the truth, confounded the rebels, and strictly commanded the people [to depart, and seperate them selues from the sedicious.] Moyses thus admonishing the cheife rebel Core, and his

Nu.16.
v. 5.

complices: [In the morning our Lord wil make it knowen, who perteyne to him, and the holie he wil ioyne to himself, and whom he shal choose, they shal approach to him.] Againe our Lord said to Moyses,

20. 21.
23. 24.

and Aaron: [Seperate your selues from the midest of this congregation, that I may suddenly destroy them.] And then to Moyses: [Command the whole people that they seperate them selues from the tabernacles of Core, Dathan, and Abiron. Wherupon

26.

Moyses saide to the multitude: [departe from the tabernacles of the impious, and touch not the thinges that perteine to them, lest you be wrapped in their sinnes.] Againe Moyses a litle before his death, amongst most principal commandements repeteth the prohibition of league, and Mariages with Infidels,

Deut.7.
v. 2. 3.

saying [Thou shalt not make league with them, nor pittie them, nor make Mariages with them. thy daughter thou shalt not geue to his sonne, nor take his daughter for thy sonne.] Likewise not to heare new

Ch. 13.
v. 1. 2.
3.

doctrines, nor false Prophets. If there rise (saith the Law) in the midest of thee a Prophet, or one that saith he hath seene a dreame, and foretel a signe, and a wonder, and it come to passe which he spake;
and

and he say to thee: Let vs goe and follow strange goddes which thou knowest not, & let vs serue them, thou shalt not heare the wordes of that Prophet, or dreamer: for the Lord your God tempteth (or proueth) you, that it may appeare whether you loue him or noe, with al your hart, and with al your soule.

True zele of good people against schisme, and heresie.

6 Such was the true zele of the people of Israel, in the time of Iosue, that when the children of Ruben and Gad, and half Tribe of Manasses, had built an Altat by the bankes of Iordan; the other Tribes suspecting that they would make a schisme, assembling together in Silo (where the Tabernacle, with the Arke then was) determined to fight against them. Of this so important danger of schisme and infidelitie, Iosue inlike maner, earnestly warned the whole people saying : [If you wil cleaue to the errour of these Nations that dwel among you, and make mariages with them, and ioyne amitie : Euen now know you, that our Lord your God wil not destroy them before your face; but they shal be a pitte and a snare, for you, and a stumbling block at your side, & stakes in your eyes, til he take you away, and destroy you from this excellent land, which he hath deliuered vnto you.]

Iof. 22. *v.* 10. 11. 12. *&c.*

Iof. 23. *v.* 12. 13.

Al true seruants of God, refrained from Ieroboams schisme.

7 When Ieroboam made the schisme of the tenne Tribes of Israel [al the Preistes and Leuites that were in those partes, came to Roboam king of Iuda, out of al their seates, leauing their suburbes & their possessions, and passing to Iuda and Ierusalem, remained in the vnitie of the Church : and manie other of those Tribes, geuing their hartes to seeke our Lord God of Israel, came into Ierusalem to immolate their victimes before our Lord the God of their fathers] because Ieroboam vanting la vsal Preistes, made vnto him self new ministers, of the excelces of diuels,

3 . *Reg.* 12. *v* . 28. 2. *Par.* 11. *v.* 13. 14. 15. 16.

and

3 . *Reg*. and of the calues which he had made.] King Iosa-
22.*v*.7. phat iustly suspecting schismatical false Prophets,
2 . *Par*. sought to be instructed by some true Prophet of our
18.*v*.6. Lord . So Micheas was consulted , and prophecied
13 . 16 . the truth . Neuertheles the same king Iosaphat was
reprehended for ioyning with king Achab in vnlaw-
2. *Par*. ful actions by the Prophet Iehu saying to him : [To
19.*v*.2. the impious man thou geuest aide, and to them that
hate our Lord, thou art ioyned in frendshippe : and
therfore thou didest deserue indeede the wrath of
our Lord ; but Good workes are found in thee ; for
that thou hast taken away the groues out of the land
of Iuda, and hast prepared thy hart to seeke our Lord
the God of thy fathers] So that ciuil conuersation,
and lawful temporal affaires, are permitted with Infidels, but no communication in Religious cases, nor
cooperation in sinne .

4 . *Reg*. 8   For wheras the Prophet Elizeus allowed Naa-
5 .*v*.18. man a Sirian , to doe his accustomed temporal seruice
19 . to an infidel king within the Temple of an Idol ; that
case differeth much, from the question of personal presence in heretical conuenticles, at seruice or sermons .
First because Naamans fact was neither a reuolt from
true Religion, nor profession of falshood, as now it
is in England by shewing conformitie to the wicked
law, by which Catholique Religion is abandoned ,
and heretical abomination, brought in place therof.
1 . *Esd*. Secondly this noble mans fact, was not scandalous to
4 . *v*.2. anie man, because in that place, true Religion was
3 .*Ch*.9. not knowne, nor anie controuersie concerning the
v.1.*Ch*. publique profession therof moued, as now there is
10.*v*.2. amongst vs . Lastly Naaman tooke direction of Eli-
2 .*Esd*. zeus in his particular case : and so must Christians doe
13.*v*.3. now in our case, not folowing the iudgement of priuate men, but of the cheife Pastor of Goddes Church,
or of such an approued Prophet of God, as Elize-

Wherin Naa-
mans case dif-
fereth from
personal pre-
sence in here-
tical conuen-
ticles.

D d d   us was

us was.

9 But for Examples like vnto our cafe, we haue manie in holie Scriptures, as Daniel, and the other children in the captiuitie, [who would by no meanes be polluted by eating of the kinges table : nor would adore his ftatua.] Iudith being in Holofernes houfe [profeffed the true God, and abftained from vnlawful meates.] After the captiuitie [thofe that builded the Temple, would not admitte the fchifmatical Samaritanes to ioine with them in that work.] Efdras and Nehemias were very diligent [in correcting the fault of manie Iewes, making mariages with infidels .] In the perfecution of Antiochus, when [manie confented to leaue Goddes Law, and to obey him : Manie alfo were moft conftant, determining not to eat the vncleane thinges, but chofe rather to dye, then to be defiled with vncleane meates] And [they would not breake the holie Law of God, and fo were murdered] For Antiochus fufpecting, that the Iewes would refufe to obey his wicked lawes [tooke the Citie of Ierufalem by force of armes, & bade the fouldiers kil, and not fpare them that came in their way ; and there were flaine in three dayes, fourfcore thoufand, and fourtie thoufand imprifoned, and no leffe number fold] And [manie retired into a defert place, liuing amongft wild beaftes eating herbes, that they might not be partakers of the contamination.] With no leffe wickednes, but with more politique pretence of iuft proceding, as by forme of law [manie were brought to trial ; accufed, and condemned for tranfgreffing the new wicked lawes. Amongft which, [two women were accufed to haue circumcifed their children. whom whē they openly led through the Citie, with their infants hanging at their breftes, they threw them downe headlong by the wales. others coming together to

the next

Examples more like to our cafe in England, touching conformitie to heretical procedinges.

Dan. 1 . v.
8. Ch. 3. v.
6. 16.
Iudith. 11.
v. 14. Ch.
12. v. 2.
19.
1. Mac. 1.
v. 45. 65.
66. 2. Mac.
5. v. 11.
12. 14.

27.

2. Mac. 6.
v. 1. 10.

the next caues, & secretly keping the day of the Sabbath; when they were discouered, were burnt with
fire, because they feared for Religion and obseruance,
to help them selues with their hand.] Renowmed
Eleazarus, cheif man of the Scribes; at the age of
nintie yeares, being commanded to eate swines flesh,
contrarie to Gods Law, would neither do it, nor suffer
his worldly frendes to say that he had done it [lest
others through his dissimulation, might be deceiued :
And so sustained glorious death, to the honour of
God, and memorable example to al men of vertue,
and fortitude.] After him, others also [especially
seauen brethren, and their mother (with admirable
courage) suffered exquisite tormentes, and by their
deathes finished their noble martyrdome. Seing therfore it was necessarie rather to suffer death, then to o-
mitte circumcision of infantes, or celebration of the
Sabbath, or to eate swines flesh, or to make shew so
to doe against Goddes Lawes, and with scandalous
example to others : it is no lesse, but more necessarie, in these times of heresies, and of persecution for
the Catholique faith, to suffer temporal losses, tormentes, and death; then to yeld conformitie vnto
wicked lawes, made in derogation of Catholique Religion, & for practise of heresie, by personal presence
at their seruice or Sermons. Neither can it be lawful to breake Ecclesiastical fastes, or abstinence, or o-
ther Catholique Obseruances, when therby tryal
is made of our faith and Religion. For then such
Christian Lawes, are to be sincerely obserued, not
only as ceremonial sacred Rites, which ordinarily
bind al Christians, but also, because in this case, they
become moral diuine Precepts, pertaining to Religion, and therfore the transgression therof, is a reuolting from God, a participation with Infidels, and
a breach of the first Commandement, concerning

D d d 2   the

11.

2. Mac.
6. v. 18.

25.

31.
Ch. 7. v.
1. 2. 8.
ad 41.

Ceremonial
Rites, become
moral pre-
cepts, when
breach therof
is exacted for
trial of our
Faith, and Re-
ligion.

the feruing of God, and not feruing falfe Goddes.
And fo is abfolutely and ftrictly forbidden; and al
fuch conformitie to Paganifme, Idolatrie, Herefiie,
or other infidelitie, is very often condemned in holie Scriptures : As both wicked in it felf; dangerous
to the tranfgreffors, of more and more corruption,
and fcandalous to others by pernicious example : &
therfore to be auoided by al the true feruantes of
God.

Manie euident
textes of the
Pfalmes, & o-
ther Prophets,
doe condemne
al fhew of con-
formitie to
the practife of
herefie or
other infideli-
tie.

10   So doth the Royal Propet admonifh vs to flee,
and abhorre al participation, and affociation with
the wicked, faying : [with the holie thou fhalt be holie : and with the innocent thou fhalt be innocent:
with the elect thou fhalt be elect; and with the peruerfe thou fhalt be peruerted. I haue hated (faith
he) the Church of the Malignant : and with the impious I wil not fitte. I haue hated iniquitie, and a-
borred it : but thy law I haue loued. But thofe that
decline into obligations, our Lord wil bring with
them that worke iniquitie. Did not I hate them that
hate thee o Lord, and pyned away becaufe of thine
enemies? with perfect hatred did I hate them : they
are become enemies to me : I wil not communicate
with the cheife of them. the iuft fhal rebuke me in
mercie, and fhal reprehend me : but let not the oyle
of a finner fatte me.] Wife Salomon teacheth the
fame neceffitie of auoiding felowfhippe with the wicked, in excercife of Religion, faying : [the hoftes of
the impious are abominable ; becaufe they are offered
of wickednes. He that is partaker with a theefe, hateth his owne foule. He heareth one adiuring, and
telleth not. He that feareth man, fhal foone fal :
he that trufteth in our Lord, fhal be lifted vp.]
Vnder the name of Babilon, Ifaias admonifheth al
Chriftians, to flee from communicating with infidels
{ Depart, depart, go ye out from thence : touch not a
polluted

Pf. 17. *v.*
26. 27. *Pf.*
25. *v.* 5.
Pf. 118. *v.*
163. *Pf.*
124. *v.* 5.
Pf. 138. *v.*
21. 22. *Pf.*
140. *v.* 4.
5.

Pron. 21. *v.*
27. *Ch.* 29.
v. 24. 25.

If. 52.
v. 11.

polluted thing ; goe out of the middeſt of her : be
clenſed ye that carie the veſſels of our Lord] Which
S . Paul applieth to the ſhunning of falſe Apoſtles ,
2 . Cor . [Thus ſaith the Lord of hoſtes (by the mouth of Ie-
6 . v . 17 . remie) Heare not the wordes of the Prophets , that
Iere. 23. Prophecie vnto you and deceiue you : they ſpeake
v. 16. 21. the viſion of their owne hart , not from the mouth
of the Lord . I ſent not the Prophets , & they ranne :
Ezech . I ſpake not to them , and they prophecied .] Ezechiel
23 . v . 16. inſtructeth thoſe that wil learne the truth , firſt to depart from Idolatrie & falſe doctrine of ſuch as preach
without right miſſion [Conuert (ſaith he) and depart from your Idols , and from al your contaminations , turne away your faces .] Our Lord threatning al vaine temporiſers by his Prophet Sophoni-
Soph . 1. as ſaith : [I wil deſtroy them that ſweare by the
v . 5 . 6. Lord , and by Melchom , and them that turne away
from after the backe of our Lord , & haue not ſought
our Lord , nor ſearched after him .]

11 Al which admonitions and threates , our Sauiour
and his Apoſtles often confirme by their doctrine.
Mat . 6 . [No man can ſerue two Maiſters (ſaith Chriſt) God
v . 24. and Mammon] that is , God , and this world , truth
Ch. 10. and falſitie , the ſpirit and the fleſh . [Euerie one
v . 32. that ſhal confeſſe me before men , I alſo wil confeſſe
33. him before my Father which is in heauen : but he
that ſhal denie me before men , I alſo wil denie him
before my Father which is in heauen . Doe not you
thinke that I came to ſend peace into the earth : I
came not to ſend peace , but the ſword] meaning ,
that he wil not haue peace , betwene faith , and in-
38. fidelitie , betwene oppoſite enemies [He that taketh
Luc . 12. not his Croſſe , and foloweth me , is not worthie of
v . 8 . 51 . me .] Our Lord [would not ſuffer the diuel to ſpeak
Mar . 1 . the truth , but compelled him to hold his peace , and
v . 25. to goe out of the man] whom he poſſeſſed & vexed .

The ſame is
much inculca-
ted in the new
Teſtament .

D d d 3

S . Paul

S. Paul likewise [commanded silence to a Pithoni- *Luc. 4. v.*
cal spirit, and expelled him out of the person whom *35. Act. 6.*
he possessed.] He taught the Corinthians that [they *v. 18.*
could not drinke the chalice of our Lord, and the cha- *1. Cor. 10.*
lice of diuels : you can not (saith he) be partakers *v. 21.*
of the Table of our Lord, and of the table of diuels. *2. Cor. 6.*
Beare not the yoke with Infidels ; for what partici- *v. 14. 15.*
pation hath iustice with iniquitie ? or what societie *16. 17.*
is there betwene light and darknes ? and what a-
grement betwene Christ and Belial ? or what part
hath the faithful with the Infidel? And what agremét
hath the Temple of God with Idoles ? For you are
the Temple of the liuing God. For the which cause
goe out of the middest of them, and seperate your
selues saith our Lord, and touch not the vncleane]
the same which was recited euen now out of Isaias.
In the very same maner S. Paul admonisheth the
Thessalonians saying : [we denounce vnto you bre- *2. Thes. 3.*
thren in the name of our Lord Iesus Christ, that you *v. 6.*
withdraw your selues from euerie brother walking
inordinately, & not according to the tradition which
they haue receiued of vs.] He instructeth Timothee
a Bishoppe that [there wil be manie heretikes] in *2. Tim. 3.*
this time of the new Testament, describing their wic- *v. 1. 2. 3.*
kednes, and noteth some euen then seducing whom *4. 5. 6.*
they could [hauing an appearance in deede of pietie,
but denying the veritie therof. and these (saith he)
auoide. For of these be they that craftely enter into houses : and leade captiue seelie women loaden
with sinnes ; which are led with diuers desires, alwayes learning and neuer attaining to the knowlege
of the truth.] In likesort instructing Titus an other
Bishoppe, how to preach and conuerse with al the
faithful especially warneth him, and in him al others
to haue no felowshippe with heretikes saying : [A *Tit. 3. v.*
man that is an heretike, after the first, and second *10. 11.*
admonition

admonition, auoide: knowing that he that is such an
one (persisting obstinate after two admonitions by
the spiritual Superior) is subuerted, and sinneth, being condemned by his owne iudgement] in that he
knoweth his error , is condemned by the Church, &
rather runneth out of the Church , then he wil submitte his iudgement . S. Iohn in his second Epistle
which he writte to a Ladie, and her sonnes, willeth
them to hould fast the faith which they had learned,

2. Ioan . and to haue no societie with an heretike; saying :[If
v.10.11. anie man come to you and bring not this doctrine ,
(once taught and receiued in the whole Church)
receiue him not into the house, nor say *God saue you*
vnto him . For he that saith vnto him : God saue
you, communicateth with his wicked workes] when
it is done in fauoure of his heresie . For otherwise
in diuers cases ciuil conuersation is permitted with
heretikes , but neuer in religious causes . And therfore our Sauiour by the penne of the same Apostle S.
Iohn in the Epistles to seueral Bishoppes of Asia ,
comendeth or taxeth them for their more or lesse proceding against heretikes . where noting some defect
in one of them, yet commendeth him for his hatred

Apoc. 2 . of heresie saying: [this (good thing) thou hast :
v. 4 . 6 . that thou hatest the factes of the Nicolaites, which
I also hate.] Commending an other for his owne
constant fortitude, yet blameth him for his couldnes

13 . 14 . in suppressing heretikes, saying: [I haue against thee
a few thinges, because thou hast there, them that hold
the doctrine of Balaam ; who taught Balac to cast a-
scandal before the children of Israel , to eate, & committe fornication : so hast thou also that hold the doctrine of the Nicolaites .] He also highly commen-

15 .   deth an other Bishoppe saying : [I know thy workes,
19 .   and faith, and thy charitie, and ministerie, and thy
patience, and thy last workes, moe then the former,
yet

yet reprehendeth his toleration of some heresie saying : [I haue against thee a few thinges : because 20,
thou permittest the woman Iezabel, who calleth herself a prophetesse, to teach, and to seduce my seruants,
to fornicate, and to eate, of thinges sacrificed to I-
dols.] An other he rebuketh, admonishing him to
be more vigilant [For I finde not (saith he) thy *Ch. 3. v.*
workes ful before my God] and commendeth some 2. 4.
of his flocke for their constancie in confessing their
faith saying : [But thou hast a few names in Sardis,
(which was his prouince) which haue not defiled
their garments : & they shal walke with me in whites,
because they are worthie.] But of al most sharply
reproueth an other Bishoppe for his want of zele in
cause of religion saying : [I know thy workes that 15. 16.
thou art neither cold, nor hote; I would thou wert
could, or hote. But because thou art lukewarme, &
neither could, nor hote, I wil beginne to vomite thee
out of my mouth. Because thou saiest : I am rich, & 17.
enriched, and lacke nothing : and knowest not that
thou art a miser, and miserable, and poore, & blinde,
and naked. Be zealous therefore and doe penance.] 19.
Ch. 2. v.

Our Sauiour
foreshewing
that Christians
shal be strong-
ly tempted, &
tryed for pro-
fessing their
faith; forewar-
neth al to be
constant, and
zealous.

12   After these admonitions to al Pastors, (for so 11. 17. 29.
our Sauiour concludeth al his seuen Epistles, that al *&c.*
Churches should take them as written to them selues)
he foretelleth manie great troubles, and persecutions
by Infidels, especially by Antichrist, warning al true
Christians by no meanes to yeld consent by word,
nor deede, vnto the practise of heresie, and in regard
that al conformitie to heretical proceedinges is honour, and adoration of the great beast Antichrist, &
the diuel; he denouncing by the loud voice of an An- *Ch. 14. v.*
gel, that if anie man adore the beast, and his image, 9. 10.
and receaue the character in his forehead, or in his
hand, he also shal drinke of the wine of the wrath of
God, which is mingled with pure wine in the cuppe
of his

of his wrath; and shal be tormented with fire, and brimstone, in the sight of the holie Angels, and before the sight of the lambe.] For preuention of which so intolerable eternal torments, our louing Sauiour eftsonnes, & often warneth his children to flee out of wicked Babilon, by an other voice from heauen saying: [Goe out from her my people: that you be not pertakers of her sinnes; and receaue not of her plagues.]

Ch. 18.
v. 4.

From the Church and Communion of Sainctes, are excluded excommunicate persons.

ARTICLE. 46.

SVch is the enormitie of some sinnes, together with the danger of infecting others with like contagion: and so noysome they are to the whole bodie wherof the malefactors are members, that God by his law ordained to punish them with corporal death. And so [take away euil from amidest the good.] Namely for wilful murther, for striking, or cursing their parents; for sorcerie; bestialitie; idolatrie; adulterie; incest; sodomie; heresie; disobedience to the cheife Iudge; & the like. Which course of Iustice al temporal Princes doe imitate, for the saiftie of the common wealthes. But in place therof, Christ our Sauiour hath established in his Church a spiritual punishment of enormious offenders, that aswel they may be corrected, as the rest preserued, and the whole bodie purged of pestiferous humors, by excommunication, and seperation of vnworthie members, from participating with the Church in holie Sacraments, publique prayers, and other spiritual felowshippe.

Exo. 21.
v. 12.
14. 15.
16. 17.
23. *Ch.*
22. *v.*
18. 19.
20.
Leuit.
20. *v.* 9.
10. 13.
Deut. 13.
v. 5. 9.
15. *Ch.*
17. *v.*
12.

Some sinnes are iustly punished with death, by temporal Magistrates.

Christ hath geuen his Church a spiritual sword, of excommunication, and of other censures.

2 A figure of this Ecclesiastical discipline, was in the auctoritie

Which Ecclesiastical power,

E e e

was prefigured
in the old Law.

auctoritie of Preiftes in Moyfes Law, to whom it
perteyned not onlie to iudge of leprofies, but alfo to
feperate the lepers from the focietie of other people :
[The man in whofe fkinne, and flefh, fhal arife the *Leuit*. 13.
plauge of leprofie, fhal be brought to Aaron the high *v*. 2. 3. 44.
Preift, or to one of his fonnes : at his arbitriment 45. 46.
(faith the Law) he fhal be feperated, he fhal haue
his cloathes hanging loofe, his heade bare, his mouth
couered with a cloath, he fhal crie him felf polluted
and vncleane. Al the time that he is a leper and vncleane, he fhal dwel alone without the campe.]
And this was done though the leprofie came of natural infirmitie without finne. And for execution
therof, the people were bound [to bring the fufpected to the Preifts, and being iudged to be leprofie, *Nu*. 5. *v*.
to caft out of the campe euerie leper, as wel man, as 2. 3.
woman, left they contaminate it.]

Diuers offen-
ders were pu-
nifhed by God
with leprofie,
and fo exclu-
ded from con-
uerfation with
others.

3 No maruel therfore if it were exactly obferued
when it happened for punifhment of finne. As when
Marie (the fifter to Moyfes, and of Aaron) for mur- *Nu*. 12. *v*.
muring againft Moyfes, was ftriken with leprofie, 2. 10. 13.
though meeke Moyfes prayed our Lord to heale her : 14.
yet our Lord commanded to punifh her for a time
faying : [Let her be feperated feuen dayes without
the campe, & afterwardes fhe fhal be called againe.]
More feuerely was Ozias King of Iuda, punifhed for 2. *Par*. 26.
his facrilegious pride. who vfurping preiftlie functió *v*. 16. 17.
to offer incenfe, and perfifting in his purpofe, and 18. 19. 20.
threatning the high Preift, and others that refifted
him [forthwith there rofe a leprofie in his foreheade,
before the Preiftes, in the houfe of our Lord, vpon
the Alter of incenfe. And when Azarias the high
Preift had beheld him and al the reft of the Preiftes,
they faw the leprofie in his foreheade, and in haft they
thruft him out : yea and himfelf being fore afraide 21.
made haft to goe out : becaufe he felt by and by the
                                                    plague

plague of our Lord. Ozias therfore the king was a
leper vntil the day of his death : and ful of leprosie
(for the which he had bene caſt out of the houſe of
our Lord) he dwelt in a houſe a part ; and his ſonne
Ioathan gouerned the kinges houſe, and iudged the
people of the land. And dying they buried him (not
in the proper ſepulchre of kinges, but) in the kinges

23 . ſepurchres fielde : becauſe he was a leper.] How greuous puniſhment this ſeperation from ſocietie of the
faithful was eſtemed, doth further appeare by continual practiſe among the people of God. As when
al the people returning from Babilon were called to
Ieruſalem, it was proclamed with this comminato-

1 . Eſd. rie warning [Euerie one that ſhal not come within
10 . v . 7. three dayes, according to the councel of the Princes,
3 . and the Auncients, al his ſubſtance ſhal be taken away,
and him ſelf ſhal be caſt out of the companie of the
tranſmigration.] And the parents of the blinde man,
Io . 9 . v . whoſe ſight Chriſt reſtored [durſt not confeſſe who
22 . had opened their ſones eyes, for feare leſt they ſhould
be put out of the Sinagogue.]

4   Our Sauiour miraculouſly clenſing diuers lepers
Mat . 8. [ſent them to the Preiſtes that they might reſtore
v . 4. them into their former conuerſation with the people,
Leuit . 14. finding them cleane from leproſie, according to the
v . 2 . 3. Law] which law being ſhortly to ceaſe, he inſtitu-
Luc . 18. ted in the meane time the thing therby prefigured ,
v . 14. which is Apoſtolical power of ſpiritual binding and
looſing in earth, as the ſame ſhould be ratified in hea-
Mat . 18. uen, ſaying to S. Peter [I wil geue to thee the keyes
v . 19. of the kingdome of heauen ; And whatſoeuer thou
ſhalt binde vpon earth, it ſhal be bound alſo in heauen : and whatſoeuer thou ſhalt looſe in earth, it ſhal
be looſed alſo in heauen.] Which power our Saui-
Ch . 18. our afterwardes declareth to haue this effect in earth,
v . 7. that he which wil not heare the Church is (for that

Chriſt fulfilled
the old Law :
and gaue grea-
ter power to
his Church, of
binding, and
looſing ſinnes,
by Iudicial ſen-
tence.

reſiſtance

refiftance to be excluded from the faithful) as the Heathen, and Publicans] For that by the word Chur-ch, in this place, he meaneth neither the vniuerfal mi-litant Church, confifting of the Cleargie, and Laitie, nor the fupreme vifible head only in whom this auc-toritie principally refideth : but al the Prelates of the Church is manifeft by the next wordes faying to al his Apoftles, & in them, to their fucceffors, al Ecclefi-aftical Prelates, as yelding the reafon why fuch difo-bedient perfons are to be auoided as the Heathen, and Publicans, [Amen I fay to you, whatfoeuer you fhal binde vpon earth, fhal be bound alfo in heauen.]

v. 18.

A cleare ex-ample of auc-toritie in Pre-lates to excom-municate, and abfolue, by S. Paules prac-tife.

5   Againe it is cleare by S. Paules practife, that he (being an Apoftle yet none of the twelue to whom Chrift then fpake) had this power of Iurifdiction to feperate obftinate offenders from the felowfhippe of other Chriftians, where he both threatneth, & pu-nifheth certaine Corinthians faying: [I wil come to you quickly if our Lord wil, and wil know, not the wordes of them that be puffed vp, but the power. For the kingdome of God is not in wordes, but in power] (not only in preaching, but alfo in gouer-ning) and fo expoftulating with them, that either committed, or carelefly tolerated fcandalous finnes, concludeth his fatherly admonition faying: [what wil you? that I come to you in rodde : or in chari-tie, and the fpirit of mildnes?] premonifhing that as they fhould deferue, fo he would deale, either with feueritie, or with mildnes. And euen then being ab-fent proceeded againft one notorious malefactor, by rigour of Excommunication, blaming, and correc-ting others flaknes and want of zele, in not feeking the offenders punifhment, that was otherwife incor-rigible [There is heard (faith he) among you fuch fornication, as the like is not among the Heathen: that one hath his fathers wife. And you (his frendes,

1 . *Cor* . 4 . *v* . 19 . 20.

21.

Ch . 5 . *v* . 1. 2.

and

and neighbours) are puffed vp : and haue not mourned rather, that he might be taken away from among
you, that hath done this deede .] Then suppoſing by
his owne iuſt zele, that which others ought to haue
ſolicited, but did not , the holie Apoſtle denounced
ſentence of Excommunication in this maner [I in-

3 . 4 . 5 . deede abſent in bodie , but preſent in ſpirit, haue alreadie iudged as preſent, him that hath ſo done ; in
the name of our Lord Ieſus Chriſt, you being gathered together, and my ſpirit with the vertue of our
Lord Ieſus Chriſt, to deliuer ſuch an one to Satan, for
the diſtruction of the fleſh , that the ſpirit may be
ſaued in the day of our Lord Ieſus Chriſt .] Againe
by the ſame power of Iuriſdiction, after the delin-
quents humble penance, he looſed that which he had
formerly bound ; abſoluing the penitent from excommunication, and withal imperting vnto him by way
of indulgence, the reſt of ſatisfaction not performed ;
and that vpon the good reſtimonie, & ſute of others ;
writing thus to them ; and to ſuch alſo as ſemed ouer

2 . Cor . ſeuere [To him that is ſuch a one (him that is excom-
2 . v . 6 . municated for inceſt) this rebuke ſufficeth that is geuen of manie : ſo that contrariwiſe you ſhould rather
pardon, and comfort him, leſt perpaps he be ſwalow-

8 . ed vp with ouer great ſorrow . For the which cauſe
I beſech you, that you confirme charitie towards him .

9 . For therfore alſo haue I writen, that I may know the
experiment of you : whether in al thinges you be obe-

10 . dient. And whom you haue pardoned (or wiſh to be
pardoned) I alſo (doe pardon) For that which my
ſelf pardoned, if I pardoned anie thing, for you (for
your ſakes) I did it .] And to ſignifie to what po-

11 . wer he did it he addeth [in the perſon of Chriſt] &
what cauſe moued him [that we be not circumuented of Satan.]

6 Thus we ſee by S. Pauls fact, and doctrine, aſwel

S. Paules ſen-
tence of excō-
munication a-
gainſt an inceſ-
tious perſon. ｜

The excom-
municate are

depriued of the
communion of
the faithful, til
they be abſol-
ued.

wel his, as other Prelates auctoritie, to excommunicate, and to abſolue; and that the effect of excommunication, is an excluſion from the Church, & from
the Communion of Sainctes. Becauſe whiles a perſon
remaineth excommunicated, he is in the power of the
diuel, as being for his fault, and for his correction,
deliuered to him for the good of his ſoule [that the
ſpirit may be ſaued] by his repentance. [For the
weapons of our warfare (ſaith the ſame Apoſtle) are
not carnal, for our power, which our Lord hath geuen
vs, is vnto edification, and not to deſtruction.] To
the end therfore that the offenders might doe penance
before hand he ſtil inculcateth, that vnleſſe they ſo
did, he would aſſuredly lay this rodde of excommunication vpon them [I foretold (ſaid he) & doe foretel as preſent, and now abſent, to them that ſinned, &
al the reſt, that if I come againe I wil not ſpare. therfore theſe thinges I write abſent: that being preſent
I may not deale hardly according to the power which
our Lord hath geuen me vnto edification, and not vnto deſtruction.] To the ſame purpoſe he admoniſhed
the Theſſalonians; both to informe him of ſuch as
were diſobedient, and to auoide their companie, writing thus to them [If anie obey not our Lord, note
him by an Epiſtle. And doe not companie with him,
that he may be confounded: and doe not eſteme him
as an enemie, but admoniſh him as a brother.]

S. Paul willed
S. Timothee
to practiſe E-
piſcopal aucto-
ritie in puni-
ſhing where
neede requi-
red.

7 As he exerciſed his power for the ſpiritual good
of al: ſo he willed S. Timothie being alſo a Biſhop
with corage and according to good conſcience, to
vſe his auctoritie in puniſhing, propoſing vnto him
for example [ſome that repelling good conſcience,
had made ſhipwracke about the faith, of whom (ſaid
he) is Himenæus, and Alexander, whom I haue deliuered to Satan, that they may learne not to blaſpheme.] Euen the ſame inſtruction he gaue to S. Titus an

Ch. 10. *v.*
4. 8.

Ch. 13. *v.*
2.
10.

2. *Theſ.* 3.
v. 14. 15.

1. *Tim.* 1.
v. 20.

Tit . 1.

v . 10.

11.

13.

15. 16.

tus an other Bifhop, to vfe feueritie where it was needeful faying : [There be manie difobedient vaine fpeakers and feducers, efpecially they that are of the Circumcifion, who muft be controuled, who fubuert whole houfes, teaching the thinges they ought not for filthie lucre ; for the which caufe, rebuke them fharply, that they may be found in faith , not atten ding to the Iewifh fables (that was then the fault wherto the Cretenfians much inclined) and commã dements of men, auerting them felues frõ the truth .] Now the dangerous crime wherwith manie are temp ted, is worldlie feare, or filthie lucre [wherby their mindes, and concience are polluted, (as the fame A poftle there fpeaketh) that albeit they confeffe they know God : yet in their workes they denie him : wheras they be abominable, and incredulous, and to euerie good worke reprobate .]

Whofoeuer falleth into mortal finne, loofeth the par ticipatiõ of good workes vntil he be truly penitent .

A R T I C L E. 47.

Not only thofe which neuer entred into the Catholique Church, or by herefie, or fchifme are gone forth , or for anie crimes are caft out ; but alfo al thofe that fal into mortal finne, though they remaine within the Church, yet they doe loofe the benfite which al the liuing members reciue by mutual communication, and participation of good workes, each one with others . For as the bodie & euerie member therof liueth by the vital fpirit of the foule ; and as that member is deade, which wanteth the influence of the foule : euen fo the foule, and e uerie good action therof, liueth fpiritually by grace ; and without grace the foule is fpiritually deade . In
which

As the bodie is deade without the foule : fo the foule is dead without fanctifying grace .

which ſtate we were al borne: as S. Paul teacheth
ſaying: that [we were by nature the children of
wrath.] And being regenerate by Chriſt in Baptiſme,
whoſoeuer falleth againe by breach of Gods commandement, into mortal ſinne, ſo dieth ſpiritually, that
he can neither merite by anie worke, though morally good, nor participate of the meritorious workes
of others, vntil he be reſtored by new grace, to ſpiritual life. Wherfore that ſacrifice might be more a-
uaileable, it was commanded in the old Law that
[neither leauen, nor honie ſhould be burnt in Sacri- *Leuit*. 2.
fice] ſignifying that the ſinne, and carnal delectation, *v.* 1.
hinder the furict of good workes. The ſame was prefigured in Sampſon: frō whom ſupernatural ſtrength
departed, when the rule of his profeſſion was viola-
ted [If my head ſhal be ſhauen (ſaid he to Dalila) my *Iudic*. 16.
ſtrength ſhal depart from me, and I ſhal faile, & ſhal *v.* 17.
be as other men.] And being ſhauen (contrarie to *Nu.*6.*v.*5.
the Nazarites rule) immediatly his ſtrength departed 19. 27.
from him, and the Philliſtians preuailed againſt him. 30.
But receiuing againe his former ſtrength [he killed
moe of his enemies dying, then before he had killed
liuing.]

2. The Pſalmiſt in the perſon of a ſinner deſtitute of *Pſ.* 101.
grace, ſaith [My dayes haue vaniſhed as ſmoke, & *v.* 4. 5.
my bones are withered as a drie burnt fire brand. I am
ſtriken as gras & my hart is withered. My dayes haue
declined as a ſhadow: & I am withered as gras] Cōfeſ-
ſing that ſo long as he is in the ſtate of mortal ſinne, al
his workes are fructles, and vaniſh as ſmoke: fitte
for no better vſe then to kindle the fire. Becauſe being ſeperated from God, by ſinne they wanting the
radical moiſturre of Gods grace, doe wither as graſſe
that is cutte from the roote. To the ſame purpoſe *Eccle*. 10.
ſaith the wiſe man [Flies dying doe marre the ſweet- *v.* 1.
neſſe of ointment.] For ſo deadlie ſinnes in mans *Eccle*. 34.
soule *v.* 23.

Sampſon loſt
his ſtrength
when his
haire was cut,
contrarie to
the Nazarites
rule.

Holie Scriptu-
res teſtifie that
tħe ſoule with-
out quickning
grace, is fruict-
leſſe.

Ephes. 2.*v.*
3.

foule make his workes (otherwise vertuous) to be vnfauorie in the fight of God, becaufe he that remaineth in affection of finne, can not pleafe God [for the Higheft alloweth not the giftes of the wicked, neither haith he regard to the oblations of the vniuft : neither wil he be made propitious for finnes by the multitude of their facrifices] It is impoffible to be

Mat. 6.
v. 24.

the feruant of God, and the feruant of finne [no man can ferue two maifters (faith our Sauiour) you can not ferue God and Mammon .] Yet are not al great finners alfo feperated from the Church, but manie doe remaine therin as dead members, doe fticke to the liuing bodie, and may be more eafelie reuiued, then the feperated members can be reunited.

3   For that there be fuch dead mēbers in the Church, is clearly proued by our Sauiours difcourfe in an other place faying : [Euerie branch in me not bea-

Io. 15.
v. 2.

ring fruict, fhal be taken away. But euerie one that beareth fruict, fhal be purged that it may bring more fruict] So diftinguifhing two fortes of branches, in him felf as head, both members of his Church ; the one forte fruictles, which if they fo continue, and be not reuiued, fhal be foner, or later, cut of ; the other fort fruictful, which are purged or pruned, & fo fhal bring forth more fruict. But neither the one can be reuiued, nor the other increafe in grace, ex-

4 · 5 ·

cept they abide in him. For [as the branch (of a vinetree) can not beare fruict of it felf, vnles it abide in the vine : fo you neither vnles you abide in me ; For without me you can doe nothing] Thofe therfore that are in Chrift, and in his Church, and yet be fruictles ; are fuch as haue only faith, and not good workes but liue in mortal finne : and thofe which are in Chrift and in his Church, and be fruictful, are fuch as haue both faith and good workes ; being vnited to Chrift, and to al his holie members by Cha-

F f f   ritie

Two fortes of members in Chrifts myftical bodie: fome fpiritually liuing, fome dead.

citie voide of al mortal sinne, keping al goddes commandementes [for he that offendeth in one, is guil- *Iac. 2.*
tie of al] that is to say, kepeth none fruictfully, but *v. 10.*
he that kepeth al , bringeth forth fruict , and hath
his part of al good workes in the holie societie of the
Church : Otherwise, neither beareth fruict, nor participateth with others, but deceiueth himself : As S.
Iohn teacheth saying [If we shal say that we haue *1. Io. 1.*
societie with God, and walke in darknes , we lie, *v. 6. 7.*
and doe not the truth . But if we walke in the light ,
as he also is in the light ; we haue societie one towardes an other (and so the good that anie doth , is
profitable to al that are liuing members of the same
societie) and the bloud of Iesus Christ his Sonne,
clenseth vs from al sinne] to witte, from al sinne
that doth frustrate the fruict of good workes , that
seperateth from the holie societie, that hindreth the
participation of others good workes . which is breifly to say : it cleanseth al the iustified liuing members ,
from al mortal sinne : though in this transitorie life,
euen the iust , and holie , are not voide of al venial
sinnes .

A plaine di-
stinction of
mortal , & ve-
nial sinnes by
S. Iohns doc-
trine.

4　Which distinction of greater and lesse sinnes, cal
led mortal, and venial, is here by the way manifestly
proued, by conference of the wordes now cited, with
the wordes next folowing . For here the Apostle speaking of himself , and others of the holie societie, and
hauing said [that the bloud of Iesus Christ cleanseth *7.*
vs from al sinne :] he immediatly addeth [If we shal *8.*
say we haue no sinne, we seduce our selues, and the
truth is not in vs] which two speaches so ioyned together, might seme to be contrarie, and except there
were distinction of diuers kindes of sinnes, it might
seme that the holie Apostle (which were horrible
blasphemie to say) did contradict himself , saying :
[Christes bloud clenseth vs from al sinne] and yet [we
can not

can not truly say that we haue no sinne] For certanly they that are cleansed from sinnes, haue not those sinnes from which they are clensed. How then doth the Apostle say, that they were clensed from al sinne : and yet confesseth that they haue sinnes? The answer and clere solution is. They were clensed from al sinne that seperated from God, and from the godlie societie of the liuing fruictful members; from al sinne, that spiritually killeth the soule; for which it is called mortal sinne: yet he truly confesseth, that himself and others of his societie had sinnes, to witte, which diuide not from God, nor from the godlie societie; which onlie wound, and blemish the soule, but kil not: and therefore are not mortal sinnes, but are called venial, because they are more easily remitted, and pardoned. But of this point more is to be said in the holie Sacrament of Penance. Here thus much may suffice to verifie the distinction of mortal, and venial sinnes : for better declaration that only mortal, not venial sinne, doth hinder the merite of other workes, and the participation of the good workes of others.

Euerie sinne doth blemish, and wound the soule : but euerie one doth not kil the soule.

5 As for moral good workes done in the state of deadlie sinne, though they doe not merite an eternal reward, yet doth God of his bountiful goodnes, reward thē temporally, as with bodily health, strength, riches, dominion, power, humane wisdome, honour, and other commodities of this world. Of which sortes of temporal blessinges, the Iewes had particular promises, and receiued singular benefites. As multiplication of children, and seruants; long and prosperous life, possessiō of a land flowing with milke and honie, abundance of wine, oyle, & other fruictes of the earth. In particular Iehu king of Israel, for his zealous exploites against certaine Idolaters for destroying the house of Achab, and Iezabel, with the

Good workes done in state of mortal sinne, not meriting eternal glorie, yet are rewarded temporally.

Exo. 3. *v.* 8. 17. *Leuit.* 26. *v.* 5. &c.

F f f 2   temple

temple of Baal, and those that worshiped him; was temporally rewarded both in him self and in his progenie: though he persisted in the state of mortal sinne, holding Ieroboams schisme, and mantaining his golden calues. For thus saith the holie Scripture: [Iehu *4. Reg. 10.* destroyed al that were left of Achab in Samaria, til *v. 17. 28.* there was not one: according to the word of our *29. 30.* Lord, which he spake by Elias: he destroed the Idol *3. Reg. 21.* Baal, out of Israel. But yet departed not from the *v. 21. 20.* sinnes of Ieroboam, the sonne of Nabat, who made Israel to sinne: neither forsooke he the golden calues that were in Bethel, and Dan. Wheras therfore our Lord said to Iehu [Because thou hast diligently done that which was right, and that pleased in myne eyes; and done al thinges that were in my hart against the house of Achab: thy children shal sitte vpon the throne of Israel to the fourth generation.] And wheras Iehu neither after this promise, reigning prosperously, twentie eight yeares, did not serue God rightly [nor walked in the Law of our Lord the God *31.* of Israel in al his hart: for he departed not from the sinnes of Ieroboam who made Israel to sinne.] Ne- *4. Reg. 13.* uertheles God performing his word [Ioachaz Iehu *v. 1. 10.* his sonne reigned for him seuentene yeares. His *Ch. 14. v.* sonne Ioas sextene yeares. Then his sonne Ieroboam *23.* one and fourtie yeares. Lastly his sonne Zacharias, being in the fourth generation after Iehu, reigned in Israel] But he and the rest before him followed the bad steppes of the first Ieroboam. And this king *Ch. 15. v.* [Zacharias hauing reigned only sixe monethes, was *8. 9. 10.* slaine by Sellum, the sonne of Iabes]of an other race, *12.* others conspiring with him. Thus was king Iehu temporally rewarded for his moral good workes, not being in the state of grace, to merite eternal reward.

Pagane Infidels were also   **6** And likewise manie others, yea al heathen men

receiued

receiued temporal rewardes at Gods hand for their

Art. 45.
parag. 3.

Is. 45.
v. 1. 2.
Iere. 25.
v. 11.
22.

2. Par.
36. v.
20. 22.
1. Esd. 1.
v. 1. 2.
3. 4.
&c.

moral good workes. As Syrus king of Perfians (as
we touched once before) was aduanced temporally
for his fingular fauoures fhewed to Goddes people,
releafing them from the captiuitie of Babylon, and
yet he neither dulie ferued God, nor rightly knew
God, which was fo prophecied by Ifaias long before
Cyrus was borne, wel neare two hundred yeares before it came to pafle faying : [Thus faith the Lord
to my Chrift Cyrus, whofe right hand I haue taken
to fubdue the Gentiles before his face, & to turne
the backes of kinges, and to open the doares before
him, and the Gates fhal not be fhutte. I wil goe before thee, and wil humble the glorious of the earth.
I wil breake the brafen gates, and wil burft the iron
barres.] When therfore king Cyrus poffeffed Babylon, and al the kingdomes of the Chaldees, Affirians, Medes, and Perfians &c. [Our Lord raifed vp
the fpirit of Cyrus king of the Perfians, and he made
proclamation in al his kingdomes, yea by writing faying : [Thus faith Cyrus king of the Perfians : Al the
kingdomes of the earth, hath the Lord the God of
heauen geuen me; and he hath commanded me that
I fhould build him a houfe in Ierufalem which is in Iurie. Who is there among you, of al his people ?
His God be with him. Let him goe vp into Ierufalem which is in Iurie, and build the houfe of the Lord
the God of Ifrael. He is the God that is in Ierufalem]
So he confeffed one God, the Lord God of heauen,
and fauoured his peculiar people, the children of Ifrael, and was for the fame aduanced in temporal power; yet was he not conuerted in al pointes of Religion, neither ferued God according to that general
knowlege that he had. For which defect, God by
the fame Prophet Ifaias, thus taxeth him faying : [For
my feruant Iacob and Ifrael mine elect, I haue cal-

F f f 3   led thee

led thee by thy name: I haue reſembled thee, & thou
haſt not knowne me.] By theſe and manie other examples, aſwel of the Iewes as Gentiles, eſpecially of
Philoſophers which liued morally wel, it is cleare,
that they receiued great giftes of God, but temporal only, not eternal ; becauſe they neither knew God
rightly, by faith, nor ſerued him according to that
knowlege which they had of him, as S. Paul teacheth
in his Epiſtle to the Romanes. And therfore theſe
are workes which he excludeth, as not auailable to
iuſtification, nor ſaluation, being without faith. For
that is the ſcope of his doctrine, to ſhew, that neither workes without faith, nor faith without workes,
doe iuſtifie ; neither can anie haue faith, or doe good
but by grace, that is, by Goddes free gift, before
anie workes cā be meritorious ; neither yet are workes
with faith meritorious, that are done in ſtate of mortal ſinne, but neceſſarily it is required to beleue rightly, to decline from deadlie ſinne, and to doe good
works [So ſhal euerie one receiue, according as he
hath done, either good or euil.]

Iſa. 45.
v. 4.

Rom. 1. v,
20. 21.

Ch. 11. v. 6,

2. Cor. 5.
v. 10.

In the Catholique Church is remiſſion of ſinnes, &
Iuſtification by Grace.

ARTICLE. 48.

Seing no ſinne
can enter into
heauen, the
way for ſinners
to be ſaued is
by remiſſion of
ſinnes.

IN the former Articles is ſhewed, that neither a-
nie can be ſaued out of the true Church, nor in
the Church, dying in mortal ſinne, neither can
anie defiled with venial ſinne, enter into heauen, vntil al his ſinnes be remitted, and his ſoule purged.
For [there ſhal not enter into the celeſtial Citie, a-
nie polluted thing] how then ſhal anie ſinners be
ſaued ? Trulie none as ſinners, can poſſeſſe life euerlaſting, nor be ſaued. For al ſinnes pollute the ſoule,
and

Act. 45.
46. 47.

Apoc. 21.
v. 27.

and fo long as the finne remaineth, it hindreth the
foule from entrance into heauen. But the remedie
of this impediment, is the remiſſion of finnes, with
iuftification of finners, & fanctificatiō of their foules.
which moft bountiful benefites, God imparteth vnto mankind through his grace offered to al, fufficient for al, and effectual in manie, as the holie Scriptures doe copiouſly witnes, both in the old and new

Gen. 3. Teftament. Our mother Eue was the firſt of man-
*v.*6.12. kind that finned, and Adam the fecond. They both
13. incurred, and we al in Adam, contracted, the guilt
of death temporal, & eternal.

2 Yet our Lord God by his grace reduced them to | God gaue
repentance, which is proued by the text. For wher- | grace of repen-
Gen. 2. as before in their innocencie, being then alfo [naked | tance, and re-
v. 2.5. they were not afhamed] but after that they had fin- | miſſion of
Ch. 3. ned [they made them felues aprones of leaues to couer | finnes to A-
v. 7.8. their nakednes, & hidde thē felues (for fhame) amidſt | dam, and Eue.
9. 10. the trees of Paradiſe . And our Lord God called A-
12. dam ſayıng : where art thou ? I heard thy voice
(faid he) and I feared] fo was he through Godd es
grace, neither obdurate in finne, nor deſperate of
mercie, as al the diuels were. But confeſſing the
13. truth, [our Lord faid to the woman ; why haft thou | Proued by the
done this ?] She likewife confeſſing the truth, God | facred text.
without more examining, condemned the diuel (in
the ferpent) that had malicioufly tempted, and ouer- | 1.
come them. And fecondly, by enioyning temporal | 2.
penance to Adam and Eue, fignified the remiſſion of
their finne, which otherwife deſerued eternal death.
Thirdly [God put alfo enmities from that tıme for- | 3.
ward, betwene the diuel and the woman, betwene
his feede, and her feede] which fheweth that fhe was
no longer the diuels feruant, but his perpetual ene-
miie ; and confequently alfo Adam was the diuels e-
nemie, not his feruant. Fourthly our Lord declared | 4.
that

that the woman by her seede, should bruise the serpentes head in peeces. Fiftly of Adam, the wisemã
saith, that [wisdome brought him out of his sinne .] *Sap. 10.*

5.

Other exam-
ples of Goddes
seruantes.

3   Some others also were the true seruantes of God, *v. 2.*
which presupposeth remission of sinne. For Abel *Gen. 4. v.*
so [offered Sacrifice, that our Lord had respect therto . *4. 26 . Ch.*
Enos inuocated the name of our Lord . Enoch wal- *5 . v . 22.*
ked with God, and God tooke him .] from the con- *24. Ch. 6.*
uersation of other mortal men . [Noe was iust and *v . 9. Ch.*
perfect in his generation] so [Abraham, Isaac, Iacob, *12 . v . 1.*
were such seruantes of God, that he vouchsaifed to *&c.*
be called their God] Al which presupposeth the remission of their sinnes, as wel original, as actual .

External sig-
nes of remissiõ
of sinnes, & of
increase of
grace.

4   The Sacrament of Circumcision was directly in- *Exo . 3 . v.*
stituted as a signe, of the remission of sinne ; not as *6. Gen . 17.*
the cause, for that is the difference betwene the Sacra- *v .10 . Rom.*
mẽts, of the old Law, and of Christ. For the same pur- *4 . v . 11.*
pose were the old Sacrifices also instituted, for signes of *Leuit . 2 . v.*
remission of sinnes & of sanctification : which yet they *3 . 13. 22.*
wrought not , but only signified; as a shadow of *27. Heb.*
thinges to come . And as the Sacraments of Circum- *10. v . 1.*
cision, of diuers sortes of washinges, & purifications , *Col. 2. v.*
of legal vncleanes, with sundrie Sacrifices for sinne , *17.*
were then instituted to signifie remission of sinne, and
iustification of sinners : So the Paschal lambe; Loa- *Gen.17.v.*
ues of Proposition, Ordination of Preistes , and Le- *10 . Leuit.*
uites , and the like figures of Christian Sacramentes, *4 . 5 . 6. 7.*
and Sacrifice, did signifie increase of grace, and more *14 .15. 16.*
sanctification of the iust . *17. Exo. 12.*

Real remission
of sinnes, and
inherẽt grace ,
proued by ho-
lie Scriptures .

5   For so much therfore as Protestantes denie that *16 . 25 . v.*
anie sinne can be really taken away, holding opinion *30. Leuit.*
that they are only couered, or not imputed ; denying *8 .*
also that sinners can be purged from mortal sinne, &
made iust and holie; but onlie that beleuing in our
Redemer they are reputed iust, not by iustice (say
they) inherent in their soules, but only by the iustice
of Christ

of Chrift imputed vnto them. we fhal here fhew the contrarie Catholique doctrine, that finnes are indeed remitted, taken away, deftroyed; and finners in very deede cleanfed from al mortal finne, made iuft, and fanctified by grace, & iuftice inherent, in their foules. Which our beleefe and doctrine befides the places alreadie here alleaged, is more abundantly proued by manie other holie Scriptures. yea euen by thofe facred textes, by which Caluin, and other Proteftants efpecially impugne, and endeuoure to difproue the fame doctrine. Of Abraham it is written in the boke of Genefis, that [he beleued God, and it was reputed to him vnto iuftice] which wordes S. Paul citeth in his Epiftles to the Romans, and the Gallacians: prouing therby that Abraham had no iuftice, nor eftimation of iuftice before God, by anie workes done, that proceded not of faith and Goddes grace. For if Abraham did commendable workes before he beleued in Chrift (as manie Philofophers did) men might account him iuft therfore; but in Goddes fight he fhould not haue had the reputation of a iuft man for thofe works. And therfore whofoeuer prefumeth of his owne workes as done of him felf without faith, without the grace and helpe of God, imagining that grace and iuftification were geuen him for fuch workes, and fo chalenge his iuftification as debt, imputing the reward as debt; doth grofly erre. For God doth not efteme or repute him iuft. But beleuing as Abraham did, & therupon doing good workes [it is reputed to him vnto iuftice, and he is made the frend of God] as S. Iames teacheth by the example of Abraham, and S. Paul confirmeth this doctrine, by the Royal Prophet Dauid, calling it [the bleffednes of a man, to whom God reputeth iuftice] without workes (done before) becaufe Dauid faith [Bleffed are they whofe iniquities be forgeuen, and whofe

Example in Abraham.

finnes

sinnes are couered. Blessed is the man to whom our
Lord hath not imputed sinne] making it al one to
repute a man iust, and not to impute sinne vnto him.
But in this whole passage, Protestantes replying,
vrge the wordes *reputed, imputed, & couered,* arguing
against Catholiques, that by these termes, is signified the continuance of sinnes, not indeede taken a-
way, but only couered and not imputed, and that a
man is not really made iust, but only reputed iust, remaining wicked after his sorow or contrition, receiuing of anie holie Sacrament, or anie thing els that
he can doe, adding withal, that there is no inherent
iustice in anie faithful soule ; but that the most faithful and best man, is only reputed iust by the iustice of
Christ imputed vnto him.

That the wor-
des: IMPV-
TED, REPV-
TED, COVE-
RED: proue
not the Prote-
stantes opiniō.
but the Catho-
lique doctrine
is declared.

6 For clearing of which Controuersie, consisting
especially in the signification of the wordes, and
termes euen now recited; First it is to be obserued,
that these termes *reputed, & imputed,* doe nomore
diminish the veritie of Iustice inherent in the soule,
then the word *esteme,* (being the same word in greke)
diminisheth the ministerie of S. Paul, & the other A-
postles, where he willeth the Corinthians [so to *e-*
steme of them, as the ministers of Christ] Neither
doth the word *couered,* anie more proue, that the
sinnes remaine in him whom God reputeth iust, then
where S. Peter saith [Charitie *couereth* the multitude of sinnes] which must needes signifie, that the
sinnes are taken away ; for mortal sinne can not consist with Charitie, the one being the spiritual death,
the other the spiritual life, of the soule . As it is impossible, that the same soule, should be at the same
time, both dead and aliue. Secondly obserue the
word *forgeuen* in the same sentence, which being of
a cleare signification, doth explaine the word *couered*
rather then contrariwise the same plaine terme *forge-*
uen

I. Cor. 4.
v. I.

I. Pet. 4.
v. 8.

Rom. 6.
v. 6. II.

I.
By examples
of like termes.

2.
By cleare ter-
mes, concer-
ning the same
point of doc-
trine.

men, can be explicated or wrested by the more ambi-guous word *couered.* Thirdly confider the like phrafe in anie other affaires. As when it is faid. A prince or Father, hath forgeuen, couered, and not imputed the former offences of his fubiect or child, al men tru-ly vnderftand, that thefe offences are quite taken a-way, and remaine no longer. When our Saniour faid to the woman accufed of adultrie [neither wil I con-demne thee] it was eafely and clearly vnderftoode, that by not condemning, or not imputing, he did forgeue her, and fo tooke away her finne, that it was not now remaining. And fo our Lord then admoni-fhed her as one void of finne faying : [goe, & now finne nomore.] Fourthly let the indifferent reader iudge, whether the doctrine that finnes be taken a-way, or that they remaine only couered and not im-puted, be more to Goddes honour, and glorie of his name ; Nay let a Proteftant declare, how his doc-trine is not iniurious to Goddes power, if he fay that God can not quite take away finnes; or to his mer-cie if he wil not ; or to his iuftice, if he neuer punifh them, and yet they alwaies remaine ; or to his truth, if he repute a man iuft, who indeede is not iuft. Let a Proteftant Doctor alfo tel you, how his doctrine is not iniurious to Chrift our Redemer, if his bloud and death be not effectual to wafh away the finnes of the penitent. And how it is not iniurious to the glorified Sainctes in heauen, arguing them as ftil infected with finnes. For if their finnes were not ta-ken away before they entred into heauen, they fhould ftil remaine therin, which is moft abfurd, for the death of finners is moft badde, *Mors peccatorum peſſima.* Finally this doctrine of Proteftantes drawne as they fuppofe from the places before recited, or fom few others, is indeede contrary, to very manie expreffe, and plaine textes of holie Scriptures, teftifying that

God

Ioan. 8.
v. 11.

Pſ. 33.
v. 22.
Pſ. 36.
v. 20.

3.
By the like man-ner of fpeach in other cafes ;

4.
By the abfurdi-tie of Prote-ftantes doc-trine : which is iniurious to God, to Chrift, to glo-rified Sainctes, and to al ho-neft people.

5.
By conference of other textes, farre moe in number which plainly teach

God by his grace, doth take away sinnes, wash them, wipe them away, heale the infirmitie or sicknes, create a cleane hart, renew a right spirit, make the dead soule to liue, make it white, iustifie, sanctifie, that is, make iust, & holie, & the like.

the Catholique doctrine.

Example of Dauid; who speaking of him self, and others, testifieth the Catholique doctrine.

7　So the Prophet Nathan denounced to king Dauid confessing his sinne, that [God tooke away his sinne] which the same Dauid thankfully acknowleged in a Psalme saying: [Our Lord hath heard the voice of my weeping: our Lord hath heard my petition, our Lord hath receiued my prayer.] And he prayed in these termes [Haue mercie on me o God: take away mine iniquitie, wash me more amply from mine iniquitie, cleanse me from my sinne. thou shalt sprinckle me with hyssope, and I shal be cleansed, thou shalt wash me, and I shal be made whiter then snow. Turne away thy face from my sinnes, & wipe away al mine iniquities. Create a cleane hart in me o God; and renew a right spirit in my bowels.] The same Royal Psalmist teacheth that sinners are made white and innocent [with snow (saith he) they shal be made white in selmon: our Lord wil not depriue them of good thinges that walke in innocencie; the people that shal be created (that is, made a new creature) shal praise our Lord (but praise is not glorious in the mouth of a sinner) who healeth al thine infirmities, who redemeth thy life fró deadly falling. As farre as the East is distant from the West, hath he made our iniquities farre from vs.] God selected a peculiar people, placed them in a plentiful land, bestowed on them manie special benefites, spiritual, and temporal, alto this end, that they might kepe his iustifications. Wherfore euerie faithful seruant of God knowing his owne insufficiency, praieth, that God by his grace, wil direct and strengthen him. [Would God (saith he) my waies may be directed to kepe thy

2. Reg. 12.
v. 13.

Ps. 6.
v. 9. 10.

Ps. 50. v.
3. 4. 9. 11.
12.

Ps. 67. v.
15. Ps. 83.
v. 13.
Ps. 101. v.
19. Gal. 6.
v. 15.
Eccle. 15.
v. 9. Ps.
102. v. 3.
4. 12. Ps.
104. v. 45.
Ps. 118. v.
5. 8. 12.
16. 20. 23.
&c.

thy iuftifications] becaufe the Law of God maketh
iuft ; which word *Iuftifications*, is nere thirtie times
in the fame pfalme, with other *Synonima* names of
Goddes Law, as *Teftimonies*, *Iudgementes*, *Iuftice*, *E-
quitie*, and *Veritie*, likewife verie often recited : Al
fignifying an abfolute taking away of finnes, and a

Pf. 142.
v. 11. 12.
real inherent Iuftice . So doth Goddes [good Spi -
rit conduct a penitent finner [into the right way,
for his owne names fake quicken him] that before
was dead; and that neither in fole imputation, nor i-
magination, but as the pfalmift confidently faith of
him felf [in equitie deftroying al enemies that afflict
the foule of his feruant.]

8   Yet let vs fee more teftimonies of other prophets.

If. 6. v.
5. 7. Ch.
33. v.
24. Ch.
43. v.
25.
An Angel of the high order [of Seraphims, touching Ifaias his mouth with a burning cole, faid vnto
him, thine iniquitie fhal be taken away, and thy finne
fhal be cleanfed.] Ifaias faith of other finners in the
Church of Chrift [Iniquitie fhal be taken away from
them.] By the penne of the fame Prophet, Chrift our
Lord faith, to his elect of mankind [I am he, I am he
that take cleane away thine iniquities for mine owne
fake : and I wil not remember thy finnes] So per -
fectly doth our Sauiour forgeue, and as it were for-

Iere. 2.
v. 22.
Ch. 33.
v. 6. 8.
geate. God by his Prophet Ieremie, recalling his
people from finne, faith : [returne ye reuolting children, and I wil heale your reuoltinges. Behold I wil
bring to them a ftarre, and health, and wil cure them;
and I wil cleanfe them from al their iniquitie wher -
in they haue finned to me.] In like maner by Eze-

Ezech.
18. v.
21.
chiel our Lord promifeth [If the impious fhal doe penance from al his finnes, which he hath wrought, &
fhal kepe al my precepts, and doe Iudgement & Iuftice ; liuiug he fhal liue, and fhal not die : al his iniquities which he hath wrougt, I wil not remember

22.
them; in his iuftice which he hath wrought, he fhal

The fame is
confirmed by
other Pro-
phets.

liue

liue : He shal viuificate his soule] make his soule to
liue , which by mortal sinne was spiritually dead.
[Make your selues a new hart and a new spirit ; and   3 **1**.
whie wil you die o house of Israel ? Because I wil   3 2.
not the death of him that dieth, saith our Lord God,
returne ye and liue . Our Lord wil returne (saith
Micheas the Prophet) and wil haue mercie on vs .
He wil lay away our iniquities : and he wil cast al   *Mich.* **7.**
our sinnes , into the botome of the sea . Come   *v.* 19.
together (saith the Prophet Sophonias) be ye ga-   *Soph.* 2.
thered o nation not beloued : ye that deserue to be   *v.* 1.
reiectted, repent, and God wil receiue you.] An
Angel said to the Prophet Zacharias [Take away   *Zach.* 3.
the filthie garment from the High Preist (defiled with   *v.* 4.
sinne) And the Angel said, Behold I haue taken a-
way thine iniquitie , and haue cloathed thee with
change of garmentes] signifying remission of sinne ,
with grace of faith, and good workes . For al is done
not by mannes power, but by diuine grace, and merites of Christ, whom al the Prophets foretold, and
S. Iohn Baptist shewed with his finger saying : [Be-   *Ioan.* **1.**
hold the Lambe of God, behold him that taketh a-   *v.* 29.
way the sinnes of the world] he saith not , behold
him that only couereth, dissembleth, winketh at, imputeth not, but simply and directly [taketh away the   8 . 9 . 12 .
sinne of the world] He gaue testimonie of the light :   *Io.* 5 . *v* . 21.
Christ our Sauiour [who is the true light, which
lightneth euerie man; who geueth power to be made
the sonnes of God .] who quickneth the dead in
soule .

Our Sauiour
did perfectly ,
& wholly cure,
bodie & soule.

9   In signe of true taking away of sinnes, and perfect curing of the soule, our Sauiour so perfectly healed the man sicke of the palsey, that immediatly ri-   *Mat.* 9.
sing he caried away his bed , wherin he was before   *v.* 2.
caried by others, him self not able neither to goe, nor
stand, and withal said to the man so cured [thy sinnes

are

are forgeuen thee] which was the farre greater worke, and benefite, and doubtles no leſſe perfect. yea and our Lord did the corporal cure [that the Scribes, & Phareſees] and al other incredulous, both then and euer after, euen our Proteſtant aduerſaries [might know that the ſonne of man hath power in earth to remitte ſinne] not imaginarie, as not to impute them, and yet they remaine, or to impute a man iuſt, that hath no iuſtice, but as our Lords maner was [to cure the whole man] wholly bodie, and ſoule perfectly :

Io.7. v. which the good [people then beleuing glorified God
22. (as the Euangeliſt writeth) that gaue ſuch power to
Mat.9. men] wel & rightly conſidering, that Chriſt the ſóne
v.7. of man, would alſo cómunicate this **power of remit-**ting ſinnes to ſome other [men.]

10   Which indeede he performed after his Reſurrection; when breathing vpon his Apoſtles, he ſaid :
Ioa. 20. [Receiue ye the holie Ghoſt : whoſe ſinnes you ſhal
v. 23. forgeue they are forgeuen] And that forgeuing importeth aboliſhing and taking away of ſinnes ; S. Peters wordes doe plainly teſtifie, exhorting the people
Act. 3. [to repent, & to be baptiſed : that your ſinnes (ſaith
v. 19. he) may be put out] S. Paul teaching that no man can be iuſtified by his workes without faith, addeth
Rom. 3. that ſome are iuſtified [*gratis*, by grace, by the Re-
v. 24. demption that is in Chriſt Ieſus] and ſo their former
25. ſinnes are remitted : for it is an vniuſt, and vntrue
Ch.4. v. thing, to account a wicked man iuſt. Therfore Chriſt
5. 25. iuſtifying the impious, doth indeede make him iuſt.
Ch 5. Be cauſe Chriſt [being deliuered for our ſinnes, roſe
19. Ch. againe for our iuſtification] For [as by diſobedience
6. v. 19. of one man, manie were made ſinners : ſo likewiſe by
22. the obedience of one man, manie ſhal be made iuſt]
1. Cor. euen as really the one as the other. [Doe not erre
6. v. 9. (ſaith he in an other Epiſtle) neither fornicators, nor
10. 11. ſeruers of Idols, nor adulterers (nor ſuch other malefactors

He gaue power to men to remitte ſinne, by their miniſterie.

The effect wherof, is iuſtification, & ſanctification.

Iefactors) fhal poffeffe the kingdome of God. And *Gal . 6 .*
fuch certes you were : but you are wafhed, you are *v . 16 .*
fanctified, you are iuftified] A moft real change from
finnes, to iuftice, and fanctitie, [made a new crea- *Ephef . 1 . v.*
ture, holie and immaculate in Goddesfight, in cha- *4 . Ch . 2 .*
ritie : when we were dead by finne, God quickned *v . 5 . Ch .*
vs in Chrift : clothed vs with the breft-plate of iuftice . *6 . v . 14 .*
Not iuftice in the law (of Moyfes) but that which *Phil . 3 . v.*
is of faith in Chrift, fpoyling your felues of the old *9 . Col . 3 .*
man, with his actes; and doing on the new hart .] *v . 9 .*
Chrift fo fanctifieth his faithful children, that [they
are fanctified, they are dead to finne, and liue to iu-
Chrift calleth ftice .] Againe that al are not wicked but fome holie,
fome iuft, and Chrift by his Angel fignifieth faying : [He that is in *Heb . 2 . v.*
holie . filth, let him be filthie yet : and he that is iuft, let him *11 . 1 . Pet .*
be iuftified yet : and he that is holie, let him be fancti- *2 . v . 24 .*
fied yet] made more iuft , made more holie. *Apoc . 22 .*
v . 11 .

Al mankinde fhal rife from death, at the day of ge-
neral iudgement.

ARTICLE. 49.

Al mens foules, God, whofe workes are perfect, whofe iudge- *Deut . 32 .*
and bodies , ments are right : creating man of bodie, and *v . 4 .*
muft be parted foule, which for iuft punifhment of fin, are to
by death, and be parted by death, hath ordained by his diuine pro-
reunited by the uidence , & omnipotent power, that our foules being
Refurrectió of immortal and naturally requiring vnion with our bo-
the bodies . dies, fhal receiue againe ech one their proper bodies :
and fo al mankinde fhal be conferued, and euerie one
receiue in foule and bodie together, according as *2 . Cor . 6 .*
they haue done, either good or euil . A point of faith *v . 10 .*
to fenfe, and natural reafon, fo hard, that no other
Article of Chriftian beleefe may feeme more ftrange .
Neuertheles is made credible by the ineffable power *Luc . 1 .*
of God *v . 37 .*

of God, to whom nothing is impoſſible. And is reueled to the Church, by his infallible word : beleued by al true Chriſtians, and not denied by Iewes, Turkes, nor Heretikes at this day; but only by ſome Paganes, and Atheiſtes.

2   Againſt which Miſcreants, this truth is firſt proued by the nature of mannes ſoule which is immortal, and hauing natural inclination to the bodie, mannes natural perfection requireth the coniunction of ſoule and bodie ; for that neither the ſoule, nor the bodie ſeperated, but both ioyned in one ſubſiſtāt perſon, is a man ; ſo that mankind ſhould periſh, & the immortal ſoule ſhould lacke his natural perfection if the bodie ſhould not riſe from death. But in cōfirmation of this truth, we haue firſt figuratiue examples in Enoch a Patriarch, and Elias a Prophet, conſerued without corruption in their corruptible mortal bodies, aboue the courſe of nature [Enoch waiked with God, and was ſeene nomore, becauſe God tooke him. he was tranſlated, that he ſhonld not ſee death. Elias aſcended in a firie chariot by a whirlewind into the aire ; of whoſe returne before the day of Iudgement, God haith foretold, by his Prophet Malachie ſaying [Behold I wil ſend you Elias the Prophet, before the day of our Lord come, great & dreadful. Theſe two being as yet preſerued aliue & are to dye in the end, may here ſuffice for example of Goddes power in this behalfe. Other examples of Goddes wil and power in this kind, we haue in diuers raiſed from death : A poore widowes ſonne raiſed by Elias ; And an other poore widowes ſonne by Elizeus ; an other dead man reuiued by touching Elizeus his bones. Our Sauiour raiſed an Archiſinagogues daughter being newly dead ; a widowes ſóne being caried towardes the ſepulchre ; and Lazarus being four daies dead, and alreadie buried. S, Peter

Gen . 5 .
v . 24 .
4. Reg. 2.
v . 11 .

Mat. 4 .
v . 5 .

3. Reg.
17 . v .
22 . 4 .
Reg . 4.
v . 25 .
Ch . 12 .
v . 21 .
Mat . 9 .
v . 25 .

The Reſurrection is proued to be conuenient by natural reaſon.

It is proued to be certainly true by holie Scriptures. It is prefigured in Enoch, and Elias.

It is ſhewed to be poſſible, by the raiſing of ſome from death.

raised a deuout woman called Tabitha from death. *Luc*. 7. *v*.
S. Paul restoared a yong man to life that was dead 13. *Io*. 11.
by a fal from an high place ; besides others, for al are *v*. 39. *Act*.
not written . Moreouer in reguard of Resurrection, 9. *v*. 40.
the Patriarch Iacob called this transitorie life, a pil- *Ch*. 20. *v*.
grimage saying to Pharao king of Egipt [the daies 9. 12. *Io*.
of the Pilgrimage of my life, are an hundred & thir- 20. *v*. 30.
tie yeares, and they are not come to the daies of my *Gen*. 4. *v*.
fathers, in which they were pilgrimes .] The same 9.
thing did king Dauid often meditate, and vtter in his
praiers to God saying : [I am a stranger with thee *Pf*. 38. *v*.
(o Lord) and a pilgrime as my Fathers . Thy iustifi- 13. *Pf*.
cations were song by me, in the place of my peregri- 118. *v*. 54.
nation . Woe to me, that my seiorning is prolonged :
my soule hath bene a seiorner.] Lastly on his death-
bed [We are pilgrimes before thee, and strangers as *Pf*. 119.
al our fathers] which he spake aswel of the soule as *v*. 5.
bodie, reioycing that at last, man shal be whollie re- 1. *Par*. 29.
stoared in the Resurrection, being as it were made *v*. 15.
yong : as the youth of an Eagle semeth to be renew- 2. *Cor*. 5.
ed ; so shal men be indeede from thenceforth immor- *v*. 8.
tal. Holie Iob in his great affliction, was singular- *Pf*. 102. *v*.
ly comforted, considering that at last his flesh & bo- 5.
die shal rise againe from death saying : [I know that *Iob* . 19. *v*.
my Redemer liueth, and in the last day, I shal rise 25. 26. 27.
out of the earth. And I shal be compassed againe with
my skinne, and in my flesh I shal see God : whom I
my self shal see, and mine eyes shal behold and none
other : this my hope is laid vp in my bosome.
3 God by his Prophet Isaias, denouceth to the Church, that al me shal rise fro death, som in glorie ; others
in miserie saying [Thy dead shal liue, my slaine shal
rise againe : a vake, and praise ve that dwel in the dust *If*. 26. *v*.
because the dew of the light, is thy dew, and the land 19.
of the Giantes, thou halt pluck do vne into ruine .]
Of the glorious in particular [Al flesh shal come to *Ch*. 66. *v*.
adore 29.

In reguard of the Resurrecti-on, this life is called a pilgri-mage.

Iob professed his beleefe of the Resurrecti-on.

The Prophets teach the Re-surrection of al mankind.

Ezech.
37. v. 3.

adore before my face : faith our Lord.] Ezechiel together with other Myfteries of the reduction of the Iewes from the captiuitie of Babylon, & of the Gentiles from Idolatrie; prophecieth the general Refurrection of al mankind, the Spirit of our Lord faying thus to him concerning dead bones prefented in a vi-

4. 5.

fion [Sonne of man, thinkeft thou thefe bones fhal liue ? Prophecie of thefe bones ; and thou fhalt fay to them; Drie bones, heare ye the word of our Lord. Thus faith our Lord God to thefe bones : Behold I wil put fpirit vnto you, and you fhal liue . And I prophecied as he had commanded me ; & there was made a foūd, & behold a cómotion, & bones came to bones,

7. 8.

euerie one to his iuncture . And I faw, and beholde vpon them finewes and flefh was growne vp, and a

10.

skinne was ftretched out in them aboue . And fpirit entred into them, and they liued : and they ftoode vpon their feete , an armie paffing great.] Daniel

Dan . 12.
v. 2.

prophecieth alfo of the Refurrection [of fome vnto life euerlafting, of others vnto reproach .] Iudas

2. Mac.
12. v.
43.

Machabeus [Religioufly thinking of the Refurrectiō, confidered that they which had taken their flepe with godlines, had very good grace laid vp for them.

4 Our Sauiour proued this Article of faith againft the Sadduces by fuch Scripture as they acknowleged, (for they denied greateft part of the old Teftament)

Mat. 22.
v. 31. 32.
32.
Exo. 3.
v. 6.

[Haue you not read (faid he) that which was fpoken of God faying to you : I am the God of Abraham, and the God of Ifaac, and the God of Iacob? He is not God of the dead, but of the liuing] So auouching that the holie Patriarches Abraham, Ifaac, & Iacob, though dead in bodie, yet are liuing , in that their foules being immortal, doe ftil ferue God , no leffe then they did, when they were in their bodies.

Mat. 22.
v. 29.
33.

And that by the power of God (which the Sadduces did not know, nor vnderftand the holie Scrip -

Chrift preached, and proued the Refurrection.

tures

tures) they fhould receiue, and reuificate their bodies
againe. For al liue to God. And not only the mul-   *Luc.20.*
titudes hearing it, nierueled at his doctrine, but alfo   *v.38.*
certaine of the Scribes anfwearing, faid to him ; Mai-   *39.40.*
fter, thou haft faid wel ; And further the Sadduces
durft not then aske him anie thing more. At an other
time our Sauiour auouched, that [the houre cometh   *Ioan. 5.*
and now it is (for this time of grace is come) when   *v. 25.*
the dead fhal heare the voice of the Sonne of God, &
they that haue heard fhal liue.] In confirmation wherof [he rofe him felf from death the third day, the firft
fructes of them that fleepe] as al the Apoftles & Euã-
geliftes doe abundantly teftifie.

Al the Euan-
gelifts teftifie
Chrifts Refur-
rection.

5   Which S. Paul preaching among the learned A-
thenians, they wondred, thinking [that he preached   *Act. 17. v.*
new goddes ; becaufe he preached to them Iefus, &   *18.24.31.*
the Refurrection] But [he preached God omnipotent
that made the world, and al thinges that are in it.
The Lord of heauen and earth; and that he wil iudge
the world in equitie, by a man whom he hath appointed, geuing al men faith, raifing him vp from the dead.
And when they had heard the Refurrectió of the dead,   *32.*
certaine indeede mocked; but certaine faid ; we wil
heare thee againe concerning this point .] By occa-
fion alfo of this doctrine [the Pharefes defended him   *Act. 23. v.*
againft the Sadduces.] Efpecially and at large, the   *8. Ch. 24.*
fame Apoftle confirmeth this doctrine of the general   *v. 15. 21.*
Refurrection, in his Epiftle to the Corinthians , by   *Ch. 26. v.*
Chrifts Refurrection, fhewing that [al men fhal rife]   *8.*
but with great difference in their ftates, of the iuft, &

As wel Chrifts
Refurrection,
as the future
general Refur-
rection of al
men, is pro-
mulgated as a
principal point
of faith.

vniuft, al fhal haue their bodies immortal and incor-   *1. Cor. 15.*
ruptible, but the wicked fubiect to vnfpeakable tor-   *v. 12. 51.*
ments, deformities, & al kind of miferies.

The bodies of
the wicked fhal
be immortal,
but moft mife-
rable.

6   Contrariwife the bleffed fhal haue their bodies indued with moft excellent qualities, as dowries of e-
ternal glorie, defcribed by the Apoftle in the fame
                                                        place

The bodies of
the bleffed fhal
be glorious, &

42. place, which are especially these foure. First *Impas-*
sibilitie, signified by these wordes [the bodie is sown
in corruption (and so is corrupted in the earth) but
shal rise in incorruption] not only inconsumptible,
for so likewise the bodies of the damned shal neuer
be consumed; but also impassible of anie greife, hurt,

Apoc. 21. or deformation [no mourning nor crying ; neither
v. 4. shal there be sorow anie more .] The second is *Cla-*
ritie or shyning brightnes, signified by the next wordes

43. [It is sowne in dishonour; it shal rise in glorie .]
The bodie dying, is pale, darke, obscure, but shal
rise most faire, cleare, and glistering, the glorie of
the soule redounding into the bodie, as Moyses face
shined like to an excellent lampe, or candle through

Exo . 34. a bright Lanthorne ; and shal so shine, that it shal not
v. 29. neede Sunne nor Moone to shine in it [they shal not
30. 33. neede the light of lampe (saith Christ in his Apoca-
35. lipse) nor the light of the Sunne, because our Lord
God doth illuminate them .] The third is *Agilitie*,

Apoc. 21. signified by the Apostle saying [It is sowne in infir-
v. 23. mitie ; it shal rise in power] Mortal Bodies, are
Ch. 22. weake, heauie, vnwealdie ; but rising from death,
v. 5. shal be strong, nimble, readie to moue in a moment
42. whether, and how farre soeuer, at the wil of the glo-
Sap 3 . rified soules [The iust shal shine, and as sparkes in
v. 7. a place of reedes, they shal runne abroade .] The
fourth, is *Penetrabilitie*, expressed by these wordes,
[It is sowne a natural bodie ; it shal rise a spiritual
bodie] Not that the bodie shal be changed in substance, from a corporal, into a spiritual substance, but
the same substance rising to glorie, shal be changed
in qualitie, and haue the power of a spirit, to penetrate an other bodie . As our Sauiour rising from

Mat. 28. death, penetrated [the monumēt wherin he was buri-
v. 2. ed . And entred into the house, the doares being shut,
Io. 20. v. where his Disciples were gathered] so likewise o-
19. 26.

ther

indued with
excellent qua-
lities.
Impassibilitie .

Claritie.

Agilitie.

Penetrabilitie.

ther glorified bodies of Sainctes, ſhal penetrate and paſſe through the ſolide firmament or anie other bodies, by the power of this ſpiritual qualitie. Yea their bodies alſo that ſhal be found aliue, when our Lord cometh to iudge, ſhal preſently dye, and reuiue againe [and be taken vp with the reſt into the cloudes to meete Chriſt in the aire : and ſo ſhal the bleſſed alwaies be with our Lord.]

Some ſhal both dye, and riſe againe the very laſt day.

1. Theſ. 4. v. 17.

The bleſſed ſhal enioy eternal Glorie ; according to their Merites.

ARTICLE. 50.

Mens purpoſes often faile, but Gods neuer.

Ennes intentions doe procede to execution, if they be not hindred by mutabilitie of wil, nor imbecilitie of power. Goddes purpoſes are infallibly performed, becauſe his wil is immutable, and his power is almightie. But how then doth it happen, that manie men doe periſh and are eternally damned, ſeeing, as S. Paul writeth, [God wil al men to be ſaued ?] For anſwear to this demand, and for explication of this, and other Scriptures, which may ſeme, but indeede are not, contrarie one to an other ; we muſt diſtinguiſh this ambiguous word, *Goddes wil* ; which is ſomwhere vnderſtood abſolutely, as when Iob ſaith [God is alone, & no man can turne away his cogitation ; and whatſoeuer his ſoule would, that hath he done.] The ſame ſaith the Royal Prophet [Our Lord is in heauen : he hath done al thinges whatſoeuer he would.] God him ſelf ſaith by his Prophet Iſaias [My counſel ſhal ſtand, and al my wil ſhal be done.] Likewiſe S. Paul ſaith : [On whom he wil he hath mercie ; for who reſiſteth his wil ?] ſignifying that none can reſiſt it. And in manie other places, the holie Scriptures

1. Tim. 2. v. 4.

Gods wil is either abſolute, or conditional.

Iob. 23. v. 12.
Pſ. 112. v. 11. Pſ. 134. v. 6.

Iſa. 46. v. 10. Rom. 9. v. 18. 19.

tures shew, that Goddes wil is alwaies performed, that is to say, *his absolute wil*. Neuerthelesse Goddes wil, is somewhere conditional ; so him self speaketh by his Prophet Ezechiel [Is the death of a sinner my wil saith our Lord God, and not that he conuert from his waies & liue ?] Againe in an other place [Liue I saith our Lord God, I wil not the death of the impious, but that the impious conuert from his waie & liue : conuert conuert ye from your most euil waies : and whie wil you dye o house of Israel ?] It is therfore Gods conditional, & antecedent wil, that al men should be saued : but his absolute & consequent wil, that iust men liuing and dying his true seruants shal be saued : wicked men, liuing and dying in mortal sinne, shal be damned. Euen as a good Prince, and other iust Iudges, would haue al subiectes to liue so long as they can by nature, but wil haue traitors, murderers, and other egregious malefactors, put to death : so God would haue al men to flee from sinne, doe good workes, and be eternally saued ; but wil neuerthelesse condemne al obstinate and impenitent sinners to euerlasting paine for their sinnes. Both which are manifestly testified by innumerable holie Scriptures. We shal first recite some places concerning the blessed which shal be glorified, & then touching the wicked which must be damned.

2 In the old Testament, this doctrine is plainly signified, first by Goddes merciful procedinges towardes mankind, by whose sinne, though heauen was shutte that none could enter ; and [Adam and Eue were cast out of Paradise] yet was not that place destroyed, but the gate therof kept by Angels] And [a Redeiner was promised] by whom men should be ransomed, and haue new accesse vnto life euerlasting in the kingdome of heauen. Goddes special care of Abel to reuenge his innocent [bloud, which cried to

him

*Ezech.
18. v.
23. Ch.
33. v.
11.*

*Gen. 2.
v. 8. Ch.
3. v. 23.
24. Ch.
3. v. 15.
Ch. 4.
v. 9.*

God hath manie wayes signified, that al shal be eternally saued: which wil cooperate with his grace.

him out of the earth] gaue vs to vnderſtand, that he
would reward the ſame holie Martyr, with an eternal crowne of glorie. And as the conſeruation of E-
noch in fleſh without corruption, ſignifieth the Reſurrection : So his preſent eſtate wherin he contem-
plateth God and diuine Myſteries ; repreſenteth the
ioyes of heauen , which he, and al other Sainctes ſhal
poſſeſſe, in perfect fruition of God . To other holie
Patriarches our Lord promiſed an eſpecial inheritance , a land flowing with milke and honie ; in figure of the true land of the liuing . To Moyſes he
promiſed the thing it ſelf more expreſly ſaying : [I
wil ſhew thee al good] But that he might vnderſtand, that it ſhould be performed in the life to come,
not in this preſent world, he added ſaying : [Man
ſhal not ſee my face and liue .] To his whole people
in general our Lord promiſed manie temporal & earthly bleſſinges, as to a carnal people, in figure of ſpiritual and heauenly rewardes, to his perfect ſeruantes .
Yet with expreſſe conditions [If you walke in my
preceptes, and kepe my commandementes and doe
them ; I wil geue you raine in their ſeaſons, and the
earth ſhal bring forth her ſpring : and the trees ſhal
be repleniſhed with fruictes : the threſhing of your
harueſt, ſhal reach vnto vintage ; and the vintage,
ſhal reach vnto ſowing time ; and you ſhal eate your
bread to your fil , and without feare ſhal you dwel in
your land. Thou ſhalt know (ſaith Moyſes to the
ſame peohle) that the Lord thy God, is a ſtrong and
faithful God ; keping his couenant and mercie , to
them that loue him, and to them that kepe his Preceptes, vnto a thouſand generations . Benediction if
you obey the commandements of the Lord your God,
which I command you this day] and manie the like
in the Law of Moyſes .

Ch. 5. v.]
24.

Ch. 15. v.
18. Ch. 26.
v. 3 . Ch.
28. v. 13 .

Exo. 33. v.
19. 20.

Leuit. 26.
v. 3. 4. 5.

Deut. 7.
v. 9.

Ch. 11. v.
27.

The ſame is proued by the Prophets. 3. To theſe proſes we may further adde predictions
of the

of the Prophets : who speake more directly of eternal rewards for good workes . Esdras hath prefixed this title to a certaine Psalme [vnto the end] which signifieth that the Psalme perteyneth to thē that beleue in Christ, who is in the end of thé law [for her that obteyneth the inheritance] that is, the faithful iust soule, that ouercometh her spiritual enemies, and gaineth the inheritance of eternal glorie in heauen . And the Psalmist inuiteth al the faithful to reioyce in Christs iust Iudgements saying : [Let al be glad that hope in thee ; they shal reioyce for euer : and thou (o Christ) shalt dwel in them . And al that loue thy name shal glorie in thee, becaufe thou wilt blesse the iust] when our Sauiour shal say [Come ye blessed of my Father possesse you the kingdome prepared for you, from the fundation of the world.] In an other Psalme after description of the meanes to attaine eternal life, which are comprised in these two pointes, to flee frō euil, and to doe good; he concludeth saying : [He that doeth these thinges shal not be moued for euer] he shal not dwel in a transitorie tabernacle, which is purpofely made to be remoued from place, to place , but in the euerlasting firme [habitation of God, worldes without end] where God him self is the inheritance . [Our Lord (saith he) the portion of mine inheritance ; and of my cuppe] the reward of suffering, and of drinking the cuppe of tribulations for iustice sake. [I, in iustice, shal appeare in thy sight : I shal be filled when thy glorie shal appeare] this is [to passe into a meruelous Tabernacle, euen to the house of God. Man shal say : If certes there be fruict to the iust ; there is a God certes iudgeing them on the earth.] If God punish sinne, as assuredly he wil ; then wil he also reward the iust, though iustice be likewise Goddes free gift, without merit. For [our Lord wil geue both grace and glorie] grace, wherby

Pf. 5. v. 1.

Rom. 10. v. 4.

Apoc. 21. v. 7.

Pf. 5. v. 13.

Mat. 25. v. 34.

Pf. 14. v. 1. 2. 5.

Pf. 15. v. 5. Pf. 16. v. 15.

Pf. 41. v. 5. Pf. 57. v. 12.

Pf. 61. v. 13. Pf. 83. v. 12.

to merite, and glorie for merite [Our Lord became   *Pf*. 93 . *v*.
my refuge : and my God, the help of my hope.] The   22.
faithful by Goddes fpecial grace, paffe through manie tribulations [of the torrent in the way he fhal   *Pf*. 109.
drinke : therfore fhal he exalt the head] for fuffe-   *v*. 7.
ring perfecution in a iuft caufe, fhal be highly exalted in glorie [they that fow in teares, fhal reape in   *Pf*. 125.
ioyfulnes . Going, they went and wept cafting their   *v*. 5. *Pf*.
feedes : but coming, they fhal come with exultation   138. *v*. 17.
carying their fheaues] To me [to my conceipt (faih
the fame Royal Pfalmift) thy frendes (o God) are be-
come exceedingly honorable; their principalitie is ex-   *Pf*. 139 . *v*.
cedingly ftrengthned . the righteous fhal dwel with   14 .
thy countenace] fighifying that beatitude confifteth
in feing God, being made cleane in hart [al faire with   *Cant*. 4. *v*.
out fpotte.] For [he that findeth me (faith eternal   8 . *Pro*. 8.
wifdome) fhal finde life] which is euerlafting [For   *v* . 35 .
the iuft fhal liue for euer ; and their reward is with our   *Sap* . 5 . *v* .
Lord, and cogitation of them , with the higheft :   16 . 17.
therfore fhal they receiue a kingdome of honour, &
a crowne of beautie, at the hand of our Lord] As alfo an other diuine writer coucludeth his booke, ad-
uifing al men to labour for this crowne [work your   *Eccle*. 51.
work (faith he) before the time : and our Lord wil   *v* . 39.
geue you your reward in his time .] God by his o-
ther Prophets, doth likewife much inculcate the future punifhment of the wicked : and reward of the
iuft. Let one place ferue for example of manie ,
where by Ifaias, he expoftulateth with the Iewes for
their wilful obftinacie, contemning his frequent admonitions; and preferring their owne willes before
his . For which he denounceth their temporal ruine,
with loffe of his grace; and withal forefheweth the
calling of the Gentiles; therin fignifying the eternal damnation, and faluation, of his enemies, & feruantes, according to their diuers defertes [Becaufe   *Ifa*. 65 . *v*.
                                          faith   12. 13. 14.

(ſaith he) I called, and you haue not anſweared ; I ſpake, and you haue not heard, and you did euil in mine eyes ; & you haue choſé the thinges that I would not. For this cauſe , thus ſaith our Lord God : Behold my ſeruantes ſhal eate, and you ſhal be hungrie ; behold my ſeruantes ſhal drinke, and you ſhal be thirſtie. Behold my ſeruantes ſhal reioice, and you ſhal be confounded : behold my ſeruantes ſhal praiſe for ioyfulnes of hart , & you ſhal crie for ſorow of hart, & for contrition of ſpirit, you ſhal howle . But al that (are truly penitent and) conuert to God, he wil ſpare as a man ſpareth his ſonne , ſeruing him. then you ſhal ſee (ſaith our Lord) what is betwene him that ſerueth God, and ſerueth him not. And there ſhal riſe to you that feare my name, the Sunne of Iuſtice, and health in his winges . And you ſhal treade the impious, when they ſhal be aſhes vnder the ſole of your feete, in the day that I doe, ſaith the Lord of hoſtes] meaning the day of general Iudgement, which wil be the day, doing al that , wherof in the meane time he premoniſheth al men .

Mal . 3 .
v . 17 .
18 .

Ch .4. *v* .
2 . 3 .

4   In this meane while alſo, ſince Chriſt redemed mankind, he hath opened the gates of heauen , that iuſt and purified ſoules, doe enter in, and receiue the reward of eternal glorie. And therfore, aſwel his Precurſor, as him ſelf [preached, that the kingdome of heauen was at hand] And our Sauiour taught the way and meanes to obtaine it, by the perfection of vertues, of which, the kingdome of heauen is the reward [Bleſſed (ſaith he) are the poore in ſpirit, for theires is the kingdome of heauen] And for great vertues, very great rewardes [Bleſſed are ye when they ſhal reuile you, and perſecute you, and ſpeake al that nought is againſt you, vntruly for my ſake : be glad and reioice, for your reward is very great in heauen.] Exhorteth expreſly to doe almes-deedes, to pray and

Mat . 3 .
v . 2 . *Ch* .
4. *v* .17 .

Ch .5. *v* .
3 . *&c* .
10 . 11 .
12 .

Iuſt retributiō ſhal be in the end, both to Gods ſeruants, and his enemies.

Since Chriſts Aſcenſion al purified ſoules aſcend into heauen .

faſt

falt, and that in perfect maner, fincere intention, *Ch.6.v.*2.
without al hipocrifie [fo to heape vp to your felues 9. 16. 20.
treafures in heauen] Our Lord alfo teacheth in par- 1. *Tim.*6.
ticular, that [he which receiueth a Prophet in the *v.*19. *Ch.*
name of a Prophet, fhal receiue the reward of a Pro- 10. *v.* 41.
phet : and he that receiueth a iuft man, in the name 42. *Mar.*
of a iuft man; fhal receiue the reward of a iuft man. 9. *v.* 41.
And whofoeuer fhal geue drinke to one of thefe litle
ones, a cuppe of cold water, only in the name of a
Difciple, Amen I fay to you, he fhal not loofe his reward. When thou makeft a feaft, cal the poore, fee- *Luc.* 14. *v.*
ble, lame, and blind; and thou fhalt be bleffed, be- 13. 14.
caufe they haue not to recompence thee : for recom- *Mat.* 16.
pence fhal be made thee in the refurrection of the *v.* 27.
iuft. For the Sonne of man fhal come in the glorie of 2. *Cor.* 5.
his Father, with his Angels; and then wil he render *v.* 10. *Ch.*
to euerie man according to his workes.] And by vi- 20. *v.* 2.8.
gour of a couenant made with the faithful workmē: *Ch.* 25. *v.*
they fhal receiue their hire, the Iudge alfo declaring 35. 46.
the reafon why they receiue it faying : [for I was an *Luc.* 6. *v.*
hungred, and you gaue me to eate; I was a thirft, & 38. *Mat.*
you gaue me to drinke. Geue and it fhal be geuen 13. *v.* 8.
to you; good meafure, and preffed downe, and fha- 23. *Io.* 14.
ken together, and running ouer, they fhal geue into *v.* 2. *Mat.*
your bofome. Some yeldeth fruict an hundred folde; 19. *v.* 29.
fome three-fcoare, fome thirtie. In my Fathers houfe *Mar.* 10.
(faith our Sauiour) there be manie manfions. And *v.* 30.
euerie one that hath left houfe, or brethren, or fifters,
or father, or mother, or wife, or cliildren, or landes
for my name fake, fhal receiue an hundred folde in
this time (that is increafe of grace, fpiritual comfort
and ftrength, which infinitly counterpofeth al worldly commodities) and in the world to come, life e-
uerlaftiug.] So was poore Lazarus, made ftrong in *Luc.* 16.
patience, and { dying, was carried by Angels into A- *v.* 22. *Ch.*
brahãs bofom.] They [that fhalbe coũted worthie of 20. *v.* 35.
                                                that 36.

Heauen fhal be
geuen for good
workes, done
with true faith,
by Gods grace.

Ioan. 5. that world and glorious Refurrection, can dye no-
v. 29. more, for they are equal to Angels; and they are the
Ch. 16.v. Sonnes of God, feing they are the fonnes of the Re-
22. furrection. For they that haue done good thinges,
shal come forth into the Refurrection of life . Now
indeede you haue forow, but I wil fee you againe, &
your hart shal reioice, and your ioy no man shal take
from you .] Thefe and manie like fpeaches did our B.
Sauiour vtter, which his holie Apoftles haue diligent-
Rom. 2. ly promulgated by their preaching and writing [God
v. 6. 7. in his iuft iudgemencts (faith S. Paul) wil render
8. to euerie one according to his workes . To them truly that according to patience in good worke, feeke
glorie, and houonr, and incorruption, life eternal.
But to them that are of contention, and that obey
not the truth, but geue credite to iniquitie; wrath,
9. 10. and indignation . Tribulation and anguish vpon euerie foule of man that worketh euil : but glorie, and
honour, and peace, to euerie one that worketh good .
Ch. 6.v. Now being made free from finne, you were made fer-
18. 19. uantes to iuftice . I fpeake an humane thing becaufe
of the infirmitie of your flesh : For as you haue exhibited your members to ferue vncleannes and iniquitie vnto iniquitie : fo now exhibite your mem-
22. bers to ferue iuftice vnto fanctification . Now being
made free from finne, and become feruantes to God ,
you haue your fruict vnto fanctification : but the end
Ch. 8.v. life euerlafting. If you liue according to the flesh ,
13. 14. you shal dye : but if by the fpirit you mortifie the
deedes of the flesh, you shal liue . For whofoeuer are
led by the fpirit of God, they are the fonnes of God.
And if the fonnes, heires alfo; heires truly of God ,
17. and coheires of Chrift : yet if we fuffer with him, that
18. we may alfo be glorified with him . For I thinke that
the paffions of this time, are not condigne to the glo-
2.Cor.4. rie to come that shal be reueled in vs . For that our
v.17.18. 						I i i 3 						tribulation

tribulation which presently is momentanie and light, *Ch.5.v.1.*
worketh aboue measure excedingly, an eternal weight
of glorie in vs, we not considering the thinges that
are seene, but that are not seene. For the thinges *1.Cor.2.*
that are seene, are temporal, but those that be not *v.9.Is.64,*
seene, are eternal. For we know that if our earthly *v.4.*
house of this habitation be dissolued, we haue a building of God, a house not made with hand, eternal
in heauen ; that which eye hath not seene, nor eare
hath heard, neither hath it ascended into the hart of
man, what thinges God hath prepared for them that
loue him. Euerie one shal receiue his owne reward, *Ch.3.v.8.*
according to his owne labour. I doe al thinges (saith *Ch.9.v.*
the same Apostle) for the Gospel, that I may be made *23.24.25,*
partaker therof. So runne, that ye may obteine a *Ch.15.v.*
crowne incorruptible. As there is one glorie of the *41.42.*
Sunne, an other glorie of the Moone, and an other
glorie of the Starres ; and starre differeth from starre in
glorie : so likewise the Resurrection of the dead. Ther *58.*
fore my beloued brethren, be stable and immoueable, abounding in the worke of our Lord ; alwaies
knowing that your labour is not in vaine in our Lord.
He that soweth sparingly, sparingly also shal reape: *2.Cor.9,*
and he that soweth in blessinges, of blessinges also *v.6.*
shal reape. He that soweth in his flesh, of the flesh *Gal.6.v.*
also shal reape corruption : but he that soweth in the *8.*
spirit, of the spirit shal reape life euerlasting. ser- *Ephes.6.*
uing with a good wil as to our Lord, and not to men, *v.8.*
knowing that euerie one, what good soeuer he shal
doe, that shal he receiue of our Lord: The retributi- *Colos.3.v.*
on of inheritance ; that you may be counted worthie *24.*
of the Kingdome of God ; for the which also you suffer.] Of him self he saith [There is laid vp for me *2.Thes.1.*
a crowne of Iustice, which our Lord wil render to me *v.5.*
in that day a iust Iudge. (where he addeth touching *2.Tim.4.*
al other blessed seruantes of God saying) And not on- *v.8,*
ly to

S. Paul did good workes ; and exhorted al the faithful to doe good workes, for the ganing of eternal reward.

Heb. 6. ly to me, but to them also that loue his coming . For
v. 10. God is not vniuſt, that he ſhould forgeat your work
and loue which you haue ſhewed in his name; which
haue miniſtred to the Sainctes, and doe miniſter.] So
this great Apoſtle teacheth in al his Epiſtles, theſe
v. 2. *Ch.* fundamental pointes of faith, that [God wil iuſtly
11. *v.* 6. iudge al this world : that he is a rewarder to them
26. that ſeeke him] And that his ſeruantes may confi-
Ch. 12. dētly in their good workes and ſufferinges [loke vnto
v. 1. 2. the remuneration] And therfore [we hauing ſo great
abundance of witneſſes, laying away al ſinne, that
compaſſeth vs; by patienſe let vs runne to the ſight
propoſed, looking on the auctour of faith, and the
conſummator Ieſus Chriſt, who (ioy being propoſed vnto him) ſuſteined the Croſſe, contemning confuſion; & ſitteth on the right hand of the ſeat of God.]

5 Likewiſe the other Apoſtles preached this
Article of euerlaſting life; encoraging the faithful,
in regard therof, to doe good workes, and patiently
Iac. 1. to ſuffer tribulations for iuſtice ſake [Bleſſ.d is the
v. 12. man (ſaith S. Iames) that ſuffereth tentation : for
when he hath bene proued, he ſhal receiue the crowne
of life, which God hath promiſed to them that loue
1. *Pet.* 1. him.] S. Peter praiſeth God [for his ineſtimable
v. 3. 4. mercie in regenerating vs, vnto this liuely hope, vnto an inheritance incorruptible, incontaminate, and
that can not fade. That the probation of faith, much
7. more pretious then gold (which is proued by the fire)
may be fonnd vnto praiſe, and glorie, and honour,
Ch. 4. in the reuelation of Ieſus Chriſt. Cōmunicating with
v. 13. the paſſions of Chriſt, be glad : that in the reuelation
Ch. 15. alſo of his glorie, you may be glad reioycing. And
v. 4. when the Prince of Paſtors ſhal appeare, you alſo may
2. *Pet.* 1. receiue the incorruptible crowne of glorie. Wher-
v. 10. 11. fore brethren labour the more, that by good workes
you may make ſure your vocation and election. for
doing

Other Apo-
ſtles often
teach the ſame.

doing thefe thinges, you fhal not finne at anie time. For fo there fhal be miniftred to you abūdantly, an entrāce into the euerlafting kingdome of our Lord & Sauiour Iefus Chrift.] S. Iohn exhorteth al to admire with him, confidering [what maner of Charitie the heauēly Father hath vouchfaifed vs, that we fhould be named, and be (by grace and adoption) the fonnes of God [My dearest (faith he) now we are the Sonnes of God, and it hath not yet appeared what we fhal be, we know, that when he fhal appeare, we fhal be like to him, becaufe we fhal fee him as he is .] For this is al in al, the very effential & perfect Beatitude, to fee God. And therfore he aduifeth by al meanes, to perfeuer in this grace [Looke to your felues (faith he to a chriftian Ladie , & her fonnes, and in them to al the iuft in this life) that you loofe not the thinges which you haue wrought , but that you may receiue a ful reward .] The very fame doth S. Iude the Apoftle alfo inculcate faying : [Keepe your felues in the loue of God, expecting the mercie of our Lord Iefus Chrift , vnto life euerlafting .]

1. Tim. 3. v. 1. 2.

2. Ioan. v. 8.

Iude. v. 21.

Chrift our Lord againe confirmeth his promife of eternal glorie to the iuft .

6 Our B. Sauiour againe in his reuelation to S. Iohn, willeth him to write to the Bifhoppes of the feuen Churches of Azia, admonifhing them, and in them al the faithful, to fight manfully in fpiritual warfare againft finne : promifing in diuers formes of fpeach, but al in one fenfe that they fhal receiue for their reward in heauen euerie one euerlafting life. [To him that ouercometh (faith he) I wil geue to eate of the tree of life, that is in the paradife of my God . He that fhal ouercome, fhal not be hurt of the fecond death . To him that ouercometh I wil geue the hidden Manna. He that fhal ouercome, & kepe my workes vnto the end; I wil geue him power oucr the nations. He that fhal ouercome, fhal be vefted

Apoc. 2. v. 5. &c.

7.

11.

17.

26.

Ch. 3. v. 5.

sted in white garments, and I wil not put his name
out of the booke of life. He that shal ouercome, I
wil make him a piller in the temple of my God: &
he shal goe out no more. He that shal ouercome I wil
geue vnto him, to sitte with me in my throne: as I
also haue ouercome, and haue sitten with my Father
in his Throne.] After this he signifieth in like vision, that certaine are signed which shal be saued of the
Tribes of Israel. But incomparably manie more of
the Gentiles, which no man can number, of al Nations and Tribes, and peoples, and tongues, cloathed
with white Robes, and Palme in their handes. In
particular, amongst manie other mysteries, pertaining
to the Churches spiritual warfare, and victorie, our
Lord hath foreshewed, that his two special witnesses
which shal be slaine by Antichrist, shal rise frō death,
be called into heauen, and ascend thither in sight of
their enemies. Finally al the elect, shal be prepared
and called to the mariage feast of Christ, and his glorious Spouse the Church. [Bookes shal be opened,
al mens workes made knowne, and al indeede of
those thinges which are written in the bookes, according to their workes.] Then wil our B. Sauiour
[wipe away al teares from the eyes of his Sainctes ; &
death shal be nomore, nor mourning, nor crying ;
neither shal there be sorow anie more ; which first
thinges are gone, and he that sate in the Throne said
[Behold I make al thinges new. He that shal ouer -
come, shal possesse these thinges : I wil be his God,
and he shal be my sonne. Blessed are they that wash
their stoales, that their power may be in the tree of
life, and they may enter by the gate into the Citie.

12.

21.

Ch. 7.
v. 4. 5.
&c.
9.
Ch. 11.
v. 3. 7.
11. 12.

Ch. 19.
v. 7. 8.
9.
Ch. 20.
v. 12. 13.
Ch. 21.
v. 4. 5.

7.
Ch. 22.
v. 14.

The

The wicked ſhal be eternally puniſhed:
for their ſinnes.

ARTICLE. 51.

Al penitent ſinners are puniſhed temporally. and al which are finally impenitent, are damned eternally.

NOw we are to declare in like maner, the ſecond part of the general Iudgement. For as [Eternal life is the fruict of grace, and the reward of good workes (by vertue of the ſame grace) ſo [the ſtipend of ſinne is death.] And the ſame is general, that for the firſt ſinne of Adam, he, and al his progenie, became ſubiect therto. Yea though God gaue him grace of repentance, with remiſſion of ſinne; yet temporal death remained a iuſt debt for the ſinne remitted, and that in al mankind. Seing therfore euen thoſe which through grace are trulie penitent, [waſhed, ſanctified, and iuſtified] and ſo made free from eternal damnation, which is the ſecond death; muſt neuertheleſſe, by the iuſtice of God, dye temporally: by the ſame diuine iuſtice, thoſe which dye impenitent, muſt nedes be eternally puniſhed, becauſe they perſiſt obſtinate in their ſinne, for euer inconuertible from the guilte therof, and incorrigible in minde.

Rom. 6. v 4
23.

1. *Cor.* 6.
v. 11.
Apoc. 21.
v. 8
1. *Cor.* 15.
v. 22.
Pſ. 113. v.
25.
Iſa. 9. v.
12. 17. 21.
Ch. 10. v.
14.

Examples of puniſhment for ſinnes.

2 Of which iuſt puniſhment of obſtinate and impenitent ſinners, we haue very manie memorable examples, and expreſſe teſtimonies in holie Scriptures. For enormious ſinnes, the whole world was drowned, only iuſt Noe, and his familie, in al but eight perſons, excepted. The preſumptuous builders of a Towre in Babel were confounded in their tongues, and diſperſed vpon the face of the earth, to ſeeke new habitations. The Cities of Sodome and Gomorrha, with other three townes adioyning, were ſudenly burned with fire and brimſtone rayning from

Gen. 7. v.
23.
Ch. 11. v. 7.
Ch. 19. v.
24.

heauen

Exo. 7. *v*.	heauen. The Egiptians were plagued tenne times,
20. *Ch*. 8.	in the space of few daies; and at last, Pharao their
v. 6. 16.	king, with al his armie, not one escaping, were
24. *Ch*. 9.	drowned in the redde sea. Manie of the children of
v. 6. 10.	Israel, for murmuring, for gluttonie, and adultrie,
23. *Ch*. 10.	and other sinnes, were punished with fire, with ser-
v. 13. 22.	pentes, and other plagues, that al aboue the age of
Ch. 14. *v*.	twentie, which came out of Egipt, in number aboue
27. 28.	sixe hundred, & three thousand men, able to beare
Nu. 1. *v*.	armes, and twentie two thousand Leuites, died in the
46. *Ch*. 3.	desert, except two only persons, Iosue, and Caleb.
v. 39. *Ch*.	Amongst the rest, Core, Dathan, and Abiron, with
11. *v*. 2.	their complices and folowers, for their rebellious
33. *Ch*. 14.	schisme, were partly swalowed vp in the gaping earth
v. 23. 24.	and so descended quick into hel, partly were burnt
30. 38.	to death by fire from heauen, fourtene thousand, se-
	uen hundred of the vulgare sort, besides the capital
Ch. 16. *v*.	schismatikes. The seauen Nations that inhabited the
30. 31. &c.	land of Chanaan, were destroyed for their abomina-
49.	ble Idolatrie, & other execrable sinnes.
Leuit. 18. *v*.	3 Neither did God omitte, to punish the sinnes of
24. 25.	his peculiar chosen people, but often suffered them
Deut. 7. *v*.	to be oppressed by their enemies, and be caried into
10. *Ch*. 8.	captiuitie, by the Assirians, and Babilonians. which
v. 19. 20.	temporal punishmentes by Goddes mercie, are whol-
Iosue. *	some medicines to manie persons, and some peoples
Iudic. *	bringing them to repentance; to others, a begin-
Reg. *	ning of their damnation. And such as liued wickedly
4. *Reg*. 17.	and yet prospered in this world; escaped not the iust
4. *Reg*. 25.	hand of God, but as holie Iob writeth of carelesse
Iob. 21. *v*.	worldlinges, and carnal Epicures [they lead their
13. *Ps*. 1.	daies in wealth, and in a moment they goe downe
v. 5. 7.	to hel.] The same doth the Royal Prophet Dauid
Ps. 48. *v*.	teach saying [The impious shal be as the dust, which
15. *Ps*. 93.	the winde driueth from the face of the earth. the way
v. 1. 23.	of the impious shal perish. As sheepe (that can not

Punishment is sometime as a medicine bringing to repentance: sometime a beginning of hel.

Worldlings, not punished in this world, dying, descend into hel.

helpe

helpe them felues) they are put in hel; death fhal
feede vpon them. The God of reuenges, wil repay
them their iniquitie · In their malice he wil deftroy
them; the Lord our God wil deftroy them. Our iuft
Lord wil cutte the neckes of finners. The head of
their compaffe (the fumme of their wicked deuifes)
the labour of their lippes (their fweete wordes of
futtle perfuafions) fhal couer them (ouerwhelme
them with perdition) Coles fhal fal vpon them, thou
fhalt caft them downe into fire of hel.] Then at laft
fhal the wicked [know, that by what thinges a man
finneth; by the fame alfo he is tormēted.] In reguard
of which miferable and eternal perdition, the wife
man faith : that [the wicked in al their fubtilties,
and fweete inticementes wherwith they flatter them
felues, and allure others to finne, doe nothing els in
effect, but lie in wait againft their owne bloud, and
practife deceipt againft their owne foules. His owne
iniquities doe take the impious; and he is faft bound
with the ropes of his finnes. He fhal dye. becaufe
he hath not had difcipline, and in the multitude of
his folie he fhal be deceiued . He that fhal finne a-
gainft me (faith wifdome) fhal hurt his owne foule.
Al that hate me loue death.] So the Prophets cal
eternal damnation, death, becaufe it is an euerlafting
death : wherin the damned are as if they were alwaies
dying in extreme torments, & neuer find end therof.
the foule being immortal, the malice of the damned
perpetual, and Goddes iuftice eternal. [Topheth
(enlargement, fignifying hel) is prepared (faith I-
faias) fince yefterday (from the beginning of finne
for the diuel and his Angels) prepared of the King,
deepe and wide. the norifhmentes therof, fire, and
much wood : the breath of our Lord, as a torrent of
brimftone kindling it.] Al [that hold the Law,
(faitg the Prophet Baruch) fhal come to life; but

Pf. 128.*v*:
4. *Pf.* 139.
v.10.11;

Sap. 11.*v*:
17.

Prou. i.*v*:
11.12.13.
14.18.
Ch. 5.*v*.
22.

23.

Ch. 8.*v*:
39.

Ezech. 18:
v.23. &*c*.

Ifa. 30.*v*:
33.

Mat. 25:
v.41.

Bar. 4.*v*:
1.

they

Mat. 3.
v. 5.
16. 18.
they that haue forſaken it, into death. I wil come to you (ſaith our Lord) in iudgement, and wil be a ſwift witnes to ſorcerers, and adulterers, and to the periured] and other wicked ſinners. As for the penitent, he ſaith to them [You ſhal ſee what is betwene the iuſt & the impious ; betwene him that ſerueth God, & ſerueth him not.]

Mat. 3.
v. 12.
Luc. 3.
v. 17.
4   Of this Iudge, and general Iudgement, S. Iohn Baptiſt preached to al ſinners ſaying : [His fanne is in his hand, and he ſhal cleane purge his floore, and wil gather his wheate into his barne, but the chaffe he wil burne with vnquencheable fire.] Our Sauiour alſo admoniſhed al [not to feare them that kil the bodie, and are not able to kil the ſoule, but feare him that can deſtroy both ſoule, and bodie into hel] For

Luc. 16.
v. 22.
an example declareth that when [poore Lazarus for his patience was caried by Angels into Abrahams boſome ; the rich glutton was buried in hel] moſt ex-

Mat. 25.
v. 31. 41.
46.
preſly foretold vs that [the ſonne of man (him ſelf) wil, at the laſt day, come in Maieſtie with his Angels, and then wil ſeperate one from an other, as the Paſtor ſeperateth the ſheepe from the goates ; on his right hand, and left] where after he ſhal haue called the iuſt vnto eternal glorie ; he wil iudge the wic-

Mat. 13.
v. 42.
50.
ked ſaying [Get ye away from me ye curſed into fire euerlaſting ; and theſe ſhal goe into torment euerlaſting. then ſhal the Angels caſt them into the fournace of fire ; there ſhal be weping, and gnaſhing of teeth.]

2. Theſ.
1. v. 8.
9.
Iac. 1.
v. 15.
5   S. Paul deliuered the ſame doctrine to the Gentiles ſaying : [Our Lord Ieſus wil come in flame of fire, geuing reuenge to them that know not God, & that obey not the Goſpel, who ſhal ſuffer eternal paines in deſtruction.] S. Iames teacheth, that [ſinne, when it is conſummate (committed by deliberate conſent of the wil) engendreth death.] If

Side notes:

S. Iohn Baptiſt, and alſo Chriſt, admoniſhed to flee from ſinne for feare of hel.

The Apoſtles often admoniſhed the ſame.

the iuſt man (ſaith S. Peter) ſhal ſcarcely be ſa- *1. Pet. 4.*
ued ; where ſhal the impious & ſinner appeare ? For *v. 17. 18.*
iudgement beginneth at the houſe of God] ſignifying that puniſhment is alſo due for ſinnes remitted.
And that wicked men ſhal not eſcape ; he further
ſheweth by Goddes iuſtice towardes Angels, and
firſt ſinners . [for (ſaith he) if God ſpared not An- *2. Pet. 2.*
gels ſinning, nor the original world, nor Sodome & *v. 4. 5.*
Gomorrha, deliuering neuertheleſſe the iuſt, but re- *9.*
ſerueth the vniuſt vnto the day of Iudgement to be
tormented .] By the ſame example of Sodome and
other Cities, S. Iude alſo confirmeth the doctrine *Iude. v. 7.*
of eternal fire ordained for the wicked . Finally the
whole troupe of the wicked, ſignified by Babilon de- *Apoc. 18. v.*
priued of al maner of ioy, conſolation, or content- *21. 22. Ch.*
ment [ſhal be throwne into the bottomles pitte of *20. v. 13.*
hel with ſuch violence, as if a milſtone were throwne
into the ſea, and ſhal be found nomore : So ſhal their *Ch. 21. v. 8.*
portion be for euer and euer, in the poole burning
with fire and brimſtone, which is the ſecond death .]
Contrariwiſe, the portion of the bleſſed, is God him
ſelf, whoſe eternal fruition they ſhal enioy, through *Ch. 22. v.*
[Chriſt his Sonne, the tree of life] who thus conclu- *2. 12.*
deth the viſion ſhewed to S. Iohn [Behold I come
quikly, and my reward is with me, to render to euerie
man according to his workes.]

*It was foreſhewed, & there haue bene, are, & wil
be, Hereſies againſt the true Faith.*

ARTICLE. 52.

Notice of euil,
is a warning to
ſeke remedie.

WArning beforehand of miſcheif to come
is a good kind of arming : Likewiſe the
record of euils paſt, is a good document
to be watchful, leſt the ſame returne vnwares ; but
moſt

most especially present irruption of anie pestilent maladie, is a singular admonition to flee from it, to vse preseruatiues against it, strongly to resist it, and neuer by consent of mind to geue entrance nor way vnto it, For so much therfore as to erernal saluation which al desire, the true faith is absolutely necessarie, as is declared in the first Article of this Christian doctrine, & particularly confirmed in the rest of this first part : it remaineth consequently to be considered, that whereas heresie is most ranke poisen of christian soules, [the worst kind of al infidelitie] it hath pleased God of his singular prouidence, not only to foreshew by holie Scriptures, that there should come heresies, false and peruerse opinions against the true faith ; but also to note certaine such, which haue bene raised, both in the time of the old Testament ; and in the Apostles time, before al the New Testament was writen ; and withal so to describe heresies and heretikes, most strictly forbidding al participation with them : that al which wil, may sufficiently know them to be false, and are bound vnder paine of damnation, to auoide al spiritual communication with them.

2. *Pet.* 2. *v.* 21.

marginal note: Heresie is the poyson of true faith.

2 The first figures, or rather examples of heretikes, were Cain before Noes floud, and Nemrod after. But the whole race and complices of the former, were vtterly destroyed by the floud, and the others were dispersed when their tongues were confounded, and presently deuided into manie sectes of Infidels ; multiplying false goddes, and imaginarie religions ; the true Church of God continuing without interruption, or change of faith, euen vnto Abraham ; and so to Moyses ; and to Christ : sundrie sortes of schismatikes, heretikes, and other infidels in that long time, breaking from it ; stil more and more deuising and holding manie, no lesse absurde, then execrable, errors.

Gen. 4. *v.* 16. *Ch.* 10. *v.* 10.

Ch. 5. *v.* 3. *ad* 31. *Ch.* 11. *v.* 10. *ad* 31. *Exo.* 3. *v.* 2. 6. *Ch.* 6. *v.* 16. 26.

marginal note: There were heresies, or errors, against true faith, before Noes floud. And more after it.

God

Deut. 12.
v. 31. Ch.
18. v. 10.
Exo. 20.
&c.

Lenit. *
Deut. 12.
v. 32. Ch.
13. v. 1.
ad 12.

Heresies, & al other Infidelities, are condemned by the law of Moyses.

3 God therfore, nere two thousãd & fiue hũdred yeares frõ the beginning of the world, geuing his people a written Law, most especially commanded them, neither to make, nor admitte, anie false god, nor false Religion; but to serue and adore him, the only true God; and that in prescript maner, as he then instructed them by particular preceptes. Often inculcating, that they should neuer harken to false prophets, nor folow new doctrine in matter of Religion [If there rise in the midest of thee (saith our Lord to his people) a prophet, or one that saith, he hath seene a dreame, and foretel a signe and wonder, and it come to passe which he spake; and he say to thee, let vs goe and folow strange goddes which thou knowest not, & let vs serue them; thou shalt not heare the wordes of that prophet or dreamer. For the Lord your God tempteth you, that it may appeare whether you loue him or noe, with al your hart, & with al your soule. And that prophet or forger of dreames shal be slaine, because he spake, that he mgiht auert you from the Lord your God, that he might make thee to erre from the way that the Lord thy God cõmanded thee; and thou shalt take away the euil out of the midest of thee. with stones shal he be stoned to death, because he would haue withdrawne thee from the Lord thy God.] And as particular men

Cities, or coũtries were punishable for heresie, by the same law of Moyses.

being false prophets, heretikes, or sowers of new doctrine, were punished by the Law: so likewise whole Cities, that mantained false religion amidest the people of God, were either to be corrected, or destroyed. Which diuine ordinances, did presuppose, and forewarne, that both priuate persons, and tumultuous people, would somtimes reuolt from the true faith; and make seperation from the faithful : some auouching false thinges in the name of the true God, which are properly heretikes; and some prea-

12.
12. &c.
Ch. 18. v.
20.

Heretiks falsly pretended Gods word.

ching

ching the like falſitie in the name of ſtrange goddes, which are plaine Apoſtataes. As Moyſes relateth,

Ch. 22. that ſome [prouoked God in ſtrange goddes, and in

v. 18.19. abominations ſtirred him to anger. they immolated to diuels, and not to God; to goddes which they knew not.] Yea they inuented new, and newer goddes, as Sectaries doe now daily coine new hereſies [There came new and freſh goddes, whom their fathers worſhipped not] euen ſo doe Puritanes hold new conceiptes, which neither Luther, Zuinglius, Cranmer, nor Iuel, euer knew, or allowed. They

Iob. 32. were herein very liuely repreſented, by the yong &

v. 18.19. laſt diſputer againſt holie Iob, vaunting [Eliu, whoſe belie, (as him ſelf proteſted) was as new wine without a vent, which breaketh new veſſels] who round-

12. ly condemned both Iob, and his other three aduerſaries [For I ſee (ſaid he) here is none of you that can reproue Iob, and anſwear to his wordes] And ſo he talketh at randome calumniating Iobes wordes, falſly charging him with thinges that he did not ſay. But Iob hauing conuinced the former three with ſolide reaſons; ouercame this laſt, and moſt arrogant, with ſilence. which their errour, was not for al this

Ch. 42. an hereſie, nor they heretikes for defending it, be-

v. 7.9. fore God him ſelf reſolued the caſe; but they were

10. figures reſembling heretikes, in holding and mantaining erronious opinions, touching goddes iudgement, in ſuffering the iuſt to be temporally afflicted.

4 Diuers other perſons, and peoples, were alſo figures of heretikes : eſpecially ſuch as deſcended of Abraham and his nere kindred, and neighbours, and diſſented in religion, and perſecuted the true Church. vnder whoſe names the Royal Pſalmiſt Dauid, pro-

Pſ. 82.*v.* phecied of heretikes, and other perſecuters of Chri-

2.3.4. ſtians; ſpeaking thus in his prayer to God [O God

Apoſtataes pretend falſe goddes, or falſe Chriſtes.

Eliu, Iobs laſt aduerſarie, much reſembleth a Puritane.

Vnder the name of Idolaters, king Dauid prophecied of Heretikes in this time of the new teſtament.

who

who ſhal be like to thee ? Hold not thy peace, nei‑
ther be thou appeaſed o God. for behold thine e‑
nemies haue made a ſound : they that hate thee haue
lifted vp their head. they haue taken·malignant
counſel vpon thy people : and they haue deuiſed a‑
gainſt thy Sainctes. they haue ſaid : Come and let
vs deſtroy them out of the nation (that they be no
more accounted a nation of God) and let the name
of Iſrael be remembred no more. Becauſe they haue
deuiſed with one conſent, they haue together made
a couenant againſt thee.] The [Idumians, Iſmahe‑ **7.8.9.**
lites, Moabites, Agarenes, Gebalites, Ammonites,
Amalacites, Philiſtians, Tyrians, and Aſſirians] As
if you wil now ſay ; Lutherans, Zuinglians, Anabap‑
tiſtes, Calueniſtes, Proteſtantes, Puritans, Hugo‑
nets, Browniſtes, Atheiſtes, Turkes, al Sectaries,
and other Infidels, combine in one to perſecute
Catholiques.

Salomon de‑   5   Salomon doth alſo at large deſcribe ſuch peruerſe   *Prou.2.v.*
ſcribeth here‑ ſinners, as reuolte from vertue, and veritie ; pro‑   **13.14.15.**
tikes by the   phetically heretikes, who leaue the right way, and
reſemblance of walke by darke waies [who are glad when they haue
inticing ſtrum‑ done euil, reioice in moſt wicked thinges ; whoſe
pettes.   waies are peruerſe, and their ſteppes infamous] Al
which, are very proper to hereſie, and ſo the reſt of his
diſcourſe ; calling this inuiting ſtrumpet [the ſtrange   **16.17.18.**
womã the forener which mollifieth her wordes ; for‑   **19.**
ſaketh the guide of her youth, & hath forgotté the co‑
uenãt of her God. For her houſe is bowed downe to
death & her pathes to hel. Al that goe in vnto her,
ſhal not returne, neither ſhal they apprehéd the pathes
of life] The reaſon of which difficultie, to returne
from heretical errour, is, becauſe heretikes doe wi‑
tingly adhere to a priuate opinion, els they were not
heretikes : and ſo choſing to folow either their owne,
or ſome other priuate ſpirits ; exclude the meanes
                                                from

from them selues, wherby they might be reduced to the truth, refusing to be taught, or iudged by anie other, but according to their owne vnderstanding and iudgement. Againe the same wise Salomon, describeth the maner of this womans inticing, by carnal and worldly allurementes, both to carnal & spiritual fornication (very proper to the sectaries of this time) with the destruction of those which are seduced by her. But more breifly, he compriseth al in this pithie sentence, which he thrice reciteth in his diuine prouerbes [There is a way (saith he) which semeth to a man iust, but the later endes therof lead to death.] He admonisheth also that [By three thinges the earth (or man in earth) is moued, yet susteineth them. By a seruant when he shal reigne: by a foole when he shal be filled with meat, : by an odious woman, when she shal be taken in matrimonie. But the fourth is intollerable, and can not be sustained ; A bond woman, when she shal be heire to her Mistris] most properly spoken of heresie, where it doth dominire ouer Catholique Religion. We haue the very like description of heresie vnder the figure of a wicked woman, in the booke of Ecclesiasticus [There is no head worse, then the head of a serpent : and there is no anger, aboue the anger of a woman.]

6　Al that the Prophets preached or writte concerning Idoles ; is mystically vnderstoode of heresies in the new Testament. For as Idolaters are very foolish, in that [the selues making an Idole doe imagine that the thing which they made, is their god ; them selues being witnesses, that those thinges which they made, doe not see nor vnderstand, because they were made of iron, or wood, or siluer, or gold] or of other mettal or matter which hath no sense at al, much lesse no vnderstanding, much lesse diuine power :

Marginal notes (left):
Ch. 7.
v. 10. 11.
12. ad 26.

Ch. 14.
v. 12.
Ch. 16.
v. 25.
Ch. 21.
v. 2.
Ch. 30.
v. 21.
22. 23.

Eccl. 25.
v. 22.
&c.

Isa. 44.
v. 9. 11.
12. 13.
&c.

Marginal notes (right):
The great resemblance betwixt Idolatrie, and Heresie, is further declared by holie Scriptures.

euen so heretikes deuise new doctrines & adore their owne inuentions, which they know were imagined, and framed by them selues, and so draw their simple folowers, to admitte and esteme the same fictions, for diuine doctrines, being nothing els, but phanta- sies of mens braines, and abominable blasphemies, vn- der the false title of Goddes word.

Examples of heresies in the old Testament.

7   But besides figures and Prophesies, there were also formal heresies in the old Testament. As Caines negatiue opinion, that there was no reward for ver- tue, nor punishment for sinne ; wherupon he offered the worse fruictes to God, keping the best to him self, and enuying his brothers good workes, slew him, and afterwardes [went out from the face of our Lord.] Also the like impious persuation of Nemrod that men were not beholding to God, but to them selues, and their owne strength for temporal prospe- ritie ; & so became [a valiant hunter against beastes] & a vioient tirant ouer men. And as then such errors desceded into plaine Idolatrie : so in this time of the new Testamet, heresies comoly procede to Turcisme , & paganisme , & soner or later, into Atheisme. An other particular example of the faithful degenerating into infidelitie, is recorded in the time of the Iudges, of one [*Michas*, of the Tribe of Ephraim, who toge- ther with his mother, made an Idol of siluer, and cal- led it his god. For which he furnished a seperated rowme as a chapel or litle temple, within his owne

Gen. 4. v. 5.

Gen. 10. v. 8.

Iudic. 17. v. 4. 5.

Aright paterne of Protestants Ministers.

house. So he made an *Ephod*, and *Teruphim*, that is to say, a Priestly vestiment; and Idoles [and filled the hand of one of his sonnes (after an apish imitati- on of annointing his handes with oile, but prophane for lacke of sacred) and he became his Preist] such a god, such a preist. Yet to amend the matter, with an other grosse sacrilege (for one absurditie admitted, a thousand wil folow) This *Michas*, a new maker of a of a god, and of a Preiſt, knowing al was not right,

7.10.12. [hired alſo a Leuite, and in the ſame maner ſilled (that is annointed) his hand and head, and held him for a preiſt ; glorying and preſuming, that God our

13. Lord would bleſſe him for his fact ſaying : Now I know that God wil doe me good, hauing a preiſt of the Leuitical kind] though indeede no preiſt, but an Apoſtata Leuite. Very like to this, but much more general was the ſchiſme of Ieroboam king of Iſrael, with the hereſies and Idolatries therupon enſuing.

3. *Reg.* Who in his wicked pollicie [fearing that if his peo-

12. *v.* ple ſhould goe vp to make Sacrifices in the houſe of our

27. Lord, into Ieruſalem; their hart would be turned to their Lord Roboā king of Iuda; finding out a deuiſe,

28. he made two golden calues, & ſaid to his people; Goe vp nomore into Ieruſalem ; behold thy goddes which

31. brought thee out of the land of Egipt. And he made Temples in the excelſes ; and preiſtes of the abiectes of the people, which were not of the children of Leui] And in that reſpect, more abſurd then the Leuite

Nu. 3. that ſerued Michas, and his falſe god ; wheras none

v. 10. were at that time lawful Preiſtes, but only of the ſtock of Aaron. For the honour alſo of theſe new made goddes, dedication of their temples, and exerciſe of their imaginarie preiſtes, this king the proper head

32. of ſuch a church [inſtituted a ſolemne feaſt after the ſimilitude of the ſolemnitie that was celebrated in Iuda] leſt forſoth ſuch men might forgeate to be apes, yet were they fondly ouerſeene, their great maiſter the diuel blinding their hartes, in that being one king-dome, and one only ſupreme king & viſible head, they

29. had two goddes, that is to ſay, two golden calues;

Ch. 18. the one in Bethel, the other in Dan; neither did there

v. 19. want great ſtore of falſe prophets in that ſchiſmatical

Ch. 22. kingdome. Amongſt which, one Sedecias, that he

v. 11. might ſeme like to true prophets (which prophecied

King Ieroboam made goddes, Preiſtes, feaſts, and mantained falſe Prophets, like to his new religion.

One ſchiſmati-cal kingdome had two gods.

A ridiculous
false Prophet
made him self
hornes of Iron.

both by factes and wordes [made him self hornes
of iron, and said to Achab king of Israel, thus saith
our Lord : with these shalt thou strike Syria til thou
destroy it. and al the other false prophets aboue four
hundred, said the same] not knowing the truth, because they would not beleue the true Prophet Micheas ; and so God suffered them to be deceiued, & to
deceiue Achab by a lying spirit, who offered his seruice saying : [I wil goe forth (said the diuel) and
be a lying spirit in the mouth of al his prophets] Al
which when Micheas plainly reueled to the king ; the
furious horned false prophet Sedecias , to reuenge
him self, further proceding , *a verbis, ad verbera*, together with calumnious wordes , strooke him on
the face.]

3. *Reg* . 11 .
v . 30. *If* .
20. *v* . 3 .
Iere . 13. *v* .
11 .
Ib . *v* . 6 . 8 .
17 . 21 . 22 .
24 . 2 . *Par* .
18 . *v* . 5 .
10 . 11 . 20 .
21 . 23 .

The offspring
of heresie, is
the multiplica-
tion of innu-
merable here-
sies .

8   Moreouer this king Achab, and his wife Iezabel,
not satisfied with the heresie that Ieroboam had forged out of his owne hart, teaching that golden calues
were goddes : worshiped Baal for god, building a
temple and an altar to him in Samaria. After this
when the Assirians had made the kingdome of tenne
Tribes captiue and had placed there peoples of diuers
Nations, who mixing the Israelites Religion , with
manie sortes of paganisme ; manie new heresies rose
vp amongst them, euerie Nation together with the
Israelites that dwelt with them, hauing in seueral có-
uenticles, their particular goddes, to witte, of [the
Babilonians, Cutheites, Ematheites, Heueites, Se-
pharuehemites] and the rest, who al neuerthelesse
(as they pretended) worshiped our Lord . Of the
Pharisees friuolous Traditions, and of the plaine heresies of Sadduces, and Herodians, we haue no testimonies in the old Testament . But Christ our Sauiour , and his Apostles, make cleare mention of
them .

3 . *Reg* . 12 .
v . 33 .
Ch . 16 . *v* .
31 . 22 .
4 . *Reg* . 17 .
v . 29 .

v . 30 . 31 .
32 . 33 .

Mat . 3 . *v* .
7 . *Ch* . 5 . *v* .
21 . *Ch* . 22 .
v . 15 . 16 .

Christ and his
Apostles fore-
warned that

9   And more amply foretel of other heresies to come
geuing

Act . 5 . *v* .
17 . *Ch* . 23 .

v. 6. 7.
8.
Mat. 7.
v. 15. 16.
Ch. 16.
v. 6. 12.
Ch. 24.
v. 4. 5.
11.
Mar. 13.
v. 23.
Luc. 21.
v. 8.

Act. 6.
v. 9.

Act. 15.
v. 1.

Ch. 11.
v. 16.
5.

Ch. 20.
v. 29.
30.

1. *Cor.*
11. *v.*
18. 19.

geuing some notes wherby to know them, and most heresies would molest the Church. diligently admonishing al the faithful to auoid them [Take ye great heede (saith our Sauiour) of false prophets which come to you in the cloathing of sheepe, but inwardly are rauening wolues : by their fruictes you shal know them. Looke wel and beware of the leauen of the pharisees, and Sadduces, not of the leauen of bread, but of the doctrine of the Pharisees & Sadduces. Beware that no man seduce you. for manie shal come in my name. Manie false prophets shal rise, and shal seduce manie. Take therfore heede; behold I haue foretold you al thinges, and the time is at hand; goe not therfore after them] As it came to passe shortly after Christes Ascension, and so wil the like hapen til the end of the world.

10 For first [there arose the Synagogue of the Libertines, and of the Cyrenians, of the Allexandrians, and of them that were in Cilicia, and Asia, disputing whith Stephen] against Christ. Not long after certaine Iewes which had bene conuerted to Christ, and were baptized, comming downe from Iurie (to Antioch, where Christs disciples were first called Christians) taught the brethren that vnles you be circumcised according to the maner of Moyses you cannot be saued] with whom the Pharesees in this agreed, that Christiãs must be crircumcised, & kepe the law of Moyses. In like maner S. Paul forewarned the cleargie, and Christian people of Ephesus, and other partes adioyning, that false teachers should arise amongst them [I know (said he) that after my departure, there wil rauening wolues enter in among you not sparing the flocke, & out of your owne selues shal arise men speaking peruerse thinges, to draw away disciples after them selues.] To the Corinthians he writeth thus. [I heare that there are schismes among you, and in part I beleue it. For there must

Some heresies rose very shortly after Christs Ascension.

be

be herefies alfo, that they which are approued, may
be made manifeft among you.] In particular he inftructeth S. Timothie in both his Epiftles, that [in
the laft daies, fhal approach perilous times, that certaine fhal depart from the faith, attending to fpirites
of errour, and doctrines of diuels, fpeaking lies in hipocrifie, and hauing their confcience feared ; forbidding to marie (as did the Manichees, Encratites,
Marcioniftes, Ebionites, and Patritians) and teaching to abfteine from meates which God created]
as did the fame Maniches, the Tatians, and other heritikes, faying, that they were not made of God, but
of an euil God . S. Peter alfo foretelleth vs, that [as
there were falfe prophets in the people (of the Iewes)
fo among Chriftians, there fhal be lying maifters,
which fhal bring in fectes of perdition . & manie fhal
folow their riotoufneffes, by whom the way of truth
fhal be blafphemed.] S. Iohn not only fheweth,
that heretikes fhould come in this time of the new
Teftament, which he calleth the laft hour (or laft time
and ftate of this world) efpecially that moft enormious enemie of Chrift, therof called *Antichrift*, that
is contrarie to Chrift : but alfo faith [as you haue
heard that Antichrift cometh, and now (euen in the
Apoftles time) manie are become Antichriftes] plainly teaching, that al fuch Chriftians, as departing from
the Church, hold new opinions againft the fame
Church, are the forerunners of the fingular man of
finne, the infamous Antichrift ; and fo they become
Antichriftes . Of which fingular great Antichrift,
more is to be faid in the next Article. For that S.
Iohn diftinguifheth betwene him and other heritikes
is manifeft, in that he calleth this one [the Antichrift] and none other the Antichrift, but [an Antichrift] faying [there were then manie fuch, & that
manie falfe prophets are gone out into the world] of
which

1. *Tim.* 4.
v . 1 . 2 . 3 .
2 . *Tim.* 3.
v . 1 .

2 . *Pet.* 2.
v . 1 . 2 .

1 . *Ioan.* 2.
v . 18.

Ch. 4 . v . 1.

Apoc .2. which fort were [thofe that faid them felues to be
v. 2.   Apoftles and were not.] And befides the principal
    beaft which appeared with feauen heades and tenne
Apoc .13. hornes [he faw an other beaft (a notorious wicked
v. 1.11. perfecuter) coming vp from the earth, with two
12.   hornes, who made the inhabitantes of the earth, to
    adore the firft beaft.]

    11   Now to know who are heretikes, and fo to a- Markes of He-
    uoide them, it behoueth to confider fuch markes as tikes.
    we finde them to be branded withal in holie Scrip-
    tures. Of which it may fuffice here to note fome few,
    which more peculiarly difcipher the Sectaries of this
    time; for the exact trial therof requireth the difcuf-
    fing of al matters of faith controuerfed. Of falfe Doctrine ten-
Mat .7. Prophets in general our Sauiour faith [that by their ding to neglec-
v. 16.   fruictes you fhal know them] explicating the fame ting Goddes
20.   to be badde fruictes, for that the tree and the fruict commande-
    are of the fame qualitie, both nought. wherupon we ments, and to
1. *Tim* . may rightly obferue that as thofe [which repel good corruption of
8.*v.* 19 . confcience, commonly make fhip-wrakke of faith] life.
    euen fo fuch doctrines are falfe, and being obftinatly
    mátained are heretical, as tending to loofenes of life,
    haue litle care to keepe Goddes commandements,
    leffe defire of Euangelical councels, of contempt of
    this world, of mortification of the flefh, and the like.
2. *Mac* . It is recorded in the hiftory of the Machabes, that whé
4.*v.* 14 . true Religion was oppreffed [the Preiftes were not
15.   now occupied about the offices of the Altar : but the
    Temple being contemned, and the Sacrifices neglec-
    ted, they haftened to be partakers of the gamne of
    wraftling, and of the vniuft mantenance therof, and
    in the exercife of the coyte . And fetting nougt by
    the honours of their fathers, they eftemed the Greeke
Mat .13. gloriesfor the beft] fo doth the diuel ouerfow his
v. 25 .   cocle vpon the wheate which was firft fowed. And fo
    doe euil men and feducers rife after and [profper to Rifing after,

                M m m   the

Not fent.

the worfe .] An other certaine marke of falfe prophets, is their coming not being rightly fent, which
God condemneth faying [I fent not the prophets,
and they ranne; I fpake not to them, and they prophecied . For neither doth anie man take the honour
to him felf, but he that is called. He that entreth not
by the doare into the folde of the fheepe, but climeth
vp an other way, is a theefe and a robber, he is a wolf
not a paftor.] By this marke the Apoftles declared
them to be feducers, which preached that Chriftians
muft be circumcifed, writing thus to the brethren at
Antioch [We haue heard, that certaine going forth
from vs, haue troubled you with wordes, fubuerting
your foules, to whom we gaue no commandement.]

2. *Tim.* 3.
v. 13.
Iere. 23. *v.*
21.
Heb. 5. *v.*
4.
Io. 10. *v.*
1. 2. 12.

Act. 15. *v.*
24.

ful.
bedient.

Falfe Apoftles are alfo difcouered by their difobedi-
ence to the lawful prelates. For our Sauiour counteth it al one, to difobey thofe whom he fendeth, as
to difobey him felf faying : [he that defpiceth you,
defpiceth me. If they haue kept my word; yours al-

Luc. 10. *v.*
16.

Teaching no-
uelties.

fo wil they kepe. But there be manie difobedient
(faith S. Paul) vaine fpeakers, and feducers.] A-
gaine they are to be knowne, by teaching otherwife
then the doctrine, to which Chriftians were firft
conuerted [For there is not an other Gofpel, but falfe

Io 15. *v.*
20.
Tit. 1. *v.* 10.
Gal. 1. *v.*
6.

Replenifhed
with bad qua-
lities.

preachers doe inuert the Gofpel.] S. Iude in breif
defcribeth heretikes by fundrie badde properties,
that [they defile the flefh, defpice dominiô, blafpheme
maieftie : Thefe (indeede beleuing nothing at al for
the teftimonie of the Church, but) what thinges foeuer naturally as dumme beaftes they know, in thofe
they are corrupted (they are enuious) like Cain,
(couetous) like Balaam (rebellious againft ordinarie fuperiours, and intruders into fpiritual functions
wherto they are not called) as Core. Thefe are in
their bankets, fportes, fefting together without feare,
feding them felues, cloudes witthout water which

1. *Tim.* 1.
v. 3. *Ch.* 6.
v. 3. 2. *Io.*
v. 10. *Iud.*
v. 8. 10. 11.
12. 13. 16.

are

are caried about with windes, trees of autumne, vn-
fruictful, twice dead, plucked vp by the rootes, raging
waues of the sea, foming out their owne confusion,
wandring starres, to whom the storme of darknes is
reserued for euer .] Thus sharply doth this holie A-
postle inueigh against teachers of new doctrines,
[beseching al Christians to stand fast, yea to contend
for the faith once deliuered to the faithful, and to
be mindful of the wordes which haue bene spoken
before by the Apostles of our Lord Iesus Christ, who
tould you, that in the last time shal come mockers,
walking according to their owne desires, in impieties .

3 . 17 .
18 .

12   For conseruation of which first and only true
faith, S . Paul testifieth, that Christ hath geuen his
Church, ordinarie Pastors & Doctors [that (saith he)
we be not children, wauering and caried about with
euerie wind of doctrine, in the wickednes of men,
in craftines, to circūuention of error .] Accordingly
he exhorted the Bishops in Asia [to be vigilant as
him self was .] And particularly S . Timothee [to
preach the word, vrging in al patience and doctrine.
For there shal be a time, when they wil not heare
sound doctrine ; but hauing itching eares, wil, according to their owne desires, heape to them selues maisters .] And this time euen then beginning, hath often returned . As we see in some Christians, called
after the names of their new pleasing maisters, Nicolaites; Manichees; Arrians; Pelagians; Donatistes;
Lolardes; Lutherans; Zuinglians; Caluenistes.

Ephes. 4 .
v . 11 . 14 .

Act. 20 .
v . 28 .
31 .
2 . *Tim.*
4 . *v* . 2 .
3 .
Iac. 3 .
v . 1 .
Apoc. 2 .
v . 6 . 15 .

The proper re-
medie against
al heresie, is to
hold the Reli -
gion first recei-
ued. and to fo-
low the ordina-
rie Pastors .

Antichrist, the head of al Heritikes, is to
come : nere the end of this world.

ARTICLE. 53.

It is neceffarie
to know that
fom time there
fhal be a moft
wicked enemie
of Chrift, cal -
led Antichrift.

IF it be profitable, as al men wil eafily graunt, to be forewarned, that herefies fhould come into the world, to the end Chriftians may be prepared to auoid them : more nedeful it is to know alfo before-hand, that once there wil come, the head of al here-tikes, the capital enemie of al faithful Chriftians, the profeffed aduerfarie of our Lord Iefus Chrift. who is therfore in the holie Scripture called *Antichrift*, that is, *Contrarie to Chrift*. Euen as the Apoftata Angel, which firft oppofed him felf againft God, the Crea-tor of al, was aptly called *Satan*, which fignifieth *Ad-uerfarie*. For albeit, al the other wicked fpirits, which tooke part, and fel from heauen with their ringlea-der, formally called Lucifer, are alfo aduerfaries to God, and to al good perfons, and fo are commonly and by a general name called aduerfarie fpirites, and diuels ; yet is the prince and head of them al, pro-perly, or Antonomaftically, eminently called *Satan*, & *Diabolus*, the aduerfarie, the diuel, the Calumnia-tor : As where S. Peter admonifhing al Chriftians faith [Be fober and watchful ; becaufe your Aduer-farie the diuel, as a roring Lyon goeth about, fee-king whom he may deuoure.] And as our Redemer, the Sonne of God, and Sonne of man, is properly called *Chrift, the annointed*, notwithftanding by par-ticipation of ointment ; Prophets alfo, and kinges, and Preiftes, are called Chriftes : So in like fenfe of contrary perfons, though, al notorious perfecuters of Chrift, and his Religion, and efpecially Heretikes, or falfe prophets ; are by the general name, called

Antichrifts

Iob. 1. *v.* 6.
Zach. 3. *v.*
1. 2.
Luc. 10. *v.*
18.

3. *Reg.* 5.
v. 4.
1. *Pet.* 5.
v. 8.

Al heretikes
are Antichrifts
in a general
fenfe : but
more properly
the head of

Antichrifts, yet is the fame name peculiarly appro- them is called
priated to the eminent aduerfarie of Chrift in al man- Antichrift.
kind; who is defigned and vnderftoode, when we
fay the *Antichrift*, to be a diftinct perfon frō al other
generally called Antichriftes.

2   But becaufe there is at this time, a moft notable What pointes
Controuerfie raifed about this important point of are principally
Religion; whether this Antichrift, taken in the par- to be decided
ticular fenfe, be one fingular determinate man, or touching Anti-
fome fpecial denomination of diuers men, fucceding chrift.
one to, or after an other, in fome feat of auctoritie,
and office? Likewife whether he be as yet to come
into the world; or be come alreadie? And diuers o-
ther queftions, concerning his doctrine, life, death,
time, place, and other circumftances therto pertaining. For more cleare declaration wherof, diftinguifhing thinges certaine, frō vncertaine; we fhal fhew
by the holie Scriptures, firft, that Antichrift properly
taken for the eminent aduerfarie, head of al other
vifible aduerfaries of Chrift; muft be one certaine
fingular man, not anie companie, nor diuers perfons
fucceding in place of power, or dignitie, lawful, or
vnlawful. Secondly, that he is not yet come, but
fhal come hereafter, & that nere the end of this world.
Then alfo we fhal declare, fome fpecial, and affured
thinges touching his doctrine, Idolatrie, tirannie,
death, and deftruction: with Chriftes, and his Churches victorie: the conuerfion of the Iewes to Chrift;
and that fhortly after (which no man can punctually
know) the end of this world fhal folow.

3   To procede therfore in order, that Antichrift That Anti-
muft be one determinate fingular man, is proued chrift fhal be
by the prophecie of Daniel. who hauing [feene in a one fingular
vifion four beaftes, coming vp out of the fea; the man is proued
fourth of which, had tenne hornes; amideft thofe by the Prophe-
Dan. 7. tenne, he fee an other litle horne fprang vp: & three cie of Daniel.
ɤ. 2. 3.   M m m 3   of the

ot the firſt hornes were plucked of, at the preſence of 7.8. the laſt : and loe eyes as it were the eyes of a man, 17. were in this horn, & a mouth ſpeaking great wordes] which viſion an Angel interpreted thus to the Pro- phet [Theſe four great beaſtes (ſaid the Angel) are four kingdomes which ſhal riſe vp out of the earth] A litle atter touching the fourth beaſt, in particular 23. he ſaid [The fourth beaſt, ſhal be the fourth king- dome in the earth, which ſhal be greater then al the kingdomes, and ſhal deuour the whole earth, & ſhal conculcate and breake it in peeces. Moreouer the 24. tenne hornes of that ſame kingdome, ſhal be tenne kinges, and an other ſhal riſe vp after them, and he ſhal be mightier then the former ; and he ſhal bring downe three kinges .] That this eleuenth horne, and eleuenth king, ſhal be the great Antichriſt, is cleare by this deſcription, foreſhewing, that [he ſhal be at firſt a litle one, but ſhal become mightier then the former.] And that he ſhal be one ſingular man is euident by this ſingular acte of [bringing downe (or killing) three kinges] of the tenne : which being once done, can by no meanes be the act of his ſuc- ceſſour, or predeceſſour; and ſo this deſcription, can not be verified, of more then of one man only . The ſame is alſo confirmed, by diuers other his ſingular actes of [ouercoming & ſubduing the other ſeauen *Apoc.* 17. kinges] the which can not be truly aſcribed to anie o- *v.* 13. ther but to the real conquerour, and the like of manie *Dan.* 11. *v.* other actions, wherof mention is here to be made for 21. *Ch.* 12. a proofe alſo of other pointes. *v.* 11.

The ſame is proued by Chriſtes ſpeach to the Iewes, and by his Apoſtles writinges. 4 In the meane ſeaſon, this preſent doctrine is fur- ther proued, and that moſt inuincibly by our Sauiour his owne ſpeach ſaying to the Iewes [I am come in *Ioan.* 5. *v.* the name of my Father, and you receiue me not; if 43. an other ſhal come in his owne name, him you wil receiue] where our Lord expoſtulating with the blind

and

and wilful Iewes, for not receiuing him as their true
Messias, by way of comparing himself with an other,
vrgeth the different maner of their coming, and different effect, through their, as absurd, as malicious,
preferring an other before him; so clearly opposing
one person to an other, that it can not be vnderstooue
but of one singular man, contrarie to an other; saying on the one part [I] on the contrarie part [An
other] Againe on the one part [In the name of
my Father] on the other part [in his owne name]
thirdly on the one part [you receiue not me] on the
other part [you wil receiue him] most plainlly signifying him self to be Christ, the other to be Antichrist. him self one *Person* [I :] Antichrist also one
person saying : [An other] to witt an other man, not
diuers other men in order of succession . Likewise [my
Fathers name] and [his owne name] not their owne
name , or names, lastly [me] and [him] not them .
Wherfore seing Christ is one Person, Antichrist also
must be one Person. Reason also conuinceth, that
the Iewes wil not receiue manie, no not successiue-
ly, but one only singular man, for their Messias.
S. Paul likewise speaking of this greatest Aduersarie of Christ, sheweth that he shal be one singular
man ; calling him, not by his place where he shal
reigne, or haue power, nor by the office which he
shal beare, but by his singular wickednes, aboue al

2 . *Thes.* other men, before him, or after him [the man of
2 . *v.* 3 . sinne] & [the sonne of perdition] so designing him
by this article [the] that al may vnderstand one certaine man, distinct from al other men. In the same
maner S . Iohn distinguisheth this one notorious aduersarie, from others also called Antichristes saying

1 . *Io.* 2 . [You haue heard that Antichrist cometh] which he
v. 18 . also expresseth with this Article [the] (in the greeke
text) and without Article telleth of other aduersaries

ries his members and forerunners saying [Now there are manie become Antichristes] prouing therby that the last hour, (the last age, and state of this world) was then alreadie begunne, because manie Antichristes, forerunners of the great Antichrist, who must come in the last time, were then come. From which proofe is firmely deduced, that the eminent Antichrist must be a singular man, distinct from al other Antichristes, and that he is the head of them al, and al the rest his members. Againe the proper name which Antichrist shal haue, sheweth that he shal be a singular man. For albeit the same is meruelous mistical, and no mortal man can as yet tel, what this name shal be, yet S. Iohn hath plainly written, that it is comprehended [in the number of sixe hundred, sixtie, sixe] & that [it is the number (& name) of a man] not of an office, nor of manie men, but of one man. And withal hath foretold, that [no man shal be suffered to buy, or to sel, but that hath the character, or the name of the beast, or the number of his name.] By which it wil also appeare, (when this prophecie shal be fulfilled) both what his name is, and by the same name, amongst manie other signes concurring, Antichrist shal be knowne, to al that shal not be wilfully blind.

Apoc. 13.
v. 18.

17.

That Antichrist is not yet come, is proued by the signes that shal come before him, with him, and shortly after him.

5   Now for proofe, & explication of the next point, that Antichrist is not hitherto come, we may obserue, that as his comming, and extreme persecution, shal be a signe that the end of the world shal then be nere at hand: for our Sauiour saith [Immediatly after the tribulation of those dayes, the sunne shal be darkned &c] and concluding saith: [when ye shal see these thinges, know ye that it is nigh, euen at the doares.] So our experience that the end of the world is not yet come, is a demonstratiue signe that Antichrist is not come manie hundred yeares since: according to
            to the

Mat. 24.
v. 29.
33.

the common opinion of Proteſtantes, who generally ſay, that he was reuealed aboue a thouſand yeares agoe, either in the time of S. Gregorie the great, or ſtreight after: about the ſix hundred yeare of Chriſt. But let vs alſo conſider of other ſignes, as wel coming before Antichriſt, as occurring together with him: which are alſo for moſt part, ſignes of the nere approaching conſummation of the world. One ſigne of them both, is by S. Paules doctrine, the deſtruction of the Romane Empire, which, though much decaied, is not hitherto deſtroyed [nor (as the Apoſtle ſpeaketh) taken away.] For the plaine ſenſe of which miſtical wordes, ſeing S. Paul remitted the *Theſſalonians* [to that which he had told them before when he was with them] we alſo remitte the reader to other larger diſcourſes written of this matter. An other ſigne which muſt come before the end of the world, our Sauiour foretelleth, that [his Goſpel of the kingdom, ſhal be preached to the whole world, for a teſtimonie to al Nations. and then ſhal come the conſummation.] And in the very next wordes interpoſeth an other ſigne, nearer adioyned to the end of the world: which is [*the Abomination of deſolation*] and extreme perſecution [ſuch as neuer was before, nor ſhal be after] which can be none other, then that which Antichriſt ſhal make. Wherupon is clearly gathered, that the preaching of Chriſtes Goſpel to al Nations, in the whole world, muſt be fulfilled before Antichriſt come. Wheras therfore it is certaine, that in a great part of the world, now called by the general name of *America*; Chriſtes Goſpel is but very lately within theſe laſt hundred yeares firſt preached; neither is yet to this day preached in manie great kingdomes therof: it is hereby manifeſt that Antichriſt did neither preach long ſince, nor is as yet come, at leaſt is not yet reuealed. But when the

holy

2. Theſ. 2. v. 7.

Mat. 24. v. 14.

15.
21.

This world ſhal end ſhortly after Antichriſt.

The Romaine Empyre ſhal be vtterly deſtroyed before Antichriſt come.

The Goſpel ſhal be preached in al the earth.

Abomination of deſolation ſhal be in Antichriſtes time.

holie Gospel shal be propagated in al the nations, in which hitherto it neuer yet was preached; then may the great Antichrist be expected; and with him assuredly cometh the horrible great persecutió, described by the Prophets, by Christ him self, & his Apostles.

Enoch, and Elias, shal preach in the time of Antichrist.

6   In the same time also of Antichristes tyranical reigne; Enoch and Elias shal come againe amongst mortal men, resist his most wicked doctrine, and mantaine the truth of Christes Gospel. As the holie Scriptures doe clearly witnesse of Enoch. Moyses (writing that the other first Patriarches dyed)saith that [he walked with God, and was seene nomore, because God tooke him.] Agreable wherto the Auctor of Ecclesiasticus writeth, that [Enoch pleased God and was translated into Paradise, that he may geue repentance to Nations.] S. Paul also saith more plainly [Enoch was translated, that he should not see death : and he was not found, because God translated him.] Of Elias it is likewise written, that [When he and Elizeus going, talked together, behold a fyrie chariot, and fyrie horses, parted them two asunder ; & Elias ascended by a whirlwind into heauen. And Eliseus saw him and cried : My father, my father, the chariot of Israel, and the guider therof. And he saw him nomore. And [their Disciples sent fiftie men, who, when they had sought three daies found him not.] Of him also it is written in Ecclesiasticus, that [he was receiued in a whirlwind of fire, in a chariot of fyrie horses : who is written in the Iudgementes of times, to appease the wrath of our Lord; to reconcile the hart of the father to the sonne, and to restoare the Tribes of Israel.] Likewise God him self saith by the penne of Malachias [I wil send you Elias the Prophet, before the great & dredful day of our Lord come; and he shal conuert the hart of the fathers to the children, and the hart of the children

Gen. 5. v. 24.

Eccle. 44. v. 16.
Heb. 11. v. 5.

4. *Reg.* 2. v. 11. 12.

16. 17.

Eccle. 48. v. 9. 10.

Mal. 4. v. 5. 6.

dren

dren to their fathers, left perhaps I come and strike the earth with Anathema] By which prophecie it is certaine, that Elias shal come before the day of Iudgement, called there [the great and dreadful day] Not at our Sauiours first coming, wherof the Disciples *Mat.* 17. demanded ; and our Saui our answered [*Elias indeede* *v.* 10. 11. *shal come*, and restoare al thinges .] But concerning their expectatió of Elias at Christes first coming, 12. he answeared them further, that [Elias is alreadie come (mening S. Iohn Baptist) who came in the *Luc.* 1. spirit and vertue of Elias (as S. Luke explaneth it) *v.* 17. & they did not know him, but wrought on him what *Mat.* 11. soeuer they would] which the disciples then wel yn- *v.* 14. derstoode to be spoken of S. Iohn Baptist . And so it is cleare, that Elias was not to come in his owne person, but in spirit, at our Sauiours first coming; & that he is indeede to come in his owne person before the second coming of our Lord . And that this shal be performed in the time of Antichrist, is further proued by the testimonie of S. Iohn, writing our Saui- *Apoc.* 11. ours reuelation made thus vnto him [It is geuen to *v.* 3. the Gentiles (that is to say, it is permitted to the persecuters, Antichrist and his ministers) that they shal treade vnder foote the holie Citie, fourtie two monethes : and I wil geue to my two witnesses ; & they shal prophecie, a thousand two hundred sixtie daies, cloathed in sacke-cloathes] what other two witnefes can these be, but *Enoch*, and *Elias* ? who are so plainly recorded in the aboue recited holie Scriptures, to be extraordinarily reserued aliue, which must needes be for such an important purpose : for that the necessitie of the Church, in that most desolate hard time, requireth such preachers . Goddes prouidence is neuer wanting ; and al these diuine Scriptures are written, for the confolation of the elect, to assure vs of his diuine protection in al distresses.

Whiles therfore, these two so special witnesses, are not come into the world; neither is it possible that Antichrist should be come.

7 More proofe of so cleare a thing, may indeede to reasonable men seeme needelesse : but because our aduersaries are so peremptorie in auouching the contrarie fiction, that he is come long since, & yet reigneth, we presse them yet further to tel vs, and that by the auctoritie of holie Scriptures, by which only they pretend to trie, and decide al doubtes in religion, how long he shal reigne, and what maner of end he shal haue? The holie Scriptures to vs are plaine in this point, that he shal reigne a very short time : but three yeares and a halfe, and then shal come to a most miserable destruction in the sight of the whole world. Christ our Lord who is truth it self, hath plainly foretold vs, that his persecution wil be so extreme [that vnlesse those dayes had bene shortned (by Goddes sweete prouidence) no flesh should be saued: but for the elect the dayes shal be shortned.] which wordes alone, though they be spoken in general, doe clearly conuince their folie that dare auouch Antichristes persecution, to haue alreadie continued a thousand yeares; neither know they how long it may indure. Moreouer other sacred textes in particular, describe the space of his persecution, to be but three yeares and a half. In the prophecie of Daniel, it is foreshewed, that [the last springing horne of the fourth beast] to witte, that king which shal subdue tenne kinges, shal be suffered [to speake wordes against the high one; and to destroy the Sainctes of the *Highest* (persecute the faithful) euen to a time, and times, and half a time] for that by one time, he signifieth one yeare, is gathered by his like prophecie, concerning the transfiguring of Nabuchodonosor into the shape of a beast, the space of seauen

yeares

Antichrist shal reigne but a short time.

It shal be only three yeares & a halfe.

Mat. 24.
v. 21. 22.
Apoc. 17.
v. 10.

Dan. 7.
v. 25.

Ch. 4. *v.* yeares, which he expressed by the terme of [seauen
13. *Ch.* times] and by the same wordes, he also describeth
12. *v.* 7. the continuance of Antiochus his persecution, who
22. was a figure of Antichrist saying [it should be vnto
a time, and times, and half a time .] So likewise the
Apoc. 12. Angel signified to S. Iohn, that [the woman (the
v. 14. Church of Christ) shal be nourished in the desert, for
a time, and times, and half a time, from the face of the
serpent] which is yet more plainly expressed by the
Ch. 11. number of [fourtie two monethes] which are iust
v. 2. *Ch.* three yeares and a half. And by the number of daies,
13. *v.* 5. the Prophet Daniel saying : that [from the time,
Dan. 12. when the continual Sacrifice shal be taken away, &
v. 11. the abomination of desolation set vp, a thousand two
hundred, ninetie daies] which make very nere three
yeares and a half. Our Lord also saying, that his
Apoc. 11. [two witnesses, whom he wil send, shal prophecie a
v. 3. thousand two hundred sixtie daies] And S. Iohn
Ch. 12. saw in his vision, that the woman, whom the dragon
v. 6. would deuoure, shal be fedde in the wildernes, (the
Church in her most distressed state) a thousand two
hudred sixtie daies.] Which so exact agrement, in
number of daies sheweth wel that the afflicted Church
shal especially be comforted and strengthned against
Antichrist, by these two extraordinarie seruantes of
God, the Patriarch Enoch, & the Prophet Elias. As
for the other thirtie daies of Antichristes reigne, longer then their preaching, no man may neede to doubt,
but the Church shal also be protected, conserued, &
more & more sanctified, by her Spouse our Sauiour,
whose hande is neuer weakened.

8   These being the principal things, necessarie for
al Christians to know concerning Antichrist, that he
shal be one singular man, and that he is not come
into the world : it may suffice our present purpose,
aswel for more ample declaration of the same, as for

It is probable
that Antichrist
shal be a Iew
borne.

further

further notice of his badde qualities, and al circumstances of his person; to obserue also, that it is very
probable, but not certaine, he shal be a Iew borne,
which wil make the Iewes more readie to receiue him;
probable also, that he shal be of the Tribe of Dan;
as it may seme by the prophecie of Iacob saying : [Be   *Gen.* 49. *v.*
Dan a snake in the way, a serpent in the path. byting   17.
the hoofes of the horse, that his rider may fal backward.] And for that in the recital of the Tribes of
Israel in the Apocalipse , where, of euerie one of the   *Apoc.* 7.
other Tribes, S. Iohn had heard [that twelue thou-   *v.* 4. *&c.*
sand were signed] the Tribe of *Dan* is omitted. what
soeuer is the meaning of the former prophecie, & of
this Mysterie; it is certaine by the holie Scriptures
It is certaine, that the Iewes wil receiue him for their Christ, in
that the Iewes Hebrew called *Messias* . Daniel calleth Antiochus E-   *Dan.* 11.
wil receiue piphanes, or rather him that was prefigured which   *v.* 22.
him . is Antichrist [Prince of the league] For this Antiochus was their vtter enemie, and had not anie league
with the Iewes . Most expresly our Sauiour said to
the Iewes, that [they wil receiue that other man (his   *Ioan.* 5. *v.*
opposite) which wil come in his owne name] S.   43.
Paul testifying the same thing , yeldeth the reason,
that God in punishment of their sinne , in refusing ,
and impugning Christ our Sauiour, who came in the
name of his Father, wil suffer them [to beleue lying   2. *Thes.* 2.
that al may be iudged which haue not beleued the   *v.* 11. 12.
truth, but haue consented to iniquitie] As whē they
cried with open mouth before Pilate [Crucifie him,   *Mat.* 27.
crucifie him : his bloud be vpon vs, and vpon our chil-   *v.* 22. 23.
dren; If thou release this man, thou art not Cesars   25. *Io.* 19.
frend : we haue no king but Cesar :] And for their   *v.* 12. 15.
inueterate malice against Christ & Christians . Which
iust punishment, the Royal Prophet foreseing, in form
of praier, prophecied thus of them saying : [Appoint   *Ps.* 9. *v.* 11.
o Lord a Law-geuer ouer them, that the Gentiles may
know

know that they are men.] The same thing also Zacharias foretelleth saying : [I wil raise vp a Pastour
saith our Lord in the land, which shal not visit thinges
forsaken, the thing dispersed he shal not seeke,, & the
broken he shal not heale, and that which standeth he
shal not nourish ; & he shal eate the flesh of the fatte
ones, & their hoofes he shal dissolue.]

Zach. 11.
v. 16.

9   It is also certaine that he shal haue a proper name,
which is comprised [in the number sixe hundred sixtie sixe :] But very vncertaine what that name shal
be. Likewise it is certaine, that he shal haue a special [*character*, (badge, or coignisence) which he wil
make al, litle and great, rich and poore, free men &
bond men to haue in their hand, or in their forheades.
And that no man may buy or sel , but he that hath
the character, or the name of the beast, or the number
of his name] but very vncertaine it is, what this character shal be, vntil it shal come in practise.

Apoc. 13.
v. 18.
Ibid. *v*.
16. 17.

He shal haue a
proper name.
And a special
character,

10   He shal rise from very base state, to exceeding great temporal dominions, and power, and that
through wonderful craft , and deceipt: wherin he
shal be most cunning by the diuels art, and instruction, so that he shal be a notorious *Oedipus*, a Ridle
reader, [Impudent of face (saith Daniel) and vnderstanding propositions] (hard obscure speaches.) His
vile condition at first, the same Prophet sheweth saying : [I considered the hornes (the tenne hornes of
the fourth beast) and behold an other litle horne
sprang out of the midest of them.] And hauing described the ruine of a certaine king he saith: [there
shal stand in his place one despised, and kingly honour
shal not be geuen him: and he shal come secretly, &
shal obteyne the kingdome by fraud.] The same
Prophet further saith that [three of the first hornes
were plucked of at the presence of this last litle horne :
and loe eyes, as it were the eyes of a man were in this
horne

Dan. 8 .
v. 23.
Ch. 7.
v. 8.

Ch. 11.
v. 21.

Ch. 7.
v. 8.

He shal rise
from base state.

horne, and a mouth speaking great wordes] which
is afterwardes thus explicated [the tenne hornes shal **24.**
be tenne kinges : and an other shal rise vp after them,
and shal be mightier then the former, and he shal
bring downe three kinges . And he shal speake wor - **25.**
des against the high one] Further explaining his progresse in enlarging his dominion, the Prophet addeth
that [he shal lay his hand vpon the landes, & the land *Ch.* 12. **v.**
of Egipt shal not escape . And he shal rule ouer the **42. 43.**
treasures of gold, and of siluer, and in al the precious
thinges of Egipt. Through Lybia also , and Ethiopia he shal passe.] When therfore Antichrist shal
haue ouercome, pulled downe, and slaine, these three
kinges of Egipt, Lybia, and Ethiopia, and haue có-
quered their kingdomes ; then wil the other seauen
kinges, submitte them selues with their kingdomes,
to his dominions As may appeare by that which S.
Iohn prophecieth of al the tenne saying : [These haue *Apoc.* 17.
one counsel and force, and their power they shal de- **v. 13.**
liuer to the beast.] Thus shal he be made the greatest Monarch that euer was or shal be in this world .

It is probable
that his cheefe
residence shal
be in Ierusalé. 11 Where his cheif Imperial seate shal be, is vncertaine ; though it seme more probable that it shal
be in Ierusalem. Because the holie Scripture saith that
[he shal sitte in the Temple of God] By which may
wel be vnderstoode, that he wil in some sort repaire
Salomons Temple to please the Iewes, as king Herode did : And because it is expresly written in the
Apocalipse, that [he shal kil the two especial witnesses of Christ, in the great Citie, which is called spi- *Apoc.* 11.
ritually Sodome and Egipt . where their Lord also **v. 8.**
was crucified .]

He wil reigne
tyrannically in
al the earth. 12 But whersoeuer his principal seate shal be , he
wil dominire in al partes of the earth ; and most tyrannical y persecute, al Catholique Christians : vrging them by al maner of subtiltie, and crueltie, to
renounce

renounce their faith; and to become conformable to his most impious heresies, and Apostasie against al Christian Religion. Wherof also he shal be called *Abaddon, Appollyon, Exterminans,* a destroyer, especially in these four capital pointes. First that our Lord Iesus of Nazareth, is not Christ, wherin he had some forerunners in the Apostles time, of whom S. Iohn maketh mention, and calleth them Antichristes, & preparers of of the way to the Antichrist which co-meth, but was not yet come saying: [you haue heard that Antichrist cometh] And in confirmation that he wil come indeede, he addeth [now manie are become Antichristes] And a litle after he expresseth this special point saying: [who is a lyer, but he which denieth that Iesus is Christ? this is Antichrist.] And for this cause he wil impugne, and also abolish al the ordinances of our B. Sauiour; namely his Sacraments of Baptisme, Confirmation, Eucharist, Penance, and the rest, especially the most holie Sacrifice: and wil bring in place therof, Circumcision, with some other Iudaical Rites, keepe the Sabbath day, not our Lords day, nor anie feast of our Lord, nor of anie Sainct. Secondly he wil auouch him self, to be the promised Messias: And not only the Iewes, but also the whole troupes of the sinful people, Turkes heritikes, worldly and fearful christians, wil receiue him; making that general reuolt wherof S. Paul speaketh saying: that [euen then in his time, the mysterie of the iniquitie did worke] that is, iniquitie did then worke in secret; as when heritikes preach false doctrine in the name of Christ: But when Antichrist shal come and shal be reueled, he and his ministers wil teach iniquitie and falshood, openly and pubikly preaching an other Christ [him that shal come in his owne name] Thirdly therfore, he wil proclame him self to be God, as S. Paul foretelleth vs [He wilsitte in the Temple

Apoc. 9. v. 11.

Ioan. 2. v. 18. 22.

2. Thes. 2. v. 7.

He wil auouch foure capital errors against the Church.

1.
That our Lord Iesus is not Christ.

2.
That him self is the promised Messias: Christ, the Annointed.

3.
That him self is God.

O o o   of

of God, shewing him self as though he were God.] *Ibid.*
And fourthly he wil arrogate, to be the only God ; *v .4.*
denying and reiecting, not only the true God almightie, creator of al thinges : but also al false gods
besides him self. For he wil be the singular [man of *Ibidem.*
sinne ; the sonne of perdition ; the aduersarie which
is extolled aboue al that is called God , or that is
worshipped] Fulfilling that thing, wherof king Nabuchodonozor was but a figure [when he commanded his captaine Holofernes, to destroy the Goddes
of the earth, that he alone mighr be called God of
those Nations which could be subdued. And that e- *Iudith .3.*
uery Nation might know, that Nabuchodonozor is *v. 13. Ch.*
God of the earth; and that besides him, there is no *5. v. 29.*
other.] But Antichrist wil surpasse al this so farre ,as
heauen is aboue earth. For that Pagan king was content to be called the only God of the earth : but Antichrist wil be accounted the only God both of heauen
and earth. For as Daniel hath prophecied [He wil *Dan. 11. v.*
not account of the God of his fathers : and he shal be *37 . 38.*
in the concupiscences of women (carnally, and spiritually) neither shal he care for anie of the Goddes ,
because he shal rise vp against al thinges, but god *Ma-*
ozim he shal worship in his place] that is (according
to the probable coherence of this whole prophecie)
he wil glorifie his owne strength, as paganes honour
Iupiter their imagined greatest only omnipotēt God.
For so *Maozim* signifieth, fortified strengthes and re-
fuges. which sense is confirmed by this reason. For
that Antichrist publikly contemning both the only
true God, and al false goddes ; must and wil secretly
adore the diuel, the great dragon, of whom he lear-
neth al this craft, and receiueth his force; for which
he must needes doe him correspondent seruice. And
so it appeareth by the next wordes of Daniels prophecie saying [And he shal doe it to sense *Maozim* *39.*
(to fortifie

9.
He wil denie
the true God
the B . Trini-
tie .

Yet secretly he
wil adore the
diuel . by
whose power
he shal reigne,
and doe al his
vilanies .

to fortifie him self) with a strange god (to witte with the diuel) whom he acknowlegeth, and he shal multiplie glorie .]

13 By which meanes, he shal become the most diuelish sorcerer, that can be imagined, hauing al the diuels skil and power; which shal also be communicated to his cheif ministers, according as our Sauiour hath forewarned saying [there shal rise false Christes and false prophets, and shal geue signes and wonders, so that the elect also (if it be possible) may be induced into errour.] And S. Paul saith particularly of Antichrist, that [his coming is according to the operation of Satan, in al power and lying signes and wonders, and in al seducing of iniquitie .] S. Iohn also saith : that [the Dragon wil geue him his owne force, and great power.] And foretelleth three special examples of lying miracles. The first, that [one of the dragons heades (most like the great Antichrist him self) shal be as it were slaine to death; & the wound of his death cured . And al the earth was in admiration after the beast. The second, that he, or rather his cheif seruant (a great nigromancer) shal make fire to come downe from heauen vnto the earth, in the sight of men.] The third, that [he shal make the Image of the beast to speake .]

14 Thus therfore being armed with al worldlie, & diuelish power, he shal become a most execrable Tyrant [For his strength (saith Daniel) shal be made strong, but not in his owne strength: and more then can be beleeued shal he wast al thinges, and shal prosper and doe. And he shal kil the strong, and the people of the Sainctes (holie people) according as he wil ; and craft shal be directed in his hand: and he shal magnifie his heart, and in the abundance of al thinges he shal murder very many: and against the Prince of princes he shal arise : but without hand he

Margin notes:

Apoc. 13.
v. 12.
Mat. 24.
v. 24.
2. Thes.
2. v. 9.
Apoc. 13.
v. 2.

12.

13.

Dan. 8.
v. 24,
25.

He shal be a most diuelish sorcerer.

And the most execrable tyrant that euer was, or afterwardes shal be.

shal

shal be destroyed.] In the meane while to this his sauage most cruel purpose , [the diuel hauing great wrath, knowing that he hath but litle time] and Antichrist seing some to stand constant against al his impietie , notwithstanding the worldes applause, & multitudes seruing him, he wil leauie in al partes of the world, and send abrode manie huge armies [For Satan shal be loosed out of his prison, and shal goe forth and seduce the nations, that are vpon the foure corners of the earth : *Gog* , and *Magog* , shal gather them into battle ; the number of whom, is as the sand of the sea . And they ascended vpon the breadth of the earth, and compassed the campe of the Sainctes , & the beloued Citie .] In this prophecie we may obserue diuers thinges . First, that Antichristes armies shal consist of al sortes of men, and diuers Nations , especially of such as are most cruel, described by [*Gog* and *Magog*] as the barbarous Saytirs descended from *Magog* the sonne of Iapheth, and the like, with their Princes or Captaines signified by *Gog* . Secondly, that these armies shal be in al partes of the world [vpon the four corners of the earth , ascending vpon the breadth of the earth .] Thirdly, that [they shal côpasse the campe of the Sainctes] that is of faithful holie Christians . Fourthly of this it necessarily foloweth, that there shal be euen in that hottest and most general persecution, manie visible good Christians , knowne Confessors of Christ . Els they could not be compassed by manie armies . but are called [one campe] because they are al vnited by one faith , one Baptisme, in one Christ, and one God . therfore also here called [the beloued Citie .] Further we may obserue, that for the time permitted, Antichrist and his wicked princes and peoples shal outwardly preuaile against the bodies and persons of the godlie . Yet so, that the proud and insolent persecuters , shal **be**

Apoc . 12. *v* . 12.

Apoc . 20. *v* . 7. 8.

Gen . 10. *v* . 2.

be excedingly vexed, by the constancie of the good.

15. And namely by the most diligent, zelous, and *Dan.* 7. *v.* 21. 22. powerable preaching of Enoch and Elias. So Daniel beheld in his vision [Loe (saith he) that horne, (the eleuenth horne which sprange after the tenne, & ouercame them) made warre against the Sainctes, & preuailed ouer them, til the Ancient of daies came,& gaue iudgement to the Sainctes on high ; & the time came , and the Sainctes obtained the kingdome.] More amply S. Iohn writeth this very thing, rather *Apoc.* 11. *v.* 2.3. 4. as an historie, then a prophecie ¿ It is geuen (that is to say permitted) to the Gentiles (the troupes of the wicked) that they shal treade vnder foote the holie Citie fourtie two monethes . And I wil geue (saith our Lord by the penne of S . Iohn) to my two witnesses ; and they shal prophecie a thousand two hun- *Zach.* 4. *v.* 3. 14. *Cant.* 3. *v.* 5. *Ch.* 8. *v.* 4. 3. *Reg.* 17. *v.* 1. 7. dred sixtie daies, cloathed in sack-cloathes. these are the two oliue trees, and the two candle-stickes, that stand in the sight of the Lord of the earth. And if anie man wil hurt them, fyre shal come forth of their mouth and shal deuoure their enemies : And if anie man wil hurt them, so must he be slaine . These haue power to shutte heauen, that it raine not in the daies of their prophecie : and they haue power ouer waters, to turne them into bloud; and to strike the earth with al plagues as ofte as they wil .] And when they haue finished their testimonie, the beast which ascendeth from the depth , shal make warre against them, and shal ouercome them, and kil them. And their bodies shal lye in the streetes of the great Citie, 8. 9. which is called spiritually Sodome and Egipt ; where their Lord also was crucified. And there shal of Tribes & peoples, & tongues, & Gentiles, see their bodies for three daies & a half; and they shal not suffer their bodies to be laid in monumentes. And the inhabi- tantes of the earth, shal be glad vpon them, & make

True Christias shal stil resist him.

Enoch, and E- lias, shal con- firme their doctrine by miracles.

In the end he shal kil them.

merie

merie, and shal send giftes one to an other, becaufe 10.
thefe two Prophets tormented them that dwelt vpon
the earth . And after three daies and a half, the fpi- 11.
rit of life from God, entred into them ; and they
ftoode vpon their feete : and great feare fel vpon
thofe that faw them . And they heard a lowde voice 12.
from heauen faying vnto them : Come vp hither.
And they went vp into heauen in a cloude ; & their
enemies faw them ; and in that hour there was made 13.
a great earthquake, and the tenth part of the Citie fel,
and there were flaine in the earthquake names of men,
feauen thonfand, and the reft were caft into a feare, &
gaue glorie to the God of heauen .] Thus writeth the
Apoftle S . Iohn, and concludeth this pagent thus ; 14.
[The fecond woe is gone, and behold the third woe
wil come quickly] which may be thus vnderftoode.
It wll be a miferable greif & torment vnto Antichrift,
and his adherents, that fo manie bleffed Confeffors,
efpecially thefe potent Prophets, Enoch and Elias ,
fhal refift them . Secondly, that thefe two vifibly ,
fhal gaine the victorie againft them al, & againft the
diuel and death . The third woe wil be, when Antichrift him felf, fhal quickly after be flaine , and fo-
danly deftroyed .

16 Of which his final ruine, diuers Prophets haue
foretold . Ifaias defcribing Chriftes excellencie, and *If. 11. v. 4.*
victorious power againft al enemies, particularly a-
gainft Antichrift, faith [He fhal ftrike the earth with
the rodde of his mouth ; and with the fpirit of his
lippes, he fhal kil the impious .] Ezechiel faith thus *Ezech. 39.*
to Gog and his armie [I wil ftrike thy bow in thy left *v. 3. 4. 5.*
hand ; and thine aroewes wil I caft downe out of thy
right hand faith our Lord ; vpon the mountaines of
Ifrael fhalt thou fal, and al thy troupes, and thy peoples that are with thee, to the wild beaftes , to the
birdes, and to euerie foule ; and to the beaftes of the
earth

But they fhal rife againe af-ter three dayes and a half, and afcend into heauen .

Antichrift fhal then be fuden-ly deftroyed .

earth haue I geuen thee to be deuoured; thou shalt fal vpon the face of the feild, becaufe I haue fpoken faith our Lord .] To this iuft Iudge Chrift our Redemer, thus faith the Prophet Abacuc, congratulating his victorie [Thou wentft forth, the faluation of thy people ; faluation with thy Chrift : thou ftrokeft the head out of the houfe of the impious.] To al which accordeth the aduertifment of S. Paul faying, that [he which fhal be reueled, fhal be deftroied, the man of finne, that wicked one, whom our Lord Iefus fhal kil with the fpirit of his mouth ; and fhal deftroy with the manifeftation of his Aduent.] The fame thing did the Angel reuele vnto S. Iohn faying [The beaft which thou faweft, was, and is not ; and fhal come vp out of the bottomleffe depth , and goe into deftruction . And the inhabitantes of the earth, fhal meruel, feing the beaft that was & is not.]

*Abac.*3. *v.*13.

2. *Thef.* 2. *v.* 3. 8.

*Apoc.*17. *v.* 8.

17   But whiles they fhal meruel at the fudaine deftruction of the great Antichrift, his whole armies, fhal in like fudaine maner, miferably, & moft ftrangely perifh. As is fignified in the fame vifion [when they compaffed the campe of Sainctes, and the holie Citie (faith the Angel) there came downe fyre from God out of heauen and deuoured them, and the diuel which feduced them, was caft into the poole of fyre and brimftone.

Ch. 20. *v.* 8.9. 10.

Al his armies, and folowers, fhal prefently fal to nothing.

18   Finally, an other moft certaine and cleare figne, not of Antichriftes coming, but whē he fhal be come and gone, is the general conuerfion of the Iewes, who as manie holie Scriptures doe witneffe, fhal at laft be conuerted to Chrift our Sauiour. So Moyfes faid to that Nation [In the later time, thou fhalt returne to the Lord thy God; and fhalt heare his voice. [The remnant (faith Ifaias) fhal be conuerted, the remnant, I fay, of Iacob, to the ftrong God. For if thy people o Ifrael, fhal be as the fand of the fea; the

Then fhal the Iewes generally be conuerted to Chrift

Deut. 4. *v.* 30. *If.* 10. *v.* 22.

remnant

remnant therof fhal be conuerted; confummation abbridged, fhal make iuftice ouerflow .] Likewife faith Ezechiel : [Thou and thy daughters, fhal re - *Ezech*. 16. turne to your antiquitie.] Alfo Micheas foretelleth *v*. 55. the fame faying : [In that day, faith our Lord, I wil *Mich*. 4. gather her that halteth, and her that I had caft out, *v*. 6. 7. I wil gather vp ; and her whom I had afflicted. And I wil make her that halted, into a remnant, and her that had laboured, into a mightie Nation. And our Lord wil reigne ouer them in mount Sion, from this time now & for euer.] Againe faith our Lord (by his prophet Zacharias) [I wil ftrengthe the houfe of Iu- *Zach*. 10. da, and the houfe of Iofeph I wil faue; and I wil con- *v*. 6. uert them, becaufe I wil haue mercie on them, and they fhal be as they were when I had not caft them of, for I am the Lord their God, and wil heare them. Thefe are the remaines of the Iewes, that fhal be a- gaine ingrafted in their owne oliue] as S. Paul ex- *Rom*. 9. *v*. poundeth the Prophets, adding for the inftruction of 27. 28. the Romane Chriftians faying : [I wil not haue you *Ch*. 11. *v*. ignorant brethren of this Myfterie, that blindnes in 24. 25. part hath chaufed in Ifrael , vntil the fulnes of the *Ifa*. 59. *v*. Gentiles might enter, and fo al Ifrael might be faued : 20. as it is written: there fhal come out of Sion, he that fhal deliuer ; and fhal auert impietie from Iacob.]

After al thefe fignes the end of this world fhal be nere. But the houre, nor day, none can know.

19   Which Myfterie when it fhal be accomplifhed, then affuredly the end of this world wil aproach. But of the verie day albeit fome doe coniecture by the prophecie of Daniel, that it wil be [fourtie fiue *Dan*. 12. *v*. dayes after Antichriftes deftruction] yet certaine it 12. is that no man, nor Angel can certainly know it. Daniel him felf faith [I haue heard, and vnderftood 8. not. And I faid (to the Angel) my Lord what fhal be after thefe thinges? And he faid: Goe Daniel 9. 13. becaufe the wordes are fhutte vp, and fealed vntil the prefixed time.] The Apoftles alfo demaunding to *Mat*. 24. know *v*. 37. 38.

39.
Mar. 13.
v. 32.
33. 35.
36. 37.

know this day our Sauiour anſwered, that [neither man, nor Angel can know it. But as in the dayes of Noe, ſo likewiſe ſhal the coming of the Sonne of man be. For as they were in the dayes before the floud, eating, and drinking, marying, and geuing to mariage, euen vnto that day in which Noe entred into the arcke, and knew not til the floud came, and tooke them : ſo alſo ſhal the coming of the Sonne of man be. Take heede (ſaith our Lord) watch, and pray, for you know not when the time is. Watch ye therfore (for you know not when the Lord of the houſe cometh, at euen, or at midnight, or cocke crowing, or in the morning) leſt coming vpon a ſoden, he find you ſleeping. And that which I ſay to you, I ſay to al, watch.]

1. *Theſ.*
5. *v.* 1.
2. 3.

20 Wherfore S. Paul admoniſhed the Theſſaloni- ans, not to be ouermuch inquiſitiue, when the day of general Iudgement, and Reſurrection ſhal be, ſaying to them : [Of the times and moments, you neede not brethren that we write to you, for your ſelues know perfectly, that the day of our Lord ſhal ſo come, as a theefe in the night. For when they ſhal ſay, peace and ſecuritie, then ſhal ſoden deſtruction come vpon them, as the paines to her that is with child, & they ſhal not eſcape. But you brethren are not in darknes, that the ſame day may, as a theefe, ouertake you.] Euen ſo doe I confidently exhort you that ſhal read this Treatiſe, not to be curious to know, when your owne death and particular Iudgement ſhal be. For your ſelues aſſuredly know, that as death is moſt cer- taine : ſo the day of our death is vncertaine. Ther-

Mat. 24.
v. 44.

fore be you al readie [becauſe at what hour you know not, the Sonne of man wil come] firſt in particular to euerie one ; and at laſt to al in general.

It is in vaine to be inquiſitiue when the day of Iudgement ſhal be.

But neceſſarie for al to watch.

The end of the firſt Part. DEO GRATIAS.
P p p

You may please, curieous Reader, to correct the
faultes with your penne, by making it thus :

Page . 36 . lin 14 . conferued .
39 . lin . 4 . Lutherans reiect .
40 . lin . vlt . And the laft .
48 . lin . 16 . perfons & cafes .
56 . lin . 8 . this hardnes confifteth .
59 . lin . 33 . part : efpecially .
73 . lin . 12 . their hearers .
76 . lin . 31 . he drew nigh to .
77 . lin . 31 . conformable .
85 . lin . 20 . in the .
88 . lin . 31 . How long halt .
128 . lin . 21 . inuiteth .
139 . lin . 5 . of pleafure .
142 . lin . 11 . actually .
145 . *in margine* ; al mankind .
161 . lin . 28 . *Dele* 4 .
166 . *in marg* . of his coming .
167 . lin . 7 . accept him .
  In margine ; The fame .
179 . lin . 19 . three Diuine Perfons .
189 . lin . 30 . anie other name .
193 . lin . vlt . laft night .
197 . lin . 5 . Dele , natures .
lin . 6 . is moft truly and prop .
208 . lin . 24 . his vfe .
210 . lin . 4 . heareth him .
  lin . *vlt* . *in margine* , of fquadron .
212 . lin . 21 . only .
213 . lin . 3 . carying .
229 . lin . 11 . of the word .
230 . lin . 32 . to true .
235 . lin . 22 . waters .
242 . lin . 16 . of thinges infinitly .
  F I N I S .

265 . lin . 2 . finners therof .
lin . 26 . folded .
267 . lin . 34 . fhal be .
282 . lin . vlt . aray .
295 . lin . 12 . He faluted alfo .
301 . li . 33 . Phaleg, Reu, Sarug
302 . lin . 1 . Aran .
303 . lin . 26 . prefidents .
304 . lin . 21 . al the princes .
305 . lin . 34 . of Iuda ; caufing .
326 . lin . 9 . greater pleafure .
327 . lin . 35 . vpon anie one .
330 . lin . 5 . To him .
314 . lin . 14 . Generally in al .
350 . lin . 1 . yea that .
358 . *in margine* . Art . 42 .
369 . lin . 25 . then alfo .
372 . lin . 2 . and his fonnes .
373 . lin . 2 . wifdom crie .
379 . lin . 12 . his breft .
380 . *in marg* . temporal prince .
385 . lin . 32 . fignifying that the .
386 . lin . 12 . but the other .
390 . lin . 22 . procedeth .
398 . lin . 14 . life were .
408 . lin 34 . they had .
409 . lin . 5 . a cheefe man .
419 . lin . 2 . then fupplying .
lin . 17 . releafing vnto him .
lin . 32 . by what power .
431 . lin . 26 . reputing .
442 . lin 31 . bodies in a forte .
455 . lin . 21 . al iudged .
480 . lin . 10 . witnes . Of Enoch .

To the right welbeloued
ENGLISH READER.

ECAVSE the former parts of this worke, and thefe latter, being printed at diuers times, wil hardly perhaps come toge-ther, to the fame perfons handes; I haue thought it mete (Welbeloued Reader) here to repete the fummarie contents of the former Preface. Wherby you may fee the caufes, why after fo manie excellent Bookes, written in our language, for clearing al pointes of Chriftian Doctrine, this alfo is written in an other forme; prouing the fame by holie Scriptures only. Which thing is vndertaken (as alfo the Holie Bible is for the fame reafons, fet forth in vulgar tongues) firft to fatisfie al fuch, as vntruly fuppofe that we preferre anie other auctoritie aboue the holie Scriptures. Secondly to ioyne iffue of trial with our Aduerfaries, who imagine that herein they haue fome aduantage againft vs. And withal to geue contentment, if it be poffible, to al thofe, which at this time, wil admitte no other proofes in matter of Faith, and Religion, but the onlie Scriptures: that fo it may appeare, who are beft grounded therein.

VVhy this Treatife is written.

The firft caufe.

2.

3.

For although our English Proteftants in the be-ginning of Quene Elifabeths reigne, very boldly pro-uoked al Roman Catholiques to trie the true Reli-gion, not only by the holie Scriptures, but alfo by the Ancient Councels, and Fathers of the firft fix hudred yeares after Chrift: as M. Iohn Iuel publikely proclamed at S. Pauls Croffe in London; yet shortly after, finding by experience, that they were not able to maintaine that chalenge, they generally euer fince fay plainly, that they wil not ftand to anie other au-

Proteftants fometime pro-mifed to ftand to the iudge-ment of an-cient Fathers.

Anno 1559.

Now they require onlie Scriptures.

† 2 &ctoritie,

&toritie, but to the onlie written Word of God . And
holding opinion that the Church ean erre in Faith,
they endeuour to bring the very Church it felf(theirs *Ifa. 54. 7.*
and our proper Iudge) to be iudged as a partie. *17.*
Wherby they draw al Controuerfies to this one queftion: Who amongft al pretenders, rightly vnderftand the holie Scriptures? Wherupó we might moft
iuftly require, that they by onlie Scriptures, should
firft difprone our long eftablished Religion;and then
alfo proue their owne, newly pretended.

We agree to
proue by onlie
Scriptures,
which is the
true Religion.

But feing they can not doe it; we, for the more manifeftation of truth, and for better reducing thofe
that erre, into the right way, doe condefcend to trie
this important caufe,by this fpecial, & onlie meanes,
to which, you our Aduerfaries, feme fo confidenrly
to appeale. Only befeching you, that we may in
fober maner, by word, or by writing, without cla-
morous contention, or vncharitable railing,procede
herein; according to thefe, or other reafonable conditions. For without reafonable conditions (as both
ancient and prefent experience teacheth) it is but
lofe of time, to difpute with contentious fpirites, out
of only Scriptures. Firft therfore you muft ftil remember, that we doe not grant your exclufion of other
proofes, to be iuft; but that we are content to abftaine from them, vntil you shal find it needeful, to
repaire vnto them againe. Secódly, that in the meane
while you be alfo limited, to the fame onlie meanes
of holie Scriptures. Thirdly, that it may fuffice for
either partie (which wil be as neceffarie for you, as
for vs) to proue the thing it felf, which we beleue,
by neceffarie confequence, of the holie Scriptures,
though the verie wordes be not there expreffed.
Fourtly, when in our conference, fome wordes, or
fentences of holie Scripture, may feme hard, or
contrarie to other places, that then the fame may be
explaned, by the more cleare: or the more in number

Prefuppofing
reafonable có-
ditions.

1. Condition.

2.

3.

4.

See Manu-
ductions
to the true
Church.ch.
9.10.

(pertey-

(perteyning to the fame matter) may explicate the fewer. Alwayes confidering that euerie word in holie Scripture, is affuredly true: al being indited by the Holie Ghoft. Thefe conditions we fuppofe, al lo-uers of truth, and ftudious of concord, wil approue for reafonable. In confidence whereof, we here proue not only matters of Controuerfie, but alfo al principal pointes of Chriftian Doctrine: becaufe ma-nie Controuerfies depend vpon other Articles, at this time not called into queftion. Becaufe alfo new errors doe dayly rife, which haue like nede, to be confuted. Thirdly, to shew by experience, that old Heretikes drew as plaufible arguments from the holie Scriptures, for their errors, as anie Sectaries doe now for their new opinions. Fourtly, for our further inftruction by holie Scriptures, as wel in al pointes of Faith, which we are bond to know: as in Precepts of life, which we are bond to performe: according to the Apoftles doctrine [Be ye doers of the word, and not hearers only] For better explica-tion fake, we diuide this whole worke into foure parts. In the firft part are explained the Articles of the Apoftles Crede. In the fecond part, the feuen holie Sacraments of Chrift. In the third, the tenne Commandments. And in the fourth part, the necef-farie vfe of Prayer: Efpecially Our Lords Prayer.

VVhy other points are here proued, which are not now in con-trouerfie. 1. Reafon. 2.

3.

4.

Iac. I.v.22.

The whole worke is diui-ded into foure parts.

To God be al glorie.

From Arras College in Paris. 25. Martij. 1622.

Yours euer in Chrift our Lord:

THOMAS VVORTHINGTON
Seminario Prieft.

† 3

THE CONTENTS OF
THE FIRST PART.
Concerning the Articles of Faith: comprised in the Apostles Crede.

Credo   F Aith is necessarie to saluation. *Article 1.*
     Mans witte, nor reach of natural reason, can not attaine faith: neither is mans testimonie sufficient to assure it, but Gods word onely. *Article 2.*

Gods word is partly written in the holie Scriptures: partly knowen, and kept by Tradition. *Art. 3.*

Some Scriptures are hard, and require authentical interpretation. *Article 4.*

True miracles are an assured proofe of faith: and of other truth, for the which they are wrought. *Art. 5.*

In Deum   God is one: and there can not be anie other God. *Art. 6.*

Patrem   In God is Trinitie of Persons, the Father, the Sonne, and the Holie Ghost. *Article 7.*

Omnipotenté   God is Omnipotent. *Article 8.*

God knoweth al thinges. *Article 9.*

God is absolute Goodnes: & al his actions rre good. *Art. 10.*

Creatorem Cæli   Angeles, the first creatures, are, the most part, in glorie: manie are damned. *Art. 11.*

Holie Angeles by their ministerie, & prayers, protect & helpe men. Diuels seeke mens ruine. *Art. 12.*

Et terræ   Man at first receiued original Iustice: which he lost by transgressing Gods commandment. And therby infected al his progenie with Original sinne. *Art. 13.*

Mans vnderstanding, and free wil are weakned by sinne: but not lost. *Article 14.*

Et in Iesum   After the fal of man, God promised a Redemer: who was also foreshewed by manie figures: and by al the Prophets. *Art. 15.*

Christum.   Our Lord Iesus of Nazareth is Christ, our Redemer. *Art. 16.*

Filium eius vnicum   Our Lord Iesus Christ is God, the Second Person of the B. Trinitie. *Article 17.*

Dominum nostrum   Our Lord Iesus Christ is truly man. *Art. 18.*

Christ

Chrift our Lord, from the inftant of his Incarnation, had fulnes of Grace, Knowlege, and Power. *Art.19.*

Chrift our Lord tooke al mans infirmities, not opofite to perfection. *Articlt 20.*

The B. Virgine Marie is the Mother of God: and moft excellent of al created perfons. *Art.21.*

Chrift our Sauiour after thirtie yeares priuate life, preached his Gofpel: confirming it diuers wayes. *Art.22.*

Chrift our Redemer fufferted manie greuous torments: Death on the Crofle: and was buried. *Art.23.*

The glorious foule of our B. Sauiour, parting from his bodie, defcended into hel. *Art.24.*

Our Sauiour Iefus Chrift rofe from death the third day. *Article 25.*

Chrift our Lord appeared often after his Refurrection. And ordeined diuers thinges, perteyning to his Church. *Art.26.*

Chrift our Lord afcended into heauen: fitteth on the right hand of God. *Article 27.*

Chrift our Lord wil come in Maieftie: and Iudge the world. *Article 28.*

God the Holic Ghoft (with the Father, and the Sonne) infpireth: & fanctifieth the Church, & the members thereof. *Art.29.*

The vniuerfal Church confifteth of holie Angeles, with other Sainéts in heauen, and the faithful in earth: of al which, Chrift as man, is Head. *Art.30.*

The militant Church conteyneth two general members: The Clergie, and Laitie; vnder one vifible head. *Art.31.*

As wel the Clergie, as Laitie conteine particular bodies, with feueral heades, al fubordinate in one bodie, to one Supreme Vifible Head. *Article 32.*

The true Church of God is knowen by fpecial markes. The firft of which is Vnitie. *Art.33.*

In the old Teftament there was euer one Supreme Vifible Head of the Church. *Art.34.*

Chrift our Sauiour ordained S. Peter cheefe of the Apoftles: and Vifible Head of the militant Church. *Art.35.*

Chrift our Sauiour alfo ordayned a continual Succeffion of S. Peters Supremacie, to the end of this world. *Art.36.*

The

[marginal Latin notes:] Qui cóceptus eft de Spiritu Sancto. Natus. Ex Maria Virgine. Paffus fub Pont. Pil. cruci.mort. & fepult. Defcendit ad inferos. Tertia die refurrexit à mortuis. Afcendit ad cælos fedet ad dext.Dei. Pat. Omnipot. Inde ven.eft Iu.viu.& mor. Credo in Spiritum Sanct. Ecclefiam.

Sanctam
Catholicam.

The true Church of Christ is Holie.   Art. 37.
The true Church is Catholique.   Art. 38.
The true Church is Apostolique.   Art. 39.
The true Church is Perpetual, from the begining of the
world to the end.   Article 40.
   The true Church of God euer hath bene, and wil be Visible.
                                                                   Article 41.
The Church can not erre, in doctrine of faith: not of maners.
                                                                   Article 42.

Sanctorum
Communio-
nem.

In the whole Church is Communion of Sacrifice, Sacra-
ments, Praiers, and other good workes.   Art. 43.
   Soules in Purgatorie doe participate of the Communion of
Sainctes: receiuing releefe by the holie Sacrifice, and other suf-
frages.   Article 44.
No Infideles doe partipate of the communion of Sainctes.
Neither is it lawful to communicate with them, in practise of
Religion.   Article 45.
   Excommunicated persons are excluded from the Church, and
communion of Sainctes.   Article 46.
   Whosoeuer doe fal into mortal sinne, lose the participation
of good workes, vntil they be truly penitent.   Art. 47.

Remissionem
peccatorum
Carnis Resur-
rectionem.

In the Catholique Church is remission of sinnes : and Iustification by grace.   Article 48.
Al mankind shal rise from death, at the day of General Iudgement.   Article 49.

Vitam æter-
nam.

   The blessed shal enioy eternal glorie: according to their merites.   Article 50.
The wicked shal be in euerlasting payne, for their sinnes.
                                                                   Article 51.

Amen.

It was foreshewed, and there haue bene, are, and wil be Heresies, against the true Faith.   Art. 52.
   Antichrist the head of al Heretickes, is to come: nere the end
of this world.   Article 53.

THE

THE CONTENTS OF
THE SECOND PART.
Concerning the Holie Sacraments of Chrift.

† †

It fuffi-

It sufficeth, and is more conuenient, that al communicants, be-sides the Priest that celebrateth, receiue vnder one kind only.
Article 20.

Al Christians hauing vse of reason, are bond to receiue this most holie Sacrament. *Article 21.*

Sacrificium. The holie Eucharist is also a Sacrifice propiciatorie. *Article 22.*

The holie Eucharist is the complement of al the old Sacri-fices. *Article 23.*

Sacrifice is due to God onlie : and to no creature, how excel-lent soeuer. *Article 24.*

Pœnitentia. Penance consisting of Contrition, Confession, and Satisfa-ction, is a true Sacrament. *Article 25.*

Contrition or (at least) Attrition is necessarie, as the first part of Penance. *Article 26.*

Confession of al mortal sinnes is necessarie, for remission thereof. *Article 27.*

Venial sinnes are sufficient, & conuenient matter of Sacramen-tal Confession: though also remissible otherwise. *Article 28.*

Secresie of Sacramental Confession is necessarie, by the Law of God, and of natnre. *Article 29.*

Satisfaction for the guilt of sinne, and for eternal payne, is made by Christ only. *Article 30.*

Eternal punishment being remitted with the sinne, there re-mayneth ordinarily temporal punishment. *Article 31.*

True penitents enabled by grace, doe satisfie the debt of tem-poral punishment, due for sinnes remitted. *Article 32.*

Praying, Fasting, and Almesdeedes, are special satisfactorie workes, for sinnes remitted. *Article 33.*

One may satisfie for an other; being both in state of grace.
Article 34.

Temporal paine due for sinnes remitted, may be released by Indulgence. *Article 35.*

The residue of satisfaction, not made in this life, is to be fulfil-led in Purgatorie: by suffering, or by suffrages, after death. *Art.36.*

The proper effect of the Sacrament of Penance is remission of actual sinnes, after Baptisme. *Article 37.*

Extrema Vnctio. Extreme Vnction of the sicke with holie Oile, by a Priest, is a true Sacrament. *Article 38.*

The

The proper effect is strengthning of the soule in the agonie of death: with remission of sinnes if anie remayned: and restauration to bodlie health, if it be expedient for the soule. *Article* 39.

It behoueth al penitents, being by sicknes in peril of death, to receiue this Sacrament of Extreme Vnction. *Article* 40.

Ordination of Priestes; and of other Clergie men; is a true Sacrament. *Article* 41. Sacer Orde.

None can be made Clergimen, but by Ordination of the Apostles successors. *Article* 42.

Competent qualities; especially of Age, Maners; and Learning, are conueniently required in Clergimen. *Article* 43.

The principal power of Holie Orders, is to consecrate, & offer Chrifts Bodie and Bloud, in the holie Sacrifice. *Article* 44.

An other power of holie Orders is Iurisdiction: to feede, & gouerne the Church. *Article* 45.

There are diuers degrees of spiritual Paftors, subordinate to one cheefe visible Head. *Article* 46.

Mariage rightly contracted betwen a Christian man & a Christian woman, is a true Sacrament. *Article* 47. Matrimonium

Diuers iuft impediments doe debarre some persons from contracting Mariage. *Article* 48.

The bond of Christian Mariage can not be diffolued, so long as both parties liue in this world. *Article* 49.

Christ gaue his Church power to institute sacred Rites, & Ceremonies: which are called Sacramentals. *Article* 50. Sacramétalia.

THE CONTENTS OF
THE THIRD PART.
Concerning the tenne commandments.

Gods commandments are possible: and necessarie to be kept. *Article* 1. Locutus est Dominus cunctos sermones hos: Ego sum Dominus Deus tuus &c.

By keping Gods commandments, the faithful please God: and merite eternal glorie. *Article* 2.

Al men are bond to serue God with diuine honour. And first to beleue in him. *Article* 3.

Al are bond to hope in God. And confidently to relie vpon his diuine prouidence. *Article* 4. Decem verba, quæ scripfit in duabustabulis. Deut. 4. 7. 13.

Al are bond to loue God aboue al other thinges. And consequently

† † 2 quently

quently their neighbours as themselues.' *Article 5.*

Al are bond to serue God with internal deuotion, & external declaration thereof, by the vertue of Religion. *Article 6.*

It is forbidden to serue anie creature as a God. *Article 7.*

Sorcerie, Nigromancie, Witchrie: & al pactes with diuels, expresse, or secrete, are execrable. *Article 8.*

Al are bond to honour holie Angeles; and other Sainctes. And to reuerence holie Reliques, and Images. *Article 9.*

An oath (when iust cause requireth) must be made by Gods name: or by some creature as depending on God. *Article 10.*

It is forbidden to sweare anie false thing: or vncertaine as certaine. *Article 11.*

It is likewise forbidden to sweare without iust necessitie, & important cause. *Article 12:*

It is also forbidde to sweare, or to promise with an oath, anie vnlawful thing. And it is duble sinne to performe such a promise. *Article 13.*

Wittingly to breake a lawful promise, made with an oath, is periurie. *Article 14.*

Blasphemie is an enormious sinne: iniurious to Diuine Maiestie. *Article 15.*

The Sabbath day was kept holie in the old Testament, by Gods ordinance. *Article 16.*

Christians are bound to kepe Sunday (called our Lords day) holie: not the Sabbath. *Article 17.*

Prudence, and the verrues annexed; Right Counsel, and mature Iudgement, are necessarie. *Article 18.*

Iustice, & other vertues annexed; Pietie, Reuerence, Obedience, Gratitude, Liberalitie, & Freindshipe, are necessarie. *Article 19.*

Fortitude, & other vertues annexed, Magnanimitie, Patience, Longanimitie, and Perseuerance are necessarie. *Article 20.*

Temperance, & other vertues annexed, Continencie, Meeknes, Humilitie, and Modestie, are necessarie. *Article 21.*

Al are bond to honour their Father & Mother. Especiallie to assist them in necessitie, spiritual and temporal. *Article 22.*

Al are also bond to honour, and obey spiritual, and temporal Superiors. *Article 23.*

Al Christians are bond sometimes to abstaine from certaine meates;

meates; And to faſt; by Diuine, & Eccleſiaſtical Lawes. *Art.24.*

It is forbidde to kil anie man: except by lawful auctoritie, & in due maner. *Article 25.* **5.** Non occides.

It is vnlawful to ſtrike, or to impriſon anie perſon, Without iuſt cauſe, and auctoritie. *Article 26.*

Reuengeful wordes, & anger without cauſe, are alſo forbidden. *Article 27.*

Al are bond, ſo much as lieth in them, to haue peace with al. And to loue their enimies. *Article 28.* **6.** Non mæchaberis.

Adultrie, fornication, & al venereous actes, are greueous ſinnes. And after vowed chaſtitie, are Sacriligious. *Article 29.*

Al are bond to eſteme chaſtitie. And to chaſtice the bodie, that it may ſerue the ſpirite. *Art clc 30.* **7.** Non furtum facies.

Al vniuſt getting, or holding of others goodes, is forbidde by the law of God, and of nations. *Article 31.*

Iniuſtice committed in ſacred thinges, is ſacrilege. And bying or ſelling ſpiritual thinges, is Simonie. *Article 32.*

Prodigalitie in ſuperfluous expenſes: and Niggardnes in miſerable ſparing, are forbidden by Gods Law. *Article 33.*

It is ſpecially forbidde to hurt the fame of anie perſon vniuſtly. *Article 34.*

Suſurration is an eſpecial iniurie, & a deteſtable ſinne. *Article 35.*

Al are bond ſometimes to practiſe workes of mercie; ſpiritual and temporal. *Article 36.* **8.** Non loqueris contra proximum tuum falſum teſtimonium,

Al are bond, when lawful auctoritie requireth, to teſtifie the truth which they know. *Article 37.*

It is forbidde to beare falſe witneſſe, or to lie, or iudge raſhly. *Article 38.*

Falſe accuſation, & condemnation of the innocent: & iuſtification of the guiltie, are damnable ſinnes. *Article 39.*

It is a particular wickednes to praiſe, or flatter anie for their ſinne. *Article 40.*

if anie be demanded of a ſecrete thing, by reuealing whereof vniuſt hurt is like to enſue, it is not lawful to reueale it. *Art. 41.*

They that are vniuſtly demanded, may lawfully anſwer in an other ſenſe, then he demander vnderſtandeth it. *Article 42.*

Whoſoeuer doe vniuſtly hurt others; or be in debt; are bond to reſtitution. *Article 43.*

†† 3   It is

It is forbidden to consent in mind, vnto vnlawful carnal thoughtes.   *Article* 44.

9.
Non concu-
pisces vxorem
proximi tui,

It is forbidde to consent in mind, vnto vnlawful desires of worldlie goodes.   *Article* 45.

10.
Non concu-
pisces domum
proximi tui:
non agrũ &c.

Christians are bond to obserue Ceremonial Precepts of Christ, and his Church.   *Article* 46.

Christians are also bond to obserue Iudicial Precepts of Temporal Superiors.   *Article* 47.

Docete eos
seruare omnia
quecunque
mãdaui vobis.

Good workes of supererogatiõ are possible, pious, & profitable.
And when they are vowed, doe binde in conscience.   *Article* 48.

Vniuersal obedience to a determinate Superiour, is piously vowed.   *Article* 49.

Si vis perfe-
ctus esse vende
quæ habes, &
da pauperib.
& sequere me.

Vow of perpetual chastitie is an holie, & meritorious act. *Art.* 50.
Vow of volũtarie pouertie, to possesse no worldlie goodes in proper, is godlie, and meritorious.   *Article* 51.

THE CONTENTS OF THE
FOVRTH PART.
Concerning Prayer. Especially the Pater Noster.

Dixit Iesus
Discipulis suis:
Sic vos ora-
bitis.

IT is necessarie to pray often : actually desiring good thinges of God.   *Article* 1.

Thankesgeuing for Gods benefites is a special, and necessarie kind of prayer.   *Articl* 2.

Praises of God, by Confessing his singular Excellences, is also a necessarie kind of prayer.   *Article* 3.

Meditation, & Contemplation is the best priuate prayer. *Art.* 4.

Vocal prayer is also necessarie. Especially publique prayer. *Art.* 5.

Priuate prayer may be in any language : though not vnderstood.   *Article* 6.

Publique prayer must be in a sacred tongue : common to manie nations, of diuers vulgar languages.   *Article* 7.

Faith, Hope, Humilitie, Repentance, and other vertues, are required in prayer.   *Article* 8.

Reuerent, modest, and comelie disposition of the bodie, is also required, as an helpe to deuotion.   *Article* 9.

Attention is so necessarie, that the more or lesse it is, the more or lesse is the fruite of prayer.   *Article* 10.

Prayer with due conditions is meritorious. And is alwaies granted by God.   *Article* 11.

We

We are bond to pray for the whole militant Church. And particularly for the ſpiritual Paſtors thereof. Article 12.

We are alſo bond to pray for al Chriſtian Princes, and Magiſtrates. Eſpecially for thoſe, vnder whom we liue. Article 13.

We are bond to pray for the ſoules in Purgatorie. Eſpecially for our parentes, benefactors, and other nereſt freindes. Article 14.

In the preface of our Lords prayer, we inuocate Almightie God: Pater Father of al men, by creation, conſeruation & redēption. Ar. 15.

God is more peculiarly the Father of the faithful. And moſt Noſter eſpecially of the iuſt. Article 16.

God being euery where; Heauen as the moſt excellent place, Qui es in cæ- is called his Seate, and Kingdome. Article 17. lis.

In the firſt petition we pray, that Gods name may be honored Sanctificetur by al, and dishonored by none. Article 18. nomen tuum,

We pray more particularly, that we which beleue in God, may euer haue grace to glorifie his name. Article 19.

Al true Chriſtians doe alſo pray, that themſelues, & al others may loue, honour, & inuocate the holie name, IESVS. Art. 20.

In the ſecond petition we pray, that God wil accompliſh his Adueniat reg- kingdome of al the elect. Article 21. num tuum.

We alſo pray that God wil propagate, and euer conſerue his militant Church, to the end of this world. Article 22.

We likewiſe pray that God wil reigne in vs, by his ſanctifying grace. Article 23.

In the third petition we pray that Gods wil, not our owne pro- Fiat voluntas per wil, be ſo fulfilled in earth, as it is in heauen. Article 24. tua: ſicut in

Gods abſolute wil, called his good pleaſure, is euermore ful- cælo & in ter- filled. Article 25. ra.

Gods conditional wil, which is knowne by ſignes, is often not fulfilled. Article 26.

In the fourth petition we pray our heauenlie Father, to geue Panem noſtrū vs al neceſſarie ſpiritual and corporal foode. Article 27. (superſubſtan-

We pray in particular that we may frutefully participate of the tialem) quoti- B. Sacrifice, and Sacrament of the Altar. Article 28. dianum da nobis hodie.

We pray alſo for al thinges neceſſarie in this temporal life.

Article 29.

In the fifth petition we pray God, to forgeue vs our ſinnes: & Et dimitte no- the debtes therof. Article 30. bis debita no-
ſtra:

For

Sicut & nos dimittimus debitoribus nostris.

For obtayning remission of sinnes, we must forgeue in our harts, al iniuries done vnto vs. *Article* 31.

It is also necessarie to loue our enimies, doing good to them for euil. *Article* 32.

Et ne nos inducas in tentationem;

In the sixth petition, we pray for strength of grace, to resist al tentations of sinne. *Article* 33.

We also pray God, that he wil not suffer vs to be assaulted, with ouer great tentations. *Article* 34.

We likewise pray for grace, to repel first motions tending to sinne. *Article* 35.

Sed libera nos à malo.

In the seuenth petition, we pray our heauenlie Father, to deliuer vs from temporal euils. Especially from al the diuels power. *Article* 36.

We pray also to be deliuered from euil habites, gotten by sinne: and from imperfections. *Article* 37.

Likewise we pray to be deliuered from dangerous afflictions, which may hurt the soule. *Article* 38.

Amen.

The Conclusion, *Amen*: is a confirmation of our part, that we truly desire, that which we aske in wordes. *Article* 39.

This word Amen, is also a confirmation on Gods part, that he granteth whatsoeuer is duly asked in prayer. *Article* 40.

Aue Maria &c.

The Angelical Salutation of the B. Vergine, Mother of God, is lawfully, and profitably recited by good Christians. *Art.* 41.

Sancta Maria, Mater Dei ora pro nobis.

The second part of the Aue *Maria*: Holie Marie, Mother of God &c. is a godlie prayer, agreable to holie Scriptures. *Article* 42.

Holie Angels doe offer mens prayers to God: doe pray for men: and are profitably inuocated. *Article* 43.

Æquales Angelis sunt.

Other glorious Saintes vnderstand the affaires of mortal men: and doe pray for them. *Article* 44.

It is lawful, and profitable to pray the glorious Saintes, that they wil pray for vs to God. *Article* 45.

Orate pro inuicem vt saluemini.

It is no derogation to Christ, & is very profitable to mortal persons, that one pray for an other. *Art.* 46.

F
I N I
S

THE SECOND PART OF
THE ANKER
OF CHRISTIAN DOCTRINE:

THE FIRST ARTICLE.

God geueth his grace to men, not only by inui-
sible meanes : but also by external signes.

IKE as it pleafed the Diuine Omnipotent Goodnes, fo to difpofe his creatures, that inferior bodies of this lower
world, fhould receiue certaine natural
influence, of the higher cœleftial planetes, & other ftarres ; & that amongft other corporal liuing thinges, mans temporal life fhould be fu-
fteined by the helpe of diuers elements; as by vfe of
the ayer, through which we breath; of food, wherwith we are fedde ; of clothing, wherewith we are
couered ; of fire, of water, & of manie other thinges,
without which we could not fubfift: euen fo it alfo
hath pleafed the fame Diuine fountaine of al goodnes, that his feruantes in this tranfitorie life fhould
receiue fupernatural grace, not only by his immediate infufion thereof into their foules, as he firft
imparted his fpiritual giftes, in the ftate of mans innocencie, but alfo by inftrumental fecondarie caufes, which his Diuine wifdom hath ordayned as vifible fignes, of his inuiffible operation. Which fpiritual vertue, becaufe Proteftants denie to be in the
holie Sacrifice, Sacraments, or anie other external
holie Rites, we fhal here through Gods fpecial grace
(whereof we now treate) manifeftly fhew, according to the Catholique doctrine in this behalf: firft
Artic. I. in general *a* that God imparteh his manifold fpiri-

B   tual

As God ordai-
ned in nature
that one crea-
ture receiueth
profite by an
other : fo it
agreeth to his
diuine wifdó,
that mã (efpe-
cialy after his
fal) fhould re-
ceiue fpiritual
grace by fenfi-
ble meanes.

What pointes of doctrine are to be proued in this second part.

tual giftes, & graces, by diuers *b* visible meanes; & *b Artic.* 2. also requireth, & accepteth mans seruice by exter- 3. nal actes, & Ceremonies, *c* especially by those most *c Artic.* 4. diuine Mysteries, which Chrift our Redemer hath 5. 6. 7. ordained, *d* as sacred instruments *e* to be admini- *d Artic.* 8. stred by men, to Gods special honour, & mans spi- *e Artic.* 9. ritual good. *f* And so we shal procede to proue &*f Artic.* 10 declare in particular, the seuen holie Sacraments, 11. *&c.* *g* with the one most dread Sacrifice of the Christian *g Artic.* 22. Catholique Church. The necessitiæ, profite, and 23. 24.

Al as clearly proued by the Scriptures as those Sacraments, and Rites, which Proteftants acknowlege.

proper effectes of euerie one in their due place, & order. And this we shal doe for most part, by the expresse written word of God, in cleare & manifest termes; the rest also, no lesse assuredly by other holie Scriptures: not only according to the vnderstanding and iugement of the piller of truth, the only knowen Church for manie ages (which we doe not so much vrge in this present trial) but also, we shal verifie our beleefe herein, by the most apparent sense, & conference of other places, againft al, that our Aduersaries can alleage of the sacred text, to the contrarie. And alwayes as directly & inuincibly, as they can proue those Rites, Ceremonies, or Sacraments, which they hold, & confesse for lawful before God: & profitable to Christian soules.

Exaples of supernatural effects wrought by sensible creatures.

2. Touching therefore the first poinct, it is euident in the holie text, that also in the state of mans innocencie, God gaue such vertue to a special tree in paradise, that whosoeuer should eate of the fruite therof, should become immortal, & liue for euer. Neither was that tree depriued of the same vertue after the fal of man, but left man by eating thereof, after his sinne, should haue liued for euer in this world, God remoued him out of Paradise, saying:

The tree of life in Paradise.

[lest perhaps he reach forth his hand, & take also of *Gen.* 3. the tree of life, & eate, & liue for euer.] Seing ther-*v.* 22. fore man, though he had not sinned, was to receiue

so graso gracious a gift, as immortalitie, by eating the fruite of a tree, it is not to be marueled, that sinners are in some sorte made subiect to sensible creatures, for recouerie, and increase of grace. In confirmation wherof we haue cleare testimonies in holie Scriptures, of Gods benefites & blessinges bestowed by the vse of sundrie creatures, designed by him for such purposes. So when the children of Israel, had no other water to drinke in the deserte, but that

Exod. 15. which was bitter; [Moyses cried to our Lord (for
v. 23. 24. remedie) & he shewed him a peece of wood, which
25. when he had cast into the waters, they were turned into swetenesse] Againe God did the like to other vnprofitable water, by the vse of salt, which the
4. *Reg.* 2. Prophete [Eliseus cast into it, & said: Thus saith our
v. 21. 22. Lord: I haue amended these waters, & death shal no more be in them, nor barrennesse. And the waters were amended, according to the word of Eliseus, which he spake.] And as God imperted benefites by wood, and salt, together with the faith and prayers of his Prophetes, so he gaue the like by the blessinges of Parents, & Priestes. For according to

Gen. 9. *v.* Noes blessing, & cursing of his children, & their pro-
25. 26. 27. genie, it happened afterwards vnto them diuersly. It appereth also to haue bene a general custome with the Patriarches, to blesse their children, especially before their death, though it be not expresly recor-
Gen. 27. ded of al. For [Isaac waxing old, called Esau his
v. 1. 2. 3. elder sonne, & said to him : Thou seest, quoth he,
4. that I am old, and know not the day of my death. Take thyne instruments, thy quiuer & thy bow, &c. bring that I may eate, and my soule may blesse thee before I dye.] And when (by Gods secrete proui-dence, for Mysterie sake) Iacob his younger sonne had gotte the principal blessing, Isaac perceiuing it
v. 33. v. to be done according to Gods wil [said : I haue
39. *Ch.* 48. blessed him, & he shal be blessed] & finally gaue Esau
v. 15. 19. an other

A peece of wood.

Salt.

Fathers blessing.

an other fecondarie bleffing. The fame Patriarch
Iacob, bleffed the two fonnes of his fonne Iofeph;
& that in fpecial manner, croffing his armes, & laying his right hand vpon the younger brother his
head, & his left hand vpon the head of the elder, fignifying literally that Ephraim the younger of thofe
bretheren fhould be preferred before Manaffes the
elder,& myftically fignifying (which was likewife
fignified, by the bleffing of Iacob before Efau) that
the Gentiles fhould be preferred before the Iewes,
in the Church of Chrift:Infinuating alfo by croffing
his armes the fpecial vertue of the Croffe of Chrift.
After this, Iacob alfo prophecied of al his owne *Ch. 49. v.*
twelue fonnes, including therein manie great My- *3. 5. &c.*
fteries of Chrift,& his Church; for as the text reporteth, [He bleffed euerie one of them, with their *v. 29.*
proper bleffinges.] Alfo Mathathias the zelous god- *1. Mach.2.*
lie [Highprieft, a litle before his death, after moft *v. 49. &*
holie inftruction, & exhortation to obferue & main- *69.*
taine the law of God, bleffed his fiue fonnes, & was

Prieftes blef-
fing.

laide to his fathers.] Concerning Prieftes bleffing of
the people God prefcribed a fette forme of wordes,
with which they fhould doe it, faying to Moyfes:
[Speake to Aaron and to his fonnes; thus fhal you *Num. 6.*
bleffe the children of Ifrael, & you fhal fay to them: *v. 23. 24.*
Our Lord bleffe thee, & kepe thee: Our Lord fhew *25. 26.*
his face to thee ; and haue mercie vpon thee : Our
Lord turne his countenance vnto thee, & geue thee
peace] Moyfes did alfo bleffe Iofue (when he was *Deut. 34.*
ordained to fuccede him in the temporal gouuerne- *v. 9.*
ment) with impofition of his handes, and he therwithal receiued fpecial grace, the fpirite of wifdõ,
as it is recorded in the end of Deuteronomie,by thefe wordes [Iofue the fonne of Nun was replenifhed
with the fpirite of wifdom, becaufe Moyfes did put
his handes vpon him.]

3.   Generally in the written law of Moyfes, God
fignified

signified his spiritual benefites, by manie Ceremonial ordinances, & external Rites, which were instituted for three special causes: First to withdraw, &
kepe the people from Idolatrie, wherto they were
very prone. Secondly to induce them therby to internal vertues: for that by visible thinges, men enter
into conceipte of inuisible. Thirdly to signifie, more
excellent, and more effectual Mysteries of the new
Testament. So when God had deliuered his tenue
moral precepts, he gaue also ceremonial, saying:

External Ri-
tes were insti-
tuted to keepe
the people
from Idolatrie
To induce the
to internal
vertues, & to
signifie grea-
ter Mysteries
in the new
Testament.

Exod. 20.
v. 24.
v. 25.

[An Altar of earth you shal make to me, & you shal
offer vpon it, your Holo caustes, & Pacifiques, your
sheepe, & oxen, in euerie place, where the memorie
of my name shal be, I wil come to thee, & wil blesse
thee. And if thou make an Altar of stone vnto me,
thou shalt not builde it of hewed stones: for if thou
lift vp thy knife ouer it, it shal be polluted.] Where
it is cleare that the vse of an Altar is to offer Sacrifice theron, of diuers sortes: as here is mention of
two kindes: Holocaustes in which the whole hoste
was burned & consumed in the honour of God; &
Pacifiques, which were either of thankesgeuing for
benefites receiued; or petitatorie for obtaining thinges needful. The third kind was Sacrifice for sinnes. Which being duly offered, was an external
signe of Gods inuisible grace, remitting sinnes: as

Leuit. 17.
v. 11.

God himself testifieth saying: [I haue geuen the
bloud to you, that vpon the Altar you may make expiation with it, for your soules, & the bloud may be
for an expiation of the soule] which was the ceremonial reason, why the faithful seruants of God
were so strictly prohibited, not to eate anie bloud,
for so it foloweth in the next wordes, [therfore
(said our Lord) haue I said to the children of Israel:
No soule of you, shal eate bloud; nor of the strangers
that seiourne with you] an other reason was (as it
also foloweth in the sacred text) because the life of

It was forbid
to eate bloud,
because it was
to be offered
in sacrifice.

And to make
more horror
of manslaugh-
ter

B 3   al

al flesh is in the bloud [whereupon I said to the chil- *Gen.* 9. *v.*
dren of Ifrael : the bloud of no flesh shal you eate: 4. 5.
becaufe the life of the flesh is in the bloud : & whofoeuer eateth it, shal dye.] Not for anie natural caufe
as though there were anie il in the bloud , or natural power in the Sacrifice , for remiffion of finnes,
but that it pleafed God by thefe fignes to exercifehis
people in feruing him, to eleuate their mindes & coo
perate with his grace , & to forfignifie the gracious
effects of future Myfteries , which should be inftitu-
teth by Chrift our Sauiour. And therfore God ftrictly
forbade, to offer anie other Sacrifice, or in anie other
maner , then according to his owne inftitution.

Onlie God ap- [What I command thee (faid God to his chofen *Deut.* 12.
pointed what people) that only doe to the Lord : neither adde anie *v.* 32.
should be of- thing, nor diminish.] & therefore exactly defcribed
fered in Sacri- what thinges fould be offered , of what qualites , in
fice, and with what place, what times , by what perfons, to what
what Rites. end, & other circumftances. For example , in a certaine particular Sacrifice for finne, it was appointed
Though befo- [to take a redde cow , of ful age , without blemish, *Num.* 19.
re the written that had not caried yoke, to bring her forth without *v.* 2. 3. 4.
Law there the campe , there to immolate her in the fight of al ; 5. *&c.*
was neither that the Prieft dipping his finger in her bloud, should
matter , nor fprinkle it, againft the doores of the Tabernakle feuē
maner of Sa- times : that he should burne her in the fight of al,
crifice pre- committing as wel her fkinne , and the flesh, as the
fcribed. bloud, & her dung to the fire : wood alfo of the Cedar , & hyffope , & fcarlet twife died, did the Prieft
caft into the flame, that wafted the cow.] Al which
was neceffarie to be done, and then the Prieft, with
others that affifted, wafhed their garmēts, & bodies.
And yet [were they for al that polluted,& vncleane *v.*8. 10.
vntil euen] fignifying that not the Sacrifices, & Sacraments of the old Teftament , but others of the
new, should both fignifie remiffion of finnes , & as
inftrumental caufes remitte them : but thofe of the
old

old law fhould only fignifie, and not worke the effe Δ.

4. Manie other external fignes of Gods benefites, were ordained in the Law of Moyfes; In which God, who is, & worketh euerie where, did of his diuine wifdome and goodnes, appropriate certaine workes & effeftes vnto fpecial placcs, times, perfons, & with fpecial Rites. So he defigned the inner part of the Tabernacle called *Sancta Sanctoru*, for the peculiar place of diuine oracle, where he would be confulted, & would geue anfwer. [Thou fhalt frame an Arke of the wood fetim (faid God to Moyfes) thou fhalt make a Propitiatorie of pure gold, wherwith the Arke is to be couered. Two Cherubins alfo thou fhalt make of beaten gold, on both fides of the oracle. Let them couer both fides of the Propitiatorie, fpreading their winges, & couering the Oracle. Thou fhalt fette the Propiciatorie vpon the Arke of teftimonie, in the *Sancta Sanctorum*, thence wil I command, & wil fpeake to thee ouer the Propiciatorie, & from the middes of the two Cherubins, vvhich fhal be vpon the Arke of teftimonie, al thinges which I wil command the children of Ifrael by thee.] Accordingly when the Tabernacle with al the appertinences, was made, & erected, in the Dedication therof the Princes of the twelue Tribes offered both ioyntly, and feuerally manie and great oblations [before the Altar, when it was annointed. And when Moyfes entred into the Tabernacle, to confult our Lord, he heard the voice of him, that fpake to him, from the Propiciatorie, that was ouer the Arke, betwen the two Cherubs, from whence alfo Moyfes fpake to our Lord.] By vfe of the fame holie Arke of couenant, diuers notable exploites were accomplifhed. To fhew that God by his owne hand, not by the power, nor prudence of men, geueth victories, he faid to Iofue. [Behold I haue

geuen

Exod. 25. *v.* 10. 17. 18. 20.

Ch. 26. *v.* 34. *Ch.* 25. *v.* 22.

Num. 7. *v.* 1. 2. *&c.*

v. 88. 89.

God defigned a fpecial place where he would fpeake to *Moyfes* & to other Highpriestes.

By vfe of the Arke, & by proceffió God deliuered Iericho to his people.

geuen into thy handes, Ierecho (a strong fensed
citie) & the King therof, & al the valiant men.] Not
by battering & assaulting of the walles] which maner of warre God also prospereth for the benefite
of his faithful seruants, but in this special conquest
by an extraordinarie meanes. [Goe round about *Ios.6.v.*
the citie (said our Lord) al you that be men of warre 2. *&c.*
once a day : so shal you doe six dayes, with the Arke
of the couenant, & Iubilee trumpettes. Al the armed hoste went before, the rest of the common *v. 9.*
people folowed the Arke,& the trumpettes sounded
round about the citie,so did they six dayes euerie day
once, but the seuenth day, seuen times. At last al *v.15.16.*
making a great shoote, the walles fel downe, & they
entred in,euerie man going vp by the place that was
ouer against him, & killing the inhabitauts possessed   20.
The Arke was the citie.] And so proceding conquered the land
a comforth to of Chanaam. In distresses likevvisse [the Arke was 1. *Reg.* 4.
the faithful: their singular conforth, terrour to the Philistins,& *v.* 3. 5.
& a terrour to other enimies, destruction to Dagon the Idol. For *Ch.* 5.*v.*3.
Infidels. irreuerent vsage therof, both the Infidel nations, & 2. *Reg.* 6.
careles Bethsamites, were sore plagued. Oza for *v.* 7.11.
rashly touching it, was sudainly slaine. For their
Religious re- religious respect vnto it [our Lord blessed Obede- *Leuit.*8.
spect vnto it dom, & al his house] Priestes, Kinges, & sometimes *v.* 12. 30.
was rewarded Prophetes were annointed with holie oyle, and so 1. *Reg.*10.
Vse of holie enabled to their seueral functions. [A Serapphical *v.* 1.*Ch.*
oyles, and a Angel, taking a hote cole from the Altar, touched 16.*v.*13.
hote cole. therwith the lippes of Isaias the Prophete, and his 3. *Reg.*19.
iniquitie was taken away,& his sinne cleansed.]The *v.* 15.16.
Ieremie pro- Prophete Ieremie was commanded to vse a certaine *Isa.*6.*v.*7.
phicied by linnen girdle for a while, then to hide it in a hole *Iere.*13.*v.*
signes. of the rocke in Euphrates, afterwards to take it vp, 1. 4. 6. 7.
when it was rotten, to signifie therby that the peo- 10.11.*Ch.*
ple vvhich vvas fast ioyned to God, should become 19.*v.* 1.
vnprofitable, & fitte for no vse, til God should recal *Ch.*27.*v.* 2
them againe. By an earthen bottel broken in peeces *Ch.* 43.*v.*9
he pro- *Ch.*24.*v.*1.

he prophecied their captiuitie. The same he also prophecied by bādes, & chaines;& by stones, hidden in a wal. By good & bad figges he foreshewed what should befal, to the penitent and impenitent. At an-

Ezech. 9. other time, & to an other Prophete, God reuealed
v. 4. 6. in a vision , that true penitentes being marked in their foreheades with the letter T. (Tau) which is formed like a Crosse, shal be saued from the destru- ction, wherin al other perish, that are not so signed: which vision perteyned especiaily to the new testament. Where God also requireth visible signes , as is cleare in the examples folowing.

The signe of the Crosse.

5. S. Iohn , Christs Precursor, together with his preaching of penance, did also baptize in water,
Mat. 3. v. forshewing that Christ, being now come into this
1. 2. 11. world , would wash away sinnes , by Baptisme in water, & the Holie Ghost. Christ also commanded his Disciples to preach,that the kingdome of God is
Mar. 6. v. at hand. [And going forth (saith S. Marke) they
12. 13. preached, that they should doe penance, & they cast out manie diuels : and annointed with oyle manie sicke, and healed them.] Which annoiling of the sicke was not without warrant, as appeareth by the effect , for therby they healed those that were sicke. And our Lord himself both approued , the deuout vse of external signes : & vsed the like in manie cu-
Mat. 9. v. res,& other actions. He imperted health to a deuout
20. 22. [woman that touched the hemme of his garments.] He tooke one that was deafe & dumme , from the
Mar. 7. v. multitude apart , put his fingers into hss eares , and
32. 33. spitting touched his tongue, & looking vp into heauen, he groned, and said to him : *Ephphela.* which is, *Be thou opened.* And immediatly his eares were opened , & the string of his tongue was loosed, and he
Mar. 8. v. spake right.] They brought an other to him that
22. 23. 24. was blinde [desiring that he would touch him.
25. And taking the hand of the blinde, he led him forth

S. Iohn Baptized in water

The Apostles annointed the sicke, and so cured them.

Other approued external Rites.

C out

out of the towne : & spitting into his eyes, imposing
his handes, he asked him, if he saw anie thing ? And
looking vp he said : I see men as it were trees walking. After that againe, he imposed his handes vpon
his eyes, & he begane to see, & was restored , so that
he saw al thinges clearly.] So he that could doe al
thinges , vvith a vvord, yea vvith a tought , vvould
for our instruction vse external meanes , sometimes
moe, sometimes fewer, sometimes more significant,
sometimes lesse , yea sometimes such as might seme
to mans iudgemen rather hurtful, then healthful. As
when he gaue sight to one that was borne blinde,
[he spitte on the ground & made clay (or morter) *Ioan.* 6. ℣.
of the spittle, & spred the clay vpon his eyes, & said 6. 7.
to him : Goe, wash in the poole of *Siloe* : which is
interpreted, *Sent.* He went therfore, & vvashed; &
he came seeing] Our Lord [imposed his handes *Luc.* 13.
vpon a woman, that was crooked, neither could ℣. 13.
she looke vpward at al, & forthwith she was made
straight, and glorified God.] Such examples, not
only of the power of Christs handes, but also of his

**Power geuen
to creatures
to worke su-
pernatural
effectes.**

seruants, by vse of other creatures, are innumerable.
[Whosoeuer, entred first into the pond of Proba- *Ioan.* 5.
tica, after the stirring of the water by an Angel, was ℣. 4.
made whole , of whatsoeuer infirmitie he was hol-
den.] S. Petres shadow cured infirmities. And S. Pau- *Act.* 5. ℣.
les hand cherchefe, being laid vpon the sicke, cured 15. *Ch.* 14.
them. So God maketh his visible creatures, as wel 1. 12.
naturally , as supernaturally to serue men by his
owne power and ordinance, vvhich otherwise they
could not doe.

Men

Men doe rightly serue God, both by internal, &
external sensible meanes.

ARTICLE. 2.

BEing sufficiently shewed that God in bestowing
benefites on men, vseth oftentimes other creatures, & external signes, as his Instruments; it foloweth consequently to be in like maner declared,
that men are bond to acknowlege their gratful acceptance therof, to render thankes, & to exhibite
their seruice to his soueraine Diuine Maiestie, both
by sincere deuotion of the hart, & by extecnal actes
& signes, conformable to humane nature, consisting
of a spiritual soule, & terrestial bodie.

*God is hono-
red by exter-
nal signes.*

2.   So holie Abel sincerely [offered giftes to God,
*Gen. 4. v.
4.* of the first begotten of his flocke, & of their fatte:
& our Lord had respect to Abel, & to his giftes.] And
albeit Cain of peruerse minde offered not the first

v. 3. fruits of the earth, but of the worse sorte, yet by this
external act, he acknowleged, that oblation was
due to God, the Supreme Dominatour, & it had bene
acceptable, if it had bene rightly sorted of the best

v. 26. fruites. [Enos did inuocate the name of our Lord]
doubtles by vocal prayer, & external Rites. [Noe
Ch. 8. v. built an Altar to our Lord, & taking of al catle, and
20. 21. foules that were cleane, offered Holocaustes vpon
the Altar, and our Lord smelled a swete sauour.]
Ch. 12. v. Abraham erected Altars in sundrie places, wherso-
7. 8. euer he pitched his tentes. [He planted an especial
Ch. 21. v. groue in Bersebee, & called therupon the name of
33. Ch. 26. our Lord God eternal.] He obserued the Ceremo-
v. 5. nies of our Lord, not only moral commandments,
Ch. 28. v. & lawes, but also Ceremonial Rites. [Iacob arising
10. 12. 18. in the morning (after that he had seene the ladder,
19. which reached from the earth to heauen) tooke
the stone, which he had laid vnder his head, and

*Sacrifice is
gratful to
God.*

C 2   erected

erected it for a title, pouring oile vpon the toppe : & he called the name of the Citie *Bethel* (that is, the house of God) which before was called Luza.] *Exod.* 3. *v.* Moyses seing the bush on fire, not burnt; and going 4. 5. nerer to view it, was commanded to loose of his shoes, from his feete [for the place (said our Lord vnto him) wherein thou standest, is holie ground.] The same Moyses, with al the childrē of Israel, after *Ch.* 15. *v.* their passage through the redsea [sang a Canticle 1. 20. to our Lord : & Marie (his sister) a Prophetesse tooke a timbrel in her hand, & al the wemen went forth after her, with timbrels, & dances To whom she   21. begāne the song, saying : Let vs sing to our Lord, for *v.* 1. *&c.* he is gloriously magnified, the horse, & the rider he hath cast into the sea.] Whilest Iosue fought against Amelech, Moyses praying [lifted vp his handes, & *Ch.* 17. *v.* Iosue with his armie ouercame : but if he did let 11. them downe a litle, Amelech ouercame. And the handes of Moyses were heauie : therfore they tooke   12. a stone, & put vnder him, wherupon he sate. And Aaron & Hur stayed vp his handes on both sides. And it came to passe, that his handes were not wearie vntil sunne sette. And Iosue put Amelech to flight   13. & his people, by the edge of the sword.] So effectual was the ceremonie of lifting vp of Moyses his handes, that otherwise his prayer auailed not against their eminie in the battle.

3.   Likewise it was to the singular honour of God, *Ch.* 25. *v.* that the Princes & people of Israel, offered so great 2. 3. *&c.* store of gold, siluer, & precious giftes, to the making and furnishing of the Tabernacle, with al thinges therto belonging : which were excellent & costlie. For manie thinges were of pure gold, others of sil- *Ch.* 28. *v.* uer, purple cloth, scarlete, hyacinth, precious stones 9. 17. 18. of sundrie kindes. Which oblations were offered in *Ch.* 35. *v.* such abundance, that the ouerseers of the worke & 5. 6. *&c,* the artificers, were cōstrained to tel Moyses, that the

                                                                                                people

Marginal notes:

Oyle poured on the Altar.

Moyses put of his shoes in a holie place.

Lifted vp his handes in prayer.

Great & precious giftes bestowed in making the Tabernacle, & thinges perteyning therto.

people offered more then was neceſſarie. Wherupon [he commanded proclamation to be made, by
the criers voice, ſaying: Let neither man nor woman offer anie more,in the worke of the Sanctuarie.
And ſo they ceaſſed from offering giftes : becauſe
the thinges that were offered , did ſuſſice, & were
ouer much.]

Amongſt the reſt ofthe Highprieſts ornaments,
one was called [The plate of ſacred veneration ,
made of moſt pure gold, wherin was written, with
the worke of a lapidarie : *The Holie of our Lord.* And
was tied to his Miter, with a lace of hyacinth, as our
Lord had commanded Moyſes.] Other ornaments
were the Ephod, & Rationale. [In the Ephod were
two Onyx ſtones,in which were engrauen the names of the children of Iſrael,ſix names in one ſtone,
& the other ſix in the other : according to the order
of their natiuitie. After the worke of a grauer, and
the grauing of a lapidarie, thou ſhalt graue them
with the names of the children of Iſrael, ſette in
gold, & compaſſed about : & thou ſhalt put them on
both ſides of the Ephod, a memorial for the childrē
of Iſrael. And Aaron ſhal beare their names before
the Lord vpon both ſhoulders, for a remembrance.
Thou ſhalt make alſo hookes of gold , & two litle
cheynes of moſt pure gold,lincked one to an other,
which thou ſhalt put into the hookes.] In the Rationale (which the Highprieſt caried on his breaſt,
lincked to the Ephod with golden cheynes aboue, &
with hyacinth lace beneath)were ſette [foure rewes
of precious ſtones : In the firſt were the ſardius , the
topazius & the emeraud : in the ſecond the carbun-
cle,the ſapphire,& the Iaſper: In the third a ligurius
an achates,& an amethyſt: In the fourth a chryſolith
an onyx, and a beryllus. Al ſette in gold by their
rewes. And in them likewiſe were grauen the
twelue names of the ſonnes of Iſrael,in euerie ſtone

Ch. 36. v.
6. 7.

Ch. 39. v.
29. 30.

Ch. 28. v.
9. 10.

v. 17. 18.
&c.

Ornaments of
rhe Highprieſt
were moſt
precious.
The plate of
ſacred vene-
ration.

The Ephod.

The Rationale

one name, according to the twelue Tribes.] An
other Prieſtlie ornament was a Tunike, made of   **v.31.**
hyacinth; at the edge wherof beneth, were hung
the formes of pomegranetes, & litle belles of gold
round about: ſo interpoſed, that there was a bel of
gold, & a pomegranete, & agane a bel & a pomegranete. And ſo the ſound of the belles was heard,
when the Highprieſt went into the Sanctuarie, &
came forth. The Highprieſt had alſo a ſtraict linnen
garment, next to his ordinarie apparel, vnder the
Tunike, then a girdle of ſilke, a mitre on his head, &   **v. 39. Ch**
the plate of ſacred veneration tyed therunto, which   **39. v. 2.**
hang downe ouer his forehead. Al very precious   *ad* **31.**
to the more honour of God: and withal ſignifying
myſtically the like ornaments to be vſed in the
Church of Chriſt. And both then, & now morally
ſignifying the vertues, which are eſpecially requi-   *See* S. Tho-
red in Biſhoppes, & other ſpiritual Paſtors. As puritie   *mas. p.* 1.
of life, ſincere intention, diſcretion, contemplation   *q* 100.
of God, & of diuine Myſteries, ſupportation of the   *S. Ierome*
peoples infirmities, ſolicitude of their ſpiritual good,   *de veſtitu.*
ſound doctrine, the ſtudie of vnion, & alwayes ex-   *Sacerdotū.*
amplar life.   *to.* 3.

A linnen gar-
ment, a ſilke
girdle, mitre,
& plate of
veneration.

5.   It pleaſed God alſo to chooſe particular places,
where he would be more ſolemnely inuocated, &
more eſpecially honored: & the faithful people were
accordingly commanded to reſorte therunto, by
theſe expreſſe wordes of the law: [To the place,   *Deut.* 12.
which the Lord your God hath choſen of al your   *v.* 5.6.
tribes, to put his name there, & to dwel in it, ſhal
you come : & ſhal offer in that place, your holocauſtes, and victimes, the tithes, and firſt fruites of your
handes, & your vowes, & donaries, the firſt borne
of your oxen, & ſheepe.] The firſt ſolemne deſigned
place, after the peoples entrance into the land of
Chanaan, was the citie of Silo, as appeareth in the
booke of Ioſue, where it is recorded, that [al the   *Ieſ.* 18. *v.* 1
children

children of Ifrael were affembled in Silo, & there
they pitched the Tabernacle of the teftimonie.]
From which time therfore Silo was the proper
chofen place of Sacrifice , and other folemne Rites.
And there the Sanctuarie remained , til the time of
Heli the Highprieft , and Samuel the Prophete (the
fpace of three hundred& fiftie yeares) as is euident
in the firft booke of Kinges , where it is written,
that when the Philiftims had preuailed in battle
1. *Reg.* 4. againft the Ifraelites [The Ancients of Ifrael faid :
v. 3, Let vs fetch vnto vs , the Arke of the couenant of
1. *Reg.* 7. our Lord from Silo.] Afterwards the Sanctuarie
v. 5. 6. remained fome while in Mafphath , where Samuel *Mafphath*.
the Prophete called together al Ifrael , prayed for
v. 10. 11. them , and offered Sacrifice ; where the people alfo
faited, and confeffed their finnes, and had victorie
2. *Reg.* 6. againft the Philiftimes. Finally [the Arke of our
v. 12. 14. Lord, & the whole Sanctuarie , was with great fo- *Mount Sion,*
lemnitie brought into Ierufalem , King Dauid, *in Ierufalem.*
amongft other deuouteft perfons, dancing before it;
& fo it was placed in the middes of the Tabernacle
in mount Sion.] Where the Temple was fhortly
*Gen.*23.*v*. after built by Salomon. The onlie ordinarie place
4. *Ch.* 49. of Sacrifice during the reft of the Old Teftament.
v. 29. *Ch.* There were moreouer manie Synagogues in fundrie *Manie Syna-*
50. *v*. 24. places , whither the people affembled together to *gogues in fun-*
Iof. 24. *v*. pray, & to heare the word of God. Sichem was one *drie places.*
32. fpecial holie place , by occafion of the burial of
principal Patriarches. where the famous fepulchre
of Iofeph, remained venerable , not only to the Iewes, but alfo to Chriftians. By reafen alfo of Gods
fpecial benefites & apparitions of Angels, places be-
Exo. 3. *v*. came holie , and required external reuerence : for
5. *Iof.* 5. *v*. which caufe [Moyfes & Iofue were commanded
16, tor put of their fhoes.]
6.   In Like manner fpecial times were fanctified,
& folemnly obferued to Gods more honour : firft
of al

Special times
sanctified and
made feastes
by the Law of
Moyses.

of al the Sabbath, or seuenth day of the weke, was
kept holie, from the beginning of the world, til
Christ., who being Lord of the Sabbath, hath now
taken it away: & made Sunday holie, which is ther- *Gen.* 2. *v.*
fore called our Lords day. In the Law of Moyses 3. *Exo.* 20.
were also obserued the feastes of *Neomenia,* the first *v.* 8. 9.
of euerie moneth: the Phase or Pasch, the fiftenth *Leuit.* 23.
day of the first moneth in the spring: also other six *v.* 3. 12.
dayes folowing were obserued, with oblation of 16. 24. 28.
special Sacrifices: the first & seuenth with rest from 35. 36.
seruile workes: & al the seuen with abstinence from *Nu.* 28. *v.*
leauen bread, eating only Azimes, or swete bread. 9. 11. 16.
The fourth ordinarie feast was Pentecoste, seuen 20. *Ch.* 29.
weekes after Pasch. The fifth was the feast of Trum- *v.* 1. 7. 12.
petts. The sixt the feast of Tabernacles. The seuenth 35.
the feast of Assemblie. And the eight was the feast *Est.* 16. *v.*
of Expiation, with strict fast from euening to eue- 22.

Two others
added vpon
special occa-
sions.

ning. To which [Mardocheus added an other feast, 1. *Mach.* 4.
in memorie of the whole peoples deliuerie from *v.* 56.
danger of vtter destruction.] By the good meanes of 2. *Mach.*
Quene Ester. Likenise [Iudas Machabeus instituted 10. *v.* 8.
an other feast of the Dedication of a new Altar] after *Io.* 10. *v.*
the persecution of Antiochus. 22.

Great costes
in making &
furnishing of
the Temple,

7. As there were great costes bestovved in making,
& adorning the Tabernacle, with al thinges therto
apperteyning: so was there much more imployed
in making the Temple, & in prouision for Diuine
Seruice, to be performed therin. King Dauid being
most desirous, but for Mysterie sake, not suffered to 2. *Reg.* 7.
build that glorious house to God, neuertheles pre- *v.* 2. 5. 12.
pared al thinges necessarie, for the building therof.
Prouiding also perpetual mantenance, for a great
multitude of Priestes, Leuites, Musitians, & of other
men to serue in & about the Temple. Also for musical Instruments of diuers sortes, & for whatsoener
might be requisite for greatest solemnitie. And before his death gaue charge to Salomon his sonne, &
other

other principal men, that al ſhould be accordingly

1.*Par.* 22.
y. 5.
accompliſhed: ſaying in preſence of them al: [Sa-
lomon my ſonne is yet a litle childe, & delicate, &
the houſe which I would haue to be builded to our
Lord, muſt be ſuch, as may be renowmed in al countries. I therfore wil prepare him neceſſaries, & al

y. 6.
7.
8.
the expenſes. And he called Salomon his ſonne, &
ſaid to him: My ſonne it was my wil to haue built
a houſe to the name of our Lord my God. But the
word of our Lord was made to me ſaying: Thou
haſt ſhed much bloud, & fought very manie battles,
thou canſt not build a houſe to my name, ſo much
bloud being ſhed before me. The ſonne which ſhal
be borne to thee, ſhal be a moſt quiet man. For I wil

9.
make him reſt from al his enimies round about: &
for this cauſe he ſhal be called *Peaceable.* He ſhal build

10.
11.
a houſe to my name. Now therfore my ſonne: Our
Lord be with thee, & doe thou proſper, & build the
houſe to our Lord thy God, as he hath ſpoken of

14.
thee. Behold I in my pouertie haue prepared the
charges, of the houſe of our Lord: of gold an hundred thouſand talents: & of ſiluer, a thouſand thouſand talents: but of braſſe, and of yron, there is no
weight, for the number is ſurpaſſed with the greatnes: timber, and ſtones, I haue prepared to al the

15.
charges. Thou haſt alſo very manie Artificers:
Hewers of ſtones, & Maſons, & Carpenters, & of al

16.
occupations moſt skilful, to make worke in gold,&
ſiluer, & braſſe, & yron, wherof there is no number.
Riſe therfore & doe it, & our Lord wil be with thee.

17.
18.
Dauid alſo commanded al the Princes of Iſrael, that
they ſhould helpe Salomon his ſonne. You ſee (quoth
he) that our Lord your God is with you, and hath
geuen you reſt round obout; and hath deliuered al
your enimies into your handes: & the land is ſub-

19.
dued before our Lord, & before his people. Geue
therfore your hart, & your ſoules to ſerue our Lord

your

your God: & arife, and builde a Sanctuarie to our
Lord God. That the Arke of the couenant of our
Lord, & the veſſels confecrated to our Lord, may be
brought into the houſe, which is built to the name
of our Lord.] Thus farre holie King Dauid his moſt
godlie oration to his ſonne, and the Princes of his
Kingdom. Touching the renowmed Temple, which
was to be builded, for the ſeruice of God. To the ſame
purpoſe for the deuout performance of diuine Ser-

Multitudes of Prieſtes, Leuites, Muſitians, & muſical Inſtrumēts for Diuine Seruice in the Temple.

uice, with al poſſible ſolemnitie, he alſo ordayned
meanes, for foure & twintie whole families of Prieſtes, to doe Prieſtlie functions; alſo for an other great
multitude of Leuites, to ſerue in ſeueral offices: and
for foure and twentie companies of Muſicians, in
euerie companie twelue: in al two hundred eightie
eitght, to ſing, & play on diuers ſortes of Inſtrumēts:
as Pſalter, Harpe, Timbrel, Nable, Cymbal, Organ,
Pipe, Vial, Symphonie, Shalme, & Trumpete. Moreouer he prouided for treſurers, watchmen, & por-
ters of the Temple, in ful numbers to diſcharge
euerie office.

1. *Par. 24.*
v. 4. 5.
Ch. 25.

Ch. 26.

The Booke of Pſalmes compoſed for Gods daylie ſeruice in the Temple, and Synagoges, & eſpecially in the Church of Chriſt.

8.   And aboue al other prouiſions, this admirable
deuout King, & excellent Prophete, being ſingularly inſpired by the Holie Ghoſt, compoſed the Diuine
Pſalmodie, of an hundred and fifetie Pſalmes, conteyning the Summarie of al Diuine Scriptures: with
very manie particular praiſes of God, to be ſoung,
not only in the Temple, & Synagoges of the Iewes,
but alſo much more in Chriſtian Temples & Churches. In which holie Booke therfore this Royal
Pſalmiſt often inuiteth, & earneſtly exhorteth, as
wel Gods people of the old Teſtament, as alſo more
eſpecially al faithful Chriſtians, to ſing and declare
Gods moſt high praiſes: prophecying withal, that
ſo it ſhould be duly performed, in the Church of
Chriſt. As theſe cleare textes amongſt others, doe
abundantly teſtifie. [Reioyce ye iuſt (ſaith he to al
Gods

Pfal. 32.
v. 1. 2.
3. 4.

Gods true feruantes) in our Lord; praifing becometh the righteous. Confeffe to our Lord *on the
Harpe , on the Pfalter* of tenne ftringes, fing to him.
Sing ye to him a new fong: fing wel to him *in iubilation.* Becaufe the word of our Lord is right : & al
his workes are in faith (performing al his promifes)

King Dauids frequent inuitation; & moft godlie example, to prayfe God by al poffible meanes.

Pfal. 46.
v. 1. 2. 3.
Pfal. 65.
v. 2.

Al ye nations *clappe handes , make iubilation* to God in
the voice of exultation. Becaufe our Lord is high,
terrible, a great King ouer al the earth. *Make ye
iubilation* to God, al the earth : fay a Pfalme to his
name , geue glorie to his praife. Before him fhal the
Æthiopians *fal downe,* & his enimies fhal *licke the earth.*

Pf. 71. *v.*
9. 10.
Pf. 80. *v.*
1. 2. 3. 4.

The Kinges of Tharfis and the Ilandes *fhul offer pre-
fentes,* the Kinges of the Arabians, & of Saba fhal *bring
gifts.* Reioice to God our helper : *Make iubilation* to
the God of Iacob. Take ye *Pfalme,* & geue *Timbrel:*
pleafent *Pfalter* with the *Harpe.* Sound ye with Trumpete in the *New moone,* in the notable daye of your fo-

Pfal. 91.
v. 4.
Pf. 94. *v.*
1. 2.

lemnitie. In the Inftrument of tenne ftringes , in
Pfalter, with Canticle on the *Harpe.* Come let vs
reioice to our Lord, let vs *make iubilation* to God our
Sauiour. Let vs preuent his face in confeffion (of
praife) *in Pfalmes :* let vs *make iubelation* to him. Make

v. 6.

ye *iubilation* to God al the earth. Chaunt, & reioice, &
fing. Come let vs adore , & *fal downe,* & *weepe* before

Pf. 97. *v.*
4. 5. 6.

our Lord that made vs. *Make ye iubilation* to God al
the earth : chaunt, and reioice, and fing. Sing to our
Lord on *Harpe:* on *Harpe* & voice of Pfalme. On *long
drowne trumpets,* & voice of *cornete of horne.* Make *iubi-

Pf. 98. *v.*
5. *Pf.* 131.
v. 7. *Pfal.*
133. *v.* 2.
Pfal. 137.
v. 2.
Pfal. 140.
v. 2.

lation,* in the fight of the King, our lord, Exalt ye
the Lord our God, & *adoore his footeftoole,* becaufe *it is
holie.* We wil entre into his Tabernacle: we wil
adore in the *place, where his feete ftood.* In the nightes
lift vp your *handes* vnto the *holie places:* I wil adore
toward the holie Temple. Let my prayer be directed *as
incenfe :* in thy fight: the *eleuation of my hvndes,* as euening facrifice. I haue *ftretched forth my handes* to thee.

D 2 In the

In the *Pſalter of tenne ſtringes*, I wil ſing to thee. Let the *Pſal.* 143.
children of Sion praiſe his name in the quire : on *v.* 9.
Timbrel , & *Pſaltir* let them ſing to him. Praiſe ye our *Pſal.* 149.
Lord in the ſound of *Trumpete* , praiſe ye him on *v.* 3.
Pſalter , & harpe; praiſe ye him on *Timbrel* & quire: *Pſal.* 150.
praiſe ye him on ſtringes , & *Organ.* Praiſe ye him on *v.* 3. 4. 5.
wel ſounding *Cymbals*: praiſe ye him on *Cymbals of* 6.
Inbilation. Let euerie ſpirite praiſe our Lord. *Alleluia,*]
In al which inuitation , & feruent deſire to praiſe
God, you ſee the Royal Prophete doubted not, but
that God is much honoured , & praiſed by ſinging,
by vſe of Muſical Inſtruments , & other external ſignes; by ſtretching forth , and by lifting vp handes,
towardes holie places , towardes the place , where
the Temple was afterwards to be built : by falling
downe proſtrate: by weeping; by kiſſing or licking
the earth; by offering giftes , by adoring Gods foote
ſtoole, & ſteppes of his feete ; by ſaying , or ſinging

Alleluia , doth *Alleluia*; That is, by honouring God, with ſpirite, hart,
not only ſig-   voice , geſture , inſtruments , & in al other poſſible
niſie *Prayſe ye*   maner. And that al this perteyneth to Chriſtians, no
our Lord ; but   leſſe , but in deede more, then it did to the Iewes,
Praiſe our   manie of the textes here recited doe plainly côuince
Lord by al   expreſly ſhewing that this holie Prophete, dire-
poſſible mea-   &ed his exhortation, to al peoples, al nations, al ge-
nes internal &   neratiôs, of al future times, to the end of this world.
external.   Likewiſe the notorious great ſolemnitie , with the *3. Reg.* 8.

The great ſo-   multitude of hoſtes or victimes: two and twentie *v.* 1.2. 10.
lemnitie and   thouſand oxen , an hundred and twentie thouſand 15. 22.
multitude of   ſheepe, & other thinges ſacrificid in the Dedication 63.
victimes vſed   of the Temple, when it was built by King Salomon,
in Dedication   & the holie Arke , and Propiciatorie were brought
of the Tem-   into it. Al which, as alſo King Salomons long and *v.* 65.
ple.   deuout prayer, wirh the Prieſtes, Leuites , & people,
& al other religious Actes, doe clearly teſtiſie that
God is rightly honoured by ſuch viſible thinges , &
withal doe inſtruct Chriſtians , how to imitate the
same,

fame : & condemne thofe of groffe errour, which imagine that Gods honour in fpirite, & veritie, is diminifhed by honoring him alfo in fuch maner, as this holie Prophete exhorteth.

9.   In like maner other Prophetes fignifie, that God is honored by fuch external meanes. Ifaias fo affuredly fuppofed this kinde of diuine worfhipe to be good, that he expoftulated with carnal careleffe people, vfing mufical inftruments for their owne delectation, and not to the houour of God, faying:

Ifa. 5. *v.* 12.
[Harpe, & Vial, & Timbrel, & Shalme, & Wine, in your feaftes : and the worke of our Lord you regard not, nor confider the workes of his handes:] fhewing that thefe inftruments vainely vfed, in drunken feaftes, haue a religious vfe in Gods feruice. God alfo faith by his Prophete Ieremie, [I wil build thee againe, & thou fhalt be builded, ô virgin Ifrael: thou fhalt yet *be adorned with thy timbrels*, & fhalt goe forth in the quire of them that play.] But we come now to the time of Chrifts appearing, and conuerfing in this world.

Iere. 31. *v.* 4.

10.   The very fame night, in which our Lord was borne, [the Shepheardes nere to Bethlem, came with fpeede *to fee the Infant* : & when they had found him, returned glorifying & praifing God, in al thinges, that they had heard, & fene, as it was faid to them by an Angel.] The three Sages (commonly called Kinges) held it for a religious act, and for fuch an one, the Euangelift hath written it in the holie Gofpel, that [they came a long voyage, with great fpede, to vifite, and adore the new borne child, in the land of Iurie.] Which homage they exhibited, both with internal deuotion, & external declaration therof. For when they found the childe [they falling downe adored him : & opening their treafures, offered to him (myftical) giftes, gold, frankencenfe, and myrrh.] When our Lord was prefented

Luc. 2. *v.* 8. 16. 20.

Mat. 2. *v.* 1. 11.

v. 12.

Otherprophetes alfo commend the vfe of mufical inftruments in Diuine Seruice.

In the new Teftamét God is alfo honored by external fignes, & Rites. The Shepheardes vifited Chrift in the manger. The Sages came to Iernfalem, and to Bethleem, to adore Chrift.

sented

fented in the Temple, the fourtith day from his
birth, holie old Simeon [*tooke him into his armes*, and *Luc.* 2. *v.*
bleffed God] with a diuine Canticle. In the pro- 28,
greffe of the Euangelical hiftorie, manie examples
are recited, of fincere faith & deuotion, declared by
external factes, of fuch as fought to fee our Lord
Iefus: fome to touch him, or his garment: others to
aproch fo nere as they ccula vnto him. [Zacheus *Luc.* 19.
did climbe into a tree to fee him. A woman which *v.* 4.
had bene twelue yeares trubled, with an iffue of
bloud, comming behind him, touched the hemme *Mat.* 15.
of his garment. For fhe faid within her felf: If I *v.* 20. 21.
fhal touch only his garment, I fhal be fafe: and fhe 22.
became whole, from that houre.] Marie Magdalen
declared her penitent hart: & did fruie worthie of
penance, [by falling downe at Chrifts feete; by
wafhing them with teares; by wiping them with *Luc.* 7. *v.*
the heares of her head; by kiffing them; & by anoin- 38. 44.
ting them with ointment.] Againe fhe fhewed her *Mat.* 26.
fingular deuotion, [bringing a box of precious oint- *v.* 7. 8. 9.
ment, & powring it vpon his head, as he fate at the 13.
table.] For which [fome hauing indignatio againft *Mat.* 14.
her, faid: wherto is this waift? this might haue bene *v.* 3. 4. 5.
fold, for more then three hundred pence, & geuen
to the poore: and they murmured againft her. But
Iefus knowing it, faid to them: Why doe you moleft
this woman? for fhe hath wrought a good worke
vpon me. Amen I fay to you, wherfoeuer this Gof- *v.* 9.
pel fhal be preached, in the whole world, this alfo
which fhe hath done, fhal be reported for a memorie of her.] A litle before this, when our Lord came
riding into Ierufalem [His Difciples, & the people. *Mat.* 21.
fpred their garments in the way: & other did cutte *v.* 8. 9.
boughes from the trees, & ftrowed them in the way: *Mar.* 11.
& a great multitude tcke the boughes of palmes, and *v.* 8. 9.
went forth to meete him: & the multitude that went *Luc.* 19.
before, & that folowed, cried, faying: Hofanna to *v.* 36.

the

Margin notes:

Simeon tooke Chrift into his armes.

Others fought to fee him: to touch his garment.

To wafh, and kiffe his feete.

To beftow coft on him.

Clothes, and boughes fpred in his way. Proceffion with palmes in their handes.

Io. 12. v. the fonne of Dauid, bleffed is he that cometh in the
12.13. name of our Lord, the King of Ifrael, Hofanna in
Mat. 27. the higheft.] When our Lord was dead on the
v. 57. Croffe [Iofeph of Arimathea a noble Senatour, & Honorably
Ioa. 19. v. Nicodemus a Prince of the Pharifees, bringing a buried.
38. 39. mixture of Myrrh & aloes, about an hundred poun-
40. 41. des, tooke downe the bodie of Iefus, and bond it in
finne linnen clothes, with the fpices: & fo laid it in
a new moniment, hewed in a rocke, wherin none
Mar. 16. had yet bene buried. Then alfo Marie Magdalen, &
v. 1. Luc. Marie of Iames, & Salome, brought fpices, that co-
2. v. 56. ming, after the Sabbath were paft, they might an-
Ch. 24. v. noint the bodie of Iefus. For on the Sabbath they
1. refted according to the commandment of the Law.
And in the firft of the Sabbath (on Sunday) very
early they came to the mominêt, carying the fpices,
which they had prepared.] Al which, and the reft
tended greatly to the feruice of Chrift our Lord.

11. Neither only the external aĉtes, of deuotion Chrifts Difci-
done to Chrift himfelf, but thinges done to his holie ples were re-
& glorious feruantes, redound likewife to the ho- fpeĉted with
nour of God. The primitiue Chriftians, which were great reue-
firft conuerted, fo refpeĉted the Apoftles, that when rence.
they brought the price of their landes, & poffeffions,
to the Apoftles (to ferue in common, as euerie one
had neede) they deliuered not the fame, as vulgar
almes into their handes, but as gooddes dedicated
Aĉt. 2. v. to God, with al humble and reuerent maner [*Laid*
44. 45. *it downe at the Apoftles feete*] as S. Luke diligently ex-
Ch. 4. v. 35 preffeth, in his facred hiftorie. And in publique af-
37. Ch. 5. femblies, al others fo reuerenced the Apoftles, that
v. 13. none [of the reft (faith the fame S. Luke) durft ioyne
themfelues vnto them: but the people magnified
them.] And although it was moft conuenient, &
neceffarie, that the Apoftles fhould haue the cheefe
power to difpofe of the Churchs treafure, & to ordaine what was to be donne therin, yet becaufe it
was

was not meete,that they should be encombred with the particular diſtributions of ſuch temporal goodes,that office was deſigned to an other order of Clergimen, namely to Deacons, together with their *Act. 6. v.* ſpiritual funcion of preaching, and baptizing. A- 3. 6. mongſt whom S. Steuen became the *Protomartyr*, that is,the firſt Martyr,after Chriſts Aſcenſion. Who hauing gayned that glorious crowne,to his ſoule in heauen, his holie bodie alſo was ſpecially regarded by the faithful. For notwithſtanding the furious perſecution,& general diſperſion of the new gathe- *Ch. 8. v.* red flock of Chriſt,yet [deuout men had ſpecial care, 1. 2. & toke order, for S. Steuens funeral, & made great mourning vpon him.]

9. Steuens bo-die carefully buried.

12.   Breefly touching ſpecial places, ſette times,& al ceremonial Rites, inſtituted by the Catholique Chriſtian Church,which our Aduerſaries côdemne as Iudaical (though themſelues obſerue ſome ſuch, according to their owne particular liking) they are clearly iuſtified to be religious, & not ſu-perſticious, by theſe manifeſt examples of the Apo-ſtles, and expreſſe teſtimonies of holie Scriptures. [S. Peter & S. Iohn went vp into the Temple, at the *Act. 3. v. 2.* ninth houre of prayer,] according to the publique maner in the Temple. And S. Peter obſerued at an other time,the accuſtomed houre of prayer,priuatly out of the Temple, praying [about the ſixt houre.] *Ch. 10. v.* According to which obſeruations, the Apoſtles in- 9. ſtituted the Canonical houres, of Matines Prime, Third,Sixt,& Ninth houre : Euenſong, & Compline, to be obſerued as wel publiquely in Churches, as priuatly by Clergiemen,and other deuout perſons. [S. Paul and Silas did praiſe God,ſo praying at mid-night in the priſon, that the reſt which were in the *Act. 16. v.* ſame priſon heard them.] S. Paul concluding his 25. Epiſtles, to the Romanes; the Firſt & ſecond to the *Rom. 16.* Corinthians,& the Firſt to the Theſſalonians,willed *v. 16.* them

Chriſtian Rites though in part boro-wed of the Iewes, are ve-ry religious.

Holie places.

Obſeruation of houres for prayer.

1. _Cor._16. them [to falute one an other in a holie kiffe:] The
v. 20. fame doth S. Peter, in the end of his former Epiftle,
2. _Cor._13. wherof the whole Church vfeth the Ceremonie of
v. 12. the Paxe, towards the end of the Publique Sacrifice,
1. _Theff._5. efpecially when it is celebrated with folemnitie:
v. 20. which hath alfo warrant from Chrifts folemne fa-
1. _Pet._ 5. lutation, faying to his Apoftles [Peace be to you.] S.
v. 14. Paul teftifying that he prayed for the Ephefians,
Io. 20. v. fignifieth it by thefe termes. [For this caufe (faith
19. 21. he) I bow my knees to the Father of our Lord Iefus
Ephef. 3. Chrift.] Defcribing the exaltation of the name of
Philip. 2. Iᴇsᴠs, he faith to the Philippians [That in the name
v. 10. of Iᴇᴇᴠs, euerie knee doth bow, of the celeftials ter-
Luc. 22. reftrials & infernals.] Our Sauiour himfelf [prayed
v. 41. kneeling.] S. Iohn beginning to write his Apoca-
Apoc. 1. v. lypfe, exactly noteth that the vifion was fhewed to
10. him, on our Lords day, faying: [I was in fpirite on
the Dominical day.] The figne, wherwith he writeth
that [the faithful feruants of God are figned in their
foreheades] can not with probable reafon be vn-
Apoc. 7. derftood to be anie other figne then the figne of the
v. 3. &c. Croffe, which Chriftians receiue in Babtifme. And
manie other holie Rites haue bene inftituted, by the
Church, in vertue of Chrifts general commiffion:
moft of which are the fame in the whole Chriftian
world; fome doe varie, according to the diuerfitie
of times, places, peoples, and other circumftances
Al, as S. Paul writeth, are to the more honour of
1. _Cor._ 14. God, being ordained [to edification; done decently,
v. 26. 40. & according to order] not by particular mens pri-
Mat. 23. uate fpirites, but by the publique fpirite of the
v. 5. &c. Church. For otherwife external fignes, are Phari-
1. _Tim._ 4. faical: & [corporal exercife is profitable to litle: but
v. 8. pietie is profitable to al thinges.]

Kiffing the paxe.

Kneeling.

The name of Iefus honored

The Sunday called our Lords day.

The figne of the Croffe.

Other Rites are ordained by general commiffion geuen to the Church.

E

Of

Of al external holie Rites, Sacrifice, & Sa-
craments are most principal.

ARTICLE. 3.

IN the former two Articles is shewed, by manie
textes of holie Scriptures, that God imperteth his
gracious benefites to men, not only immediatly by
himself, but also by secondarie causes: and that he
likewise requireth & accepteth mens seruice, both
by internal operation of the minde, & by external
sacred Ceremonies. It foloweth to be in like maner

The definitiō
of Sacrifice.

declared, that aboue al other external holie Rites,
Sacrifice, and Sacraments are the most excellent.
First therfore touching Sacrifice, which is an obla-
tion of some external thing, offered to God, in

Al nations
hold that
Sacrifice is
due to God.

acknowlegement of his supreme dominion ouer al
creatures: al nations doe esteme it, to be the most
principal homage, that man can exhibite to God.
For it is hard to finde anie people so barbarous, excepting some few heretikes, but they did this kind
of seruice in some sorte, either to the true God omnipotent, or to some falsly imagined diuine powre.

Proued by
examples of
Cain.

2.   More especially this truth is proued by holie
Scriptures. Cain wel knew that Sacrifice was a
principal dutie, which he owed to God. And *Gen.* 4. *v.*
therfore [offered it] though peruersly, not of the 3. 4 5.

Abel.

best, but of the worse fruites. Abel rightly [offered
of the first begotten of his flocke, & of their fatte:
& our Lord had respect to Abel, & to his giftes. But
to Cain & to his giftes, he had not respect.] Noe, as a
first dutie of thankesgeuing to God, after their deli-

Noe.

uerie from the diluge [built an Altar to our Lord, *Ch.* 8. *v.*
& taking of al cattle, & foules, that were cleane, 20 21.
offered Holocaustes vpon the Altar. And our Lord *Ch.* 12. *v.*

Abrahrm,

smelled a sweete sauour.] Abraham [built Altars in 7. 8. *Ch.*
sundrie

13. v. 18. sundrie places] & offered gratful Sacrifices theron.
Ch. 26. v. [Isaac also built an Altar in Bersabee, & called vpon
25. Ch. 35. the name of our Lord.] God said to Iacob [Arise, &
v. 1. 7. goe vp to Bethel, & dwel there, & make an Altar to
God, that appeared to thee, when thou diddest flee
from Esau thy brother] which he performed [and
called the name of that place, *The House of God.*] The
same Iacob consulted our Lord at the wel of oath in
Ch. 46. v. Bersabee, about his iourney into Ægypt, [killing
1. 2. 3. there victimes to the God of his father Isaac.] And
had answer by a vision to goe, & feare not. So God
most especially required Sacrifice, aboue al other
external seruice, that he commanded Moyses, and
Aaron to alleage that particular cause to Pharao
King of Ægypt, why he should dismisse the chil-
Exod. 5. dren of Israel. Who therupon [said to Pharao: Thus
v. 1. saith the Lord God of Israel : Dismisse my people,
That they may sacrifice to me in the desert.]
And at their departure from Ægypt [God institu-
Ch. 12. v. ted the perpetual Sacrifice of the Pascal lambe] to
6. 17. 18. be offered euerie yeare, in memorie of that sin-
24. gular great benefite. And shortly after, amongst
other Ceremonial precepts, our Lord first of al pre-
Ch. 20. v. scribed, [how they should make an Altar, and offer
24. 25. therupon Holocaustes, & Pacifiques] And afterwards expresly declared the proper vse & end, for
which an Altar is made, saying to Moyses, & by him
Ch. 29. v. to Aaron, & to euerie Priest : [This is it which thou
38. 39. shalt doe vpon the Altar : Two lambes of a yeare
old, euerie day continually: one lambe in the morning, & an other at euen] And besides this daylie
duble Sacrifice, our Lord also ordained manie other
sacrifices of diuers victimes, with their libaments of
oyle, wine, & other liquors : as wel ordinarie at certaine feastes, & for certaine purposes ; as extraordinarie, vpon occasions which might happen. In al
there were three kindes of Sacrifices. The first was

Side notes:

Isaac.
Iacob.

Moyses Aaron
& al the peo-
ple of Israel.

The proper
vse of Altars
is to sacrifice
theron.

E 2   *Holocaust*

Three kindes of Sacrifices. Holocaustus Sacrifice for sinne. Pacifique Sacrifice

Holocaust : wherin the hostes were wholly consu- *Leuit.* I. med to the honour of God. The second were Sa- *v.* 3. 9. 13. crifices for sinne. Wherof part was burnt, & part 17. *Ch.* 4. alloted to the Priestes The third were Pacifique *v.* 2. 5. Sacrifices : either of thankesgeuing for benefites re- *Ch.* 6. *v.* ceiued, or of obsecration, for obtayning thinges ne- 26. cessarie. In which one part was burnt, an other part perteyned to the Priestes, & the third part to the persons, that prouided the hoste. And al these were *Ch.* 7. *v.* principally required, & were the most excellent of 31. 37. al ceremonial Rites, in the old Testament, And that external Sacrifice is also the most excellent Diuine Seruice in the new Testament, is not only proued by

Sacrifice of the new Testament excelleth the old, as the bodie excelleth the shadow.

the Law of nature, & iudgement of al nations; but also is as necessarily confirmed by the holie Scrip- tures, as it is certaine that the shadow importeth a bodie, & the figure requireth the thing figured. yea and no lesse assuredly by the prophecies of the old Testament, & testimonies of the new. As we shal *Artic.* 22. euidently shew in the proper place; where we are 23. to proue, and declare the Christian beleefe, and do- ctrine, touching the most souereigne Sacrifice of Chrifts bodie & bloud, in the blessed Eucharist.

Sacraments next after Sacrifices, excel other ceremonies.

3. Next to Sacrifice, are Sacraments, which are visible signes of inuisible grace. In the old Testa- *Gen.* 17. ment there were manie Sacraments. As Circumci- *v.* 10. sion, Ordination of Priestes, & Leuites. Al hostes & *Lenit.* 8. Sacrifices for sinnes : & diuers purifications of legal *Num.* 8. vncleanes were Sacraments, signifying either re- *Leuit.* 4. mission of sinne, or increase of grace. It is probable *v.* 3. 13. that the loaues of propoiition : and the Pascal lambe *&c.* were also Sacraments. At least they were figures *Ch.* 14. 15. of the most blessed Sacrament of the Altar. 16. 17.

The eminent excellencie of Sacrifice and Sacraments is proued by

4. The excellencie of Sacrifice, and Sacraments, aboue al other external Ceremonies, consisteth in *Exod.* 12. this, that Sacrifice is the proper external worshipe *Exod.* 25. of God, which can not lawfully be done to anie *Gen.* 1. *v.* 1. creature:

Exod. 3.
v. 14.

creature : becaufe God is the onlie Creator of al reafon, dedu- other thinges , which are befides himfelfe : and ced from therfore hath the fupreme dominion ouer al : is the holie Schrip- firft beginning of al, & the end , wherto al ought to tures. be directed , in acknowlegement wherof Sacrifice is due to him onlie. And the next excellencie is of Gods Sacraments, becaufe without them none can be admitted either to offer Sacrifice, or to participate the benefite therof. We fpeake of al times fince Sacraments were firft inftituted. For when Circumcifion was firft comanded to Abraham, God withal ordained it as a Sacramental figne, to diftinguifh his peculiar people from others : & for an entrance of And by ex-

Gen. 14. v. al that fhould be adioyned in fpiritual felowfhipe to preffe Schrip-
ro. 11. the fame vifible Church [This is my couenant (faid tures. God to Abraham) which you fhal obferue, betwen me and you : and thy feede after thee. Al the malekind of you fhal be circuncifed, & you fhal circun-

v. 14. cife the flefh of your prepuce , that it may be for a figne of the couenant betwen me & you. The male Sacraments whofe flefh of his prepuce , fhal not be circuncifed had relation that foule fhal be deftroyed out of his people.] And to Sacrifices,

Exod. 12. afterwards God faid to Moyfes, at the departure of
v. 48. 49. the Ifraelites from Ægypt. [If anie of the foiorners (ftrangers) be willing to dwel among you, & make the Phafe of the Lord, firft al the male that he hath, fhal be circuncifed, & then fhal he celebrate it, according to the Rites : & he fhal be as he that is borne in the land : but if there be anie man vncircuncifed, he fhal not eate therof. Al one Law fhal be to him, that is borne in the land, & to the Profelyte, that foiourneth with you.] Where it is to be vnderftood by the way, that the malefexe being circumfifed, the female of the fame kindred, were alfo adioyned, profeffing the fame faith & religion. By other Sacra-

Levit. 14. ments of the old Law, as wafhinges, & Purifications
v. 4. &c. impedimenis were remoued, which hindered from

E 3   the

the feruice of God. By ordination, Prieftes were *Leuit.* **8.**
made apt Minifters : to offer Sacrifice, to pray for *v.* **1.** *&c.*
the people, and to difcerne, & iudge their fpiritual *Ch.* **9.** *v.*
caufes. And Leuites were addicted by an other fpecial **22.**
Confecration, to their feueral functions, fubordinate
to the Prieftes. Al directed to the offering of Sacrifice. Other holie thinges, perteyning alfo to the

So had other
holie thinges.

Ceremonial Law, as the Tabernacle, & afterwards *Num.* **8.**
the Temple, the holie veffels, Prieftlie attyre, and *v.* **6.**
ornaments, were thinges acceffarie to the Sacrifices *Num.* **3.**
& Sacraments. Yea the holie Altar it felf (as wel of *v.* **6.9.10.**
other oblations, as of Incenfe) were fanctified by *Mat.* **23.**
the Sacrifice, & by reafon of the Sacrifice, it fancti- *v.* **19.**
fied the giftes, that were offered therupon. Alfo the
ceremonial obferuances, of feaftes at fette times, as

And al legal
obferuances.

the Sabbath, the New mone, Pafch, Pentecoft, and
the reft, were fpecially folemnized with prefcribed *Leuit.* **23.**
Sacrifices. And the continual abftinence from cer- *v.* **2.8.**
taine meates legally vncleane, had particular rela- *Num.* **28.**
tion to the offering of Sacrifices, & receiuing of Sa- *v.* **2.** *&c.*
craments. For neither anie thing reputed by the *Ch.* **29.**
Law vncleane, could be offered in Sacrifice, nor *v.* **1.** *&c.*
anie perfons being vncleane, could be partakers of *Leuit.* **11.**
Sacrifices, or Sacraments, til they were firft cleanfed. *Ch.* **12.13.**
So by the vfe of al other holie Ceremonies it is ma- **14. 15.16.**
nifeft that Sacrifice is the cheefeft external feruice, **17.**
& worfhipe of God. And that next to them are
Sacramentes.

Internal ver-
tues are pre-
ferred before
Sacrifice, as
before the
cheefeft ex-
ternal feruice
of God.

5. Moft true it is, that internal vertues, & fpiritual
Sacrifices, are much more required, then external,
as both reafon teacheth, and holie Scriptures doe
often teftifie, perferring them exprefly before external Sacrifice it felf; which alfo confirmeth our prefent purpofe. For that, when God by his Prophetes,
& by Chrift our Lord, required true repentance of
the hart, iuftice in al actions, obedience, mercie,
gratitude, with praifes of God, & the like vertues,
                                        faying

saying he wil rather haue them, then Sacrifice; he plainly shewed, that Sacrifice is the principal of al external diuine Seruice, & rightly so esteemed of the faithful. As when King Saul pretending excuse of his disobedience, in that he reserued the better thinges taken in praye, that the same might be offered in Sacrifice, the Prophete Samuel reprehen-

1. Reg. 15. v. 22. ding him said: [Why, wil our Lord haue Holocaustes & victimes, & not rather, that the voice of our Lord be obeyed? For better is obedience then victimes, & to hearken rather, then to offer the fatte of rames] In like manner God by his Prophete Osee, admonished such people, as neglecting workes of mercie, thought to escape punishment, by offering

Osee. 6. v. 6. Sacrifices, that it would not auail them: [Because (saith our Lord) I would mercie, and not Sacrifice, and the knowlege of God, more then Holocaustes.] Which doctrinal sentence Christ our Sauiour alleageth, & applieth to this same purpose, saying to the Pharisees, when they calumniated him, for shewing

Mat. 9. v. 13. mercie to sinners. [Goe your wayes (saith hee) and learne, what it is: *I wil mercie, & not Sacrifice.*] By which & the like sayinges, external sacrifice is not excluded, but other vertues are rather required, then the very best external ceremonies. It is cleare also that spiritual Sacrifices are more necessarie, and better then onlie external. In comparison wherof the Royal Prophete in his penitential Psalme, saith to

Psal. 50. v. 18. 19. God. [with holocaustes thou wilt not be delighted. A Sacrifice to God is an afflicted spirite: a contrite, & humbled hart, ô God thou wilt not despise] This spiritual Sacrifice of contrite & penitent spirite, is first in order of al spiritual Sacrifices, and prepareth the way to the second; which is Sacrifice of Iustice; wherof the same Psalmist speaketh, exhorting al faithful soules, to render vnto euerie one that which is due; saying: [Sacrifice ye the Sacrifice of iustice:

& hope

[marginal notes:]
Obedience.

Workes of mercie, and knowlege of God.

Spiritual Sacrifices of contrite hart of iustice, & of praise, doe al excel external Sacrifice.

& hope in our Lord.] The third spiritual Sacrifice, *Pſal.* 4. but not the leaſt, is of praiſe, &gratful minde towards *v. 6.* God, the Auctor of al good, yelding thankes for al his beneſites beſtowed, & promiſed: which is more to Gods glorie, then the immolating of oxen, buckgotes, rammes & the like. [Immolate to God the *Pſal.* 49. Sacrifice of praiſe; & pay thy vowes to the Higheſt. *v. 9. 10.* The Sacrifice of praiſe ſhal glorifie me] ſaith our *&c. v. 14.* Lord: that is, ſhal moſt eſpecially glorifie me: as 23. being the complement of al ſpiritual Sacrifices, & perfect fruite of both internal, & external ſeruice of God. By al which compariſons is ſufficiently ſig- nified, that Sacrifice rightly offered, excelleth al other external workes. And when there is no im- *Gen. 8. v.* pediment, of their partes, for whom it is offered it 12. *Leu.* is (as holie Scriptures often aſſure vs) a ſweete I. *v.* 9. 13. ſauour to our Lord, & he therby becometh propici- *Ch.* 4. *v.* ous, & merciful. [I wil not rebuke thee in thy Sa- 20. *Ch.* 23, crifices (ſaith God to al his true ſeruants) and thy *v.* 28. Holocauſtes are in my ſight alwayes.] *Pſal.* 49. *v.* 8.

Al which compariſons preſuppoſe that Sacrifice excelleth al other external actes.

*In the Church of Chriſt are diuers Sacraments:
which here we preſuppoſe, & in their ſeueral
places, proue to be ſeuen.*

ARTICLE 4.

THus much touching al diuine Sacrifices, and Sacraments, eſpecially of the old Teſtament. Now we are to declare others, of the new Teſta- ment, & Chriſtian Church. And firſt in General, that Chriſt our Sauiour hath inſtituted ſome holie Sacraments, al that wil ſeme to be Chriſtians, doe confeſſe in wordes at leaſt. But becauſe certaine pretending to reforme ſuppoſed errors, doe vtterly denie, that there is anie proper external Sacrifice, in the

The ſumme of the contro- uerſie betwen

in the Church of Christ : and not only denie fiue, of
the seuen Sacraments, which the whole Christian
World, of more then a thousand yeares by our Aduersaries confession, and the farre greater part of
Christendom stil beleueth : but also denie, that
those two which they hold for Sacraments, doe
remitte sinne, or conferre grace; it wil be necessarie
to shew how manie Sacraments there be, & which
they are; likewise of what necessitie, and efficacie
euerie one is. And withal in the proper place, that
there is a proper propiciatorie, most excellent external sacrifice in the Law of grace, the complement
of al old, true, & lawful Sacrifices, that were from
the beginning of the world, before Christ.

2. First therefore it is proued both by figures, and
prophecies of the old Testament, & by testimonies
of the new, that Christ instituted certaine holie Sacraments, that is to say, *Visible signes of inuisible grace.*
Or as Protestants confesse, External Rites with special promise of spiritual grace, & remission of sinnes.
For as the Tabernacle prefigured the Church of
Christ, being as S. Paul calleth it [a parable of the
time present] euen to the thinges done therin, by
the Priestes of the same old Law, and by other ceremonial obseruances [in meats, & in drinckes, and
diuers baptismes, & iustices of the flesh] were figures of Christes, and his Priestes actions, and of Christian Rites: the same Apostle teaching in the same
place, that these thinges [were laid on them (enioyned to the Iewes) vntil the time of correction]
not that al external Rites should be taken away, and
al quite abolished, but changed, & bettered. For so
the next wordes doe plainly testifie, that the Law
of grace, is not without other religious external
actions. [But Christ (saith this Apostle) assisting
an Highpriest, of the good thinges to come, by a
more ample, & more perfect Tabernacle, not made

F   with

Margin notes:

vs & Prote-
stants, tou-
ching Sacri-
fice & Sacra-
ments.

The definitiō
of a Sacra-
ment.

Christs Sacra-
ments were
prefigured by
Sacraments &
other Rites
of the old
Testament.

Exo. 25.
v. 8 *&c.*
1 *Cor.* 1.
v. 1. 3 *&c.*
Heb 9. *v.*
9.

v. 10.

v. 11.

with hand, that is, not of this creation : neither by   *v.* 12.
the bloud of goates , or of calues , but by his owne
bloud entered in once, into the Holies : eternal redemption being found] to witte, by Chrifts death
on the Croſſe, al mankinde being redemed : which
could not be done, by anie other Sacrifice. But as it
was prefigured by the former old Sacrifices , Sacraments , & other Rites of the old Teſtament : ſo is it
repreſented by religious Rites , of the Chriſtian
Church, & alſo applied in particular, to thoſe faithful
ſoules, which are from time to time actually iuſtified , and ſanctified by the onlie merite of Chriſt , 1. Io. 2.

Thoſe only
are iuſtified,
to whom
Chriſts re-
demption is
applied.

dying in deede for al mankinde , and ſufficiently re- *v.* 2.
deming al , yet effectually only iuſtifying thoſe to
whom the ſame infinite price, and ranſome is really
applied. For vnles by applying , & not applying of
our Redemers ranſome , the iuſt were diſtinguiſhed
from the wicked , and finally the elect from the reprobate; you ſhould ſay : that ſeing Chriſt died for
al, & redemed al , ſo al ſhal be iuſtified , & al ſaued.
which is moſt falſe. For the farre greater part of *Mat.* 7.
men are wicked, and the farre greater number wil *v.* 13.
be eternally damned. And as this application of
grace, was ſignified by Sacraments , & Sacrifices,
wherof the faithful in the old Teſtament, beleuing
in Chriſt then to come were participant: ſo now the
application of grace is alſo ſignified , by other greater and better ſignes , [in a more ample, and more *Heb.* 9.
perfect tabernacle] in the preſent Church of Chriſt. *v.* 11.
The ſame may alſo be exemplified in the figure of *Gen.* 17.
Circumciſion, the Paſcal lambe, Manna, the Loaues *Exo.* 12.
of propoſition, ordinatiō of Prieſtes,& Leuités, diuers 16.25. *v.*
ſacrifices, with manie particular Rites, as the ſprink- 30.
ling of bloud vpon the vpper ſtranſom, & cheekes *Leuit.* 8.
of the doore of the houſes, where the Paſchal lambe *Nu.* 8.
was firſt immolated , whileſt the Iſraelites were *Ex.* 12. *v.*
yet in Ægypt, the ſprinkling of bloud of the Teſta- 22.

                                                        ment

Ex. 24 v. ment vpon the booke, and people, sprinkling bloud
8. Heb. 9. seuen times, in cleansing a house infected with
v. 19. leprosie, seuen times sprinckling bloud towards the
Leuit. 14. doore of the tabernacle, & the like; which did not
v. 51. only signifie gracious benefites of God, in those
Nu. 19. times; but also prefigured thinges to come, in the
v. 4. time of grace [and were parables of greater myste-
Heb. 9. ries] which can be no other then the external signes
v. 9. of spiritual grace, the holie Sacraments of Christ,
instituted by him in his Church.

3. The Royal Prophete very often in his Psalmes **The same was**
Psal. 22. foresheweth the abundant grace to be imparted by **prophecied in**
v. 1. 2. 3. Christs Sacraments. Prophecying of Christs ordi- **the Psalmes.**
narie benefites, he saith in the person of euerie faith-
ful soule. [Our Lord ruleth me, & nothing shal be
wanting to me: in place of pasture there he hath
placed me. Vpon the water of refection he hath
brought me vp: he hath conuerted my soule] Di-
v. 5. recting his speach to God, he addeth. [Thou hast
prepared in my sight a table: against them that truble me. Thou hast fatted my head with oyle: and
my chalice inebriating, how goodlie is it?] Thou
Psal. 64. hast visited the earth, & hast inebriated it, thou hast
v. 10. multiplied to inrich it. The riuer of God is replenished with waters: thou hast prepared their meate;
because so is the preparation therof. We haue passed
Ps 65. v. through fire, and water, & thou hast brought vs into
12. 13. 14. refreshing. I wil goe into thy house, with Holocaustes, I wil render to theem my vowes: which my
lippes haue distnguished, & my mouth hath spoken
in my tribulation.] In which and other like places,
though the Prophete alludeth to the Rites of Moyses
Law, yet he foresheweth the blessinges, which
Christ hath bestowed vpon the Gentiles: succee-
ding after that the Iewes were reiected, for their
reiecting of him. As is cleare by the wordes going
v. 7. 8. before [God, who ruleth in his strength, for euer his

F 3 eyes

eyes looke vpon the Gentiles. They that exaſpera-
ted him (the Iewes) let them not be exalted in them
ſelues. Ye Gentiles bleſſe our God, and make the
voice of his prayſe heard.] More clearly where he
reioyceth in Gods promiſe, that Chriſt ſhould be
borne of his ſeede, he foretelleth alſo that Chriſt
wil bleſſe his Church with ſpecial grace. [Our
Lord hath ſworne truth to Dauid, and he wil not *Pſ.* 131.
diſopoint it. Of the fruite of thy wombe, I wil ſet *v.* 11.
vpon thy ſeate.] And a litle after, concerning the
Chriſtian Church [Becauſe our Lord hath choſen *v.* 13 14.
Sion: he hath choſen it for an habitation to himſelf.
This is my reſt (ſaith our Lord) for euer and euer, 15. 16.
here wil I dwel, becauſe I haue choſen it. Bleſſing *Pſ.* 147.
I wil bleſſe her widow, her poore I wil fil with *v.* 3.
breades. Her Prieſtes I wil cloth with ſaluation, &
her ſainctes ſhal reioyce with ioyfulnes.] In general alſo Salomon ſaith, that [Wiſdom hath built *Prou.* **9.**

Alſo in gene-
ral by Salo-
mon.

herſelf an houſe, ſhe hath cut out ſeuen pillers.] that *v.* 1.
is, ſtrengthned, and furniſhed the ſame houſe, the
Chriſtian Church, with competent fortifications, &
munition, neceſſarie for the inhabitants. Our Lord

And by Iſaias,

ſaith by his Prophete Iſaias. [I wil powre out wa- *Iſa.* 44.
ters vpon the thirſtie ground, & ſtreames vpon the *v.* 3 4.
drie land. I wil powre out my ſpirite vpō thy ſeede,
and my bleſſinges vpon thy flocke. And they ſhal
ſpring the herbes as willowes, beſyde the waters
running by.]

The ſame was
inſinuated by
S Iohn.

4. It can not be without ſingular great Myſterie,
which S. Iohn the Euangeliſt writeth, and ſo ſe-
riouſly teſtifieth, that [out of Chriſts ſide (being *Ioan.* 19.
dead on the Croſſe) incontinent came forth bloud *v.* 34 35.
& water. And he that ſaw it, hath geuen teſtimonie, and his teſtimonie is true.] This doubtles ſignified the grace of Chriſt, as a riuer flowing into *Ioan.* 7.
life euerlaſting, deriued into faithful ſoules, by vi- *v.* 39.
ſible Sacramental ſignes, as here it vvas viſibly
fore

foresignified. Finally that there are such visible Sacraments in the Church: S Paul presupposed, as a thing vniuersally knowen, when he auouched him *selfe & others, to be [the Ministers of Christ : and the dispensers of the Mysteries of God.]* Which may here suffice for proofe in general, that there are some holie Sacraments, & a proper Sacrifice in the Church of Christ. Which are to be further proued in particular, in their proper places.

1. Cor. 4. v. 1.

And supposed by S. Paul.

5. In the meane season, that there be seuen such holie Sacraments, in the Church of Christ, is made apparent, by the conuenient resemblance of mans temporal life to his spiritual. For as to our temporal life, it is first necessarie that we be borne into this world : so to liue spiritually, it is necessarie to be borne againe, that is, to be regenerate by the Sacrament of Baptisme. Secondly, as it is requisite for an infant, to grow in stature, & strength: so it is no lesse requisite, that the baptized be also confirmed by the Sacrament of Confirmation : without which the faithful, are but as infantes in Gods Church. Thirdly as it is impossible to liue anie while temporally in humane bodie, without corporal nutriment: so it is as impossible for the soule of man, to liue anie long time spiritually, without the spiritual foode of grace; which is the bread of life, in the most blessed Sacrament of the Altar. Fourtly, as mans bodie being subiect to infirmitie, may sometimes fal into sicknes, or happen to be wounded, & to nede phisike or surgerie : so the soule falling at anie time into sinne, by yelding to tentations, needeth in that case, spiritual cure, and medicine; which is ministred by the Sacrament of Penance : euen as necessarie for remission of actual mortal sinne, as Baptisme is for original. Fiftly, as after curing of the sicke bodie, for preseruing the same from recidiuation, former noysome humors are to be purged; and the vital

Ioan. 3. v. 3. 6.

Act. 8. v. 15 16.

Ioan. 6. v. 51. 53.

Ioan. 20. v. 23.

Resemblance betwen mans spiritual life & temporal.

A Christian is borne by Baptisme,

Groweth by Confirmation.

Is nourished by the B. Sacrament of the Altar.

Is cured by Penance.

F 3 spirite

spirite to be conforted : fo after that the foule is cured by Penance , it behoueth to ftrengthen it , with
more grace , againft the fpiritual affaultes of the
enemie ; efpecially in the laft conflict before death,
which fpiritual helpe is geuen by the Sacrament of
Extreme Vnction. And thefe fiue Sacraments per-   *Iac. 5. v.*
teyne to euerie Chriftian in particular. Befides   *14. 15.*
which there are other two, which belong to the
whole Church in common. For as the temporal
commonwealth neceffarily requireth ciuil Magiftrates to rule , & direct the whole bodie in temporal affaires : fo the militant Church requireth fpiritual Gouernours, & Paftors, which are prouided , &   *Act. 20. v.*
appointed ouer the flocke , by the Sacrament of   *28.*
Holie Orders. Moreouer as it is neceffarie to the
due propagation of new offfpring , that men and
wemen contract Mariage : fo amongft Chriftians,
where neither pluralitie of wiues, nor folution of
the contract can be lawful , during life of both parties. Matrimonie is made a Sacrament , conferring   *Ephef. 5.*
fpecial grace, for better difcharge of the burdens   *v. 31. 32.*
incident to that ftate, and for conferuing mutual
concord, and loue betwixt man and wife, with
holie education of their children.

Margin notes:

More purged & ftrengthned by Extreme Vnction.

The whole Church is fpiritually gouerned by the Clergie.

And pioufly propagated by the Sacrament of Matrimonie.

Chrifts Sacraments , & daylie Sacrifice, excel al Sacrifices & Sacraments of the old Teftament.

ARTICLE 5.

Fiue other pointes concerning the Sacraments in general.

YEt before the declaration of euerie Sacrament in particular, thefe other pointes are to be breefly difcuffed, perteyning to them al in general. Firft the excellencie of Chrifts Sacraments , & Sacrifice, aboue al thofe of the old Teftament. Secondly how
God

God himself; thirdly how Chriſt as man; fourtly
how the Sacraments; and fiftly how the Miniſters
therof, are in true, and peculiar ſenſe, the efficient
cauſes of Sacramental grace.

2. Touching the firſt point; the principal difference betwen the Sacraments of the old and new
Teſtament is, that the former were only ſignes, at
the preſence and vſe wherof, God gaue his ſpecial
grace, remitting ſinnes, and ſanctifying the ſoule:
and theſe new Chriſtian Sacraments are both ſignes
and inſtrumental cauſes of iuſtifying and ſanctifying
grace. The reaſon of which difference is becauſe
al vertue of Sacraments procedeth from the merite
of Chriſt, in whom the faithful of the old Teſtament
beleued, as being to come, and by his Paſſion to
redeme mankinde, and to merite this grace; which
merite being not extant, could not be applied by
anie inſtrumental cauſe, but only be a ſigne without
cooperation to the effect: but now Chriſt being
come, & hauing redemed man, and merited mans
iuſtification, his merite being really extant, worketh the effect by ſuch inſtruments, as he hath inſtituted for ſignes therof, and ſo they are inſtrumental
cauſes, & not only ſignes, of grace; as ſhal be further
ſhewed in due place. An other difference is, that
the old Sacraments of the Law of nature, & of Moyſes, were figures of greater Sacraments, to be inſtituted by Chriſt, & ſo Chriſts Sacraments doe excel
the others, as the thing prefigured ſurpaſſeth the
figure; & as grace geuing ſtrength to kepe the commãdments, excelleth the Law, which only gaue notice of the cõmandments, but not abilitie to obſerue
them: according to the doctrine of the Euangeliſt,
ſaying: [The Law was geuen by Moyſes: grace and
veritie was made by Ieſus Chriſt.] Our Sauiour
himſelf ſignifying this good change of the ſhadowes
and figures, into the true thinges prefigured, ſaid:
[The

Pſal. 39.
v. 7. 8.
Heb. 10.
v. 6. 7. 9.

Artic. 8.

Ioan. 1.
v. 17.

*Sacraments of
the old Teſta-
ment did only
ſignifie grace.
Chriſts Sacra-
ments doe
both ſignifie
& geue grace.*

*The old were
figures, the
new are the
thinges prefi-
gured.*

*The old Sa-
crifices and
Law are cea-
ſed, and new
ſuccede which
are better.*

[The houre cometh, and now it is, when the true *Ioan. 4.*
adorers shal adore the Father, in spirite & veritie] *v. 23.*
For hauing said in the next wordes before, that
shortly there should neither be adoration, (that is *v. 21.*
Adoration oblation of Sacrifice) in the schismatical temple of
strictly taken Garizim, nor in the true Temple of Ierusalem. And
signifieth that in the meane time the schismatical Samaritans, *v. 22.*
oblation of adored that they knew not ; but the Iewes adored
Sacrifice. that which they knew, he signifyed, that the Iewes
offered sacrifice, & adored lawfully ; & the Samaritanes vnlawfully [for saluation (said he) is of the *Ibid.*
Iewes] he then added that there should be adoration (by offering Sacrifice) in other places; and in
other maner ; not in the flesh, and bloud of lambes.
calues, & other terrene creatures, not hauing in them
veritie, grace, spirite, & life ; and therfore such sacrifices should be taken away, and an other Sacrifice
should succede, which should be in it self, celestial &
diuine, ful of veritie, grace, spirite, & life ; which Sacrifice therfore is the veritie it self, wherof the former were figures. And this is called [Spirite & veri- *Ch. 4. v.*
tie, grace & veritie] in respect of the other sacrifi- *23. Ch. 1.*
ces, which were indede true sacrifices, yet but sha- *v. 17.*
dowes of Christs bodie and bloud, sacrificed once on
the Crosse, nere to Ierusalem, & dayly in al nations : *Mal. 1. v.*
as Malachias prophecied ; and our Lord instituted, & *11.*
Largely taken commanded to be done, vntil he come againe in the *Luc. 22.*
al Sacraments end of the world. Adoration also more largely *v. 19.*
and al diuine signifieth, al whorshipe of God, not only by Sacri- *1. Cor. 11.*
Seruice are fice, but by al Sacraments of the new Testament : *v. 26.*
adoration. and so they likewise are veritie, grace, and spirite,
both signifying & geuing grace, which the old Sa-
Christian Sa- craments did only signifie but not geue. And ther-
craments are fore Christian Baptisme is water and the Holie
external signes Ghost. Confirmation is holie Chrisme, & the Holie
& true inter- Ghost. The Eucharist is the formes of bread & wine,
nal grace. and Christs very bodie and bloud : the true bread of
life.

life; And so the other Sacraments are external signes, & true sanctifying grace. Because Christ hath so
merited, and so instituted, that they should worke

Iob. 6. v. effectually, that which they signifie [the wordes
63. that I haue spoken to you be spirite & life] said he
to his Disciples. And S. Peter in the name of them

v. 68 al said againe to him. [Thou hast the wordes of
eternal life.] By reason of which power in Christ
al the Apostles (except Iudas Iscariote) beleued the
efficacie of his word, touching the B. Sacrament.
And likewise in other Sacraments his wordes worke
that grace which they signifie, and therin excel the
old Sacraments.

3. Likewise S. Paul writing against certaine false
Apostles, which endeuored to bring Christians to
obserue the Law of Moyses, teacheth that the Mi- As the Law of
nisterie of the new Testament, so farre excelleth the Christ excel-
old, as the quickening spirite is better then the kil- leth the Law

2. Cor. 3. ling letter, saying [God hath made vs meete Mi- of Moyses:
v. 6. nisters of the new Testament, not in the letter, but
in the spirite, for the letter killeth, but the spirite
quickneth.] Aud prosecuting the same comparison,

v. 7. 8. addeth [if the ministration of *death*, with letters figured in stones, was in glorie, so that the children

Exod. 34. of Israel, could not behold the face of Moyses, for
v. 33. 35 the glorie of his countenance, that is made voide;
how shal not the ministration of *the Spirite* be more
in glorie? For if the ministration of *damnation* be in
glorie, much more the ministrie *of iustice* abundeth
inglorie] where the Apostle manifestly ascribeth
the effect of making iust, to the ministerie of the
new Law, which could not be done by the old.
And further sheweth that the old Law is ceased, &

v. 10. the new abideth. [If that which is made voide
(saith he) is by glorie, that which abideth is in glorie.] Vpon the like occasion of false Apostles, he
also sheweth the excellencie of Christian Sacra-

G   ments:

So Chriſtian Sacraments excel al the Rites of the old Teſtament.

ments and other Rites aboue thoſe of the old Law, calling the former [weake, & poore elements] ge- *Gal. 4.* uing the Chriſtians therby to vnderſtand, that we *v. 9.* haue now in place of them, others, which are ſtrong & rich, in ſanctifying grace. Agane to the ſame pur- *v. 21. 22.* poſe he putte them in minde which pretended [to know the Law, that the old Teſtament is reſembled by the bondwoman Agar, and the new by the free-woman Sara,] Where he concludeth that Chriſtians are borne of the quickning ſpirite, not of the dead fleſh : [not the children of the bondwoman, but of *v. 29. 31.* the free; by the freedom, wherwith Chriſt hath made vs free] by grace merited by his Paſſion, and applied by his Sacraments.

Chriſts excellencie is proued by the excellencie of his Sacraments.

4.   Where as alſo the ſame Apoſtle in his Epiſtle to the Hebrewes, auoucheth that Chriſt farre excelleth the Angels, and Moyſes, and al the Prophetes, amongſt diuers other prooſes, he declareth this aſſured truth, for that the new Law & Teſtament, wherof Chriſt is Mediator, excelleth the old, in reſpect of Sacrifice, & Sacraments, ſaying that [Chriſt *Heb. 8. v.* hath obtained a better miniſterie, by ſo much as he *6. 7. 8.* is Mediator of a better Teſtament, which is eſtabliſhed in better promiſſes. For (ſaith he) if that former had bene void of fault (that is, of defect,) there ſhould not certês a place of a ſecôd haue bene ſought For blaming them ſaith our Lord (by his Prophete Ieremie) I wil conſummate a new Teſtament, not *Iere. 31.* according to the teſtament, which I made to their *v. 31.* fathers. And in ſaying *a new*, he hath made the for- *v. 13.* mer *old*, & that which groweth ancient, & waxeth old, is nigh to vtter decay.] Of which old he likewiſe ſaith that [Giftes & hoſtes offered in the Ta- *Heb. 9. v.* bernacle could not make perfect, concerning the *9. Ch. 10.* conſcience, him that ſerueth. For the Law hauing *v. 1.* a ſhadow of good thinges to come, not the very image of the thinges, it was impoſſible that with *v. 4.*

the

v. 10.

the bloud of oxen & goates, sinnes should be taken away.] But Christ hauing offered his owne bodie and bloud once, on the crosse, the same Sacrifice is dayly offered in an other maner, but the same thing:

Mat. 26. then bloudie, now vnbloudie [vnto remission of
v. 28. sinnes.] wherupon S. Paul saith [we haue an Altar,
Heb. 13. wherof they haue not power to eate, which serue
v. 10. 15. the Tabernacle] & concludeth [By him therfore let vs offer the hoste of praise, alwayes to God] especially the holie Eucharist, which is the principal hoste of praise, & thankesgeuing.

God is the principal efficient cause of grace, in al the Sacraments.

ARTICLE 6.

When the ancient Fathers, & Schoole Doctors teach, that the Sacraments, and Ministers of Sacraments, doe forgeue sinnes, it is farre from their cogitations, to thinke, that God, or Christ doe not more especially worke that effect. But because our Aduersaries, not distinguishing the diuers maners of operations, vse to inferre of one assertion the denial of an other, and by one truth to impugne an other, as when they charge Catholiques, to detract from God, & from Christ, & to denie their power to forgeue sinnes, by saying that the holie Sacraments & Priestes doe remitte sinnes; to take away this calumniation, it is necessarie to declare, by the holie Scriptures, that according to the Catholique faith, & doctrine, in remission of sinnes, and collation of grace, yea in al natural, and supernatural workes, God is alwayes the principal cause efficient.

There may be manie causes of the same effects, in diuers maners,

2. Which is euident in examples of al actions, wherin it pleaseth God to vse either Ministers, or

God is euer the principal

G 2 Instru-

cause of al effectes natural and fupernatural.

Inftruments. One may ferue for manie. In the deliuerie of the children of Ifrael from Ægypt, God commanded that bloud of the Paſchal lambe ſhould be ſprinkled on the doores , where the Ifraelites remained , & commanded an Angel to kil the firſt- *Exo.* **12.** borne in euerie houſe of Ægypt , where the bloud *v.* **22.** was not ſprinkled ; paſſing ouer the houſes , where he ſhould ſee the bloud. This being done : It is truly faid , that the ſprinkled bloud, faued the Ifraelites from death that night, as the inftrumental figne of their ſafetie : it is alſo truly faid : that the Angel killed the firſt borne of the Ægyptians, and ſpared the Iſraelites : It is neuer the leſſe moſt true : that [our Lord ſtroke euerie firſt begotten in the land of *v.* **29.** Ægypt.] Againe, when the children of Iſrael were al paſſed through the read ſea, by the drie channel, *Ch.* **14.** *v.* Moyſes by Gods commandment [ſtreatched forth **22. 26.** his hand againſt the ſea, & it returned to the former **27.** place , and the Ægyptians fleing , the waters came vpon them , & our Lord enwrapt them in the middes of the waters.] Where it is moſt cleare that in this action, Moyſes was Gods miniſter , the hand & rodde of Moyſes an inſtrument, vſed to this purpoſe, the waters firſt ſupernaturally ſtayed , then (being permitted to their natural courſes) ouerwhelmed the Ægyptians : and ſtil God himſelf in the whole action , & in euerie parcel , was the principal cauſe & actor. And ſo in miracles, which are Gods only *Pſal.* **71.** workes, as the principal Agent , yet Moyſes, and *v.* **18.** other Prophetes, alſo the Apoſtles , and other holie men, were his Miniſters. And Moyſes his rodde, the braſen ſerpent, the Arke of couenant , the water of **1.** *Reg.* **5.** the poole called probatica , & the like, were inſtru- *v.* **3. 4.** ments, & inſtrumental cauſes. Neuertheles, God *Ioan.* **5.** is euer the principal Agent in al actions. And ſo it is *v.* **4.** moſt true that God onlie can forgeue ſinnes , As al Chriſtians aſſuredly know, & acknowlege. Which

is yet

is yet further confirmed by these and the like holie Scriptures.

Iob. 14.
v. 4.
Exo. 34.
v. 7.

3. Who [can make him cleane, that is conceiued of vncleane seede, (said holie Iob) is it not thou (ô God) which onlie art? It is God the Dominatour of al, which taketh away iniquitie, & wicked factes, & sinnes, and no man of himself is innocent before

That only God remitteth sinnes, is proued by other holie Scriptures.

Isa. 43.
v. 25.

him] God himself by his Prophete Isaias saith [I am, I am he, that take cleane away thyne iniquities, for myne owne sake.] For this cause, Dauid (& euerie true penitent) crieth to God [Haue mercie on me ô

Psal. 50.
v. 3.

God: according to thy great mercie. And according to the multitude of thy commiserations, take away myne iniquitie.] Men, as Gods ministers preach, instruct, perswade, baptize, impose handes, annoint, & doe manie spirituall functions (as shal be particularly shewed in the Articles folowing) but God is alwayes the principal Agent, the onlie fountaine of grace, & Auctor of al good giftes, for [they

Iac. 1. *v.*
17.
1.Cor. 3.
v. 6. 7.
2.Cor. 5.
v. 17. 18.

al descend from the Father of lightes.] And S. Paul saith of himself & other Ministers of Christ. [I planted, Apollo watered, but God gaue the increase. Therfor neither he that planted is anie thing, nor he that watered, but he that geueth the increase, God. Behold al thinges are made new, but al of God.]

Chrift as man, is the meritorious cause of grace, by the Sacraments.

ARTICLE. 7.

NExt after God, he that is next vnto God, Christ as man, is the cause of grace, in al other men, that euer were, or shal be sanctified. For he onlie being of himself, by reason of his Personal vnion to God, innocent, and endued with al fulnes of grace,

Onlie Christ could merite grace for al mankinde.

G 3   was

was able, & hath merited grace, for al mankinde by
his Paſſion. As the holie Scriptures doe abundantly
witneſſe, both in the old, and new Teſtament. A-
mongſt other figures of this veritie, the bloud of the *Exod.* **12.**
Paſchal lambe, ſprinkled vpon the doores of thoſe *v.* **22.**
houſes, where it was immolated, & eaten, did fore-

Chriſts death signifie that Chriſts bloud ſhould redeme, and ſaue
for mans re- his faithful true ſeruants: as the Apoſtle expoundeth
demption was it, ſaying [our Paſch is immolated, Chriſt.] So did **1.** *Cor.* **5.**
prefigured in the daylie Sacrifice, & generally al other Sacrifices *v.* **7.**
the old Teſta- of the old Teſtament, prefigure the ſame Redemp- *Exo.* **24.**
ment. tion of mankinde, in that the bloud therof was ordi- *v.* **8.**
narily poured out about the Altar, and part therof *Leuit.* **1.**
ſprinkled vpon the people, as is expreſſed in manie *v.* **5. 15.**
places, not needful to be often repeted. Al for ſhew- *Nu.* **19.**
ing the remiſſion of ſinnes, and iuſtification by his *v.* **4.**
death, whom S. Iohn Baptiſt declared to be preſent
in ſight of manie, when pointing with his finger, he *Ioa.* **1. v.**
ſaid [Behold the lambe of God: behold him that **29. 33.**
taketh away the ſinne of the world. This is he, that
baptizeth in the holie Ghoſt.] In compariſon therfore of Chriſts death, and oblation, al the former
Sacrifices of the old Teſtament, were refuſed, as of
no valew [Sacrifice, and oblation (ſaith Chriſt to *Pſal.* **39.**
God) thou wouldeſt not, but eares (of obedience to *v.* **7. 8.**
dye for mans redemption) thou haſt perfited to me. *Heb.* **10.**
Holocauſt, & (ſacrifice) for ſinne, thou didſt not *v.* **5. 6. 7.**
require : then ſaid I : Behold I come] wheras ther-
fore, thoſe old ſacrifices did not ſuffice, Chriſt hath
ordained that which is ſufficient; by his paſſion meriting grace, which he applieth to his ſeruants, by
ſuch meanes, as pleaſed him to ordaine, in his
Church.

The offence, 2.   The neceſſitie of this merite aroſe, both for that
of Gods infi- Gods iuſtice required a competent ranſome, for
nitie Maieſtie mans ſinne, which iuſtly deſerued eternal puniſh-
required infi- ment, for offending Gods infinite Maieſtie; and for
that

that no other man, nor anie mere creature, was able to pay this ranſom, but onlie Chriſt, who is both God & Man; al others being by corrupted nature ſinners, and needing an other to redeme them. But Chriſt being of himſelf (as no other was) wholly innocent, ſaith to God [me thou haſt receiued, becauſe of innocencie, and thou haſt confirmed me in thy ſight for euer.] By whoſe iuſt ranſom therfore, both Gods iuſtice is fully ſatisfied, ann his mercie abundantly ſhewed, & al thoſe his faithful ſeruants are effectually iuſtified, and ſanctified, to whom Chriſts merite is actually & particularly applied. In them Gods [mercie & truth haue mette each other: iuſtice & peace haue kiſſed. Truth is riſen out of the earth, & iuſtice hath looked downe from Heauen] Which merite of Chriſt, for others, God alſo witneſſeth by his Prophete Iſaias, ſaying [Behold my ſeruant (Chriſt in his humanitie) I wil receiue him, myne elect, my ſoule hath pleaſed it ſelf in him. He is clothed with iuſtice, as with a breaſt plate, and there is an helmet of ſaluation, on his head: he is clothed with garments of reuenge (againſt the diuel and ſinne) and is couered with a mantel of zele] to redeme, & ſaue mens ſoules.

3. Vpon this onlie merite of Chriſt, is iuſtly therfore grounded his ſingular power to remitte ſinnes which power he ſignified himſelf to haue, when he ſaid to the ſicke man, that ſouhgt his helpe [Haue a good hart ſonne, thy ſinnes ar forgeuen thee.] And he proued the ſame auctoritie, by a preſent miracle. [That you may know (ſaid he to the Scribes) that the Sonne of man hath power in earth, to forgeue ſinnes (then ſaid he to the ſicke of the palſey) Ariſe, take vp thy bedde, and goe into thy houſe. And he aroſe, and went into his houſe.] The ſame wordes did our Sauiour alſo ſpeake to Marie Magdalen [Thy ſinnes are forgeuen thee.] And inuited al ſinners to parti-

Exod. 34.
v. 7.
Pſal. 40.
v. 13.

Pſal. 84.
v. 11. 12.

Iſa. 42. *v.*
1. *Ch.* 59.
v. 16. 17.

Mat. 9. *v.*
2. *Mar.* 2.
v. 4.

Luc. 7. *v.*
48.

nite ſatiſſaction, which none but Chriſt could make.

Gods wiſdom ordained that his mercie & iuſtice ſhould concurre in mans redemption.

Chriſt proued by a miracle that he had power to forgeue ſinnes.

participate of the fame benefite, faying [Come ye to Mat. 11.
me, al that labour, & are burdened, & I wil refresh v. 28.
you.] Further alfo promifing what grace foeuer is
needful; faying [If you aske the Father anie thing Ioan. 16.
in my name, he wil geue it you.] Diftinctly tea- v. 27.
ching, both that God is the principal geuer of al
grace, & that he geueth the fame, for the merite of
his Sonne: for his fake, & in his name therfore, the
Church alwayes asketh, concluding generally al
her petitions, *Per Chriftum Dominum Noftrum. Through
Chrift our Lord.* Which S. Peter accordingly auou-

S. Peter prea-
ched that
mans falua-
tion is only
by Chrifts
merite.

ched euen to them, that perfecuted him, and al the
Apoftles, for preaching Iefus Chrift, faying plainly
to the Princes of the people, and the Ancients: that
[There is not faluation in anie other: for neither is Act. 4. 7.
there anie other name vnder heauen, geuen to men, 8. 12.
wherin we muft be faued.]

4.   In S. Paules doctrine, nothing is more frequent,
then that al iuftification and fanctification, is only by

S. Paul tea-
ched the fame
in al his
Epiftles.

Gods mere grace, & Chrifts merite. [For al haue Rom. 3. v.
finned (faith the Apoftle) & doe neede the glorie of 23. 24. 25.
God. Iuftified *gratis*, by his grace: by the redemp- Gal. 5. v.
tion, that is in Chrift Iefus, in whom God hath pro- 6. Ch. 6. v.
pofed a propiciation, by faith, in his bloud, to the 15. 1. Cor.
fhewing of his iuftice, for the remiffion of former 7. v. 10.
finnes.] And that none other, nor manie others,
ioyning their vertues together, could make redemption for fine, he proueth by the promife which God
made, vrging the forme of Gods wordes, faying:
[To Abraham were the promifes faid, & *to his feede. Gal. 3.
He faith not: And to feedes,* as in manie: but as in one, v. 16.
And to thy feede: which is Chrift.] The fame he ite- Gen. 22.
rateth in manie places. [In Chrift (faith he) we v. 18.
haue redemption by his bloud (the remiffion of Ephef. 1.
finnes) according to the riches of his grace. We v. 7. Ch.
were by nature the children of wrath, as alfo the 2. v. 3. 4.
reft, but God (who is rich in mercie) for his exce- 5. 6.

ding

ding charitie, wherwith he loued vs, euen when we were dead by sinnes, quickned vs together in Christ, by whose grace you are saued, and raised vp with him; and hath made vs sitte with him in the celestials, in Christ Iesus. By him we haue accesse, both (Iewes & Gentiles) in one Spirite, to the Father. For as there is one God: so one also Mediator of God & men, man Christ Iesus: who gaue himself a redemption for al. Euen the same, [that was a litle leassened vnder the Angels, because of the passion of death, we see is crouned with glorie and honour, that through the grace of God he might taste death for al. That he might repropiciate the sinnes of the people.] That is, make a reconciliation for their sinnes: [who being consummate was made, to al that obey him, cause of eternal saluation.] This smal Abstract, out of much more, which may be collected in S. Paules Epistles, doth sufficiently shew, that Christ by his death & passion merited the grace, wherby mankinde is redemed, and wherby al the elect are, and shal be eternally saued.

v. 18.

1. Tim. 2. v. 5.6.
Heb. 2. v. 9.17.

Ch. 5. v. 9.

Christ merited the glorie of his owne bodie, & the remission of other mens sinnes, and their glorie in soule and bodie.

Iac. 1. v. 18.
1. Pet. 1. v. 3. Ch. 2. v. 21.
1. Io. 1. v. 7. Ch. 2. v. 2.
Apoc. 2. v. 5. Ch. 12. v. 11.

5. The other Apostles teach the same. [Voluntarily hath God begotten vs (saith S. Iames) by *the word* of truth] by Christ, the *Eternal word*, and *Truth* it self. [God according to his great mercie (saith S. Peter) hath regenerated vs vnto a liuelie hope, by the Resurrection of Iesus Christ from the dead. Who also suffered for vs.] S. Iohn saith [The bloud of Iesus Christ cleanseth vs from al sinne. He is the propiciation for our sinnes, & not for ours only, but for the whole worlds] sinnes. In the Apocalypse he testifieth that [Christ hath washed vs from our sinnes. And that the glorious Sainctes ouercame (the assaultes of al enimies) by the bloud of the lambe] that is, of Iesus Christ. S. Iude, though not expresly, yet as supposing that al Christians know, that Christ is our onlie Redemer, and meritorious

The other Apostles teach the same.

H   cause

caufe of our reconciliation to God [exhorteth al *Iud*. v.
theiuſt, to kepe themſelues in the loue of God, ex-   21.
peſting the mercie of our Lord Ieſus Chriſt, vnto
life euerlaſting] concluding his Epiſtle with eternal
thankes, & praiſe [To the onlie God our Sauiour,   v. 25.
by Ieſus Chriſt our Lord.]

Sacraments are the inſtrumental cauſe of grace.

ARTICLE 8.

THeſe former two Articles, being without controuerſie confeſſed to be moſt certaine, by al
Chriſtians : That God is the principal Auſter of al

Gods grace is ordinarily applied to mens ſoules by the vſe of Sacraments.

grace; & that he geueth it for the merite of Chriſt:
it foloweth to be declared, that the ſame is accompliſhed by ſecondarie cauſes; by ſpecial inſtruments,
& miniſters, appointed of God for this purpoſe, as
the ordinarie meanes, by which Gods grace, and
Chriſts merite, being ſufficient for al, are effectually applied to ſome, & not to al. For it is cleare, that
albeit [God would haue al to be ſaued] offering his   1. *Tim.* 2.
grace to al; & that Chriſt redemed al, paying abun-   v. 4.
dát ranſome for al, yet manie are eternally damned;   1. *Ioa.* 2.
either perſiſting ſtil in ſinne, or not perſeuering in   v. 2.
iuſtice, to the end. The cauſe of which different
effectes, can be no other, then the vſe, or not vſe, of
the meanes, that God hath ordayned: which is ordinarily, by receiuing of his holie Sacraments.

2.   The conueniencie wherof is very manifeſt, by
like examples, in the moſt part of Gods prouidence,   *See Arti-*
in gouerning this whole world : eſpecially his pe-   *cle* 1.

The conuenien-cie of ſa-craments, is proued by ex-

culiar people the Church. For ſo God multiplieth
al liuing corporal creatures, by generation in euerie
kind, which he could doe by his only word, as he
firſt

Gen. 1. v.
22. 28.
29. 30.

Ch. 6. v.
17. Ch. 7.
v. 1.

Exod. 3.
v. 2.
Ch. 4. v.
17. v. 31.

Ch. 14. v.
31.
Ch. 7. v.
17. 20.
Ch. 8. v. 7.

Num. 21.
v. 9.

4. Reg. 5.
v. 14.

Tob. 6. v.
8. 19. Ch.
8. v. 2.

 amples of Gods prouidence in other workes.

first created only two of euerie forte: and fo he alfo conferueth them by foode, though he could make them liue, as wel without meate, as with it. Likewife when God would deftroy men, with beaftes, & foule for mans finnes, he did it by water, rayning fourtie dayes, and nightes; and referued thofe few, which he pleafed, by the meanes of an Arke, & by the induftrie of Noe. When he would deliuer his people from Ægypt, he fent Moyfes; confirming his miffion by miracles, & geuing him power to worke miracles, and that with a rodde, which he caried in his hand; faying to him: [This rodde alfo take in thy hand: wherwith thou fhalt doe the fignes.] And accordingly [Moyfes wrought the fignes before the people, & they beleued God, & Moyfes his feruant.] With the fame rodde [he ftroke the water before Pharao, and other Ægyptians, which was turned into bloud.] By the fame meanes [frogges were multiplied, & fciniphes] & other plagues vpon the Ægyptians. And contrariwife [the rockes (being ftrooken with the fame rodde) yelded plentiful fwete waters, to Gods people in the defert.] Thofe [which were ftoong with ferpents, were cured by looking vpon the brafen image of a ferpent. Naaman the Affirian was cleanfed of leprefie, by wafhing himfelf feuen times in Iordan. The diuel was driuen away from young Tobias, and from his fpoufe Sara, by the fmoke of a fifhes hart, and liuer broiled on the coales. And old Tobias being blind, was cured by the gall of the fame fifh.] By which, & by innumerable other examples it is euident, that God both in natural, & fupernatural workes vfeth, fecondarie caufes, and external fignes. As is more amply fhewed in the former Articles of this fecond part: as alfo that Sacrifice, and Sacraments are the moft principal facred fignes, and holie Rites. And withal, that the Sacraments and Sacrifice of the new Law, farre excel thofe of the old Teftament.

3. Now therfore that Chriftian Sacraments, are
not only fignes, but alfo inftrumental caufes of iuftification, and fanctification, is directly and clearly
proued by holie Scriptures. Firft here in general, &
breefly : afterwards particularly of euerie Sacrament, in their proper places. Touching them al in
general, the Royal Prophete forefhewing the fingular grace of the new Teftament, defcribeth it, by the
fimilitude of a riuer, which floweth from a perpetual botomles fountaine, faing : [The riuer of God *Pfal.* 64.
is replenifhed with waters. Thou ô God, haft pre- *v.* 10.
pared their meate (fpiritual nutriment of faithful
foules) becaufe fo is the preparation therof] Euen
by the diuine inftitution of Chrift, geuing power of
operation to what external fignes, it pleafed his
infinite wifdom. For albeit the Sacraments of the
old Teftament were only fignes, & feales, as S. Paul
teacheth, faying : [Abraham receiued the figne of *Rom.* 4.
Circumcifion, the feale of the iuftice of faith, that *v.* 11.
is in prepuce] becaufe Abraham beleued, & obeyed
God, & fo was iuftified before he was circumcifed,
& then receiued circumcifion: yet the Sacraments of
the new Teftament, doe both fignifie, and geue the
grace which they fignifie, as is euident, by the Apoftles comparifon, calling the former [weake, and *Gal.* 4. *v.*
poore elements, which could not bring to perfe- 9. *Heb.* 9.
ction] & afcribing life of the foule, & death of finne, *v.* 9.
to the vertue of Baptifme, faying : [We are buried *Rom.* 6. *v.*
together with Chrift, by Baptifme, into death (of 4. 5. 6.
finne) that as Chrift is rifen from the dead, by the
glorie of the Father, fo we may walke in newneffe
of life. For if we be become complanted to the
fimilitude of his death, we fhal be alfo of his Refurrection. Knowing this, that our old man is crucified with him, that the bodie of finne may be
deftroyed

Chriftian Sacraments are proued by holie Scriptures to be inftrumental caufes of grace.

Sacraments of the old Teftament could not be inftruments of Chrifts grace, which was not then extant, as now it is, and fo the Sacraments are inftruments therof.

Proued by S. Paul exemplifying in Baptifme.

v. 7. deſtroyed, to the end, that we may ſerue ſinne no longer. Fot he that is dead (to ſinne) is iuſtified from ſinne.] Neither doth only faith iuſtifie, but the Sacraments together with faith in Chriſt, make vs aliue to God, by the merite of Chriſts death and reſurrection, applied to our ſoules. For as Chriſt once dead in bodie, and riſen againe liueth to God. [So **v. II.** thinke you alſo (ſaith this Apoſtle) that you are dead to ſinne, but aliue to God, in Chriſt Ieſus our Lord.] And ſo this change from the ſtate of ſinne, to the ſtate of iuſtice, is wrought by faith and Baptiſme, the firſt Sacrament ; as is plaine by the Apoſtles doctrine in this place, And by faith and other Sacraments, ſoules are alſo iuſtified, and ſanctified, after Baptiſme. As ſhal be declared in the enſuing Articles, concerning euerie Sacrament in particular. Here it only reſteth to ſhew in general : How Chriſts Miniſters doe cooperate in his Sacraments.

Nor faith alone bnt with Baptiſme, or other Sacrament, doth iuſtifie.

Chriſts Miniſters are the miniſterial cauſe of grace, in the Sacraments.

ARTICLE. 9.

SO doth euerie Deputie repreſent him, whoſe office he executeth, that albeit the act which he doth, and ſentence which he geueth, taketh force from the principal, that geueth commiſſion, yet is not the Deputie a mere meſſenger to declare, or denounce, the wil of him, by whom he is deputed, but a true actor of the thing, which is done, by him in the name of an other : to witte, with this declaratiue diſtinction, that one is the principal, the other the miniſterial Agent. And in ordinarie ſpeach, the thing done hath denomination of both the actors. So the old Law is called the Law of God,

A deputie is not a mere meſſenger, but an actor of the thing which he doth by commiſſion of an other.

Examples.

H 3   and

and also the Law of Moyses. The Gospel is called Christs Gospel, and seuerally that is called S. Matthewes Gospel, which he writte; & so to the other three Euangelistes are ascribed the Gospels which they writte, by this title [According to Mathew, to Marke, to Luke, and to Iohn.] And S. Paul calleth it his Gospel, which he preached, saying: [According to my Gospel] nothing derogating from Christ, who is the proper, & principal Auctor of the Gospel. And so al other holie Scriptures, are Gods word, and also (in this true & ordinarie sense) are the wordes of the Prophetes, of the Apostles, and of the Euangelists. And so in al other actions, God being euer the principal Agent, diuers thinges are his instruments, and Agents, and men are often his ministers: so that the effectes are truly ascribed to al those Agents, & they are al truly called the efficient causes, of the same effectes. For euen as properly, and truly as it is said; that a man writeth, his hand writeth; & his penne writeth; and that a Scribe, or Secretarie writeth the wil of an other, so no lesse true and proper is it to say: God geueth grace, and remission of sinnes, as the principal Agent; Christ as Man, doth the same, as Gods instrument vnited in Diuine Person. The Sacraments doe the same, as instruments prepared to such vse: & Christs Ministers doe also the same, as his deputies. Through his merite, and power, inuisibly working by the same instruments, & ministerie. Which is further declared, as wel concerning the conueniencie, as the assured certaintie therof, by these holie Scriptures.

2.   God by the ministerie of Moyses deliuered his people from Ægypt (as is noted before) bringing them through the redde sea, making them drie passage, where Pharao, & al his hoste were drowned; so that they saw & acknowleged [the mightie hand which our Lord had excercised.] Acknowleging

Rom 2. v. 16. Ch. 16. v. 25. Ch. 15. v. 19.

A similitude.

This doctrine is proued both to be conuenient & certaine, by holie Scriptures.

Exo. 14. v. 31.

also

Ch. 32.
v. 1.
Ex. 20. *&c*
Leuit. 1.
&c.

also [That Moyses had brought them out of the land of Ægypt; and beleued our Lord, & Moyses his seruant.] Likewise by the ministerie of Moyses God gaue them the written Law, with Sacrifices, Sacraments, & other Rites, ordayning proper Ministers of al. Which we shal not nede here to recite. Also in temporal gouernment of the same people, God vsed Ministers: General Captaines, Iudges, and Kinges. Amongst which, when Gedeon the Iudge fought

Iudic. 7.
v. 18. 20.

the battles of our Lord, against the enimies, the faithful good people cried, victorie [To our Lord, & to Gedeon. The sword of our Lord, & of Gedeon]

God is honored for his power geuen to his Ministers.

Rom. 13.
v. 1. 2.

So in the Law of Christ, temporal Princes, & other Magistrates, are Gods ministers in temporal affaires; & as Actors therof, if they be good, are renowmed, though the principal glorie perteyneth to God, who is alwayes the principal Agent. But touching our present, and special purpose, it is no lesse euident that the Ministers of Christs Sacraments, whether themselues be in the state of grace, or no, so they be Christs true Ministers, are the ministerial cause, of that grace, which God geueth to them, that rightly receiue the same Sacraments. For, that Christ not only hath power in earth, as he is the Sonne of man, to forgeue sinnes, but also communicateth the same to other men, is cleare by the testimonie of the Eu-

Christ as Man not only hath power, but also geueth power to men to forgeue sinnes.

Mat. 9.
v. 8.

angelist S. Matthew, expresly saying that [the multitudes seing (the visible miracle, by which our Lord proued his inuisible power, to forgeue sinnes) glorified God, that gaue such power to men.] Not to one man, Christ; but also to other men, by his imparting therof. If anie Aduersarie shal perhaps replie, that this was but the conceipt of the vulgar people, not the true beleefe of the more prudent; let him know, that God is not glorified, by erronious mistaking, or wrong interpreting his factes, and sayinges; but by the certaine truth, & right beleefe.

An obiection is preuented.

In

Confirmed by
other Scrip-
tures, And
a friuolous
euasion cutte
of by the text.

3. In further confirmation that Chrifts Minifters
can by their minifterie forgeue finnes, himfelf faid *Ioan.* 20.
plainly to his Apoftles:[Receiue ye the Holie Ghoft: *v.* 22. 23.
whofe finnes you fhal forgeue, they are forgeuen
them.] He faith not : whofe finnes you fhal denounce, or declare to be forgeuen: but [whofe finnes you fhal forgeue] which neceffarily importeth,
that Chrifts Minifters doe in deede forgeue finnes,
and fo are the minifterial caufe of grace, and of the
effects of his Sacraments, and of other diuine Rites

Chrifts Mini-
fters are Gods
coadiutors,
helping to
faue foules.

[we are Gods coadiutors (faith S. Paul of him felf, 1. *Cor.* 3.
and other Apoftolical men) you (Chriftian people) *v.* 9. *Ch.*
are Gods husbandrie, you are Gods building. So let 4. *v.* 1.
a man efteme vs, as the Minifters of Chrift, and the
difpenfers of the Myfteries of God. God hath geuen 2. *Cor.* 5.
vs the minifterie of reconciliation, *VVe helping,* doe *v.* 16. *Ch.*
exhorte, that you receiue not the grace of God in 6. *v.* 1.
vaine.] In al which, and the like textes of holie

The Apoftles
in very deede
wrought mi-
racles, & for-
gaue finnes by
power recei-
ued of God.

Scriptures it is manifeft, that Chrifts Minifters are
not only meffengers, but real *Actors, Coadiutors,* doe *Iac.* 5. *v.*
reconcile, doe *forgeue finnes,* doe *helpe, to faue* foules (as 20.
S. Iames fpeaketh) in the very fame fenfe, as the
Councel of the Iewes truly faid, of S. Peters and S.
Iohns miracle, when they had healed a lame man. *Act.* 3. *v.*
[A notorious figne, in deede *hath bene done by them.*] 16.
And as S. Luke alfo faith. [By the handes of the Apo- *Ch.* 4. *v.*
ftles, were manie fignes, and wonders done among 16. *Ch.* 5
the people] that is, by the powerable minifterie of *v.* 12.
the Apoftles. And euen fo the fame, and other Apoftles did forgeue finnes, & other Priefts doe in deede
forgeue finnes, by power & commiffion receiued of
Chrift, as they are the Minifters of his holie Sacraments. And thus much may here fuffice, of Sacraments in general.

Baptiſme, the firſt of Chriſts Sacraments, is neceſſarie to ſaluation.

ARTICLE 10.

TO enioy the vſe of this life, it is neceſſarie to be borne into the world, for before a childe be borne, he is not accounted as one of this world: Euen ſo to enioy the glorie of heauen, it is neceſſarie to be made one of Gods faithful flocke

1. Ioa. 1. a member of the Church, [That we haue ſocietie
v. 3. with the heauenlie father, & with his Sonne Ieſus Chriſt.] As therfore ſome were ingraffed in the ſ ocietie of the faithful, & made members of Gods
Gen. 17. Church, in the old Teſtament by Circumciſion, and
v. 10. before that, by Sacrifices, or other Rites: So in the
Gen. 4. Church of Chriſt a farre more excellent meanes is
v. 4. 26. ordained, that men be borne againe by ſpiritual re-
Ch. 5. v. generation, by baptiſme in water, and the Holie
22. Ch. 6. Ghoſt. As we ſhal here declare by the holie
v. 8. Scriptures.

2. This Sacrament of Baptiſme was firſt prefigured in the beginning of this world, by that which Moy-
Gen. 1. ſes writeth: that [the Spirite of God moued ouer
v. 2. 10. the waters.] For as the waters then receiued vital vertue of the Holie Ghoſt, to produce fiſhes, and birdes: ſo Baptiſme in water receiueth ſpiritual ver-
Gal. 4. v. tue of the Holie Ghoſt, to procreate new men, as
15. Ch. 4. [new creatures] wherupon Chriſts children are
v. 19. called fiſhes: and [his Apoſtles fiſhers of men] for
Mat. 4. v. that he ſent them with auctoritie [to teach al na-
19. Ch. 28. tions] of this vaſt world, & to geue them ſpiritual
v. 19. life, by the quickning water of baptiſme. Another
Gen. 7. figure foreſignifying Baptiſme, was the vniuerſal
v. 23. diluge [in which onlie Noe and they that were

Men are in-
graffed in the
ſocietie of
God by ſpe-
cial Rites.

Diuers figures
of Baptiſme.

The water
ſpringing
fiſhes and
birdes:

The diluge,
And manie
other waters:

I   with

with him in the Arke: eight foules, were faued by 1. *Pet.* 3.
water, wherunto Baptifme (faith S. Peter) being of *v.* 20. 21.
the like forme, now faueth vs alfo.] Manie other *Ex.* 14. *v.*
waters; the Redde fea, through which the children 16. *Cb.* 15.
of Ifrael paffed from Ægypt; the water which was *v.* 25. *Ch.*
made fwete by Moyfes, cafting into it, a peece of 17. *v.* 6.
wood; the waters drawen out of rockes; the water *Iof.* 3. *v.* 13
of Iordane, through which Iofue with al the people 4. *Reg.* 5.
paffed; in which afterwards Naaman the Syrian *v.* 15. *Ch.*
was wafhed, & cleanfed from leprofie; the water 6. *v.* 6.
on which Elifeus the Prophete made yron to fwime: *Exo.* 3. *v.*
and fundrie baptifmes in water, prefcribed by the 18. *Leuit.*
Law, did forefhew that Chrift would inftitute this 22 *v.* 6.

Circumcifion is a moft proper figure of Baptifme. moft neceffarie holie Sacrament in water. Circun- *Gen.* 17.
cifion, though of an other forme, was in other *v.* 10. 23.
refpects the moft proper figure of our Baptifme: as
by which, the faithful were incorporated in the
Church of God, made capable of other Myfteries, *Exo.* 12.
and diftinguifhed from al other nations. For euen *v.* 48.
fo Baptifme is now *Ianua Sacramentorum.* The gate

No Chriftian Sacrament before Baptifme. of al other Chriftian Sacraments. Before which
there can not be anie other, & by which Chriftians
are diftinguifhed from al other people. Wherupon
S. Paul faith, that Chriftians [are circuncifed with *Colof.* 2. *v.*
Circuncifion not made by hand, in fpoiling of the 11. 12.
bodie of the flefh, in the Circuncifion of Chrift, buried with him in Baptifme.]

Baptifme is proued alfo by the Prophetes By Dauid. 3. Befides which prophetical figures, fo expounded in the new Teftament, Baptifme was alfo fore- *Pfal.* 105.
fhewed by other Prophetes. The Royal Pfalmift, *v.* 10.
alluding to the hiftorial deliuerie of the Ifraelites
from Ægypt, faith that our Lord [redemed them 1. *Tim.* 2.
out of the hand of their enemie] Which more pro- *v.* 6.
perly perteyneth to Chriftians, deliuered from captiuitie of finne, by vertue of Chrifts redemption,
applied in Baptifme, then to the children of Ifrael,
for whom no price, nor ranfome, was payed, at
their

their departure from Ægypt; in regard wherof the Prophete fhould fay that God[redemed them]when he in a mightie hand, without payment of ranfome, brought them from captiuitie. But now in Baptifme foules are deliuered from captiuitie of finne, by application of Chrifts death for our ranfome. Be-

Heb. 2. *v.* 17. caufe [he gaue himfelf a redemption for al. He tafted death for al, that he might repropiciate the finne of the people] as the Apoftle fpeaketh, that is, reconcile them from finne. Of Chriftian Baptifme also are moft properly vnderftood two Prophecies **By Ezechiel.** of Ezechiel, by whofe penne in one place, God faith to fuch of his people, as fhal be reduced from captiuitie. [I wil powre out vpon you cleane wa- ter, and you fhal be cleanfed from al your conta-

Ezech. 36. *v.* 25, 26. minations: and from your idols wil I cleanfe you, And I wil geue you a new hart, and vvil put a nevv fpirite in the middes of you: & vvil take avvay the ftonie hart out of your flefh, and I vvil geue you a flefhie (or foft tender) hart: and I wil put my fpirite in the middes of you.] What other vvater, but the vvater of Baptifme vvorketh fo excellent effectes, in *cleanfing from al contaminations*, and in *making a new fpirite*, in men foules, and tender harte? At another time God fhevved to the fame Prophete a vifion, concerning diuers Myfteries: Amongft vvhich he

Ch. 47. *v.* 1. *ad* 12. favv vvaters, iffuing from vnder the Temple. [Be- hold (faith he) vvaters iffued forth vnder the thre- fhold of the houfe tovvard the Eaft.] Certaine it is, that no hiftorie maketh anie mention, of vvaters iffuing from anie part of the Temple, vvhich vvas build by Salomon, or renevved by Zorobabel and others, after their captiuitie in Babylon. Moreouer

1. *Efd.* 1. *v.* 5. *&c.* 2. *Efd.* 1. 2. *&c.* at this time, vvhen Ezechiel prophecied, Salomons Temple vvas deftroyed, & this Prophete and others, foretold that it fhould be reedified. And Efdras and Nehemias vvritte aftervvards, that it vvas accor-

dingly

dingly performed: but no word at al, of such waters issuing forth from the same Temple. Notwithstanding that the Prophete here describeth a very admirable water strangely issuing forth, & mightly increasing: first knee deepe, [euen to the knees] *Ezech.* 47. then [euen to the reynes] lastly it was such [a torrent, which (saith the Prophete) I could not passe *v. 4 5.* ouer, because (saith he) the waters were risen of the deepe torrent, which can not be passed ouer.] He addeth of the fruitfulnes of the ground, which was watered with the same torrent, that [he be- *v. 7.* held in the banke therof exceding manie trees, on both sides] & further touching the benefite of this water he saith, that [euerie liuing soule that cree- *v. 9.* peth, withersoeuer the torrent cometh, shal liue, & there shal be very manie fishes, after that these waters are come thither, and they shal be healed, and al thinges shal liue, to which the torrent shal come.] How al this, and the residue of this passage, may be interpreted of Baptisme the first of Christs Sacraments, and consequently of other Christian Mysteries, the studious may search, and al the faithful may admire the profunditie of Gods word.

3. Iohn Baptist did both prefigure. and foretel the Sacrament of Baptisme.

4.   A more cleare & certaine, both figure, & prophecie of Christian Baptisme, was the Baptisme of *Mat.* 3. *v.* S. Iohn, & his preaching ioyned therwith. For [he 5. 6. baptized in water, and manie came to him, from Ierusalem, & al Iewrie, and al the countrie about Iordan, & were baptized of him. And he preached the *Mar.* 1. *v.* baptisme of penance vnto remission of sinnes.] He 4. *Luc.* 3. that could not baptize, vnto remission of sinnes, yet *v.* 3. preached the Baptisme of penance, to witte, the Baptisme, which Christ would geue vnto remission of sinnes: expresly teaching that as Christ did farre excel him: so Christs Baptisme should haue much *Mat.* 3. greater vertue, and effect, then his Baptisme had. *v.* 11. And therby amongst other differences, declared his
                                                                owne

owne meannesse in respect of Chrits excellencie.
For [the people imagining (saith S Luke) and al
men thinking in their harts of Iohn, lest perhaps he
wereChrist (the expected Messias) Iohn answered
saying vnto al: I in deede baptize you with water,
but there shal come a mightyer then I, whose latchet
of his shoes, I am not worthie to loose: he shal baptize you in the Holie Ghost, & fire] shewing plainly
that his Baptisme was but a preparation, and presignification in water only, of Chrits Baptisme, which
should be both in water, & the Holie Ghost, sanctifying the baptized, and inflaming their soules with
the fire of charitie. Againe that S. Iohns Baptisme
was only a figure of Chrits Baptisme, and not the
same in vertue, and effect, is cleare: for that it sufficed not to saluation. As S Paul, & others teach vs,
by their practise, causing them to be baptized with
Chrits Baptisme, that had bene already baptized
with S. Iohns Baptisme, which had neither bene
necessarie (as they iudged it to be) nor lawful (but
sacrilegious rebaptization) if the two Baptismes had
bene of equal vertue, & effect.

5. Further concerning the necessitie of Christian
Baptisme, our Lord himself said expresly to Nicodemus. [Amen, amen I say to thee: Vnles a man be
borne againe, he can not see the kingdome of God.]
And Nicodemus not vnderstanding the Mysterie, &
demanding, [How a man can be borne againe? Iaf-
ter that he is once borne, from his mother wombe?]
our Sauiour explicating his former speach [an-
swered, & said: Amen, amen I say to thee: Vnles a
man be borne againe of water, and the Spirite, he
can not enter into the kingdome of God] The reason
wherof our Lord explained, saying: [That which
is borne of flesh (of natural parents, by ordinarie
generation) is flesh (is in the state of humane nature,
which is corrupted; and so he is borne the childe of

Luc. 3 *v.*
15. 16.
Marc. 1.
v. 1.
10. 1. *v.*
33.

Act. 19. *v.*
4. 5.

Ioa. 3.
v. 3.

v. 4.

v. 5.

v. 6.

Ephef. 2.
v. 3.

After S. Iohns
Baptisme,
Chrits Bap-
tisme was
necessarie,

Christ ex-
presly taught
that Baptisme
is necessarie.

I 3   wrath)

wrath) & that which is borne of the Spirite´ (spiritually borne againe of water, & the Holie Ghoſt) is ſpirite] that is, liueth ſpiritually. And ſo he willing Nicodemus to learne this point of doctrine, ſaid vnto him [Maruel not, that I ſaid to thee: You muſt be borne againe.] Al one, as if he had ſaid : You muſt be baptized in water and the Holie Ghoſt : els you că neither *ſee* nor *enter into the kingdome of God.* Which is euident by the plaine wordes of the ſacred text.

1. *Iuan. 3.*
v. 7.

v. 3. 5.

6.   Agreeable wherunto, our Sauiour after his Paſſion, and Reſurrection, gaue commandment to his Apoſtles, when he appeared to them in Galelee, ſaying: [Al power is geuen to me, in heauen and in earth : going therfore teach ye al nations: baptizing them in the name of the Father, and of the Sonne, and of the Holie Ghoſt.] Laſtly to the ſame Apoſtles, and others, at the time of his Aſcenſion, he ſaid [He that beleueth, and is baptized, ſhal be ſaued] diſtinctly ſignifying that both Faith, & Baptiſme are neceſſarie to ſaluation. And what els is neceſſarie, as Hope, Charitie, and other vertues, with perſeuerance therin to the end, is to be declared in other places.

And comman-ded to baptize al nations.

Mat. 28.
v. 18. 19.

Mar. 16.
v. 16.
1. *Cor.* 13.
v. 13. *Mat.*
10. *v.* 22.
Ch. 24. *v.*
13.

7.   That the Apoſtles, and other faithful perſons held Baptiſme to be neceſſarie, together with faith, repentance, and other vertues, is further manifeſt by their diligent, & conformable practiſe to Chriſts doctrine. S. Peter hauing perſwaded a great multitude, that Chriſt our Lord, whom they had denied, & cauſed to be crucified, was riſen from death, and they being compunct in hart, and demanding what they ſhould doe; [Doe penance (ſaid he) and be euerie one of you baptized in the name of Ieſus Chriſt, for remiſſion of your ſinnes.] S. Philippe the Deacon inſtructing the Eunuch (the Quenes Treaſurer of Æthiopia) amongſt other poinctes of Chriſtiă faith, taught him the neceſſitie of Baptiſme;

The Apoſtles did execute this comand-ment, as ne-ceſſarie to ſaluation.

Act. 2. *v.*
37. 38.

as ap-

*Act.*8. *v.* as appeareth by the Eunuches demanding to be
27.35.36. baptized; saying, when they came by the way to a
certaine water [Loe water, who doth let me, to be
*v.*38. baptized? And they went downe into the water, &
Philippe baptized him.] S. Paul being miraculously
conuerted from a hote persecutor, to a faithful ser-
*Act.*9. *v.* uant of our Lord Iesus Chrift, was cured of blindnes,
1. 6. 18. by Ananias a disciple of Chrift: and by Baptisme adioyned to the Church. Cornelius a Gentil being
Ch. 10. *v.* wel disposed, & religiously affected [fearing God,
1. 2. 3. with al his house, doing manie almes deedes to the
v. 25. people, and alwayes praying to God] was appointed by a vision, to send to S. Peter, and by him to be
v. 35. *&c.* further instructed, which S. Peter, by warrant of
an other like vision from God, performing, and finding him, & diuers others with him, already indued
*v.*44. 46. with Gods special grace [the Holie Ghost also co-
48. ming in visible signes vpon them, so that they spake
with tongues, & magnified God] yet S. Peter caused
them to be baptized. So necessarie it is by Chrifts
owne doctrine, & Apostolical practise, that *al must
be borne againe*: that is to say, be baptized, both for remission of sinnes, & though some be iustified before,
yet they also, must (by this Sacrament) be associated
to the visible Church of Chrift.

Though some
be iustified
before Baptis-
me, yet it is
necessarie for
other effectes.

8.   In case that anie sincerly desiring Baptisme,
happen without their owne fault, to be preuented
with death, before they be baptized, then their good
desire is to them, *Baptismus Flaminis*: Baptisme of the
Holie Ghost, inflaming their hartes, & supplying the
effect, to eternal saluation. Some also before Baptisme, haue yelded their liues; & others may yeld their
liues, for Chrifts sake, in testimonie of Chriftian Catholique Religion, & to them, Martyrdom is *Baptismus Sanguinis*, Baptisme of bloud. Because they are
baptized in their owne bloud. But the ordinarie
Baptisme is *Baptismus Fluminis*, Baptisme of water.

Three sortes
of Baptisme.

Flaminis.

Sanguinis.

Fluminis.

Baptisme

Baptifme is more especially necessarie for Infants.

ARTICLE. II.

IF the inueterate malice, and enuie of the subtil ferpent, were not know en to be infatiable, we migh maruel, why the Pelagianes long fince, and fome Sectaries at this time, namely Anabaptiftes, defraude infants of Baptifme. Especially feeing, that although it were not neceffarie, yet al Chriftias confeffing at leaft, that it is not hurtful, and that Infants being baptized, & fo parting from this life, before they committe anie actual finne, are affuredly faued. But the cruel enimie of mankinde, befides al thofe, whom through their actual confent, by yeelding to falfhood; or other mortal crimes, he bringeth to eternal perdition, laboreth alfo to depriue children of eternal glorie, by feducing their parents, to omitte their Baptifme, as not neceffarie for their faluation. Which is the doctrine of Caluin,& practife of Anabaptiftes, and of fome English Puritanes. Againft whom therfore we are to proue, that it is not only lawful to baptize Infants (which few or none dare denie) but alfo moft neceffarie for them : becaufe they, not hauing the vfe of reafon, can not actually defire, & feeke it [nor otherwife enter into *Ioan. 3.* the kingdome of God] without it.　　　　*v. 5.*

2. And firft this Catholique doctrine, that Infants ought neceffarily to be baptized, is more then probable, by the fimilitude of Circuncifion : which God inftituting, commanded exprefly, to circumcife childi en in their infancie, faying : [An Infant *Gen. 17.* of eight dayes, fhal be circuncifed among you : as *v. 12.* wel the homeborne fhal be circucifed, as the bought feruant] whether the parents were Hebrewes, or

Gentiles

Gentiles, Abraham was commanded, to cauſe al
that belonged to him, to be circunciſed. [the male
whoſe fleſh of his prepuce ſhal not be circumciſed,
that ſoule ſhal be deſtroyed out of his people.] That
this was a figure of Baptiſme is noted in the precedent Article. S. Paul ſo expounding it. Comparing
therfore the figure, & the thing prefigured together,
you ſee, that by Circumciſion the people of God
were not only diſtinguiſhed from the Heathen Infidels, but alſo that Infantes were to be circumciſed, and puniſhment inflicted for omiſſion therof, at
leaſt vpon them, by whoſe fault it was omitted.
Euen ſo therfore by Baptiſme, Chriſtians are not
only diſtinguiſhed from Iewes, & Paganes, but this
diſtinction alſo perteyneth to children: & they wanting Baptiſme, loſe the benefite therof, and al thoſe
offend, by whoſe default it is omitted.

3. But to paſſe from the figure to the thing it ſelf.
Our Sauiours wordes are general without limitation of age, or ſexe, without exception of Infants.
[Vnles a man (*niſi quis*, man, woman, or childe) be
borne agane of water, & the Spirite (water & the
Holie Ghoſt) he can not enter into the kingdom of
God.] Yea ſo farre doe they erre, from Chriſts
wordes & practiſe, which would exclude Infants
from Baptiſme, that our Lord corrected his Diſciples, for endeuoring to hinder children, from other
grace, & ſpiritual benefite, imparted by external ſignes, ſaying to thē in plaine termes [Suffer the litle
children, & ſtay them not from coming to me: for
the kingdom of heauen is for ſuch. Let them come
to me] not only, be commended to me (by the faith
of others) but be perſonally brought to my preſence: ſhewing that by ſo coming to him, they ſhould
be made apt to enioy the kingdom of heauen, which
is ordayned for ſuch. And being ſo brought vnto
him [he embracing them, & impoſing handes vpon
them,

v. 14.

Art. 10.
nu. 2.
Coloſ. 2. *v.*
11. 12.

Proued by
Chriſts wor-
des.

Ioan. 3.
v. 5.
Mat. 3. *v.*
11. *Luc.* 3.
v. 16.

And by his
fact, in a be-
nefite of leſſe
neceſſitie.

Mat. 19.
v. 14. 15.

Luc. 18. *v.*
15. 16.

Marc. 10.
v. 16.

K

them, bleſſed them.] If Chriſts Actions be for our
inſtruction (as doubtles they are, for he begane to
doe, & then to teach) in that, he admitted infantes, *Act.* I. *v.* I.
he did plainly teach vs, that they are as capable of
his Baptiſme, as of his bleſſing, by embracing, and
impoſition of handes. And are not his wordes general, that al muſt be baptized, not excluding Infants? Did he not yelde this reaſon why they ſhould
be brought vnto him, becauſe the kingdome of heauen is for ſuch. And conſequenly that they muſt
come (or be brought) vnto him, to this end, that
they may enioy the kingdom of heauen?

4.   Againe that children are capable of Baptiſme,
and the grace therof, is proued, becauſe our Sauiours
prouidence is ſufficient to al, which are in ſinne, &
that children are borne in original ſinne, S. Paul
teacheth, ſaying [By one man ſinne entred into *Rom.* 5. *v.*
this world, & by ſinne death, & ſo vnto al men death 12.
did paſſe, in which al ſinned] directly affirming
that we al ſinned in Adams tranſgreſſion, and that
in him al his future progenie was infected: his actual
preuarication, originally perteyning to al his poſteritie, becauſe he repreſented al mankinde. for though
the diuels ſinned firſt, and alſo Eue ſinned before
Adam, & manie doe imitate both them & Adam, in
ſinning actually, yet death, which is the puniſhment
of ſinne, came not vpon al men, for the ſinnes of
diuels, or of Eue, but [it entred by the ſinne of one
man (to witte of Adam) euen on them alſo (ſaith   *v.* 14.
the Apoſtle) that ſinned not, after the ſimilitude of
the preuarication of Adam] that is ſinned not actually, as it is certaine that Infantes doe not, who yet
are iuſtly ſubiect to death, which were not iuſt, if
humane nature were not generally ſubiect to ſinne,
& therfore it is cleare, that they are borne in original
ſinne. And ſo doe nede remiſſion of ſinne, becauſe
[Iudgement in deede is of one (ſaith the Apoſtle) to   *v.* 16.
                                                    con-

Al men are
borne in ori-
ginal ſinne,
which can not
be otherwiſe
remitted in
children then
by Baptiſme.

v. 17. condemnation : for in the offence of one, death reigned by one] Wherfore feeing Infantes neede remiffion of original finne, & that Chrift hath ordayned Baptifme to be the regeneration, or new birth,

Ioan. 3. v. without which [none can fee God, nor enter into
3. 5. the kingdome of God] it foloweth by good confequence of Chrifts fpecial care of al, & amongft the reft of Infants, that this fpecial helpe by Baptifme, perteyneth alfo to them. And fo much the rather, others ought to procure that they be baptized, becaufe they can neither procure it to themfelues, nor by actual defire fupplie the effect, as thofe may doe in cafe of neceffitie, which haue vfe of reafon.

5.   As for the euafion which fome Caluinifts make Solution of an obiečtion. pretending, that Chriftians children, are holie

I. Cor. 7. from their mothers wombe, & nede not Baptifme,
v. 14. becaufe S. Paul faith [The man an infidel is fanctified by the faithful woman : & the woman an infidel, is fanctified by the faithful husband : otherwife (faith he) your children fhould be vncleane, but now they are holie] therfore, fay our Aduerfaries : Children are holie by the faith of their parents. Obferue here by the way diligent reader, firft how Our aduerfaries contradiċt their owne doċtrine. egregioufly the new mafters contradiċt their owne moft common doċtrine, denying that anie can merite holines for them felues, much leffe for others, & yet fay they : Chriftians children are holie for their parents faith. Secondly how fleightly they fearch They doe not fearch the fenfe of holie Scriptures, but wreft them to their owne purpofe. the fenfe, and meaning of this holie Scripture, catching the wordes, & applying them to their owne imagination, contrarie to the Apoftles doċtrine in

Ephef. 2. other places, where he faith that [we are borne the
v. 3. 4. children of wrath : and by regeneration, become the children of God.] The true fenfe of the Apoftles wordes is manifeft by the fcope of his difcourfe. He The true fenfe of the Apoftles wordes hauing taught how ftrict & indiffoluble, the bond of Matrimonie is betwen two Chriftians, exhorteth

K 2   alfo

also such Chriftians , as were formerly maried to Infidels, rather to continue with them , then to be feparatead,if the infidel be alfo content to remaine. And for the better perfwading them in this cafe, he propofeth the fpiritual good , which may enfue , as wel to the maried partie, not yer conuerted, as to their children, faying [If anie brother (that is , if *v.* 12. anie Chriftian) haue a wife, an infidel ,and fhe confent to dwel with him , let him not put her away. And if anie woman haue a husband, an infidel, and he confent to dwel with her , let her not put away her husband] his reafon why he geueth this counfel foloweth [For (faith he) the man an infidel is *v.* 14. fanctified by the faithful wowan, and the woman an infidel is fanctified by the faithful husband] which can no otherwife be vnderftood , but that the good conuerfation of the faithful, may he occafion of conuerting the infidel. And likewife that their children may be fanctified. In confirmation of which probable good effect, he alleageth the example of their children, which by this fame occafion , were already , made cleane, cleanfed from finne, which [otherwife fhould be vncleane . but *Ibid.* now they are holie] *now* (faith he) not fo borne, but *now are holie*, which were borne the children of *Ephes.* 2. wrath. Neither doth the Apoftle affure them , that *v.* 3. this effect fhould folow , nor deliuereth his aduife *v.* 15. as a precept, but commending it to their confideration , concludeth , faying : [How knoweft thou *v.* 16. woman, if thou fhalt faue thy husband? or how knoweft thou man, if thou fhalt faue the woman?] fignifying that there may be good hope ,but no certaintie, of the parties conuerfion,that is yet an infidel, & of the childrens cleanfing from finne by this occafion,to witte,by Baptifme,as by the inftrumental caufe.

6. Finally when the facred Hiftorie reporteth in general

---

is gathered by the fcope of his exhortation.

The faith of one may be occafion, but not the caufe of an others conuerfion.

And of the fanctification of children.

Act. 16. v. 15. 31. 33. general, that whole families were baptized, [The deuout woman Lidia, & her house: The keper of a prison, & al his house] and the like, who can doubt but children are comprised, & were baptized, seing no exception is made of children? Els let our Aduersaries shew by expresse Scriptures, that it is not lawful, or not necessarie to baptize Infantes. And so this being sufficient, touching the necessitie of Baptisme, let vs likewise declare the effectes therof.

Whole families were baptized, without exception of children.

By Baptisme the soule is cleansed from sinne, & sanctified with grace.

ARTICLE 12.

Like as in the former Articles, our Aduersaries denie the necessitie of Baptisme, especially to Infants: so they dissent from vs, rather more concerning the effectes of Baptisme, & other Christian Sacraments: holding them to be only signes, or seales of iustification: such as were Circumcision, and other Sacraments of the old Testament, & denying the Sacraments of Christ, to be instrumental causes of the remission of sinnes, & of sanctificatió through Christs grace, applied by them, to the soules of men, as the Catholique Church beleueth, and teacheth. Which beleefe & doctrine, besides the former proofes, touching al Christs Sacraments in general, is here further declared of Baptisme in particular.

The state of the controuersie.

Art 8.

2. A plaine figure, & presignification wherof, was that fauour of God which happened by his mightie power, to the children of Israel, passing through the reade sea: where Pharao, and al his armie of the Ægyptians being entred into the reade sea, were destroyed [neither did there so much as one of them remaine. But the children of Israel marched through the

As the Ægyptians were drowned in the reade sea so al sinnes are destroyed in Baptisme.

Exo. 14. v. 28. 29. 30.

K 3

the middes of the drie fea, & the waters were vnto
them, as in ftede of a wal, on the right hand, and on
the left: and our Lord deliuered Ifrael in that day,
out of the hand of the Ægyptians.] Euen fo Baptifme applying the merite of Chrifts bloud, to the baptized, al their finnes are deftroyed, & wafhed away,
not one remayning. For it is cleare by S. Pauls ex-
pofitiõ, that this Myftical diuine worke, was a figure
of Chriftian Baptifme, where he not only faith, that
al the Ifraelites (in the time of Moyfes gouernmẽt)
[were vnder the cloud, & al paffed through the fea, *1. Cor.* 10.
& al in Moyfes were baptized, in the cloud, and in *v.* 1. 2. 5.
the fea: and that in the more part of them, God was
not wel pleafed] but he alfo addeth, that [thefe thin- *v.* 6.
ges were done in a figure of vs: & chanced to them
in figure.] And fo inftructed the Corinthians, & in *v.* 11.
them al Chriftians, that Myfteries of the old Teftament, are figures of Chriftian Myfteries, namely the
paffage of the Ifraelites through the fea, to be a figure
of Chriftian Baptifme; their eating of Manna, and
drincking water of the rocke, a figure of the holie
Eucharift; their fafe deliuerie from the Ægyptians,
& yet deftruction of manie in the deferte, a figure of
manie Chriftians, once deliuered from al finnes in
Baptifme, and nourifhed by the B. Sacrament, yet
perifhing through other finnes, committed afterwards.

Thinges done in the old Teftament were figures of Chriftian Myfteries.

3.   Further more, touching our prefent purpofe,
the Royal Pfalmift reciting this benefite of the peoples deliuerie from Ægypt, by paffage through the
readfea, interpofeth (as the maner of Prophetes is)
fomething not conteyned in the hiftorie, but apperteyning to the thing prefigured, faying [Our Lord *Pfal.* 105.
faued them, from the hand of thofe that hated them: *v.* 10. 11.
& he redemed thẽ out of the hãd of the enimie. And
the water ouerwhelmed thofe, that afflicted them,
there did not one of them remaine] where the Prophete

King Dauid prophecied this effect of Baptifme, al- luding to the deliuerie of Ifrael, and deftruction of the Ægypti- ans in the readfea.

phete foreſeing the Redemption of mankinde, to be
made by Chriſt, & to be applied to Chriſtians by Sa-

v. 10. craments, as firſt by Baptiſme, ſaid [our Lord redemed them] paying a great price, an abundant ranſome, his owne bloud, by which we are ranſomed
from bondage of ſinne, & the diuel, & that alſo applied by Baptiſme, ſignified not by euerie ſea, but moſt
aptly by the *readſea* ; hauing vertue to waſh away
ſinnes by Chriſts bloud : yea al ſinnes what ſocuer

v. 7. 8. contracted, or committed before : euen from al
ſinnes, that enter with them, into this readſea, as
the hiſtorie conteyneth in the figure, & the Prophete

v. 11. expreſſeth in his prophecie : [The water ouerwhelmed thoſe that afflicted them, there did not one of
them remaine.]

Art. 10. 4. Agreable wherto our Lord alſo ſaith by his Pro-
nu. 3. phete Ezechiel, vnto future Chriſtians (as we allea-
Ezech. 36. ged befoae) [I wil powre out vpon you cleane wa-
v. 25. ter, & you ſhal be cleanſed from al your contaminations, and from al idols wil I cleanſe you.] Further
concerning ſanctification, and holines, after the remiſſion of ſinnes, he addeth, ſaying [And I wil geue

v. 26. you a new hart, & wil put a new ſpirite in the middes of you: and wil take away the ſtonie hart out of
your fleſh, and wil geue you a fleſhie hart] a tender
hart, prone to mercie, flexible to Gods wil, and apt
to embrace good inſpirations.

5, Doubtles our Sauiour in his ſpeach to S. Peter,
vpon occaſion of an other waſhing, alluded to Baptiſme, ſignifying the effect therof, to be waſhing and

Ioan. 13. cleanſing from al ſinnes: when he ſaid [He that is
v. 10. waſhed (that is baptized) needeth not but to waſh
his feete (his affections or inclinations, which are
not ſinnes, for it foloweth [but is cleane wholly]
being rightly waſhed by Baptiſme: to witte, if the
perſon baptized was ſincerely diſpoſed, to receiue
the grace, & effect of the Sacrament. For otherwiſe
if anie

*An other pro-
phecie of re-
miſſion of
ſinnes, and
ſanctification
by Baptiſme.*

*The ſame is
proued by
Chriſts doc-
trine.*

if anie be impeniteut, forstering wickednes in his
hart, though he be baptized, yet the Sacrament is
hindered from producing the effect, either of sanctitie,or remission of sinnes. As it was in Iudas Isca-
riotte. In regard of whom our Sauiour added [you   *v.* 11.
are cleane (speaking to the college of his Apostlrs in
general) but not al. For he knew (saith the Euangelist) who it was that would betray him: therfore
he said : You are not cleane al.] By al which it is
euident, that the proper effect of Baptisme is to remitte sinnes,and to make the soule cleane & holie.

By S. Peters
exhortation.

6.   Most plainly did S. peter declare this effect of
Baptisme saying to a great multitude of Iewes new-
ly conuerted by his first Sermon [Be euerie one of   *Act.* 2. *v.*
you baptized,in the name of Iesus Christ,for remissio   38.
of your sinnes.& you shal receiue the gift of the Holie

By Ananias
his speuch to
S. Paul,

Ghost.] The same did Ananias,the discipel of Christ
signifie , when he said to Saul (in Damascus, before
that he was called Paul) [Rise vp, and be baptized,   *Act.* 22.
and wash away thy sinnes.]   *v.* 17.

And by S.
Paules Epi-
stles.

7.   As clearly the same S. Paul explicateth this duble effect of Baptisme, in remitting sinnes , & sanctifying the soule , writing thus to the Romanes. [Al
we which are baptized in Christ Iesus , in his death   *Rom.* 6.
we are baptized. For we are buried together with   *v.* 3. 4,
him by Baptisme into death : that as Christ is risen
from the dead,by the glorie of the Father;so we also
may walke in newnes of life.] A litle after shewing
the destuction of sinne by Baptisme. [Knowing this   *v.* 6.
(saith he) that our old man is crucified with him,
that the bodie of sinne may be destroyed,to the end,
that we may serue sinne no longer. For he that is   *v.* 7.
dead (mystically dead by Baptisme) is iustified from
sinne.] And interposing a further effect of eternal
glorie in the resurrection, concluding this point of
iustification by Baptisme,saith [So thinke you also,   *v.* 11.
that you are dead to sinne, but aliue to God in Christ
Iesus

Iesus our Lord.] Likewise in other places he often repeteth and confirmeth this point of doctrine. [As manie of you (saith he to the Galatians) as are baptized in Christ, haue put on Christ.] And to the Ephesians speaking generally of the whole Church [Christ (saith he) loued the Church, and deliuered himself for it, that he might sanctfie it, cleansing it, by the lauer of water in the word.] Elswhere he saith to other Christians [You are buried with Christ in Baptisme : in whom also you are risen againe by the faith of the operation of God, who raised him vp from the dead. Christ saued vs by the lauer of regeneration, and renouation of the Holie Ghost, whom he hath poured vpon vs abundantly, by Iesus Christ our Sauiour.] In al which, and the like sacred textes of diuine Scriptures, Iustification Sanctification, and Saluation are ascribed to diuers kindes of causes, in true and proper senses, to God, to Christ our Redemer, to the lauer of water, that is to baptisme, & so to other Sacraments: as to the principal, meritorious, and instrumental causes, of the selfsame effectes.

Gal. 3. *v.* 27.

Ephes. 5 *v.* 26.

Colos. 2. *v.* 12. *Tit.* 3. *v.* 5.

The same eff. & is ascribed to diuers causes in diuers senses.

Concupiscence remayning after Baptisme, is not sinne.

ARTICLE 13.

AGainst this so confirmed truth, that al sinnes are remitted by Baptisme, our Aduersaries obiect, that concupiscence stil remaineth, which (say they) is sinne. We answer: It is true that cōcupiscence remaineth in the baptized: and did generally remaine in al mankinde since Adams fal: also in those which were iustified : but it is not sinne without consent of the wil, yelding to il suggestion. As shal here be shewed by those special places of holie Scripture,

Concupiscence, without consent of the wil, is not sinne.

L

ture, which our Aduerfaries commonly produce
for their contrarie opinion,& by diuers o.her places,
where fpecial mention is made of concupifcence:
or of the luft of finne, v. hich is an other name of
the fame thing.

In the wicked
it is a diftinct
thing from
finne before
confent be
yelded.
2.   Firft in the cafe of the wicked, in whom the
queftion may feme to be more difficult, namely in
Cain, finne, and the luft therof, are plainly diftinguifhed, to be two different thinges in themfelues.
For touching finne, [our Lord faid to him: If thou *Gen.* 4.
doeft il, fhal not thy finne forthwith be prefent at *v.* 7.
the doore.] where you fee, that the act of doing il,
bringeth forth finne, making it prefent, which was
not at al, before the act of confent. Touching concupifcence, appetite, or luft of finne, he faid: [The   *Ibid.*
luft therof fhal be vnder thee, & thou fhalt haue dominion ouer it:] What more manifeft difference
can be required,then that a wicked perfon by doing
il(to witte in thought,word,or deede) maketh finne
to be prefent, wherby it is cleare, that he is now
fubiect to finne: and yet concupifcence, or luft of
finne, is fubiect to the finner, & vnder his dominion, that he may further confent, or not confent
vnto it.

Concupifcen-
ce remained
in Dauid be-
ing contrite,
and confe-
quently iufti-
fied from his
finnes.
3.   Much more is concupifcence fubiect to the iuft.
Example in King Dauid, being hartely contrite for
his finnes committed, & therby reftored to iuftice,
and Gods fauour through grace ; yet feeling the
combate of concupifcence ftil in his flefh, humbly
acknowleging that infirmitie, & lamenting for the
moleftation which he therby fnffered, prayed to
God faying [I am become miferable, & am made *Pfal.* 37.
crooked, euen to the end: I went forowful al the *v.* 7. 8.
day,becaufe my loynes are filled with illufions: &
there is no health in my flefh.] But this weaknes
being in the flefh,his mind not côfenting,he prayed
for helpe & for more ftreingth [I am afflicted (faith
he) &

v. 9. he) & am humbled exceding: I rored for the grouing of my hart.] So great was the forow of his hart, that from the abundance therof, his voice broke out into clamour, and as he calleth it, into roring. And fo perſeuering in reſiſtance, conſented not in minde, to concupiſcence alluring by illuſions in his loynes, but deſired to be freede from tentation.

v. 10. 11. [Lord (ſaid he) before thee is my deſire, and my groning is not hid from thee. My hart is trubled, my ſtrength hath forſaken me: & the light of myne eyes, & the ſame is not with me.] Agane in an other penitential Pſalme, where it is more cleare by the teſtimonie of Nathan the Prophete, that his ſinne was remitted, he prayed, that God would

Pſal. 50.
v. 4.
amply waſh him, & cleanſe him: ſaying, [waſh me ô God, more amply from myne iniquitie, & cleanſe me from my ſinne] Which muſt nedes be vnderſtood of ſome other thing then of the guilt of ſinne it ſelfe, which was already remitted, but as the temporal puniſhment, was not al taken away, ſo alſo there remained concupiſcence, common to al men, contracted together with original ſinne, and increaſed by actual, from which therfore he prayed

v. 7.
to be more waſhed, & cleanſed, [For behold (ſaith he) I was conceiued in iniquities, and my mother conceiued me in ſinnes] But if concupiſcence were a ſinne, it were not true which the Prophete affir-

2. Reg. 12. med [our Lord hath taken away thy ſinne] vnles
v. 13. anie wil ſay (which is moſt falſe, and abſurde) that God forgeueth part of a penitents ſinnes, and not al his ſinnes, which ſeparate him from God. But becauſe we ſpeake here particularly of concupiſcence after Baptiſme, omitting the like examples of the old Teſtament, we come to the doctrine of Chriſt and his Apoſtles.

Ioan. 13. 4. Our Sauiour (as is noted in the precedent Ar-
v. 10. ticle) teſtifying [that he which is waſhed (to witte
L 2 by

Yea after that the Prophete had ſaid, that his ſinne was taken away, yet corcupiſcence remayned.

Proued by our Sauiours doctrine.

by Baptisme) is wash-d wholly] that is from al kind of sinne : for els he were not wholly washed, yet addeth [that the same person needeth to wash his feete] that is, some euil inclinations, tempting to sinnes. And therfore there is some euil in a iust man, which is not sinne, but tempteth to sinne, And this is properly concupiscence. For so soone as consent of mans wil is geuen to the tentation, as when anie man wittingly applieth his minde, or sense, desiring to committe the thing, or willingly delighteth in the thought, he doth then sinne in his hart, & it is more then concupiscence, for then concupiscence reigneth & is sinne, which before consent of the wil was not sinne.

Mat. 5. v. 29.

More largely by S Pauls doctrine.

5.   Wherof S. Paul treateth largely, laying first this ground : that Baptisme resembling the Death, and Resurrection of Christ, so complainteth, or ingraffeth Christs seruants into him, that [the bodie of sinne is destroyed, to the end that we may serue sinne no longer.] He then admonished to resist, and ouercome tentations, and allurements of concupiscence, saying [Let not sinne therfore reigne in your mortal bodies, that you obey the concupiscences therof] signifying that concupiscence in deede remaineth, but that it is in the power of the iust (assisted by Gods grace) to resist it. Els his exhortation were in vaine, if it were vnpossible to resist concupiscence. And so he further prosecuting his admonition saith. [But neither doe ye exhibite your members, instruments of iniquitie vnto sinne : but exhibite your selues to God, as of dead men, aliue : & your members instruments of iustice to God. For sinne shal not haue dominion ouer you, for you are not vnder the Law, but vnder grace] Which most important difference betwen the Law of Moyses, conteyning the commandments, and not geuing grace to kepe them ; and the Law of Christ, confirming

Rom. 6. v. 3. 4.

v. 6.

v. 12.

v. 13.

v. 14.

ming

ming the fame commandments, & geuing grace to
obferue them, the Apoftle explaineth in the next
chapter, by the fimilitude of a woman maried firft
to one husband, and after his death, to an other : that
feing our former husband (finne with the power
which it had before) is dead, thróugh Chrifts grace
applied in Baptifme, & that now we are maried to
an other hunsband Chrift, he therfore willeth vs to
bring forth children, to God : that is, good workes.

eb 7. v. 2. [The woman (faith he) that is vnder a husband :
her husband liuing, is bond to the Law, but if her
husband be dead, fhe is loofed from the Law of her
v. 4. husband &c. Therfore my brethren you alfo are
made dead to the Law, by the bodie of Chrift, that
you may be an other mans, who is rifen againe
from the dead, that we may fructifie to God] which
before Baptifme we could not. [For when we
v. 5. were in the flefh, the paffions of finnes that were by
the Law did vvorke in our members, to fructifie
v. 6. vnto death (becaufe concupifcence then reigned)
But now vve are loofed from the law of death,
vvherein vve vvere deteyned : in fo much we ferue
in newnes of fpirite, & not in the oldnes of the letter]
v. 12. or vvritten law of Moyfes. [Which Law not vvith-
ftanding vvas in it felfe iuft and holie, and the commandment holie, and iuft and good] yet concupifcence then reigning, the Lavv not geuing grace,
vvrought finne, novv concupifcence remayning,
reigneth not in the iuft, Chrifts grace geuing ftrégth
to refift. As the Apoftle further confirmeth in the
reft of this chapter, fhevving the greuous affaultes,
and moleftations of concupifcence, and paffions of
the flefh, but the greater vertue and force of grace,
v. 15. vvheras therfore he faith [Not that vvhich I vvil
the fame doe I, but vvhich I hate, that I doe] he can
not meane that he committeth finne againft his wil,
neither doth he condemne the Law, for his wil vvas

Concupifcen-
ce had more
force in the
olde law then
now it hath
in the law of
grace.

Chriftians by
Baptifme re-
ceiue domi-
nion ouer the
paffions of có-
cupifcence.

L 3   to kepe

That in deede is an humane act, and is either sinne which is done by consent of thewil.

Euel motions of the flesh, without consent, are not humane actes.

to kepe the Law : and so both his wil, and the Law are good, as he explaineth in the next wordes [If that which wil not, the same I doe, I consent to the Law, that it is good] and where he repeteth the same. [Not the good which I wil, that doe I, but the euil which I wil not, that I doe] he also explicateth it, saying : [And if that which I wil not, the same I doe: now not I worke it, but the sinne (the inclination of the flesh, concupiscence) that dwelleth in me.] Againe he saith [I am delighted with the Law of God according to the inward man : but I see an other law in my members repugning to the Law of my minde, and captiuing me in the law of sinne, that is in my members.] So that concupiscence how much soeuer striuing, and alluring, so long as consent of the wil, and minde is not yelded, is not sinne. Which is yet further confirmed by the wordes folowing : where exemplifying in his owne person, in behalf of al the iust, he saith [Therfore I myself with the minde serue the Law of God, but with the flesh, the Law of sinne.] As certaine therfore, as a manslefe with the minde is himselfe: and his flesh without his minde, is not himself : so certaine it is, that concupiscence without consent of the vvil, is not sinne.

v. 16.

v. 19.

v. 20.

v. 22.

v. 25.

S. Iames also distinguisheth concupiscence from al sinne.

6 In plaine termes also S. Iames distinguisheth concupiscence from sinne, shewing the maner how sinne is produced, and whence man is tempted to euil saying [Let no man when he is tempted say, that he is tempted of God : for God is not a tempter of euils, and he tempteth no man. But euerie man is tempted of his owne concupiscence, abstracted & allured. Afterward concupiscence, when it hath conceiued bringeth forth sinne] what can be said more directly, to signifie, that concupiscence tempting doth not at first bring forth sinne ? so that the first motion to sinne is not sinne, but tentation only : &

Iac. 1.
v. 13. 14
15.

v. 2. 3.

ly : & as wel the occasion of good as of euil wherupon the same Apostle said before [Esteme it al ioy, my brethren, when ye fal into diuers tentations: knowing that the tentation of your faith, worketh patience] But in case the person that is tempted, linger and resist not, then [Afterward

v. 15.

(saith the Apostle) concupiscence, when it hath conceiued bringeth forth sinne] by getting consent of the wil, bringeth forth sinne, but without consent can not bring furth, because alone without the wil it can not conceiue. Neither is euerie sinne mortal. But as it foloweth in the next wordes [Sinne

Art. 28.

when it is consummate, ingendereth death] Which point perteyneth to an other place. It resteth here to know an other effect of Baptisme.

And venial sinne frō mortal.

Baptisme imprinteth a spiritual character in the soule.

A R T I C L E 14.

SOme pointes of Christian doctrine, as is noted in the Preface of this worke, are not exptesly, and immediatly written in the holie Scriptures, but supplied in those thinges, which the Apostles lerned otherwise, either of Christ, or of the Holie Ghost.

Ioan. 16.

Who, as our Sauiour promised, should teach them

v. 13. *ch.*

al truth, and remaine with his Church for euer.

14 *v.* 16.

Neither did the Apostles write al, which they lerned, and taught. For the greatest part of them

Mat. 28.

writte nothing at al, that is now extant. And S.

v. 20.

Iohn in the very last wordes of his Gospel (which was written last of al the holie Scriptures, yea after his Apocalypse) testifieth in these plaine wordes, that

Ioan. 21.

[There are manie other thinges also, which Iesus

v. 25.

(our Lord) did, which if they were written in particular,

Al pointes of faith and Religion are not expresly writtē in holie Scripture, yet prouet by expresse Scripture, remitting is to Traditions.

ticular, neither the world it self I thinke were able to conteyne thofe bookes that fhould be written] So amongft other thinges not exprefly written in particular, Tradition teacheth this beleefe and doctrine of the Church, that the Sacrament of Baptifme, befides the remiffion of finnes, and fanctification of the foule, imprinteth a certaine fpiritual figne or marke, called a *Character* in the foule of the baptized which can neuer be taken away, nor blotted out by herefie, apoftafie nor other finne, or meanes, but remaineth indelible in their foules, for a cognifance of their once entring into Chrifts fold: and for a diftinction from thofe which neuer were chriftened. By which alfo they are made capable of other Sacraments, & Rites of the Church.

2. Neuerthelesthis doctrine being not expreffed in the holie Scripture, yet is it deduced from thēce. For firft the proper figure of Baptifme, the old Sacrament of Circumcifion made a diftinct marke in the flefh [You fhal circumcife the flefh of your prepuce (faid God to Abraham) that it may be a figne of the couenāt betwē me & you.] Therefore the figuratiue Sacramēt hauing fo indeleble a marke, diftinguifhing the circumcifed from the vncircuncifed; the fpiritual Sacrament of Chrift, being the thing prefigured, requireth alfo an indeleble marke: & that in the foule which is fpiritual. Which can be no other in al the baptized, but this fpiritual Character. For the other effectes of Iuftification, and Sanctification are deleble in this life, and are loft in manie, by finnes after Baptifme: but this figne and effect ftil remayneth, alfo in moft enormious finners: by vvhich, fo long as they are in this vvorld, they haue povver, and poffibilitie, by repentance, and other Sacraments, to recouer grace with remiffion of finnes & fanctification. This Character alfo eternally remaineth to the greatter glorie of the bleffed, and greatter torment of the damned.   3. Of

Character of Baptifme.

As Circumcifion made a marke iu the bodie, fo Bap. tifme maketh a figne in the foule.

Gen. 17.
v, 11.

Other effectes of Baptifme may be loft: but the character can not.

3. Of this indeleble diſtinctiue marke, and ſeale of the couenant betwen Chriſt and Chriſtians, S. Paul ſemeth to ſpeake in his Epiſtle to the Corinthi-
2. Cor. 1. ans, ſaying [God alſo hath ſealed vs, & geuen vs
v. 22. the pledge of the Spirite in our hartes.] For ſeale, pledge, marke, ſigne, or character is al one in ſenſe, Except we ſhal contend about the word, or terme when the ſacred text ſufficiently proueth the thing it ſelf. Againe the ſame Apoſtle admoniſhing the Chriſtian Epheſians not to prouoke the Holie Ghoſt with new ſinnes, by whom they (& conſequently al other Chriſtians) were marked, to witte in Bap-tiſme, putteth them in mind of ſome general inde-
Epheſ. 4. leble ſigne, ſaying [Contriſtate not the Holie Spi-
v. 30. rite of God: in which you are ſigned vnto the day of redemption.] calling the day of general Iudge-ment, the day of redemption: in which it ſhal ap-peare, what effect Chriſts Redemption ſhal haue in al, as wel the iuſt, as the wicked.

Proued by S. Pauls teſti-monie, more probably then it can be im-pugned by anie holie ſcripture,

Solemne Rites are requiſite, and profitable in the adminiſtration of Baptiſme: & of other Sacraments.

ARTICLE 15.

FOr due obſeruation & moſt benefite of Lawes, & good Ordinances, it much auaileth to procede in practiſe & execution therof with ſuch order, and ſo-lemnitie, as may bring iuſt terrour to malefactors, edification to the wel diſpoſed, & general good to the whole commonwealth. And no leſſe it behoueth in adminiſtration of holie Sacraments, to remoue ſuch impediments, as may hinder the fruite of Gods mercie, and to prepare the way to the participation of the ful effect of diuine grace. For both which

Solemnitie in execution of Lawes, and adminiſtratiõ of Sacraments is profitable.

M   purpoſes,

purpoſes, in the Sacrament of Baptiſme, are required
certaine ſolemne ſignificant Rites, as wel to repreſſe
the power of the malicious enimie, as to diſpoſe the
perſons coming to the ſeruice of Chriſt, by renoun-
ciation of the ſpiritual aduerſarie of mankinde, with
al his pompe & wickednes, and by profeſſion of the
Chriſtian faith : either by them ſelues, if they haue
competent age, and vſe of reaſon, or by others anſwering & promiſing for them, which are ordinarily annexed, as requiſite and profitable : though in
caſe of neceſſitie it ſufficeth to ſaluation, to be baptized without other ceremonies, in natural elemental, water in the name of the Father, and of the
Sonne, & of the Holie Ghoſt, which are the eſſential
partes of Baptiſme.

2. Concerning therfore the acceſſarie Ceremonies
of Baptiſme, the firſt part is Chriſtian Exorciſme,
by which the diuel is diſpoſſeſſed, & his powre reſtrained, which he hath in al that are in ſtate of
mortal ſinne, whether it be original or actual : and
ſo it is requiſite for Infantes, borne in original ſinne,
that the diuel be expelled by diuine power, exerciſed by the Church, & the lawful Miniſters. Which
ſpiritual power differeth ſo farre from magical con-
iuration practiſed by Nicromancers, commonly called coniurers, as pact and couenant with the diuel,
differeth from auctoritie, and dominion ouer him.
For al that Magical coniurers can doe, is by conſent
and helpe of diuels, with whom they either make
expreſſe pact, geuing them bloud, or other thing,
which they require, as ſorceres, & wiches doe practiſe, or els they pleaſe the diuel by ſuperſticious
aſcribing ſpiritual vertue & holines to wordes, actes,
or other thinges, wherto it belongeth not, which is
a ſecrete pacte : wherupon he worketh to their contentment, nouriſhing their wicked errour. But
Gods miniſters command, & compel diuels by power
receiued

Exorciſtes
expel diuels
by power of
their holie
Order.

Sorcerers
deale with
diuels by pact,
either expreſ-
ſe or ſecrete.

receiued of God, to depart from perfons, or places, which they infeſt, & to ceaſe from that euil, which they would doe. So the Phariſees knew that euil men can do wonderful thinges, by the diuels power,

Mat. 12. *v.* 24. When they calumniating our Sauiour, ſaid [that he caſt out diuels in the power of Beelzebub, the prince of the diuels.] But our Lord confuted their wicked calumniation, ſhewing that ſome men caſt out diuels by diuine power, in the Holie Ghoſt, the finger of

v. 21. God. And he gaue this power to his Apoſtles, yea alſo to the ſeuentie two diſciples, who returned

Luc. 11. *v.* 20. with ioy (after that they had preached ſome while, and exerciſed their auctoritie ouer the vncleane

Mat. 10. ſpirites, ſaying [Lord, the diuels alſo are ſubiect to

v. 1. *Luc.* vs in thy name.] By this holie Exorciſme therfore

10. *v.* 17. the diuel is forced to geue place to Chriſt, & to depart from thoſe, that are to be baptized. And this is the firſt Rite. The ſecond is Cathechiſme, or Profeſſion of faith in Chriſt.

3. For by our Lords commandment thoſe that are

Mar. 16. to be baptized muſt firſt beleue, and profeſſe their

v. 16. faith, which is done alſo for al children in the faith of the Church, others anſwering for them. For as they contracted ſinne by the act of Adam, ſo the new Adam Chriſt accepteth their beleefe, and profeſſion therof by others : ſo that the Sacrament be admini-

Art. 11. ſtred. As is declared before. Other Rites and Cere-monies which the Church vſeth, are alſo confor-mable to Chriſts owne actions, either the ſame, or the very like. As when he cured one that was borne

Ioan. 9. blinde, [he ſpitte on the ground, & made clay of the

v. 6. 7. ſpittle, & ſpread the clay vpon his eyes.] In imitation wherof Catechumes are touched with ſpittle, and anointed with holie oyle, & after they are baptized, that is, waſhed in Chriſt, Sent of God, ſignified by [the water of Siloe, which is interpreted, Sent.] Againe when he cured an other man, that was deafe and

As Infantes contract ori-ginal ſinne by Adam ſo they beleue & pro-feſſe the Ca-tholbue faith by others.

Other cere-monies are alſo by imita-tion of Chriſts actions.

dumme, he did not only touch h m with his hand,
which was only requeited (and his leaft word, or
thought alone had bene fufficient) but alfo he vfed
al thefe Rites: Firft [taking the infirme man from *Mar.* 7. *v.*
the multitude apart (fecondl,) he put his fingers 31. *ad* 37.
into his eares thirdly) fpitting, touched his tongue
with the fpitle (fourthly) looking vp into heauen,
(fiftly) he groned (fixtly) he faid *Ephpheth4,* and this
word (the Holie Ghoft fo directing him) The Euangelift would haue to remaine in the fame language:
which is : *Be thou opened,* (feuently) the fame word
had operation in two members at once, the eares &
the tongue, for it foloweth : [And immediatly his
eares were opened, and the ftring of his tongue was
loofed, & he fpake right] wherupon though our
Lord (to teach his Minifters, not to defire vaine praife
of men) forbade them to fpeake therof, yet the gratful people, glorified God [and fo much the more
a great deale, did they publifh this fact, and fo much
the more did they wonder, faying : He hath done al
thinges wel: he hath made both the deafe to heare,
and the dumme to fpeake.] Holie Church therfore
vfeth thefe folemne holie Rites, to the glorie of
Chrift, edification of Chriftians, and great benefite
of the faithful, when they are baptized. God open
alfo the eares of our deafe Aduerfaries, which neglect or contemne fuch facred Rites, and loofe their
tongue to confeffe the truth, and fhame the diuel,
who as yet ftoppeth their eares, from hearkening
to Catholique doctrine, tyeth their tongues from
fpeaking that truth, which they can not but fee: &
holdeth them captiues in finne. For Proteftants
acknowlege Baptifme to be a Sacrament, but erre
and contradict them felues, in denying it to remitte
finne, which is the proper effect of al Chrifts Sa- *Art.* 8.
craments, as we haue already proued, both in gene- *Art.* 12.
ral, & of this in particular. They are content to vfe
in ad-

Proteftants
confeffing
Baptifme to
be aSacramēt,
denie the
effect therof,
and vfe fome

in adminiſtring therof, the ſigne of the Croſſe. They admitte alſo Godfathers, & Godmothers, to anſwer for children in Baptiſme, & exaɕt that the Baptized ſhal afterwards ratifie, profeſſe, & performe al that was done in their behalfe, as if themſelues had aɕtually deſired Baptiſme: & made the ſame profeſſions, & promiſes by their owne willes & mouthes. Puritanes alſo are content with al, but the Croſſe, therin croſſing their elder brethren, & ſuperiour auɕtoritie, which cōmandeth them to vſe it. Seing therfore our Aduerſaries vſe ſome accidental Ceremonies, for more decencie & order: it is very manifeſt by that which hath bene here ſaid, that al the Rites which are vſed by the Catholique Church, are as wel grounded in holie Scriptures, & iuſtified therby, as either Proteſtants can defend the vſe of the Croſſe, againſt the Puritanes, or both (ioyntly together Proteſtantes and Puritanes) can proue the whole forme which they vſe, beſides the only water, & eſſential wordes.

1.Cor. 14.
v. 26.

ceremonies therin. As the ſigne of the Croſſe which Puritenes contemne.

Confirmation is a true, & proper Sacrament, geuing ſpecial grace.

ARTICLE 16.

Next after Baptiſme, in order of Chriſtian Sacraments, foloweth Confirmation. For as a childe temporally borne into this world, in ſmal ſtature, & weake in bodie, groweth bigger & ſtronger by courſe of nature: ſo a Chriſtian ſoule ſpiritually borne into the Church of God, by Baptiſme, as a new planted graſſe, groweth in grace towards perfeɕtion, & is ſtrongly fortified by Confirmation, geuing ſpecial grace to hold faſt, & conſtantly to confeſſe the Chriſtian Catholique faith, & religion, notwitſtanding whatſoeuer tribulations, reproches,

Confirmation ſhould be receiued next after Baptiſme, before anie other Sacrament.

M 3

reproches, feares, threates, & perfecutions for the
fame. Which we fhal here breefly fhew, firft by
Proteftants owne groundes, & practife, if they wil
hold conformable doctrine in their principles, and
in conclufions neceffarily deduced from the fame.
But efpecially by the holie Scriptures, we fhal inuincibly proue, that Confirmation rightly admini-
ftred is a true, & proper Sacrament of the New Teftament of Iefus Chrift.

It is proued
to be a Sacra-
ment, by al,
that Prote-
ftants require
in a Sacramēt.

2.   Firft therfore, Proteftants require not more in
anie Sacrament, but that it be a vifible figne inftituted by Chrift, with fome fpiritual promife annexed.
Which three thinges they alfo acknowlege to be in
this folemne Ceremonie. Firft they hold that impofition of handes, & fome forme of wordes, are here
required, as an external holie figne. Secondly they
confeffe, that the Apoftles did practife it, and that by
Chrifts Inftitution, and commandment. And by the
fame, themfelues pretend to practife it, not by euerie
Minifter, of lower degree, but only by their cheefe
Elders, or Superintendents, called Bifhopes. And
thirdly they account it fo neceffarie, that they haue
made an efpecial Decree, or Canon, to admitte none
to receiue their Communion vntil they haue lerned
their Catechifme, and *be confirmed.* which plainly
fheweth that they thinke there is fpiritual benefite
annexed vnto it. Al which their eftimation of this
external Rite, exprefly appeareth, in their Booke of *Proteſt.*
common prayer, and of Adminiftration of Sacra *Ritual.*
ments, & other Ecclefiaftical Rites, where is particularly fet forth a prefcript forme, how, & by whom
the faithful being formerly baptized, muft alfo be
confirmed, before they may receiue the Communion. It is very ftrange therfore, & hard for them
to yeeld anie good reafon, why they vcutfafe not to
cal it a Sacrament, feeing it hath al the conditions,
partes, & proprieties, which they neceffarily require
in a Sacrament.   3. But

3. But this proofe made of the Aduersaries owne Proued by the confession, and pretended practise, being only of Prophetes. force against them that lay these insufficient groundes, & so is but *Argumentum ad hominem*, we shal further proue against them, by the holie Scriptures, that Confirmation being rightly ministred, is according to the true definition of a Sacrament, a visible signe of inuisible grace, both signifying, and to the worthie receiuers geuing as the instrumental cause, the grace which it signifieth. Amongst other senses of the Psalmists wordes saying to God [Thou hast

Psal. 22. fatted my head with oyle] it semeth most probable
v. 5. that he vttered them in the person of faithful Christians, rendering thankes to God, for benefites by this external signe in the forehead, receiued by the vse of diuers Sacraments, which are conduites of grace: more especially by that Sacrament, in which the forehead is signed, and annointed with holie Chrisme, made of oyle & balme. For albeit Sacred oyle is also vsed in the Rites of Baptisme, in the ordination of Priestes, and Bishopes: in Extreme vnction, & in the vnction of some Christian Kinges, likewise in cosecration of holie Altares, & Chalices: Yet this particular mention [of fatting the head with oyle] may be most properly applied to the grace, geuen to euerie Christian after Baptisme, that he may not feare, nor be ashamed to confesse Christs true Religion. If our Aduersaries wil say, this text is obscure, & proueth not our purpose, we grant that both this place, & innumerable others are hard, to be rightly vnderstood, which they comonly denie, let them therfore produce an other sense, and we wil ioyne issue of trial with them, that either it is not so proper, or excludeth not this, which we haue proposed. More clearly the Prophetes, Isaias and
Isa. 44. Ioel, signifie the great effect of Confirmation. God
v. 3. speaking thus by them [I wil power out waters
vpon

vpon the thirstie ground, and streames vpon the drie *Ioel. 2. v.*
land : I wil poure out my Spiritie vpon thy seede, & 29.
my blessing vpon thy stocke. I wil poure out my *Act. 2. v.*
Spirite vpon al flesh] which S. Peter expoundeth to 16. 17.
be in part verified & fulfilled, when the Holie Ghost
coming in visible signes vpon the Apostles, & other
faithful, in Ierusalem on whit sunday, they were al
confirmed by increase of grace, then geuen extraordinarily, in miraculous maner, and to be geuen to
others by imposition of handes, after that they should
be baptized, saying in the end of his sermon to the
multitude that beleued [Be ye baptized in the name   *v. 38.*
of Iesus Christ, for remission of your sinnes, and
you shal receiue *the gift of the Holie Ghost*] expresly
teaching that as the former disciples with the Apostles, had receiued the Holie Ghost, according to the
prophecie of Ioel, so also others that would beleue,
and be baptized, should by Baptisme receiue remission of their sinnes, and also receiue this other grace
of the Holie Ghost, which was & stil is performed by
the Apostles, and their Successors vpon the baptized.
As we shal further declare by and by, reciting first
one other prediction, & then Chrifts owne promise
of this great Sacrament, & performance therof.

Proued by S.   4. S. Iohn our Lords precursor, baptizing in water,
Iohn Baptists   and preaching the remission of sinnes, which he
prediction.   could not geue, declared that there was one among
them (meaning our Sauiour Christ) who should
geue an other Baptisme, not only in water, but also
in the Holie Ghost, with remission of sinnes, and
sanctifying grace, yea should geue abundance of
grace. [In deede I baptize you (said S. Iohn) in wa-   *Mat. 3. v.*
ter vnto penance, but he that shal come after me, is 11.
stronger then I, he shal baptize you in the Holie *Luc. 3.*
Ghost, & fire.] To haue shewed great difference *v. 16.*
betwen his owne Baptisme, & Chrifts, it had bene
sufficient to say : I baptize in water, and he shal
baptize

baptize in the Holie Ghoft, but adding more, he said [in the Holie Ghoft, & fire] which importeth a further augmentation of grace, fignified by fire.

5. Which doctrine is alfo confirmed by our Sauiours owne wordes, faying [I came to caft fire on the earth (that is to fay, zele and fernour) and what wil I, but that it be kindled, and burne] and accordingly the Holie Ghoft came vpon the multitude, in the figne [of parted tongues, as it were of fire, & it fate vpon euerie one of them.] Of this greater grace, no doubt our Sauiour alfo fpake, when promifing to fulfil the prophecies (of Ifaias and Ioel) he cried faying [If anie man thirft, let him come to me, and drinke. He that beleueth in me, as the Scripture faith, out of his bellie fhal flow riuers of liuing water. And this he faid (faith the Euangelift) of the Spirite that they fhould receiue, which beleued in him. For as yet the Spirite was not geuen: becaufe Iefus was not yet glorified] What better Interpreter may we require? Doth not the Euangelift tel vs, that by the flowing waters prophecied in former Scripture, & promifed here by Chrift, to thofe that beleue in him, is to be vnderftood [the Spirite, that they fhould receiue, which beleued in him?] Doth he not alfo explaine Chrifts promife, to be meant of an other gift, and increafe of grace, greater then grace of Baptifme, which greater fhould not be geuen til after Chrifts Afcenfion. For the Apoftles, to whom amongft the firft, this promife was made, were baptized before Chrifts death. As is manifeft by our Lords wordes vnto them, as to men already wafhed, by Baptifme, faying [They that are wafhed, nede but to wafh their feete and are cleane wholly. And you are cleane] to witte by meanes of Baptifme. For obtaining therfore this greater grace, Chrift alfo commanded his Apoftles immediatly before his Afcenfion [to tarie in the

Luc. 12. v. 49.

Act. 2. v. 3.

Ioan. 7. v. 37. 38.

v. 39.

Ioan. 13. v. 10. 11.

Luc. 24. v. 49.

Proued by our Sauiours doctrine, and promife.

N   citie

citie til you be endued (faith he) vvith power from
High.] Againe he sayd to them [you shal be baptized *Act.* 1.
with the Holie Ghost, after these few dayes] cal- *v.* 5.
ling this gift, an other Baptisme, but improperly, as
he called his Passion & Death baptisme : saying [I *Luc.* 12.
haue to be baptized vvith a Baptisme.] And to tvvo *v.* 49.
of his Disciples [Can yuu be baptized, vvith the *Mar.* 10.
Baptisme vvherwith I am baptized.] For speaking *v.* 38.
properly [There is but one Baptisme.]   *Eph.* 4. *v.* 5.

6.   Moreouer as it is manifest, that the Apostles with
others, receiued this promised special grace of the
Holie Ghost, by other visible signes, of a vehement
winde, & of parted tongues, as it were of fire, sitting
vpon euerie one of them: which God then wrought
extraordinarily without a Sacrament : so it is no
lesse euident, that S. Peter affirmed to al, which
would be baptized, for remission of their sinnes,
that they should also receiue the gift of the Holie
Ghost : & likewise that he, and other Apostles did
impose their handes vpon the baptized, for this very
purpose, & effect, that they might receiue the same
gift of the Holie Ghost, a new grace, & distinct spiritual benefite after Baptisme. S. Peters wordes are
these, vnto such as were penitent for their offence
against Christ [Be euerie one of you baptized, in *Act.* 2. *v.*
the name of Iesus Christ, for remission of your 38.
sinnes. And you shal receiue the gift of the Holie
Ghost.] So that they not only receiued the Holie
Ghost by Baptisme, vnto remission of sinnes, but
also were after Baptisme to receiue an other special gift of the Holie Ghost.

7.   Which is yet more cleare by the practise of the
Apostles. For [when manie in Samaria beleued *Ch.* 8. *v.*
Philippe the Deacon, euangelizing of the Kingdom 12. 14.
of God, and of the name of Iesus Christ, and were
baptized; & that the Apostles; who were in Ierusalem had heard, that Samaria had receiued the
word

That special grace which was geuen to the faithful on whitsunday by other visible signes, was also geuē to others by imposition of Apostolical handes after Baptisme.

S. Peter and S. Ihon went to Samaria to administer Cōnfirmation.

word of God : they ſent vnto them Peter and Iohn.

v. 15. who when they were come prayed for them , that
16. they might receiue the Holie Ghoſt. For he was
not yet come vpon anie of them : but they were only
17. baptized in the name of our Lord Ieſus. Then did
they impoſe their handes vpon them , & they receiued the Holie Ghoſt.] Is not this a manifeſt teſtimonie , that they which in Samaria were baptized of
Philippe the Deacon , hauing receiued Chriſts Baptiſme , & could not be baptized anie more, yet wanted ſome thing , which was done by S. Peter , and
S. Iohn : to witte, that by their prayer, and impoſition of handes, the Holie Ghoſt might be powred
vpon them, & geuen to them againe after Baptiſme ?
The very ſame thing which the Catholique Church
beleueth, & teacheth, that they which are baptized,
doe by Confirmation receiue the Holie Ghoſt, with
increaſe of ſpecial new grace. Againe we haue in
this ſame Hiſtorie of the Actes of the Apoſtles, how

Ch. 19. *v.* [S. Paul coming to Epheſus, and finding certaine
1. 2. 3. diſciples, that were only baptized in S. Iohns Baptiſme, cauſed them to be baptized with Chriſts Bap-
v. 5. 6. tiſme. And then himſelf impoſed handes on them,
and the Holie Ghoſt came vpon them.] Here you
v. 4. ſee three diſtinct holie Rites. Firſt [theſe men were
already baptized in S. Iohns Baptiſme (which was
5. no Sacrament) Secondly [they were baptized in
the name of our Lord Ieſus (which is the firſt
6. Chriſtian Sacrament) Thirdly [S. Paul impoſed
handes vpon them, and the Holie Ghoſt came vpon
them , and they ſpake with tongues & prophecied.]
Shal we yet doubt, but that with this external viſible
ſigne, they alſo receiued the internal effect, to witte,
increaſe of grace , being immediatly before baptized ? How then can it be denied, but this Holie Rite
is a true and proper Sacrament?
8. But if anie wil obiect, that becauſe theſe viſible

*So Paul alſo
adminiſtred
Confirmation
to thoſe that
were already
baptized.*

N 2   miracles

An obiection
is solued by
the practise
& doctrine of
Proteſtants.

miracles doe not now folow, it is a ſigne, that this
is not a Sacrament, nor anie longer to be practiſed.
For anſwer touching practiſe, we firſt aske them,
why Proteſtants make reſemblance to practiſe it?
Secondly touching both the efficacie, & practiſe, they
may as wel ſay, that becauſe the viſible miracles,
which our Sauiour promiſed [ſhould folow them *Mar.* 16. 7.
that beleued & were baptized] doe not now folow, 17. 18.
therfore none doe now beleue. Baptiſme muſt alſo
ceaſe to be practiſed, & thatBaptiſme is no Sacramēt.
which conſequences were both wicked & abſurde,
alſo in Proteſtants owne doctrine. Finally therfore

An other an-
ſwer.

we anſwer, as wel in reſpect of beleefe, & Baptiſme,
as of Confirmation; that viſible miraculous ſignes
are wrought of God rather [for Infidels, then for
the faithful] as S. Paul teacheth, & ſo were necef- *1. Cor.* 14.
ſarie in the firſt preaching of Chriſts Goſpel, and *v.* 22.
founding of his Church, & ſtil are neceſſarie, where
Chriſtian Religion is to be firſt planted. But when,
& where it is once receiued, and firmely fixed in the
hartes of the faithful, ſuch miracles commonly
ceaſe. As when greue plantes are firſt ſette, they
nede watering, but not after that they haue taken
faſt roote in the earth: euen ſo the viſible miracles
ceaſing, the inuiſible grace, the principal & moſt
proper effect of Sacraments, remaineth annexed
vnto them. And ſo notwithſtanding miracles are
now more rare in the Chriſtian world, yet there be
(God be therfore glorified) innumerable perſons of
al ſortes and degrees, which rightly beleue in Ieſus
Chriſt, & the inuiſible gracious effectes doe vndoubtedly folow the due adminiſtration, and worthie
receiuing of Baptiſme, & Confirmation. And ſo of
other holie Sacraments.

9.　S. Paul alſo beſides his practiſe, writeth in his

S. Paul reci-
teth Confir-

Epiſtles (as is neceſſarily gathered) of Confirmation, *2. Cor.* 1.
& the eſpecial effect therof, which is further to be *v.* 22.

declared

Ephef 1.
v 13.
Heb. 6. v.
1.2.

declared in the next Article. For admonifhing the
Hebrewes, that they ought to behaue themfelues as
Chriftians already inftructed, & not needing to lerne
againe the firft principles of Chriftianitie, he repeteth for example [Penance from dead workes;
Faith towards God ; the Doctrine of Baptifmes; &
of Impofition of handes; and of the Refurrection;
and of general Iudgement.] And fo exhorteth them
to procede to perfection: where, by Impofition of

v.4.

handes (which he alfo calleth the heauenlie gift)
& gift of the Holie Ghoft, he can not but meane an
other Sacrament after Baptifme, belonging to al
Chriftians, to vvitte Confirmation. Els fuch diftinct
mention needed not of the Doctrine of Baptifmes,&
of Impofition of handes.

10. It remaineth yet touching this Sacrament of
Confirmation, to fhew here, by what auctoritie the
Church vfeth holie Chrifme in the adminiftration
therof. We anfwer, that Holie Church doth it by
Chrifts Inftitution; though it be not expreffed in

Act. 1.
v. 3.

holie Scripture. For manie thinges were done, and
faid by Chrift, & receiued by his Apoftles, and by
them deliuered, and taught by word without writing. Amongft which this is euident to be one, not
only by teftimonie of moft ancient, authentical
recordes (vvhich yet we vrge not in this Encounter)
but alfo by continual practife therof, no Aduerfarie
being able to fhevv, vvhen it firft begane, or was
brought into vfe, as a new thing. And fo it is proued
by Apoftolical Tradition, to be inftituted by Chrift.
For the Apoftles did not neither could they, or anie
of them, inftitute the matter, or forme of anie Sacrament. And that fuch perpetual Tradition & general

Part. 1.
Art. 3.

practife, is an infallible proofe of Chriftian doctrine,
is euidently declared in the firft parft of this worke,
by manie expreffe textes of the Holie Scriptures.

mation or im-
pofition of
hands amogft
the principles
of Chriftian
doctrine.

That Chrift
inftituted
Confirmation
to be admini-
ftred with
holie Chrifme
is proued by
Apoftolical
Tradition:
warranted by
expreffeScrip-
tures.

Confirmatiõ alſo imprinteth a ſpecial Character.
And in that, & other reſpectes, it behoueth
al Chriſtians to receiue it.

ARTICLE. 17.

**Seing al Chri-
ſtians are in a
ſpiritual war-
re, it behoueth
that they be
armed againſt
the enimies.**

Mans life is a warrefare vpon the earth (ſaith **Iob. 7.**
holie Iob) and his dayes, as the dayes of one **v. 1.**
that is hyred.] S. Paul more particularly admoniſheth vs Chriſtiãs, of our danger in this warrefare,
both in reſpect of our ſuttle ſtrong enemie, ſaying
[our wreſtling is not againſt fleſh & bloud (only) but **Eqheſ. 6.**
againſt the princes & poteſtates, againſt the rectors **v. 12.**
of the world, of this darkenes, againſt the ſpiritual
of wickednes] and in reſpect of our obligation to
worke diligently, for erning the promiſed penie, or
reward, ſaying [No man ſhal be crowned, vnles **2. Tim. 2.**

**By Baptiſme
we are chil-
dren of Chriſt
& by Confir-
mation we are
made ſoul-
diars.**

he fight lawfully] that is, ſtrongly reſiſting al **v. 5.**
firce aſſaults. Wherfore as the combate is great and
dangerous, & our obligation ſtrict: ſo the grace of
Chriſt is potent, & readie to al that wil vſe it. For
he doth not only remitte our ſinnes, & ſanctifie our
ſoules by Baptiſme, but hath alſo prouided this other
Sacrament of Confirmation, by which an other
ſpiritual indeleble Character is geuen vs, as it were
à Militare gyrdle, with armour of ſpecial ſtrength,
& fortitude : ſo making vs complete ſouldiars of this
Chriſtian warrefare, as formerly we were made
children, & citizens of the Church by Baptiſme.

**That Confir-
mation im-
printeth an
indeleble cha-
racter is de-
duced from
S. Pauls doc-
trine.**

2.   Of this ſecond indeleble Character, receiued by
Confirmation, S. Paul ſemeth to ſpeake in his Epiſtle to the Epheſians, where magnifying the grace
of God, by which ooth Iewes & Gentiles are called
into the way of ſaluation, he congratulateth with
them, for that they beleued the Goſpel of Chriſt, and
receiued

Ephef. I.
v. 13.

receiued fruite therby saying : [You also, when you
had heard the word of truth, in which also beleuing
you were signed, with the Holie Spirite of promise]
which wordes necessarily proue, that Christians
were spiritually signed with the Holie Ghost, according to former promise: and therfore most like it
was in Confirmation : because the gift of the Holie
Ghost, was both specially promised, & afterwards
geuen by imposition of Apostolical handes.

3.   In regard also of these permanent spiritual
markes, and indeleble Characters, as wel of Baptisme, as of Confirmation, the same Apostle auoucheth, that such as are baptized, and confirmed,
and fal from grace, can not receiue the same Sacra- **As Baptisme,**
ments againe [For it is impossible (saith he) for **so also Con-**
them, that were once illuminated (that is baptized) **firmation can**
haue tasted also the heauenlie gift, and were made **not be itera-**
partakers of the Holie Ghost (by Confirmation) & **ted.**
are fallen ; to be renewed againe to penance] that
is, to be borne againe by Baptisme, or confirmed

See Part. I.
Art. 48.
& infra.
Art. 37.

againe. Not that anie sinne is irremissible, so long as
the sinner is in this world (for it is cleare in manie
places of holie Scriptures, that stil there is meanes
for al sinners, to be restored to grace in this life, if
they wil ; but it is impossible to be renewed, by
either of these two Sacraments of Baptisme, or Confirmation. Which sheuueth that they are irreitera-
ble, by reason of their indeleble characters, stil remayning : & distinguishing their soules from others,
that neuer receiued the same markes.

4.   Al which sheuueth the excellent, & permanent
benefite, of these two first Sacraments. Baptisme
most necessarie of al : & Confirmation though not
so absolutely necessarie, as Baptisme, and Penance, **Confirmation**
nor so great as the B. Sacrament of the Altar (which **is a greater**
infinitely excelleth al the rest) nor so great as Holie **Sacramēt then**
Orders, yet is it the greatest of the other fiue, and no **Baptisme, or**
Penance.

lesse

And is more neceſſarie alſo then Extreme Vnction, or Mariage to euerie Chriſtian.

Foure cauſes why it is re-quiſite to al Chriſtians.

1.
To auoide pride, ingra-titude, and other ſinnes.

2.
Deſire of per-fectiou.

3.
Deſire of more grace, & more glorie.

4.
Neceſſitie of ſtrengthning ſpecial grace in time of perſecutiŏn.

leſſe requiſite but rather more then either Mariage, or Extreme vnction. And therfore is to be deſired & ſought for, by al Chriſtians. As may further ap-peare by theſe foure important reaſons. Firſt, in that it pleaſed our B. Sauiour to inſtitute ſo behoofull a meanes of ſpecial grace, it bringeth with it, an obligatiŏ to al his ſeruants, for whoſe ſpiritual good *Mat. 3.* it is prouided, to ſhew our gratful humble minde, *v.* 15. for ſo great a benefite by ſeeking to receiue it: els *Luc.* 7. *v.* may we be worthily condemned, of diſdaynful in- 29. 30. 35. gratitude, negligence, and arrogancie, in light eſte-ming ſuch diuine ordinance. Secondly, as in al *Matt 5.* other poinctes of Religion, we ought to tend to per- *v.* 48. fection; ſo in Chriſtianitie it ſelf, the ground of al happines, it behooueth to be complete Chriſtians. And therfore is it requiſite (ſo much as lieth in euerie one) to receiue this great Sacrament: becauſe with-out it, al the baptized are but as infantes in reſpect of men: therfore called (by the Canon Law) half- *Lib.* 5. Chriſtians. Thirdly, this greatSacramĕt importeth *Decret.* al Chriſtians in regard of more glorie in heauen. Be- *Tit. 39,* cauſe grace and glorie are correſpondĕt: ſo that the *cap. 43.* want, or diminution of the one, is want or dimi-nution of the other, yea though it be without our 1. *Cor.* 15. owne fault: eſpecially in reſpect of the Character, *v.* 41. 42. which none can haue without the Sacramĕt. Fourt-ly, & moſt eſpecially this Sacrament is moſt needful, in time, and place of perſecution for the Catholique Faith, & Religion. Which is now the proper caſe of this Iland of Great Britanie: where only of al King-domes, & Prouinces within the precinctes of Chri-ſtendom, at this day, and theſe manie yeares, the ad-miniſtration of this Sacrament is wholly wanting. Where notwithſtanding innumerable deuoute ſou-les moſt hartely deſire it: not vnlike to thoſe, for whom the Prophete Ieremie lamented, ſaying [The *Lamen.* 4. litle ones asked bread: & there was none, that brake *v* 4. it vnto them.]

In the

In the B. Sacrament of the Eucharist, Christ is really & substantially present.

ARTICLE 18.

COncerning the Articles of Faith, comprised in the Apostles Crede, Protestants differ from vs in very manie special pointes, as appeareth in the first part of this present worke: though they acknowlege it al in general termes. But in this second part, touching the holie Sacraments, they dissent from vs in almost al particulars. For albeit they confesse that Baptisme is a Sacrament, as in deede it is, also with them, so long as they applie the right matter & forme, with intentention to doe that, which Christ instituted to be done therin. Yet they denie both the necessitie, & effect therof. And by condemning the Sacred Rites belonging therunto, and by administering it, in heretical maner, both the minister, and al that consent, or anie way cooperate therwith, committe great sacrilege, and in fact denie the Catholique Religion, by their external conformitie to heretical procedings. The second Sacrament which is Confirmation, they vtterly denie to be a Sacrament. And in deede it is none with them, though they pretend to doe. them selues know not what, but committe also herein egregious sacrilege; and so do al that concurre therunto. The third Sacrament which is the B. Eucharist, they cal a Sacrament, but with them it is none at al, no better then most high sacrilege, not only in the ministers by peruerting Christs Institution, but also in al others that communicate with them, or make resemblance so to doe. The other foure Sacraments they plainly denie to be Sacraments, as in

Part. 1.
Artic. 45.
§. 5. *&c.*

There is great difference betwixt Catholiques & Protestants touching the Articles of beleefe, but much more concerning the holie Sacraments.

They denie fiue of the seuen holie Sacraments, & the effects of the other two.

O　　　　　　dede

dede with them, three of the fame are none. Onlie
Matrimonie, when it is made betwen perfons apt
to contract, hauing no effential impediment is à true
Sacrament: buih wanteth the effect of grace, which
it fhould haue, & the contracters, & al that confent
to the folemnizatió therof in heretical maner, committe facrilege, by their conformitie to heretical
practife in a Sacrament. Al which we haue fhewed,
in the firft two Sacraments, & fhal further declare
of the reft in particular.

2.   Wherfore being now to fpeake of a moft high
Myfterie, the greateft Sacrament, & onlie Sacrifice
of the Law of grace, & to difcuffe one of the cheefeft
controuerfies of this time : what we are to beleue

The ftate of
the Contro-
uerfie, concer-
ning the B.
Sacrament.

touching the moft holie Sacrament of Chrifts bodie
& bloud. For more cleare notifying the ftate of this
controuerfed queftion, it is firft to be obferued, that
al which wil feme to beare the name of Chriftians,
doe acknowlege that the holie Eucharift, otherwife
called the Supper of our Lord, is a Sacrament of the
new Teftament, inftituted by Chrift, though it be
no where in the holie Scripture called à Sacrament.

What al con-
feffe.

Secondly, Catholiques doe beleue, and hold that in
this holie Sacrament, bread and wine are tranffub-
ftantiated, that is, fubftantially changed into the very
bodie and bloud of Chrift, really and fubftantially
prefent; but inuifibly vnder the vifible accidents

What Catho-
liques beleue.

of bread & wine. Thirdly, Lutherans fay that the
very bodie and bloud of Chrift are really, and fubftantially prefent, together with bread and wine,
ftil remayning in their natural fubftance. Fourtly,

What Luthe-
ans hold,

other Proteftantes, namely Zuinglians, and Englifh
Caluiniftes denie that Chrifts bodie, or bloud is really & fubftantially prefent, or anie way extant in
this Sacrament, but only to be fignified, or reprefented by the bread & wine, without anie fubftantial change in them. Yet fay they, that Chrift is

What Zuin-
glianss, & En-
glifh Prote-
ftants ima-
gine.

really

really & substantially present, when the bread and wine are actually receiued, into the mouth of the communicant, and not before: and that Christ is so made present, by the faith of the receiuer, if he doe so beleue, els not. Thus doe they, in their opinion ascribe an imagined power to the faith of the receiuer, denying anie power at al to be in the wordes of consecration, nor in the Priest that pronounceth them, by vertue of Christs institutiõ. Fistly, you must obserue, that though we doe al agree, in general wordes, that the holie Eucharist is a Sacramēt; yet al doe meane, that then only it is a Sacrament, when it is ministred according to Christs Institution, and that otherwise it is no Sacrament, but horrible, and most wicked sacrilege. And so it resteth for vs to shew, that our Catholique beleefe in this poinct, is true & certaine; & consequently both Lutherans, & other Protestans doe grosly erre. Which we shal here declare by manie holie Scriptures, both of the old, & new Testament.

Al doe agree that there only, it is a Sacrament, where it is according to Chrifts institution.

3.   First then to satisfie the doubtful conceipte of some, & to remoue the greatest difficultie, which is the cheefest ground of our Aduersaries opinion. How it can be possible, that anie accidents should be, or remaine, without their proper subiect? wherupon both Luther, and Zuinglius, and al Protestants suppose, that there must needes be bread and wine, so long as their accidents remaine. To this we answer, in one word, sufficiently to al Christians, which doe in deede beleue in God [that nothing is impossible with God] according as we al professe in the beginning of our Crede [that we beleue in God the Father Almightie.] But for more ample satisfaction, that God not only can doe whatsoeuer he wil, but also hath done other potent workes, aboue the course of al creatures, we haue a particular example (at least according to the expresse wordes

It is most certaine, & confessed of al Christians, that God is omnipotent,

Mat. 19. v. 26. Luc. 1. v. 37.

O 2   of diuine

An example
of accident
existing with-
out subiect.

of diuine Scripture) in this very kinde. of accident existing without the proper subiect ; We read in Genesis, that light was made the first day, and the Sunne, the proper subiect of light (which distinguisheth the day from night) was made the fourth day, together with the Moone, and other starres, which are lightned by the Sunne. And so there was light, which is an Accident , three dayes existing without the subiect. Why then shal it be harder for Christians to beleue, that the accidents of bread and wine, may remaine without their subiects; then, for the children of Israel to beleue, that which Moyses writte? They in deede saw the wonderful effectes of Gods blessing, in the multiplication of mankinde, and of other creatures, both in the beginning of this world, & after the floud & Gods omnipotent power in plaguing the Æpyptians, and præseruing them selues, bringing them through the redsea [and they beleued our Lord, & Moyses his seruant.] And shal not we, that beleue al which the people of Israel then beleued, vpon Moyses worde , and writing, beleue the word of Christ, written by his Apostles, and Euangelistes, that our Lord taking bread and wine into his handes, & blessing them , and saying : [This is my bodie: This is my bloud] did therby make them to be that, which he so plainly sayde that they were? Though we see, that the accidents of bread & wine remaine? Innumerable other examples occurre in the holie Scriptures , of the creation of al thinges of nothing ; of producing some creatures from others ; changing one creature into another ; & the like miraculous workes of God, aboue al natural power of creatures, which shew Gods omnipotent power , that it is not impossible, that Christ our Lord, God & man, could change the subbstance of bread and wine , the accidents stil remayning, into the subbstance of his owne bodie, & bloud.

Gen. 1.
v. 3 5.
v. 15. 16.

Exod. 14.
v. 31.

Mat. 26.
v. 27. 28.

Other exam-
ples of Gods
omnipotent
power.

Gen. 1.v.
11. 20.
Exod. 4.
v. 3. &c.

And

And so the obiection of suppofed impoffibilitie is folued, as of no force in matters of faith, where we are to beleue Gods word. Though fometimes, the thinges appeare otherwife to our external fenfes, or to natural reafon.

4. Seing therfore it is certaine, that Chrift could, if it was his wil, make his owne bodie and bloud really, & fubftantially prefent, vnder the accidents of bread & wine, & it is an affured Maxime, cleare in euerie reafonable mans vnderftanding: That what foeuer Chrift (yea or anie other man) both can doe & wil doe, he in deede doth the fame thing: it is only to be difcuffed, whether Chrift our Lord had an actual wil to doe it, or no? for of his power none but plaine Infidels make anie doubt. And that it was his wil, is fhewed by manie diuine Scriptures. By figures, and prophecies therof in the old Teftament: and by his promife, and performance, and by his Apoftles teftimonie, and practife therof in the new Teftament. The Pafchal lambe was doubtles a figure of Chrift, & of fomething done by Chrift: witnes S. Paul, faying [Our Pafch Chrift, is immolated.] In that the fame lambe was flaine, it was a figure of the holie Euchariſt wherin Chrift is facramentally eaten. In that the lambe vvas prepared the tenth day of the moneth, fiue dayes before the feaft of Pafch, was prefigured Chrifts coming into Ierufalem, fiue dayes before his Paffion, which the Church reprefenteth on Palme funday. In that the lambe vvas eaten vvithin the houfe, vvhere it vvas immolated and nothing therof caried forth, out of the houfe, that no ſtranger ought to eate therof, til they vvere by Circuincifion, adioyned to the peculiar people of God, it prefigured the holie Euchariſt: which perteyneth only to the faithful, vvithin the Church: and did not fo properly fignifie Chrifts death on the Croffe, which was without

the

Marginal notes:

What foeuer anie man can and wil doe, that thing he doth in deede.

Chrifts real prefence in the B. Sacrament is proued by the figure of the Pafchal lambe.

1. *Cor.* 5. v. 7. *Exod.* 12. v. 3.

v. 45. 46. 48.

the houſe, yea vvithout the gates of Ieruſalem : and the price of his Paſſion, is extended not only to thoſe that are vvithin the Church , but alſo to al that ſhal therby be brought into the Church. In that the lambe was not only to be immolated that one night, vvhen the children of Iſrael vvere deliuered from death, vvhervvith the firſt borne of the Ægyptians *v. 24. 25.* vvere ſtriken, but alſo the like to be yearly obſerued for commemoration of the former benefite , it directly prefigured the holie Euchariſt, inſtituted by our Redemer , the ſame night before his Paſſion , to be continually done in like ſorte , for a commemoration of his death, vntil he come againe, in the end of this world. For his death it ſelfe was the very *Luc. 22.* price of our Redemption , & not a commemoration *v. 19.* therof. By al which , and other circumſtances, of *1. Cor. 11.* time, place, maner of immolating & eating, and by *v. 25.* our Sauiours fact , inſtituting this B. Sacrament im- *Exo. 12.* mediatly after his ſolemne immolating and eating *v. 6. 7. 8.* the Paſchal lambe with his Diſciples , it is euident, *9. 10. 11.* that it was a ſignificant figure, not only of Chriſts Sacrifice on the Croſſe, but alſo of the ſacred Euchariſt , which he inſtituted the night before his death, and commanded to be obſerued in his Church , for commemoration of his death , & ſingular benefite of

The thing prefigured farre excelleth the figure

his faithful ſeruants. And therfore the ſame muſt neceſſarily be farre more excellent, then the figure, which can not be verified , if it conteyne no other ſubſtance, but bread and wine, which indeede are not better , or not ſo much more excellent , as alwayes the thing figured is better, & more excellent, then the figure. Neither ſufficieth it to ſay , that *Coloſ. 2.*

Proteſtants euaſions ſuffice not.

bread and wine in the vſe of this Sacrament, dœ *v. 17.* ſignifie Chriſts death, for ſo did the Paſchal lambe, *Heb. 10.* nor to ſay, that they ſignifie, and repreſent Chriſts *v. 1.* death now performed , which the lambs death ſignified as to come: for that maketh not ſuch different excellencie,

excellencie, as is betwen the thing figured, and the figure. So also they might say, that the picture of Christ crucified, signifieth, & representeth the death of Christ, vpon the Crosse, as in deede it doth, and yet doth it not so farre excel the figure of the Paschal lambe, as a Sacrament of the new Testament, excelleth the figuratiue Sacrament of the old, by Protestants owne iudgement: confessing that the holie Eucharist is a Sacrament, and so is not the picture of Christ crucified.

5. An other figure of this holie Sacrament, was

Exod. 16. Manna, as is cleare by our Sauiours comparing them,
v. 14. 15. & much preferring this aboue the admirable excel-
16. *&c.* lencie of the other, which was an excellent meate, conteyning manie great miracles, wherby amongst other proofes, it is manifest, that the Protestants communion, hauing no miracle in it at al, being no other thing in substance, then bread and wine, only signifying Christs bodie & bloud, can not possibly be the thing prefigured. And by the same miracles being more emmently in Christ, it appeareth that he himselfe is really present in his owne substance (the spiritual meate of faithful soules) in this most blessed Sacrament: which otherwise could not be the thing prefigured. For whereas Manna, was

Psal. 77. made by Angels, wherof it is called [the bread of
v. 24. 25. Angels] this new Manna was first made by Christ the Sonne of God, and is continually made by himself, geuing power to Priestes, as to his Ministers: but if it stil remained bread in substance, then were the making of it, lesse then the Angels action in making Manna. Secondly Manna was not produced from the earth, nor water, as ordinarie meates originally are, and namely bread from graine, wine from grape, both from the earth: but Manna was

v. 24. from the ayre, as the Psalmist saith [bread of heauen he gaue them to eate] yet not from the Empyrial heauen,

In Manna were twelue special miracles.

The first miracle in Manna.

2.

heauen, but from the ayre called heauen. For so our
Sauiour expoundeth it, saying to the Iewes [Moyses *Ioan. 6.*
gaue you not the bread from heauen (but of our *v. 32.*
Manna, which is geuen in the militant Church, he
saith) my Father geueth you the true bread from
heauen] which is himself the Sonne of God, who
in his Diuine Person, came from the Empyrial heauen. & that this true bread which came from heaue,
is geuen in this Sacrament, is cleare by Christs whole
discourse, comparing that which he here promiseth,
with Mana, & teaching that it is better then Manna.

3. Thirdly how diligently or flowly soeuer anie gathe- *v. 17. 18.*
red Manna, when it came to measuring, euerie one *2. Cor. 8.*
had the same measure ful, called a gomer, and no *v. 15.*

4. more nor lesse. Fourtly, the sixth day (which was *Exo. 16.*
next before the Sabbath) that which euerie one *v. 22. 23.*
gathered was two gomors, & so did serue them for

5. the same day, & for the Sabbath. Fiftly, there fel no *v. 25. 26.*
Manna in the Sabbath, as there did in al other dayes:

6. for that of the former day sufficed. Sixtly, if in the *v. 20.*
other dayes of the weeke, anie part of Manna was
reserued at night it putrified, & was corrupt in the *v. 24.*
morning : only the night before the Sabbath, it re- *v. 16.*

7. maned souud and good. Seuently, notwithstanding *v. 21.*
diuersitie of stomakes in so great a multitude, the *Num. 11.*
same measure of a gomor, was sufficient, and no *v. 8.*
more, to euerie one, young, & olde, and midle age. *Deut. 8.*

8. Eightly the heate of the Sunne did melt & consume *v. 16.*
that which was lefr in the filde, though the heate of *2. Esd. 9.*
the fire, seething in water, grinding in the milne, & *v. 20.*
beating in the morter, did not hurt it. Nintly, Manna *Nu. 11. v. 7*

9. tasted to euerie one that was wel disposed, what *v. 6.*

10. they desired. Tently, to euil minded persons it semed *Exod. 16.*
loathsome, and light meate, but was pleasant to the *v. 32. 33.*

11. good. Eleuenthly, that part of Manna, which was *Ch. 40. v.*
kept in the Arke of testimonie, by Gods command- 18.
ment, remained there incorrupt manie hundred *Heb. 9. v. 4*
yeares.

yeares. Twelftly, this ſtrange extraordinarie meate The twelft miracle in Manna.

Exod. 16. continued fourtie yeares, that is, til the children of
v. 35. Iſrael came into the promiſed land, & then ceaſed,
Ioſ. 5. *v.* Al which miraculous, & ſupernatural proprieties,
12, of Manna being a figure of the holie Euchariſt, doe
neceſſarily importe, & inuincibly proue, the thing
prefigured to be the very ſame in proper termes,
which our Lord and Sauiour expreſſly ſaith it is his
owne true bodie, & bloud, in very deede, not only
a figure or ſigne therof, as faithles new maſters haue

Gen. 14. imagined. Other figures, of bread and wine offered Other figures alſo proue the ſame.
v. 18. by Melchiſedech: the bloud of the Couenant ſprin-
Ex. 24. *v.* kled vpon the people by Moyſes: the loaues of pro-
5. 8. *Ch.* poſition, of ſingular ſanctitie: the bread brought to
25. *v.* 3. Elias by an Angel: and the like, foreſignifying the
3. *Reg.* 19. holie Euchariſt, the former two as it is a Sacrifice,
v. 5. 8. the other as it is a Sacrament: we wil here omitte
& procede to the prophecies.

6. Iacob the Patriarch, bleſſing his ſonnes before Prophecie of the B Sacra-
his death, in the benediction of Iudas, of whom men, in the
Gen. 49. Chriſt deſcended, prophecied that [the ſcepter
v. 10. 11. ſhould not be taken away from Iudas, til he came, Law of nature,
that ſhould be ſent] to witte Chriſt our Redemer:
& by and by addeth, that [He ſhal waſh his ſtole in
wine, & in the bloud of the grape his cloke] what
other wine can this be, but the Chalice which our
Lord conſecrated at his laſt ſupper? when he ordained his new Teſtament in his bloud. Wherin
he then myſtically waſhed his ſtole, & cloke, that is,
his fleſh, in the bloud of the grape, which before
his bleſſing, was wine of the grape. If perhaps ſome Obiection.
wil ſay it is to be vnderſtood of Chriſts death on the
Croſſe: we anſwer, that Chriſts bloud, as it was Anſwer.
ſhed on the Croſſe, came not from wine, nor grape:
& therfore this prophecie can not be ſo wel applied
to his death on the Croſſe, as to his myſtical death
in the holie Euchariſt, where bread & vvine are by

his powreful bleſſing, changed into his bodie and bloud, and ſo this prophecie was really fulfilled, vvhen our Lord inſtituted the new Teſtament in his bloud, as ſeparated from his bodie, repreſenting his real death on the Croſſe : vvhere the ſame Teſtament vvas made complete, & confirmed.

7.   The Royal Prophete as of other Chriſtian Myſteries, ſo of this heauenlie foode, maketh frequent mention. Who deſcribing diuers particular pointes of Chriſts Paſſion, interpoſeth the ſpecial benefite of this B. Sacrament, inſtituted the euening before his death. [The poore ſhal eate (ſaith he) and ſhal be *Pſal. 21.* filled : & they ſhal praiſe our Lord, that ſeeke after *v. 27. 31.* him, their hartes ſhal liue for euer, and euer. Al the fatte ones of the earth, haue eaten, & adored.] None vvil denie but this meate is the B. Sacrament of the Euchariſt. And it is alſo manifeſt, that manie faithful *Pſal. 22.* Chriſtians doe eate it, & adore it, both the poore, and *v. 5.* fatte ones, that is both the humble, which are poore *Pſal. 33.* in ſpirite, and ſome that diſdaine to be humble : but *v. 1.* vvith this difference, that they al eate, and adore, beleuing that Chriſts bodie is there preſent, els they could not lavvfully adore : but onlie the humble are filled. The ſame Royal Pſalmiſt, by vvay of inuiting Chriſtians to praiſe God, for benefites receiued by Chriſt, exhorteth them to adore his footſtoole, ſaying [Exalt ye the Lord our God, and adore his *Pſal. 98.* footſtoole, becauſe it is holie] which can not of anie *v. 5.* other thing be ſo properly vnderſtood, as of Chriſtians adoring this B. Sacrament. For the Arke of the old Teſtament called Gods footſtoole, to which the Hebrew Rabbins referre it, perteineth not to Chriſts ſeruice, of whom the ſame Rabbins interprete the reſt of this Pſalme. Neither ſufficeth it to ſay, that Chriſt was adored in his humanitie, taken of the earth, which is alſo Gods footſtoole : for this adoration was performed only of a few, and for a
ſhorte

shorte time in this world : but his humanitie as his footstoole , is to be perpetually adored of al true Christians, as it is performed in the holie Eucharist. For that this adoration, and praise perteyneth to the B. Sacrament, which is the spiritual foode of Christian soules, is further confirmed by the same Prophete , recounting this meate , as a most special, and perpetual memorie, of al his meruelous workes,

Psal. 110. *v.* 4.
saying [He hath made a memorie of his maruelous workes, a merciful and pitiful Lord : he hath geuen meate to them, that feare him.] This therfore being the singular meate , is the memorie of al his maruelous workes, a most principal Mysterie amongst al other diuine Mysteries. Of this Diuine foode also

Osee. 14. *v.* 8.
the Prophete Osee semeth to speake, saying [They shal liue with wheate , & they shal spring as a vine] Hebrew Rabbins acknowlege here, that in the time of our Redemer Christ, there shal be made mutation

Ibidem.
of nature in wheate. And [this memorial (saith the Prophete) as the wine of Libanus] signifying, that this benefite, & mysterie is not ordinarie, but singular, and most excellent. To the same purpose the Prophete Zacharias foreshewing that God wil geue manie good thinges to the faithful Christians, extolleth one special benefite more excellent then others,

Zach. 9. *v.* 17.
saying [What is his good thing , & what is his beautiful thing, but the corne of the elect, & wine springing virgins :] which no doubt is to be vnderstood of Christ. And may be applied to him , not only in his proper and natural forme: but also as he is in the B. Sacrament, in the formes of bread and wine , because the diuine benefite here mentioned, is deriued in the Prophetes speach from *Corne*, and *VVine*. For most prophecies be hard to be vnderstood , & manie haue diuers true senses. But now we wil repayre to the new Testament, which in this especial matter, is more cleare then either figures , or prophecies.

The same is proued by the Prophecie of Osee.

And of Zacharias.

8. Our

8. Our Sauiour in the prescript forme of prayer, deliuered to his Church, teacheth vs to aske, our heauenlie Father, that he wil voursafe [to geue vs *Mit. 6.* our supersubstantial, daylie bread.] In one Euange- *v. 11.* list (as we haue it in the Latine text) called *supersub-* *Luc. 11.* *stantial*, in the other, *daylie bread.* By which prayer *v. 3.* we aske al maner of necessarie sustenance for soule and bodie: & most especially the singular spiritual foode, which our Lord then intended to ordaine, farre surpassing natural bread, therfore called super-substantial, and also daylie, for our daylie benefite. Which bread he shortly after more expresly pro-mised to geue. For hauing fedde fiue thousand men with fiue loaues, yet the Iewes at Capharnaum, re-quired an other signe, wherby they might be indu-ced to beleue in him: and proposed the example of *Ioa. 6. v.* Manna, saying [What signe doest thou, that we *11. 12.* may see, & may beleue thee? what workest thou? Our fathers did eate Manna in the desert, as it is *v. 30. 31.* written: Bread from heauen he gaue them to eate] our Lord answered to their demand, & particularly touching Manna, that he would geue a better bread then Manna, from an higher place then Manna came, & that the same is him self, and yet should be meate in deede. [Amen amen (said he to them) *v. 32.* Moyses gaue you not the bread from heauen, but my Father geueth you the true bread from heauen. For the bread of God it is, that descendeth from *v. 33.* heauen, and geueth life to the world.] Wherupon they requesting this bread, he told them plainly, *v. 34.* that himself is this bread, saying [I am the bread of *v. 35.* life: he that cometh to me, shal not hunger: and he that beleueth in me, shal not thirst] with further promise that he wil both quicken his faithful ser-uants, spiritually in this life, and raise them to life euerlasting in the last day. [The Iewes therfore *v. 41.* murmured at him, because he had said : I am the
bread,

Christ our Lord taught his Church to pray, that they may receiue supersubstan-tial daylie bread.

He promised to geue him-self to be eate.

bread, which defcended from heauen &c.] Our
Sauiour againe anfwered faying [Murmur not one
to an other. No man can come to me, vnles the
Father, that fent me, draw him] fignifying, that
none can beleue in him, or beleue anie high Myfterie, without fpecial grace from God. And interpo-
fing more to the fame purpofe, he eftfownes repeted, and confirmed his former wordes, [I am the
bread of life] adding further touching the different
effectes of Manna, and of this bread, he faid. [Your
fathers did eate Manna in the defert, and they died,
This is the bread, that defcended from heauen, that
if anie man eate of it, he die not.] Againe he faid,
[I am the liuing bread, that came downe from
heauen. If anie man *eate of this bread*, he fhal liue for
euer.] Thus hauing made mention of eating this
heauenlie bread, which is himfefe, he yet further
telleth what bread it is, that is to be eaten, faying,
[And the bread which I wil geue, is my flefh, for
the life of the world.] Here the incredulons murmured, and contended more & more. [The Iewes
therfore (faith the Euangelift) ftroue among themfelues, faying: How can this man geue vs his flefh
to eate?] Our Lord againe (not telling them of eating a figure or figne of his flefh, as Zuinglius would
expound it, but iterating the fame thing, vrgeth the
neceffitie of eating his flefh) faying to them [Amen
amen I fay to you: Vnles you eate the flefh, of the
Sonne of man, & drinke his bloud, you fhal not haue
life in you] and concerning the fruitful effect of this
diuine foode, he addeth further faying [he that eateth
my flefh, & drinketh my bloud, hath life euerlafting:
and I wil raife him vp in the laft day] Yet more amply our Lord declareth that his very flefh is to be
eaten, and his very bloud to be drunken, yelding the
reafon of fo great effect, as rifing vp therby to life
euerlafting, in foule & bodie [For (faith he) my flefh

v 43. 44.
&c.

v. 48.

v. 49.

v. 50.

v. 51.

Ibid.

v. 52.

v. 53.

v. 54.

v. 55.

Nothwith
ftanding the
people did
murmure,
Chrift ftil
affirmed &
confirmed
the fame
doctrine.

The greatnes
of the promi-
fed effect re-
quireth infi-
nite excellen-
cie of the
meate.

P 3   is meate

is meate in deede: and my bloud is drinke in deede.]
If our Lord Chriſt, God and Man, were not really,
& ſubſtantially preſent in his owne fleſh and bloud,
& were not ſo receiued, his fleſh were not *meate in
deede*, nor his bloud *drinke in deede*, his wordes were
not true, Chriſt our Bleſſed Lord were not truth it
ſelf, as he is. But his word being moſt true, his
fleſh is meate in deede, his bloud is drinke in deede.
And by the worthie receiuing of this moſt Diuine
meate: the faithful ſoule is myſtically ioyned with
Chriſt himſelf, as he againe affirmeth, ſaying [He   *v.* 56.
that eateth my fleſh, & drinketh my bloud, abideth
in me, & I in him] Yet more in confirmation of his
real preſence, of real eating, & real effect, our Lord
ſaith [as the liuing Father hath ſent me, and I liue   *v.* 57.
by the Father; & he that eeateth me, the ſame alſo
ſhal liue by me. This is the bread that came downe   *v.* 58.
from heaeun. Not as your fathers did eeate Manna,
& died. He that eateth this bread, ſhal liue for euer.]
By al which ſo frequent aſſeueration of our Sauiour,
that he is the bread, which came from heauen, that   *v.* 51. 52.
Our Lord   the bread which geueth is his fleſh, that his fleſh 55. 57.
auouching the   muſt be eaten, that his fleſh is meate in deede, & that
ſame doctrine   himſelf wil be eaten, is abundantly confirmed, that
ſheweth that   he meant as he ſpake, to geue his very bodie, really
he ſpake in   preſent in the moſt B. Sacrament, to be eaten. And
proper termes   though manie murmuring ſaid [This ſaying is hard, *v.* 60. 61.
not in figures.   and who can heare it?] he ſtil confirmed the ſame,
and blamed the incredulous, ſaying to them [Doth
this ſcandalize you?] plainly ſignifying, that they
ought not to be ſcandalized. And further inſinuated, that after his Aſcenſion, they would take more
occaſion of ſcandal, ſaying [If then you ſhal ſee the
Sonne of man aſcend, where he was before [As if
he ſaied, Seing you are ſcandalized with my doctrine, whyles I am preſent with you in earth, you wil
be more ſcandalized, when I ſhal be aſcended from
                                                    you

you into heauen. Neuertheles he told them, that the
lacke of humble spirite, & their carnal conceipt, was
v. 63. the cause of their scandal, saying [It is the spirite
that quickeneth : the flesh profiteth nothing] It is
the humble spirite, illuminated & moued by Gods
special grace, that beleueth his word. Carnal imagination conceiueth not, aboue sense & natural reason, according to that, which our Lord said twise
v. 44. in this chapter. [No man can come to me, vnles
v. 65. the Father that sent me, draw him: vnles it be geuen
him of my Father.] So certaine it is that no man
of himself, by his owne sense, or natural reasen, can
beleue this, or other high Mysteries, but by special
grace, through which the humble spirite, beleueth
and confesseth, al highest pointes of Christian doctrine. And this explication of our Sauiours wordes,
is further confirmed, by his like speach afterward,
Mat. 16. saying to S. Peter [Blessed art thou Simon Bar-Iona ;
v. 17. because flesh & bloud hath not reuealed it to thee; but
my Father, which is in heauen.] And by the like
1. Cor. 2. sentence of S. Paul, saying [The sensual man per-
v. 14. 15. ceiueth not those thinges, that are of the spirite of
God; for it is foolishnes to him, and he can not vnderstand: beeause he is spiritually examined. But the
spiritual man iudgeth al thinges] discerneth, beleueth, & approueth al diuine Mysteries, though they
be aboue the reach of his natural sense, and vnderstanding.

9.   As for the Protestants wresting of our Sauiours
wordes [The flesh profiteth nothing] by which
they would exclude Christs real presence from
this B. Sacrament, it is an interpretation, against his
whole discourse, as though by these wordes he recalled that, which he had plainly said before, that
[his flesh is meate in deede and the rest.] As though
he denied his sacred flesh to be present. Which can
with no reason be gathered of his wordes. For

The want of an humble true spirite is the cause of not beleuing Christ word.

The Prote-stants sense of Christs wor-des, contra-dicteth his whole doctri-ne, often repe-ted and con-firmed.

first

Their gloſſe
corrupteth
the text.
It impugneth
alſo Chriſts
Incarnation,
his Paſſion, &
al his actions
in humane
fleſh.

firſt it is a farre other thing to ſay [The fleſh profi-   *v. 63.*
teth nothing] & to ſay, My fleſh is not there, as they
would haue him to haue ſaid. Againe it were moſt
abſurde, yea horrible to heare, that Chriſts fleſh
profiteth nothing: for then his Incarnation, Paſſion,
and Death, ſhould profite nothing, which no Chriſtian dare to ſpeake: except he be as wicked, and
impudent, as the old condemned heretike Neſtorius:
and then we anſwer, that Chriſts fleſh redemed vs,
quickeneth vs, wil raiſe vs vp from death to glorie:
becauſe it is the fleſh of God and Man, vnited to
the eternal Word, the Sonne of God. For in deede
the fleſh of a mere man, could not quicken. And
yet that heretike did confeſſe, that the fleſh of Chriſt
as man, is in the holie Euchariſt, but not the fleſh
of God and Man: which hereſie then trubled the
Church, now the Zuinglians, and others. Al which
notwithſtanding it is cleare by the Euangeliſt S.
Iohn, that [Chriſt promiſed to geue his fleſh to be *v. 52. 55.*
eaten; and that the ſame is meate in deede.]

The ſame real
preſence of
Chriſt in the
B Euchariſt,
is moſt cleare
by his wordes
when he in-
ſtituted the
ſame B. Sacra-
ment.

10.   Let vs ſee alſo his diuine performance, which
is recorded by the other three Euangeliſtes, and S.
Paul, in theſe expreſſe wordes [Ieſus tooke bread, *Mat. 26.*
& bleſſed, & brake; & he gaue to his Diſciples, and *v. 27. 28.*
ſaid: Take ye, and eate: This is my bodie, which is *Mar. 14.*
geuen for you, which ſhal be deliuered for you. Doe *v. 22. 23.*
this for a commemoration of me. In like maner *24. Luc.*
the chalicie alſo, after he had ſupped, ſaying, This is *22. v. 19.*
my bloud, of the new Teſtamen, which ſhal be ſhed *20.*
for you, & for manie, vnto remiſſion of ſinnes. This *1. Cor. 11.*
is the chalice, the new Teſtamēt in my bloud, which *v. 24. 25.*
ſhal be ſhed for you. This chalice is the new Teſta- *26.*
ment in my bloud. This doe ye, as often as you ſhal
drinke it, for the commemoration of me. For ſo
often as you ſhal eate this bread, and drinke the
chalice, you ſhal ſhew the death of our Lord, vntil
he come.] Theſe are the ſpecial wordes, reporting
how

how our Lord and Sauiour inſtituted the holic Sacrament of the Euchariſt , and ordained his owne
Teſtament. In the Syriake Edition , S. Matthew
ſaith: This is the ſubſtance of my bodie. S. Marke
ſaith : This truly is my bodie. Al which according
to the very ſacred letter , and expreſſe termes ,
doe teſtifie the Catholique beleefe , and doctrine, ſo
manifeſtly, that onr Aduerſaries are forced to flee
vnto diuers interpretations , and to frame manie
anſwers, in excuſe of their incredulitie : eſpecially
vſing two euaſions. Firſt they hold it to be impoſſible. Wherunto we haue anſwered in the beginning of this preſent Article , that al thinges are
poſſible with God, who hath done,& ſtil doth other
workes , aboue the ordinarie courſe of al creatures. Secondly they pretend our Lords ſpeach, and
wordes in this whole paſſage, to be like to his figuratiue ſpeaches in other places, & times, when he
ſaid : [I am the doore of the ſheepe, I am the true
vine: and my Father is the husbandman : I am the
vine, you are the branches ,] and ſuch others. It is
eaſyly , and firmely anſwered , that there is great
diſparitie in manie reſpectes. Firſt in the wordes
aboue rehearſed , Chriſt our Lord made his Teſtament: and in euerie teſtament, plaine & proper ſignificant termes are neceſſarily required. Metapho-
rical, Allegorical , and al obſcure ſtrange ſpeaches
are auoided [This is my bloud of the new Teſtament (ſayde our Lord) The new Teſtament in my
bloud] Secondly Chriſt here inſtituted a Sacrament,
as our Aduerſaries acknowlege. And in that reſpect
alſo, proper & vſual termes are requiſite. As were
his wordes to his Apoſtles , concerning Baptiſme.
[Teach al nations , baptizing them in the name of
the Father , & of the Sonne , & of the Holie Ghoſt]
In the other places, where our Lord ſaid, that [he is
a doore, & a vine] he neither inſtituted Teſtament,

Margin notes:

The Syriake Edition plain-ly teſtifieth the Catholi-que doctrine.

Our Aduerſa-ries flee from the expreſſe word of God, pretending impoſſibilitie, in the literal ſenſe.

Nu. 3.

Ioan. 10. *v.* 7. *Ch.* 15. *v.* 1.5.

Al teſtaments require plaine and vſual ter-mes.

Mat. 26. *v.* 28. *Luc.* 22. *v.* 20.

So doth the Inſtitution of a Sacra-ment.

Mat. 28. *v.* 19.

Chrift alfo
declared that
he gaue his
very bodie &
bloud in the
B. Sacrament
the fame
which he
gaue in his
death.

nor Sacrament. Thirdly, when our Lord faid [This is my bodie (which are moft plaine words, though the thing expreffed by thefe wordes, is an high Myfterie aboue the natural capacitie of our vnderftanding) he explained, and confirmed his affirmation, that he meant in deede, his very bodie, faying [This is my bodie, which is geuen for you (now in this Sacramēt) which fhal be deliuered for you] for both are true [is geuen] as S. Luke writeth, & [which fhal be deliuered] as S. Paul witneffeth. For euerie one doth not write al, which our Lord fpake. In like maner he faid: [This is my bloud, of the new Teftament, which fhal be fhed. This chalice is the new Teftament in my bloud] affirming as certaine, that his felf fame bodie, which was deliuered on the Croffe, his felf fame bloud, which was fhed, was alfo in the B. Sacrament. But our Lord did not explaine his other fpeaches [I am a doore: I am the vine, you the branches] and the like Allegories, to fhew that they were to be vnderftod, of an artificial doore, or natural vine of the vinneyeard. For they were in deede Allegorical fpeaches, and fo vnderftood, & applied to his meaning. And therfore thefe euafions of Proteftants, can not excufe their incredulitie, nor fatiffie faithful Chriftians, which beleue and hold Chrifts wordes to be true, as he fpake them in plaineft termes.

Luc. 22.
v. 19.

1. *Cor.* 11.
v. 24.

Mat. 26.
v. 28.

3 Luke and
S. Paul did fo
vnderftand
Chrifts wordes, and beleued his real
prefence in
the B. Sacrament, as Catholiques
now doe.

11.   Yet further it is proued by the teftimonie of S. Luke, and of S. Paul, that they, & confequently the other Apoftles, & al true Chriftians, beleued Chrifts real prefence, in the B. Sacrament. S. Luke writeth not only that our Lord faid: This is my bloud, which fhal be fhed, though that were fufficiently euident, but alfo that the thing conteyned in the chalice fhal be fhed. His wordes are thus [This is the chalice, the new Teftament in my bloud, which (chalice) fhal be fhed for you] By which ordinarie maner of

Luc. 22.
v. 20.

speach

speach [This chalice shal be shed] euerie man vnderstandeth, that the thing conteyned in the chalice,
shal be shed. Wherfore it is manifest, that S. Luke
beleued, that Chrifts bloud, which was shed for our
redemption, was conteyned in the chalice, when
our Lord pronounced those wordes. Els he would
not haue writtē as he did [This is the chalice, which
shal be shed.] And this is fo cleare in the Greke, Beza oppo-
wherin S. Luke writte the Gospel, that Beza very feth himfelf
impudently faith, that either S. Luke writte not these againft the
wordes; or committed a Solecifme in falfe Greke : Euangelifts
falfely imagining that the word [*Shal be shed*] ought wordes.
to be referred to the word [*bloud*] and not to the
word [*chalice*] For fo the Latine might be conftrued,
with Grammatical congruitie, becaufe in the Latine [Calix, in fanguine meo, qui effundetur] the
Relatiue [qui] might agree either with the word
[*Calix*] or with [*fanguine*] but in the Greeke it is [*To*
poterion, en to aimati mou, to ecchynomenon] as if it were
in Latine, *Poculum in fanguine, quod effundetur*. So that
neceffarily it is faid, *The cuppe, or chalice shal be shed,*
to witte, the contents of the chalice. And moft cleare
it is, that the thing which was shed, for mans redemption, is not wine, but Chrifts owne bloud.
Wherupon we forme this perfect Sylogifme : That Otherwife he
which was shed, for our redemption, is Chrifts is conuinced
bloud. But that which is in the chalice, was shed for by an euident
our redemption. Ergo, That which is in the chalice, demonftra-
is Chrifts bloud. The Maior propofition is confeffed tion.
Ch. 22. *v.* by al Chriftians. The Minor is S. Lukes narration.
20. And fo the Conclufion neceffarily foloweth, of the
Premiffes.

12. S. Paul likewife sheweth his beleefe of Chrifts
real prefence, in this B. Sacrament, where he fo carefully inftructeth, and exhorteth the Corinthians
(and in them al Chriftians) how to come therunto
rightly prepared, not only reciting Chrifts inftitu-

tion cherof, as the Euangelistes doe, but also admoniſhing them of errors, touching the behauiour of ſome, in the vſe of this great Myſterie: wherupon he ſaith plainly, that [Who ſoeuer ſhal eate this bread, or drinke the chalice of our Lord vnworthily, he ſhal be guiltie of the bodie, & of the bloud of our Lord.] By which particular guilt of ſinne, he euidently ſheweth, that Chriſts bodie & bloud, are abuſed by vnworthily receiuing this holie Sacrament. But vnles his bodie & bloud, be there really preſent, they could not be particularly abuſed in this act, of receiuing vnworthily. The groſſe abuſe of anie holie thing, is ſacrilege. So bying, & ſelling of holie thinges, is ſimonie. Falſely or vnlawfully ſwearing is periurie; but the offenders in ſuch actes, & the like, are not ſaid to be guiltie of the bodie, and bloud of our Lord For the thing abuſed, geueth the denomination to the ſinne, in particular. As one can not be guiltie of manſlaughter, except the thing that is ſlaine be a man: no more can one be guiltie, of abuſing Chriſts bodie, except Chriſts bodie be there, where it is ſaid to be abuſed. Againe S. Paul in the ſame place, admoniſhing that euerie one, which cometh to this holie Sacrament [proue himſelf (that is, examine himſelf in his conſcience, preparing himſelfe in ſoule) and ſo let him eate of this bread, and drinke of the chalice] repeteth what ſinne it is, to receiue vnworthily [For he that eateth and drinketh vnworthily (ſaith he) eateth & drinketh iudgement to himſelf: *not diſcerning the bodie of our Lord*] So declaring why this probation, & due preparation is neceſſarie, becauſe he that cometh vnworthily, diſcerneth not the bodie of our Lord, Which reaſon neceſſarily preſuppoſeth, that our Lords bodie is there preſent. Els the vnworthie receiuer, could not be charged, with this particular ſinne, of not diſcerning, not duly honoring, eſteming,

1. Cor. 11.
v. 27.

v. 28.

v. 29.

Vnworthie receiuing this B Sacrament, is wicked abuſing of Chriſts bodie and bloud.

The Apoſtles admonition to diſcerne, and regard Chriſts bodie in the B. Sacrament preſuppoſeth that the ſame bodie is there preſent.

ming, or respecting the bodie of our Lord: but only of not discerning the figure, or signe of his bodie.

13.   Seeing therfore, that Christ our omnipotent Lord, could change bread & wine, into his owne real bodie & bloud, & that it is abundantly shewed, first by pregnant figures, and prophecies of the old Testament; more especially by his owne promise, that he would doe it; and likewise declared by his solemne action, & most plaine wordes; and by the Apostles beleefe, practise, and doctrine, that he hath done it: what greater infidelitie, what more manifest heresie, can be imagined, in such as wil be called Christians, then to reiect that truth, which Christ hath so manie wayes vttered: and to say, It is stil bread & wine, which he saith, is his bodie, & his bloud?

Seing Christ both could & would make himselfe really present in the B. Sacrament, it is plaine heresie to denie it.

Vnder each forme of bread, & of wine, in this B. Sacrament, is whole Christ, Bodie, Bloud, Soule, & Diuinitie.

ARTICLE 19.

Other Controuersies, concerning this most holie Sacramēt, doe almost al depend, vpon the principal Article, of Christs real presence therin. For al those difficulties, which our Aduersaries obiect against other pointes, either tend to the impugning of the same chefe ground, falsely supposing that Christ is not really present in this Sacrament: or els with Luther they imagine, that Christ being in deede really present, bread and wine doe also remaine. And so they gather as they thinke, diuers absurdities, in the Catholique beleefe, & impute to vs much errour, & idolatrie. Al which quarel, is accusations fal to nothing, the maine point standing firme, as it doth: by the groundes produced in the

Diuers Controuersies depending vpon Christs real presence in the B. Sacrament, are in general decided by the same principal point. Yet are here also further discussed, & proued in particular.

Q 3   precedent

precedent Article. Neuertheles , as wel for more
abundant satisfaction to their common obiections,
as for further explication of the Catholique doctrine , we shal here breefly shew by the holie Scriptures, that Christ is wholly in euerie part , of this B.
Sacrament : then declare the reasons of communi- *Article.*
cating vnder one kinde ; also the obligation to com- 20. 21. 22.
municate sometimes : and that this holie Sacrament 23. 24.
is also à Sacrifice : the complement of al old Sacrifices : and that it is due to God only.

By concomi-
tance Christ
is wholly ,
wheresoeuer
anie part of
him is.

2.   Touching the first of these particular pointes :
albeit by vertue of the sacred wordes of consecration , in the former part , vnder the accidents of
bread, onlie Christs bodie is present ; & in the other
part , vnder the accidents of wine , is onlie Christs
bloud : yet by concomitance of al thinges in Christ :
(now glorified) where hisbodie is , there also is
his bloud , & where his bloud, there his bodie , and
where either of both, there also his soule , & where
al three, yea or anie of them (as in the time, betwixt
his Death & Resurrection) there also is his Diuinitie,
because they are al vnited to his Diuine Person. And
so in each of the accidents of bread, & of wine , and
in euerie least particle therof, Christ is wholly , in
Bodie, Bloud , Soule , & Godhead. A figure of this

It was so pre-
figured in
Manna.

was foreshewed in Manna [of vvhich the children *Exod.* 16.
of Israel gathered, one more, and an other lesse, and *v.* 17. 18.
they measured by the measure of a gomor, neither
he that gathered more, had aboue : nor he that prouided lesse found vnder] And the same measure
(which vvas an other miracle) did iust suffice to
sustaine euerie one, as it folovveth in the next vvordes [euerie one gathered, according to that which *Ibidem.*
they were able to eate] Wherupon S. Paul saith
[He that had much, abounded not , & he that had 2. *Cor.* 8.
litle, wanted not] Why shal à Christian then, make *v.* 15.
scruple to beleue, that Christ is whole , & that there
is the

is the same spiritual fruite, in one part of the accidents, of this holie Sacrament (which infinitely
excelleth Manna) as in both partes. and the very
same, in lesse forme, which is in the greater? In an
other place the same Apostle speaking of the old Sacrifices saith, that [They which eate the hostes, are
they not partakers of the Altar?] without anie mention of drinking, of the libaments: which ordinarily were adioyned to euerie Sacrifice, as a part therof. The Apostle hereby signifying, that they which
did only eate of the hostes, did as wel participate of
the Sacrifice, as if they had also drunke of the libaments. And the reason is, because in spiritual thinges, the effect, & fruite is the same in euerie part, as
in the whole. Thus it was in the figure, much
rather it is so in the thing prefigured.

3. Which is yet more cleare by our Sauiours doctrine in the Synagogue at Capharnaum. For in that
his diuine discourse, he attributeth the same effect to
one part of this B. Sacrament, as to both the partes.
Sometimes saying [Vnles you eate the flesh of the
Sonne of man, and drinke his bloud, you shal not
haue life in you. He that eateth my flesh, & drinketh
my bloud, hath life euerlasting, & I wil raise him vp
in the last day] sometime saying [This is the bread,
that descendeth from heauen, that if anie man eate
of it, he dye not. I am the liuing bread, that came
downe from heauen: If anie man eate of this bread,
he shal liue for euer: & the bread which I wil geue,
is my flesh for the life of the world] Aagane [This
is the bread, that came downe from heauen. Not as
your fathers did eate Manna & died. He that eateth
this bread, shal liue for euer] Which self same effect
could not be ascribed, to one part, of this holie Sacrament, which is the whole effect of both partes,
except, the self same efficient cause (Christ geuing
life) were as wholly in one part, as in both partes.
And

Margin notes (left):
1 Cor 10.
v. 18.
Exo. 25.
v. 29.
Leuit. 6.
v. 14.
N. 6. v.
15.

Ioan. 6.
v. 53. 54.

v. 50.

v. 51.

v. 58.

Margin notes (right):
In the old Sacrifices, he that receiued anie part, was made partici-pant of the whole.

Christ attri-buteth the same effect to the receiuing of one part, of the B. Sa-crament, as of both parts.

And that our Lord here fpeaketh not only of receiuing fpiritually, but alfo of receiuing facramentally,
and fpiritually together, is manifeft: as wel by the
mention here of Manna (to which he compareth, &
preferreth this holie Sacrament) as by the termes of
eating & drinking, with diftinction of eating his bodie,
& drinking his bloud, which plainly fheweth that
he fpeaketh of facramental communicating, & not
only of fpiritual.

The fame ir
proued by
S. Paules
doctrine.

4.   Againe by S. Paules doctrine, this truth, that
Chrift is in each part, of the feueral accidents, of
bread & of wine, is euidétly proued, where he faith
[Whofoeuer fhal eate this bread, or drinke the cha- *1. Cor. 11.*
lice of our Lord vnworthily, he fhal be guiltie of *v. 27,*
the bodie, and of the bloud of our Lord.] In the former wordes touching the crime of an vnworthie
communicant, the Apoftle fpeaketh difiunctiuely
[Whofoeuer fhal eate or drinke vnworthily] in the
other wordes, touching the guilt of finne, he fpeaketh coniunctiuely [he fhal be guiltie of the bodie,
and of the bloud of our Lord.] So that the fault committed, in vnworthily receiuing, the one, or the
other part, of the holie Sacrament, to witte in the
forme of bread, or in the forme of wine, maketh
the offender guiltie both of the bodie, & of the bloud
of our Lord. Which could not be faid, vnles both
the bodie, and the bloud, be in each of the kindes:
wholly vnder the accidents of bread, and wholly
vnder the accidents of wine. And confequently,
Chrift is whole in each part of this B. Sacrament,
his facred Bodie, Bloud, Soule, and Deitie. Which
is not hard, for anie true faithful Chriftian to conceiue, that beleeueth Chrifts real prefence, in this *Rom. 6,*
holie Sacrament: becaufe Chrift our Lord, being *v. 9.*
glorious, his bodie, bloud, & foule, can not be anie
more feparated, one from an other. Likewife when
our Lord was mortal, according to his manhood, &
confe-

consecrated this same holie Sacrament, his bodie, bloud, and soule were in each forme, of bread, and of wine, and al stil vnited to his Godhead. From which nothing, that his Diuine Person once assumpted, euer was, or euer shal be separated. But in the time betwixt Christs Death & Resurrection, his Godhead was with his bodie in the sepulchre, without his bloud & soule; with his bloud on the Crosse, and other places, without his bodie and soule; and with his soule in *Lumbus Patrum*, without his bodie and bloud. His Godhead euer being where his Humanitie was or anie part therof. But not his Humanitie whersoeuer his Deitie. For that is a new coyned heresie, by certaine Sectaries, therof called Vbiquitarians, or Vbiquists.

Though God be euerie where, yet Chrißts humanitie is not euery where.

It sufficeth, & is more conuenient, that al com-
municants, besides the Priest that celebra-
teth, receiue vnder one kinde only.

ARTICLE 20.

VPon the assured truth, that Christ our Sauiour is really present in the B. Sacrament; and wholly in each of the accidents of bread, and of wine: this other truth is also grounded; that it sufficeth for receiuing the benefite of this holie Sacrament, to receiue it, vnder one kinde only. For as in the Protestants opinion, falsely supposing, that there is no other substance, but bread, signifying Christ bodie, & of wine, signifying his bloud, it were in deede a defrauding of the communicants, togeue them only one kinde: because in their sense, they should haue but half of the Sacrament, & but halfe of the benefite: so on the other side, seing that according to the Catholique faith, Christ is really, & wholly in each

Being proued that Christ is really, and wholly present in the B. Sacrament, it neccessarily foloweth, that the whole fruite is receiued in one kinde of the accidents.

R   kinde

kinde of the accidents, it is al one fruite, and effect, by receiuing one only kinde, and by receiuing both kindes. And if the Proteſtants would beleue, the truth of Chriſts real preſence, they would neither ſtand, vpon his being wholly in euerie kinde of the accidents, nor vpon their imagined neceſſitie, that al muſt receiue both kindes. It being therfore proued, that Chriſt is both really, & wholly in each kinde, *Art.18.19.* it is therby euident, that the communicants receiue whole Chriſt, and ful fruite of this Sacrament, by one kinde only, and ſo it is not neceſſarie, that they receiue both. But reſteth to be ſhewed, that to receiue vnder one kinde only, is both lawful, & more conuenient.

2. For declaration wherof, our Sauiours owne fact, is a pregnant example. Who after his Reſurrection

Chriſt miniſtred this B. Sacrament in one kinde only, to two diſciples, at Emaus.

gaue this holie Sacrament in the one kinde only, to the two Diſciples, into whoſe companie he put himſelf, in the way from Ieruſalē to Emaus. Where [it came to paſſe, whiles he ſate at the table vvith *Luc. 24.* them, he tooke bread, & bleſſed, and brake, and did *v. 30. 31.* reach to them. And their eyes vvere opened, and they knew him.] That this was the B. Sacrament, appeareth by our Sauiours action, taking bread, then bleſſing it, thirdly breaking it, fourtly geuing it to them to eate; & finally by the preſent effect wrought in them, as themſelues reported to the Apoſtles. [How they knew him in the breaking of bread.] *v. 35.* In which termes of breaking of bread, the ſame S.

The celebration of this B. Sacrament is often called, The breaking of bread.

Luke alſo relateth, the holie exerciſe of the faithful, preſently after the coming of the Holie Ghoſt ſaying [They were perſeuering in the doctrine of the Apo- *Act. 2. v.* ſtles, and in the communication of the breaking of 42. bread, & prayers.] Likewiſe he writeth of S. Paul and him ſelf, with manie others, aſſembling together on the firſt of the Sabbath (or weeke) which is our Lordsday (called with vs Sunday) to the celebration

Ch. 20.
v. 7.

bratton of this Sacrament, saying [In the first of the Sabbath, when we were assembled to breake bread] Where we may obserue by the way, that the principal Diuine Seruice, and cheefe function, for which Christians assembled together on our Lords day, was to breake bread: and therto was adioyned preaching, as the holie Historiographer declareth, thus

Ibid.

connecting his narration [when we were assembled to breake bread, Paul disputed with them (at Troas) being to depart on the morow, & he continued the sermon vntil midnight] Likewise that this diuine function is called breaking of bread, and not by the name of a Sacrament was (no doubt) to conceale the high Mysterie, from the derision of Infidels, and doth nothing preiudice the real presence of Christs bodie: being called bread, in the same

Why it is called bread, after the consecration,

Gen. 2. *v.*
23.
Exo. 7.
v. 12.
Io. 2. *v.* 8.

sense, as Adam called Eue [bone of his bone, flesh of his flesh] and as serpentes were called roddes, and wine, at the mariage in Cana of Galilee, was called water, after their mutation; by the names of the thinges, which they were, before they were changed. Wherfore concerning our present purpose, you see by the fact of our Sauiour, & by the practise of the primatiue Church, that it is lawful to administer this holie Sacrament, in one kinde only. And that in the thing itself it is indifferent, whether it be receiued in one kinde only, or in both. And so the holie Church hath in subsequent ages, sometimes administred it, to al Christians in both kindes: but more generally in one kinde only, as wel to al secular persons, as also to Clergiemen, yea to Priestes, except him onlie, that celebrateth the same Diuine Mysterie. For otherwise there is no difference betwen the Clergie & Laitie in this behalfe.

The B Sacrament hath sometime bene ministred in both kindes to al communicants, but more generally in one kinde only,

3   The reasons of which more general practise, & of the Ecclesiastical Decree made therupon, are especially these (still considering, in euerie reason of

It is not only lawful but also more

R 2   more

conuenient,
that the com-
municants re-
ceiue vnder
one kinde
only for diuers
seasons.

1.
2.

3.

4.

5.

more conuenience, that there is no necessitie of both
kindes to al communicants, as is declared) First
there is great danger of sometimes sheding the most
sacred Bloud, by mishappes which might chance, in
great troupes of people, in so manie chalices, or
other vessels, as would be necessarie : with peril
also in keeping the residue, after the communicants
were serued. Secondly, there would be difficultie,
in manie places, to prouide so much wine, as might
serue great multitudes, frequently reparing to this
most holie Sacrament. Thirdly some persons, either
of natural, or accidental infirmitie, doe not wel indure the taist, or streingth of wine ; & therfore it is
not so conuenient, with danger of reluctatió, or vomite, or with corporal hurt of the communicants,
without necessitie, to administer to al in both kindes.
Fourtly it is most conuenient, that Christian people
receiue this B. Sacrament in one kinde only, that
they may more exactly be instructed, and know, that
Christ our Lord, is wholly in each part, & least parcel of the accidents ; & that therfore they reape the
same fruite, by receiuing vnder one kinde, as if they
receiued vnder both. Fiftly, to require both kindes,
is a foule signe of grosse errour, & want of faith, not
beleuing that Christ is in deede, wholly in each part,
of the accidents of bread & of wine, after consecration therof. Which kind of ignorant incredulous *Exo. 16.*
people, were aptly prefigured, by those that stroue *v. 16. 18.*
to gather more of Manna, then the ordained mea-
sure, which was neither more, nor lesse, then suffi- *Sap. 16.*
cient for euerie one. And as it was in quantitie com- *v. 20.*
petent for euerie one, so also it was qualified, that to *Exo. 17.*
the wel disposed it serued for bread, flesh, drinke, & *v. 2. 3.*
what they desired. But manie through their volup- *Nu. 11. v.*
tuous concupiscence murmured for want of water, *4 5. 6. 31.*
and desired flesh. Of which murmurers the Royal *Ps. 94. v.*
Prophete speaking, exhorteth others (not to harden *8 9.*

It is hardnes
of hart and
defect in faith

their

their hartes, as thofe did in the defert.] Euen fo it is hardnes of hart, and defect in beleefe, that moueth anie to require participation of this Sacrament, in both kindes, hauing it wholly in one.

that fome doe require to re-ceiue vnder both kindes.

4. Finally to anfwer the cheefe obiection touching this controuerfie : where our Sauiour commanded his Apoftles, that they fhould al drinke of the confe-crated chalice, faying [drinke ye al of this] It is cleare that none els were prefent, but the Apoftles onlie. [And they al dranke of it] as S. Marke exprefly wri-teth. wherby it is euident, that the wordes [Drinke ye al of this] were fpoken to al the Apoftles only. And that it is not a general commandmēt to al men, appeareth further, by our Sauiours geuing this holie Sacrament in one kinde only , & by practife of fome primatiue Chriftians, as is already fhewed in this Article. Neuertheles both kindes muft generally be confecrated together , to make the complete figni-fication, & commemoration of Chrifts death. And fo the Prieft, that celebrateth, muft alwayes receiue both kindes. For although the holie Sacrament is perfect, and the fruite therof is whole, to them that receiue but in one kinde, yet the Sacrifice is not com-plete, but in both formes together.

Mat. 26. v. 27. Mar. 14. v. 23.

Anfwer to the Proteftants cheefe obiec-tion.

Nu. 2.

Both kindes muft be con-fecrated, that the Sacrifice may be com-plete.

Al Chriftians hauing vfe of reafon , are bond to receiue this moft holie Sacrament.

ARTICLE. 21.

COnfidering that this B. Sacrament , of Chrifts very bodie, and bloud (conteyning the Foun-taine it felf , & Auctor of grace, Chrift God & Man) is moft gracioufly ordayned by him, to be the foode, and nutriment of our foules, no man can doubt, but his diuine wil & pleafure (though it were not other-

Chrifts infti-tution is a

wife

Sufficient incitation to al greatful Christians.

wise intimated vnto vs) sufficiently obligeth al true Christians, with gratful minde to repayre to so inestimable a benefite, preparing themselues so much as in them lieth, to the worthie receiuing therof. Yet lest anie of slouth, pusillanimitie, scrupulositie, or other impediment, should thinke to be excused, omitting to participate, our Lords so bountiful benignitie, in due time, and maner, he hath further bond vs, not to neglect this admirable releefe of our soules, foreshewing also our obligation herein, as wel by the figure of the old Pasch, as by his premonition of the losse, if we doe it not, declared when he promised to geue himself vnto vs; and finally when performing the same, both figure & promise, he gaue an expresse precept therof, the night before his Passion & Death.

The Iewes were commanded to make their Pasch once euerie yeare.

2. The precept of celebrating, and eating the Paschal lambe, was clearly geuen to the Iewes, which as the shadow instructeth vs in these wordes. [Al the assemblie of the children of Israel (saith the Law) *Exod. 12,* shal make the Phase.] The time also was prescribed, *v 47.* to be euerie yeare once: Our Lord saying to Moyses [Let the children of Israel make the Phase in his *Num. 9.* time. The fourtenth day of this moneth (the first *v. 2. 3.* moneth, called Nisan, which is our March) at euen, according to al the ceremonies, & iustifications therof.] In case of impediment, at the proper time, there was this prouision [The man that shal be vncleane *v. 9. 10.* vpon a soule, or in his iourney, farre of in your na- *11.* tion, let him make the Phase to the Lord, in the second moneth, the fourtenth day of the moneth, at euen, with azimes, & wilde lettice, shal they eate it] Touching the punishment for omission, without iust impediment, the Law saith [If anie man both *v. 13.* being cleane, & was not in his iourney (which two cases were put for examples of iust impediments, for there might be others) and yet not make the Phase, that

Vnder the paine of death or other great punishment.

that foule fhal be deftroyed, out from amongft his peoples, becaufe he offered not facrifice to the Lord, in his due time : he fhal beare his finne] So ftrict was the precept concerning the figure: which punifmēt whether it was corporal death, which is more probable, or feparation from the faithful people, it did wel fignifie Excommunication amongft Chriftians, & eternal death, as for a mortal finne, if the offender dye impenitent, for his omiffion.

3. Which is more affured by our Lords wordes, touching the thing prefigured. Who being the true

I. *Cor.* 5. *v.* 7. *Ioan.* 6. *v.* 51.

Pafch, & heauenlie Manna, promifing to geue his owne flefh, the true bread of life, and the Iewes not beleeuing his word, but murmuring againft that, which they vnderftood not, at laft he told them the loffe, & punifment to al that fhould not both beleue, and receiue this diuine foode, faying to them, and in them to al that fhould liue in his Church (after the performance of his promife, and eftablifhment

v. 53.

therof, by the coming of the Holie Ghoft [Amen, amen, I fay to you: Vnles you eate the flefh of the Sonne of man, and drinke his bloud, you fhal not haue life in you.] And likewife declared the fruitful effect, which thofe fhould reape, that fhal fo beleue,

v. 54.

& receiue him, faying in the next wordes [He that eateth my flefh, and drinketh my bloud, hath life euerlafting, and I wil raife him vp in the laft day,

v. 58.

And he that eateth this bread fhal liue for euer.] Finally performing this his promife, by geuing his owne bodie, and bloud, in the formes & accidents of bread and wine, to his Apoftles, he commanded them, to doe the fame thing, which he then did,

Luc. 22. *v.* 19. I. *Cor.* 11. *v.* 24. 25.

faying [Doe ye this] That is, Doe ye confecrate this great Myfterie, & minifter it to others. For fo our Lord then did. By al which we fee the diuine precept, binding al that are capable of precept, to witte al Chriftians that haue vfe of reafon, fometime to

Chriftians are bond to receiue the B. Sacrament vnder the paine of loofing life euerlafting.

And Paftors are bond to minifter it, to their flocke.

receiue

receiue this heauenlie meate, for releefe of their ſoules, vnder the paine, neuer otherwiſe to enioy eternal life, & with aſſurance, receiuing it as they ought,
to haue life euerlaſting, & to riſe in glorie,

4.   As for the time when & how often, this affirmatiue precept bindeth Chriſtians, to receiue this moſt
bleſſed, & greateſt Sacrament, is not otherwiſe expreſſed in holie Scripture; then that the Apoſtles
were commanded to teach al nations, & baptizing
ſuch as ſhould beleue in Chriſt, ſhould alſo [Teach *Mat. 28.*
them to obſerue al thinges, whatſoeuer (ſaith our *v. 20.*
Lord) I haue commanded you] Amongſt which
general vnwritten commandments deliuered to the
Apoſtles, and by them to the Church, no doubt there
was ſome precept, concerning this ſo ſingular great
Myſterie. In vertue wherof, it is by the Ordinance,
and Commandment of the ſame Church, decreed
that al Chriſtians ſhal vpon paine of Excommunication, receiue this B. Sacrament, at the leaſt, once
in euerie yeare. And that within eight dayes before,
or after the feaſt of Eaſter, or Chriſtian Paſch. And
likewiſe whenſoeuer anie ſhal finde themſelues in
probable danger of imminent death. Becauſe this *Ioa. 6. v.*
moſt ſacred meate, is the proper foode of Chriſtian *33. 50. 51.*
ſoules, wherby to conſerue ſpiritual life, and ſo in- *54.*
creaſe their grace: and eſpecially it is the proper
viaticum, or wayfayring prouiſion, in the iourney
of the ſoule, from earth towards heauen. This is
the wholſome, & neceſſarie commandment of holie
Church, determining the times, of putting our Lords
general commandment in particular execution. To
this therfore al are no leſſe bond, vnder paine of
mortal ſinne, & of Excommunication, & of eternal
puniſhment due therunto, then vnto our Lords
owne general precept. Els in vaine, did our Sauiour
ſay to his Apoſtles [He that heareth you, heareth me, *Luc. 10.*
and he that deſpiſeth you, deſpiſeth me, & he that *v. 16.*
                                          deſpiſeth

*When & how
often to re-
ceiue this B.
Sacrament, is
not particular-
ly expreſſed
in holie Scrip-
tures: but a
general pre-
cept was ge-
uen to the A-
poſtles, to
teach the peo-
ple manie
thinges not
expreſſed,*

*Often com-
municating*

despiseth me, despiseth him that sent me.] And this
is said concerning the necessarie precept. But it is
most conuenient, to communicate often. As best
Christians vse to doe. According to their diuers states, at least in al principal great Feastes. Some also,
as it were monethly, others weekely, and some
almost dayly.

is very con-
uenient,
though not
commanded.

The holie Eucharist is also a Sacrifice propiciatorie.

ARTICLE 22.

OF the three general kindes of Infidelitie,
Paganisme, Iudaisme, & Heresie, the worst
is Heresie. Because Heretikes once professed (at least implicitely in Baptisme) to beleue the
true Catholique faith, from which they reuolt by
obstinatly denying anie special Article therof: and
so become worse then Turkes, Iewes, or anie sorte
of heathen Paganes, which neuer receiued the Christian faith, & Religion [For (as S. Peter teacheth) it
had bene better for them, not to haue knowen the
way of iustice, then after the knowlege, to turne
backe, from that holie commandment, which was
deliuered to them. For that of the true prouerbe is
chanced to them: The dogge returned to his vomite:
and, The sowe washed, into her wallowing in the
mire.] And as heresie is the worst kind of Infidelitie
so also amongst manie grosse heresies of these dayes,
it is one of the obsurdest, to denie that there is anie
true, and proper Sacrifice in the Law of grace, and
Church of Christ: which is in effect to say: that
there is no external religious Action, by which anie
thing is offered to God, in acknowlegement of his
supreme Dominion: which most principal publique
maner of Diuine Seruice, was neuer wanting in Gods

Heresie is the
worst kinde
of infidelitie.

2. Pet. 2.
v. 21.

v. 22.

It is a most
grosse heresie
to denie that
there is anie
true & proper
Sacrifice in
the Chutch
of Christ.

S   faithful

faithful people. Yea it is a thing so necessarily required by the light of reason, and Law of nature, that
scarse anie nation, or people was euer, before this
time, so barbarous. but they knew, that this special
homage is due to God: & in some sorte performed
it, offering external sacrifice to such, as they erroniously thought, or imagined to be geddes. And the
faithful true seruantes of God, in al ages rightly offered to him, exteanal true Sacrifices, which were to
him most pleasing, & to the offerers, & others for
whom they were offered, most profitable of al reli- *Art. 3.*
gious external actions. And therfore it can not with
reason be imagined, that Christians should want this
ordinarie meanes, to serue God, & to impetrate his
mercie, & fauour, which the Law of nature taught
not only the holie Patriarches, but also most other
nations: & which God by his written Law, exactly
prescribed to his peculiar people.

2. Yet because our Aduersaries denie it, & for that

Melchise-
dechs Sacrifice
was a plaine
figure of the
holie Eucha-
rist.

it is a principal point of Catholique Religion, we
shal euidently proue it by auctoritie, both of the old
& new Testament. That which Melchisedech did, *Gen. 14.*
when he mette Abraham, is so manifest a figure *v. 18.*
of the holie Sacrifice of Christs bodie, and bloud, in
the formes of bread and wine, that Protestants haue
no better euasion, but to denie that Melchisedech
did offer Sacrifice, in that bread & wine, wherof he
made Abraham, and his companie participant: but
wil needes imagine, that he brought that bread and
wine, only to refresh, and releue that campe, after
their trauel, & victorie; which their inuention hath
neither coherence with the text, nor probabilitie of
reason. For the text saith, that those souldiars, had *v. 11. 24.*
then taken great plentie of victuals in the praye. &
had eaten therof. And vvheras they denie, that
Melchisedech did here anie Priestlie function, vvith
the bread and vvine, the contrarie affirmation is
cleare,

cleare ; especially by the wordes interposed, that
[He was the Priest of God most high] so immediatly
adioyned to the narration, of his bringing of bread
& wine, and not to his blessing of Abraham, and receiuing tithes of him [Melchisedech the King of
v. 18. Salem (saith Moyses) bringing forth bread & wine,
for he was the Priest of God most high; blessed A-
v. 19. braham, and said: Blessed be Abraham to God the
highest, which created heauen & earth. And Abra-
v. 21. ham gaue him the tithes of al] So the holie text most
euidently sheweth, that he did the office of à Priest
Psal. 109. in the bread & wine. And consequently Christ being
v. 4. a Priest according to the order of Melchisedech, did
Heb. 5. fulfil this propheticall figure, most directly, in the
v 6. 10. holie Eucharist, where he consecrated bread and
Art. 18. wine, changing them (as is already declared) into
his owne bodie, and bloud: & so offered the same
vnder the accidents of bread & wine. The selfsame
Sacrifice in vnbloudie maner, which he offered the
Heb. 10. next day bloudily on the Crosse. For as his Sacrifice
v. 14. was offered on the Crosse, it was once only offered,
1. Cor. 11. & neuer to be iterated in that maner: but that which
v. 25. 26. he instituted in the Eucharist, is done often in commemoration of his death, euen til he shal come
againe, in the end of this world.

3. Likewise the Paschal lambe being not only à
Exo. 12. Sacrament, but also a Sacrifice, as is manifest in the
v. 6. 27. Law, saying [The whole multitude of the children
Num. 9. of Israel shal sacrifice the lambe : It is the victime of
v. 13. our Lords passage] & in other places, expresly called
Mat. 14. a Sacrifice, it was both in respect of Sacrament, and
v. 12. of Sacrifice, a very significant figure of the holie Eu-
Exod. 25. charist, For in that it was offered at euen, within the
v. 30. Ch. house, with azime bread, & eaten; al these circum-
29. v. 38. stances agree with our Sauiours Action in his mystical oblation, in the formes of bread & wine. A third
figure were the loaues of proposition continually

The Paschal
lambe was an
other figure.

Likewise the
loaues of
proposition.

S 2   sette

sette vpon the table in the Sanctuarie. A fourh the daylie Sacrifice. And al the other Sacrifices at special times, & for special purposes, did importe some continual Sacrifice in the Church of Christ, commemoratiue of that one bloudie Sacrifice on the Crosse, which in that maner can not be offered anymore: & so doth not in that respect, answer to the figures, as the holie Eucharist doth.

4. Of this also the Prophetes doe speake, and not only of the same as it was offered on the Crosse. Isaias faith [The Lord of hostes shal make to al peoples, in this mount, a feast of fatte thinges] according to the Seuentie Interpreters [Shal sacrifice oyntment] which proueth that Christ the Annointed should be offered in Sacrifice [in the Church of al peoples] not only amongst the Iewes, but also amongst the Gentiles, of whom especially his Church consisteth, & is here signified by this mount called [The citie of strong nations.] Daniel necessarily presupposeth, that there shal be a daylie Sacrifice, euen til the end of this world, where he prophecieth, that Antichrist wil endenour to abolish it, saying [From the time, when the continual Sacrifice shal be taken away, & the abomination of desolation shal be sette vp, a thousand two hundred nintie dayes] which prophecie our Sauiour applieth to the persecution, which shal be nere the end of this world. And the time here described, agreeth to other places, foreshewing that Antichrist shal reigne three yeares and a half. How then shal this prophecie be verified, if there were no continual Sacrifice, in the Church of Christ, against which Antichrist wil so fircely bend his forces, and so farre as God shal permitte, wil hinder the publique oblatió of Sacrifice: as now his forerunners doe in al the places, vvhere they haue that povver? And of this perpetual Sacrifice in al places, & nations, our Lord
further.

Mal. 1, *v.* 11. further saith by his Prophete Malachias, that [From the rising of the sunne, euen to the going downe, great is my name among the Gentiles : & in euerie place there is sacrificing, and there is offered to my name, a cleane oblation : because my name is great among the Gentiles, saith the Lord of hostes] Seing therfore this prophecie was vttered of a new, & perpetual Sacrifice, most pure in comparison of the former Sacrifices of the old Law, which the Priestes did not offer so pure, as they ought to haue bene (not

v. 8. of the best hostes, but of the lame, and feeble) foreshewing a Sacrifice, that can not be polluted, how can so cleare wordes be anie way wrested to improper Sacrifices of prayers, and thankesgeuing, as Protestants contend, & not be vnderstood of external Sacrifice, of Christ himself the must pure Hoste, and eternal Priest offering himself, by the handes of his Priests, who although sinful, can not pollute the immaculate Sacrifice.

These prophecies can not be vnderstood of improper Sacrifices.

5. As therfore the figures foresignified, and the Prophetes foretold : so our B. Sauiour instituted the most excellent daylie Sacrifice, after the celebratiō of the Paschal lambe, the night before his death.

Mat. 26. *v.* 26. 27. *Luc.* 22. *v.* 19. 20. *1. Cor.* 11. *v.* 24. 25. 26. For then [He tooke bread, & blessed, and brake, & he gaue to his Disciples &c. & taking the chalice, he gaue thankes, and gaue to them, &c.] and said seuerally of each part: [This is my bodie: This is my bloud] Lastly he said [*Hoc facite.* Doe ye this.] In which diuine Action, our Sauiour did so represent his owne death, by consecrating, and geuing his bodie in the accidents of bread, & his bloud in the accidents of wine, that by the power of his wordes making his bodie in the one forme, and his bloud in the other (to witte, by vertue of the consecration : though by concomitance, both were in each forme) that he offered a perfect Sacrifice : and withal signified that the same should also be done by his

That our Sauiour instituted a daylie Sacrifice, the night before he dyed, representing his owne death, is proued by his wordes.

Priestes

Priestes, saying [Doe ye this] That is, Doe ye conſecrate, and offer this, as now I haue done, For ſo the
ſame word [*Facite*] ſignifieth in diuers other places,
Namely in the booke of Leuiticus: [*Faciet vnum pro* Leuit. 15,
peccato, & alterum in Holocauſtum : he ſhal make(or doe) v. 30.
one for ſinne, and the other for an Holocauſt] ſpeaking of ſacrificing turttles, or pigions. And [you Ch. 23.
ſhal make, a buck goat for ſinne, & two kiddes of a v. 19.
yeare old, for pacifique hoſtes.] Elias alſo ſaid to his 3. Reg. 18.
aduerſaries [Chooſe you one oxe, and make it firſt] v. 25.
that is ſacrifice it. Further S. Luke maketh it euident,
that the ſame hoſte (Chriſts bodie) was offered in
the holie Euchariſt, which was offered on the Croſſe
ſaying in the preſent tenſe, [My bodie which is Luc. 22.
geuen] and of the other part, in the future tenſe v. 19.
[My bloud, which ſhal be ſhed.] And S. Paul ſaith 1. Cor. 11,
of the bodie [which ſhal be deliuered] becauſe it v. 24.
is the ſame in ſubſtance, which was offered in both
places : but in diuers maners, bloudily on the Croſſe,
and vnbloudily in the holie Euchariſt,

Proued alſo
by S. Paules
comparing it
with other
Sacrifices.
5.   Againe this vnbloudie Sacrifice is proued, by S.
Pauls large diſcourſe, admoniſhing the Corinthians,
not to participate with Infidels in meates, & drinkes
offered to Idols. To which purpoſe he putteth them
in minde (as of a Myſterie wel knowen to them) of
the participation, and communication of Chriſts
bodie & bloud. [My dearest (ſaith he) flee from the 1. Cor. 10.
ſeruing of Idols. I ſpeake as to wiſe men, your ſelues v. 14. 15.
iudge what I ſay; The chalice of benediction, which 16.
we doe bleſſe : is it not the communication of the
bloud of Chriſt ? & the bread which we breake, is it
not the participation of the bodie of our Lord ? For v. 17.
being manie, we are one bread. (that is, by this
meanes, we are vnited to Chriſt, the true bread of
life) one bodie (vnited alſo among our ſelues) al
that participate of one bread] to witte of Chriſt,
by receiuing the holie Euchariſt. This example
being

being proposed, he addeth an other, in the Sacrifices of the old Law, as a thing knowen to the Israelites, saying [Behold Israel according to the flesh (I appeale to the Israelites my countrimen.) They that eate the hostes, are they not partakers of the Altar?] as if he should say: Certes they are partakers of the Altar, by eating of the sacrifices, which were offered on the Altar. By these two examples the Apostle teacheth, that although the thing which is immolated to Idols, is neither better nor worse therby in it self: and although the Idol in it self, is nothing: yet in regard that the heathen doe immolate such thinges to diuels, & not to God: they that (wittingly) eate of the same thinges, doe therby participate with diuels, which is also cleare by his next vvordes, saying [I vvil not haue you become felovves of diuels] vvherupon the Apostle then further vvarneth them, that they must either forsake the sacrifices, & felovvshipe of the Idols, & Idolaters, or els refuse the participation of Chrifts bodie & bloud, in the Church of Chrift: saying [You can not drinke the chalice of our Lord, & the chalice of diuels: you can not be partakers of the table of our Lord, & of the table of diuels.] In al which discourse, & doctrine of the Apostle, you see, that our Christian holie Eucharift, the moft sacred bread & chalicie, the holie table and altar, & the participation of our B. Sacrament, are so compared, & resembled to the altars, hostes, sacrifices, immolations, & participations of the Iewes, and heathen Gentiles, that vnles our moft bleffed Sacrament of the Altar, be a true, and proper Sacrifice, S. Paules admonition to the Corinthians, to refraine from eating meates offered to Idols, and his cheefe proofe that the same was necessarie, should haue no true ground nor coherence, but be wholly impertinent to his purpose. For vnles this be a true and proper sacrifice, as the Iewes Sacrifices

v. 18.

v. 19. 20.

v. 21.

If the holie Eucharift were not a Sacrifice, the comparing of it with other sacrifices were vnfittee.

crifices, and alſo heathen ſacrifices were, and had
their effectes, the good Sacrifices making felowſhipe
with God, the bad making felowſhipe with diuels,
the ſimilitude, reſemblance, and compariſon were
no fitte examples, as the B. Apoſtle knew them to
be moſt fitte, & ſo vſed them.

7.   Yea if this B. Sacrament, of Chriſts bodie and
bloud, were not a true & proper Sacrifice, an other

impoſſible inconuenience, and moſt wicked abſur-
ditie muſt be granted by Proteſtants (who denie
anie Sacrifice to be now in the Church) that Chriſt
ſhould ceaſe to exerciſe his function of Prieſthood,
by the miniſterie of his vicarial Prieſtes, contrarie to
the Royal Prophete, and to S. Paul, affirming that
Chriſt is a Prieſt, not only according to the order of
Melchiſedech (which requireth a Sacrifice fulfilling
his figuratiue, in bread & wine,) but alſo [for euer] *Pſ.* 109.
which requireth a perpetual daylie Sacrifice, to the *v.* 4.
end of this world. Contrarie alſo to S. Pauls doctrine *Heb.* 5.
in an other place, where doubtles he ſuppoſed *v.* 6.
that there is true Prieſthood in the Church of the
new Teſtament, as aſſuredly, as Chriſts Law conti-

nueth, when he ſaid [The Prieſthood being tranſla- *Heb.* 7.
ted, it is neceſſarie that a tranſlation of the Law be *v.* 12.
alſo made] And in a third place, affirming that [we *Ch.* 13. *v.*
haue an Altar, wherof they haue not power to eate, 10.
which ſerue the Tabernacle] Becauſe an Altar likewiſe importeth a Sacrifice. For theſe three thinges,

Prieſthood, Altar, & Sacrifice, does ſo neceſſarily concurre, and depend one of an other, that ordinarily
in what ſoeuer Law and Religion, anie one of them
is, there they are al. For as there can not be Sacrifice without Prieſthood, nor can be rightly offered
without an Altar: ſo Prieſthood wanteth the moſt
Principal function, and an Altar wanteth the proper
vſe, without Sacrifice. And therfore amongſt Engliſh Proteſtants, & other Caluiniſtes: becauſe there
· is no

is no Sacrifice, there are no Prieftes, nor Altars: but
Minifters, and communion tables. But feing in the
Law of grace, in the new Teftament, there is by S.
Pauls teftimonie, Priefthood, and an Altar, there is
alfo a true & proper Sacrifice.

8.　The fame truth is yet further confirmed by the
practife of other Apoftles, & Apoftolical men together with S. Paul : who (as S. Luke writeth) did offer
Sacrifice at Antioch [As they were miniftring to
our Lord (faith he) or (according to the Greke text)
As they were facrificing. *Lytourgounton auton.* Sacrificantibus illis. or, *Publicum Minifterium Domino
celebrantibus.* Celebrating the publique Minifterie
to our Lord] which can not poffibly be wrefted to
anie other thing, but muft neceffarily, be the publique celebration of that Diuine Minifterie, for
which Chriftians [affembled together the firft of
the Sabbath, to breake bread.] The fame Adminiftration, and folemnitie, for which the Corinthians
reforted together. Wherof S. Paul writeth to them,
correcting fome diforders, & admonifhing them to
celebrate the fame with due preparation, & in godlie
maner: concluding thus [The reft I wil difpofe
when I come] This moft Diuine publique Seruice,
practifed in the Church at Antioch, when the Holie
Ghoft, defigned S. Paul & S. Barnabas to be confecrated Bifhoppes: S. Luke exprefly calleth [Sacrificing. By which one word *Lytourgounton, Sacrificantibus.*
Sacrificing, if there were no other proofe in holie
Scriptures (as you fee there is ftore) doth fufficiently
conuince, & confute our Aduerfaries, denying that
there is anie publique proper facrifice in the Church
of Chrift, comemoratiue of the Same offered by him
on the Croffe. And that this therfore is the holie
Eucharift, they can not ftand in denial: becaufe no
other was euer pretended. As for the exception
which they make, becaufe our Latine text hath

Act. 13.
v. 2.

Act. 20.
v. 7.
1. Cor. 11.
v. 17. 28.
29.

v. 34.

The Apoftles
did offer Sa-
crifice.

An obiection
anfwered.

Mini-

Ministrantibus, not *Sacrificantibus:* Ministering, not Sacrificing, it sufficeth that the thing it self is proued, and confirmed. Contention about the word, or the name, auaileth litle. For to say in general, Ministring, denieth not in special, Sacrificing.

9. Howbeit concerning the name, it resteth to be briefly obserued, that this greatest Sacrament, and onlie Sacrifice in the Christian Church, for better notification to al the faithful (and withal to conceale the high Mysterie from contumelie, and blasphemie of the Infidels) hath bene, & is yet diuersly called. Sometime, The breaking of bread, as hath bene already noted. Also *Lyturgia,* of S. Lukes word in Greke, which is Publicum Ministerium Diuini officij: Publique Diuine Seruice. Likewise *Eucharistia,* that is, *Bona gratia,* Good grace. A terme common to al the holie Sacraments, but peculiarly attributed to this most excellent aboue the rest; because it containeth most principal sanctifying grace: yea Christ himself, the fountaine of al grace. It is also interpreted, Tankesgeuing: for in it, praise and thankes are offered to God, in most special maner, Christ being both the Priest, and Hoste of this Sacrifice. In Latine it is called *Missa,* Masse, deriued of *Mitto* to send. Because by a most ancient custome, the Sacrifice being offered, some sacred hostes were sent to others absent to receiue, and so be made participant. Also called *Missa,* of the solemne dimission, and sending away, of such as beleued, but were not baptized, when part of the Diuine office is ended, before the Offertorie and Consecration, the Deacon then denouncing that those should depart, as not admitted to the more diuine Mysterie, saying: *Ite Missa est.* Goe ye, the Masse is now ended, which perteyneth to you, & the rest perteineth to the baptized. Wherof cometh the distinction, of *Missa Catechumenorum,* and *Missa Fidelium,* the Masse of them that as yet learne their

[margin: Christian Sacrifice is called.]
[margin: Breaking of bread.]
[margin: Liturgie or Publique diuine Seruice.]
[margin: Eucharist.]
[margin: Masse.]
[margin: Art. 20. Nu. 2.]

their Catechifme, and the Maffe of the faithful. But fince that there are no fuch Catechumes commonly in Chriftian Churches, this denounciation of *Ite Miſſa eſt*, is made in the end of the whole Maffe. It is likewife called *Sacrum*, The Holie Myfterie, becaufe it is the moſt Sacred of al Diuine offices.

Sacrum.

10. Whether S. Paul meant this moſt Holie Sacrament and Sacrifice, or rather a certaine other feaſt, called *Agapæ*, a charitable banket, fometimes vfed in Churches, when he faid: [It is not now to eate our Lords fupper]is not fo certaine. For that other feaſt or banket might be called *Cana dominica*, becaufe it was made in, or nere to the Church, the houfe of our Lord. And it is cleare that the Apoſtle there fpeaketh of abufes, which fome of the richter forte, committed, with confufion of the poore, in the feaſt, before the holie Eucharift. So that Proteſtants commonly calling their communion, the Supper of our Lord: neither haue fo certaine a ground, as to preferre this name before other names, nor fo fmal ground, as to be refufed of Catholiques. But we fay as before, we ſtand vpon the thing, & wil not contend about the name.

1. Cor. 11.
v. 20.

The Supper of our Lord is a doubtful name: neither to be preferred before others, nor to be reiected from amongſt the others.

The holie Eucharift is the complement of al the old Sacrifices.

ARTICLE. 23.

IN the Law of nature before Moyfes, the Patriarches, & other feruants of God offered Sacrifices, of diuers kindes, by diuine inſtinct, and by tradition, without other prefcript rule. In the wꞃiten Law, though there is no expꞃeſſe mention therof, in the tenne commandments, yet nothing is more exactly commanded, in al the Ceremonial precepts, then the offeꞃing of Sacrifices, for diuers purpofes. There

Gen. 4. v.
4. Ch. 8.
v. 20. Ch.
12. v. 7.
Ch. 14.
v. 18.

In the old Teſtament were three kindes of Sacrifices.

T 2 were

were in al three kindes (as is declared before) The *See Artic.*
firſt was Holocauſt, in which the whole hoſte was 3. *nu.* 2.
burnt in honour of God. The ſecond was Sacrifice *Exo.* 20.
for ſinne, in diuers maners, for ſund. ie offences, in *v.* 24.
which the one part of the oblation was conſumed *Leuit.* 1.
in honour of God, the other part ordinarily belon- *v.* 9. *Ch.*
ged to the Prieſtes. The third kinde was Pacifique 4. *v.* 2. 13.
Sacrifice: wherof one part was conſumed in Gods *&c.*
ſpecial honour, an other part perteyned to the Prie- *Ch.* 3. *v.*
ſtes, & the third part remained to them that prouided 5. 9.
the hoſte. And of this kinde there were two ſortes,
the one of thankeſgeuing to God, for benefites receiued: the other of obſecration to procure his diuine
fauoure in anie good deſire, or enterpriſe. Al which
did prefigure, and foreſhew one onlie Sacrifice of

Chriſtian Sa- **Ch**riſts bodie and bloud, offered by him in two ma-
crifice is the ners, once bloudie on the Croſſe; & dayly vnbloudie
complement in the holie Eucharist, inſtituted after his laſt ſupper, *Mat.* 26.
of al old Sa- the night before his death, in his owne bodie and *v.* 28.
crifices. bloud, vnder the formes of bread & wine, which he 14. *v.* 24
expreſly called [His new Teſtament in his bloud: &, *Luc.* 22.
His bloud of the new Teſtament] alluding to the *v.* 20.
dedication of the old Teſtament, & [Law, which he 1. *Cor.* 11.
came not to breake, but to fulfil] And ſo not to take *v.* 25
away al Sacrifice, but to ordaine a better, and the *Exo.* 24.
ſame a continual Sacrifice, the complement of al the *v.* 8.
old Sacrifices, farre excelling them al, being al in *Mat.* 5.
one, our Holocauſt, & Sacrifice for ſinne, and Paci- *v.* 18.
fique, for al purpoſes.

2.   Of this change of the old Sacrifices, God ſpake
Proued be the by his Prophetes, firſt and moſt eſpecially requiring
Prophetes. internal vertues, and for obteyning therof, promiſed
a better external Sacrifice, then thoſe of the old
Teſtament. Firſt ſaying thus by the Royal Pſalmiſt to
the Iewes [I wil not take calues out of thy houſe, *Pſal.* 49.
nor buckgoates out of thy flockes. Immolate to God *v.* 9. 14.
Dauid. the Sacrifice of praiſe, and pay thy vowes to the
                                                    Higheſt

v. 23. Higheſt The Sacrifice of praiſe ſhal glorifie me.]
not denying external Sacrifice in the Law of grace,
but admoniſhing his people, to bring therwith internal vertues, & right affection of their hartes, repentance for their ſinnes, with honour and praiſe to
God, adoring him, not only by external Sacrifice
(which he alſo commanded) but more eſpecially
Pſal. 50. to ſerue him, with a contrite humbled hart, in ſpi-
v. 18. 19. rite, and veritie. true internal deuotion, which the
Pſalmiſt here prophecied, and our Sauiour ſignified,
ſhould be more perfectly performed, in his new
Ioan. 4. Teſtament, ſaying [The houre commeth, and now
v. 23. 24. it is, when the true adorers ſhal adore the Father in
ſpirite, & veritie. For the Father alſo ſeeketh ſuch
to adore him, God is a ſpirite, & they that adore him,
muſt adore in ſpirite, and veritie] Not in figuratiue
Sacrifices, but in the veritie prefigured : in a more
excellent Sacrifice, then thoſe of the old Law : in
which, then alſo conſiſted the principal maner of
adoring God. As both the Iewes & the Samaritanes
wel knew. But the Samaritanes contended about
the place, where they ought to offer their Sacrifices.
Vpon occaſion of which queſtion (concerning the
right place of adoring by the way of Sacrifice) our
v. 21. Lord foretold that [Neither in the mount Garizim,
nor at Ieruſalem, is the place, where men muſt
adore] Yet withal affirmed, that ſtil there ſhal be
adoring, to witte, by Sacrificing, for of that adoration did our Sauiour there ſpeake, as it is manifeſt in
the Goſpel. Our Lord ſaid likewiſe by his Prophete
Iere. 33. Ieremie [There ſhal not faile from before my face,
v. 18. a man to offer Holocauſtes, & to burne Sacrifice, &
to kil (or immolate) victimes, al dayes] which Prophecie muſt needes be myſtically vnderſtood of the
new Teſtament, ſeeing it is cleare that the old Sacrifices, continue not al times nor dayes, but are
wholly ceaſſed : and ſo to verifie this, and the like

T 3   prophe-

Marginal notes:

External adoration conſiſteth eſpecially in Sacrifice.

Chriſt fore-told that there ſhal be adora-tion of God, by offering Sacrifice in the new Law,

Ieremie.

Prophecies, other perpetual Sacrifice muſt, and doth
ſucceede in place of them : for ſo they faile not, but
are fulfilled : which is moſt plainly written by the
Prophete Malachias, by whom our Lord ſaith to

Malachie. Leuitical Prieſtes : [I haue no wil in you, ſaith the *Mal. 1.*
Lord of hoſtes : and gift I wil not receiue at your *v. 10. 11.*
hand. For from the riſing of the ſunne, euen to the
going downe, great is my name among the Gentiles,
and in euerie place is ſacrificing, and there is offered
to my name a cleane oblation.] Thus doe the Prophetes tel vs, that the old Sacrifices ſhould ceaſe, &
that an other better Sacrifice ſhould ſuccede, and
continew.

3. In further profe, and declaration wherof let vs
ſee the ending of the former, and dedication of the
new, namely the old Paſch ending, and the new

Chriſt inſtitu- beginning. Our Sauiour that very time & euening,
ted the new when he would make this memorable happie
Sacrifice im- change, firſt ſignified to his Apoſtles, his eſpecial
mediatly after deſire of eating with them his laſt old Paſch, now at
the old Paſ- the time of inſtituting his new, ſaying [with deſire *Luc. 22.*
chal lambe. I haue deſired to eate this Paſch with you (at this *v. 15.*
time more then in other yeares) before I ſuffer. For
(ſaith he) I ſay to you, that from this time, I wil not *v. 16.*
eate it, til it be fulfilled in the kingdom of God] to
witte in the new Law, & teſtament, euen by and by
to beginne. And at the ſame ſupper drinking the
libament, which belonged to the old Paſch, he
ſaid : [Take and diuide among you, for I ſay to you: *v. 17. 18.*
that I wil not drinke from hence forth, of the generation of the vine, til the kingdom of God doe come]
When ſupper was done (as S. Ihon writeth) our *Ioan. 13.*
Lord waſhed his Diſciples feete. After which he *v. 2. &c.*
ſate downe againe, exhorted them to humilitie,
ſignified in general that one of them would betray *v. 12. 21.*
him; and gaue a particular ſigne, to S. Iohn, who it
was. Then as the other three Euangeliſtes, & S Paul *v. 26.*

doe

doe relate (which S. Iohn writing laſt of al omitteth)

Mat. 26.
Mar. 14.
Luc. 22
1.*Cor.* 11. Ieſus [tooke bread, and bleſſed, and brake (in like maner taking the chalice) he gaue to them, & ſaid : [This is my bodie : This is my bloud, of the new Teſtament] as S. Matthew and Marke doe write; S. Luke and S. Paul, thus : [This is the chalice, the new Teſtament in my bloud.] Al teſtifying that our Lord called this high Myſterie, his new Teſtament, & that in his bloud, as ſhed, & ſeparated from his bodie. Agreable wherto the ſame Apoſtle S.

Heb. 9. *v.*
16. *&c.* Paul alſo teacheth [that no teſtament is dedicated without bloud] Vpon al which is demonſtratiuely inferred, that ſeeing Chriſt our Lord, dedicated his new Teſtament, in the holie Euchariſt (as himſelf ſo plainly affirmeth) & that no Teſtament is dedicated without bloud(as S. Paul alſo affirmeth)therfore Chriſts bloud is in the holie Euchariſt. And therfore alſo the holie Euchariſt is a true, & proper Sacrifice, the complement of al the old Sacrifices : and commemoratiue of the ſame which Chriſt offered, both as he inſtituted it in vnbloudie maner, in the formes of bread and wine, and as he offered it in bloudie maner, once for euer vpon the Croſſe.

4. Againe at large in a great part of his Epiſtle to the Hebrewes, this Apoſtle proueth by manie arguments, that the old Law and teſtament, with the *Heb.* 5. *v.*
9. 10. Sacrifices therof are ceaſſed, and that the new Law & Sacrifice are ſucceded; Chriſt hauing fulfilled al thoſe thinges, which by Moyſes, and others were prefigured. Namely performing the figure of Melchiſedech, who in manie reſpectes reſembled our Sauiour; & particularly in that our Lord is a Prieſt of the ſame order,& for euer, which appeareth eſpecially in this Sacrifice,inſtituted in the formes of bread and wine, and ſecondly in that it is ſtil offered, by Chriſts Prieſtes for euer, to the end of this world. For where as the Sacrifice on the Croſſe, is moſt

S. Paul ſheweth that the new Sacrifice ſuccedeth in place of al the old ſacrifices.

sufficient

ſufficient for the redemptiõ of al mankinde, not only of the elect, but alſo of the reprobate (becauſe Chriſt died for al ; gaue himſelf a redemption for al ; is the propiciation for our ſinnes, and not for ours only, but alſo for the whole worlds) yet thoſe onlie are ſaued to whom the ſame redemption, and propiciation is applied : & none els haue remiſſion of ſinnes, but thoſe, to whom this vniuerſal price is in particular applied by Sacraments, Sacrifice, and other meanes. And this application is made by meanes of his Prieſthood, and performed eſpecially by this Sacrifice of the holie Euchariſt, which is ſtil offered, & ſo the general price applied. And therfore thoſe that denie a daylie Sacrifice, denie not only that the daylie Sacrifice of the old Law is fulfilled, in the Church of Chriſt; but alſo denie, that Chriſt ſhould ſtil exerciſe his Prieſthood after the order of Melchiſedech.

2. Cor. 5.
v. 15.
1. Tim. 2.
v. 6.
1. Ioan. 2.
v. 2.

If There were not a daylie Sacrifice in the Church, the old daylie ſacrifice were not fulfilled.

Neither ſhould Chriſt for euer, exerciſe his Prieſthood according to the order of Melchiſedech

Sacrifice is due to God onlie : & to no creature, how excellent ſoeuer.

ARTICLE 24.

Diuine honour being due to God onlie : as ſupreme Lord of al, an other Spiritual honour (infinitely inferior) being due to Sainctes, and ſpiritual perſons, in reſpect of their ſpiritual giftes, & graces; and Ciuil honour being due to temporal perſons, in reſpect of temporal power, auctoritie, or dignitie ; we doe oftentimes, & that lawfully, exhibite the ſame external actes of honour, to al theſe three diſtinct Excellences. For examples, we bow our knees, and kneele downe, not only to God, but alſo to our King: and Catholiques kneele to Sainctes : but with mental diſtinction, geuing to God Diuine honour ; to Sainctes, ſpiritual honour not diuine; and to our King ciuil

Three kindes of honour.

Diuine : an other Spiritual not diuine : & Ciuil : are diſtinctly exhibited to three kindes of exlencie.

ciuil honour. So we pray to God, for fpiritual, and
temporal good thinges, and we pray mortal men,
to pray for vs to God, & that they wil doe vs temporal pleafures, and benefites: we alfo yeelde thankes to God, and to men, with like wordes, and
geftures: and manie other, the very fame external
actes, are done to God, and to fome creatures. But
Catholiques haue one fpecial external religious act,
to wit external Sacrifice, which is due to God onlie,
and is not done to anie creature, mortal or immortal, how excellent foeuer. As we fhal here breefly
declare by the holie Scriptures, for better fatiifaction
to al, that either of fimple ignorance thinke, or of
malice falfely impute vnto vs, that we offer Sacrifice to Sainctes.

2.   After recital of the tenne cõmandments, where
it is ftrictly forbidden to haue, or to honour ftrange
goddes, or anie creature whatfoeuer as God, for
more explanation therof, the fame diuine Law,
amongft other particular precepts, hath this [He
that Sacrificeth to goddes, fhal be put to death, but
to the Lord only] which paine of temporal death,
implieth the guilt of mortal finne, and of eternal
damnation. Neither is it only vnlawful to facrifice
to Idols, which are falfe goddes, but alfo vnlawful,
to offer facrifice to fuch holie creatures, as are otherwife to be refpected, with fpiritual reuerence, and
deuotion. As the picture of a ferpent made in braffe,
by Gods commandment, [fette vp for a figne, that
the people being ftrooken with ferpents, might
looke vpon it, and efcape death, which when they
that were ftriken looked on, they were healed.]
and fo the thing was a long time, rightly efteemed
and honored. But when the people by exceffe of
refpect, towards the fame brafen ferpent [burnt
incenfe to it] the good religious King Ezechias brake
it in peeces, auouching, as truth was, that it had no

*Sacrifice may
not be offered
to anie crea-
ture.*

Exo. 22.
v. 20.

Num. 21.
v. 8. 9.

4. *Reg.* 18.
v. 4.

V   diuine

diuine power. But was merely in substance, a peece of brasse, called therfore by him in Hebrew *Noheftan.* And so if at anie time, in anie place, Christian people should imaginie Deitie to be in a creature, or presume to offer sacrifice to it, the abuse is to be corrected, and if neede be, the thing it self to be taken away: and al iust occasions of idolatrie or superstition, or of other euil, especially in faith & religion, are to be remoued: but the right vse of holie thinges, & due respect to holie persons, is stil to be obserued. The Holie Apostles of Chrtst were righly estemed [as the dispensers of the Mysteries of God: the co-adiutors of God. The shadow of S. Peter, and S. Pauls napkines, were respected, because they cured infirmities, being deuoutly vsed, but when some men attempted to offer sacrifice to S. Paul, and S. Barnabas, it could in nowise be tolerated, because Sacrifice is due to God onlie [that made the heauen and the earth, & the sea, & al thinges that are in them.]

1. *Cor.* 3.
v. 9. *Ch.*
4. *v.* 1.
Act. 5. *v.*
15. *Ch.* 19.
v. 12.
Ch. 14. *v.*
12. 14.

3.   Neuertheles Sacrifice is rightly offered to God, in memorie of glorious Sainctes. In signe and figure wherof [Moyses builded an Altar at the foote of the mount, & twelue titles according to the twelue tribes of Israel.] And there offered Sacrifice to God: and by those twelue titles, stirred vp the people to deuotion, putting them in minde, to imitate the vertues of their Progenitors. And so the liues, and monuments of Sainctes, are proposed to faithful people, when Sacrifice is offered to God onlie: to moue Christians to folow the godlie examples of holie persons, now glorious in heauen. Which is no other thing, then that which S. Paul aduised the Hebrewes, saying [Remember your Prelates, which haue spoken the word of God to you: the end of whose conuersation beholding imitate their faith.] And seeing the faith of S. Gregorie, & S. Augustine, our first Prelates, moued them, to build Altars in
memorie.

Exo. 24.
v. 4.

Heb. 13.
v. 7.

Al occasion of Idolatrie, or superstition is to be auoided but due honour to be obserued.

Sacrifice is offered to God in memorie of his Sainctes, proued by the fact of Moyses.

And doctrine of S. Paul.

memorie of former Sainctes, and to offer Sacrifice
vpon them to God onlie: and withal to pray thofe
Sainctes, to pray for them, and for their faithful
freindes. Thofe alfo that now erect Altares to God,
in memorie of glorious Sainctes, and pray them, to
pray to God for our prefent neceffities, doe rightly
according to the Apoftles doctrine, remember their
Prelates, & imitate their faith.

4. If anie incredulous wil suppofe, that glorious
Sainctes can not know, nor vnderftand mortal
mens prayers, Chrifts telleth vs [that other Sainctes,
are as Angels in heauen.] And he that wil alfo denie,
that holie Angels in heauen can know our ftate, or
vnderftand, our affaires, let him remember that our
Sauiour alfo faith: that [the Angels in heauen reioyce vpon a finner that doth penance] & confider
how they fhal reioice, if they cã not know it. And fo
let him repent of his errour, that holie Angels may
reioice for his repentance. Seing alfo no Chriftian
doubteth but diuels vnderftand, and know, when a
mortal man curfeth, or blafphemeth, fhal a Chriftiã
thinke, that holie Angels, & other Sainctes know not
as wel what we doe, & fay, as wicked diuels doe: This
by way of digreffion, touching prayer to Sainctes,
which point is to be difcuffed in his proper place.

5. Yet remember one other example, perteyning
to our purpofe of erecting Altars. An Angel appearing to Gedeon, in fhape of a man, fent him to deliuer, and defend the people, being fore oppreffed,
by their enimies the Madianites. And Gedeon firft
doubting, and afterwards beleuing the meffage,
prayed the Angel to tarie, whileft he might fetch an
hofte for Sacrifice. The Angel ftayed, and when
Gedeon came with al thinges prepared, fauing fire,
the Angel directed him what to doe: and fo other
thinges being made readie [The Angel of our Lord
ftretched forth the tippe of the rodde, which he

(margin notes left)
Mat. 22.
v. 30.

Luc. 15.
v. 10.

Part 4.
Art. 44.
45.

Iud. 6. v. 4
11. 12.

v. 13.

(margin notes right)
Angels and
other Sainctes
can know the
affaires of
mortal men.

Diuels alfo
doe know
mens wordes
and actions,
much more
glorious
Sainctes.

An Angel
cooperated
with Gedeon
in offering
Sacrifice to
God.

held in his hand, & touched the flesh, and the vnleauened loaues, & there arose a fire from the rocke, &
consumed the flesh, & the vnleauened loaues. And
the Angel of our Lord vanished from his eyes.]   *v. 23.*
Wherupon Gedeon, being mnch astonished, and
frighted, but finally conforted, and strengthned

In memorie [Built there an Altar to our Lord] for gratful memo-   *v. 24.*
wherof Ge- rie of the Angels apparition, & cooperation in offe-
deon built ring of the Sacrifice, so miraculously performed.
an Altar. And called the Altar : Our Lords peace. And so Ge-   *v.25. &c.*
deon proceded to warre against Madian [destroying
first the Altar of Baal the Idol, ouetrhrew the enimie,
and brought peace to Israel.]

Penance consisting of Contrition, Confession, & Satisfaction, with Priestlie Absolution, is a true Sacrament, institnted by Christ.

ARTICLE. 25.

As man natu- EVerie corporal liuing creature, feeling it self
rally desireth at anie time bodily diseased, seeketh to be
corporal cured, being moued by instinct of nature to
health, so he desire a good state. Amongst al other thinges in
ought to seeke earth, Man hauing vse of reason, & therby conside-
spiritual ring that the paine, which he feeleth, not only doth
health of the presently molest him, but also that his infirmitie
soule. tendeth to corruption, of his temporal life; to conserue himself, applieth such remedies, as he supposeth requisite for ease, or cure of the bodie. Much
more it behooueth a reasonnable mortal person, if
the soule be sicke, to seeke, & vse spiritual medicine,
because euerie least sinne defileth, and spotteth the
soule with some blemish; and euerie mortal sinne
depriueth the soule of spiritual life, by losse of grace,
and separation from God: and if the soule so depart
from

Iſa. 49.
v. 15.

Ezec. 18.
v. 23. Ch.
33. v. 11.
1. Tim. 2.
v. 4.

from the bodie in that ſtate, it falleth into eternal
damnation, & into euerlaſting torment. For auoiding wherof, and attaining of eternal life, our merciful good Lord, not willing that anie ſhould periſh,
but returne to him, & be ſaued, offereth new grace
to al ſinners in this world, that if they wil, they
may repent, & doing that, which for this purpoſe
he hath ordained, may haue remiſſion of al their
ſinnes, be reſtored to his fauour, and liue for euer,
in vnſpeakable glorie. Which meanes of recouerie
from ſpiritual ſicknes of the ſoule, was alwayes by
hartie repentance, with a willing minde to doe, or
ſuffer temporally, that which Gods wil appointeth,
for puniſhment of tranſgreſſion paſt. So God did
not only lay temporal afflictions vpon al mankinde,
for the ſinne of Adam our firſt parent, but alſo in
particular, put vpon him, and others, long penance,
ordayned more ouer in the written Law, certaine
Sacraments, and Sacrifices for ſinne; & in the new
Teſtament, Chriſt hath inſtituted more effectual Sacraments, to witte of Baptiſme for remiſſion of original ſinne, as is already declared: and for remiſſion of actual ſinnes after Baptiſme, hath ordayned
the Sacrament of Penance. Which conſiſteth of
Contrition, Confeſſion, and Satiſfaction, with Abſolution of a Prieſt, as Iudge in this ſpiritual court of
conſcience, and as the Miniſter of Chriſt, who is the
Supreme Iudge. Which ſpecial point of Catholique
faith and doctrine, we ſhal here proue by the holie
Scriptures, of the old & new Teſtament.

Art. 10.
11. 12.

Repentance is neceſſarie for the reco-uerie of ſpi-ritual health being loſt by ſinne.

2. Of this ſo neceſſarie, & wholſome a Sacrament,
we haue a very examplar figure in both Adam and
Eue, our firſt parents, the firſt ſinners of mankind,
and firſt penitents. Who when they had ſinned,
and [perceiued them ſelues to be naked, they ſowed
togeather leaues of a figge tree, & made themſelues
aprons, to couer their nakednes, and hid themſelues

Adam & Eue, were ſorie for their ſinne.

Gen. 3.
v. 7. 8.

V 3   amiddes

amiddes the trees of paradiſe. But God (of his gratious mercie) called Adam, and ſaid to him : where
art thou ? Adam anſwering ſaid : I heard thy voice   *v.* 10.
in paradiſe, and I feared, becauſe I was naked, and
I hid me] Where as before ſinne [they were both   *Ch.* 2. *v.*
naked, to witte Adam, and his wife : and were not 25.
aſhamed] now after that they had diſobeyed God,
tranſgreſſing his commandment, they were aſhamed of their nakednes (which not before but after
ſinne gaue cauſe of ſhame) then [they feared, & hid
them ſelues] Which ſhewed remorſe of conſcience
for ſinne, with feare and ſorow. Which is the firſt
part of Penance, called Contrition. The ſecond part,
They confeſ- which is Confeſſion folowed. For our Lord char-   *Gen.* 4.
ſed their ging them, with the breach of his commandment,   *v.* 9.
ſinne. they confeſſed, the ſimple truth : (farre otherwiſe
then Cain afterwards did) Adam ſaying [The wo-   *Ch.* 3. *v.*
man which thou gaueſt me, to be my felow com-   12. 13.
panion, gaue me of the tree, & I did eate.] And the
woman being asked [why ſhe had done this, anſwered : The ſerpent deceiued me, and I did eate]
wherupon our Lord, without examination, condemned the impenitent ſerpent, ſaying [Becauſe   *v.* 14.
thou haſt done this thing, accurſed art thou among
al catle, and beaſtes of the earth. &c.] But enioyned
temporal puniſhment, to our parents, as to penitents.
[Of multiplied trauels, in bearing of children, to   *v.* 16.
Eue; with ſpecial ſubiection to her husband : and of
much toyling in the earth, to Adam al the dayes of
his life, with the ſweate of his face, to eate his bread
til he returned to the earth; & laid alſo other penal-
And willingly ties of this life vpon them both, and vpon al their
accepted the natural progenie, & finally temporal death. Saying
puniſhnents to Adam : [Duſt thou art, and to duſt thou ſhalt   *v.* 19.
enioyned for returne.] Al which they indured as temporal Sa-
temporal ſa- tiſfaction for ſinne. which is the third part of Pe-
tisfaction. nance.

                                         3. An

3. An other very fignificant figure, of this holie Sacrament, was fhewed, when after that the firft tables of the Decalogue were broken, new tables

Exo. 24.
v. 9.

were writen, our Lord faying to Moyfes [Cutte thee two tables of ftone, like vnto the former, and I wil write vpon them, the wordes which the tables had, which thou haft broken] for euen fo after Baptifme (by which original finne, is remitted with other finnes, if anie be comitted before) it pleafeth God to graunt againe, remiffion of actual finnes to the penitent, by an other Sacrament, called therfore

Leuit. 4.
v. 5. Ch.
13. v. 2.

The fecond table after fhipwrake. The fame was alfo prefigured by diuers Sacrifices for finne, and by fundrie wafhings, and cleanfings from leprofies, & other legal vncleannes, where alfo the iudgement, & minifterie of Prieftes was required, in figure of the power geuen to Priftes in the Law of Chrift, to remitte finnes, as his onlie Minifters in this behalf.

4. Likewife touching this point, the Auctor of Ecclefiafticus, admonifheth al men, of the neceffitie, both of medicine, & of phifition, as wel for the foule, as for the bodie, confidering that God hath orday-

Eccli. 38.
v. 1. 2.

ned them both [Honour the Phifition for neceffitie (faith he) for the Higheft hath created him. For al medicine is of God] And touching phifike for the

v. 9. 10.
11.

foule, he faith [Sonne in thyne infirmitie contemne not thyfelf; but pray our Lord, & he wil cure thee. Turne away from finne, and direct thy handes; and from al offence cleanfe thy hart. Geue fweetnes, and a memorial of fine floure, and make a fat oblation, and geue place to the Phifition. For our Lord created him] Where firft prefuppofing that the foule may fal into infirmitie of finne, the wifeman teacheth, that diuers thinges are required to the curing therof. Firft that a finner muft not defpare, but confide in God, faying [Contemne not thy felf, but (with hope) pray our Lord.] Secondly that he muft

[turne

Sidenotes:

The fecond tables of the tenne commandments were a figure of this Sacrament.

So were the old Sacrifices for finne, and the power of Prieftes figures of the fame Chriftian Sacrament.

As corporal medicine, fo alfo fpiritual was alwayes neceffarie.

Diuers thinges are required to cure finners.
1. Hope of remiffion.
2. repentance.

[turne away from finne, and direct his handes] to good workes. Thirdly purge his foule by confeffion,

3. Sacrifice, & prayer.
and Sacrifice [from al offence cleanfe thy hart: Geue fweetnes, a memorial of fine floure, and make a

4. Confeffion.
fatte oblation.] Fourtly, humble himfelf to the fpiritual Phifition [Geue place to the Phifition. For our Lord created him] ordayned him for the cure of

5. Alfo of fecrete finnes.
foules. Fiftly though the finnes be fecrete, they muft be reueled to the phifition [He that finneth in his   *v.* 25. sight, that made him (though it be fecrete from men) fhal fal into the handes of the Phifition] playnly teaching, that finners haue neede, both of fpiritual phifike, and Phifition: alfo for fecrete finnes. As therfore the firft medicine of finful foules, is the Sacrament of Baptifme, & the ordinarie phifirions, and minifters therof are Prieftes, and in cafe of neceffitie, al other men and wemen, for none can baptize themfelues: fo the fecond ordinarie medicine, to cure finners after Baptifme, is the Sacramen of Penance, wherof onlie Prieftes are the Minifters·

This Sacrament of Penance is moft clearly proued by expreffe wordes of the Gofpel.
5. The inftitution and neceffitie of which Sacrament, is fo clearly written by the Euangelift S. Iohn, with diuers circumftances, that it is a wonder, anie pretending to beleue Chrifts Gofpel, wil denie it. The facred wordes, touching Chrifts apparition to his Apoftles, his action, and fpeach, in the day of his Refurrection are thefe: [When it was late that day,   *Io.*:*n.* 20. the firft of the Sabbath, and the doores were fhutte,   19. 20. where the Difciples were gathered together, for   21. 22. feare of the Iewes: Iefus came and ftood in the mid-   23. des, and faith to them: Peace be to you. And when he had faid this, he fhewed them his handes, and fide. The Difciples therfore were glad, when they faw our Lord. He faid therfore to them againe: Peace be to you. As my Father hath fent me, I alfo doe fend you. When he had faid this, he breathed vpon them, and he faid to them: Receiue ye the

Holie

Holie Ghoſt: whoſe ſinners you ſhal forgeue, they
are forgeuen them: & whoſe you ſhal reteyne, they
are reteyned.] Let anie faithful perſon ſincerly conſider theſe few pointes in the Euangeliſts narration.
Firſt our Lord appearing vnto his Diſciples, as yet
not al of them beleuing, that he was riſen from
death: he not only ſaluted them, ſaying [Peace be
to you] but alſo to make them know, that it was
himſelf, & not a ſpirite; as they imagined [he ſhewed
them his handes & ſide.] Secondly when they were
fully aſſured, that he was riſen, and viſibly preſent
in his natural bodie amongſt them [and were glad]
then with the ſame ſalutation as before [he ſaid to
them againe : Peace be to you.] Thirdly, he added
this preface to that which he would now doe further vnto them, and to others, by their miniſterie,
ſaying : [As my Father hath ſent me, I alſo doe ſend
you.] Fourtly [when he had ſaid this, he breathed
vpon them.] Fiftly explaining his intention what
he meant, by this ceremonial breathing vpon them,
[he ſaid to them : Receiue ye the Holie Ghoſt.]
Sixtly he alſo expreſly ſignified, to what ſpecial vſe,
and purpoſe, he now gaue them the Holie Ghoſt,
ſaying [Whoſe ſinnes you ſhal forgeue, they are
forgeuen them, & whoſe you ſhal reteyne, they are
reteyned.] Seuently therfore you ſee, that Chriſt
our Lord by geuing his Apoſtles the Holie Ghoſt, in
this maner of act, and wordes, gaue them power &
auctoritie, as his Miniſters, ſent by him, to forgeue,
and to reteyne ſinnes. And therby it is moſt euident, that he made them his miniſterial Iudges, in
the court of conſcience, and ſpiritual tribunal, ſo to
abſolue, or not abſolue ſinners, from the guilt of
ſinnes, that their ſentence in earth, is ratified and
confirmed in heauen: Eightly in this diuine ordinance is further implied, what ſinners muſt neceſſarily doe on their part, to haue their ſinnes forgeuen,

Luc. 24.
v. 37. 39.
45. 16. 20.
&c.

Mat. 18.
v. 18.

Conſider wel
this ſacred
paſſage with
the circum-
ſtances of
Chriſts wor-
des & actions.

1.

2.

3.

4.
5.

6.

7.

8.

W   that

Not the peniten's but their Paſtors, are Iudges in the cauſe of remitting ſinnes.

that is, to be truly penitent, ſubmitting themſelues to Chriſts Prieſtes, as his appointed miniſterial Iudges, in this iudicial act, for remiſſion of their ſinnes. For otherwiſe their incapacitie hindereth the effect of abſolution, becauſe it is impoſſible, & implieth contradiction, to perſiſt in ſinne, and to be looſed from the ſame ſinne. Al Therfore that wil haue the benefite of this Sacrament, muſt firſt be made capable therof, by performing ſuch conditions, as are required of them : not being Iudges of their owne

And ſo it is a true Sacrament.

cauſe; but reparing to the Iudge, ordayned by Chriſt, with true repentance, Which not only conſiſteth in ſorow for ſinnes paſt, but alſo in ſincere declaration of the offences, that the Iudge may know the cauſe: and in their preparation of minde, to make what ſatiſfaction is required for their faultes: which are the three partes of penance. As we touched before, and ſhal further proue, and declare in ſeueral Articles folowing. Vnto which religious actes of the penitent, Prieſtlie abſolution, being adioyned, ſinnes are forgeuen, by this external Ceremonie, inſtituted by Chriſt, for this very end: and therfore the ſame is a proper and true Sacrament of the new Teſtament. And as the inſtrumental cauſe, worketh the effect of remiſſion of actual ſinnes, after Baptiſme, as ſhal alſo be further ſhewed, after the explication of the three propoſed partes of penance.

§. 1.

Artic. 35.

Contrition, or (*at leaſt*) *Attrition, is neceſſarily required, as the firſt part of Penance.*

ARTICLE 26.

What contrition is neceſſarie to be deſired by penitents.

Contrition, which is a vehement ſorow for hauing offended God, with loue of Gods honour, aboue al worldlie, and proper pleaſure, or commoditie, and with deteſtation of ſinne aboue al other euiles,

euiles, is neceſſarie to be deſired of al penitents. And in caſe Contrition be not thus perfect, at leaſt it is neceſſarie to haue actual Attrition : which is a true ſorow for ſinne committed, becauſe it is foule and deformed, and deſerueth puniſhment : & that, with a reſolute purpoſe neuer againe to committe mortal ſinne : and with intention to confeſſe : and make ſatisfaction, or ſuffer puniſhment, according as the Law of God requireth. For albeit God remitteth ſinnes, of his mere mercie, not for anie act, or condigne merite of ſinners; yet as he geueth his grace for the merites of Chriſts, which no other can condingly merite : ſo he alſo requireth right diſpoſition in the penitents, that they haue due ſorow for their ſinnes committed: which ſorow likewiſe procedeth from his gift of grace, ſtirring them vp to remorſe, and repentance, and ſo is a congruent diſpoſition to ſanctifying grace, as is clearly to be ſhewed by examples, and teſtimonies, both in the old and new Teſtament,

At leaſt actual attrition is neceſſarie with the Sacramēt,

2. Of Adam and Eue is already noted, that they, after their ſinne, were aſhamed, and feared God, were ſorie for their tranſgreſſion of Gods cōmandment. Contrariwiſe Cain wanting due ſorow, & repentance, went out from the face of our Lord, & ranne into more ſinne. Alſo innumerable other ſinners, both before & after the floud, for their ſinnes, wanting repentance periſhed: and true penitents were pardoned, and reconciled to God. For this cauſe Ioſeph ſpake to his bretheren [as it were to ſtrangers, ſomewhat roughly ; & put them in priſon three dayes] dealing hardly with them for ſome time, not for reuenge of the iniurie done to himſelf, but to bring them into conſideration of their former faultes, and ſo to neceſſarie ſorow, or contrition for the ſame : without which, although iniuries be remitted by men : yet the offenders are not abſolued

Art. 25.
§. 2.
Gen. 3.
v. 10.
Ch. 4. v.
13, 16.

Gen. 42.
v. 17.
Ch. 44. v.
2. 3. &c.

True penitents obtaine remiſſion of ſinnes.

Impenitents fal further into ſinnes.

Ioſephs pietie & prudence to bring his bretheren to true repentance,

W 2 before

God afflicted his people to make them more penitent for their sinnes.

before God. After some punishment of the people of Israel in the desert, for their abominable Idolatrie, worshipping the image of a calfe for God, they were also threatned, to be left without Gods protection, and assistance; wherby they were brought to more fruitful repentance, and so God did not leaue them, but stil protected them as before. Yet wrought not so great miracles til al those were dead, which had so greuously sinned in idolatrie, and manie murmurations [I wil not goe vp with thee (sayd God) because thou art a stiffenecked people, lest perhaps I destroy thee in the way. And the people hearing this very il saying, mourned: and no man put on his ornaments after the custome.] In like maner when this people possessed the promised land of Chanaan, they very often (manie of them) declined from God, fel to Idolatrie, were afflicted, then repented, and were releeued. But alwayes by true repentance, as Moyses had premonished, saying [when thou shalt seeke the Lord thy God, thou shalt finde him. Yet so , if thou seeke him with al thy hart, & al tribulation of thy soule.]

Exod. 32. *v.* 4 5. 6. *v.* 27. 28.

Ch. 33. *v.* 3. 4. 5. *Nu.* 14. *v.* 28. *Ch.* 26. *v.* 64.

Iudic. 4. *v.* 2. 3. &c.

Deut. 4. *v.* 29.

Gods faithful seruants some times sinned & repented.

King Dauid by word and example inuiteth sinners to repentance.

3. Also the better sorte, and more faithful seruants of God, sometimes offended : & by Gods new grace repenting, sorowfully mourned. King Dauid fel into some enormious crimes, for which he much lamented. As appeareth in diuers of his Psalmes, & in other places [Dauids hart strooke him, after the people was numbred, & he said to our Lord : I haue sinned very much in this fact : but I pray thee Lord to transferre the iniquitie of thy seruant: because I haue done exceding foolishly.] Yet wat this sinne but a simple vanitie. For al his sinnes (in general, and particular) this true penitent mourned , & cried often to God for mercie [Heare me ô Lord (said he) because al my bones be trubled. And my soule is trubled exceedingly , I am afflicted , & am humbled exceedingly.

2. *Reg.* 24. *v.* 10. 2. *Reg.* 12. *v.* 4. 9. 13. 14. 15. &c.

Psal. 6. *v.* 3. 4.

excedingly. I rored for the groning of my hart. Lord

Pf. 37. *v.* before thee is al my defire : and my groning is not

9. 10. 11. hid from thee. My hart is trubled, my ftrength hath

Pfal. 50. forfaken me: and the light of myne eyes is not with

v. 3. 10. me. Haue mercie on me ô God, To my hearing thou

11. 19. fhalt geue ioy, and gladnes, and the bones humbled

Pfal. 118. fhal reioyce. A Sacrifice to God is an afflicted fpirite

v. 136. a contrite and humbled hart, ô God thou wilt not

Pfal. 129. defpife. Myne eyes haue gufhed forth iffues of wa-

v. 2. ters: becaufe they haue not kept thy Law. From

Pfal. 142. the depthes I haue cried to thee ô Lord: Lord heare

v. 4. my voice. My fpirite is in anguifh vpon me, within

me my hart is trubled.] The fruite of which hartie

compunction for finne, the fame Royal Prophete

Pfal. 33. teftifieth, faying [Our Lord is nigh to them that

v. 19. are of a contrite hart: and the humble of fptrite he

Pro. 28. wil faue.] Salomon alfo faith [Bleffed is the man,

v. 14. that is alwayes fearful ; but he that is of an obftinate

Ecclef. 7. minde fhal fal into euil. The hart of wifemen, where

v. 5. fadnes is : & the hart of fooles where mirth.] Other

Ifa. 31. Prophetes inculcate the fame admonitiôs [Returne

v. 6. as you reuolted, depely (faith Ifaias) ô children of

Ifrael, Conuert, and doe penance from al your ini-

Ezec. 18. quities (faith Ezechiel) and iniquitie fhal not be a

v. 30. ruine to you. You fhal remember your wayes, and

Ch. 20. al your wicked deedes, in which you are polluted :

v. 43. and you fhal miflike your felues, in your one fight :

in al your malice, which you haue done.] Ioel crieth

Ioel. 2. to al finners [Rent your hartes, and not your gar-

v. 13. ments : and turne to the Lord your God.]

> Salomon and
> other Prophe-
> tes exhorte
> alfo to repen-
> tance.

4.   Chrift our Sauiour, vpon occafion of temporal

affliction, which fel on certaine Galileans, by the

crueltie of Pilate : admonifhed al the Iewes, to hartie

Luc. 13. and perfect repentance, faying [Vnles you haue

v. 2. 3. 5. penance, you fhal al likewife perifh] S. Peter moft

feuerely admonifhed the Iewes, of their enormious,

finne, in crucifying our Lord, to moue them to

> Our Sauiour
> admonifheth
> al finners to
> repent.

W 3   hartie

hartie forow, for the fame: and perceiuing manie
to be compunct in hart required yet more declara-　*Act.* 2.*v.*
tion therof, faying to them [Doe penance] and this　23.
alfo before Baptifme: much more is hartie forow　*v.* 37.38.
neceffarie in the Sacrament of Penance. S. Paul of
purpofe, writte in fuch maner to the Corinthians,　2. *Cor.* 7.
as might bring them into forow for their faultes, &　*v.* 8. 9.10.
when his purpofe had effect, he acknowleged the　11.
fame, and reioiced therin, faying in his other Epiftle
to them : [Although I made you forie in an Epiftle,
it repenteth me not, and albeit, it repented me; feing
that the fame Epiftle (although but for a time) did
make you forie. Now I am glad : not becaufe you
were made forie, but becaufe you were made forie
to penance. For you were made forie according to
God, that in nothing you fhould fuffer detriment
by vs. For the forow that is according to God, worketh penance vnto faluation, that is ftable: but the
forow of the world worketh death. For behold
this very thing, that you were made forie, according to God, how great carefulnes it worketh in
you: yea defence, yea indignation, yea feare, yea
defire, yea emulation, yea reuenge.] Obferue here
manie particular good effectes of forow according
to God: Carefulnes, not to finne againe : defence,
againft new tentations : indignation, againft our
felues for hauing yelded to tentatiós: feare, of lofing
Gods grace: defire, to perfeuere in grace : emulation,
hatred of finne: yea reuenge, by voluntarie punifhment, and penance for finne committed. The gene-
ral and ful effect is remiffion of finnes, & faluation,　*Art.* 27.
if it be perfect contrition, which yet includeth purpofe to confeffe: for fo Chrifts ordinance requireth.
And if the penitents forow be vnperfect: which is
Attrition, the fame with the Sacrament, worketh　*v.* 10.
remiffion of finnes, & as the Apoftle fpeaketh [Penance vnto faluation] As is further to be declared in
the Articles folowing.　*Con-*

S. Peter ex-
horted peni-
tents to be
more forow-
ful for their
finnes.

S. Paul did
wiſingly make
offenders pen-
fiue.

Difference of
Godlie, and
worldlie fo-
row.

Special fruites
of contrition,
and forow for
finnes,

Confession of al mortal sinnes, is necessarie for remission therof.

ARTICLE. 27.

GReater and lesse sinnes are distinguished, by the iudgement of most men, though certaine Stoical Philosophers singularly held opinion, that al transgressing from the right rule of reason, should be of equal enormitie; which paradoxical doctrine, al other Philosophers reiected. And the general Lawes of al Nations doe diuersly punish diuers offences; which were not iust, if al faultes were equal. Neuerthelesse certaine Sectaries of this time called Anabaptistes, incline much to the errour of the old Stoikes. And al Protestants generally hold, that al sinnes are mortal: and al sinners guiltie of eternal damnation, by Gods Law, & diuine Iustice.

Mat. 5. v. 23.
1. Cor. 3.
v. 12. 13.
15.
Iac. 1. v.
13. 14.
Ch. 3. v. 3.
4. 7. 8.

Directly against our Sauiours owne doctrine, teaching that some are guiltie of hel fire; others of lesse punishment [Whosoeuer (saith our Lord) is angrie with his brother, shal be in danger of iudgement. And whosoeuer shal say to his brother, Raca; shal be in danger of a councel. And whosoeuer shal say: Thou foole; shal be guiltie of the hel of fire.] By which, and other textes of holie Scriptures it is euident that al sinnes doe not bring the guilte of eternal death; but such as are more greuous, doe spiritually kil the soule, which are therfore called

Rom. 6. v. 23.

mortal: of which S. Paul saith] the stipends of sinne is death.] These necessarily require remission in this world, & so perteine to the iudicial power geuen to the Apostles, to be practised in this Sacrament of Penance. And therfore must be made knowen to the Iudge, who otherwise can not geue iuridical sentence, in the cause to him vnknowen.

2. That

Marginal notes:

Most Philosophers, and Lawes of al nations doe iudge that some sinnes are greater, others lesse, against the Stoikes, and Sectaries of this time.

Al sinnes are not mortal by Chrisis doctrine.

Mortal sinnes must necessarily be confessed.

Conueniencie
hereof is pro-
ued by the old
Testament,
The necessitie
by Chrifts
Inftitution.

2.　That this is moft conuenient, is manifeft by examples, and teftimonies in the old Teftament; from
whence we fhal firft recite fome fpecial textes, and
then proue that it is neceffarie by Chrifts Inftitution.
For this purpofe we may againe remember, that
euen God himfelf, who moft perfectly knoweth al
fecreetes, required the expreffe confeffion of Adam, *Gen.* 3. v.
and Eue feuerally, that they had eaten of the tree, 11. 12. 13.
which was forbidden them. God demanded alfo
of Cain [Where is Abel thy brother] but he an- *Ch.* 4. v. 9.
fwering peruerfly, remayned in his finne [a rogue 12. 16.
and vagabond vpon the earth, & went forth from
Examples be-
fore Chrift.
the face of our Lord.] In the written Law it was *Leuit.* 4.
commanded, to offer fpecial Sacrifices, for fpecial v. 2. 3.
finnes, yea for offences of omiffion, fo that by the *Ch.* 5. v.
fpecial Sacrifices, it appeared what the faultes were. 1. 6. *Ch.*
Neither thus only, but more expreffly the fame Law 7. v. 27.
faith [Man, or woman, when they fhal doe anie of *Num.* 5.
al the finnes, that are wont to chance to men, and v. 6. 7.
by negligence haue tranfgreffed the commandment
of the Lord, and haue offended, they fhal confeffe
their finne.] King Dauid not only acknowleged
the finnes, wherwith he was iuftly charged by the
Prophet Natham ; but alfo his other finne of vainly 2. *Reg.* 2t.
numbering the people, fo fowne as he was ftrooken v. 13. *Ch.*
with remorfe for it, in his hart, confeffing & faying 24. v. 10.
[I haue finned very much, in this fact : I haue done
exceding foolifhly.] Touching al his finnes, wherof
he knew himfelf guiltie he profeffed plainly, that he
would confeffe them, faying [I wil declare myne *Pfal.* 37.
iniquitie.] And touching finnes which he remem- v. 19.
bred not, or knew not in himfelf, but only fufpected,
he prayed, faying [Who vnderftandeth al finnes ? *Pfal.* 18. v.
from my fecrete finnes cleanfe me ô Lord, & from 13. 14.
other mens, fpare thy feruant. The finnes of my *Pfal.* 24.
youth, and myne ignorances, doe not remember ô v. 7.
Lord.] The neceffitie alfo of confeffing finnes, Salomon

Prou. 28.
v. 13.

mon teacheth, saying [He that hideth his wicked deedes, shal not be directed : but he that shal confesse and shal forsake them, shal obtayne mercie.] Those sinners that came to S. Iohn Baptist, wel obserued this rule of confession, though he had not Iurisdictiõ to absolue, the same penitents, by vertue of a Sacrament. For they did not only acknowlege themselues sinners, or in general, that they had manie wayes sinned, as Protestants doe in the beginning of their common prayer : but also confessed their sinnes, the

Mat. 3.
v. 5. 6.

Euangelist saying [They went forth to him ; & were baptized of him, in Iordan, confessing their sinnes.] And so did penitents at Ephesus, as it appeareth, also before they were baptized : of whom S. Luke writeth thus [Manie of them that beleued (hauing seene

Act. 19.
v. 18.

a miracle) came confessing, and declaring their deedes.] Yet none of these were so much obliged to declare the estate of their conscience (by confessing their former deedes, and actions) as Christians are, which committe mortal sinnes, after Baptisme.

Heb. 6.
v. 6.

whose ingratitude [as it were crucifying againe to themselues the Sonne of God, and making him a mockerie] must needes be chasticed, and their later heynous sinnes, cured by more humiliation, of the relapsed sinners, in their reconciliation to God, by an other Sacrament of Penance, then was required in their first regeneration by the Sacrament of Baptisme: which first Sacrament, as the same Apostle

Ibidem.
v. 4.

S. Paul teacheth, can not possibly be iterated.

3. Wherfore our B. Redemer, and Sauiour, whose

Psal. 144.
v 9.
Isa. 40.
v. 13.
Mat. 18.
v. 22.

[mercie is aboue al his workes : & whose wisdome, and iustice inscrutable] willing stil to saue sinners, hath reserued further grace, that not once only by Baptisme [nor only seuen times, but seuentie times seuen times] that is how often soeuer a sinner is truly penitent, he may be reconciled to him, & haue againe remission of his sinnes. [For he is our perpe-

Other examples since Christ of confession before Baptisme, doe shew that it is much more necessarie after Baptisme.

Christ stil reserueth grace for remission of al sinnes to penitents,

X   tual]

tual Aduocate, as S. Iohn witnesseth, saying to al
Christians [My litle children, these thinges I write 1. Ioá. 2.
to you, that you sinne not. But and if anie man shal *v*. 1. 2.
sinne, we haue an Aduocate with the Father. Iesus
Christ the iust: and he is the propiciation for our sinnes: and not for ours only, but also for the whole
worlds] sinnes. Yet doth not our merciful iust Aduocate, otherwise plead for our pardon, but by the
ordinarie meanes, which himself hath ordained:
that in the Sacrament of Penance, greuous sinners
must humbly confesse al their mortal sinnes, to the
Iudge. And as this obligation is iustly necessarie, so

Manie rea-
sons why
penitents
confesse al
their mortal
sinnes.
1.
2.
3.
4.

is it also very profitable for diuers good respectes,
as wel for right disposition in penitents, to receiue
remission of their sinnes: as for terrour, to make
them more warie in their actions, considering the
bond of confession, if they offend againe mortally.
It diminisheth also some part of the due satiffaction, by how much it is made with more humilitie,
and sorow for hauing offended Gods goodnes. And
finally it is meritorious of more glorie, in eternal
life. So vnspekable is Christs prouidence in ioyning
manie benefites together. Al such sinners therfore
must (if they wil be saued.) make vertue of this necessitie; wherinto they haue brought themselues.
For seing they are fallen into mortal infirmitie, in
their soules, if they wil liue againe spiritually, and
so liue for euer, they must vse the necessarie designed medicine, that is they must repayre to the spiritual Phisition, designed by Christ, who only can
cure sinnes: and hath ordained this meanes and
remedie, that for remission therof, the guiltie persons must come to the spiritual court, doing there,
that which to them perteineth. If they beleue
Christs wordes before recited, saying to his Apostles [whose sinnes you shal forgeue, they shal be Ioa. 2*0*.
forgeuen them: and whose you shal reteyne, they *v*. 23.

are

are reteyned] Much more, if they obserue alſo, and
duly conſider the reſt of his wordes, and actions at
the ſame time (as is likewiſe recited) it is cleare, that
Chriſt made the Apoſtles his miniſterial Iudges, to
forgeue, or to reteyne ſinnes. And it is no leſſe certaine, that our Sauiour, ordained this meanes: for
remiſſion of ſinnes, for his faithful people, euen til
the end of this world: and therfore gaue this iudicial power to others : which ſhould ſuccede the A-
poſtles: & to al thoſe, whom they, & their Succeſſors
ſhould impert the ſame power, and iuriſdiction, ſo
farre as it ſhould be enlarged or limitted.

3. And thus much being clearly ſhewed by the holie
Scripture, and being manifeſt, both by light of reaſon, and by practiſe alſo of al nations, that al Iudges
muſt firſt know the cauſe which they are to iudge,
before they can rightly geue ſentence (either abſolue
or puniſh) It is therfore moſt certaine that the penitent which deſireth remiſſion of his mortal ſinnes, through Chriſts mercie, and redemption, muſt
repayre to ſome Prieſt auctoriſed by Chriſts ordinance, for this purpoſe, a ſpiritual Iudge : and by plaine,
and ſyncere confeſſion of al his mortal ſinnes, declare his conſcience, ſo wel as he morally can, and
is able. For God requireth mans good wil, & diligence ſuch at leaſt, as the penitent hinſelf, would
reaſonably require of his ſeruant, or freind, in ac-
counts for temporal goodes, and other affayres of
this world. And he that wil not doe thus much, for
the eternal ſaluation of his ſoule, is neither worthie
nor capable of remiſſion of his ſinnes. He may perhaps ſay, that he is ſorie for his ſinnes, but aſſuredly
he is not ſo ſorie as he ought to be, who wil not in
this life confeſſe his great ſinnes to one onlie Prieſt,
with al poſſible ſecreſie, and ſecuritie, which ſhal
otherwiſe be layed open vnto al Angels, and men,
and diuels, in the general day of Iudgement to his

This ordinan-
ce continueth
to the end of
this world.

And therfore
who ſoeuer
wil haue re-
miſſion of
mortal ſinne,
muſt by con-
feſſion declare
the ſame ſinne
to the ſpiritual
Iudge.

Mortal ſinnes
not remitted
in this life
ſhal be reuea-
led in the day
of Iudgement,

X 2 euer-

to the eternal confuſion of the wicked.

euerlaſting confuſion, beſides his other eternal torments. [The worke of euerie one ſhal be manifeſt: 1. *Cor.* 3. for the day of our Lord wil declare, becauſe it ſhal *v.* 13. *Ch.* be reuealed in fire.]   4. *v.* 5.

Venial ſinnes are ſufficient, & conuenient mater of Sacramental Confeſsion. Though alſo remiſsible otherwiſe.

ARTICLE 28.

Some ſinnes are venial, & not mortal.

FOr declaration of this Article, it is firſt to be obſerued, that ſome ſinnes are venial, not mortal. that is, not deſeruing eternal death; becauſe they doe not depriue ſinners of iuſtice, nor make them enimies to God, nor ſlaues of the diuel. Of which forte of ſinners Salomon ſaith, that [Seuen times *Prou.* 24. (that is often times) ſhal the iuſt fal, and riſe againe] *v.* 16. In that the iuſt falleth, he committeth ſome ſinne, yet committeih not mortal ſinne, for then he ſhould loſe grace, and iuſtice: but remaineth the childe of God, riſeth againe, and is eaſyly pardoned. [But the *Ibidem.* impious ſhal fal into euil] not eaſyly riſe againe, but more commonly, falleth into more ſinne: becauſe by mortal ſinne he loſeth iuſtice, & becometh impious. Chriſt our Lord (whoſe wordes touching §. 1. this point, are recited in the precedent Article) plainly diſtinguiſheth ſmal and great ſinnes, by the *Mat.* 5. diuerſitie of puniſhments due vnto them. He that is *v.* 23. angrie (without iuſt cauſe, for ſome angre is no *Pſal.* 4. ſinne) is to be iudged, & puniſhed. He that by ſome *v.* 5. obſcure word (as Raca) vttereth his vniuſt angre, is in danger of a councel, to decide what puniſhmēt is to be inflicted for his ſinne. But he that contumeliouſly calleth his brother a foole: is guiltie of hel fire. Which clearly ſheweth that not al ſinnes, but only onlygreat finnes, deferue eternal punifhment in hel.

See Art.
13. §. 6.

S. Iames alfo teacheth that al concupifcence is not finne, but that only, which conceiueth, to witte, which getteth confent of the mind [bringeth forth

Iac. 1. v.
14. 15.

finne. But finne when it is confummate, ingendreth death] manifeftly diftinguifhing, that fome finne is deadlie, fome not. Likewife S. Iohn, not doubting to account himfelf, and other holie perfons, to haue focietie with God, & that they walked in the light:

1. Io. 1. v.
2. 7.
v. 8.

yet faith [If we fhal fay that we haue no finne, we feduce our felues, and the truth is not in vs.] Which holie Scriptures, and manie others euidently proue, that al finnes are not mortal, but fome of an other kinde: called venial.

2. Now for remiffion of venial finnes, although there be manie other meanes, of cooperating with Gods grace to this effect; as prayer, fafting, almes, a Bifhops bleffing, taking holie water, and euerie feruent act of charitie, with repentance, for the finnes committed, and purpofe not to committe them againe: yet the cheefeft, and moft effectual meanes, is by Sacramental Confeffion. For feing, this Sacrament of Penance, is directly inftituted for remiffion of finnes, committed after Baptifme, and feeing, it wafheth the foule from mortal, and greateft crimes, much more it cleanfeth thofe penitents, which confeffe alfo venial, & leffe offences, from which they are facramentally abfolued, when they are declared, & fubiected to the fpiritual Iudge, although the fame penitents, be formerly free from al mortal finne. And therfore it is very conuenient, that faithful penitents confeffe fuch leffe faultes: as wel for more fecuritie, left perhaps they be vnwiting guiltie of fome fecrete mortal finne, to themfelues vnknowen, or forgotten, which in fuch cafe is implied in confeffion; as alfo for more fatiffaction, of the temporal debt of punifhment, for al finnes, at

Venial finnes are remitted by diuers means.

But the cheefeft way is by Sacramental Confeffion.

Reafons why confeffion of venial finnes is conuenient, though it be not neceffarie.

1.
2.

the

3.

4.

5.

6.

the same time or formerly remitted: especially also for obteyning sacramental grace to resist future tentations: and for more cleansing of the soule from al spotte: reliques of sinnes, and euil habites: and for better correcting of imperfections: because [nothing polluted (nor imperfection) shal enter into the kingdom of glorie] but must be first purged. & corrected [that Christ may present to himself a glorious Church, not hauing spotte, or wrinkle, or anie such thing, but that it may be holie, & vnspotted] Which ordinarie practise of deuout Catholiques, much frequenting this wholsome Sacrament, hauing no others, but venial sinnes to confesse, being a special worke of counsel, without precept, or necessitie, is clearly approued, and commended, by the like pious examples, & exhortations recorded in holie Scriptures.

Apoc. 21.
v. 27.

Ephes. 5.
v. 27.

Holie Prophetes by example & doctrine admonish al to wash away the smalest sinnes.

3.   Isaias a most holie Prophete said: [Woe is me because I haue held my peace, because I am a man of polluted lippes] Ieremie, though sanctified in his mothers wombe, yet cried [A a a, ô Lord God: Behold I can not speake, because I am a childe.] Holie Dauid, after that his more greuous sinnes were remitted, yet prayed [wash me more amply from myne iniquitie, & cleanse me from my sinne.] The same Royal Prophete denounceth them [Blessed, that shal dash the little children of wicked Babylon, against the rocke.] Morally signifying that it is a blessed good thing, to kil lesse sinnes, & to mortifie passionate il motions in themselues, by often confession, and renouation of good purpose, to amend al lesse faultes, therby to grow more perfect [because account must be rendered for euerie idle word in the day of Iudgement.

If. 6. *v.* 5.

Iere. 1.
v. 6.
Psal. 50.
v. 4.

Psal. 136.
v. 9.

Mat. 12.
v. 36.

The Apostles doe the same.

4.   But if we iudge ourselues, we shal not be iudged] saith S. Paul. And S. Iames sayth, that [In manie thinges we offend al. If anie man offend not in

1. Cor. 11.
v. 31.

word:

Iac. 3. v.
2. Ch. 5.
v. 16.

word : this is a perfect man.] Againe where he exhorteth [to confesse our sinnes, one to an other] either he admonisheth to confesse sacramentally, which is very probable, or if he iudgeth it profitable to acknowlege sinnes, one freuid to another, without Sacrament, much more it profiteth, by the vertue of the Sacrament. S. Iohn likewise aduiseth, al euen such as haue societie with God (and consequently are free from mortal sinnes) to confesse their sinnes, (to witte such sinnes, as consist with iustice, saying of him self, and of others, of the same holie societie,

1. Io. 1.
v. 3. 8. 9.

[If we shal say that we haue no sinne, we seduce our selues, and the truth not in vs. If we confesse our sinnes, God is faithful and iust, for to forgeue vs our sinnes, and to cleanse vs from al iniquitie.]

Secresie of Sacramental confession is necessarie, by the Law of God, & of nature.

ARTICLE. 29.

Sap. 8. v.
7. Ch. 15.
v. 1.

WIsdome increated (Christ Iesus the Sonne of God, and Sonne of man) reaching from end to end, disposing al thinges swetely] amongst his other diuine ordinances, did so institute the holie Sacrament of Penance, that albeit penitents are bond, for the remission of mortal sinnes, committed after Baptisme, to confesse the same to some Priest, which hath auctoritie to absolue them, yet are not anie penitents further bond, to confesse secrete sinnes, then secretely: in the eare of their ghostlie father, who is most strictly bond, by the Law of God, and of nature, and vnder most seuere censures also of the Church, for euer to conceale the same : and in no case whatsoeuer, to reueale anie thing heard vnder the sacred seale of Sacramental Confession. For that such reuealing is vtterly vnlawful, & contrarie to diuers necessarie vertues. 2. The

margin: It sufficeth by Christs ordinance, and is most conuenient to confesse secrete sinnes, secretly.

Reuealing of
Sacramental
Confeſſion
were the vio-
lation of ma-
nie vertues.

Fidelitie.

Iuſtice,

Charitie.

Religion.

2. The vertue of Fidelitie, or truſt, requireth to kepe ſecrete what ſoeuer is told, and receiued in ſecrete. For [he that is faithful (ſaith Salomon in his Prouer- *Prou. 11.* bes) concealeth the thing committed of his freind.] *v. 13.* As contrariwiſe [He walketh fraudulently that re- *Ibidem.* uealeth ſecretes.] And this is ſpokē of ciuil humane conuerſation grounded in the Law of nature : and here confirmed by Diuine Scripture , which is a moſt ſufficient obligation, if there were no other, to kepe al thinges ſecrete, which are only knowen by Sacramental Confeſſion. Detraction alſo is a very deteſtable ſinne, againſt the moral vertue of Iuſtice, and therfore iuſtly hated of al good men, worthily condemned by the Royal Prophete, ſaying [Him *Pſal. 11.* that ſecretly detracteth from his neighbour , did I *v. 5.* perſecute.] The Law expreſly forbiddeth calum- niation, al kind of vnlawful defamation, or ſclander ſaying [Thou ſhalt not calumniate thy neighbour.] *Leuit. 19.* Moreouer, reuealing of Confeſſion ſhould not only *v. 13.* diminiſh the fame of the penitent, but alſo would ſcandalize manie , & be occaſion of their perſiſting in ſinne, by hindering them from Sacramental Con- feſſiin, if they were not ſecure of ſecreſie : al which ſcandals are againſt the Theological vertue of Cha- ritie. And therfore [woe to that man, by whom the *Mat. 18.* ſcandal cometh : It were better for him (ſaith our *v. 6.7.* Sauiour) that a milne ſtone were hanged about *Mar. 9.* his necke, and he were drowned in the ſea.] And *v. 42.* yet is the vertue of Religion a greater bond. For he that ſhould reueale that, which he heard in Con- feſſion, beſides wicked fraud, deteſtable detraction, iniuſt defamation, and damnable ſcandal; ſhould alſo committe great ſacrilege, by abuſing the holie Sacrament, violating the ſacred ſeale therof. In re- gard therfore of al theſe neceſſarie great vertues. Fidelitie. Iuſtice, Charitie, and Religion, no Prieſt can lawfully, for anie cauſe ; nor in anie caſe, of

feare,

feare of death, or of manie mens deathes, in danger of anie mifcheefe, or imminent ruine, of greateſt perſons, or whole kingdomes, detect anie thing, which he hath heard in Sacramental Confeſſion.

3. Which Chriſtian doctrine is yet further con-firmed by Gods ſpecial promiſe, made to al true penitentes, ſaying by his Prophete Dauid [Bleſſed are they whoſe ſinnes be couered] And more clear-ly by his Prophete Ezechiel [If the impious ſhal doe penance, from al his ſinnes which he hath wrought and ſhal kepe al my precepts, and doe iudgement, & iuſtice, liuing he ſhal liue, and ſhal not dye. Al his iniquities, which he hath wrought, *I wil not remember them*: in his iuſtice, which he heth wrought, he ſhal liue.] Seing then, God himſelf ſaith, that he wil not remember a penitents former ſinnes, ſignifying that after due repentance, they are no longer ſinnes, it is clearly Gods wil, that no man wholoeuer, ſhal re-ueale that which he knoweth only, as he is Gods miniſter, and not as a mortal, and priuate, or pub-lique perſon of the temporal common wealth, but [The diſpenſer of the Myſteries, of God (ſaith the Apoſtle, adding withal) Here now is required, among the diſpenſers, that a man be fond faithful.] Surely in nothing, wel immaginable, can religious fidelitie, or chriſtian iuſtice, and charitie be more requiſite, then in this holie Sacrament, wheron ſo generally dependeth the eternal ſaluation of ſoules. For if this ſecreſie were not ſtrictly enioyned, ma-nie would perhaps thinke, that Chriſts Law were not [a ſwete yoke, and light burden] & would not therupon ſubmitte themſelues vnto it: which yet they ought, though it were harder. For although this prouiſion of ſecreſie were not ordayned, yet could they not with anie reaſon pretend, ſuch an excuſe. For, that ſinners muſt confeſſe their mortal ſinnes, for remiſſion therof, is not to be imputed to the

Pſal. 31. *v.* 1.

Ezech. 18. *v.* 21. 22.

1. *Cor.* 4. *v.* 1. 2.

Mat. 11. *v.* 30.

This doctrine is further con-firened by Gods promiſe.

And by S. Pauls doc-trine.

And by rea-ſon,

If ſecreſie were not or-dayned, yet Chriſts yoke

Y

were not hard but seing it is ordayned, his yoke is very swete. the Law of Chriſt, which is ful of al mercie, but to their owne wilfulnes, in falling into ſuch ſinnes. But the right & beſt way to be free from this bond, or burden of Confeſſion, is not to fal into mortal ſinne, for then ſhal you not haue anie neceſsitie, to confeſſe at al. But if you wil confeſſe venial ſinnes, for the cauſes before mentioned (wherto none is *Art.* 28. bond) or if you fal into mortal, then euerlaſtingly §. 2. thanke God, who of his milde mercie admitteth of ſecrete Confeſſion, and ſo ſtrictly bindeth his Miniſter to kepe it moſt ſecrete. Yea that Prieſt, which ſhould be ſo wicked (which to this day, hath not bene heard, that euer anie did) but if anie ſhould breake

If a Prieſt ſhould breake this ſacred ſeale he were therby made alſo infamous and not to be credited, Gods owne ſeale, beſides his guilt of eternal damnation, degradation from his Prieſtlie function, and other ſeuere puniſhment, he ſhould alſo be depriued of al credite: ſo that no Chriſtian Law can take notice by ſuch a witnes: nor anie honeſt perſon is to beleue, that thing to be true, which ſo vnfaithfully, vniuſtly, vncharitably, and ſacrilegiouſly ſhould be reported.

Satisfaction for the guilt of ſinne, & for eternal paine, is made by Chriſt only.

ARTICLE 30.

No other man, nor anie creature, but onlie Chriſt, can ſatiſfie Gods iuſtice for the guilt of ſinne. DEbt is not payed, without equiualent recompence rendered, by or for the debter, and receiued by the creditor. Mans debt incurred by ſinne in reſpect of Gods infinite Maieſtie therwith offended, is alſo infinite: and not only mans power, but al power alſo of mere creatures, is finite, and limited, & therfore vnable by anie poſsible meanes, to ſatiſfie Diuine Iuſtice, for the treſpaſſe of tranſgreſsing his commandment. Which inſufficiencie of al men, to ſatiſfie for their ſinnes, is often teſtified in holie in holie Scriptures, together with the necessitie of a sufficient Redemer, to pay this debt, and to ransome mankinde, being generally captiue in sinne, and iustly subiect to eternal death. This merciful potent Redemer is Iesus Christ the Sonne of God, and Sonne of man, who in Diuine Person, assuming humane nature, hath by his temporal death, payed the price of al mens redemptiõ, euen in rigour of iustice, which no other man, Angel, nor other creature, could possibly haue payed. As is before declared in other Articles. Wherunto we may here adde, a few other sacred textes, for better satisfaction to our Aduersaries, who vntruly charge vs, to derogate from Christs Redemption, in that we also beleue that penitents, through Christs grace so enabling them, can and must pay, or suffer temporal punishment, after that by Christ the sinne is remitted, and the eternal paine changed into temporal.

Part. 1.
Art. 15.
Part. 2.
Art. 7.

2   Concerning therfore the former point, of mans insufficiencie, to redeme himself, and necessitie of our Redemption by Christ: The Royal Psalmist, prophecying Christs Incarnation, for the redemption of mankinde, first sheweth the insufficiencie of al others, saying [There is not that doth good, no not one. Our Lord hath looked forth from heauen, vpon the children of men, to see if there be anie that vnderstandeth, and seeketh after God. Al haue declined, they are al become vnprofitable together, there is not, that doth good, no not one.] In this desolate case, he saw in prophetical spirite, that God would send a Redemer, and that through his grace some were made iust: for he saith a litle after, [Our Lord is in the iust generation: you (that are wicked) haue confounded the counsel of the poore man: because our Lord is his hope.] And then praying, that the Redemer wil come, saith [Who wil geue from Sion the saluation of Israel?] And as answering

Psal. 13.
v. 1. 2. 3.

v. 6.

v. 7.

Mans insufficientie, & the necessitie of a potent Redemer is proued by holie Scriptures,
By the Psalmist.

Y 2   answering

answering to his pious desire, addeth [When our
Lord shal haue turned away the captiuitie of h's
people, Iacob shal reioyce, and Israel shal be glad.]
Thus the Royal Prophete in this and manie other
Psalmes, which are wholly of Christ, testifieth th's
Catholique doctrine. Isaias likewise declareth the
insufficiencie of mans workes, without our Redemer, saying [There is none that doth inuocate iustice,
neither is there anie, that iudgeth truly: but they
trust in thinges of nothing, and speake vanities] A
litle after [Their webbes shal not be for clothing,
neither shal they be couered with their workes:
their workes are vnprofitable workes:& the worke
of iniquitie is in their handes.] So the Holie Prophete lamented, for that most mens workes were
wicked: and none able to auert Gods wrath, nor to
satisfie for sinnes. Then prophecieth thus of Christ.
[And our Lord saw, that there is not a man; and he
was astonied, because there is none to oppose himself: and his owne arme saued to himself, and his
iustice it self confirmed him. He is clothed with
iustice, as with a brestplate; and as an helmete of
saluation on his head, he is clothed with garments
of reuenge: & is couered, as with a mantel of zele.]
The same Prophete describing the greuousnes of
our Lords Passio, plainly sheweth that he only could
satisfie the infinite debt, for mans sinne, saying [He
surely hath borne our iniquities: and our sorowes
he hath caried: and we haue thought him; as it were
a leper, and striken of God, and humbled. But he
was wounded for our iniquities, he was broken for
our sinnes: the discipline of our peace vpou him, and
with the waile of his stripe, we are healed. Al we
haue strayed, as sheepe, euerie one hath declined
into his owne way: and our Lord hath put vpon
him, the iniquitie of al vs. He was offered, because
himself would.] Thus the Prophete. And the very
same

By Isaias.

Margin notes:
Ibid.
Psal. 2. 8.
16. 20.
&c.
Isa. 59. v.
4.
v. 6.
v. 16.
v. 17.
Ch. 53. v.
4. 5. 6. 7.

same our Lord speaketh in his owne Person, by the
same Prophete, saying [I haue troden the preſſe
alone: and of the Gentiles there is not a man with
me: I haue troden them in my furie, and haue troden them downe in my wrath: and their bloud is
ſprinckled vpon my garments: and I haue ſtayned
al my rayment. For the day of reuenge (againſt ſinne) is in my hart: the yeare of my redemption is
come. I looked about, and there was no helper, I
ſought and there was none to ayde: and myne arme
hath ſaued, and myne indignation itſelf hath holpen me.]

*Ch.*63.
*v.*1. 4. 5.

3. This therfore ſo mightie Conquerour, is our only
Redemer, Chriſt the Annointed of God, ſingularly
aboue al others. And is alſo [called Ieſus, becauſe he
ſaueth his people from their ſinnes.] And [there is
not ſaluation in anie other (ſaith S. Peter) for neither
is there anie other name vnder heauē geuen to men,
wherein we muſt de ſaued.] For both Iewes and
Gentiles were vnder ſinne, ſaith S. Paul, confirming his doctrine by the wordes of the Pſalmiſt,
euen now recited, concluding that [al haue ſinned,
and doe neede the glorie of God. So that none but
Chriſt onlie, could ſatiſfie for the guilt of ſinne. Al
that are iuſtified, are iuſtified gratis, by his grace, by
the Redemption, that is in Chriſt Ieſus, whom God
hath propoſed a propiciation by faith in his bloud, to
the ſhewing of his iuſtice, for the remiſſion of former ſinnes.] Stil inculcating the ſame, ſaying [Ieſus
Chriſt was deliuered vp for our ſinnes. When we
were enimies, we were reconciled to God by the
death of his Sonne. As by the offence of one, vnto
al men to condemnation: ſo alſo by the iuſtice of
one, vnto al men, to iuſtification of life. Who ſhal
deliuer me from the bodie of this death? The grace
of God by Ieſus Chriſt our Lord. God ſpared not
his owne Sonne, but for vs al, deliuered him.

Pſal. 4.
v. 8. *Heb.*
1. *v.* 9.
Mat. 1.
v. 21.
Luc. 1. *v.*
31. *Ch.* 2.
v. 21.
Act. 4.
v. 12.
Ro. 3. *v.*
9, 10.
v. 23, 24.
25.

Ch. 4. *v.*
25. *Ch.* 5.
v. 10.
v. 18.

Ch. 7. *v.*
24. 25.
Ch. 8. *v.*
32.

Chriſt our
Redemer is
alſo called
IESVS, that
is to ſay Sa-
uiour, be-
cauſe he only
is our Saui-
our.

Y 3   The

The Iewes not knowing the iustice of God, & seeking Ch. 10. v.
to establish their owne, haue not bene subiect to the 3, 4.
iustice of God. For the end of the Law is Christ, v. 5.
vnto iustice to euerie one that beleueth. For Moyses
wrote that the iustice. which is of the Law, the man
that hath done it, shal liue in it.] The iustice of the Gal. 3.
Law of Moyses going no further of it selfe, but to v. 24.
saue a man from punishment by death, prescribed Mat. 28.
for transgressors therof. And so [was our pedagogue v. 19.
to Christ.] By al which it is certaine, that none can Io. 3.
haue remission of sinnes, except they beleue in Iesus v. 1.
Christ. And doe also those thinges, which are like- Rom. 8,
wise required, for they must also be baptized; they v. 24.
must hope in Christ; which is an other distinct the- 1. Cor. 13.
ological vertue, of which S. Paul saith [By hope we v. 1. 2. &c.
are saued] they must haue [charitie the third, and v. 13.
greatest theological vertue] they [must suffer with Rom. 8.
Christ, (which implieth penal workes, to be done, v. 17.
or paine to be suffered) that they may also be glori- Mat. 10.
fied with him.] And breefly, they must auoide v. 22. Ch.
mortal sinnes; or if they fal into anie, repayre to this 24. v. 13.
Sacrament, in due maner for absolution : they must 1. Cor. 7.
perseuere in good life : that finally they obserue v. 19.
Gods commandments. [For circumcision (with the Gal. 5.
rest of Moyses Law) is nothing: and prepuce (al that v. 6. Ch.
man can doe of him self) is nothing, but the obser- 6. v. 15.
uation of the commandments of God.]

Manie other chinges are required besides true faith.

*Eternal punishment, due for mortal sinne, being
remitted with the sinne, there remaineth
ordinarily temporal punishment.*

ARTICLE. 31.

Three thinges are conteyned in the punish-

PVnishmēt due for mortal sinne, conteyneth three
thinges : Paine of losse that is, losse of seeing God,
answerable to the sinners auersion from God : The
paine

paine of fenfe; that is, fenfible torment, anfwerable to the finners inordinate conuerfion to creatures : and the eternitie of them both, anfwering to the infinitenes of mortal finne, offending the infinite Maieftie of God : and perpetually perfifting in the fame malice, alfo after death: becaufe the foule after this life, remaineth inflexible, according to that

Eccle. 11. *v.* 3.

doctrine of Salomon [If the tree fhal fal to the South, or to the North, in what place foeuer it fhal fal, there fhal it be.] If therfore the foule depart from the bodie in ftate of grace, it is then confirmed therein, that it can not finne anie more : if it depart in ftate of mortal finne, it remaineth obftinate therein, and can neuer repent. But when mortal finnes are remitted, the eternal punifhmēt, as wel of *pæna damni*, as of *pæna fenfus*, is changed into temporal : which temporal paine the penitent is to fuffer, for particular fatiffaction, that he may participate Chrifts abundant fatiffaction, made for al mankind.

2. Againft this Catholique doctrine, our Aduerfaries pretend, that it derogateth from the fufficiencie of Chrifts Paffion, arguing (as their maner is, in manie pointes of Religion) by one truth to difproue an other. For being an affured truth, that onlie Chrift hath fatiffied Gods iuftice for al finnes, as is fhewed in the precedent Article, they would inferre therupon, that al other fatiffaction is fruitles, fuperfluous, and derogatorie to Chrifts fatiffaction, as if the fame were not fufficient: which is as fophiftical, and falfe a confequence, as if they fhould fay : Chrift hath redemed al mankind, therfore it is nedeles, fuperfluous, and derogatorie from his Redemption, to beleue in him, to hope in him, to loue him, to be

Rom. 8. *v.* 17. *Mat.* 16. *v.* 24.

baptized, to receiue anie Sacrament; or to doe, or fuffer anie thing for the loue of God : and namely it fhould be derogation from Chrift [to fuffer with him, or to take vp anie croffe (that is anie maner of ne-

ment, which is due for mortal finnes.
Pæna damni :
Pæna fenfus :
Æternites vtriufque.

Temporal fatiffaction of penitents is conformable, not derogatorie, to Chrifts fatiffaction for al.

of neceſſarie or voluntarie afflictiō, and to folow him.] The anſwer therfore (as wel to their argument, as to theſe other arguments,& the like)is, that Chriſts Redemption , and Satiſſaction , being abundantly ſufficient for al mankinde, is not effectual, that is , worketh not the effect of ſaluation in anie other, but [in al that obey him] in thoſe to whom it is applied in particular. As if there were one moſt potent medicine , able to heale al ſores, and to cure al infirmities in the whole world , yet ſhould only thoſe infirme perſonr be cured therby, to whom the medicine ſhould be applied. But a Proteſtant wil ſay, that Chriſts Satiſſaction is applied , by onlie faith. To this we anſwer. Firſt, that theſe wordes: Onlie faith doth iuſtifie,or doth applieChriſts iuſtice or ſatiſſaction to the faithful: are nowhere , in the holie Scriptures. Further we anſwer, that Baptiſme and manie other thinges are alſo neceſſarie together with true faith. And that in particular , penal workes, are neceſſarie in al penitents, that haue committed ſinne after Baptiſme, we ſhal here proue by manie exemples, & teſtimonies of holie Scriptures.

3.   For beſides temporal death inflicted vpon al men for ſinne, God enioyned other penalties vpon Adam [That with much toyling he ſhould laboure in the earth, al dayes of his life] and to Eue [that in trauel ſhe ſhould bring forth her children] and the like afflictions common to al men and wemen. More particularly , our Lord ſending an Angel to conduct his people in the deſerte, forewarned them that the ſame Angel ſhould puniſh their offences temporally ſaying [he wil not forgeue , when thou haſt ſinned] which can not be vnderſtood of the guilt of ſinne, for al ſinnes were remiſſible vpon repentance , but of the puniſhment due for the ſame. Neither did only mourning in hart, and wordes ſuffice, but alſo other external penance was required of the people,

after

Chriſts ſatiſfaction is only effectual to whom it is applied in particular.

A manifeſt ſimilitude.

An anſwer to the Proteſtants replie.

Temporal death, and other penalties are inflicted vpon al men notwithſtanding that Chriſt died for al.

Heb.5.
v. 9.

Mar. 16.
v. 16.
Io. 3.v. 4.

Gen. 3.
v. 16. 17.
19.

Exo.23.
v. 21.

Exod. 32. after that they had made, and adored a molten calf,
v. 14. 28. for though [our Lord was pacified] yet manie were
Ch. 33. slaine. And further [our Lord said to Moyses: Speake
v. 5. 6. to the children of Israel. Thou art a stiffnecked people, once I shal goe vp in the middes of thee, & shal
destroy thee. Now presently, lay away thyne ornaments, that I may know, what to doe vnto thee.
Therfore the children of Israel layde away their
ornaments, from mount Horeb] It was also ordayned by the Law of Moyses, that besides restitution of al thinges gotte by fraude, the offeder should
Levit. 6. [render the fift part more, to whom the damage
v. 5. 6. was done, and should offer a ramme without spotte
in sacrifice to God, for his sinne.] For a general
satisfaction for al sinnes forgotten, or vnknowen
Num. 5. [The people once euerie yeare kept the feast of Ex-
v. 7. piation, fasting, & offering Sacrifice] which could
not be meant for only admonition, or terrour, to
auoide sinne, but for satisfaction also for their sinnes,
which the people knew not themselues, to haue
Levit. 23. committed. Likewise in particular [Marie the sister
v. 27. 28. of Moyses & of Aaron, was not only strooken with
32. leprosie, for the sinne of detraction, & murmuring
Num. 12. against Moyses, but also was separated from the
v. 14. 15. campe seuen dayes. [After that the people had often
murmured against God, notwithstäding they were
(at least manie of them) restored to his fauoure by
remission of their sinnes, yet they were temporally
punished, as it is more particularly recorded in these
wordes [Forgeue I besech thee (said Moyses to our
Num. 14. Lord) the sinne of thy people, according to the
v. 18. greatnes of thy mercie, as thou hast bene propi-
19. cious to them, since their going out of Ægypt, vnto
20. this place. And our Lord said: I haue forgeuen it,
21. according to thy word, liue I, and the whole earth
22. shal be replenished, with the glorie of the Lord. But
yet al the men that haue seene my Maiestie, and the

Marginal notes:
Likewise other particular punishments were inflicted for particular offences.

God being pacified yet punished temporally.

Z   signes,

fignes, that I haue done in Ægypt, and in the wildernes, and haue tempted me, now tenne times,
neither haue obeyed my voice; they shal not see the   *v.* 23.
land, for the which I sware to their fathers, neither
shal anie of them, that hath detracted me behold it.]
Accordingly [al that came from Ægypt aboue the   *Ch.* 26. *v.*
age of twentie yeares, dyed in the wildernes, within   64. 65.
the space of fourtie yeares, except only two, Iosue
and Caleb] who were free from that sinne of murmuring, and concupiscence of flesh : for though (as
the text is cleare) God had forgeuen the sinne, yet he   *Num.* 20.
punished them temporally. [Neither is Gods indig-   *v.* 13.

Holie meeke
Moyses was
also tempo-
rally punished
for his offence
though it was
smal.

nation against the people to be marueled at (said   *Deut.* 1. *v.*
Moyses) wheras our Lord being angrie with me   32. 33.
also for you said to me : Neither shalt thou enter thi-   *v.* 26.
ther] Which he repeteth twise more, intimating   *Ch.* 4. *v.*
that neither their great, and manie sinnes, nor his   21.
owne smal sinnes, were remitted without temporal
punishment.

4.   Another pregnant example was in king Dauid,

A particular
example in
king Dauid.

vvhose sinnes being forgeuen, as the Prophete Nathan expresly declared, yet the same Prophete told
him vvithal, that he must be punished, vvith the
death of his sonne, saying [Our Lord hath taken   2. *Reg.* 12.
away thy sinne, thou shalt not dye. Neuerthelesse,   *v.* 13. 14.
because thou hast made the enimies of our Lord to
blaspheme, for this thing the sonne that is borne to
thee, dying shal dye.] Neither could Dauid by his
voluntarie fasting weeping, praying, & lying vpon   *v.* 16. 18.
the ground, obtayne the life of his childe. After his   21.
other sinne, in numbering his people, and after his
hartie repentance for it, and remission therof, he was   *Ch.* 24. *v.*
also temporally punished [by the death of seuentie   2. 10. 12.
thousand men. And Dauid lifting vp his eyes, saw   15. 17. 18.
the Angel of our Lord standing betwen heauen &   1. *Par.* 21.
earth, and a sword drawen in his hand, turned   *v.* 14. 16.
against Ierusalen; & he, with the ancients, fel flatte   17. 18.
on the

on the earth clothed in hearcloth. And Dauid said
to God : Am not I he that commanded the people
to be numbred, it is I that haue sinned: it is I that
haue done the euil, this flocke what hath it deserued?
Lord my God, let thy hand be turned, I besech thee,
vpon me, and vpon my fathers house : and let not
the people be striken.] Finally [our Lord said to the
Angel, that stroke the people: It is sufficient : now
hold thy hand] and the same Angel commanded
Gad the Prophete, to bid Dauid offer Sacrifice;which
he performed accordingly.

2. Reg. 2,
v. 16.
Ibidem,

5. When Iosias the good King of Iuda, and al his
people, corrected the former faultes of their predecessors, and serued God sincerly [yet our Lord was
not auerted from the wrath of his great furie, wherwith his furie was wrath against Iuda: for the pro-
uocations, wherwith Manasses had prouoked him]
although also the same king Manasses repented before his death, and [did penance excedingly, before
the God of his fathers: and earnestly praying was
heard of God, and was brought againe to Ierusalem
into his kingdom.] Neuertheles our Lord punished
the former sinnes, and so foretold these penitents,
saying [Iuda also wil I take away from my face, as
I haue taken away Israel; and I wil reiect this citie,
which I chose Ierusalem, and the house, wherof I
said: My name shal be there] which so came to passe,
about twentie yeares after, when Ierusalem was
taken, the Temple destroyed, and the Kinges, and
people, ledde captiues into Babylon. Which kind
of punishment for sinnes, holie Iudith rightly considering, iudged the peoples former sinnes, to be the
cause of their present tribulations, aduising al to
beare them patiently, shewing by ancient examples
that impacience would increase the iust wrath of
God, and patience would mitigate the same: [They
that did not (saith she) receiue the tentations (or

4. Reg. 23.
v. 2. 3. ad
v. 25.
v. 26.
Iere. 15.
v. 4.
2. Par. 33.
v. 12. 13.
14. &c.
4. Reg. 23.
v. 27.

Againe the
people repen-
ting were
temporally
punished for
sinnes remit-
ted.

Others were
afflicted for
sinnes not
remitted to
bring them
to true re-
pentance.

Z 2   tribula-

tribulations) with the feare of our Lord, & vttered *Iudith.* 8.
their impatience, and reproch of their murmuring v. 24 25.
against our Lord, were destroyed of the destroyer, 26. 27.
and perished by serpents. And we therfore, let vs
not reuenge our selues for these thinges, which we N*u.21. v.
suffer lesse then our sinnes, but reputing the very 4. 5.6.
punishments to be the scourges of our Lord, wherwith as seruants we are chastised, let vs thinke them
to haue chanced to our amendment, and not to our
destruction.]

The Prophe-
tes generally
teach that God
forgeuing
sinnes, doth
punish peni-
tents tempo-
rally.

6.   Generally al the Prophetes preached, that God
being alwayes readie to forgeue al sinnes, vpon true
repentance, doth not forthwith forgeue al the due
punishment. [Returne vnto me saith our Lord (by *Iere.* 3. v.
his Prophete Ieremie) and I wil receiue thee. Re- 1. 12. 13.
turne ô rebellious Israel, saith our Lord, and I wil 14.
not turne away my face from you : because I am
holie, & I wil not be angrie for euer. But yet know
thou thyne iniquitie, that thou hast transgressed
against the Lord thy God. Returne ô ye reuolting
children, saith our Lord, because I am your husband]
But touching the punishment, God also forewarned
them, by the same Prophete, that he would not
wholly remitte it, not only whiles they persisted incorrigible, but neither when they should repent.
No though also the same Prophete Ieremie should
pray for them : and therfore our Lord said to him
[Thou therfore pray not for this people, neither *Ch.* 7. v.
take vnto thee praise, and prayer for them, & resist 16.
me not, because I wil not heare thee.] No nor [in *Ch.* 11. v.
the time of their crie, & affliction] Yea [when they 14. *Ch* 14.
shal fast I wil not heare their prayers : & if they shal v. 11. 12.
offer holocaustes and victimes, I wil not receiue
them, because with sword, and famine, and pestilence I wil consume them] Not only for present or
future sinnes, but for sinnes past, and forgeuen, as is §. 5.
noted before [I wil geue them into rage to al Kingdomes

Iere. 15. domes of the earth (faith God) becaufe of Manaffes,
v. 4. the fonne of Ezechias the king of Iuda: for al thinges, that he did in Ierufalem.] Likewife by his Prophete Ezechiel God promifeth prefent remiffion of
Ezech. 18. finnes [If the impious fhal doe penance from al his
v. 21. finnes, which he hath wrought, and fhal kepe al my
precepts, and doe iudgement and iuftice, liuing he
fhal liue, and fhal not dye] but withal requireth that
the penitent fhal doe penance, and fo forwards fhal
kepe al his precepts. Neither can a Proteftant make   God requireth
euafion, by turning the wordes, doe penance, into   both repen-
fimple repenting, which is only conuerting to God,   nance.
without anie worke of penance, or fatiffaction: for
God requireth both the one and the other; & by his
v. 30. Prophete expreffeth both, faying [Conuert, and doe
Ch. 21. penance, from al your iniquitie.] Againe he faith
v. 3. [Behold I to thee (land of Ifrael) and I wil draw
forth my fword out of his fcabbart, and wil kil in
thee, the iuft, and the impious] moft affuredly God
doth not punifh the iuft eternally, but only temporally: neither would God punifh anie iuft man temporally, if Adam had not finned. God ftil threatned,
Ch. 20. *v.* that he would punifh Ierufalem, and al the people,
40. 41. yea though fome did truly repent, and did workes
&c. of penance, and that he would afterwards, reduce
them from captiuitie. Daniel accordingly confeffing Gods iuft punifhment, when he vnderftood,
that the captiuitie of the Ifraelites fhould be releafed,
after feuentie yeares, and that the time was com-
plete, he confidently prayed, in faftinges, fackcloth,   Prayer, fafting
Dan. 9. *v.* and afhes, faying [I befech thee, ô Lord God, great,   fackcloth and
2. 3. 4. and terrible, which kepeft couenant, and mercie to   afhes perteyne
them that loue thee, and kepe thy commandments,   for finnes re-
v. 5. we haue finned, we haue done iniquitie, we haue   mitted.
dealt impioufly, and haue reuolted, and we haue declined from thy commandments, and iudgements,
v. 6. we haue not obeyed thy feruants, the Prophetes,
Z 3   that

that haue spoken in thy name, to our Kinges, to our
Princes, to our fathers, and to al the people of the
land.] Thus the holie Prophete in the name of the
whole nation, confessed their general sinnes, and
euil desertes, and withal acknowleged, that iust
punishment is due for the same: & that therin God
sheweth his iustice, saying to God [To thee iustice,   *v. 7.*
but to vs confusion of face, as is to day, to the man
of Iuda, and to the inhabiters of Ierusalem, and to
al Israel: to them that are nere, and to them that
are farre of, in al the landes, to which thou hast cast
them out, for their iniquities, in which they haue
sinned against thee, ô Lord to vs confusion of face,   *v. 8.*
to our princes, and to our fathers, that haue sinned.

God exerci-
seth mercie
and iustice
together, in
that he both
forgeueth &
punisheth
sinnes.

But to thee, Lord our God, mercie, & propiciation]
so he prayeth that God wil mitigate his iustice, with
mercie, not omitte the one vertue, nor the other,
but to shew both [Iust(saith he)is the Lord our God,   *v. 14.*
in al his workes, which he hath done] and therfore
addeth in his humble prayer, that their sinnes haue
iustly deserued, much more punishment, not pleading that their afflictions in the destruction of cities,
and temple, and seuentie yeares captiuitie in Babylon, may be accounted sufficient satisfaction, but
prayeth that God of his mercie wil accept al this in
part of due punishment, and remitte the rest [For   *v. 18.*
(saith he) neither in our iustifications doe we prostrate prayers before thy face, but in thy manie
commiserations] In al which it is manifest, that
this temporal punishment was both medicinable,
to reduce the people to sincere repentance; and sa-

Affliction
bringeth to
repentance &
being suffered
with patience
is satisfactorie.

tisfactorie, in part of greater due debt. For both
which causes Gods mercie sent afflictions, els his
people must haue bene vtterly destroyed. So also the
Prophete Amos ascribeth it to Gods Goodnes, that *Amos 3.*
temporal euils doe happen to his people, saying *v. 6.*
[Shal there be euil in the citie, which our Lord hath
not

not done?] ſpeaking of that euil, wich is called *malum pæna*, the euil of paine, for otherwiſe, God is neuer the doer of euil, which is *malum culpæ*, the euil of fault, and ſinne. But puniſhment is ſent of God for the good of al. And the iuſt doe ſo acknowlege it, as did the holie Prophetes. And ſo did the worthie Machabees Martyres, ſaying: [We ſuffer this for our owne ſakes, ſinning againſt God, & thinges worthie of admiration are done is vs] ſaid one of the glorious brethren. An other, which was the yongeſt likewiſe ſaid: [we for our ſinnes ſuffer theſe thinges. And if the Lord our God hath bene angrie, with vs a litle, for rebuke and correction, yet he wil be reconciled againe to his ſeruants.] In regard alſo, both of due puniſhment, and of inclination to fal againe, through il habite gotten by cuſtome of ſinne, the wiſeman admoniſheth penitents to puniſh themſelues with daylie care, and feare, ſaying [Of ſinne forgeuen be not without feare. If thou hold not thyſelf inſtantly in the feare of our Lord, thy houſe ſhal quickly be ſubuerued. As in the ſhaking of a ſieue, the duſt wil remaine: ſo the perplexitie of a man (the intricate diſcourſe of the mind) in his cogitations] inſtructing vs in the former place to haue iuſt feare, becauſe ſinnes forgeuen muſt be puniſhed: and in the other place, to feare and watch, leſt we fal againe.

7.   Of the new Teſtament few textes may here ſuffice, becauſe the old Teſtament hath yelded good ſtore: and there wil be alſo occaſion to recite ſome more, touching the ſpecial kindes of penal ſatiſfactorie workes. For here we only ſhew, that temporal puniſhment remaineth due, and is inflicted, after the remiſſion of ſinnes, as wel for amendment, as for ſatiſfaction. S. Iohn Baptiſt in his preaching to penitents, willed them, that ſeing they had lerned to flee the danger of eternal puniſhment (which he
calleth

Margin notes:

vt ſupra.

2. Mach.7.
v. 18.

v. 32. 33.

Eccli. 5.
v. 5.

Ch. 27. v.
4. 5.

Artic. 33.

Holie Martyrs accept their afflictions as temporal puniſhments for former ſinnes.

Al are to mortiſie themſelues.

S. Iohn Baptiſt exhorted penitents to doe penance.

calleth the wrath to come)to doe temporal penance (which he calleth the fruite of penance) saying [Ye vipers brood, who hath shewed you to flee, from *Mat.* 3. *v.* the wrath to come? Yeld therfore fruite worthie of 7.8.10. penance. Euerie tree therfor that doth not yeld good fruite, shal be cut downe, & cast into the fire]

Our Sauiour preached the same.

The same did our Sauiour also preach, saying [Doe *Ch.* 4. *v.* penance : for the kingdome of heauen is at hand.] 17. The kingdom of heauen is purchased by Christ, for al his true seruants, but to enioy it, they must doe penance. And now in the time of grace, as it is more fruitful, so it is no lesse necessarie. Els it brideth a new sinne of negligence : as S. Paul warneth the

And. S. Paul inculcateth and vrgeth Christians to die the very same.

Corinthians [we helping doe exhorte(saith he)that 2. *Cor.* 6. you receiue not the grace of God in vaine. For he *v.* 1. 2. saith : In time accepted haue I heard thee, and in the *Isa.* 49. day of saluation, haue I holpen thee. Behold now is *v.* 8. the time acceptable, behold now is the day of saluation.] In the same Epistle he threatned some, that himself should be forced to punish them, not only that did persist in their sinnes, but also those that did not requisite penance [I feare (saith he) lest when 2. *Cor.* 12. I come, I finde you not such as I would, and that I *v.* 20. 21. be found of you, such a one as you would not. Lest againe God humble me among you, and I mourne manie of them, that sinned before, & haue not done penance, for the vncleanes, and formication, and in continencie, that they haue committed.] The Christians at Ephesus not only [confessed their deedes] *Act.* 19. their particular sinnes, but in way of satisfaction, *v.* 18. burnt naughtie Bookes, of Magike and sorcerie, in presence of manie, in detestation of former offences : for though al peril of corrupting others, and of abusing the same bookes, by anie afterwards, might haue bene auoyded by defacing, and spoyling them, sauing some part of the damage, being [of great *v.* 19. price, of fiftie thousand pence] nere about two
hundred

hundred fiftie poundes, yet they burned al for edification to the Church, and satisfaction to God. S. Paul againe admonished other Christians, to be alwayes readie to doe, and to suffer penance for their sinnes, seing Christ our Lord suffered exceding much.

Heb. 12. [Thinke diligently (saith he to the Hebrewes) vpon
v. 3.4. him, which susteyned of sinners, such contradiction
5.6. against himself, that you be not wearied, fainting in your mindes. For you haue not yer resisted vnto bloud, repugning against sinne, and you haue forgotten the consolation, which speaketh to you: as it were to children (not to enimies) saying: My
Prou. 3. sonne, neglect not the discipline of our Lord: neither
v. 11.12. be thou wearied, whiles thou art rebuked of him. For whom our Lord loueth he chasticeth, and as a father in the sonne, he pleaseth himself, and he scourgeth euerie childe, that he receiueth. Perseuere
v. 7. ye in discipline. As vnto children doth God offer himself vnto you, for what sonne is there, whom
v. 8. the father doth not correct. But if you be without discipline wherof al (children) be made partakers, then are you bastards, and not children.] These termes; Discipline, rebuketh, correcteth, chasticeth, scourgeth, doe presuppose sinnes past, corrected, and remitted, not obstinacie in sinne, for in that state, sinners are not children, but enimies. And al these sacred textes inuincibly declare, that some penalties, and punishments remaine, after that sinnes are forgeuen. Christs satisfaction is most sufficient, but for application, compassion, and cooperation is also required. Neither doth Gods inflicting of punishment awarrant penitents, to endeuour nothing at al: for Christ in the Apocalyps maketh the contra-
Apoc. 3. rie conclusion, and inference [Whom I loue, I doe
v. 19. rebuke, and chastise. Be zelous therfore, and doe penance.]

Christ by punishing, admonisheth vs also to punish our selues.

A a

True

True penitents enabled by grace, doe satisfie the debt of temporal punishment, due for sinnes remitted.

ARTICLE 32.

Being already proued that God requireth that penitents shal doe some penance, in part of satisfaction, it is necessarily presupposed that they can doe it, els God would not require it.

OVr Aduersaries, besides their obiection, that satisfaction of penitents should be superfluous, and derogatorie to Chrifts Satisfaction, because he hath most abundantly satisfied for al, wherunto we haue now answered, and by holie Scriptures, euidently shewed, that penal workes are also required of penitents: they further denie it to be possible, that anie man, though iustified by Gods special grace, can make anie part of satisfaction, for sinnes formerly committed, and forgeuen. To which we first breefly answer; that Chrift our Sauiour: whose [Yoke is swete and burden light] requireth nothing impossible of his seruants. Seing therfore it is already proued, that temporal punishment remaineh due, and is required of penitents, after the remission of actual sinnes, and our Aduersaries wil easyly grant, that our Lord requireth nothing impossible, it is manifest that some satisfaction is possible. *Mat. 11.* *v. 30.* *1. Io. 5.* *v. 3.*

Which is further proued by more holie Scriptures.

2. Neuertheles we shal here further declare, by holie Scriptures, that penitents haue done, & can doe penal workes, gratful to God, and satiffactorie for their sinnes: not by mans owne power, without Gods special grace [for we are not sufficient of our selues, as of our selues, to thinke anie good thing, but our sufficiencie is of God] yet by his gift this sufficiencie is made ours: so that, it is truly said: man is made able by Gods grace, both to thinke, and doe that which is good. Gods Grace is the principal cause, but the same excludeth not the secondarie, & partial cause *2. Cor. 3.* *v. 5.*

cauſe. The ſecondarie in deede, can doe nothing, without the firſt: & the principal doth not ſome good thinges, without the ſecondarie cauſe cooperating :
1. *Cor.* 15.
v. 10.
[Now not I (ſaith S. Paul) but his grace with me] not his grace (to witte in ſome action) without me, but with me. And ſo mans ſatiſfaction is neither derogatorie to Chriſt, but ſheweth his power and goodnes, in making mans wil able to cooperate, which otherwiſe it could not: neither is impoſſible, being made poſſible by him, that made al thinges. And hereby Chriſts Satiſfaction is applied to the iuſt and elect; and for lacke of cooperating, is not applied to the wicked and reprobate.

3. Obſerue here alſo, that penitents ſatiſfaction is not an act, or worke of iuſtice, for no humane act, though done by Gods grace, doth render equal recompence, to the leaſt offence, againſt Gods Maieſtie, which is infinitie; but it is the proper act of repentance, proceding from Gods mercie, ſhewed to vs, of his mere grace without our deſerte, and is by him accepted, not for ful payment of the debt, or for equal recompence of the offence, but becauſe it is adioyned to Chriſts Satiſfaction, God is herewith contented, pleaſed, and ſatiſfied. For wheras it is poſſible amongſt men, that one, euen in rigoure of iuſtice may repay, and render equal recompence, to an other man, for iniurie done to him : yea to an enimie exacting the vtmoſt due: ſo that ſuch an enimie is bond to accept it. Yet is it neuer poſſible, for man to render equal to God, ſo that God ſhould be bond to accept it, for recompence, but we alwayes neede his mercie. But whereas ſometimes a man, not being poſſibly able to make equal recompence for treſpaſſe, or iniurious offence done to an other man, yet doing according to his abilitie, and the other accepting his good endeuour, therwith contenteth himſelf, remitting the reſidue, no man can doubt,

Penitents ſatiſfaction is not properly the act of Iuſtice, but of Penance.

Man may ſatiſfie an other man, either according to iuſtice, or to his ſufficient contentment, But neuer to God according to iuſtice, but only to his ſufficient contentment.

but

but this is iust satisfaction, though not iust payment. Euen so in our case towards God, though man is neuer able to render equal, and so God is not bond to accept it, in respect of the penitents act, yet God benignly accepting it in respect of Christs satisfactió, mans satisfaction is enabled by Christs, and so becometh sufficient to God, our merciful Creditor, for sinnes mercifully remitted.

Iob. 9. v. 1. 2.

King Dauids desire to be punished was acceptable to God.

4.   King Dauid without presumption, both lawfully, & frutfully prayed that the punishment, which fel on his people, might fal vpon himself and his fachers house. Which his desire God so accepted, that he commanded the Angel to strike no more, saying [It is sufficient, now hold thy hand: And the Angel commanded Gad the Prophete, to tel Dauid in the name of our Lord, that he should goe vp and builde an Altar to our Lord God, in the floore of Ornan the Iebusite] which he performed, paying for the place six hundred sicles of gold, for [I may not (said he to Ornan) take it from thee, and so offer to our Lord, Holocaustes geuen gratis. And he built there an Altar to our Lord, and offered Holocaustes, and Pacifiques, and he inuocated our Lord, and our Lord heard him in fyre from heauen vpon the Altar of Holocauste.] God declaring by miracle, that Dauids penance was gratful, & his satisfaction acceptable. Yet did not this penitent king cease from doing penance al his life, as appeareth in manie places: especially in his Psalmes called Penitential, where he often cried to God stil for mercie in these, and like humblest prayers [Lord rebuke me not in thy furie; nor chastise me in thy wrath. Haue mercie on me Lord, because I am weake: heale me Lord, because al my boness be trubled. And my soule is trubled exceeingly : but thou Lord how long? I haue labored in my sighing: I wil euerie night wash my bed, I wil water my couch with my teares

2. Reg. 24. v. 16.

1. Par. 21. v. 18. 19. 24. 25.

v. 26.

Yet he ceased not to doe more satisfactoire workes during his life especially by prayers, and lamentations for his sinnes.

Psal. 6. v. 2. 3. 4. 7. &c.

Pſal. 31.　teares. Becauſe I held my peace, my bones are inue-
v. 3. 5.　terated, whiles I cried al the day. *I haue made my
　　　ſinne knowne to thee, & myne iniuſtice I haue not
　　　hid. I ſaid: I wil confeſſe againſt me, myne iniuſtice
　　　to our Lord: and thou haſt forgeuen the impietie of
Pſal. 37.　my ſinne. There is no health in my fleſh, at the face
v. 4. 18.　of thy wrath: my bones haue no peace, at the face
　　　of my ſinnes. I am readie for ſcourges, & my ſorow
　　　is in my hart alwayes. Haue mercie on me ô God,
Pſal. 50.　according to thy great mercie. Waſh me more
v. 3. 4.　amply from myne iniquitie, and cleanſe me from
　　　my ſinne. Becauſe I know myne iniquitie, and my
Pſal. 101.　ſinne is before me alwayes. Becauſe my dayes haue
v. 4. 5. 6.　vaniſhed as ſmoke: and my bones are withered, as
　　　a drie burnt fire brand. I am ſtriken as graſſe, & my
　　　hart is withered: becauſe I haue foregotten to eate
　　　my bread. For the voice of my groning, my bone
Pſal. 129.　hath cleaued to my fleſh. From the depthes I haue
v. 2.　cried to thee, ô Lord: Lord heare my voice. If thou
　　　ſhalt obſerue iniquities ô Lord: Lord who ſhal ſu-
Pſal. 142.　ſteine it? Enter not into iudgemēt with thy ſeruant;
v. 2. 4.　becauſe no man liuing ſhal be iuſtified in thy ſight.
　　　My ſpirite is in anguiſh vpon me; within me my
　　　hart is trubled.] Thus and much more, holie Dauid
　　　did penance in hart, word, and worke, ſtil ioyning
　　　confident hope with penal workes, concludeth his
v. 9. 10.　prayers with deſire of merciful helpe. [Deliuer me
　　　from myne enimies ô Lord: to thee I haue fledde:
　　　teach me to doe thy wil: becauſe thou art my God.
　　　Thou wilt bring forth my ſoule out of tribulation:
　　　and in thy mercie thou wilt deſtroy myne enimies.
v. 12.　And thou wilt deſtroy al, that affliĉt my ſoule: be-
　　　cauſe I am thy ſeruant.] So Gods ſeruants merci-
　　　fully aſſiſted with grace, doe ſatiſfaĉtorie workes of
　　　repentance, not of iuſtice but by acceptation ſuffi-
　　　cient for ſatiſfaĉtion through Gods mercie.
　　　5. Wiſe Salomon in his Prouerbes inſerteth this

*Though al
ſinnes are
knowen to
God, yet muſt
a penitent
confeſſe and
acknowlege
them, as accu-
ſing himſelf.

　　　　　　　　　　leſſon

The iuſt doe penance with ioy.

leſſon, perteyning to voluntarie, and fruithful puniſhment of ſinne, ſaying [It is a ioy to the iuſt to doe iudgement; & dread to them that worke iniquitie] *Prou.* 21. *v.* 15. Yea king Achab otherwiſe a wicked man, wel knew that doing of penance would mitigate Gods iuſt wraih, when [He rent his garment, & couerd his fleſh with heartcloth, and faſted, and ſlept in ſackcloth, and walked caſting downe his head. And

God alſo reſpeĉted the voluntarie affliĉtion of ſome wicked men.

the word of our Lord came to Elias the Thesbite, ſaying: Haſt thou not ſene Achab humbled before me? Therfore becauſe he hath humbled himſelf, for my ſake, I wil not bring in the euil in his dayes : but in his ſonnes dayes, wil I bring the euil vpon his houſe.] Much more if Achab had alſo rent his hart with true contrition, he might then by adioyning penal workes to his inward ſorow, haue more pacified Gods wrath, ſeing ſo ſhorte, and vnperfeĉt penance obtained delay of puniſhment, for his great and obſtinate ſinnes. King Manaſſes more effeĉtu-

Much more their penance, that doe it ſincerly with hartie repentance.

ally repenting in Babylon, and [doing penance excedingly before the God of his fathers, deſired and beſought God earneſtly, and he heard his prayer, & brought him againe to Ieruſalem into his Kingdom] A plaine figure of true penitents attayning poſſeſſiõ of the kingdome of heauen, when ſufficient ſatiſfaĉtion is made. The Niniuites beleuing Ionas, repented, and to eſcape deſtruĉtion (which otherwiſe had then fallen vpon them) did great penance, in hope [That God would conuert, and forgeue, and returne from the furie of his wrath, and they not periſh. And God ſaw their workes, that they were conuerted from their euil way : and did not the euil] which he had threatned. Which manner of penance (by faſting in ſackcloth) Chriſt commending, propoſeth it for an example to be imitated: yea affirmeth, that their faĉt ſhal condemne others which doe not penance.

Prou. 21. *v.* 15.

3. *Reg.* 21. *v.* 27. 28. 29.

Iere. 14. *v.* 12.

2. *Par.* 33. *v.* 11. 12.

Ione. 3. *v.* 7. 8. 9. 10.

Mat. 12. *v.* 41.

6. S. Marie

6. S. Marie Magdalen ſtriken with repentance for
her ſinnes [fel downe at the feete of our Sauiour,
begane to water his feete with teares, wiped them
with the heares of her head, and kiſſed his feete, &
annointed them with ointmēt.] Al which our Lord
not only accepted, but alſo defended her fact againſt
the Phariſees that diſdayned her : compared alſo her
hartie and humble penance, with the Phariſees en-
tertainent of him in his houſe, in al reſpectes much
preferring her deede before his. When S. Peter of
humane frailtie, had denied Chriſt to be his Maſter,
going forth of Caiphas his houſe [he wept bitterly]
waſhing away his fault with bitter teares. [If we
did iudge our ſelues (ſaith S. Paul) we ſhould not be
iudged. But whiles we are iudged (temporally puniſhed) of our Lord, we are chaſtiſed: that with this
world we be not damned.] In al thinges (ſaith he)
let vs exhibite our ſelues, as the Miniſters of God, in
much patience, in tribulations, in neceſſities, in
diſtreſſes, in ſtripes, in priſons, in ſeditions, in laboures, in watchinges, in faſtinges.] S. Iohn the
Apoſtle writeth to the Biſhop of Epheſus (& in him
to al Biſhopes, Prieſtes, and other perſons in the like
caſe) that albeit he did manie good workes, had
great patience, and great zele againſt heretikes, yet
[hauing left his firſt (more abundant) charitie] for
this he muſt doe penance, ſaying : [Be mindful from
whence thou art fallen, and doe penance, and doe
the firſt workes. But if not (ſaid Chriſt by the penne
of his Apoſtle) I come to thee, and wil moue thy
candleſticke out of his place, vnleſſe thou doe pe-
nanca. He that hath an eare, let him heare, what
the Spirite ſaith to the Churches.]

Luc. 7.
v. 28.

v. 44. 45.
46.

Mat. 26.
v. 75.

1. Cor. 11.
v. 31. 32.
2. Cor. 6.
v. 4. 5.

Apoc. 2. v.
2. 5. 6.

v. 7.

Examples of
S. Marie Ma-
gdalen.

And S. Peter.

S. Paul exhor-
teth al ſinners
to iudge, and
puniſh them-
ſelues,

The ſame
doth Chriſt
againe by the
penne of S.
Ihon the
Apoſtle,

Praying

Praying, Fasting, & Almes deedes, are especial
satisfactorie workes, for sinnes remitted.

ARTICLE. 33.

More in particular the holie Scriptures doe also
instruct vs, that prayer, fasting, and almes, are
three especial satisfactorie workes of penance. Alwayes presupposing faith, which is the first ground,
then true repentance, which is syncere remorse of
conscience, for the offence of God, for the deformitie of sinne, defiling the soule, and for the punishment and separation from God, which sinne iustly
deserueth. And so from this faith and repentance
procedeth the fruite of penal workes, done with
right intention of the mind, special grace assisting,
without which al mans workes, and sufferinges,
are dead of themselues, and insufficient.

2. The first and cheefest of these three is Prayer,
an act of the minde eleuated to God. Wherunto
when Fasting, or Almes are adioyned, they serue as
winges, by which prayer more effectually ascendeth into heauen. As the holie Angel Raphael testifieth, saying [Prayer is good with fasting and almes: *Tob.* 12.
rather then to lay vp treasures of gold.] And so *v. 8.*
deuout persons doe often conioyne them al three
together, especially fasting and prayer. So the Prophete Esdras by word and example directed the
children of Israel, which were come from Babylon, to pray that God would sette them, and their
children in a right way of seruing him, and withal
to fast at a special time; as himself hath recorded in
his historie, saying [I proclamed a fast beside the *1. Esd. 8.*
riuer Ahaua, that we might be afflicted, before the *v. 21.*
Lord our God, and might desire of him a right way
for vs, & our children, & al our substance. And we *v. 23.*
fasted

Marginal notes:

True faith, and repentance presupposed, Prayer, Fasting & Almes deedes are especial satisfactorie workes.

By prayer man conuerseth with God.

fafted, and befought our God hereby: and it fel out profperoufly vnto vs.] Neither did they pray and faft, for Gods direction only (which was one good caufe) but alfo for more fatiffaction, for finnes remitted, to which they were alfo obliged. For albeit

Ch. 9. v.
23. 15.
the Prophete faid to God [Thou ô God haft deliuered vs from our iniquitie] yet he faith withal, [behold, we are before thee in our finne, which two fpeaches muft needes be vnderftood with this diftinction: that God had deliuered them from the guilt of finne, but not from al the guilt of punifhment. Otherwife if you fay, that they were deliuered from finne, and yet were in the fame finne, and that in the fame refpect, it is a flatte contradiction:

Ch. 10.
v. 1.
from which al holie Scripture is moft free. [Efdras therfore thus praying, and befeching, and weeping, and lying before the Temple of God, there was gathered to him of Ifrael, an exceding great companie of men, and wemen, and children; and the people wept with much lamentation.] To prayer alfo per-

3. Reg. 24.
v. 18.
2. Par. 21.
v. 18.
Mat. 6.
v. 12.
teyne al Sacrifices for finne, and are more properly for fatiffaction, then for remiffion of finnes. Becaufe God immediatly forgeueth the guilt of finne, when the finner is truly penitent, and his prayers, & other good workes folowing, are in way of fatiffaction. Chrift our Lord prefcribed that al fhal pray for remiffion of finnes. Which prayer is ftil to be faid of euerie one, alfo after that his finnes are remitted, for remiffion of the punifhment remaining vnfatiffied.

Sacrifice is a principal kind of prayer.

3. Fafting was directly inftituted in the Law of Moyfes, for fatisfaction: and the feaft in which it was fpecially prefcribed, was called the Feaft of

Lewit. 23.
v. 27. 29.
32.
Nu. 29.
v. 7.
expiatió [Vpon the tenth day of the feuenth moneth fhal be the day of Expiation moft folemne: and it fhal be called holie: and you fhal afflict your foules in it, and fhal offer holocauft to the Lord. Euerie foule that is not afflicted this day, fhal perifh out of

The feaft in which the Iewes did efpecially faft was called the feaft of Expiation.

Bb his

his people] which fast begane from euening of the
minth day, and continued al the tenth. Besides this
ordinarie fast penitent people, did voluntarily vse
fasting amongst other satisfactorie workes. So [Sa-   *1. Reg. 7.*
They fasted   muel assembling the people together into Masphath,   *v. 4. 5. 6.*
also vpon spe-   they cast away their idols, and serued our Lord only,
cial occasions.   and Samuel prayed for them, and they al fasted. Cer-   *1. Reg. 31.*
For their sin-   taine men of Iabes Gallaad fasted seuen dayes for   *v. 13.*
nes.   King Saul, and his sonnes] being slaine by the Phi-   *2. Par. 20.*
For soules   listimes. King Iosaphat being in distresse, and feare   *v. 3.*
departed.   of his enimies, betooke himself wholly to besech
our Lord, and proclamed a fast to al Iuda. In the
captiuitie of Babylon, saith Ieremie the Prophete
And for other   [It came to passe, in the fifth yeare of Ioakim the   *Iere. 36.*
causes.   sonne of Iosias the King of Iuda, in the ninth mo-   *v. 9.*
neth, they proclamed a fast in the sight of our Lord,
to al the people in Ierusalem.] Likewise after the
captiuitie, such as had put away their vnlawful wi-   *2. Esd. 9.*
ues [came together in fasting, and sackcloth, & earth   *v. 1.*
vpon them.] Tobias, Iudith, & Ester, amongst other
pious, and penal workes, fasted much, & exhorted   *Tob. 12.*
others to fast, not only to chastise their bodies, which   *v. 8.*
is also most godlie and necessarie, but also to pacifie   *Iud. 4. v.*
Gods wrath prouoked by sinnes, and forgeuen. Al   *8. Ch. 8.*
which fasting was only acceptable in those, which   *v. 6.*
were truly penitent, whose sinnes vpon their sin-   *Est. 4. v.*
cere repentance, were remitted. And so fasting is   *16.*
most properly for satisfaction, and not only for remission of the sinne it selfe. Therfore the Prophetes
Fasting with-   Isaias, and Zacharias earnestly admonished such as
out true re-   persisted in sinne, that their fasting was not accep-
pentance hath   table before God, who by the same Prophetes, thus
smal or noe   expostulateth with such hypochrites. [Is this such   *Isi. 58.*
fruicte.   a fast, as I haue chosen, for a man by the day to afflict   *v. 5.*
his soule? Is this it, to winde thy head about like a
circle, and to spread sackcloth and ashes? Wilt thou
cal this a fast, and a day acceptable to the Lord?]
Likewise

Zach. 7.
v. 5.
Mat. 6.
v. 16. 18.
Ch. 9. v.
15.
Luc. 5.
v. 33.
Luc. 2.
v. 37.

Rom. 8.
v. 12. 13.

Likewise [when you fasted, & mourned in the first, and seuenth moneth, for these seuentie yeares, did you fast vnto me?] Thus Christ also teacheth to fast in synceritie, not in hypocritie, or other sinnes. And fortold that his Disciples should fast in due times, and right maner. And that fasting rightly [The Father of heauen wil repay thee.] Holie Anne the religious [widow by fastinges, and prayers serued God night and day.] S. Iohn Baptist, and his Disciples fasted much. In like maner, as fasting, so al other voluntarie afflictions of the bodie, are satisfactorie: as watching, discipline, wearing hearcloth, traueling to holie places, kneeling, and the like [for mortification of the flesh, that the spirite may liue.]

> *Christ also teacheth vs to fast with synceritie, not with hypocrisie.*

> *Right fasting is an act of religion.*

Dan. 4.
v. 24.

v. 26.

Tob. 2.
v. 3. Ch. 4.
v. 9.
Ch. 12.
v. 9.

4. Almes deedes, & al workes of mercie, spiritual and corporal, are also of special value, in way of satisfaction for sinnes remitted, & doe in some forte dispose the person to true repentance, for remission of sinnes. The Prophete Daniel aduised King Nabuchodonosor, to vse this meanes for redeming of his sinnes, saying to him: [O King let me counsel thee: and redeme thou thy sinnes with almes, and thyne iniquities with the mercies of the poore: perhaps God wil forgeue thee thyne offences.] At least such almes procureth diminution, or delay of punishment for sinnes, which the Prophete here calleth, redeming of sinnes. For this King continued twelue monethes after this, in prosperitie. Holie Tobias knew wel the inestimable valure of almes deedes, & therfore wholly imployed himself therin [leauing his owne dinner, that he might burie the dead bodies of his faithful brethren, went fasting to take away a bodie newly slaine] because [almes (as the Angel Raphael afterwards witnessed) deliuereth from death, & that is it, which purgeth sinnes and maketh to finde mercie, and life euerlasting.] Our Lord and Sauiour teacheth vs to doe al these

> *Almes deedes, and al workes of mercie are satisfactorie.*

> *Holie Tobias merited much by workes of mercie.*

three

three special workes sincerly. Touching almes he admonisheth [Let not the left hand know what the *Mat. 6.* right hand doth. That thy almes deede may be in *v. 3.* secrete, and thy Father which seeth in secrete, wil reward thee.] Touching spiritual almes he saith ; If you wil forgeue men their offences, your heauen- *v. 14.* lie Father wil forgeue you also your offenses. But if you wil not forgeue men, neither wil your father *v. 15.* forgeue you your offenses.] Againe touching temporal almes, our Lord aduiseth, that [he which hath *Luc. 3.* two coates geue to him that hath not : and he that *v. 11.* hath meate, let him doe likewise] Finally our Lord wil in such maner iudge the world, that euerie one of the faithful, which beleueth in him, & shal come to the discussion of their actes, shal receiue sentence of life, or death euerlasting, as they shal be found to *Mat. 25.* haue done, or not done workes of mercie, almes *v. 35.* deedes spiritual, and corporal. [Religion cleane and *v. 41.* vnspotted with God, and the Father is this (saith S. *Iac. 1. v.* Iames) to visite pupils, & widowes in their tribula- 27. tion : & to kepe himself vnspotted from this world.] 5. These are the especial satisfactorie workes, for the debt of sinnes remitted. Patience also in suffering meekly., and thankfully al tribulations, worketh to the very same effect. Especially in suffering of temporal death, disgrace in the world, losse of landes, goodes, and other possessions for truth sake, for true Faith and Religion. It is Gods special goodnes, to lay, or suffer afflictions, to be layde vpon the iust, that albeit they be colde, and slow to punish themselues, and to pay part of their debt to him, yet by patiently susteyning (that which we can not escape, and auoid) some satisfaction is made, and the *Heb. 10.* debt diminished, & merite also increased [Patience *v. 36.* therfore is necessarie] saith S. Paul. And our Lord *Luc. 21.* hath pronounced to al his elect, that [In your pa- *v. 19.* tience, you shal possesse your soules.]

One

Marginal notes:

Christ exhorting al to doe workes of mercie, teacheth to doe them with alacritie and sinceritie.

And wil iudge the faithful according as they doe, or omitte such workes.

Patient suffering is very satisfactorie.

One may satisfie for an other, being both in state of grace

ARTICLE 34

EVen as in the natural bodie, one member assisteth an other: the handes worke for the good of themselues, and al the rest; the feete susteyne the other members; the eyes direct the feete and legges where to goe; and so of the rest, each part is profitable to an other: and sometimes one member supplieth the defect, or otherwise doth the function of an other: as when the hand, or the eye, signifieth, that which the tongue should speake: As also in a ciuil bodie, one man by commission, executeth the office of an other, payeth, satisfieth, or answereth for the debt of an other: so in the mystical bodie of Christ, which is his Church, the liuing members therof, may in the case of temporal satisfaction, for the debt of sinne remitted, pay or satisfie some part therof, by vertue of the communication, and participation, which is among the same members of the whole bodie. So that it be intended, & applied to that end, or purpose; and so that both parties be in state of grace. For otherwise neither the worke of anie in state of mortal sinne, is meritorious, nor satisfactorie before God, nor anie persisting in mortal sinne is capable of such benefite, but both being in spiritual life, one may satisfie for the other. As is proued by these holie Scriptures.

Ephes. 3.
v. 25.

2. After that the people of Israel had made, and adored a molten calf, God said to Moyses [I see that this people is stiffenecked, suffer me that my furie may be angrie against them, and that I may destroy them.] But Moyses praying for them [our Lord was pacified from doeing the euil, which he had

Exod. 32.
v. 8.9.10.
11. &c.
v. 14.

spoken

As in the natural, & ciuil bodie: so in the mystical, one member supplieth for an other.

Moyses first Praying that God would remitte the peoples sinne

prayed after-wards for re-mission, or mitigation of the punish-ment.

spoken against his people] that is, from wholly de-stroying them. Yet some were punished: for [there were slaine about three thousād men.] After which [Moyses returning to our Lord, besought him to forgeue them this trespasse] that is to forgeue the residue of temporal punishment, for [our Lord was pacified] already, and so had forgeuen the sinne, but not al the punishment. For this therfor Moyses now prayed: and desired rather to be punished him-self, then that al due punishment should be inflicted vpon the people, saying [Either forgeue them this trespasse, or if thou doe not, strike me out of the booke, that thou hast written] What punishment this was, which Moyses in most feruent zele, desired to susteyne, for the people, is not easyly explaned, & perteyneth to an other point of Christian doctrine. But by this passage it is manifest, that Moyses could by suffering punishment, satisfie part of Gods wrath for the peoples sinne already remitted, & not suffici-ently punished. Holie Iudith, by her austere life, & penal workes, wearing hearcloth, much fasting, frequent praying, auerted Gods wrath from puni-shing the people, as they iustly feared, and had deser-ued: so that for her great penance, & by her meanes, God of his mercie spared, and deliuered his people, now penitent for their sinnes; by her hand destroy-ing their enimie, which being done, she willed them to render thankes, and praise to God, saying to them [Praise yee the Lord our God, who hath not forsa-ken them, that hope in him: and in me his hand-maide he hath fulfilled his mercie, which he pro-mised to the house of Israel: and he hath killed by my hand, the enimie of his people, this night.] The constant suffering of certaine zelous Machabees, also pacified the wrath of God, by their dying, & inuo-cating Gods mercie towards themselues, and their nation: saying [Our Lord wil behold the truth, and

And offered to suffer for them, or with them.

Holie Iudith by penal wor-kes mitigated Gods wrath for the peo-ples sinnes.

The Machabee Martyres did also appeaze Gods wrath.

v. 28.

v. 31.

v. 14.

v. 32.

Part. 3.
Art. 5.

Iudith. 8.
v. 5. 6.
Ch. 9. v. 1.
Ch. 13. v.
6. 7. &c.

Ch. 13. v.
17. 18.

2. Mach. 7.
v. 6.

wil

wil take pleasure in vs (said the first : and an other
said) Our stocke is not forsaken of God. We suffer
for our owne sakes, sinning against our God, and
thinges worthie of admiration, are done in vs. For
we for our sinnes, doe suffer these thinges. And if
the Lord our God, hath bene angrie with vs a litle,
for rebuke and corrcction ; yet he wil be reconciled
againe to his seruants.] And considering that their
deathes should helpe for satiffaction of their nation,
the last and youngest of these Martyres said to the
Tyrant[My bretheren hauing now susteyned shorte
paine, are become vnder the testament of eternal
life. And I, as also my bretheren, doe yelde my life,
& my bodie for the Law of our fathers; inuocating
God, to be propicious to our nation, quickly. But in
me, and in my bretheren, shal the wrath of the Almightie cease : which hath iustly bene brought
vpon al our stocke].

3. S. Paul confirmeth this doctrine, that he actions
and sufferinges of the liuing members of Christ, doe
profite, & satisfie one for an other, when he exhorted the Christian Corintians, to impert of their temporal goodes, to them which suffered want in Iurie;
that such benefactors might matually be made partakers of their suffering in persecutions : that as the
one companie helping the other temporally, so the
other might helpe them spiritually [Let in this present time (saith he) your abundance supplie their
want, that their abundance also may supplie your
want : that there be an equalitie.] And the same
Apostle being himself in prison, doubted not to
write in his Epistle to the Colossians, that he now by
his sufferinges, helpt to supplie that which wanted
in their sufferinges for themselues : first witnessing
to them, that the Gospel which they had receiued
by the preaching of Epaphras, is the same, which is
the Gospel of the vniuersal Church:& for which he

now

Marginal notes (left): v. 16. / v. 18. / v. 32. / v. 33. / v. 36. / v. 37. / v. 38. / 2.Cor. 8. / v. 14. / Coloss. 1. / v. 5. 6. 7. / 23.

Marginal notes (right): S. Paul tea-cheth that as some helpe others tempo-rally, so they doe spiritu-ally. / And that his owne suffe-rings did in part, supplie the want of others.

now suffered, and reioyced therin, affirmeth plainly, that they also were partakers of his suffering, euen for the same Gospel [Wherof (saith he) I Paul *v. 24.* am made a Minister, who now reioyce in suffering for you: and doe accomplish those things, that want of the passions of Christ, in my flesh for his bodie, which is the Church] What more cleare wordes can be required, then these, to shew that both some suffering of temporal paines, is wanting in some members of the Church ; and also that the same may be accomplished by other members ? But

One hard place of holie Scripture explained by an other.

where at first sight these wordes [those thinges that want of the passions of Christ] are more obscure, you may explaine them by the same Apostles wordes, in an other place, where speaking of his owne tribulation, and comfort therin by Christ, he calleth his owne passions, the passions of Christ, saying:

Passions of the faithful are called Chrifts passions.

[As the passions of Christ, abound in vs : so also by *2. Cor. 1.* Christ doth our comforth abound] And in this very *v. 4. 5.* place, and in manie others, the Church is called *Colos. 1.* Christs bodie. And Christ also calleth his faithful *v. 24.* members, himself, for the most straite coniunction *Act. 9.* that is betwen him and them. So that the necessarie *v. 4.* sense of the wordes aboue recited is, those thinges *Mat. 25.* that want of the passions of Christs members, were *v. 35. 40.* accomplished, or in part supplied, by S. Pauls suffering. And consequently the want in some, may be supplied by others.

Temporal paine due for sinnes remitted, may be released by Indulgence.

ARTICLE. 35.

The doctrine of Indulgences is groun-

VPon the same foundamental doctrine, that the *See part 1.* good workes of the iust are communicated, and *Art. 43.* participated, amongst the liuing members of the Church.

Church, through the spiritual vnion, which al haue ~~ded in the Communion of Sainⓒts, & of none things in the whole Church.~~

Pſal. 118. *v.* 63.

Art. 34.

with Chriſt, and in him euerie one with others: is also grounded the doⓒtrine of Indulgences, or Pardons. As is already ſhewed, that one may ſupplie ſatiſfaⓒtion for an other. The ſpecial difference is, that in the former caſe one doth actually in his intention applie his worke, or ſuffering (as prayer, faſting, diſcipline, going on pilgremage, geuing almes, or the like) for ſome particular perſon, or companie: but moſt commonly ſuch ſatiſfaⓒtorie workes, as are abundant in Gods merciful acceptation, for the perſon that doth them, are ſtored vp for the whole militant Church in general: and ſo perteyne to the common treaſure (which is therby alſo increaſed, and by Chriſts Satiſfaⓒtion is made infinite) from whence is diſpenſed, and ſatiſfaⓒtion made for the debtes of others, which by them ſelues doe not, or can not ſo ſowne diſcharge the ſame.

To the effeⓒtual fruite, and benefite wherof, three ſpecial conditions are neceſſarily required, and that they rightly concurre together, which are theſe: Auⓒtoritie, in the Diſpenſer of this treaſure. Conuenient cauſe mouing him to grant the pardon: and Capacitie in the penitent, that is to receiue it.

That Indulgences may be effeⓒtual, are required, Auⓒtoritie, Cauſe & Capacitie.

2. Touching the firſt requiſite condition, which is auⓒtoritie in the geuer, it can not be in anie other but in the head, & cheefe ſtuared, the Supreme ſpiritual Gouernour, and Paſtor of the militant Church. For to him only it muſt needes perteyne, to diſpenſe the common treaſure of the whole bodie, vnto the members therof. Al other Biſhoppes, Paſtors, or Prelates, and inferior ſubordinate Prieſtes, can only diſpenſe, ſo much of this treaſure, & in ſuch maner, as the Supreme Diſpenſer aſſigneth, and limiteth. The ſecond condition (which is conuenient, and reaſonable cauſe) requireth, that it be done to edification, and not to deſtruⓒtion. And ſo, of the

Onlie the ſupreme Paſtor hath power to grant plenarie, Indulgences.

Others by his commiſſion.

The cauſe muſt be pious, and to edification.

Cc Popes

Popes part, and likewife of others , to whom he
communicateth anie part of this power, it is requi- *Mat* 24.
red, that they be faithful Difpenfers, not Diffipaters; *v.* 45.
that they be not moued of humane fauoure, natural
affection, partialitie, filthie lucre, lightly, rafhly, or
by other vnlawful motiue:but fyncerly to Gods honour, fpiritual profite of the Church, common good
of manie, or good of fuch perfons, as may redound
to the fpiritual good of others , and of them felues.
As when they wil pray for othets, releue the poore,
or to draw men to repaire to the holie Sacraments,
or by whofe example others wil be fturred vp, to
repentance,deuotion or other vertues, & good wor-

None are ca- kes. The third condition (which is capacitie, in the
pable, that parties, to whom Indulgences are granted) neceffa-
perfift in mor- rily requireth, that they be in the ftate of grace, that
tal finne. is , free from mortal finne. For fuch as perfift im-
peñitent , are fubiect to euerlafting punifhment, du-
And the con- ring which ftate , no part of due punifhment can be
ditions affig- releafed. But euen their venial finnes alfo, if they dye
ned, muft be in anie mortal, by that occafion (which is called
performed in *Per accidens*) are eternally punifhed : becaufe fuch
the ftate of perfons are neuer rightly penitent. Neither can they
grace. therfore, being fpiritually dead in finne, participate
of anie good workes, or fatiffaction done by the
liuing members : for that there is no fpiritual influence , or communication of holie thinges, betwen
the huing and dead members. For the branch cut *Io.* 15. *v.*
of, or otherwife dead , can receiue no iuce of life, 4.6.
til it be vnited, or reuiued : which is neuer poffible
without due repentance. But by grace returning and
rightly repenting,that is, vfing the meanes ordained
by Chrift, for remiffion of mortal finnes , then and
not otherwife, they are made able to fatiffie for the
debt of temporal punifhment, and capable of others
fatiffaction,and of Indulgence : performing alfo the
conditions affigned by the geuer for this purpofe.

3. Practife

3. Practise hereof is cleare in holie Scripture, which necessarily proueth that it is true, & found doctrine. And so we shal not nede to repete the groundes of this kinde of satisfaction practised in Gods Church, hauing declared them already in the precedent Articles. Two examples therfore may here suffice for this purpose. Our B. Sauiour on the Crosse gaue a plenarie Indulgence, & free pardon, to the penitent theefe, who being truly, and hartely sorie, for his owne sinnes, with iust indignation reprehended the other theefe, for his obdurate hart, and insolent blasphemie, saying [Neither doest thou feare God, wheras thou art in the same damnation? And we in deede iustly : for we receiue worthie of our doings; but this man (Christ our Redemer) hath done no euil.] And the same penitent also humbly besought Christ our Sauiour, to releue his soule, after it should be departed, when our Lord himself should be in his heauenlie kingdom (for it appeareth that he thought when Christ should be in glorie, his owne soule, should neede releefe) praying thus to him : [Lord, remember me, when thou shalt come into thy kingdom.] To which humble petition, our merciful Sauiour answering, graunted more then the penitent presumed to aske, saying vnto him: [Amen, I say to thee : this day thou shalt be with me in paradise.] A most plaine, and free relaxation, not only from al his sinnes, but also from punishment due for the same after death.

4. An other example is in the practise of S. Paul, who hauing first excommunicated a certaine incestious sinner, and bond him to penance; afterwards released him by way of pardom, from the residue, before that al was performed. For wheras the Apostle [in the name of our Lord Iesus Christ, had deliuered the sinner to Satan, for the destruction of the flesh, that the spirite might be saued, in the day of our

Art. 25.
31.32.34.

Luc. 23.
v. 39. 40.
41.

v. 42.

v. 43.

1. *Cor.* 5.
v. 4. 5.

The same is proued by practise, testified in holie Scriptures.

Christ gaue a plenarie pardon to the penitēt theefe on the Crosse.

S. Paul also gaue a pardon to a penitent Corinthian, to whom he had formerly enioyned temporal penance.

Cc 2   of our

of our Lord Iefus Chrift.] In his other Epiftle to the
fame people, hauing in the meane time vnderftood,
that the finner humbly proceded in doing his enioyned penance, vpon fuch information, and at the
requeft of fome, he graunted relaxation . from the
reft of his penance : faying [Of much tribulation, 2. *Cor.* 2.
and anguifh of hart, I wrote to you by manie teares ; *v.* 4.
not that you fhould be made forie, but that you may
know, what charitie I haue more abundantly towards you] fhewing that as wel in punifhing, as
pardoning, he had great charitie toward them, and
fo being now to releafe the penitent, whom he had
formerly bond, touching him, he faith : [To him *v.* 6. 7.
that is fuch a one (in the cafe as you know) this re- *ad* 11.
buke fufficeth, that is geuen of manie : fo that contrariwife you fhould rather pardon, & comfort him,
left perhaps fuch an one be fwallowed vp, with
ouer great forow. For the which caufe, I befech
you, that you confirme charitie toward him. For
therfore alfo haue I written, that I may know the
experiment of you, whether in al thinges you be
obedient. And whom you haue pardoned anie thing,
I alfo. For my felf alfo, that which I pardoned, if I
pardoned anie thing, for you in the parfon of Chrift:
that we be not circumuented of Satan, for we are
not ignorant of his cogitations.] Thus the Apoftle
both bond, and loofed finners. And by this particular fact of pardoning, it may euidently be feene, that
as fome femed too feuere againft the penitent, them
the Apoftle exhorted to compaffion, & to confirme *v.* 7. 8.
their charitie towards him. Others entreated for

his relaxation, vnto whofe requeft he agreed. His *v.* 10.
auctoritie he auouched to be [In the power of *Ibidem.*
Chrift.] The caufe mouing him to remitte the reft
of penance not performed, was [left perhaps the *v.* 7. 11.
penitent fhould haue bene ouerwhelmed, or fwallowed vp with ouer great forow, & becaufe Satans
cogitations

▼ 9.

cogitations are futtle and cruel.] And by the way also to exercife the obedience of the faithful in conforming their iudgements to h¹s. The penitent alfo was now capable of pardon, hauing fuffered rebuke with patience, and being content to fuffer more, the Apoftle denounced that this fhould fuffice.

v. 6.

And fo the partie being truly penitent did paticipate the benefite.

The refidue of fatisfaction not made in this life, is to be fulfilled in Purgatorie : by fuffering, or by fuffrages after death.

ARTICLE 36.

Reafon directeth, that delay of paying debtes, doth nothing at al difcharge, nor diminifh the debters oblihation, but more and more bindeth him to make at laft due fatisfaction to his creditor: which happeneth efpecially by not paying in this life, the temporal debt of paine for finnes remitted. For a iuft foule departing from the bodie, before ful fatisfaction be made, muft then without more delay, fuffer much more punifhment, then would haue fufficed, whiles it was in the bodie. Becaufe penal workes voluntarily performed, by the penitent in this world, whiles it is in his power to doe them, or to differ them, are more fatisfactorie, then the punifhment, which is inflected in the next world; where it can be no longer differred. For albeit the penitent foule doth then willingly fuffer iuft paine, that it may be purged, and fo come to fee God, yet this fuffering is more properly called fatifpaffion, then fatisfaction, and for that it was not performed, in the due, & more acceptable time, is finally exacted with more feuere iuftice, yet ftil mixed with Gods mercie. For feing euerie fmalleft offence, muft be punifhed; and euerie mortal finne deferueth eternal

Delay of paying debtes dimifheth not, but augmeteth the obligation to pay them.

2. Cor. 6.
v. 2.
Rom. 6.
v. 23.

Cc 3   death;

death; and seing God of his goodnes geueth grace of repentance to al that wil accept it, & so changeth eternal punishment into temporal: seing also the penitent by Gods further grace, may it he wil, *Art. 31.* make acceptable satisfaction, by prayers, fastings, 32. 33: 34. almes deedes, or other good workes; may likewise & 35. be assisted herein by others; and may gaine Indulgences, for release of his debt: if be al these meanes, that which is requisite be not performed in this life, it is exceding great mercie, that yet in time and conuenient place, the soules, which remaine in debt of temporal paine, may be purged by due punishment, *Ephes. 5.* after their parting from their bodies, and be presen- *v. 27.* ted immaculate to their spous Iesus Christ, and so *Apoc. 21.* enioy eternal glorie, in the heauenlie Ierusalem, *v. 27.* whither nothing can enter, that is polluted with anie spotte or blemish, but must first be cleansed, purged, and made perfect.

2.   Against which Catholique doctrine Protestantes seeke diuers euasions, al very friuoulous. First they say, the name Purgatorie is not in al the holie Scriptures. We answer, that neither is the word Trinitie, nor Person, in that sense as Christians confesse Trinitie of Persons, in one God. Neither are Baptisme, and the Eucharist called Sacraments, in the whole sacred Bible. Yet the thinges themselues are there signified, and proued. Secondly they denie that there is anie other place for soules, departed from the bodies, but only heauen for the blessed, & hel of eternal torments, for the damned, and so they would exclude Purgatorie. But their opinion is euidently confuted by the Article of Christs descen- *Part. 1.* ding into hel. Which is a distinct place both from *Art. 24.* heauen, and from hel of the damned. As we haue declared by manie holie Scriptures in the explication of that Article. Thirdly they would exclude *Part. 2.* Purgatorie, by denying anie temporal punishment *a Art. 31.*

to remaine

to remaine due for finnes remitted; and by denying anie punifh-
that anie fatisfaction of penitents is either necefarie, ment is due
b Art. 32. or *b* poffible to be made, by the fame penitents; *c* or for finne re-
c Art. 34. by others for them; by denying alfo that there is mitted : al
d Art. 35. anie *d* common treafure of fatisfactorie workes, with which are
auctoritie to grant Indulgence, & fo (fay they) there former Ar-
is neither neede, nor poffibilitie of Purgatorie in an ticles.
other world. Al which their negatiue no faith, is
confuted, and the contrarie Catholique beleefe, and
doctrine manifeftly proued in the next precedent
Articles: for their better fatisfaction, who wil be
fatisfied in pointes of Religion, by true Chriftian
Pfal. 92. credibilitie, according to the holie Scriptures. For
v. 5. our Aduerfaries, which haue anie meane lerning,
doe eafyly fee, that thefe controuerfies haue fpecial
dependence, and coherence, each with others. And
fo the proof of the former pointes, proueth Purgatorie. And contrariwife their denial of Purgatorie,
maketh them to denie al the reft. Neuertheles that
there is in deede a Purgatorie: & that faithful foules
departing from this world in ftate of grace, but not
fufficiently purged, muft there remaine, til fatisfaction be made for their finnes, by their fuffering, or
by fuffrages of the Church, is further proued by thefe
fpecial places of holie Scripture.

3. Our B. Sauiour admonifhing al, to fatisfie, for Purgatorie is
wronges in this life, teacheth that thofe which doe further pro-
it not, fhal be conftrained, with more feueritie, ued by our
Mat. 5. *v.* when they come to the Iudge, to pay al, faying [Be Sauiours
26: 27. at agreement with thy aduerfarie betimes, whiles doctrine.
Luc. 12. thou art in the way with him: left perhaps the ad-
v. 58. 59. uerfarie deliuer thee to the Iudge, and the Iudge
deliuer thee to the officer (to the exactour, faith S.
Luke) and thou be caft into prifon. Amen I fay to
thee : thou fhalt not goe out from thence, til thou
repay the laft farthing, the very laft mite] plainly
fignifying, that the laft part, and parcel of the debt
muft,

must, and fhal be payed : and then the debter fhal
goe out from thence. Wheras in hel of the damned,
there is no payment made, but eternal punifhment
neuer ended, neuer diminifhed, no counting of far-
thinges, and mites: for the whole debt, and punifhment ftil continueth, neither fhal anie be euer deliuered from thence. Becaufe from hel (of the damned) there is no redemption. [For it is the hel of *Ifa. 66.*
vnquenchable fire, where their worme (of confci- *v. 24.*
ence) dieth not,& the fire quencheth not.] Therfore *Mar. 9. v.*
the place of payment,wherof our Sauiour here fpea- 45. 46.
keth, is a temporal,not an eternal prifon. And what *Mat. 25.*
other temporal prifon can there be, after this life, *v. 46.*
but this place of payment, by purging of foules,
called Purgatorie? At an other time Chrift our Lord
diftinguifhing the greater difficultie of fome finnes

The fame is confirmed by like doctrine, in an other place.

to pe remitted, then of others, faith that fome finne
fhal not be forgeuen [neither in this world, nor in *Mat. 12.*
the world to come] Wherof it is inferred by very *v. 32.*
good confequence, that fome finnes fhal be forgeuen after this life. And S. Marke relating this doctrine of our Sauiour, that fome finne fhal neuer be
forgeuen, calleth the fame [an eternal finne] fig- *Mar. 3.*
nifying that fome finnes are eternal, and fome not *v. 29.*
eternal.

4.   S. Paul likewife teacheth that fome workes

Likewife by S. Paules doctrine,

being vnperfect, fhal not only be tried, but alfo purged by fire [The worke of euerie one fhal be mani- 1. *Cor.* 3.
feft (faith he) for the day of our Lord wil declare *v.* 13.
(in the particular iudgement of euerie one, at their
death) becaufe it fhal be reuealed in fire : and the
worke of euerie one, of what kinde it is, the fire fhal
trie. If anie mans worke abide, which he built *v.* 14.
therupon (vpon Chrift the foundation) he fhal re- (11.)
ceiue reward. If anie mans worke burne, he fhal *v.* 15.
fuffer detriment : but himfelf fhal be faued : yet fo
as by fire] where we fee that fome workes being
                                            built

built vpon the true fundation Chrift Iefus and vpon
true faith in him, are perfect, and therfore refembled by the Apoftle, to [gold, filuer, and precious
ftones] the fame fuffer no detriment in the fire, but
prefently receiue reward : & other workes being
built alfo vpon the fame fundation, are vnperfect,
refembled to [wood, hay and ftuble] thefe fuffer
detriment (not eternal damnation) but himfelf (he
that hath fuch workes) fhal be faued : yet fo as by
fire.] And thus according to our Sauiours, and the
Apoftles doctrine, thofe fhal fatisfie for their debt
by fuffering after this life, which departing from
this world in Gods fauoure and grace, had not fatisfied fufficiently before.

v. 12.
v. 14.

5. An other ordinarie meanes of fatisfaction, after
death, in Purgatorie. befides fuffering, is by the holie
Sacrifice, and by other prayers, and fatisfactorie
workes done by others : and by application of Indulgence (which is alfo by the way of fuffrage) offered for releefe of foules departed. For albeit they
are not vnder the Iurifdiction of the militāt Church,
and therfore can not be abfolued by the ordinarie
keyes therof ; yet when fatisfaction is offered for
them, being in the ftate of grace, the fame is vndoubtedly accepted, for payment of their debt, as
prayers of the faithful are profitable, of one for an
other in earth. And fo al prayers, & other fatisfactorie workes offered, by the faithful in this world, are
profitable to foules, departed in ftate of grace : and
euer fo were, from the beginning of the world. As
is clearly gathered by the diligent [performing of
obfequies for Sara, the wife of Abraham, for Abraham himfelf, for Ifaac, for Iacob, for Aaron, for
Moyfes] and others. Which Exequies was a diftinct
religious office from their burial. And though fome
of thefe holie perfons, needed not prayers, after
their death, yet the fruite therof, remained in the

Satisfaction is
alfo made by
Sacrifice, and
other fuffrages
for foules in
Purgatorie.

Gen. 23.
v. 3. Ch.
25.35.50.
Num. 20.
Deut. 34.
v. 8.

Exequies
were celebra-
ted for the
faithful foules
departed in
the old Tefta-
ment.

Dd   common

common treasure of satisfactorie workes, applicable
to others, which haue nede. It is also recorded, that 1. *Reg.* 31
King Dauid, and others mourned, and fasted for v. 12 13.
King Saul, and his sonnes being slaine. Iesus the 2. *Reg.* I.
sonne of Sirach exhorteth al to extend their charitie v. 12.
towards the departed, saying [The grace of a gift is *Ec. li.* 7.
in the sight of al the liuing: And from the dead stay v. 37.
not grace. Iudas Machabeus the High Priest, and
General Captaine of Gods people, caused Sacrifice
to be offered in Ierusalem, for the souldiars slaine in
battle [because he considered, that they which had 2 *Mach.*
taken their slepe, with godlines, had very good grace 12. v. 42
laid vp for them.] Doubtles neither he, nor Dauid, 43. 45.
nor Abraham instituted the first office for the dead,
but obserued the godlie ancient custome of other
holie Patriarches, Priestes, and Prophetes. And the
Iewes to this day, obserue a Rite of Praying for the
dead, wheresoeuer they dwel, as in Rome, Venice,
Amsterdam, Frankford, and in other places.

6. Finally S. Iohn the Apostle, considering that
some sinners dye obstinate in their sinnes: and some
are penitent, before, or at their death; as he would
not aduise anie man, to pray for the impenitent, so
he exhorteth to pray for them, that dye penitent,
saying [He that knoweth his brother to sinne a sinne 1. *Io.* 5.
not to death, let him aske, and life shal be geuen him, v. 16.
sinning not to death. There is a sinne to death, for
that I say not, that anie man aske] By which doctrine it is most manifest, that prayer is profitable for
some soules after this life. Wherfore hauing also
elswhere alleaged some of these, and other textes
of holie Scriptures, concerning the communication *Part.* I.
and participation of spiritnal good workes, betwen *Art.* 44.
the soules departed, and the faithful in this world,
we may with al assurance conclude this pointe,
with the holie Auctor of the Booke, of Machabees,
(yea though the same Booke were not Canonical
Scripture

The Wiseman exhorteth to vse mercie towards the dead.

Iudas Machabeus caused Sacrifice to be offered for souldiars slaine in battle.

The Iewes stil pray for the dead.

Prayer for the dead is inuincibly proued by S Iohns doctrine.

Scripture, as it is also proued to be) at leaſt vpon the

2.*Mac.*12.
v. 46.
other proofes we may ſay with him [It is therfore a holie, and healthful cogitation to pray for the dead, that they may be looſed from ſinnes.] And ſo it is fully proued that al true penitents, through Gods abundant mercie, ſhal be ſaued : but with this difference, that ſome committing in this life few and ſmal ſinnes, and doing great, and long penance: others committing manie and great ſinnes, & doing very litle penance, or none at al, til the laſt houre before their death, ſhal al enioy eternal glorie, albeit not al in like meaſure, nor ſo ſpeedily. Al ſhil re-

Mat. 20.
v. 2.9.
10.14.*v.*2.
1. *Cor.* 15.
v. 4.42.
2. *Cor.* 3.
v. 15.
ceiue the penie : which is their hyre. But [In my Fathers houſe (ſaith our B. Sauiour) there be manie manſions.] Thoſe, whoſe workes are perfect, ſhal preſently receiue reward : as S. Paul teacheth, but if anie mans worke burne, he ſhal ſuffer detriment, but himſelf ſhal be ſaued, yet ſo as by fire.] And thus hauing proued that Penance is a true Sacrament, and declared alſo the three partes therof, which are Contrition; Confeſſion; and Satisfaction, either in this life, or in Purgatorie: It reſteth breefly to adde, ſome more ſacred textes of holie Scriptures, in further confirmation of the effect of this holie Sacrament.

Al true penitents ſhal be ſaued, but not al with like ſpede.

The proper effect of the Sacrament of Penance, is remiſſion of actual ſinnes, after Baptiſme.

ARTICLE 37.

Amongſt the general Articles of our Beleefe, expreſſed in the Apoſtles Crede, we confeſſe that in the Church there is Remiſſion of ſinnes. In the explication of which, and other Articles, we haue more particularly declared, that God onlie is the principal efficient cauſe of remiſſion of ſinnes; and

Part. 1.
Art. 43.

Manie loſe the benefits of Chriſts Redemption for

lacke of application therof. by true faith and Sacraments.

Christ as Man, the meritorious cause. Who by his Part. 2. Passion redeming al mankinde, hath payed a most Art. 6. 7. sufficient, yea superabundant ransom for al; which notwithstanding is onlie effectual vnto those, to whom it is applied. As must be stil remembred, and therfore I repete it often, because manie doe lose the benefite of Christs Redemption, for lack of application therof by right faith in Christ, and of due repentance, with the vse of holie Sacraments, the Art. 8. proper Instruments of sanctifying grace. For first by Baptisme (which is the doore, and entrance to al

Baptisme is the first ordinarie instrument of grace remitting sinne.

Christian Sacraments) original sinne is fully washed away, and also actual sinnes committed before Baptisme. And for remission of sinnes after Baptisme

The Sacrament of Penance is the ordinarie instrument after Baptisme.

the Sacrament of Penance is the ordinarie meanes. The other fiue Sacraments doe also geue first grace, with remission of sinnes, if perhaps anie sinnes remaine vnwitting to the penitent: but they are directly ordained for increase of grace, & more sanctification, not so purposly for remission of sinnes. And therfore none ought to receiue anie of those fiue, knowing themselues guiltie of mortal sinne, but must first be absolued in this Sacrament of Penance; whose proper effect is the remission of sinnes committed after Baptisme. As is before declared, where Art. 25. we proued it to be a Sacrament. Wherunto may be here added some other particular textes of holie Scriptures, in further declaration of this so necessarie an effect.

2.   In the old Testament no Sacrifice, nor Sacrament had the vertue to remitte sinnes, nor to geue grace, but only to signifie the same, as geuen by God,

Sacraments of the old Testament did only signifie iustifying grace.

if the persons were rightly disposed to receiue it, yet was it then foresignified, that our Redemer, in his new Testament, would both merite such grace, and conferre it by Sacraments, as by external Instruments, instituted by him for this purpose. For
besides

besides the old significant Sacrifices , and Sacra- *Art. 5. 23.* ments, as is already declared , the whole maner of Gods proceding from time to time , with his peculiar people , foreshewed , that in the time of grace, sinnes should be remitted , not only once, to each one (that would receiue it) by Baptisme , but againe and againe, so often as neede should require , by the Sacrament of Penance , the penitent doing his endeuour. For as God alwayes most iust , and most propicious,specially admonished al to walke rightly before him , keeping his commandments , so likewise he admonished them , that if they sinned, his wil is,that they be cleansed, but not without repentance,and punishment,especially the relapsed. And to bring them to repentance, he often sent them afflictions, and so reducing them from their wicked sinnes , releued them , and receiued them into new grace. As is manifest in their written Law , and in the Prophetes writinges, and other Histories of that people. In the Law, our Lord thus warned them,

Leuit. 26. [If you walke in my precepts, and kepe my com- *v. 3. 4.* mandments,and doe them , I wil geue you raine in their seasons , and the earth shal bring forth her spring, & the trees shal be replenished with fruites] and manie like temporal benefites, according to the state of that people. Contrariwise our Lord threat- *v. 14.* ned them, saying [But if you wil not heare me , nor doe al my commandments,if you dispise my Lawes, *v. 15.* and contemne my iudgements , that you doe not those thinges , which are appointed by me , & bring *v. 16.* my couenant to nothing worth : I also wil doe these thinges to you; I shal quickly visite you with pouertie, and burning heate, which shal waist your eyes, and consume your liues : you shal sow your seede in *v. 17.* vaine, which shal be deuoured of the enimies. I wil set my face against you, and you shal fal downe before your enimies , & shal be made subiect to them,

Sacraments of Christ both signifie and geue grace.

God promised benefites to those that kept his Lawes, and threatned punishment to those that transgressed, with remission of sinnes to the penitent.

Dd 3 that

that hate you : you shal flee, when no man pursueth
you. But if you wil not obey me so neither, I wil *v.* 18.
increase your chastisements seuen fold for your sinnes] And more to the same purpose, al for chastise-
ment, to bring them to repentance, and confession *v.* 21.
of their sinnes. As it foloweth in the same place:
[They and their Children shal be afflicted vntil they *v.* 39.
confesse their owne, and their ancesters iniquities, *v.* 40.
wherby they haue preuaricated against me, & walked contrary vnto me, I also therfore, wil walke *v.* 41.
against them, and bring them into their enimies
land, vntil their vncircuncised minde be ashamed:
then shal they pray for their impieties. And I wil
remember my couenant, that I made with Iacob,
and Isaac, and Abraham &c.] Thus we clearly see,

God stil desi-
reth that sin-
ners wil re-
pent, puni-
sheth them to
bring them to
repentance, &
then remitteth
their sinnes.

Gods readie wil to remitte al sinnes, but not without
repentance, and confession : and to bring them therunto, Gods good prouidence suffered their enimies
to afflict them. Which yet further Moyses repeteth,
assuring them of release and remission, when they
should be truly penitent [Therfore (saith he) when *Deut.* 30.
al these wordes shal be come vpon thee, the blessing *v.* 1.2.&c.
or cursing which I haue sette forth before thee, and
thou be touched with repentance, of thy hart, in al
nations, into which our Lord thy God dispersed thee;
and shalt returne to him, and obey his commandments, as I this day command thee, with thy children, in al thy hart, and in al thy soule : Our Lord
thy God wil bring thee againe from thy captiuitie,
and haue mercie vpon thee : and gather thee againe,
out of al the peoples, into which he dispersed thee
before.]

3.   Euen as it was foreshewed, so the sacred Historie reporteth al to be performed. For after the death *Iudic.* 2.
of Iosue, vnder whom the children of Israel con- *v.* 11.12.
quered, and possessed the promised land of Canaan
[manie did euil in the sight of our Lord, and serued
　　　　　　　　　　　　　　　　　Baalim,

The sacred
Histories re-
late that it so
hapened to

Baalim. And they left our Lord the God of their this people,
fathers, that had brought them out of the land of as Movfes had
Ægypt, and folowed ftrange goddes, & the goddes foretold them,
of the peoples that dwelt round about them, and
adored them, and they prouoked our Lord to anger;
leauing him, and feruing Baal, and Aftaroth. And

v. 13. our Lord being wrath againft Ifraél, deliuered them
into the handes of ranfackers, who tooke them, and
v. 14. fold them to the enimies, that dwelt round about,
v. 15, neither could they refift their aduerfaries: but whither foeuer they had meant to goe, the hand of our
Deut. 29. Lord was vpon them, as he fpake & fware to them,
v. 12. and they were vehemently afflicted.] In the meane
Iudic. 2. time [God raifed vp Iudges (General Captaines, &
v. 16, cheefe temporal Gouernours) that fhould deliuer
them, from the handes of the waifters, but neither
would they heare them, fornicating with ftrange
goddes, and adoring them] Thefe Iudges, & manie
with them, ferued God fincerly. But for the idolatrie of the greateft multitude: the whole nation
was vehemently afflicted. At laft, thefe idolaters
Ch. 3. v 2, repenting, they with the reft [cried to our Lord, who
10. 11. raifed them vp a Sauiour, and deliuered them, to
witte Othoniel, and the fpirite of our Lord was in
him, he ouerthrew the enimie, and the land refted
fourtie yeares.] But the people fel againe, & againe.
And were very often afflicted, at laft repented, and
fo were releeued, and reftored to grace, during the
times of the Iudges.

4. In like forte when the ftate was changed into a
Kingdom, for diuers finnes, efpecially for idolatrie, The like ha-
the Kingdom was diuided into two kingdomes, pened in the
times of the
wherof the one, greater in circuite, and number of Kinges,
tribes fel prefently into fchifme, fo into idolatrie,
was at laft ouerthrowne by Paganes, and made captiue to the Affirians. The other Kingdom, where
the Temple was, and the High Prieft, with other
Prieftes,

Priestes, continued longer, but was alſo made captiue to the Babylonians, in which affliction, the *Baruc. 3.*
people repenting for their ſinnes, were after ſeuentie *v. 7.*
yeares captiuitie releaſed, and ſo returned into their
countrie. Now comparing together al this, as the

These thinges figure with the thing therby prefigured (for to this
chanced to very purpoſe S. Paul ſaith, the ſinnes & puniſhments
them in figure
& are written of this old people of God [are written to our cor *1. Cor. 10.*
for our admo reption] and admonition) it manifeſtly appeareth, *v. 11.*
nition, cor that God is alwayes readie, & willing to remitte al
reption, and
erudition. ſinnes, euen Idolatrie, and whatſoeuer is greateſt,
but not without repentance, vnto which is euer adioyned puniſhment, either before remiſſion or after,
or both before and after, eſpecially in al remiſſions
after the firſt: which wel ſheweth that remiſſion of
mortal ſinnes committed after Baptiſme, requireth
harder penance, and the oftener that anie ſo falleth,
the greater ought his penance to be, for the ingratitude in recidiuation. But ſtil the Sacrament of Penance hath grace ſufficient, through the merites
of Chriſt, to remitte al, and to reſtore the penitents
to Gods fauoure, and to true iuſtice. For [God is *Heb. 13.*
the ſame, yeſterday and today] as S. Paul ſaith, of *v. 8.*
Chriſt: euen the ſame merciful louing God, who

Gods readines ſaid by his Prophete Ieremie, that he wil ſtil receiue
to remitte ſin al that ſyncerely returne vnto him, in due maner, as
nes is further
teſtified by he requireth. [It is commonly ſaid (ſaith our be *Iere 3.*
the Prophe nigne Lord) if a man put away his wife, and ſhe de *v. 1. 12.*
tes. parting from him, marie an other man, wil he returne to her anie more? ſhal not that woman be *Oſe. 14.*
polluted, and contaminated? But thou haſt com *v. 2. Ioel. 2.*
mitted fornication with manie louers, neuertheles *v. 12.*
returne vnto me, ſaith our Lord, and I wil receiue *Zac. 1. v. 3.*
thee] And in innumerable other places holie Scrip *Iſ. 1. v. 18.*

But ſtil with tures teſtifie, that al ſinnes are remiſſible, but alwayes *Ezec. 18.*
condition of vnderſtood with this condition [If the impious ſhal *v. 21. Iſ.*
repentance,
& penance. doe penance] otherwiſe [there is no peace to the *48. v. 22.*
impious, ſaith our Lord.]   **5. To**

5. To this same purpose, that al which wil, may
be absolued from their sinnes, our Sauiour crieth

Mat. II.
v. 28. 29.

[Come ye to me, al that labour, and are burdened,
and I wil refresh you] Our Lord here promiseth
to refresh such as haue hartie sorow for their sinnes,

Mat. 7.
v. 21.

not such as doe only [crie: Lord, Lord, but such as
doe the wil of his Father.] For those that wil be
refreshed by him, must doe that which foloweth
in the next wordes [take vp his yoke vpon them, &
lerne to be meeke and humble] Christs yoke is his

I. Ioan. 2.
v. I. *Ch.*
I. v. 9.

Law: which requireth [that we sinne not] and
when we haue at anie time sinned, [to confesse our
sinnes] and so he promiseth remission, by their ministerie, to whom he hath geuen commission, and

Io. 20. *v.*
23.

power to absolue: saying [whose sinnes you shal
forgeue, they are forgeuen them.] This you see, is
the yoke and crosse which sinners must take vp, and
this is to come to him, and so he wil disburden them,
and refresh them. Our Lord also teacheth that al
sinners may be receiued into Gods fauour, and be
pardoned, if they wil returne in due maner, by the
parable of a prodigal childe, who after a dissolute

Luc. 15.
v. 17. 20.

life returning penitently [when he was yet farre
of, his father saw him, and was moued with mercie,
and running to him, fel vpon his neck, and kissed
him] so wonderful and tender is Gods mercie towards penitent sinners: neuertheles the penitent

v. 21.

said [Father, I haue sinned against heauen, & before
thee, I am not now worthie to be called thy sonne.

v. 22.

And the father said to his seruants (so doth God
our heauenlie Father say to Priestes his seruants)
Quickly bring forth the first stole, and doe it on him,
and put a ring vpon his hand, and shoes vpon his

v. 23.

feete: and bring the fatted calf, and kil it, and let vs
eate, & make merrie,] signifying that with remission
of sinnes, not only the first stole, of innocencie from
the guilt of former sinnes, but also grace of other

*Christ inui-
teth al to
come vnto
him, doing
penance, &
so promiseth
to refresh
them.*

*The prodigal
childe by ma-
nie humble
actions shew-
ed his true
repentance,
and receiued
remission of
sinnes.*

E e   vertues,

vertues, abilitie to walke in Gods commandments, and capacitie to receiue more grace by other Sacraments, namely by the moſt bleſſed Sacrament of the Altar (ſigniſied by the ring, ſhoes, and feaſt), are receiued of true penitents. And although this parable is ſpecially vnderſtood of the returning of the Gentiles to God, which the Iewiſh nation diſdayneth, yet it perteyneth alſo to the conuerſion of al particular greate ſinners, as we ſuppoſe Proteſtants wil not denie. And it ſheweth that al ſinnes, ſo long as the ſinners are in this life, if they returne by true repentance, may be remitted, & grace geuen them, by the miniſterie of Gods ſeruants, firſt in Baptiſme (which alſo, is alwayes miniſtered by another, for none can baptize themſelues) and afterwards in the Sacrament of Penance. But therein more penance is required, becauſe the ſtate of ſuch ſinners is worſe, then it was before.

Luc. 11.
v. 26.
2. Pet. 2.
v. 21. 22.

6. But ſome man may perhaps doubt, that certaine great ſinnes, namely the ſinne againſt the Holie Ghoſt, can not be forgeuen; becauſe Chriſt ſaith [He that ſhal ſpeake againſt the Holie Ghoſt, it ſhal not be forgeuen him, neither in this world, nor in the world to come.] And S. Paul ſaith: [It is impoſſible for them, that were once illuminated, haue taſted alſo the heauenlie gift, and were made partakers of the Holie Ghoſt &c. and are fallen: to be renewed againe to penance] and [If we ſinne willingly, after the knowlege of the truth receiued: now there is not left an hoſte for ſinnes.] Vpon which wordes, Nouatus an old heritike grounded his hereſie, that none falling into anie mortal ſinne, after Baptiſme, could be receiued vnto mercie, or penance in the Church. And Caluin holdeth that it is impoſſible, for one that forſaketh his faith, and becometh an Apoſtate, or an Heretike, to be receiued to penance, or to Gods mercie. For anſwer, and explication of theſe,

Mat. 12.
v. 32.
Mar. 3.
v. 29.
Heb. 6.
v. 4. 6.
Ch. 10 v.
18. 26.

An obiection ſolaed, touching ſinne againſt the Holie Ghoſt, & other great ſinnes after Baptiſme.

I. is euer to be obſerued,

these, and other difficulties, which seme to haue apparance of contradiction, to other holie Scriptures; We must necessarily obserue, that in deede there is not, neither can be anie contradiction in al the holie Scriptures. And the holie Church (the piller and ground of truth) so vnderstandeth, and expoundeth such hard places, as the true sense of al may be verified. And so the former place importeth, that sinnes of mere malice, against the Holie Ghost, are harder to be forgeuen, then sinnes of ignorance, or frailtie As the sinne of the Pharisees, attributing the euident workes of the Holie Ghost, in casting diuels out of men, to the diuel himself, was harder to be forgeuen, then the sinne of those, that only said, that Christ the sonne of man, was a glutton, a drinker of wine, a freind of the Publicans and sinners, a breaker of the Sabbath, and the like, as he is a man. And the wordes of S. Paul haue this most true sense, that if the Christian Hebrewes, to whom he then wrote, should reuolt to Iudaizme; or they, or anie other should fal into mortal sinne after Baptisme, they can not possibly be renewed to the same penáce, which is in Baptisme: that is, they can not haue that first great, & large remedie applied vnto them, through anie other penance, as it was by Baptisme. Because the Sacrament of Penance, is a more painful medicine, requiring more punishment, by fasting, more praying, more particular confession, and other penal workes. And so the oblation of Christs death & passion, may stil be applied, with stricter penance, vnto the remission of anie sinnes, how great soeuer. And our Sauiours word & promisse, is most true & assured, which he vttered to his Apostles, saying without exception of anie sinne [Whose sinnes you shal forgeue, they shal be forgeuen them] & that which he said to S. Peter, & to the rest [Whatsoeuer you shal loose in earth, shal be loosed also in heauen.]

1. Tim. 3. v. 15.

Io. 20. v. 23. Mat. 16. v. 19. Ch. 18. v. 18.

Sidenote: that no sentence, nor word, in holie Scripture is contrarie to anie other.

Sidenote: Sinnes against Christ as he is God, are more hardly, and more rarely forgeuen, then sinnes committed against him, as he is Man.

Sidenote: Sinnes after Baptisme can not be remitted with so litle penance, as sinnes are first remitted by Baptisme.

Sidenote: Al sinnes, without exception, are remissible in this life, by the Sacrament of Penance.

Ee 2   *Extreme*

Extreme Vnction of the ficke , with holie Oyle,
by a Prieft, is a true Sacrament.

ARTICLE 38.

Our B. Saui-
our according
to his feruants
fpecial neede,
geueth them
his fpecial,
helpe,

CHrift our Lord louing his feruants vnto the *Ioan.* 13.
end, continually fendeth to them his fpecial *v.* 1.
affiftance, as their daylie neceffities require.
And fo wheras in their ficknes tending to death, and
departing from this world , their bodies and fenfes
being weake, and ftil decaying , their fpiritual eni- *1. Pet.* 5,
mie alwayes defiring, and in that time moft bufie, *v.* 8,
to inuegle and ouerthrow them : our merciful Sauiour hath ordayned for this our laft, and moft dangerous confl &, an efpecial Sacrament of fpiritual
counfort , and ftrength. Which confifteth in annointing with facred oyle, thofe partes of the bodie,
and proper inftruments of fenfes , by which finnes
often haue acceffe into the foule, as wel for more

So hē geueth
them Extreme
Vnction in
their ficknes
tending to
death.

fully cleanfing the faithful penitent , from al formerly contracted euil·habites, and reliques of finne,
as for more ftrength of the minde againft al new
affaultes, and tentations in the agonie of death : that
the fonle may pioufly depart, purged from al finne,
and ftrongly fortified by grace , and fo haue more
fpeedie entrance, into the Kingdom of heauen.

It is proued
by the holie
Scriptures to
be a Sacra-
ment.

2.   But becaufe Proteftants denie this holie Sacrament, as they doe moft of the others, we fhal here
proue by the holie Scriptures , that this alfo is a true
and proper Sacrament, inftituted by Chrift, and very
profitable to Chriftian foules. Holie Dauid tending
to old age , and weaknes of bodie , with thankes to
God for his continual protection , prayed him in
fpecial maner, that he would ftil defend, & ftrengthen him in minde, and fpirite, to the laft end of his *Pfal.* 70.
tranfitorie life, faying [In thee ô Lord I haue hoped, *v.* 2.

let me

let me not be confounded for euer in thy iustice deliuer me, and receiue me. Becaufe thou art my patience, ô Lord: ô Lord my hope from my youth.
Vpon thee haue I bene confirmed from the wombe,
from my mothers bellie, thou art my protector; let
my mouth be filled with praife, that I may fing thy
glorie: al the day thy greatnes. Reiect me not in the
time of old age; when my ftrength fhal faile, forfake
me not. Becaufe myne enimies haue faid to me, and
they that watched my foule confulted together, faying: God hath forfaken him; purfue, and take him,
becaufe there is none to deliuer] thus doe the diuils
watch the time, confpire, and affaulte faithful foules
in their greateft diftreffes, which the holie Prophete
confidering, procedeth in this prayer. [O God be
not farre from me: my God haue refpect to myne
ayde. Let them be confounded, & faile, that detract
from my foule. But I wil alwayes hope in thee. O
God thou haft taught me from my youth, and vntil
now: I wil pronounce thy meruelous workes. And
vnto ancient age, & old age, ô God forfake me not.]
So the holie Pfalmift prayed for himfelf, & alfo left
this prayer in writing, as a figure, or rather a prophecie, of this fo nedeful deprecatorie Sacrament,
in the Church of Chrift. But more clearly Chrift
himfelf forefignified to his Apoftles, the holie vfe
of oyle towords the ficke. For albeit the Euangelift
doth not exprefly relate our Sauiours commandment to them in this behalf, yet is it moft certaine
by his narration of their annointing the ficke, and
of the miraculous effect therof, that the Apoftles did
the fame vpon our Lords commiffion, as they alfo
caft out diuels [Going forth (faith he) they preached, that they fhould doe penance. And they caft
out manie diuels: and annointed with oyle manie
ficke: and healed them.] Yet was it not then a Sacrament: for neither is it like, that thofe ficke per-

v 5.

6.

8.

9.

10.

11.

12.

13.
14.
17.
18.

Mat. 6. *v.*
12. 13.

Prefigured
& propheci-
ed by Dauid.

The Apoftles
annointing of
the ficke with
oyle, before
Chrifts Paffi-
on, was a
figure, and
preparation
to the Sacra-
ment of Ex-
treme Vncti-
on.

Ee 3   fons

sons, whom they instructed, and miraculously healed, were baptized; neither were the Apostles at that time Priestes. But this ceremonial annointing with oyle, was a manifest preparation to this Sacrament: as S. Iohns baptizing was to Christs Baptisme.

3. When it was instituted, is not eypressed in holie Scripture: but included amongst those [manie other thinges, which Iesus did (as S. Iohn testifieth in the last wordes of his Gospel) and are not written in particular.] And most like it was ordayned after the Sacrament of Penance, within the space [of those fourtie dayes, in which Christ appearing to his Apostles, after his Resurrection, spake with them of the Kingdom of God,] to wit, concerning his Church, & thinges belonging therunto. For as it is certaine that no man euer could, nor can institute anie Sacrament, but Christ onlie : so it is also assured, by S. Iames his promulgation, in his Catholique Epistle, writen to al the faithful in the world, that before that time, this holie Rite was vsed in the Church. Els he would not haue written in such maner, as of a thing knowen to manie, and not newly ordayned by him: but must haue declared the Auctor, and Institutor therof : which (as being already knowen to the Church) he omitted, admonishing al Christians, to vse it in due time, and maner: telling them the benefite therof. His wordes (adioyned to an other exhortation of praying; & singing in certaine cases) are these [Is anie man sicke among you? let him bring in the Priestes of the Church, & let them pray ouer him, annointing him with oile, in the name of our Lord. And the prayer of faith shal saue the sicke: and our Lord shal lift him vp : and if he be in sinnes, they shal be remitted him. Confesse therfore your sinnes, one to an other : and pray one for an other, that you may be saued.] In this whole passage we may

When this Sacrament was instituted, is not expressed in holie Scripture.

Ioa. 21.
v. vlt.

Act. 1.
v. 3.

S. Iames omitting to declare the institution of this Holie Rite, therby sheweth that he spake of a thing already knowen, and so expresseth other circumstances perteyning to the practise.

Iac. 5. v.
14.

v. 15.

v. 16.

§ 15.

may first obserue, though they be not the first wordes, that if the person thus annoiled [be in sinnes, they shal be remitted him] which effect of remission of sinnes, by an exterdal Ceremonie, doth inuincibly shew that it is an holie, and perfect Sacrament. In further declaration wherof, let vs also consider al the other wordes, before and after : by which other effectes, with the state of the person to be releeued, the Minister, the matter, and forme of this holie Sacrament, are likewise declared. By the first wordes [Is anie man sicke among you] it is signified, that this Sacrament perteyneth only to the sicke : not to others that haue bodilie health , and competent strength to pray, and doe other spiritual exercises, for their owne soules health, and to resist the enimies assaultes. Secondly we see by the Apostles wordes, that Priestes are the Ministers of this Sacrament: whom the partie diseased must desire to pray, not only for him, which might be done absent, but [ouer him] that is, in presence by him. Thirdly that the Priest, together with his prayer, must annoint him with oyle[pray ouer him, anointing him with oyle.] Fourtly the forme of this Sacrament is deprecatorie, as is euident by the wordes [let them pray ouer him.] And so the Church practiseth in administring it, by this sette forme of wordes vttered by the Priest, applying the holie oyle to the seueral partes of the bodie, where the senses haue their most proper function. As, touching the eyes he saith: [By this holie vnction, and by his most pious mercie, our Lord pardon, and forgeue thee, whatsoeuer thou hast sinned by sight.] And so in like forme annoiting the other visual partes, the special organes of the external senses. Al agreable to S. Iames his declaration, though not al expressed by him. And, that so manie partes of the bodie are annoiled (which some may perhaps imagine to be superfluous) doth nothing

By the effect of remitting sinnes, it is most especially proued to be a Sacrament.

Who is to receiue it.

Who is to minister it. and where ?

What is the external matter of this Sacrament ?

And what is the forme.

An obiection is solued.

nothing at al disproue this holie action, nor hinder it, from being a perfect Sacrament. For the Prieft annointing anie one part only, adioyning therwith the deprecatorie forme, with intentio there to complete the Sacrament, it is in dede complete. And may lawfully be fo adminiftered, in cafe of neceffitte, when the ficke perfon is in the laft extremitie, like to depart from this world, before the reft (which is otherwife required) can be performed. And therfore, whether only one part of the ficke bodie, or more partes be annoiled, here are fufficient matter, forme, minifter, promife of gracious effect, and al other thinges requifite to a true, and perfect Sacrament. And

The Apoftles practife prefuppofeth Chrifts Inftitution.

Chrifts Inftitution is alfo clearly proued by the practife. For as the Apoftles fact, in annoyting the ficke, prefuppofed Chrifts commiffion fo to doe: euen fo S. Iames his admonition, to vfe this facred Rite, to fo great effect, prefuppofeth Chrifts Inftitution therof, as of a proper Sacrament: becaufe the Apoftles could not inftitute anie external Rite, to fo great effectes. As is yet further declared in the next Article.

Mar. 6. v. 13.

The proper effect, is ftrengthning of the foule in the agonie of death; with remiffion of finnes, if anie remained; & reftauration to bodilie health, if it be expedient for the foule.

ARTICLE 39.

IN thefe wordes of the Apoftle [The prayer of faith fhal faue the ficke: and our Lord fhal lift him vp; and if he be in finnes, they fhal be remitted him] are conteyned three effectes of this holie Sacrament, one proper, & abfolute; which is ftrengthning of the foule, in the agonie of death. An other effect

Iac. 5. v. 15.

Three effectes of this Sacrament; one common to al Chrifts Sa-

effect is common to this Sacrament , with al other Sacraments of Christ , which is remission of sinnes conditionally, if anie remained. The third effect is also proper to this Sacrament : which is restauration of corporal health, but conditional, if the same be more expedient for the soule. Al which we shal here further explicate, and declare in order.

craments : the other two proper to this.

2. First, by these wordes [Prayer of faith] no doubt the Apostle meaneth the same prayer, whereof he spake immediatly before, to witte the Priestes prayer ioyned with the action of annoiling , & so the word and external element, that is, the forme and matter, doe ioyntly worke special effect in the sicke person, either in his soul, eor bodie, or both, signified by those wordes [shal saue the sicke.] For as in other places of holie Scripture , so here [to be made whole , and safe] sometimes signifieth both spiritual, and bodilie health, for so it is our Saviours maner [to cure men wholly] and especially the soule, which is the more principal part. And so the proper, & peculiar effect of this Sacrament, is the strengthning of the soule, with special grace and comfort , as wel to beare more patiently , the bodilie paine, and pangues of death : as to resist , and withstand the tentations of the enimie , who then most busily assaulteth the sicke, with divers suggestions, to drive them into damnable state, or to kepe them therein : as sometimes into presumption of imagined securitie, without due repentance, & without helpe of Sacraments: sometime into desperation, & distresse of mind, without hope of Gods mercie, by aggerating the horrour of their sinnes, & terrifying them with Gods iustice. Our Lord therfore most iust, & most merciful , hath ordained this special supplie of grace , in the time of most neede, besides other holie Sacraments : that as the spiritual combate is then most dangerous , so new helpe, & succursse of more strength is afforded,

Mat. 9.
v. 2. 6. 7.
22. Ch.
14. v. 36.
Iv. 7. v.
23.

The proper & absolute effect is strengthning of the soule in the agonie of death.

F f   by our

by our propicious Lord, and Sauiour, who [neuer 1.*Cor* 10. suffereth his seruants to be tempted aboue their *v.* 13. strength, but geueth also fruite (or good issue) with tentation.]

3.   An other spiritual effect is expressed in these wordes [If he be in sinnes, they shal be remitted him] which is the common effect of al Chrifts Sacramento, that if they be worthily receiued, they remitte sinnes, geuing first grace of iustification, if the soule was not actually iuft, but only disposed therto by attrition: and if the soule be iuft, it is [yet *Apoc.* 22. iuftified more] by increase of grace. These wordes *v.* 11. therfore (if there were no other proofe) doe clearly shew (as is noted before) and inuincibly confirme, *Article.* that this is a true, and proper Sacrament. For that 38. no other Ceremonie, nor Ecclesiaftical Rite, nor external signes, doe remitte al kinde of actual sinne, but only true Sacraments. And therfore the Apoftle speaking generally of al such sinnes, as are committed by anie Chriftian after Baptisme (for to al such persons he writte his Epiftle) he affirmeth plainly, that the vertue of this prayer, together with the annoiling, doth remitte sinnes, if anie remaine in the sicke person so annoiled. By adding of which condition [if he be in sinnes] he sheweth that it is not the proper effect of this Sacrament, but that the penitent muft seeke remiffion of his sinnes, by the Sacrament of confeffion: and so expresly he exhorteth in the next wordes, saying [Confeffe *p.* 16. therfore your sinnes, one to an other, and pray one for an other, that you may be saued.] So the circumftance of the sacred text moft apparently signifieth. And if after confeffion, or by anie defect in confeffion (against the penitents wil, being willing to confeffe al, if they were knowen vnto him, and in his memorie) there remaine anie sinnes, they are al remitted by Extreme vnction, whether they be
mortal

An other effect is remiffion of sinnes, if anie remaine, and if the sicke person be attrite.

mortal or venial: for here the Apostle speaketh indefinitely without restriction.

4. The third effect expressed by the Apostle in these wordes [Our Lord shal lift him vp] is assuredly true, no lesse then the other two : but only the first is absolute, without condition, and the other two conditional. For as the effect, of remission of sinnes, which is last expressed, is conditional, if he be in sinnes: so this which is expressed in the midde place, must nedes to be vnderstood, to be also conditional; in respect of corporal health, if the same be more expedient for health of the soule. Because otherwise the lesse benefite should preiudice the greater, which can not be in Gods workes, for they are alwayes perfect in themselues. And we see by experience, that albeit some are restored to corporal health, after this Sacrament, yet manie are not; Gods prouidence ordayning to euerie one of his seruants, that which is best for them, alwayes hearing and granting the deuout prayers of the iust, though not alwayes in that sense, as they demand, yet to such effect, as his diuine wisdom knoweth to be better. For as the same Apostle teacheth [some aske, and receiue not, because they aske amisse.] And so if they should pray absolutely for corporal health, by vertue of this holie Sacrament, they should in that point pray amisse. Because we must neuer pray absolutely, for anie temporal or corporal thing, but conditionaliy, if it be (and so farre as it may be) to Gods more honour, and the good of soules. As remission of sinnes is alwayes most necessarie, where they remaine: for otherwise the soule is not capable of other grace. And therfore the forme of this deprecatorie Sacrament, is a direct prayer for pardon, and remission of sinnes, which haue bene committed of the sicke person, by abuse of al, or anie of his senses. And so accordingly, as the wordes

V. 15.

Deut. 32. v. 4.

Luc. 11. v. 9. 10. 33.

Iac. 4. v. 3.

The third effect is restauration to corporal health, conditionally if it be expedient for the soule.

We must not pray for temporal, nor corporal thinges, but with condition, if they be to Gods more honour, and health of soules.

Ff 2   signifie,

fignifie, it hath effect, of ftrengthning the foule, in
the conflict before death : alfo remiffion of finnes,
if anie remained : and of corporal health. if it be beft
for the foule : at leaft of fo much bodilie ftrength,
as is neceffarie for the foules health.

*It behoueth al penitent Chriftians , being by
fiknes in peril of death, to receiue this holie
Sacrament of Extreme Vnction.*

ARTICLE. 40.

Not to fecke
things pro-
fitable to our
foules, is the
finne of im-
prudence, of
negligence,
& often grea-
ter finne.

English Pro-
teftants allow
of particular
Confeffion,
but not of
Extreme
Vnction.

Neceffitie in things poffible and of importance,
bindeth vnder paine of great finne. Vtilitie in
like things poffible , and of importance bindeth in
prudence , and in fome cafes induceth obligation,
vnder paine of other finne, more or leffe. For fo
much therfore , as al the feuen Sacraments , are of *Artic.*10.
great importance , we haue hitherto declared , in 11.
their feueral places, of what neceffitie, and fpecial *Art.* 17.
vtilitie the former foure are:& it is alfo very needful *Art.* 21.
to explicate the fame point , touching this Sacra- *Art.* 27.
ment, becaufe it likewife perteyneth to euerie Chriftian penitent , in particular : and is rather more reiected, then the reft, by Proteftants , who wil feme
to make fome fhew of al the other, but none at al of
Extreme Vnction. For although they haue a new
deuifed maner of vifiting the ficke , where they
allow of particular Confeffion of finnes , with a
prefcript forme of Abfolution from al finnes, to be
geuen by the Prieft, which highly offendeth Puritanes : yet they neuer fpeake of annointing the ficke,
nor deale therwith : but by diuers very friuolous
obiections impugne it, neither admitting the Sacrament it felf, nor anie refemblance in fhew therof.
2. Their firft euafion from fo cleare teftimonie of
S. Iames,

S. Iames, is the denial, or calling into doubt, that S.Iames Epistle should not be Canonical holie Scripture. Luther in plaine termes denieth it, & calleth it, *Stramineam Epistolam : & Apostolico spiritu indignam :* A straw Epistle : and vnworthie an Apostolical spirite. Some other Protestantes wil only doubt of it, and so wil not admitte it, for an assured ground of proofe in matter of faith. English Protestants doe admitte it with Caluin, to be Canonical Scripture : and so flee to other shiftes. In the Bibles which they commonly read in their Churches, in stead of the word [Priestes] is Elders, of the Church (and in one Bible, Elders of the congregation) as if this annoiling of the sicke, were no Priestlie function, and that the Apostles meaning were, that ancient old men, whether they be Clergie men, or Laimen, were in this case to be called for [to pray ouer the sicke, annointing them with oyle.] But when it is proued, that their translation is corrupt, and fraudulent (for not only both Latine & Greke texts haue Presbyteros) which they sometimes translate Priestes : but also they here auoide the word Ministers, lest it might appeare, that the Apostle meaneth Ecclesiastical persons. Againe when this sleight is also detected, they haue an other, which is a mere imagination, that the Apostle should speake, only of a miraculous maner of curing the sicke, which is long since ceassed, and so no more vse therof, Which their inuention hath diuers, and great absurdities. First this glosse hath neither warrant of holie Scripture (by which they wil haue al trial made) nor is proued by Tradition (if perhaps in some case they wil repaire therunto) for neither anie holie Scripture doth witnes, that this annointing of the sicke should in time ceasse, & be no more in vse ; neither doth Tradition helpe them : but both the Apostles promulgation of it, is in plaine and general wordes, perteyning to al times,

margin notes:

Their chefe obiections are answered.

Lutherants denie S.Iames Epistle to be Canonical.

Other Protestants translate *Elders,* for *Priestes.*

3552.

1. *Tim.* 4. v. 14.

They also pretend that the Apostle speaketh only of a miraculous gift, not of anie perpetual Rite in the Church.

Manie absurdities in this inuention.

1. It hath no warrant,

times,

times, and places of the Christian world. And by tradition it is most cleare, that in al the Church of Christ it hath bene stil in vse. Secondly it is false, and absurde to say, that al sicke persons were then directed to seeke corporal health by miraculous meanes, as the principal benefite: for so these glossers plainly shew that they esteme it, in that they would haue this holie action to cease, because al are not visibly cured therby in bodie. Thirdly it is also false, and absurde to say, that either al Priestes (or Elders) generally, or they onlie, had this peculiar gift to cure sicke bodies, but some had this gift, as wel others, as Priestes, and some Priestes had other like giftes, and not this, and some had no extraordinarie giftes at al. [Al were not Apostles, al Prophetes, al Doctors, al did not miracles, al did not cures, al did not speake with tongues, al did not interprete] euen so albeit Priestes were the Ministers of this Sacrament, yet they did did not alwayes cure al the sicke therby. For some died shortly after, as wel in the primitiue Church, as now. Fourtly, they doe manifestly contradict their owne general doctrine, denying that anie Sacrament remitteth sinnes, and are here forced to confesse that by this external action (consisting in praying, & annoiling) their sinnes are remitted, to whom it is ministred: and yet denie it to be a Sacrament. What can be more absurde, then to graunt greater effect, to an other external action, that is no Sacrament, then to anie Sacrament?

3. Wherefore seing in al true diuinitie, Extreme Vnction is in dede an holie Sacrament, geuing grace and remitting sinnes, though ordinarily it be not so necessarie, as without it the soule should eternally perish, yet is it necessarie in an other degree, *ad melius esse*, to the bettering of the soules estate: for more strength in the last combate against the firce enimie.

Net

margin notes: 2. Corporal health is not the principal effect. 3. Neither al, nor onlie Priestes had the gift of curing infirmities by miracles. 4. Protestants denying that anie Sacrament remitteth sinne, confesse that this external action (which they say, is no Sacrament) remitted sinnes. Extreme Vnction is requisite for great benefites of soules. 1. Cor. 12. v. 28. 29.

Not to esteme it, therfore is incredulitie: to persist in opinion that it is of smal importance, is plaine heresie: knowing it to be a Sacrament profitable for the soule, not to desire it, is great imprudence: to omitte it for anie temporal respect, is [prudence of the flesh] which is a greuous sinne: to vse no ende-uour to receiue it, is grosse negligence: to refuse it, when it may be had in case requisite, is contempt. Finally in some case, as if for lacke or speach, or of perfect memorie, the penitent sicke person, can not sufficiently confesse his mortal sinnes, especially if he can not confesse anie of his sinnes at al, then this Sacrament is most necessarie; for procuring of more grace, and spiritual supplie of the penitents imbecilitie, to cooperate in cleansing his soule, and for remission of sinnes, if he haue only Attrition, not Contrition.

Rom. 8. v. 6.

Art. 26.

What sinnes are incurred by omitting this holie Sacrament.

In some case it is necessarie.

Ordination of Priestes, & of other Clergimen, is a true Sacrament.

ARTICLE 41.

After declaration of the fiue Holie Sacraments, which perteyne to euerte faithful person, in respect of their owne particular spiritual state, we are in like maner to declare the other two, which are ordayned to the spiritual good of the whole communitie of Gods Church: which are Holie Orders, and Matrimonie. Wherfore concerning Holie Orders, we shal first shew, that it is a true and proper Sacrament, instituted by Christ. By which some are taken from the Laitie, made Clerkes, and ordained Ecclesiastical Ministers of Christ, to execute spiritual functions in the Church: according to their diuers powres, of seuen distinct Orders, lesse & greates. Of which also some (of the greatest Order,

Six particular pointes are here proued concerning Holie Orders.

1.

Order, which is Priefthood) are confecrated Cheefe Prieftes, called Bifhopes. Secondly that neuer anie man fince Chrifts Afcenfion could be promoted to anie of thefe Orders, or be made a Clergiman, but by Ordination of the Apoftles, or their Succeffors.

2.

3. Thirdly that neither ought anie man to be admitted,

4. without certaine requifite qualities. Fourtly that the principal functions, of al the feuen Orders, doe tend, to the confecration and oblation of the holie

5. Eucharift, which onlie Prieftes can performe. Fiftly, that an other function of holie Orders, is fpiritually to feede, & gouerne the faithful flocke of Chriftians.

6. And fixtly that the fame is, in facred fubordination of one cheefe vifible Superior. Al which we fhal here proue in feueral Articles.

2. Touching the firft point, in al congregations, which pretend anie Religion, there are fome orders of men, deputed to fpiritual offices, whom they account as Ecclefiaftical perfons. Pureft Caluiniftes haue onlie Minifters, or as they cal them, Preachers of the word: with an Elder, or Superintendent, in euerie citie, or prouince. Lutherans haue alfo Superintendents, & Minifters, whom they cal Prieftes. Which pretend to confecrate Chrifts real bodie and bloud in the Eucharift. Englifh Proteftants ordaine in their peculiar maner Bifhopes: keping the title, and external habite of Catholique Bifhopes. And thefe doe ordaine certaine Readers, Deacones, and Minifters: which title of Minifters is either al one with Deacones (for Διαconos in Greke, is in Latine *Minifter*) or els it is common to Readers, Deacones, Bifhopes, and whatfoeuer other Ecclefiaftical Order. But they vfe this name of Minifter, for the Degree next aboue a Deacon: becaufe they wil haue no Prieftes: wel knowing that euerie true Prieft, is a Maffing Prieft: and that his moft proper office is to offer Sacrifice: which they abhorre, & fo farre as

lieth

Not onlie true Religion, but alfo al falfly pretended religions depute fome men to fpiritual functions.

Proteftants haue neither Prieft, nor Sacrifice, nor Altar.

Leuit. 8. v. 2. &c. Ch. 9. v. 2. 7. 2.Par. 26. v. 18.

lieth in them, haue abolished. As also they wil haue no Altar, for that, it importeth a Sacrifice, & Priest-hode, but in place therof they haue a communion table. And so for lacke of a proper terme, they cal him a Minister, that ministreth their communion: miserably confounding themselues in their practise, and new doctrine, which admitteth a Deacon of the Catholique Romane Church, for a sufficient Mini-ster, and also maketh al Christianes, men, wemen, and children, to be Priestes alike. And therfore it is no maruel, that they denie Holie Orders, to be a Sacrament. as in deede it is not with them.

They hold a Catholique Deacon equal to their owne Minister, and al Christians to be Priestes alike,

3. Which neuertheles is euidently proued to be a true, & great Sacrament, in the Catholique Church. And first by the figure therof in the Law of Moyses, Where it is manifest, and I suppose our Aduersaries wil not denie, that Ordination of Priestes & Leuites, was a Sacrament. For God expresly instituted the same, in external Ceremonies, with sanctification of the persons. [Thou shalt speake to the wise of hart (said our Lord to Moyses) that they make Aarons vestments, wherin he being sanctified, may minister to me. Thou shalt bring Aaron & his sonnes, to the doore of the Tabernacle of testimonie. And when thou hast washed the father, with his sonnes in wa-ter: thou shalt vest Aaron with his vestments, &c. And thou shalt powre the oile of vnction vpon his head: and by this Rite shal he be consecrated. His sonnes also thou shalt bring, & shalt inuest them, &c. Seuen dayes shalt thou consecrate their handes: and thou shalt offer a calf for sinne, euerie day, for expia-tion. And thou shalt cleanse the Altar, when thou hast offered the hoste of expiation: & shalt annoynt it vnto sanctification.] As it was thus ordained: so with al the prescribed solemnitie, it was perfor-med: before al the people, at the doore of the Taber-nacle, where they were washed, reuested, annointed

Holie order is proued to be a true Sa-crament. First by the figure of or-dination of Priestes in the old Law, which was a Sacrament,

Exo. 28.
v. 3.
Ch. 29.
v. 4.

v. 7.
v. 8.

v. 35.

v. 36.

Leuit 8.
v. 2. 3.
6. 7. 12.

Gg   Sacrifice

Sacrifice was alſo offered, Aaron and his ſonnes 14. 18.
putting their handes vpon the hoſtes, which were
immolated. The Leuites alſo had a ſpecial ordination. [Take the Leuites out of the middes of the chil- *Num.* 3.
dren of Iſrael (ſaid our Lord to Moyſes) and thou *v.* 10.
ſhalt purifie them, according to this Rite: Let them *Ch.* 8. *v.* 5.
be ſprinckled with the water of luſtranon, & ſhaue *v.* 6.
al the haires of their fleſh: and when they haue wa-   7.
ſhed their garments, and are cleanſed, they ſhal take
an oxe out of the heardes, and his libament, &c.   8.
And thou ſhalt bring the Leuites before the Taber-   9.
nacle of couenant. The children of Iſrael ſhal put   10.
their handes vpon them. And Aaron ſhal offer the   11.
Leuites a gift, in the ſight of the Lord, from the 13. 14.
children of Iſrael, that they may ſerue in his mini- 15. &c.
ſterie] Al this (with more ſolemnitie, in ordayning
both Prieſtes, and Leuites, purifying, cleanſing, and
ſanctifying them, for the miniſterie of God in the
old Teſtament, doth not only ſhew, that their Ordination was then a Sacrament, but alſo proueth, that
much more the Ordination of Prieſtes, and other
Clergimen, now in the Law of Chriſt (to a farre
more excellent miniſterie) is a true and proper Sacrament, by as much as the bodie excelleth the ſhadow, and the veritie ſurpaſſeth the figure. [For the *Ioan.* 1.
Law was geuen by Moyſes, grace and veritie was *v.* 17.
made by Ieſus Chriſt.] Wherfore as the former ordination was a Sacrament, ſignifying grace, but not
geuing it; ſo this now, both ſignifying, and as an
inſtrumental cauſe geuing grace, which it ſignifieth; muſt neceſſarily be a true Sacrament of the
Chriſtian Church.

4.   Yet more clearly it is proued to be a true Sacrament, by the new Teſtament: and that according to
thoſe groundes, which Proteſtants require, to witte
that it is an external ſigne (or *ſymbolum*) with promiſe
of grace; inſtituted by Chriſt. The firſt of theſe is
                                        euident,

Alſo the Or-
dination of
Leuites.

The ſame is
inuincibly
proued by
the new Te-
ſtament.

euident, which is Impofition of Apoftolical, or Epi-
fcopal handes, with wordes fignifying the power
geuen, and with deliuerie of fome thing, wherin External
the fame power is to be practifed. As to him that is figne.
made a Prieft, are deliuered bread and wine, with
power to confecrate them. To a Deacon is deliuered the Booke of the Gofpels, with impofition of
handes. And in other Orders other thinges. So the
AB. 6. Apoftles made the feuen Deacons, by impofition of
v. 6. handes: and although in the fame place, there is
not mention of power to preach the Gofpel, yet it
Ch. 7. is manifeft, that S. Steuen, & S. Philippe did preach,
Ch. 8. v. 5. and baptize, and the fame is to be vnderftood of the
reft, which prefuppofeth that they had commiffion
Ch. 13. fo to doe. And S. paul and S. Barnabas were orday-
v. 3. ned Bifhopes, and Apoftles, by impofition of handes.
The fecond thing required is grace, to be geuen, Collation of
which S. Paul teftifieth, was geuen to S. Timothee, grace.
1. Tim. 4. when he receiued holie Orders, faying to him [Ne-
v. 14. glect not the grace, that is in thee, which is geuen
thee, by prophecie, with the impofition of the handes of Priefthood.] In that the Apoftle faith [by pro-
phecie] he fignifieth, that by prophetical fpirite, or
reuelation he knew Timothee to be fitte, & worthie
to be promoted, as he was, to facred function in the
Church. In faying [with impofition of handes of
Priefthood] he plainly fignifieth, that grace was
geuen him, by that external figne of impofition of
handes, that is by Ordination. Againe S. Paul witneffeth the fame, in his fecond Epiftle, fignifying
his great and continual care, of S. Timothees pro-
2. Tim. 1. greffe in al vertues. [For the which caufe (faith he)
v. 3. &c. I admonifh thee, that thou refufcitate the grace of
v. 6. God, which is in thee, by the impofition of my handes,] what can be more clearly faid, to fignifie.
that the grace of God was geuen, by impofition
of S. Paules handes, ordaining S. Timothee a Prieft,

Priesthood was instituted by Christ.

and a Bishope? The third thing requisite in euerie Sacrament, is Diuine Institution, which is both manifest by Chrifts wordes, (faying to his Apostles *Luc 22.* (after that he had confecrated the B Sacrament of *v. 19.* his owne bodie and bloud) Doe ye this] therby making them Prieftes, and fo inftituting the holie order of Priefthood. And the fame is alfo neceffarily vnderftood, by the other two requifite conditions, becaufe no other man but onlie Chrift, who is God & Man, can annexe grace to an external figne. And therfore whenfoeuer a vifible external figne. hath grace adioyned vnto it, the fame is a true Sacrament of Chrift, inftituted by him: whether his Inftitution therof be expreffed or no. And fo being *Vifibile fignum inuifibilis gratiæ:* A vifible figne of inuifible grace: it is a complete Chriftian Sacrament.

5   There was alfo in the old Sacrament of Leuitical Orders, an other efpecial refemblance of the holie Orders, which are in the Church of Chrift.

The other orders of the Clergie were also prefigured in the Law of Moyfes.

For there were then not only Prieftes, and amongft them an High Prieft, but alfo diuers degrees of Leuites, fuperior, and inferior: fo difpofed that al the *Nu. 3. v.* power of the inferior, was in the fuperior, and in *17.18.45.* him fome more, which was not in the inferior. The *Nu. 4. v.* firft and cheefeft order of the Leuites were the Caathites; the fecond the Gerfonites; and the third the *15.24.31.* *1. Par. 24.* Merarites: who al ferued in, and about the Tabernacle, & Temple, al fubordinate to the Prieftes, who *v. 4. 7.* onlie could offer Sacrifice. Which figure is fulfilled *Ch. 25.26.* in the thing prefigured, with fpecial excellencie. *2. Par. 26.* For wheras in the Law of Moyfes, al that were *v. 18.* borne of the Tribe of Leui perteyned to the Clergie, and none others: now in the Church of Chrift, neither by birth, nor of one only Tribe, or kindred, *Ifa. 66.* but by fpiritual vocation [of al Chriftians] fuch as *v. 21.* are iudged fitte, and [voluntarily defire this ftate] *Pfal. 15.* are taken from the Laitie, & by a fpecial ceremonie, *v. 5.*

By firft tonfure laimen

called, Firft Tonfure, are made Clergimen, & fo are

made capable of Ecclefiaftical Orders. And wheras are made Clerques.
in the old Law there were four diftinct Orders, to
witte, Priefthood, & three degrees of Leuites, in the
Chriftian Church are Seuen Ecclefiaftical Orders, Befides which there are se-uen diftinct Orders.
which are (in order of afcending) Oftiarius, Lector,
Exorcifta, Acolytus (called *Minores Ordines*) and Subdeacon, Deacon, & Prieft, called *Maiores*. Amongft
which, for complement of the facred Ecclefiaftical
Ierarchie, fome are chefe Prieftes, called Bifhopes. And Bifhopes cheefe Prie-ftes.
Al which (by reafon of the fubordination, euerie
greater prefuppofing and including al the leffe) are
comprehended in the general name of Holie Order,
and fo are one, of the feuen Chriftian Sacraments.

Act. 14. Howbeit confidered diftinctly euerie Order, efpe-
v. 22. Ch. cially euerie one of the greater (called Maiores) is
15. v. 2. a Sacrament. And although only Bifhopes, Prieftes,
Ch. 20. and Deacons are exprefly named in holie Scripture:
v 28. yet by authentical Tradition (to which holie Scrip-
1. Tim. 3. ture afcribeth infallible affurance of truth) the reft
v. 1. 8. alfo, haue ftil bene in the Catholique Church, fince
Tit. 1. v. 5. Chrifts Afcenfion.

6. And it is alfo gathered in the holie Gofpesl, that
our B. Sauiour, the Cheefe Eternal Prieft, exercifed Chrift exer-cifed al the Ecclefiaftical Orders.
al thefe holie Orders, as occafion ferued : moft of
them very clearly recorded by the Euangeliftes.
Twife we read, that our Sauiour practifed the office
of Oftiarius : driuing vnworthie perfons out of the
Ioan. 2. Temple of God. [When he made as it were a whip
v. 15. of litle cordes, and caft them, that folde oxen, and
fhepe, and doues, and bankers of money, out of the
Temple, and poured out the money of the bankers,
v. 16. and ouerthrew their tables, & faid vnto them : Make
not the houfe of my Father, a houfe of marchan-
dife.] This he did at his firft beginning to preach.
Likewife three yeares after, a litle before his Paffion,
Mat. 21. finding the fame fault to be committed againe [he
v. 12. 13. caft out of the Temple, al that folde, and bonght

there:

there: and the tables of the bankers, and the chayres of them that folde pigions, he ouer threw: and faid to them: It is writen: My houfe fhal be called, the *Ifa* 56. houfe of prayer; but you haue made it a denne of *v.* 7. theeues.] The office of Lectorfhippe, or Reading, our Sauiour fometimes exercifed, in the Synagogue at Nazareth [where (as S. Luke writeth) he entred ac- *Luc.* 4. cording to his cuftom on the Sabbath day, & he rofe *v.* 16. 17. vp to read, and the Booke of Ifaias the Prophete was *v.* 20. 21. deliuered vnto him] And fo he both read, which is the proper office of Lectoratus: and expounded the Prophecie, which is one fpecial office of Subdeaconfhipe. And he very often proued himfelf to be Meffias, which is an other office of Deaconfhipe. Likewife the office of Exorcift, our Lord practifed *Mat.* 8. very much, cafting diuels out of men: and gaue that *v.* 31. 32. power to his Apoftles, and other Difciples, making *Ch.* 10. *v.* 8 them Exorciftes. Sometimes vfing external cere- *Luc.* 10. monies, and corporal creatures, touching the eares, *v.* 17. & tongue of the infirme perfon, with fpitle: which *Mar.* 7. *v.* maner of Rites perteyne to Exorcifme. The Aco- 33. 34. lytes office, which is to bring light: and to ferue in *Luc.* 12. time of Sacrifice nere the Altar, our Lord exercifed *v.* 49. al his life, for he brought himfelf, the true light of the world. In particular he prefented himfelfe to his perfecutors, in the houre appointed for his apprehenfion, when he would the next day offer himfelfe vpon the Croffe, going to them, and faying: [Whom feke you, I am he.] Againe, when the eni- *Ioan.* 18. mies were fallen downe on the ground, he fuffered *v.* 4. 7. them to rife, and faid [Whom feeke ye? I am he] The other three greater Orders our Lord practifed, in the inftitution of the B. Sacrament of his owne bodie and bloud [Whiles they were at fupper] Iefus *Mat.* 26. firft taking bread, and afterward the chalice, de- *v.* 26. 27. figned the matter for the holie Sacrament and Sacri- *Mar.* 14. fice, feparating it from the reft, as determinate to *v.* 22.

this

Luc. 22.
1. Cor. 11.

this purpose: which is the proper office of the Subdeacon. The office of Deacon he performed, in taking the bread and wine, which were vpon the Altar into his owne handes, and mixing water into the wine, which perteyneth to the office of the Deacon (besides preaching, and baptizing) and so to put it into the Priests handes, & also to minister it. The principal office of Priesthod, he performed in consecrating, and offering his owne bodie & bloud, in Sacrifice to God: himself as Man being the Priest, and Hoste, sacrificed to God, the B. Trinitie. Lastly he exercised also the office of the Bishope, in making his Apostles Priestes, when he said to them: [Doe ye this] & againe, when after his Resurrection

Joa. 20.
v. 22. 23.

he said to them [Receiue ye the Holie Ghost: whose sinnes you shal forgeue, they shal be forgeuen them] which is an other special function of Priestes, committed to them by the Bishope. Al which textes of holie Scriptures, though not al expresly, yet by agreable deduction, may suffice, together with the Apostolical Tradition, to proue & defend, al the distinct Orders of this holie Sacrament, as the Catholique Church beleueth, holdeth, and teacheth, against whatsoeuer our Aduersaries can alleage in expresse holie Scriptures to the contrarie. If anie man wil contend that these are not sufficient proofes, nor defence of al the Catholique Ecclesiastical Orders: we auouch to defend them al, by better warrant, then English Protestantes, or Puritanes, can iustifie their new terme of Elders, or shal proue the lawful institution of their Readers, or of anie, their pretended Ecclesiastical Orders. And more manifestly then they shal shew an essential, or real difference betwen their Deacon, and Minister. Now we shal shew, that they haue none of al these holie Orders at al.

We proue al these by better warrant, then our Aduersaries can defend their new terme of Elders &c. or difference betwen their Minister and Deacon.

None

None can be Clergimen, but by Ordination of the Apostles Successors.

ARTICLE. 42.

King Ierobo-
am vpon false
imagination
of temporal
danger to his
Kingdom, ma-
de schisme in
Religion, and
false Priestes.

WHen Ieroboam was by Gods permission, law- 3. *Reg* 11. fully made King ouer tenne Tribes of Israel, *v.* 31. *Ch.* he falsely imagining that his temporal state could not 12. *v.* 24. be secure, vnles he separated himself, and his people from the High Priest, and Temple, which were in Ierusalem, he altered among themselues, the whole state of Religion. [For he sayd in his hart: If this 3 *Reg.* 12. people shal goe vp to make Sacrifices in the house of *v.* 26. 27. our Lord, into Ierusalem: the hart of this people wil be turned to their Lord Roboam, the King of Iuda, and they wil kil me, and returne to him. And finding out à deuise, he made two golden calues, *v.* 28. and said to the people: Goe vp no more into Ieru-salem: Behold thy goddes Israel, which brought thee out of the Land of Ægypt. And he put one in *v.* 29. Bethel, and the other in Dan. And he made Temples in the excelses, and Priestes of the abiectes of the *v.* 31. people, which were not of the children of Leui.] And being admonished by a Prophete [which was sent from Iuda to Bethel, he returned not from his *Ch.* 13. wicked way, but on the contrarie part, he made of *v.* 1. 2. the most abiect of the people, Priestes of the excel-ses: whosoeuer would, he filled his hand (annoin- *v.* 33. ted their handes with oyle, as Schismatikes apishly imitate some holie rites) and he was a Priest of the *Ex.* 29. *v.* excelses] not of the true Church, but of the places, 9. *Leu.* 8. where idols were worshipped. A most proper re- *v.* 7. *&c.* semblace of the present English Ministerie. For after *Iud.* 17. that King Henrie the Eight, had (for imagined tem- *v.* 5. poral danger, & gaine) separated himself & his peo ple from the Sea Apostolique, he made himself Head

of the

of the Church, or cheefe Prieſt. And 20 yeares after,
ſix of the Clergie, and ſix temporal Lawyers were
appointed, in the time of King Edward the Sixt, to
deuiſe a forme of making Clergiemen. But as it is
certaine that thoſe of King Ieroboams creatiõ, were
not Prieſtes, but falſely ſo called, euen ſo manifeſt it
is, that Engliſh Miniſters are neither Prieſtes, nor
Clergimen, but mere Laimen. Becauſe, as in the
Law of Moyſes, none were Prieſtes (no though they
were of the familie of Aaron, who only were then
capable of Prieſthod) neither were others of the
Tribe of Leui, right Leuites to ſerue in the miniſterie
of the Tabernacle, and Temple: vntil they were admitted, conſecrated, & ordayned by ſpiritual auctoritie, with due Rites: ſo abſolute neceſſarie it is, and
euer was in the Church of Chriſt, that ſuch as ſhal be
Clergimen muſt be lawfully called, ordayned, and
conſecrated to ſacred functions, by the Apoſtles Succeſſors: as the Apoſtles them ſelues were called, and
ordayned by Ieſus Chriſt: and others by them, and
ſo continually by right ſucceſſion, al Clergimen
haue their Ordination deriued from Chriſt. And
therfore al others, otherwiſe pretending Eccleſiaſtical miſſion, vocation, or ordination, are mere
laimen, intruders, and vniuſt vſurpers.

2. Lacking better pleas, the Sectaries of this time
vſe two ſpecial ſhiftes to defend their pretended
Eccleſiaſtical functions. Sometimes they ſay that al
Chriſtians (men, wemen, and children) are Prieſtes:
and therfore nede not anie other ordination, but
may be deſigned, by the Prince, or people, to exerciſe ſpiritual power. And vpon this, or no better
ground, a ſecular Laiman, King Henrie the Eight:
alſo his ſonne, a childe ſcarſe tenne yeares of age,
King Edward the Sixth: and after them a woman,
Quene Eliſabeth, haue bene taken for Prieſtes, and
made High Prieſtes, the Supreme heades of the

Margin notes:

Anno. Ed.
5. & 6.
Eliſ. 2.
& 8.

Leuit. 8.
v. 2 &c.
Nu. 8. v.
14. 15.

Proteſtant Mi-
niſters are no
more Prieſtes,
nor Clergie
men, then
thoſe of Iero-
boams ma-
king.

Sectaries of
this time vſe
two falſe
ſhiftes, to
defend their
pretended
miniſterie.

Firſt they
ſay that al
Chriſtians
are Prieſtes

Church of England, and Ireland: and vnder them haue bene pretended Bishopes, Ministers, Deacons, and Readers, al of the same creation; as being Priestes in their sense, by Baptisme: & put into possession, to practise spiritual power; the Prince by himself, and the people; and the rest. by the same Prince, and by his commission. And this new doctrine, they would maynteyne by the holie Scripture: alleaging sacred textes, for their purpose: For that S. Peter saith to al Christians. [Be ye also your selues *1. Pet. 2.* superedified, as it were liuing stones, a spiritual *v. 5.* house, a holie Priesthod, to offer spiritual hostes, acceptable to God, by Iesus Christ. You are an elect *v. 9.* generation, a Kinglie Priesthod, a holie nation, a people of purchase: that you may declare his vertues, which from darkenes hath called you into his maruelous light.] S Iohn like wise saith that Christ hath *Apoc. 1.* made vs a Kingdom, and Priestes to God his Father. *v 6.* And the blessed say to Christ [Thou hast made vs to *Ch. 5.* our God a Kingdom and Priestes.] Thus they finde *v. 10.* in the written word of God, to serue their turne, if themselues may vnderstand, and applie it as they list. But if they wil consider the whole passage, and search the true sense, they may see, that the Apostles *Io. 5. v.* and other blessed Sainctes, speake not of Priesthod, *39.* as it is properly taken: no more then of proper Sacrifices, and of proper Kinges. For S. Peter saith, that al Christians ought to be such Priestes, as may offer spiritual hostes, not external proper Sacrifices. And consequently he speaketh of spiritual, vnproper Priesthod. Albeit therfore such spiritual Priesthod was in the Iewes, of al the tribes, and is more excellently in al good Christians: yet could not anie lawfully offer hostes, and immolate Sacrifice in the *Leuit. 28.* old Law, but such as were of the familie of Aaron, *v. 17. &c.* and were consecrated Priestes, and had no other *Nu. 3.* legal defectes. [Who only were appointed by God, *v. 10.*

They pretend to proue their doctrine by holie Scripture, but wrong vnderstood.

So did Core and his complices alleage

ouer

ouer the seruice of Priesthod.] So that Core, Dathan and Abiron, with their complices did falsly, and wickedly denie the proper Priesthod of Aaron, pretending [That al the multitude consisted of holie ones, and our Lord is among them.] Likewise S. Peter withal saith, that [Christians are a Kinglie Priesthod] & S. Iohn, as also the other Sainctes say, that [we are a Kingdome, and Priestes] Yet are not al Christians Kinges, and Quenes, but al are spiritually so called, that haue the dominion & superioritie ouer conpiscences, and sinnes, and doe not yelde to tentations : especially those which are wholly free from al concupiscece, as the glorified are in heauen: and so al these are as Kinges in a Kingdom. And so whosoeuer imploy themselues, and their laboures, to the seruice of God, and offer al their actions, as spiritual hostes, an acceptable sacrifice to him, are spiritually Priestes. But as he, that denieth proper Kinglie power to be only in consecrated terrestrial Kinges, Quenes, & other ordinarie supreme Princes, and maketh al men Kinges alike : so he that denieth proper Priestlie power, to be only in consecrated sacrificing Priestes, and accounteth al to be Priestes alike : erreth grosly, & sediciously opposeth himself against especial power ordayned by God.

3. But this shift fayling, English Protestants haue found an other Plea for themselues, contrarie to their former defense, and contrarie to al their other brethren and neighbours, in France, Germanie, Sweserland, Holland, and Scotland : and wil nedes deriue their present Ecclesiastical Ministerie, from the Apostles, by the Apostolical Seat of Rome. To auerre this, they plead succession, without anie interruption, since the conuersion of our countrie to Christianitie: which they confesse was immediatly from the Pope of Rome. And therfore their new inuention is, that their first Protestant bishopes of

Nu. 16.
v. 3.
Exo. 29.
v. 45.
Leuit. 26.
v. 11. 12.

the word of God in defence of their rebellious schisme.

Perfect Christians, and Sainctes, are spiritually Kinges, and Priestes.

Their second shift is newly deuised, pretending to deriue their imagined Clergie from the Apostolical State of Rome.

Quene Elifabeths time, were Canonically confecrated by true Catholique Bifhopes : which is a moft
newly raifed controuerfie: not of doctrine (for euen
by this new plea, they approue the abfolute neceffitie, both of Apoftolical ordination, and of continual
fucceffion) but in matter of fact. For proofe wherof
there can be no alleaging of holie Scriptures expected, neither from them, nor vs. But that this late
found defenfe, is both falfe, in refpect of the thing
by them auouched, and alfo foolifh, or very imprudent, in refpect of their differing in opinion, from
not only other Proteftants, but alfo from themfelues, thefe laft yeares paft, is declared by inuincible
proofes, in fundrie lerned Booces, lately fet forth,
fince they pretended the auctoritie of a Regifter of
their owne, which they fay, reporteth, that Mafter
Parker, M. Young, M. Pilkington, Grindal, Horne,
Sandes, Iuel, and others were confecrated with al
due Rites, by Mafter Barlow, M. Scorie, and others.
A wonderful Myfterie, that fuch a thing fhould be
fo long concealed, efpecially at firft, when Catholique writers, Doctor Harding, Doctor Sanders, Doct.
Stapleton, Doct. Briftow, and others, in their printed Bookes, expreffy auouched that they were not
Bifhopes. And Doctor Edmund Bonner, the true Catholique Bifhope of London, openly pleaded in publique Court, before the Quenes Highcommiffioners,
that M. Grindal vniuftly vfurped his Seat : and that
the fame M. Grindal was not only an vniuft Intru-
der, but alfo that neither he, nor anie of the reft, was
a Bifhope, for lacke of neceffarie confecration. Neither did M. Iuel anfwering Doct. Harding ; nor M.
Horne in his anfwer to D. Stapleton; nor M Grindal
in iuftification of himfelf, or of anie of his felowes,
nor anie other for them, once alleage, that they were
confecrated by anie Bifhope, formerly confecrated.
Truly fome of them fhould, & would then, without
al doubt

Proteftants
and we are
now agreed,
that Apofto-
lical ordina-
tion withcon-
tinual fucceffi-
on is necefla-
rie.

So depe filen-
ce in fuch a
cafe is a very
fufficient con
feffion hat
there was
then no fuch
regifter.

al doubt, haue auouched the fact, and so haue produced their proofe, and appealed to witnesses: and namely to the late pretended Register, if there had bene anie such. For they knew very wel, what was done. And indeede manie did know, when & how the new pretended Bishopes were made. And amongst others, M. Stowe, the ordinarie Historiographer then in London, knew and said (though the time suffered him not to write it) that these men, nominated by the Quene to be Bishopes, endeuoured by al possible meanes, to haue bene consecrated by one special Catholique Bishope (of Landaffe) who finally refusing to doe it, and no possibilitie remaining, to ouertreate anie other, themselues being together, not in anie Church, nor Chapel, nor before manie witnesses, but such as they best trusted, in a priuate chamber, of an Inne, the Nagsehead in Cheape side, there M Parker, M. Scorie, & the rest, euerie one shewing the Quenes Patentes, for their Nomination, M. Scorie (who had bene named, a Bishope, but not consecrated in King Edwards time) taking the Bible (or some other Booke) laide it vpon the heade, or shoulders, of euerie one, and said: Take thou power, and auctoritie to preach the word of God sincerly. And so they were esteemed to be Bishopes, and among the people went for Bishopes. Which when Catholiques denied them to be, especially Bishope Bonner hauing publiquely pleaded, and others in wordes, and in print had auouched, that they were not Bishopes, to cure so desperate disease, with a violent medicine, at last the Parlament, in the eight yeare of Q. Elisabeth, enacted, that al such as had the Quenes Letters Patentes to be Bishopes, & were by her admitted into possession, should be so taken, helde, and esteemed, notwithstanding anie omission, defect, impediment, of due consecration, or of what other thing soeuer

See D. Kellisons Examen Religionis reformatæ· part. 1 cap. 2. and D. Champenes Treatise of the Vocation of the Clergie ch. 14.

A new deuised forme signifying no more power in a Bishope then in an other Preacher.

Anno Elisabethæ Octauo.

to the

to the contrarie. This in dede is in record amongst the Actes of Parlament. But the pretended Register, imagined to be so long concealed,& now auouched, hath no probabilitie at al to be true. But if anie wil nedes thinke (which in dede is false , if a matter of feaned fact can be shewed to be false) that the first Bishopes, nominated by Quene Elisabeth, were canonically consecrated , and others folowing them, & so their Protestants whole Clergie, by the power and auctoritie, deriued from the Bishope of Rome, let them also (for vtter reproch of their present pretended clergie) change their opinion , concerning the same Bishope, and Seate of Rome, and confesse that Bishope, and Seate of Rome to be right Christian Catholique, and Apostolical , and Supreme visible head of the militant Church in earth.

Saing they say their ordination is deriued from the B. of Rome, they must acknowlege that Seate to be Christian and Apostolical.

4.   In the meane time in further confirmation, that Clergimen must necessarily, besides Baptisme , and designation of the Layprince , or people, also haue spiritual mission, & ordination by the Apostles Successors : it is very certaine, and English Protestants wil not denie,that as the Priesthod of the Leuitical, and Aaronical Order, was instituted with manie special Rules, and holie Rites, and therin differed from the former Priesthod of the first borne , in the Law of nature : so Priesthod of the new Testament, which is instituted by Christ, by participation of his owne Priesthod, according to the Order of Melchisedech, doth farre excel al other Priesthod, either of the Law of nature , or of the written Law of Moyses. And yet in the former Law of nature , it was not sufficient to be the first borne , but his fathers ordination was also required by his blessing,or other declaration , & younger brothers also became Priestes, and sometimes preferred before the elder , and al, when they maried & had issue, were the Priestes of their owne families, but alwayes by order, some

Priestes in the Law of nature had special Vocation.

In the writen Law , their vocation was more exact.

And is most perfect in the Law of Christ

Gen. 25.
v. 5. Ch.
27. v. 4.
33. 36.

Rule

Rule was obſerued. More exactly when this order was changed, Prieſthod was not only reſtrayned, to the familie of Aaron, and the other Miniſterie in the Tabernacle, and Temple, to the Tribe of Leui, but alſo a preſcript forme of conſecrating thoſe, that were without other impediments, was ſet downe in the Law: as is noted before. And namely that Prieſtes muſt be conſecrated by the High Prieſt, and alſo the Leuites: & doe al their functions in ſubordination to the Prieſtes. For Moyſes being extraordinarie HighPrieſt, conſecrated Aaron, and his foure ſonnes And ſo Aaron was the ordinarie HighPrieſt, to whom ſucceded his ſonne Eleazar: & ſo the reſt. And al that wanted this ordination, and ſucceſſion were vnlawful vſurpers: as after that Manaſſes, the High Prieſt fel into apoſtaſie, who built the ſchiſmatical temple in Garizim, he & his folowers, were al ſchiſmatical vſurpers. So was in like maner Iaſon, making an other ſchiſme in Ægypt, where ſome Iewes, remained after the Captiuitie. And alſo Menelaus, Liſimachus, and Alcimus, were vniuſt vſurpers, for lacke of ſucceſſion, & ordination. And the others were the true High Prieſtes, which rightly ſucceded. To witte, Onias the ſecond, Simon the ſecond, Onias the third, Matthathias, Iudas Machabeus, Ionathas, Simon, Ioannes Hyrcanus, and ſo to Caiphas. Who, though he vvas vvicked, yet vvas the right Highprieſt of that order.

5. There is an other Miſſion extraordinarie, without ſucceſſion, but that neceſſarily requireth extraordinarie confirmation, by Miracles. So Moyſes vvith his miſſion, receiued povver to vvorke miracles, els the Iſraelites vvould not haue beleued him, neither had they bene bond to beleue him. God alſo ſent Samuel, extraordinarily (vvho vvas borne rather by miracle then by common courſe of nature, of his mother long barren) of the Tribe of Ephraim.

He was

Art. 41.
§. 2.

Num. 8.
v. 6. 11. 21
Pſal. 98.
v. 6.
Nu. 18.
v. 4.
Leuit. 8.
v. 6. &c.

Nu. 8. v.
7. &c.
2. Mach. 4.
v. 7. 10. 11

Io. 11. v.
49. 51.

Miſſion without ſucceſſion neceſſarily requireth to be proued by miracles.

Exo. 4.
v. 2. &c.

1. Reg. 1.
v. 10. 20.

He was miraculousls endewed with giftes. He pro- *Ch. 3. v. 4.* phecied being a childe, and was ordayned of God, *11. 18. 20.* to admonish Heli, the High Priest of his fault, in not correcting his sonnes. He also offered Sacrifice by special warrant from God, yet was no Priest, of Aarons order. Of whom the Royal Prophete saith [Moyses, and Aaron in the Priestes of our Lord, and *Psal. 98.* Samuel among them, that inuocate his name.] King *v. 6.* Saul presuming to offer Sacrifice, as he thought in case of necessitie, greatly offended God. So al the true Prophetes proued their mission from God, by *3. Reg. 18.* miracles, & false prophets hauing no mission, could *v. 23. 24.* neuer worke anie miracle: but when they were vrged so to iustifie their falsely pretended mission, failed therin, and were confounded. So that al the

Protestants can neither proue their pretended mission by right ordination, as ordinatie: nor by miracle, as extraordinarie.

power of Priestes, & wholeClergie dependeth vpon *Iere. 14.* lawful diuine mission, and ordination, either ordi- *v. 14.* narie by succession, and ordination of thoe, whom God instituted, and declared by miracles to be of his owne sending, and ordinance: or els, by new miracles. By neither of both which proofes, can Protestants shew themselues to be anie Clergie men at al except such as being ordained, and consecrated in the Catholique Apostolique Church, & are Apostates, from their Order: and so can not lawfully execute anie Ecclesiastical function, but sacrilegiously in heresie, or at least in schisme, and mortal sinne, to their owne, and their complices greater damnation. Of al such intruders and vsurpers, our

※ Michas thought himself wel sped, with an Apostate Leuite, in place of a Priest. Iudic. 17. v. 13.

Lord, by his Prophete Ieremie saith: [The Prophe- *Ch. 23.* tes prophecie falsely in my name: I sent them not, *v. 21.* and I commanded them not, neither haue I spoken *Ch. 27.* vnto them: lying vision and deceiptful diuination, *v. 15.* guilfulnes, & the seduction of their owne hart, they prophecie vnto you] Where he also denounceth vtter ruine, both to false Prophetes, or preachers,

Ruine threatned to al false preachers and to al that heare them.

which come without seding, & to the people which heare them.

6. Much

6.   Much more the fame neceſſitie of miſſion, and ordination is proued in the new Teſtament. S. Iohn Baptiſt gaue this for a general rule, to his owne diſciples, that [A man can not receiue anie thing vnles it begeuen him from heauen] ſpeaking of Chriſt himſelfe, that he had his miſſion, & ſpiritual power from heauen. Our Lord alſo confirmeth the ſame, ſaying [He that entreth not by the doore into the folde of the ſheepe, but climeth vp an other way, he is a theefe, and a robber. But he that entreth by the doore, is the Paſtor of the ſheepe] Cōformably hereunto, when Chriſt our Lord would ordaine true Paſtors. [He called his diſciples, & he choſe twelue of them: whom alſo he named Apoſtles.] That is in Englifh, Men ſent, Meſſengers or Legates. [Afterward he deſigned alſo other Seuentie two, and he ſent them, two and two before his face, into euerie citie and place, u hither himſelf would come.] Further ſhewing the neceſſitie of miſſion deriued from God, he willed al to pray God to ſend ſpirttual Paſtors, ſaying: [The harueſt truly is much, but the workemen few: Deſire therfor the Lord of the harueſt, that the ſend workemen into his harueſt] Againe after his Reſurrection, ſending his Apoſtles into al the world, he declared firſt his owne power, by meanes of heauenlie miſſion: & in vigour therof, ſent them ſaying [As my Father hath ſent me, I alſo doe ſend you.] At an other time, a litle before his Aſcenſion, he ſaid [Al power is geuen to me in heauen, and in earth: going therfore, teach ye al nations.] S. Paul ſpeaking of the ſame neceſſitie of miſſion, as of a doctrine wel knowen to al Chriſtians, faith confidently to the Romanes [How ſhal they preach, vnles they be ſent?] And declaring Chriſts Prieſthod, ſaith that he (as Man) was alſo called therto of God. [Neither doth anie man (ſaith he to the Hebrewes) take the honour to himſelf,

Ioa. 3.
v. 27.

Ioa. 10.
v. 1. 2.

Luc. 6.
v. 13.

Luc. 10.
v. 1.

v. 2.

Ioa. 20.
v. 21.

Mat. 28.
v. 18. 19.

Ro. 10.
v. 15.

Heb. 5.
v. 4.

Neceſſitie of due ordination is further confirmed by the new Teſtament.

So S. Iohn Baptiſt taught.

So Chriſt ſent his Apoſtles.

And the other ſeuentie two Diſciples.

S. Paul inculcateth the ſame neceſſitie of miſſion.

Ii   but

but he that is called of God: as Aaron. So Chriſt *v.* 5.
alſo did not glorifie himſelf, that he might be made
a Highprieſt: but God that ſpake to him: My Sonne
art thou, I this day haue begotten thee: Thou art a *v.* 6.
Prieſt for euer, according to the order of Melchiſedech] The very ſame Chriſt being according to his
Deitie, the onlie Sonne of God, yet according to his
humanitie, was called of God, in maner as Aaron
was, and was made a Prieſt, according to the order
of Melchiſedech. Thus by ordinarie calling, ordina- *Mat.* 28.
tion, and miſſion, the Apoſtles were ſent by Chriſt. *v.* 19.

Particular
Apoſtles, of
ſpecial na-
tions.

S. Matthias was afterward ordayned by the other *Act.* 1.*v.*
Apoſtles. Likewiſe S. Paul, and S. Barnabas were 26.*Ch.*13.
ordayned by others. Epaphraditus was made a par- *v.* 2.3.
ticular Apoſtle of the Philippians: and Epaphras of *Phil.* 2.
the Coloſſians, not by themſelues, but by the other *v.* 25.
Apoſtles, S. Timothee, and S. Titus were ordayned *Coloſ.* 1.
by S. Paul. And they ordayned others, in cities and *v.* 7.
prouinces, as appeareth by S. Pauls Epiſtles, written 1.*Tim.* 5.
to them afterwards. Such Preachers, and particular *v* 22.
Apoſtles were S. Fugatius, and S. Damianus ſent by *Tit.*1.*v.*5.

As of Britanes
and Engliſh.

S. Eleutherius Biſhop and Pope of Rome, into our
Iland of great Britanie: King Lucius requeſting the
ſame of the Pope. Such an Apoſtle was S. Auguſtin,
ſent into the ſame Iland to our Engliſh, and Saxon
nation, by S. Gregorie the Great, alſo Biſhope and
Pope of Rome. From whence al our true Engliſh
Paſtors, and Clergie had their calling, ordination, &
miſſion. And from the ſame Apoſtolique Seate muſt
ſtil haue it. Els it is cleare that they can not poſſibly
be of the true Clergie.

7. And therfore Proteſtants, Puritanes, & al others,
that can not proue themſelues to be ſo ordained, and
ſent, want the very eſſence, and ſubſtance of Cler-

Such as haue
attempted to
proue their

gimen. But if they wil pretend extraordinarie ordination, and miſſion from God, then muſt they
proue it, and make it manifeſt by miracles. Yet let
them

them beware withal, if they ſhal attempt to make
this proofe, leſt it fal to them, as it did to [certaine
Iudaical Exorciſtes, who(after the promulgation,&
receiuing of Chriſts Goſpel, and new Law) aſſayed
to inuocate the name of our Lord Ieſus, vpon them
that had euil ſpirites, ſaying [I adiure thee by Ieſus,
whom Paul preacheth. And there were certaine
ſonnes of Sceua a Iew, cheefe Prieſt, ſeuen, that
did this. But the wicked ſpirite anſwering ſaid to
them: Ieſus I know, & Paul I know; but you, what
are you? And the man in whom the wicked ſpirite was, leaping vpon them, and maſtring, both
(the Iudaical Exorciſtes, and the Highprieſtes ſonnes) preuailed againſt them : ſo that they fled, out of
that houſe, naked, and wounded] The like ſucceſſe
is authentically recorded, to haue fallen vpon Martin Luther, the Apoſtate frere : who was in deede a
Prieſt, but by apoſtaſie being degenerate, had loſt al
his power, and iuriſdiction ouer diuels, and ſo became the diuels ſlaue. This by the way. And now
we precede to declare, that beſides vocation, ordination, and miſſion (which are ſo eſſential, that
without them, none can be of the Clergie) there be
alſo other thinges required, as accidental qualities,
that they may be good, and ſitte Clergimen, in the
Church of Chriſt.

*Competent qualities; eſpecially of age, maners,
and lerning, are conueniently required
in Clergimen.*

ARTICLE. 43.

Qualities are of ſuch importance, that wheras al
thinges are good by their creation, and proper
nature, if alſo their qualities be good, they do adorne
the ſame thinges, and make them better; but if the

Ii 2 qualities

Sidenotes (left margin):
Actor. 19.
v. 13.

14.
15.
16.

3. Reg. 18.
v. 26. &c.

Anno De.
1545.

See Sta-
philus. &
Coeleus:
in Actis
Lutheri.

Sidenotes (right margin):
falſe preten-
ded miſſions
by miracles,
haue alwayes
failed therein,
and bene con-
founded.

By good or
bad qualities
the thinges,

which by na-
ture are good,
due become
better, or
worse.

qualities be euil, they depraue the thinges; and the
better a thing is by nature, so much the better, or
worse it is made, by accesse of good, or bad qualities.
As we see in the blessed Angels, and wicked diuels:
in holie men, and impious: and in al states of men,
as euerie one is qualified, so are they good or bad.
And therfore in designing of men to be made Clerkes (which ought by word and example, to teach
and direct the Laitie, in the way of God, and good
life) manie thinges are required, which may al be
reduced to three special heades. That they haue
competent age; knowen good maners, and vertues:
and suhcient knowlege and lerning, in the Law of
God, for that state, wherto euerie one is calld.

2.   Concerning age, there is no expresse Rule in the
new Testament. But in the Law of Moyses, which
was a figure, the Leuites were at first numbred, euerie *Num. 3.*
male from one moneth and vpward: and then de- *v. 15. 41.*
signed for the seruice of the Sanctuarie, and made
participant of the benefites & priuileges, perteyning
to that Tribe: but were not consecrated to their seueral functions, vntil the age of twentie fiue yeares.
And thence forth did execute al the offices, belon- *Ch. 8. v.*
ging to their seueral orders, vntil they were fiftie *7.24.*
yeares of age: from which time they were deliuered, from al burdenous seruice, and were only [to *25.*
kepe the thinges, that were commended to them, *26.*
but not to doe the very workes] The children also
of Aarons familie, were made participant of benefites, and priuilegies, with their fathers, from their
birth: and were consecrated Priestes, at competent
age, when they were able to kil the victimes, dresse,
and sacrifice them; whether before or after twentie
fiue yeares, is not expressed in the written Law. But
the Iewes had an ancient Decree, that none should
read certaine hard partes of holie Scriptures, vntil
they came to thirtie yeares of age. Wherof I here
make

The Leuites
in the old
Law, were
paticipant of
priuilegies,
from their
infancie: but
consecrated
to their seue-
ral offices, at
the age of
twentie fiue
yeares.

The Iewes
were forbid
to read cer-
taine partes

Luc. 3.
v. 23.
Ch 2. *v.*
42. 47.

make mention, becaufe Chrift our Sauiour, begane firft to preach publiquely about that age : only once before, at the age of twelue yeares, making manifeft fhew of his Diuine wifdom. Now by ordinance of the Catholique Church, children hauing no other impediment, and hauing lerned to read Latine diftinctly (or in Grecian countries, to read Greke) may be admitted, by firft Ecclefiaftical Tonfure, into the ftate of the Clergie, from the age of feuen yeares complete, fo that they be firft confirmed; and doe incline in wil, rather to procede in that ftate, then to depart from it : yet without obligation, to the one or the other. But more ordinarily they are differred, til they come to twelue yeares. The foure leffe Orders may be receiued at the age of eightene yeares. Subdeaconfhipe, at ful one and twentie. Deaconfhipe at twentie three complete. And Priefthod at complete twentie foure. And thirtie yeares of age are required, before anie be confecrated bifhope

Eccli. 32.
v. 1. *&c.*

becaufe maturitie of Iudgement, Vertues, and lerning, fitte for fo high power, and dignitie, can not ordinarily, be wel fuppofed in younger age. Yet may the Church difpenfe, in the want of age, with anie, in whom fufficiencie is otherwife found, other iuft caufe therwith concurring.

3. In the next requifite condition, of competent perfection in maners, there can be no lawful difpenfation : but due examination is to be made, and good teftimonie to be geuen, by fuch as know their approued vertues : not only by Clergimen, but in fome cafe alfo by fecular perfons. According as S. Paul willed S. Timothee, in that time, when Chriftians liued, and conuerfed in temporal caufes, amongft

1. Tim. 3.
v. 6
v. 7.

Infidels, not to geue holie Orders to [a Neophite (one lately conuerted to Chriftianitie) left puffed into pride, he fal into iudgement of the diuel. And, he (that vvas in thofe dayes to receiue holie Orders)

of holie Scripture, before the age of thirtie yeares.

Children may be made clerkes at feuen yeares of age, more conueniently at 12. yeares.

Clergues may receiue the foure leffe Orders at 18. yeares.

May be made Subdeacons at 21.
Deacons at 23 Prieftes at 24 Bifhopes at 30. complete,

Good maners are neceffarily required.

muſt haue alſo good teſtimonie, of them that vvere vvithout: that he fal not into reproch, and the ſnare of the diuel·] Becauſe the diuel intrappeth manie ſoules, by the ſcandalouſe life, or doctrine, of bad Clergimen. It is therfore prouidently foreſene by the Church, & exact Rules are ſet downe, that none de admitted, contrarie to the ſame rules, but are re-fuſed, as irregular, or not ſufficiently approued. And this Irregularitie is contracted, not only by certaine enormious crimes, but alſo by natural defectes, and by ſome iuſt, and lawful actions. As by vvilful mur-ther, manſlaughter, obſtinate hereſie, and apoſtaſie: thoſe that are illegimate by birth: or haue notorious deformitie in bodie: thoſe that haue maried tvviſe, or haue maried widowes: thoſe that haue coopera-ted to the death, or maming of anie perſon, although lavvfully, vvhich is no ſinne: yet is a defect of ſuch lenitie, as is required in Clergimen. Theſe and ſome other faultes, and defectes, doe hinder from being made of the Clergie, vvithout ſpecial diſpenſation, vpon iuſt cauſe. As is largely declared in particular Bookes, vvritten for this purpoſe, to vvhich vve re-mitte them, vvhom it concerneth. The groundes of theſe Eccleſiaſtical Lavves, appeare to be iuſt con-uenient, & moſt agreable to holie Scriptures: partly by example of the old Lavv; more eſpecially by ſome particular aduertiſments, and by general au-ctoritie, geuen to the Church in the nevv Lavv of Chriſt.

4. In the Law of Moyſes, which was but a ſhadow of Chriſtian perfection, diuers vvere excluded, euen of Aarons familie, from offering Sacrifice (Speake to Aaron (ſaid our Lord to Moyſes) The man of thy ſede, through out their families, that hath a blemiſh, ſhal not offer breades to his God, neither ſhal he ap-proch to his miniſterie. If he be blinde, if lame, if he haue a litle, or a great, or a crooked noſe: if his foote

Leu. 21.v. 16.17.18

Diuers Irre-
gularities hin-
der the lawful
taking of ho-
lie Orders.

The conueni-
encie of theſe
Eccleſiaſtical
Lawes is ſhe-
wed by holie
Scriptures.

20. foote be broken, if his hand, if he be crooke backed Diuers coror bleareyed, or naue a pearle in his eye; or a con-poral blemi-
tinual fcabbe or drie fcurfe, in his bodie, or be burnt. fhes made
21. Euerie one that hath a blemiſh, of the feede of Aaron Prieſtes irre-
the Prieſt ſhal not approch to offer the hoſtes to the gular in the
old Law.
22. Lord, nor offer the breades to his God He ſhal eate
notwithſtanding of the breades, that are offered in
23. the Sanctuarie Yet ſo that he enter not within the
veile, nor approch to the Altar, becauſe he hath a
blemiſh, & he muſt not contaminate my Sanctuarie.
I the Lord that fanctifie them.] Some thinges did
alſo debarre Prieſtes from participation of thinges
Ch. 22. fanctified [Say to them, & to their poſteritie: Euerie
v. 3. man of your ſtocke, that approcheth to thoſe thinges, that are conſecrated, and which the children of
Iſrael haue offered to the Lord, in whom there is vncleannes, ſhal periſh before the Lord. I am the Lord.
v. 4. The man of the ſeede of Aaron, that is a leper, or hath
a fluxe of feede, ſhal not eate of thoſe thinges, that
Mat. 12. are fanctified to me, vntil he be healed &c.] Theſe The Law of
v. 4. impediments, as they were ordinances of the old Moyſes doth
Law, doe not binde Chriſtians: but ſuch are now not binde
Chriſtians,
Irregularities, as the Church of Chriſt, directed by but by exam-
his Spirite, declareth to be ſuch, as I touched euen ple of it the
now. Al kinde of mortal ſinne remayning in the Church of
foule doth much more hinder, from lawful recei- Chriſt orday-
uing anie holie Order, or anie other Sacrament (ex- neth Lawes
cept Baptiſme, and Penance) and from miniſtering conuenient
for this time.
anie Sacrament, vntil ſuch ſinners be cleanſed from
Pſal. 49. their ſinne. To ſuch greuous ſinners [God hath ſaid
v. 16. (by his Prophete Dauid) Why doeſt thou declare my
iuſtices, and takeſt my teſtaments by thy mouth?]
And becauſe the Sacrifice, and Sacraments of the
Law of grace, are moſt pure in themſelues, Chriſt
Mal. 3. requireth much puritie in his Miniſters [For he is
v. 2. 3. (faith the holie Prophete Malachias) as it were purging fire, and as the herbe of fullers: and he ſhal ſitte
purging,

purging, and cleanfing the filuer, and he fhal purge
the fonnes of Leui, and wil ftreyne them as gold, &
as filuer, and they fhal be offering Sacrifices to our
Lord in iuftice.

5.   Further alfo the vertues required in clergimen

Vertues requi-
red in Clergi-
men are figni-
fied by the pa-
raments of
the Clergie.

(efpecially of the new Law) were fignified in the
holie veftments of Aaron, and the other Prieftes, &
are reprefented by the confecrated paraments of the
Chriftian Clergie, and holie Altars. As being made
by Gods appointment [of gold, and hyacinth, and *Exo.* 28.
purple, and fcarlette twife dyed, and filke; adorned *v.* 5. 9. 17.
alfo with manie, & excellent precious ftones] which 18. 19.
in general fignified, puritie of life, difcretion in iudgement, fincere intention, contemplation of God, *See before*
fupportation of the peoples infirmities, folicitude of *Art.* 2.
their fpiritual good, examplar life, found doctrine, *Page.* 22.
and band of vnion.

6.   S. Paul expreffeth alfo fome fpecial conditions

S Paul fpeci-
fieth certaine
qualities re-
quifite in the
Clergie.

in particular requifite, in the Chriftian Clergie:
comprifing Prieftes, vnder the name of Bifhopes *Act.* 20. *v.*
(for in the primitiue Church moft part of Prieftes 17. 28.
were alfo Bifhopes)and vnder the name of Deacons, *Tit.* 1. *v.*
al other inferior Orders, he writeth thus to S. Timo- 5. 7.
thee [If anie man difire a Bifhopes office (or confe- 1. *Tim.* 3.
quently a Prieffs office) he defireth a good worke. *v.* 1.
It behoueth therfore a Bifhope (& likewife a Prieft) *v.* 2.
to be irreprehenfible, the husband of one wife (for
a man that hath bene once maried, might receiue
holie Orders, but not if he haue maried twife)fober,
wife, comelie, chaft: a man of hofpitalitie, a teacher, 3.
not geuen to wine, no fighter, but modeft, no qua- 4.
reler, not couetous, wel ruling his owne houfe, hauing his children fubiect withal chaftitie.] Deacons *v.* 8.
in like maner (and fo Subdeacons, Acolytes, and the
reft) chaft, not duble tongued, not geuen to much 9.
wine, not folowers of filthie lucre: hauing the Myfterie of faith, in a pure confcience. And let thefe 10.
                                                                also

also be proued firſt, and ſo let them miniſter, hauing no crime.] Againe he ſaith in the ſame Epiſtle [Impoſe handes on no man lightly, neither doe thou communicate with other mens ſinnes.] The very ſame in ſubſtance, he writte to S. Titus, an other Biſhope, ſaying [For this cauſe I left thee in Crete, that thou ſhouldeſt reforme the thinges that are wanting: and ſhouldeſt ordaine Prieſtes by cities, as I alſo appointed thee; If anie be without crime; the husband of one wife (not *bigamus*) hauing faithful children, not in the accuſation of riote, or not obedient. For a Biſhope (ſo he calleth the ſame perſons, Biſhopes, whom in the ſentence before he called Prieſtes) muſt be without crime, as the ſtuard of God, not proud, not angrie, not geuen to wine, no ſtriker, not couetous of filthie lucre; but geuen to hoſpitalitie, gentle, ſober, irſt, holie, continent: embracing, that faithful word, which is according to doctrine, that he may be able to exhorte, in ſound doctrine, and to reproue them, that gayne ſay it.] Moſt agreably S. Peter exhorteth al Biſhopes, and Prieſtes (vnder the name of Seniors, as common to both) ſaying [Feede the flocke of God, which is among you: prouiding not by conſtreynt, but willingly according to God : neither for filthie lucre ſake, but voluntarily: neither as ouerruling the Clergie, but made examples, of the flocke from the hart] Finally Chriſt himſelf by his Angel, commendeth ſuch Prelates, as are formerly deſcribed by his Apoſtles, for their wel doing, and by threates recalleth others to penance, ſaying to the Biſhope of Epheſus: [I know thy workes, and labour, and thy patience; and that thou canſt not beare euil men, & haſt tried them, which ſay themſelues to be Apoſtles, and are not, and haſt found them liars. And thou haſt patience, and haſt borne for my name, and haſt not fainted. But I haue againſt thee a few thinges: be-

Ch. 5. v. 22.

Tit. 1. v. 5. 6.

v. 7.

v. 8.

v. 9.

1. Pet. 5. v. 2.

Apoc. 2. v. 2.

3.

4.

S Peter requireth the ſame good qualitie in Clergimen.

Chriſt our Lord requireth the ſame.

becaufe thou haft left thy firft charitie. Be mindful *v. 5.*
therfore from whence thou art fallen, & do penáce,
and doe the firft workes. But if not, I come to thee,
and wil moue thy candlefticke out of his place,
vnles thou doe penance. But this thou haft, becaufe *v. 6.*
thou hateft the factes of the Nicolaites, which I alfo
hate.] To the Bifhope of Smyrna he faith [I know *v. 9.*
thy tribulation, and thy pouertie, but thou art rich,
and thou art blafphemed of them, that fay themfelues to be Iewes; & are not, but are the fynagogue
of Satan. Feare none of thefe thinges, which thou 1c.
fhalt fuffer. Behold the diuel wil fend fome of you
into prifon, that you may be tried, aud you fhal haue
tribulation ten dayes. Be thou faithful vntil death:
and I wil geue thee the crowne of life.] In like *v. 12. 18.*
maner to the other fiue particular Bifhopes of Perga- *Ch. 3. v.*
mus, Thyatiria, Sardis, Philadelphia, and Laodicia: 1. 7. 14.
praifing their vertues, and admonifhing them to
amend their faultes.

7. For better attayning, and conferuing neceffarie
vertues, in Clergimen, efpecially of the greater Or-

Perpetual cha- ders, Subdeacons, and fo vpward. The holie Church
ftitie is requi- hath decreed, that before Clerkes be admitted, to the
red in thofe fame greater Orders, they doe voluntarily promife,
that take the to kepe perpetual chaftitie, embracing herein the
greater holie Euangelical counfel [Making themfelues Eunuches *Mat. 19.*
Orders. for the Kingdom of Heauen (our Sauiour faying to *v. 12.*
his difciples) He that can take, let him take] this
ftate vpon him. Which holie Inftitution was prefigured, and in part obferued, by the Prieftes of the

It was prefi- old Law: in that they being maried, liued feparatly
gured in the from their wiues, al the fpace of times, whiles they
old Law. executed their Prieftlie functions, in the order of *1. Par. 24.*
their courfes before God, to offer incenfe entring *v. 8. 19.*
into the Temple of our Lord. As appeareth by Za- *Luc. 1. v.*
charias the Prieft. Who doing this Prieftlie functi- 8. 9.
on in his proper courfe, remayned in the Temple.
vntil

v. 23.

vntil [the dayes of his office were expired] then, & not sooner [He departed into his houfe] How much more conuenient is it, that Prieftes of the new Teftament, doe liue in perpetual chaftitie, without cumber of wife, and children; feing their function is not by courfe only of interrupted times, but continually, euerie day to ferue at the Altar, of a farre more excellent Sacrifice? This ftate of life was alfo prophecied by Ifaias, faying [Let not the Eunuch fay Behold I am a drie tree. Becaufe thus faith our Lord to the Eunuches: They that fhal kepe my Sabbathes, and fhal choofe the thinges that I would, and fhal hold my couenant: I wil geue vnto them, in my houfe, and within my walles, a place, and a name, better then fonnes, and daughters; an euerlafting name wil I geue them, which fhal not perifh.]

Ifa. 56. v. 4.

v. 5.

It was alfo forefhewed by Ifaias the Prophete.

8. Al the Apoftles according to this prophecie, & to our Sauiours counfel, though it was no precept, fuch as were vnmaried fo remained, & fuch of them as were maried, parted with their wiues: as appeareth by Chrifts anfwer to S. Peter, demanding what reward he and his felowes fhould haue, which had left al, and folowed him: our Lord [faid to them: Amen I fay to you; that you which haue folowed me, in the regeneration, when the Sonne of man fhal fitte in the feate of his maieftie, you alfo fhal fitte vpon twelue feates, iudging the twelue tribes of Ifrael. And euerie one that hath left houfe, or brethren, or fifters, or father, or mother, or wife, or children, or landes for my names fake, fhal receiue an hundred fold, and fhal poffeffe life euerlafting] where you fee, that amongft other thinges, they had left their wiues, to folow Chrift, and that the fame is both lawful, and meritorious of reward [an hundred fold, in this time(faith S. Marke, to witte abundance of grace) and in the world to come life euerlafting.] S. Paul likewife gaue the fame counfel,

Mat. 19. v. 27 v. 28.

The Apoftles and primitiue Prieftes of Chrift obferued perpetual chaftitie.

v. 29.

Mar. 10. v. 30.

K k 2   declaring

S. Paul by word and example taught the same.

declaring withal, that it is no precept (before it be 1. *Cor.* 7. promifed) and both propofed his owne example, *v.* 25. 29. and his reafon, why it is better to liue fingle, faying [I would haue you to be without carefulnes. He *v.* 8. 32. that is without a wife, is careful for the thinges, 33. that perteyne to our Lord; how he may pleafe God.

The Church compelleth none to promife, but only admitteth fuch as wil promife.

But he that is with a wife, is careful for the thinges, that perteyne to the world, how he may pleafe his wife; and he is diuided.] Seing therefore, fo manie of their free wil, through Gods grace are difpofed to make this promife of perpetual chaftitie, it is moft conuenient, only to admitte fuch to the greater holie Orders, they being both fufficient in number, that there is no want : and more apt for facred functions·

By the like voluntarie promife they are alfo bond to the Canonical houres

9.   Thefe adde alfo of their owne accord, without compulfion, an other holie promife, eiter to fing dayly in the Quire with others, or in fupplie therof, to read euerie day, the Diuine office of the feuen Canonical houres, which is compofed of the Holie Pfalmes, and other holie Scriptures, with facred *Pfal.* 118. Hiftories, Sermons, and Homilies, of the ancient, *v. 62 164.* Fathers, and Doctors of Gods Church But of thefe and other Euangelical Counfels, which are not precepts, til they be promifed by free, and voluntarie *Part.* 3. vow, more is to be faid after the explication of the *Art.* 48. ten commandments.

Competent lerning in euerie Order is alfo required.

10.   Competent lerning, is the third neceffarie, and fpecial qualitie, required in the feueral orders of the Clergie. For the firft entrance to be made Clerkes   §. 2. it fufficeth by the ordinance of the Church, that they can read Latine, or in the Grecian contries, Greke, as is noted before. Before they be promoted to the foure leffe Orders, it behoueth that they vnderftand Latine, or Greke. It is moreouer requifite, that Subdeacons be able to catechize, and inftruct the *Luc.* 10. people in the principal pointes of Catholique Faith *v.* 1. 9.

and

and Religion. Deacons ought to be able to preach,
or at leaſt priuately to teach, and exhort, both in
matter of faith, and good life : in thoſe eſpecial vertues wh ch perteine, to euerie eſtate of Chriſtians, &
ſo to aſſiſte Prieſtes alſo in that office. In Prieſtes is
required ſufficient knowlege to diſcerne, and iudge
al ordinarie caſes, touching ſinnes, and matters of
conſcience : to reſolue the people in ſuch ſpiritual
doubts ; eſpecially ſuch Prieſtes, as haue the paſtoral
charge of ſoules. Biſhopes ought to be indued with
ample, and exact knowlege, in al the ſacred Scriptures of the old, and new Teſtament. [For the lippes of the Prieſt (ſaith Malachias) ſhal kepe knowlege, and the Law they ſhal require of his mouth :
becauſe he is the Angel of the Lord of hoſtes] which
is ſpecially meant of the cheefe Prieſtes, that is, of
Biſhopes in the Church of Chriſt. For to them it
properly perteyneth, to define in holie Councels, &
Conſiſtories, al pointes of faith, and general cauſes
of ſpiritual controuerſies amongſt Chriſtians, together with the Supreme Biſhope, in greateſt difficulties. And it behoueth al Biſhopes to be able, to teach,
and decide, ſuch doubtes as commonly occurre [ac-
cording to ſound doctrine, and to reproue them,
that gaynſay it.]

Mat. 28.
v. 19.

Oſea. 4,
v. 4. 6.

Mal. 2.
v. 7.

Tit. 1.
v. 9.

In Paſtors, &
eſpecially in
Biſhopes mo-
re exact kno-
wlege in al
Chriſtian do-
ctrine is re-
quired.

The principal power of Holie Orders, is to con-
ſecrate, and offer Chriſts bodie and bloud,
in the Holie Sacrifice.

ARTICLE. 44.

TO what both general, and eſpecial purpoſe,
ſome men are taken from their former ſtate of
the Laitie, and made of the Clergie, S. Paul teacheth
ſaying [Euerie Highprieſt taken from among men,
is appointed for men, in thoſe thinges, that perteyne
to God :

Heb. 5.
v. 1.

to God : that he may offer giftes, and Sacrifices for
sinnes.] In this sentence are breefly cōteyned diuers
particular pointes. For vnder the name of Highpriest, the Apostle declareth in general the function
of al Priestes, and of Leuites also,in the old Law,and
of al Clergimen in the new Testament. For they are
al ordained Ministers in those thinges, that peculiarly perteyne to God, and Diuine Seruice. In that
he saith : they are taken from men, it is euident that
Ecclesiastical Ministers, are of Mankinde,not of Angelical spirites; secondly that they are separated in
state from other men : from the state wherin they
were borne, and made of an other state, wherof
they were not before. In saying,they are appointed
for men, he plainly sheweth that the Clergie is instituted for the benefite of al mankinde, themselues
and others. Saying : in those thinges that perteyne
to God : he declareth, that their office is to haue the
charge of diuine thinges, to deale as mediators be- *Deut 5.*
twen God, and his people. Lastly saying [that he *v. 5.*
may offer giftes, and Sacrifices for sinnes] he telleth
the principal function of the whole Clergie, to be
the oblation of Sacrifice. For albeit onlie Priestes, *Leu. 9. v.*
can offer Sacrifice,yet al other inferior Orders are *2.7. &c.*
subordinate to Priesthod, and are especially to assist
for the performing of Sacrifice, as the Leuites were
subordinate to the Priests of Aarons Order. For so
God commanded Moyses, saying [Thou shalt geue *Nu. 3.*
the Leuites, for a gift to Aaron and to his sonnes, *v. 9.10.*
to whom they are deliuered of the children of Israel. But Aaron, & his sonnes, thou shalt appoint oner
the seruice of Priesthod [to burne incense, vpon the *1. Reg. 2.*
Altar] and to offer al other Sacrifices [The stranger *v. 28*
that approcheth to minister shal dye] Wherfore, as *2. Par. 26.*
in the Law of Moyses: so in the Law of Christ,onlie *v. 18.*
Priestes can offer Sacrifice:& al otherClergimen are
specially deputed to assist them, in the most sacred
Action

Al the infe-
rior Orders
are subordi-
nate to Priest-
hod.

Action, of confecrating Chrifts bodie and bloud, & offering the fame in Sacrifice.

2. Being therfore abundantly proued already, that Priestes haue powre to confecrate the true and real bodie and bloud of our Lord Iefus Chrift, in the formes of bread and wine: and to offer the fame in Sacrifice, it necessarily foloweth, that this is the moft excellent of al whatfoeuer offices, and facred fun-&ions, which are in the whole militant Church of God: in fo much that if our Aduerfaries would beleue it, as it is declared by the plaine wordes of Chrift himfelf, written in his new Teftament, they would eafyly alfo grant, and confeffe, that the fame is of al others, the moft fufferegne powre, which God hath geuê to mortal men. For the greatnes therof(which they falfely cal an impoffibilitie) is the cheefe, and maine difficultie, which moueth them fo peremptorily to denie, that there is, or can be fuch powre in anie man, yea in Chrift himfelf, fo to change, and transfubftanciate bread, & wine, into his owne fubftantial bodie, and bloud. For if they wil once acknowlege this powre to be in Chrift, & to be communicated by him to his Priestes, they wil then moft eafily graunt, that it is abfolutely the greateft, & moft excellent powre of al powers in this world.

3. Which is further declared, by thefe two manifeft Theological demonftrations. Firft, feing al fpiritual fun&ions (which farre excel al temporal, and ciuil powre) doe either apperteyne immediatly to our dutie towards God Omnipotent, the moft B. Trinitie: or to our dutie towards Chrift, as Man: or towardes the Church his myftical bodie; it is cleare that the confecration of his bodie, and bloud, in the formes of bread and wine, perteyneth dire&ly to his owne real bodie and bloud, which confift in his Diuine Perfon: and therfore this facred fun&ion fo farre excelleth al fun&iôs perteyning to his myftical bodie

Art. 18.
Art. 22.

Pfal. 110.
v. 4. 5.

Art. 18.
§. 3.

Whofoeuer beleueth the Catholique do&trine that Priestes can confecrate & offer the B, Sacrifice of the Altar, wil eafily confeffe that it is the moft excellent fun&ion in the Church of God.

Which is further proued, becaufe it concerneth Chrift himfelf in his owne bodie and bloud.

bodie, the Church, as himself the Head excelleth *Ephef.* 5.
the fame Church, his myftical bodie. Secondly feing *v.* 23.
Sacrifice is the moft principal, and moft excellent
external Act of Religion (due to God onlie) and the
cheefe external dutie, which man oweth, or can ex- *Exod.* 22.
hibite to God. And feing that Prieftes are conftituted *v.* 20.
the onlie Minifters of Chrift, to confecrate, & offer
this onlie proper Sacrifice of the new Teftament, *Art.* 23.
which infinitely excelleth al Sacrifices of the old
Law, being the very fame, with that vpon the croffe,
not differing in the hoft, which is offered, but only
in maner of oblation (to witte, there bloudily, here
vnbloudily) it is euident, that the moft principal
function, of al holie Orders, confifteth in confecrating, and offering the fame moft bleffed Sacrament,
and Sacrifice of Chrifts bodie & bloud, in the vifible
formes of bread, & wine. So let vs procede to fpeake
of an other Prieftlie, and Ecclefiaftical function.

An other power of holie Orders is Iurifdiction :
to feede and gouerne the Church.

ARTICLE 45.

Spiritual power perteyneth, & is directed to thefe
two general purpofes : to the better performing
of mens feruice towards God : and for better obteyning the health of foules, which two endes are alwayes fo conioyned, that when the one is rightly
done, the other alfo is implied. For whatfoeuer
feruice pleafeth God, the fame is profitable to the
foule, becaufe [God is a remunerator, or rewarder, *Heb.* 11.
to them that feeke him] by duly feruing him. And *v.* 6.
the health of foules is of al thinges moft gratful to
God. [For this is the wil of God (faith S. Paul) your 1. *Thef.* 4.
fanctificatiō.] To this duble purpofe, Chrift our Lord *v.* 3.
hath ordayned Prieftes, & other Clergimen, for the
better performing of al **Gods** due Seruice , wherby
soules

And becaufe
Sacrifice is
the moft ex-
cellent exter-
nal Act of Re-
ligion.

Al fpiritual
powre is ge-
uen for two
endes.

For the ferui-
ce of God,

And health of
foules,

foules may alfo receiue his grace; and for the fanctifying of foules, wherby God may be more glorified, whiles his fpiritual Minifters, as officers betwixt him and men, doe thofe efpecial thinges, for themfelues and others, which others can not perforthe. As to offer the dread Sacrifice, which is the cheefeft function (as is now declared) and next therto, is the power to abfolue from finnes, by the Sacrament of Penance: a power only geuen to Prieftes: as alfo to be the ordinarie Minifters of al the other Sacraments, yea and the onlie Minifters of the moft part, of them. Likewife fpiritually to feede, and gouerne the militant Church generally: as S. Paul fpeaketh in the place before recited [to doe thofe thinges for men, that perteyne to God] to witte, mens fpiritual affayres, which Laimen can not doe, but Clergimen onlie, being taken for this purpofe, from the Laitie. For fo it is euident by the Apoftles doctrine, that as temporal affayres are managed by temporal Princes, Magiftrates, and other fecular perfons: fo fpiritual caufes, whatfoeuer perteyning to the principal Seruice of God, and fpiritual health of foules, belong to fpiritual Prelates, Prieftes, and other Clergimen. Which is further declared by other like teftimonies, of the old and new Teftament, as the one is a figure, or examplar fhadow of the other.

2.   God hearing the crie of his people, fore afflicted in Ægypt, and intending to deliuer them, could haue done it, by manie other meanes, yet would releue them, by the minifterie of Moyfes. Whom therfore he called from the keeping of fheepe, made him an extraordinarie Prieft, for this extraordinarie purpofe, not only by him to deliuer the whole people from their feruitude in Ægypt, but alfo by him, to lead them in the deferte, and there by him, to geue them a written Law. And withal ta make Aaron and his fonnes, and fucceffiuely their fonnes, the

See §. 6.

Heb. 5.
v. 1.

Exo. 3.
v. 1. &c.

Other offices, of the Clergie are to teach Chriftian doctrine, to minifter al Sacraments, and to gouerne the Church fpiritually.

God who can doe al thinges without fecondarie caufes, yet vfeth the minifterie of his creatures.

He fent Moyfes extraordinarily. Aaron

Ll   Ordinarie

with other
Priestes and
Leuites, or-
dinarily.

ordinarie Priestes : and the rest of the Tribe of Leui,
to assist the Priestes, in the seruice of the Sanctuarie,
so long as the same Law should continew. [Come   *v.* 10.
(said our Lord to Moyses)and I wil send thee to Pharao, that thou maist bring forth my people, the children of Israel out of Ægypt.] And although Moyses
should be cheefe in this worke : yet should he not be
alone, but haue assistame, which he also desired: and
therupon , our Lord said further [Aaron thy bro-   *Ch.* 4. *v.*
ther the Leuite, I Know that he is eloquent, behold 14.
he cometh forth to meete thee , and seing thee shal
be glad at the hart. Speake to him , and put my wor-   *v.* 15.
des in this mouth: and I wil be in thy mouth , and
in his mouth, and wil shew you what ye must doe.]
After that by Gods mightie hand, and ministerie of
Moyses, and Aaron, the people were deliuered, and
had also receiued the tenne moral precepts,the principal part of the Law , our Lord then further commanded Moyses, to consecrate Aaron the ordinarie *Leuit.* 8.
Highpriest , and al his sonnes Priestes. Likewise to *v.* 1. 2.
ordaine Leuites, of the rest of Leiues Tribe, to assist *Nu.*8. *v.*5.
the Priestes.

3.   Which being done , and the principal Priestlie
function of offering Sacrifice, being first prescribed,

Leprosie pre-
figured here-
sie, and other
errors in faith:
wherof Prie-
stes were
made the
Iudges.

an other office was declared,concerning the iudgement of Leprosie,our Lord speaking ioyntly to Moyses and Aaron, saying [The man , in whose skinne, *Leuit.* 13.
& flesh, shal rise a diuers colour, or a blister, or anie *v.* 1. 2.
thing as it were shining, that is to say,the plague of
leprosie, shal be brought to Aaron the Priest,or anie
one of his sonnes , who seing the leprosie in his
skine, at his arbitrement,he shal be separated] from   *v.* 3.
ordinarie conuersation with other people [Al the   *v.* 46.
time that he is a leper, and vncleane , he shal dwel *v.* 13. 17.
alone without the campe.] His restauration,when 29. 34.
the leprosie should cease, was also by the Priestes *Ch.*14. *v.*
iudgement. [The Priest shal view him, & shal iudge 2. 3.
                                                    him

Luc. 17.
v. 14.
Mat. 8.
v. 4.

him to be cleane.] Which Law our Sauiour obseruing (in testimonie that it was of God, and signified
Priestlie power, in the old Law, of separating and
restoring lepers) sent such as he cleansed from leprosie, to the Priestes. That they might iudge by their
auctoritie, according to the Law. Which is therby
plainely proued to be a figure, of Priestlie power in
Chrilts Priestes, to binde, or loose sinners, according
to Chritts Law, geuen to them in earth, that the same
is in like maner bond, or loosed in heauen.

Ch. 18.
v. 18.

4. An other office of Aaronical Priestes, was by
sound of trumpette, to cal assemblies, and by diuers
maner of sounding, as occasions diuersly required,
to admonish and direct the people. [The sonnes of
Aaron the Priestes (said our Lord to Moyses) shal
sound with the trumpetes: and this shal be an ordinance for euer in your generation.] Which Rite of
sounding appropriated to the Priestes: was as wel
to warne the people of their dangers, to prouide &
looke to themselues, calling to God for his helpe, &
so it was vsed in case of warres: as also to sturre vp
their deuotions to the seruice of God, and so it was
vsed in their feastes and solemnities, especially in the
Iubilee yeare, for which there were special trumpettes. Moreouer that this sounding with trumpets
signified preaching & spiritual admonition, is cleare
by Ezechiel the Prophete, vsing the same Allegorie
in these wordes [If the watchman see the sword
comming vpon the land, and sound with trumpette,
and tel the people; and he that heareth the sound of
the trumpet, whosoeuer he be, and doth not looke
to himself, and the sword come, and take him, his
bloud shal be vpon his head, &c. but if he shal looke
to himself, he shal saue his life. And if the watchman see the sword come, and sound not with the
trumpet; and the people loke not to themselues, and
the sword come, & take a soule from among them,

Nu. 10.
v. 8.

v. 9.

Ios. 6. *v.*
10.
Leu. 25.
v. 9.

Ezech. 33.
v. 3.4.

v. 5.

v. 6.

An other
Priestlie of-
fice was to
warne, and
direct the
people,

Sounding
with trum-
pets prefigu-
red reaching.

The Pastors
fault condem-
neth himself,
but excuseth
not the peo-
ple.

he certes is caught in his iniquitie, but his bloud I
wil require at the hand of the watchman] The same
Ezechiel, a good watchman, both a Priest, and Prophete, seing and foreseing, the great harme, of bad
Pastors, and great necessitie of good Pastors, crieth
thus to the bad ones [Thus saith our Lord God: woe Ch. 34 v.
to the pastors of Israel, which fede themselues: are 2.3.4. &c.
not the flockes fed of the Pastors? You did eate the
milke, and were couered with the wool, and that
which was fatte ye killed: but my flocke you fed
not. That which was weake, you strengthned not:
& that which was sicke, you healed not: that which
was broken, you bond not vp: & that which was cast
away, you brought not againe; and that which was
lost, you sought not: but with austeritie, you did rule
ouer them, and with might.] A most plaine testimonie that the function of Priestes, of greater, and
lesse Iurisdiction, is to feede, & spiritually to gouerne
their seueral flockes. Bishopes must strengthen the
weake, with the Sacrament of Confirmation: other
Pastors must also heale the sicke sinners, with the Mat. 5.
Sacrament of Penance. They must reconcile men v. 25.
at variance by making peace, that they may fruitfully receiue the B. Sacrament of Vnion. Those that
seme wholly lost, good Pastors must seeke, by godlie
preaching, with mildnes beseching, & gently inuiting them to returne to God. Obstinate contemners
they must correct and punish, with the rodde of discipline. Which iudicial power our Lord also foreshewed should be in the Church of Christ, saying
to her, by his Prophete Isaias [Euerie vessel, that is Isa. 54
made against thee, shal not prosper: & thou in iudge- v. 17.
ment, shalt iudge euerie tongue resisting thee] euidently auouching, that the Church is not, as her rebellious aduersaries would make her, a partie against
them, and so to be iudged, as wel as they, but is their
Iudge, & must iudge them: as this sacred text doth
necessarily

Particular duties of Pastors.

The Church is Iudge of al her rebellious children.

neceſſarily conuince. Breefly in two wordes, our
Lord againe ſheweth, that the function of Prieſtes is
to feede, & correct, ſaying by his Prophete Micheas
Mich. 7. to Chriſt, & in him to euerie Chriſtian Paſtor [Feede
v. 14. thy people, with thy rod] with Sacraments, and puniſhments, with doctrine, and diſcipline. The ſingular good fruite of feeding is thus deſcribed by Ma-
Mal 2. v. lachias [ô Ye Prieſtes, you ſhal knowe (ſaith our
1.4.5.6. Lord) that I ſent you this commandment, that my
7. couenant might be with Leui, ſaith the Lord of
Hoſtes. My couenant was with him, of life & peace:
and I gaue him feare, and he feared me; and at the
face of my name he was afrayde. The Law of truth
was in his mouth, and iniquitie was not found in his
lippes, in peace, and in equitie he walked with me:
and turned away manie from iniquitie. For the lippes of the Prieſt ſhal kepe knowlege; and the Law
they ſhal require of his mouth: becauſe he is the Angel of the Lord of Hoſts.] So God alwayes conſerued ſome good Paſtors, for his couenant ſake, made
to Abraham, Iſaac, and Iſrael. Such were Phinees,
1.Eſd. 10. and manie both Prieſtes, and Prophetes. Namely
v. 4. 5. this Prophete Malachias, otherwiſe (as ſome ſup-
6. 14. poſe) called Eſdras: who both exhorted, and cor-
2.Mach 3. rected the Princes, Prieſtes, and people, which had
v. 1. offended, by marying ſtrange wemen, of infidel na-
1. Mac. 2. tions. And ſuch were after him Onias, Matthathias,
&c. Iudas Machabeus, Ionathas, Simon, and others.

5. In the new Teſtament, Chriſt himſelf teſtifieth,
what Prieſtes are by their function, and ought to be
in their liues, and laboures, ſaying to his Apoſtles:
Mat. 5. v. [You are the ſalt of the earth. But if the ſalt leeſe his
13 14. vertue, wherwith ſhal it be ſalted? It is good for
Luc.14. v. nothing, anie more, but to be caſt forth, and to be
34 35. troden of men. It is profitable neither for the ground
Mat. 5. nor for the dunghil: but it ſhal be caſt forth. You are
v. 15. the light of the world. A citie cã not be hid, ſituated

L1 3   vpon

Marginal notes:
To feede with the rodde, is to teach, and where nede it to puniſh.

God ſtil pro-uided Paſtors both to teach, and to puniſh.

The Clergie is the ſalt of the earth, the light of the world, and a citie vpon a mountaine.

vpon a mountaine. Neither doe men light a candle,   v. 16.
and put it vnder a bushel, but vpon a candlestticke,
that it may shine to al, that are in the houfe. So let   v. 17.
your light shine before men, that they may fee your
good workes, and glorifie your Father which is in
heauen.] The first point therfore of Pastoral charge
is to teach by good example. The next to preach the
word of God: then to minister Sacraments, & other
thinges needful to al fortes: spiritual foode, medicine, discipline, correction. For as by the il life of
hyrelinges, & by false doctrine of falfe pretending
pastores, sheepe receiue pestilent poyfon:fo without
pasture, they sterue by famine. Christ the true good
Pastor [seing the multitudes pitied them, becaufe Mat. 9. v.
they were vexed with infirmities: & lay like fhepe, 35. 36.
that haue not a shepeheard: and faid to his difciples: 37. 38.
The harueit furely is great, but the workmen are
few. Pray therfore the Lord of the harueit, that he
fend forth workemē into his harueit.] Accordingly
our Lord and Sauiour fent his Apostles: and after Mat. 10.
them other Difciples, to preach: fift to the lewes . v. 5. 6.
to doe penance, becaufe the Kingdom of heauen is Luc. 10.
at hand. After that he fent to al the Gentiles: [Al v. 1.
power is geuen me, going therfore teach ye al nati- Mat. 18.
ons: preach the Gofpel to euerie creature: teaching v. 19 20.
them to obferue al thinges, whatfoeuer I haue com- Mar. 16.
manded you. And lest they should doubt of fuccesfe, v. 15.
he addeth, promising perpetual affistance of his Spirite [behold I am with you al dayes : euen to the
confummation of the world.] At an other time Luc. 10.
confirming their commiffion he faid [He that hea- v. 16.
reth you heareth me. He that receiueth you, recei- Io. 13.
ueth me. He that receiueth anie that I fend, recei- v.20. Ch.
ueth me. You fhal geue teftimonie of me in Ierufa- 15. v.27.
lem, and in al Iewrie, and in Samaria, and euen to Act.1. v.8.
the vtmoft of the earth.

6.   Vpon al which S. Paul faith to the Corinthians.
                                          [We

Euil Pastors
kil their peo-
ple, either
with poyfon,
or by famine.

1. *Cor.* 3. [We are Gods coadiutors, you are Gods husbandrie: *Paſtors are*
7. 9. 10. you are Gods building. According to the grace that *Gods coad-*
is geuen me, as a wiſe workmaiſter, haue I laide the *iutors.*
foundation, and another buildeth therupon.] The
1. *Cor.* 4. ſame office of preaching he often auoucheth, to be-
v. 1. long to none els, but to thoſe only, that are deſigned
Epheſ. 3. therto. [The Myſterie of Chriſt (ſaith he) which
v. 5. was not knowen in other generations, to the ſonnes
of men, is now reuealed to his holie Apoſtles, and
7. Prophetes in the Spirite: wherof I am made a miniſter, according to the gift of the grace of God, which
is geuen me, according to the operatiō of his power.
8. To me the leaſt of al the ſainctes is geuen this grace,
among the Gentiles, to euangelize the vnſearchable
riches of Chriſt.] In like ſorte the adminiſtration of *They are the*
al Sacraments, ſo perteyneth to the Clergie, that *ordinarie ad-*
fiue of the ſeuen are no Sacraments at al, except they *miniſtrators*
be miniſtered by Prieſtes. Baptiſme in neceſſitie may *of al the Sa-*
be miniſtered by anie man or woman. And in that *craments.*
caſe alſo, it ought rather to be miniſtered by a Clergiman, or childe, that hath onlie firſt Tonſure, then
by anie laiman. And if Mariage be contracted without the preſeme of a Catholique Prieſt, it is in ſome
places no true Mariage. And whenſoeuer it is ſo
contracted, though it be valide, yet is it a greuous
ſinne ſo to contract. Eſpecially when it is done in
2. *Cor.* 6. hereſie, or ſchiſme. [For there is no participation
v. 14. 15. betwen Chriſt and Belial: betwen the faithful and
the infidel.]

7. Againe that al ſpiritual charge, & gouernment *It perteyneth*
of the Church, apperteyneth only to the Clergie, is *to the Clergie*
a moſt cleare thing, both by the doctrine, & practiſe *to reſolue and*
of the Apoſtles. When a doubt aroſe about Circun- *decide doub-*
Act. 15. ciſion, and other Rites of the old Law [The Apoſtles *tes in Reli-*
v. 6. and Ancients aſſembled to conſider of his word] or *gion.*
thing. And reſoluing the queſtion, decreed in theſe
v. 28. termes [It hath ſemed good to the Holie Ghoſt, and
to vs.]

to vs.] S. Paul in an other assemblie of Bishopes, and
other Prieites, exhorting them to see to their charge,
said [Take heede to your selues, and to the whole, *Act.* 20.
flocke, wherein the Holie Ghost hath placed you *v.* 28.
Bishopes, to rule the Church of God.] He also signified his owen coercife power, to command, and
by punishment to compel : writing thus to the Corinthians [What wil you? In rod that I come to you, 1. *Cor.* 4.
And by com- or in charitie, and the spirite of mildnes?] Plainly *v.* 21.
pulcite power intimating that if mildnes would not serue, he must
to correct of- vse the rod. In his other Epistle to the same people
fenders. he saith [Therfore haue I written vnto you, that I 2. *Co.* 2.
may know the experiment of you, whether in al *v.* 9.
thinges you be obedient.] He admonisheth the
Thessalonians to obey their Pastors, not only as those
that feede them spiritually, but also as their Gouerners, saying [we besech you brethren, that you wil 1. *Thes.* 5.
know them, that labour among you (by preaching *v.* 12. 13.
and ministring Sacraments, and other Rites) & that
gouerne you in our Lord] Writing to S. Timothee
he saith [The Priestes that rule wel, let them be 1. *Tim.* 5.
eitemed, worthie of duble honour] wheras Priestes *v.* 17.
may, & doe sometime offend, they are to be corrected
yet with respect of their vocation [Against a Priest *v.* 19.
(saith he) receiue not accusation, but vnder two or
three witnesses.] To S. Titus likewise he writeth
thus [These thinges speake, and exhorte, and rebuke *Tit.* 2.
with al auctoritie. Let noe man contemne thee] In *v.* 15.
Gods cause, Bishopes must vse their auctoritie, and
suffer no resistance, because contempt of them, is
the contempt of God [He that despiseth you despi- *Lnc.* 10.
seth me] said Christ to his Disciples. As S. Paul ad- *v.* 16.
The people monished Bishopes to feede, rule, and punish, where
must obey it is needful : so he also admonished the people to
their Pastors obey spiritual Superiors [Obey your Prelates (saith *Heb.* 13.
in al spiritual he to the Hebrewes) and be subiect to them. For *v.* 17.
causes. they watch, as being to render account for your
soules]

foules.] Confider wel this reafon; why al muft be fubiect, and obedient to their Prelates, becaufe the Prelates muft render account, for the foules of their flocke. For it were againft iuftice, & againft reafon, that anie fhould be bond to render an account , for thofe, ouer whom they haue not power, not only to admonifh, but alfo to correct. If therfore the Prelates be not obeyed, the account wil not be expedient, for the fubiects: as the Apoftle here concludeth. [If they doe it with mourning (faith he) this is not expedient for you]

Otherwife Paftors were not bond to render account.

Ibidem.

There are diuers degrees of fpiritual Paftors : fubordinate to one cheefe vifible Head.

ARTICLE. 46.

ORder is required in al thinges : and in nothing is more neceffarie, then in Holie Orders themfelues, the Ecclefiaftical ftate. Which confifteth in a Sacred Subordination of Superiour Prelates, and other inferiour Clergimen, called the Ecclefiaftical Ierarchie : hauing one Supreme vifible Head, which was S. Peter in his time, & after him his Succeffors, as is fhewed in the firft Part. Vnder which one head are conftituted certaine Patriarches, in diftinct partes of the Chriftian world : next to them are Primates, or Archbifhopes, in their feueral Prouinces ; then Bifhopes, in their proper Diocefes : and vnder them other Paftores, in particular Parifhes. With other Clergimen affifting : as Chancelers, Deanes, Archdeacons : and other Prieftes, Deacons, Subdeacons, and the reft. Some defigned onlie to the adminiftration of holie Sacraments, and other Rites ; or to affift the proper Minifters therof : others haue alfo Iurifdiction, belonging to the Regiment of the Church. Touching the power of holie Orders, as they may

The Ecclefiaftical Ierarchie confifteth of manie Superiors & fubiectes al fubordinate to one Supreme Head.

Artic. 35. 36.

Ecclefiaftical auctoritie confifteth in the power of holie Order, and of Iurifdiction.

be exe-

Power of Order, is equal in al that haue the same Order.

be executed without Iurisdiction, euerie Clergiman can as fully performe the function of his owne Order, or Orders, as he that hath greatter Orders. So euerie Priest can as really consecrate, and offer the holie Sacrifice, as a Bishope, or Chefe Bishope. Likewise in Actes of Iurisdiction, the inferiour Pastor, as perfectly performeth that which is within his power, as the superior can doe it. So a Pastor of a Parish as absolutly absolueth his penitent subiect, from his sinnes, as if the Bishope, or Pope should doe it. But al haue not Iurisdiction extended a like, in respect of

Iurisdiction is greater in some, & lesse in others.

places, persons, & causes. Onlie the Supreme Head Pastor, hath vniuersal Iurisdictiō in the whole Christian world, in al persons, and causes, being Christs vicar General in earth. Other Pastors haue more, or lesse Iurisdiction, according to their limited circuites of places, or persons, or causes. And thus spiritual Iudges are assigned in Ierarchical Order, and sacred Subordination by diuine ordinance. As appeareth by the holie Scriptures, and authentical practise of Gods Church, both in the old Testament, and in the Church of Christ.

There was diuersitie of Iurisdiction in the Law of nature.

2.   So we see in the ancient Church of the Law of nature, long before Moyses, there was subordination of superior, and inferior Priestes, and Pastors, in spiritual causes. Melchisedech as superior Priest, blessed *Gen* 14. Abraham (who was also a Priest) & receiued Tithes *v.* 19. 20. of him. By which two special actes, amongst other excellences in Melchisedech, S. Paul sheweth, that *Heb* 7. he was the superior Priest, and of greater power, *v.* 1. 2. & that Abraham was subiect to him. [Behold (saith *v.* 4. S. Paul) how great this man (Melchisedech) is, to whom also Abraham the Patriarch, gaue tithes of the principal thinges: and who blessed him, that *v.* 6. had the promises. But without al contradiction, that *v.* 7. which is lesse, is blessed of the better.] Moyses also was constituted by God, in superior auctoritie, both

spiritual

spiritual & temporal: and so Aaron was subordinate More expresly in the written Law. to Moyses : that he should be mediator , betwen him and the people , and betwen him and King Pharao. [He shal speake in thy steed, to the people (said our Lord to Moyses) and shal be thy mouth ; but thou shalt be to him, in those thinges that perteyne to God.] Againe [Our Lord said to Moyses : Behold I haue appointed thee the God of Pharao: and Aaron thy brother, shal be thy Prophete. Thou shalt speake to him al thinges, that I command thee ; and he shal speake to Pharao.] Moreouer Moyses also constituted inferior Iudges [to heare, and determine lesse matters only, and easyer cases : reseruing the greater to himself.] And this he did vpon the prudent suggestion, of Iethro his father inlaw, the Priest of Madian, without expresse warrant from God. Which by this example we see , is supposed in so cleare, and needful cases. After this, Moyses also commended special cases to be decided by Aaron, & Hur [If anie question shal rise (to witte of more difficultie) you shal referre it , to them] appointing Aaron of the tribe of Leui, Hur of the tribe of Iuda, as it were the one a spiritual Iudge, the other a temporal, his owne deputies, who was supreme in al causes. But more particularly, for the seruice of the Tabernacle, al the Leuites being to minister vnder the Priestes , had their particular Superiors in euerie Order ; of Caathites, Gersonites, and Merarites. And the same were subiect to one Principal of the same Order ; and al the three princes were subiect to one of the Priestes, called the Prince of the Princes of the Leuites. And the same Priest , and al other Priestes, and Leuites , and the whole people were subiect in spiritual causes to the Highpriest , who was also called the Grand Bishope, that is to say : The Priest that is greatest among his brethren. And he was commanded by the Law, to mainteine his high state,

Exo. 4. *v.* 16.

Ch. 7.*v.* 1. 2,

Ch. 18. *v.* 14. 22.26.

v. 19.

Ch. 24. *v.* 14.

Nu. 3. *v.* 6. 30. 32. 35.

Leuit. 21. *v.* 10.

Superiors may substitute coadiutors to themselues, without particular commission from their owne Superior, in some cases.

Al according to the Law.

Mm 2   and

and dignitie in al respectes, as singularly priuileged, v. 11. 12. and eminent aboue al. By whom also it pleased God 13. &c. to impart his diuers graces, as deriued from him, to others. Witnes the Royal Prophete [As oyntment Pfal. 132. (faith he) on the head, ranne downe vpon the beard, v. 2. the beard of Aaron: which ranne downe vnto the hemme of his garment] From the hieghest to the next subordinate, by him to others, so to the meanest, euen to the hemme of Aarons garment. For this diuine ordinance being set in the house of God, the same Royal Pfalmist, inuiteth al men, especially the Clergie, that by their spiritual functions serue the Church, to praise God day and night [Loe now Pfal. 133. (faith he) blesse our Lord, al ye the seruants of our v. 1. 2. Lord, which stand in the house of our Lord: in the courtes of the house of our God. In the nightes lift vp your handes vnto the holie places, and blesse ye our Lord] To the whole Church he saith [Ye house Pfal. 134. of Israel blesse our Lord] To the Priestes, [Ye house v. 19. of Aaron blesse our Lord.] To al others of the Cler- gie [Ye house of Leui blesse our Lord.] Againe to al   v. 20. the faithful in general : [You that feare our Lord, blesse ye our Lord]

3.   Seing then, as wel in the Law of nature, as in the written Law, there were degrees of spiritual gouerners, to the great strengthning, and also orna- ment of Gods Church: and that temporal kingdo- mes are especially established, by the meanes of Ma- giltrates, gouerning the whole ciuil bodie : much Cant. 6. more hath Christ our Lord, set his Church in strong, v. 3. 9. and comelie order, disposed in aray of Ecclesiastical Pastors, & people: with plenitude of spiritual power Mat. 16. in one cheefe for vnitie sake: with great power also v. 18. in other principal Pastors: and with competent, and Ch. 18. conuenient power, in al that haue charge of soules, v. 18. to direct & gouerne their flockes. For so our Sauiour, Ch. 25. deliuered his talentes to some more, to some lesse. v. 15.

Amongst

Power of the inferior was deriued from the superior.

Much more the Church of Christ, is both fortified and adorned, by Ierarchical gouernment, of one visible Head, with manie subor- dinate Supe- riors, & sub- iectes,

Mar. 3. v. Amongſt manie Diſciples he made but twelue Apo-
14 *Luc.* ſtles : and among them made one the Head, to hold
6. *v.* 13. al in vnion. At firſt he limited their commiſſion,
ſending them to preach the Goſpel, to the Iewes
Mat 10. only [into the way of the Gentiles (ſaid he to his
v. 5. Apoſtles) goe ye not, and into the cities of the Samaritanes enter ye not.] In like maner [The Seuentie
Luc. 10. two diſciples were ſent into euerie citie, and place,
v. 1. whither himſelf would come] with direction to
got two and two together ; what they ſhould ſay
v 4 5. coming to euerie houſe, how alſo to behaue them
6. *&c.* ſelues, where to take their temporal neceſſarie releeſe ; to take nothing of ſuch, as would not heare
v. 10. 11. their doctrine : but [to ſhake alſo the duſt from their
Mat. 28. feete, in teſtimonie againſt them.] By which exam-
The eleuen
v. 19 *Iu.* ples, and the like : and by the general commiſſion
Apoſtles or-
20. *v.* 21. geuen to S. Peter, and the other Apoſtles, they ordai-
dained S. Mat-
Act. 1. *v.* ned S. Matthias an Apoſtle. And ſhortly after, ſeuen
thias the
15. *Ch.* 6. Deacons. Likewiſe other Biſhopes, Prieſtes, Deacons,
twelſt Apo-
v. 6. and Clergimen for diuers functions. [For there are
ſtle.
1. *Cor.* 12. (ſaith S. Paul) diuiſions of graces, diuiſions of mi-
The ſame A-
v. 4. 5 6. niſtrations, diuiſions of operations, but one Spirite,
poſtles : and
one Lord, one God, which worketh al in al.] For
alſo S. Paul,
though we haue not al the holie Orders of the Cler-
ordayned
gie, expreſſed in the holie Scriptures, yet vnder the
other Cler-
titles of Biſhopes, Prieſtes, and Deacons, the reſt are
gimen.
compriſed : as we ſee that ſometimes, Prieſtes are
conteyned vnder the name of Biſhopes. So S. Paul
writing to the Philippians ſaluteth al the faithful
Philip. 1. [with the Biſhopes, and Deacons] and ſometimes
As Prieſtes
v. 1. Biſhopes vnder the name of Prieſtes : for writing to
are ſometimes
S. Titus, a Biſhope of Crete, he ſaith, that he left him
contained vn-
Tit. 1. in the prouince of Crete, that [He might ordaine
der the name
v. 5. Prieſtes by cities] that is, both Biſhopes and Prieſtes,
of Biſhopes :
yea alſo Deacons, and inferior Clergie, for al Eccle-
ſo other infe-
ſiaſtical offices to ſupplie, ſaith he [Whatſoeuer was
rior Orders
wanting.] The reaſon of comprehending Biſhopes,
are conteyned vnder
the name of

and

Deacones
which signi-
fieth Mini-
sters.

and Priestes vnder one name was, becaufe for most part, al Priestes were then Bishopes, the necessitie so requiring: and becaufe the fame qualities, & vertues were required in both. Neuertheles their power, & auctoritie was differēt, as appeareth in that none but Bishopes could make Bishopes, or anie other Cler-gimen. And Bishopes were alwayes of greater dig-nitie. As Likewife, the Apostles did excel other Bishopes, both in power, and dignitie. S. Paul called Timothee, and Titus his fonnes, being Bishopes, and directed them in the Churches affaires, as their Su-perior. In like maner, speaking of Epaphroditus, who was alfo a Bishope, and the particular Apostle of the Philippians, shevveth his ovvne auctoritie, & eminencie aboue him, saying [I haue thought it ne-cessarie, to fend to you Epepaphroditus my bro-ther, and coadiutor, and felovv fouldiar; but your Apostle, and minister of my necessitie] where he calleth him his brother, in that they vvere both Prie-stes, both Bishopes, both Apostles in a general fenfe: he calleth him his coadiutor, in that S. Paul vvas a more principal Apostle, the other his helper, and assistant: he calleth him his felovv fouldiar, both feruing one Master, Christ our Lord: he calleth him minister of his necessitie (vvhich importeth fuperior and inferior) but your Apostle (faith he) for as S. Paul vvas an Apostle in al the vvorld, fo Epaphroditus vvas an Apostle, of that particular citie, and countrie of Philippi. The like Apostle vvas Epaphras, of the Colossians. S. Gregorie the Great, and S. Augustine of vs Englishmen. But the tvvelue Apostles, S. Paul and S. Barnabas, vvere vniuerfal Apostles of the vvhole earth, in al nations vvherfoeuer they came. But S. Peter being the ordinarie Supreme Head of al, and the other Apostles extraordidarie founders of Churches: their Succeffors vvere limited, to their circuites. And now (fome fowner, fome later)

Tim. 1.
v. 1. *Tit.*
1. *v.* 1.

Philip. 2.
v. 2.

Colof. 1.
v. 7.

Al the Apo-
stles were
founders of
the Christian
Church: but
S. Peter was
the ordinarie,
the other A-
postles were

are

are al fayled. Only S. Peters Succeſſors do continew, **extraordina**-
without interruption. And ſo his Seate, is the onlie **rie. See the**
Apoſtolical Seate, and the Biſhope therof the Apo- **firſt part Art.**
ſtolical Biſhope. Others alſo are truly and proper- **35. 36.**
ly Biſhopes, Archbiſhopes, and Patriarches. Who
with al other ſubordinate Paſtors, vnder the one
Supreme viſible Paſtor, and Head, make a perfect
and formal Eccleſiaſtical Ierarchie in earth., reſem-
Part. 1. bling the Celeſtial Ierarchie of heauen. Chriſt our
Art. 36. Lord the Supreme Head of both : al making one
complete vniuerſal Church, in heauen and in earth.

Mariage rightly contracted betwen a Chriſtian man, and a Chriſtian woman, is a true Sacrament.

ARTICLE 47.

TWo of the ſeuen holie Sacraments, doe per-
Art. 41. teyne to the whole communitie of Chriſti-
§. 1. ans, as we noted before : which are Holie-
Order, wherof ſufficiét for our purpoſe is ſaid in the **What is here**
precedent Articles : and Matrimonie, which is now **to be declared**
to be in like maner explicated. Firſt ſhewing that it **touching Ma-**
is a true Sacrament : then what perſons may con- **trimonie.**
tract : laſtly that the contract is indiſſoluble, during
life of both parties. Concerning the firſt point, it is
very ſtrange, that Proteſtants wil denie Mariage to **It is ſtrange**
be a Sacrament, ſeing they preferre it before vowed **that Prote-**
chaſtitie, accounting it the more holie ſtate of life; **ſtants denie**
ſeing they alſo confeſſe it to be conſecrated by God, **Matrimonie**
to ſuch an excellent myſterie, that it ſignifieth, and **to be a Sacra-**
repreſenteth the ſpiritual Mariage, & vnitie betwixt **ment.**
Chriſt and his Church; and ſeing it is expreſly called
Epheſ. 5. a Sacrament, in the holie Scripture; which title is not
v. 32. there geuen to anie of the other Sacraments. Againſt
their

their denial therfore, we shal clearly proue, that it is not only in name, but also truly & properly an holie Sacrament, of the Christian Church, instituted by Christ, reducing it to the first perfection, & annexing therunto Sacramental grace.

2.   Wherfore it is specially to be obserued, that Mariage was instituted by God in paradise, in the state of Innocencie. For when God had first created one man [he tooke a ribbe from his side, and built the *Gen. 2. v.* same into a woman.] Then he blessed them, & said *21. 22.* [Increase and multiplie, and replenish the earth] *Ch. 1. v.* but it was not then a Sacrament. Because in that *28.* state of innocencie, by the vertue of Original Iustice, the soule had perfect dominion ouer the bodie, and the superior power of the soule, ouer the inferior. And therfore whiles they had not committed anie sinne, there was no neede of anie Sacrament. Neither was it conuenient, that man should then be perfected in his soule, by the vse of sensible creatures. To which by his fal he became to be subiect. Neither was it made a Sacrament in the old Testament, but only a figure of Christian Matrimonie, and an holie state, for the due propagation of mankinde. And so of godlie Mariage came the progenie of the holie Patriarches, and other faithful people, which were called the Sonnes of God. And of lasciuious fornication and adultrie. rose vp the wicked generations, of Cains race: called the children of men. For some of the better societie degenerating from their godlie parents, and declining to vice, matched themselues with the wicked [The sonnes of God (saith Moy- *Gen. 6. v.* ses) seing the daughters of men, that they were faire, *2. 3. 4.* tooke to themselues wiues out of al, which they had chosen, and they brought forth children, giants the mightie of the old world, famous men.] For which *v. 5.* and other enormious sinnes, God sent the vniuersal *Ch. 7. v.* diluge [The inundation of waters, which preuailed *17. 18. 19.*

out of

Mariage was first instituted in paradise: where there was no neede of anie Sacrament.

In the old Testament it was a figure of Christian Mariage.

By lawful Mariage, Gods people prospered; by fornication manie degenerated; and fel into grosse sinnes.

Ch. 7. v.
19. 20.

out of meafure, vpon the earth: and al the high mountaines vnder the heauens, were couered fiftene cubites, higher was the water, aboue the mountaines, which it couerd.] So that the huge mightie

Iob. 26.
v. 5.
Sap. 4.
7. 1.

[giants groning vnder the waters (faith Iob) were drowned] and deftroyed. Contrariwife [O how beautiful is the chafte generation, for the memorie therof is immortal.] As we fee in Noe, Sem, Abraham, Ifaac, Iacob, Iofeph, and others, whofe chafte Mariages, adorned with manie vertues, were figures of Chriftian Mariage. As farre therfore as the thing prefigured excelleth the figure, fo much Chriftian Matrimonie is more excellent, then Mariage in the old Teftament. And is reduced by Chrift our

Christian Matrimonie excelleth that of the old Law, and is like to that which was inftituted in paradife.

Mat. 19.
v. 4. 5. 6.

Sauiour, to the forme of that mhich was in paradife: that one man fhal haue but one wife, and not be deuorced fo long as both parties liue in this world: and therfore is made a Sacrament of the new Law.

1. Io. 5.
v. 3.

3. For it is an affured Rule, that whatfoeuer Chrift our Lord commandeth anie to doe, he geueth therwith fufficient grace to performe the fame. In ftead

Cer. 10.
v. 13.

therfore of [the old permiffion to difmiffe their wiues, geuing them a bil of diuorce (to auoide greater inconuenience) becaufe of the hardnes of mens hartes] now Chrift by Sacramental grace, mollifieth their hartes. Otherwife he would not haue made the Law of Mariage ftraiter, then it was before, but as this ftate is more perfect, fo it is alfo a more eafie yoke, by the helpe of Sacramental grace. In regard of which grace, S. Paul likewife prefcribeth perfect and ftrict precepts, both to husbandes, and wiues,

Chrift reducing the ftate of Mariage to a ftricter rule then it was in the old Teftament, gaue withal fpecial grace to obferue his ordinance.

Eph. 5.
v. 22.
23.
24.

faying [Let wemen be fubiect to their husbandes, as to our Lord: becaufe the man is the head of the woman: as Chrift is the head of the Church. As the Church is fubiect to Chrift, fo alfo the wemen to their husbandes in al thinges.] On the other partie

v. 25.

he faith alfo [Husbandes loue your wiues, as Chrift
Nn   alfo

v. 28.
v. 29.
v. 31.
(Gen. 2.
v. 24)
v. 32.

v. 33.

1. *Pet. 3.*
v. 1.2.

3.

4.

5.

6.

Gen. 18.
v. 12.

Also S. Pauls strict precept presupposeth sacramental grace in that state.

also loued the Church, and deliuered himself for it. So also men ought to loue their wiues, as their owne bodies. He that loueth his wife, loueth himself For no man euer hated his owne flesh, but he nourisheth & cherisheth it, as also Christ the Church. For this cause, shal man leaue his father and mother, and shal cleaue to his wife, and they shal be two in one flesh. This is a great Sacrament, but I speake in Christ, & in the Church.] Mariage is called a great Sacrament, because it signifieth Christs perpetual, & indissoluble coniunction, with his Church, his one onlie general spouse. For whose loue, he as it were left his Father, exinaniting himself by his Incarnatió, & left the Synagogue his mother, ioyning himself to his Church: which sprong out of his side sleeping on the Crosse: prefigured by Eue, who was built of the ribe, taken from Adams side, in his sleepe. For which great resemblance sake, amongst other reasons the Apostle exhorteth al maried persons, to honour, cherish & loue each other : concluding thus [you also euerie one, each man loue his wife, as himself, and let the wife feare her husband] not with seruile, but reuerential feare. The very same teacheth S. Peter [Let the wemen (saith he) be subiect to their husbandes, that if anie beleue not the word, by the conuersation of the wemen, without the word, they may be wonne : considering your chaste conuersation, in feare : whose trimming let it not be outwardly in the plaiting of heare, or laying on gold round about, or of putting on vestures : but the man of the hart, that is hidden, in the incorruptibilitie of a quiet and modest spirite, which is rich in the sight of God. For so sometime the holie wemen, also that trusted in God, adorned themselues, subiect to their owne husbandes; As Sara obeyed Abraham, calling him Lord.] Thus doth he exhorte wemen, which haue husbandes. And in the next wordes admonisheth

S. Peter teacheth the same touching maried persons.

maried

v. 7. maried men, saying [Husbandes likewise, dwel with them (to witte with your wiues) according to knowlege: as vnto the weaker feminine veſſel, imparting honour, as it were to the coheyres alſo of the grace of life; that your prayers be not hindered.] Al which perfection of vertues being required of maried perſons, among the manifold burdens of that ſtate of life, doth plainly ſhew, that ſpecial grace is neceſſarie for them: and conſequently proueth that Chriſt our Sauiour, together with the obligation, and indiſſoluble knotte of Mariage, geueth correſpondent grace, to performe the duties, wherunto they are bond, and therfore the Apoſtles doe admoniſh them to cooperate with the ſame grace, which is alwayes requiſite in euerie Sacrament.

Special grace being neceſſarie for the ſtate of Mariage, Chriſt hath therfore made it a Sacrament.

4. Breefly therfore to conclude this point, ſeing our Sauiour voutſaffed to honour Mariage, by his Perſonal preſence, and by working there his firſt notorious miracle in Cana of Galilee, before it was a Sacrament, and afterwards declared the reformation of that, which was permitted by Moyſes Law, concerning diuorce, and pluralitie of wiues: it is therby made ſufficiētly credible to the holie Church of Chriſt, and ought to ſuffice al Chriſtians to beleue, that Matrimonie rightly contracted by Chriſtians, is a true Sacrament. But is further confirmed againſt our Aduerſaris ſo to be, not only becauſe S. Paul ſo calleth it, which is a greatter proofe, then anie they haue to the contrarie; but alſo, becauſe the ſame Apoſtle in an other place, teſtifieth moſt plainly, that it geueth ſanctification, or ſanctifying grace. For admoniſhing the Theſſalonians to abſtaine from fornication, he telleth them that Mariage (which amongſt the Heathen is in paſſion, and luſt of vncleanes) doth ſanctifie Chriſtians, rightly contracting and ſo maketh matrimonial ſtate to be in ſanctification. [You know (ſaith he) what precepts I haue

Ioā. 2. v.
2. 11.

Epheſ. 5.
v. 32.

1. Theſ. 4.
v. 2.

It is further inuincibly proued, becauſe it geueth ſanctifying grace: by the teſtimonie of S. Paul,

Nn 2   geuen

geuen to you, by our Lord Iesus. For this is the wil
of God, your sanctification : that you absteyne from
fornication : that euery one may know (by contracting lawful Mariage) to possesse his vessel, in sanctification , and honour : not in the passion of lust , as
also the Gentiles, that know not God] so not only
teaching, that Christian Mariage excelleth the mariage of Infidels, but also that it maketh the persons
more holie , as the word Sanctification importeth,
which the Apostle againe inculcateth saying in the
same place [God hath not called vs into vnclean-
nesse, but into sanctification.] So that of lawful
Mariage lawfully contracted in the Catholique
Church, resulteth this threefold benefite : the auoiding of fornication ; the vertue of fidelitie betwen
husband and wife ; and sanctifying grace . which
maketh it a Sacrament.

v. 3.

v. 4.

v. 5.

v. 7.

Three espe-
cial benefites
in Christian
Mariage : to
auoid forni-
cation : the
vertue of fide-
litie : & Sacra-
mental grace.
If God send
Issue , it is the
fourth benefi-
te, or blessing.

Diuers iust impediments doe debarre some per-
sons from contracting Mariage.

ARTICLE 48.

Protestants
also admitte
more impe-
diments hin-
dering the
contract of
mariage, then
are expressed
in holie Scrip-
tures.

TOuching impediments of Mariage , only some
more principal pointes are expressed in holie
Scriptures; the rest depēd vpon Tradition, & Decrees
of the Church, directed by the Holie Ghost : as not
only Catholiques hold, but also Protestants must necessarily confesse. For albeit in the beginning of the
world, brothers did marie their owne sisters, Adams
children , because then there were no others : Yet
afterwards, both in the Law of nature , and in the
written Law of Moyses, as it was ordinarily vnlawful to marie either in the first degree, or in the first
and second, of consanguinitie, or affinitie : so was it
not only dispensed withal sometimes , but also was
expresly ordayned by Law, & custome, that in some
case

Leuit. 18.
v. 6 &c.
Ch. 20. *v.*
14. &c.

case they should marie in the degrees otherwise prohibited. So Abraham by way of dispensation maried Sara, as some thinke his owne sister, at least, (which is more probable) his brothers daughter. Iacob maried two sisters, Lia, & Rachel, both liuing together, Amram (the father of Moyses & Aaron) maried Iocabed his aunt, to witte his fathers sister, before the Law of Moyses. And after the same Law Othoniel (the first of the Iudges which gouerned the people of God after Iosue) maried Axa his brother Calebs daughter, no doubt lawfully, by dispensation. And it was expresly ordayned by the written Law, that in a special case the brother should marie the widow, of his brother deceassed; in these wordes [when brethren shal dwel together, and one of them dye without children, the wife of the deceased shal not marie to anie other, but his brother shal take her, and raise vp the seede of his brother.] And if the brother, or nerest kinseman, refused such mariage, they were punished with special disgrace. By vigore of which Law [Booz maried Ruth, the widow of Mahalon, the sonne of Elimelech, of Bethleem Iuda.] From whom descended King Dauid, & Christ our Lord. Which Law of marying the brothers wife, is now abrogated, that it bindeth not Christians, as al confesse: and consequently al the other Lavves of Moyses, concerning Mariage, are likevvise abrogated, and of no other force, nor obligation, then as they are renevved and established by the Lavv of Christ, and his Church. It resteth therfore to see, vvhat Christ, & his Apostles haue taught in this behalfe. And in the rest, vve must relie vpon that Church, vvhich by the infallible assistance of the Holie Ghost, teacheth al necessarie truth, and nothing but truth.

2. Amongst other Rules belonging to Matrimonie, it is cleare by Christs doctrine, that pluralitie of

Gen. 11.
v. 29. Ch
32. v. 13.
Ch. 29. v.
23. 28.
Exod. 6.
v. 20.
Nu. 26.
v. 59.
Ios 15.
v. 17.
Iudic. 3.
v. 9.
Deut. 25.
v. 5.

v. 7. 8. 9.
10.
Ruth. 4.
v. 4. 5. 9.
10. 22.

Io. 14. v.
26.

Mat. 19.
v. 5. &c.

Examples of holie men testifie, that they maried, in some cases such as the Law, and custome of those times did not ordinarily permitte.

MoysesLawes are abrogated, and binde not Christians, but Christian Lawes bind them.

Nn 3   vviues

By the Law of vviues is taken avvay. Which vvas lavvful in the
Chrift, who- old Teftament. Abraham had tvvo vviues, Sara and *Gen.* 16.
foeuer is ma- Agar. Iacob had foure, Lia, Rachel, Bala, & Zelpha. *v.* 3 *Cb.*
ried can not Dauid had alfo diuers, and that lavvfully: though 29. *v.* 13.
marie an other Salomon finned in exceeding multitude, for he had 28. *Ch.* 30.
til the former a thoufand vviues, and concubines, contrarie to the *v.* 3.
be dead. Lavv, prefcribing that [The King fhal not haue ma- 1 *Reg.* 18.
nie vviues: that may allure his minde.] As for plu- *v.* 27.
Pluralitie of ralitie of husbandes to one vvife, it vvas neither *Deut.* 17.
wiues was lavvful, nor tolerated at anie time. And nature, and *v.* 17.
permitted in reafon abhorre it, becaufe it vvould rather hinder
the old Tefta- propagation then further it [They fhal be tvvo (faid *Gen.* 2. *v.*
ment, but ne- God in the beginning) in one flefh] not three, nor 24. *Mat.*
uer pluralitie more, but tvvo. To vvhich ftate our Lord reftoring 19. *v.* 4. 5
of husbandes. Mariage, repeted the fame firft inftitution, and efta- *Rom.* 7.
blifhed it, in his Church of the nevv Teftament. *v.* 3.
Whofoeuer therfore, man or vvoman is already 1. *Cor.* 7.
maried, can by no meanes, marie anie other, during *v.* 11.
the natural life of the former: vvhich if anie doe attempt, the fame is no Mariage, but adultrie. And this
is the firft impediment: commonly called *ligamen.*

3.   An other impediment is called *Difparitas eultus,*
An other im- Difparitie of diuine vvorfhipe, and Religion. As if
pediment is, one be a baptized Chriftian, the other a Ievv, Turke,
if one partie or Pagane, they can not contract Mariage. And if
be not bapti- anie Chriftian fhould attempt it, he committeth high
zed. facrilege, neither is it a Sacrament, in that cafe, becaufe one partie vvanteth Baptifme, vvhich is the
gate, or entrance of al Chriftian Sacraments. And
as Mariage can not be betvven more then tvvo perfons, one man, and one vvoman: fo neither can the
Sacrament confift in leffe then tvvo. For they muft
be tvvo in one flefh. This impediment vvas prefi-
It was prefi- gured by the fact of Abraham, prouiding that his
gured by the fonne Ifaac fhould not marie a Chananite, but fent *Gen.* 24.
fact of Abra- his feruant vnto the houfe of Nachor, to take a vvife *v.* 3. *&c.*
ham & Ifaac. of his ovvne kinred, that is of his ovvne faith and
religion.

religion : and so Isaac maried Rebecca the daughter
of Bathuel , the sonne of Nachor , Abrahams brother Isaac commanded his sonne Iacob [not to take
a wife of the stocke of Chanaan : but goe (said he)
and make a iourney into Mesopotamia of Syria , to
the house of Bathuel thy mothers father , and take
thee a wife thence, of the daughters of Laban thyne
vncle.] Esau offended his parents by marying the
daughters of Infidels.

4. After this, in the written Law it is expresly said
[Enter not trafficke with the Amorrheites, Chana-
neites (and other Infidels) lest when they haue fornicated with their goddes , and haue adored their
idols, some man cal thee to eate of the thinges immolated. Neither shalt thou take a wife for thy sonnes of their daughters : lest after themselues haue fornicated, they make thy sonnes also to fornicate with
their goddes] Which precept is repeted amongst
the principal commandments of God, in the repetition of the Law [Thou shalt not geue thy daughter
to his sonne, nor take his daughter for thy sonne : for
he wil seduce thy sonne, that he folow not me, and
that he rather serue strange goddes.] And although
God dispensed with some in this positiue Law , in
whom there was no danger to be peruerted, as with
Samson marying Dalila a Philistian : with Dauid
marying Maacha daughter of the king of Gessur :
with Esther marying king Assuerus, & with others :
yet the general Law stood firme. In so much that
when the Israelites in their captiuitie of Babylon had
taken strange wemen for wiues , they vvere compelled to dismisse them , being first brought to due
repentance for that sinne, by Gods grace, & godlie
endeuour of Esdras. Who vnderstanding by relation of the princes, of the people, that very manie
had herein transgressed Gods commandment, begane first of al himself to lament , and due penance

Cb. 28.
v. 1.2.

Cb. 26.
v. 35.

Exo. 34. *v.*
11. 15. 16.

Deut. 7.
v. 3. 4.

Indic. 14.
v. 4.
2. *Reg.* 3.
v. 3.
Est. 2. *v.*
8. *Ch.* 14.
v. 15.
Mal. 2.
v. 11.
1 *Esd* 9.
v. 1. 2.

The Law ex-
presly forbade
to marie with
Infidels.

Gods people
were compel-
led to dismisse
the Infidels,
whom they
had presumed
to marie,

for

for other mens finnes [When I had heard this word   *v. 3.*
(faith he) I rent my cloke, and my coate, and plucked of the heares of my head, and beard, and fate
mourning. And there affembled to me al that fea-   *v. 4.*
red the God of Ifrael, for the tranfgreffion of them,
that were come from the captiuitie, & I fate forowful, vntil the euening Sacrifice. And at the euening   *v. 5.*
Sacrifice I rofe out of my affliction, and my cloke, &
coate being rent, I fel vpon my knees, & fpred forth
my handes to our Lord my God.] And in moft humble maner acknowleging this fpecial finne of the
people [in ioyning matrimonies with the infidel *v* 14. 15.
peoples, cried for grace, & remiffion, that the whole
people fhould not fal into vtter deftruction, but fome
remnant be left, and faued.] Efdras therfore thus *Ch. 10.*
praying, and befeeching, and weeping, and lying *v. 1.*
before the Temple of God, there was gathered to
him of Ifrael an exceeding great companie of men,
and wemen, and children, & the people wept with
much lamentation. And Sechenias (an appointed *v. 2. & 4.*
prolocutor for al) faid to Efdras: We haue tranfgreffed againft our God, & haue taken to wiues ftrange
wemen, of the peopls of the land, and now if there
The penitents be penance in Ifrael vpon this, let vs make a coue-
put away tho- nant with the Lord our God, to put away al the
fe whom they wiues, and them that are borne of them, accord ng
had vnlaw- to the wil of our Lord, and of them that feare the
fully maried. precept of the Lord our God: be it done according
to the Law. Arife, it is thy part to difcerne, and we
wil be with thee, take corege, and doe it. Efdras
therfore rofe vp, & adiured the princes of the Prieftes, and of the Leuites, and al Ifrael, that they fhould
doe according to this word: and they fware. Then
Efdras faid: You haue tranfgreffed, and taken ftrange *v. 10.*
wemen to wife, to adde vpon the finne of Ifrael.
And now geue confeffion to our Lord, the God of *v. 11.*
your fathers, and doe his pleafure: and be feparated
from

from the peoples of the land: and from your wiues. the strangers And al the multitude answered, and
v. 12. said with a loude voice: Acording to thy word vnto vs, so be it done.] And so it was performed, by the diligence of designed officers for this purpose, with consent of al the people. As Nehemias testi-
2. *Esd.* 9. fieth, saying [The children of Israel came together
v. 1. 2. in fasting and sackcloth, and earth vpon them. And the seede of the children of Israel, was separated from euerie strange childe, and they stood and confessed their sinnes, & the iniquities of their fathers.] Then renewing their promise, and oath: that they would walke in the Law of God, which he gaue in the hand of Moyses, that they would doe, and kepe al the commandments, iudgements, & ceremonies, made special mention of this particular sinne, in which they had lately and greuously offended, say-
Ch. 10. *v.* ing. [They would not geue their daughters to the
29. 30. people of the land, and their daughters, they would not take to their sonnes. And it came to passe, when
Ch. 13. they had heard the Law (that Ammonites, Moabi-
v. 3. tes, and other Infidels, should not enter into the Church of God) they separated euerie stranger from Israel.]

They did also other penance for this transgression.

5. A third impediment, or prohibition of Mariage among the Iewes, by an other positiue diuine ordinance, was that none should marie without their
Num. 36. owne tribe. [Lest the possession of the children of
v. 7. 8. 9. Israel be mingled, from tribe into tribe (saith the
10. Law) al men shal marie wiues of their owne tribe, and kinred: and al vvemen shal take husbandes of the same tribe: that the inheritance may remayne in the families: and that the tribes be not mingled among themselues, but remaine so, as they were separated by our Lord.] So that al vvere limited neither to marie vvith ouer nere kinred, nor vvith further of, then their ovvne tribe. Neuertheles the

An other prohibition was made, for a temporal respect.

A speciall priuilege that the Tribe of Leui might marie with the Tribe of Iuda,

tribe of Leui vvas exempted, from this particular Lavv: as appeareth by the factes of holie persons, though not otherwise expressed in the holie Scripture. For Ioida the Zelous, and godlie Highpriest maried Iosabeth, the daughter of king Ioram, the sister of Ochozias, and aunt of Ioas, of the tribe of Iuda. And Elisabeth of the daughters of Aaron, and tribe of Leui (S Iohn Baptists mother) vvas cosine to our B. Ladie, of the tribe of Iuda, and familie of Dauid.

2. Par. 22.
v. 11.

Luc. 1.
v. 5.

6. These vvere the especial Lavves of the old Testament, touching impediments of Mariages, vvherin vve may obserue these particular pointes for our present purpose. First that by the strict Lavv of nature, Mariage can neuer be contracted in the right line of consanguinitie, ascending and descending, nature it self abhorring it, and light of reason so directing euerie mans vnderstanding, & so there vvas no nede to expresse the same in the vvritten Lavv, but in affinitie only. By this rule Adam could not marie anie other vvoman then Eue, nor she anie other man but Adam: because al others descended directly from them. Secondly, by the secondarie Lavv of nature, it vvas not lavvful to marie in the first degree of collateral lines, that is, betvven brother & sister, by both parents, nor by one. In this degree God dispensed vvith Adams children, for that there vvere no others, to propagate mankind. Thirdly there being no other degree of kinred, forbid by the Lavv of nature, God by positiue Lavv forbade also to make mariage in the first and second degree, as vvel in consanguinitie, as affinitie, but so, that he sometimes dispensed therin, and in one special case of raysing seede, to the dead without issue, ordayned that the brother, or next in kinred, of the deceassed, should marie the widow. Fourthly pluralitie of wiues vvas lawful in the old Testamen, and diuorce

1.
By the first Law of nature none can marie in the right line of ascending & descending.

2.
By the secondarie Law of nature brother & sister can not marie.

3.
By the positiue Law deliuered by Moyses, mariage was forbid in the first and second degree but in a special case it was ordayned that they should marie in the first degree of affinitie,

Leuit. 18.
v. 8.
1. Cor. 5.
v. 1.

Leu. 18.
v. 9.

diuorce permitted, for the hardnes of some mens hartes, but both are now taken away: & for a better remedie, Sacramental grace is geuen to mollifie Chriſtian hartes. But pluralitie of husbands, nor multiplication of manie wiues, was neuer lawful, nor permitted by the Law of God. Fiftly mariages betwen the faithful, and heathniſh infidels was forbidde generally: yet diſpenſed withal, where no danger appeared of ſpiritual peruerſion to the faithful. Sixtly the degrees prohibited by the written Law, as perteyning only to the Iewes, as figures of the new Law of Chriſt, doe not otherwiſe binde Chriſtians, but as they are either forbid by the Law of nature, or renewed, and eſtabliſhed by Chriſt, and his Church. Which Church hath power by Chriſts commiſſion, to make conuenient Lawes, and conſequently to diſpenſe in the ſame, as iuſt cauſe may require: to decree what degrees, and other impediments, ſhal make Mariage inualide, and vnlawful; our Lord ſaying to his Apoſtles, and in them to their Succeſſors. [He that heareth you, heareth me: whatſoeuer you ſhal binde vpon earth, ſhal be alſo bond in heauen, & whatſoeuer you ſhal looſe vpon earth, ſhal alſo be looſed in heauen.]

7. An other impediment, proper to the new Teſtament, is the ſolemne vow of perpetual chaſtitie, either voluntarily made, by ſuch as enter into anie approued Religious Order: or doe voluntarily accept, the Churches propoſed condition, to al thoſe that taking the three greater Holie Orders, promiſe to kepe perpetual chaſtitie. To neither of vvhich vowes, none are forced, but hauing once by ſolemne promiſe to God, and his Church, ſo bond themſelues, they can not afterwards contract Mariage: and if they doe pretend to marie, it is voide, & inualide. As is cleare by S. Pauls doctrine, concerning vowed virgines, & widowes. For the ſame rule perteyneth

Luc. 10. v. 16.
Mat. 18. v. 18.

4.
Pluralitie of wiues, & alſo diuorce are taken away by Chriſt.

5.
Mariage with Infidels was forbide.

6.
Moyſes Law bindeth not Chriſtians.

A ſpecial Ecclefiaſtical impediment is the ſolemne vow of Religion, which bindeth before God.

Proued by S. Paules doctrine.

to al that make the like vowes. Concerning virgines, he faith, that there is no precept, that they fhal
kepe virginitie, yet he fo counfelleth, for the better   1. Cor. 7.
feruing of God:& addeth,that [not hauing neceffitie   v. 25.
but hauing power of his owne wil (fignifying that
by vowe, the wil hath bond it felfe) he doth wel   37.
that kepeth his virgine, yea better then to geue her
in Mariage] And of widowes vvhich hauing promifed chaftitie, and afterwards haue a wil to marie,
he faith moft plainly, that [They haue damnation   1. Tim. 5.
(are in damnable ftate) becaufe they haue made   v. 11. 12.
voide their firft faith.] that is, haue broken their
fidelitie, and promife geuen to God [And are turned

S. Paul calleth
the breach of
vow, a retur-
ning to Sa-
tan.

backe after Satan.] Thofe therfore that after fuch
vowes of perpetual chaftitie returning backe, prefume to match themfelues in wedlocke, are ftil
bond by a former, and greatter promife to God,
then is anie promife made to mortal perfon, and fo
the later promife is vtterly voide, and fuch pretenfed Mariage, is merely nought els but facrilegious
adulterie. But of the lawfulnes, & obligation of this
and other vowes, we fhal fay more after the explication of the tenne commandments. And of other
impediments you may fee the Doctors, which write
particulai ly therof.

The bond of Chriftian Mariage can not be diſſolued, ſo long as both parties liue in this world.

ARTICLE. 49.

WHeras in the old Teftament, Mariage wanting facramental grace, to mollifie the hardnes of mens hartes, they were permitted by the Law
of Moyfes, to dimiffe their wiues, & to marie others,   Deut. 24.
by thefe wordes of the Law [If a man take a wife,   v. 1.
and.

Divorce was
permitted by
the Law of

and haue her, and she finde not grace before his
eyes, for some lothsomnes, he shal write a bil of
diuorce, and shal geue it in her hand, and dismisse
her out of his house] By the Law of Christ this tolle-
ratiō is reformed, & a farre better remedie brought
in place therof, sanctifying grace is geuen, wherby
the maried parties are enabled, not only to beare
with Christian patience, the ordinarie difficulties of
their estate, but also with mutual loue to affect each
other, performing their solemne promise, & perfect
bond of cohabitation, as husband and wife, so long
as they shal both of them liue in this world, according to the conceiued wordes expresly vttered, as
the accustomed maner is : Vntil death shal them depart. Which indissoluble knotte of Christian Matrimonie, is manifestly proued, and confirmed by the
holie Scriptures of the new Testament. And first by
Chrifts owne doctrine.

2. For our Sauiour Christ, teaching that we must
kepe the commandments, more exactly then the
Scribes and Pharisees did, sheweth that their iustice,
was vnsufficient in manie precepts. Amongst others
in the matter of diuorce, declaring that it is neither
lawful for anie man to dismisse his wife, excepting
the cause of fornication ; nor to marrie an other [It
was said (saith Christ) whosoeuer shal dismisse his
wife, let him geue her a bil of diuorcement. But I
say to you; whosoeuer shal dismisse his wife, excepting the cause of fornication, maketh her to commite
aduoutrie. And he that shal marie her that is dismis-
sed, committeth aduoutrie.] Which same doctrine
our Lord repeted, in his answer to the Pharisees, demanding : Why Moyses did command to geue a bil
of diuorce, and to dismisse the married wife, telling
them [that Moyses did this, for the hardnes of their
hart: but from the beginning it was not so] adding
also as before [that whosoeuer shal dismisse his

Mat. 5.
v. 21.

v. 32.

v. 33.

Ch. 19.
v. 7. 8.
v. 9.

Moyses, with
licence to take
an other, but
is not lawful
by the Law
of Christ.

As in manie
other pointes
so in the mat-
ter of diuorce
the Scribes &
Pharisnes Iu-
stice was not
sufficient.

There is onlie
one cause of
diuorce, none
at al, to take
an other, the
former liuing,

Oo 3   wife,

vvife, but for formication, and shal marie an other, doth committe aduoutrie, & he that shal marie her, that is dimissed, committeth aduoutrie.] vvherupon, his Disciples considering the case to be so strict, be- *v. 10.* tvven the husband and vvife, presently [said vnto him: If the case of a man vvith his vvife be so, it is not expedient to marie] vvhich their iudgement our Sauiour approued, for the more perfect state, vvhich yet none are bond to folovv, except they *v. 12.* vvil, for better gaining the kingdom of heauen. But Protestants supposing this Apostolical remedie of single life, to be ouer hard, and vvith most men im- possible, vvould make the state of Mariage more easie, by applying the excepted case of fornication, not only to the Pharisees question, vvhether [it *v. 3.* vvere lavvful for a man to dismisse his vvife for eue- rie cause? but also to the last part of our Sauiours an- svver, concerning mariage of an other: vvhich they account lavvful, not only for the innocent partie, but also for the guiltie: most absurdly making that lavvful by the meanes of adultrie, vvhich can not be done for anie honest cause: as necessarie long ab- sence, imprisonment, captiuitie, leprosie, infectious sicknes, barrennes, or the licke more iust causes, of marying an other, then for adultrie.

3.   For explication therfore of this holie text of the Gospel, vvhether the excepted case of fornication, perteyneth to both the partes of our Sauiours an- *Lib. 3. ca.* svver, as Caluin, and his felovves vvould haue it, *19. Inst.* or only to the former part, touching diuorcement, and not to the vvordes folovving, touching their mariage vvith others; as al Catholiques vnderstand it: the circumstances of the vvhole passage are to be vveyed; as the occasion of our Lords doctrine at this time, the persons to vvhom he ansvvered, the con- cordance also of this Euangelist, vvith S. Marke, and S. Luke; vvho vvrite the same discourse: likevvise

S. Pauls

In regard of which diffi- cultie his Disciples iud- ged it expe- dient not to marie, which Christ did commend, but not com- mand.

Whether the case of forni- cation pertei- neth to both partes of Chrifts an- fwer, or to the former part only: is decided by the text.

S. Pauls doctrine, touching the bond of Mariage, wil geue vs fome light, for better vnderftãding the true fenfe of Chrifts wordes. For al are affuredly true, and none of their wordes, contrarie to others. The occafion why Chrift declared, that perfect obferuation of Gods commandments is neceffarily required, was the fuperficial infufficient iuftice of the Scribes and Pharifees, as is manifeft by his general wordes, vttered as a preface, to diuers inftru- ctions, when he faid [Vnles your Iuftice abound more, then that of the Scribes and Pharifees, you fhal not enter into the Kingdom of heauen] & then in particular he taught, that Pharifaical iuftice, (which feemed the beft amongft the Iewes) was infufficient, in the precepts concerning murder, aduoutrie, diuorce, fwearing, reuenge, vfurie, and enimies, requiring more perfection in them al, then the Pharifees obferued. The occafion of fpeaking againe concerning diuorce, permitted by Moyfes Law, was the Pharifees temting him, and alleaging the Law againft his doctrine, wherupon he auou- ched, that albeit Moyfes did permitte diuorce, for anie great diflike, or lothfomenes, for the hardnes of their hart, left a greater euil (as the murder of the wife) fhould happen : yet there is in deede, but one onlie iuft and Lawful caufe, to feparate man and wife, by perpetual diuorce, which is fornication : and as for marying an other, the firft liuing, he faid : that [he which marieth an other, doth committe aduoutrie, & he that fhal marie her, that is difmiffed, committeth admoutrie] which cleare wordes can not admitte former fornication, for an excufe of marying an other : becaufe fo to imagine, that after adultrie, it were lawful, to marie an other, yea for the guiltie partie difmiffed, to marie an other, is to make filthie finne, an excufe, & defence for flefhlie libertines, to finne of purpofe, that they may haue their

Mat. 5.
v. 20.
v. 21. 28.
32. 34.
38. 42,
43.

Mat. 19.
v. 4.

v. 9.

The occafion of this doctrine, was to fhew the infufficiencie of Pharifaical iuftice.

The occafion of repeting the fame was the Pharifees obiecting of Moyfes Law againft Chrifts doctrine.

The abfurditie of Proteftants expofition, fheweth it to be falfe,

and not agrea-
ble to Chrifts
meaning.

their pleafure, and that with pretence of lawful mariage, only made lawful by committing adultrie. Then the which what can be more abfurde, yea more vnpoffible? Wheras therfore our Aduerfaries contend, that the accepted cafe of fornication, perteyneth alfo to the wordes folowing, for marying an other, it is both an extorte & abfurde extention, moft hardly applyed to S. Marke, and S. Luke, who

Their expo-
fition is alfo
contrarie to
the wordes
of S. Marke,
and S. Luke.

without anie word, or figne of exception, relate our Sauiours wordes, concerning Mariage after fuch diuorce, abfolutely faying [whofoeuer dimiffeth his wife (faith S. marke) and marieth an other committeth aduoutrie vpon her. And if the wife dimiffe her husband, and marie an other, fhe committeth aduoutrie.] Which doth clearly agree with S. Matthew, according to al Catholiques vnderftanding, but were cleane repugnant by the Proteftants gloffe. S. Luke alfo relateth the fame without anie exception, as S. Marke doth, and doubtles they both agree in fenfe with S. Matthew. [Euerie one (faith S. Luke) that dimiffeth his wife, & marieth an other, committeth aduoutrie, & he that marieth her that is dimiffed from her husband, committeth aduoutrie.] Thus the three Euangeliftes teftifie Chrifts doctrine, touching this caufe without al iarre or cotradiction.

Mar. 10.
v. 11.
v. 12.

Luc. 16.
v. 18.

4.   And the fame is further explicated by S. Paul, writing thus [The woman that is vnder a husband, her husband liuing is bond to the Law, but if her husband be dead, fhe is loofed from the Law of her husband. Therfore her husband liuing, fhe fhal be

Rom. 7.
v. 2. 3.

S. Paul alfo
fhould con-
tradict S. Mat-
thew, if Pro-
teftants gloffe
were true.

called an aduoutreffe, if fhe be with an other man : but if her husband be dead, fhe is deliuered from the Law of her husband : fo that fhe is not an aduoutreffe, if fhe be with an other man] What can be fpoken more clearly, to fhew that neither adultrie, nor anie other thing, but onlie death diffolueth Mariage? The onlie euafion againft this Apoftolical doctrine,

is to

is to fay: The Apoftle affirmeth not, that a woman once maried, & liuing with another man, her former husband yet being aliue, is an aduoutreffe, but fhal be called an aduoutreffe: as if S. Paul made a *Their euafion is as wicked as friuolous.* difference in being fo, and being called fo, which in dede is not to expound, but to delude holie Scripture. Wheras the Apoftle faith plainly both here,

1. Cor. 7 & in another Epiftle, that [a woman is bond to the
v. 39. Law (of her husband) fo long time, as her husband liueth: but if her husband fleepe, fhe is at libertie] where alfo a wrangler may cauile, & fay : The Apoftle fpeaketh not of death, but of fleepe, & fo a wife *S. Paul teacheth the fame doctrine in another Epiftle.* is at libertie from the Law of Mariage, when her husband hath once flept, after their mariage. Let

Iude. goe therfore thefe mockries : and fee yet one place
v. 18. more, of the fame holie Apoftle faying a litle before
1. Cor. 7. [To them that be ioyned in matrimonie, not I, geue
v. 10. 11. commandment, but our Lord, that the wife depart not from her husband : and if fhe depart, to remaine vnmaried, or to be reconciled to her husband. And let not the husband put away his wife.] Obferue wel, and conferre this with our Sauiours doctrine, which he here vrgeth, as greater then his owne. For firft he faith it is not his owne only iudgement, *He alfo profeffeth to teach Chrifts doctrine touching this point.* but our Lords commandment, that the wife depart not from her husband : nor the husband difmiffe his wife from him, as was permitted by Moyfes Law. Secondly that if anie depart, or be difmiffed

(Mat. 5. (which may be only for adultrie) then to remaine
& 19. vt without marryinge an other, or to be reconciled to
fupra.) her husband. Thirdly it is euident, that if there could be a new mariage made during the life of the parties once maried, the Apoftle would haue made mention therof, by adding one claufe more, feing he profeffed here to deliuer our Lords commandment, touching this point. And fo this may fuffice our purpofe, concerning the indiffoluble bond of Chriftian

Mariage

Mariage, by anie humane power, but by death only.
5. Neuerthelesse God himselfe, by his diuine power, looseth the bond of Mariage contracted, but not consummate: when one partie, after the contract, choseth the better state of life, to kepe perpetual chastitie, in some approued Religious Order. After whose solemne profession, the other partie may marie. And in this case not man, but God doth separate them, by this spiritual calling of one to renounce this world: which is a holie kinde of spiritual death.

6. But Mariage made before Baptisme, not being a Sacrament, hath not so strict bond. Touching which the Apostle in the same place, geueth his aduise by way of counsel, without precept, saying [To the rest I say, not our Lord: If anie brother haue a wife an infidel, & she consent to dwel with him, let him not put her away. And if anie woman haue a husband, an infidel, and he consent to dwel with her, let her not put away her husband.] In case therfore that two Infidels being maried, the one become a Christian, the same partie may if he wil, depart from the other, yet the Apostle counseleth such to remaine in that mariage, so that the infidel partie wil dwel peaceably: that is, without contumelie of God, and reproch of Religion. His reason is, for that by peaceable, and godlie conuersation of the faithful partie, the infidel may be gained, to become also faithful, and so be made a Christian. [For (saith he) the man an infidel is sanctified by the faithful woman (by occasion & meanes of her good example, is perswaded & gained to Christ, & by Baptisme is sanctified) and the woman an infidel is sanctified (brought to sanctitie) by the faithful husband. Otherwise your children should be vncleane, but now they are holie] that is to say, are become Christians, by meanes of their parents cohabitation: which is like vvould not so sowne

Marginal notes:

In case of solemne religious vow, God solueth the bond of Mariage not consummate.

Mariage before Baptisme may either be continued or dissolued.

1. Cor. 7.
v. 38.

1. Thes. 5.
v. 19.

1. Cor. 7.
v. 12.

v. 13.

v. 14

so sowne haue happened, if their parents had bene
v. 15. separated, [But if the infidel depart (saith the Apostle to the faithful) let him depart: for the brother,
or sister (the Christian) is not subiect to seruitude in
such: but in peace hath God called vs] shewing that
the ciuile contract before Baptisme, may be either
kept or broken: as the parties can agree, or doe disa-
gree. Yet againe, the Apostle exhorteth the Christian partie, so much as lieth in their power, rather
to remaine in their mariage, then to depart, for the
hope of spiritual good to the infidel partie, saying:
v. 16. [For how knowest thou woman, if thou shalt saue
thy husband? or how knowest thou man, if thou
shalt saue the woman?] Thus the great Apostle aduiseth, and counseleth, not abriging the libertie of
Christians, but only exhorting for the more glorie
of God, edification of the faithful, and benefite of
others, which may be wonne to Christ.

7. What the Church ordayneth in this, or anie
other Sacrament, is by commission from Christ, limited within her bondes, not extended to alter the
essential partes, neither to ordaine, nor take away
the proper matter, or forme of anie Sacrament. And
therfore wheras it is ordayned that al Christians
must obserue the ordinances of God, and the Holie
Church : It is alwayes to be vnderstood, that God
principally maketh the Law, and that the Church
Mat. 18.
v. 18. doth expresse and declare Gods wil, & that which
the Church so declareth, doth loose and bind, accor-
ding as the same Church declareth: and by power
geuen to her by God decreeth, and so accordingly
God ratifieth the same in heauen, as the Church de-
termineth in earth : which Protestants, especially
the English, ought not to calumniate. Who most
absurdly, in place of holie Church, intrude temporal
power, of Prince and Parlament: as appeareth in
their Communion Booke: where among other Rites,

*The Church hath commis-
sion from Christ, to or-
dayne Lawes touching al
circumstan-
ces, but not
to alter the
substantial
partes of anie
Sacrament.*

*Also to dispo-
se of the ciuil
contract, de-
termining
what persons
can or can not
make it.*

in the

in the publique solemnization of Mariage, they appoint their Minister, to denounce al those Mariages, and only those to be lawful, which are so approued (say they) by the Law of God, and of this Realme. Wel knowing, and thereby confessing, that Gods Law, concerning Mariages, doth neede and require to be declared by the vocal sentence of visible Iudges. But they erre grosly by intruding temporal Iudges, and Lawes of the Realme, or temporal kingdom, in place of the Church, & Ecclesiastical power. For albeit they haue certaine pretended spiritual courtes, in euerie Dyocese: yet al these haue relation, & in some cases by way of appealing, al controuersies must finally be decided, by the pretended Supremacie of the Laiprince: which no other Sectaries doe admitte. And so in al other Sacraments, & al matters of faith & Religion, that is only holden by them for truth, and that for errour, and heresie, which is, or shal be so declared by their Parlament, their highest Tribunal.

English Protestantes remitte al cases of Mariages (yea and al other spiritual causes) to temporal Iudges.

8.   And thus much may suffice our present purpose, concerning al the seuen holie Sacraments, and B. Sacrifice of Christ. Wherunto for complement of this Second part, we shal here adde one Article more, concerning some special Rituals, holie Blessinges, and sacred Ceremonies: which are no Sacraments, but for the external similitude, are commonly called Sacramentalia. Which doe not geue first sanctifying grace, with remission of mortal sinnes, as Sacraments doe: but yet by right vse whereof grace is increased, and [the iust is made more iust, and the holie more holie.]

Grace is increased by right vse of Sacramentals.

Apoc. 22. v. 11.

Christ

Chriſt gaue his Church power to inſtitute ſacred Rites, and Ceremonies : which are called Sacramentals.

ARTICLE 50

AFter declaration of the ſeuen holie Sacraments, it reſteth to ſhew , that as Chriſt himſelfe vſed diuers ceremonial Rites , which he made not Sacraments: ſo he alſo gaue power to his Church , to ordaine external Ceremonies , as wel in the adminiſtration of the diuine Sacraments, as by adding other ſacred Rites, to the more honour of God, & ſpiritual good of Chriſtians. Eſpecially by bleſſing and conſecrating creatures, to holie vſes, to the comforth of the faithful, and for repreſſing the malice of wicked ſpirites. But omitting other Rites, partly proued already , againſt the contemners therof : partly confeſſed, and in ſome ſorte practiſed by Engliſh Proteſtants, as the vſe of their Publique prayers, in ſette forme for ſundrie purpoſes; their wearing of Surplices, Rochettes, Copes , and other Eccleſiaſtical paraments, the ſigne of the holie Croſſe in Baptiſme; their kneeling , when they make their general acknowlegement of ſinnes; and when they receiue their Communion; and the like : it may here ſuffice to proue certaine principal , and moſt vſual Sacramentals, for example ſalke : becauſe from the ſame groundes of holie Scriptures, al the reſt are likewiſe deduced.

2. To beginne therfore with Holie water, which was inſtituted in the firſt age after Chriſts Aſcenſion by S. Alexander Pope and Martyr. Whoſe fact in inſtituting it, and the whole Churches general practiſe in vſing it, are abundantly warrented by like examples both in the old & new teſtament. For ſo it hath

margin notes:

Chriſt vſed ſome other ſacred ceremonies beſides the Sacramenta.

Artic. 15.

Engliſh Proteſtants doe allowe of ſome few.

Holie water was inſtituted about fourſcor yeares after Chriſts Aſcenſion.

pleaſed

pleafed God at al times, by the minifteric of his feruants, and vfe of external elements, to worke fupernatural effedes. So vvere bitter waters made fwete,
by cafting into them a peece of wood As vve reade
in Exodus, vvhen the people of Ifrael vvere nevvly
parted from Ægypt, and found no other but bitter
vvater in the defert, therupon murmuring againft
Moyfes [He cried to our Lord, who did fhevv him a *Exod.* 15.
peece of vvood: vvhich vvhen he had caft into the *v.* 25.
vvaters, they vvere turned into fvveteneffe.] Like-
vvife Elifeus the Prophete amended vnprofitable
vvaters, by his prayer, and cafting falt into them.
For when the people of a certaine citie, lamenting
faid [The vvaters of this citie are very il, and the 4. *Reg.* 2.
ground barren.] The fame Prophete faid: [Fetch *v.* 19. 20.
me a nevv veffel, and put falt into it, vvhich vvhen
they had brought, he going out to the fountaine of
the vvaters, caft falt into it, and fayde: Thus fayth
our Lord: I haue amended thefe vvaters, and death
fhal no more be in them, nor barrenneffe.] Alfo by
vvater fandified vvith fpecial Rites, God ordayned
an extraordinarie meanes of trial, in the cafe of ielofie, faying: [If the fpirite of ielofie ftir vp the hufbãd *Num.* 5.
againft his vvife, vvhich either is polluted, or char- *v.* 14. 14.
ged vvith falfe fufpition, he fhal bring her to the
Prieft, and fhal offer an oblation for her. And the *v.* 17.
Prieft fhal take holie vvater in an earthen veffel, and
he fhal caft a litle grauel of the pauement, of the tabernacle into it. And he fhal adiure her, and fhal fay: *v.* 19.
If an other man haue not flept vvith thee, & if thou
be not polluted, by forfaking thy hufbands bedde,
the moft bitter waters fhal not hurt thee, vvherupon
I haue heaped curfes. But if thou haft declined from *v.* 20.
thy hufbãd, & art polluted, & haft lien with an other
man, thou fhalt be fubiect to thefe maledictions. Our
Lord geue thee for a malediction, and an example of
al among his people, make he thy thigh to rotte, and
thy

It is warren-
ted by like
examples, ap-
proued in ho-
lie Scriptures.

The cafe of
ielofie tried
by a kinde of
holie water.

thy bellie swelling burst asunder: the cursed water
enter into thy bellie, & thy wombe being swollen,
let thy thigh rotte. And the woman shal answer:
Amen, amen. And when she hath drunke this wa-

v. 27. ter [if she be polluted, and by contempt of her husband, guiltie of adultrie, the waters of malediction
shal goe through her,& her bellie being puft vp, her
thigh shal rotte withal : and the woman shal be for
v. 28. a malediction, and an example to al the people. But
if she be not polluted, she shal be blamelesse, & shal
beare children.] This was the Law of ielosie, for
trial of the truth, by a special kinde of holie water,
Num. 8. ordained for this purpose. By water also of lustra-
v. 7. Ch. tion (which was mixed with ashes of a redde cow,
19. v. 2. sacrificed with special Rites) the Leuites were consecrated, together with other Ceremonies. And the
v. 9. &c. same water [was reserued, for water of aspersion]
that is, was reserued to be sprinkled, for diuers purposes, then in religious vse : as holie water is now
in al the Catholique Church. S. Iohn Baptist also by
Mat. 3. special instinct of the Holie Ghost, did baptize in
v. 3. water, which was no Sacrament, but a figure of
Ioa. 13. Christian Baptisme. Our Sauiours washing of his
v. 45. Apostles feete : his imposition of handes vpon chil-
Mar. 10. dren, and imbracing them. The Apostles ordinarie
v. 16. ceremonies, prayers, benedictions of creatures, ex-
orcismes, & al religious actions, besides Sacraments,
were sacramentals, instituted by Christ : or his Apostles, by power receiued of him, not only for themselues, but also for their Successors. And so by this
power and auctoritie S. Alexander instituted Holie
water, to be continually in the Church, for the spiritual benefite of al faithful Christians, against the
diuels diuers,& manifolde molestations:that wheras
he endeuoreth by the meanes of creatures, to deceiue, allure, and hurt Gods seruants, by other creatures, faithful deuout Christians may resist, & repel
his

Marginal notes: Water of lustration vsed in consecrating of the Leuites. / S. Iohn baptized penitents in water. / Our Sauiour washed his Apostles feete. / Imposed his handes vpon children: and the like.

his tentations, and wicked attempts. Not by anie maner of yelding to him, or by anie pact made with him : as Nigromancers, Sorcerers, Witches, & other execrable miscreantes vse : but by diuine power, by the vertue of God , working by holie creatures, which are blessed by Gods Church, faithful Christians may ouercome the diuels, expel them from their persons , and places, auoide their malice , and procede in vertues , by vse of such sanctified creatures, Gods grace so strengthning his childrē, which cooperate with the same grace, not trusting to their owne strength, nor presuming of their owne merites, but only in God, from whom as the eternal immense fountaine, al riuers of grace doe flow, and procede. Amongst which external meanes of spiritual helpes , next after holie Sacraments , as none is more frequent, so scarce anie other, is more potent, then Holie water.

It is a most wicked thing to intreate the diuel.

It is alwayes necessarie to resist him.

1. Tim. 4. v. 4. 5.

3.　An other principal Ritual Ceremonie , is the Consecration of Churches , & Altars. Which is also very ancient , and hath bene continually in the Catholique Church, euer since S. Siluesters time. Who first instituted the solemne maner of erecting Christian Altars, annointed with sacred Oyle & Chrisme, in publique Churches, representing Christ our Lord the Annointed of God : who is our Altar , Sacrifice, and Priest. For albeit euen from the Apostles time, special places were dedicated to God, and Diuine Seruice : of which some were called Oratories, others Churches, where Christian people mette together to pray , to heare Gods word preached , and to receiue the B. Sacrament of the Eucharist , which S. Luke calleth [breaking of bread] & where [collections were made , the first day of the Sabbath] which is our Lords day : yet vntil Constantine the Great was conuerted to Christ (who first both by example, and publique decree inuited al Christians

Consecration of Churches and Altares instituted by S. Siluester, is agreable to holie Scriptures.

Anno Do. 306.

Act. 20. v. 7.
1. Cor. 16. v. 2.

to build

to build Churches) the Apoftles, & their Succeffors, with other Prieftes and Chriftian people, reforted together fecretely in priuate houfes, and criptes, to auoide perfecution, very often changing places. But when this holie Emperour was once conuerted to Chriftianitie, Churches, and Altares were erected, and folemnly confecrated, as now we fee: and our Aduerfaries denie not, though they feeke manie euafions to difalow the facred dedication of Churches: and efpecially they contemne, and deftroy confecrated Altars. And therfore feeing the fact is cleare, it refteth only to proue that the fame is agreable to Gods word, and true religion, and in no wife, as they wil nedes contend, infected with anie fuperftition. Which is manifeftly fhewed, by practife in the felected people of God, as wel in the Law of

Gen. 8. nature, as in the written Law of Moyfes. For Noe
v. 20. immediatly after the floud erected an Altar to God, and vpon the fame offered holocauftes to our Lord. Abrahā not only built manie Altars, but alfo bought
Ch. 23. *v.* a peculiar place for burial: where (it is probable)
9. 13. he erected fome houfe: and doubtles dedicated the fame, to that and other Religious vfes. Iacob alfo in
Ch. 28. his prayer, when he had feene Angels defcending
v. 16. and afcending by a ladder, which reached from the earth to heauen, vowed to build, & dedicate a houfe to God in the fame place, & afterwards performing
v. 19. *Ch.* his holie vow, called the place Bethel, that is, The
33. *v.* 20. houfe of God: which before was called Luza.

4. In the written Law nothing was more exactly commanded, amongft the ceremonial precepts, then
Exod. 25. the building of the Tabernacle, with the thinges
v. 10. 17. perteyning therto. As the Arke of teftimonie; the
18. 23. Propiciatorie; and Cherubimes; the Table for the
31. *&c.* louaes of propofition; the Candlefticke for feuen
Ch. 30. *v.* lampes, Snufters of pure gold: a Lauer of braffe (for
18. 19. the greatnes) called a Sea; which ftood vpon the

Marginal notes:

Approued by the example of Patriarches.

The making and erecting of the Tabernacle, was an efpecial figure of Temples, in the Church of Chrift.

Qq   pictures

pictures of twelue oxen, as vpó twelue feete. Diuers **3. *Reg. 7.***
other veſſels, and inſtruments, ſome of gold, ſome ***v. 25.***
of ſiluer, others of braſſe, iron, marble, wood of
diuers ſortes : and ſpecial Prieſtlie attyre, adorned ***Exo. 35.***
with precious ſtones. Al to ſette forth the worthie ***v. 2. 9.***
eſtimation of true Religion. For accompliſhing ***Ch. 36.***
wherof, the deuoute people contributed ſo abun- ***v. 6. 7.***
dantly, that their voluntarie oblations did not only
ſuffice, but being ouer much, publique proclamation
was made, that they ſhould offer no more. [The gold ***Ch. 38.***
that was ſpent in the worke of the Sanctuarie, which ***v. 24.***
vvas offered in donaries, vvas nine and tvventie talents, and ſeuen hundred thirtie ſicles, according to
the meaſure of the Sanctuarie. There vvere moreo- ***v. 26.***
uer an hundred talents of ſiluer, vvhich made the
hundred feete of the pillers (that bore vp the Tabernacle.) And a thouſand ſeuen hundred, ſeuentie ***v. 28.***
fiue talents made the heades of the pillers. A ſicle of
ſiluer being in value, about fifetene pence ſterling,
and ſo ſixtene ſicles making a pound, & an hundred
ſicles making a talent, the vvhole ſumme of ſiluer
beſtowed only in making the feete, and the heades
of the pillers, amounted aboue eleuen thouſãd ſeuen

A ſicle being hundred pounds ſterling. The gold was much more
fifetene pence, in value. The whole charges therfore in gold, ſiluer,
ſo a talent 6. braſſe, and other thinges in making the Tabernacle,
pondes fiue vvere exceding great. Al being finiſhed, & the Ta- ***Ch. 40.***
ſhillinges, the bernacle erected, God repleniſhed it with maieſtie] ***v. 32.***
whole ſumme This excellent Tabernacle vvas continually remo- ***Ch. 13. v.***
was very ued vvith the vvhole campe, as God directed by a ***21. 22.***
great. cloude in the day, and by a piller of fire in the night, ***Ioſ. 18.***
ſo long as the Iſraelites vvere in the deſert. After ***v. 1.***
vvhich peregrination, it vvas placed ſometime in ***1. Reg. 7.***
Silo, then in Maſphath, and other places, and finally ***v. 5.***
in Ieruſalem.

5.   Yet vvould King Dauid, of his zelous deuotion ***2. Reg. 7.***
haue built a more excellent Temple [vvhich God ***v. 2. 12. 13.***
vvould

would not haue him, but his sonne Salomon (for
mysterie sake) to performe] Which Temple [God
also replenished with glorie, and sanctitie, aboue al
places in the earth.] The same being destroyed by
the Babylonians, God so permitting, for the peoples
sinnes, it was [reedified after the captiuitie by Zorobabel, Esdras, and others.] Againe being prophaned
and in part destroyed by Antiochus, [It was purged,
& repared by Iudas Machabeus, with new Altars]
and other apurtenances, and [a yearlie feast instituted of the new dedication therof.] It was also enlarged, and much adorned by Herod Ascolonita, to
gratifie the Iewes. There were also manie Synagogues, or litle temples in cities, and townes, built
and dedicated to God, for his seruice: the one principal Temple in Ierusalem, being à liuelie figure of
the head mother Church, and the Synagogues figures of other Churches, Temples, and Chapels.

6.   More particularly concerning Altars, which
Protestants denie, as they doe al proper Sacrifice, &
Priesthod, in the Church of Christ: not only the
necessarie vse, but also the consecration therof, is
proued, by the figures in the old Testament. To
which the Protestants Communion tables are nothing answerable. For in the Law of nature [Noe,
Abraham, and other Patriarches, built Altars for
Sacrifice. Iacob erected à stone for a title, powring
oyle vpon it,] which afterwards he perfected by
Gods special commandment [annointing it with
oyle.] Likewise in the written Law, Aaron and his
sonnes offered Sacrifices, vpon consecrated Altars,
King Salomon at the dedication of the Temple made
an Altar of gold, tenne candlestickes for lampes, &
snuffers, al of pure gold. Yet was the Altar more
excellent for the sanctification, then for the mettal,
wherof it was made. For as our Sauiour teacheth
[not the giftes vpon the Altar, but the Altar doth

Marginal notes (left):
3. Reg. 8.
v. 10.
1. Esd. 3.
v. 8, Ch.
5. v. 1.
1. Mach. 4.
v. 36, 43.
v. 56.
2. Mach.
10. v. 3.

Gen. 8.
Ch. 12.
&c.
Ch. 28.
35. v. 7.
Ibidem.
v. 1. 14.
Nu. 7. v. 1.
3. Reg. 7.
v. 48.

Mat. 23.

Marginal notes (right):
Salomons Temple, and diuers Sina-gogues, were more exam-plar figures of Christian Churches.

Consecration of Altares more particu-larly proued by the holie Scriptures.

Erection and consecration of Altares was expresly commanded in the Law of Moyses.

God feuerely
punisheth
facrilegious
robrie.

fanctifie the giftes, and al thinges that perteyne vnto *v.* 18. 19.
it] and that by vertue of the Sacrifice offered theron. 20.
The example of King Baltafars destruction, may *Dan.* 5. *v.*
teach al prophane contemners of holie thinges, 2. 3. *ad.*
what hortible punishment hangeth ouer them, for *v.* 30.
the abuse of Altars, and other thinges dedicated to
God, and his Diuine Seruice.

Inunction of
kinges though
not prescribed
by the Law,
yet religiously
instituted, and
obferued in
the old Testa-
ment.

7.   Inunction of Kinges is an other holie Rite, boro-
wed from the old Testament, not instituted by the
Law, deliuered to Moyses: but brought in afterwards. The Prophete Samuel, by Gods special or- *1. Reg.* 10.
dinance annointed Saul, King of Israel. And after *v.* 1. *Ch.*
him Dauid. Likewise [Sadoch the Priest, and Na- 16. *v.* 13.
than the Prophete, annointed Salomon king] to suc- 3 *Reg.* 1.
cede his father. And when the kingdom was diui- *v.* 34.
ded into two kingdomes, not only the successors of
Dauid, and of Salomon, in the kingdom of Iuda, but 3. *Reg.* 19.
also the other Kinges of Israel were annointed, as *v.* 15. 16.
appeareth [in Iehu] yea some other kinges also, as 4. *Reg.* 9.
[Hazael king of Syria] Of these therfore it semeth, *v.* 3.
that some Christian kingdomes, namely England,
& France, borow the sacred Ceremonie of annointing their Kinges, with Holie oyle, at their Corona-
tion. And English Protestants kepe euen to this day,
the external resemblance therof. As they doe of
diuers other Sacramentals: for which there is no
expresse special warrant, in the new Testament.
But only general power geuen to the Church; and
particular Customes, and Tradition.

Protestants
defend exter-
nal Ceremo-
nies againft
Puritanes, by
Chrifts gene-
ral commiffi-
on.

8.   To which maner of defense, they are forced to
repaire, when Puritanes impugne their Iniunctions
of Ecclesiastical Rites, and practife. And Puritanes
also in their formes of Baptifme, Communion, Mariages, Preachinges, Publique exercifes, and other
actions in their conuenticles: and al Sectaries plead
general auctoritie geuen by Chrift, to inftitute diuers
particular formes, which are not expreffed in the
holie

holie Scriptures: prefuming, and euerie forte fuppofing that themfelues are the true Church. So that al
conclude and agree in this : that the true Church
hath the true faith, and Religion, the true vfe of Sa-
See the firft craments, and Sacramentals. But which is the true
Part from Church ? remaineth ftil amongft them, an endles
Art. 33. to circular queftion. Which to Catholiques is clearly
43. knowne by the Markes therof, declared by expreffe
holie Scriptures.

margin: Puritanes alfo
& al Sectaries
plead general
auctoritie ge-
uen by Chrift
to his Church,
for diuers rites
not expreffed
in holie Scrip-
ture.

.9 Of other Sacramentals therfore, we fhal not
1 *Reg.* 21. nede to fpeake in particular. As the Benediction of
v. 4. 6. Agnus Dei, Holie bread, Beades, Croffes, Medals,
Exo. 25. Candles, Afhes, Palmes, Firft fruites, Belles, New
v. 37. *Ch.* houfes, New fhippes, and the like. Al which crea-
28. *v.* 34. tures being good, as S. Paul teacheth, & no creature
is to be reiected, but to be vfed with thankes geuing:
are made more profitable by benedictions, & [fan-
1. *Tim.* 4. ctified by the word of God, and prayer] For fo the
v. 4. 5. Church bleffeth al fuch thinges, by expreffe inuocation of God, alwayes vfing this Preface: *Adiuto-*
Pfal. 123. *rium noftrum in nomine Domini.* Our helpe is in the
v. 8. name of our Lord.] And fo befecheth God to bleffe,
confecrate, and fanctifie his creatures, by the vertue
of his Paffion & Death, fuffered on the Holie Croffe:
that the fame may be free from the power of the
1. *Cor.* 10. enimie, beneficial to men, and (which is the cheefe
v. 31. *Ch.* end, wherunto al actions ought to be directed) to the
14. *v.* 26. more glorie of God : and to edification. As S. Paul
inftructeth. Euer concluding *Per Chriftum Dominum*
Pfal 150 *Noftrum*, By Chrift our Lord. Amen, Adding alfo, as
v. vlt. we adde here, and fo end this fecond part: *Benedi-*
camus Domino. Deo gratias.

margin: By which
confeffed ge-
neral aucto-
ritie al Sacra-
mentals are
clearly iufti-
fied in the
Catholique
Church.

Al being done
in the name, &
through the
merites of
our Lord Ie-
fus Chrift.

The end of the Second Part.

You may pleaſe, courteous Reader, to correct the faultes, with your penne, by making it thus.

Page 10. line 1. and 2. *b* requireth
Page 31. line 11. bought
    line 16. moniment
Page 32. line 31. publiquely
Page 38. line 12. was ſanctified
Page 48. line 29. al worſhipe
Page 83. line 1. excedingly
Page 86. line 3. which I wil not
Page 101. line 35. part
Page 106. line 4. but wanteth
Page 109. betwixt the 23. & 24. line:
was a figure of Chriſts death. In that it was eaten, it
Page 112. Marg. line 31. *Sap. 16. v. 20. 21.*
Page 119. line 7. natural reaſon
Page 127. line 35. crament (which &c.)
Page 142. line 21. 6.
Page 161. line 1. whoſe ſinnes
Page 184. line 11. perſons
Page 215. Marg. remitted &c. Al which
Page 256. line 1. miraculouſly
Page 268. line 17. either

Other leſſe faultes are eaſily amended.

FINIS

THE THIRD PART
OF
AN ANKER
OF
CHRISTIAN DOCTRINE
CONCERNING THE
TENNE COMMANDMENTS.

THE FIRST ARTICLE.

Gods commandments are possible: and necessarie
to be kept.

OR so much as al which beare the name of Christians, doe confesse, that only true Religion is the meanes (through the merites of CHRIST our Sauiour) to attaine eternal life; and for so much as some wil admitte no other trial of true Religion, but the only written word of God; we haue for their sakes, and for the more manifestation of the truth proued, and declared by this special way, which they require, the principal points of the Christian Faith: and in like maner the seuen holy Sacraments; in the two former Partes of this worke. Now it foloweth in this third Part to explicate in like sorte the Tenne Commandments of God.

The connexiō of this third Part with the rest.

A

God. And so in the fourt Part to declare the necessity,
and efficacie of Prayer : according to the Methode
proposed in the Preface. To procede therfore in this
present subiect, as in the matters of Faith, and of the
holy Sacraments ; so likewise concerning the Commandments, our Aduersaries haue in these latter dayes
raysed diuers Controuersies, though not so many in
number, as in the former Partes: yet some of especial
importance: which we shal discusse, as they occurre.
And first touching al the Commandments in general,
Protestants hold that it is vnpossible for any mortal
person, by any meanes to kepe them, or any of them.
And that it is not necessarie, that they should be obserued. But that only Faith doth iustifie. Neither doe
they meane the whole Faith, of al Christian Articles,
but an especial assured perswasion of euery one, that
whosoeuer beleeueth, that himself is reputed iust by
CHRIST, and that he shal be saued, his soule shal vndoubtedly be in heauen, so sowne as it shal be parted
from the body. None of which their Assertions can
either be found, in expresse holy Scripture, nor be deduced from thence : nor otherwise proued by any
good ground, of sacred text or reason. But the direct
contrarie Propositions are clearly proued, and abundantly confirmed by many sacred textes, both of the
old and new Testament. Vpon al which we ioyning
issue of trial doe thus proceede.

Protestants haue no good proofe, that the commād-ments are im-possible : or not necessarie, nor for only faith; nor for their special faith &c.

2.   God, who is alwaies the same, and whose iustice
is immutable, not only commanded Adam the first
man, in the state of Innocencie, to abstaine from eating of a certaine fruite, and punished him for transgressing the same commandment : but also after the
losse of original Iustice, particularly punished Cain,
for murdering his brother Abel. Which punishments
had not bene iust, if either Adam in Paradise, could
not haue obserued Gods precept; or Cain in the state
of sinne, could not haue abstained from killing Abel.
Because

Gods com-mandments, presuppose possibilitie to kepe them, both in the state of inno-cencie, and af-ter the fal of man.

Gen.2.v.17. ca.3.v.17. 18.19.ca.4. v.8.10.11.

Becaufe by the rule of reafon, none can be bond to a thing vnpoffible. And where is no obligation, there is no tranfgreffion; and where no tranfgreffion, there can not be iuft punifhment. But Adam knowing by Gods commandment, that he was bond to kepe it: And Cain alfo knowing by the light of nature, that he ought to haue refrained from manflaughter: and confequently both Adam, and Cain knowing that their obligations were poffible: were therfore iuftly punifhed; and fo neither Adam, nor Cain, replied to the contrarie, by pleading impoffibilitie. For Adam in humble repentance, accepted the inioyned punifhments: and Cain defpairing of mercy, acknowleged his iuft defert, faying to our Lord [Myne iniquitie is greater, then that I may deferue pardon.] Further this poffibilitie of obferuing Gods commandments, is confirmed by examples of Adam in the reft of his life. For [he was finally faued] and of Enoch who [walked with God, & was fene no more, becaufe God tooke him. For before his tranflation he had teftimonie, that he had pleafed God] of Noe, who [was a iuft and perfect man, in his generation, he did al thinges which God commanded him] concerning the making of an Arke, and preaching iuftice by his life, and doctrine. [For I haue fene thee iuft in my fight] faid our Lord vnto him. And S. Peter calleth him [the Preacher of iuftice] Likewife by the example of Abraham who [went forth of his countrie as our Lord had commanded him.] He walked before God and became fo perfect, that vpon Gods comandment he was ready, without reply, [to kil, and offer his beloued fonne Ifaac in Sacrifice.] For which prompt obedience our Lord by his holie Angel gaue him teftimonie, of iuftice, and promife of reward; faying [Now haue I knowne that thou feareft God: and haft not fpared thyne only begotten fonne for my fake. By my owne felfe haue I fworne, faith the Lord, becaufe

v. 13.

Sap. 10.*v.*2.
Gen 5. *v.* 24.
Heb. 11.*v.*5.
Gen. 6.*v.*9.
21.

c4. 7. *v.* 4.
et
2. *Pet.* 1. *v.* 5.

Gen. 12. *v.* 4. *c4* 17. *v.* 1.
C4. 22. *v.* 2. 3. 4 *& c. v.* 12. 16. 17.

Examples of fulfilling Gods commandments.

A 2 caufe

cause thou haſt done this thing, and haſt not ſpared
thyne only begotten ſonne, for my ſake; I wil bleſſe
thee, and I wil multiplie thy ſede, as the ſtarres of
heauen: and as the ſand, that is in the ſea ſhore. Thy
ſeede ſhal poſſeſſe the gates of his enimies. And in thy
ſeede ſhal be bleſſed, al the nations of the earth, becauſe thou haſt obeyed my voice.]

Like examples of other Patriarches, and faithful perſons.

3.   Other examples abund in the ſacred Hiſtorie of
Iſaac, Iacob, Ioſeph, al which walked rightly before
God, and of other Patriarches, and faithful people,
which ſometimes obſerued Gods wil, and ſo proue it
to be poſſible:& ſometimes offending were puniſhed,
which preſuppoſeth their obligation to haue fulfilled
it: and conſequently the poſſibilitie therof. God commanded his whole people, when he had brought
them forth of Ægypt, to kepe his precepts, with promiſe of protection, and other reward, if they would
obey, and with threates of puniſhment, if they diſobeyed, ſaying: [If thou wilt heare the voice of the
Lord thy God, and doe that is right before him, and
obey his commandments, and kepe al his precepts,
none of the maladies, that I laid vpon Ægypt, wil I
bring vpon thee: for I am the Lord God thy Curer.]
For ſo ſowne as there was want of meate, they murmuring: [Our Lord ſaid to Moyſes: Behold I wil
raine to you bread from heauen. Let the people goe
forth, and gather that ſufficeth for euerie day: that
I may proue them, whether they wil walke in my
Law, or no. But the ſixt day, let them prouide to
bring in (for the ſeuenth) and let it be duble, to that
they were wont to gather euery day. Gather it ſix
duies: but in the ſeuently day is the Sabbath of our
Lord. Therfore it ſhal not be fond] which precept
ſome obſerued, and ſome tranſgreſſed: going forth
on the Sabbath to gather Manna, but fond none.
[And our Lord ſaid to Moyſes (and by him to the
people) How long wil you not kepe my commandments,

Marginal references: Gen. 24.v. 62.63. ca.25. v.27. ca.28. v.13 ca.40. v.15.   Exo. 15. v.26.   Ca.16.v.3. 4.5.   v.26.   27.   28.

mandments, and my Law?] Wherby it is manifest
that some obseruing this commandment, it was not
vnpossible: and some transgressing it, were bond to
haue obserued it;els they had not bene iustly blamed.
And the same is the nature, and condition of euery
commandment of God, that al are bond, and al can,
if they wil, through Gods grace, kepe it.

4.   Againe this doctrine as wel of possibilitie, as of
necessitie to kepe Gods commandments, is proued
by the threates, and promises. As where our Lord
immediatly after the first of the tenne commandments, sayth [I am the Lord thy God, mightie, ielous
visitie the iniquitie of the fathers, vpó the children,
vpon the third, and fourth generation of them, that
hate me: and doing mercy vpon thousands, to them,
that loue me, and kepe my precepts.] To strike also
more reuerence, and feare of God in this people;they
heard [the voices, and saw the flames, and the sound
of the trumpet, and the mount smoking; and being
frighted, and strooken with feare they stood a farre
of: saying to Moyses: Speake thou to vs, and we wil
heare: let not our Lord speake to vs, lest perhaps we
dye. And Moyses said to the people: Feare not: for
God came to proue you, and that his terrour might
be in you, and you should not sinne.] Here Moyses
saith plainly, that God sent this terrour, to make
them afeard to sinne. Which necessarily proueth, that
if they would, they could obserue the thinges commanded: and that al this was done, to incline their
willes to good, and to terrifie them from euil:leauing
it in their power and wil,to doe the one,or the other.
And therfore albeit manie did presently after these
admonitions, fal most wickedly, making, and adoring golden calues, yet they did it voluntarily,not necessarily. As also manie other holie Scriptures doe
abundantly declare.

5.   For that none should pretend ignorance,or obli-

Margin notes:

Gods threates
and promises
shew it to be
both possible
and necessarie
to kepe his
command-
ments.

Ex. 10.7.
5.6.

7.18.

19.
20.

God againe by commanding to write the same thinges often : & often to read them, sheweth that they mist be kept.

uion, God commanded his Couenant to be written. Yea some thinges often repeted, and al to be often read . As when Moyses ascended the second time into the mount , and had receiued diuers precepts, Moral, Ceremonial, and Iudicial [Our Lord said to him : Write thee these wordes in which I haue made a Couenant, both with thee, and with Israel] Vpon an other occasion our Lord said againe [You shal doe my Iudgements , and shal obserue my Precepts: and shal walke in them. I the Lord your God. Kepe my Lawes,and Iudgements : which a man doing shal liue in them. I the Lord.] Againe he saith [Doe my precepts,and kepe my iudgements , and fulfil them, that you may dwel in the land,without any feare] In the repetition of the Law , Moyses againe and againe admonisheth, & vrgeth the people to kepe the com- mandments. Which were al in vaine, if it were vnpos- sible. And if onlie Faith would suffice, he would haue vrged that cheefly, or only. But he stil crieth : [Now Israel heare the Precepts , and Iudgements , which I teach thee (and neuer sayth:that thou maist only know them, or only beleue them. No not in al the Law, neither in al the holie Bible:but he addeth [that doing them , thou maist liue. And entring in maist possesse the land , which the Lord the God of your fathers wil gene-you.] Thus was a terrestrial reward promised to that people , in figure of heauenlie re- ward to Gods spiritual children. But the one, and the

Ex.34 v.27.

Leuit.18.v. 4.5.

ca.25 v 13.

Dent.4.v.1.

The same againe is con- firmed by the maner of deli- uering the Law,

other, to those that kepe his precepts. After recital of special benefites, Moyses putteth them in minde in what maner the commandments were geuen, saying [You came to the foote of the mount,which burned euen vnto heauen : and there was in it darknes , and a cloud, and mist. And our Lord spake to you from the middes of the fire. The voice of his wordes you heard , and forme you saw not at al. And he shewed you his couenant, which he commanded you to doe.

v.11.

11.

13. &c.

And

And the tenne wordes that he wrote in two tables
of stone. And he commanded me at that time, that I
should teach you the Ceremonies, and Iudgements,
which you should doe, in the land that you shal possesse. Kepe therfore yourselues carefully. You saw
not any similitude, in the day that our Lord spake to
you in Horeb from the middes of the fire: lest perhaps
deceiued, you might make you a grauen similitude, or
image of male or female : the similitude of al cattel
that are vpon the earth; or of birdes, that flie vnder
heauen, and of creeping beastes, that moue on the
earth, or of fishes, or of the Sunne, Moone, Starres,
&c. and deceiued by errour you adore, and serue
them.] These were the false imagined goddes, which
some Iewes sometimes, and the heathen Paganes generally adored for goddes. But now in place of Idolatrie, the iewes hold their obstinate malice against
Christ. The Turkes esteme their Mahomete for a singular diuine Prophete, and many grosse absurdites
for sound Religion. Al Heretikes esteme and adore
their owne deuised new doctrines, as their proper
Idoles. Amongst the rest Protestants hold Gods commandments to be vnpossible, and not necessarie to be
kept. Wherof there is no similitude at al in the holy
Scriptures, but the quite contrarie doctrine. Therfore deare freindes, haue patience to search the Scriptures. [Heare Israel (saith Moyses againe) and obserue that thou doe the thinges, which our Lord hath
commanded thee, and it may be wel with thee. Now
Israel, what doth our Lord thy God require of thee,
but that thou feare the Lord thy God, and walke in
his wayes? and loue him, and serue the Lord thy God,
with thy whole hart, and with thy whole soule, and
with thy whole strength. And kepe the commandments of our Lord, and his ceremonies which I command thee this day, that it may be wel with thee. Circumcise therfore the prepuce of your hart: and your

necke

*Zach.*13
*v.*2.

*Deut.*6.*v.*
3.5.
*ca.*10.*v.*12.

*v.*13.*v.*16.

Iewish, Tur-
kish, and He-
retical errours
in Religion,
are as detesta-
ble as Pagans
false goddes.

Besides faith,
God especially
requireth that
his seruants
doe fulfil his
command-
ments.
Mãs coopera-
tion to cir-
cumcise his
owne hart
is required.

necke indurate no more.] The faithful people did not reply to Moyſes his admonitions, as holding it vnpoſſible, or vnneceſſarie to kepe Gods command-ments: but freely accepted the couenant, as Moyſes further teſtifieth ſaying to the ſame people [Thou haſt *ca.16. v. 17.* choſen our Lord this day to be thy God; and to walke 18.19. in his wayes: and to kepe his Ceremonies, and Precepts, and Iudgements, and to obey his commandment. And our Lord hath choſen thee this day, that thou ſhouldeſt be his peculiar people : as he hath ſpoken to thee, that thou ſhouldeſt kepe al his com- *(ca.27 v.1.)* mandments : and make thee higher then al nations: which he created to his praiſe, and name, and glory: that thou maiſt be a holie people, of our Lord thy God, as he hath ſpoken.] In regard alſo that man can *(2. Cor. 3.*

God promiſeth ſufficient grace to mollifie the hardnes of mans hart.

not (of himſelf, as of himſelf) performe this coue- *v. 5.)* nant, God promiſeth euer to aſſiſt with his grace, enabling his faithful ſeruants by mollifying, and inclining their hartes to obey: as Moyſes teſtifieth ſaying [Our Lord thy God wil circumciſe thy hart, and the *Deut. 30. v.* hart of thy ſeede, that thou maiſt loue our Lord thy 6. v. 7. 8. God, in al thy hart, & in al thy ſoule, that thou maiſt liue. And al theſe curſes he wil turne vpon thine enimies, and them that hate, and perſecute thee. But thou ſhalt returne, and heare the voice of our Lord thy God: and ſhalt doe al the commandments, which I command thee this day] Wherupon he inferreth euen the ſame which Catholiques beleue, and teach [This *v. 11. 17.* commandment which I command thee this day, is *&c.* not aboue thee (how then dare any man ſay, it is vnpoſſible?) nor farre of, nor ſituated in heauen, that thou maiſt ſay: which of vs is able to aſcend vnto heauen, to bring it to vs, that we may heare, and fulfil it in worke? nor placed beyond the ſea, that thou maiſt pretend (excuſe) and ſay: Which of vs can paſſe ouer the ſea, and bring it euen vnto vs, that we may heare, and doe that which is commanded? But the
word

v.15. word (the thing commanded)is very nere thee,in thy mouth,and in thy hart to doe it. Consider that I haue sette before thee, this day life and good : and contra-

16. riwise death and euil: that thou maist loue our Lord, thy God, and walke in his wayes, and kepe his commandments, and ceremonies, and iudgements, and thou maist liue: and he multiplie thee, and blesse thee in the land which thou shalt enter to possesse.] By al which it is most cleare that through Gods grace , the faithful can if they wil, kepe al,& euerie one of Gods comandments. Neuertheles they can also if they wil,

17. transgresse and breake them , according to the next wordes [But if thy hart (saith Moyses) be auerted and thou wilt not heare; and being deceiued with errour, thou adore strange goddes , and serue them (or choose and folow false opinions in Religion) I fortel thee this day, that thou shalt perish , and abide litle time in the land,which passing ouer Iordan,thou shalt enter to possesse,]Likewise passing by Baptisme into the Christian Church , and falling into heresie, thou shalt perish;no wāt nordefect on Gods part,geuing alwayes sufficient grace, according to Moyses conclusion, saying[I cal for witnesses this day,heauen and earth,that I haue proposed to you, life and death,

v.19. blessing and cursing. Choose therfore life, that both

20, thou maist liue, and thy seede; & maist loue our Lord thy God, and obey his voice, and cleaue to him : for he is thy life, and the length of thy dayes.]

6.   As Moyses in his time; so al good Gouernors, Priestes and Prophetes admonished the people,of the necessitie (and consequently they presupposed it possible)to kepe Gods commandments. Iosue conserued the people, for most part, in the seruice of God . And

Ios.24. at his death exhorted them to the same,saying [Feare

v 14. you our Lord, and serue him with a perfect, and very true hart: and take away the goddes , which your fathers serued in Mesopotamia, and in Ægypt; & serue

God geuing power to kepe the commandments,leaueth it in mens power to breake them if they wil.

The couenant betwen God and his people was renewed by Iosue , and is stil to be kept.

B   our

our Lord . But if it like you not to ſerue our Lord,   15.
choiſe is geuen you (therfore it was in their power)
chooſe this day, that which pleaſeth you whom you
ought eſpecially to ſerue whether the goddes, which
your fathers ſerued in Meſopotamia, or the goddes of
the Amorrheites , in whoſe land you dwel: but I and
my houſe wil ſerue our Lord. And the people anſwe-   16.
red and ſaid : God forbid we should leaue our Lord,
and ſerue ſtrange goddes . We wil ſerue our Lord be   18.
cauſe he is our God. And Ioſue ſaid to the people: you   21.
are witneſſes, that yourſelues haue choſen to you our   22.
Lord, for to ſerue him. And they anſwered: witneſſes .
Now therfore, quoth he , take away ſtrange goddes   23.
out of the middes of you ; and incline your harts to
our Lord, the God of Iſrael. And al the people ſaid to
Ioſue : We wil ſerue our Lord God : and wil be obe-   24.
dient to his precepts . Ioſue therfore in that day made   25.
a couenant, and propoſed to the people precepts and
Iudgements] This renouatiõ of the couenant betwen
God, and his people , as it was morally in confirmation of the peoples actual dutie , and purpoſe ſtil to
ſerue God, by keping his cõmandments: ſo myſtically
it prefigured the like couenant to be made with Chriſtians [To obſerue al thinges, whatſoeuer Chriſt com-   *Mat. 28.*
mandeth by himſelf, and his Paſtors.]   *v. 20.*

Luc. 10,
God circum-   7. Obſerue now, ye that read theſe wordes of Ioſue,   *v 16.*
ciſeth and in-   & the like of other Prophetes. How conformable the   *Deut 30.*
clineth mans   Catholique doctrine is to the expreſſe ſacred text   *v.6.ca.10.*
hart: and man   [God circũciſeth the hart of man] by his ſpecial grace   *ca,16.*
muſt alſo cir-   [Man circũciſeth his owne hart] by cooperating with   *3.Reg. 8.*
cumciſe and   Gods grace . We pray with Salomon, and with al the   *v.58.Pro.2,*
incline his   faithful, that [God wil incline our hartes to him, that   *v.2.3.*
owne hart.   we may walke in his wayes, & kepe his cõmandmẽts]   *Ioſ.24.v.23.*
Ioſue exhorted the people [to incline their hartes to
our Lord the God of Iſrael] the Royal Prophete
prayed [Lord incline my hart into thy teſtimonies.]   *Pſal.118.*
And in the ſame Pſalme confidently profeſſeth of   *v.36.112.*
himſelf [I haue inclined my hart to doe thy iuſtifications

tions for euer.] In like maner, our Lord inuiteth al to incline their hartes, and diligent ly to kepe his commandments. And expostulateth with those that dòe not [Incline your eare (saith he by his Prophete Isaias) and come to me: heare, and your soule shal liue, and I wil make an euerlasting couenant with you] By Ieremie he saith [I commanded them, saying: Heare ye my voice, and I wil be your God, and you shal be my people: and walke ye in al the way, that I haue commanded you, that it may be wel with you. And they heard not nor inclined their eare: but haue gone in their pleasures, and in the peruersitie of their wicked hart: & haue bene made backward, & not foreward.] So that by Gods grace first stirring vp the hart, and stil assisting, and by mans cooperation with the same grace, Gods commandments both can, and must be obserued: els man hath not spiritual life, nor can possibly attaine eternal life. Further that (by these meanes) the commādments are possible is testified by the same Prophetes [Al his commandments are faithful (saith the Psalmist) confirmed for euer and euer: made in truth, & equitie] If they were vnpossible, how could they be in truth, & equitie? Which can not be imagined, in commanding thinges vnpossible. [But thou ô God (saith the same holie Psalmist) hast very much commanded thy commandments to be kept] And therfore they are both possible, and necessarie to be kept. To the same purpose Salomon, and by him the Eternal wisdom, crieth [Hold discipline, leaue it not: kepe it, because the same is thy life] And against our Solifidians, the same diuine Preacher concluding his Booke, saith [Let vs al heare together the end of speaking: Feare God, and obserue his commandments: for this is euerie man.] As if you wil say: In fearing God, and in keping his commandments, consisteth the means of mans felicitie; & côtrariwise in presuming of securitie, & breaking the commandments consisteth the cause of mans

Isa.55.v 3.

Iere.7. v.23. 24.26.

ca.11.v.8. ca.17 v.23. ca.25,v.4.

Psal.110. v.8.

Ps.118.v.4.

Prou.4. v.13.

Ecle.12. v.13.

miserie.

miserie. [Kepe ye iudgement, and doe iustice] saith   *Isa 56.*
our Lord againe by his Prophete Isaias . And by Ie-   *v. 1.*
remie:[Make your wayes good, and your studies (de-   *Iere. 7.*
sires, and affections) and I wil dwel with you in this   *v. 3.*
place. Trust not in wordes of lying , saying: The
Temple of our Lord, the temple of our Lord, it is the
temple of our Lord. For if you shal wel direct your   4.
wayes, and your studies, if you shal doe iudgement,   5.
betwen a man and his neighbour : to the stranger,   6,
and to the pupil, and to the widow shal doe no op-
pression, nor shede innocent bloud (doe good , and   7.
flee from euil) I wil dwel with you] Wisdom (saith
Baruch the Prophete) is the Booke of the command-   *Bar. 4.*
ments of God , and the Law that is for euer : al that   *v. 1.*
hold it shal come to life, but they that haue forsaken
it, into death] Ezechiel threatneth false Prophetes,   *Ezech. 13.*
and the people that are deceiued by them . [for that   *v. 10. 11.*
they had deceiued the people, saying: Peace, & there
is no peace: God builded the wal (saith the Prophete)
and they daubed it with morter without straw. Say
to them that daub without tempering, that it shal
fal : for there shal be a shower ouerflowing , and I
wil geue very great stones, falling violently from
aboue, and the wind of a storme dissipating : shal
it not be said to you: Where is the daubing, that   13.
you daubed ? Therfore thus saith our Lord God:
I wil destroy the wal, that you haue daubed with-
our tempering ; and I wil make it euen with the
ground; and the fundation therof shal be reuealed;
and it shal fal, and shal be consumed in the middes
therof: and you shal know that I am the Lord.] By
which Metaphore of daubing, without tempering of
straw with the morter, the Prophete sheweth , how
vaine the imagination of securitie is, to saluation,
without due repentance, and other good workes:and
how fouly the careles wil be deceiued, which presume, that their sinnes stil remaining, are not imputed,
as if

as if onlie faith, yea onlie perſwaſion of imputed iuſtice, would iuſtifie, and ſaue them. Which damnable imagination the ſame Prophete yet further confuteth by the example of Sodome and Gomorrhe, which were deſtroyed in their pertinacie of ſinnes, proceeding of proud preſumption of ſecuritie, and of idlenes from good workes, ſaying [Loe this was the iniquitie of Sodome thy ſiſter : Pride, Fulnes of bread, and Abundance, and Idlenes of her, and of her daughters. And they raught not their hand to the needie, and the poore.] For omiſſion therfore of good workes, and committing euil, no maruel that deſtruction came at laſt, ſudainly and violently vpon them : liuing quite contrarie to the general Law of God, and nature, which preſcribeth theſe two general precepts [To decline from euil, and to doe good] they contrariwiſe declining from good, and doing euil. And therfore the like, deſtruction (though perhaps not temporal, yet which is worſe, eternal) muſt needes remaine to al ſuch, as runne the ſame courſe, how much ſoeuer they preſume of imagined ſecuritie. Al becauſe they wil not incline their harts and eares, to doe that, which on mans part is required, in the couenant betwen God and his people. For on Gods part (which muſt ſtil be remembred) there is neuer any defect: Whoſe grace is alwayes readie, if men wil accept it : Wherby euerie one may if he wil, kepe Gods commandments. As God yet further teſtifieth by the ſame Prophete, ſaying [I wil put my ſpirite in the middes of you, and I wil make (by my grace) that you (may if you wil) walke in my precepts, and kepe my iudgements, and doe them.] Daniel, and the other three renowned children and ſeruants of God, with excellent fortitude obſerued Gods commandments, notwithſtanding the terrour of the hote burning furnace, & of deuouring lions, which together with the

*ca.*16. *v.*49.

*Pſal.*36. *v.*27.

*Ezech.*36. *v.*27.

*Dan.*1.*v.*8. *ca* 3.*v.*12. *ca.*6.*v.*16.

Preſumption of ſecuritie, & omiſſion of good workes brought the Sodomites to moſt deteſtable ſinnes and vtter deſtruction.

Other examples, and teſtimonies.

conſtancie

conſtancie of old Eleazarus, & the young ſeuen brethren Machabees, and others of diuers ſtates and
ages, may ſerue for examples vnto al Chriſtians, in
times of perſecution, And in times of peace, godlie
Zacharias, and his wife Eliſabeth with others doe teſtifie, that al the commandments of God are poſsible
to be kept, Becauſe they al were inuironed with fleſh
and bloud, with the world, and ſpiritual enimies, as
we are, and the helping grace of God, throng Chriſts
Paſſion, is now greater, then it was in the old Teſtament. Finally let one teſtimonie more of thoſe times
ſuffice for manie. The Prophete Micheas hath this
cleare doctrine [I wil shew thee ô man (ſaith he)
what is good, and what our Lord requireth of thee.
Verily to doe iudgement; and to loue mercie; and to
walke ſolicitous with thy God] Which breefe leſſon
conteyneth three ſpecial pointes of good life [To doe
iudgement] by confeſsing our owne ſinnes, doing
penance for them [for the iuſt is firſt accuſer of himſelf] Secondly [to loue mercie] by doing good
workes, with good wil and alacritie [for God loueth
a chereful geuer.] Thirdly [to walke ſolicitous with
thy God.] by carefully conſidering euerie thought.
Word, and deede; that it be agreable, and not contrarie to Gods commandmets. As holie Iob ſaith of himſelf to God [I feared al my workes: knowing that
thou didſt not ſpare the offender.]

2. Mac 6.
v. 18, ca.
7. v 1. &c.
Luc. 1. v.
6.

Mich. 6.
v. 8.

Prou. 18.
v. 17.

2. Cor. 9,
v. 8.

Iob. 9.
v. 28.

Obſeruation of the commandments is more exactly required in the Law of Chriſt, then the Iewes obſerued them.

8. Now that al theſe examples, precepts, and admonitions of the old Law, and Prophetes, concerning
Gods commandments, perteyne no leſſe, but rather
more to al Chriſtians, then to the Iewes, our Sauiour
expreſly teacheth, ſaying [Doe not thinke that I am
come to breake the Law, or the Prophetes: I am not
come to breake, but to fulfil. For aſſuredly I ſay to
you, til heauen and earth paſſe, one iote, or one tittle
ſhal not paſſe of the Law: til al be fulfilled. He ther
fore that ſhal breake one of theſe leaſt commandments,

Math 5.
v. 18.
19.

20.

ments, shal be called the leaſt in the kingdom of
heauen (that is, ſhal not enter into the kingdom of
heauen) But that ſhal doe, and teach (by word, or
example) he ſhal be called great in the kingdom of
heauen. For I tel you, that vnles your iuſtice abund
more then that of the Scribes and Phariſees you ſhal
not enter into the kingdom of heauen.] And after
that our Lord and Sauiour had explicated, by diuers
examples, wherin the Scribes and Phariſees were defectiue in keping the commandments; exacting of
his diſciples to kepe them rightly, he ſaith to them
[Be you perfect therfore: as alſo your heauenlie Father is perfect.] And ſo proſecuting his doctrine
ſaith. [Not euerie one that ſaith to me: Lord, Lord,
ſhal enter into the kingdom of heauen; but he that
dith the wil of my Father, which is in heauen, he ſhal
enter into the kingdom of heauen. Manie ſhal ſay to
me in that day: Lord, Lord, haue not we prophecied
in thy name, and in thy name caſt out diuels? and in
thy name wrought manie miracles? And then I wil
confeſſe vnto them (plainly tel them,) that I neuer
knew you; depart from me, you that worke iniquitie.] As therfore it is neceſſarie to beleue in Chriſt,
ſo likewiſe to kepe the commandments. Not only to
know them, but alſo to doe them, [Take vp my yoke
vpõ you (ſaith our Lord at an other time) and learne
of me: becauſe I am meeke and humble of hart: and
you ſhal finde reſt to your ſoules. For my yoke is
ſwete, and my burden ligth] If light, then not vnpoſſible. More and more doth our Sauiour declare in his
Goſpel, that this yoke, and burden, of keping the
commandments, is neceſſarie to ſaluation. Very directly and moſt expreſly by occaſion & a demand propoſed vnto him [Behold (ſaith the Euangeliſt) one
came to him, and ſaid: Good Maſter, what good ſhal I
doe, that I may haue life euerlaſting? (as an other Euã-
geliſt relateth it) By doing what, ſhal I poſſeſſe euerlaſting

21.

48.

*Cb.*7.
*v.*21.

22.

23.

*Cb.*11.
*v.*29.
30.

*Cb.*19.
*v.*16.
17.

Manie euident
textes of the
Goſpel doe
ſhew that
onlie faith
doth not iuſti-
fic.

lafting life. And IESVS faid to him: If thou wilt enter *Luc.18.*
into life, kepe the commandments. This doe, and *v.18.*
thou shalt liue] What can be faid more exprefly ? And *ca.10.*
becaufe al the commandments are brefely reduced to *v 18.*
two heades [To loue God aboue al other thinges; *Mat.22.*
and to loue thy neighbour as thy felf] yea al compri- *v.40.*
fed in loue, as the roote from which the bräches procede: our Sauiour faith in an other place [If you loue *Ioan.14.*
me, kepe my commandments . He that hath my *v.15.21.*
commandments, and kepeth them, he it is that lo- *ca.15.*
ueth me.] Againe faying [If you kepe my precepts, *v.10.*
you shal abide in my loue] he sheweth that to
loue him, and to kepe his commandments, is fo
one, and the fame thing, that thofe which kepe not
his cömandments, doe not loue him, but by breaking
any commandment, doe fal from louing him. Euerie
one of thefe, and the like textes of the hölie Gofpel,
doth euidently proue, that only Faith doth not iuftifie
without obferuafion of al Gods commandments.

The fame is
proued by the
doctrine of S.
Paul.

9.   The fame both poffibilitie & neceffitie, of keping
Gods commandments is further declared by the doctrine of Saint Paul . Who shewing at large, the
weaknes of man, without Gods fpecial grace: and
that in the ftate of finne, none could fulfil the Law,
teacheth the poffibilitie therof, by the merite, and
grace of Chrift, faying [That which was impoffi- *Rom.8.*
ble to the Law (before Chrift) in that it was weake- *v.3.*
ned by the flesh. God fending his Sonne, in the fimilitude of the flesh of finne, euen of finne damned
finne, in the flesh (that now concupifcence in the
regenerate hath not dominion) that the iuftification of the Law might be fulfilled in vs, who walke
not according to the flesh, but according to the fpirite] And fo the Law can now, through Chrifts grace,
be fulfilled, which could not be kept without his
grace. For therfore the Law was geuen, that grace
might be knowen to be neceffarie, and fo be defired;

                                                                4.

fired; and grace is geuen that the Law may be fulfilled
For [they that are in the flesh can not pleafe God. But

8. you (faith the Apoftle to the regenerate) are not in
the flesh, but in the fpirite: yet if the Spirite of God

9. dwel in you] If in dede you kepe the cōmandments,
and part not from the loue of God, and fo his Spirite
remaine in you. And agreable to Chrifts former recited doctrine; the Apoftle, in regard that the loue of
our neighbour, prefuppofeth the loue of God aboue
al; faith that [He which loueth his neighbour, hath

cd. 13. fulfilled the Law] becaufe the loue of our neigbour,
v. 8. 9. prefuppofeth the loue of God; and thefe two are the
10. fumme of the whole Law. And fo concludeth, faying
[Loue therfore is the fulnes of the Law] In otherplaces
he writeth touching the neceffarie obferuatiō of the

Rom. 2. commandments; that [not the hearers of the Law are
v. 13. iuft with God; but the doers of the Law shal be iufti-
3.Cor. 7. fied] Againe he faith: [Circumcifion is nothing, and
v. 19. prepuce is nothing, but the obferuation of the com-
Gal 5. v. mandments of God. For in Chrift Iesvs neither cir-
6, c4.6. v. cuncifion auaileth ought, nor prepuce, but faith that
15. worketh by charitie; But a new creature] that is, iuftification of the foule by grace, renewing and reui-

Pf. 50. uing the finner to fpiual life [creating a cleaue hart
v. 12. (as the Pfalmift prayed) and renewing a right fpirite]
This quickning, and liuing grace is it, which enableth
man, and moueth the iuft to obferue the commandments. Wherupon the fame S. Paul, confidently
writeth thus to S. Timothee[I command thee before
1.Tim. 6. God, who quickeneth al thinges, and before Chrift
v. 13. 14. Iefus, who gaue teftimonie vnder Ponnus Pilate,
a good confeffion, that thou kepe the commandment
without fpotte, blamelesse vnto the coming of our
Lord Iefus Chrift.]

10. Touching the fame neceffitie of obferuing the **And of other**
commandments, S. Iames in the very like wordes **Apoftles.**
to S. Paules, admonisheth al Chriftians, faying [Be

C   doers

doers of the word, and not hearers only: deceiuing *Iac.*1. *v.*22.
your selues, for he that only heareth the word, & doth (23.24.)
it not, is like to him that hauing sene his owne face in   *v.*25.
a glasse, & by and by forgetteth what an one he was.
But he that hath looked in the Law of perfect libertie
and hath remained in it, not made a forgetful hearer,
but a doer of the worke; this mã shal be blessed in his
deede.] And touching the possibilitie, or rather the
facilitie of carying the swete yoke, and light burden
of Gods commandments, S. Iohn saith in planest 1. *Ioan.* 5.
termes[Gods commandments are not heauie]He also *v.*3.
agreable both to S. Paul, and to S. Iames, and to the
Catholique beleefe, teacheth that al are bond to kepe
the commãdments, in that they are bond to beleue in
God, & to loue God, saying[He that saith he knoweth *Ch.*2. *v.*4.
God, & kepeth his word (his commandment) in him
in very deede the charitie (or loue) of God is perfited:
in this we know that we be in him. For (saith he in *cap.*5.*v.*3.
the same Epistle) this is the charitie of God, that we
kepe his commandments: and his commandments
are not heauie] They are not heauie saith S. Iohn the
Apostle. Detest therfore the grosse, & blasphemous
paradox of Iohn Caluin, saying: They are not only
heauie, but also impossible to be kept. But the holie
Apostle declareth also the reason, why they are not
heauie. [Because al that is borne of God, ouercometh   *v.* 4.
the world: and this is the victorie which ouercometh
the world, our faith] God geueth grace to beleue in
Christ by faith, the first vertue: to be borne in him, by
Baptisme; to loue him by charitie, to confide in him *Ch.*2.*v.*12.
by hope, and to ouercome the would, the flesh, and 13. *&c.*
the diuel, by faith, hope, charitie, christian fortitude,
& other vertues: al springing frõ his grace. For which
grace also S. Iude the Apostle rendreth thankes, and *Iude v.*24.
praise to God, in the behalf of al good christiãs, saying
[To him that is able to preserue you without sinne:
and to sette you immaculate before the sight of his
                                            glorie:

glorie:be glorie, & magnificéce for euermore. Amen]
By al which is fufficiently proued that the obferuatió
of Gods cómandméts is both poffible & neceffarie.

11. As for the newly imagined fhorte way, by
which fome perfons, properly called Libertines,
wil affure themfelues of eternal faluation, by their
owne fingular faith, or phanfie; by euerie ones owne
perfwafion, that he, or fhe fhal affuredly be faued, it
is no faith at al, but a moft vaine illufion. For if it
were any point of true faith, then an Anabaptift fo
perfwading himfelf, fhould infallibly be faued:
then a Lutheran, and a Caluinift were bond to beleue
that the fame Anabaptift fhal vndoubtly be faued.
And fo euerie one that holdeth fuch a perfwafion, to
be a point of faith, muft beleue that euerie Sectarie
holding this point, fhal be affuredly faued, whatfoeuer he holdeth, or denieth in other points of Chriftiá
faith: & howfoeuer they depart fró this life in ftate of
other finne. Which, befides the abfurditie, & cótradi-
ction of diuers Sectaries, condéning each others, and
only iuftifying théfelues, is euidétly confuted by holie
Scriptures, which affirme that [many fhal fay to Chrift
in the day of iudgemét, Lord, Lord haue not we prophecied in thy name, & in thy name caft out diuels; &
in thy name wrought manie miracles? And then wil
Chrift our Lord fay to thé: I knew you not: depart fró
me, you that worke iniquitie.] And to the foolish virgins which fhal come late [faying: Lord Lord opé the
gate to vs: he wil fay: I know you not] Al thefe haue
both faith, & hope, & are in their owne conceipt per-
fwaded, that they fhal be faued: no leffe then Proteftants fuppofe themfelues are iuft, & fhal be faued by
their onlie faith in Chrift, and by their particular beleefe, that they are affured of their owne eternal faluation. Neither haue they any holie Scripture to confirme this their perfwafió. The moft probable they cá
produce is the faying of S. Paul [The Spirite himfelf

Mat.7.v.22.
23.

Ch.25.v.11.
12.

Rom.8.
16.17.

The new ima-
gined phanfie,
that al fhal be
faued which
fo perfwade
themfelues,
hath no fun-
datió in holie
Scripture.
And is con-
trarie to ex-
preffe Scrip-
tures.

An obiectioa.

C 2   geueth

geueth teſtimonie to our ſpirit, that we are the ſonnes of God. And if ſonnes, heyres alſo: heyres truly of
God, and coheyres of Chriſt] we anſwer. That this
teſtimonie being only internal, can be no more aſſu-

Anſwer.
rance then a good and confortable hope, of our iuſtifi-   *Ibidem.*
cation, and future ſaluation[yet if we ſuffer with him   *v. 17.*
(ſaith the Apoſtle, in the next wordes) that we may
be alſo glorified with him.] But this is not an aſſuráce
of faith. For it is manifeſt by other expreſſe holie
Scriptures, that together with good hope, we muſt   *Prou. 28.*
haue iuſt feare. [Bleſſed is the man (ſaith Salomon)   *v. 14.*
that is alwayes fearful. There are iuſt men and wiſe,   *Eccle. 9.*
and their workes are in the hand of God: and yet man   *v. 1.*
knoweth not, whether he be worthie of loue, or ha-   *1. Cor. 4.*
tred. I am not guiltie in conſcience of any thing (ſaid   *v. 4. Phil.*
S. Paul) but I am not iuſtified herein. He that iudgeth   *2. v. 12.*
me is our Lord. With feare and trembling worke
your ſaluation.] ſaith he to al Chriſtians. Likewiſe
ſaith S. Peter [Brethren labour the more that by good   *2. Pet. 1.*
workes, you may make ſure your vocation, and ele-   *v. 10. Iac.*
ction. By workes (ſaith S. Iames) a man is iuſtified,   *2. v. 24.*
and not by faith only.] No not by the true, and intire
Chriſtian faith alone, without good workes. Much
leſſe by heretical opinion, by particular beleefe, phanſie, or perſwaſion of euerie one for himſelf, that he
ſhal vndoubtedly be ſaned.

The opinion,
that the com-   12.   Seing then it is manifeſt, by their owne confeſ-
mandments   ſion, that Proteſtants doe not fulfil the command-
are impoſſible   ments of God: for they hold opinion; that none can
is abſurde, in   poſſibly kepe them, or anie one of them, it falleth ne-
common   ceſſarily vpon them, that the iuſt Iudge muſt ſay to
iudgement of   euerie one, that not only confeſſeth (as al penitents
moderate   truly doe) that they haue ſinned, but alſo that it is im-
Proteſtants.   poſſible to kepe anie cómandment; to him the Iudge
muſt needes ſay [By thyne owne mouth I iudge thee,   *(1. Io. 1. v. 9.)*
naughtie ſeruant; thou didſt know, that I am an auſte-   *Luc. 19.*
re man, taking vp, that I ſette not downe, & reaping,   *v. 22. 23.*

that

that which I fowed not : why didft thou not geue my money to the banke, that is; why didft thou not cooperate with my grace? Why didft thou not endeuour to kepe my precepts, but holding them impoffible, prefumeft, to be rewarded without working at al, by thy onlie faith, or perfwafion of fecuritie? [thou knoweft, that I haue very much commäded my commandments to be kept.] thou faift thou couldeft not

Pfal. 118. v. 4. 9. &c.

kepe anie, and thou haft kept none. Then if thy felf faift truth: Thou art a mifcreant Infidel; a perfidious Turke; an obftinate Iew; an abominable Idolater; an apoftata Heretike; thou art a Sorcerer; a Nigromancer, a Witch, a Blafphemer, a periured perfon, a prophaner of holie feaftes. Thou haft reproched thy parents. Thou art a traitor to thy prince, and countrie. Thou haft refifted fpiritual, and temporal Superiors. Thou art a wilful murderer, and manflayer. Thou art a facrilegious, and an inceftious aduouterer, a robber, a theefe, a falfe witnes, a liar. Thou doeft carnally defire al fleshlie, and beaftlie pleafures in thy hart. Thou doeft alfo vniuftly couete thy neighbours houfe, landes, and al his goodes. There is no finne, but thou doeft committe it in thy peruerfe wil, at leaft. Thy fetled opinion fo holdeth, that thou fulfilleft none of the commandments, but breakeft them al: the imagined religion which thou holdeft, fo telleth thee. If Proteftants opinion were true in this point, then were euerie one guiltie of al thefe, and of al other innumerable crimes, But when a moderate perfon rightly confidering, that himfelf by Gods grace, is free from manie enormious finnes : for example, from adoring Iuppiter, or the Sunne for a God : from hating God, and the like; he, therby feeth that the doctrine is falfe, which holdeth that none can poffibly kepe anie of the commandments. And if he can kepe one by Gods grace, by his grace alfo (which is potent to euerie good worke) he can kepe

Protestants, by their owne opiniõ, should be guiltie of al finnes.

Euerie one may fee in his owne confcience, that he can obferue fome of the commandments.

an other , and fo euerie one [we are not fufficient to   2.Cor.3.v.5.
thinke anie good thing,of our felues,as of our felues,
but our fufficiencie is of God] And by this grace euerie one can if he wil,and maift if he wil be faued,kepe
the commandments. Now by the like holie Scriptures is confequently to be proued , that fpiritual , and
eternal fruite, euerie one shal reape , that finally departeth from this life , in due obferuation of Gods
commandments.

By keping Gods commandments the faith-
ful pleafe God : and merite eternal
glorie.

ARTICLE 2.

The general   HOlie Scriptures doe as abundantly teftifie, this
couenāt betwē   point of doctrine, as the former : or any other
God and men   Article of Chriftian Religion. Very often repeting the
is, that he wil   couenant made betwen God and his faithful feruāts.
reward them,   In which God on his part promifeth to gene them his
if they wil   grace, protectiō,& final reward of eternal life, if they
ferue him.   on their part (cooperating with his grace) wil kepe his
cōmandments. Forewaring them alfo , that he wil vi-
fite , & punish the iniquitie of al,not only in the firft
offenders , but alfo in al that folow their euil fteppes
[vpon the third & fourth generatiō,of them that hate   Exo.20.v.5.
me (faith our Lord) & wil doe mercie vpō thoufands,   6 ch.25. v.
to them that loue me, and kepe my precepts.] More   22.
particularly this couenant is declared in thefe facred
textes,which we shal here recite, both of the old and
new Teftament.

Diuine iuftice   2.   God himfelf faid to Cain [If thou doeft wel,shalt   Gen.4.v.7.
rewardeth   thou not receiue againe ? but if thou doeft il, shal not
good workes,   thy finne forthwith be prefent at the dore ? Which
and punisheth   sheweth as wel that reward shal be receiued for wel
ſinnes.   doing;

doing; as punishmeut shal be inflicted for finne.

Exo.1.v.21. Moyfes writeth that [Becaufe the midwiues (of Ægypt) feared God (preferuing the Hebrewes chil-dren, whom the king commanded them to kil) God built them houfes] by multiplying their iffue: or o-therwife bleffing their families, at leaft temporally, which was a figure of eternal reward, for workes doue in true faith, & ftate of fanctifying grace. More expresly the written Law promifeth reward, for the

Ex.34,v.27.
Leuit. 18.
v.5.
ch.26. v.12.
14.15.16.17.
&c.
obferuation of Gods commandments [Write thefe wordes (faid our Lord to Moyfes) in which I haue made a couenant both with thee, and with Ifrael: Kepe my Lawes, and iudgements; which a man doing shal liue in them. I wil walke among you, and wil be your God, and you shal be my people. But if you wil not heare me : nor doe al my commandments, if you difpife my Lawes, and contemne my iudgements, that you doe not thofe thinges, which are appointed by me; and bring my couenant to nothing worth : I alfo wil doe thefe thinges to you: I shal quickly vifite you with pouertie, & burning heate, which shal waift your eyes, and confume your liues.] Spiritually figni-

v. 25.
Ro.1.v.21.
24.
fying fubftraction of grace, and leauing them to their hote paffions of carnal, and worldlie pleafures [And I wil bring in vpon you, the fword, a reuenger of my couenant] Which téporal punishmét is alfo inflicted,

Ifa. 28.
v.19.
that [vexation may gene vnderftanding.] In al which God of his mere grace, & mercie, without any merite of men (which muft ftil be remébred) electeth whom he wil, making them capable of his benefites. As Moyfes exprefly teftifieth, faying to the people of If-

Deut. 7.
v.6.7.
rael [The Lord thy God hath chofen thee, to be his pe-culiar people, of al peoples that are vpon the earth. Not becaufe you paffed al nations in number, is our Lord ioyned vnto you, and hath chofen you; wheras you are fewer, then al peoples : but becaufe our

8.
Lord hath loued you, and hath kept the oath,
which

Election is only of Gods mercy, coope-ration is prin-cipally by Gods grace fecondarily by free wil affi-fted with the fame grace.

which he fware to your fathers, & hath brought you
forth in a ftrong hand, and redemed you from the
houfe of feruitude, out of the hand of Pharao, the
king of Ægypt. And thou fhalt know, that the Lord   9.
thy God, he is a ftrong, and a faithful God, keping his
couenant, and mercie, to them that loue him, and to
them that kepe his precepts: vnto a thoufand generations.]Againe touching punishment of tranfgreffors,
he addeth [And rendring forthwith to them that   10.
hate him] immediatly rendring to them that they deferue. For immediatly greuous finners lofe Gods fauour, and fanctifying grace: though the eternal due
punishment, is often differred, that they may if they
wil repent [Kepe therfore (faith Moyfes) the pre-   11.
cepts, and iudgements, which I command thee this
day, to doe them. If after thou haft heard thefe iudge-   12.
ments, thou kepe & doe them, the Lord alfo thy God   *ch.*8.9.10.
wil kepe the couenant vnto thee,& the mercie which   11.*&c.*
he fware to thy fathers.] So Moyfes affuring the
people of the ful performance of this couenant, on
Gods part, which he declareth by reciting Gods benefites, and perpetual protection; and earneftly admonishing them that the defect is often on their part, by
their often finning, and fo forfaking him: he denounceth plainly that God wil neither profper them, without their owne cooperation, nor deftroy them, if they
wil kepe his commandments, or at leaft repent from
the hart, when they happen to finne, faying [Behold

Benediction &
malediction
are propofed
to al men to
choofe which
they wil, by
doing good or
euil.

I fette forth in your fight this day, Benediction, and   *Ch.* v. 26.
Malediction: Benediction if you obey the command-   27 28.
ments of the Lord your God, which I command you
this day. Malediction, if you obey not the commandments of the Lord your God, but reuolt from the way,
which now I doe shew you, and walke after ftrange
goddes, which you know not] In the whole written
Law nothing is more exactly, and largely expreffed
then bleffinges, and curfes, reward, and punishment,
                                                for

Chapter. 17. for keping or breaking Gods precepts. More particu-
28.29.30. larly in foure whole chapters of Deuteronomie. In
ch.30.*v*.1.2. the laft of which is fpecial promife to true penitents,
3 *&c.* that God wil receiue them againe into his fauour, &
reftore them to his bleffings : yet o leauing it in their
power to ferue him if they wil, that they can refift his
v.10.15.17. grace if they wil. And therfore the Prophete warneth
&c. al men, that the impenitent fhal affuredly perish [be-
caufe hauing life and death, bleffing and curfing pro-
pofed] they choofe the worfe.

3. Manie cleare examples are recorded of diuers
faithful feruants of God, which receiued fpecial rewards for obferuing his commandments: and of others
punished, for tranfgreffing. Of both which we fhal
No. 13. here recite fome few [When Moyfes had fent twelue
v.18.19. men, of euerie Tribe one, to view the ftate and
qualitie of the land of Chanaan, and to obferue,
and reporte, whether the inhabitants, and cities,
and townes therof, were ftrong, or weake, few in
number, or manie.] With other inftructions: at their
returne after fourtie dayes, tenne of thefe difco-
v.29.33.34. uerers falfely reporting [that they faw there men,
as it were monfters, the fonnes of Enac, of the
Giants kind, to whom being compared (faid they)
we femed, as it were locuftes] and fo making the
v.31. people to murmure : Caleb one of the twelue, as
(*ch* 14. *v.* alfo Iofue (formerly called Ofee) an other of the
30.8. fame difcouerers: appeafing the murmuring of the
ch.26.*v*.65.) people, that rofe againft Moyfes, faid [Let vs goe
vp, and poffeffe the land : becaufe we may ob-
ch.14.*v*.11. taine it.] Wherupon our Lord punishing thofe de-
12.22. 23. tractors, and al that murmured vpon their falfe re-
24. porte, promifed to reward Caleb, faying [My
feruant Caleb, who being ful of an other fpirite, hath folowed me, wil I bring into this
land, which he hath circuited, and his feede
ch.27.*v*.18. fhal poffeffe it.] And our Lord with al ordayned
19.*&c.*

Examples of
vertues rewar-
ded, and finnes
punished.

Iofue & Caleb
rewarded for
their truth and
good zele.

Tenne other
difcouerers, &
the murmu-
ring people
punished for
falfe repor-
ting, and diffi-
dence.

D   Iofue

Iosue the Duke, and General Captaine, that should conquire the same Land. And accordingly when the Land was conquired [Iosue deliuered Hebron in possession to Caleb, because he had folowed our Lord, the God of Israel] And by free consent of al the people [special possession was geuen to Iosue in the middes of the children of Israel] This couenant of rewarding good workes, was also performed to Ruth a Gentile for her pietie : as Booz wel considering, and testifying her merite, cooperated to her remuneration, saying to her [Al thinges haue bene told me, which thou hast done to thy mother in law, after the death of thy husband: and thou hast left thy parents, and the land, wherein thou wast borne, and art come to a people, which before thou knewest not. Our Lord render vnto thee for thy worke: and God grant thou mayst receine a ful reward, of our Lord the God of Israel, to whom thou art come, and vnder whose winges thou art fled] which renowmed man Booz, the principal heyre of the tribe of Iuda, maried the same Ruth, which was an especial temporal reward ; cheefly for that of her descended the royal race of Dauid, and al the kinges after him of Iuda ; and finally the king of kinges Christ Iesus : but the ful reward, which Booz prayed that she might also receiue, importeth increase of spiritual grace in this life, and eternal glorie in heauen. Samuel a childe, borne of godlie parents, more by miracle, then force of nature, his mother hauing bene long barren, was brought vp in the feare of Go among the Priests, and seruing God in puritie, was made the Admonitor to Heli the High priest, and Gouernour of the people, And in shorte time ordained by God to succede Helie, in the temporal gouernment. For Heli was punished, for not correcting his sonnes faultes [But the child Samuel prospered, & grew, and pleased both our Lord, and men] Became a Prophete to the comforth, and

Ruth a gentile rewarded for her pietie.

Samuel a childe rewarded for manie vertues. Heli punished for not correcting his sonnes.

Ios. 14.
v. 13 14.

ch. 19 v.
49. 50.

Ruth 2.
v. 11. 12.

ch 4, 1. 10.
13.
v. 18. &c.
Mat. 1.
v. 5.

1. Reg. 1.
v 22. 11.
20. 27.

ch. 2, v.
11. 12. 26.
ch 3. v. 20.
21.

good

good of al Israel. And Heli at the age of ninetie eight
yeares dying, Samuel gouerned the people. After
this, in the life time of the same Samuel, king Saul
being at first so innocét, húble and obedient to God,
that he was described [to be a childe of one yeare,
when he begare to reigne] and so continuing some
while, prospered in gouerning the kingdom: And if
he had perseuered in keping Gods commandments,
had bene confirmed in his kingdom, but for transgressing, was reiected of God: and an other of sincere
hart was chosen for the place : which was King
Dauid, of whom Samuel testifieth, that [our Lord
had found a man according to his owne hart.] which
Dauid was not only aduanced to the kingdom, and
prospered against al his enimies, but also for his sake
the kingdom of Iuda, was long conserued in his
seede, and stil in eminent reputation, euen to Christ
our Sauiour, the sonne of Dauid, Againe amongst
Dauids successors in the kingdom, those that were
of more special vertue, and good zele (which were
Iosaphat, and Ezechias, and Iosias) were especially
rewarded. As at large is recorded in the sacred
Historie, and we shal touch the same by and by. And
contrariwise, Ieroboam (who by wicked schisme,
and idolatrie, made Israel to sinne) and al his
successors, were iustly punished, their whole families extirpated, and that kingdom of Israel, caried
into captiuitie, nere two hundred yeares before the
kingdom of Iuda was captiue vnder Babylon. In like
maner particular persons, Tobias, Iudith, Mardocheus Esther, and others proceding in vertue,
increased in grace. And others liuing wickedly, fel
into more and more sinnes, and into vtter ruine.

4. But most pregnant examples of al those kinges
of the Iewes, are of Salomon, who for his sinnes lost
from his successors the greater part of the whole
kingdom and of Ieroboam, who; with his whole familie, and diuers other like kinges, his successors,

king Saul was rewarded for vertues: and punished for sinnes.

ch. 13.
v. 1. 3. 4.
&c.

v. 8. 13.

v. 14.

Mat. 1.
v. 1. ch. 20.
v. 30. ch. 21.
v. 9. 15. &c.

3. Reg. 12.
v. 28. ch.
13. v. 34.
ch. 5. v. 29.
30.

Tobias.
Iudith.
Esther.

D 2   with al

An especial example in king Salomõ.

with al their feueral families, were vtterly deftroyed. Firft Salomon, both very vertuous, and excedingly wife, a knowleged fincerely Gods iuftice, as wel in his rewards, as in his punifhments, faying in his prayer to our Lord [Thou ô God fhalt heare in *3. Reg. 8.* heauen, and fhalt doe and indge thy feruant, con- *v. 32.* demning the impious, rendring his way vpon his head: and iuftifiyng the iuft, rewarding him accor- ding to his iuftice] In confirmation wherof our Lord himfelf faid to the fame king Salomon [Thou alfo *ch. 9. v. 4.* if thou wiltwalke before me, as thy father walked, in fimplicitie of hart, and in equitie, and wilt doe al thinges, which I haue commanded thee, and wilt *v. 5.* kepe myne ordinances, and indgements: I wil fet the throne of thy kingdom ouer Ifrael for euer: as I haue fpoken to Dauid thy father, faying: There fhal not be taken away a man of thy ftocke, from the throne of Ifrael. But if by reuolting, you and your children *6.* fhal turne away, not folowing me, nor keping my commandments and my ceremonies, which I haue propofed to you: but fhal goe, and worfhipe anie ftrange goddes, and adore them: I wil take away Ifrael from the face of the land, which I haue geuen them; and the Temple, which I haue fanctified to my name, I wil caft away from my fight, and Ifrael fhal be for a prouerbe, and for a fable to al peoples. And *8.* this houfe fhal be for an example. Euerie one that fhal paffe by it, fhal wonder, and hiffe, and fay: Why hath the Lord done thus to this land, and to this houfe? And they fhal anfwer: Becaufe they haue *v. 9.* forfaken the Lord their God: which brought their fathers out of the land of Ægypt, and haue folowed ftrange goddes, and adored them, and worfhipped them: therfore hath the Lord brought vpon them al this euil.] According to this forewarning it happe- ned, as wel to Salomon in particular, as to al the kingdom in general. For whiles Salomon rightly

serued

ch. 10.
v. 1. 2.*&c.*
2. *Par.* 1.
ad cap. 10.
3 *Reg.* 11.
v. 1. *&c.*

v. 9.

10.

11.

12.

33.

v. 33.

34.

serued God, he prospered excedingly, in wisdome, wealth, power, and singular renow in al the world. But afterwards falling into sinne of the flesh he became sottish; and benig depriued of Gods fauour, and former grace, he fel also into idolatrie, seruing manie false goddes, to please his multitude of wiues, and concubines. [And therfore our Lord was wrath with Salomon: because his mind was turned away from our Lord, the God of Israel; who had appeared to him, the second time: and had commanded him concerning this word, that he should not folow strange goddes, and he kept not the thinges, which our Lord commanded him. Our Lord therfore said to Salomon: Because thou hast done this, and not kept my couenant, and my precepts, which I haue commanded thee, breaking I wil rent asunder thy kingdom, and wil gene it to thy seruant. Neuertheles in thy dayes I wil not doe it, because of Dauid thy father. Out of the hand of thy sonne I wil rent it. Neither wil I take away the whole kingdom, but one tribe I wil geue to thy sonne, for Dauid my seruant, and Ierusalem, which I haue chosen. And this I wil doe to Salomon, said our Lord; because he hath forsaken me, and hath adored false goddes] which was the greatest crime, but not the onlie, for he brake also some other comandments [Because he hath not walked (said our Lord) to doe iustice before me, and my precepts and iudgements, as Dauid his father did.] And so it came to passe. For Ieroboam possessed tenue tribles, there remagning to Roboam, Salomons sonne, only two tribes, Iuda and Beniamin, wherin Ierusalem was situated. As for the tribe of Leui, they had no distinct portion, but were dispersed among al the twelue tribes. And in the whole time of schisme, al the Priestes and Leuites, stil adioyned themselues to the kingdom of Iuda, and to Ierusalem: where the Temple was, and only lawful Sacri-

And in his Successors.

D 3   fice

fice. [Our Lord also proposed (and conditionally
promised) to the new king Ieroboam , protection
and prosperitie, if he would kepe the cōmandments,
saying to him [If therfore thou wilt heare al thinges, *3. Reg. 11.*
that I shal command thee , and wilt walke in my *v.38.*
wayes, and doe that which is right before me, keping
my commandments , and my preceps , as Dauid my
seruant did , I wil be with thee , and wil build thee a
faithful house, as I bnilt a house to Dauid , and I wil
deliuer Israel to thee.]

King Iero-
boams race
was qnite ex-
tirpated for
their profane
wickednes.

5.   But this profame king Ieroboam , preferring *3. Reg. 12.*
his temporal kingdom before Religion , and falsely *v.28. 29.*
imagining that they could not stād to gether]finding *31.*
out a deuise , made two golden calues, and setting
them vp in two partes of his kingdom , said to his
people ; Goe vp no more to Ierusalem : behold thy
goddes, Israel, which brought thee out of the land of
Ægypt.] And made like false imaginarie priests , to
serue their false goddes. Which schisme, and idolatrie,
God iustly punished , also in this world , besides
eternal damnation, to al that consented, and dyed *ch. 15. v.29.*
impenitent. For this kingdom standling about the *ch 16. v. 9.*
space of two himdred and fiftie yeares , had in that *11.12.15.*
time marie ciuil , and forraine warres , with misera- *4. Reg. 9.*
ble change of kinges, in al twentie : of nine different *v. 21.22.*
families, euerie one inuading an other. The first fami- *ch.10. v.30.*
lie (which was cut of in Nadab, Ieroboams sonne) *ch.15. v. 12.*
held the scepter and kingdom , but four and twentie *&c.*
yeares. The second familie held it twentie six yeares. *ch 17.v.1.6.*
9. &c.

Also the other
kinges of the
tenue schisma-
tical tribes
with their fa-
milies, extin-
guished for
their like im-
pietie.

The third but seuen dayes. The fourth, fourtie eight
yeares. The first three, yeares of which time , two
Antikings reigned in ciuil warre : one chosē by the ar
mie, the other by the people. The fifth an hūdred and
three yeares (in king Iehu, and his issue to the fourth
generatiō : for his zele against Achab and Iesabel. The
sixth , but one moneth. The seuenth twelne yeares.
The eight, twentie yeares. And the ninth , which was
the

the laſt, nine yeares. Then was this ſchiſmatical kingdome ouerthrowne by the Aſſirians, al the principal perſons caried away captiues, and the reſt alſo kept in bondage. Which afflictions fel vpon them

ch.17 v. 7. 8, 11. 13. 14. [becauſe they had ſinned againſt our Lord their God: and walked according to the rite of the Gentiles; and did wicked thinges, prouoking our Lord. And our Lord teſtified by his Prophetes, ſaying: Returne from your moſt wicked wayes, and kepe my precepts, and ceremonies, according to al the law, who heard not, but hardned their neck, according to the neck of their fathers, who would not obey our Lord their God] After which ruine of the kingdom of Iſrael, the kingdom of Iuda yet ſtood, aboue an himdred

ch. 25. v. 1. 8. 15. 20. 2. Par 36. v 15. 16. ad. 20. ch. 3. v. 15. 16. &c. and fourtie yeares more. But was at laſt alſo ſubdued by the Babylonians, for their tranſgreſſions of Gods commandments, and couenant Neuertheles al thoſe of each kingdom, which kept true Religion, and other commandments, pleaſed God therby, and were rewarded accordingly.

Both the king domes fel into captiuitie for grenous ſinnes.

6. Likewiſe after the captiuitie of the two tribes in Babylon (by which occaſion manie alſo of the other tenne tribes, enioyed more freedome then before) according as euerie one obſerued, or tranſgreſſed Gods commandment, doing good workes, or euil, they merited reward, or puniſhment. So holie Nehemias confidently prayed for reward of his good

2. Eſdr. 13. v. 14. workes, ſaying [Remember me, my God for this thing, and wipe not out my mercies (my workes of mercie) which I haue done, in the houſe of my God,

Nehemias prayed for reward of his good workes.

v. 22. and in his ceremonies.] Namely for correcting the prophanation of the Sabbath [For this alſo (ſaid he) remember me my God, and ſpare me (diminiſh the puniſhment due for my ſinnes) according to the multitude of thy mercies.] Finally for al his good workes, done trough Gods grace, concludeith his Booke,

v. 31. praying thus [Remember me, my God, vnto good. Amen.]   Tobias

Tobias
prayed, that
patient suffe-
red might
procure Gods
clemencie.

Tobias in his affliction of corporal blindnes (in
the former captiuitie of Israel) wel considering that
most commonly such afflictions are punishments
for sinnes , besought God for mitigation therein,
saying [Now Lord be mindful of me , and take not *Tob.3. v.3. 4.*
reuenge of my sinnes, neither remember the sinnes of
me, nor of my parents . Becaufe we haue not obeyed
thy commandments; therfore we are deliuered into
spoile, and captiuitie, and death: and into a fable, and
into reproche to al nations, in which thou hast dif-
perfed vs.] Alfo Sara the daughter of Raguel, being   *Ibidem*
afflicted by vniuft reproch , both confessed Gods iuft   *25.*
punishment, for sinnes, and confidently auouched
her owne sincere mind , free from carnal concupifcence, and therupon prayed to be deliuered from a

Sara confided
in the inno-
cencie of her
life.

false sclander, saying [Blessed is thy name ô God, of   *v. 13.*
our fathers, who when thou hast bene angrie, wilt
doe mercie, and in the time of tribulation forgeueft
them their sinnes, that inuocate thee . To thee ô Lord   *14.*
I turne my face: to thee I direct myne eyes. I desire   *15.*
Lord, that thou loofe me from the bond of this re-   *16.*
proch, or els take me away from the earth. Thou
knoweft Lord, that I neuer coueted a hufband , and   *17.*
haue kept my foule cleane from al concupifcence. Neuer haue I companied myself with sporters : neither
haue I made myself partaker with them that walke   *18.*
in lightneffe. But a hufband I confented to take, with
thy feare, not with my luft] And both these godlie
perfons Tobias, and Sara, receiued reward for their
merites . As alfo young Tobias, and others of their   *24.*
kinred, receiued comforth , by the miniʃterie of the   *25.*
holie Angel Raphael.

Merite of
good workes
is proued by
manie testi-
monies in the
Psalmes.

7.   The Royal Pfalmift abundeth in teftifying, and
praysing Gods iuft rewarding of vertues, & punishing
of sinnes. And that the iuft doe in deede merite increafe of grace, and eternal glorie . Gods grace firft
preuenting, and alwayes affifting them. As on the
other

other fide the wicked deferue punifhment, for their
finnes cómitted through their owne naughtie willes.

Pfal.1.v.1. [Bleffed is the man (faith he) that hath not gone
in the counfel of the impious : and hath not ftood in
the way of finners : and hath not fitte in the chaire of
v.2. peftilence. But whofe wil is in the way of our Lord,&
in his Law wil meditate day and night. And he fhal
3. be as a tree, that is planted nigh to the ftreames of
waters: which fhal geue his fruite, in his time] In this
preface of the diuine Pfalter, is firft denounced the
happie ftate of fuch iuft perfons, as neuer yelded to
fuggeftion of any finne [Which haue not gone into
the counfel of the impious] Secódly of fuch as fhortly repéted after their fal [Which haue not ftood in the
way of finners.] Thirdly of fuch as at laft haue returned to God [Which haue not fitte in the chaire of peftilence.] Laftly of al that declining from euil, imploy
themfelues diligently in doing good workes [Whofe
willes are occupied, in the way, and Law of our
Pfal.4.v.7. Lord, day and night.] The reafon of which happines
8.9. is, for that by wel vfing Gods grace, they procede in
vertue [fructifying as the tree that is planted by the
ftreames of waters, which fhal geue fruite (of eternal
Pf.5.v.13. glorie) in his time] In like maner in an other Pfalme,
the fame holie Prophete, and by him euerie iuft foule,
meditating vpon this moft happie reward, and the
meanes wherby to attaine vnto it, demandeth of
Pf.14.v.1. God, faying [Lord, who fhal dwel in thy tabernacle, or who fhal reft in thy holie hil?] And therto anfwereth, by warrant of Gods couenant, faying [He that
walketh without fpotte, and worketh iuftice. He
2.3. that fpeaketh truth in his hart : that hath not done
guile in his tongue. Nor hath done euil to his neigh-
v.5. bour. &c. He that doth (not euil, and doth good) fhal
not be moued for euer.] Shal receiue eternal, and immortal glorie. Againe, and againe repeting the fame
Pf.17.v.21. in other wordes, he faith [Our Lord wil reward me
22.
23.

according

according to my iustice: and according to the puritie
of my handes, he wil reward me. Becaufe I haue kept
the wayes of our Lord:neither haue I done impioufly
from my God. Becaufe al his iudgements are in my   Pf.18.v. 8.
fight : and his iuftices I haue not repelled from me.   9.10.11, 12.
The law of our Lord is immaculate : the iuftices of
our Lord be right; the precept of our Lord lightfome:
the feare of our Lord is holie, the iudgements of our
Lord be true, iuftified in themfelues . To be defired
aboue gold, and much precious ftone; & more fwete
aboue honie , and the honie combe . For thy feruant
kepeth them. In keping them is much reward. Come   Pf.33. v 12.
children (faith the fame holie Pfalmift) heare me : I
wil teach you the feare of our Lord . Who is the man   13,14.
that wil haue life: loueth to fee good dayes ? Stay thy   15.
tongue from euil, and thy lippes that they fpeake not
guile . Turne away from euil, and doe good : feke
after peace, and purfne it . Decline from euil and doe   Pf.26.v. 27.
good : and inhabite for euer and euer . The vniuft   28.
shal be punished: and the feede of the impious shal   29.
perish . But the iuft shal inherite the land : and shal   35.36.
inhabite for euer and euer vpon it . I haue fene the   37.
impious highly exalted , and aduanced , as the cedars
of Libanus. And I paffed by, and behold he was not:
and I fought him, and his place was not found . Kepe
innocencie, & fee equitie; becaufe there are remaines
(rewardes) for the peaceable man. Power is Gods, &   Pf.61.v 13.
mercie ô Lord is to thee : becaufe thou wilt render to
euerie one, according to his workes.Mercie & iudge-
ment I wil fing to thee o Lord . But the mercie of our   Pf.100.v.1.
Lord from euerlafting, and vnto euerlafting, vpon
them that feare him. And his iuftice is vpon the childrens children, to them that kepe his teftament. And   Pf.102.v.17.
are mindful of his commandments to doe them.Blef-   18.
fed is the man that feareth our Lord : he shal haue
great delight in his cômandments. Bleffed are the im-   Pf.111.v.2.
maculate in the way : which walke in the Law of our   Pf.118. v.
                                                    1.2.
                            Lord.

Lord. Bleſſed are they that ſearch his teſtimonies; that ſeke after him with al their hart. For they that worke iniquitie; haue not walked in his wayes. Thou (o God) haſt very much commanded thy cōmandments to be kept. Wherin doth a young mā correct his way? in keping thy wordes. I haue inclined my hart to doe thy iuſtifications for euer, for reward.] What can be ſpoken more clearly for merite of good workes, then this holie King and Prophete in expreſſe termes, ſaid [In keping the commandments is much reward, that he inclined his hart to kepe them, for reward? &c.]

8. To the ſame purpoſe, in reſpect of reward due for keping Gods cōmandments. Diuine wiſedom, exhorteth, and al the Prophetes admonish al men, to lerne and kepe Gods Law. [My ſonne (ſaith Eternal wiſdom by the penne of Salomou) heare the diſcipline of thy father; and leaue not the Law of thy mother, that grace may be added to thy head: & a chaine of gold to thy necke. He that ſhal heare me, ſhal reſt without terrour, and ſhal enioy abundance, feare of euils being taken away. He that kepeth the commandmēts, kepeth his ſoule: but he that neglecteth his way ſhal dye. He lendeth to our Lord, that hath mercie on the poore (reward is ſo due for meritorious workes, as repayment is due for lent money) and our Lord wil repay him the like. The feare of our Lord (ſaith an other diuine preacher) is glorie, and gloriation, and ioy, and a crowne of exultation (to write the cauſe of a glorious crowne.) The feare of our Lord is religioſitie of knowlege. Religioſitie ſhal kepe and iuſtifie the hart: ſhal gene gladnes and ioy. With him that feareth our Lord, it ſhal be wel, & in the dayes of his conſummation, he ſhalbe bleſſed. Worke your worke before the time, and he wil geue you your reward in his time] Plainly ſignifying that merite is in this life, & reward in the next. Other Prophetes ofté teſtifie the ſame fruite of keping Gods

3 4.
v. 9.
v. 112.

Pſ. 18, v. 12.

Prou. 1. v. 8.
9.

33.

ch. 19. v. 16.
17.

Sap. 10.
v. 17.
Eccli. 1.
v. 11.
v. 17.
18.
19.

ch. 51. v 38.

The ſame doctrine is confirmed by the ſapiential Bookes.

And by other Prophetes.

commandments : and punishment for breaking them
[Your iniquities (faith Ifaias) haue diuided betwen
you and your God, and your finnes haue hidde his
face from you, that he would not heare] But to thofe
that returne to God and ferue him, he faith [They fhal
inherite the land. The Lord fhal be vnto thee for an
euerlafting light, and thy God for thy glorie] Likewife our Lord both threatneth offenders with punifhment, and promifeth gracious giftes to penitents,
by his Prophete Ieremie, faying [Shal I not vifite
vpon thefe thinges (their manifold finnes) and on
fuch a nation fhal not my foule take reuenge?] But to
the conuerted he faith [This fhal be my couenant,
which I wil make with the houfe of Ifrael: I wil geue
my Law in their bowels, and in their hart I wil write
it:and I wil be their God, and they fhal be my people]
By his Prophete Ezechiel he faith [Myne eye fhal not
fpare, neither wil I haue mercie: I wil require their
way vpon their head. The foule that fhal finne the
fame fhal dye. The iuftice of the iuft fhal be vpon
him : and the impietie of the impious fhal be vpon
him. But if the impious fhal doe penance from al
his finnes, which he hath wrought, & fhal kepe al my
precepts, liuing he fhal liue, and fhal not dye] By his
Prophete Amos, our Lord warneth al finners, that although he expect long, the conuerfion of finners, yet
if they be ftil obftinate, at laft he wil punifh feuerely,
repeting eight times thefe wordes[Vpõ three wicked-
neffes) & vpon foure, I wil not conuert]the obftinate
finner. Signifying that for the multitude of finnes, infinuated by three (for three are manie) God ftil offering grace of repentance, during this temporal life, pu-
nifheth not eternally, vntil the fourth kinde of finne,
which is obdurate abftinacie, be ioyned to the former
and becometh final impenitence, and then there is no
more poffibilitie of conuerfion. For then [as the tree
fhal fal] to the South, or to the North: in what place

Ifa.59.v.2.

ch.60.v.

19.21.

Iere.5.v.9.
29 ch.9.v.
9.10.
ch 31.v.33.

Ezech 9.
v.10.

ch 18.v.4.
20.21.

Amos 1.v.3.
6.9.11.13.
ch. 2.v.1.
4.6.

Eccle.11.v.3

foeuer

foeuer it shal fal, there shal it be] At that day, & houre
of death, whē euerie one shal receiue sentence of eternal life, or death (euen the same in particular, which
they shal receiue againe, in the general day of Iudgement) God who is iuft, & merciful, both meke & also

Nahum. 1.
v. 27.
ielous, wil come as the Lord rewarding, & also [reuē-
ging & hauing furie: the Lord reuēging on his aduerfaries, & angrie with his enimies. Our Lord is good, &
ftrēgthning in the day of tribulation, & knowing thē

Soph. 1. v 7.
15.
that hope in him. The day of our Lord is nere, our
Lord hath prepared an hofte, he hath fanctified his
called (or elect) that day, a day of wrath, a day of tri-
bulatiō, & diftreffe, a day of calamitie & miferie, a day
of darkneffe, & mift, a day of cloud, and whirlewind.

Malach. 1.
v. 1.
For behold the day shal come kindled as a furnace, &
al the proud, & al that doe impietie, shal be ftubble, &
the day coming shal inflame them, faith the Lord of
hofts, which wil not leaue them roote, & fpring (no
more time of repentance, for recouering new grace)

v. 2.
But to the iuft, and bleffed, it is said [There snal rife
to you, that feare my name, the Sunne of iuftice, and
health in his wing es and you shal goe forth, and shal
leape as calues of the: heard. And you shal tread the
impious, when they shal be ashes vnder the fole of
your feete, in the day that I doe: faith the Lord of
hofts] Now that this great difference of reward, and
punishment dependeth vpon keping, and not keping
Gods commandments: the Propete teacheth vs, by
Gods owne final admonition, adding thus in the next

4.
wordes [Remember ye the Law of Moyfes my feruāt,
which I commanded him in Horeb, to al Ifrael, precepts and iudgements.] And that al this perteyneth

1. Cor. 10.
v. 11.
also to vs Chriftians, S. Paul teacheth, faying [Al thefe
thinges (admonitions, rewardes, and punishments)
chanced to them (the Iewes) in figure: but they are
written to our correption, vpon whom the endes of
the world are conce.]

E 3   9. Neuer-

Moſt eſpe-
cially this do-
ctrine is con-
firmed in the
new Teſta-
ment.
By S. Iohn
Baptiſt.

9. Neuertheles this Catholique beleefe, and doctrine is rather more manifeſtly teſtified in the new Teſtamét. Firſt it is auouched in expreſſe wordes by S. Iohn Baptiſt, that penitents muſt both doe workes of penance, & euerie one doe that perteyneth to their ſtate and condition. To al ſortes he ſaid [Doe penance, for the kingdom of heauen is at hand. Yelde fruite worthie of penáce. Now the axe is put to the roote of the trees. Euerie tree therfore that doth not yeld good fruite, ſhal be cutte downe, and caſt into the fire. To the multitudes he ſaid: He that hath two coates, let him geue to him that hath not: & the that hath meate, let him do likewiſe. He ſaid to the Publicanes: Doe nothing more then that which is appointed you. And he ſaid to the Souldiars: Vexe not, neither calumniate any man: & be content with your ſtipends.] And the the like precepts he taught, for auoiding of the wrath of fire & damnation, and for gayning of heauen. Becauſe (ſaid he) The kingdom of heauen is at hand.] And barren trees, that is, idle perſons, which yeld not fruite of good workes, much more thoſe that perſiſt in al workes. [ſhal be cutte downe, and caſt into the fire] Further our Sauiour himſelf expreſly affirmeth, that life euerlaſting is attained by obſeruing the commandments [If thou wilt enter into life (ſaid he) kepe the commandments. This doe, & thou ſhalt liue] And in his Sermó in the Moút he teacheth that, The poore in ſpirite, and thoſe which are indued with other vertues, haue right, & iuſt title to the kingdom of heaué [for theirs (ſaith he) is the kingdom of heauen.] And to thoſe that patiently ſuffer perſecutió, for the truth, he ſaith [Be glad, and reioice: for your reward is very great in heauen.] And to euerie one, that rightly geueth almes, rightly prayeth, or rightly faſteth, he ſaith [Thy father which ſeeth in ſecrete, wil repay thee. Heape vp to yourſelues (ſaith he) treaſures in heauen] Againe he teacheth the ſame by diuers very ſignificát

By Chriſt our
Lord.
In expreſſe
wordes.

*Mat.3.v.2.
8.10.
Luc.3.v 8.9.
v.11.
13.
14.*

*Mat.19.
v 17.
Luc.10.v.
28.*

*Mat 5 v.
3. 12.*

*ch 6.v. 4.6.
18. 20.*

*Mat.20.
v.1.*

parables

2.
3. &c.
8.

parables [The kingdome of heauen (faith he) is like And in fignifi-
to a man, that is an houshoulder which went forth- cantpērables.
early in the morning, to hire worke men into his
vineyard. And hauing made couenant with the
workmen, he fent them into his vineyard.] So hyring
others at diuers houres, euen to the laft houre of the
day [And when euening was come, the Lord of the
vineyard faith to his balife: Cal the workemen, & pay
them their hyre, beginning with the laft, euen to the
firft.] Is not this a plaine couenant; or bargaine, made
and performed, in hyring for wages : working and

ch.25.v.14. paying; merite, and reward ? In an other parable our
15. Sauiour faith, that the Lord which deliuered to one
feruant fiue talents, to an other two, and to an other
one, finding that fome had labored, & gained, others
had not labored, nor gained, faith to each of them

v.21. which had gained [Wel faire thee, good and faithful
feruant, becaufe thou haft bene faithful ouer a few
25. thinges, I wil place thee ouer manie thinges : enter
into the ioy of thy Lord] And to the idle feruant, he
v.26. shal fay [Naughtie, & flouthful feruant, thou oughteft
to haue committed my money to the bankers.] And
v.30. wil command [to caft the vnprofitable feruant into
the vtter darkenes. There shal be weeping and
ch. 21. v. gnashing of teeth.] In figure alfo of this iuft iudge-
19.20. ment,it pleafed our Lord, to curfe a figgetree,becaufe
[he found no fruite on it, but leaues only. And incóti-
nent the figtree was withered] Againe concerning di- Diuerfitie of
uerfitie of reward, proportionable to diuers merites: reward,accor-
by an other parable our Lord teacheth, that to him. ding to diuerfitie ofmerite.
Luc.19 v.13. which of one pound gained téne poundes,was geuen
16.17.18.19. power ouer téne cities. To him that of one, gained
22.24. fiue poundes, was geuen power ouer fiue cities. And
he that gained nothing, was depriued of that which
was deliuered vnto him, & iuftly iudged a naughtie
feruant] In al his doctrine our Sauiour teacheth the
necessitie,

necessitie, and reward both of beleefe in him, and of observing his other commādments [He that beleueth *Ioan. 3. v. 17.* in the Sonne of God (performing also other thinges requisite) is not iudged but he that doth not beleue, is already iudged, becaufe he hath not beleued in the name of the onelie begotten Sonne of God] which sheweth that faith is absolutely necessarie, but not alone sufficient to saluation. For faith only sufficying to make the faithful to be branches of Christ, the true vine, and a member of his Church, it is no lesse necessarie to saluation, that the same branches must bring forth fruite [I am the true vine (saith Christ our Re- *ch.15. v.1.s* demer) & my Father is the husbandman. Euerie brāch in me, not bearing fruite he wil take it away, & euerie one that beareth fruite, he wil purge it, that it may bring more fruite. In this my Father is glorified; that *v. 8.* you bring very much fruite. As my Father hath loued *9.* me, I also haue loued you. Abide in my loue. If you *10.* kepe my precepts, you shal abide in my loue] And in *Artic.1.* loue (as is before declared) al the commandments *§.8,* are comprised. Vpon obseruation therfore, or transgression therof dependeth saluation or damnation, [For the Sonne of man shal come in the glorie of his *Mat.16.* Father, with his Angels, and then wil he render to *v.27.* euerie man, according to his workes. Watch therfore, *Luc.21.* praying at al times, that we may be accoūted worthie *v.36.* to escape al these thinges that are to come· & to stand before the Sonne of man.]

Againe in plaine termes reward is promised, for good workes.

10.   Against this manifest doctrine, collected of the expresse wordes of the Gospel, our Aduersaries haue neither plaine text, nor better reason, then to say, that al S. Iohn Baptists preaching, was only to *Luc.14.* perswade men to beleue in Iesvs Christ. And Chrifts *v.47.* owne preaching, to the same only purpose. Most *Act.4.* true it is, that both Christ, and his Precursor, and *v.12. & c* al the Prophetes, and Apostles, doe preach this principal point, that al must first beleue, that Iesvs of Nazareth

The cheefest arguments of Protestants against merite, are answered.

zareth the Sonne of the Bleſſed Virgine Marie, is Chriſt, our onlie Redemer. But they preach not this point aloue. As the manie holie textes here recited, and innumerable others, doe euidently shew: teſtifying that together with true faith of other Myſteries, beſids Chriſts Incarnation, and Paſſion, the couenant, and obſeruation of al Gods cōmandments is required, and trhough Chriſts ſpecial grace, bringeth to ſaluation. Other euaſions alſo our Aduerſaries vſe, as to ſay; the Figures of the old Teſtament, Prophecies, and Parables are obſcure, and may haue diuers ſenſes, granting by this occaſion, which commonly they denie, that ſome Scriptures are hard to be vnder ſtood, are ſometines vttered by figuratiue ſpeach; and ſo they interprete al, as ſemeth beſt to their owne ſpirites, and preiudicate opinions. And therfore we vrge them to trie al doubts, by the moſt cleare wordes, or by more places in number. Namely this preſent controuerſie. Whether obſeruation of Gods commandments, and good workes done in Chriſts grace, by his faithful ſeruants, be meritorious of eternal glorie, or no? Proteſtants holding the negatiue part, doe eſpecially alleage two places of holie Scriptures: the one, of the Goſpel vttered by Chriſt himſelf; thother of S. Paul. The former is a parable, or ſimilitude propoſed by our Sauiour, ſaying to his diſciples: Which of you hauing a ſeruant, plowing, or keping cattle, that wil ſay to him, when he is returned out of the field: Goe thee way quickly, and reſt: but wil rather ſay to him [Make readie ſupper, and gyrd thyſelf; and ſerue me whiles I eate, and drinke: and afterward thou ſhalt eate, and drinke. Doth he geue that ſeruant thankes, for doing the thinges, which he commanded him? I trow no. So you alſo, when you ſhal haue done al thinges that are commanded you, ſay: *We are vnprofitable* ſeruants: we haue done that which we ought to doe.] Hereupon Proteſtants

Luc. 17.
v. 7. 8. 9.
10.

Our Sauiours wordes make againſt Proteſtants, not for them.

F   would

would inferre, that the good workes of the faithful, namely the keping of Gods commandments, deserue not heauen, or anie reward at Gods hand. As if our Sauiour had said: that the keping of Gods commandments is vnprofitable, or doing al which we ought to doe, is vnprofitable. But he said not so. He teacheth, what true and humble conceipt euerie one ought to haue of himself, when he hath done that, which God commandeth him. That is, to ackowlege and say, that he is an vnprofitable seruant. towitte, vnprofitable to God. Neuertheles he is profitable to himself, & shal receiue the wages of his master, due for his worke. Neither is his master bond to thanke him, but only to pay him his hyre, according to couenant. But the seruant is bond to thanke his master, for entertening him, imploying him, promising, and paying him his hyre; which he could not haue earned, except he had bene called, hyred, and sent to labour in the vineyard. And so God our heauélie Father, and Master accounteth such a seruant [a good, and faithful seruant, and biddeth him enter into ioy, because he hath bene faithful: and by how much more the seruant humbleth himself, the more he is exalted. Neither doth God accout him vnprofitable, that confesseth himself vnprofitable: but as S. Paul saith [If anie man shal cleanse himself, from sinful workes, he shal be a vessel vnto honour, sanctified, and *profitable* to our Lord.]

Mat 25. v.21.

2.Tim.2. v.21.

11. The other obiection is drawen from the S. Pauls wordes, saying [That the passions of this time, are not condigne (or worthie) to the glorie to come] Wher-vpon our Aduersaries would inferre as before, that the workes, or sufferinges, of this life, are not merito-rious, or worthie of eternal glorie. Where they doe both corrupt the text, by false tranflation: for the Apostle saith; they are not *condigne to the glorie* (as it is both in Greke, & Latine in this place) not, *of glorie*: and

Likewise S. Pauls doctrine is against them, and not for them.

Rom. 8. v.18.

and peruert the fenfe. For S. Paul comparing temporal afflictions, which are fhorte, and in their owne
nature of fmal value, with the glorie of heaué, which
is eternal, and moft excellent, in refpect of fo great recompence for fmal fuffering : he exhorteth al the
faithful [to fuffer patiently, & willingly with Chrift,

v.17.

that they may be alfo glorified with him] For fo
he affirmeth immediatly before [that the adoptiue
children of God, fhal be heyres of God, and coheyres
of Chrift; if they fuffer with him.] And therfore to
encorege good Chriftians, willingly to fufteyne tribulations, he affirmeth, that the workes, or fufferinges, of this time, are not comparable to the glorie to
come; but he faith not, that they are not meritorious,
or not worthie of eternal glorie : as our Aduerfaries
would haue him to fay. Which could not agree with
his former wordes [that if Gods children fuffer with
Chrift, they fhal be alfo glorified with him] For that
fuch fuffering, although it be not in itfelf, cóparable
to the glorie of heauen, yet through Chrifts grace, it is
the meanes to attanie eternal glorie; as the coherence
of the whole fentence, conuincerh. And the fame

2. *Cor.* 4.
v. 17.

Rom. 5.
v. 15.
1. *Cor.* 15.
v. 10.

Apoftle more exprefly declareth the fame in an other
place, faying [that our tribulation, which prefently
is momentanie, and light, worketh aboue meafure excedingly an eternal weight of glorie in vs.] Which
great effect rifeth not of the value of the workes in
them felues, but of the grace, wherby they receiue
value. For as the value of Chrifts actions rifeth not of
the length or greatues of them in themfelues (though
fo alfo they paffed al other mens actions) but of the
worthines of the Perfon: fo the value of our actions
rifeth not of the greatnes, or multitude therof, in
themfelues, but of the grace of our adoption: which
maketh thofe actions (that of their owne natures,
are not meritorious, nor anfwerable to the ioyes of
heauen, in them felwes) to be meritorious, and

Other wordes
of S. Paul are
more cleare
for our Ca-
tholique do-
ctrine.

Great differé-
ce of workes
in their owne
natures, and as
they procede
from grace, or
from malice.

worthie of heauen. This great difference of workes
in their owne natures, & as they procede from grace,
may further appeare, by considering the like great
difference in euil workes, in their owne nature, and as
they procede from the mind auerted from God. Because the very action of a mortal sinne in itself, and
proper natuie, considering the time, and the quantie
of the pleasure, is not comparable to the eternal
paine of hel; but for the auersion from our omnipotent eternal Creator, whom we ought to obey, it deserueth eternal damnation. And therfore the wilful
greuous act of Gods enimie against his commandmét
is iustly damnable. And so the voluntarie good act of
Gods childe (according to his cómandments) is meritorious. Neither of them, in respect of their proper
value considered in themselues, but as proceding
from malice, and from grace.

'eue. 2.
v. 19.
2 Tssess. 1.
v. 8.

Merite of
keping Gods
command-
ments is fur-
ther proued
by S. Pauls
doctrine.

12. Thus hauing answered our Aduersaries obiectiós,
wherby it is euidét that the holie Scriptures by them
most alleaged for this purpose, and consequently al
others, which they can produce, being wel cósidered,
make more against their opinion, then for it: we shal
yet recite some more testimonies of al the Apostles,
which left anie thing in writing. And first of S. Paul,
because they most pretend his doctrine. Who so
preached the worthie fruite of faith in Christ, that he
taught also eternal saluation to depéd no lesse vpon
the obseruation of al the commandments, and vpon
al vertues requisite in true Christians: affirming that
those which want either faith in Christ, or other necessarie vertues, and persist either in infidelitie, or in
other wicked workes, shal vndoutedly misse of eternal saluation [Fo we know (saith he) that the iudgement of God is according to veritie vpon them that
doe wicked thinges] such as he had named before:
fornication; auarice, murder, and the like. And that
such as persist impenitent [heape vnto themselues
                                                    wrath,

Rom. 2.
v. 2.
(ch.1.v. 29)
v. 5. 6.

wrath, in the day of wrath, and of the reuelatiõ of the
iuſt iudgement of God. Who wil render to euerie
mã, according to his workes.] Speaking in particular
of himſelf, & other Miniſters of God, he ſaith[Euerie
one ſhal receiue his owne reward, according to his
owne labour.] He likewiſe teacheth the eſpecial
good fruite of diuers vertues; and how one vertue
bringeth an other[We glorie (ſaith he) in tribulations:
knowing that tribulation worketh patience; and patience probation; and probation (approued fortitude, worketh hope : and hope confoundeth not,
becauſe the charitie of God is powred forth in our
hartes, by the Holie Ghoſt, which is geuen vs] By
which gift of grace, he donounceth to al Chriſtians,
that now, life & death, is more in their powre, then it
was in the people of old Teſtament [Therfore if you
liue according to the fleſh, you ſhal die: but if by the
ſpirite you mortifie the deedes of the fleſh, you ſhal
liue.] Often adminiſhing that it is of Gods grace (as
the principal cauſe) and alſo of mans cooperation
(as the ſecondarie cauſe) that the faithful doe anie
good workes [For we are his fabrique, created in
Chriſt Ieſus, in good workes, which God hath prepared, that we ſhould walke in them] Againe ſhewing
that mans owne intention, and attention is neceſſarie,
he ſaith [Whatſoeuer you doe, in word, or in worke,
doe al in the name of our Lord Ieſus Chriſt. Whatſoeuer you doe, worke it from the hart, as to our
Lord, and not ro men: knowing that you ſhal receiue
of our Lord the retribution of inheritance. Serue our
Lord Chriſt. For he that doth iniurie, ſhal receiue
that which he hath done vniuſtly.] Breefly, that
the wilful, and groſſe breaking of Gods commandments deſerueth damnation, the Apoſtle reciting
manie wicked crimes, for example of al the reſt,
denounceth plainly, that al which dye in guilt therof, though they beleue al points of faith, ſhal neuer

F 2   enter

1. *Cor.* 3. *v.* 8.
Rom. 5. *v.* 3. 4. 5.
ch. 8. *v.* 9. 10. 12.
v. 13.
Epheſ. 2. *v.* 10.
Coloſ. 3. *v.* 17. 23.
24.
25.
Heb. 11. 2. 1. 26.

enter into the kingdom of heauen. [The workes of
the flesh be manifeſt (ſaith he) which are, fornica-   *Gal.* 5. *v.*
tion, vncleannes; impudicitie, lecherie, feruing of   19. 20.
idols, witchcraftes, emnities, contentions, emulatiōs,
angers, brawles, diſſentions, ſectes, eniuies, mur-   21.
ders, ebrieties, comeſſations, and ſuch like: which
I foretel you, as I haue foretold you, that they which
doe ſuch thinges, ſhal not obtaine the kingdom of
God.]Contrariwiſe for examples of al vertues, required for the attayning of heauen, he reciteth certayne,
ſaying [But the fruite of the Spirite is : charitie, ioy,   *v.* 12.
peace, patience, benignitie, goodnes, longanimitie,   23.
mildnes, faith, modeſtie cōtinencie, chaſtitie. Againſt
ſuch there is no Law] And cōcerning the ſame merite
of the iuſt, and reward of glorie due therunto, exem-   2 *Tim.* 4.
plifying in himſelf, he ſaith [I haue fought a good   7. 7. 8.
fight; I haue conſummate my courſe; I haue kept the
faith. Concerning the reſt, there is laid vp for me, a
crowne of iuſtice; which our Lord wil render to me,
in that day, a iuſt Iudge : and not only to me, but to
them alſo that loue his coming.] In reſpect alſo of
which iuſt reward, he exhorted the Chriſtian Hebrewes, to perſeuere in good workes, vpon Gods aſſured couenant, and iuſtice [For God (ſaith he) is   *Heb.* 6.
not vniuſt, that he ſhould forgete your workes, and   *v.* 10 11. 12
loue, which you haue ſhewed in his name, which
haue miniſtred to his ſainctes (other faithful) and   *ch.* 10. *v.*
doe miniſter. And our deſire is; that euerie one of you   39. *&c.*
ſhew forth the ſame carefulnes, to the accōpliſhing
of hope, vnto the end: that you become not ſlouthful,
but imitators of them, which by faith and patience
ſhal inherite the promiſſes.] Much more in the ſame
Epiſtle to this purpoſe. And concluding, ſtil putteth
them in minde of merite by good workes, ſaying [Be-   *ch.* 13.
neficence, and communication doe not forgete: for   *v.* 16.
with ſuch h oſtes God is promerited.] That is, Gods
fauour, and his reward of euerlaſting life (which is
                                                        himſelfe,

himselfe, that we may eternally see, and enioy him in glorie) is procured by workes of almes, and charitie. But our Aduersaries by al meanes auoide the word *Merite*. And here translate [God is pleased.] which also conuinceth them. For if God be pleased with such workes, and shew more fauour for them, then are they meritorious, and by them, the faithful doe merite. And not faith alone, but also other good workes doe procure Gods fauour to men. In as plaine termes this Apostle also affirmeth, that Christiãs are counted, or holden worthie of the kingdom of God, for their constancie in true Religion: congratulating with the Thessalonians for the same [we glorie in you, in al Churches of God (saith he) for your patience, and faith, in al your persecutions and tribulations, which you sustaine: for an example of the iust iudgement of God; that you may be coũted worthie of the kingdõ of God, for the which also you suffer.] Seing therfore the faithful are accounted worthie of the kingdom of God, because they patiẽtly suffer for it, it is euidẽt, that by obseruing the commandments, they please God, and are worthie of heauen: by the doctrine of S. Paul.

Protestants owne translationproueth the Catholike doctrine of merite.

2. Thes. 1. v. 4. 5.

13. It resteth to see some few testimonies of manie, written by the other Apostles. S. Iames purposely, against Solifidians in his time, proueth that not onlie faith, but good workes with faith, doe iustifie, and merite saluation. [The probation of your faith (saith he to al the faithful) worketh patience. And let patience haue a perfect worke: that you may be perfect, and intyre, failing in nothing. Blessed is the man that suffereth tentation: for when he hath bene proued, he shal receiue the crowne of life, which God hath promised to them that loue him] True and vnspotted Religion consisteth in doing workes of mercie, with other good workes; & [in keping thyself vnspotted from this world] And that we must kepe al and, euerie

Iac. 1. v. 3. 4.

v. 12.

v. 22. 27.

ch. 2. v. 10.

Perfection in al vertues is required that the faithful may receiue the crowne of life.

And that onlie
faith doth not
saue is pro-
ued by S. Iames

rie one of the commandments. And touching the   *v.14.*
opinion, that onlie faith should iustifie, he discourseth thus:[What shal it profite (my brethren)if a man
say,he hath faith, but hath not workes: Shal faith be
able to saue him? Faith,if it hath not workes, is dead
in itself. But wilt thou know ô vaine man, that faith   17.20.
without workes is dead? Abraham our father, was   21.
he not iustified by workes, offering Isaac his sonne
vpon the Attar?Seest thou, that faith did worke with   22.
his deedes:and by the workes,the faith was consum-   24.
mate?Doe you see, that by workes a man is iustified,
and not by faith only? And in like maner also Rahab,   25.
was not she iustified by workes, receiuing the messengers, and putting them forth an other way? For   26.
euen as the bodie without the spirite is dead: so also
faith without workes is dead.]Yet may it be a true
faith, as a dead bodie is a true bodie : but by charitie, and good workes it is a liuing faith : and
then it is not onlie faith. For faith, which worketh   *Gal.5.v.*
by charitie, is more then onlie faith. It is ,in an   6.1 *Cor.7.*
other place, al one in sense, with [the obseruation   *v.19.*
of the commandments of God.] In the rest of his
Epistle besides condemnation of errors in faith , and
maners, he exhorteth to practise vertues,for the gay
ning of heauen. Namely that [He which is wise, and   *ch.3 v.13.*
hath knowlege, shew by conuersation his working   *ch.4.v.9.*
in mildnes of wisedom,that euerie one doe mourne,   10.
and wepe, punishing themselues for their sinnes. Be
humbled in the sight of our Lord ,that he may exalt
them]In sicknes to seeke the benefite of Sacraments,   *ch.5.v.14.*
Holie Annoiling, and Confession, for remission of al   16.20.
sinnes. And in al their life , to endeuour the conuersion of those,that erre in opinion,& of other sinners,
to amédment of life, which procureth great grace,&

Also by S.
Peter.

reward to thé that doe it. S. Peter in both his Epistles
exhorteth the Christian Iewes, which were dispersed
in diuers coútries, & had receiued the same true faith

in

2. Pet. 1. v. in Chrift[equally with himfelf and others : to perfe-
1. ch.3.v.1. uere conftantly, both in the fame faith, and fame precepts of our Lord, and Sauiour,] notwithftanding
the great perfecution, and alfo feduction : by which
they might be tepted, as though either faith in Chrift,
were not neceffarie(as the Perfecutors vrged) or were
alone fufficient(as the Seducers pretended) requiring
therfore of them, nor only to perfift in faith: but alfo
1. Pet. 1 v. in good workes. To be in al converfation holie. And
15.17 ch.2. fo invocate God, who iudgeth according to euerie
v.19. ch.4. ones worke. For this is thanke (worthie) if for con-
v.8.19. fcience of God a man fuftaine forowes, fuffering vniuftly. But before al thinges hauing mutual charitie,
becaufe charitie couereth the multitude of finnes.
Therfore they that fuffer let the comend their foules
to the faithful Creator in good deedes.] In fumme he
requireth with faith, the affociation of other vertues.
2. Pet. 1. [You imploying(faith he) al care, minifter ye in your
v.5.6.7. faith vertue:and in vertue knowlege; & in knowlege
abftinence;and in abftinence,patience: and in patiece
pietie:and in pietie,loue of the fraternitie & in loue
v.8. of the fraternitie,charitie. For if thefe thinges be prefent with you, and abound; they shal make you not
vacant, nor without fruite, in the knowlege of our
9. Lord Iefus Chrift. For he that hath not thefe thinges
ready, is blinde, and groping with is hand, hauing
forgotten the purging of his old finnes. (forgetting
the grace by which he is made able, and obligation
v.10. by which is bond to doe good workes.) Therfore,
brethren, labour the more, that by good workes, you
may make fure your vocation, and election:for doing
11. thefe thinges, you shal not finne at anie time. For fo
there shal be miniftred to you abundantly an entrace
into the euerlafting kingdom of our Lord & Sauiour
Iefus Chrift.] Thus and much more S. Peter. S. Iohn By S. Iohn.
moft agreably alfo teacheth,that the keping of Gods
comandments, is fo pleafing to him;that it procureth

G   what

what good thing foeuer is asked , by fuch his feruants
[what foeuer we shal aske (faith he) We shal receiue of God , becaufe we kepe his commandments:
& doe thofe thinges, which are pleafing before him]
In al his three Epiftles he exhorteth to perfift in true
faith , and to doe good workes ; often affirming that
[the true knowlege (and feruice)of God , confifteth
in keping of his commandments] And that [He
which doth iuftice is iuft in dede] And fo continuing
may affuredly expect eternal reward. Likewife S.

And by S.Iude, Iude the Apoftle teftifieth , according to the prophecie of Enoch , that our Lord wil come in his holie
thoufandes , to doe iudgement , and to reproue the
impious (not only which goe aftray from true faith
firft receiued , but alfo) of al the workes of their impietie, wherby they haue done impioufly: & of al the
hard things , which impious finners haue fpoken

That God wil againft him. But you my deareft building your felues,
render to euerie vpon your moft holie faith , in the Holie Ghoft,
one accor-
ding to his praying kepe your felues in the loue of God; expe-
workes: is cting the mercie of our Lord Iefus Chrift, vnto life
often repeted euerlafting.] Plainly teftifying that iudgement of
in holie damnation, or life euerlafting;shal procede as Gods
Scriptures. precepts are kept or not kept. And that [God wil
render to euerie one , according to his workes.]
which doctrine is very often vttered in the fame
fenfe: yea very often in the fame wordes in the holie
Scriptures. At leaft tenue times.

1.Ioan.3.
v.22.
ch.1.v.6.
ch.2.v.5 29
ch.3.v.7.8.
9.24.
ch 11 v 17.
ch 5.v.3.
Ep.2.v.8.
Ep.3.v.5.6.
11.
Iuda v.14.
15. (v.3. 4)
v.10.21.
Pf.61.v.13.
Mat 16.v.
27.
1.Cor.3. v.8.
21.Apoc 2.
v. 23.
2.Cor. 11.
v.15.
ch.18. v.6.
2 Tim. 4.
v.14.
ch.20.v. 12.
13.
1.Pet.1.v.
17.
ch.22.v.12.

Al men are bond to ferue God with diuine honour. And firft to beleue in him.

ARTICLE 3.

Some contro-
uerfies con-
cerning the
command-
VV E haue bene more large in the two firft
Articles, concernig the commandments
ingeneral; becaufe it is called into queftion at this time, how poffible,neceffarie, and profitable

table the obſeruatiõ of them is, to eternal ſaluation. And therfore I iudged it better to be rather too abũdant, then too ſparing in ſo important controuerſies. But theſe pointes being diſcuſſed, we may more conueniently be brefe, in declaring the ſame commandments in particular. Which I purpoſe in al that foloweth: eſpecially where no Controuerſie occurreth. As in this firſt point, that al men are bond to honour and ſerue God aboue al other thinges. Which none wil denie but either Atheiſts, which thinke there is no God, or the deſperate damned ſoules, which are already in hel; and diuels, which ſeke to be honored in place of God. For the very light of nature, which is in euerie reaſonable man, teacheth that the Supreme Diuine Power is to be ſerued by al creatures: As [The ſonne ought to honour the father: and the ſeruant his Lord, and the creature the Creator] By al which tittles euerie man is bond to honour God, as Father, Lord, and Creator, & that ſingularly aboue al other thinges; becauſe there is but one beginning of al thinges, one omnipotent conſeruer, vpon whom al depẽd; one ſupreme dominatour, whom al miſt ſerue, and ought to obey. Al this the holie Patriarches, and other iuſt perſons wel knew, & generally obſerued in the Law of nature. As the ſacred hiſtorie witueſſeth, of Adam (after his repentãce) of Seth, Enos, Cainan. Malaleel, Iared, Henoch, Mathuſale, Lamech, Noe, Sem, &c. Abraham, Iſaac, Iacob; and their ſpecial progenie, to Moyſes and Aaron.

2. Afterwards God gaue his peculiar people a writtẽ Law, by the miniſtrie of Moyſes: conteyning three ſoites of precepts. Moral, Ceremonial, and Iudicial. Yet ſo that al are reduced to the Moral: which are cõpriſed in two Tables, and in Tenne Commandments. For the Ceremonial perteyne to the obſeruation of the three commandments of the firſt table; concerning mans durie towards God: and the Iudicial perteyne to the better obſeruation of the other ſeuen,

Pſ.13.v.1.
Pſ.52.v.1.

Pſ.4.v.7.
Mal.1.v.6

Gen.5.v.3.6. &c.
1.Parab.1. v.1,24.

Exo 20.v.1. &c.
v.24.
ch 21.v.1. &c.
ch.24.v.12.
Deut 4.v. 13.
chap. 10. v 1.4.

ments in general, being diſcuſſed: the ſame cõmandmẽts in particular may be more breſely explaned.

God alwayes conſerued ſome, that truly ſerued him.

Al the commandments are compriſed in tenne.

The Ceremonial, and Iudicial are for the better obſeruation of the Moral.

in

in the second table, touching mans dutie towards
his neighbour. In obseruing of al which, through the
especial grace of God, with concurrence of mans
wil (which is free to choose or refuse) confiteth the *(Deut 30.*
obtayning of eternal glorie, in life euerlafting. And *v.15)*
contrariwife in tranfgreffing of the fame commandments, or of anie of them enormioufly, and perfifting
therin at the departing of the foule from this world,
confifteth the fole and true caufe of eternal punifhment, in euerlafting death. As is declared in the two
former Articles.

Euerie com-
mandment
conteineth
both an affir-
matiue, and a
negatiue pre-
cept.

3.   Now therfore in particular, it is firft to be obferued, that euerie one of the renne Commandments,
conteineth two precepts: one negatiue forbidding
that which is vnlawful; an other affirmatiue, commanding to doe the contrarie good. In which affir-   *Pfal. 33.*
matiue forme, it pleafed God to deliuer only two of   *v. 15.*
the tenne. (Which are the laft of the firft table, and   *Pf 36.*
the firft of the fecond table) The other cight are   *v.27.*
expreffed in the negatiue maner. And fo the firft
exprefly forbiddeth to ferue anie falfe god; including the affirmitiue Precept: Our firft and greateft
dutie, of rightly honoring and feruing our Lord, &

God is efpe-
cially ferued
by Faith,
Hope, Chari-
tie, and Reli-
gion.

Creator: One God Omnipotent. Which is efpecially
performed, by foure moft principal vertues; which
are, Faith, Hope, Charitie, and Religion. For firft of al
we are bond to beleue in God, by the Theological
vertue of Faith. Which we haue fufficiently declared
in the firft Article of the firft Part of this worke, by
abundance of holie Scriptures. Al agreable to that

The neceffitie
of faith is
proued in the
firft part.

fundamental principle, vrged by S. Paul [Becaufe   *Heb. 11.*
without faith it is impoffible to pleafe God. For he   *v. 6.*
that cometh to God muft beleue that he is, and that
he is a rewarder to them that feeke him.] And fo we
are here to shew in like maner, the neceffitie, and
efficacie of the other three vertues, in the next
enfuing Articles.

Al are bond to hope in God. And confidently to relie vpon his diuine Prouidence.

ARTICLE 4.

Gen. 3.
v. 10. &c.

MAnie examples and other teſtimonies of holie Scriptures, doe inſtruct vs, that as we muſt firmely beleue in God; ſo we muſt confidently repoſe al our truſt in him. Adam and Eue after that they had Examples of tranſgreſſed Gods commandment, deſpared not, but ſuch as truly hoping in Gods mercie, anſwered when he called hoped in God, them, confeſſed their fault, and willingly accepted

ch. 4. v.
13 16.

punishment inioyned. Cain deſpared, and therupon adding more ſinne to his former [Went forth And of others from the face of our Lord ; and dwelt a fulgitiue on that deſpared; the earth.] His generations, and manie others, fel at and preſumed. laſt to the contrarie extreme ſinne of preſumptiõ not fearing punishment, which iuſt Noe preached; but perſiſted careles, and preſumptuous [in the dayes before the floud, eating and drinking, marying and

ch. 6. v. 1.
2. &c,
Mat. 24.
v. 38. 39.
Luc. 17. v. 2.

geuing to mariage, euen vnto that day, in which Noe entred into the arke: and knew not til the floud came and tooke them al.] So were both deſperation, and preſumption iuſtly punished, with other enourmious ſinnes. The true vertue of Hope, confiſting in the right meane betwen extremes, both ſaued the penitents, and iuſtified the hopeful. [Abraham (as

Rom. 4.
v. 18. Gen.
22. v. 3. 5.
9. 10. (Heb.
11. v. 19.)
v. 11. 13.

S. Paul writeth) contrarie to hope, beleued in hope] that is, aboue al humane probabilitie, truſting in Gods prouidence, beleued and hoped in God. And therupon obeying his commandment, tooke his ſonne Iſaac to the place appointed, bond him, and laid him ou the Altar, ready to ſacrifice him [accounting that God is able to raiſe vp euen from death.]

And

And God accepting of this fact, a ramme was facrificied in place of Ifaac. The parents alfo of Moyfes, in the perfecution of Pharao king of Ægypt, trufting in Gods prouidence, expofed their fonne Moyfes, an infant [in a baskette of bulrushes, in a fedgie place, by the riuers brinke] From whence according to the parents confidence in God, the childe was taken vp, by Pharaos daughter, and nurced by his owne mother, and for a time (fo long as himfelf would) was accounted the adopted fonne of the kings daughter.

Exo. 2. *v.* 3.
5. 9. 10.
Heb. 11. *v.*
24. 25.

2.   which Moyfes, afterwards gouerning the whole people of Ifrael, often in his life, and againe a litle before his death, exhorted al to hope in Gods protection, by examples of former experience in themfelues [Thou shalt remember(faith he)al the iourney, through the which, the Lord thy God hath brought thee, and that the thinges which were in thy hart, might be made knowne, whether thou worldeft kepe his commandments, or not. He afflicted thee with penurie, and gaue thee Manna for meate, which thou kneweft not, nor thy fathers : for to shew vnto thee, that not in bread only, a man liue, but in euerie word, that procedeth from the mouth of God. Thy rayment wherwith thou waft couered, hath not decayed for age : and thy foote is not worne : loe this is the fourtith yeare. That thou mayft recount in thy hart, that as a man difciplineth his fonne; fo thy Lord, thy God hath difciplined thee; that thou shouldeft kepe the commandments of our Lord thy God, and walke in his wayes, & feare him,] Thus fearing and hoping in God, they neded not do doubt of his continual protection, and prouifion of al thinges neceffarie. Holie Iob by his great confidence in God, ouercame three fortes of vehement tentations; The loffe of al his childrea, and great abundance of wordlie goodes, in one day; the greuous bodilie afflictions; and the contentious

Deut. 7. *v.*
17. *& c.*
Dout. 8.
v. 2.

3.

4.

5.

6.

v. 7. *& c.*
ch. 29. *v.* 2.
3. *& c.*

Moyfes exhorted the faithful to truft in God.

Iob, by his confidence in God, ouercame manie and great afflictions.

falfe

false accusations of particular freindes: firmely hoping, and confidently saying to God in his prayer
[Sette me beside thee (nere to thee) and let the hand
of whosoeuer fight against me] By such confident *So did Dauid.*
hope, Dauid, as yet young, ouercame & slew a lion,
a beare, and great Goliath, the chalenging Philistian.
And afterwards gotte manie other wonderful victories. By the like hopeful confidence, were the victories of Elias the Prophete, against foure hundred and *Elias.*
fiftie false prophetes: and against Achab & Iezabel.
By like confidence in God, king Ezechias preuailed *Ezechias.*
against the Assirians, with a huge armie beseging Ierusalem : where fourscore and fiue thousandes were
slaine by an Angel in one night, and Senacherib their
king, departing went away, with the rest that were
left aliue. Iudith preuailed against Holofernes : *Iudith.*
Whose head she cutte of, whiles he was in a depe
drunken slepe. Mardocheus, and his nece, Quene *Mardocheus.*
Esther, preuailed against wicked Aman. Who had pro- *Esther.*
cured king Assuerus his Edict, to destroy al the Iewes,
Which were in that kingdom. But by confident
prayer [the lotte was changed] and cruel Aman
was hanged on the high gibbette, which he had prepared for faithful Mardocheus. By like confidence
in God, Daniel the Prophete, was preserued from *Daniel, and*
seuen hungrie lions. And the other tree Hebrew chil- *the other*
dren, Ananias, Misael, and Azarias, from anie hurt in *three children.*
the burning furnace. And chaste Susanna, by her con- *Susanna.*
fidence in God, choosing rather in her innocen-
cie to fal into the handes of wicked Iudges, then
to consent vnto greuous sinne, ouercame her false
accusers, and auoided both sinne, and the ignominious death, to which she was vniustly condemned. So Mathathias, and his sonnes, with *Matthathias*
other faithful people, through their assured confi- *and other Ma-*
deme in God, saued themselues from contamination *chabees.*

of

Iob. 17.
v. 3.

1. Reg. 17.
v. 4 34.
35 45.46.
2 Reg. 22.
v. 1. 2. &c.
3. Reg. 18.
v. 21. 22.
4. Reg 19.
v. 19 32.3.
36. Isaith.
4. v. 11. 12.
ch.13.v.7 8.
10. 27.31.

Est. 7 v. 6.

ch.16. v.19.
20.

Dan. 6. v.
16. 21. ch.
3. v.23. &c.
ch.13. v. 22.
60. 62.

11. Mach. 2.
v. 15. 21.
ch. 4. v. 36.
2. Mach. 6.
v. 18 ch. 7.
v. 1. 2. &c.

of idolatrie, in the perſecution of king Antiochus.
And manie of them gotte the glorious crowne of
Martyrdom. Others being alſo ſtout champions
of the Church, and happie Confeſſors of God, reſtored againe the free vſe of true Religion in their
countrie.

The Prophe-
tes teſtifie
the neceſſitie,
and excellen-
tie of hope.

3. The ſame neceſſitie, and excellent fruite of hopeful confidence in God, which ſo glorioully ſhineth
in the actes of renowmed Sainctes, is in like ſorte
confirmed, by the doctrine, and frequent exhortations of the holie Prophetes, and of Chriſt our
Lord, and his Apoſtles. The Royal Pſalmiſt abundeth in commending this great vertue. [In peace Pſal 4.v.6.
(ſaith he) I wil reſt. Becauſe thou Lord haſt ſingular 9. 10.
ly ſetled me in hope. Our Lord is Protector of al that Pſ 17.v.31.
hope in him. Although I ſhal walke in the middes Pſ.22.v.4.
of the ſhadow of death, I wil not feare euils: becauſe

Eſpecially
king Dauid,
in his Pſalmes.

thou art with me. Thy rodde, and thy ſtaffe (thy
right direction, and ſtrong aſſiſtance) haue comforted me. Our Lord is my illumination, and my
ſaluation : whom ſhal I feare ? Our Lord is the Pſ.26 v.1.
Protector of my life: of whom ſhal I be afrayde?
Hope in our Lord and doe good: and inhabite the Pſ.36.v.3.4.
land, and thou ſhalt be fedde in the riches therof. 5. 6.
Be delighted in our Lord, and he wil geue thee the
petitions of thy hart. Reueale thy way to our
Lord, and hope in him, & he wil doe it. He wil bring
forth thy iuſtice, as light; and thy iudgement as
midday. Why art thou ſorowful ô my ſoule, and Pſ. 42. v.
why doeſt thou truble me? Hope in God : becauſe 5. 6.
yet I wil confeſſe to him, the ſaluation of my countenance, and my God (that is, I wil euer praiſe him,
whoſe countenance I hope to ſee face to facie)
Our God is a refuge, and ſtrength : an helper in tri- Pſ 45. v.
bulations, which haue found vs excedingly. Ther- 2.3.
fore wil we not feare, when the earth ſhal be trubled,

and

and mountanes tranſported into the hart of the ſea.
The Lord of hoſts is with vs: the God of Iacob is our
defender. I as a fruitful oliue tree in the houſe of
God, haue hoped in the mercie of God for euer : and
for euer, and euer. Caſt thy care vpon our Lord ; and
he wil nouriſh thee ; he wil not geue fluctuation (not
ſuffer the iuſt to remaine in doubtful : dangerous, wauering thoughts, or perplexitie , but wil geue quiet
repoſe of mind) to the iuſt for euer. I haue hoped in
God, I wil not feare, what man can doe to me. Thou
(ô God) haſt conducted me , becauſe thou art made
my hope: and a toure of ſtrength from the face of the
enimie. My hope is in God. Hope in him al ye the congregation of people : powre out your harts before
him: God is our helper for euer. It is good for me to
cleaue to God: to put my hope in our Lord God. Saue
thy ſeruant (my God) that hopeth in thee. He that
dwelleth in the helpe of the Higheſt, ſhal abide in the
protection of the God of heauen. He ſhal ſay to our
Lord: Thou art my Protector, and my refuge, my
God I wil hope in him. With his ſhoulders ſhal he
ouerſhadow thee: and vnder his winges thou ſhalt
hope. With ſhielde ſhal his truth compaſſe thee: thou
ſhalt not be afrayde of the feare of the night. Of the
arrow flying in the day : of buſines walking in
darkenes: of inuaſion, and the midday diuel. Becauſe
he hath hoped in me (ſaith God) I wil protect him,
becauſe he hath knowen my name. He ſhal crie to
me, and I wil heare him. With him I am in tribulation:
I wil deliuer him, and wil glorifie him. From tribulation I inuocated our Lord, and our Lord heard me in
largenes. Our Lord is my helper: I wil not feare what
man can doe to me. Our Lord is my helper : and I
wil looke ouer myne enimies. It is good to hope in
our Lord, rather then to hope in man. It is good to
hope in our Lord, rather then to hope in princes. I
haue cleaued to thy teſtimonies ô Lord : doe not

H   confound

v. 8, et 12.
Pſ. 51. v. 10.

Pſ. 54. v. 23.

Pſ. 55. v. 11.
Pſ. 60. v. 4.
Pſ. 61. v. 8. 9.

Pſ. 72. v. 28.

Pſ. 85. v. 2.

Pſ. 90. v. 1.
2. 4.

5.

6.

14.
15.

Pſ. 117 v. 5.
6, 7. 8. 9.

Pſ. 118, v. 31.
v. 42.

confound me. (suffer me not to be confounded) I shal
answer a word to them that vpbrade me: becauʃe I
haue hoped in thy wordes. I haue lifted, vp myne eyes *Pʃ.120.v.1.*
vnto the mountaines: from whence helpe shal come 2.
to me. My helpe is from our Lord; who made heauen *Pʃ.124.v.1.*
and earth. They that truʃt in our Lord, as mount *Pʃ.130.v.3.*
Sion. He shal not be moued for euer, that dwelleth
in Ieruʃalem. Let Iʃrael hope in our Lord, from hence *Pʃ.141.v.6.*
forth, now, and for euer. I haue cried to thee ô Lord, *Pʃ.145.v.2.*
I haue ʃaid: Thou art my hope: my portion in the 3.v.5.6.
land of the liuing. Put not confidence in princes: in

There is no
ʃaluation but
in God onlie.

the ʃonnes of men, in whom there is no ʃaluation.
Bleʃʃed is he whoʃe helper is the God of Iacob, his
hope in our Lord, his God: Who made heauen, and
earth, the ʃea, and al thinges, that are in them. Our *Pʃ.146.v.11.*
Lord is wel pleaʃed towards them, that feare him: &
in them, that hope vpon his mercie.] By theʃe, and
other like diuine ʃpeaches the Royal Prophete inʃtru-
ʃteth vs, both how neceʃʃarie, and how excellent, and
profitable the vertue of Hope is, to al the faithful ʃer-
uants of God.

Salomon tea-
cheth the
ʃame.

4.   No otherwiʃe doth wiʃe Salomon teach the ʃame
in his Sapiential Bookes. Wherof we shal alʃo recite
ʃome ʃpecial ʃentences. [Haue confidence in our *Prou.3.v.5.*
Lord with al thy hart (ʃaith he to euerie one, that wil
ʃerue true wiʃdom) and leane not vpon thyne owne 6.
prudence. In al thy wayes thinke on him, and he wil
direct thy ʃteptes. Dread not at ʃudaine terrour: and 25.
at the power of the impious falling vpon thee. For 26.
our Lord wil be at thy ʃide, and wil kepe thy foote,
that thou be not taken. Our Lord wil not afflict with *ch.10.v.3.*
(ʃpiritual) famine, the ʃoule of the iuʃt: and the deceiptful practiʃes of the impious, he wil ouerthrow.
He that hopeth in our Lord, is bleʃʃed. Lottes are caʃt *ch.16.v.20.*
into the boʃome, but they are ordered of our Lord. 33.
A moʃt ʃtrong tourre the name of our Lord: the
iuʃt

ch.18, v.10.
ch.21. v.30.
ch.29. v.25. iuſt runneth to it, and ſhal be exalted. There is no wiſdom, there is no prudence, there no counſel againſt our Lord. He that feareth man ſhal ſowne fal: he that truſteth in our Lord ſhal be lifted vp. There are iuſt men to whom euils happen, as though they had done the workes of the impious: and there are Eccle. 8.
v.14. impious men, which are ſo ſecure, as though they had the dedes of the iuſt. But this alſo I iudge moſt Sap.1. v.13.
14.15,
(Ezech.18.
v.23.32.) vaine. God made not death, neither doth he reioyce in the perditiõ of the liuing. For he created al thinges to be: and he made the nations of the earth to health. There is no kingdom of hel in earth (none are condemned whiles they are in this world.) But the impious with handes, and wordes, haue prouoked it ch.2. v.23.
24. (brought damnation vpon themſelues) For God created man incorruptible, and to the image of his owne likenes he made him. But by the enuie of the diuel, Eccle 32. v.
23. death entred into the world. He that truſteth in God ſhal not be leſſened.]

5.   Other Prophetes teſtifie the ſame neceſſitie of Hope, and truſt in God, againſt al that truſt in So doe other Prophetes. humane helpes. And againſt Soliſidians, which aſcribe al to faith, without other vertues. Of ſuch as truſted in the helpe of Æthiopians, and Ægyp- Iſa.20. v.5.
6.
ch.31. v.1.
2. tians, our Lord ſaid by his Prophete Iſaias [They ſhal, feare, and be aſhamed of Æthiopia, their Hope; and of Ægypt their glorie. Woe to them that goe downe into Ægypt, for helpe, hoping in horſes, and hauing confidence vpon chariottes, becauſe they be manie; and vpon horſemen, becauſe they be very ſtrong: and haue not truſted v.4. vpon the holie one of Iſrael, and haue not ſought after our Lord. Becauſe thus ſaith our Lord: As a lion: ſo ſhal the Lord of hoſts deſcend, to fight ch.41. v.14. vpon mount Sion, and vpon the litle hil therof. Feare not thou worme of Iacob, ye that are dead of Iſrael. I haue holpen thee, ſaith our Lord, and thy

H 2   Redemer,

Redemer, the holie one of Ifrael. Heare me, ye that *ch.51.v.1.*
folow that which is iuft, and that feke our Lord, attend to the rocke, whence you are hewen out: & the
caue of the lake, from the which you are cutte out.]
To Ieremie, being fent to admonish others, our Lord *Iere 1.v.17.*
faid [Be not afrayde of their face: for I wil make thee *v.19*
not to feare their countenance. And they shal fight *ch.20.v.11.*
againft thee, and shal not preuaile: becaufe I am with
thee, faith our Lord, to deliuer thee] Ieremie being
thus encoreged, admonished the people, amongft
other vertues, to truft in Gods heipe, doing their
owne endeuours[Not to truft in wordes of lying(as if
it were yuough to fay) The temple of our Lord, the *ch.7 v 4.*
temple of our Lord, it is the temple of our Lord]Nei- *ch.17.v.5.*
ther to truft in any man [Curfed be the man that trufteth in man : and maketh flesh his arme, and his hart
departeth from our Lord. Bleffed be the man, that *7.*
trufteth in our Lord, and our Lord shal be his confi- *8.*
dence. And he shal be as a tree that is planted vpon
the waters, that fpreadeth his rootes towards moi-
fture: and it shal not feare, when the heate cometh.
And the leafe therof shal be grene, and in the time
of drought, it shal not be carreful (not neede to feare) *9.*
neither shal it ceafe to bring forth fruite. Feare not at *ch.42.v.11.*
the face of the King of Babylon, of whom you(being
fearful) are afraide: feare him not faith our Lord, becaufe I am with you, to faue you, and to deliuer you
out of his had. And thou my feruant Iacob feare not: *ch.46.v.27.*
and be not thou afraide Ifrael, becaufe loe I wil faue
thee from a farre, and thy feede out of the land of thy
captiuitie: and Iacob shal returne, and reft, and profper: and there shal be none to terrifie him] For albeit
for their finnes, they were temporally punished with
captiuitie, yet being brought by this meanes to repentance, and to confide in God, they were in time releafed. As the Prophete Baruc, Ieremies Scribe, did fur- *Bar.4.v.21.*
ther affure them, faying [Be of good comforth my
children:

children: cry to our Lord, and he wil deliuer you, out
of the handes of the princes your enimies. For I haue
hoped in the euerlasting, for your saluation: and ioy is
come to me from the holie one, vpon the mercie,
which shal come to you, frō our euerlasting Sauiour]
To draw the faithful people into true confidence, our
Lord said further vnto them by his Prophete Ezechiel
[When no eye had mercie on desolate soules (saith he)
I passing by thee, saw thee to be troden downe, in thy
bloud: & I said to thee, when thou wast in thy bloud:
Liue. I said to thee, I say; In thy bloud, liue.] Daniel, &
the other three children, captiues in Babylon, wholly
reposing their confidence in God, said to their keper:
[Proue, we besech thee, vs thy seruants, for tenne
dayes: and let pulse (beanes, pease, &c.) be geuen vs
to eate, and water to drinke: and looke vpon our
faces, and the faces of the children, that eate of the
kings meate, & as thou shalt see, thou shalt doe with
thy seruants. And after tenne dayes, their faces appeared better, & more corpulent, then al the children,
that did eate of the kings meate] And so they continued, with confidence in God, obseruing his Law immaculate, and stil prospered. Osee, and other Prophetes, admonished the people, concerning the same
vertue of Hope, amongst other vertues necessarie besids faith [Kepe (saith he) mercie, and iudgement, and
hope in thy God alwayes.] Who please to see more testimonies of the Prophetes, in a matter so cleare, may
read innumerable. Especially these here noted in the
margine.

6. Christ more especially teacheth, and requireth
this vertue of Hope, in al the faithful. [Be not careful
(saith he) for your life: What you shal eate; neither for
your bodie. what rayment you shal put on. For your
heauenlie Father knoweth, that you nede these
thinges. Seke therfore first the kingdom of God, and
the iustice of him, and al these thinges shal be geuen

Marginal notes (left column):
v. 12.
Ezech.16.v.
56.
Dan.1.v.12.
13.
15.
&c.
Osee.12.v.6.
Ioel.3.v.16.
Nu.1.v.7.
Ab.2 v.4.
Soph.3.v.12.
Zach.5.
v.12.
Mat.6.v.25.
32.33.34.

Marginal note (right column):
Christ exhor-
teth, and enco-
regeth his chil-
dren to cōfide
in him.

H 3 you

you befides. Be not careful therfore for the morow.
For the morow day fhal be careful for it felf: fufficiét
for the day, is the euil therof. Behold I fend you as *ch.10.v.16.*
fhepe in the middes of wolues. Be ye therefore wife *17.19.20.*
as ferpents, and fimple as doues. When they fhal de- *Luc.10.v.5.*
liuer you vp (to perfecuters) take no thought, how or *ch.21 v.14.*
what to fpeake: for it fhal be geuen you in that houre, *15.*
what to fpeake. For it is not you that fpeake, but the
fpirite of your Father, that fpeaketh in you. Let not *Io.14. v. 1.*
your hart be trubled; you beleue in God, beleue in *2.&c.*
me alfo. In my Fathers houfe there be manie man-
fious. If not, I would haue told you. Becaufe I goe *2. 3. 4.*
to prepare you a place. And if I goe, and prepare you
a place, I come againe, and wil take you to myfelf,
that where I am, you alfo may be. And whither I goe,
you know, and the way you know] Further inftru- *v.6 14.*
cting, and comforting his difciples, that himfelf is *v.10.11.*
the way to life euerlafting (according to his Humanitie) and alfo the end (according to his Diuinitie) euen as the Father, becaufe they are confubftantial. And inftantly before his apprehenfion, he
exhorted them againe to kepe corege, and confidence, faying: [Behold the houre cometh, and it is
now come, that you fhal be fcattered, euerie man *v. 32.*
into his owne, and me you fhal leaue alone: and
I am not alone, becaufe the Father is with me. Thefe *33.*
thinges I haue fpoken to you, that in me you may
haue peace. In the world you fhal haue diftreffe: but
haue confidence. I haue ouercome the world.]

Hope is no
leffe neceffarie
then Faith:
yet they both
are infufficiét
without cha-
ritie.

7.   S. Paul in order of the Theological vertues, next
after Faith, teacheth the neceffitie of Hope, and
therto addeth, the perfecteft of al, Charitie: which
is the forme, perfecting al other giftes, and vertues
[Being iuftified therfore by faith (faith he, as by the *Rom.5 v.*
firft beginning and meanes) let vs haue peace (that is *1.2.*
confidence) toward God, by our Lord Iesvs Chrift:
by whom alfo we haue acceffe, through faith, into this
grace

grace, wherin we ftand, and glorie in the Hope, of the glorie of the fonnes of God. And Hope confoundeth not: becaufe the charitie of God is powred forth in our hartes, by the Holie Ghoft, which is geuen vs.] So doth the Apoftle afcribe faluation fome time to Faith, fome time to Hope, as a partial caufe, faying [we account a man to be iuftified by faith, without the workes of (Moyfes) Law. By hope we are faued.] But neither to any of thefe two alone, nor to them both together, without other vertues, efpecially charitie. For al iointly are neceffarie, as the total meanes. Therfore in the conclufion of his Epiftle he prayeth faying [The God of Hope replenish you with al ioy, and peace in beleuing: that you may abound in hope, and in the vertue of the Holie Ghoft.] In al vertues namely the three, which tend directly to God [Faith Hope, and Charitie, but the greater of thefe is charitie.] Againe of Hope in particular he faith [If in this life only we be hoping in Chrift, we are more miferable then al men] And exhorteth al Chriftians faying [Let vs not flepe as others: but let vs watch, and be fober; hauing on the breaftplate of faith, and charitie: and a helmet, the Hope of faluation. Chrift (God and Man) hath geuen vs good Hope in grace, of eternal confolation. Wherein God meaning more abundantly to shew to the heyres of the promife (to Chriftians indued with grace of the new Teftament) the ftabilitie of his counfel, he interpofed an oath: that by two thinges immoueable, wherby it is impoffible for God to lie, we may haue a moft ftrong comfort, who haue fled to hold faft the Hope propofed: which we haue, as an Anker of the foule, fure, and firme. Hauing confidence in the bloud of CHRIST. Doe not therfore leefe your confidence, which hath a great remuneration] Thus S. Paul in diuers places auoncheth the neceffitie, and fruite of Chriftian Hope S. Peter brefely [admonisheth

v. 5.

ch. 3. v. 28.
ch. 8. v. 24.
1. Cor. 13. v.
1, 2. &c.

Ro. 15 v. 13.

1. Cor. 13.
v. 13.
ch 15 v. 19.

1. Thef. 5.
v. 6. 8.

2. Thef. 2.
v. 16.
Heb. 6. v. 17.

18.

19.

ch. 10. v. 19.
v. 35.

Faith and charitie are the breaftplate; & Hope is the helmet of a true Chriftiã.

monisheth

monisheth al the faithful, that God by raising Christ from the dead, hath geuen glorie, that our faith, and hope might be in God.] But falsely imagined hope to be saued, without other vertues conioyned, is mere Presumption; and contrariwise; so to be terrified with greatnes, and number of sinnes, as to diffide in Gods mercie (which is aboue al his other workes) is plaine Desperation. The meane betwen which two gulfes of perdition, is true hope in God.

Presumption and Desperation are gulfes of perdition.

Phil. 2. v. 12.

Ps. 144. v. 9.

Al are bond to loue God aboue al other thinges. And consequently their neighboures, as themselues.

ARTICLE 5.

BEsides faith and hope in God, which are the first, Charitie is no lesse necessarie: without which al other vertues are insufficient to iustification, or saluation, because it perfecteth, and connecteth al others, in the loue of God, referring them al to the chefe End; which is God himselfe, and in God eternal saluation. Wherupon S. Paul commending, manie other vertues as necessarie, addeth, saying [But aboue al these thinges, haue Charitie: which is the band of perfection.] Perfectly directing al good workes to Gods honour, & perfectly vniting al the faithful iust persons among themselues. The superexcellencie of which vertue is proued, and confirmed by manie holie Scriptures.

Charitie maketh al other vertues perfect. and so is most necessarie.

Colos. 3 v. 14.

2. And first by the Moral precepts; which are the same in the Law of nature, & writté Law of Moyses, and in the Law of Christ. Abraham (as other holie Patriarches both before, and after him) obserued, & taught others to obserue [the way of our Lord, doing

The first, and most principal com nandmét is to loue God aboue al other thinges.

Gen. 18. v. 19.

doing iudgement, and iustice] louing God aboue al, seruing him, and abhorring al false goddes. Which thing God inspired into their mindes, and at last expressed the same, by the ministrie of Moyses, to his peculiar selected people, saying [I am the Lord thy God, mightie ielons, visiting the iniquitie of the fathers, vpon the children, of them that hate me: and doing mercie vpon thousands of them that loue me. Thou shalt loue the Lord, thy God, with thy whole hart, and with thy whole soule, and with thy whole strength, and with al thy minde. Thou shalt loue thy freind as thy self: Thy neighbour as thy self. And now Israel what doth the Lord thy God require of thee, but that thou feare the Lord thy God, and walke in his wayes, and loue him, and serue the Lord thy God, with al thy hart, and with al thy soule? Loue therfore the Lord thy God.] Which is often repeted, and that with explication, that loue consisteth in keping al his commandments: & with promise of Gods assistance: by which we may kepe them, if we wil, saying [Our Lord God wil circumcise thy hart, and the hart of thy sede, that thou maist loue our Lord thy God, in al thy hart, and in al thy soule, that thou mayst liue. But if thy hart be auerted (if thy self wilt not withal circumcise thyne owne hart) and thou wilt not heare, I foretel thee this day, that thou shalt perish. This diligently beware (saith Iosue) that you loue our Lord your God. And incline your harts to our Lord] said he, in his last admonition to the people.

3.   The Royal Prophete very often professeth, & comendeth to others, the most bonden dutie of louing God aboue al, and our neigboures as ourselues. And so doe other Prophetes. [I wil loue thee ô Lord my strength (saith Dauid) Praysing I wil inuocate our Lord: and I shal be saued from myne enemies. Loue our Lord al ye his sainctes: because our Lord wil require truth. They that loue his name shal dwel in Sió. You that loue our Lord, hate euil. He shal rest in the holie

The Psalmist, and other Prophetes teach the same.

Ex.10.v 5. 6.
Deut.5.v 10.
ch.6. v.5.
Luc.10.v. 27.
Leuit.19.v. 18.
Deut. 10.v. 12
ch.11.v.13. 22.
ch.19.v.9.

ch 30.v 6.
16.17.18.
(ch.10.v. 16.)

Ios.22.v 5.
ch.23.v.11.
ch.24.v 23.

Ps.17.v.1.

Ps.30.v.24.
Ps.68.v.37.
Ps.96.v.10.

I

holie hil, that doth not euil to his neighbour . Behold *Ef.14.v3.*
how good, and how pleasant a thing it is, for bre- *Pf.132.v.1.*
thren to dwel in one. I loue them that loue me (saith *Pro.8.v.*
eternal wisdom)and them that watch toward me shal *17.21.*
finde me. That I may enriche them that loue me, and
may replenish their treasures. Oyle powred out is thy *Cant.1.v.3.*
name : therfore haue young maides (faithful soules) *ch.2 v.4.*
loued thee. He hath ordered in me charitie. I haue *ch.3.v.1.2,3,*
sought him, whom my soule loueth. I wil seeke him, *4.*
whom my soule loueth.Haue you sene him,whom my *ch.8.v.6.*
soule loueth? I haue found him , whom my soule lo- *v.7.*
ueth.I held him, neither wil I let him goe.The middes
(of the Church, Christs throne) he hath paued with
charitie, for the daughters of Ierusalé. Loue is strong
as death. Manie waters can not quench charitie : neither shal floudes ouerwhelme it: if a man shal gene al
the substance of his house for loue,as nothing he shal
despise it]he shal not esteme the price,which he gaue,
in comparison of charitie purchased.

It is moſt ab- 4·   Isaias expostulateth with Gods people , for that
furde ingrati- they loued not God, with so hartie affection, as they
tude, not to were bond [Heare ye heauens(saith he)and geue eare *Isa.1.v.2. 3.*
loue God be- ô earth: because our Lord hath spoké:I haue brought
fore al crea- vp children, and exalted them: but they haue despi-
tures. sed me. The oxe hath knowne his owner, and the asse
his masters cribe: but Israel hath not knowne me, and
my people hath not vnderstood] By his Prophete Ie- *Iere.1.v 5.6*
remie thus saith our Lord. [What iniquitie haue your *ch. 3.v.6.*
fathers found in me, that they haue made themselues *ch.4 v.5.*
farre from me? And they haue not said : Where is our *ch.5.v.9.*
Lord, that made vs come vp, out of the land of *&c.*
Ægypt.] In the greatest part of al his prophecie he *Ezech.2.v.5.*
foreshewed afflictions,& plagues, by sword, famine, *9.*
pestilence, & captiuitie, because they loued not God, *Dan.9.v.5.*
nor kept his cõmandméts, but hardned their neckes, *ad 15.*
and would not heare the admonitions. And the same *Osee 1.v. 4.*
other Prophetes. *5. &c.*

                              5.   In

Mat.22 v.
37.38.39.
Mar.12.v.
1.

5. In the new Teftament, Chrift our Sauiour teacheth moft plainly, that [to loue God from thy whole
hart, and with thy whole foule, and with thy whole
minde, is the greateft, and the firft commandment,
And that the fecond is like to this : Thou shalt loue
thy neighbour as thy felf. An other commandment
greater then thefe, there is not.] Though faith be the
firft vertue, yet this duble charitie of louing God, and
our neighbour, is the greateft, as it is here expreffed,
And of thefe two it is cleare, that to loue God aboue
al, is the greater: and to loue our neighbour as ourfelf,
is like to the firft, and is the fecond in greatnes. And
[on thefe two commandments dependeth the whole
Law, and the Prophetes.] And fo he that hath this
duble charitie, fulfilleth al that is commanded, by the
Law, & the Prophetes: neither doth Chrift our Lord
command any more, but the felf fame. In further
explication wherof our Lord commadeth to beleue,
and Hope in God, yea and in himfelf, as he is God,
and Man [You beleue in God, beleue in me alfo] faith
he: and the like touching other vertues. And concerning loue, and charitie, he being both our Creator in his Diuinitie, and our neighbour in his Humanitie, he is to be loued before, and aboue al others.
[Whofoeuer (faith he) loueth father, or mother, more
then me, is not worthie of me : and he that loueth
fonne or daughter aboue me, is not worthie of me]
Which he fpeaketh not only, in refpect of his Deitie,
but alfo of his Humanitie: becaufe he is our Redemer. To thofe therfore that impugned him, not accepting him for their Redemer, he faid [You wil not
come to me, that you may haue life. Glorie of men I
receiue not (for he had al glorie of his Father, and
neded not to receiue glorie of men) But I know you,
that you haue not the loue of God in you] becaufe
they did not loue their neighbour: no not Chrift, our
Redemer.

Mat.22.
v.40.

Io.14.v.1.
Mat.5.6.7.

Mat. 10.
v.37.

Ioan.5.v.
40.41.42.

The duble
charitie, of lo-
uing God,
and our
neighbour,
conteyneth al
the Law of
God.

I 2   Of

6. Of the most eminent excellencie of this vertue S.

S. Paul most plainly teacheth, that charitie is the greatest of the three Theological vertues.

Paul often discourseth largely. Yelding the reason why Hope confoundeth not, he saith [Because the charitie of God is powred out in our harts, by the Holie Ghost, which is geuen vs] In an other place he testifieth [that to the that loue God, al thinges cooperate vnto good. If any man loue God (saith he to the Corinthians) the same is knowne of him. If I speake with the tongues of men, and of Angels, and haue not charitie, I am become as sounding brasse, or a tinkling cymbal. And if I should haue prophecie, and knew al mysteries, and al knowledge, and if I should haue al faith (also that which worketh miracles) so that I could remoue mountanes, and haue not charitie, I am nothing. And if I should distribute al my goodes, to be meate for the poore, and if I should deliuer my bodie, so that I burne, and haue not charitie, it doth profite me nothing. Charitie is patient, is benigne: Charitie enuieth not, dealeth not peruersly: it is not puffed vp, is not ambicious, seketh not her owne, is not prouoked to anger, thinketh not euil: reioyceth not vpon iniquitie; but reioyceth with the truth; suffereth al thinges, beleueth al thinges, hopeth al thinges, beareth al thinges.] In summe you see that Charitie presupposeth, and includeth al vertues. And is so absolute perfect, that it continueth eternally [neuer faileth] as Prophecie, Faith & Hope, being in this life vnperfect, are to be changed into perfect knowledge, and possession of eternal felicitie : but charitie continueth the same in nature. So there remane manie vertues, Moral and Theological, namely. [Faith, Hope Charitie these three: but the greater of these, is charitie.] Againe vpon other occasions shewing the differéce or value of charitie, & other diuine giftes, which are also or sometime were very profitable, this Apostle sayth [In Christ IESVS (for attaining eternal life in Christ IESVS) neither circuncision auaileth ought, nor

Rom.5.v.5.

ch.8 v.28.
ch.15 v.14.
1.Cor.8.v.3.
ch 13.v.1.
2.

3.

4.
5.
6.
7.

8.

v.13.

Gal.5.v.6.

prepuce,

Colof.3.v.
14.

Iac.1.v.12.

1.Pet.1.v.
21.22.

1.Io 2.v.15.
ch.4.v.16.
19.

v.10.

21.

Iudæ v.21.

Cant.2.v.4.

prepuce, but faith, that worketh by charitie. Aboue al thinges haue charitie, which is the band of perfection] The crowne of glorie (faith S. Iames) is promifed by God [to them that loue him] God hath raifed Chrift, and geuen him glorie (faith S. Peter) that the faith, & hope of Chriftians, might be in God. Making their foules chafte in obedience of charitie: in the fincere loue of the fraternitie, from the hart. loue ye one an other ferioufly. Loue not the world (faith S. Iohn) nor thofe thinges, which are in the world. If any man loue the world, the charitie of the Father is not in him. God is Charitie, and he that abideth in charitie, abideth in God: and God in him. Let vs therfore loue God, becaufe God hath firft loued vs. If any man shal fay, that I loue God, and hateth his brother, he is a liar. For he that loueth not his brother, whom he feeth: God whom he feeth not, how can he loue? And this commãdment we haue from God, that he which loueth God, loue alfo his brother. Kepe yourfelues in the loue of God (faith S. Iude) expecting the mercie of our Lord Iesvs Chrift vnto life euerlafting.]

7. In the precept, & bond of louing our neighbour as our felues, it is fufficiently infinuated, that euerie one is bond alfo to loue himfelf, in the way of fpiritual life, and honour of God: and by this example of ourfelues, we muft loue our neighbours, and that in due order of charitie. For [God hath ordered charitie] in his faithful people. To witte: to loue God firft, and aboue al; Then Chrift our Redemer: as Man. Then the whole Church, the myftical bodie of Chrift Iefus the Head. After thefe & in thefe, in refpect of fpiritual good, and health, of foules, euerie one is bond to prefer his owne good ftate, before any other: and by example of himfelf, to defire the like to al others. But in refpect of temporal good, either corporal, or external; the common good muft in order of charitie, be

Other Apoftles, of purpofe teach the fame, againft Heretikes in their time.

In the precept of louing our neighbour, is fuppofed the loue of our owne foules.

And both in ourfelues, and neighbours, fpiritual good muft be preferred before temporal.

I 3 preferred

The bodie before external goodes.
And the publique before priuate.

preferred before priuate, yea before euerie ones pro-pee, being a priuate person. And in regard of the communitie, the temporal good of a publique person, must be preferred before anie priuate. And amongst publique persons, the Superiors case before an other publique, subordinate vnder him. The reason is, because in the Common, and Superior, the priuate, and inferior is conteyned, and hath his part (at least spiritually, for his temporal damage) and the Communitie, and Superior is not conteyned in the priuate, or inferior : except such as can profite the communitie, and so promote the common : for then such a one is reputed as publique. Againe when the question is betwen the spiritual good, of one, or of manie, and the temporal of others, then must the spiritual good of eternal saluation, be preferred in charitie (though not sometime by rigour of iustice) before the temporal good, or profite of anie. For as we must yelde our goodes, to releue an others bodie, in extreme necessitie : so we must yeld our life (if that case shal happen) for the eternal saluation of an other. In so much, that a true charitable Christian, must yelde (if nede be, and shal haue that effect) his temporal goodes, yea and temporal life, for the eternal saluation of his neighbour; that is, of any other man, or woman, if such be the case. This in dede is right charitie : commended by our B. Sauiour, in an high degree, saying [Greater loue then this, no man hath, that a man yelde his life, for his freindes] More special obligation is in such, as haue pastoral charge of soules, commended and imposed by Ecclesiastical Iurisdiction : which special obligatiō of spiritual Pastors, our Sauiour by word, and example teacheth, saying [A good Pastor geueth his life for his shepe] In more general cases, circunstances doe geue light, what is due. And holie Scriptures witnesse [That God hath geuen commandment to euerie one, concerning his

1.Io.3, v.17.

Io.15 v.133.

Ioan. 10.11.

Eccli. 17. v.12.

neighbour]

Pſal.121.v.
8. neighbour]Holie King Dauid ſaith[For my brethren,
and for my neighbours ſakes, I ſpake peace of thee]
Iſa.41.v.6. Iſaias ſaith [Euerie one ſhal helpe his neighbour, and
ſhal ſay to his brother: Be ſtrong.] If in ciuel workes,
by inſtinct of nature, one doth aſſiſt, and conſpire
with an other : much more the ſame mutual helpe
ought to be in ſpiritual good thinges.. Becauſe this is
the complement of al the commandments, as S. Paul,
Rom.13.v.8.
Gal.5.v.13. ſaith [He that loueth his neighbour, hath fulfilled the
Law. By charitie (ſaith he) ſerue one an other.]

8. Examples of ſuch, as truly and ſincerly haue loued their neighbours, are ſo innumerable, as are al
the Sainctes of God. For al and euerie one, that pleaſed God, loued their neighbours : becauſe otherwiſe
they had not loued, nor pleaſed God, Yet in particular, remember the extraordinarie great charitie of
Exo.32.v.
32. Moyſes, in the old Law,[who deſired rather that God
would ſtrike him out of the booke of life, then that
he should deſtroy al the people] for the enormious
ſinne of idolatrie, committed by moſt of them: and
Rom 9.v.3. of S. Paul in the new Teſtament [who wiſhed himſelf
to be an anathema from Chriſt (ſeparated from
Chriſt) for the ſaluatiõ of his brethren the Iſraelites]
Which their zele for their neighbours, was no doubt
principally, for the more honour of God: that he
might be glorified in manie. But how theſe, their ſo
charitable deſires, were not againſt due order of charitie, which they were bond to haue, in louing their
neighbours as themſelues, not before themſelues,is no
ſmal difficultie to decide. For explication of which
profound textes of holie Scripture, there be foure
probable expoſitions. The firſt is, that theſe be hyper-
bolical ſpeaches: a frequent figure, in holie Scriptures,
to make vs vnderſtand, or conceiue, that the greatnes
of the thing affirmed, ſurpaſſeth humane capacitie, ſo
their ſincere deſires of the peoples ſaluation, were
farre greater then ordinarie men could comprehend.

Moyſes and
S. Paul ſheued
extraordinarie
charitie to-
wards others,

Foure pro-
bable expoſi-
tions of
Moyſes, and
S. Paules ma-
ner of praying
for others.

Secondly

Secondly some thinke that they meant only, that
they were willing and content, to be for a time separated from God, for part of satisfaction for others.
Thirdly some suppose that in dede they were content conditionally, if so it pleased God, to be eternally punished, that manie others might be saued.
Speaking therein according to the affection of their
mindes, not according to their iudgement of reason.
Lastly it is also probably expounded, that they knowing, by special reuelation, that themselues were elected to eternal glorie, and so determined by God, that
it should not be altered, they prayed instantly that
seing God would not separate them, he would also
extend his mercie vnto those others: the granting of
which request, should be more gratful to them, then
was their owne particular saluation. Both in dede desired, but the greater the more desired.

*Al are bond to serue God vvith internal
deuotion, and external declaration therof,
by the vertue of Religion.*

ARTICLE 6.

By religion
the greatest
moral vertue
we referee al
honour to
God.

REligion is the fourth principal vertue comprised
in the first commandment. For as al men are
bond to beleue in God with true faith: to confide in
him with firme hope; and to loue him aboue al other
thinges, with sincere charitie: so al are likewise obliged to exhibite to him diuine honour, and seruice,
both by internal and external actes of deuotion,
prayer, sacrifice, other oblations, and ceremonial
Rites, due to his supreme Excellencie, as the omnipotent sole Creator, Gouernour, and Lord of al
thinges, from whom al good procedeth, and to whom
al good

al good tendeth. Which moft excellent moral vertue
of Religion, and our neceſſarie obligation to performe the ſame dutie, is partly declared in the ſecond

Part 2.
Artic.2.22.
23.
Part. 4.
Art. 1. &c.

part of this worke, eſpecially concerning Sacrifice: &
is further to be explicated touching Prayer in the
fourth part. Neuertheleſſe we ſhal here alſo recite
ſome ſpecial textes of holie Scriptures; which clearly
teſtifie this obligation.

2.   Al the holie Patriarches, & other godlie perſons,
by diuine inſtinct ſerued God religiouſly, in thoughtes
wordes, and deddes: with mutual examples and inſtructions, the elder ordinarily ſo euer teaching the
younger: that when the written Law was geuen,
this obligation was preſuppoſed to be knowne in
general, and now further particular maner was expreſſed, how it ſhould be continued, and increaſed: as appeareth in the ſame Law at large, amongſt
other precepts. Where our Lord ſaid to Moyſes:
[Speake to the children of Iſrael, that they take firſt
fruites for me of euerie man that offereth of his owne
accord, you ſhal take them. And theſe are the thinges
which you muſt take: Gold, and ſiluer, and braſſe,
hyacinth, purple: &c. And they ſhal make me a Sanctuarie, and I wil dwel in the middes of them] When
the whole Tabernacle was made, and erected, in
confirmation that God was rightly honored therwith [A cloud couered the Tabernacle of teſtimonie,
and the glorie of our Lord filled it] And during
their fourtie yeares abode in the deſerte, a cloud by
the day, and a pillare of fire by night, hanging ouer
the ſame Tabernacle, directed them to remaine in
the ſame place: and leauing the Tabernacle it went
before, and ſo guided them, whither to remoue
their manſions. The ſame Law preſcribed the matters,
places, times, and maner, of offering Sacrifices:
how to make other oblations; to pay tithes, to make

It is proued
to be a neceſ-
ſarie vertue.

Gen.4.v.4.
26.
ch.8. v 20.
ch.18. v.19.
&c.

Exo.25.v.1.
2.3.8.

ch,40 v.32.
34.35 36.

Leuit.6.v.2.
&c.

ch. 23.
ch. 27.

K   holie

holie vowes , with obligation to performe them . Deut.6.v.
Al which Moyſes often , and earneſtly admonished 13.
the whole people to obſerue; God promiſing reward, ch 31.
and threatning puniſhment , as euerie one ſhould 32.
deſerue. Other nations generally running their owne
wayes , fel vnto multitudes , of falſe goddes: had in
deede no religiō becanſe they honored not our onlie
true God. Manie alſo of the children of Iſrael often Num.25.v.
reuolting from God, loſt(for the time) the true vertue 1.2.
of Religion , firſt falling into other ſinnes, and ſo to
idolatrie.

Interual and external actes of Religion muſt cōcurre.

3.   But euer ſome godlie perſons , eſpecially Prophetes, by word and example , conſerued true Religion, with internal, and exteral actes of deuotion [Sa-
crifice ye (ſaith the holie Pſalmiſt) the ſacrifice of iu- Pſ.4.v.6.
ſtice: the ſacrifice of praiſe (and firſt of al) the ſacri- Pſ.49.v. 14.
fice of an afflicted ſpirite, a contrite, & humbled hart.] Pſ.50.v. 19.
which internal ſacrifices being rightly offered to Pſ.146.149.
Cod, doe geue life to the external, and by the ſame, 150.
external are more inkindled. And ſo nor onlie holie
cogitations of the hart , but alſo voices , and inſtruments ſerue to Gods more honour, in religious Actes
Yea alſo external goodes beſtowed to Gods honour,
are helpes to religious exerciſes [Honour our Lord Prou.3.v.9.
with thy ſubſtance (ſaith Salomon) and geue to him Iſa.29 v.13.
of thy firſt fruites.] Alwayes ſuppoſing that the inten- Deut.16.v.
tion directeth al to God. Otherwiſe God himſelf doth 20.
ſay [This people approcheth with their mouth , and Mat 6,v.2.
with their lippes glorifieth me: but their hart is farre 5.16.
from me. Iuſtly thou ſhalt purſue that which is iuſt]
ſo alſo almeſe deedes, faſting, and prayer, without ſincere intention are hypocriſie.

Examples of external reli-gious actes in the ſeruants of Chriſt.

4.   Which is more manifeſtly declared by Chriſt,
not only in that diuine ſermon in the mount , but alſo
in other places [charging the Scribes and Phariſies Mat.23 v.
with hypocriſie, becauſe they pretended holines be- 13.14.15.
fore men: but meant it not in their hartes . Whereas &c.

[True

Io.4.v.23. [True adorers doe adore God in spirite, and veritie.
Gen.8.v.21. For the Father of heauen seketh such to adore him]
Neither doth this exclude external actes, but both together are a swete odour [When Christ our Sauiour
Luc.2.v.10, was borne in Bethleem, the shepheardes were dire-
Mat.2.v.11, cted by an Angel to visite the litle Childe in the
cribbe. And the Sages moued by God, and guided by
a strange starre, came from a farre countrie, with
great spede, to the same infant, and adoring him, offered to him giftes; gold, frankencense, and myrrh]
Luc 2.v.36. The deuout ancient widow, and Prophetese Anna
37. [with fastings and prayer (religiously) serued God,
night and day] S. Iohn Baptist preaching penance
Mat.7.v.33. [baptized in water] Our Lord besides his preaching,
Mat.26.v. vsed external ceremonies. And instituted holie Sa-
26. craméts. After the visible coming of the Holie Ghost,
ch.28.v. 19. manie thousandes were baptized, in water:and so are
Act.24.v. more and more euer since, Al which and the like are
41. religious actes.[If any man thinke himself to be reli-
Iac.1.v. 26. gious (saith S. Iames) and bridleth not his tongue (or
27. otherwise offendeth God) this mans religion is vaine.
Religion cleane and vnspotted with God, is to doe
good workes (to the honour of God) and to kepe
himself vnspotted from this world.]

VVorkes of mercie done to Gods ho- nour, and with pure con- scie[n]ce, are re- ligious Actes.

Jt is forbidde to serue any creature,
as a God.

ARTICLE 7.

Art.3.§.3. According as is noted before, that euerie one of
the tenne commandments ; conteyneth two
precepts: one affirmatiue, the other negatiue; being
sufficently proued, for the affirmatiue part of the first
commandment ; that al men are bond to beleue, and

to hope in God our Lord, and to loue & honour him
aboue al other thinges; it here foloweth to declare
Gods negatiue precept: Not to haue, nor ferue anie
other God: that is, Not to honour any creature as a
God, God himfelfe faying [Thou shalt not haue *Exo.20.v.3.*
ftrange goddes before me. Thou shalt not make to *4.5.*
thee a grauen thing, nor anie fimilitude, that is in *Deut 5.v.7.*
heauen aboue, and that is in earth beneth: neither of *8.9.*
thofe thinges, that are in the water vnder the earth.
Thou shalt not adore them, nor ferue them.] In confirmation of which fundamental diuine Law, God
very often repeteth the fame, with threates, to the
tranfgreffors, of greuous punishment temporal and
eternal. So he adioyneth to this firft precept thefe ad-
monitorie wordes [I am the Lord thy God, mightie, *v.5.*
ielous, vifiting the iniquitie of the fathers, vpon the
children, vpon the third and fourth generation, of
them that hate me.] And after recital of al the tenne
general precepts he repeteth againe the fubftance of
this firft, faying [You shal not make goddes of filuer *v.23*
nor goddes of gold shal you make to you] Againe
shortly after touching the feruing of falfe goddes,
with diuine honour he faith, that [He which facrifi-
ceth to goddes, shal be put to death] According to
which Law [there were flaine in one day, about three *ch.22.v.26.*
thoufand men, which had offered facrifice to the *ch.32.v.28.*
molten calfe, which they had made] Againe our *v.4.*
Lord faid [they shal no more immolate their hoftes to *Leuit.17.v.7.*
diuels, with whom they haue committed fornicatió. *ch.19.v.4.*
Turne not yourfelues to idols, neither make you to *ch.26.v.1.*
yourfelues molten goddes. I the Lord your God. You
shal not make to yourfelues an idol, & thing grauen;
neither shal you erect titles, nor fet a notorious ftone
in your land, for to adore it. For I am the Lord your
God] when manie of the people were feduced by the
Moabits wemen, and were profeffed to Beelphegor,
Moyfes commanded the Iudges of Ifrael, to kil the
                                                    fame

*The firft com-
mandment as
it is negatiue,
forbiddeth al
fortes of Ido-
latrie.*

Num.15.v.
1 3 5.9.
Deut.4.v.
15.16.&c.
ch.7.v.2.5.
ch.10 v.20.
ch.12,v 2.3.
ch.13,v. 1,2.
3.

same Idolaters. [And there were slaine foure and twentie thousand men] Againe in the repetition of the Law, our Lord most especially condemneth Idolatrie, and al false doctrine, and the auctors therof saying [If there rise in the middes of thee a Prophete, or one that saith he hath sene a dreame, and fortel a signe, and a wonder: and it come to passe, which he spake, and he say to thee: Let vs goe & folow strange goddes, which thou knowest not, and let vs serue them: thou shalt not heare the wordes of that Prophete, or dreamer: for the Lord your God tempteth you, that it may appeare, whether you loue him or no, with al your hart, and with al your soule. And that Prophete, or forger of dreames shal be slaine: because he spake that he might auert you from the Lord your God. If thy brother, the sonne of thy mother, or thy sonne, or daughter, or thy wife, that is in thy bosome, or thy freind, whom thou louest, as thy soule, wil perswade thee secretly, saying: let vs goe & serue strange goddes which thou knowest not, nor thy fathers: consent not to him, nor heare him: neither let thyne eye spare him, to pitie and hide him: but forthwith (by order of Law) thou shalt kil him. Let thy hand be first vpon him, and after thee, let al the people lay hand on him. With stones shal he be stoned to death: because he would haue drawne thee from the Lord thy God. That al Israel hearing may feare, & may doe no more any thing like to this. If thou finde that a citie harkning to the children of Belial, comitte abomination, thou shalt forthwith strike the inhabitants of that citie, in the edge of the sword, and shalt destroy it: and al thinges that are in it: vnto the very beastes. And there shal nothing sticke in thy hand of that anathema: that our Lord may be turned from the wrath of his furie.] When there shal be found man or woman, that serueth strange goddes, & adore the Sunne, or the Moone, or the hoste of heauen,

v.5.
v.6.

v. 8.
9.

10.
11.
12. 13.
14. 15.
17.
ch. 16.
v.22.

ch.17.v.2.3.
4.5.6.

The auctors of Idolatrie, or false doctrine, were stoned to death by the Law of Moyses.

K 3   being

being found to be true (vpon diligent inquirie) that a-
bomination is committed in Iſrael, they ſhal be ſtoned. At the mouth of two, or three witneſſes ſhal he
perish, that is to be ſlaine.] More to the ſame purpoſe ch.18.v.20.
in the reſt of the Law. [The prophete that being de- ch.17.v.15.
praued with arrogancie, wil ſpeake in my name, the ch.31 v.16.
thinges that I did not command him to ſay, or in the 17.18.
name of ſtrange goddes, ſhal be ſlaine.] And the ch.32.v.15.
like. 16.17.&c.

Examples of Idolaters pu-
niſhed, & the whole people afflicted for that ſinne moſt eſpe-cially.

3.   In the Hiſtorical bookes is often recorded, how
ſome fel into Idolatrie, and were ſowner or later punished. [Manie (in the times of the Iudges) did euil in Indic.2.v.1.
the ſight of our Lord, and forgate their God, ſeruing 2.11.13.14.
Baalim, & Aſtaroth. And our Lord being wrath againſt ch.3.v.7.8.
Iſrael, deliuered them into the handes of ranſakers. ch.4.v 1.
who tooke them, and ſold them to the enimies, that ch.6.&c.
dwelt round about] In particular [there was a man of ch.17.v.14.
mount Ephraim, named Michas, who with his mo- 5.9.10.13.
ther made a molten, and grauen idol of ſiluer, and ch.18.v.2.3.
made one of his ſonnes as a Prieſt of the ſame idol. 14.30.31.
And with al hyred a Leuite (for want of a true Prieſt)
falſely reputing him for a Prieſt.] This idol shortly
after was taken from this man, by the tribe of Dan, &
they ſette vp idolatrie, and made alſo falſe Prieſtes]
which were Apoſtata Leuites. So from time to time
idolatrie crept in amongſt that people, and was 1.Reg.7.v3
eſſownes extirpated by good Iudges, Othoniel, 3.4.
Gedeon, Iephte, Samſon, and others. Moſt effectually 2 Reg 6.v.
by Samuel the Prophete; [who reduced al from ido- 2.ephes.&c.
latrie, cauſing them to take away Baalim, and Aſta- 3.Reg.6.&c.
roth, and to ſerue our Lord only] So that Idolatrie 4.Reg. 15.v.
was often vtterly deſtroyed amongſt the Iſraelites in 11.13.
the times of good kinges, Dauid, Aſa, Ioſaphat, Eze- ch.22.v.43.
chias, Ioſias, and others: and the Church was neuer 4.Reg.18.
at any time, wholthy ſuppreſſed, though ſore affli- v.3.4.
cted, eſpecially in the tenne tribes, after Ioroboams ch.22.v.22.
schiſme. Par 15.v.16.
ch.23.v.16.
17.&c.

4.   Al

4. Al the Prophetes most diligently (as occasions required) preached against Idolatrie, and against al false doctrine. Dauid King and Prophete plainly denounceth that [Al the goddes of the Gentiles are diuels, the Idols of Gentiles are (in material substance) siluer, and gold (and other mettal) the workes of mens handes. They haue mouth and shal not speake; they haue eyes, and shal not see. They haue eares and shal not heare: they haue nosthreles, and shal not smel. They haue handes, and shal not handle: they haue feete, and shal not walke: they shal not crie in their throte. Let those that make them become like to them: and al that haue confidence in them] This sinne of Idolatrie, was the most especial cause of the captiuities, first of the tenne tribes, and lastly of the other two: As Ieremie the Prophete witnesseth saying [Because your fathers haue forsaken me, saith our Lord, and gone after strange goddes, & serued them. But you also haue wronght worse then your fathers: for behold euerie one walketh after the peruersitie of his euil hart, that he heare me not.] The extreme vanitie, and sensles madnes of which crime, the same Prophete Ieremie in his Epistle sent by Baruch: as also Isaias: and the Auctor of the Booke of wisdome, most amply declare that al may shunne, and detest so wicked, and foolish abomination.

Ps.95.v.5.
Ps.113.v.12.
Ps.134.v.15.
Iere 16.v.11.
12.
ch.44.v.4.5.
ca.10.v.11.
14.15.&c.
Baruch.6.v.
7.&c.
Is.44.v.13.
Sap.13.v.10.
11.&c.
ch.14.
ch.15.
Dan 3.14.

The Prophetes admonished and threatud Idolaters. And shew the sottish vanitie of al that beleue, or worshippe false goddes.

5. Satan notwithstanding, of his singular proud ambition, presumed to tempt our Eternal Lord and Sauiour, to this enormious sinne of Idolatrie. But then did our Lord command him away, saying [Auant Satan: for it is written: The Lord thy God shalt thou adore: and him only shalt thou serue] S. Paul seuerely reprehendeth the Painims, for their foolish Idolatrie [The Gentiles (saith he) changed the glorie of the incorruptible God, into a similitude of the image of a corruptible man; and of foules, & fourfooted beastes, and of them that crepe. And haue changed the veritie

Mat.4.v.9.
10.
Rom.1.v.23.25.v.8.1.
Cor.1.v.4.
&c.
1.Thes.1.v.9.

Christ and his Apostles aboue al other sinnes, condemne idolatrie.

veritie of God into lying : and haue worshipped, and
serued the creature, rather then the Creator] He congratulateth with al Christiãs, for their faith in Christ,
and for that [they are turned to God, from Idols, to
serue the liuing and true God. And to IESVS Christ,
his Sonne : our Redemer, and Sauiour. *Alpha* and *Apoc.1.v.8.*
Omega. The beginning (from whom is al good) & end, *ch.22 v.13.*
(wherto al thinges are to be directed.) He hath geuen *1 Io.5.v.*
vs vnderstanding, that we may know the true God: & *20,21.*
may be in his true Sonne. This is the true God, and
life euerlasting saith S. Iohn : and so concludeth with
admonition to flee from al false goddes , saying [My ἀπὸ' τοῦ
litle children, kepe yourselues from Idols.] εἰδ᾽ ολων.

Sorcerie, Nigromancie, Witcherie: and al pactes vvith diuels, expresse or secrete, are execrable.

ARTICLE 8.

A T what time Moyses and Aaron in Ægypt, tur- *Exo.7 v.11.*
ned a rodde into a serpent [Pharao the King of *12.*
Ægypt called the wisemen, and the enchanters, and
they also by Ægyptian enchantments, and certaine secretes did in like maner . But Aarons rodde deuoured
their roddes.] Againe when Moyses and Aaron had
turned the waters of Ægypt into bloud [the enchan- *v.22.24.25.*
ters with their enchantments did in like maner.] And
for seuen dayes the Ægyptians could not drinke of
the riuers. Likewise Moyses and Aaron bringing in- *ch.8.v.6.7.*
numerable frogges in the land of Ægypt, [the en- *8.*
chanters brought also more frogges] But could not *13.*
take away anie. For Pharao was forced [to request *v.17.*
Moyses , and Aaron to pray to God, to take them *18.*
away] Which they did. In the third plague of the *19.*
Ægyptians , by dust turned into sciniphes, [The
enchanters

Particular
sortes of Ido-
latrie are par-
ticularly con-
demned in
holie Scrip-
ture.

Diuels can doe
wonderful
thinges, but
not true mi-
racles.

enchanters attēpting to doe the like, could not doe it]
And then confeſſed the power of God[ſaying to Pharao: This is the finger of God.] And cōſequently their
enchantement, were not of God, but of the diuel.

Exo.22 v.
18.
Leuit.19 v.
26,31.
ch.20.v.6.
27.

2. Againſt which diuelish arr, and practiſe, God gaue
expreſſe commandment vnder paine of death: ſaying:
[Enchanters thou shalt not ſuffer to liue. You shal not
diuine, nor obſerue dreames. Decline not to Magicians, neither aske anie thing of ſoothſayers. The
ſoule that shal decline to Magicians, and ſoothſayers,
and shal committe fornication, I wil ſette my face
againſt it, and deſtroy it, out of the middes of his
people. Man or woman, in whom is a pythonical, or
diuining ſpirite, dying let them dye: they shal ſtone

Deut.18.v.
10.

II.

12.

14.

them: their bloud be vpon them. Neither let there be
foūd in thee anie, that shal expiate (ſacrifice) his ſonne,
or daughter, making them to paſſe through the fire:
or that demandeth of ſoothſayers, and obſerueth
dreames, & diuinatiōs: neither let there be a ſorcerer;
nor inchanter, nor that conſulteth with pythons, or
diuiners, & ſeeketh the truth of the dead. For al theſe
thinges our Lord abhorreth: & for theſe abominatiōs
wil he deſtroy theſe nations, whoſe land thou shalt
poſſeſſe. but thou art otherwiſe inſtructed of our Lord
thy God.]

Al Magique is
condemned by
Gods Law.

1.Reg.28.v.
3.7.8.9.
10.
11.
13. 14.
15.

v.19.
ch.31.v.1.2.
4.6.
1.Par.10.v.
24.6.

3. King Saul according to Gods Law tooke al the
Magicians, & ſoothſayers out of the land] But falling
into diſtreſſe, and being ouercome with diuelish tentation [he ſaid to his ſeruants: Seeke me a woman that
hath a pythonical ſpirite; and I wil goe to her, and wil
aske by her] And learning where ſuch a one was, he
went vnto her, promiſing her ſafetie, from danger of
punishment. She therfore attempting to raiſe vp
Samuel the Prophete (lately departed from this life)
Samuel appeared (or at leaſt a ſpirite repreſenting
Samuel) who blamed Saul for his attempt, and foretold him, that [he with his ſonnes should be ſlaine]

King Saul
ſometime pu-
niſhed Magi-
cians, but af-
terwards fel
into that
crime, and
periſhed.

L   And

And he perished accordingly the next day . Ochozias   4. *Reg.1.*v.
King of Israel [sent messengers to consult Beelzebub,   2.3.4.
the false God of Accaron, whether he should recouer   *ch.*21 *v.*8.
his health, or no (being hurt by a fal from a window)   2.*Par.*33.*v.*
and Elias the Prophete mette the messengers, and sent   4.*Reg.*23 *v.*
them back to tel the King: that he should not reco-   24.*v.*26.
uer, but dying should dye] King Manasses (amongst
other sinnes of Idolatrie) vsed sooth saying , and obserued diuirations, and made (allowed) pythones, &
multiplied inchanters.] Al which at last repenting, he
lamented; yet were both he and others, punished for
the same sinnes. And his sonnes sonne [King Iosias
tooke away, and destroyed the pythones, and sooth-
sayers: and the images of Idols] and al occasions of
idolatrie, or superstition.

The Pro-   4.   The Royal Psalmist, and other Prophetes, in like
phetes in-   maner testifie , not only the wickednes of idolatrie,
veigh against   but also of al superstition. [Thou hast hated them (o   *Ps.*30.*v.*7.
al Magique, &   God, saith Dauid) that obserue vanities : But I haue
superstition,   hoped in our Lord] The spirite of Ægypt shal be
broken in the bowels therof (saith our Lord by his
Prophete Isaias) and I wil ouerthrow their counsel   *Isa.*19.*v*3.
headlong: and they shal aske their idols, and their di-   4.
uiners, and pythons, and sooth sayers. And I wil deliuer Ægypt into the hand of cruel masters.] So our
Lord forewarned Ægypt. And to Babylon he said:
[These two thinges shal come to thee sudainly: Bar-   *ch.*47.*v.*9.
rennes, and widowhood. Al thinges are come vpon
thee, because of the multitude of thy sorcerers: and
for the vehement hardnes of thyne inchanters. Euil   *v.* 11.
shal come vpon thee, and thou shalt not know the rising therof: & calamitie shal fal violently vpon thee,
which thou canst not auoide: miserie shal come vpon
thee sudainly, which thou shalt not know. Stand (if   12,
thou canst) with thyne inchanters, and with the multitude of thy sorcerers, in which thou hast traueled
from thy youth, if perhaps it may profite thee any
thing,

13.

thing, or if thou maift become ftronger. Thou haft failed in the multitude of thy counfels : let the Aftro logers of the heauen ftand, and faue thee ; which did contemplate the ftarres, and count the monethes, that by them they might tel thinges, that shal come to

14.

thee. Behold they are become as ftubble, fire hath burut them, they shal not deliuer their foule from the hand of the flame] Againft which heathnish imagination of diuine powre in ftarres, or in imagies of

Iere 10.*v.*2. idols, the Prophete Ieremie alfo admonisheth the

3. faithful, faying [According to the wayes of the Gentiles learne not: and of the fignes of heauen, which the heathen feare, be not afraide : becaufe the lawes of

*ch.*27.*v.*9. fuch people are vaine. Heare not your Prophetes (which are not fent) nor diuiners, and dreamers, and footh fayers, and forcerers, that fay to you : you shal not ferue the king of Babylon] or fay any other thing, contrarie to that, which Gods true Prophetes teach

v 10. [Becaufe they prophecie lies vnto you] With thefe

*Mal.*3.*v* 5. admonitious of Ifaias, and Ieremie, agreeth the do-

*Eccli.*34.*v.*1. ctrine of an other diuine Preacher faying: [Vaine

2. hope, and lying is to a foolish man: and dreames extol the vnwife. As he that apprehendeth a shadow, and purfueth the winde; fo is he alfo that attendeth to

3. 5. lying vifions. According to this is the vifion of

6. dreames. Diuination of errour, and lying foothfayings, and the dreames of them, that doe euil, are

7. vanitie. Vnles it be a vifion fent forth from the Higheft, fet not thy hart vpon them. For dreames haue made manie to erre, & they that hoped in them haue failed.]

*Gen.*37.*v.*6. 5. Neuertheles fome dreames are of Gods infpira-

9.10 tion As in Iofeph the fonne of Iacob; whofe dreames

*ch.*40.*v* 12. were fignificant, forefhewing what should happen to

13.18. him, and his brethren. He alfo had the gift to in-

ch 41.*v.* 16. terprete the dreames of two Eunuches, and of King

15. Pharao. Daniel the Prophete had the fame gift, and

L 2 inter-

And efpecially againft falfe Prophetes.

Some dreames are approued by holie Scripture.

interpreted the dreames of King Nabuchodonofor. Mardocheus had a dreame fignifying what should come to paffe, concerning Quene Efther, & himfelf, and Aman, and the people in captiuitie. Likewife Iudas Machabeus had a comfortable true dreame: wherby himfelf, & the good people were encoreged to procede in battle, againft their enimies. And Iofeph the holie fpous of the moft bleffed Virgine, Mother of God, was diuers times inftructed by dreames in his flepe, what he should doe. Brefely manie Prophetes, and other holie perfons (amongft others S. Paul the Apoftle) had reuelations from God in flepe, shewing to them, Gods fecrete wil. And by his Prophete Ioel, our Lord faith [I wil powre out my fpirite vpon al flesh: and your fonnes, and your daughters shal pro-phecie; your ancients shal dreame dreames, and your youngmen shal fee vifions. Yea & vpon my feruants, and hand maides, in thofe dayes wil I powre out my fpirite. And I wil geue wonders in heauen, and in earth, bloud, & fire, & vapour of fmoke] Also ominous fpeaches are fometimes from God, importing true prefages. As Abrahams feruant had a fpecial, and true inftinct, what wordes should be vttered vnto him, by Rebecca, the maide, whom God had ordained to be the wife of Ifaac. And [by certaine wordes of the Philiftians, Ionathas knew, that he should preuaile againft them. By a Madianites dreame, Gedeon was encoreged to fight againft the enimies, & ouerthrew them.] But more generally obferuation of dreames, and of ominous fpeaches, and of obfcure vifions, is fuperfticious, and vnlawful. And therfore not to be credited, without approbation of holie Scripture; or of the Church, and ordinarie Paftors therof.

6. For it is a moft dangerous thing left the diuel (who ean transforme himfelf, into an Angel of light, and neuer ceafeth, like a roaring lion, feeking whom he may deuour) may at anie time delude the vnwarie, &

by futtle

Margin notes (right):
Dan.2.v.19.
ch.4.v.16.
17.
Efth 11 v.2.
2.Mach.15.
v 12.
Mat.1 v.
20.
ch.2.v 13.
Act 2.v.16.
&c.
Ioel.2.v.28.

Gen.24.v.
14 18.19.
1.Reg.14.v.
9.10.

Iudic.7.v.9.
13.15.20.22.

2.Cor.11.v.
14.
1.Pet.5.v.8.

Margin notes (left):
Likewife fome ominous fpea-ches,

Ordinariely dreames are not to be re-garded: fur-ther then the Church ap-proueth in particular.

by futtle pretended holines, intangle them in his fnares. And therfore his malice confidered, together with his craft, al true faithful Chriftians muft, euen as we are bond to thinke the beft we may, of other mortal men, fo muft we iudge the worft of the diuel: becaufe he alwayes meaneth mifchefe, and endeuoreth to worke mans ruine. And it is fo execrable a crime, to haue dealing, or conuerfation with the diuel, that Chrift our Sauiour (for our inftruction) fuffered not the diuel, to tel the truth [but threatned him, faying: Hold thy peace: and goe out of the man.] The Pharifees alfo knowing it to be a moft enormious finne, to deale with the diuel, and by his meanes to doe that is otherwife good, did calumniate our B. Sauiour therwith, faying [This felow cafteth not out diuels, but in Beelzebub, the prince of the diuels] At an other time they faid [that he had a diuel, & that they knew that he had a diuel.] Then the which, nothing could feme more opprobrious, nor more wicked among the better Iewes, And for that reafon, the fchifmatical Samaritanes, were the more hateful. For manie of them were feduced by diuelifh fuperftitions: in fo much that the Pharifees reprochfully ioyned thefe two falfe accufations together, faying [Thou art a Samaritane, and haft a diuel] S. Luke alfo writeth that amongft other feducers [A certaine man named Simon, a Magician, feducing the nation of the Samaritanes, was held to be a great one: vnto whó al harkened, frõ the leaft to the greateft, faying: This man is the powre of God, that is called great. And they were attét vpon him, becaufe a long time he had bewitched them, with his magical practifes] Some of thefe Magicians were alfo conuerfant among the heathen Pagaines. For [S. Paul with others coming to Paphos in Cypres, found there a certaine man, that was a Magician, a falfe Prophete, a Iew: who was with the Proconful Sergius Paulus, a wifeman: Which refifted them,

The diuel muft not be heard though he faith the truth.

Mar.1.v.25.

Mat.12.v.24.

Io.7.v.20.
Io.8.v.48.
52.
sh 10.v.20.

v. 48.

Act.8.v.9.
10.

11.

Act.13.v.6.7.
8.

feeking

seeking to auert the same Proconsul from the faith]
which sorcerer therfore S. Paul very sharpely reproued; and punished him with corporal blindnes: as he
was blinde before in his diabolical errour. In an
other place, in Macedonia he cast a pythonical spirite
out of a young woman, that brought great gaine to
her masters by diuining:whose testimonie S. Paul contemned, thought it was most true, that she said, and   *ch.16.v.16.*
proclamed him, and his folowes [to be the seruants   17.
of the High God, and that they preached the way of
saluation] because the diuel spake in her. who is in
no case to be heard, whether he speake truly or fal-
sely. S. Paul further warneth al Christians, that [An-   *2.Thes.2.v.*

Antichrist shal
doe strange
thinges, but
not anie true
miracle.

tichrists coming is according to the operation of Sa-   9.10.
tan, in al powre, and lying signes and wonders:and in
al seducing of iniquitie,to them that perish]Of which
sorte of people S. Iohn likewise prophecieth in his
Apocalypse, saying: [they adored the dragon, which   *Apoc.13.v.*
gaue powre to the beast, and they adored the beast,   4.11.
saying: who is like to the beast? and who shal be able   12.
to fight with it? And an other beast did al the powre
of the former beast, in his sight: & he made the earth,   13.
and the inhabitants therof, to adore the first beast,   14.
whose wound of death was cured. And he did manie
signes, so that he made also fire to come downe from   15.
heauen vnto the earth, in the sight of men.And he se-
duceth the inhabitants on the earth, through the
signes which were geuen him to doe,in the sight of
the beast: saying that they should make the image of
the beast, which hath the stroke of the sword, and liued. And it was geuen him to gene spirite to the image
of the beast: and that the image of the beast should
speake] Finally amongst other heynous sinners: Sor-   *ch.21.v.8.*
cerers, and Idolaters, and al execrable liars, shal be
damned in the poole burning with fire & brinstone:
which is the second death.]

Al are

Al are bond to honour holie Angels : and other Sainsts. And to reuerence holie Reliques, and Images.

ARTICLE 9.

Touching the falfe imputation of Idolatrie, wherwith Proteftants charge Catholiques, for the honour which we doe to glorious Sainctes, and their Reliques and Images, the Chriftian reader may pleafe to fee the Annotations vpon the twentith Chapter of Exodus, in the Catholique Edition of the English Bible: where our Aduerfaries calumnious fclander is brefely confuted, in three refpectes. Firft in that they belie Catholiques; vntruly charging them to gene diuine honour to creatures, which is falfe. As may appeare in al Catholique Bookes, & Inftructions concerning this point. Which clearly teach, that diuine honour called *Latria,* is due to God onlie: & that ciuil honour is due to humane, and temporal excellencie: and a midle honour called *Dulia* (which is infinitely leffe then diuine, yet greater then ciuil) is due to holie Angels, and other Sainctes: as Gods efpecial feruants: and to holie Reliques, and Images, as to thinges perteyning to glorified Sainctes. But to Chrift himfelf as God, our Lord, and Creator, diuine honour is due, and is religiouſly geuen vnto him. Secondly Proteftants bewray their falfe accufation of Catholiques, by corrupt tranflation of the Hebrew word *Pefel,* into a grauen Image, reftrayning the general fignification (which is in Latine *sculptile,* in English, *a grauen thing*) to ferue their owne purpofe, againft Images in particular. Wheras it is manifeft, that al grauen thinges are not vnlawful, nor forbidde by Gods commandment, but only fuch grauen thinges,

and

see Part. 2.
Article 24.
§. 1.

3. Reg. 6. 7.
23. 27. 29. 32.
35.

Proteftants falfely charge Catholiques to gene diuine honour to Sainctes & to other creatures.

English Proteftants corrupt the facred text in their tranflation.

and such similitudes of thinges, in heauen aboue, or
in the earth beneth, or in the waters vnder the earth,
are forbidde to be made, or kept, which men doe
adore, and serue with diuine honour, as goddes. And
so the Seuentie two Interpreters (singularly inspired
by the Holie Ghost) translate the Hebrew word *Pesel*,
into εἰδωλον, in Greke. Which is in English, *an Idol*.
According to which Greke text, we should translate
thus [Thou shalt not make to thee an Idol.] But because the Latine hath *sculptile*. We say in English *a
grauen thing*. Which is a true and sincere translation,
leaning it to be discussed, what graue thing is forbid,
seing it is cleare by other holie Scriptures, that al
grauen thinges are not forbid. And the Protestants
translation is corrupt and partial, abridging the sense
to Image, which word is not here expressed. Thirdly
the Protestants accusation is also false: in that they
say: Catholiques cut of one of the tenne commandments: because we adioyne the prohibition of making
a grauen thing to be adored, in the same commandment, with the former wordes [Thou shalt not haue
strange goddes] Which the Protestants say, are two
distinct commandments: vainly contending about the
maner of diuiding al the commandments into tenne:
which is no matter of faith, seing we agree vpon the
number, and acknowledge al the wordes. Yet that
our maner is more conuenient, we yeld this reason.
Because to geue diuine honour to the Image of a
Sainct, or to the Sainct himself, were manifest idolatrie: and were to worshippe a strange God, and so
perteyneth to the prohibition of the first commandment, as an explanation therof: & is not distinct from
it in sense, and substance. But the prohibition of internal consent to carnal concupiscence of the flesh, is
really as distinct, from the prohibition of internal
consent, to vnlawful concupiscence of wordlie
goodes, as the external act of theft, is distinct from
the

*Exo.25.v.18.
3.Reg.6.v.
23.
ch 7.v.28.
35.&c.*

*Exo.34.v.
28.
Deut.4.v.13.
ch.16.v.4.*

Againe they
calumniate
Catholiques,
And ignorātly
contend, that
to worshippe
an idol, and to
worshipe a
Sainct for God
are distinct
kindes of ido-
latrie.

the external act of adultrie. And therfore we doe
more rightly count these two prohibitions of internal concupiscences, of the flesh, and of temporal
goodes, to be two commandments(the ninth,and the
tenth) then others doe ioyne them, in one command-
ment:and to make vp the number of tene, doe diuide
the first into two: which we hold to be but one.

2. Larger Apologie needeth not,to cleare Catholiques from imputatió of idolatrie,falsly obiected vnto
them, for honoring holie Angels, and other Sainctes,
and holie Reliques, & Images,or other holie thinges,
perteyning to Gods seruice.Al which is proued both
to be lawful,and a necessarie dutie of al faithful Christians,by manie holie Scriptures.Wherof we shal here
recite a competent number. And first in regard that
holie Angels, by their ministrie and prayers, doe protect & helpe vs mortal men (as it is proued in the first
part of this Booke) we are mutually bond,not only to
loue them, though in farre lower degree vnder God,
but also to honour them,though with an other kinde
of honour, then that wherwith we loue and honour
God aboue al. So Abraham adored the Angels,which
appeared to him in Mambre.Moyses was bid to loose
his shoes from his feete : because the place was holie.
Iosue being newly entred , with the people of Israel,
into the land of Chanaan, which they were to conquere: seeing a man standing against him,with a
drawne sword,went to him, and (after a few wordes
passed betwixt them) knowing him to be an Angel
[a prince of the host of our Lord : fel flatte on
the ground . And adoring said : what speaketh
my Lord to his seruant? Loose, saith he, thy shoe
from thy feete: for the place, wherein thou doest
stand is holie. And Iosue did as it was commanded
him.] Where you see that Abraham adored Angels,
Moyses honored an holie place. Iosue honored an

M　　　　　Angel

Part.I.
Art.12.

Gen.18.v2.
Exo.3.v.5.

Iosue.5.v.13.

v.14.

15.

16.

Honoring of Sainctes,and other holie things is proued by the holie Scripture,

Abraham, Moyses and Iosue honored Angels.

Angel [a Prince of the hoſt of our Lord] with adoration, falling flat on the ground, and put of his shoes,
in reſpect of the holines of the place, where the Angel
appeared. Which honour muſt needes be diſtinct fró
ciuil honour, as being ſpiritual, and yet much leſſe, &
of an other kinde, then diuine honour. Manue alſo a
faithful ſeruant of God (the father of Samſon) vnderſtanding by an Angel, that he should haue a ſonne: &
being inſtructed that the childe should be a Nazareite, and should doe wonderful thinges, deſired to
honour him (in caſe his ſpeach should proue true)
eſteming him as Gods meſſenger, that repreſented
God. According to that which God had commanded
the whole people of Iſrael [to obſerue the Angel
(whom he would ſend) to heare his voice, and not
contemne him] Likewiſe Daniel the Prophete receiuing manie comfortable inſtructions, and reuelations
from God, by S. Gabriel the Archangel, for reueréce
ſake, ſometimes [lay proſtrate on the ground, ſometime ſtood, ſometime looked downe to the ground,
afterwards receiuing ſtrength, he ſaid to the Angel:
Speake my Lord, becauſe thou haſt ſtrengthned me]
In like maner Zacharias, with ſpecial reuerence, ſpake
to the Angel, which he ſaw in a viſion, ſaying. [What
are theſe, my Lord?] So diuers other Prophetes, in
wordes & behaniour, honored holie Angels, as Gods
meſſengers, and glorious ſeruants. Al which honour
redounded to Gods more honour.

3. Which If Proteſtants would conſider, they muſt
nedes be aſhamed to denie, that anie religious honour is due to holie Angels, or to accuſe Catholiques,
that they geue diuine honour to Angels, and other
Sainctes. But ſo contencious they are, in holding their
owne errours, and ſo great is their ſplene againſt vs,
that rather then they wil confeſſe the true diſtinction
of the honour due to God, and the honour due to
his holie, and glorious ſeruants, they ſtick not to

accuſe,

So ded other ſeruants, and Prophetes of God.

Iudic.13.v. 3.5.

v.16.17.21. 23.

Exo.23 v. 20.21.

Dan.9.v.21. ch.10.1.5 8. 15.19.&c. Zach.1.v.8. 9.&c. Iob.33 v.23.

Apoc. 19. v.
10.
ch. 22. v. 8.
accuse, euen S. Iohn himselfe, of idolatrie : not only Protestants
once, which is very absurde, but also the second time blasphemously
(which is more insolent impudencie)after that he had accuse S. Iohn
bene warned before (as they falsely imagine)of a fault the Apostle to
in adoring the Angel. Wheras it is certaine, that the haue commit-
Blessed Apostle in this fact, committed no fault at al. ted idolatrie,
For whether he erred in the person, thinking the
Angel to be Christ our Lord, and so honored him as
God, with diuine honour, it was no idolatrie ; being
onlie an errour in fact, not in iudgement, and wil (as
if one thinking some noble mā to be the King, should
knele to him, as to the King; it were in dede no trea-
son, because he had no cogitation, nor wil to make
that subiect, his King) Or that S. Iohn honored the
Angel, as an Angel with other inferiour honour, due
to an holie Angel; so it was right, and lawful: notwithstanding, the Angel refused it; in regard of S.
Iohns like excellencie, being also a great seruant of
Christ: manie wayes most deare to God, and renowmed in the Christian Church: an Apostle, an Euangelist: a Prophete, and a perpetual Virgin. As the same
Angel affirmed, saying [I am thy felow seruant, and
of thy brethren, that haue the testimonie of IESVS.]
And so shewed himself by his wordes, highly to
esteme of S. Iohn, and the other Apostles, and Prophetes, which had so great a function, to testifie in the
world, that IESVS is Christ: and that he, and the rest;
must stil, and aboue al [adore God] to witte, with
diuine honour. Which nothing hindereth, but that an
other kinde of honour is due, and is to be geuen to
Gods seruāts. Yea Christ said to the Angel or Bishope
Apoc. 3. v.
9.
of Philadelphia [Behold I wil make them (thy diso-
bedient subiectes) come, and adore before thy feete:
and they shal know that I haue loued thee.]
Sec. Part. 4.
Art. 44.
4. Albeit therfore this which is said, concerning
honour of holie Angels, might suffice touching other
glorious Sainctes: yet the same is further proued by

M 2 other

other holie Scriptures: besides the expresse general Mat.21.v.
testimonie, and promise of Christ, that Sainctes of 30.

Other glo- humane kind [shal be like to the Angels of God, in Luc. 20.v.
rious Sainctes heauen. And equal to Angels] it is necessarily deduced 36.
are like and from the examples of faithful people in the old Te-
equal to An- stament, who as they honored holie Angels, so did
gels. they also honour their Patriarches, by making, and
reuerently keping memories of them. To this pur-

Moyses hono- pose [Moyses erected twelue Titles (pillars) accor- Exo.24.v.4.
red, and taught ding to the twelue tribes of Israel] for honorable me- ch 28.v.9.
the people to morie of the twelue sonnes of Iacob. He caused also 10.12.
honour the fa- the names of the same children of Israel, to be grauen
thers of the in two onix stones: six names in one stone, and the
twelue tribes. other six in the other, according to the order of their
natiuitie: and put them on both sides of the Ephod (a
sacred ornament, which the High priest bare on his
shoulders) a memorial for the children of Israel] To
the same purpose, Iosue caused twelue men, one of
euerie tribe, to carie twelue great stones, out of Iordan, and to set them vp for a memorie of the miraculous passage through the drie chanel of Iordan [ac- Iosue 4.v.4.
And Abraham cording to the number of the children of Israel] The 5.6.7.
Isaac, & Iacob, honorable memorie of Abraham, Isaac, and Iacob,
their holie was most frequent in the mindes, and mouthes of al
progenitors. deuout Iewes, continuing to Christs time, with often
mention therof in the new Testament, sometimes also Apci.7.v.5.
of the twelue sonnes of Iacob: the heades of twelue 6.&c.
Tribes. There was also a special sepulcher made, and a
Title set vp in the honorable [memorie of that Prophete, which was sent from Ierusalem, to reproue Ie- 3 Reg 13.v.
roboam, for making an Altar of idolatrie in Bethel] 1.2.30.
The famous sepulchres also of Abraham, and his wife 4.Reg.23.v.
Sara, of Isaac, Rebecca, Iacob, Lia, Rachel, Ioseph, 17.18.
and others doe euidently testifie the special honour Gen.23.v.19.
done to such holie persons, after their departure from ch.49 v 31.
this world, in regard that they were more special true ch.50. v.24.
seruants of God. Exo 13.v.19.
Ios.24.v.32.
Heb.11.v.

5. Moreouer 22.

5. Moreouer in figure of the honour due to glorious Sainctes in heaué, holie perſons were alſo reſpectiuely honored in their tranſitorie life. A few examples may ſuffice for manie. [Abdias a noble man, gouernour of King Achabs houſe, meeting Elias the Prophete [fel on his face, and ſayd: Art not thou Elias?] This honour, in falling on his face, before the Prophete of God, was neither diuine; for Abdias was a true ſeruant of God, and [feared our Lord from his infancie] nor ciuil, and worldlie honour; for in the world, this Abdias was a farre greater perſon, then Elias (a hearie man girded about his reines with a girdle of lether) and therfore it was a diſtinct ſpiritual honour, neither diuine nor ciuil, called *Dulia:* due to ſpiritual holie perſons, and thinges. Likewiſe certaine religious diſciples, called [the children of the Prophetes, coming to mete Eliſeus, adored him, flatte to the ground] Amongſt the holie ornaments of the High prieſt, there was one called [The plate of ſacred veneration, wherin was written: The Holie of our Lord] Which when he did carie on his forehead [others did adore.] In the new Teſtament, not only the faithful people reuerently reſpected Sainct Iohn Baptiſt: but alſo [King Herod feared him, knowing him to be a iuſt, and holie man. And he heard him gladly] After Chriſts Aſcenſion, & apparition of two Angels, the Apoſtles [adoring went backe into Ieruſalem] The faithful people did ſo eſteme the Apoſtles that [bringing their goodes (to ſerue al in common) they laide the ſame, before the feete of the Apoſtles,] The religious Centurion Cornelius came to meete S. Peter, and falling at his feete, adored] which honour though S. Peter humbly refuſed, lifting him vp: & left Cornelius might thinke him to be more in nature thē a man, declared vnto him, ſaying [Ariſe, myſelf alſo am a man] yet Cornelius did no other thing, then was

M 3

conue-

Marginal notes:

3.Reg.18 v. v.12.

4.Reg.1.v.8.

4.Reg.2.v. 3.15.

Exo.39.v. 29.

Mat.3.v.4. 5. Mar.6.v.20.

Act.1.v.10. Luc.24.v. 52.

Act.4.v.35. ch.10. v.25. v.26.

Holie perſons were alſo honored in this life for their ſpiritual excellencie.

Cornelius rightly honored S. Peter.

conuenient, and lawful. For the ordinarie laipeople *ch 5.v.15.*
[durſt not ioyne themſelues vnto the Apoſtles : but
magnified them] And Chriſt our Lord ſaith, that he *Apoc.3.v.9.*
wil haue his Biſhopes to be honored . And promiſeth *Mat.10.v.*
reward to them that receue, & reſpect his Prophetes: 40.41.
Apoſtles, and other his iuſt ſeruants. And wil alſo reward al with ſuch difference of powre , and glorie as *Luc.19.v.*
their merites be diuers: ſhewing the ſame , by an ap- 17.19.

Different power is ge-uen to Saincts for diuerſitie of merites. parent parable of him [which by one pound gayning
tenne poundes, for his reward , received power ouer
tenne cities. And of an other , by one pound gayning
fiue poundes, who received power ouer fiue cities]In *Ioan 14.v.2.*
plaine termes, ſaith alſo [In my fathers houſe there
be manie manſions] S. Paul ſaith as clearly , that as *1.Cor.15.v.*
[ſtarre differeth from ſtarre in glorie : ſo alſo the re- 41.42.
ſurrection of the dead] Which future difference of
glorifird bodies, procedeth from the different glorie
of bleſſed ſoules. And therfore as honour is due to
excellencie: ſo is more honour due to more excellencie. Very great honour is due to the leaſt in the
kingdom of heauen, for [the leaſt there, is greater
then S. Iohn Baptiſt] was in earth . Moſt great ther- *Mat 11.v.*
fore is the honour , which is due to the ſame S. Iohn, 11.
and to al the Prophetes, Martyrs, and Apoſtles in
heauen. And moſt excellent to the moſt glorious Mother of God.

Honour of Reliques re-dundeth to the Sainctes, whoſe Re-liques they are. 6.   Concerning Reliques , and other thinges per- *Eccli. 44.v.*
teyning to Gods ſpecial ſeruants, and ſeruice; as the 1.2 &c.
ſame are memories , and viſible teſtimonies of holie
perſons ſanctitie, and glorious victories : ſo the ſame
victorious perſons, doe geue a reſpectiue ſanctitie to *Mat 23.v.*
thoſe memorable ſignes, and ſo are a ſpecial cauſe of 29.
deuout and honorable eſtimation, which the faithful
haue of ſuch places, and Reliquer. For who ſeing
the holie Sepulchre, where Chriſt our Sauiour was
buried , or anie other monument of his actions , *Iſa.11.v.10.*

and

and fufferings, wil not therby eleuate his mind to
pious cogitations ; to gratful memorie, to hartie
thankes, and interual defire to honour, and ferue
him, for fo merciful, and vnfpeakable benefites,
beftowed vpon mankinde? And fo in right proportion, by the memorie of anie Sainct, euerie faithful Chriftian wil be fturred vp to confider, to admire, to loue, and to defire, to imitate their vertues, to paffe by the way of good life, as they did,
that fo he may come to the like eternal reft & glorie,
where they are. Such memories were the fepulchres
aboue mentioned, of Abraham, and of other Patriarches, Prophetes, and holie perfons. Such a
memorie of a fingular benefite, was a part of the
Manna, kept as a Relique, of fo ftrange, and excellent meate, wherwith the whole people of Ifrael was
fedde, fourtie yeares together in the defert, which
was moft honorably [referued in a golden potte,
and kept in the Arke of the couenant, with the
rod of Aaron, and the tables of the teftament.
And ouer the fame holie Arke, were the Cherubins
of glorie, ouershadowing the propitiatorie] It is
recorded by the Euangelift for fingular great deuotion, proceding from a liuelie Faith, and firme
Hope, that [a ficke woman, preffing amiddes the
multitude, touched the hemme of our Sauiours gar-
ment] and the effect of her curing iuftified her religious cogitation, of fuch vertue in a corporal thing,
belonging to Chrift. Yet did our B. Sauiour fortel,
that greater workes fhould be done, then his owne
ordinarie cures, and miracles were. Fulfilled by
leffe Reliques, then was his owne garment: to witte
[by S. Peters fhadow, as he paffed by in the ftreate.
And by S. Paules napkins, or handkerchefs brought
from his bodie: By which both the ficke were
cured of their difeafies: and wicked fpirites were

The fhadow
of S. Peter, and
S. Paules hand
kercheefe
were reli-
gioufly efte-
med, the per-
fons being yet
mortal.

Mat.27.v.
60.
Ioan.19.v.
38.39.

§. 4.

Exo 16.v.
32.
Heb 9.v.4.
5.

Mat 9.v.
20.21.23.

Io.14.v.12.

Act 5.v.15.
16.
ch.19.v.12.

expelled

expelled from the bodies, which they possessed] He
therfore that shal thinke, there is lesse vertue in the
bodie, or part of the bodie, of S. Peter, or S. Paul, or
other glorious Martyr or other Sainct, or in S. Peters,
S. Paules, or other Saincts chaines, wherwith they
were bond, for professing Christ: or of other garment, or relique perteyning to them, who are now
glorious, then of their shadowes, or handkechefes,
whiles they were mortal, is not only incredulous, for
want in faith; but also without the ordinarie vnderstanding of a reasonable man: in that he not only
doubteth, or feareth that for his owne vnworthines,
or for other cause knowne to God, such a cure shal
not be done, by a holie Relique, with the prayer of
the Sainct, whose Relique it is, but absolutely denieth,
that it can so be done: in this doubtles he wanteth
faith, and without reason also, against experience, limiteth the power & wil of God, besides his base conceipt of glorious Sainctes: as if they either had not so
great fauour with God, or not so great charitie towards the faithful. Because a reasonable man wil consider, that Sainctes both are in high fauour with God,
& wish al good to the faithful in earth, and doe also
esteme of their owne bodies, ot ashes, which they shal
againe receiue in glorie: for [no man neglecteth his *Ephes* 5, 7.
owne flesh, but nourisheth, and cherisheth it] and 29.
consequently he loueth, & estemeth a Sainct, & also
must loue, and esteme the Relique, that perteyneth to
the same Sainct.

Images are 7.   Holie Images, which Turkes, and Caluinistes
clearly appro- impugne, as grosse idolatrie, are clearly approued by
ued by holie holie Scriptures. For God expresly commanded *Exo.25.7,*
Scriptures. Moyses [to make two Cherubims of beaten gold, 18. 19.
on both sides of the Oracle. Let one Cherub be on 20.
the one side, and the other on the other. Let them
couer both sides of the Propitiatorie, spreading
their

their winges, and couering the Oracle, and let them looke one towards the other; their faces turned vnto the Propitiatorie, wherwith the Arke is to be couered.] And so Moyses set vp two Images, represen- Cherubims. ting Angels, as they appeared inuisible shape (with faces and winges) for otherwise there can be no similitude framed of them, being pure spirits. Againe, vpõ special occasion, God also commanded Moyses [to make a brasen serpent, and to set it for a signe] which Brasen serpẽt. was an image of a serpent made of brasse, and was a remedie to cure the people, when anie were hurt by serpents. [He that being striken (saith our Lord) looketh on it, shal liue] This Image was also a figure of Christ our Sauiour, as himselfe interpreteth it, saying [As Moyses exalted the serpent in the desert: so must the Sonne of man be exalted: that euerie one, which beleeueth in him, perish not, but may haue life euerlasting] When King Salomon built the Temple, amongst other ornaments [he made in the oracle, two Cherubs of oliue trees, of ten cubites in height. And he put the Cherubs in the middes of the inner Temple. And al the walles of the Temple round about he engraued with diuers engrauings, and caruing: and he made in them Cherubs and Palme trees, Palme-trees, and diuers pictures; as it were standing out of the wal, and comming forth] And he set doores of oliue timber [the graued pictures of Cherubs, and figures of palme trees: and grauen workes standing out very much. Likewise, [the great brasen lauatorie (called a sea) stood vpon twelue oxen] that is, pictures of Oxen. oxen. [And betwene the litle crownes and plaites (which were about the lauar) were other pictures of lyons, and oxen, and cherubs. In the seelings also of the lauatorie, were grauen Cherubs, and lyons, and palme-trees.] Of what religious estimation, these Lions. Images were (at least some of thẽ, especially the Cherubims ouer the Oracle) is further proued, by Osee

N   the

Nums.21.
7, 8.

Ioan.3 v.
14.15.

3 Reg.6.
v 23.
27.
29.

32.
35.
Ch.7.v.25.
29.
v.36.

the Prophet. Who thus forshewed and lamented the

The want of images, lamēted amongſt principal loſſes. want of them, amongſt principal loſſes, ſaying [Manie daies ſhal the children of Iſrael ſitte, without King, & without Prince, ſacrifice, altar, ephod, and *theraphim*] that is, without Images. For ſo the Word *Theraphim*, ſignifyeth Images, good, or euil. But here being ioyned with King, Prince, Sacrifice, Altar, & Ephod muſtnedes import lawful Images; the want wherof is laméted.

Oſee.3. v. 4.
Gen 31. v 19.
1. Reg. 19.
v. 13.

The ſigne of the Croſſe and Crucifixe proued by figures thereof. 8. But becauſe amongſt al holie pictures, the ſigne of the Croſſe, and Crucifixe is eſpecially deſpiſed by Puritanes, and but coldly eſteemed of Proteſtāts, ſome particular holie Scriptures may be here repeted, by which this holie ſigne is prefigured, prophecied, and declared, to be honorable, cōfortable, & profitable, to Chriſts true ſeruants : And contrariwiſe hateful, terrible, and diſpleaſant to his enemies [The holie Patriarch Iacob, bleſſing the two ſonnes of Ioſeph, made the ſigne of a Croſſe with his armes.] Not by chance, not by errour, but wittingly to ſignifie two great Myſteries, beſides the firſt literalſenſe, that Ephraim being the yonger, ſhould be preferred before Manaſſes the elder. Which preeminćnce of the younger brother, did Prophetically prefigure, firſt that the Gentiles being Chriſts yonger people, ſhould excel his elder people, the Iewes, after that the Redemption of al mankind ſhould be made. And ſecondly, that this Redemption ſhould be performed, by Chriſt our Redeemer, his death vpō a Croſſe. [For whē Ioſeph had ſet his elder ſonne Manaſſes, before the right hand of Iacob, & Ephraim his younger ſonne, before Iacobs leſthand: Iacob not only laide his right hand vpon the yonger, & left vpon the elder, to ſignifie that the yonger ſhould excel the elder (which he might haue done, by cauſing thē to change their places, or by laying his right hand firſt vpō the one; & afterward vpō the other) but alſo to foreſignifie a further Myſterie of the Croſſe, with his armes, laying the one ouer the other. In which ſolemne action, neither the different reſpect of the right hau & left, nor the croſſing of his armes, was

Sec. Part. 1.
Arts: 2; §.
5. &c.

Gen 48. v.
13. 14. 17. 18.

with.

without myſterie. An other figure of our Redemptiō
by Chriſts death on the Croſſe, was by [the peece of
wood, which Moyſes caſt into bitter waters, which
made them ſwete] For ſo the wholſome wood of the
Croſſe, hath by Chriſt dying theron, made the bitter
ſea, to become ſwete. Moſt true it is, that Chriſt our
Sauiour, could haue redeemed vs, by any other maner
of death: yea & without death, by ſheding leaſt droppe
of blood, or leaſt meritorious actiō of his diuine Perſon in his Humanity: but his diuine prouidence ſo ordayned: that as the malicious enemie ouercame man,
by the fruit of a tree: ſo the ſame malignāt aduerſarie,
ſhould be ouercome, by Chriſt in his manhood, dying
vpon the tree. Moreouer of this ſigne of the Croſſe, & **By Prophecie.**
fruit therof is prophecied in Ezechiel, where [Our lord
ſaid to a certaine Scribe; Paſſe through the middes of
the citie, in the middes of Ieruſalem, & ſigne *thau* (the
letter T.) vpon the forheads of the men that mourne]
And then cōmanding to kil al others, ſaid [But euerie
one, vpō whom thou ſhalt ſee *thau*, kil not] which Hebrew letter *thau*, hath the forme of a Croſſe, as the
Greeke letter *Tau*, and our Latin *T*. And ſo it did foreſhew the Croſſe, on which Chriſt ſhould die: as now
the ſame ſigne doth repreſēt the ſame Croſſe, on which
Chriſt did dye Our Sauiour expreſſely fortold that he
[muſt be Crucified.] And that in the generall Iudgemēt;
the ſigne of the Sonne of man ſhal appeare in heauen] **It ſhal appeare**
What other ſigne is more propable to be meant, then **in the general**
this ſpecial Enſigne, or Cogniſcence of the Croſſe? in **Iudgement.**
which he deſtroyed death, ouerthrew the diuel, conquered the world, obtained glorie of his owne bodie,
& of al the elect? S. Paul contemplating this ſo excellent a Myſterie of Chriſt, dying on the Croſſe [iudged
himſelfe not to know anie thing, but Ieſus Chriſt, and
him crucified:] Againe declaring the ineſtimable honor
due to Chriſt our Redeemer, & to his moſt glorious
name I ᴇ s ᴠ s, teſtifyeth, that it is honored aboue al
names: becauſe [he hath humbled himſelfe, made

Exo.15.v.
25,

Gen.3.v 7.
11.

Ezech 9.v.
4.5 6.

Mat.20. v,
19.ch.24.
v.30.

1.Cor.2.v.2

Philip. 2.v.
7 8.9.

obedient vnto death : euen the death of the Croffe.]
Moft honorable therefore is this figne of the Croffe,
with al true Chriftians, and to them moft comfortable, though contrariwife it be wickedly defpifed, by
[the enemies of the Croffe of Chrift] Diuels, Here- *ch 3.v 18*
tikes, and Iewes. Thus much may here fuffice, becaufe
more of this particular figne is declared, in the firft *Art. 23.*
part of this worke. And concerning the Inuocation of *§ 5.6 7.*
holie Angels, and other glorious Saints, we remitte
you (courteous Reader) to the ende of the fourth
part, which is the proper place to declare, that it is
both lawful, and very profitable, to pray vnto Saints, *Artic. 41*
that they wil pray for vs to God, the giuer of al good *42 &c.*
things.

Prayers of
Saints, and to
Saints, is pro-
ued in the
fourth part.

An oath (vvhen iuft caufe requireth) muft be made by Gods name: or by fome creature, as depending on God.

ARTICLE 10.

Examples of
lawful oathes.

AS in other commandments, fo in this fecond, *Artic. 5*
befide the negatiue precept, forbidding vnlaw- *§ 3.*
ful oathes, is alfo conteyned an affirmatiue
precept to fweare, when iuft caufe requireth, in due
maner. Which we shal briefely declare by authentical
examples, and teftimonies of holie Scripture, and fo
procede to the other part. Abraham dwelling in Ge-
raris, the king of that countrie called Abimalech, making league of peace with him, in confirmation therof
required an oath, faying [Sweare therefore by God, *Gen. 21. 7.*
not to hurt me, and my pofteritie: and my ftocke. And *23.24.31.*
Abraham faid; I wil fweare. And fo boath did fweare.]
Abraham fending his feruant into Mefopotamia to
take a wife for his fonne Ifaac, faid vnto him [Put *ch.24.v.3.9.*
thy hand vnder my thigh, that I may abiure thee by
our

our Lord God of heauen and earth , that thou take not a wife for my fonne, of the daughters of the Chananites, amongft whom I dwel, but that thou goe vnto mine owne countrie, and kindred, and thence take a wife for my fonne Ifaac. The feruant therefore put *v. 9.* his hand vnder the thigh of Abraham his lord, and fware to him vpon this word.] After this , Ifaac and Abimelech making the like league , in confirmation *ch.16.v.28.* therof, [they fware one to another] Alfo Iacob requi-*31.* red an oath of his brother Efau [in confirmation of *ch.25.v.33.* *ch.42.v.15.* his yeelding his birth-right to Iacob.] Iofeph in afteueration of his wordes, fware [by the health of Pharao] as by a thing much defired by him, and depending vpon Gods prouidence. Rahab in Ieri-*Iof.2. v. 12.* cho lawfully reqnired an oath of the difcouerers, whom she afsifted, and deliuered from danger [and they fware] and performed their oath , by fauing her, and her familie, when others were deftroyed, and fpoyled.

2. It was alfo commanded by the written Law, that in fome cafes, the faithful muft fweare.   As in trial, whether one haue vniuftly done damage to an *Ex.22.v. 7.* other, or no? If a man (faith the law) commit money, or veffel to his friend to keepe, and they be ftollen a-*8.* waie from him, that receiued them: if the thiefe, be not knowne, the maifter of the houfe shal be brought to the goddes (to witte the Iudges) and shal fweare, *9.* that he did not extend his hand vpon his neighbours good, to doe anie fraud, and whatfoeuer may bring *v.10.* damage. If a man commit an affe, an oxe, a sheepe , or any beaft, to his neighbours cuftodie, and it die, or be hurt, or be taken of the enemies, & no man faw: there shal be an oath betwene them , that he did not put forth his hand, to his neighbours good: & the owner shal admit the oath: and he shal not be compelled to make reftitution] And the like is required in trial of other right, to decide the controuerfed caufe by an

The law dire-cteth to fweare by the name of God, not by falfe goddes.

oath

oath. And by an oath to confirme some promises of
special importance, as in the former examples, and *ch 33. v. 13.*
the like. Alwaies obseruing that it be made in due *Deut 6 v.13.*
maner. For [by the name of forren goddes, thou shalt *ch 10. v. 20.*
not sweare, thou shalt feare the Lord thy God, and
him onlie shalt thou serue: and by his name shalt thou
sweare. To him thou shalt cleaue, and shalt sweare
in his name.] Whereby is shewed, that by a lawful
oath God is serued, honored, and his name sanctifyed;
and by the name of good things, as depending vpon
him, is a signe that we *cleaue vnto God.* And swearing
by false goddes, by wicked or vndecent things, is seruice to the diuel, and dishonour to God.

The Prophets
admonish the
faithful to
sweare in law-
ful maner, whē
iust cause re-
quireth.

3. In regard therefore, of the honour done to
God, by lawful oathes, the same are commended by *Psal. 62 v.*
the Royal Psalmist, and other Prophets [Al shal be *11. Psf 14. v.*
praised (saith Dauid) that sweare by our Lord.] He *1. 4.*
that sweareth to his neighbour, and deceiueth not,
shal dwel in the tabernacle of our Lord.] Isaias fore- *Isa. 19. v. 18*
shewing the conuersion of the Gentils to Christ, saith *ch 65. v. 16*
[In that day there shal be fiue cities in the land of
Ægypt, speaking the tongue of Chanaan, and swearing by the Lord of Hosts. He that sweareth in the
earth, shal sweare by God. Ieremie saith [Thou shalt *Iere 4 v. 2.*
sweare: Our Lord liueth: thy children haue forsaken *ch. 5. v. 7. ch.*
me, and sweare by them that are not goddes. If being *12 v. 16.*
taught, they will not learne the waies of my people,
that they sweare in my name: Our Lord liueth.] Daniel describing Christ our Sauiour, as a man decla- *Dan. 12. v.*
ring how long his great aduersarie, should remaine, *6. 7.*
saith, that [he swore by him which liueth for euer, that
vnto the time, and times, and the halfe of a time.] *Amos. 8. v.*
Amos condemneth those [that swoare by the sinne *14.*
of Samaria, saying: Thy God of Dan liueth: and the
way of Bersebee liueth] And Sophonias no lesse condemneth those, that ioyning God, and the diuel together

Soph 1.ⱴ 5. gether [sweare by our Lord, and sweare by Melchom.]

5. Our Sauiour, and his Apostles teach the same,
that lawful othes made by the name of God, or good Chrift and his
Mat 23 ⱴ.
20 21.22. things, perteyning to God, are to his honour. [He that Apoftles teach
sweareth by the Altar, (saith Christ) sweareth by it, the same.
and by al things that are vpō it. And whosoeuer shal
sweare by the Temple, sweareth by it, & by him that
dwelleth in it. And he that sweareth by the heauen,
sweareth by the throne of God, & by him that sitteth
therein] S. Paul sweareth often in confirmation of
Rom.1. ⱴ. 9.
10 ch 9.ⱴ.1.
2
2 *Cor*,1.ⱴ.
23. truth, saying to the Romanes [God is my witnes, whō
I serue, that without intermission, I haue a memorie of
you, alwaies in my prayers.] To the Corinthians, touching his not returning to them, according to his promise, or purpose, he saith, [I cal God to witnes vpon
my soule, that sparing you, I came not any more to
Phil.1. ⱴ. 8. Corinth] Of his great affection towards the Philipiās,
he saith [God is my witnes, how I couet you al, in the
bowels of Iesus Christ] In defence of himself, he saith
1 *Thef*.2. ⱴ.
5.10. to the Thessalonians [Neither haue we bene at anie
time in the Word of adulation, as you know, nor in
occasion of auarice, God is witnes] His doctrine also
Hæb 6.ⱴ.16. is cleare, writing thus to the Hebrewes [Men sweare
by a greater then themselues, and the end of al their
controuersie, for a confirmation, is an oath] Yea, an
oath is so religious, & so important an act before God,
that amongst other profes of Chrifts most excellent
Priesthood, according to the order of Melchisedec,
ea.7.ⱴ.20.
21. aboue Leuitical Priesthood, of the Order of Aaron,
the Apostle vrgeth this difference, that [The other
truly without an oath, were made Priests: but this
with an oath: by God, that said vnto him : Our
Pf.109. Lord hath sworne, and it shal not repent him, thou art
a Priest for euer, according to the Order of Melchisedec.] The same Apostle further affirming that [God
because

because he had none greater, by whom he might
fweare, he fware by himfelfe. For meaning more a-
boundly to fhew to the hearer of his promife, the ftabilitie of his counfel, he enterpofed an oath.] The Angel alfo whom S. Iohn faw [lifted vp his hand to heauen, and fware by him that liueth for euer and euer]
Al which, and innumerable other holie Scriptures,
teftifying that God doth fometime fweare, and alfo
approueth oathes, may abundantly fuffice againft
the franticke fantafie of Anabaptifts, denying anie
man to be lawfull at al.

ch.6.v.13.
17. Gen. 22.
v.16. &c.
Apoc.10.
v.6.

The Anaba-
ptifts obie-
ctions are fol-
ued.

5. Whofe arguments are drawne from fome words
of the holie Scripture, efpecially thefe of our Sauiour [I fay to you, not to fweare at al; neither by heauen, becaufe it is the throne of God: neither by the
earth, becaufe it is the footeftoole of his feete: neither by Ierufalem, becaufe it is the citie of the great
King: neither fhalt thou fweare by thy head, becaufe
thou canft not make one heare white, or blacke. But
let your talke be: Yea, yea: No, no: and that which is
ouer, and aboue thefe, is of euil] S. Iames repeating
the fame precept, faith in like maner [Before al things,
my brethren, fweare not: neither by heauen, nor by
earth: nor other oath whatfoeuer. But let your talke
be: Yea, yea: No, no: that you fal not vnder iudge-
ment] Therefore, fay the Anabaptifts, and fome Puritanes, A Chriftian muft not fweare at al. For anfwere to this obiectio, & better vnderftading of thefe
wordes. We muft remember and confider, that euerie
worde in holie Scripture is true, and no contradiction
can be in al the whole Bible, being al infpired by the
Holie Ghoft. And therfore al muft be fo vnderftood
and explained, that al be verified. And when fome
wordes feme contrarie to others, by conference of
al, the truth muft be fought. The examples, and teftimonies before recited make euident proofe, that
fome oathes haue bene, and may be lawfully made:

Mat.5 v.34.
35,36.
37.

Iac.5.v.12.

yea

yea in fome cafes are neceffarie. And it is impoffible by anie gloffes or interpretations to verifie fo plaine wordes, if it were true, that no oath were lawful. But feing fome are lawful, how doth Chrift our Lord fay [Sweare not at al?] And why doth S. Iames fay [Sweare not anie oath whatfoeuer?] Their meaning, and true fenfe is gathered, by confidering the occafion of their fpeach, and admonition adioyned. Our Sauiour teacheth againft the Pharifees, that there is much finne committed by often fwearing, and by not rightly performing that which is promifed by oath. And Sainct Iames amógft other vifes particularly dehorteth from vnlawful oathes. But they both fpeake of fwearing in common talke and vfual conuerfation; as fufficiently appeareth by the laft wordes [let your talke be: Yea, yea; No, no.] They fpeake not in thofe places of trial in matters of right before Iudges; of confirming couenants, and leagues of peace betwen principal perfons: nor of affuring truthes in Chriftian doctrine, and of other great importance. For in fuch cafes oathes are requifite, lawful, and religious actes. As is before declared. Now we fhal further fhew. What oathes are vnlawful and forbidden.

It is forbidde to ſweare anie falſe thing: or vncertaine as certaine.

ARTICLE II.

Exo 20.v.

OVr Lord fpake thefe wordes [I am the Lord thy God: Thou fhalt not take the name of the Lord thy God in vaine.] In this general prohibition of not vainly vfing the holie name of God, which al are bód to honour, is neceffarily vnderftood, that Gods name muft not be vfurped to maintaine vntruth, which is farre worfe thé fimple vanitie. And therfore our Lord

O   in further

Abuse of Gods holie name is sinne, especially in vnlawful oathes.

further explication of this commandment, saith more expresly in an other place [Thou shalt not forsweare *Leuit.19.v.* thy self, in my name : nor pollute the name of thy 12. God. I the Lord] He also that knoweth, and concealeth an others periurie, is guiltie of the same crime [If a soule sinne (saith the Law) and heare the voice of *ch.5.v.1.* one swearing, & be witnes: because either he himself saw, or is priuie to it: vnles he vtter it, he shal beare his iniquitie. Let him doe penance for his sinne] Be-*v. 5.* sides which penance, before God, and the Church, if damage fel therby to others, the Law bond the periured person to restitution: with further recompence, thus ordayning [He that shal finde a thing lost, and *ch.6.v.3.* denying it, be also foresworne: he shal render al 5. thinges, which by fraude he would haue obtayned, whole, and the fifth part besides to the owner, vnto *v. 6.* whom he did the damage. And for his sinne he shal offer a ramme without spotte.]

Three special conditions are required in an oath, the first is Truth,

2. Ieremie the Prophete admonishing the people *Iere.4.v 2.* neuer to sweare by false goddes saith; [Thou shalt sweare. Our Lord liueth] And withal expresseth three special conditions necessarie in euerie oath: that it be [in truth: and in iudgement, and in iustice] which three are further explaned in other places, as we shal brefely note in distinct Articles. The first is the certaintie of truth, which is first to be regarded. For as lying is a foule, and reprochful sinne; so addition of an oath vpon a lie, calling God (who is truth it self) to testifie an vntruth, or an vncertaine thing as certaine, is very heynous and execrable, often exemplarly punished. (As in King Achab, Quene Iezabel, Alcimus the Apostata) And is alwayes dānable. Of this perni-*3.Reg.21v.* cious wickednes God warneth al by his Prophete Za-*10.19.&c.* cherias saying [These are the wordes (or thinges) *Zach.8.v.* which you shal doe: Speake ye truth, euerie one with *16.17.* his neighbour : truth and iudgement of peace, iudge ye in your gates. And thinke ye not euerie man in your

your hart euil againſt his freind: and lying oath loue ye not: for al theſe thinges are ſuch as I hate: ſaith the Lord.] The wiſeman inuening againſt Idolatrie noteth manie extreme [euils which procede from it, & tend vnto it, exemplifiing in periurie, as not the leaſt, for that Idolaters doe quickly fore ſweare theſelues, not only ſwearing by falſe goddes, but alſo ſwearing vniuſtly, in guile contemning iuſtice.]

3. Chriſt our Lord correcting the Phariſees doctrine, about ſwearing, approueth ſo much as they taught rightly, [Thou ſhalt not committe periurie] Which conſiſteth moſt comonly, either in ſwearing an vntruth, or in not performing that which is lawfully promiſed with an oath. Sainct Paul reciteth periurie amongſt greuous ſinnes, of manſlaughter, paricide, & the like. And ſeing euerie pernicious lyé, and falſe teſtimonie is great ſinne, as is proued by the holie Scriptures: it is much greater to auouch the ſame by an oath.

It is peruirie to ſweare an vntruth, or not to performe that which is lawfully promiſed with an oath. See Article 38.

It is likevviſe forbidde to ſvveare vvithout iuſt neceſſitie; of important cauſe.

ARTICLE 12.

AN other condition neceſſarily required in an oath (after the certaine truth of the thing which is ſworne) is [to ſweare in iudgement] as the Prophete admoniſheth, that is to ſay: Not raſhly, nor vnaduiſedly vpon bad cuſtome & for ſmal matter: but vpon iuſt neceſſitie, with good conſideration, and mature iudgement, when ſimple teſtimonie without an oath, ſufficeth not to gene aſſurance of the truth: and that the matter be alſo of good importance. For els the holie name of God muſt not be vſed, to teſtifie a ſmal, or needles thing, but when it may be to Gods more

The ſecond condition required in an oath is mature conſideration of important neceſſitie. Declared by the law of God.

O 2 honour

Sap.14.v.
25 28 29.
30.

Mat.5.v.
34.

1.Tim 1.v.9.
10.
Prou.21.v.
28.

Iere.4.v.2.

honour, the good of foules, & maintenance of truth, and equitie. And this condition is moſt expreſly declared in the fundamental Law of God, ſaying [Thou Exo.20.v. shalt not take the name of the Lord thy God, in vaine. 7. For the Lord wil not hold him innocẽt, that shal take the name of the Lord his God vanely.] Againe in the repetition of the ſame Law is ſignified, that in reſpeẽt of the Diuine Maieſtie (which in an oath is called to witnes) not only the thing which is ſworne muſt be true, and iuſt, but alſo of importance [Thou shalt not Deut.5.v vſurpe the name of the Lord thy God in vaine. For he 11. shal not be vnpunished, that taketh his name vpon a vaine thing] that is, vpon a ſmal, or needles thing.

Confirmed by other Scriptures.

2.   Moſt prudently doth Salomon admonish [not Prou.24.v. to be witnes without cauſe, againſt thy neighbour. 28. Haſt thou ſene a man ſwiſt to ſpeake? Follie is rather ch.29.v.20. to be hoped, then his amendment.] Much leſſe hope is of him, that is ſwift to ſweare. Wherupon an other Eccli.23 v.9, diuine Preacher warneth to abſtaine frõ rash oathes, 10. ſaying [Let not thy mouth be accuſtomed to ſwearing: for there be manie falles in it. Let not the naming of God be vſual in thy mouth: and meddle not with the names of ſainẽtes [in idle, or vaine talke] becauſe thou shalt not eſcape free from them. For as a ſeruant 11. dayly examined (often faultie) lacketh not the marke therof: ſo euerie one that ſweareth, and nameth (God or Sainẽt rashly) shal not be purged from al ſinne, for 12. a man that ſweareth much, shal be filled with iniquitie; & plague shal not depart from his houſe. And if he ſweare in vaine, he shal not be iuſtified: for his houſe shal be filled with retribution] He shal be pu· 14. nished as he deſerueth.

3.   Chriſt our Lord correẽteth (amongſt other ſinnes) rash and nedeles ſwearing [I ſay to you: not Mat.5.v.35. to ſweare at al] to witte, in common conuerſation 37.

without

without iuft caufe for that to be his meaning is euident, by his admonition adioyned, faying: [Let your
talke be, Yea, yea. No, no:] as is noted before, in
anfwer to the Anabaptiftes, who againft manie expreffe holie Scriptures, condemne al oathes whatfoeuer, which is a groffe errour. And the truth confifteth in the right meane, betwen both extremes. For
fometimes oathes are lawful, neceffarie, and religious
actes. But oathes vpon euerie fmal occafion, of careles
bad cuftom, rashly made in cómon talke, of paffion
or pride, are irreligious, & very greuous finnes. Neither can other idle refemblance of an oath be iuftly
excufed: as to fay: I wil fweare; or: I may fweare; when
in deede there is no fufficient caufe of fwearing: for
fuch fpeaches are in dede, more then Yea, yea: or. No,
no. And our Lord faith plainly [that which is ouer,
and aboue thefe, is of euil.] And fure fuch idle termes,
protefting that he may fweare, though he meane not
to fweare, is worfe then other ordinarie idle wordes
[for which alfo account muft be rendered in the day
of Iudgement] And euerie idle oath is fo much worfe
in proportion, then an idle word, or an officious
lie, as a pernicious oath is more greuous, then a
pernicious fimple word, or fimple lie. Remember therfore Chrifts, and his Apoftles admonition
[Not to fweare at al (in common vfual fpeach) But
let your talke be, Yea, yea: No, no: that you fal not
into iudgement.]

Marginal notes:
v. 37.
Artic. 10.
§ 5.

v. 37.

Mat. 12. v. 36.

Iac. 5. v. 12.

Rafh and idle oathes are có-demned by our Sauiour.

S. Iames ad-monifheth the fame.

O 3   *It is*

It is alſo forbidde to ſuueare, or to promiſe
vuith an oath, anie vnlavuful thing.
And is duble ſinne to performe
ſuch a promiſe.

ARTICLE 13.

Some thing may ſeme to be good or lawful, after long deliberation, which in dede is vnlawful.

To ſweare ſuch a thing is periurie, for lacke of iuſtice.

THe third ſpecial condition required in an oath, *Iere. 4. v. 2.* [is Iuſtice] that the thing which is ſworne be iuſt. For althrough i₂ be in it ſelf true, and long conſidered of, and doth ſeme to be ſo true, and maturely conſidered, that it appeareth neither falſe, nor raſh : yet if it be in dede vniuſt, or vnlawful, it is a pernicious oath. As if a man deliberatly thinking ſome thing to be his owne, which is not his owne, ſweareth that it is his owne : his oath appeareth neither falſe, becauſe he ſweareth not contrarie to his minde (which is properly called a lie) nor raſh, becauſe he thinketh long *Mentiri, eſt* vpon it, and then ſweareth wittingly : yet is this oath *contra mentem ire.* vnlawful, becauſe it is vpon an vniuſt chalenge, affirming that which in it ſelf is vniuſt. Likewiſe if vpon long deliberation, one purpoſeth to murder an other, & then ſweareth that he wil ſo doe : it is neither falſe becauſe in dede he ſo interdeth; nor ſemeth to be raſh, becauſe he doth not ſudainly, but debitately ſo reſolue : yet this oath is pernicious, becauſe it is vniuſt, and tendeth to wilful murder, already committed in the hart . And if it be alſo committed in act, is then a more greuous ſinne ; and moſt wicked of al, being perpetrated vpon pretéce of an oath : becauſe [Feaned *Simulata* ſanctitie is duble iniquitie] So it is one heynous crime *ſanctitas eſt* in ſwearing to doe a wicked thing : and a greater in *duplex iniquitas.* performing it.

    2.   In further declaration wherof, may be conſidered the differéce betwixt a ſinne cómitted in thought only,

only, and the same vttered in word; and afterwardes maintaned by an oath, and lastly put in practise in regard of the same oath. True it is that errour in opinion of anie thing, which we are bond to know, is a sinne, when the minde wittingly consenteth therto. [For peruerse cogitations separate from God] To vtter the same cogitation, as of a true, or good thing to make others to thinke, or doe the same, is a greater sinne, geuing scandal [for euil cōmunications (or speaches) corrupt good maners .] Further to auouch the same with an oath , is farre greater offence, because Gods name is vsurped, and called to testifie, a false or vniust thing. And therfore he that so sweareth a wicked, or false thing, [buildeth his sinne vpon Gods backe] Yea albeit he doth not sweare that the thing is true or iust, bnt only that he thinketh it so to be. Which is true, because in dede he so thinketh : yet his thought being erromous, it is a sinne, because it is in dede a false opinion, or vncertaine : and it is a wicked oath , because he ought not so to thinke , much lesse to auouch it in word, least of also to sweare . For the greater asseueration of an errour (or of an vncertaine thing as certaine) not only aggrauateth the sinne, making it worse, but also by reason of the oath, changeth the sinne into a worse kinde . That wheras at first it was an errour of iudgement in the hart only , and a scandal being spoken to draw others to the same opinion, it is grosse periurie , and sacrilegious abuse of Gods holie name, when it is protested and maintaned by an oath, that he thinketh it to be true : which he holdeth, being in deede either false , or vncertaine. Albeit therfore such an oath be not false , because he that sweareth, in dede thinketh as he sweareth ; nor properly rash, because he sweareth deliberatly : yet it is vniust, because it is an vniust asseueration. For example a Lutheran, a Zuinglian, or Caluinist, swearing that he thinketh, that Sacraments doe not remitte sinnes, as

inftrumental

An errour in thought is a sinne, the same mainteyned by word is a greater sinne, and mainteyned by an oath is the greatest of the three.

inſtrumental cauſes inſtituted to that effect by Chriſt, although he ſweare truly, becauſe in dede he ſo thinketh : and with how much ſo euer deliberation, he ſweareth wittingly, yet he ſweareth wickedly, becauſe the thing is falſe which he thinketh, and is a greuous ſinne of hereſie, ſo to thincke : and a greater ſinne of blaſphemie ſo to ſpeake : and greateſt ſinne of blaſphemous periurie, ſo to ſweare.

Examples of periurie, by ſwearing vnlawful things.

3.   Take alſo other examples, of thinges done, and recorded in holie Scripture. Thoſe Iewes offended greuouſly [which ſware, that they would take partie with the perſecutors of the good people (in the time of Eſdras and Nehemias) after their relaxation from the captiuitie in Babylon.   And ſinned more greuouſly, in adhering vnto the wicked, reporting odious thinges, againſt Nehemias.   Likewiſe King Herod greatly offended God [in ſwearing an vniuſt thing, that he would geue whatſoeuer the danſing damaſel should aske him; and much worſe in beheading the great Prophete, Chriſts Precurſor. S. Iohn Baptiſt, hypochritically pretending his oath.   And thoſe fourtie men ſinned very wickedly, which [conſpiring ſware, and vowed, that they would kil S. Paul] It was not a falſe oath, for they meant to doe, as they did ſweare, nor ſo raſh as obſtinate; for they earneſtly thought and reſolued vpon it, but was moſt wicked, and directly againſt Iuſtice, contriuing, conſpiring, vowing, and ſwearing to kil an innocent.

2. Eſd, 6.v. 18,19.

Mat.14.v.8. 9. Mar.6.v.19. 23.

Act.23.v.12 14,21.

Wittingly to breake a lavvful promiſe made vvith an oath, is periurie.

ARTICLE 14.

A lawful promiſarie oath bindeth in conſcience.

IN the written Law beſides the prohibition of ſwearing by falſe goddes, or anie thing falſly, rashly, or vniuſtly, it was commanded to performe
lawful

lawful promisarie oathes, and vowes: the breach
Levit.5. v.4. therof was punished, as great sinne [The soule that
5. sweareth, and vttereth with his lippes, that he would
doe either il, or wel (what lawful thing soeuer, dis-
pleasant or pleasant) and bindeth the same with an
oath, and his word, and hauing forgotten, afterwards
vnderstandeth his offence, let him doe penance for
his sinne.] Which holie text though some what obscure, sufficently proueth, that a lawful promisarie
Num. 30. oath must be performed. Which is further declared by
v. 3. these textes [If anie man make a vow to our Lord, &
bind himself by an oath, he shal not make his word
v. 4. frustrate, but al that he promised, he shal fulfil. If a
woman vow anie thing & bind her self with an oath,
she that is in her fathers house, and as yet in maidens
v. 5. age, if her father know the vow, that she promised,
and the oath wherwith she bond her soule, and hold
his peace, she shal be bond to the vow, whatsoeuer
she promised, and sware, she shal fulfil in dede] The
like concerning maried wemen, whose voluntarie
vowes, and oathes depended vpon their husbands
v.7.8. consent: but being once ratified, did bind the wife
in conscience, to performe them [The widow, and
v. 10. she that is deuorced, whatsoeuer they vow they shal
render.]

Ios.9. v. 3 4.   2. Iosue the Duke, and other Princes of Israel
14.15.16.18. [being deceiued by the Gabaonites, made a league
with them, and sware that they should not be
slaine. But three dayes after, they vnderstood
that they were circumuended, by the same Gabaonites, yet stroke them not, because the Princes
of the multitude had sworne in the name of our
Lord the God of Israel. The people murmured a-
gainst the Princes. Who answered: We haue sworne
to them, and therfore we may not touch them.
23. Iosue therfore (punishing them more lightly for
26.

Promisarie
oathes must be
performed in
things not
vnlawful,
though with
temporal da-
mage.

P   their

their deceipt) deliuered them from the hand of the children of Israel, that they should not be slaine, lest the wrath of God be stirred againt vs (said *v. 20.* the Princes) if we shal be forsworne] After this; eleuen tribes of Israel, vpon occasion of a crime committed, hauing sworne not to geue their daughters in Mariage to the children of Beniamin, though [They lamented, that they had sworne, they carefully kept their oath, and gane not anie of their daughters to the distressed tribe of Beniamin, being *Iudic.21, v.* almost extinguished] but found other meanes to *7.18.19.* repaire it. King Sedecias was iustly, and seuerely *&c.* punished for breach of his oath, reuolting from *4. Reg.24.v.* Nabuchodonosor, to whom he had sworne fide- *17 21.* litie, and true allegeance, [Our Lord saying (by *2, Pro.36.v.* his Prophete Ezechiel) shal he prosper, or gette *13.* saluation, that hath done these thinges? And he *Ezech 17.v* that broke the couenant shal he escape? Liue I, *13.15.16.* saith our Lord God, that in the place of the King, that made him King, whose oath he made frustrate, and brake the couenant: that he made with him: in the middes of Babylon shal he dye.] Of this sinne a diuine Preacher admonisheth [If a man *Eccli 23.* frustrate his oath, his sinne shal be vpon him: *v. 13.* and if he dissemble (by anie tergiuersation) he offendeth duble] in periuring and in excusing it, as a smal offence which in dede is great.

3. Euen Scribes, and Pharisees, whose iustice was in manie pointes defectiue, condemned the breach of oathes: teaching that [Thou shalt not *Mat.5.v.34.* committe periurie: but thou shalt performe thy oathes to our Lord] Which our Sauiour approuing added other pointes also requisite, and necessarie. As *Artic 12.* is declared before.   *§. 3.*

Blas-

Blafphemie is an enormious finne; iniurious to Diuine Maieftie.

ARTICLE 15.

BY lawful oathes God is honored, and by vnlaw- ful great wrong is done to his holie name. But by blafpemie Gods proper Maieftie is more contemned: by denying to him Power, Wifdom, Goodnes, Truth Iuftice, Mercie, or other Attributes: or by afcribing to him imperfections, weakenes, ignorance, malice falfehood, or tne like: or by detracting from his Church, his General fpoufe, by auouching anie vntruth, contrarie to true Religion. Which albeit none but the damned crew, of defperate mifcreants wil denie to be horrible crimes, yet for more edi- fication of the faithful, we shal here recite fome fpecial examples, and teftimonies of punifhing blafphemers, as wel againft God himfelfe, as againft his peculiar people, Church, and his cheefe fer- uants, whofe defpite redoundeth to the contempt of God.

2. A certaine man, whofe father was an Ægyp- tian, and his mother an Ifraelite, blafphemed the name of Ifrael (that is, of the whole people in ge- neral) and curfed it.] For whofe examplar punifh- ment [Our Lord faid to Moyfes: Bring forth the blafphemer, without the eampe, and let al that heard him, put their handes vpon his head, and let al the people ftone him] This man did not dire- ctly, and immediatly blafpheme God, but Gods people, yet was he punifhed with death. And vpon this occafion a Law was made touching al fortes of blafphemies, as iniurious to God himfelf, & his moft holie name, our Lord further faying to Moyfes [And

2. Pet. 2. v. 10. 12.

Leuit. 24. v. 10, 11. 13, 14.

Euerie falfe, & irreuerent af- fertion con- cerning God, or holie thinges is blafphemie.

Blafphemers were ftoned to death by the Law of Moyfes.

P 2　　　　to the

to the children of Israel thou shalt speake : The man v.15.
that curseth his God, shal beare his sinne, and he that
blasphemeth the name of our Lord, dying let him v.16.
dye : al the multitude of the people shal stone him :
Whether he be a natural , or a stranger . He that
blasphemeth the name of our Lord , dying let him
dye] The rebellious contempt, and the opprobrious
speach of Chore , Dathan , and Abiron , against Num.16 7.
Moyses and Aaron, saying: Why lift you vp your 1 2.
selues aboue the people of our Lord?] Was condemned and punished by the name of blasphemie :

Opprobrious
speach against
Gods princi-
pal Ministers
is blasphemie. Moyses saying to the people [You shal know that v 30.
they haue blasphemed our Lord] yet did not those
schismatical Rebelles directly speake blasphemie : a-
gainst God, but rather honorably of God, and of
the whole people, or multitude saying [let it suffice
you, that al the multitude consisteth of holie ones :
and our Lord is among them] Only they said to v.3.
Moyses, & Aaron [why lift you vp yourselues aboue
the people of our Lord.] And to Moyses in particular 13.
they said [why, is it a smal matter to thee , that thou
hast brought vs out of a land, that flowed with milke
and honie to kil vs in the desert, vnles thou rule also
like a Lord ouer vs:] So they murmured and ca-
luniated Moyses, and Aaron, vttering swete wordes
of our Lord, and of his people : yet Moyses said ,
and the euent proued, that [they had blaspemed our
Lord . For immediatly as Moyses ceased to speake, v.30.
the earth brake insunder vnder the rebelles feete, and
opening her mouth deuoured them, with their ta- 31,
bernacles , and al their substance ; and they went 32,
downe into hel quicke, couered with the ground, 33.
and perished out of the middes of the multitude]

Other exãples
of blasphemie. More directly against God in himself [Rabsaces a
Pagane captaine (in the name of the Asirians bele- 4.Reg.18.7.
ging Ierusalem) blasphemed God, comparing false 33.ch.19.7.
goddes with him, auouching that as false goddes had 10.11.12.7.
                                                   16. 22.
not,

not, nor could not defend, and deliuer their people:
so neither could God Almightie defend, and deliuer
Ierusalem, with King Ezechias & the faithful people
from the same Assirians armie] So did the Assirians
vpbraide and blasphemie the onlie liuing God, and in
one might, were slaine by an Angel of our Lord, an
hundred eightie fiue thousand Assirians: and their
King Sennacharib shortly after was murdered, by
his owne sonnes, whiles he was sacrificing to his
Idols [Baltassar King of Babylon with his thousand
Nobles, and his wiues, and concubines, drinking in
the holie vessels, which his father Nabuchodonosor
had taken away from the Temple of Ierusalem, and
praising their goddes of gold, and of Siluer, of Brasse,
Yron, Wood, and stone, was the same night slaine;
and the Medes and Persians possessed his kingdom.]
The cruel persecutor also of the Church Nicanor,
threatning swearing and saying [Vnles you wil deliuer Iudas Machabeas prisoner vnto me, I wil beate
downe this Temple of God to the flatte ground, and
I wil digge downe the Altar, and this Temple I wil
consecrate to Liber Pater : and for his blasphemous
bragging of his power in earth, as God is potent in
heauen, he was in the next conflict, slaine in the
middes of his armie . And then were his head,
hande and shoulder, cutte of and caried to Ierusalem; and his blasphemous tongue cutte out, and
geuen peecemeale to the birdes : and the hand of the
furious man hanged against the Temple.]

3.　Of such a swearing and cursing blasphemer,
holie Dauid denounceth sentence, saying : [He loued cursing, and it shal come vnto him : and he
would not blessing, and it shal be farre from
him.] An other example was King Herod Agrippa : who in the height of his pride, accepted of
the blasphemous flattrie of the people, accounting
him

Marginal notes (left):
v. 36.
37.

Dan 5. v. 2.
3. 4.

v. 30. 31.

2Mach 14. v.
32 33. ch. 15.
v. 5.
v. 28.
30.
33.

Psal. 108. v.
18.

Marginal note (right):
Condemned
by other holie
Scriptures.

him a God after his oration: they making to him this *Act.12.v.*
acclamation: The voices of a God, and not of a man. *21.22.23.*
And forthwith an Angel of our Lord ſtrooke him:be-
cauſe he had not geueu the honour to God:and being
conſumed with wormes, he gaue vp the ghoſt.

    4.   Finally S. Peter writing againſt certaine He- *2.Pet.2.v.*
retikes, riſen in his time noteth them with blaſphe- *10.*
mie, in that [they walking after the fleſh, in concupiſcence of vncleanneſſe, contemned dominion,

Eſpecially in
the new Teſta-
ment,
bold, pleaſing themſelues, they feare not to bring in
ſertes, blaſpheming. Theſe men (ſaith he) as vnrea- *v.12.*
ſonable beaſtes, naturally tending to the ſnare, and
into deſtruction, in thoſe thinges, which they know
not, blaſpheming, ſhal periſh in their corruption]
which obſeruation of the ſame blaſpheming Heretikes, S. Iude writeth almoſt in the ſame wordes,
ſaying [Theſe men, what thinges ſoeuer, certes they *Iude.v.10.*
are ignorant of, they blaſpheme: and what thinges
ſoeuer naturally, as dumme beaſtes, they know, in
thoſe they are corrupted.] Theſe, and al other Heretikes are moſt iuſtly charged with blaſphemie, in
that they vtter anie falſe doctrine, againſt true faith,
and religion, and there in are forerunners of the great
Antichriſt, of whom S. Iohn forewarneth, that [He *1 Ioan.2.v.*
ſhal come, and that now there are become manie an- *18.*
tichriſts] The great, and ſingular Antichriſt called
[The beaſt, (as S. Iohn ſaw in the viſion) hath vpon *Apoc.12.v.*
his ſeuen heades, the names of blaſphemie. And there *1.5.ch.17.v.*
was geuen to it, a mouth ſpeaking great thinges, and *3.*
blaſphemies: and power was geuen to it, to worke
two and fourtie monethes. And he opened his mouth
vnto blaſpemies, againſt God, to blaſpheme his name:
and his tabernacle, and thoſe that dwel in heauen]a-
gainſt the Church militant in earth, and glorious
Sainctes in heauen. And ſuch blaſphemers, ſhal blaſ- *ch.16.v.9.*
pheme perpetually [boiling with great heate.]

The

The Sabbath day vvas kept holie in the old Teſtament, by Gods ordinance.

ARTICLE 16.

A S wel by the forme of wordes, in expreſſing this precept, as a thing already in practiſe, ſaying: [Remember that thou ſanctifie the Sabbath day:] as alſo by the reaſon, why this Ceremonial precept was to be ſtil kept: [becauſe the ſeuenth day God ended his worke, which he had made, and reſted the ſeuenth day from al the worke which he had done] it appeareth that the ſeuenth day was by Tradition kept holie, from the beginning of the world. Neuertheles this Ceremonial precept, was expreſly repeted amongſt the Moral precepts, becauſe by the Law of nature it is required, that ſome ſpecial times, and dayes be aſſigned to Gods peculiar ſeruice, with reſt from other workes, though the deſignation of the ſeuenth day, rather then an other day, perteyned to a Ceremonie of the old Teſtament: as the eight day properly perteyneth to the new Teſtament. And ſo this precept of keping the ſeuenth day holie, was confirmed to the Iewes, with expreſſe explication, in what maner they ſhould kepe it, ſaying [Remember that thou ſanctifie the Sabbath day. Obſerue the Sabbath day, to ſanctifie it. Six dayes ſhalt thou worke, and ſhalt doe al thy workes. But on the ſeuenth day, is the Sabbath of the Lord thy God: thou ſhalt doe no Worke in it: thou and thy ſonne, and thy daughter, thy man ſeruant, and thy woman ſeruant, thy beaſt, and the ſtranger that is within thy gates. Moreouer this precept in the Law of Moyſes did ſtrictly forbidde, that [you ſhal not kindle fire in al your habitations, on the Sabbath day.] Neither was it lawful to bye, or ſel anie thing on the Sabbath day. As appeareth by the

practiſe

Exo 20.v.8. 11. *Gen.*2,v,2. 3.

*Exo.*20.v. 8.9. *Deut.*5.v. 12,13.14.

*Exo.*35.v.3.

2.*Eſd.*13.v. 15 &c.

The Sabbath day was kept holie by tradition before the Law was written.

It is ceremonial in reſpect of the day.

The obſeruation therof conſiſted in abſtayning from worke.

from captiuitie of Babylon . For then correcting errors whereinto they were fallen , amongst other thinges [they promifed not to bye anie thing in the Sabbath day.] And confequently not to fel . And in the Gofpel it is recorded that the deuout wemen [Marie Magdalene, and Marie of Iames, and Salome bought fpices, and ointments in the euening before the Sabbath: and on the Sabbath they refted , according to the commandment:& the next day very early, they came to the monumét, carying the fpices, which they had prepared,that they might annoint IESVS]To the celebration alfo of the Sabbath perteyned oblation of Sacrifices [On the day of the Sabbath (faith the Law) you shal offer two lambes of a yeare old, without blemish, and two tenthes of floure tempered with oile in Sacrifice; and the libaments . Which are ritely powred euerie Sabbath , for an euerlafting Holocauft.]

Mar.16. v.
1.2.
ouc.23.v 56.
ch.24.v.1.

And in offe-
ring Sacrifice.

Num. 28.
v. 9.
10.

Breach of the
Sabbath was
feuerely pu-
nifhed.

2.   The punishment for breaking this command ment was feuere[See that you kepe my Sabbath(faith our Lord) becaufe it is a figne betwen me and you, in your generations, that you may know, that I am the Lord, which fan&ifie you. Kepe you my Sabbath, for it is holie vnto you. He that shal pollute it,dying shal dye: he that shal doe worke in it, his foule shal perish out of the middes of his people . Six dayes shal you doe worke, in the feuenth day is the Sabbath, the holie reft to the Lord . Euerie one that shal doe anie worke in this day shal dye.] According to this Law [A man for gathering stickes on the Sabbath day, was prefented to Moyfes, and Aaron, and to the whole multitude . Who shutte him into prifon, not knowing (at firft) what they should doe with him. (For if it had bene ignorance , or vnwitting: then repentaing , and offering the appointed Sacrifice, the offender had bene pardoned: but being done of pride and contempt , he was flaine.) And

Exo.31.v.13.

14

15.

Num.15.v.
31.33 34.
v.22.27.28.

30.31.35.

our Lord said to Moyses: Dying let this man dye: let
al the multitude stone him without the campe. And
when they had brought him out, they stoned him, &
he dyed, as our Lord had commanded.]

3. Others were so obedient, and zelous in keeping
this precept, amongst the rest, that [whē king Antiochus, had made, and promulgated a most cruel Edict,
that al nations (vnder his dominion) should leaue
their owne Law: and prohibited Sacrifices to be offered in the Temple of God, the Sabbath to be celebrated, nor other solemne dayes: Manie cōming together to the next caues, secretly kept the day of the
Sabbath. And being discouered, were burnt with fire;
because they feared for Religion, and obseruance, to
helpe themselues with their hands] Againe [when manie were fled into the mountaines, the persecuters
pursuing them in the Sabbath day, said vnto them:
Come forth and doe according to the word of King
Antiochus, and you shal liue. They answered: We wil
not come forth; neither wil we doe the kings word,
to pollute the day of the Sabbaths. Then did the enimies hasten battle against them. And they answered
them not, neither did cast a stone at them, nor stopped the secrete place; but said: Let vs dye in our simplicitie: And heauen and earth shal be witnsses vpon
vs, that you vniustly destroy vs. And they gaue them
battel on the Sabbaths: and there dyed, they and their
wiues, and their children (and their cattel) euen to a
thousand soules of men] simple as doues, meeke as
Lambes among Wolues.

4. But after this [the residue said one to an other:
If we shal al doe, as our brethren haue done, and shal
not fight against the Heathen, for our liues, and our
Iustifications (our Lawes) now wil they quickly destroy vs, from the earth. And they thought in that
day, saying: [Euerie man whosoeuer shal come vnto
vs in battel, on the day of the Sabbaths, let vs fight

Q   against

*r.33.
36.*

*1.Mach.1.
r.43 47.48.*

*2 Mach. 6.
v.11.*

*1.Mach 2
v 28.29.32.
33.
34.
35.
36.
37.
38.*

*Ibidem v.
40.*

41.

The faithful
were very ze-
lous in kee-
ping the Sab-
bath.

A thousand
Martyrs dyed
in the simpli-
citie of doues.

Others as pru-
dent serpents,
defended the
Church from
ruine, by bat-
tle on the Sab-
both day.

against him : and we wil not al dye, as our brethren dyed in secret places] In like maner [Nicanor
(General Captaine of King Antiochus armie) with
al his violence, purposing to ioyne battel against Iudas Machabeus, on the day of the Sabbath; the Iewes
that folowed him saying: Doe not so fiercely and bar-
barously: but giue honour vnto the day of sanctification, and honour him, that beholdeth al thinges: that
vnhappie man asked: If there were a power in heauen, that commanded the Sabbath to be kept? And
they answering: There is the liuing Lord himselfe in
heauen; the Potent, that commanded the seuenth
day to be kept: But he said: And I am potent vpon the
earth, that commanded armes to be taken, and the
Kings affayres to be accomplished.] Which his Luciferian proud, and blasphemous contempt of the holie Sabbath, cōmanded by Almightie God, was forthwith reuenged (besids his eternal torments in hel)
with the death of the same Nicanor, and of thirtie
fiue thousand his folowers, in battel the same holie
day. His head, hand, and shoulder hanged vp nere to
the holie Temple: and his tongue geuen pecemeal to
the rauening birdes.] Thus was the seuenth day of
the weke, which is our Saturday, blessed, sactified, instituted, and obserued the Sabbath; that is, the day of
Holie rest, in the old Testament: from the beginning
of the world, til Christ our Lord.

2 Mach. 15.
v. 1.

2.

3.
4.

5.

7. 27.
28.
30.
35.

Chtiſtians are bound to kepe Sunday (called our Lords day) Holie ; not the Sabbath.

ARTICLE 17.

So far as the
obseruation of
the Sabbath

THe other nine commandments, being al Moral
precepts; doe no lesse binde Christians now,
then they did the Iewes in the Old testament. But this
commandment concerning the Sabbath, being in respect

spect of the seuenth day of the weke, a Ceremonial
precept is ended, and taken away by Christ. Neuertheles being also a Moral precept, in respect of some
one daie of euerie weke, to be kept holie, it continueth
stil: and is designed to the first day of the weke, made
holie, & properly called, Our Lords day. Which abro-
gation of the old Sabbath, is euidently proued by the
holie Scriptures: and from thence also the obligation
to kepe this new feast, is sufficiently deduced, though
not in expresse wordes.

4. Touching the former point of abrogating the old
Sabbath; it may be first obserued, that albeit the commandment was strict, & the punishmēt for transgressing it, was seuere: especially being done wittingly, &
of cōtempt: yet diuers workes were lawfully done in
the Sabbath day, for pious, and necessarie causes. So
[the beastes & birdes were killed on the Sabbath day,
which were then offered in Sacrifice. Children were
Circumcised on the Sabbath, if that were the eight
day of their birth. Mē might trauel by the way, a Sabbaths iourney: Cure the sicke: Draw a shepe, or an
oxe, or an asse out of a pitte: Loose thē frō the manger, and lead them to water.] Our Sauiour also defended his Disciples fact, when [the Pharises blamed thē
for plucking eares of corne on the Sabbath day] the
reason whereof in general he geueth, saying, [The Sabbath was made for man, & not man for the Sabbath]
Adding moreouer [Therfore the Sonne of mā is Lord
of the Sabbath also.] And at an other time [I tel you
(said he) that there is here a greater then the Temple]
insinuating that he would disanul the Sabbath, for
the greater good of man (for whom the Sabbath was
made) And so by the Lord of the Sabbath, and Sauí-
our of man, Christians are so deliuered from keping
the Sabbath, that they should greuously offend God;
by keeping it. As S. Paul declareth to the Christian
Colossians. Whom certaine false Apostles endeuoured

Q 2   to se-

Marginal notes:

was cereme-
nical, it is a-
brogated.

VVorkes of
pietie, and of
necessitie were
lawfully done
in the Sabbath.

Christ signi-
fied that Chri-
stians should
not keepe the
Sabbath day.

Num 28.
v 9. Gen 17.
v 12.
Act 1. v. 12.
Mat. 12. v.
1.5 &c.
Mar. 2. v. 23.
24.
Luc. 13. v.
14.15.16.
Io. 5. v. 9.11.
ch. 7. v. 22.
ch 9. v. 14.
16.

to feduce, pretending that they ought wholly to abftaine from certaine meates, and drinkes: and muft keepe feftiual dayes, according to the Law of Moyfes] The Apoftle therfore alleageth & vrgeth againft thofe feducers, the merite, and power of Chrift, in redeming man, and geuing a new better Law. And fo admonisheth al Chriftians, faying [Let no man therfore iudge you in meate, or in drinke, or in part of a feftiual day, or of the New moone, or of Sabbaths: which are a shadow of thinges to come: but the bodie is Chrifts] fignifying that Chrifts law, excelleth the old Law, as a bodie excelleth the shadow thereof.

Colef.2 v. 13.16.17. Leuit.23.v 3.

The caufes of keeping the Sabbath.

3. Now concerning the caufes, by which the difference wil better appeare, and efpecially by their effects: the old Sabbath was inftituted in memorie of the creation of al things, as it wete in fixe dayes of trauel, and of reft in the feuenth day. As Moyfes relateth the Hiftorie. And afterwards denounceth the Law, faying [The heauens and earth were fully finished, and al furniture of them. And God refted the feuenth day, and fanctifyed it, becaufe in it he hath ceafed from al his worke. The feuenth day, is the Sabbath of the Lord thy God; thou shalt doe no worke in it (Againe he faith) Let the children of Ifrael kepe the Sabbath, and celebrate it, in their generations. It is an euerlafting Couenant, betwen me, and the children of Ifrael; and a perpetual figne. For in fixe dayes the Lord made heauen and earth, and the fea, and al things that are in them, and refted the feuenth day: therfore the Lord bleffed the feuenth day, and fanctified it; becaufe in it he ceafed from al his worke.] This was the firft reafon, pertaining to al the feruants of God, from the beginning of the world. The fecond, perteining particularly to the people of Ifrael, was in grateful memorie of their deliuerie from feruitude in Ægypt. Wherof Moyfes faith to the fame people [Remember that thou alfo didft ferue in Ægypt: and

Gen. 2.v.1. 2 3.

Exod. 20: v 10. ch 31. v.16. 17.

Deut.5.v. 15.

the

the Lord thy God, brought thee out from thence, in a ſtrong hand, and ſtretched out arme. Therfore hath he commanded thee, that thou ſhouldeſt obſerue the Sabbath. But the cauſes & reaſons of inſtituting our Lords day, are farre greater. One is a perpetual memorie, of our happie Redemption, from ſeruitude of ſinne, and of Chriſts glorious victorie ouer death, which is perfected by his Reſurrection, the firſt day of the weke. An other cauſe, is an aſſured ſignification of the general Reſurrection of al mankinde, which ſhal be moſt glorious to the bleſſed, and elect: repreſented by the day after the Sabbath; in reſpect wherof, it is the eight day; and neuertheles the firſt day. For as the Sabbath was the ſeuenth of holie reſt, after trauel: ſo our Lords day, is the eight day, of eternal life and glorie, after both trauel and reſt. So it is both the firſt & the eight; the complement of glorie; not tranſitorie, but ſtil in prime, not waxing old, by proceſſe of time, but alwayes continuing in endles eternitie.

4. This therfore[is the day, which the Lord hath made: Let vs reioyce, and be glad therin]In this firſt day of Chriſts corporal glorie (for his bleſſed ſoule was alwayes glorious) our Redemer triumphed ouer death: he appeared in bodie (after his death and burial) to his B. Mother, and other holie ſeruants in that one day, ſeuen times. In this day of Our Lord (being the ſeuenth Octaue, and fiftith day from his Reſurrection [the Holie Ghoſt came in viſible ſignes vpon the faithful, repleniſhing them with his ſeuen gifte; of Wiſdome, Vnderſtanding, Counſel, Fortitude, Knowledge, Pietie, and Feare of our Lord] In this day (as recurring euerie eight day) S. Paul with other Apoſtolical men, and faithful people, more eſpecially [aſſembled together to Diuine Publique Sacrifice (which S. Luke calleth) Breaking of brea d] In this day the Chriſtians(namely at Corinth) vſually aſſembled, for the ſame ſolemne religious purpoſe.

Rom.6.v.5.
10.

1 Cor.15. v.
v 21.22,
1 Pet 3.v.
18,21.

See Part 1.
Ar.ic 26.

Pſal.117. v.
24.

Mat.28.
Mar.16.
Luc.24.
Ioan.20.

Act.2. v.1.
2.3.

Iſa.11.
Act.20,
v.7.
1.Cor.16.
v.2.

The cauſes of inſtituting our Lords day.

Other important reaſons, why the ſeuenth day is abrogated, & the eight day (which is alſo the firſt day of the weeke) is made the ordinarie Holie daye. And called OurLords day.

Al which being euident in the holie Scriptures, who shal doubt, but that al the Apostles, and other Apostolical first founders, and Pastors of the Christian Church, with their faithful flockes, obserued the same day sacred euerie weke, with holie solemnitie: Which being for some while, called [The first of the Sabbath] was shortly after, euen in the Apostles time, cōmonly called [Our Lords day. *Dies Dominica*]. As may be gathered by that S. Iohn thus beginneth to write his Reuelation [I was in Spirit (saith he) on the Dominical day.] Which apparantly semeth to be our weekely holie day, vulgarly called Sunday. And so by these authentike proofes, al good Christians hold themselues boūd to kepe this day holie, as ordained by Christ our Lord; & made knowne to vs, by Apostical Tradition.

Apoc. 16. 7. 10.

Prudence, and the vertues annexed, Right counsel, & Mature Iudgemēt, are necessarie.

ARTICLE 18.

The foure Cardinal vertues, with others annexed, are necessarie

AS to the obseruing of the commandments in the first table, conteining mans dutie towards God, are required the three Theological vertues, Faith, Hope, and Charitie; and Religion the most principal Moral vertue: so for obseruing the commandmēts of the second table, conteyning our dutie towards our neighbours, are required al the other moral vertues. Which are reduced to foure fundamental, called Cardinal, to wit, Prudence, Iustice, Fortitude, and Temperance. Which with the other vertues annexed, are proued to be necessarie by manie examples, and other instructions of holie Scriptures.

Rom. 13. v. 8. Gal. 5. v. 14.

Examples of true prudence in Abraham.

2. Prudence, which is the first, & consisteth in rightly discerning, & resoluing what to desire, & what to auoide; did eminētly appeare in Abraham [who going into Ægypt, prudently foresaw danger of his life: & to auoide the same, caused his wife Sara to say, that she

Gen 12. v. 12 13. ch. 20. v. 2.

was

was his fifter (which was indede true, according to the cómon vſe of ſpeaking amongſt the faithful, ſhe being otherwiſe his kinſwomā)Iacob fearing his brother Eſaus wrath, prudently diuided his people, and flockes into two troupes,ſaying:If[Eſau come to one troupe,and ſtrike it:the other troupe,that remaineth ſhal be ſaued]When Ioſeph told his dreames,his brethren ennying hᵒm [his father prudently conſidered the thing with himſelfe]The ſame Ioſeph being ſolicited to follie by his myſtreſſe[prudētly left his cloke in her hand, & fled frō her]In al his way[Dauid dealt wiſely,& our Lord was with him. Saul therfore ſaw, that he was exceding wiſe,& begā to beware of him.]

ch.37 v. 10. 11.ch.39. v.12. — Iacob.

1.Reg.18. v.14 15. — Ioſeph.

— Dauid.

3. My mouth ſhal ſpeake wiſdome (ſaid the ſame Dauid)& the meditation of my hart prudence.Aboue myne enemies thou (ô God)haſt made me wiſe, by thy commandements.Aboue al that taught me,haue I vnderſtood:Aboue Ancients,haue I vnderſtood:becauſe I haue ſought thy cōmandments] God alſo gaue wiſdome to Salomō,& prudence exceding much[If thou wilt learne wiſdome (ſaith the ſame Salomon)incline thyne hart to know prudence. Children attend that you may know prudence. Poſſeſſe wiſdome,poſſeſſe prudence : in al thy poſſeſſion purchaſe prudence. In the hart of the prudent,reſteth wiſdome:& it ſhal inſtruct al the vnlearned]Chriſt our Lord the eternal Increated Wiſdome,inſtructing his Apoſtles,& in them al Chriſtians,ſaith [Be ye wiſe as ſerpents,& ſimple as doues. And take hede of mé.For they wil deliuer you vp.And to Preſidents & Kings ſhal you be led for my ſake.He that ſhal perſeuere to the end,he ſhal be ſaued. And when they ſhal perſecute you in this citie, flee into another.]

Pſ.48.v.4. Pſ.118,v.98 99 100. 3.Reg.4. v 29. — Commendation of prudence,

Pro.2,v.2. ch.4.v 1.5. 7.ch.14.v. 33.

Mat.10.v. 16.17.18. 22.23.

4. Worldlie policie is reproued by manie holie Scriptures.Moyſes in his laſt Cāticle, taxing thē for manie faults,called thē [A nation without counſel, & without wiſdome: O that they were wiſe (ſaith he) and vnder-

Deut.32. v. 28.29. — Right counſel,

vnderſtood, and would prouide for their laſt] ſignifying, that prudent men doe conſider things paſt, vnderſtand thinges preſent; and prouide for thinges to
come: according to Right Counſel, & Mature Iudgement. Which are the ſpecial vertues, annexed to the
Cardinal Vertue of Prudence. Salomon teacheth the *Pro. 13. v. 16.*
ſame, ſaying, [The prudent (or warie man) doth al *ch. 14. v. 15.*
thinges with counſel. The diſcrete man conſidereth *16. 18.*
his ſteppes. A wiſe mã feareth & declineth from euil.
The childiſhman ſhal poſſeſſe follie, and the prudent
ſhal expect knowledge. There is no wiſdome, there *ch. 21. v. 30.*
is no prudence, there is no counſel againſt our Lord.
Woe to you (ſaith Iſaias) that are wiſe, in your owne *Iſ. 5 v. 21.*
eyes, and prudent before your ſelues. Conferre no
counſel with fooles (ſaith the Preacher) for they can *Eccli. 8. v.*
not loue but ſuch thinges as pleaſe them (that is, *20.*
worldlie men, taiſt not ſpiritual good thinges; The
children of this world (ſaith Chriſt) are wiſer then *Luc 16. v. 8.*
the children of light, in their generation] The whole *Mat. 25. v.*
militant Church, is like to ten Virgins [Of which fiue *1. 2.*
are fooliſh, and fiue wiſe] The wiſdome of the fleſh *Ro 8 v. 6.*
is death (ſaith S. Paul) but the wiſdome of the ſpirite *1. Cor 1.*
life, and peace. It is written: I wil deſtroy the wiſ- *v 19.*
dome of the wiſe, and the prudence of the prudent, I
wil reiect. Bleſſed is the man that hath not gone in the *Pſal. 1. v. 1.*
counſel of the impious. Counſel ſhal kepe thee, & *Pro. 2. v. 11.*
prudence ſhal preſerue thee. There is health, where *Eccli. 25. v.*
is much counſel. A man of counſel wil not deſtroy *5 7.*
vnderſtanding. Gold and Siluer are the eſtabliſh- *ch. 32. v 22.*
ment of the feete: and Counſel is wel accepted aboue *ch 40. v. 25.*
them both. Seeke counſel alwayes of a wiſe man.] ſaid *Tob. 4. v 19*
Tobias to his ſonne. The ſame al prudent men ob-
ſerue, and teach by word and example.

5. Of imprudent men, and bad ſucceſſe, examples
abund. King Saul being tempted with fooliſh emula- *1 Reg. 18. v.*
tion, becauſe greater praiſe was giuen by ſimple we- *6. 7. 8 &c.*
men, to Dauid, then to him, yealed to the paſſion *v. 11 ch. 19.*
of *v. 1. 9. 11.*

Mature iudge-
ment.

Examples of
imprudent
worldly poli-
tiques.

of enuie, and loſt both grace, and wit, erred often in

ch.13 v. 19. iudgement, and conſequently in his actions. He at-
ch.18.v.1. tempted often to kil Dauid, and cruelly perſecut him,
ch.31.v.4. but neuer preuailed againſt him. He fel into extreme
diſtreſſes, conſulted a Pythonical ſpirite, and peri-
3.Reg.12. ſhed in battel. [King Roboam anſwered his people
v.13. with rough wordes, leauing the counſel of the Ancients, which they had geuen him:& he ſpake to them
Luk.7.v. according to the counſel of the yong men. The Pha-
30. riſces and the Lawyers] deſpiſed the counſel of God
againſt themſelues, being not baptized of Iohn Bap-
Mat.16.v. tiſt] To both Phariſes and Sadduces, our Lord ſaid:
3. [The face of the element, you ſhal ſkil to diſcerne:
and the ſignes of times can you not?]

Iuſtice; and other vertues annexed, Pietie, Reuerence, Obedience, Gratitude, Liberalitie, and Freindſhip, are neceſſarie.

ARTICLE 19.

IVſtice in a large ſignification, importeth al right
performing of humane actions. And ſo it comprehendeth al vertues, as the Philoſopher deſcribeth it,
Gen.6.v.8. ſaying[*Iuſtitia in ſe virtutes continet omnes.*] And our Sauiour in this general ſenſe, vſeth the ſame word Iu-
Mat.5.v.21. ſtice: where teaching the perfect obſeruation of al the
commandments, and good workes, he ſaith [Vnles
your Iuſtice abound more then that of the Scribes
and Phariſees, you ſhal not enter into the kingdome
of heauen] But in more ſtrickt ſence, it is one of the
foure Cardinal vertues : by which euerie one poſſeſſeth, and yeeldeth to others, that which is theirs, according to equitie, in due and equal portion. And to
this principal vertue, are annexed other particular
vertues, which render alſo to euerie one, that which
is due, yet not in equal, but more or leſſe proportiõ,

Iuſtice in ge-
neral, contey-
neth al ver-
tues; in ſpecial
is one of the
foure cardinal
vertues.

R   according

according to the diuersitie of persons, and states. As Pietie, Reuereuce, Obedience, Gratitude, Liberalitie, and Frienship. Al which, are seuerally required in their due times, places, occasions, and other circum-stances, diuersly occurring: and sometimes manie of these vertues are requisite in the same action.

Abraham in one and the same act, exercised diuers vertues.

2. As when Abraham to appease strife, betwixt his owne, and Lots heardsmen: not only granted to them al that was iust, but also of his Pietie towads Lot, being his brothers sonne, recounting him as his owne brother: with great kindnes besought him to kepe Freindship with him, and his seruants; and of his bountiful Liberalitie, gaue him leaue to choose what land he liked best [Let there be no brawle, I *Gen.13.v.5.* beseech thee, betwen me and thee (said Abraham to *6.* Lot) and betwen my heardsmen, and thy heardsmen: *7.* for we are brethren. Behold, the whole land is be-fore thee: goe apart from me, I pray thee; If thou wilt goe to the left kand, I wil take the right: if thou choose the right hand, I will passe to the left.] Also Heathen Kinges moued by moral vertue, did that which was iust, when their seruants had done wrong. For [when *ch.21.v.25.* Abraham rebuked Abimelech, King of Gerara, for a wel of water, which his seruants had taken awaie by force, Abimelech answered: I knew not who did *26.* this thing: yea, and thy selfe didst not tel me, and I heard not of it, but to day. Abraham therfore tooke sheepe and oxen, and gaue to Abimelech, for a testi- *27.* monie, that the wel perteyned to Abraham, and both of them made a leage] Likewise Isaac, after some in-iuries susteyned, was peaceably petmitted to dwel in Gerara, and to enioy his welles, which he had digged. And so [he and Abimelech made a league] Iacob *ch.26.v14* made a couenant with Laban, saying [My iustice shal *22.31.* answer for me to morow before thee, when the time of the bargaine shal come] Innumerable other *ch.30.* exemples occurre in the holie Scriptures, commen- *v.33.* ding

-ding the neceſſitie, and excellencie of iuſtice.

3. Abundance alſo of admonitions doth confirme the ſame. Of Iuſtice in general, Salomon ſaith [The treaſures of impietie ſhal profite nothing; but iuſtice ſhal deliuer from death. The bleſſing of our Lord, is vpon the head of the iuſt : but iniquitie couereth the mouth of the impious. The worke of the iuſt vnto life : but the fruite of the impious vnto ſinne. As a tempeſt paſſing, the impious ſhal not be : but the iuſt as an euerlaſting foundation] Of the ſpecial vertue of Iuſtice, he ſaith [A deceiptful ballance, is abomination before God; and an equal weight is his wil. Weight and weight, meaſure and meaſure, both are abomination before God] He that gathereth treaſures, with a lying tongue, is vaine, and witleſſe, and ſhal ſtumble in the ſnares of death.] And the like of the vertues annexed.

4. Pietie (ſaith S. Paul) is profitable to al thinges: hauing promiſe of the life that now is, and of that to come. If anie hath not care of his owne, eſpecially of his domeſticals, he hath denied his faith, and is worſe then an Infidel Pietie with ſufficiencie, is a great gaine. Purſue Iuſtice and Pietie] Honour of Parents, requireth both Pietie in releeuing their neceſſities, and Reuerence to their perſons. Likewiſe, Reuerence is due to al other perſons, according to order and degree. [Before the hoare head riſe vp (ſaith the Law) and honour the perſon of an old man; and feare the Lord thy God. Rebuke not a Seniour (ſaith S. Paul) but beſech him, as a father. The Seniours which are among you, I beſech (ſaith S. Peter) my ſelfe, a felow ſeniour] Sara obeyed Abraham, calling him lord] Performing both due reuerence, and obedience. As God ordayned, [that the wife ſhal be vnder her huſ-

Marginal notes (left):
Pro. 10. v.
2.
6.
16.
25.
ch. 11. v. 1.
ch. 20. v. 10.
23.
ch. 21. v. 6.
Ex. 21. 22.
Eccli. 4. &c.
1. Tim. 4. v.
ch. 5. v. 8.
ch. 5. v. 11.
Leuit. 19. v.
32.
1. Tim. 5. v. 1.
1. Pet. 5. v. 1.
ch. 3. v. 6.
Gen. 18. v. 12

Marginal notes (right):
Commendation of Iuſtice in the holie Scripture.
Pietie.
Reuerence.
Obedience.

bandes power : and he shal haue dominion ouer
her. According to the common knowne dutiful obedience of the sonne to his father, and of the seruant to
his lord, or master, God requireth, at least the same respect to be had of himselfe, which supposition sufficiently proueth the necessitie of obedience towards
al Superiors, whereof more is to be said in the proper

Gratitude.

place. Of Gratitude to Benefactors, Salomon saith
[He that rendreth euil thinges for good; euil shal not
depart from his house.] And S. Paul exhorting to gratitude, saith [Let the peace of Christ exult in your
hartes, and be thankful] And much commendeth the
gratefull affections of the Galatians towards himselfe,
though they were faultie in other respects, saying to
them [I giue you testimonie, that if it could be done,
you would haue plucked out your eyes, and haue ge-

Libetalitie.

uen them to me] Liberalitie is the meane vertue, be-
tweene the two extreme contrarie vises, of Auarice
and Prodigalitie. And is worthily commended in
holie writte [Some diuide their owne goodes (saith
Salomon) and are made richer: others take violently
not their owne, and are alwayes in pouertie. He that
trubleth his house (by waste and prodigalitie) shal
possesse the windes] shal shortly blow al away , like
chaffe in the winde [He that pursueth auarice, disturbeth his hous: but he that hateth giftes, shal liue. Manie are freindes of him that geueth gifts. He that is
iust, wil geue, and wil not cease. It is a more blessed
thing (said our Sauiour) to geue, rather then to take]
Of the liberal Almeseman it is said [He distributed, he
gaue to the poore: his iustice remaineth for euer.]

Amitie.

Trne & perfect Amitie, maketh a freind to be euen
as much an others mans as his owne. *Amicus est alter
idem.* [He loueth at al time (saith Solomon) that is a
freind : and a brother is proued in distresses. A man a-
miable to societie, shal be more freindlie, then a bro-

ther

*ch.3. v.
16.*

Mal.1.v.6.

Artic.23.

*Prou 17.
v.13*

Colos 3.v.15

Gal.4,v.15.

*Pro.11.v.24
29.*

ch.15.v.27.

ch.19.v.6.

Ch.2:6.

*Act.20.v.
35.*

Psal.11.v.9.

*1.Cor.9.v.
9.*

*Pro.17.v.
17.ch.18.v.
24.*

ther. A man that with fayre, and feaned wordes, speaketh to his freind, spreadeth a nette to his steppes. There is a freind in name only a freind. A companion is pleasant with his freind in delictations : and in the time of tribulation, he will be an aduersarie] So the wiseman aduiseth to be a true freind, not a feaned. To beware of a feaned freind : and to esteeme much a sincere freind.

ch.29.v.5.

Eccli:37.v.4

Fortitude, and other vertues annexed, Magnanimitie, Patience, Longanimitie, and Perseuerance, are necessarie.

ARTICLE 20.

FOrtitude consisteth in doing and suffering hard, and lawful thinges. By which vertue Abraham feared not, with three hundred .nd eightene stout men of his owne people, to assault foure Kings with their armies, which had newly ouercome fiue other Kings, and their armies, and had caried away manie captiues, and amongst the rest, had led away Lot, Abrahams brothers sonne, with al his familie, & substance, and so pursuing the victorers, stroke them, and brought backe al the substance, and Lot his brother, with his substance, the wemen also and the people] By greater Fortitude, and heroical Magnanimitie, which excelleth the ordinarie corege of valient men, the same Abraham obeyed Gods commandmét, being willing & readie to sacrifice his beloued young sonne Isaac, which God most highly commended and rewarded, with manie great blessings to him, and his issue, and al that imitate him, in faith, obedience, and fortitude, against difficult tentations to the contrarie: With verie great fortitude, accompanied with other vertues. Ioseph the Patriarch, being yet young,

Gen.14.v. 10.11.12. 14 25.16.

ch 22. v 3. 4.9.16.17.

ch.39.v.10. 11.

Fortitude, and Magnanimitie were admriable in Abrahã.

Great in Ioseph.

R 3 con-

conſtantly refuſed to committe aduoutrie, wherto his
Myſtreſſe day by day importunely ſolicited him]
Young Dauid armed with admirable fortitude, vndertooke the ſingle combate againſt Goliath, ſaying;
[Our Lord which hath deliuered me from the hand
of the lion, and of the beare, he wil deliuer me from
the hand of this vncircumciſed Philiſtian] So euerie one that ouercommeth the ſpirite of pride, and
of carnalitie (ſignified by a lion, and a beare) is able
alſo to ouercome al tentations, of the world, the
fleſh, and the diuel.

Likewiſe in Dauid,

1.Reg.17. v.37.

2 The hand of the ſtrong (ſaith Salomon) ſhal rule,
but the hand which is ſlouthful ſhal ſerue vnder tributes. The ſluggard wil and wil not: but the ſoule of
them that worke, ſhal be made fatte. Feare caſteth
downe the ſlouthful, and the ſoule of the effeminate,
ſhal be hungrie. The ſlouthful ſaith: A lion is without,
in the middes of the ſtreetes, I am to be ſlaine. If thou
deſpayre, being wearie in the day of diſtreſſe, thy
ſtrength ſhal be diminiſhed] Manie like ſentences are
written by the wiſeman. And wiſdome it ſelfe admoniſheth al] Not to feare them that kil the bodie, and
are not able to kil the ſoule]

Praiſe of Forti-tude in holie Scriptures.

Prou.12. v.24.

ch.13.v.4.

ch.18.v.8.
ch.22.v 13.
ch.24.v.10.

Mat.10.v. 28.

3, To the better accompliſhment of true fortitude,
perteyne theſe vertues: ſeuerally commend in holie
Scriptures. Patience of the poore (ſaith the Royal Pſalmiſt) ſhal not periſh in the end. My ſoule (ſaith he) be
ſubiect to God, becauſe my patiece is frō him. The doctrine of a man, is knowne by patience (ſaith Salomō)
& his glorie is to ouerpaſſe vniuſt things. By patience
the Prince ſhal be pacified: and a ſoft tongne ſhal
breake hardnes. In your patience you ſhal poſſeſſe
your ſoules] ſaith our Sauiour. S. Paul teacheth, that
[Tribulation worketh patience: Patience probation;
probatiō hope: & hope confundeth not. We expect
by patience. In al things, let vs exhibite our ſelues, as
the Miniſters of God, in much patience, tribulation, in

Vertues an-nexed to For-titude,

Patience.

Pſ 9.v.19.

Pſ.61.v.6.
Pro.19.v. 11,
ch.25 v.15.
Luc.21.v. 19.
Rom.5 v.8.
ch.8.v.25.
2.Cor.6.v. 4.
Gal.5 v.22.
Eph.4.v.2.1
Tim.6.v.1.2.

diſtreſ-

2.Tim.3.
v.10. diftreffes, in ftripes, in prifons. The fruite of the Spirite, is charitie, ioy, peace, patience, benignitie, goodnes, longanimitie, with al humilitie and mildnes: with
Heb.10.v.
36. patience and longanimitie, with ioy. Purfue iuftice,
pietie, faith, charitie, patience, mildnes, longanimitie.
Patience is neceffarie for you: that doing the wil of
ch 12.v.1.
Iac.v.4. God, you may receiue the promife. By patience, let vs
runne, to the fight propofed vnto vs. Let patiéce haue
a perfect worke (faith S.Iames) that you may be per-
Mat.10.v.
22. fect, & intyre, failing in nothing] Againe, our Sauiour
faith; [He that perfeuereth to the end, fhal be faued]
ch.24.v. 13. Therfore againe S.Paul admonifheth, not only to haue
patience, but alfo to perfeuer in Gods feruice, and to
Heb 12.v.6.
7.
Pro.3.v. 11 fuffer eué to the end, faying according to the doctrine
of Salomon. & of Chrift our Lord [Be thou not wea-
rie, whiles thou art rebuked of our Lord. Perfeuere ye
in difcipline. As vnto childré doth God offer himfelf
to you. For what fonne is there, whom the father doth
not correct?]

Longanimitie
is patiéce with
ioy, and con-
ftancie.

Perfeuerance
perfecteth pa-
tience.

Temperance, & other vertues annexed; Con-
tinencie, Meekenes, Humilitie, and Mo-
deftie, are neceffarie.

ARTICLE 21.

TEmperance, the fourth Cardinal vertue, confifteth in the moderation of meate, drinke, and of
other corporal thinges, perteyning to mans bodie, or
appetite. That this is a true moral vertue, is cleare by
the light of nature, which taught Affuerus a Heathen
King, to prouide that in a great feaft, which he made
to the Princes of his Kingdome, none fhould be compelled to drinke more then they defired [But as the
Efther,1.v.
7.8. King had appointed, making each of his Princes ouer-
feer of euerie table, that euerie one might take what
he would.] By which Royal ordinance, it feemeth that there was then amongft the more barbarous people, the like drunkardes cuftome, as is

Examples of
more tempe-
rance in fome
heathen peo-
ple, then is
now in fome
that beare the
name of Chri-
ftians.

now

now againe reigneth,efpecially in countries infected
with herefie, not only to drinke excefsiuely, but alfo
to vrge, and force others to anfwere them with
like intemperance, worfe then beaftly. For brute
beaftes can not be compelled to drinke more then
they lift, by anie meanes that man can vfe: much leffe
doth anie beaft conftraine an other, to excede the
bondes of nature; but becaufe brutish men paffe al
beaftes in this kinde, both in themfelues, & towards *Efth.1.v. 8.*
others;the more ciuil heathen Princes, corrected the
inhumane and vnnatural prefling of others to fuch
exceffe. Much more ought good Chriftians to auoide
the filthie crimes of intemperance, as wel in their
owne perfons, as in drawing others into fclowshipe
of wickednes.

Intemperance is greater in fome men, then in anie beafts. (margin)

2. Againft this fo fotish vife of drunkennes, and
gluttonie, and for due moderation in eating, drinking, and other humane conuerfations, Salomon geueth manie neceffarie admonitions, telling the bad
fucceffe of the one, and good fruite of the other [He
that is delighted with much quaffing of wine, leaueth *Pro.12.v.*
contimelie in his munitions]that is, leaueth shame in *11.*
his memorie and poftcritie[The iuft eateth and filleth *ch.13.v. 25.*
his foule, but the bellie of the impious is vnfatiable. *ch.20. v.*
Wine (and euerie liquor that can make drnnke)is a *1.ch.21.v.*
luxurious thing,and drunkennes tumultuos:whofoe- *17.*
uer is delighted therwith, shal not be wife. He that
loueth good chere, shal be in pouertie:he that loueth
wine, and fatte thinges,shal not be rich.Be not in the *h.23.v. 20.*
feafts of great drinkers, nor in their comeffations, *21.*
which contribute flesh together to eate:becaufe they
that are geuen to drinking, and that pay shottes,shal
be confumed: and droufineffe shal be clothed with
ragges. To whom is woe? to whofe father is woe? *29.*
To whom browles? to whom ditches? to whom *30.*
woundes without caufe? to whom bloud-shedding *31.*
eyes? Is it not to them, that paffe their time in wine?
and

Admonitions to vfe tempe- rance, (margin)

v. 31.

and ſtudie to drinke out their cuppes? Behold not
wine when it waxeth yelow: When the colour therof

32.

ſhal ſhine in the glaſſe, it goeth in pleaſantly; but in
the end, it wil bite like a ſnake: and as a baſiliske it
wil powre abrode poyſons. Thou haſt foūd honey; eate
that which ſufficeth thee (and no more) leſt perhaps

ch. 25.*v.*16.

being filled, thou vomitte it vp.] And further exhor-

*ch.*31.*v.* 4.5.

teth not only to abhorre al exceſſe, but alſo to ſhunne
al danger therof, ſaying [Geue not to kinges, ô La-
muel, geue not wine to kinges: becauſe there is no ſecrete, where drunkenes reigneth: and leſt perhaps
they drinke, and forgete iudgements; and change the
cauſe of the children of the poore] An other diuine

Eccli. 19.*v.*1.
2.

preacher ſaith [A workeman that is a drunkard ſhal
not be rich, and he that contemneth ſmal thinges,
ſhal fal by litle & litle wine, & wemen make wiſemen
to apoſtatate, & ſhal reproue the prudēt. Woe to you

*Iſa.*5.*v.*22.

that are mightie to drinke wine (ſaith Iſaias) & ſtout
men in drunkenes.]

3. Sobrietie and al temperance are moſt eſpecially
required in Chriſtians, becauſe we are not borne of

*1 Pet.*1.*v.*23.

the fleſh, but regenerate of the Spirite, hauing re-
nounced the world, the fleſh, and the diuel, who by
intemperance firſt ſeduced Eue, and ſhe then allured
Adam, in whom al mankind fel. And for ſo much
as al men muſt eate, drinke, couer their bodies, ſlepe,
reſt, and vſe other refreſhing of bodie, and minde:
there is more danger of exceding, in theſe thinges
which neceſſarily muſt be done, then in other
thinges, from which men may wholly abſtaine. And

*Luc.*21.*v.*34.

therfore our Sauiour ſaith: [Looke wel to yourſelues,
leſt perhaps your hartes be ouercharged, with ſur-
feiting, and drunkemes, and cares of this world.]
Not forbidding the neceſſarie vſe, but warning to

*Ro.*13.*v.*13.
14.

beware of anie exceſſe. Alſo S. Paul exhorteth to ſo-
brietie, ſaying [As in the day, let vs walke honeſtly:

In thinges ne-
ceſſarie muſt
be ſpecial care
to kepe mode-
ration.

S   not

not in banketinges, and drunkcnnes, not in cham-
beringes, and impudicicies; and make not prouision
for the flesh in concupiscences. Be not drunke with
wine, wherein is riotoutnes. They that be drunke,
be drunke in the night (in darkenes of sinne) But we
that are of the day (in light of grace) are sober.]

*Vertues ad-
joyned to Té-
perance.*

4. Vnto this vertue of Temperance belong also
the necessarie vertues of Continencie, and Chastitie,
in due degree of euerie state. As in maried persons
matrimonial chastitie, and temporal continencie for
the special times of prayer. In single persons per-

*Continencie
and Chastitie.*

petual, during the same state of life. Example of
temporal chastitie is corspicuous in young Tobias,
and his spouse Sara, by the counsel of S. Raphael
the Angel [who were continent, three dayes, geuing themselues to prayer.] The wiseman desiring
to be made partaker of wisedome, and knowing
that he could not so be, but by the gift of God,
earnestly prayed God for the same, and for al vertues. S. Paul numbreth the vertue of Continencie
amongst other special vertues, saying [The fruite of
the Spirite is charitie, mildnes, modestie, continencie, chastitie] And speaking of al vertues in general,
maketh special mention [of iustice and chastitie:
faith and chastitie: pietie and chastitie] testifying that
chastitie is an especial companion, and very nere
adioyned to other greatest vertues. An other vertue

*Clemencie &
Mekenes.*

annexed to Temperance is Clemencie [which vertue (saith Salomon) prepareth life.] Againe saith
he [The kinges Clemencie is as the later showre.
Mercie and Truth kepe the King: and his throne
is strengthned by Clemencie. The seruant of our
Lord must not wrangle, but be milde, towards al
men: apt to teach: patient with modestie, admonishing them that resist the truth: lest sometime
God geue them repentance to know the truth: and
                                    they

*Ephes. 5. v.
18*
*1 Thes. 5. v.
7.8.*

*Tob 6 v.18.
ch.8.v 2.&b.
8.v 45.*
*Sap 8 v.2.
ch.9 v. I.
Gal.5 v 23.
Act.24. v.
25.*
*I.Tim.2 v.
2.ch 4 v.12.*

*Prou. 11.v.
19 ch.16.v.
5 ch.20.v.
28.*
*2 Tim 2.v.
24.25.26.*

they recouer themſelues from the ſnares of the diuel: of whom they are held captiues at his wil]
Humilitie in like maner is an indiuidual compa- Humilitie.
nion of Temperance, a moſt neceſſarie and an highly
commended vertue [Before I was humbled (ſaith
the Royal Prophete) I offended . It is good for me
ô God , that thou haſt humbled me . Our Lord
(ſaith the moſt bleſſed Virgine) hath regarded the
humilitie of his hand-maide. He hath diſperſed the
proude in the conceipt of their hart : He hath de-
poſed the mightie from their ſeate , and hath exalted the humble] Our Lord himſelfe ſaith [Whoſoeuer ſhal humble himſelf, as this litle childe, he
is greater in the kingdom of heauen . Bleſſed are
the poore in ſpirite ; for theirs is the kingdom of
heauen . Bleſſed are the meeke : for they ſhal poſſeſſe the land . Lerne of me, becauſe I am meeke,
and humble . He that exalteth himſelfe , ſhal be
humbled : and he that humbleth himſelfe ſhal be
exalted] For better tempering al humane conuerſa- Modeſtie.
tion in countenáce, ſpeach, & geſture, Modeſtie is no
leſſe neceſſarie then the other vertues mentioned [In
much talke (ſaith wiſe Salomon) there wil not want
ſinne: but he that moderateth his lippes is moſt wiſe.
A ſoft anſwer breaketh anger. He that moderateth his
wordes, is lerned and prudent . And he lerned man
is of a precious ſpirite . The foole alſo , if he hold his
peace, ſhal be reputed wiſe : and if he cloſe his lippes,
a man of vnderſtanding . The end of modeſtie , the
feare of our Lord, riches, and glorie, and life. Let your
modeſti be knowen to al men (ſaith S. Paul) Put ye
on the bowels of mercie, benignitie, humilitie, modeſtie, patiéce. Be not litigious, but modeſt. The wiſdom
that is from aboue (ſaith S. Iames) is chaſte, peaceable, modeſt, ſwaſible, conſenting to the good, The
inward (ſpiritual) man of the hart (ſaith S. Peter) is

Pſal. 118. v.
67. 71.

Inc 1. v 48.
51. 52.

Mat. 18. v. 4.
ch. 5 v. 4.
ch. 11. v. 29.
Inc. 18. v.
14.

Pro 10. v.
19. ch. 15 v.
1. ch. 17. v
27. 18. ch. 22
v. 4.

Philip. 4 v.
5. Coloſ 3. v.
12. Tit. 3. v. 2.

Iac. 3. v 17.

1. Pet. 3. v. 4.

S 2   hidden

hidden in the incorruptibilitie of a quiet, and modest
spirite : which is riche in the fight of God.] S. Iohn   *3 Ioan. 7. 10*
taxeth the immodeftie of Diotrepes, a trublefome Pre-
late, faying of him, that [he with malicious wordes
chatting againft vs : and as though thefe thinges fufficed him not; neither himfelf doth receiue the brethré:
and them that doe receiue, he prohibiteth, and cafteth
out of the Church] And S. Iude alfo chargeth a Sect   *Iuda. v. 4.*
of Heretikes for immodeftly [contending with the   *8. 9.*
teachers of truth] & for their contemning, and [defpi-
fing Dominion, and blafpheming Maieftie. When
Michael the Archangel difputing with the diuel,
made altercatió for the bodie of Moyfes; he durft not
inferre iudgement of blafphemie, but faid: Our Lord
command thee.]

Al are bond to honour their fathers, and mo-
thers: especially to affift them in necessitie,
spiritual and temporal.

ARTICLE 22.

THus much being interpofed concerning the
foure Cardinal vertues, with the others annexed; al which perteyne to mans dutie toward
himfelf, and his neighbour: we procede to the more
expreffe commandments of the fecond table. The
firft of which is, that euetie one muft honour, and if
neede require, muft affift his father and mother, fpiritually and temporally. As al pious children haue done
in the Law of nature : in the written Law; and more
efpecially in the Law of grace. For declaration wherof
it wil fuffice moft breefly, and as it were barely to recite certaine holie Scriptures, as wel inftructing vs by
way of example, and of precept : as by the threatned
punishment

punishment of offenders in this behalfe, & of promifed reward to the obferuers . In the Law of nature

Gen.9.v.22.
23.

[Sem & Iapheth shewed their dutiful refpect, & performed their bonden dutie, towards Noe their father, by couering his imperfection . Contrariwife his
other fonne Cham dishonored his father, deriding
him] For which the firft two were bleffed, and Cham

th.45.v. 16,
th.46.v.29.
th.48.v.2.
th.50.v.1.

was curfed . Iofeph with fingular care both prouided
temporal relefe for his father, and his whole familie,
in time of fcarfitie; and with very great refpect honored his father, in al his life, and after his death. So
did Iacob honour his father Ifaac. Ifaac honored A-
braham: and Abraham his progenitors.

Examples of honoring, and dishonoring parents.

2. God alfo exprefly commandeth by his written

Exo.20.v.
11.

Law, faying [Honour thy father, and thy mother :
that thou maift be long liude vpon the earth : which
the Lord thy God wil geue thee] Touching tranfgref-

th.21.v.15.
17.
Levit. 19. v.
3.ch.20.v 9.
Deut 21.v.
18 19.21,

fors, the fame Law faith : [He that ftriketh his father,
or mother, dying let him dye. He that curfeth his father or mother, dying let him dye . Let euerie one
feare his father, and mother, If a man begette a ftubborne frowatd fonne, that wil not heare the commandments of his father and mother; and being cha-
ftined, contemneth to be obedient : they shal take
him, and bring him to the Ancients of the citie, and
to the gate of Iudgement, and shal fay to them : This
our fonne is froward, and ftubborne: he contemneth
to heare our admanitiós: he geueth himfelf to comef-
fation, and to riote, and to banketinges: the people
of the citie shal ftone him , and he shal dye : that you
may take away the euil out of the middes of you : and
al Ifrael hearing it, may be a fraide.]

The Law of God & nature bindeth children to honour their parents.

Prou. 15.v.
20.ch.17.
v.25.

3. A wife fonne (faith Salomon) maketh the father
ioyful: and the foolish man defpifeth his mother . A
foolish fonne is the anger of his father: and the forow
of the mother, that bare him . He that afflicteth his

Other admonitions to obferue this cõmandment,

father

father, and fleeth from his mother, is ignominious
and vnhappie. He that curseth his father, and mo
ther, his lampe shal be extinguished in the middes of
darkenes. The inheritance, whereunto haste is made
in the beginning, in the latter end shal lacke blef-
sing. He that pilfereth anie thing from his father;and
from his mother : and saith : This is no sinne : is the
partaker of a mankiller] comitteth like sinne, as if he
should kil an other man . [Heare your fathers iudgement, o children (saith the diuine preacher) and so
doe, that you may be saued. As he that gathereth
treasure; so be also that honoreth his mother. He that
honoreth his father, shal haue ioy in children; and in
the day of his prayer he shal be heard . He that honoreth his father shal liue the longer life ; and he that
obeyeth the father shal refresh the mother. He that
feareth our Lord honoreth his parents : and as his
lordes, he wil serue them that begate him . In worke
and word, and in al patience honour thy father, that
blessing may come vpon thee from him : and his blef-
sing may remaine in the latter end . The fathers blef-
sing establisheth the houses of the children : but the
mothers curse rooteth vp the fundation. Glorie not
in the contumelie of thy father:for his confusion is no
glorie to thee. For the glorie of a man is by the honour of his father : and the father without honour is
the dishonour of the sonne . Sone receiue the old age
of thy father, and make him not sorowful in his life.
And if he faile in vnderstanding, pardon him, and
despise him not in thy strength . For the almes to the
father, shal not be in obliuion. For good shal be restored thee , for the sinne of thy mother (if thou with
compassion and reuerence be forie, and pray for her)
and in iustice it shal be builded to thee: and as yce
in the cleare wether shal thy sinnes melt away. Of
what an euil fame is he, that forsaketh his father ?
and

ch.19. v.26
ch 20, v 20.
21.
ch.28. v.24

Eccli.3 v 2.

5.

6.

7.

8.

9.

10.

11.

12.

13.

14.

15.

16.

17.

18.

Fathers blef-
sing is of great
value.

and he is curſed of God, that doth exaſperate his mother.]

4. Chriſt our Saniour sharply reprehendeth the
Scribes and Phariſees, for peruerting this commandment to their lucre, with pretence of Religion ſaying,
to them [God ſaid: Honour thy father and thy mother: He that shal curſe father, or mother, dying let
him dye. But you ſay: Whoſoeuer shal ſay to father, or
mother: The gift (of Sacrifice, or oblation) whatſoeuer procedeth from me, shal profite thee; and shal not
honour (helpe and releue) his father and mother; And
you haue made fruſtrate the commandment of God,
for your owne tradition]. S. Paul admonisheth Chriſtians carefully to fulfil this commandment, ſaying
[Children obey your parents in our Lord, for this is
iuſt. Honour thy father, and thy mother, which is the
firſt commandmet in the promiſe, that it may be wel
with thee, and thou maiſt liue long, vpon the earth.
And you fathers, prouoke not your children to anger,
but bring them vp in the diſcipline, and correption of
our Lord. Children obey your parents in al things:
for that is wel pleaſing to our Lord. Fathers prouoke
not your children to indignation, that they become
not diſcouraged. Children lay not vp treaſures for
the parents (ordinarily) but the parents for the
children. This command (parents) that they be blame-
leſſe. If anie man haue not care of his owne: and eſpecially of his domeſticals, he hath denied the faith: &
is worſe then an Infidel.]

*Mat.*15.v. 4.
5

v. 6.

*Ephes.*6.v.
12 3 4.

*Coloſ.*3.v.
20.21.

2 *Cor.*12.v.
14.

1 *Tim.*5.v.
7.8.

*Chriſt explai-
neth this com-
mandment:
teaching that
children are
bond to helpe
their parents
in al neceſſi-
ties.*

*Parents are
likewiſe bond
to helpe their
children.*

Al are bond to honour, and obey, ſpiritual and temporal Superiors.

ARTICLE 23.

VVE haue exáples in the Iewes, both of obedience & diſobedience, toward Superiors.
Some-

Vnder the name of parēts al other superious are conteyned.
Betwen them also is a bond of mutual helpe, when neede requireth.

Sometimes they obeyed Moyses very diligētly. As whē they made their first Pasch, immolating in euerie familie a lambe, in such time, place, and maner, as was commanded. Also in marching and lodging, where God directed them by his signes, of the cloud by the day, and pillar of fire in the night, & the like: as God commanded them by the mouth of Moyses, & Aaron. Sometimes manie disobeyed, murmuring against their Superiors, yea some breaking into schisme, and open rebellion. Namely Core, Dathan, and Abiron, enuying the functions, and auctoritie of Moyses, and Aaron. Also Hon of the tribe of Ruben, and two hundred and fifetie other principal men, rose against Moyses and Aaron, and drew manie into murmuration, & rebellion. Which God punished, by the earth swallowing them into hel, and fire from heauen, consuming fourtene thousand seuen hundred of the cōmon people, for adhering vnto the captaine Rebels. It was also ordayned by the written Law, that [whosoeuer should be proud, refusing to obey the cōmandment of the High priest, for the time bearing that office, should be punished with death.]

Exo 12.v 3. 4. & c.ch.13. v.17. ch.14. v.4. ch.33.v. 8.

Ex.16, v.1 2 31.32.

Num.16.v. 1 2. & 6.

Deut.17.v. 12.

Power and auctoritie remaine in euil Superiors.

2.   Which power and auctoritie Christ auouched to remaine in the Priests, though they were degenerate in maners, not doing the good thinges, which they taught: yet [becaufe they sate vpon Moyses chayre, al were bond to doe, and obserue al thinges, which they taught, but according to their workes doe ye not: for they say, and doe not] And establishing his Disciples with special auctoritie, he said to them in plaine termes [He that heareth you, heareth me: and he that despiseth you, despriseth me: and he that despiseth me, despiseth him that sent me.] S. Paul speaking of his owne, and other Apostles auctoritie saith [He that despiseth these thinges, despiseth not men, hut God, who also hath
geuen

Mat 23.v.2 3.

Luc 10.v. 10.

1.Thes.4. v.8.

2.Thef.3.7. geuen his Holie Spirite, in vs. And if anie obey not
14   our word; note him by an Epiftle.] To S. Titus a
7it.2.7.15. Bishope, he said [Rebuke with auctoritie. Let no
man contemne thee] The Hebrew Chriftians he ad-
Heb.13.7.17. monished saying [Obey your Prelates, and be fubiect to them: for they watch, as being to render account for your soules.]

3. In like maner, al subiectes are bond to obey
tem poral Princes, and Superiors. So the Israelites
Iof.1.7.17. promised obedience to Iosue, saying to him [As
we obeyed Moyses in al thinges, so wil we obey
thee also. He that shal gainesay thy mouth, and
not obey thy wordes, that thou doest command
Pro.15.7.28. him, let him dye] Salomon saith [The minde of
ch.20.7.2. the iuft, meditateth obedience: the mouth of the im-
ch.24.7.21. pious redundeth with euils. As the roaring of a lion:
so also the terrour of the King: he that prouoketh
him, sinneth againft his owne soule. Feare our Lord
my sonne, and the King.]

Subiects are also bond to honour and obey temporal Superiors.

4. Our Sauiour confirmeth the same due obedience to Princes, yea though they erre in Religion,
Mat.22.7. saying [Render the thinges that are Cæsars, to Cæ-
21. sar: and the thinges that are Gods, to God.] euidently diftinguishing that some thinges perteyne to
temporal Princes, which are enimies to God, and
to truth; which muft be rendered vnto them But
spiritual thinges perteyning to Religion, muft be
rendeed to God, not to Cæsar. Yea to Pilate,
Io.19,7.11, Cæsars deputie, our Lord, said [Thou shouldeft
not haue anie power againft me, vnles it were geuen thee from aboue. Therfore he that hath be
trayed me to thee, hath the greater sinne] Al which
Sainct Paul further explaneth, saying [Let euerie
Ro.13,7.1. soule be subiect to higher powers. For there is no
power, but of God. And those that are: of God
are ordayned.] Becaufe God either geueth, or permitteth al auctoritie, that is in the whole world. And

Also Chriftiãs, & Catholiques are bond to honour and obey Infidel Princes in tẽporal caufes.

T   draweth

draweth good from both lawful, and vnlawful vse of
auctoritie. [Therfore (faith the fame Apoftle) he that
refifteth the power, refifteth the ordinance of God.   *v. 2.*
And they that refift, purchafe to themfelues damna-
tion] In particular he faith [Seruants be obedient to   *Eph.6 v.*
your lordes, according to the flesh(in temporal & bo-   6.
dilie feruice) with feare and trembling, in the fimplicitie of your hart, as to Chrift. Not feruing to the eye,   7.
as it were pleafing men: but as the feruants of Chrift,   8.
doing the wil of God from the hart; with a good wil
feruing as to our Lord, and not to men, knowing that
euerie one, what good foeuer he fhal doe, that fhal he
receiue of our Lord; whether he be bond or free. We-   *Colof 3.v.*
men be fubiect to your husbandes, as it be houeth in   18. 20.
our Lord. Children obey your parents in al thinges:
for that is wel pleafing to our Lord] He willeth Titus   *Tit.3 v.1.*
the Bishop of Crete, amongft other inftructions [to
admonish his people, to be fubiect to Princes, and Potentates, to obey at a word, to be readie to euerie
good worke] The fame doth S. Peter teach al Chri-
ftian people, faying [Be fubiect to euerie humane crea-   *1.Pet.2 v.*
ture, for God (that is, to euerie Prince, Magiftrate, &   13. 14.
Superior, whom God appointeth, or fuffereth to haue
dominió among men: fo farre as Gods Law is not violated) whether it be to the King, as excelling: or to Rulers, as fent by him, to the reuenge of malefactors, but
to the praife of the good. For fo it is the wil of God,   17.
that doing wel, you may make the ignorance of vn-   18.
wifemen to be dumme. Feare God. Honour the King.
Seruants be fubiect iu al feare (in reuerential feare) to
your mafters: not only to the good, and modeft, but
alfo to the waward. For this is grace (or the effect of   19.
grace, and caufe of thanke, and reward) before God:
if for confcience of God (for confcience, or iuftiee
fake) a man fuftaine forowes, fuffering vniuftly.] Al   *Rom.13.v.5.*
therfore, as the holie Apoftles teach, and admonish
[muft be fubiect of neceffitie (that they may auoide
                                              finne

finne, and punishment, and gaine reward of God) not only for wrath, but alfo for confcience fake. Render therfore to al men their due: to whom tribute is due, render tribute: to whom cuftom is dur, réder cuftom: to whom feare is due, render feare: to whom honour is due, render honour.] And fo to al Superiors. To fpiritual Prelates, fpiritual obedience, to temporal, Princes, temporal obedience.

5.   In this fundamental doctrine therfore, as wel of the old Law, as of Chrift, and his Apoftles, al good Chriftian Lawes, both Ecclefiaftical, and Ciuil are grounded, warranted, and confirmed.

The Lawes of the Church, and common wealthes are grounded in Gods Law.

The more efpecial Precepts of the Church are thefe fiue.

1.   To kepe al Sundayes, and certaine other feftiual dayes holie: by abftayning from feruile, & gainful workes: and by perfonal prefence at the holie Maffe, the Chriftian Sacrifice. Which is further proued, & declared in this third Part. Article 17. and 46.

2.   To receiue the moft bleffed Sacrament, at leaft euerie Eafter, or within feuen dayes before or after. Proued in the fecond Part. Article 21.

3.   To confeffe facramentally, at leaft once euerie yeare. Alfo proued in the fecond Part. Article 27.

4.   To faft, and kepe other abftinence, in certaine appointed times. As is proued in the next enfuing Article 24.

5.   Not to folemnize Mariage within certaine times prohibited. Al which Precepts: and others perteyning to particular perfons, and purpofes, are proued by the holie Scriptures, recited in tnis, and other Articles here mentioned. And further confirmed in the fourtie fixt Article folowing. The Lawes, & Statutes: of temporal kingdomes: Common wealths: Cities, Princes, & other Ciuil Magiftrates, are moe in nuber, then can be recited; very diuers, in diuers places,

and

and times. And are alſo proued in general, by the
former groundes,& further confirmed in the fourtie
ſeuenth Aiticle.

Al Chriſtians are bond, ſometimes to ab-ſtaine from certaine meates; and to faſt: by Diuine, and Eccleſiaſtical Lavves.

ARTICLE 24.

CoNcerning therfore the particular Precept of
Abſtinence, and Faſting (which our Aduerſaries of this time much impugne; it is proued to be
iuſt, wholſome, and religious in this preſent Article,
here for this purpoſe inſerted. Almightie God our Gen 1. v 1.
Creator hauing made [al ſortes of herbes that ſeede, 30 ch.9.v.
and al trees that bring fruire, to be the meate of
man] as alſo fleſh of beaſtes, and birdes, at leaſt
after the general floud; yet from the very beginning of the world, euen in Paradiſe, he excepted one
tree: commanding man to abſtaine from it, vpon
paine of death, ſaying to Adam [Of euerie tree (of Gen.2.v.16
al other trees) of Paradiſe, eate thou. But of the 17.
tree of knowledge, of good and euil, eate thou not.
For in what day ſoeuer thou ſhalt eate of it, thou
ſhalt dye the death.] And according to this premonition, ſo ſowne as Adam had tranſgreſſed this
precept of abſtinence, though he was by and by
penitent for it; yet both he, and al his future pro- ch.3 v.16.
genie, beſides other penalties, were ſubiect to death; 17.18.
euerie one decaying, and dying, as Gods former
threatning, and ſubſequent ſentence iuſtly require,
ſaying [Duſt thou art, and into duſt thou ſhalt re- v.19.
turne] Againe after the floud, our Lord expreſſly
gaue an other commandment of abſtinence, ſaying
to Noe; [Al that moueth,and liueth ſhal be yours,
for

Marginal note: Certaine ab-ſtinence from meate was commanded iu the ſtate of innocencie.

for meate; euen as the grene herbes, haue I deliuered al to you : Sauing that flesh with bloud you
shal not eate. For I wil require the bloud, of your
soules, at the handes of al beastes, and at the hand
of man.] Which precept was geuen, as wel to make
man, the more to abhorre manslaughter : as to exercise the faithful seruants of God, in obedience :
and for Ceremonie sake , as the same, and manie
other ceremonial Lawes , were afterwards added.
For it was lawful to kil beastes , and to eate their
flesh, but not anie bloud. So we see, there was a
precept of abstinence in the state of Innocencie; and
also in the Law of nature, after mans fal.

2. In the written Law of Moyses, not only abstinence from bloud was againe commanded in these
wordes [If thou wilt eate, and the eating of flesh
delight thee, kil, and eate according to the blessing of the Lord thy God. Only without eating of
the bloud, which thou shalt powre out vpon the
earth, as water. Whosoeuer shal eate bloud, I wil
sette my face against his life: and wil destroy him,
out of his people.] but also other precepts of abstinence, and fasting were added. It was precisely
commanded to abstaine from leauened bread, in the
feast of Pasch, seuen dayes together [Seuen dayes
shal you eate azimes: in the first day there shal be
no leuen in your houses: whosoeuer shal eate leuen,
that soule shal perish out of Israel, from the first
day vntil the seuenth day] In the feast of Expiation , euere yeare , the tenth day of the seuenth
moneth, was ordayned a perfect fast, from al meate
euen vntil night. [Vpon the tenth day of the seuenth
moneth, shal be the day of Expiation most solemne
(said our Lord to Moyses) and it shal be called
holie: and you shal afflict your soules in it, that your
Lord your God may become propicious vnto you.
Euerie soule that is not afflicted this day, shal perish

T 3   out

b. 9. v. 4. 5.

Deut. 12 v.
15. 16.

Leuit. 17. v.
10.

Exo 12. v.
15.
ch. 13. v. 7.

Leuit. 23. v.
27. 28. 29.
Nu 29. v. 7.

*An other pre-
cept of absti-
nence was ge-
uen after the
floud.*

*Manie other
abstinences
from certaine
meates were
added in the
written Law.*

out of his people. The ninth day of the month, from euen vntil euen, shal you celebrate your Sabbathes.] & other feastes. Vpon particular occasions also which might happen, abstinence from certaine meates was forbidde extraordinarily [If an oxe with his horne *Exo.11.v.* strike a man, or a Woman, and they dye: he shal be *28.ch.22. v.* stoned: & his flesh shal not be eaten. (Likewise) The *31.* flesh that beastes haue taisted of, before, you shal not eate, but shal cast it to the dogges] Manie kindes also of beastes, fishes, and birdes, were by the Law reputed vncleane, with strict prohibition, not to eate anie of *Leuit. 6 7.* them, which are not vnlawful by nature, but only be-*11.17.19.22.* cause they were prohibited in that time, for significa-*23.* tion sake, and for exercise of obedience. And are now lawful to be eaten. As porke, rabbites, puddings, and the like.

Faithful peo-
ple were very
diligent in ob-
seruing these
precepts of ab-
stinence.

3. In obseruing of which ceremonial lawes, of per-petual abstinence from certaine meates, faithful good people were very careful, and zelous. Holie Tobias *Tob.c 1.v.* kept himselfe free from being contaminate, by eating *12,* of meates, which were forbidden by the Law.] Iudith *Iudith.12.v.* said to Holofernes [I can not eate of the things which *2.* thou commandest to be giuen me] Daniel and the *Dan.1.v 8.* other three Hebrew children, in the captiuitie of Ba-bylon, would not eate of the meates, which were pro-uided for them, by the Kings commandment; because the Law of God commanded not to eate such thinges. Old Eleazarus, and seuen young men brethren, and *2.Mach.6.* their mother suffered death, and are glorious Mar-*v 18.ch.7.v.* tyrs, because they would not, contrarie to Gods Law, *1.2.3.&c.* eate swines flesh. Yea S. Peter, after Christs Ascension, *Act 10.v.* durst not eate of such prohibited meates, til it was by a *13.14.15.* vision declared vnto him, that God had altered that Law, the signification therof being fulfilled. And so he was therupon commanded, to receiue penitent Gentiles, into the Church of Christ. By which figura-*Leuit.23.v.* tiue abstinence: & moral obseruation of some fastes *28.*

[to

[to make God propitious for sinnes] did sufficiently foreshew, that in the new Testament, should be both fasting, and other abstinence, at special times: for Religion sake, for mortification, and for satisfaction.

4. S. Iohn Baptist (amongst other workes of penance) with his disciples, observed certaine fastes [Religious old Anne, the widow, serued God night & day, in fastings and prayers] The Pharisees also fasted often, which vnles it were an holie worke, they had not therby fallen into hypocrisie. Therfore our Sauiour correcting their hypocritical fasting, teacheth the right maner of fasting with sinceritie, and humilitie. And further forshewed expresly [that his Disciples should fast, after that the bridgrome (himself) should be taken from them (said he) they shal fast] Neither can his wordes be wrested, to signifie only fasting frō sinne. For that fast, his disciples were bound also to obserue, whiles he yet remained with them. He also calleth this future [fasting, by the name of mourning] At an other time he said: that [there is a kinde of diuel, which is not cast out, but by prayer, and fasting.]

5. As for the determinate times of fasting, there is no expresse precept in the newTestament. But by imitation of one special fasting day in the Law of Moyses: of other fastes vpon occasions occurring, as of the Niniuites, of other deuout persons, Tobias, Iudith: diuers Prophets; namely of Moyses fasting fourtie dayes together. When he first receiued the Law, and againe when he receiued the same, in the new tables, the first being broken. Likewise of Elias, fasting fourtie dayes. And of our Sauiour himselfe fasting fourtie dayes: his holie Apostles instituted, & obserued the holie & solemne fast of Lent: fourtie dayes before Easter. As it is manifest by perpetual Tradition. Because al Christians doe so obserue it, or know that others doe so obserue it, and haue done in al former times: no Aduersarie being able to shew, anie

other

Margin left: 2 Esd.9.v.1. &c. Isa 58 v.3. Ioel.1.v.14. &c. Matt.3.v 4. ch.11.v.18. Luc.2.v.37. Mat.5.v.16.17. ch.9.v.14.15.16. v.15. ch.17.v.21. Leuit.23.v.28. Ione3.v.5. Iudith.8.v.6 Tob.12.v.8. Exo.24.v.18.ch.34.v.28. Deut.9.v.18. 3.Reg.19.v.8. Mat.4.v.2.

Margin right: S.Iohn Baptist and his disciples, & others obserued voluntarie fastes. Christ foretold that his disciples should obserue some fastes: after his departure from them. The determination of time, and maner of fasting is left by Christ to his Church. Fast of Lent, and Ember dayes were instituted by the Apostles,

other beginning of Lents faſt. Which is a plaine,
and an aſſured proofe, that it was begune by the
Apoſtles of CHRIST : & doubtles by Chriſts warrant
Els the beginning of ſo vniuerſal an obſeruation,
would haue bene noted, and recorded, When, and
by whom, it had bene firſt ordayned. Likewiſe the
obſeruation of the Ember dayes, foure times, euerie
yeare (called . *Quatuor Tempora* : wherof Temper
dayes, and by a litle mutation: Ember dayes:) by
the ſame Rule of vniuerſal obſeruation, without o-
ther record, when the ſame begane, is inuincibly
proued to be an Apoſtolical Tradition, inſtituted
by the Apoſtles, by Chriſts commiſſion. The Vigiles
alſo of the more ſolemne feaſtes, obſerued in al places
of Chriſtendom, are confirmed by the very ſame
Rule of Apoſtolical Tradition. Some other Vigiles,
and faſtes, not obſerued in al places, but only in particular countries, or places, doe ſo farre bind, as
the cuſtome therof is approued, by the Ordinarie
Prelates of the ſame places. Which may alſo be altered, according to times, perſones, and other circum-
ſtáces, by auctoritie of the ſame particular Churches:
the Supreme viſible Head, approuing, or not contradicting the ſame.

2. Theſ. 2. v: 15.
2. Tim. 1. v. 14.

Vigiles were inſtituted by the Church.

VVith ſome difference in particular Prouinces.

Heb. 13. v. 17

*It is forbidde to kil anie man : except by
lavvful auctoritie, and in due maner.*

ARTICLE 25.

MAnſlaughter eſpecially wilful murder, is one
of thoſe enormious ſinnes, which crie to
God, into heauen for reuenge. As our Lord
himſelfe witneſſeth, ſaying to Cain, when he had
ſlaine his brother [Where is Abel thy brother? What
haſt thou done? The voice of thy brothers bloud cry-
eth to me, out of the earth. Now therfore curſed
ſhalt thou be vpon the earth, which hath opened her
mouth,

VVilful mur-der crieth to heauen for re-uenge.

*Gen. 4. v. 9.
10. 11. 15.
Apoc. 6. v.
10.*

mouth, and receiued the bloud of thy brother at thy hand] Yea it is also greuous sinne to kil a murderer, without right order of iustice. God also saying[Whosoeuer shal kil Cain, shal be punished seuen fold.] After Noes floud, arose manie cruel murderers, as Nemrod, surnamed the Valiant, or violent hunter. And his complices, the Scythians, and other Tyrants. Also king Pharao in Ægypt, and others in diuers places, which being knowne, and holden by the light of nature, to be a most greuous, no maruel that God, Iust, and Mightie, amongst other moral Precepts, expresly commandeth, saying [Thou shalt not murder] Which is often repeted, and punishment of iust death designed by God, for vniustly bereuing others of life [He that striketh a man wilfully to kil him, dying let him dye. If a man, of set purpose kil his neighbour, and by lying in waite for him, thou shalt pluck him out from mine Altar, that he may dye. He that striketh & killeth a man, dying let him dye]

Al vniust killing is condemned by the Law of God, and of nature

2. Because iustice must be done iustly, God not only ordained punishment by death, for the more saftie of innocéts liues, to terrifie & hinder the wicked, fró murder(& fró other heynous sinnes of idolatrie, blasphemie, cursing or striking of parents, and the like)but also prescribed a due course of trial, and processe of iudgement, in al causes;and namely, in the question of life or death[the murderer (saith the Law) shal be punished by witnesses. None shal be condemned at the testimonie of one man. At the mouth of two or three witnesses, shal he perish, that is to be slaine.Let none be killed, one only geuing witnesse against him. When there shal be found in the land, the corps of a man slaine, & he that is guiltie of the murder is not knowne, thy Ancients and Iudges, shal goe forth, and measure from the place of the corps, the distance of euerie citie round about : and the Ancients of the citie that shal be nerer, together with the Priestes, shal come to

Punishment by death is ordained, for the safetie of other mens liues, & for safetie of soules.

v.15.

ch. 10. v. 8. 9. 10.

Exod. 1. v. 10. 16. 22.

ch. 20 v. 13. Deut. 5. v. 17.

Ex. 21. v. 12. 14. Leuit. 24. v. 17. Deut. 19. v. 11.

Deut. 16. v. 20.

Num. 35. v. 30. Deut. 17. v. 6. ch. 21. v. 2. 3. &c.

the slaine person : and shal by Sacrifice of an Heffer, cleare the innocent, from the innocent bloud, that was shed. And if the murderer be found, procede a- *ch.19. v. 11.* gainst him. Thou shalt not pittie him: and thou shalt 12.13. take away the guiltie bloud out of Israel: that it may be wel with thee.]

3. Wheras sometimes holie zelous persons, haue kil-led, or intended to kil others, without due processe of ordinare iustice, it must be obserued that such special instinct of God, making their actions lawful, doth not warrant, nor excuse priuate persons to doe, nor to at-tempt the like, but ordinarie persons must obserue, & kepe the ordinare rule; and so admire, but not imitate so rare, and extraordinarie examples. The great and holie Patriarch [Abraham, vpon Gods especial com- *Gen.22.v.* mandment, purposed, & was readie with his sword in 2. 9.10. his hand, and lifted vp to that end , to kil Isaac his *Exo.2.v. 12* owne sonne.] Moyses especially moued by Gods Spi-rite]killed an Ægyptian, & hid the corps in the sand, that had done greuous wrong to an Israelite] As is re-corded in the sacred Historie; and was approued by *Act.7.v.24* God, as witnesseth S. Steuen] Phinies slew suddainly 25. two aduouterers, stabbing them both with a dagger] *Nu.25.v.8.* at one blow. For which iust zele he was highly com- 10. mended and rewarded of God [Aod, the Iudge of *Iudic.3.v.* Israel, iustly & lawfully killed Eglon king of Moab, 20.21. their enemie, with a dagger, secretly in his chamber] Iudith [iustly killed Holofernes] an infidel wicked *Iudith.9 v.* enimie of Gods people, and Religion. Al which a- 12. ctions were lawful, and pleased God: yet being extra-ordinarie, doe neither alter the ordinarie law of God, and nature , which condemne manslaughter, nor ex-cuse anie person from greuous sinne, in killing men. otherwise then in lawful warre, or by other publique iustice. Of some other particular examples, there is *ch.13.v.6.* more doubt. As of Iephte his fact in sacrificing his 10. &c. daughter. For though it is certaine, that he sinned in rashly

The extra-ordinarie fact of some, is no warrant for priuate per-sons, to doe the like.

Iephte is pro-bably excused

rashly vowing, that he would offer to God in sacrifice, whatsoeuer liuing thing should first meete him,
in his returne from battel with victorie. Yet in performing this incōsiderate vow, he is by manie probably excused, for that he supposed it to be Gods wil,&
sure it was not pleasant, but very greuous to himself,
As it was also greuous to Abraham, according to nature,to kil his beloued sonne Isaac, but to the good
contentment of his minde, hauing Gods expresse
commandment so to do. It is also more probable
that Samson did wel in killing himself,with manie
Philistians. Not directly in that he killed himself,
but in that he resolued rather to dye himselfe,at that
time, being captiue in the handes of his,and Gods
enimies, then not to kil somanie of them. For [there
were al the Princes of the Philistians, and the whole
multitude were about three thousand.] God also
concurred in his act, restoring to him that miraculous strength to shake the pillars,and to pul downe
the house vpon them (as a trappe vpon so manie
Rattes) And so he killed manie moe dying,then before he had killed liuing.] Both which renowmed
Iudges,Iephte & Samsō,are registred by S.Paul,in the
Catologue of the Sainctes of the old Testament.
But King Saul doubtles sinned greuously in killing
himselfe,through errour, and weaknes of mind,not
susteyning the iust punishment of God, with due patience. His esquire also vnlawfully bereueed himself
of life,through his pusillanimitie. The case of Razias
a Noble Iew, one of the Ancients of Ierusalem, killing himselfe in distresse, is very doubtful. Whose admirable stout courege, holie Scripture reporteth,but
praiseth it not. Howsoeuer therfore these, and such
other singular persons, in special cases, did some very
wel,some doubfully, some very il,in killing others,or
themselues, the general Commandment is the ordi-

narie

Sidenotes: Iudic. 11. v. 30.31.36.39. — ch. 16. v. 26. &c. — v. 30. — Heb. 11. v. 32 — 1. Reg. 31. v. 4. 5. — 2. Mach. 14. v. 37. 41. 42.

Margin: from sinne, in killing his daughter. — Samson is more proba-bly defended, in killing him-selfe, with three thou-sand enimies of God. — King Saul and his esquire, sinned gre-uously in kil-ling theselues, — The stout cou-rege of Razis as is more ad-mirable,then imitable.

narie Rule. That[thou shalt not murder] nor kil anie
person, otherwise then by order of publique iustice;
and in due maner.

4. Amongst other kindes of manslaughter, and
wilful murder, scarce anie is more greuous sinne, then
priuate combate. Which some (deluded by the diuel)
would exeuse by pretence of defending their estimation in manhode. As if such fighting were an act of
manlie valure, or militarie fortitude: to which vertue,
it is in deede, directly opposite: proceding of a weake
minde, not able to sustaine supposed wrong, for vertues sake. For by true fortitude, man is valiāt against al
tentations of the diuel, the flesh, and the world. And
so according to Gods precept, against his owne wrath
ful inclination, & passion of priuate reuenge. For [Bet-
ter is the patient, then a strong man: & he that ruleth
his minde, then the ouerthrower of cities] As for
warlike fortitude, and corege in iust battel, vndetta-
ken by lawful auctoritie, or of lawful defence of himself, being inuaded by theeues, or murderers, it hath
no affinitie with priuate combate, wittingly chalenged, or accepted vpon passionate quarels : which in
true Christian doctrine, is wilful murder, before God,
whether death happen to ensue therof or no. Because
the wil cōsenteth to geue, or to take deadlie woundes,
and so they make themselues guiltie of al, that either
doth, or may probably happen therby. For that they
geue cause vnto such effect. And the Law of God saith
expressely [He that striketh a man wilfully to kil him,
dying let him dye] appointing the same punishmēt for
actual attempting, as for actual killing And though
the common Lawes of some countries, only so punish
the effect, yet before God it is no lesse sinne. It is also
wilful damnation of their soules, because their
soules being, euen for this attempt (howsoeuer they
are otherwise) in state of mortal sinne, so parting from
their bodies, do vndoubtedly, and instantly fal into
the

Priuate com-
bate, is wilful
murder before
God: whether
actual death
ensueth or no.

And wilful
damnation of
al their soules,
that consent
thereto.

Pro.16.v.
12.
Mat.5.v.39.
ch.26 v.52.
Ro.13.v.4.
Iac.4.v.1.
13.

Mat.5.v.29.

Exod 21.v.
12.

the diuels iawes, and into eternal torments of Hel. Al through a madde humour, false imagination, and diuelish illusion, accounting wilful wicked audacitie, to be true Christian fortitude, and true fortitude to be cowardlie dastardnes; that is, vise to be vertue; and vertue to be vise [Woe to you that cal euil good, and good euil.]

Isa 5 v. 20, 21.

It is vnlavuful to strike, or imprison anie person, vvithout iust cause, and auctoritie.

ARTICLE 26.

VNto the sinne of maslaughter, perteyne al kindes of vniust hurting anie mans bodie. And it is greater or lesser offence, according to the iniurie, which is done, and so is diuersly to be punished, as appeareth in the Lawes of God, and of nations [If men fal at wordes, (saith the Law of Moyses) and one strike an other with a stone, or with his fist, and he dye not, but lye in his bedde, if he rise, and walke vpon his staffe, he that did strike shal be quitte; yet so that he make restitution for his worke, and for his expenses vpon the Phisitions] Generally al offences in this kinde, were condemned by the Lawe (besides incurring Gods wrath for their sinne) to render [life for life; eye for eye, tooth for tooth; hand for hand; foote for foote; adustion for adustion; wound for wound; stripe for stripe] wherof it is called, *Lex talionis.* The law of like penaltie [If Iudges shal see that the offender be worthie of stripes, they shal cast him downe, and shal cause him to be beaten before them. According to the measure of the sinne, shal the measure also of the stripes be: yet so that they excede not the number of fourtie.]

2. Not only al Persecutors of truth, doe offend in killing, but also in striking, and otherwise vexing

Al bodelie iniuries are forbidden by this precept.

Exod. 21. v. 18. 19.

23. 24. 25.

Deut. 25. v. 2.

v. 3.

Oppressing, Imprisoning,

V 3

and banishing ing the innocent. So [king Pharao greuouſly ſin- *Exod 1.v.*
of innocents ned in oppreſſing the children of Iſrael, with workes, *11.16.22.*
is againſt this with ſtripes for not working ſo much as he requi-
precept. red, in commanding to kil, and to drowne their in- *1.Reg.18.x.*
fants. King Saul offended, not only in attempting *11.25.*
to kil Dauid, but alſo in expelling him from his *ch.19.v.10.*
houſe. King Aſa offended againſt this Precept, in ca- *v 18.*
ſting Hanan the Prophete into priſon, for telling the *2.Par.16.*
truth. Achab king of Iſrael, tranſgreſſed this com- *v.7.10.*
mandment, in puniſhing Micheus, with vniuſt im- *3.Reg.22.v.*
priſonment, commanding to feede him with bread *26 27.*
of tribnlation, and water of diſtreſſe. Thoſe offended, that caſt Ieremias the Prophet into a dyrtie *Iere 37.v.*
lake, and darke dungeon, and al thoſe that ſtroke *13.14.*
him.] And innnmerable the like. Iſaias blamed the *ch.38.v.7.*
vulgar people of the Iewes, for this crime ſaying [Be- *Iſa.58.v.4.*
hold you faſt to debates, and contentions, and ſtrike
with the fiſt impiouſly] S. Iohn Baptiſt, exhorting al
ſinners to repentance, admoniſheth ſouldiars [Not to *Luc.3.v.14.*
calumniate anie man.]

Al Chriſtians   3. Generally, al Chriſtians muſt rather ſuffer, then
are bound to doe violence. Our Sauiour commandeth [Not to re- *Mat.5.v.39.*
vſe clemencie, ſiſt euil: but if one ſtrike thee on the right cheeke,
and meeke- turne to him alſo the other.] Be you rather content
nes. to take a ſecond blow, then by priuate auctoritie, to
reuenge the firſt. In no wiſe to ſtrike thy fellow ſeruants [Not reuenging your ſelues, my deareſt (ſaith S. *Rom. 12.v.*
Paul) but geue place vnto wrath. For it is written: *19.*
Reuenge belongeth to me: ſaith our Lord.]

Reuengeful vvordes, and anger vvithout iuſt cauſe, are alſo forbidden.

ARTICLE 27.

Anger with   ANger being in it ſelfe, neither vertue, nor viſe,
reaſo is a helpe   but a paſſion of the mind, grounded in the
natu-

natural power of the foule, which is called *facultas* to vertue; with
irafcibilis: When it is rightly vſed, perteyneth to the out iuſt reaſon
vertue of fortitude: whereby hard thinges ate be tter is a ſinne.
put in execution, notwithſtanding impediments, that
hinder the ſeruice of God, or anie other iuſt thing. But

Gen.4.v.4.
5.v.6.
when it reſiſteth, or excedeth reaſon, it becommeth
a hurtful ſinne, often and much condemned in holie
Scriptures. [Cain ſeeing Abels Sacrifice to be re
ſpected, and his owne not reſpected of God; he
was exceding angrie, and his countenance abated:

ch 37.v.4.
8.9.&c.
(Wherupon) our Lord ſaid to him: Why art thou
angrie? and why is thy countenance fallen?] Io
ſephs brethren, ſeing that he was beloued of his
father, more then al his ſonnes, were ſo ouercome
with the paſſion of anger, that they [hated him: neither could they ſpeake anie thing to him peace

1.Reg.17.
v 50,
ch 18.v.8.
9.
ablie] When Saul heard the wemen ſinging, in the
triumph of Dauids victorie ouer Goliath [Saul
ſtrooke a thouſand, and Dauid tenne thouſand: he
was exceding angrie, and did not looke vpon Dauid with right eyes from that day.]

Exod.15.
v 20.
Num.12.v.
3.
Exod.32.v.
19.
2. But anger ruled with reaſon, is very commendable, and neceſſarie [So Moyſes (though he was the
mildeſt man aboue al men that dwelt vpon the earth)
was angrie againſt them, that contrarie to his commàndment, had left ſome Manna vntil the morning]
Alſo when he ſaw the golden calfe, and the people
dācing, he [being very wrath, threw the tables out of
his hand, & brake them, at the foote of the mount]

Nu.16.v.15.
ch.31.v.14.
15.16.
Likewiſe againſt the rebellious ſchiſmatikes, Core,
Dathan, and Abiron, being[very wrath, he ſaid to our
Lord: Reſpect not their ſacrifices] Againe he was very
angrie with the Princes of the Hoſte, the Tribunes, &
Centurions, becauſe they had reſerued the wemen of
[the Madianites, which had ſeduced the children of

4.Reg.13.v.
18.19.
Iſrael, by the ſuggeſtion of Balaam]Eliſeus the man of
God, was angrie with Ioas King of Iſrael(who hauing
ſtrooken

Examples of
commendable
anger.

strooken the earth three times,(stood stil)and said to
him:If thou hadst strooken fiue,or six,or seuen times,
thou hadst strooken Syria euen to destruction] King
[Assuerius was angrie with Aman, for complotting *Est.7.v.6.7.*
mischefe against the whole nation of the Iewes] Manie examples occurre of iust anger against sinnes, and
imperfections. Wherupon the Royal Prophet , and S.
Paul, doe admonish Gods seruants to be angrie for *Psal.4.v.5.*
iust cause, saying [Be angrie,and sinne not] Which in- *Eph.4.26.*
cludeth two good lessons [Be angrie] when cause re- *27.*
quireth, els you doe sinne in pusillanimitie: and [Be
angrie] with moderation, els you doe sinne in passionate furie. For auoyding wherof, the same Apostle
saith[Let not the sunne goe downe vpon your anger. *Ibid.*
Geue not place to the diuel. Anger(saith Salomon)is
better the laughter: because by sadnes of the counte- *Eccle.7.v.*
nance, the mind of the offender is corrected. But be *4.*
not quickly angrie: because anger resteth in the bo- *v.10.*
some of a foole.]

Gods anger is
not passion,
but perfect iu-
stice.

3, It is also most frequently said in the holie Scrip-
tures:that God is angrie with sinners. But Gods anger
is properly called *propaßion*,not passió,because his perfection admitteth not anie passion, nor imperfection.
He is said to be sorie, angrie, and the like, when he
doth such thinges, as men vsually doe, when they
are iustly moued with sorow, anger,and the like. As
where it is said, that [it repented God, that he made *Gen.6.v.6.*
man on the earth: And touched inwardly with sorow *7.*
of hart, I wil,saith he, cleane take away man, whom I
haue created, from the face of the earth] signifying,
that as men repenting that they haue done something,
vse to reuerse,or vndoe that which they had done , &
like not:so[God seing mans cogitation wholly bent to *v.5.*
euil; decreed,by an vniuersal floud,to take away man
from the face of the earth] as if he were penitent,so-
rowful, or angrie, which in dede is vnpossible, that he
should be. Because he is immutable. So there is infinite
diffe-

difference-betwen Gods anger,sorow, furie, &c: and these passions in men. When therfore it is said, that [God in the spirite of his furie,destroyed sinners: His furie wil take indignation: wil strike with the sword: His furie is angrie against his people. Let thyne anger cease ô Lord,] and the like: it is therby signified;that God so punished,or wil punish sinnes,as his iustice requireth. And to expresse it the better, it is declared by the similitude of mens indignation,anger,wrath,and furie, iust or vniust, moderate, or immoderate: but so to be vnderstood, that in God it is alwayes most iust, and most moderate, lesse then sinners descerue. And these passions in man ought alwayes to be moderate: and so anger is often necessarie,to correct vises in our selues, and in others. Otherwise it is sinne.

Exod.15. v.7.8. ch.22.v.24. ch.32.v.11.12.&c. Leuit.26.v.28.29. Apoc.19.v.15. Iac.1.v.20.

4. Against immoderate anger therfore holie Scripture, hath manie wholsome admonitions. Holie Iacob the Patriarch iustly reprehended the vndiscrete [furie of his sonnes Simeon and Leui, in killing manie Sichimetes] with danger to themselnes, and whole familie. Ioseph aduised his brothers [not to be angrie in the way.] To which passion trauelers are much subiect, by occasion of wearines, want, and frequent molestations. The Royal Prophet admonisheth so to haue iust indignation against the wicked, that we hurt not our owne soules [Cease from wrath, and leaue furie: haue not emulation, that thou (thyself) be malignant. For so a man by his passionate emulation, falleth into that sinne, which he condemneth in others[A foole by and by sheweth his anger (saith Salomon) but he that dissembleth iniuries is wise. A soft answere breaketh anger, and a hard word raiseth vp furie. A peaceable tongue is a tree of life: but that which is immoderate, shal breake the spirite. He that is swete in speach, shal finde great thinges. Better is a drye morsel with ioy, then a houseful of victimes with browling. He that moderateth his wordes, is learned and prudent. A spi-

Admonitions against vnbridled anger.

Gen.34.v.25.26.30. ch.49.v.5.6.7. ch.45.v.24. Psal.36.v.1.8. Rom.2.v.21.22. Pro.12.v.16. ch.15.v.1. v.4. ch.16.v.21. ch.17.v.1. v.27.

rite that is eafie to be angrie , who can fufteyne?Say
not I wil requite euil,expect our Lord,and he wil de- *ch.18.v. 14.*
liuer thee. It is better to dwel in a defert land, then *ch.20.v.12.*
with a brawling, and angrie woman. Say not : As he *ch 21.v.19.*
hath done to me, fo wil I doe to him. As a citie being *ch 24.v.29.*
ch.25. v. 15.
open, and without compaffe of walles: fo a man that *18.*
can not represse his spirite in speaking. Anfwere not a
foole according to his follie(that is foolishly)left thou *ch.26.v 4.*
be made like to him.Anfwere a foole according to his *5.21.*
follie (as his follie may be corrected) left he feme to
himself to be wife. As coales to burning coales,and *ch.27.4.6.*
wood to fire;fo an angrie man raifeth brawles. Drop- *15.*
ping through, in the day of cold, and a brawling woman,are compared together. A wife man, if he con- *ch.29.v.9.*
tend with a foole, whether he be angrie, or whether
he laugh, shal not finde reft. A fwete word multiplieth friendes, and appeafeth enimies : and a gratious
tongue in a good man abundeth.] bringeth good *Eccl.6. v.5.*
fruite . Other Prophets, by wordes and examples
teach the fame.

Immoderate anger is forbidde by this commandement,

5. Chrift our Lord, teaching the true fenfe of this
commandment againft murder:explaneth clearly that
[whofoeuer is angrie with his brother(without iuft
caufe) shal be in danger of iudgement. And whofoe- *Mat.5.v. 22*
uer shal fay to his brother: Raca (that is, anie litle *23.*
word, or found of word,tending to reproch, or reuenge,) shal be in danger of councel (shal be punished more or leffe) And whofoeuer shal fay: Thou
foole(a manifeft calumnious word,notoriously dimi-
nishing his fame) shal be guiltie of the hel of fire]Nei-
ther did our Lord approue the zele of his difciples,S.
Iames, and S. Iohn, demanding [If they should pray
that fire might come downe from heauen & confume *Luc.9.v 53.*
certaine (difdainful Samaritans) but turning, he re- *54.55.*
buked them,faying:You know not of what fpirit you
are] And accordingly when his Apoftles had receiued
the Holie Ghoft, with his diuine giftes,they vfed,and
taught

taught al mildnes, ioyntly with zele of truth, and of
other vertues. [Bleſſe them that perſecute you (ſaith
S. Paul) bleſſe, and curſe not. Let euerie man be ſwift
to heare (ſaith S. Iames) but ſlow to ſpeake, and ſlow
to anger. For the anger of man, worketh not the iuſtice of God]S. Peter exhorting to meekenes ſaith[To
this are you called: Becauſe Chriſt alſo ſuffered for vs,
leauing vs an example to folow his ſteppes. Who did
no ſinne, neither was guile found in his mouth. Who
when he was reuiled, did not reuile; when he ſuffered,
he threatned not: but deliuered him ſelfe to him, that
iudged him vniuſtly. Be ye louers of fraternitie (that
is, of al your brothers, and neighbours) merciful, modeſt, humble : for vnto this you are called; that you
may by inheritance, poſſeſſe benediction] So theſe &
other Apoſtles, in manie places, admoniſhed to beware of immoderate wrath, and anger, from reuengeful wordes, as from other ſinnes; though euerie inordinate paſſion, or haſtie word is not mortal, but more
commonly a venial ſinne. [For in manie things (ſaith
S. Iames) we offend al. If anie man offend not in
word, this is a perfect man.]

Ro.12.v.14.
Iac.1.v.19.
20.

1.Pet.2.v.21
22.23.

ch.3.v.8.9.

Gal.5.v.20.
Coloſ.3.v.8.
1.Tim.2.v.
8.

Iac.3.v.2.
Eccli.14.v.1
ch.19.v.17.

*Al are bound, ſo much as lieth in them, to haue
peace vvith al: and to loue their enimies.*

ARTICLE 28.

IT is the Law of nature, directed by the light of
reaſon, that we muſt doe to others as we would,
that they ſhould doe to vs. Wherupon holie Tobias,
exhorting his ſonne, amongſt manie particular good
leſſons, geueth this general rule[That which thou ha-
teſt to be done to thee by an other: ſee thou doe it not
to an other at anie time]Seing therfore we would not
that anie ſhould hate vs, we muſt not hate anie. And
as we would that al ſhould loue vs, ſo we muſt loue al.

As we would
be loued of al
men: ſo we
muſt loue al.

Tob.4.v.16.

W 2   More

More expresly God commanded [Thou shalt not
hate thy brother in thy hart, but controlle him openly (if he be in fault) left thou (by silence seming to
consent) incurre sinne through him. Thou shalt loue
thy friende as thy selfe, I the Lord. If a stranger dwel
in your land, and abide among you, doe not vpbraide
him : but let him be among you, as the same contri-
man : and you shal loue him as your selues; for you also haue bene strangers, in the Land of Ægypt. I the
Lord your God] Againe, [Doe you threfore loue
strangers; because you also were strangers in the land
of Ægypt].

Leuit. 19. v.
17,
18.
33.
34.

Deut. 10. v.
18.19.

2.   Enimies are also neighbours; sometimes of our
kindred, or brothers. But whether so or not, the Law
prescribed, that [If thou mete thine enimies oxe, or
asse, going astray, bring it backe to him. If thou see
the asse of him that hateth thee, lye vnder his burden,
thou shalt not passe by, but shalt lift him vp with the
burden] So wilfully blinde were the Pharisees, that
vpon the holie text [thou shalt loue thy freind as thy
selfe] they falsely, and maliciously inferred, as an other
precept [Thou shalt hate thyne enemie] directly opposite to the other text [Thou shalt reduce the asse go
ing astray to his owner [and, lift vp the asse fallen vnder his burden] belonging to him that hateth thee.
King Dauid by fact and word, teacheth Christians to
loue their enimies. Who [when he might haue killed
King Saul in a caue, and an other time in the campe,
he would not. Neither would he kil Semei : scorne-
fully reuiling him : nor suffer others to kil him. Wherupon, and vpon like patience, and loue towards particular enimies to his owne person, he most truly testified of himself, saying [With them that hated peace,
I was peaceable : When I spake to them, they impugned me gratis] without cause; without effect. For they
did not moue him to emnitie, in reuenge of himselfe.
But in reuenge of Gods enimies, he as truly auouched,

VVe must also
loue enimies,
that loue not
vs.

Exod 23. v.
45,

Mat. 5. v. 43.

1. Reg. 24. v.
54.

ch. 26. v. 7.
9.

2. Reg. 16. v.
5. &c.
Ps. 119. v. 7.

and

and reioyced therin before God, saying [Did not I hate them, that hate thee, ô Lord; & pined away; becaufe of thyne enimies? With perfect hatred did I hate them: they are become enimies to me.] Salomon preacheth the fame doctrine I [Ioy (faith he) foloweth them that geue counfels of peace. Côtend not with the wicked, nor emulate the impious. If thyne enimie fhal hunger geue him meate: if he thirft, geue him drinke. For doing this, thou fhalt heape hote coales of fire vpon his head] This is the way to mollifie his hard hart, with the feruour of thy charitie.

3. Bleffed are the meeke (faith the true peace makere our B. Sauiour) for they fhal poffeffe the land. Bleffed are the peace makers: for they fhal be called the children of God . If thou offer thy gift at the Altar, and there thou remember, that thy brother hath ought againft thee; leaue there thyne offering before the Altar: and goe firft, to be reconciled to thy brother: and then coming thou fhalt offer thy gift. I fay to you, loue your enimies, doe good to them, that hate you, pray for them that perfecute, and abufe you: that you may be the children of your Father, which is in heauen: who maketh his funne to rife, vpon good & bad: and rayneth vpon the iuft, and vniuft. For if you loue them that loue you, what reward fhal you haue? Doe not alfo the publicanes this? And if you falute your brethren only, what doe you more? Doe not alfo the heathen this? Be you perfect therfore , as alfo your heauentie Father is perfect. You muft forgeue feuentie times feuen times (that is how often foeuer) Vnles you forgeue others, my heauenlie Father (faith Chrift) fhal deliuer you fo the tormenters, vntil you repay al the debt: If you forgeue not euerie one his brother, from your hartes.] Our Lord alfo himfelf prayed for thofe that crucified him . And S. Steuen prayed for them, that ftoned him to death.

4. Bleffe them that perfecute you (faith S. Paul)

Pf.138.v. 21.
22.
Pro.12.v.20
ch.24.v.19.
ch.25.v.21.
22.
Rom. 12. v. 20.

Mat.5.v.4.
9.
v 24.
25.
v. 44.
45.
46.
47.
48.
ch.18.v.22.
33. 34.
Luc.23.v.34.
Act.7.v.60.
Rom. 12.
v. 14.

Readie minde to remitte iuriès, is necef-farie.

W. 3 To

To no man rendering euil for euil. If it may be, as 17.18.19.21. much as is in you, hauing peace with al men. Not reuenging yourselues, my dearest, but geue place vnto wrath. Be not ouercome of euil, but ouercome the euil in good. Certes there is plainly a fault in you 1, *Cor.6.v.7.* (saith he to the Corinthians) that you haue iudgemēts among you. why doe you not rather take wrong? why doe you not rather suffer fraude? Al the Law is fulfilled in oue word. Thou shalt loue thy neighbour as thy self] saith the same Apostle to other Christians. *Gal.*5.l.14 15 [But if you bite and eate one an other; take heede you be not consumed one of an other] And reciting *v.*19.20.21. workes of the flesh, which are (among other) enmities contentions, emulations, angers, brawles, dissentions, sectes, enuies, murders, and the like. [I fore tel you (saith he) as I haue foretold you, that they which doe such thinges, shal not obteyne the kingdom of God. 15. 16. If we liue in the spirite, in the spirite also let vs walke. Let vs not be made desirous of vaine glorie, prouoking one an other, enuyiug one an other. If there be *Phil. 2. v.1.* anie consolation in Christ, if anie solace of charitie, if 2.3 4. anie societie of spirite, if anie bowels of commiseration; fulfil my ioy, that you be of one meaning, hauing the same charitie of one minde, agreing in one, nothing by contention, neither by vaine glorie: but in humilitie, each counting others better then themselues: euerie one not considering the thinges, that are 1. *Thes.*5. v. their owne, but those that are other mens. we besech 14 15. you brethren, admonish the vnquiet, comforte the weake minded, beare vp the weake, be patient to al. See that none render euil for euil to anie man: but alwayes that which is good, pursne towards each other, and towards al.] S. Iames vrgeth the same loue, and concord amongst al saying, [Grudge not brethren, one against an other, that you be not iudged. Behold the *Iac.*5. v.9. Iudge standeth before the gate] The like S. Peter: admonisheth al [to make their soules chaste in obediēce 1. *Pet.*1.v. 22.

of

Let al good Christians direct their consciences by these admonitions of Christ, and his Apostles.

Let both chalengers and accepters of cōbates, and al

ch. 2 v. 1. 2
ch. 3. v. 9. 10
ch. 4. v. 7. 8.

of charitie, in the sincere loue of fraternitie, from the hart, loue ye one an other earnestly. Laying away therfore al malice, and al guile, and simulations, and enuies, and detractions: as infants euen now borne, reasonable milke without guile desire ye, that in it you may grow vnto saluation. Before al thinges hauing mutual charitie, continual among yourselues: because charitie couereth the multitude of sinnes] S. Iohn most diligently inculcateth the very same necessitie of louing al men, saying [He that saith he is in the light, and hateth his brother, is in darkenes euen til now. He that loueth his brother, abideth in the light, and scandal is not in him. But he that hateth his brother, is in the darkenes, and walketh in the darkenes, and knoweth not whither he goeth: because the darkenes hath blinded his eyes. He that loueth not abideth in death. Whosoeuer hateth his brother, is a murderer. And you know that no murderer hath life euerlasting abiding in himself.] He hath not sanctifying grace, by which euerlasting life should be obteyned.

1. Ioan. 2.
v. 9 10 11.

ch. 3. v. 14. 1
15.

that kepe enmitie in their hartes remember, that the Iudge standeth before the gate.

Adultrie, fornication, & al venerious actes, are greuous sinnes. And after vowed chastitie as sacrilegious.

ARTICLE 29.

LVxurie abunded much in the first age of the world. For [after that men begane to be multiplied vpon the earth, and had procreation of daugters: the sonnes of God (the better sorte of people. Which were of Seths progenie) seing the daughters of men (especially of Cains race, which were more wicked) that they were fayre, tooke to themselues wiues out of al. Which they had chosen] without order, at their pleasure. Wherof came the generation of Giants (an huge great, lascinious, and cruel people)

Gen. 6. v.
2.

v. 4.

The whole world was drowned especially for sinnes of the flesh

people.) And the earth was corrupted before God, &   v. 11.
was replenished with iniquitie. And God said to Noe: 13.
The end of al flesh is come before me. I wil destroy
them with the earth] So that especially for carnal sin-   ch.7.v 7.21.
nes al were drowned, with an vniuersal floud, sauing   23.
                                                          ch.18.v.
eight persons. After wihch againe, for the abominable   20.

Likewise So- sinne of Sodom and Gomorre, with other cities ad-   ch.19.v.24.
dom and Go- ioyning [Our Lord rained vpon them brinstone and   52.
morre. fire, & wholly consumed them. And they were made   Iud.v.7.
VVere burnt an example, susteyning the paine of eternal fire.] Like-   Gen.12.v.17
for carnal sin- wise carnal sinnes were condemned in al other Na-   18.20.
nes, not to be tions. Pharao in Ægypt, and Abimelech in Gerara,   ch.26.v.10.
named. heathen kinges, knew that adultrie is a great sinne: &   11.
                                                                        ch.34.v.2.
therefore commanded their people, that none should   23.25.
touch Sara the wife of Abraham, nor Rebecca Isaacs   ch.35 v.22.
wife. The Sichemetes were iustly slaine for rauishing   ch.49.v.4.
Dina, Iacobs daughter, though the maner of reuenge
was not discrete. Incest was worthely contemned in
Ruben, for which his father Iacob depriued him of   ch.38. v.24.
his birth right. Simple fornication was iudged in   ch.49. v. 7.
Thamar to be worthie of death. Holie Ioseph the Pa-   20.
triarch would in nowise assent vnto his mystresse to
committe the crime of adultrie. For which his constant chastitie he was vniustly cast into prison. But by
that occasion, shortly after aduanced.   Exo.20.v.

The written 2.   In the written Law, al kindes of fleshlie vene-   14.
Law punished rious sinnes, are forbidde, by the common name of   Deut.5.v 18
diuers carnal aduoutrie. God saying to his people [Thou shalt not   Leu.20. v.
sinnes with committe aduoutrie] And that vnder paine of death   10.11.12 13.
death. [If anie man committe adultrie with an other mans   &c.
wife, dying let him dye: both the adulterer, and the ad-
uoutresse] Likewise incest with kindred, or alied;   ch.21.v.9.
beastialitie; and fleshlie sinnes against nature, were punished with death: some stoned, some burnt. For
fornication with pagane people [twentie foure thou-   Nu.25.v.1.5.
sand Israelites were slaine, hanged on gibbets, by the
handes of the Iudges. God so commanding, that his
furie might be auerted from Israel.]

3.Manie

3. Manie holie examples, and wholſome admonitions are written in the holie Scriptures, commending chaſtitie, and condemning fleſhlie ſinnes, eſpecially in theſe places of the old Teſtament, beſides the former recited and others. Iob 24.v.15.ch.31.v.1.Tob. 4.v.13.2. Reg.11.v.2.ch.12.v.7.3. Reg.11.v.1.2.&c. Pſal. 49.v.18. Prou.6.v.32. Eccli.23.v.24.Mal.3.v.5. Dan.13. v.8.9.&c.

Deut. 22.
v.20 21.
ch 23 v 17.
Iudic.19.
v.21.&c.

4. Al which is much more confirmed in the new Teſtament, where al puritie is required, in ſoule and bodie: in act, word, and thought. Againſt carnal cogitatiõs our Sauiour expreſſly denounceth that [Whoſoeuer ſhal ſee a woman to luſt after her, hath already committed aduoutrie with her in his hart] If the hart yeeld ful conſent to ſuch cogitation. And therfore commandeth al to auoide al occaſions, of ſuch tentations, by the eyes, yea [rather to plucke out that eye, that ſcandalizeth. For it is expedient that one of the parts periſh, rather then that the wholebodie goe into hel] Againſt ſimple fornication (which the Gentiles commonly held for no ſinne) the Apoſtles in their Councel made an expreſſe Decree, declaring it to be vnlawful: much more are al other greater ſinnes of this kind, more damnable. S. Paul teſtifieth that diuers Gentiles [not honoring God, as they knew him, became vaine in their cogitations, changed the glorie of the incorruptible God, into a ſimilitude of the image of a corruptible man, and of foules, and fourfooted beaſtes, and of them that crepe, haue worſhipped, and ſerued the creature, rather then the Creator. Therfore God deliuered them into paſſion of ignomie, and into a reprobate ſenſe, repleniſhed with al iniquitie, malice, fornication] and al vncleanes. For this kind of ſinne he puniſhed ſome, & admoniſhed al to auoid the ſame. Yea to ſhunne the companie of ſuch Chriſtians, as became fornicators. [Conſidering that their bodies being (by profeſſion) the members of

Mat 5.v.
29 30.

ch.18.v.9.
Act.15.v.
20.
ch.21.v. 25.

Rom.1.v.21
23.25.26.
28.29.

1.Cor.5.v.1.
3.11.
ch.6.v.15.
18.

X   Chriſt

Manie holie
Scriptures doe
much condemne al carnal ſinnes.

Eſpecially the
Law of Chriſt
requireth al
puritie of mind
and bodie.

Chrift, are by fornication made the members of har-
lottes] noting with al that fornication is not only a
finne againft the foule, but alfo [againft the bodie]
which it defileth, weakneth; corrupteth, wafteth, &
deftroyeth, much more al impudicicie, and leacherie
being workes of the flesh, deftroy the spirite. And
therfore [ought not fo much as to be named among
Chriftians] And fo in ftead of reciting more facred
textes, I rather remitte those, that shal nede to fee
more (for this purpofe) vnto these fpecial places. v.5.
1.Thef.4.v.3. Heb.12.v.16. ch.13.v.4. Iac.4.v.4.Apoc.
21.v.8.

*2.Cor.12.v.
21.
Gal.5.v.19.
Eph.5.v.3.4
Colof.3 v.5.*

Violation of vowed chaftitie is facrilege.

5. Only here we adde, that whatfoeuer fleshlie
venerious finne is anie way committed in act, word,
or deliberate thought, with confent of the minde, by
fuch as haue vowed chaftitie, is fpiritual inceft, and
facrilege. In fo much, that the very purpofe, and wil
to marie, after promife to God, of perpetual chaftitie,
is more damnable [becaufe they haue made voide
their firft faith (that is to fay, their promife and vow,
to God)& are turned back after Satan] [faith S. Paul.
If the vow was folemne, fuch pretended mariges are
no mariges at al, but facrilegious adultrie. If the vow
was only priuate, then the Mariage is valide : but the
breach alfo of fuch a vow is damnable.

*1 Tom.5.
v.11.12.
v.15.*

*Al are bond to efteme chaftitie; as a precious
thing. And to chatife the bodie, that it may
ferue the fpirite.*

ARTICLE 30.

Al are bound to kepe cither perpetual chaftitie or matrimonial.

ALbeit none are bond to kepe their virginitie, or
perpetual continencie, wholly abftaining from
Mariage, but fuch as voluntarily accept of that Euangelical counfel, and binde themfelues therto by free
vow: yet not only those that doe fo promife vnto
God

Gòd, are thenceforth ſtrictly obliged: to performe the ſame: but alſo al others are bond to eſteme much of chaſtitie, & euer to obſerue it ſo far, as their ſtate requireth: either in Matrimonie, as the Law of that Sacrament preſcribeth, or in ſingle life, vntil they ſhal lawfully contract Mariage. Both which ſortes of chaſtitie, according to their diuerſe degrees, are often commended in holie Scripture.

Iob.31.v.1

Exemples of chaſtitie.

2.   I haue made a couenant with myne eyes (ſaid holy Iob) that I would not ſo much as thinke of a virgine] By whoſe ſo chaſte, and prudent example, others may lerne that to auoide carnal cogitations, it much auaileth to reſtraine the eyes, and other ſenſes from geuing occaſion to concupiſcence of the minde; & ſo to conſerue chaſtitie, in thonght, word, & dede: according to the ſtate of eurie one. And this ſo diligét care of ſo holie a man wel ſheweth the greatntes and neceſſitie of the ſame verrue. Other exemples doe alſo côfirme the ſame. Ioſeph the Patriarch was an eſpecial paterne of chaſte life, nor yelding to tentatiô, but prudently fleeing, & conſtantly ſuffering the affliction of impriſonment, and loſſe of fauour, and commoditie, with preſent diſpleaſure both of maſter, and myſtreſſe, where he liued, as a bought & ſold ſeruant, in a ſtrange countrie. Iudith the godlie widow, for the loue of chaſtitie, much chaſtiſed her owne bodie [who in the highet part of her houſe made herſelf a ſecrete châber, in which ſhe abode ſhut vp with her maides, and hauing cloth of hare vpon her loynes, ſhe faſted al the dayes of her life, but Sabbathes, & new moones and the feaſtes of the houſe of Iſrael] So ſhe liuing in widoual chaſtitie, wel nere ſenentie yeares, adioyning other vertues vnto her chaſtitie, became the helpe and ſafetie of al the people, in extreme diſtreſſe not only the deliuerer of Bethulia, but conſequently of al the conutrie (As Ioachim the High prieſt teſtified in her iuſt praiſe, ſaying to her) Thon art the glorie

Iob. a maried man.

Gen 39.v. 8.10.12.

Ioſeph in ſingle life.

Iudith.8. v.5.b.

Iudith a widow.

ch.13.v.10 ch.15.1.3. 10.11.

X 2   rie

rie of Ierusalem: thou the ioy of Israel: thou the honour of our people: becaufe thou haft done manfully
& thy hart was ftrengthned, for that thou haft loued
chaftitie: and after thy husband not knowne anie o-
ther. Therfore alfo the hand of our Lord hath ftreng-
thened thee, and rherfore shalt thon be bleffed for
euer. And al the people said: So be it, fo be it] Of this
vertue of chaftitie fee more exemples in the fiftith Article, where we are to declare the lawfulnes, and worthines of vowed chaftitie.

v. 12. *ch.* 16.
v. 25. 26.
Artic 50.

The flesh is to the foule as a bondman to his mafter.

3. In the meane while confider here, the neceffitie &
vtilitie, of duly chaftifing the bodie, that it may ferue
the fpirite. The bodie is or ought to be the feruant of
the foule. In regard wherof Salomon faith [A feruant (a bondflaue) can not be taught by wordes (a-
lone) becaufe he vnderftandeth that, which thou
faift, and contemneth to anfwer] that is, obeyeth
not: and therfore muft be made, with due ftripes to
obey. And therfore he admonisheth thofe that doe
not rightly chaftife their owne bodies, of the inconuenience which foloweth, faying [He that nourisheth his feruant delicatly from his childhood, afterward shal feele him ftubborne] To the fame purpofe
in commendation of chaftitie, an other wifemen faith
[O how beautiful is the chafte generation, with glorie: for the memorie therof is immortal : becaufe it is
knowne both with God, & with men. When it is prefent, they imitate it, and when it hath withdrawne it
felf, they defire it. And it triumpheth, crowned for
euer: winning the reward of vndefiled conflictes.]

Pro. 29.*v.* 19

v. 21.

Sap. 4.*v.* 1, 2.

4　Two thinges doth our Sauiour neceffarily require, in al faithful foules, by the parable of wife virgins [Lampes, and Oyle] for lampes without oyle,
faith without workes, are shut out from the mariage
of glorious foules with Chrift the heauenly fpoufe.
And oyle without lampes, that is, workes without
faith, neuer approch at al, to the gate of heauen. Euen

Mt. 25.*v.* 4.
11. 12.

so chaftitie,without other good workes,fufficeth not Chaftitie ae-
to faluation, but other workes without due chaftitie cording to the
auaile nothing at al: can no fo much as pretend anie ftate of euerie
reward at al. Chaftitie therfore according to euerie one, is moft
ones proper ftate, is firft required,euen as faith it felf, neceffarie.
and then are other good workes to be adioyned[Let
your loynes be gyrded (faith our Lord) and candles
burning in your handes.] What is gyrding of the
loynes, but chaftifing of the whole bodie? for if the
panch be ful, the loynes wil be inflamed;if al the bodie be pampered,the loynes wil firft rebel.Yea though
the bodie be competently, and temperatly fedde; yet
wil the loynes be fcarfly,or hardly kept in order, and
fubiection. Concupifcence remaineth in the iuft, for
Chriftians exercife. The flesh ftriueth againft the fpi-
ritet.If the fpirite ftriue not, if it refift not, the battle
is quickly loft. S. Paul doubtles liued with al temperance, yet was not without his combate. He was enriched fpiritually, with moft excellent giftes,with vnfpeakable knowledge of diuine Myfteries, with admirable power to worke miracles,with moft burning
zele of Gods glorie, and health of foules, with al vertues, efpecially with perfect charitie , the fame that
geueth life to al the reft:yet for his better exercife, for S. Paul for his
his greater victorie, for his more glorious crowne: more merite,
left other incomparable gifts [might extol him,there fuffered tenta-
was geuen him a pricke of the flesh, an angel of Sa- tions.
tan to buffete him. For the which he often befought
our Lord, that it might depart from him,but receiued
anfwere; that Chrifts grace fuffieeth him:for power,
and vertue is perfected in infirmitie.] What did he And therfore
therfore more befides his earneft, and frequent pray- both prayed]
er; him felf telleth vs, what els he did; faying [I doe and chaftifed
runne (the courfe of warefare, to gaine the victorie) his bodie.
not as it were, at an vncertaine thing:fo I fight,not as
it were beating the ayre (with wordes only) but I
chaftife my bodie, and bring it into feruitude,left per-

haps

Matt.12.v.35

2 Cor.12.v.
7.

8.

9.

1.Cor.9.v.
26.27,

haps, when I haue preached to others, my self become
reprobate.] Thus by example teaching what al should
doe: he alſo writte the ſame, for inſtruction to al poſteritie; and further addeth [In al thinges (ſaith he) let
vs exhibite our ſelues, as the Miniſters of God, in much
patience, in tribulations, in neceſsities, in diſtreſſes, in
ſtripes, in priſons, in ſeditions, in labours, in watch-
ings, in faſtings, in chaſtitie;] Alwaies among neceſſarie vertues, naming *chaſtitie* for a ſpecial one, in al degrees: as wel in chaſte Mariage, which muſt be honorable in al fidelitie, loue, concord, & al other reſpects,
[The bed vndefiled] free from aduoutrie: as in ſingle
life, that chaſtitie be perfect in dede, word, & thought.

Chaſtitie is an
eſpecial vertue
of edification.
Likewiſe S. Peter admoniſheth to loue and kepe chaſtitie, not only for the perfecting of euerie ones ſoule,
but alſo for edification to others, ſaying [Let the wemen be ſubiect to their huſhandes : that if any beleue
not the word, by the conuerſation of the wemen,
without the word, they may be wonne; conſidering
your chaſte conuerſation in feare] With care to geue
no leaſt cauſe of ielouſie, touching chaſtitie.

2. *Cor. 6. v.*
4. 5. 6.
Gal 5. v. 22
23.
1. *Tim.* 4. v.
12.
ch. 2. v. 2.
ch. 3, v 3.
4.
ch. 5. v. 2. 22.
Tit. 2. v. 5.

Heb. 13. v. 4.

1. *Pet.* 3. v. 1
2.

Al vniuſt getting, or holding of others goods,
is forbidde by the Lavv of God; and
nations.

ARTICLE 31.

Al iniurie in
teporal goods
is forbidde by
the name of
theft.
VNder the name of theft, are comprehended al
iniuries, done to anie other in their temporal
goods, eſtimation, and fame. As by ſecrete ſtea-
ling, by violent robbing, by fraudulent deceiuing,
by vſurie, oppreſſion, tyrannie, by not paying debts,
by deſtroying vniuſtly others goods: by calumniation,
detraction, deriſion: by anie vniuſt maner depriuing
an other of that thing, which belongeth vnto him. Al
which are forbidde by theſe general wordes of Gods
Law [Thou ſhalt not ſteale.] More particularly the
ſame

Exod 20. v.
15.

same diuine Law, adioyned due punishmēt for tranſ-greſsing in certaine caſes, conuenient for that time and people, ſaying [He that ſhal ſteale a man, and hold him, being conuicted of the treſpaſſe, dying let him dye. If anie man ſteale an oxe, or ſhepe, and kil, or ſel it: he ſhal reſtore fiue oxen for one oxe; and foure ſhepe, for one ſhepe] So greater ſinnes are more ſe-utrely puniſhed, aboue the proportion of the damage: which Iudicial penal precepts may be changed, or ta-ken away, or others made by Princes, & Common wealths, as is declared before, and more hereafter. But the Moral precepts euer did, and ſtil doe bind al men. Of which we eſpecially ſpeake here, prouing the ſame as wel by the old, as by the new Teſtament.

2. Touching vſurie therfore, which is too much vſed, and by manie defended, or cloked, the Law of God ſaith [If thou lend money to my people being poore, that dwelleth with thee, thou ſhalt not vrge them, as an exactor, or oppreſſe them with vſuries. If thy brother be empoueriſhed, and weake of hand, & thou receiue him as a ſtranger, and ſeiourner, & he liue with thee, take not vſuries of him, nor more then thou gaueſt. Feare thy God, that thy brother may liue with thee. Thou ſhalt not geue him thy money to v-ſurie: and ouerplus of the fruites, thou ſhalt not exact of him. I the Lord your God. If thy brother conſtrai-ned by pouertie ſel him ſelf to thee, thou ſhalt not oppreſſe him, with the ſeruitude of ſeruants (that is of bondſlaues) but he ſhal be as an hyreling, and a ſe-iourner. Thou ſhalt not lend to thy brother money to vſurie, nor corne, nor anie other thing, but to the ſtranger] By ſtrangers is vnderſtood, onlie ſuch as are enimies, againſt whom is lawful warre. For al nati-ons admitted among Gods people, were by his Law, in caſe of his proper people.]

3. Vſurie is alſo condemned as a wicked iniuſtice, by the holie Prophets, and by Chriſt himſelf expreſly.

The

Deut 5. v. 19
Exod. 21 v. 16.
cb. 22. v. 1.
Deut 24. v. 7.

Artic. 23.
Art. 47.

Exod. 22. v. 25
Leuit 25. v. 35. 36. 37. 38. 39. 40.

Deut 23. v. 19. 20.
Ex. 22. v. 21 cb. 23. v. 9. &c.

Vſurie is con-demned by the written Law.

The Royal Prophete plainly affirmeth, that whofoe-

And by the Prophets. uer wil enter into heauen, muft be free from the finne of vfurie, amongft other requifite conditions, faying: [Lord, who shal dwel in thy tabernacle, or who shal reft in thy holie hil? (and therto anfwereth)He that walketh without fpotte, and worketh iuftice. (And among other greuous finnes, nameth vfurie.[He(faith the Prophet)that hath not geuen his money to vfurie: and hath not taken giftes vpon the innocent]fignify-ing that vfurie, & briberie doe exclude from heauen. Defcribing alfo the wicked conuenticle, which is op-pofite to the holie Citie of God, he faith [There hath not ceaffed out of the ftreates therof Vfurie & guile] Againe, amongft greuous finnes, from which finners can not be redemed, but by new iuftifying grace, he faith[From vfuries, and iniquitie he shal redeme their foules]Salomon admonisheth vfurers, that the goods which they gette by that trade, are not theirs, but per-teyne to the poore of whom they receiue them, fay-ing[He that heapeth together riches by vfuries, and ocker, gathereth them for him, that is liberal to the poore] Ezechiel faith [He that geueth to vfurie, and taketh more (then he lendeth) what shal he liue? he shal not liue, wheras he hath done thefe deteftable thinges, dying he shal dye: his bloud shal be vpon him]Nehemias amongft other thinges, which he con-demned, and corrected in the people, faith[I rebuked the Princes, and Magiftrates, and faid to them:Doe you euerie one exact vfuries of your brethren? and I gathered againft them a great affemblie] Chrift our Lord correcting alfo the falfe doctrine of the Scribes and Pharifees, who wrefted the fenfe of holie Scrip-tures, in excufe of their auarice, and of taking vfurie: commandeth both to lend to the needie, and to take no vfurie at al, faying [He that asketh of thee, geue to him, and to him that would borow of thee, turne not away] And directly againft the fame corrupters, who

Pfal.14.v. 1.5.

Pf.54.v.12. Pfal.71. 14.

Pro.28.v.8.

Ezech.18.v. 8.13.17.

2.Efd.5.v. 7.

And efpeciblly by Chrift.

Mat 5.v.42.

accoun-

accounted, whom they lift their freindes, and whom they lift their enimies, he faith [If ye lend to them of whom ye hope to receiue, what thanke is to you? for finners alfo lend vnto finners, for to receiue as much. But loue your enimies : doe good: and lend, hoping for nothing]by lending , nor exacting, nor expecting anie more for lending , but the fame in iuft value which is lent. For fo iuftice requireth; and bindeth him that boroweth, to pay al the debt. [Owe to no man anie thing(faith S. Paul)but that you loue one an other] fignifying that al are bound in due time and maner, to pay al other debts : and perpetually, to be only in debt of mutual loue, each one to others.

4. Other theft , roberie, & fraud, are by the fame diuine auctoritie condemned. [Hope not in iniquitie, (faith the Pfalmift) and couet not robbries. The robbries of the impious (faith Saloman) shal draw them downe. Emulate not euil men , neither defire to be with them, becaufe their minde doth meditate robberies, and their lippes fpeake deceipts. He that is partaker with a theefe, hateth his owne foule. The riches of the vniuft , shal be dryed vp, as a riuer, & they shal found as great thunder in the raine. (faith an other wifeman) The nephewes of the impious, shal not multiplie boughes : nor vncleane rootes found vpon the toppe of a rocke. They haue not knowne how to doe right((faith the Prophet Amos) trefuring vp iniquitie, and robberies in their houfes.]

5. Particularly againft bribes, the Law faith [Neither shalt thou take bribes, which doe blinde alfo the wife: and peruert the wordes of the iuft] Repeting the fame commandment, our Lord faith againe[Thou shalt not accept perfon, or gifts: becaufe that giftes blinde the eyes of the wife; and change the wordes of the iuft. Curfed be he that taketh giftes, to kil the foule of innocent bloud: and al the people shal fay: Amen. Fire (faith holie Iob)shal deuour their tabernacles

Marginal notes (left):
Luc.6.v.54. 35.
Rom.13.v. 8.
Pfal.61.v. 11.
Pro.21.v.7. ch 24.v.12. ch 29.v.24.
Eccli.40. v. 13.15.
Amos. 3. v. 10.
Exod.25.v. 8.
Deut.16.v.
ch.27.v.25.
Iob.15.v.34

Marginal notes (right):
Againft theft, robberie,and al fraude.
Againft bribes

Y   nacles

nacles, which gladly take giftes. The impious (faith
Salomon) receiueth giftes out of the bosome, that he   Pro.17.v.23.
may peruert the pathes of iudgement. He that know-
eth a person in iudgement doth not wel ; this man   ch.18.v.21.
euen for a morsel af bread, forsaketh the truth. He   ch.15.v.27.
that pursueth auarice, disturbeth his house : but he
that hateth giftes shal liue] Other Proohets threaten
punishment for this vise of bribrie; especially when   Isa.1.v.23
great persons are corrupted therewith. [Thy Princes   ch.5.v.23.
(saith Isaias to the Iewes)are vnfaithful, cōpanions of
theeues: al loue giftes, foilow rewardes. Woe to you
which inst fie the impious for giftes. He that shaketh
his handes from al gift, and stoppeth his eares, lest he   ch.33. v.15.
heare bloud, and shutteh his eyes, that he may see   16.17.
no euil: this man shal dwel on high, the munitions
of rockes shal be his highnes; bread is geuen him, his
waters are faithful. His eyes shal see the King in his
glorie] The like saith Amos [I haue knowne manie   Amos 5.v.
your wickednesses, and your strong sinnes, enimies   12.
of the iust taking bribe: and oppresiug the poore in   Mich. 3 v.
the gate. Her Princes iudged for giftes (saith Micheas)   11.12.
and her Priestes taught for wages : and her Prophets
(false Prophet) diuined for money. For this, Sion shal
be ploughed as a fielde, and Ierusalem shal be as an
heape of stones; and the mount of the Temple, as the
high places of the forests] signifying the ruine of Ierusalem and Temple, for auarice, briberie, and other
great sinnes.

 6. Aboue al other iniuries Tyrannie, by forcebly

Tyrannie and
extorsion is
most damna-
ble.

inuading mens goods, and persons, vnder pretence
of iust power, is most wicked & execrable. So[Achab   3.Reg.21.v.
King of Israel, moued with vniust indignation, and   2 4.8.13.
fretting, because Naboth (his faithful subiect) would   15.19.
not sel him his vineyard, agreed to Iesabels deuise, that   ch.22.v.34.
Naboth should be accused, & by false witnesses con-   58.
demned, and stoned to death, as for blasphemie: and   4.Reg.9.v.
so the king tyrannically possessed the vineyard of Na-   7.8.9.10.
             33.36.
            both

both] adding wilful murder of the innocent, to his
tyrannical oppreſſion. And God reuenged the ſame,
alſo in this world, vpon Iezabel, who was ſuddenly
ſlaine, & eaten by dogges: vpon Achab, whoſe bloud
alſo the dogges did eate: and vpon al Achabs familie,
and generation, which was quite ruined, and extin-
guiſhed. And [al tyrannical oppreſſion is further eternally puniſhed, in fire and brimſtone.]

Gh. 10. *v.* 17

1.Cor.6.v.
10.
Apoc. 9. *v.*
21.

Iuſtice committed in ſacred things is ſacrilege.
And bying or ſelling ſpiritual thinges,
is Simonie.

ARTICLE 32.

BEſides the ordinarie rules of iuſtice to be obſerued in temporal thinges, reaſon directeth, that as
ſpirit̃ual and ſacred thinges, perſons, and places doe
excel the reſt, ſo euerie iniurie done in them, is greater offence in the ſight of God, then theft, roberie, or
wrong commited in profane thinges. And this ſinne
is called Sacrilege, becauſe ſacred thinges are ſtollen, or violated. And both God, and his deputies in
earth, haue ſeuerely puniſhed this crime. Wherof be
manie notorious examples [God hauing commanded
the Iſraelites, in the conqueſt of Iericho, that whatſoeuer of gold, or ſiluer, there ſhould be taken, or of
braſſen veſſels; or yron, ſhould be conſecrated to our
Lord, and laide vp in his treaſures. One Achan reſeruing ſecretly to himſelf certaine money, & other precious things; the people aſſailing their enimies were
ouercome in battel, wherwith Ioſue, and the whole
campe being much afflicted [Our Lord ſaid: I wil be
nomore with you, til you diſpatch him that is guiltie
of this wicked fact. Ariſe (ſaith our Lord)ſanctifie the
people, there is anathema in thee] Trial was made by
lotte, Achan of the tribe of Iuda, being found to haue

Ioſ.6.v.18.
19.

ch.7.v.1.
2.5.10.

v. 12.13.16.

Theft & other
iniures in ſa-
cred thinges is
ſacriledge.

God comman-
ded, to appro-
priate certaine
téporal goods
vnto ſacred
vſes.

And puniſhed
transgreſſors
with death.

Y 2   tranſ-

tranfgreffed. Iofue faid to him [Becaufe thou haft di- *v.25.*
fturbed vs, our Lord difturbe thee in this day. And al
Ifrael ftoned him, and al thinges that were his, were
confumed with fire, And the furie of our Lord was   16.
auerted from th(m.]

2. Ballafar King of Babylon, fonne of Nabucho-

Terrible ex-
amples in the
King of Baby-
lon.

dofor, with his wiues, concubines, and nobles, deriding holie thinges, and blafpheming God, dranke in
the facred veffels, that were brought from the Temple of Ierufalem, and the fame night was flaine, and
his kingdome conquered by Darius the Mede, and fo
that Monarchie was tranflated from the Affirians to
the Medes and Perfians. In like maner, or rather more
miferably was Antiochus Epiphanies (a moft wicked
King of the Grecians) for perfecuting and moft fa-
crilegioufly robbing, & contaminating the holie veffels, and treafures of the Temple[was moft worthily
plagued in his bowels, with bittereft torments in his
inner parts, but not ceafing frō malice ftil threatned,
breathing fire in his minde, confeffing that he was
iuftly tormented, but neuer awhite repented, his liue
flefh falling from his bodie, in defperate maner, the
facrilegious blafphemer, with moft miferable death,
departed this life] Ananias alfo and Saphira [For facrilegious fraud, died fudenly]ftriken with the hand
of God; vpon S. Peters reprehenfiue word.

In King An-
tiochus.

And Ananias.

Dan.5.v.2.
4.30.31.

1.Mach.1.v.
13.24.
39.

2.Mach.5.
v.16.17.
18.19.20.

ch.9.v.4.5.
&c.

Act.5.v.
3.5.10.

3.   Like vnto Sacrilege, is the crime of Simonie.

Simonie is no
leffe finne.

fo named of one Simon a Magician, who falfely va-
luing fpiritual grace, with earthly thinges [offered to
giue money for fuch power, as the Apoftles had; that
vpon whomfoeuer he fhould impofe his handes, they
might receiue the Holie Ghoft] To whom therfore
S. Peter faid; [Thy money be to thee vnto perdition;
becaufe thou haft thought with money to bye the
Holie Ghoft, fo the Magitian fel into the gal of bit-
ternes] Into this finne long before, fel Giezi the feruant of Elizeus the Prophete[requiring and receiuing
tem-

Act.8.v.18
19.20.

temporal reward, of Naaman the Affirian, for a miraculous cure, wrought by the Prophete, in cleanfing
the fame Naaman from leprofie. For which wicked
finne, the Prophete punished his owne feruant, with
a perpetual plague of leprofie, faying vnto him[The
leprofie of Naaman shal cleaue to thee, and to thy
feede for euer: And he went out from him a leper, as
it were fnow]Into this enormious crime do al they fal,
that either bye or fel anie fpiritual holie thing, or anie
thing annexed vnto fpiritual power, or function. For
albeit the bodily cure, & clenfing frō leprofie in Naaman, was a temporal, & corporal benefite, valiable in
fome forte with money, if it had bene done, by induftrie and art of Phifitiones; Yet being miraculoufly
wrought by Gods Prophete, it was fo annexed to
fpiritual power, and function, that the falfe valuation
therof was wicked finne, & was punished acordingly.
And euen fo are al fpiritual benefites, & benefices ordayned for maintenance of fpiritual power, & functions. As be Church landes, tithes, oblations, & Ecclefiaftical reuenewes. The vniuft vfurpation wherof, by
intrufion, force, or other meanes by Minifters, falfe
pretended Clergimen, in heritical countries, is both
Sacrilege in the vniuft poffefsion of facred thinges:
and Simoney in the maner of obtaining them, being
annexed to fpiritual functions, and granted and gotten, for farre worfe then temporal profane labours,
of mere laimen: and therfore (befides the profeffion,
and practife of herefie) altogether vncapable of thofe
poffeffions.

4 *Reg.* 5.7.
20.

*v.*27.

See *Part.* 2.
*Artic.*42.

It confifteth
in bying and
felling fpiri-
tual thinges,
for a temporal
price.

Prodigalitie, in fuperfluous expenfes: and nig-
gardnes in fparing, are forbiddē by Gods Lavv.

ARTICLE 33.

Vertue confifting in the iuft meane, is peruerted
by either of the extremes, of too much, or of too
Y 3 litle.

Liberalitie
confifteth in

the right meane betwene Prodigalitie.and niggardnes.

little. And therfore if pretended Liberalitie do either excede in ouer much geuing, or fpending of wordlie goodes, it lofeth the nature of vertue, and is the vife of Prodigalitie: or if it be defectiue in ouer much getting or fparing; it is Auarice, or Niggardnes; which vifes are condemned by the light of reafon, & by the law of God. A few textes of holie Scripture may fuffice in confirmation therof. [He that troubleth his houfe (faith Salomon) fhal poffeffe the windes: and he that is a foole, fhal ferue the wife. A diligent woman is a crowne to her husband. A wife woman buildeth her houfe; the vnwife wil with her hand deftroy that alfo which is built. He that kepeth the Law (of reafon) is a wife fonne, but he that feedeth gluttons fhameth his father. A prince lacking prudence fhal oppreffe manie by calumnie: but he that hateth auarice, his dayes fhal be made long. He that tilleth his ground, fhal be filled witn breades, but he that purfueth idlenes, fhal be replenished with pouertie. Beggerie, and riches geue me not: geue only thinges neceffarie, for my fubftance.]

P.⋆.11.⋆.2.
29.
ch.12.⋆.4.
ch.14.⋆.1.
ch.28.⋆.7.
⋆.16.
⋆.29.
ch.30.⋆.8.

Againft Idlenes.

Prodigalitie is condemned by Ifaias the Prophet.

2. Ifaias the Prophete defcribeth the fuperfluous, vaine, & lafciuious attyre of fome wemen, faying] The daughters of Sion, are hawtie, and haue walked with ftretched out necke, & went with twingling of eyes, and clapping their handes, walked on their feete, and ietting in a fette pafe. Our Lord fhal take away the ornament of their shoes, & litle moones. And cheynes and ouches, & braceletes ; & the shedings combes, and floppes, and tablettes, and fwete balles, & earlets Ringes, and pearles hanging on the forehead. And changes of apparel, and shorte clokes. And for fwete fauour, there fhal be ftinke, and for a girdle, fhal be a corde; and for frifled haire, baldnes: and for a ftomacher, fhal be harecloth] Al which riotte, and fuperfluitie, the Prophet adonisheth prodigal perfons to auoide, otherwife iuft punishment vil fal vpon them,

Ifa 3. ⋆. 16.
17.18.⋆c.

⋆.24.

by

by the contrarie afflictious, for such vaine pleasures. True frugalitie requireth: that as we would haue no want, so we must make no wast.

3. Our Sauiour in commendation of S.Iohn Baptist, said to the people [what went ye out into the desert to see? a man clothed in soft garments? Behold they that are clothed in soft garments, are in Kinges houses] Insinuating, that in kings courtes is commonly superfluitie of expenses in costly apparel, and other delicates. Againe our Lord taxeth the like superfluitie towards mens selues; with auarice and niggardnes towardes the poore [There was (saith our Lord) a certaine rich man, and he was clothed with purple, and silke, and he fayred euerie day magnifically] who neglecting to releue a poore man, called Lazarus. When they both dyed [Lazarus was carried by Angels into Abrahams bosome (a place of rest, and plentiful comfort) and the rich glutton was buried in hel] Accordingly S.Paul teacheth that [Pietie with sufficiencie, is great gaine. Hauing foode, and wherewith to be coue red, with these al (moderat persons) ought to be content] S.Peter admonisheth that [wemens trimming ought not to be outwardly, in platting of haire, or laying on gold round about, or on putting on vestures: but in the incorruptibilitie of a quiet, and modest spirite] S.Iames seuerly reprehendeth vnmerciful rich men [that make merrie vpon the earth, and in riotousnes nourish their hartes in the day of slaughter.] When they kil and offer victimes, they pamper themselues, and neglect the poore. Of auarice & niggardnes, see more in the last commandment.

Margin notes:
Mat.11.v.8.
Luc.7.v.25.

Christ and his Apostles, condemne al prodigalitie.

Luc.16.v. 19,20,22.

1 Tim. 6.v. 6.8.

1.Pet.3.v. 3.4.

Iac.5.v.5.

And miserable niggardnes.

Artic. 45.

It is specially forbidde, to hurt the fame of anie person vniustly.

ARTICLE 34.

Pro.22.v.1.

BEtter is a good name, then much riches. Aboue siluer and gold good grace. And better then precious

Defamation is worse then theft.

cious oyntments.] And therfore in like proportion,
it is a greater sinne, to hurt anie person, vniustly in   Ecle.7.v.
their fame, then in their external goods. Which thing   2.
holie Scripture further testifieth, in regard of diuers
sortes of this kinde of iniurie. The common people of
the Israelites, when they were afflicted by king Pharao in Ægypt, greuously offended in murmuration,
and calumniation: charging Moyses and Aaron, as if
they had bene the causers, that al the people were   Exod.5.v.21
more afflicted, saying to them [You haue made our
sauour to stincke before Pharao, and his seruants: and
you haue geuen him a sword for to kil vs]   Againe   ch.15.v.24.
in the desert they calumniated Moyses, as if he had
bene careles of them, saying [What shal we drinke,   ch.16.v.3.
would to God we had died by the hand of our Lord,
in the Land of Ægypt. Why haue you brought vs in-   ch.17.v.3.
to this desert; that you might kil al the multitude
with famine? Why didst thou make vs goe forth out   Num.20.v.
of Ægypt, to kil vs, and our children, and our beastes   4.5.
with thirst. Why haue you brought forth the Church
of our Lord into this wildernes, that both we and our   v.6.&c.
cattel should dye? Why did you make vs ascend out
of Ægypt, and haue brought vs into this exceding
naughtie place, which cannot be sowen, which bringeth forth neither figge, nor vines, nor ponegranats,
moreouer also hath no water for to drinke?] Against
this malicious iniurie of calumniation, our Lord gaue   Leuit.19.
expresse commandment, saying [Thou shalt not ca-   v 13.
lumniate thy neighbour.] When therfore Gods true
seruants are vniustly charged, with crimes falsly imputed, they must first with patience and meekenes, recurre to God by prayer, as Moyses and Aaron did.
Aud also with discrete zele, in due time and place,
must answere in iustification of truth, as the Prophet
Elias answered wicked Achab, saying plainly [Not I   3.Reh.18.
haue troubled Israel, but thou, and the house of thy   v.17.18.
father: who haue forsaken the commandments of
           our

Against ca-
lumniation.

our Lord, and haue folowed Baalim] So our B. Sauiour confuted the Pharifees calumniations, with true, plaine, & modeſt anſweres [To eate with vnwaſhen handes, doth not defile a man: but they tranſgreſſe Gods commandments, that teach the people, not to releue their parents, for their owne traditions.]

2. Detraction, conſiſting in vnlawful reuealing others ſecrete faults, defectes, or imperfections, is more or leſſe ſinne, according to the wrong, and damage commonly enſuing therby. Which ouer frequent iniurie, is worthily condemned in holie Scripture [I did perſecute euerie one (ſaith holie Dauid) that ſecretly detracteth from his neighbour. The thinges which thyne eyes haue ſeene (ſaith Salomō) vtter not quickly in a brawle, leſt afterwards thou canſt not amend it: when thou haſt diſhonoured thy freind. The Northwinde (ſaith he) diſſipateth raine, and a ſadde looke the tongue that detracteth] If a ſerpent bite in ſilence, nothing leſſe then it, hath he, that detracteth ſecretly. Hedge thyne eares with thornes, and heare not a wicked tongue: and make doores to thy mouth, and lockes; & right bridles to thy mouth. And take heede, leſt perhaps thou ſlippe in thy tongue, and fal in the ſight of thyne enimies, that lye in waite for thee, and thy fal be vncurable vnto death. He that ſtoppeth his eares, leſt he heare bloud (ſaith Iſaias) and ſhutteth his eyes, that he may ſee no euil: This man ſhal dwel on high] ſignifying that none ought curiouſly, neither to vtter, nor to heare euil of others. [Detract not one from an other, my bretheren (ſaith S. Iames) He that detracteth frō his brother; or he that iudgeth his brother, detracteth from the Law, and iudgeth the Law. But if you bite, and eate one an another (ſaith S. Paul) take heede you be not conſumed one of an other.]

3. Contempt, or ſmal reſpect of others is not a ſmal ſinne: and deriſion is alſo a greater fault, and very iniurious. The wife of holie Iob derided him, ſaying:

Against detraction.

Against the hearing of detraction.

Against deriſion.

Mat. 15. v. 1. ad 20 ch. 23. v. 13. &c.

Pſ. 100. v. 5.

Pro. 25. v. 8.

23.

Eccle. 10. v. 11. Eccli. 28. v. 28. 29. 30.

Iſa. 33. v. 15. 16.

Iac. 4. v. 11.

Gal. 5. v. 15.

Z   Doeſt

[Doeſt thou yet continue in thy ſimplicitie] The wife *Tob.1.v 9,*
and kinsfolke of Tobias derided him. when he was *ch 5 v.5.6.*
blinde, ſaying[Where is thy hope, for the which thou *Tob.2.v.15.*
didſt beſtow almes, and burials. Thy hope is become *16.22.23.*
vaine manifeſtly, and thine almes now haue appea-
red] S. Paul geueth al Chriſtians a general Rule, for
mutual wordes, and exterual behauiour, ſaying [Loue *Rom.12.v.*
the charitie of the brotherhode, one towards an o- *10.*
ther: with honour preuenting one an other.] And generally, againſt al ſinnes and iniuries committed by
Againſt al the tongue. Salomõ ſaith[For the ſinnes of the lippes, *Prov.12.*
ſinnes of the ruine approacheth to the euil man.]S.Iames ſaith.[If *v.13.*
tongue. a man offend not in word, this is a perfect man(a rare *Iac 3.v.2.*
man.) The tongue is fire, a whole world of impietie. *ch.4.v.13.*
Thou, what art thou, that iudgeſt thy neighbour?
Who art thou (ſaith S. Paul) that iudgeſt an other
mans ſeruant?] As if he ſaid:It ſufficeth that euerie one *Rom.14. v.*
control, correct, and amend his owne faultes, & theirs *4.*
which by office perteyne to his charge : to aduiſe o-
thers of brotherlie charitie, and with al modeſtie:
teaching: not otherwiſe to intermedle[For who art
thou that iudgeſt an other mans ſeruant?] *Ibidem.*

Suſurration is an eſpecial iniurie, and a deteſtable ſinne.

ARTICLE 35.

Suſurration is SVſurration by ſuggeſting cauſe of diſlike, to make
the poyſon of or nouriſh diſcord, where agrement ought to be,
concord, and doth not only hurt their good name, of whom euil
oppoſite to report is made , as calumniation, and detraction doe;
pacification. but alſo diminiſheth mutual loue, and depriueth (or
indeuoureth to depriue) both parties , of that good
fauour and freindſhip, which ſhould be in charitable
perſons, and is betwene ſpecial freindes, which is
great iniurie, and a diueliſh malice; the bane & poyſon

fon of humane focietie:and therfore to be detefted of al good perfons, as it is often condemned in holie Scriptures. The Law faith [Thou shalt not be a criminator, nor a whifperer among the people.]Againft this precept of God, and nature [Doeg an Idomeite reuealed to king Saul, that Abimelech the Prieft had affifted Dauid, geuing him victuals, and a fword, and confulting our Lord for him] wherby Saul was fo incenfed againft Abimelech, that he fent for him, and flew him, & aboue fourfcore other Priefts, & fauorers of Dauid: and ftroke al the citie of Nobe, for the fame pretenfed caufe, al vpon the wicked fuggeftion of one Whifperer Doeg. Dauid therfore, finding oportunitie, to manifeft his true affection to Saul, befought him, not to geue credite, nor eare to fuch malicious Whifperers, faying to him [My Lord king: For what caufe doth my Lord perfecute his feruant? What haue I done, or what euil is there in my hand? Now therfore, heare I pray thee, my Lord King, the wordes of thy feruant: If our Lord ftirre thee vp againft me, let there be odour of facrifice (be it grateful to God, I I am wel content with Gods wil) but if the fonnes of men (haue ftirred thee vp againft me : they are curfed in the fight of our Lord, which haue caft me out this day, that I should not dwel in the inheritance of our Lord] The Princes of the Philiftims did alfo fuggeft to their king Achis, caufe of fufpition againft Dauid, faying [Is not this Dauid, to whom they fang? Saul hath ftrooke his thoufandes, and Dauid his ten thoufands.] Abfolom King Dauids owne fonne, ambitioufly, and very feditioufly, whifpered amongft the people: falfely fuggefting, as if there had bene defect in his fathers maner of gouerning, and fo folicited, and [intifed the hartes of the men of Ifrael, to fal from their allegeance, & to adhere to himfelfe in rebellion.

2. Againft fuch whifperers, the fame Royal Prophet, and euerie iuft foule prayeth thus: [Iudge me, o God

*Leuit.19.
v.16.*

*2.Reg.22.v.
9.18.19.*

*cb.26.v.18.
19.*

*cb.20.v.4.
5.*

*2.Reg.15.
v.2.3.6.*

Suffurration is condemned

by many ho-
ie Scriptures.

God, and discerne my cause, from the sinful nation:
from the vniust and deceiptful man deliuer me] And
against al such traitors, as Doeg was to Dauid, euerie
faithful seruant of God, worthily inueigheth, saying
[Why doest thou glorie in malice, which art mightie
in iniquitie? Al the day hath thy tongue thought iniustice: as a sharpe rasar thou hast done guile. Thou
hast loued malice more then benignitie: iniquitie rather then to speake equitie. Thou hast loued al words
of precipitation: a deceiptful tongue. Therfore wil
God destroy thee for euer: he wil plucke thee out, and

The enormi-
tie therof is
often descri-
bed.

wil remoue thee out of thy tabernacle: thy roote out
of the land of the liuing:] Thou shalt be vtterly destroyed, & al the race, that folow thy malignant hart,
and wicked steppes. Likewise Salomon pathetically
describeth this enormious crime of Susurration, saying [Six thinges there are, which our Lord hateth: and
the seuenth his soule detesteth. Loftie eyes; a lying
tongue; handes that shede innocent bloud; a hart
that deuiseth most wicked deuises; feete swift to runne
into euil; a deceiptful witnes that vttereth lies; (al sixe
very wicked and damnable, but the seuenth) he that
among brethren soweth discordes.] is most detestable: because it is most opposite to the cheefe vertue
charitie: it breaketh vnitie: and is the proper sinne of
the diuel. Againe saith Salomon: The impious man
diggeth euil, and in his lippes fire burneth. A peruerse
man raiseth contentions: and one ful of wordes, sepa-
rateth Princes. An vniust man allureth his freind, and
leadeth him by a way not good. He that with astonied eyes thinketh wicked thinges, byting his lippes,
bringeth euil to passe. He that concealeth offence, seeketh freindships (which is a singular good worke of
charitie) he that in other word repeteth it (making it
worse then that which he heard) seperateth the con-
federate (breaking concord, or nourishing the discord)
He that meditateth discordes, loueth brawles. The

Psal.42.7.
1.2.

Ps.51.v.3.4.

5.

6.

7.

Pro.6. v.
16,17.

18.

19.

ch.16.v.27.
28.

29.

30.

ch.17.v.9.

13.

                                          wordes

ch.18.v.8.　wordes of the duble tongued as it were simple,& the
ch.16.v.20.　same come to the inner partes of the bellie. When
22.　wood faileth, the fire shal be extinguished: and the
whisperer taken away, brawles ceafe.] To al this, an
other wife preacher addeth, to refresh the memories
*Eccli.*5.v.　of al the faithful {Be not called a whisperer (faith he)
16.17.　and be not taken in thy tongue, and so be confounded. For vpon a theefe is confusion, and repentance:
& a very euil condemnation vpon the duble tongued:
ch.21.v.31.　but to the whisperer is hatred, and enmitie, and
contumelie. The whisperer shal defile his foule, and
shal be hated in al: and he that shal abide with him
ch.28.v.15.　shal be odious. The stil man and the wife, shal be ho-
16.　nored. The whisperer and the duble tongued is ac-
curst. For he hath troubled manie, that were at peace.
A third tongue (malicious, or vndiscrete report to
17.　one, what an other hath faid) hath moued manie; and
18.　dispersed them from nation into nation. It hath destroyed the walled citie of the riche; and hath digged
downe the houses of great men. It hath cut the forces
19.　of peoples, & vndone strong nations. A third tongue
hath cast out manlie wemen, and depriued them of
their labours, (al the merite of their former good
20.　workes) He that regardeth it shal not haue rest: nei-
21.　ther shal he haue a freind, in whom he may repose.
The stroke of a whippe maketh a blew marke, but
22.　the stroke of the tongue wil break bones. Manie haue
fallen in the edge of the sword, but not so manie as
they that haue perished by their tongue. Blessed is he
that is defended from a wicked tongue.]

    3. S.Paul with no lesse zele and force, reciting whis-
*Rom.*1.v.　perers, detractors, inuentors of euils, among other
29.30.31.32.　grosest sinners, odible to God, denounceth: that not
only they which doe such things, but they also which
consent to the doers, are guiltie of death, euerlasting.
*Ephes.*5.v. 6　Admonisheth therfore al Christians, [not to be seduced with vaine wordes. Because for these thinges

S.Paul con-
demeth it
amongst other
great crimes.

cometh the anger of God, vpon the children of diffi-
dence. Become not therfore partakers with them.]

Al are bound to practise sometimes vvorkes of mercie ; spiritual, and corporal.

ARTICLE 36.

VVorkes of mercie are alwayes counselled, and in some cases commanded.

DEcline from euil, and doe good [saith the Royal Prophet: teaching that it sufficeth not to abstaine from doing wrong, but it is also necessarie to doe good. And especially, among other good workes, to helpe the needie, with spiritual and corporal relefe. Sometimes it is but counseled without obligation, sometimes it is commanded, as abilitie serueth, and others necessitie vrgeth. And in general, al are bound, sometimes to bestow almes, more or lesse, of one kinde or other. Gods prouidence so ordaining, that some doe neede, and others can helpe: at least the poorest can pray, can admonish sinners to repent, can remitte offences done to themselues, can sometimes giue a dish of cold water, or the like. [If a stráger dwel in your land (said our Lord in the written Law) and abide among yon, doe not vpbrade him. There shal not want poore, in the land of thy habitation, therfore I command thee, that thou open thy hand to thy needie & poore brother, that liueth in the land. Thou shalt not see thy brothers oxe, or shepe straying, and passe by, but thou shalt bring it backe to thy brother] In particular for the poores sake it was commanded, that [when thou reapest the corne of the land, and gatherest grapes, thou shalt leaue some to the poore and strangers to take. I the Lord your God.]

Ps.33.v.15
Ps.36.
v.27.
Mat.25.v.
35.42.

Leuit.19.
v.33.

Deut.15.v.
11.
ch.22.v.1.
23.
ch.24.v.19.

Leuit.19. v.
9.10.

Gods prouidence ordayneth that some

2. Examples of the rich and poore, which gaue and receiued, and both merited, are for instruction to others, recorded in holie Scriptures. Abraham was

so readie to releue the needie, that he earneftly inuited, and befought ftrangers paffing by the way, to enter into his houfe, to lodge, and eate, and drinke with him. And fo did Lot. And they both fuppofing that they inuited ftrange men, receiued holie Angels. A godlie widow woman in Sarepta fedde Elias the Prophete, by Gods fpecial prouidence, for her merite, rather then for his neede. For otherwife he was alfo ferued by a Crow, when God would fo haue it [Abdias (gouernour of king Achabs houfe) receiued and relieued an hundred Prophetes, whom Iefabel perfecuted. Tobias being captiue (with manie others) in Afiria, forfooke not the way of truth: but imparted that he could make, dayly to his brethren captiues with him, which were of his kindred. He went to al, and gaue them wholefome admonitions. He lent to the needie; and gaue as he was able; and he buried the dead, with danger of his owne life. He aduifed his fonne to geue almes (among other fatherlie precepts) He and his fonne, and whole familie were afsifted, comforted, and directed by an Angel, in their happie wayes, and feruice of God.] And fo innumerable others, did manie workes of mercie.

are richer, fome poorer, that al may merite.

3. Of the reward of almes dedes, the Royal Prophete teftifieth faying [The iuft fhal be in eternal memorie: he fhal not feare at the hearing of euil. He diftributed, he gaue to the poore: his iuftice remaineth for euer and euer. His horne (his crowne) fhal be exalted in glorie.] The Sapiential Bookes abund in precepts, and praifes of almes deedes [Let not mercie & truth leaue thee (faith Salomon) put them about thy throte: and write them in the tables of thy hart: and thou fhalt finde grace, and good difcipline before God, and men. Doe not prohibite him to doe good, that is able. If thou be able, thy felfe alfo doe good. Say not to thy freind: Goe, and returne, and to morow I wil geue to thee, wheras thou maift geue forthwith

The reward of al good workes is great.

with. He that hideth corne, shal be curfed among the *ch.11.v.26.*
peoples: but bleſsing vpon the head of them that fel. *30.*
The fruite of a iuſt man, a tree of life: and he that gaineth ſoules, is wiſe. He that deſpiſeth his neighbour, *ch.1   +v.*
ſinneth; but he that hath pittie on the poore, ſhal be *22 31.*
bleſſed. Mercie and truth prepare good thinges. He *ch.19.v.17.*
honoreth his Maker, that hath pittie on the poore:
and he wil repay him the like. He that ſtoppeth his *ch.21.v.13.*
eare at the crie of the poore, himſelfe alſo ſhal crie, & *14.26.*
ſhal not be heard. A gift hidde quencheth angers; & a
a gift in the boſome, the greateſt indignation. He that
is iuſt, wil giue, and wil not ceaſe. He that is prone to *ch.22.v.9.*
mercie, ſhal be bleſſed: for of his breades, he hath geuen to the poore. Deliuer them that are led to death: *ch.24.v.11.*
and thoſe that are drawen to death, ceaſe not to de- *12.*
liuer. If thou ſay, I am not of force: he that ſeeth into
thy hart, he vnderſtandeth: and nothing deceiueth
the keper of thy ſoule: and he ſhal render to a man,
acording to his workes. He that geueth to the poore, *ch.28.v.27.*
ſhal not lacke; he that deſpiſeth him that asketh, ſhal
ſuſteyne penurie. Caſt thy bread vpon the paſsing wa- *Eccle.11.v.1*
ters, becauſe after much time thou ſhalt finde it (in
eternal life.) Sonne, defraude not the almes of the *Eccli.4.v.1.*
poore (ſaith an other diuine Preacher) and turne not
away thine eyes from the poore. Deſpiſe not the hun- *2.*
grie ſoule: and exaſperate not the poore in his pouertie. Afflict not the heart of the needie, and deferre not *3.*
the gift to him that is in diſtreſſe. Reiect not the petition of him, that is in affliction, and turne not away *4.*
thy face from the needie. From the poore turne not
away thyne eyes, for anger: and leaue not to them *5.*
that aske of thee, to curſe thee behinde thy backe. *6.*
For the prayer of him that curſeth thee, in the bitter-
nes of his ſoule, ſhal be heard: and he that made him,
wil heare him. Make thy ſelfe affable to the congrega- *7.*
tion of the poore. Bow downe thyne eare to the
poore, without ſadnes, and render thy debt, and *8.*

Almes deedes
are like to
good ſeede,
ſowen in good
ground; And
are muchcom-
mended in al
the Sapiential
bookes.

answer

9.

answere him peaceable wordes in mildnes. Deliuer him that suffereth iniurie, out of the hand of the

10.

proud; and be not faint in thy soule. In iudging be merciful to pupils, as a father; and as an husband to their mother: and thou shalt be as the obedient sonne of the Hieghest: and he wil haue mercie on thee, more then a mother] If thou wilt doe good, know to

11.

ch.11.v.2.

whom thou doest it: and there shal be much thanke in thy good deedes. Doe good to the iust, and thou

3.

shalt finde great reward. And if not of him, assuredly of our Lord. For it is not wel with him, that is euer occupied in euil thinges, and that geueth not almes: because the Hieghest both hateth sinners, and hath mercie on them that are penitent] Wherfore the best and most necessarie almes for obstinate sinners, is to correct them, as Salomon often admonisheth [A

Of al sortes of almes, correction of sinners is the best.

Pro.10.v.
13.

rodde (saith he) on his backe, that lacketh witte. He that spareth the rodde, hateth the childe: but he that

ch.13.v.24.

loueth him, doth instantly nurture him. The pestilent being punished, the litle one shal be wiser. The

ch.21.v.11.
12.

iust deuiseth concerning the house of the impious, that he may drawe the impious from euil. Follie is

ch.22.v.15.

tyed together in the hart of a child: and the rodde of discipline shal driue it awaye. Be not defrauded of thy good day, and let not a litle portion of a

Eccli.14.v.
14 16.

good gift, ouer passe thee. Geue and take, and iustifie thy soule. He that lendeth to his neighbour, doth mercie, and he that preuaileth with hand, kepeth the

ch.29.v.1.
2.10.

commandment. Lend to thy neighbour in the time of his necessitie: and againe, repay thy neighbour in his time. Man e haue not lent, not because of wickednes (not of want of compassion) but they were afraid

11.

to be defrauded without cause. But yet vpon the humble, be strong of minde, and for almes differre him

13.

not. Loose money for thy brother, and thy freinde, and hide it not vnder a stone vnto perdition. Put thy

14. &c.

treasure in the precepts of the Hieghest, and it shal profite thee more then gold. Shut vp almes in the

hart

hart of the poore, and the same shal obtaine for thee
against al euil. Aboue the chield of the mightie, and
aboue the speare, it shal fight against thine enemie.
Geue to the Highest, according to his gift, and with a
good eye, doe according to the abilitie of thy handes.
Becaule our Lord is a rewarder, and wil repay thee,
seuen times so much] For he geueth grace in this life,
& glorie in heauen, for euerie good worke of mercie.

The same is urged by other Prophets.

4 Isaias, and otherholie Prophets testfie, that almes
deedes doe excel fasting, and other mortifications,
though the same also are commended in due times,
and maner. To such as fasted, and omitted workes
of mercie. God said [Is this such a fast, as I haue chosen, for a man by the day to afflict his soule? Is not this
rather the fast that I haue chosen? Dissolue the bandes
of impietie: loose the bundels that ouerlode: dismisse
them free that are broken, & breake in sunder euerie
burden. Breake thy bread to the hungrie, and the needie; and bring in the herberles into thy house; When
thou shalt see the naked, couer him : and despise not
thy flesh (for al men are of the same flesh) Then shal
thy light breake forth as the morning; and thy health
shal sooner arise, and thy iustice shal goe before thy
face: and the glorie of the Lord shal embrace thee]
Yea these workes are preferred before external Sacrifice [I would mercie & not sacrifice saith our Lord] A-
mos crieth [wo to them, that were in Sion, great men,
heades of the peoples, going stately into the house of
Israel] and had not compassion vpon the poore. Nehemias by word and example teacheth al, to practise
workes of mercie [We as you know (saith he to the
Priestes and Magistrates) haue redemed our brethren
the Iewes, that were sold to the Gentiles, according to
our abilitie : and wil you therfore sel your brethren?
(by not releuing them, suffer them to be sold a-
gaine?) and shal we redeme them? I also and my brethren, and my seruants haue lent money, and corne

35.
v.10.11.

Isa 58.v.5.
6.

7.

&

Osee. 6 v. 6.
Mat.9 v.
13.
Amos 4 v.
1.
cb.6.v.1.
2.Esd.5.v.1.
1 7.7.8.9.
10.

to

to very manie. Let vs not aske this againe in cómon: Let vs remitte them the debt, that is due to vs.]

5. Chriſt our Lord, the God of mercie, coming from heauen to doe workes of mercie : to redeme al mankinde, to teach men, to feede men ſpiritually, and temporally, to purchaſe eternal life to other men, by his owne death : teacheth, that not only for wicked deeds, & greuous wronges done, but alſo for omiſsion of good workes : euerie [vnprofitable ſeruant; ſhal be caſt into vtter darkneſſe, where ſhal be weping and gnaſhing of teeth.] And ſo requireth workes of mercie of euerie faithful ſeruant, towardes others : that vnleſſe they performe ſuch workes, he wil iuſtly exclude al that neglect to doe them, from eternal life {calling the iuſt into life euerlaſting;becauſe they doe them : & reiecting the wicked, becauſe they doe them not] In the meane time, exhorteth his children {To heape vp treaſures in heauen, where neither the ruſt, nor moth doth corrupt, and where theues doe not digge through, nor ſteale. For where thy treaſure is (ſaith our Lord) there is thy hart alſo] He came to geue; euen himſelfe, not to take : to miniſter, not to be miniſtred vnto] And S. Paul willeth al men{ to remember the word of our Lord Ieſus : becauſe he ſaid : It is a more bleſſed thing to geue, rather then to take.] So did S. Paul perſwade the Epheſians in his paſtoral Sermon:ſo did he perſwade in his ſeueral Epiſtles, the Corinthians, the Galathians, the Philippians, and al Chriſtians, to be diligent, and abundant in al workes of mercie, and that with alacritie [Becauſe (ſaith he) God loueth a chereful geuer]aſſuring al that they ſhal reape in bleſſings, as they ſow] Which is alwaies vnderſtood, according to the deuout affection, and ſincere good wil of euerie one, in proportion of their abilitie. Wherupon our Lord auoucheth, that [a poore Widow, which caſt two mites into the treaſure of the Temple, caſt in more then al the reſt,

Omiſsion of of almesdedes in caſe of neceſsitie, is damnable.

1. Ioan.3.v. 16. 17.

Mat 25. v. 30. 34. 41.

Mat. 6 v. 20. 21.

Luc.6. v. 36

Act 20 v. 35. 1. Cor 16

2. Cor. 8.

ch.9. v. 6. 7. 8. &c.

Gal. 6. v. 6. Phil. 4. v. 15.

A a 2   though

though manie riche men caſt in much:becauſe al they Luc.21.7.
of their abundance caſt in, (what to them ſemed 3. 4.
conuenient)but ſhe of her penerie, hath caſt in al that Mar.12.
she had, her whole liuing.] Her example therfore is 43.44.
not rightly pretendedby rich perſons, whē they geue
ſmal almes, and cal it the poore widowes two Mites.
For none do perfectly imitate this deuoute poore widow, but they onlie, which in dede geue al that they
haue, whether it be much or litle. Neuertheles others
doe alſo right wel, which geue more or leſſe, but few
are comparable to this moſt bountiful liberal geuer
of al that ſhe had, and of al atonce without limite, and
without delay.

Not thoſe which geue litle, but thoſe which geue al they hane, are like to the deuont poore widow.

6. Only al are bound to doe in this point, as S. 1.Tim.6.7.
Paul writeth to S. Timothie, willing him [to com- 17.18.19.
mād the rich of this world, not to be highminded:nor
to truſt in the vncertaintie of riches: but in the liuing
God, to doe wel, to become rich in good workes, to
geue eaſily, to communicate to others that nede : to
heape vnto them ſelues a good foundation, for the
time to come, that they may apprehend the true life]
The aſſurance wherof, he confirmeth alſo in an other Heb.13.7
place ſaying [With ſuch hoſtes, God is promerited] 16.
A ſacred text ſo cleare, that albeit our Aduerſaries not
induring the name of merite, doe corrupt the text, yet
confeſſe the thing it ſelf [That God is wel pleaſed
with ſuch workes]that he sheweth fauour for them.
And what is it els in true English, but merite (howſoeuer they quarrel with S.Ierom about the Latine
word, *promeretur*) ſeing they here confeſſe that ſuch
workes doe pleaſe God, and procute Gods fauour:
Why may we not ſay; that they merite God:that is,
They(through Gods grace) merite eternal life, which
conſiſteth in the ſight, and fruition of God. And alſo
ſay, as the Apoſtle here speaketh[By ſuch hoſtes God
is promerited] S.Iohn alſo teaching that the omiſſion
of ſuch worke in time and place requiſite, sheweth
the'

Though none are bonnd to geue al, yet al are bound to haue a good wil to helpe al that nede.

the want of neceſſariecharitie [He that ſhal haue the
ſubſtance of this World (ſaith he) and ſhal ſee his bro-
rher haue neede, and ſhal ſhut his bowels from him:
how doth the charitie of God abide in him?] Plainly
affirming that ſuch aman, not releuing his neighbour
in that caſe, hath not charitie. Which S. Iames further
explaineth, teaching alſo that it ſufficeth not to ſay,
vnto them that are naked, and lacke daylie foode,
[Goe in peace, be warmed & filled, if thou geue them
not the thinges, that are neceſſary for the bodie, what
ſhal it profite] ſaith he: ſigniffing that it profiteth nothing. For euen as ſuch an anſwere doth not corporally helpe them that are in neceſſitie: ſo doth it not
ſpiritually profite him, that ſo anſwereth, hauing
meanes, and not releuing the needie. The ſame thing
doth S. Peter teach, admoniſhing [Before al thinges
to haue a mutual and continual charitie: becauſe charitie couereth the multitude of ſinnes. Vſing hoſpitalitie one towardes an other, without murmuring.
Euerie one as he hath receiued grace, miniſtring the
ſame, one toward an other, as good diſpenſers of the
manifold grace of God.] Theſe and the like workes
of mercie, ſpiritual and corporal are required of euerie one, according to their abilitie, and others neceſſitie. For which our Sauiour, the iuſt Iudge wil ſay to
thoſe on his right hand, in the day of Iudgement,
[Come ye bleſſed of my Father, poſſeſſe you the kingdome prepared for you from the foundation of the
world. For I was an hungred, & you gaue me to eate:
&c. And to thoſe on the left hand: Get ye away from
me, you curſed, into fire euerlaſting, which was prepared for the diuel, and his angels. For I was an hungred, and you gaue me not to eate. &c. And theſe ſhal
goe into puniſhment euerlaſting: but the iuſt into life
euerlaſting.]

Marginal notes (left):
1. Ioan 3,
v. 17.

Iac. 2. v. 15.
16.

1. Pet. 4. v. 8.
9. 10.

Mat. 25. v.
34.
35.
41.
42.
46.

Marginal note (right):
Eſpecially to
releue thoſe
that are in
extreme ne-
ceſſitie.

A a 3

A!

Al are bound, vvhen lavvful auctoritie
duly requireth it, to testifie the truth,
vvhich they knovv;

ARTICLE 37.

Affirmatiue
precepts bind,
when due cir-
-cumstances
concurre.

Negatiue precepts doe bind at al times, not to do those thinges which are vnlawful: but affirmatiue precepts only binde, when iust causes require, and other due circumstances concurre. So al are bond to testifie the truth which they know, when a lawful Iudge, or Superior in due maner commandeth it. And also when an established iust Law prescribeth, al are bond to reueale the truth, that is necessarie to be knowen, for the common good, and for iustice sake, in euerie case of important necessitie: though they be not expresly demanded. Touching which point, the Law of Moyses ordained, that [whosoeuer knew that an other had sworne falsely, vnles he did vtter it, he should beare the iniquitie.]. *Leuit 5.v.1 2.*

Silence is somtimes a great sinne.

2. Against vnlawful silence, the holie Psalmist expostulateth as with the fautor of sinners, saying [If thou didst see a theefe, thou didst runne with him, and with adulterers, thou didst put thy portion. He that is partaker with a theefe (saith Salomon (hateth his owne soule. He heareth one adiuring, & telleth not. Sonne obserue time (saith an other diuine Preacher) and auoide from euil. For thy soule be not ashamed to say the truth. Accept no face against thyne owne face, nor against thy soule a lie. Reuerence not thy neighbour in his offence, nor kepe in a word in time of saluation. Hide not thy wisdome in the beautie therof. For by the tongue, wisdome is discerned: and vnderstanding, and knowlege, and doctrine, by the word of the wise, and stedfastnes in the workes of iustice. For iustice contend for thy soule, and vnto death striue

Psal.49.v. 18.

Pro.29.v. 24.

Eccli.4 v. 23.26.

27.
28.29.

v 33.

ftriue for iuftice : and God wil ouerthrow thyne enimies for thee.]

3. We haue memorable examples of this iuft, and
neceffarie reuelatiou of the truth , in diuers worthie
perfons [Achior an Ammanite informed Holefernes
the truth , concerning the people of the Iewes, who
though he was threatned, and banifhed, yet was he
by this occafion conuerted to true Religion, eftemed
and rewarded for his faƈt. Mardocheus a noble Iew,
difcouering & reuealing a treafon contriued againft
king Affuerus, in the citie of Sufan, was eftemed, and
finally rewarded ; and by his meanes, the people of
Ifrael, which were captiues vnder the Medes and Perfians, were deliuered from danger of ruine, plotted
againft them, by their wicked enimie Aman. Daniel
the Prophete (whiles he was very young) vnderftanding, that innocent Sufanna was vniuftly accufed, and condemned to death [cried out amongft the
people with a loud voice: I am cleane from the bloud
of this woman. Returne ye into iudgement, becaufe
they haue fpoken falfe teftimonie againft her] He then
conuinced her falfe accufers, and witneffes; wherby
fhe was deliuered , and they iuftly punifhed with
death.

4. S. Iohn Baptift came for the teftimonie of neceffarie truth, which was not knowne to the people[To
geue teftimonie of the light] which he performed
moft faithfully. Our B. Sauiour himfelfe [came to
beare witneffe of the truth] He alfo taught his difciples, to admonish fraternally priuate offenders of
their faultes: and if that should not fuffice to corre-
ƈtion, then to adioyne one or two witneffes : that in
the mouth of two or three witneffes, euerie word
may ftand]& truth be confirmed. And finally [if nede
require to tel the Church] He alfo gaue his Apoftles
commandment [to teftifie of himfelf, to al the nations of the world.]And accordingly they preached
Chrift

Marginal notes (left):

Iudith.5.v.
26
ch 6.v.7.
ch.13.v.27.
ch.14.v.6.

Heſt.2.v.
22

Dan.13 v,
46.49,

Io.1.v.7.19.
17.&c.

Io.18.v. 37.

Mat.18.v.
16,
ch.28.v.19,
20.

Marginal notes (right):

Examples of
neceffarie de-
claration of
truth.

Efpecially
Chriftian faith
and doƈtrine
muft be decla-
red, where
nede requi-
reth.

Chrift euerie where. And vpon this commiſſion and
commandment, S. Peter and S. Iohn ſaid plainly [We
can not but ſpeake thoſe thinges, which we haue ſene *Act.*4 v̄. 20
and heard] Al the twelue, and S. Paul, S. Barnabas, S.
Luke, & S. Marke, and innumerable other Apoſtolical
men, haue and ſtil doe teſtifie of Chr iſt our Redemer, *Mat.*16. v.
and Sauiour, auouching Chriſtian doctrine, notwith- 20.
ſtanding anie prohibition to the contrarie [Becauſe 2.T.*m.*2.v.
the word of God is not tyed] Al truthes are good, and 9.
to be auouched in due time, place, and maner.   But
Chriſtian faith and religion is moſt principally euer,
and euery where, with diſcrete zele is to be confeſſed, and profeſſed, & in no caſe to be denied [Becauſe *Mat.*10.v.
he that denieth Chriſt before men, ſhal be denied by 33.
Chriſt, before the face of the Father of heauen.]

It is forbidde to beare falſe vvitneſſe, or to lie, or iudge raſhly.

ARTICLE 38.

Al maner of lying is forbidde by the Law of God, and nature.

GOd being truth it ſelf, and louing truth in al
thinges, deteſteth lying, and al vntruthes. And
hath therfore expreſly amongſt other precepts, commanded ſaying [Thou ſhalt not ſpeake againſt thy *Exod* 20.
neighbour falſe teſtimonie] Further ordayning (be- v 16.
ſides pnniſhment of the ſoule) ſpecial temporal reuenge by death, or other paine, for this offence a-
gainſt our neighbour : that [If a lying witnes ſtand *Deut.*5.v.
againſt a man, accuſing him of preuarication: both of 20.
them, whoſe the cauſe is: ſhal ſtand before our Lord, *ch.*19.v.16
in the ſight of the Prieſtes, and the Iudges, that ſhal be 17.
in thoſe dayes. And when ſearching moſt diligently, 18.
they ſhal finde, that the falſe witnes hath ſaid a lye
againſt his brother: they ſhal render to him, as he 19.&
meant to doe to his brother; and thou ſhalt take away
the euil out of the middes of thee: that others hearing
may

may haue feare, and may not be bold to doe such
thinges. Thou shalt not pitie him: but life for life;
eye for eye: tooth for tooth: hand for hand: foote for
foote shalt thou exact. Thou shalt not admitte a lying voice (saith our Lord againe to euerie appointed
Iudge) neither shalt thou ioyne thy hand to say false
testimonie for a wicked person.]

Exod.23.7.
1.

2 Neither is it lawful to affirme, a bare opinion as
one thinketh to be true, not being assured vpó knowlege, nor to auouch a probable coiecture, as if it were
cectaine: which is rash iudgement, iustly reproued by
holie Iob: saying to his importune freindes, which
charged him with supposed faultes, not committed
by him [Heare ye my corrections, and attende the
iudgement of my lippes. Hath God neede of your
lyes; that for him you speake guiles? Doe you take
his person, and doe you endeuour to iudg: for God?
He shal reproue you, because in secret (indirectly)
you take his person] and office vpon you. Likewise
the Royal Prophete, and others doe often reproue
both lying, and rash assertions. [Ye sonnes of men
(saith the Psalmist) how long are you of heauie hart?
Why loue you vanities, and seeke lying? Sinners are
alienated from the matrice, they haue erred from the
wombe; they haue spoken false thinges. They loued
God with their mouth, and with their tongue they
did lye to him: The enimies of our Lord haue lied to
him] Salomon saith [Whosoeuer trusteth to lies, feedeth the windes: and the same man foloweth flying
birdes. He that speaketh that which he knoweth, is
an vtterer of iustice: but he that lieth, is a fraudulent
witnes. Lying lippes are an abomination to our Lord:
but they that doe faithfully, please him. The iust shal
detest a lying word, but the impious confoundeth,
and shal be confounded. A false witnes shal not be
vnpunished; & he that speaketh lyes, shal not escape.
The bread of lying is sweete to a man: and afterward

Iob.13.7.6.
7.8 9.10.

Psal 4.v 3.
Ps.5 v 7.
Ps.57.v 4.

Ps.77.v 36.

Ps 80.7.16.
Pro 10.7.
4.

ch 12.7.17.
22.

ch 13.v 5.
ch.19.7.5.
9.

ch.20.7.17.

*To affirme a
thing vncer-
taine, as cer-
taine, is rash
iudgement.*

*Al sortes of
lies are con-
demned by
the holie
Scripture.*

Bb   his

his mouth shal be filled with the grauel stone. He that
gathereth treasures with a lying tongue, is vaine, and
witles and shal stumble at the snares of death. A lying
witnes shal perish. Desire not his meates, in which is
the bread of lying. Cloudes, and winde, and no rayne
folowing, a glorious man, and not accomplishing his
promises. A dart and a sword, and a sharpe arrow, a
man that speaketh false testimonie against his neighbour. A Prince that gladly heareth wordes of lying,
hath al his seruants impious.] Thus did wise Solomon
preach against lying. An other holie preacher admonisheth the like, saying [Doe not gainesay the word
of truth, by anie meanes, and be ashamed of the lye of
thine vnskilfulnes (of an vntruth vttered out of errour, which the speaker supposed to haue bene truth)
Plow not (deuise not) a lye against thy brother: neither
doe likewise against thy freind. Be not willing to
make anie lye: for the custome therof is not good. (is
veriena ught) Lying is a wicked reproche in a man:
& in the mouth of men without discipline, i t shal be
continually. Better is a theefe, then the continual custome of a lying man: but both shal inherite perdition. The maners of lying men, are without honour:
& their confusion is with them, without intermission.

3. Of al damnable liars false Prophets, and Heretikes are most wicked: because they belie God, calling their errors Gods word: and speake in his name,
wheras [he sent them not, he commanded them not,
neither hath spoken vnto them. They say they are A-
postles, and are not, and are found liars.] Their false
doctrine is the word of the diuel, for of him they are
sent [The diuel is their father. When he speaketh a
lye, he speaketh of his owne: because he is a liar, and
the father of al lying] S. Paul therfore admonisheth
al seducers, & liars [to put on the new man, which according to God is created in iustice and holinesse of
the truth. For the which cause, laying away lying,
(saith

Margin references:
ch.21.v.6.
28.
ch.23.v.5.
ch 25.v.14.
18.
ch 29.v.
12.
Eccli.4.
v.3.
ch.7.v.15.
ch.26.v.26.
27.28.

Left margin note: Aboue al o-
ther lyars, false
prophetes, and
heretikes are
most detesta-
ble

Iere.14.v.
15.
Apoc.2.v.
1.Ioan.8.
v.44.
Ephes.4.v.
24.
25.

(faith he) fpeake ye truth, euerie one with his neighbour, becaufe we are members one of another] And
the Angel in the Apocalypfe reciteth the finne of lying, amongft other damnable crimes, faying[To the
fearful (fuch as feare the world more then God) to
the incredulous, and execrable, and murderers, and
fornicators, and forcerers, and idolaters, and al lyars:
their part fhal be in the poole burning with fire and
brimftone, which is the fecond death] And into the
heauenlie Ierufalem [There fhal not enter anie polluted thing, nor that doth abhominttion and maketh
lye, &c.]

Apoc.21. v. 8.

v 27.
ch.22 v.15.

4. Againft rafh iudgement, and inconfiderate affertion of anie thing vncertaine, which is a common
vife of careles perfons, efpecially of barbarous people: our B. Sauiour admonifheth al men, faying
[Iudge not, that you be not iudged. For in what iudgment you iudge, you fhal be iudged : and in what
meafure you mete, it fhal be meafured to you againe]
The barbarous common people in Mileta, firft rafhly
iudged [that S. Paul was a murderer, becaufe a Viper
inuaded his hand.] and by & by againe, rafhly iudged
[that he was a God] becaufe there was no harme done
to him by the viper.

Mat.7. v. 1.

2.

Act.28. v. 4. 6.

Chrift expref-
ly condemneth
rafh iudge-
ment of things
doubtful.

Much more al
manifeft lying.

Falfe accufation, and condemnation of the in-
nocent : and iuftification of the guiltie,
are damnable finnes.

ARTICLE 39.

VNiuft proceding in the Tribunal feate of Iuftice,
is greater wickednes then fimple lying, or priuat
wrong, becaufe publike feaned iuftice is dubled by
falfe pretence of auctoritie, and by doing iniurie: for
albeit [there is no power but of God] yet is not the
abufe of Power from God. From whom is nothing
but iuft, and good. And therfore iniuftice defended,

Rom.13. v.1.

Pretended
iuftice and
wicked pro-
ceding, as in

forme of Law, is duble iniquitie.

or cloked by pretence of auctoritie, is not only iniurious to men, but also to God. [Whose Law is immaculate] And the same Law prescribeth, that euerie Iudge shal exactly without acception of persons, in al causes geue true and iust sentence [Thou shalt not folow the multitude to doe euil: neither shalt thou in Iudgement agree to the sentence of the most part, to stray frō the truth. The poore man also thou shalt not pittie in Iudgement. Thou shalt not doe that which is vniust, nor iudge vniustly. Consider not the person of a poore man : neither honour thou the countenance of him that is mightie. Iudge iustly to thy neighbour. Doe not anie vniust thing in iudgement : in rule, in weight, or measure. Thon shalt nor decline the poore mans iudgement. The innocent, and iust thou shalt not put to death: because I abhorre the impious man. Heare them (that haue causes) and iudge that which is iust : whether he be the same countriman, or a stranger. There shalbe no difference of persons : so shal you heare the litle, as the great : neither shal you accept anie mans person ; because it is the iudgement of God.] In regard of which diuine office [Iudges are called goddes.]

Psal. 18. v. 8.

Exod. 24. v. 2.

3.

Leuit. 19. v. 35.

35
Exod. 23. v. 6.7.

Deut. 1. v. 16.17.
ch. 16. v. 18.
19.

Exod. 21. v. 6.

ch. 22. v. 8.

Examples and testimonies against corrupt Iudges.

2.   Against this Law, the sonnes of Samuel offended [Being Iudges in Bersebee, who walked not in their fathers wayes ; but declined after auarice, and tooke bribes; and peruerted iudgement] Against such peruerse Iudges, the Royal Prophet inueigheth saying [God stood in the assemblie of goddes (of Iudges called goddes) and in the middes he iudgeth goddes. How long iudge ye iniquitie, and accept ye the persons of sinners. I said: You are goddes, and the sonnes of the Hieghest al. (ye that haue auctoritie of God.) But you shal dye as men: and fal as one of the Princes.] When you dye, you shal finde, that you are mortal men : and because being Princes, you iudged not right iudgement, you shal be punished as euil prin-

1. Reg. 8. v.
2.
3.

Psal. 81. v. 1.
2.

6.

7.

ces

ces [For to the litle one mercie is granted: but the mightie, shal mightely suffer torments. To the stronger more strong torment is imminent.] Salomon further saith[He that iustifieth the impious, and he that condemneth the iust, both are abominable before God. These thinges also to the wise: To knowe a person in iudgement is not good (that is, according to the Hebrew phrase, is very badde)They that say to the impious:Thou art iust:peoples shal curse them, and tribes shal detest them. They that rebuke him, shal be praised: and blesing shal come vpon them. The king that iudgeth the poore in truth,his throne shal be replenished for euer. Loue iustice, you that iudge theearth [saith the wise man) Thinke of our Lord in goodnes, & in simplicitie of hart seeke him. Heare ye kinges,and vnderstand ;learne ye Iudges of the endes of the earth. Geue eare ye,that rule multitudes,and that please your selues in multitudes of nations : because the power is geuen you of our Lord, and strength by the Hieghest, who wil examine your workes,and search your cogitations. Seke not to be made a Iudge,vnles thou be able by power to breake iniquities; lest peahaps thou feare the face of the mightie, and put a scandal in thyne equitie. Presents and giftes blinde the eyes of the Iudges; and as one dumbe in the mouth, turneth away their chastismets. Onr Lord wil heare the prayer of him that is hurt He wil not despise the prayers of the pupil: nor of the widow,if she poure ont speach of mourning. Doe not the widowes teares runne downe to the cheke : and her exclamation vpon him, that causeth them to runne?]According to these most wholsome instructions,the good Kinges, and other Iudges carefully performed their offices, and gaue charges to others subordinate to themselues,to doe the same [Take heede what you doe (said good king Iosaphat,to the particular Iudges of his kingdome) for you exercise not

the margin notes:
Sap 6.v.7. 9.10.
Pro 17 v. 15.
ch.24 v.23 24.
25.
ch.29.v.14.
Sap.1.v.1.
ch 6.v.2.
3.
4.
Eccli.7.v.6.
ch 20.v 31. ch.35.v.14. 25.
Iudic.3.v. 10.15. &c.
L.Reg.12.v. 15.
Eccli 46.v. 13.
2Par.19.v.6

The dutie of good Kinges, and Iudges.

Bb3

the iudgement of man, but of our Lord: and whatsoeuer you shal iudge, it shal redound to you.   Let the
feare of our Lord be with you : & with diligence doe
al things: for there is no iniquitie with the Lord our
God : nor acception of persons, nor desire of giftes.]
The Prophet Micheas (as likewise other Prophets)
seuerely reprehended vniust Iudges : saying, [Heare *Mich.3.v.*
this ye Princes of the house of Iacob, and ye Iudges   *1.9.*
of the house of Israel, which abhorre iudgement, and
peruert al right thinges: which builde Sion in bloud,
and Ierusalem in iniquitie. Her Princes iudged for *v.11.*
giftes, and her Priestes taught for wages, and her Prophets (pretended prophets) diuined for money, and
the y rested (pretended to relie) vpon our Lord, saying: Why, is not our Lord in the middes of vs? euil shal
not come vpon vs.]

VVicked pre-
tended lawes,   3 Aboue al other wickednes in publike trans-
against truth gressing of Law, and Iustice : the makers of wicked
and iustice, Lawes so farre surpasse, as the principal auctors of in-
are not Lawes iustice, are more faultie then the accessorie partici-
but Tyrannie. pants. And therfor Isaias the Prophete crieth [Woe *Isa 10.v.1.*
to them that make wicked Lawes: and writing, haue
written iniustice. That they might oppresse the poore
in iudgement, and doe violence to the cause of the
humble of my people : that widowes might be their
praye : and they might spoile pupilles] A notable example of a wicked Law (most like to Heretikes pro-
ceedings against Catholiques) is written by Daniel
the Prophet, of a Decree deuised by his enimies to in-
trappe him, as if he had bene disloyal to the King.
For [when they could not finde anie occasion against *Dan. 6.v.4.*
him, on the behalfe of the King, because he was faith- *5.*
ful and no falt, nor suspition was found in him] They
suggested to the King, to make a Decree in matter of
Religion] That euerie one which should pray to God, *v.7.*
or to anie but to the King only, should be cast into
the lake of Lyons] which being enacted, and published

shed, Daniel not with anie contempt of the King, nor
wittingly prouoking the persecutors, but warily in
his owne house, prayed thrise in the day to God, as he
had accustomed before : and the malicious men curiously watching and searching, found him praying in
his vpper chamber, his window being opened towardes Ierusalem, therupon accused him, as a tranf-
greffor of the kinges Edict. Vrged the king, and by
much importunitie, forced him to geue sentence, that
Daniel should be cast into the lake of Lions, and so
it was. Wherin both the king sinned greeuously, as
wel in yelding to the wicked suggestion, as by putting
such a pretended Law in execution, through faintnes
of hart, and also the cruel craftie persecutors, more
heynously offended both God, and the King. And so
by Gods iust iudgement, fel themselues into that pitte
which they had made to catch the innocent. For God
preseruing Daniel from the Lions, the king iustly condemned the plotters of the wicked Law [to be cast
into the same denne of Lions, who were there prefently deuoured] For though it was true that Daniel
did so pray to God, contrarie to the kings Edict, as
they did charge and accuse him: yet because the Law
was vniust, and against God, and Religion, they were
iustly punished by the King, whom they had most
wickedly abufed. And the King by this meanes, came
to honour God, better then before.

4. Moreouer against both wicked Lawes, and abufe of good Lawes, our B. Sauiour, gaue diuers precepts, commanding Magistrates to abstaine from iniustice, and to doe iustice [Did not Moyses (faith he)
geue you a Law, and none of you doth the Law? Why
seeke ye to kil me? Iudge not according to the face;
but iudge iust iudgement. And to the vniust Scribes
and Pharifes our Lord cried. [woe to you hypocrites,
because you tith mint, and anife, and cummine, and
haue left the weightier thinges of the Law: iudgement,

Margin left:
7.10.

11.12.&c.

Eccli.7.7.
9.10.

7.24.

9.56.

Ioan.17.7,
19.

24.

Mat.23.7.
2.

Margin right:
Christ con-
demneth al
wicked lawes
and abufe of
iust Lawes.

ment,and mercie,and faith.These thinges you ought
to haue done, and not to haue omitted those other. *Mat 23.v.2
Blind guides, that straine a gnat, and swallow a ca-   23, 24.
mel. And passe ouer iudgement, and the charitie of *Luc.11.v.
God.] S. Iames, amongst manie other admonitions,   42.
blameth the Iudges that wrest the Law: who by pretence of good Law, in dede make wicked Lawes, to
serue their owne turne. [For he that iudgeth his bro-   *Iac.4.v.
ther (saith he) detracteth from the Law: and iudgeth   11.
the Law. But if thou iudge the Law (by false interpre-   13.
tation) thou art not a doer of the Law, but a Iudge.
But whar art thou, that iudgest thy neighbour?] that
darest iudge, that thy neighbour breaketh the Law,
because he displeaseth thee?So thou vrgest his conscience, for thyne owne comoditie: not for his amendment. Wherin thou offendest against the Law: Which
appointeth indifferent Iudges, to decide controuersies betwene parties, and neuer alloweth anie partie,
to be Iudge in his owne cause.[For there is one Law-
miaker, and Iudge (God, who auctoriseth lawful in-   *12.
different Iudges, in whom himselfe is principal)that
can destroy,and deliuer.]

It is a particular vvickednes, to praise, or to flatterr anie for their sinne.

ARTICLE 40.

Not to admo-
nish an other
of his fault is
sometime a
sinne:but to
praise anie for
his fault, is al-
vvayes a grosse
sinne.

FRaternal correction being an especial worke of
mercie, tending to the spiritual good of others,
is so necessarie in time, and place requisite, other circumstances also concurrning,that the omission therof   *Mat.18.v
is sinne, more or lesse,according to the necescitie and   15.
hope of good therby. Much more to commend ,or
praise anie person,for his fault is a farre greater crime,
tending to the obduration of sinners,and their eternal ruine. Then the which there can scarse be greater
                                        crueltie

crueltie. For this is worse then corporal iniuries, a-
gainst bodilie health or life, by so much, as the soule
of euerie one, is better then their bodie.

2. This sinne therfore of flatterie in euil actions,
is worthily reproued by the Royal Prophete, saying
[Becanse the sinner is praised in the desires of his soule:
and the vniust man is blessed (commended by others)
He hath exasperated our Lord] more and more offended, and so is depriued of Gods grace, and according
to the multitude of Gods wrath, he shal not seeke to
recouer Gods fauour by repentance: but becommeth
bolder in the sinnes committed, persisting and reioycing in them. So by taking pleasure in sinnes, and passing with impunitie, they thinke not of death, nor of
iudgement [Therfore pride holdeth such sinners, and
they are couered with their iniquitie, and impietie,
Their inquitie hath proceded as it were of fatte, they
haue passed into the affection of the hart. They haue
thought and haue spoken wickednes: they haue spoken iniquitie on high.] Boldly boasting of their euil
wordes and deedes. Such praisers therfore of wickednes, doe both participate of others sinnes, formerly committed, by praising and approuing them,
& of the iteration of the like, by their inciting others
therto. Al such parasites the same Psalmist purposed
to shunne, and willingly to heare sincere admonitors,
saying [The iust shal rebuke me in mercie, and shal
reprehend me: but let not the oyle of a sinner fatte
my head] Salomon also aduiseth the prudent to be-
wa e of a flatterer, saying [When he shal submitte his
voice, beleue him not, because there are seuen mis-
chiefs in his hart. Better are the woundes of him that
loueth, then the fraudulent kisses of him that hateth.
It is better to be rebuked of a wiseman, then to be
deceiued with the flaterie of fooles. Because as the
sound of thornes burning vnder a potte: so the laughter of a foole: but this also is vanitie.]

He that prai-
seth sinne, ma-
keth the offe-
der more ob-
stinate, and
himself parti-
cipant therof.

Psal.9.v.
7.14.
25.

Psal 72. v.
6.7 8

Psal 140.
v 5.

Pro.2.6.v.
25
b 27.v.6.

Eccle. 7 v.
6 7.

C c

3. Woe

3. Woe to them that fow cushions vnder the cubite of euerie hand (faith our Lord by his Prophete Eze- *Exech 13.v. 18.* chiel) and make pillowes vnder the head of euerie age, to catch foules; and when they caught the foules of my people, they did viuificate their foules] affirming that they were in good ftate of fpiritual life and health, when in dede they were in euil ftate of finne, and in danger of ruine, deceiuing them by fawning *Mich.3. v.5.* flatterie. Likewife [Our Lord faith (by his Prophete *6.* Michas) Vpon the falfe prophets, which feduced my people: that bite with their teeth: and preach peace: There fhal be night to you for vifion, and darknes to you for diuination.] It fhal be quite contrarie to that which flaterers fay. They praife finners, and promife good fucceffe, but calamities fhal take the finners in the end. Flatterie is the oppofite vife to finceritie, and charitable aduife. And it corrupteth the true vertues of fidelitie and freindfhipe, vnder pretence of affabilitie. [Whofoeuer feke to pleafe men (in their euil *Gal.1.v.10.* dedes, wordes, or purpofes) are not the feruantes of Chrift] as S. Paul auoucheth. And againe, faith of him- *1. Thef. 2.v.* felfe in an other place [So we fpeake, not as pleafing *4.5.* men, but as pleafing God: who proueth our hartes. For neither haue we bene at anie time in the word of adulation, as you know, nor in occafion of auarice: God is witnes: nor feeking glorie of men, but in plaine finceritie and veritie.] Let louers of flatterie remember king Herod Agrippa, who accepting of the peo- *2. Cor.1.v. 12.* ples flaterie, faying: that [his wordes were the voices of a God, and not of a man, was forthwith ftroken by *Act.12.v.* an Angel: and being confumed of woormes, he gaue *22.23.* vp the ghoft] and died a miferable wretch, for fuffering that blafphemous flatterie.

Ff

If anie be demanded of a secrete thing, by re-
uealing vuherof vniuſt hurt is like to en-
ſue, it is not lavuful to reueale it.

ARTICLE 41.

AS euerie one is bond to declare that truth which
he knoweth, when it is duly demanded, by
lawful auctoritie, for iuſtice ſake: ſo when anie thing
is vniuſtly demanded, that wrong may be done therby to himſelfe, of whom it is demanded, or to anie
other, it is not lawful to reueale it. Becauſe ſo to reueale, is to concurre to iniuſtice: which al are bond
to auoide. As is cleare by reaſon, and by authentical
examples, and inſtructions of holie Scripture.

2. The Midwiues in Ægypt, which feared God,
and did not kil the Hebrewes children: being demanded, Why they did not kil them? could not lawfully
tel the true cauſe to king Pharao: for that he would
then haue vniuſtly puniſhed the ſame Midwiues, and
terrified others from vſing the like pietie, and by ſome
other meanes haue deſtroyed ſuch children. And although they ſinned venially, by making an officious
lie (which is neuer lawful) yet they were rewarded
for their pietie [becauſe they feared God.] Likewiſe
Rahab, being commanded by the king of Iericho, to
bewray the men that were in her houſe, iuſtly conceal-
led, & hid them. For which fact, ſhe is ſpecially commended by S. Paul, and by S. Iames. But Samſons wife
offended, in bewraying her husbands ridle, for feare
of temporal harme. And ſhortly after, both ſhe, and
her father were burnt by the ſame enimies. Michol
iuſtly concealed Dauid her husband, when her father
king Saul had ſent certaine men to kil him: and made
an excuſe to her father. An other woman iuſty concealed Dauids men being in danger of Abſolom, who
would haue killed them.

Cc2   3. Sa-

Article 37.

Exod.1.v.
17.18.19.
20.

v.21.

Ioſ 2 v.3.4.
5.
Hib.11.v.
31.

Iac.2 v.
25.
Iudic.14.v.
17
ib.15.v.6.

1 Reg.19.v.
21.17.
2.Reg 17.
v.19.20.

Truth muſt
ſometimes be
concealed.

Examples of
concealing the
truth.

3. Salomon confirmeth this doctrine, of necessarie concealing the truth in some cases, in which Iustice, or Prudence, or other vertues should be violated. For al vertues are so connected, that if anie one be peruerted, the others are but false pretenses, not true vertues. To this purpose he saith [A circumspect man concealeth knowlege: and the hart of the vnwise pronoketh follie. Be not witnes without cause aganst thy neighbour. He that kepeth his mouth, kepeth his soule: but he that is vnaduised to speake, shal feele euils. A wiseman feareth, and declineth from euil, the foole leapeth ouer, & is confident. Al thinges haue a time. There is a time to kepe silence, & a time to speake] teaching that consideration, & discretion when, and what to speake, are alwaies necessarie. And namely in geuing testimonie, and reuealing secretes: lest anie should either beare witnes rashly, without sufficient cause: or vntruly affirming vncertaine, as certaine, errour for truth: or vniustly, by which anie may be wronged; and so the reuealer should cooperate to others doing iniurie; and participate in the same sinne.

Confirmed by other holie Scriptures.

Pro 12. v. 23. ch. 13, v. 3. ch. 14 v. 16.

Eccle 3. v. 7.

4. For other causes also, besides the auoiding of iniuries, truth must somtimes be concealed. As from the vnworthie, lest they should contemne it: for which reason, our B. Sauiour saith [Geue not that which is holie to dogges: neither cast your pearles before swine: lest perhaps they tread them with their feete; and turning al to teare you] He spake very much in Parables, saying: I wil open my mouth in parables: I wil vtter thinges hidden, from the foundation of the world.] But would not explaine euery thing to al, saying to his Apostles [To you it is geuen to know the Mysteries of the kingdome of heauen, but to the multitudes it is not geuen.]

Truth is not to be reuealed without probabilitie of good therby.

Ma. 7. v. 6. ch. 13. v. 34.

v. 11.

They

They that are vniuſtly demanded, may lavv-
fully anſvver in an other ſenſe, then
the demander vnderſtandeth it.

ARTICLE 42.

Artic.38.
Artic.41.

FOr ſo much as it is neuer lawful to lye (no not
venialy and ſometimes is not lawful to reueale
the truth; and that ſometimes alſo ſilence, or refuſing
to anſwere, wil be hurtful to the partie that is exami
ned or to others: he that is ſo preſſed, may lawfully in
ſuch a caſe to auoide perplexitie, anſwere in a true
ſenſe, reſerued in his owne minde, different from that
ſenſe, in which the demander, or others doe vnderſtand his anſwere. Which maner of anſwering by
equiuocation (that is by wordes which may haue diuers ſignifications) is approued by manie good examples, and teſtimonies of holie Scriptures: wherof we
ſhal here recite a competent number.

Truth muſt be
prudently cō-
cealed. when
vniuſt hurt
would enſue.
by reuealing
it

2. Abraham going into Ægypt, and foreſeing danger, which probably might happen to him, & to Sara
his wife [willed her to ſay, that ſhe was his ſiſter]
Which was true in his ſenſe, becauſe ſhe was his nere
kinſewoman, and in a general ſignification was his
ſiſter (as he called Lot his brother, being his brothers
ſonne) but was not true in that ſenſe, as the Ægyptians
vnderſtood it who vpon this affirmation thought
her to be his german ſiſter, the daughter of his owne
father and mother, and ſo not to be his wife. Againe
Abraham ſaid the ſame in Gerarts, where he dwelt
afterwards, [She is my ſiſter.] Iſaac ſaid the like of his
wife Rebecca. [She is my ſiſter. For he was afraide to
confeſſe, that ſhe was married to him, thinking leſt
peraduenture they would kil him, becauſe of her
beautie. Ioſeph ſaid to his brethren, when they were
with him in Ægypt [You are ſpies] Albeit he knew

Gen.12.v.
13.

v.8.

ch.20.v.2.
ch.26.v.7.

ch.42.v.9.

Examples of
concealing the
truth by equi-
uocation.

So did Abra-
ham.

Iſaac.

Ioſeph.

Cc 3   right

right wel, who they were,& why they came: yet they not knowing him, he called them spies:becaufe they might feme fo to be, before ftrangers, vntil they fhould proue themfelues to be comen for iuft caufe: with faithful and honeft meaning Furthermore God himfelfe bade Samuel to fay [that he was comen to Bethleem, to immulate to our Lord] wheras the particulate caufe, for the which he came thither, at that time, was to annoint Dauid ,to be King of Ifrael. The godlie zealoufe mother of the feuen brothers Martyres, in the perfecution of Antiochus, by equiuocation, deceiued the Tyrant, feming to promife him, that she would perfwade her youngeft fonne to faue his life, by yelding to the kings wil. Which she performed not wickedly, as the tyrant vnderftood her, to faue his temporal life, but pioufly to faue his foule, and fpiritual life: by perfeuering in Gods Law. And the good Prieftes of the Temple, being commanded by Nicanor, to deliuer Iudas Machabeus into his handes, did both fay and fweare [that they knew not where he was] meaning that they knew not precifely in what particular houfe he was: or knew not with intention to take him, and to deliuer him prifoner to his perfecuters, as they were vniuftly commanded: or in fome other referued fenfe.

3, Our B. Sauiour likewife very often fpake in parables, which might haue diuers fenfes, alwayes moft true in his owne fenfe and meaning. not alwayes true in the moft common fignification of the wordes, nor as the hearers vnderftood. So he faid to the Iewes that asked a figne of his power: [Diffolue this temple, and in three dayes I wil raife it] which they vnderftood of the material Temple in Ierufalem [but he fpake of the Temple of his bodie] An other time being in Galilee,& certaine men willing him to go into Iewrie, to the feaft of Scenopegia he faid [Goe you vp to this feaftiual day: I goe not vp to this feftiual day, becaufe my time

Marginal notes:

Samuel.

The mother of feuen Martyrs.

The Prieftes of the Temple.

Chrift himfelf vfed equinocation often in wordes.

Right margin references:

1. Reg. 16.v. 2.3. &c.

2. Mach.7.v. 25 26.27.

ch.14.v 30. 31.32.33.

Ioan. 2. v. 19.21.

ch.7.v. 2. 3. 8.

time is not yèt accompl.shed. But after that his brethren were gone vp, then he also went vp to the feftiual day? not openly, but as it were in fecrete.] He
faid also to his difciples concerning the day of the
general Iudgement [Of that day, and houre no bodie
knoweth, neither the Angels of heauen, but the
Father alone. Nor the Sonne, but the Father. Neuerthelesse it is certaine, that our B. Sauiour, (alfo in his humanitie) knoweth that day, in which he
shal be Iudge of al men:& that he knoweth al thinges
whatfoeuer are, or haue bene, or shal be: but he knoweth not the day of Iudgement, to reueale it before-
hand, when it shal be, as he hath reuealed manie other
Misteries. Namely that it wil come sudainly, whē most
men shal not expect it, nor thinke it to be so nere, as
they shal finde and feele it. So that, faying [the Sonne
of man knoweth not that day, and houre] was fpoken
by him in fome other fenfe, then fuch wordes doe
commonly fignifie. Likewife after his Refurrection,
our Lord vfed equiuocation in his fact, when walking
with two difciples, and drawing nere to Emmaus [He
made femblance to goe further. *Fin cit fe longus ire.*]
S. Paul fpake wlth equiuocation when he made the
Pharifees to thinke, that he was of their Sect. [For
knowing that one part of his aduerfaries was of the
Sadduces, and the other of Pharifees, he cried aloud
in the Councel: Men brethren: I am a Pharifee, the
fonne of Pharifees] In general the fame great Apoftle aduifed the Ephefians, and in them al Chriftians,
[to walke warily, not as vnwife, but as wife; redeming
the time, becaufe the dayes are euil.]

4. But we muft alwayes obferue, that equiuocation is neuer lawful in pointes of faith, nor in profeffion therof, which muft be cleare and plaine. For
vpon confeffing Chrift, and Chriftian Religion, in
word, and fact, dependeth eternal faluation, and vpon
denying, or not confeffing the fame in due time, and
place

Margin notes left:
v 10.
Mat. 14. v. 36.
Mat 13. v. 32.
Luc. 24. v. 26.
Act. 23. v. 6.
Eph 5. v. 15. 16.
I. Pet. 3. v. 15.

Margin notes right:
Some time in fact.

S. Paul vfed alfo equiuo-cation, to get lawful fauour of fome of his Adnerfa-ries.

In matters of fact, equiuo-cation is law-ful, to auoide perplexitie.

But not in pro-
fession of faith
or of Christi-
an doctrine.

place, foloweth eternal damnation [Euerie one that shal confesse me before men (saith our B. Sauiour) I *Mat. 10. v.* also wil confesse him before my Father, which is in *31.33.* heauen. But he that shal denie me before men, I also wil denie him, before my Father which is in heauen] He also is accounted to denie his faith, that in due time, when he is called to trial, maketh euasions, and doth not plainly confesse it, because Christ our Lord wil only confesse and acknowlege, those before his Father, that confesse him in word and deed before men. So S. Paul teacheth, saying [With the hart we be-*Rom. 10. v.* leue vnto iustice: but with the mouth confession is *10.* made to saluation.] Factes also must be answerable. Else if some say they are Christians, and exteriorly communicate, or practise anie act of infidelitie, with Christs enimies, they denie him worse then in word only, because deedes are more then wordes. Of such the same S. Paul saith: They confesse that they know *Tit 1. v 16.* God; but in their workes they denie. Wheras they *Ro. 1. v. 21,* know God, (and his true Religion) they doe not glo-rifie him as God] So that such knowlege, and such confession by wordes, with contrarie deedes, doe not diminish, but augment their damnation [That seruant *Luc 12. v.* that knew the wil of his Lord, and prepared not him-*47.* self, and did not according to his wil; shal be beaten with manie stripes.] Albeit therfore in temporal cau-ses, and in matters of fact, those which are vniustly commanded to reueale the truth, may equiuocate in their answeres: yet in poyntes of faith, they must speake plainly without al equiuocation.

*VVhosoeuer doe vniustly hurt others, or be
in debt, are bound to restitution.*

ARTICLE 43.

True

Tari. 2.
Artic. 16.

TRue repentance, amongst other conditions, especially requireth a resolute purpose to cease from sinne. And therfore whosoeuer hath vniustly hurt an other, must repaire the damage, by rendring al that he hath vniustly taken, or anie way withholdeth, from an other, or is by anie meanes indebted: at least he must haue a readie wil, and a true purpose to restore al, according to his abilitie, and best endeauour so sowne as he shal be able, and the creditor requireth: els he continueth in sinne, so long as he persisteth in minde, to hold, or not restore, that which right'y belongeth, and is due to an other. Whether it be temporal goodes, landes, money, or money worth: or damage done to the person or bodie of anie; or to their fame or reputation. And so this bond of restitution perteyneth to al the sinnes, committed against al the former commandments of the second table, concerning the dutie towards Parents, & other Superiours: concerning murder, adultrie, theift, false testimonie, and al the branches of the same fiue commandments.

Non dimittitur peccatum, nisi restituatur ablatum.

Of this obligation commeth the common approued *Axiome*, or general Rule, that sinne is not remitted, vnles that be restored, which is vniustly taken away, or witholden: at least (as is already said) in good wil, and true desire, with purpose when abilitie shal serue. Al which is cleare by the rule of reason, and in summe was expressed in the written Law of Moyses, perteyning to Moral precepts, and so bindeth al Christians (according to the particular Lawes of euerie nation) no lesse then the Iewes. For example it was ordayned, that (if a man strike a woman that is with childe, and she make aborte, but herselfe liue, he shal be subiect to so much damage, as the womans husband shal require, & as the arbiters shal award. But if her death doe ensue therupon, he shal render life for life. Also: Eye for eye; tooth for tooth: hand for hand; foote for

Exod. 21. v.
22.
23.
24.
25.

VVhosoeuer wil not restore that which they vniustly hold from others, remaine in sinne.

D d foote

foote:aduſtion for aduſtion: wound for wound, ſtripe
for ſtripe , &c. And he that is conuicted of anie Leuit. 6. v.
offence , ſhal render al thinges , which by fraude he ſ.
would haue obtained , whole, and the fifth part be- *ch. 24. v. 18.*
ſides to the owner, vnto whom he did the damage.]
He that ſtriketh (and killeth a beaſt, ſhal render one
for it]that is, the like in value: yea though the damage
happened by negligence only , and not of other ma- Num. 5. v. 7.
lice, they that ſo offended, were bond [to confeſſe
their ſinne, and to reſtore the principal it ſelfe, and the
fifth part ouer, to him againſt whom they ſinned] Al
which perteyneth to the firſt and ſecond partes of penance: that is, to neceſſarie ſorrow for their ſinne, and
humble confeſſion therof. For except the offender wil
recompence the wrong, he is not rightly ſorie for it,
and vnles he confeſſe it, he can not haue remiſſion. Beſides both which, it is alſo neceſſarie to make Satisfaction, which is the thirde eſſential part of Penance, diſtinct from Reſtitution.

Al are bond to pay debtes in due time and maner.

2. Thoſe alſo that contract debts by lawful meanes,
as by borrowing, by bying vpon credite , or by anie
other way , are bound to pay ſuch debts in due time,
and maner, els the delay, or withholding, is as vnlawful, as vniuſt getting [The ſinner wil borrow (ſaith *Pſal. 36. v.*
the Royal Prophet) and not pay.] ſignifying that he 21.
ſinneth, which wil not pay al that be boroweth. [Who *Pro. 13. v 13*
ſoeuer detracteth from anie thing (ſaith Salomon) he
bindeth himſelfe for the time to come.]

Chriſt wil haue iuſtice to be ſatisfied, before he wil accept of vo- luntarie ſacri- fice.

3. Touching reſtitution in general, to the ſufficient
contentment of the owner, our Sauiour declareth it
to be ſo neceſſarie, that it muſt be preferred before al
free oblations to God. [If thou offer thy gift before *Mat 5. v. 24*
the Altar (ſaith he) and there thou remember that 25.
thy brother hath ought againſt thee (that is, if thou
haſt done him wrong, and not geuen him contentment) leaue there thy offering before the Altar, and
goe firſt to be reconciled to thy brother : and then
com-

comming, thou shalt offer thy gift] Deuout Zacheus
wel confidered, that al finnes of iniurie are irremiffi-
ble, vntil that which is iuft be reftored to the owner,
in fact, or iu preparation of minde. And therfore being rich, and able to render al that he owed to anie
Luc.19.v. 8 man, he faid [Lord, if I haue defrauded anie man of
anie thing, I reftore fourfolde,] S. Paul gcueth a general admonition : fo to render al that is due to
euerie one, that onlie mutual loue and charitie, re-
Ro.13.v.7. maine a perpetual debt [Render (faith he) to al men
8. that is due, owe no man anie thing : but that you
loue one an other.]

It is forbidde to confent in minde vnto vn-
lavvful carnal thoughtes.

ARTICLE 44.

Beaufe al finful actes do procede from the minde,
yelding confent to euil fuggeftions of concupif- | **Not only ex-**
cence: and becaufe fometimes the external vn- | **ternal actes of**
lawful actes are committed, fometimes the confent is | **finne, but also**
expreffed in wordes, but not completed in factes, and | **internal côfent**
fomtimes the côfent remaineth only in the thoughts, | **of mind, is for-**
not proceding into external actes, nor wordes: after | **bidden by**
the prohibition of Adulterie, and Theft (amongft o- | **Gods law.**
Sap. 1 v.3, ther finnes in the former Precepts , in al which not
1.Ioan.v. 16 only external deedes , and wordes , but alfo internal
confent of the minde are vnlawful, and implicitely
forbidden by Gods Law) two other cômandments are
added ; concerning the internal defires of vnlawful
carnal delectation, and of vniuft vfurping other mens
temporal goodes. In which two kindes of concupifcence, there is more frequeut tentation , and more
danger of yelding mental confent , by occafion of | **VVhy confent**
mans corrupt inclination, and more prownes to thefe | **of minde is**
two vifes (for that man confifting in bodie, of flesh | **more expreffly**
| **forbid in two**

D 2 and

kindes of
finnes, feeing
it is vnlawful
in al kindes.
Sap 1 v.3.

and bloud, and liuing corporally by the vfe of temporal goodes, and by poffeffion of them, hath more
eftimation amongft men of this World) mans corrupt nature, more often defireth, and more often taketh pleafure in fuch defires, then in bare congitation
of other impietie. And therfore it femeth more neceffarie to haue expreffe commandements againft thefe
particular concupifcences of the flesh, and of the
world, that we not yeeld confent of minde vnto
them. Touching therfore concupifcence of the flesh,
God not only forbiddeth in he fixt commandement, *Exod. 20. v.*
al adultrie, & al particular finnes of that carnal kind, *54.15 17.*
in act, or word, but alfo in the ninth commandment,
forbiddeth internal confent of the minde vnto carnal
cogitations. And likewife touching concupifcence *Deut.5.v.*
of the world, not only forbiddeth al iniuries in world- *28,19.21.*
iie goodes, by fact or word, in the feuenth commandment, but alfo in the tenth, forbiddeth to geue mental
confent, vnto vnlawful defires of worldly goodes.

Examples and
admonitions
againft men-
tal confent
vnto carnal
concupif-
cence.

2. For better auoiding of the former of thefe two
mental finnes, by confenting in minde to the pleafure
of carnal thoughtes: holie Iob before this precept was
expreffed in anie written Law, fincerely teftifieth of
himfelfe, faying [I haue made a couenant with mine *Iob.31.v 1.*
eyes, that I would not fo much as thinke of a virgine.] So did he gouerne his fenfes, that his thoughtes
might be more fafe from confenting to fuch carnal
pleafure. The like did chafte Sara, the daughter of
Raguel, confidently fay of her felfe, in her prayer to
God, that she had kept her minde and thought free *Tob.3. v.16.*
from carnal delight, faying[Thou knoweft Lord, that *17.18.*
I neuer coueted a hushaud, and that I haue kept my
foule cleane from al concupifcence. Neuer haue I
companied my felf with fporters, neither haue I made
my felfe partaker with them that walke in lightnes.
But a husband I confented to take, with thy feare, not
with my luft.] To this purpofe, other diuine Scriptures

Ecli.9.
v. 1.
3.
4.
5.
6.
7.
8.
9.

tures exhort al persons, to kepe their mindes, and thoughtes pure from consenting to carnal sinnes, aduising married persons [not to be ielous] al men in general to shunne the occasions of inticemets [Looke not vpon a woman, that it desirous of manie: lest perhaps thou fal into her snares. With her that is a dancer, be not daily conuersant nor heare her, lest perhaps thou perish in her efficacie. Behold not a virgin, lest perhaps thou be scandalized in her beautie. Looke not round about in the wayes of the citie, nor wander vp and downe in the streates therof. Turne away thy face from a trimmed woman, and gaze not about vpon others beautie. By the beautie of a woman manie haue perished: and therby concupiscence is inflamed, as a fire. Goe not after thy concupiscences,

ch 18.v.
10.31.
ch.25. v.28.

and turne away from thy wil (thy lust, or carnal appetite) If thou geue to thy soule her concupiscence, she wil make thee a ioy to the enemies] to diuels which alwaies seeke mans ruine. And therfore man being weake, must both labour & pray for grace & strength against this kinde of aluremet, as this diuine Preacher instructeth in this, or like maner. [O Lord Father & God of my life, leaue me not in their cogitations. Take from me the concupiscences of the bellie: and let not the concupiscences of copulation take holde of me; and geue me not ouer to a shamelesse and foolish minde.]

3. Scribes and Pharisees, helde it sufficient to abstaine from the external act of sinnes, not caring much for badde speaches, and lesse of euil thoughts. Wherupon our Sauiour Christ said [Vnles your iustice abound more then that of the Scribes and Pharisees, you shal not enter into the kingdome of heauen.] And amongst manie correctiõs of their defects, he teacheth plainly concerning the sixt & ninth commandments, that the former alone sufficeth not, as they falsely supposed. For they said only [Thou shalt not committe

Mat. 5. v. 21.

Concupiscence getting consent of the wil, is a sinne in thought.

And therfore it is necessarie to shunne al dangerous occasions,

Christ reproueth the Scribes and Pharises for neglecting this ninth commandment.

ad-

aduoutrie.] But our Lord requireth alſo the obſeruation of the ninth commandment. [Thou shalt not v. 18.
deſire thy neighbours wife. Whoſoeuer shal ſee a wo- 29.
man to luſt after his (with conſent of wil,before either external act,or word) hath already committed
aduoutrie with her in his hart.]Conformably hereto
S. Paul admonisheth to flee from al the three ſortes
of luxurie,in act,word,& thought. Touching the act,
he sheweth , that it corrupteth both bodie & ſoule, 1.Cor.6.v.
ſaying [Euerie (other) ſinne whatſoeuer a man doth, 18.
is without the bodie (defiling only the ſoule) but he
that doth fornicate, ſinneth againſt his owne bodie.]

Carnal ſinnes defile both the bodie and the ſoule. Touching fornication in word, without act, he ſaith:
[Fornication,and al vncleannes, or auarice, let it not Epheſ.5.v.
be ſo much as named amongſt you,as it becommeth 3.4.
Sainctes: nor filthines, nor foolishnes, nor ſcurrilitie]
Touching alſo fornication in thought only, he ſaith, 1.Cor.7.v.
that thoſe, which are truly chaſte [Thinke on] the 34.
thinges that perteyne to our Lord: that they may be
holie,both in bodie and in ſpirite The flesh and the Gal.5.v.17.
ſpirit are aduerſaries,one to an other. They that be 24.25.
Chriſts, haue crucified their flesh , with the viſes and
concnpiſcences. If we liue in the ſpirite,in the ſpirite
alſo let vs walke] S.Peter very plainly teacheth,that
not only the loynes of the bodie , but alſo fleshly cogitations (which he calleth the loynes of the minde)
muſt be girded and reſtrained , that we may rightly &

Secret thoughtes, are loynes of the minde. fruitfully truſt in Chriſtes grace[Hauing (ſaith he) the 1.Pe.1.v.13.
loynes of your minde girded, ſober , truſt perfectly in ch.2.v.11.
that grace, which is offered you : in the reuelation
of Ieſus Chriſt] Againe he ſaith [My deareſt I beſeech you, as strangers and pilgrimes (trauellers towardes heauen, being as yet ſubiect to tentations)
to refraine your ſelues from carnal deſires, which
warre againſt the ſoule.]

It is forbidden to consent in minde vnto vn-lavvful desires of vvorldlie goodes.

ARTICLE 45.

IN like maner, as besides the prohibition of actual adulterie, internal consent vnto carnal thoughtes, is forbid : so besides the act of theft, mental consnet to vniust desires of worldlie goodes, is also prohibited by the expresse Law of God in these wordes [Thou shalt not couet thy neighbours house, nor seruant, nor handmaide, nor oxe, nor asse, nor any thing that is his.] Which vnlawful desire is properly Auarice, a vise condemned by the Law of nature, as may appeare by the iudgement of Iethro the Priest of Madian, who prudently counseling Moyses his sonne inlaw, to appoint subordinate Iudges, ouer the common people, aduised him to choose such as were not addicted to the vise of couetousnes. But [to prouide out of al the people men, that are wise (said he) and doe feare God, in whom there is truth, and that doe hate auarice.] He wel considered that the roote of all sinnes, is in the minde and cogitation of the hart. So that manie sinnes are comitted in the hart, which neuer come to be vttered in wordes, nor executed in factes. And therupon the wiseman in the beginning of his booke saith expresly that [Peruerse cogitations separate from God] And so either vniust desire to gette, or miserlie niggardnes in keping, or vaine pleasure of the minde in possessing worldlie goodes, produceth sinne, and offendeth God.

2. For which cause, the holie Psalmist exhorteth the faithful, saying, [Hope not in iniquitie, and couete not robberies : if riches abound, set not your hartes vpon them] Himselfe also prayed [Incline my hart, ô Lord, into thy testimonies, and not into auarice.]

Salomon

Marginal notes (left):

Exod. 20. v. 17.

Deut. 5. v. 21.

Exod. 18. v. 21.

sap. 1. v. 3.

Psal. 61. v. 11

Psal. 118. v. 36.

Marginal note (right): Vniust desire of others temporal goods, is condemned by the Law of God and nature.

Special ad-
monitions
againſt coue-
tous mindes.

Salomon geueth manie moſt excellent documents, to
moderate mans deſires of worldlie thinges [The iuſt
(ſaith he) eateth, and filleth his ſoule, but the bellie
(the deſire) of the impious is vnſatiable. Better is a
litle with the feare of our Lord, then great treaſures,
and vnſatiable. Better is a poore man that walketh in
his ſimplicitie: then a rich, writhing his lippes, and
vnwiſe. Al the day he longeth and deſireth, but he that
is iuſt wil geue, and wil not ceaſe. Labour not to be
rich : but ſette a meane to thy prudence. Hel and perdition are neuer filled : in like maner alſo the eyes of
men are vnſatiable. A couetous man ſhal not be
filled with money: and he that loueth riches, ſhal take
no fruite of them: and this therfore is vanitie. There
is alſo an other very il infirmitie, which I haue ſene,
vnder the Sunne : riches kept to the hurt of the owner. For they periſh in very euil affliction: he hath begotten a ſonne, which ſhal be in great pouertie. As he
came forth naked from his mothers wombe : ſo ſhal
he returne, and ſhal take nothing away with him of
his labour. Let not thy hand be ſtretched out to receiue, and cloſed to geue. Nothing is more wicked
then the couetous man. Why is earth & aſhes proud?
Nothing is more wicked then to loue money. For he
hath his ſoule alſo to ſel. He that loueth gold ſhal not
be iuſtified : and he that foloweth after corruption,
ſhal be repleniſhed of it. Bleſſed is the rich man that
is found without ſpotte, and that hath not gone after
gold; nor hoped in money, and treaſures. Who is this,
and we wil praiſe him : for he hath done meruelous
thinges in his life? Who is proued therin, and perfect,
ſhal haue eternal glorie. He that could tranſgreſſe,
and hath not tranſgreſſed? and doe enils, and hath
not done.]

*Pro.13.
v.25.*

ch.15.v.16.

ch.19.v.1.

ch.21.v.16.

ch.23.v.4.

ch.27.v.20.

*Ecclef.1.
9. 12. 13 14*

Eccli.4 v.36

*ch.10.v. 9.
10.*

*ch.31.v.5 8
9.
10.*

The Pro-
phetes ac-
count coue.

3. To al ſuch as yeld internal conſent vnto the
concupiſcence of others external goodes: God by his
Prophets often threatneth, not only temporal puiſh-
ments,

ments, but alſo eternal in the euerlaſting fire of hel.

Iſa.33.v.14. [Which of you (ſaith our Lord, to al couetous minds) can dwel with deuouring fire ? Which of you ſhal dwel with euerlaſting heates?]To which queſtion, the Prophet anſwering, telleth who ſhal eſcape this in-

v.15. quenchable fire, ſaying [He that walketh in iuſtice, and ſpeaketh truth, that caſteth away auarice of op-preſſion:and ſhaketh his handes from al gift;and ſtop-peth his eares, leſt he heare bloud, and ſhutteth his eyes, that he may ſee no euil.] ſignifying that thoſe which wil eſcape eternal damnation, muſt reſiſt the concupiſcence of the fleſh, & of reuenge, and of aua-rice: not lending their eyes to ſee euil, nor their eares to hearken vnto ſheeding of bloud, nor their handes to catch other mens goodes. Al which muſt be corre-

Iere 6 v.12. 25. cted in the hart, from which al euil proceedeth. And namely from auarice, our Lord ſaying[wil extend my hand vpon the inheritance of the land. For from the

ch.2.v.17. leſſer, euen to the greater, al ſtudie auarice (al folow auarice) thyne eyes(ſaith our Lord againe to his peo-

Eſ.b 33.v. 31 ple, and thy hart are to auarice, and to ſhede innocent bloud, and to craftie oppreſſion, and to the courſe of euil worke. Their hart foloweth their auarice. For

Am 9.v.2. there is auarice in the head of al: and the laſt of them wil I kil by the ſword : there ſhal be no flight for them]

4. Chriſt our Sauiour expreſly teacheth, that al ſinnes procede from the hart, and wil of man, & ther-

Mat.6.v. 22 23. fore muſt be there corrected, as in the roote.[If thyne eye (that is thyne intention) be ſimple, the whole bo-die ſhal be lightſome. But if thyne eye be naught, thy whole bodie ſhal be darkeſome].The actions procee-

v.24. ding fró the wil are good or euil, as the wil directeth wel or il. [God and Mammon are the two maſters, whom no man can ſerue. [For that thing which the hart moſt loueth, and preferreth, is to that perſon *ſummum bonum*, his God, in that action. [The thinges

Christ tea-cheth that al ſinnes procede from content of the hart.

Ee   that

that procede out of the mouth,(or from the handes, feete, or other member)come forth from the hart, and thofe thinges (being euil) defile the man. For, from *ch.15.v.18. 19.* the hart, come forth euil cogitations, murders, ad-uoutries, fornications, theftes, falfe teftimonies, bla-fphemies. Thefe are the thinges, that defile a man jbe-caufe the hart confenteth to them. Hence it is that *Colof.3.* S. Paul calleth [Auarice the feruice of Idols]becaufe, a couetous man preferreth temporal gaine, before the feruice of God.[They that wil be made rich(faith the *1.Tim.6.* fame Apoftle, of al thofe that in hart and wil yelde to *9.10.* the vnlawful concupifcence of other mens goodes) fal into tentations, and the fnare of the diuel, and ma-nie defires vnprofitable and hurtful, which drowne men into deftruction and perdition. For the roote of al euil is couetoufnes: which certaine defiring(al the mifchiefe cometh from vnlawful defiring) haue er-*v.17.* red from the faith, and haue entangled themfelues in manie forowes. Command the rich of this world, not to be hiegh minded, nor to truft in the vncertaintie *18.* of riches: but in the liuing God, who geueth vs to en-ioy al thinges abundantly) to doe wel, to become *19.* rich in good workes: to geue eafyly: to communicate (with the needie) to heape vnto themfelues a good foundation for the time to come, that they may ap-prehend the true life] He lamenteth the fal of one *2.Tim.4.9.* fpecial Clergie man, by ouer much loue of this world, *10.* faying [Demas hath left me, louing this world] A-*1.Tim.3.7.* mongft other fpecial qualities requifite in Clergimen, *8.9.* the fame Apoftle S. Paul inftructeth al Bifhops, not to admitte anie to hofieOrders[that are folowers of filthie lucre.] and warneth al the faithful in general, *Heb.13.v.5.* faying[Let your maners be without auarice] S. Iames and other Apoftles admonifh in like maner to roote out this defire of others goods, as the principal caufe of manie other greuous finnes. [From whence are warres, and contentions among you (faith S. Iames) *Iac.4.1.*

Are

Auarice is a dangerous finne in al men, but fpe-cially in the Clergie.

Are they not hereof? of your concupifcences, which warre in your members? you couet and haue not: you kil, and enuie, and can not obtaine: you contend, and warre, & cannot haue] your vnfatiable defires. He further admonifheth vnmerciful richmen of their future iudgement, faying [Goe to now ye rich men, wepe, howling in your miferies, which fhal come to you. Your riches are corrupt, and your garments are eaten of mothes. Your gold and filuer is rufted, and their ruft fhal be for a teftimonie to yon, and fhal eate your flefh as fire: You haue ftored to your felues wrath in the laft dayes. You mayt (through Chrift) be made partakers of the diuine nature (faith S. Peter) fleeing the corruptió of that cócupifcence, which is in the world] He warneth alfo al Chriftians, of the fpecial concupifcences of the flefh, and of auarice, by which vnftable foules fal from the true faith into herefie [hauing eyes ful of adultrie: and their hart exercifed with auarice: become the children of malediction: leauing the right way, they haue erred: hauing followed the way of Balaam, (the fonne of Beor (a fouthfayer, or Magitien) which loued the reward of iniquitie: but had a checke of his madneffe, the dumme beaft (an affe) fpeaking with mans voice, proh:bited the foolifhnes of the prophete] of him that pretended to be a Prophete; and loued reward for iniquitie.

ch.5.v.1.2.
3.

2.Pet.1.v.
4.

ch.2.v.14.
15.16.

Nu.22.v.5.
19.23.
28.

Chriftians are bound to obferue Ceremonial precepts of Chrift, and his Church.

ARTICLE 46.

Guliel.
Parieffien.
lib de fide.
& legib.
D. Stap.
Antidot.
in cap.15.
Act.v.10.
pog 433.B.

GOds peculiar people in the old Teftament, for the better obferuing of his Moral precepts, concerning mans dutie towards God, in the first table of the ten commandments, were alfo bond to obfe ue very manie other facred Rites (as fome haue diligently numbred, fixe hundred and thirtene Cere-

Ceremonial precepts helpe to the obferuation of the Moral.

E e 2 mo-

monial precepts. Al which are now abrogated by
Chrift out Sauiour, becaufe they did forefignifie him,
and thinges perteyning to him, as then to come, who
now is comen: and others are ordained by Chrift, and
by his auctoritie, more fitte for the prefent ftate of the
Chnrch. Which are proued to be right religious actions (to the honour of God, and fpiritual good of
foules) as wel by example of the former prefiguratiue,
as by practife of Chrift himfelf, and his primitiue
Church.

Act.7.10.
pag. 433. B.

2. Concerning therfore the figuratiue examples of
Religious external Rites in the olde Teftament, to
which the faithful feruants of God were then obliged, we fhal here recite fome obferued before the
written Law: others commanded by the Law: and
fome alfo inftituted afterwardes. Long before the
Law, euen from the beginning of the world, not only
Sacrifices were offered, as appeareth by Abel and
Cain; but alfo other publique maner of inuocating
the name of our Lord, was inftituted by Enos the
Patriarch: and confequently continued by others.
Noe obferued diftinction of cleane and vncleane, receiuing of al cattel & foule, feuen male and feuen female of thofe which were cleane, into the Arke; and
two and two, male and female, of the other fort reputed vncleane. And after the floud he offered Sacrifice vpon an Altar, of al the fame which were cleane:
but none of the vncleane. At which time, God alfo
probibited the eating of bloud. And when God had
called Abraham out of his countrie, he gaue him an
efpecial commandment for himfelfe, and for al the
male of his progenie, and focietie, to circumcife the
prepuce of their flefh, inftituting the Sacrament of
Circumcifion. Likewife the Sacrifice of the Pafchal
Lambe, was inftituted before the Law was written:
with the obferuation of eating it, with vnleauened
bread, and other ceremonies.

Diuers Cere-
monial Rites
were obfer-
ued before the
written Law.

Sacrifice.

Gen. 4. 7. 3.
4.
26.

Diftinction of
cleane and vn-
cleane.

ch. 7. 7. 2. 3.
ch. 8. 7. 10.
21.

Abftinence
from eating
bloud.

ch. 9. 7. 3 4.

ch. 17. 7. 10.
1. 27.

Circumcifion.

The Pafchal
Lambe, with
vnleauened
bread.

Exod. 11. 7.
3.

3 Then

3. Then God geuing his people a written Lawe very brefely comprifed the tenne commandements. And forthwith largely added almoft innumerable ceremonial Rites. As is manifeft in the refidue of the same Booke of Exodus: and in the greateft part of Leuiticus, concerning the making of a Tabernacle, Altars, the Arke of couenant, facred Veffels and Veftments; Sacrifices, Sacraments, Feafts, Faftes, Vowes, Tithes, and other obferances. Wherof is alfo frequent mention in the Bookes of Numeri, and Deuteronomie. Partly by way of repetition, and partly by addition. And their neceffarie obferuation, is often alfo fignified in the Hiftorical, Sapiential, and Prophetical Bookes.

4. Moreouer, after that the Law was geuen, yea after Moyfes his death, fome other Religious ordinances were made, and priuilegies, or difpenfations granted. As that Sacrifice was fometime offered lawfully in other places, befides the Tabernacle & Temple: yea and by others then Prieftes extraordinarily. So Gedeon the Iudge, being of the Tribe of Manaffes: Manue the father of Samfon, of the Tribe of Dan, offered Sacrifices in priuate places. Samuel alfo, though a Prophet, yet not a Prieft, offered Sacrifice in Bethleem. Likewife Elias the Prophete, vpon fpecial occafion, built a new Altar, in the mount of Carmel, and offered Sacrifice theron, which God approued, miraculoufly fending fire from heauen, which confumed the oblation, and confounded the fourhundred and fiftie falfe prophets of Iefabels faction, his Aduerfaries. Mardocheus alfo with other principal Iewes [ordayned a new Feaft, to be kept folemnely euerie yeare] in grateful memorie of Gods benefite, in deliuering the whole people from imminent danger of ruine. In like maner [Iudas Machabeus, when he had ouercome Antiochus, and clenfed the Temple, and built a new Altar, inftituted a yearly feaft of the

Ee 3   De-

Marginal notes (left):

Exod. 20. v. 3. ad 17. v. 24. & 6 | ch. 11. v. 29. 30. 31. ch. 27. v. 20. &c.

Lenit. v.

Iudic. 6. v. 20. 21. ch. 13. v. 19. 1. Reg. 7. v. 9. ch. 16. v. 3. 5 3. Reg. 18. v. 23. 32. 36. 38.

Efth. 9. v. 27. 28. ch. 16. v. 11. 24.

1. Mach. 4. v. 56. 59.

Marginal notes (right):

Very manie other Rites were ordayned by the written Law.

Moe alfo were added afterwardes.

the Dedication therof, eight dayes together] Esdras ²·Mach.I.v. also proclamed an extraordinarie fast, which al the 9.18. people obserued by his commandment [that they ch.10.v.5. might be afflicted before the Lord their God : and I.Esd.8.v. might desire of him to be directed in the way of God] 21.

Moral precepts alwaies continuing, Ceremonies are changed, according to the diuerse state of the Church.

5. Our Lord and Sauiour coming in flesh into this Mat 5.v. world[not to breake the Law and the Prophets, but 18. to fulfil them] did not only teach, to kepe the moral precepts, more perfectly then the Scribes and Pharisees obserued them, but also to kepe the whole Law of Ceremonial, and Iudicial precepts, according to the wil of God the Lawmaker: to witte, with this differéce, that wheras the Moral precepts are vnchangeable, they contintinue stil the same, in al times and places, Gal.3.v.24. as they were from the beginning : but the Ceremoni- ch.4.v.10. al consisting in signification of thinges to come, with memorie also of figuratiue thinges done; the thinges prefigured and foresignified, being comen and fulfilled, those former Ceremonies doe cease, for that they should now be false(so farre as they signified thinges to come, which are already comen)and others are instituted, and commanded, which represent Mysteries performed, and present: and which withal foresignifie the heauenlie glorie, that is amongst the glorified Sainctes, and to be expected by al the faithful true seruanrs of God. Euen as therfore[The old Te- Heb 13.v. stament was dedicated with Sacrifice in bloud, and 14. strictly commanded by God, to be daily offered: so Exo.24 v. Christ our new Lawgeuer, instituted his new Testa-8. ment with Sacrifice, the night before his death, in his owne most sacred bodie and bloud (the seifesame) which he gaue the day folowing, with expresse commandment to offer it vntil he come againe, saying to his Apostles [Doe ye this for commemoration of me] Luc.22.v. Which also S. Paul reciteth, repeting our Sauiours 19.20. wordes, saying[This Chalice is the new Testamét in my bloud : this doe ye, as often as you shal drinke it,

for

1. Cor. 1. v.
25.26.

for the cōmemoration of me. For as often (saith the A-
poſtle) as you ſhal eate this bread, & drinke the Chalice, you ſhal ſhew the death of our Lord, vntil he
come] So that this is the moſt principal Ceremonial
precept in al the new Teſtament, and Law of Chriſt,
to offer the dread Sacrifice of Chriſts owne Bodie and
Bloud, in the formes of bread & wine; ſeuerally conſecrated, the one from the other, by vertue of Chriſts
wordes, ſaying of the one part [This is my bodie (and
of the other part) This is my bloud] and ſo is ſhewed
the moſt bleſſed death of our Lord and Redemer,
which was by the ſeparation of his moſt holie bodie
and bloud on the Croſſe, really and bloudily on the
Croſſe, and as really, but vnbloudily, at the laſt ſupper the night before: and ſtil as really and vnbloudily
on the Altar, vntil he ſhal come, in the end of this
world.

6. Manie other ceremonial precepts, our B. Sauiour
alſo gaue, which likewiſe binde no leſſe, then the moral, becauſe by them the maner is expreſſed, how God
is to be religiouſly ſerued. For in the Inſtitution of
euerie holie Sacrament, is implied a ceremonial precept, to vſe the ſame Sacrament in due time, and maner, to Gods honour, and good of ſoules. Beſides alſo
the holie Sacramentes, there be manie other holie
Rites, partly vſed by our Lord himſelf, partly inſtituted by his Church, but al by his commiſſion: by vertue wherof, the faithful are bond, both to eſteme
them, and (due circumſtances concurring) to participate the ſame. [And to obſerue (generally and particularly) al thinges whatſoeuer (ſaith our Lord to his
Apoſtles) I haue commanded you] To them alſo he
had ſaid before [He that heareth you, heareth me: he
that deſpiſeth you, deſpiſeth me. And, Manie thinges
I haue yet to ſay to you, but you can not beare them
now. But when the Spirit of truth cometh, he ſhal
teach you al truth. You ſhal receiue the vertue of the

Christs inſti-
tutiou impli-
eth a precept
to obſerue
thoſe thinges
which he or-
dained.

See Para.
2. Artic.
30. & 82.3.

Mat. 28. v.
19.

Luc. 10. v.
16.
10.16. v. 12.
Act. 1. v. 8.

Holie

Holie Ghoſt coming vpon you, and you ſhal be wit- *Act.1.v.8.*
neſſes vnto me] Neither was this comiſſion of power,
& promiſe of truth, limited to onlie pointes of faith,
and doctrine, but alſo perteyned to the making of
Decrees and Lawes, concerning factes, and conuerſation of life, and for the gouernement of the whole
militant Church. As S. Paul witneſſeth in his Sermon,
made at Epheſus, when he ſaid to certaine Paſtors
of the people[The Holie Ghoſt hath placed you Bi- *ch.20.v.28.*
ſhops to rule the Church of God] And accordingly al
the Apoſtles, with other Apoſtolical Paſtors, made
Decrees, which bond al Chriſtians, and that by diuine *ch.15.v.28.*
auctoritie, the whole Aſſemblie thus auouching [It
ſemeth good to the Holie Ghoſt, and to vs]ſo binding
al to obey the ſame Decrees. Which againe S Paul admoniſhed in Syria & Cilicia, commanding them to *v 41.*
kepe the precepts of the Apoſtles and Ancients) And *Heb 13.*
ſaying[Obey your Prelates and be ſubiect to them.] *v.17.*

7.   Not only therfore the Moral precepts, but alſo
Ceremonial, and Iudicial, doe binde al Chriſtians
in conſcience, whether they be expreſly declared in
the holie Scriptures, or decreed by the Apoſtles, and
their Succeſſors, authorized by the word of God.
Such are al the Decrees of approued Councels and
Sea Apoſtolique, Conſtitutions of al Biſhops within
their Dioceſes. And of al Prelates within their owne
Iuriſdictions. Becauſe as it is neceſſarie, to ſerue God,
and neuer to ſerue falſe goddes: ſo it is no leſſe neceſſarie to know, and obſerue the right maner of ſeruing
God, by his viſible ordinarie Deputies, and not euerie
priuate perſon to be his owne maſter, or guide. And
when by ſuch ordinances, ſome thinges are changed,
abrogated, or newly inſtituted, as iuſt cauſes, with varietie of times, places, perſons, and other occaſions require, al are ſtil obliged to the general Rule[To obey *Mat.18.v.*
their Prelates. Al in ſubordination of Eccleſiaſtical *8*
Ierarchie. To edification, and according to order.] *1 Cor.14.v.*
16.40.
Chri-

Chriſt promi-
ſed, and ſent
the Holie
Ghoſt, to di-
rect his
Church.

As al are bond
to ſerue God:
ſo they are
bond to ſerue
him in due
maner.

Chriſtians are alſo bond to obſerue al Iudicial precepts of temporal Superiors.
ARTICLE 47.

THere were likewiſe in the old Teſtament manie particular Iudicial Lawes, ſo perteyning to
the Moral precepts of the ſecond table of the
Decalogue, as the Ceremonial perteyned to the Moral precepts of the firſt table : which in deed bind not
Chriſtians, by vertue of Moyſes Law, no more then
the Ceremonial doe ; yet are they partly eſtablished,
and partly changed by Chriſtian Princes, and Common wealthes, and ſo binde al their ſubiectes in conſcience, no leſſe then the former did binde the people
of God in the former times. Wherupen we are to conſider, that as Gods faithful people, being ſometimes
by his permiſſion, in captiuitie vnder infidel Princes,
were bound to obey, and obſerue their temporal
Lawes, not repugnant to true faith, and religion : ſo
in like maner Catholiques are bond to obey, and obſerue temporal Lawes, and ſtatutes, not only of Catholique Princes, and countries, but alſo of Heretikes
or other Infidels, ſo far as they are not contrarie, nor
preiudicial, to Gods honour, or CatholiqueReligion.

Iudicial pre-cepts doe binde Chriſti-ans, as they are ordayned by temporal Su-periours, ſo farre as they are not re-pugnant to true Religion.

2. To this purpoſe, we may firſt obſerue, that immediatly after the recital of the tenne general commandments, Moyſes together with Ceremonial precepts, declareth other particular diuine Lawes, concerning ſeruants, bargaines, offences, iniuries, controuerſies, and al doubts, which might happen among the
people [Theſe are the Iudgements (ſaid our Lord to
Moyſes) which thou ſhalt propoſe to them: If thou
bye an Hebrew ſeruant, ſix yeares ſhal he ſerue thee, in
the ſeuenth he ſhal goe out free, with what rayment
he entered in, with the like let him goe out.] And
ſo folow other Iudicial Lawes, concerning man-

Examples of iudicial Lawes in the old Te-ſtament.

*Exod. 21. v.
1.2 &c.
v.12.16. 23.
24.*

F f   ſlaugh-

slaughter, & striking;especially of cursing or striking
parents, concerning adultrie, deflouring of virgines,
bestialitie, hurting strangers, widowes, and orphanes,
theft, robberie, vsurie, with punishment for al these,
and for idolattie,blasphemie,inchanting and the like,
with a general Law called The law of like paine.

*ch.22 v.7.
16.18.
ch.23 v.1.
2 &c.*

*Lex talio-
nis.*

3. After that the Law was published and receiued
a new difficultie occurring [When a man died without issue male:Whether that his daughters should succede to his inheritance, Moyses consulted our Lord,
and a particular new Law was added, that [When a
man dieth without sonne, his inheritance shal passe
to his daughters.And so it was made a perpetualLaw]
which was not expressed before. And after Moyses
his death, Iosue commanded some thinges, not formerly expressed: and the whole people promised to
obey whatsoeuer he should command them[Al thinges
(said they)that thou shalt command vs, we wil doe.
He that shal gainsay thy mouth, and not obey al thy
wordes, that thou shalt command him,let him dye]
So the Iudges, each one in his time, had auctoritie to
command, and by punishment to compel: and the
people, euerie one in their degrees, were bond to
obey. Dauid being the General Captaine, and designed king, but not yet in possession of the kingdome
[made a new particular Law, that he which abideth
with the baggage in time of warre,should haue equal
portió with him,that went downe into battel. And e-
uer after it was decreed,& ordained as aLaw in Israel]

*Num.17.
v.1.2 4.8.*

*Ios.1.v.10.
16.18.*

*Iudic.3. v.
10.
ch.4 v 10.
1.Reg.16. v.
13.
ch.30.14.
25.*

4. When the same people were in captiuitie, first
the ten Tribes vnder the Assirians. and afterwardes
the two Tribes in Babylon, they were bound to obey
and obserue the temporal Lawes and commandments of Infidel Kinges, and Magistrates: so farre as
was not against God, and true Religion. As the holie
Prophetes in those times,by word,& example taught,
and admonished the people. And the same obligation

*Tob.1.v. 13.
14.
4.Reg. 17.
v.24.
ch.25.v. 11.*

Other like
lawes were
added after-
wardes.

Examples of
obeying infi-
del Priuces
in lawful tem-
poral causes,
but not in Re-
ligion.

tion bond the faithful people, liuing vnder the schif-
matical Kinges of Ifrael. For notwithftanding they
made a wicked fchifme, and fome of them profeffed
herefies, yet were the good people bond to obey them
in al iuſt temporal affayres : but by no meanes in matter of fchifme and herefie, or idolatrie. Witneffes
Elias, Elifeus, Micheas: Tobias, and the reſt.

3. Reg. 12. v. 24.
ch. 13. v. 2. 3. &c.

Tob. 1. v. 5.

5. In confirmation wherof, Chriſt our Lord commandeth, to render the thinges that are Cæſars to
Cæſar: and the thinges that are Gods, to God] Euidently diſtinguiſhing temporal and ſpiritual thinges:
and ſo teacheth to geue temporal thinges, and temporal ſeruice to temporal Princes; but not ſpiritual obedience in religious cauſes. S. Paul vrgeth the very ſame
neceſſarie obedience to Infidel Princes, and Potentates, ſaying to the Romane Chriſtians [Let euerie
ſoule be ſubieɕ vnto higher power: for there is no
power but of God. And they that refiſt, purchaſe to
themſelues damnation. Therfore be ſubieɕ (faith he)
of neceſſitie, not only for wrath, but for conſcience
ſake] He inſtructeth S. Titus, [to admoniſh al the
faithful people to be ſubieɕ to Princes, & Poteſtates,
to obey at a word, to be readie at euerie good worke]
which clearly includeth obligatiõ to obſerue the lawful commandments of temporal Magiſtrates. S. Peter
teacheth the very ſame, ſaying [Be ſubieɕ to euerie
humane creature for God (to Magiſtrates created by
men; and confirmed, or permitted by God) whether it
be to the King, as exeelling; or to rulers, as ſent by
him, to the reuenge (the puniſhment) of malefaɕors:
but to the praiſe of the good] S. Iude taxeth Heretikes
with diſobedience to temporal Princes, and with
contempt of Dominió [They deſpiſe dominion (ſaith
he) and blaſpheme Maieſtie] Al Maieſtie being by Gods
ordinance, or permiſſion, contempt therof with reproche is blaſphemie: ſo iudged by this holie Apoſtle.

Mat. 22. v. 21.

Rom. 13. v. 1. 2.

v. 5.

Tit. 3. v. 1. 2.

1. Pet. 2. v. 13. 14.

Iude 5. v. 8.

Chriſt and his
Apoſtles teach
the ſame.

Good

Good works of supererogation, are possible,
pious, and profitable. And when they are
vowed, doe binde in consciente.

ARTICLE 48.

Hitherunto we haue, according to our purpose,
explicated the, Ten Commandments of God,
with other Ceremonial and Iudicial precepts,
by keping wherof, through Gods special grace, the
faithful gaine the kingdome of heauen: & by wilfully
breaking anie of them, fal into the state of eternal
damnation. It resteth here brefely to speake of other
good workes not commanded, but counselled, which

A careful con- are therfore works of Supererogation. Betwen which
science ende- counsels and precepts, is so much difference, as be-
uoureth to twen good and better: betwen lesse and more merite:
doe some- and consequently lesse and more reward. Moreouer
thing more these workes of counsel doe helpe not only, for ob-
then is com- tayning more grace, and glorie: but also for the better
manded. Lest performing of the commandments, which are abso-
he omitte that lutely necessarie. Because those which wil endeuour
which is ne- no more, then that wherto they are strictly bond, are
cessarie. in great danger to transgresse sometime, that which
is expresly commanded. And they which in deede
haue iust care to fulfil Gods commandments, wil for
more securitie (lest they be deficient) rather doe a litle
more, then omitte that is necessare. And likewise wil
rather abstaine voluntarily from some thing lawful,
then not abstaine from al that is prohibited. And
wheras Protestants denie it to be possible, for anie
man, though he be iust, to doe such workes of Supererogation, they denie it, vpon the same false ground,
as they denie it to be possible, to kepe anie at al of
Gods commandments: confessing (if themselues say *Artic.1.*
true) that they transgresse al and euerie one of the ll.
commandments. They beleue not in God, they hope
not in God, they loue not God: they serue false gods:
they

they are blaſphemers, periured perſons, murderers,
adulterers, theues, & in euerie dede, word, & thought
they are moſt wicked, if their owne doctrine be true,
that none can kepe anie commandment at al. Wherfore ſeing it is cleare, that a faithful perſon, can and
doth beleue in God, which he is bound to doe by
Gods commandment: It is alſo poſſible, that he can
geue a morſel more of bread to a poore man, then he
is bound to doe, by anie comandment: which in ſuch
a caſe of free gift without ſpecial neceſſitie, is a worke
of Supererogation.

2. But forſomuch as our Aduerſaries are extreme
importune, in denying and often deriding this point
of Chriſtian doctrine; we ſhal here ſhew by abundant
teſtimonies of holie Scriptures: that good workes of
Supererogation, are not only poſſible, but alſo are
pious in the ſight of God, and ſpiritually profitable to
the faithful that doe them. No doubt it was a worke
*Gen.*18.v. of pietie, tending to brotherlie peace and concord,
8.9. amongſt freindes, that [Abraham gaue free leaue &
power vnto his Nephew Lot to chooſe which part of
land he would haue to poſſeſſe] to which free grant
Abraham was not bond in equitie, but of mere liberalitie, gaue the choyſe to Lot. For by indifferent equitie, and rule of reaſon, Abraham might haue choſen
rather then Lot. At leaſt it had bene abundant, or ful
iuſtice, that the landes had bene appropriated by caſting lottes, which part each of them ſhould haue and
poſſeſſe. Iacob an other Patriarch, in a vow made to
God, did not only promiſe, if God ſhould proſper
him, to ſerue him ſincerely, and to pay tithes of his
fruites· to both which he was formerly bond by di-
*eb,*28.v.20. uine Law: but alſo he promiſed [to builde and dedicate a particular houſe, to Gods ſpecial ſeruice] wherto he was not bond before his vow. And ſo it was a
worke of Supererogation: and it is alſo manifeſt that
God accepted it, as an act of free deuotion, ſaying to
Iacob

Iacob afterwardes [I wil be with thee, I am the God *ch.31.v.3.*
of Bethel, where thou didſt annoint the ſtone, and
didſt vow vnto me. Now therfore(becauſe thon ſo
didſt) ariſe and goe out of this land (from Meſopotamia)returning into the land of thy natiuitie] into
Chanaā. And ſo our Lord bleſſed and proſpered him,
& his progenie more & more. When the Tabernacle,
with al the appertinances, was to be made in the de- *Exo.35.v.*
ſert [The children of Iſrael moſt liberally contribu- *20.*
ted, not only ſufficient, but alſo more then was ſuffi- *ch.36.v.6.*
cient. Albeit the neceſſarie expenſes were required, *7.*
yet the ſuperabundance was of Supererogation:and
meritorious. Such a worke did the men of Iabes Ga- *1 Reg.31.v.*
laad [taking the bodies of King Saul, and his ſonnes, *5.6.*
& burying them, and faſting ſeuen dayes] Which fact
King Dauid called a worke of mercie, meritorious of *2.Reg.2.v.*
reward at Gods hand, ſaying to them[Bleſſed be you *5.6.*
to our Lord, which haue done this mercie with your
lord Saul, & haue buried him. & now our Lord certes
wil render you mercie and truth] God wil according
to his truth, reward good workes.   The ſame King *ch 7.5.2 3.*
Dauid did a worke of Supererogation, as wel in that *&c.*
he deſired to build a Temple to our Lord, as in pro- *1.Par.29.v.*
uiding meanes to doe it, though he was not permit- *3.4.*
ted to performe it. And ſo did the Princes which con- *3.Reg.7. v.*
tributed more for that purpoſe And king Salomon in *8.*
accompliſhing it, in more excellent maner, then they *2 Par.34.v.*
were bond by anie commandment. *5.&c.*

Vowesfreely made doe binde in conſcience.

3. It is manifeſt jn the written Law, that vowes
(to witte, free promiſes to God of good thinges not
commanded) are pious actes, and being made in due
maner, doe binde in conſcience, to the performance
therof, as theſe holie Scriptures doe expreſly teſtifie
[The man that ſhal haue made a vow, and bond his
ſoule to God by eſtimation, he ſhal geue the price(that *Leuit 27.v.*
is, if he geue not the thing promiſed, he ſhal geue the *2. ad 30.*
value therof) If anie man make a vow to our Lord, or
bind

bind himſelf by an oath, he ſhal not make his word
fruſtrate, but al that he promiſeth, he ſhal fulfil. When
thou haſt vowed a vow to our Lord thy God, thou
ſhalt not ſlack to pay it; becauſe our Lord thy God
wil require it; and if thou delay, it ſhal be reputed to
thee for ſinne. If thou wilt not promiſe, thou ſhalt be
without ſinne (which clearly ſheweth, that the Law
ſpeaketh of thinges not commended) But that which
is once gone out of thy lippes, thou ſhalt performe, &
ſhalt doe as thou haſt promiſed to our Lord thy God,
and haſt ſpoken with thy proper wil, and thyne owne
mouth.] In al which, the ſame diuine Law declareth,
that promiſes made by ſuch as are ſubiect to the wil
of Superiours, are not perfect vowes, nor doe binde,
vntil they be ratified and confirmed, either by the expreſſe conſent, or by interpreted conſent of ſilence,
after that the Superiours know, what is promiſed,
& doe not gaine ſay it. As the promiſes of maides in
their fathers houſes, whiles they are in maidens
age. Alſo of wiues in their husbandes time, and the
like, may be fruſtrate by their ſuperiors: which they
could not be, if the promiſes were of thinges neceſſarie, and commanded. And if the ſuperiors know and
conſent, then they are perfect vowes, and bind the ſuperiors no leſſe, yea rather more, then the parties that
made the promiſes. And ſo to bind themſelues, is a
plaine worke of Supererogation.

4. Moreouer, that ſuch vowes belonged not only
to ceremonial Lawes of the old Teſtament, as Proteſtants would interpret them, and ſo account al ſuch
vowing to be abrogated in the Law of Chriſt, is further proued by other holie Scriptures. The Royal
Prophet both exhorteth to make vowes, and admoniſheth to render them which are made [Immolate
to God (ſaith he) the ſacrifice of praiſe (that is promiſe to God ſome ſpecial thankſgiuing, & praiſes of
God) & pay thy vowes to the Hiegheſt] As thou ſhalt
pro-

Side notes left:
Num. 30. v.
3.

Deut. 23. v.
v. 21.

v. 22.

v.

Num. 30. v.
4 6 8.
12. 16.

v. 24.

Pſal. 49. v.
14.

Side note right:
Vowes doe
bind as moral
precepts alſo
in the Lawe
of Chriſt.

promise so performe [Vow ye and render to our Lord *Psal. 75. v.* your God, al ye that round about him, bring giftes. *12.* I wil render my vowes to our Lord (saith he) in the sight of al his people.] He also prayed to be rewar- *Psa. 115. v.* ded, for his vow made, and payed [Remember Da- *5. 9.* uid ô Lord (saith he) and al his meekenes. As he sware *Psal. 131. v.* to our Lord, vowed a vowe to the God of Iacob] Sa- *2.* lomon taxeth those with great crime, that performe *Pro.20.v.* not their vowes, saying [It is ruine to a man, to de- *25.* uour saintes (to pretend the honour of Saintes, vow- ing to praise them) and afterward to retract the vow. If thou hast vowed anie thing to God, deferre not to pay it. For vnfaithful and foolish promise displea- *Eccle. 5. v. 3.* seth him. But whatsoeuer thou hast vowed pay it]

Protestants arguments a-
gainst vowes,
haue no pro-
babilitie.

Now how contrarie to so expresse holie Scriptures, do they preach, that perswade votaries to break their vowes of obedience, of chastitie, and of voluntarie pouertie? And what Scriptures haue they for their warrant? forsooth say they: Salomon also teacheth *7.4.* that [It is much better not to vow, then after a vow, not to performe the thinges promised]. Ergo say they, It is not good to vow at al. As good a deducti- on, as if they should say: It is much better not to pro- mise anie thing to your neighbour, then not to per- forme that which is promised. Therfore it is not good to promise anie thing to our neighbours. Againe they argue, that it is vnpossible to kepe the vow of chasti- tie, which they would proue, because themselues haue not that gift and so inferre; Therfore none hath it. But where doth anie Scripture say: Thou shalt not make anie vow; or, Thou canst not kepe anie vowe. It is certaine, that there is no such Scripture: because as you see, there be manie which exhorte the faith- ful to make vowes, and admonish them to performe the same. By the light of nature also simple mariners of Ioppe knew that vowes are grateful to God, and *Lone. 1. v.* therfore, when by lotte Ionas was cast into the sea] *8 16.*

They

[They prayed,& immolated hostes,& vowed vowes]
Ionas also in the whales bellie vowed, and promised

ch. 2. *v.* 19. to fulfil his vowes, saying [In the voice of praise, I wil
immolate to thee (ô God) what thinges soeuer I haue
vowed, I wil render for saluation to our Lord]

5. As it were betwen the old Testament, and the
new,[S.Iohn Baptist did workes of Supererogation,
that is, good workes of his free accord, not comman-

*Mat.*3. *v.* 4. ded liuing very austerely [in the desert, with litle meate
and hard rayment] therin pleased God, and edified

*ch.*9. *v.* 14. the people[He also taught his disciples to fast much]
Which thinges were not otherwise commanded, but
taken vpon them for the better seruice of God, and
more merite. Our Sauiour in a parable of a Samaritan, that tooke compassion vpon a man spoiled, and
wounded by theues, teacheth, that a charitable man,
may if he wil, doe workes of Supererogation; & withal promiseth recompence for the same, saying in the
person of the Samaritan to the Host, that tooke care

*Luc.*10.*v.* of the infirme[Whatsoeuer thou shalt Supererogate,
35.
*Ibid.v.*42. I at my returne wil repay thee]Our Lord also saith,
that Marie(Magdalene)hath chosen the best part]sig-
nifying that she of her owne free choise, gaue her self
to contemplatiue life, to which she was not bond by
anie commandment. Against this cleare doctrine, our
Aduersaries alleage our Sauiours wordes to his disci-

*Luc.*17.*v.* ples, saying [When you shal haue done al thinges, that
10. are commanded you, say: We are vnprofitable seruants.] Therfore sayth a Protestant, there is no merite nor profite in anie good worke, for when they
shal haue done al, that is commanded, yet they are
vnprofitable. We answer first, that by this supposition,
[when you shal haue done al thinges that are com-
manded] is sufficiently proued, that the faithful can
doe al that is comended. That is, can if they wil, kepe
al the commandments. Which is yet more cleared by
the next wordes: our Sauiour affirming, that some

S.Iohn Bap-
tist, and his
disciples did
workes of Su-
pererogation.

Christ suppo-
seth that man
can doe more
then is com-
manded.

How a iust
person is an
vnprofitable
seruant.

The first an-
swere.

faithful may fay [VVe haue done that which we ought Ibid.
to do]Which Proteſtāts hold for impoſible:teaching
that none can ſo doe . Which their errour we haue
largely confuted in the firſt Article of this Part. Se-

The ſecond answere.

condly we anſwere (as before in the ſecond Article)
that Gods ſeruants doing al that is comanded them,
muſt ſtil ſay , they are vnprofitable ſeruants to God,
our Maſter , who needeth not our ſeruice, nor is
made richer therby:but God ſo accepteth of our ſeruice, that it is gratful to him , and ſo it is profitable to
ourſelues , and we ſhal receiue wages for it. Yea for
great workes [are heaped vp great treaſures in hea- *Mat.6.v.*
uen. And the vnprofitable ſernant, ſhal be caſt into ²⁰.
vtter darknes, where ſhal be weping and gnaſhing of *ch.25.v.30.*
teeth]Albeit therfore al good ſeruants muſt thinke &
ſay, that they are vnprofitable to God,yet Gods grace
maketh them profitable. Wherupon S.Paul ſaith[If a *2.Tim.2.v.*
man ſhal cleanſe himſelfe from his ſinnes,he ſhal be a ²⁰.
veſſel profitable to our Lord.] Thirdly we anſwere,

The third answere.

that although a ſeruant,doing al that is commanded
him, were vnprofitable both to his Maſter, and'to
himſelfe, yet he might be profitable,for doing alſo
more then he is commanded. And his Maſter which
doth not thanke him,for doing al that he comanded;
yet wil thanke him,for doing the ſame,and alſo more.
Which is properly a good worke of Supererogation.
wherof we ſpeake in this place.And of which S.Paul
ſaith [He that ſoweth in bleſsings, of bleſsings alſo *2.Cor.9.v.*
ſhal reape.]   6.

*Primitine
Chriſtians
without anie
commandmēt
put al their
goodes in a
communitie.*

6. A moſt cleare example of Supererogation was
in the firſt Chriſtians,when al the faithful,both Clergie and Laitie, put their temporal poſseſsions into a
common banke , for the competent maintenance of *Act.2.v.*
euerie one:as S.Luke writeth in theſe wordes[Al that ⁴⁴.
beleued were together,and had al thinges common. ⁴⁵.
They ſold their poſseſsions and ſubſtances,and diuided them to al,according as euerie one had nede:nei-
                                                    ther

ther did anie one say: that ought was his owne of those thinges which they possessed, but al thinges were common vnto them. Neither was there anie one needie amongst them. For as manie as were owners of landes, or houses, sold them, and brought the prices of those thinges, which they sold; and laid it before the feete of the Apostles. And to euerie one was diuided according as euerie one had neede] Against which communitie, when Ananias and his wife offended, reseruing in priuate to themselues, part of the money, which they had receiued for their land [S. Peter (knowing by reuelation, that they dealt fraudulently) said to Ananias: Why hath Satan tempted thy hart, that thou shouldest lie to the Holie Ghost, and defraude of the price of the land? Remaining did it not remaine to thee, and being sold, was it not in thy power? Why hast thou put this thing in thy hart? Thou hast not lied to men (only) but to God. And Ananias hearing these wordes, fel downe, and gaue vp the ghost] The same punishment fel also vpon his wife. And the like doubtles is due, to al them that doe the like. In successe of time, this voluntarie worke of Supererogation, by geuing al, and liuing in common, ceassed to be so general in al Christians, as it was at first, both in Ierusalem, and other places (namely at Alexandria in Ægypt) but stil remained in some persons and places. Especially in Clergie men. Manie also adioyned vnto this Euangelical counsel (of liuing in common, without proprietie of temporal goodes) other two religious vowes, of obedience to a special Superiour, and of perpetual chastitie. As appeareth in manie holie religious Orders, which make al the three vowes. Al Clergie men which receiue the greater holie Orders, doe voluntarily promise perpetual chastitie, with special obedience to their Ordinarie, and haue more obligatió then Laimen haue to vse workes of mercie towardes them that neede. And in particu-

Side notes:
ch. 4. v. 32. 34. 35.
ch. 5. v. 1. 2. &c.
v. 7. 10.
Philo Iudeas.

Transgression of his vow was great sinne.

VVhen this general vow ceassed, yet some stil obserued the same Rule. And some added other vowes vnto it.

lar, there remaineth practife of liuing in communitie, or of common prouifion, in al Cathedral & Col-
legical Churches, in fubordination of Superiors and
Subiectes, of Prouoftes, Deanes, and Chanons. This
forme of Communitie is alfo obferued in beft inftituted Colleges: & at this prefent in Seminaries of fcho-
lers, for the better prouifion of the Paftoral Clergie,
befides Religious and Regular Orders.

Vniuerfal obedience, to a determinat Superi-
rior, is pioufly vovved.

ARTICLE 49.

Al Religious Orders make three fpecial vowes.

VVhich being made, doe binde as much as precepts.

Figuratiue examples of Religious Orders in the old Teftamēt.

COncerning therfore the more fpecial workes of
Supererogation, which are the three folemne
Vowes of vniuerfal Obedience; perpetual Chaftitie,
and voluntarie Pouertie, made by al Religious, and
Regular Orders: we fhal here in three diftinct Articles, fhew that they are very godlie actes, profitable
to the vniuerfal militant Church, and fingular good
meanes to the vowed perfons, for attaining perfecti- M4.19.v.
on in Chriftian life. So much the more meritorious, 12.21.
as they are freely vndertaken. From which time forwards, they binde as ftrictly, as an expreffe precept of
God: becaufe promife maketh debt, and free promife Deu 23 v,
to God, of a good thing not otherwife commanded, Esc.e.5,v.3
is a Religious Act: and therfore the breach therof is
facriledge, by vniuftly taking from God, that which is
due vnto him.

    2. The firft of thefe, which is religious Obedience,
was prefigured in the old Teftament, by the Order of
the Nazareites (fo called becaufe they were fegregated
from the common forte of the faitnful) who by vow
bond themfelues, to obferue a certaine prefcript Rule
of life, vnder a Superior, either perpetually, which Act.18.v.
was more rare, or for a fette time, which was then 18.
more common. Both which God fo approued, that he ch.21.v 24.
prefcribed them a particular Rule, faying to his people, by the mouth of Moyfes[Man or woman, When

                       they

Num 6.v.
2.3.
they shal make a vow to be sanctified, and wil confe- Nazareites.
crate themselues to the Lord, they shal abstaine from
wine, and euerie thing that can make one drunke. Al

4.
the dayes wherin they are by vow consecrated to the
Lord, whatsoeuer may be of the vineyard, from the
raysen to the kernel, they shal not eate. Al the time of

5.
his separation, a rasor shal not passe ouer his head, vntil the day be expired, that he is consecrated to the

6.
Lord, He shal be holie, whiles the bush of heare doth
grow. Al the time of his consecration, he shal not en-

7.
ter in to the dead: neither shal he be cotaminated: no
not vpon his fathers, and mothers, and brothers and
sisters corps: because the consecration of his God is
vpon his head.] So by this vow some did voluntarily
bind themselues, to absteyne from thinges otherwise
lawful. Some also were more specially called by God
to embrace, and kepe this Rule of life. So Samson re-

Iudic.13.v.
4.5.
ch 16.v. 19.
20.
ceiued this special grace of God, to be a perpetual Nazareite, with other great giftes, namely, a most admi-
ble corporal streingth, & corege of minde. But [when
his heares were cutte] his former streingth departed from him. [And then the Philistians apprehended him, and manie wayes cruelly & scornfully abu-

28.30.
sed him, vntil againe God restored to him, his former
admirable strength. Also [Samuel the Prophete was a

1 Reg 1.v.
15.16.22.
28.
perpetual Nazareite, euen fro his infancie] first by his
mothers vow: who presented him to Heli the High
Priest, to remaine al his life, in the special seruice of
God, in the Tabernacle, which he (coming to mature
age) confirmed voluntarily, and duly performed.

3. Likewise Elias, and Eliseus the Prophets, and

5 Reg. 17.v.
4.6.
4 Reg. 1.v.
28.
their disciples, obserued a special religious Rule [Hea- Disciples of
rie men, girded about the reynes with girdles of le- the Prophets.
ther (as Elias was described) Their disciples were called, The children of the Prophetes: They singularly

ch.2.v.5.7.
15.
both obeyed, and reuerenced their Superior. For [cō-
ming to mete Eliseus, they adored him flatte to the
ground.] Their ordinarie diet was so meane, that

Gg 3 [a wilde

[a wilde herbe by mishappe being put into their potte
of broth, al their prouision was spoiled with bitter-
nes] til the Prophete had miraculously amended it. *ch.4.v.39.*
Their habitation was poore & straite, in such cotages
or cabinettes, as themselues could frame of boughes, *ch 6 v.1.2.*
which they cut off frõ trees] There was also an other 3 4.5.
Religious Order of Rechabites, instituted by a Holie
man called Ionadab, the sonne of Rechab: who voluntarily bond themselues to a certaine Rule of life [not *Iere 35. v.5.*
to buide: nor dwel in houses, but in tents: not to sow *6.9. 13.14.*
seed, nor to plant, nor haue vineyards: not to drinke *&c.*
wine] Al which they obserued so perfectly, that being
by Gods commandment, proued therin by Ieremie
the Prophet; he proposed their worthie example of
obedience, against other Iewes, which obeyed not the
necessarie cõmandments of God: iustly commending
these so religious obseruers of their Rule: & condemning the wilful transgressors of Gods Law [The chil- *v.16.*
dren of Ionadab, the sonne of Rechab haue firmely
kept the precept of their father, which he commanded them: but this people (saith our Lord) hath not *1.Mach 2.*
obeyed me] Like vnto these were also the Assidians, *v.42.*
other wise called Esseni; a Societie of deuout men, ob *ch.7.v.13.*
seruing a religious forme of life. Who moreouer pro- *2.Mach.14,*
fessed a special rule of militarie life, in defense of true *v.6.*
Religion. They ioyned themselues therfore, with zelous Matthathias, and his sonnes, and others in the
holie warres against King Antiochus. In whih warres
[Alcimus (an Apostata Priest) solicited, and by false *Li.1.ch.7.v.*
pretence of sinceritie, deceiued certaine Assidians, & *16.li.2.*
getting threescore of them together, slew them most
cruelly in one day] And then most maliciously accused
and calumniated their whole Order, before King De- *ch.14.v.5.*
metrius, saying [They of the Iewes that are called As *6.*
sidians, of whom Iudas Machabeus is Captaine, doe
nourish battles, & moue seditions: neither doe they
suffer the realme to be in quiet] Which his calumnious sclander, & special hatred, more against the Assi-
                                        dian;

Rechabites.

Assidians.

dians then others, is a plaine teſtimonie of their more
rare, & ſingular vertues: & ſpecial zele in Gods ſeruice

4. Moreouer, God foreſhewed by his Prophets,
that there ſhould be Religious Votaries, and Orders
of Religions perſons in the new Teſtament: obſeruers
of ſpecial Rules of life, more tending to perfection,
then other ordinarie Chriſtians. In particular Iſaias
ſaith [The Ægyptians ſhal vow vowes to our Lord,
and pay them] which is fulfilled in the multitude of
Chriſtian holie Monkes in Ægypt, amongſt which are
moſt renowmed S. Paul the Eremite. S. Antonie. S.
Hilarion, with innumerable others. In other places
S. Baſil, S. Ierom, S. Auguſtin, S. Benet. S. Bernard, and
manie others of diuers particular Rules. But in general, al are imitators of the Apoſtles, who forſaking their
natural parents and freindes, folowed Chriſt. Which
counſel he alſo propoſed to the young man [which
had kept al the commandments from his youth, aſking what was yet wanting.[Whom our Lord beholding (as writeth S. Marke] loued him, and ſaid to him:
One thing is wanting vnto thee (not wanting for attaining heauen; for to that effect the keping of the
commandements ſufficeth, as our Lord had ſaid before) If thou wilt enter into life, kepe the commandments, (and to another.) This doe, & thou ſhalt liue]
but to perfection ſome thing was wanting: and therfore our Lord ſaid [If thou wilt be perfect, goe ſel the
thinges that thou haſt, and geue to the poore: & thou
ſhalt haue treaſure in heauen, and come, folow me]
In which two wordes [Folow me] is inclnded perfect
obedience, and the beſt way to perfection. There be
therfore two ſortes of obedience, one is neceſſarie for
al Chriſtians, to be obedient to al Gods commandments, and al that ſo obey, ſhal attaine to euerlaſting
life in heauen. An other obedience is voluntarie, and
tendeth to more perfection: to be obedient, not only
in al the commandments of God, but alſo in the whole
state

Marginal notes:

Prophecies in the old Teſta-ment of Reli-gious Orders in the Church of Chriſt.

Iſa. 19. v. 21.

Mat. 19. v. 21. 27. v. 20. 21.

Mar. 10. v. 29. 21.

Mat. 19. v. 17. Luc. 10. v. 28.

ſtate of life, to a determinat Superior. And to this obedience none are bound, except they wil freely by promiſe binde themſelues therto.   This is the ſtate which al Religious Orders profeſſe, for the more ho-nour of God, and their owne better meanes to attaine perfection, and to auoide the frequent danger of fal-ling from God, by tentations of the world, the fleſh, and the diuel.   So al haue libertie to chooſe their owne ſtate of life, as God by his ſpecial grace inſpi-reth each one. For [hauing giftes (ſaith S. Paul) accor-ding ro the grace that is geuen vs, different.   To one, certes by the Spirite is geuen the word of wiſdome, to an other the word of knowlege (& ſo to others diuerſly) And al theſe thinges, one and the ſame Spi-rite worketh, diuiding to euerie one according as he wil. Not al Apoſtles; not al Prophets; not al Doctors. For God hath ſet the members, euerie one of them in the bodie, as he would. And if al were one member, where were the bodie ?] It were no perfect bodie. So if none ſhould vow particular Rules of life, then were the Church of Chriſt, leſſe [compaſſed & clothed with varieties] leſſe adorned in this reſpect, thē the Church of the old Teſtament. Which beſides the diſtinction of Clergie & Laitie, had alſo Votaries, that bound thē ſelues to ſome thinges, vnder obedience of Superiors, wherto they were not before obliged. But [whatſoe-euer thou haſt vowed pay it (ſaith Salomon) For an vnfaithful promiſe diſpleaſeth God. And it is ruine to a man to retract his vowes.

Rom.12.v.
4.5.6.

1.Cor.12.v.
8.9.10.
11.&c.v.
28.

v.18. 19.

Pſ.44.v.
11.1.

Eccleſ. v.5.

Pro.20.v.25

Diuerſitie 'of Religious Or-ders adorneth the Church of Chriſt, with comelie varie-tie.

Vovv of perpetual chaſtitie, is an holie and meritorious act.

ARTICLE 50.

Solemne vow of perpetual chaſtitie is

PErpetual Chaſtitie, is the ſecond ſolemne vowe, which is made, as a worke of Supererogation, by al Religious Orders, that profeſſe anie approued
Rule

Rule of Religion, of men or wemen. And is also promised by al Clergie men, which take the three greater Holie Orders, when they are made Subdeacons.
The reason of this promise, so required by the Church
and made by such Clergie men, is declared in the
Sacrament of Holie Orders. Here it is further confirmed, that the same vow and promise, is both lawful
and meritorious. In the old Testament this state of
single life was more rare, yet there were also some examples in that time. Holie Abel the Martyr was neuer married; and is honoured in the Church of God,
as a Virgin Martyr. Ieremie a Prophet & a Priest, was
commanded by God, not to marie [Thou shalt not
take a wife (said our Lord to him) and thou shalt not
haue sonnes and daughters in this place. Because thus
saith our Lord concerning sonnes and daughters, that
are begotten in this place : and concerning their mothers: they shal dye, and not be mourned &c. [In
this place (said our Lord) to witte, in Ierusalem & Iurie. And that he should marie afterwardes in Ægypt,
when he was elder, and suffered more and more persecution, and finally was stoned to death in Taphnes,
is not imaginable. But he is by the Church of God,
honoured also as a Virgin Martyr, by very probable
deduction from holie Scripture; & assured Tradition.

2. It is also most probable, that holie Daniel, Ezechiel, Aggeus, Zacharias, and Malachias, al Prophetes,
liuing and prophecying in captiuitie, and continual
tribulations, neuer maried, though there be no other
mention therof in the holie Scriptures. Of Iudith the
holie widow, it is cleare that [she knew not man al
the dayes of her life, after that Manasses her husband
was dead: liuing to the age of an hundred and fiue
yeares] Retired from much companie, in frequent
prayer, wearing heare cloth, and fasting much. Likewise an other holie widow, and Prophetesse, called
[Anne the daughter of Phanuel, after that she had li-

Hh   ued

Par.2.
Art.43.§.
7.8.

Gen.4.v.8.
25.
Mat.23.v.
35.
Heb.11.v.4.
Iere 16.v.
2.3.

Iudith 16.v.
26.28.

ch..8.v.4
5 &c.
Luc.2.v.
36 37.

---

made by al
that professe
anie, approued
religious rule:
and al that re-
ceiue the grea-
ter Holie Or-
ders.

Some obser-
ued perpetual
chastitie in the
old Testamēt.

Other exam-
ples of perpe-
tual chastitie.

ued with her husband ſeneu yeares, remained in the
Temple, vntil eightie and foure yeares, ſeruing God
night and day, by faſtings, and prayers] But aboue al
other: The moſt glorious Virgin Marie, Mother of
God, vowed and obſerued perpetual Virginitie; the   *Luc. 1. v. 34*
moſt ſingular example and Patroneſſe of al pure virgines, chaſte widowes, and godlie obſeruers of continent ſingle life. To theſe are added S. Ioſeph. S. Iohn
Baptiſt, S. Iohn Euangeliſt, S. Paul, and S. Iames the
younger, al their liues; al the other Apoſtles, at leaſt,
after their vocation. which may ſuffice for examples.

The ſtate of
ſingle life was
prophecied in
the old Teſta-
ment.

3. Beſides examples, God foreſhewed by his Prophete Iſaias, that this ſtate of ſingle life ſhould be
more bleſſed in the new Teſtament, then the fruite of
children, ſaying: [Let not the Eunuch ſay: Behold I   *Iſa. 56. v.*
am a drie tree, Becauſe thus ſaith our Lord to the Eu-   *4. 5.*
nuches; they that ſhal kepe my Sabbathes (with other
precepts, wherto al are bound) and ſhal chooſe the
thinges that I would, and ſhal hold my couenant, I
wil geue vnto them in my houſe, & within my walles
a place, and a name, better then ſonnes & daughters:
an euerlaſting name wil I geue them, which ſhal not
periſh.] Two thinges doe men deſire and hope for, by
the fruit of Mariage: conſolation of children, as partes
of themſelues, multiplied by lawful iſſue, & continuance of their name, or memorie, in future poſteritie.
Both which hopes, arc ſo much greater, by chaſte
ſingle life, as ſpiritual children gained to God, are
cauſe of more comfort, then can be of manie ſonnes
and daughters, that may happen to anie parents. And
ſo much more ſecure, as Gods promiſe which can
not faile, is more certaine, then mens conceipt or
imagination, which often periſheth. Yea the memorie alſo of voluntarie chaſtitie, is heauenlie and eter-

Single life is
called Ange-
lical.

nal; the fruite of Mariage, though both lawful, and
commendable, yet but terreine, and temporal. For   *Mat. 19. v.*
[after the Reſurrection, there ſhal be no marying: but   *30.*

al

al the blessed shal be as the Angels in heauen] Wherof single life is called Angelical.

4. Agreable to this prophecie', and as it were an explanation therof,is our B. Sauiours expresse counsel,proposed to al Christians,saying [There are Eunuches (persons that kepe perpetual chastitie)which were borne so from their mothers wombe: and there are Eunuches,which were made by men:&:there are Eunuches,which haue gelded themselues(not corporally, for that is not lawful, but by vow of perpetual chastitie:) for the kingdome of heauen] The former two sortes,can neithei haue children,nor anie special reward for their chastitie . But the third sort, because they are voluntarily chaste,by their free vow,not for the seruice of men, nor for worldlie commoditie, but for the kingdome of heaue, are those of whom Isaias prophe.ied.that [choose the thing which God would haue them (yet doth not command them) And shal therfore haue both a better,and a surer reward in the house of God,then sonnes and daughters. And so to this better choise, to the which is promised a better and surer reward , in the kingdome of heauen , our Lord and Sauiour inuiteth the faithful,but commandeth not, saying [*Qui potest capere,cap ait.* He that can take, let him take.] He that can so resolue with himselfe : let him make himselfe an Eunuch for the kingdome of heauen.

5. No lesse clearly S. Paul distinguishing betwen precept and counsel, exhorteth(such as wil folow his adutte) to choose single life, saying [I would haue al men to be as my selfe : but euerie one hath a proper gift of God : one so, an other so. But I say to the vnmarried,and to widowes: It is good for them, if they so abide, euen as I also. But if they doe not conteyne themselues (from fornication) let them marrie. For it is better to marrie, then to burne]that is,then to be ouercome with tentations. Plainly teaching that fornica-

*Mat.*19.v. 12.

1. *Cor* 7.7. 7.8.9.

Our Sauiour doth expresly counsel his seruants to vndertake single life. But doth not command it.

St Paul counseleth the same,explicating Christs doctrine.

nication is naught : Mariage is good , and perpetual
continencie is better. Which he further declareth
saying [As concerning virginitie : commandment of
our Lord, I haue not : but counsel I geue, as hauing   v.25.
obtained mercie of our Lord to be faithful. I thinke   16.
therfore that this is good for the present necessitie:
becaufe it is good for a man so to be(that is, to be content with his present state) Art thou tyed to a wife?   27.
Seeke not to be loosed. Art thou loose from a wife?
Seke not a wife. But if thou take a wife, thou haft not   28.
finned (in so resoluing) And if a virgin marie, she hath
not sinned] And interposing the tribulations which
commonly folow Mariage; and the commodities of a
single life, he concludeth, saying [This I speake to your   v.35.
profite:not to caft a snare vpon you, but to that which
is honeft, and that may geue you power (make you
able) without impediment to attend vpon our Lord.
Therfore both he that ioyneth his virgine (geueth
his daughter in Matrimonie) doth wel; & he that ge-   38.
ueth not, doth better. A woman if her husband dye, is
at libertie, let her marie to whom she wil; only in our
Lord(that is, a true faithful Christian, not an Infidel)
But more blessed shal she be, if she so remane, accor-   39.
ding to my counsel; and I thinke that I also haue the   40.
Spirite of God.]

And teacheth,
that after pro-
mise is made,
it bindeth, as
other pre-
cepts.

6. Thus the Apostle exhorteth al Christians, whiles
they are in consultation, whether to marie, or no; to
consider the comodities, and difficulties of each state:
but after that they are resolued, he wisheth them to be
constant in their resolution: yet with this difference,
(as appeareth by his whole discourse) that the deter-
minatiō of the lesse perfect, ought not to hinder good
motions to the more perfect: but rather to change to
the better, so long as there is no obligation. And therfore it is necessarie to discerne , betwen purpose and
promise. For where there is only a purpose, the determination may be altered, without finne, either from
inten-

intention of perpetual chastitie vnto Mariage, or from intention of Mariage, vnto perpetual chastitie. But where promise is past, there no change is lawful. Because those that promise, either perpetual chastitie, to God, or Mariage to anie marigeable partie, are bond to their promise, & can not without iust relaxation, or dispensation part from it. As the Apostle decideth this case, according as euerie one determined in his hart, saying [He that hath determined in his hart, being setled, not hauing necessitie (not hauing promised) but hauing power of his owne wil (not hauing bond himselfe) & hath iudged this in his hart, to kepe his virgine, doth wel] though there was purpose of mariege; so long as there was not promise to marie. Concerning also vowed chastitie, he teacheth clearly, that it must be obserued. And therfore admonisheth Prelates, to be wel aduised, in admitting Widowes, or Virgines, to the vow of perpetual chastitie; counselling'the vnfitte rather to marrie, then to be in danger to breake their vowes. [Honour widowes, which are widowes in deede (saith he) But the younger widowes auoide (such as are not mortified in maners) for when they shal be wanton in Christ, they wil marie, hauing damnation, because they haue made voide their first faith] Because they haue in wil violated their promise, made to God, and sinned, by consenting in wil to marie, after vowed chastitie.

Ibid. v. 37.

1. Tim. 5. 7, 9. 11. 14.

Vovv of voluntarie pouertie, to possesse no vvorldlie goodes in proper, is godlie and meritorious.

ARTICLE 51.

Voluntare pouertie, by renouncing al proprietie of worldlie goodes, which al persons of Religious Orders doe solemnly vow; helpeth much to attaining perfection in this life: for that by cutting of al loue to external possessions, a great steppe is made to

Renunciatione of worldlie goodes, and of carnal pleasures, prepare

leaue

H h 3

the way to re-
nounce alfo
the proper wil. leaue alfo the defire of corporal and worldly pleafures. And thefe two refolutions, prepare a readie way
to refigne alfo the proper wil, fubiecting it wholly to
Gods wil, by the mediation of a fpecial vifible Superior: to whofe commandment and direction, religious perfons by vow, fubmitte their owne willes. Becaufe in the intyre fubmiffion of mans wil to Gods
wil, confifteth the greateft perfection of this life,
which fhal be more perfited in glorie: and is more or
leffe perfect here, as it is more or leffe e mortified. Albeit therfore perfectió of this life may ftand together
with poffeffions of worldlie goodes, & with the ftate
of Mariage (for Noe, Abraham, & other Patriarches &
Prophets, were perfect men in their generations) yet
are vowed pouertie, and chaftitie; very good meanes
for mortification, and drawing neerer to perfection.
But forfomuch as it is not abfolutely neceffarie, but
only as the Royal Prophete admonifheth [If riehes a-
bound, fet not your hart vpon them] it is not commanded, but only counfeled [to geue al to the poore.]

Gen. 6. v. 9.
ch. 7 v. 1.
cb. 22 v 16.

Pfal. 61. v.
11.

Some in the
old Teftament
liued in com-
mon. 2. In the old Teftament, Elias, Elifeus, and their
difciples: likewife the Rechabites, had either nothing
in proper, but only in communitie, or els had leffe
then otherwife they might lawfully haue had; as is declared before. And fo though they were not direct
exemples; yet were they apparant figures of Religious Chriftian Orders, which doe vowe, and obferue
voluntarie pouertie, renouncing al priuate proprietie
of landes, and moueable worldlie goodes.

Article 49.
4 Reg. 6. v.
1.
Iere. 35. v. 7.

Our Sauiours
maner of fu-
fteyning him-
felfe and his
Apoftles, was
moft perfect. 3. But more expreffly our B. Sauiour, with his difciples, liued in comon, vpon almes geuen them, which
was put in a comon purfe, to ferue them al, according
as euerie one had neede. And when our Lord fent his
twelue Apoftles, & feuentie two difciples to preach, he
prefcribed them this Rule, faying [Gratis you haue receiued, gratis geue ye. Doe not poffeffe gold nor filuer, nor money in your purfes: nor a fcrippe, for the

Ioan. 12. v.
5. 6.
ch. 13 v. 29.
Mat. 10. v.
8. 9. 10.
ch. 19. v 16.
17. 20. 23.
29.

way:

way:neither two coates, neither shoes, neither rodde:
for the workeman is worthie of his meate] And to a

Mat. 10. v.
11. 29.
young man, inquiring what els was wanting to him,
that kepeth the commandments: Our Lord answered [If thou wilt be perfect, goe sel the thinges that
thou hast, and geue to the poore: and thou shalt haue
treasure in heauen] Wheras therfore, to obtaine some
place in heauen, it sufficeth to kepe the commandi-

Io. 14. v. 2.
ments:those which also geue al that they haue to the
poore; doe merite treasure (that is, a great reward) in

2. Cor. 9. v.
6. 8.
heauen. [For in my Fathershouse (said our Lord at an
other time.) there be manie mansions] And S. Paul
saith, [He that soweth sparingly, sparingly also shal
reap. and he that soweth in blessinges, of blessinges
also shal reape. For God loueth a chereful geuer]

4. That al the Apostles, and manie others vowed,

Eccli. 35 v. 9.
Act. 2. v.
44 45.
Act. 19. v.
27.
and obserued voluntarie pouertie, is further confirmed by that which S. Peter said to Christ, in the behalfe of them al [Behold we haue left al thinges, and
haue folowed thee] And that also S. Paul did the same
is manifest by diuers his speaches of himselfe, and
frequent exhortations to others. For amongst other
requisite qualities, and necessarie vertues in Clergi-

Tim. 2. v.
1. 2.
52 Tim. 2. v.
3. 4.
men, he requireth [That they be not couetous:not
folowers of filthie lucre] Againe he saith to S. Timothee, and in him to euerie Clergiman [Labour thou as
a good souldiar of Christ Iesus. No man being a souldiar to God, intangleth himself with secular bussines-
ses] He lamenteth also that some were parted from

ch 4. v. 10.
2. Cor. 6. v.
10.
him, and were returned to the world, saying [Demas
hath left me, louing this world] Of himself and other
Apostolical men, he auoucheth, that they were needie (or poore) but enriching manie:as hauing nothing,
and possessing al thinges] Hauing nothing of their
owne in proprietie, yet wanted nothing by Gods
prouidence, for their competent vse of temporal
goodes in this life.

Al the Apo-
stles, & manie
others vowed
and obserued
voluntarie
pouertie.

5. Finally

5. Finally, that this vow of voluntarie pouertie, *Artic.*48.
binderh in conscience, is euident by the textes before
recited. And especially by the example of Ananias, & *Act.* 5.v.1.
his wife Saphira. Concerning therfore workes of Su- 2.5.10.
pererogation, we may here conclude, & so end this
third Part; that to doe anie such worke without vow,
ouer and besides the commandments, is very good.
To vow such workes, and to performe them, is much
better. But so to vow, and not performe, is the worst.
Before al, to kepe the commandments, is absolutely
necessarie. Christ Iesus grant to vs al his grace: so to
passe through temporal goodes, that we lose not eternal.

Transgressi-
on of Vow
is damnable.

The comand-
ments are ne-
cessarie.
More is bet-
ter.

The end of the third Part.

Deo Gratias.

THE FOVRT PART OF
AN ANKER
OF CHRISTIAN DOCTRINE.

Concerning Prayer. Especially the *Pater noster.*

THE FIRST ARTICLE.
It is necessarie to pray often: actually desi-
ring, and asking good thinges of God.

Eternal saluation (which consisteth in seeing
God) is the absolute good thing, for which
man is created. This is the complete felicitie
desired of al men. This only, and nothing els
doth satiate mans mind, and filleth his desires. It is at-
tayned by doing those thinges, which God (assisting
with his grace) requireth: and is lost by defect of anie
one of the same thinges so required, according to that
general Rule of reason: *Bonum est ex integra causa; ma-*
lum ex quolibet defectu. A good thing procedeth of the
whole cause: euil of euerie defect. For obtayning therfore this singular, most eminent good thing, the fruition of God in euerlasting life, al Christians confesse
that for the first fundation, true Faith is necessarie. As
we haue abundantly declared in the first part of this
worke. It is also clearly proued in the second Part,
that holie Sacraments are necessarie, and requisite, for
remission of sinnes, & other especial effectes. Thirdly
it is likewise manifestly shewed in the third Part, that
it is necessarie to kepe Gods comandments. And for
better accomplishing al the same, it resteth to declare
in this tourt & last Part, the necessitie, & efficacie of
Prayer.

2 Io 3.7.1
sb 2 v.25.
Pf. 16 v.15.
Iac.2.7.10.

Part.1.
Artic.1.
Par.2.
Art.10.
11.17.27.
&c.
Part.3.
Artic.1.

Mans cheefe
end is eternal
glorie.

Four general
thinges are
required ther-
unto.
1.
True Faith.
2.
Vse of holie
Sacraments.
3
Obseruation
of Gods Com
mandments.

4.
Prayer,

I i Prayer.

Prayer. Especially discussing, and expla-ning in what
maner, in what tongue, with what preparation, attention; and intention; for whom, and to whom, it behoueth to pray.

The contents of this Part.

2. First then concerning the necessarie vse of prayer,
it appeareth by testimonies of holie Scriptures, that al
the faithful seruants of God, held themselues obliged
to desire and pray for Gods special grace. So Abel and
Cain sought Gods fauour by offering Sacrifice, which
is the most principal kinde of prayer, Though Cain
performed it not in good forte, as Abel did) And the
Patriarch Enos in some forme of wordes [inuocated
the name of our Lord.] Which sufficiently geueth
vs to vnderstand, that not only these which are named, but also Adam and Eue, Seth, Cainan, Enoch,
and al others, especially those which were called [The
sonnes of God] vsed both priuate and publike prayers. More particular mention is made of Abrahams
praying, for Sodome and Gomorrhe, sixe times renewing his supplication in one day, and had obtained his suite, if tenne iust persons had bene found in
those cities. Likewise, vpon manie occasions, special
prayers were often made by Gods faithful people. So
Abrahams seruant prayed for good successe, in the
particular busines, wherin his master imployed him,
about the mariage of Isaac. The same [Isaac, besought
our Lord, for his wife Rebecca, because she was barren: who heard him, and made Rebecca to conceiue.] Much more, it is to be vnderstood, that al
true seruants of God, prayed for grace, and saluation
of their soules, seeing they so carefully praied for temporal good thinges. Knowing that al good thinges,
spiritual and corporal: temporal and eternal, procede
from God, and are by praier to be obteyned of him.
3. Breefely al good workes are to be vndertaken with
prayer, that they may succede to Gods honour, health
of soules, or other good end, directed thereunto. As a
diuin

*Al the faith-
ful from the
beginning of
the world
haue inuoca-
ted God by
prayer.*

*Gen 4 v.3.
4.*

v.26.

*ch 18.1. 2s.
ad3.*

*ch. 24 v. 12.
&c.*

ch. 25 v. 21

*Prayer ought
to accompa-*

Ecclĩ.18.v.
22, diuine Preacher exhorteth, saying [Be not hindered nie al good
to pray alwaies, and feare not to be iustified, euen to   workes.
death, becaufe the reward of God abideth for euer]
For as grace and merite increafe in this life: fo is re-
eb.37.v. 19
Gen.15.v.
21.
eb 28.v. 20.
1.Reg 1.v.
11.
Sap.8.9.
&c. ward augmented in heauen. But both are the giftes of
God: to be obtayned of him, by al thofe meanes,
which he hath ordayned,&amongft other meanes by
prayer [In al thefe (faith the fame preacher) befech
the Hieghest, that he direct thy way in truth]So did
al the Patriarches, Prophets, & other godly perfons.

4. Our B. Sauiour, and his Apoftles, by word and
example teach, that frequent prayer is neceffarie, with It is necefsimple finceritie of hart, and refignation of proper tie to pray
Luc.11.v. 5.
6.8.
eb.18.v.1.2.
5.7. 8. wil:to be attentiue, and inftant, as it were with earneft often.
importunitie, like to him[that goeth to his freind at
midnight, to borrow three loaues: and continueth
knocking, and asking, vntil he obtaine his requeft:
through his importunitie.]And like to[the widow,
which ouertreated the Iudge (who femed neither to
feare God, nor to refpect man) with much foliciting
and importunitie, to heare and iudge her caufe] For
fo our heauenlie Father, knowing what we neede,
alwayes heareth, but fometime deferreth to grant;
that his feruants may know and feele their owne neceffities,and by perfeuering,become more capable of
his benefites; defiring and asking by day & by night,
with deuout & hartie prayers[Reioyce in hope (faith
Rom.12.v.
12. S. Paul) Be patient in tribulation, inftant in prayer.
Our Lord is nigh. Be nothing careful: but in euerie
thing by prayer and fupplication, with thankefgeuing: let your petitions be knowen with God (that
your felues may be more ftirred vp to feruent defire
Pf.4.v.5. 6.
Mat.6.v.8.
1.Pet 4.v.
7.8. in God) who beft knoweth what is needful for you,
before you aske him]Likewife S. Peter requireth diligent & frequent prayer in al the faithful [The end of
al shal approach (faith he) Be wife therfore & watch,
in prayers.If anic of you lacke wifdom (faith S.Iames)

let him aske of God, who geueth to al men abundantly, and vpbradeth not, and it shal be geuen him] And wheras our Sauiour admonisheth that [It behoueth alwaies to pray, and not to be wearie] And S. Paul willeth vs [to pray without iutermission] These precepts are fulfilled, if at conuenient times we doe actually imploy our selues in formal prayer, and ceassing from that exercise, haue stil intention to returne thereunto againe, from time to time, & in the meane while, whensoeuer we set our bodies or mindes to other good actions, we intend, and direct the same to Gods honour, and our owne, and our neighbours good, desiring that God wil euer blesse, and prosper vs therin, We so doing, make no interruption, nor intermission, but continuation of other good workes, with prayer, and againe of prayer, with other good workes. And thus doing, we pray alwayes, & are not wearie, but kepe the same intention to pray againe, and againe, so long as we shal liue in this world; and in the next life, hope to praise God eternally.

5. By al which it is most euident, that Prayer is the proper act of Hope (the second Theological vertue) is necessarie to Iustification, and saluatiou. Euen so necessarie, and withal so effectual, that saluation is ascribed in like maner to Hope, as it is to Fath. S. Paul saying [We account a man to be iustified by faith] and in the same Epistle saying also [By hope we are saued] Because both these vertues are necessarie, and by them both (together with other vertues, especially with Charitie, the third and greatest Theological vertue) the faithful cooperateth to his saluation. The Apostle nowhere saith : Faith onlie, nor Hope only iustifieth, or saueth. But he saith [That faith auaileth, which worketh by Charitie. Hope confoundeth not (and hope saueth) because the charitie of God is powred forth in our hartes.] And likewise al moral Vertues: the seuen Giftes of the Holie Ghost.

Marginal notes (left):

How we must alwayes pray without intermission.

Neither onlie Faith; nor only Hope doth iustifie But both are necessarie.

And do iustifie together with other vertues.

Marginal notes (right):

Iac.1.v.5.
Luc.11.v.1.
1 Thess.5.v.
17.

Rom 3.v.
28.
Rom 4.v.
5.18.
1.Cor.13.v.
13.
Isa.11.
Mat 5.
Gal.5.v 6.

Rom. 5.v.5.

Ghoſt. The vſe of holie Sacraments, and the obſeruation of al Gods commandments, together with diligent prayer (wherof we here ſpeake) are al neceſſarie.
And al theſe together, through Gods grace, doe iuſtifie, and ſaue ſoules. But the wilful, and groſſe defect
of anie one of theſe, bringeth ſpiritual death of the
ſoule : and if it ſo perſiſt vnto temporal death of the
bodie, it bringeth eternal damnation. Becauſe euerie
good thing, dependeth vpon the whole cauſe; and
euil commeth vpon euerie notorious defect. Ac cor-
ſupra §.1. ding to the Maxime, that can not be denied.

Thankſegeuing for Gods benefites, is a ſpecial
and neceſſarie kinde of prayer.

ARTICLE 2.

Holie Scriptures doe often inſtruct vs, that
thankſegeuing, and praiſes to God, are ſpecial
kindes of prayer : no leſſe neceſſarie, then direct peti-
Gen. 8. v. 18 tions for thinges needful. So Noe for his owne and
19. 20. 21. his families conſeruation, with other liuing creatures, in the general diluge of the world [built an Altar
to our Lord: and taking of al cattle, & foules that were
cleane, offered Holocauſt vpon the Altar. And our
Lord ſmelled a ſwete ſauour.] When God firſt promiſed to Abraham, that his ſeede ſhould poſſeſſe the
land of Chanaan [he builded there an Altar to our
ch. 11. v. 7. 8 Lord:] And ſo in other places [where he pitched his
ch. 14. v. tent, he builded Altars to our Lord, and called v-
18. 19. 20. pon his name] Melchiſedech alſo offered Sacrifice of
thankes to our Lord, for the victorie obtained by A-
braham ouer their enimies. Iacob very gratefully re-
ch. 32. v. 10. counteth the great benefites, which he had receiued
of Gods bountie, ſaying [I am inferiour, ô Lord, to al
thy mercies, and thy truth, that thou haſt fulfilled to
thy ſeruant. With my ſtaffe I paſſed ouer this Iordan,
and now with two troupes I doe returne] Likewiſe
Moyſes with al the people of Iſrael, in thankeſgeuing

Examples of
thankeſge-
uing and prai-
ſes to God in
the Lawe of
nature.

1i 3 for

for their deliuerie frō Ægypt,& safe passage through
the read sea,ſsang a Canticle of thankes and praises *Exod.15.v.*
to our Lord: with voices, timbrels,and dances]These 1.2.
and manie other examples are recorded of this necel- *v.20*
sarie dutie,of rendring thankes and praises,to gether
with other prayers vnto God, before the Law was
geuen.

Certaine Sa-
crifices and
Canticles, or-
dayned for
thankesgeuing by the
Law.

    2. By the written Law,diuers Sacrifices were in-
stituted, as wel for thankesgeuing, as for obtayning *Levit.7.*
benefites of God. And withal special Canticles were 12.
composed by Moyses, to be solemnly recited & song,
conteyning thankes,and praises to God: both for general and particular gracious diuine fauours,receiued
by his people. As when they had passed from the

Moyses made
in al three
Canticles.

Moabites, and Armorrheites in the wildernes, safe
vnto Arnon, they sang a Canticle,at a Wel, as it were
with duble quire : some singing this verse [Arise the *Num.21. v.*
wel] Others sang therto [The wel which the princes 10.&c.
digged,& the captaines of the multitude prepared in
the Lawgeuer,& in their staues&c.]The like thankes
and praises they rendted the same time, for their victories against Sehon,& Og,Kings of the Amorretes,
and of Basan] Againe , Moyses composed an other
larger Canticle for the people to sing often, conteyning a Summarie of manie great benefites: with ad- *v.17.*
monition to be grateful & to be [*VVise*, to consider *v.21.25.*
thinges past; to *vnderstand* thinges present , and *to* 27.28.33.35.
prouide for their last] thinges to come. In al, which *Deut 32.v.*
Moyses foreseeing the ingratitude of that people,cal- 1.2.&c.
ling it [A nation without counsel, and without wis- *v.29.*
dome]declared Gods threates, and punishmenss,and *v.28.*
prophecied the conuersion of the Gentiles, who *v.33.&c.*
should be more gratful. Yet also amongst the same *v 43.*
Iewes, were some which beleuing and hoping in
Christ then to come, rendred thankes to God for his
graces bestowed vpon the same people : and that in
forme of Canticles. So Barach a General Captaine,
                                                            and

Iudic's 1.2.
&c.

and Debora a Prophetesse, sang thankes and praises for a speciall victorie, atchiued by them, and by Iael a wise, and godlie woman. Also holie Anna the mother of Samuel, indited and sung a like Canticle of thanks to God for the same happie childe, prophecying therin speciall Mysteries of Christ, and his Church. Which Canticle is called a prayer, in these expresse termes: [Anna prayed, and said: My hart hath reioyced in our Lord] Diuers others sang Canticles, which are recorded in holie Scriptures, & often repeted in the Christian Church. Two of the Euangelical Prophet Isaias: one of King Ezechias, one of Ionas the Prophete. Another of Abacuc the Prophete, which is also called a Prayer, in the sacred text. Also the three Hebrew noble children, in a furnace of fire, accompanied, and defended by an Angel [as out of one mouth praised and glorified, and blessed God] with a large and solemne Canticle.

Other Canticles
Of Debora and Barach.

Of Anna.

Of Isaias two.

Of Ezechias.

Of Ionas.

Of Abucuc.

And of the three childien.

1.Reg.1.v. 28.
ch.2 v.1.
lj.12.
ch.26.
ch.38.v.9
4 Reg. 20. v.11.
Ione 2.v.2.
Abac.3.v.1
Daniel 1.v
25.26 &c
A versu.
51. ad 91.

3. In this kind of prayer, the Royal Prophet Dauid is also abundant. Who most humbly admiring, and as gratfully confessing Gods great benefites vpon himself, noway deseruing so singular fauours [went in (into the Tabernacle, where the Arke of God remained) & meditating before our Lord, said: Who am I, ô Lord, and what is my house, that thou hast brought me thus farre? But this also semed litle in thy sight, ô Lord God, vnles thou also didst speake of the house of thy seruant, for a long time] After this he said to his sonne Salomon, and to other cheefe Nobilitie of his Kingdome [Heare me my brethren, and my people: I meant to haue built a house, wherin the Arke of our Lord might rest: and the footstoole of the feete of our God: and to build it I prepared al thinges.] But God otherwise ordaining, that Salomon should do it, not Dauid, he addeth saying [Howbeit our Lord the God of Israel, chose me of al the house of my father, to be King ouer Israel. For of Iuda he chose

King Dauid was much replenished with the vertue of gratitude and deuotion.

2.Reg.7. v. 18.19.

2.Par.28.v. 2.3.4.5.

chofe the Princes. Moreouer of the house of Iuda, my fathers house; and of the sonnes of my father, it pleafed him to choose me King, ouer al Ifrael, yea & of my sonnes (for our Lord hath geuen me manie sonnes) he hath chosen Salomon my sonne, to sitte in the throne of the kingdome of our Lord, ouer Ifrael? These and other like benefites', this Royal Pfalmift gratefully considering, redubleth thankes, and praises to God, in his Pfalmes. [Thou Lord(faith he) art my Protector, my Glorie exalting my head. With my voice, I haue cried to our Lord, & he hath heard me, frô his Holie hil. Bleffed be our Lord, becaufe he heard the voice of my petition. Our Lord is my Helper, & my Protector; in him my hart hath hoped and I was holpen. Our Lord is my Rocke, my Strength, and my Sauiour. God is my Strong one, I wil hope in him, my Sheilde, and the Horne of my faluation, my Lifter vp, and my refug?] I wil exalt thee, ô Lord (faith he in the Pfalme of Canticle, which he made in the dedication of his owne house)becaufe thou haft receiu.d me; neither haft delighted myne enemies ouer me. O Lord my God, I haue cried to thee, and thou haft healed me. Lord thou haft brought forth my foule out of hel:thou haft faued me from them that goe downe into the Lake. Sing to our Lord, ye his Sainctes: and confeffe (render thankes and praifes) to the memorie of his Holines.]The farre greater part of the whole diuine Pfalter, confifteth of thankes and praifes to God, euer adioyned, or prefixed to other diuine Myfteries of Chrift, and his Church. As we fhal yet recite a few more of manie, in the next Article.

4. In the meane fpace, fee the confirmation of this bonden dutie; by Chrifts owne example and doctrine: whofe actions are our inftructions: whofe documéts are to vs obligations. Generally our B. Sauiour adioyned thankefgeuing to al his prayers, preachings, and other workes [I confeffe to thee (that is, I thanke and praife

Pfal.3.v. & 5.
Pfal.7.v.2. 3.
Pf.27.v.6. 7
2 Reg.22 v. 2 3 4.

Pf 29.v. 1.2.

Mat.11.v. 25.

Our Sauiour by example and doctrine, sheweth the obligation of

Mat.11.v.25 praise thee)ô Father, Lord of heauen & earth, becauſe
(ſaith he)thou haſt hid theſe thinges , from the wiſe &
Luc.14.v. 29. prudent: & haſt reuealed them to litle ones)Thus ſaid
he concerning higheſt Myſteries, which he preached.
And namely of his owne humilation, and ſufferinges.
When he multiplied, fiue loaues, and two fiſhes, he
Mat.14.v. 19. Luc.9.v.16. firſt taking them into his handes, gaue thankes to
God his Father, then bleſſed them, & ſo brake them,
& gaue them to his Apoſtles to diſtribute to the peo-
Io.11.v. 41 42. ple]When he raiſed Lazarus from death[lifting vp his
eyes towards heauen , he ſaid :Father, I geue thee
thankes, that thou haſt heard me, and I know that
thou doeſt alwayes heare me: but for the people,that
ſtandeth about, haue I ſaid it, that they may beleue
that thou haſt ſent me] When he inſtituted the moſt
holie Sacrament, and Sacrifice,taking bread & wine,
Mat.26. Mar.14. Luc.22. 1.Cor.11.v. 24. 25. he gaue thankes, vocal or Mental,to God (by whoſe
power al thinges are done)then bleſſed the ſame, &
by made them his owne ſacred bodie,&bloud:ſaying,
[This is my bodie.This is my bloud] Witneſſes three
holie Euangeliſtes, and S. Paul relating Chriſts actions & wordes. If the nine men which were cleanſed
by Chriſt from leproſie, had bene thankful,he would
haue aknowleged their gratitude: but he ſeeing
their naked thankles cogitations,iuſtly reprehended
them, ſaying[Were not tenne made cleane ? And
where are the nine?]And then ſaid to that one:which
Luc.17.v. 13 15. came and gaue thankes [Ariſe, goe thy wayes : becauſe thy faith hath made thee ſafe]*Thy faith* ſaid our
Lord: which hauing other vertues,of gratitude,hu-
militie, deuotion, confeſſion of Chriſts power, and
v.19. goodnes, to the edification of others,ioyned with it
and ſo not faith alone (but faith accompanied with
other vertues)made this man ſafe.But the faith of the
other nine: being alſo true faith , for they al beleued
in Chriſt,crying vnto him [Ieſus.Maiſter,haue mercie
v.13. on vs] was but only faith , which alone ſufficed for a

Kk   temporal

al men , to
render thanks
and praiſes to
God.

Nine Lepers
hauing only
faith, were
cleanſed in
bodie, but not
therby ſaued
in ſoule.

temporal, and corporal benefite, for their cleanfing from leprofie, but cleanfed not their foules.

S. Paul by example and doctrine admonisheth al to be diligent in rendring thankes to God.

5. S. Paul a right folower of Chrift, both practifed the vertue of gratitude, in rendring thankes, and teacheth that thankefgiuing muft be ioyned with petition in prayer. For after that, in peril of shipwrake on the fea, it was fignified to him by an Angel, that they should al arriue fafe to land [taking bread he gaue thankes to God, in fight of them al;and when he had broken it, he began to eate] Shortly after comming al fafe into Italie, approaching nere to Rome. S. Paul with S. Luke and others, finding fome Chriftians at Apij forum [Geuing thankes to God: they tooke corege. And fo coming to Rome, S. Paul was permitted to remaine to himfelfe, with a fouldiar that kept him] In al his Epiftles, he ioyntly with prayer for more grace, geueth thankes to God for grace receiued [To al that are at Rome(said he) grace to you, and peace, from God our Father, and our Lord Iefus Chrift. Firft I geue thankes to my God, through Iefus Chrift, for al you: becaufe your faith is renowmed in the whole world] He withal reprehended the incredulous, not for not beleuing, before Chrift was preached vnto them, but [becaufe, wheras they knew God (to witte, by light of reafon, that there is one God) they did not glorifie him as God, nor had geuen thankes] Difcuffing a controuerfie amongft the Chriftians, he more efpecially vrged them, to be thankful, then to be ouer curious in practife of a thing, in it felfe indifferent. [He that eateth, eateth to our Lord, (faith he) for he geueth thankes to God. And he that eateth not, to our Lord he eateth not, & geueth thakes to God.] So writing to other Chriftians, together with prayer, for grace & peace, he alwaies adioyneth thankes geuing [I geue thankes to God alwayes for you, for the grace of God that is geuen you, in Chrift Iefus] Requefting other mens prayers for himfelfe,

Act.27.v. 24.25.

ch.28.v.15.

Rom.1.v. 7.8.

v.20.21.

ch.14.v.6.

1.Cor.1.v. 3.4.

he

2.Cor.1.v.
10.11.
Ephes.1.v.
15.16.
Colos.1.v.3.
ch.4.v.2.
1.Thes.1.v.
3 ch.3.v 9.
ch.5.v.18.
2 Thes.1. v.
3.
1.Tim.1. v.
12.ch.2.v 1.
Phile.v.4.
Apoc 7.v.
12.ch.11.v.
16.&c.

he willeth them withal, to render thankes: signifying that the same is of like necessitie and efficacie. [We hope (saith he) that God wil deliuer vs, from great dangers: you helping withal in prayer for vs, that by manie mens persons, thankes for that gift which is in vs, may be geuen by manie in our behalfe] Againe to others he said [I hearing of your faith, that is in our Lord Iesus, and loue towards al the Saintes, cease not to geue thankes for you, making a memorie of you, in prayers] To al, he saith [Be instant in prayer, watching in it, in thankesgeuing] the same in manie places, testifying what himselfe did, and exhorting al to doe the like.

Praises of God, by confessing his singular Excellences, is also a necessarie kinde of prayer.

ARTICLE 3.

OVr daylie necessities forcing vs to craue manie thinges of God, doe not only induce obligation to be thankful for benefites, but also require especial acknowlegement of Gods incomparable Excellencies, hauing al absolute perfections, with want of nothing: alwayes geuing and neuer needing.

Sap.8.v.
21.

As therfore we must nedes aske al necessaries of him, that can geue al, which is only God: so it being impossible to recompence his bountiful giftes: we are bond to what we can (which is also his gift) to be thankful. And in regard of impossibilitie, to render due thankes, we must confesse the reason therof to be Gods infinite immensitie of al Excellences. Which is a third kinde of prayer, no lesse necessarie, then the other two. As is cleare by light of reason; by which we may both know, that there is one God, Creator of

Rom.8.v.
21.

al other thinges: and that [we ought to glorifie him as God.] It is also confirmed by the holie Scriptures, and espcially by examples of the faithful seruants of God, practising it in this life: and of his glorious ser-

Margin notes:
Necessitie moueth vs to aske.
Dutie bindeth to be thankful for giftes.

Impossibilitie to render due thankes, requireth confession of Gods infinite Excellences.

uants

uants more perfectly performing it , in the eternal ioyes of heauen.

2. In part of supplie therfore, of mans defect in not rendring due thankes to God, were instituted, not only Sacrifices of thankesgeuing, wherin part of the offered hoste, was consumed to Gods special honour, the rest remaining to the Priestes , and those that brought oblations ; but also the Sacrifices of Holocaustes, in which al was burnt to the honour of Gods supreme dominion, no part reserued for mans vse. So holie [Abel offered of the first begotten of his flocke, *Gen. 4. v. 4:* and of their fatte] to witte, the best thinges that he had, confessing therby that God farre excelleth al other thinges, he the Creator, and they his creatures. [Iust Noe offered Holocaust of al the cattle & foules *ch. 8. v. 28.* that were cleane] Melchisedech Priest of God most Hiegh, together with his Sacrifice, rendred both thankes to God for Abrahams victorie: and praises of Gods name, saying [Blessed be God the Hieghest, *ch. 14. v. 19.* which created heauen and earth, by whose prote- *20.* ction the enimies are in thy handes] So in al Sacrifices, is cheefely professed the praise of God, as onlie Creator, onlie Lord of al. Likewise in Canticles, Psalmes, & al Prayers, besides the petitions, & thanks, are generally inserted titles, eminently, and singularly proper to God alone, not comunicable to anie creature. In that first Canticle of thankes and praise to *Exod. 15. v.* God, al the children of Israel (when they had passed *2. 3.* the read sea, wherin Pharao with his whole armie was drowned) sang thus [My strength and my Praise is our Lord: and he is made vnto me a Saluation. This is my God , and I wil glorifie him: the God of my Father, and I wil exalt him. Our Lord is a war- *v. 11.* rier: Omnipotent is his name. who is like to thee among the strong, ô Lord, who is like to thee!] There is indeede none equal, none comparable to God. There haue bene, and may be potent, mightie men,

good,

Marginal notes:

Al Sacrifices implie thanks and praises to God; especially Pacifiques, and Holocausts.

Canticles coteyne proper titles attributed to God, not communicable (in the same eminent sense) to anie creature.

Gen.6.v.4. good and euil: also[Giants, the mightie of the old ch.10.v.9. world, famous men]for crueltie iufamous[Nemrod 1.Reg.17.v. was a valiant (and violent) hunter.] Hercules was 24 33. strong. Goliath terrible. Pharao, Nabuchodonofor, Alexander, Cæfar, and others, were great and potent. Also amongst the true feruants of God, manie were glorious: Abraham, Moyfes, Iofue, Gedeon, Iephte, Samfon, Dauid, with his valiants Iudas Machabeus, 1.Par.11. v. with his brethren: and manie others, were ftou-, 10.11.19. ftrong, valiant, mightie, victorious, and admirable amongst men: but no man, nor Angel euer was, or can be Almightie, onlie God can doe al thinges. Others may by participation of Gods power, be very mightie; but God alone, and no other is Almightie. [Omnipotent is his name] Also in al other Excellences, creatures may participate, onlie God is abfolute, Ifa 45 v.5. 6. and independent. Euen as he is One God, and there is no other: fo he onlie, Omnifcious. Al goodnes, Almercie, Al truth in him felfe, and of him felf:al creatures haue that they haue, & their very being of him.

Diuers men truly called very mightie, but onlie God is Almightie

3. Al holie Scriptnres yeld fpecial found, vpon this ftring of Gods praifes. And none more abundantly or more fwetely fhew the tenne corded Pfalter, then the Royal Pfalmift, & Prophet Dauid. Wherin he inftructeth, & by example inuiteth al to repaire Pfal 7.v. 18. vnto this diuine Melodie[I wil confeffe to our Lord (faith he) according to his iuftice; and wil fing to the name of our Lord moft High. O Lord our Lord, how Pf.8 v.1. maruelous is thy name in the whole earth! Becaufe thy magnificence is eleuated aboue the heauens. I wil Pf 9.v.2. vtter praife to thee, ô Lord, with al my hart: and I shal be faued from myne enimies Bring to our Lord Pf.17 v.4. Pf.28.v.1.2. 3. ye children of God: bring to our Lord, Sacrifice of laudes: bring to our Lord glorie, and honour, bring Pf.32.v.1. Pf.33.v.1. Pf.34.v. 28. glorie to his name: Adore ye our Lord, in his holie court. Praifing becometh the righteous. His praife alwaies in my mouth. Thy praife, ô Lord, al the day.

As King Dauid abundeth in rendring thankes to God; fo likewife in fetting forth his praifes.

Immolate to God the Sacrifice of praise. The Sacri- *Pf.49.v.14.* fice of praise (saith God) shal glorifie me. O Lord 23. (saith againe the Prophete)thou wilt open my lippes, *Pf.50.v.17.* and my mouth shal shew forth thy praise] Brefely, besides manie other great partes of diuers Psalmes, al *Pf.104 &c.* those which haue *Alleluia* in their title (which are twentie in number) are wholly composed of diuine *Psalmi.147.* praises. Of which the four last both beginne and end 148.

VVhat Alleluia signifie h, and why it is not translated, into English, with the same Hebrew wordes, *Allelu Ia*: which the 149. Greke and Latin pronounce as one word, but trans- 150. late it not: much lesse, can vular languages sufficiently expresse it so breefely. For that therby is not only signified, as our English Protestants translate, *Praise ye the Lord;* but also it importeth the endles eternal songue,wherwith al the faithful in earth,and glorious in heauen inuite themselues, and each others, with al possible, ioy, gladnes, iubilation, in hart, voice, gesture, musical instruments,and by whatsoeuer meanes can be inwardly couceiued,or outwardly expressed,to praise, and magnifie God , our Omnipotent Lord,for his infinite,immense goodnes,greatnes, and al his diuine incomprehensible Excellences.

Other Scriptures shew the necessarie dutie of praising God.   4. This obligation of al creatures, to praise our Creator, is yet further testified in the Sapiential, and Prophetical Bookes [Honour our Lord with thy *Pro.3.v.9.* substance (saith Salomon) and geue to him of the first of al thy fruites] Eternal diuine wisdome saith, to al those that haue some sparke of wisdom,or other *ch.8.v.14.* vertues, that it is not their owne, but al his.[Myne is 15.16.17. Counsel,and Equitie,Prudence is myne, Strength is myne. By me Kinges doe reigne; and the Makers of **Lawes** decree iust thinges. By me Princes doe rule, & the mightie decree iustice. I loue them that loue me; and they that watch toward me, shal finde me] Shal finde me saith God to man , that is, partly in this life by light of faith , and godlie affection of loue: but perfectly in heauen, by the light of glorie, & fruition
of

of his diuine Maiestie. Which so farre excelleth mortal mens conceipt, that in the meane while, for lacke
of capacitie; the faithful must admire it, nor ouer
curiously search into it. For [As thou art ignorant,
which is the way of a spirite (saith the diuine Preacher) and as thou art ignorant, how the bones (of a
childe) are framed together in the wombe of her that
conceiueth:so thou knowest not the workes of God,
who is the Maker of al] The right praise therefore of
Gods Excellences consist (during this life)in admiration, more then in wordes, or cogitations. The least
which beginne to serue God, may desire to praise him
worthely. Those that haue made some progresse in
vertues, may admire his greatnes. If anie be perfect,
they may further contemplate with the spouse, in the
Canticle of Canticles, the bridal songue of the Mariage, betwen God and his whole Church, saying to
him [Behold thou art fayre and comelie: our bed (of
glorious rest) is flourishing] And each saith to others
[My beloued is white and ruddie, chosen of thou-
sands] But the more anie conceiueth of God, the better they perceiue that he is incomprehensible [The
high Seraphims (whom al other Angelicial Orders
do imitate)incessantly crie one to an other:Holie. Holie, Holie, the Lord God of Hostes, al the earth is ful of
his glorie] To the faithful in earth, Isaias saith[Sing to
the Lord a new songue, his praise is from the endes of
the earth] To al both in heauen and in earth he saith:
[Praise ye o heauens, because our Lord hath done
mercie. Make iubilation ye endes of the earth: Ioy,
and gladnes shal be found in Sion:geuing of thankes,
and voice of praise. Sing ye to our Lord (saith Ieremie) praise our Lord. Blessed art thou, o Lord God,
(said the holie children in the furnace)and laudable,
& glorious is thy name for euer[Yea Nabuchodonosor, being returned into his wittes, gaue praise, & magnificence, & glorie to the only God king of heauen.]

5. In

Ecle. 11. v.
1.

Cant. 1. v.
16.
ch 5. v 10.
ib. 6. v. 4.

Isa. 6. v. 3.
an. 42 v. 10.
ib. 44. v. 33.

ib. 51. v. 3.

Iere. 20. v.
15.

Dan. 3. v.
24 52. 90.

ch. 4. v. 3 4.

The Canticle
of Canticles
excelleth al
other Canti-
cles of the old
Testament.

It perteyneth
to the per-
fect.

Especially to
the glorified.

5. In the new Testament, are also both practise,
and precepts of praising God. The most blessed Virgine Mother of God, sang the Canticle of praise [My
soule doth magnifie our Lord] Zacharias pronounced the Canticle [Blessed be our Lord God of Israel]
A multitude of Angels sang [Glorie in the Hieghest
to God] Iust old Simion sang [Now thou doest dimisse
thy seruant, ô Lord, in peace.] Religiouse Anne also a
Prophetesse praised God, speaking of Christ, to al that
expected the redemption of Israel] Our Lord himself
instructeth vs to pray in the first petition of our daylie
prayer, that [Gods name may be sanctified] by al men
honoured, and praised. After our Lords Ascension,
[The disciples were in the Temple, praising and blessing God] Being replenished with the Holie Ghost
they spake to al peoples the great workes of God.
S. Paul, as he generally beginneth his Epstles with
prayer for grace, and thankes for benefites bestowed,
& promised: so he commonly concludeth with [prai-
ses to God, through Iesus Christ, with al honour and
glorie for euer and euer, Amen] S. Iohn testifieth the
same holie actes, as wel of prayers, and thankes, as of
praises, to be continually done in heauen, saying [I
saw, when the Lambe had opened the Booke, the
foure liuing creatures, and the foure and twentie seniours, fel before the lambe, hauing euerie one harpes
and golden vials, ful of odors, which are the prayers
of Saintes. And I heard manie multitudes in heauen,
saying: Benediction, & glorie, & wisdome, & thankesgeuing, honour, and power, and strength to our God,
for euer and euer, Amen. We thanke thee Lord God,
Omnipotent, which art, and which wast, and which
shalt come: Alleluia, Praise and Glorie, and Power to
our God. Alleluia, Amen, Alleluia] Thus much côcer-
ning the three kindes of prayers: Petitions, Thankes,
and Praises. Now we procede to shew the diuers maners of praying, and other pointes.

Canticles and other praises of God in the new Testamēt

Especially in heauen.

Luc 1. v. 48.
v. 68.
ch. 2. v. 13.
29. 38.

Mat 6. v.
1. 9.

Luc 24. v.
53.

Act. 2. v. 4.
11.

Rom. 16. v.
27
Ephes. 5.

Apoc. 5. v.
8.
ch. 7. v 11.
ch. 11 v. 16.
17.

ch. 19. v. 1.

Medi-

Meditation, and Contemplation, is the best maner of priuate prayer.

ARTICLE 4.

Silent cogitation of the hart, doth so much the more approach to God, then the voice of the tongue: as the vnderstanding of a reasonable creature doth better conceiue spiritual thinges, then the external senses can know inuisible spirites. Because the operation of the minde, whether it be vttered by external wordes, or remaine secrete in thought, apprehendeth more then sense can reach vnto. And so mental prayer, whether it be vttered by voice or no, ioyneth the soule to God, conuersing with him in cogitation, but the external voice, without cogitation of the minde, doth only beate the ayer, and maketh no special coniunction, betwen God and the soule, more then when a brute creature is taught to speake. And therfore it is not voice, nor sound of wordes by themselues, but the wil, and cogitation, hartely desiring Gods honour, or other good thing, that approcheth to God. And this is truly called Prayer. Either Vocal, when the mouth vttereth that good thing, which the hart desireth: or Mental, when it is retayned in the minde only, and not vttered by voice. And the difference of these two maners is, that Vocal so dependeth vpon the Mental, that at least the minde must actually sometime intend to pray, els it is no prayer at al: but mental is truly a prayer, though no word at al be pronounced by voice. wherfore, though Vocal prayer be very good, & in regard of publique Assemblies is also necessarie, yet concerning priuate aud particular deuotion, Mental prayer properly called Meditation, is better. in al those that can performe it. And that, in al the three kindes of prayer before declared: In Petitions, Thankes, and Praises to God. The holie vse, and fruite wherof, is often cōmended in holie Scriptures.

Sap 9 ?.ⅰ5.
ⅰ4.ⅰ5.

Pſa.ⅰ9.7.ⅰ3.

By the cogitation of the mind, soules approach to God, not by wordes without good thoughtes.

2. It is recorded by Moyses, in the Historie of the Holie Patriarches, that[Isaac went forth to meditate in the fielde, the day now being wel spent] Which importeth that he vsed sometimes this maner of Mental prayer. And consequently it is to be vnderstood, that other prudent deuout persons also vsed it. Certaine it is, that Moyses prayed mentally for Gods special helpe, when he speaking with his tongue, and voice to the people [God said to him: Why criest thou to me] For whiles he and al the people, were inuironed betwen Pharaos armie and the sea; they murmuring, and he admonishing, and encoregeing them, to confide in Gods present helpe, not otherwise speaking to God, then in his minde, and depe cordial desire, with assured confidence [willing them not to feare, but to stand and see the great wonders of our Lord, that he would doe that day] God calleth his mental cogitation, and desire[Crying to him.] Holie Dauid vsed very often this maner of prayer, as himselfe witnesseth saying, to God[The meditatiõ of my hart shal be in thy sight alwaies. My hart waxed hote within me: and in my meditation, a fire shal burne. I haue bene mindful of thee, ô God, vpon my bed: in the morning I wil meditate on thee, because thou hast bene my helper. I meditated in the night with my hart, & I was exercised, & I swept my spirit] Thus the Royal Psalmist, and doubtles al the Prophets, & other seruants of God, much oftner eleuated their mindes in good desires, prayers, thankes, and praises to God, then are written: and much more is written, then shal be nedeful here to repete, for profe of so cleare a truth.

3. But for the better practise hereof, although there be most excellent instructions, compiled by manie most expert in this holie exercise, yet we may not wel omite the breefe, and pithie aduertisment of a diuine preacher, as wel concerning some special dispositions requisite in al, that wil fruitfully meditate: as certaine

prin.

Examples of Meditation.

Instructions. of holie Scripture for meditation.

Gen. 24. v. 63.

Exo. 14 v. 15. v. 12. 11.

v. 13. 14.

Psal. 18. v. 12. Ps. 38 v 4. Ps. 62. v. 7. 8. Ps. 76. v. 7. 11. 13. Ps. 118. v. 16. & c.

principal pointes, for daylie meditations. The firſt diſpoſition, or preparation is, the true knowlege of thoſe diuine Myſteries, which al the faithful are bond to learne. For otherwiſe cogitations wil be erronious, the minde wil runne into ignorant phanſies, & falſe opinions. Therfore he ſaith [The wiſeman wil ſearch out the wiſdome of the Ancients, and wil be occupied in the Prophers] And becauſe knowlege is not ordinarily gotten, eſpecially of high Myſteries, without prayer to God, and diligent induſtrie to lerne, he addeth, that he which truly ſeeketh knowlege, wil labour for it [wil geue his hart to watch early vnto our Lord, that made him: and he wil pray in the ſight of the Higheſt] The ſecond diſpoſition is puritie of the ſoule, without which, though a man may know the letter of holie Scripture, or other document hiſtorically, yet without true ſanctifying grace, no ſoule can rightly vnderſtand diuine thinges, nor applie his affection, to the pure ſeruice of God. And therfore it foloweth in this ſacred inſtruction, that he which wil conuerſe with God, muſt firſt obtaine remiſſion of ſinnes [He wil open his mouth in prayer, and wil intreate for his ſinnes. For (ſo doing) it wil pleaſe our Lord, and he wil fil him with vnderſtanding: and he wil power forth the wordes of his wiſdome, as ſhowers, and in prayer he ſhal confeſſe to our Lord] So ſhal he alſo fructifie in vertues [As Libanus, ſhal haue the odours of ſweetnes] The third diſpoſition is profound humilitie, confeſſing al knowlege and vertue to be of Gods mere grace, without former merite. [Geue magnificence to our Lord) his name, & confeſſe vnto him in the voice of your lippes: and in ſongues of the lippes, and harpes, and thus ſhal you ſay in confeſſion (of praiſe) Al the workes of our Lord are exceding good] The fourth diſpoſition is hope of eternal reward [His bleſſing (ſaith this diuine Auctor) hath ouerflowed as a ſtreame. And as a floud

hath

Margin notes:

Foure preparations requiſite in thoſe that meditate.

1. Knowlege of diuine Myſterie.

2. Puritie from mortal ſinne.

3. Humilitie.

4. Hope of reward for vertue.

Eccli. 39. v. 1. & 6.

v. 6.

v. 7.
8.
9.

v. 18.

v. 20.
21.

v. 27.

hath watte red the drie land : so his wrath shal inhe-   28.
rite the nations(possessing their landes)that haue not
sought him.Good things were created for the good,
from the beginning: so for the wicked,good things   30.
and euil] These are the special preparations of those
that will fruitfully meditate:to wit, True knowlege
of the pointes wheron they meditate,lest they erre in
iudgement;Puritie from great sinnes,els they can not
be an habitacle of the Holie Ghost: Humilitie ac-   *Sap. 1. v. 4*
knowleging that al good things are the free giftes
of God; And assured confidence , that God wil also
geue a crowne of glorie,to al that perseuer vnto the
end in his grace.

4. Apt matters of meditation , are al pointes of
Christian doctrine : particulatry , Mans creation,pre-
sent state of calamitie, and after this short life,either   *ch. 4. v. 1. &.*
eternal glorie, or euerlasting miserie [great trauel is
created to al men (saith he) and an heauie yoke vpon   *30*
the children of Adam: from the day of their coming
forth of their mothers wombe, vntil the day of their
burying, into the mother of al their cogitations and
feares of the hart, imagination of things to come,   *Eccli 7. v.*
and the day of their ending.] Also in more particu-   *40.*
lar it behoueth to meditate vpon the four last things
[In al thy workes, remember thy later endes,& thou
wilt not sinne for euer]   The first of these is death:
then the which nothing is more certaine : and no-
thing is more vncertaine,then the time,and maner of   *ch. v 1. v. 3. &*
death.Concerning which he saith [O death,how bit-   *&c.*
ter is thy memorie, to a man that hath peace in his   *10.*
riches : to a man that is at rest, and whose wayes are
prosperous in al things. The children complaine of
an impious father, because for him they are in re-
proche] The next thing after death is Iudgement,
which wil be right and iust, according to the state
wherin euerie one dieth [If the tree shal fal to the   *Eccle. 11. v*
South,or to the North,in what place soeuer it shal fal,   *3.*

there

there shal it be] The third & fourth laſt thinges to be
ſtill remembred in our tranſitorie life, are Heauen 　Heauen
and Hel. The one or the other ſhal be adiudged to 　And Hel.
euerie one; both can happen to none. For they are
both eternal: & after ſentence & iudgment are immu-
tabie. Heauen is of incomparable ioy [For no eye hath
ſene, nor eare hath heard, neither hath it aſcended into the hart of man , what thinges God hath prepared
for them, that loue him] Wherof this Preacher ſaith
[Grace is as paradiſe in bleſſings, and mercie remayneth for euer] Hel is quite cōtrarie of more then imaginable torments. Neither is anie appeale to be made
to anie higher tribunal ſeate, the ſentence is paſt already vpon them that are there. For from hel there is
no redemption: nor anie further pleading of their
cauſe. [For in hel there is no accuſing of life] Other
principal matter of godly meditation , are Gods
workes, in making & gouerning the vniuerſal world:
heauen, earth, ſea, and al thinges in them [I therfore
wil be mindful of the workes of our Lord (ſaith the
ſame wiſe man) and I wil ſhew forth which I haue
ſene. By the wordes of our Lord are his workes. The
Sunne illuminating, hath looked throughout al, and
is ful of the glorie of our Lord in his worke. Hath not 　Gods workes
our Lord made the Sainctes, to declare al his merue- 　admirable in
lous thinges: which our Lord the omnipotent con- 　nature.
firmed, to be eſtabliſhed in his glorie] So the incomprehenſible, and ineffable Excellencie of God, may be
admired in mental cogitation , by his workes in the
heauens, in the planetes, & other ſtarres, in meteours,
precious ſtones, gold, ſiluer, and other mettals, in
earth, water, ayre, fire, birdes, fishes, beaſtes, plantes,
and in innumerable particular creatures. But moſt 　His mercie
eſpecially in his workes of mercie and grace The re- 　and grace, are
demption of al men, and ſaluation of the elect. 　more ineſti-
　　　　　　　　　　　　　　　　　　　　　　　　　mable.
　5. Examples of holie perſons , much exerciſed in
ſpiritual meditations, are al the ancient Patriarches,
　　　　　　　　Ll 3　　　　　　　　and

1. Cor. 2. v.
9.
Eccli. 40. v.
27.

Iob 14 v. 13.
ch. 41. v. 7.

Eccli. 42. v.
15.

16.

v. 17.

and Prophets.Especially.S.Iohn Baptist,liuing in the

S.Iohn Baptist deserte from his infancie, to the age of thirtie yeares, *Mat.11.7.9.* in continual contemplation of God,and his workes. *11.* of al heauenlie Mysteries,and mans miseries.Of him *Luc.1.7 15.* said the holie Angel before his conception [He shal be great before our Lord;he shal be replenished with the Holie Ghost, euen from his mothers wombe.He shal goe before Christ(our Sauiour)in the spirite and *16.* vertue of Elias. He is more then a Prophet(saith our *37.* B.Sauiour) There hath not risen among the borne of wemen, a greater, then Iohn the Baptist] Al the

Our B. Ladie, same time (yea also before and after him) the most immaculate, most holie Virgin, Mother of God,seeing,reading, hearing most diuine Mysteries,and her selfe cooperating in manie of the same with God, in the Incarnation, Natiuitie. Education,Miracles,and other sacred Actes of Christ;she kept al these thinges *ch.2.7 19.* (saith the Euangelist) conferring them in her hart] *51.* Our most blessed Lord also,besides his daylie actions with litle rest [went often forth into the mountaine *Luc.6.7.12.* to pray. And he passed the whole night in the prayer *ch.21.7.37.*

And Christ of God. The dayes he was teaching(saith S.Luke)in **our Lord vsed** the Temple, but the nightes going forth,he abode in **much medita-** the mount; that is called Oliuete] Which is further **tion.** shewed to haue bene his frequent exercise,by that which is againe written by an other Euangelist, that immediatly before his Passion [Our Lord Iesus went *Ioan.18.7.* forth wilh his disciples beyond the torrent Cedron: *1.2.* and Iudas(who was then departed from them)knew

So did also the the place:because(saith S.Iohn)Iesus had often resor**Apostles.** ted thither with his disciples] Wherby is also insinuated, that our Lord trayned vp his disciples, in the same holie exercise of meditation,and mental prayer, Neither was S.Paul inferiour in this kinde. For [he *Act.9.7. 5.* was rapt into a traunce three dayes, and did neither *2.Cor.11.7.* eate nor drinke, where he saw in contemplation, so *2.4.* great thinges, as he could not in particular declare]

                                        The

The same Apostle besides daylie preaching? prayed much, and had continual sollicitude of al particular Churches, meditating diuine Mysteries, and charitables workes. To al which he exhorted others. Namely S. Timothee, writing thus to him, and in him, to al spiritual Pastors : yea and to al Christians, according to their seueral states [Neglect not the grace, that is in thee: These thinges doe thou meditate. Be in these thinges, that thy profiting may be manifest to al. Attend to thy selfe] Which diligent actual attention, referring and offering al good workes to Gods honour, and good of soules, is a godlie meditation, and euerie thought desiring anie good thing from God is a mental prayer.

1.Cor.11. v. 28.

1.Tim.4. v.14.15.16.

Euerie good desire is a mental prayer.

Vocal prayer is also necessarie. Especially publique prayer.

ARTICLE 5.

God our heauenlie Father, who knoweth al mens secrete thoughtes, euen as wel as wordes: and [knoweth what is nedeful for his seruants, before they aske him] hath neuertheles ordayned, that they shal aske the same first and principally with their hart, by offering their desire to him, which is done by mental prayer. Besides which his wil is also, that we aske the same necessarie thinges sometimes by Vocal prayer, expressing by the tongue, as by an external instrument, what the minde desireth, that so we may both by soule and bodie, cooperate with his grace, to our owne good. For so he inspired his faithful seruants to inuocate his name, as is noted before, and largely recorded in holie Scriptures: for an euerlasting testimonie, that this external religious action, amongst other, is necessarie to mans saluations.

Iere 17. v. 10 Mat.6.v.8.

Artic.1. Ge.4.v. 26. ch 18 ch.24.28. &.&c.

Though God knoweth our wants, yet we must aske the supplie therof.

2. In the written Law, besides arbitrarie prayers, which euerie one might frame, according to occasions occurring, God prescribed some special formes of pub-

Mat.6.v.25.

Some formes of vocal praiers

publique prayers. As is the set maner, how the Priest
should blesse the people in these determinate words: Nu.6.v.24.
[Our Lord blesse thee, and kepe thee. Our Lord shew 25.
his face to thee, and haue mercie vpon thee; Our
Lord turne his countenance vnto thee, and geue thee 26.
peace. And they shal inuocate my name vpon the 27.
children of Israel, and I wil blesse them] There was
also a particular prayer, and a sette forme of wordes,
when the Arke of God was lifted vp to be caried,
Moyses saying [Arise Lord, and be thyne enimes di- ch.10.v.35.
spersed, & let them flee that hate thee, frō before thy 36.
face] And when it was set downe he said [Returne
Lord, to the multitude of the host of Israel] Al the
people in thankesgeuing for a wel of water, which ch.21.v.17.
God miraculously gaue them in the desert, sang a 18.
Canticle in this maner [Some sang this verse: Arise
the wel: others sang therto: The wel which the prin- Artic.2.
ces digged. &c.] §.2.

3. The Royal Psalmist, not only prayed often, and
sincerely in his hart, but also maketh expresse mention of prayers, and praises to God, by mouth and Psal.50.v.
lippes, saying [Lord thou wilt open my lippes; and 17.
my mouth shal shew forth thy praise. In the euening Ps.54.v.18.
and morning, and midday, I wil speake and declare:
and our Lord wil heare my voice. Because thy mercie
is better then manie liues, my lippes shal praise thee.
So wil I blesse thee in my life: and in thy name I wil
lift vp my handes. And my mouth shal praise with Ps.62.v.4.
lippes of exultation] Neither only in voice and ge- 5.
sture of handes, but also he prayed, and praised God 6.
with musical instruments, inuiting al to doe the same.
[Praise ye our Lord (saith he) in the sound of
Trumpette: praise ye him on Psalter and Harpe. Praise Ps.150.v.3.
ye him on Timbrel, and Quire. Praise ye him on 4.5.6.
stringes and Organes. Praise ye him on wel sounding
Cymbals: Praise ye him on Cymbals of Iubilation.
Let euerie spirite praise our Lord. Alleluia] So the
other

other Prophets teach both to pray, and sing, in hart & spirite, & also in voice and songes: in the hearing of other men [Confesse ye to our Lord, and inuocate his name: make his inuentions (his Decrees and precepts) knowen among the peoples. Sing ye to our Lord, because he hath done magnifically.]

Isa.12.v. 4.5.

4. But did not our B. Sauiour take away vocal prayers, and praises to God, by commanding to pray and adore in spirite? Nothing lesse, For he commandeth both the one and the other. And himselfe for our further instruction practised both [You shal not pray as hypocrites doe] but with sinceritie, humilitie, and that both in hart, and in voice [Thus therefore shal you pray (saith he) Our Father which art in heauen] He prayed kneeling: and being in agonie he prayed the longer, the same wordes [Father if thou wilt take this chalice from me : But yet not my wil, but thyne be done] It is manifest by the practise of the Apostles, that the faithful obserued sette times of prayer in the Temple. For S. Luke writeth that [Peter and Iohn went vp into the Temple, at the ninth houre of prayer] Where no doubt they had as wel a sette forme of prayer, as sette times. Sure their publique prayer was not only mental, but vocal. And vpon special occasion [Al the Apostles with other faithful, with one mind, lifted vp their voice to God, saying: Lord thou that didst make heauen and earth, the sea, and al thinges that are in them: who in the Holie Ghost, by the mouth of our Father Dauid, thy seruant hast said: Why did the Gentils rage, and the people meditate vaine thinges: geue vnto thy seruants with confidence, to speake thy word] praying also in that case, that God would confirme their doctrine by miracles which was granted Further touching vocal and publique prayer in general: S. Paul directeth S. Timothee, to vse foure sortes of prayers. [I desire (saith he) first of al thinges, that obsecrations,

Ioan.4.v. 23. Mat.6.v. 7.5.9.& 6.

Luc.6. v. 31 ch.22.v. 41. 42.43.

Act.3 v.1.

ch.4.v.24. 25.

v.9. 30.

1.Tim.2. v.1.

Puritanes objection against Vocal prayer.

Christ. and his Apostles prayed, both Mentally and Vocally.

pray-

prayers, poftulations, and thankefgiuing be made for
al men] Al which fortes, are in the Holie Maffe. In the
firft part, before the Confecration, are efpecially ob
fecrations. In the Côfecration, vntil the facred Hofte
be receiued, are prayers. After the receiuing, are poftulations, And finally Thankefgeuing, wherof fee the
Annotations vpon the fame wordes of S. Paul, in the
Catholique Edition of the New Teftament.

1.Tim.1.7.1

*Priuate prayer may be in anie language,
though not vnderftood.*

ARTICLE 6.

Pant 19.
Artic.1.2.
Pant 4.
Artic.1.

IN that Proteftants afcribe iuftification, and faluation to onlie faith, confequently they fay, that
good workes are not neceffarie. And fo amongft the
reft, prayer fhould not be neceffarie at al. Which their
opinion being elfwhere confuted, & they confeffing
that it is a good thing (though it were not neceffarie)
to pray, both priuatly & in publique affemblies, haue
raifed an other côtrouerfie, that prayer muft neceffarily be in a tongue, which the people doe vnderftand:
and that otherwife they cannot haue anie fruite therof, neither of priuate nor publique prayer, wherin
though there be no fmal difference, yet in both they
erre from the Catholique doctrine: as we fhal here
breefely declare.

2, Firft therfore concerning priuate prayer, in refpect of God, to whom we pray, our Aduerfaries wil
eafyly grant, that it importeth not in what tongue we
pray, for he knoweth al tongues: Yea he knoweth,
al fecrete cogitations, and fo needeth no information.
He alfo knoweth what is needful for vs, before we
aske, and therfore nedeth no inftruction: and he is alwayes readie to grant the beft thinges, and therfore
needeth not perfwafion. But in refpect of thofe that
pray, it is doubtles better that they vnderftand the
language, in which they pray. For by attending to the

signi-

Al fortes of
prayer are in
the holie Sa-
crifice of the
Church.

If onlie faith
iuftifie then
prayer were
not neceffarie.

In refpect of
God it is not
neceffarie to
pray in a vul-
gar tongue.

signification of the wordes, they may be better instructed what to aske, and their minde may also be more sturred vp, hartely to desire the same good thinges, which are expressed in the wordes. Yet is not this helpe so necessarie, that otherwise their prayers are fruitles. For albeit they vnderstand not the words, yet ioyning their intention, with the intention of the Church. they may in general, desire whatsoeuer the same holie Church asketh by those wordes, & whatsoeuer is needful to themselues, and others, for whom they pray: and may also eleuate their mindes to God, desiring either good thinges in particular, if so it be Gods wil, or in general Gods most glorie and health of their owne, and others foules. And so (themselues being rightly disposed) their prayers are good and fruitful As likewise those that haue knowlege of the language, wherin they pray, and are not attentiue to the signification of the wordes, doe not therby lose al the fruite of their prayers, through euerie distraction & euagation of minde: no though the minde through humane infirmitie, be carried away for a while, into idle, or vaine cogitations, so that they doe not willingly consent thereunto, but perceiuing their distraction, recollect their minde, and renew their actual attention, their prayer is good, and loseth not the merite by vnwilling distractions. Much lesse is it anie losse, but is greater fruite, if the minde be eleuated to other spiritual good cogitations: which is the best attention, and may be had without vnderstanding the wordes of vocal prayers. For this kind of attention, especially feedeth the foule spiritually, and hath reward of God. [Who regardeth the wil, rather then the wordes, and knoweth what is needful for vs (which we know not) and wil geue the same best thinges] though we doe not expresly aske them, so that we desire Gods wil, and [repose our whole

Rom.8. 26.

See Art. 10.

Mat. 6. 7 7.
8.
Ps 54. v.
23.

Al fruite of prayer is not lost for lacke of vnderstanding the wordes.

Neither for lacke of actual attention to those wordes which we doe vnderstand.

care vpon him] which may be perfectly done, without vnderstanding the tongue, wherin we pray.

3. S. Paul also expresly teacheth, that prayer in a strange tongue, not vnderstood by him that prayeth, is good & profitable, saying] If I pray with the tongue, to witte, with a strange tongue, wherof he there speaketh) my spirite prayeth: But my vnderstanding (saith he) is without fruite] that is, hath not anie instruction by the wordes, which I doe not vnderstand: yet hath some other fruite, of his good intention, for he saith [My spirite prayeth] and so reapeth the fruite of my good desire, though I vnderstand not the tongue, in which I pray. Againe the Apostle saith in the same place, concerning thankesgeuing in a strange tongue [Thou indeede geuest thankes wel (where he also addeth] but the other is not edified.] Which sheweth that there is in dede lesse fruit, by reason of the strange tongue, in that kinde of exercise, wherof he there speaketh, but stil there is some good fruite. For he saith [Thou in deede geuest thankes wel] So that in this discourse of the Apostle, is plainly proued, that praying, and geuing thankes in a strange tongue, are not fruitles, but fruitful, & wel done. Howbeit S. Paul in that place, speaketh not purposely of Ordinarie prayers, nor thankesgeuing vsual in the whole Church, but of a particular spiritual exercise amongst the Corinthians. Wherin some errors were comitted, which he here correcteth. As we shal further declare in the next Article. And as for priuate prayers, the Catholique doctrine, and practise is, to pray either in sacred tongue, though not vnderstood, especially in most vsual Prayers, as the Pater noster, Aue Maria, The Office of our B. Ladie, and the like: or els in the vulgar tongues, for those that vnderstand not Latine: Especially in other Prayers, composed for particular causes. But in what language soeuer anie pray, the fruite of their endeauour, and pious worke, stil dependeth

more

S. Paul teacheth, that prayer & thankesgeuing, áre profitable in a strange tongue

1.Cor.14.
v.14.

v.17,

Priuate prayer may be either in a sacred tongue, or in a vulgar.

more vpon the wil, affection, and good defire, then vpon vnderftanding the wordes, which are fpoken. For otherwife if the cheefe ftuite depended vpon vnderftanding the wordes: how few, I pray you, not only among the vulgar people, but alfo of the wifer, and more learned, doe know the proper fenfe of al the wordes of our Lords prayer in Englifh. For exam-ample of the firft petition [Halowed be thy name] or of the fecond [Thy kingdome come] And fo of moft of the reft? It is neceffarie in dede, that al Chriftians be taught, according to their capacitie, as wel our Lords prayer, as the Crede, & Commandments, with the other parts of the chriftian doctrine. That they may both know, and doe, that which is required of euerie one. And touching this particular point, euerie difcrete perfon wil fincerely confider, that al are bond often to recite our Lords prayer, in one language or other. Whether they vnderftand the fenfe therof or no, in anie language.

side note right: Very few doe vnderftād the true fenfe of our Lords Praier, though it be in En-glish.

Publique prayer muft be in a facred tougue, common to manie nations, of diuers vulgar languages.

ARTICLE 7.

NOw concerning publique Prayer, vulgar lan-guage is not conuenient. But as the true Church euer, and euerie where obferueth, it ought to be in a facred language: which is proued diuers waies. Firft for vniformities fake, it is moft meete to be in a tongue which is common to manie nations. Such are efpe-cially the Latine, Greke, and Hebrew. Which as being moft eftemed, are learned in al countries. And are commonly called the three facred tongues: becaufe the holie Scriptures, are moft efpecially written in thē; & becaufe alfo it pleafed the Diuine prouidence that the renowmed Title of our Redemer [IESVS NA-ZARENVS REX IVDÆORVM] should be writen in al thefe

side note right: Hebrew, Greeke, and Latine, are the moft common tongues.

side note right: And are called facred tōgues.

side note left: Io.19. v.19. 20 22.

M m 3   tongues

tongues: as being most common, and most famous of al in the whole world. And being also thus consecrated to God, in the triumphant Title of Christ our Lord, redeming mankind vpon his holie Crosse, they are by this meanes, more sacred then before. Hence it is come to passe, that in al this Weast part of the world, the Holie Sacrifice, and other Diuine Seruice, are performed in the Latine tongue. Wherof this part of Christendome is called the Latine Church. And likewise in al the East part of the same Catholique Church, the same Diuine Sacrifice, & other publique Seruice, are in the Greke tongue And the Christians there are called, The Greke Church. And both parts doe singularly esteme the Hebrew tongue. But by reason, that the Hebrew people the Iewes, refusing Christ our Redemer, and persisting obstinate in their incredulitie, haue no participation with the true Church, there is no part of Christendome call d the Hebrew Church. Neuertheles in such Conuenticles and Synagogues, as they haue, they sing and read their publique seruice, for the quicke and dead, in the Hebrew tongue: notwithstanding that few of them vnderstand the Hebrew: but al commonly speake the vulgar languages of the countries, where they are borne, and dwel. As Italian in Italie Slauonian in Slauonia: German, in Germanie: and so in other places: which confirmeth our present purpose. Neither can Protestants shew, anie other reason, of calling these two general parts of Christendome, The Latine, and the Greke Churches, but because Publique Diuine Seruice hath continually bene performed, only in these two sacred tongues.

2. It is manifest also, which is no lesse proper example, that in the old Testament the Iewes (when the peculiar people of God) had their Publique Diuine Seruice, in their Tabernacle, Temple, & Synagogues, only

Diuine Seruice in the Latine Church in Latiue.

In the Greeke Church, in Greke.

The Iewes haue their publique seruice in Hebrew.

In the old Testament, Publique Diuine Seruice was in Hebrew.

4. *Reg.* 1. 7
v. 31.
ch. 25.
Iere. 43.

only in the Hebrew tongue. Also when they were in captiuitie in Aſſyria, Babylon, and Ægypt. For it is certaine that the Holie Bible, was not tranſlated into Greke, vntil the time of Plolomeus Philadelphus King of Ægypt: ſcarſe threee hundreth yeares before Chriſt. Nor into Latine, but ſince Chriſts time. Much leſſe into anie vulgar language. Moreouer the verie Hebrew text, eſpecially the Pſalmes, which were the greateſt part of Publique Diuine Seruice in the Temple, were aboue the capacitie of the vulgar people to vnderſtand, being indited in meter, & verſe. Wherof let ſincere Engliſh men be Iudges, hauing them now in Engliſh. And the ſame may be conſidered of the greateſt part of the Prophets; of the Canticle of Canticles; and of ſome of S. Paules Epiſtles: and of the Apocalypſe of S. Iohn.

Though holie Sbriptnres be in vulgar tongues, yet they are hard to be vnderſtood.

3. Where we are alſo to obſerue that amongſt the Iewes, there were admitted into the Church of God verie manie thouſands: of Proſelytes that is to ſay, people of the ſame faith, and religion with the Iewes, but of other nations and tongues, who were made participant with them in holie Sacrifices, a nd other Rites [the holie text witneſſing, that at one time, was the number of an hundred fiftie three thouſand ſixe hundred, in the land of Iſrael] in the reigne of King Salomon. And aboue two hundred yeares after, in the time of king Ezechias, is like mention made [of manie Proſelytes, both in the kingdom of Iſrael, & of Iuda: which made a great Paſch, and ſolemnized the feaſt of Azimes, with the Prieſtes, Leuites, and other people in Ieruſalem, ſo great as had not bene in that citie from the dayes of Salomon] Doubtles in al this varietie of Proſelytes, from diuers nations, and of diuers tongues, there were no other holie Scriptures read, nor ſung in their ſolemnities, but only in the Hebrew tongue, which manie vnderſtood not.

Strangers amongſt the Iewes had not publique diuine Seruic. in their vulgar tongues.

3. Par.2. v. 17.

ch. 30. v. 25. 26.

4. Againe

The people
did not heare
the Priestes
prayer in the
Temple.

4. Againe it is euident, that the people did not vnderstand, no nor heare, what the Priest said in his
prayers, for himself and them. For in dede they were
not present with him, nor saw what he did sometimes
in the Temple: especially in the most sacred place, *Exod.30.v.*
called [*Sancta Sanctorum*] where none entred but the 10.
High Priest onlie.] And [when anie Priest offered the *Heb 9.v.6.*
Sacrifice of Incence in the Temple of our Lord, al the 7.
multitude of the people was praying without, at the *Luc.1.v.9.*
houre of incense] as writeth S. Luke, reporting what 10.
was done by Zacharie the Priest. S. Iohn Baptists father. As therfore the Priestes office profited the
people, not hearing him; so did the singing and playing of Psalmes, Hymnes, and Canticles, with voices,
and on musical instruments, profite them that heard,
and vnderstood not anie word, much lesse the sense
of the wordes in particular: but only in general knew
it to be to Gods honour, and their spiritual good.

Neither did
they vnder-
stand what
was song and
plaide on in-
struments.

Moreouer, when not only the multitudes of men and
wemen, but also of children, ioyfully mette our swete
Sauiour, entring into Ierusalem with triumph, and
cried aloud to him: Ho zanna (which they, especially *Mat.21.v.9*
the children, vnderstood not) and the same in the 15.16.
Temple, they did therwith so pleate God, that (the
malignant Pharisees disliking, and reprouing both
them for doing it, and Christ our Lord for accepting

Nor the word
Ozanna,
wherwith
themselues
praised God.

it) he defended, and commended the same solemne *Psal.8.v 3.*
acclamation, saying [Haue you neuer read, that out of
the mouth of Infants, and sucklinges, thou hast perfited praise] Protestants also yet retaine the Hebrew
word, *Amen*] As the Greke and Latine Churches doe,
for the more effectual asseueration, then anie other
tongue can so brefely expresse it.

5. We come now to S. Pauls text, which Prote- *1 Cor.14.v.*
stants wil needes count their strong wal & bulworke 12.&c.
in this Controuersie. But that it maketh nothing at al
for them, euerie indifferent arbiter wil easyly see, and
iudge:

iudge: by confidering the wordes of the Apoftle,& the caufe and fcope of his difcourfe. It is cleare, that he there reprehendeth certaine Corinthians, for ab-ufing fome fpecial extraordinarie giftes of God; ad-uifing them how to vfe the fame better. In particu-lar the giftes were thefe fiue : recited by him in thefe wordes [When you come together (faith he) euerie one of you hath ¹ Pfalme; hath ² a doctrine; hath ³ a re-uelation; hath ⁴ a tongue; hath ⁵ an interpretation.] The firft was, to geue forth a Pfalme of prayer, or praife to God: the fecond, to teach fome thing which others knew not; (which the Apoftle calleth do-ctrine, and prophecie) the third, to reueale fecrete thinges prefent, or to come; (which is an other gift of Prophecie) the fourth, to fpeake ftrange tongues; the fift, to interprete ftrange tongues, tranflating them in-to their owne language. Al thefe giftes they had a-mongft them. Some had one, fome an other; fome alfo more, fome fewer, it is cleare that al had not al. For of their diuerfitie of giftes, together with the pride and indifcretion of fome, arofe emulation, conten-tion, and diforder: fome preferring one gift, & others an other: and fo ftriuing who should fpeake, manie fpeaking together, made great confufion. The fpecial comparifon, and contention was, betwen prophecy-ing (otherwife called doctrine) and fpeaking ftrange tongues. For decifion wherof, the Apoftle faith plain-ly that prophecie, or doctrine, is better then fpeaking ftrange tongues, and that both are good [Folow cha-ritie (faith he) earneftly purfue fpiritual thinges: but rather that you may prophecie. For he that fpeaketh with tongue, fpeaketh not to men, but to God. He that prophecieth, fpeaketh to men vnto edification, and exhortation, and confolation. He that fpeaketh with tongues, edifieth him felfe; but he that prophe-cieth, edifieth the Church. And I would haue you al to fpeake with tongues; but rather to prophecie. For

greater

*1. Cor.14.
7,1,1.&c.*

v.26.

v.1.3.4.5.6

v.1.

2.

3.
4.
5.

S. Paul fpea-keth, Cor.14 Of fiue fpecial gifts, which fome Chri-ftians had ex-traordinarily.

The gift of ftrange tongues is good but the gift of knowlege to teach others is better.

greater is he that propheci[th, then he that speaketh
with tongues] Which he further declareth by exam-   ♈ 7. *& 8.*
ples of instruments, by which, if they yeld a distinct
sound, men are therby directed what to doe, if their
sound be not vnderstood, men are not directed therby. And by example of prayer, in a strange tongue,
which is also good, but is better if it be vnderstood
[If I pray (saith he) with the tongue, my spirite pray-   ♈. 14.
eth: but my vnderstanding is without fruite.] And
therfore for the amending of the disorder fallen a-
mong the Corinthians, through this contention, and
comparison of giftes, he admonisheth them, saying
[He that speaketh with the tongue let him pray that
he may interprete] And so one gift is made better by   ♈ 13.
an other. Yea in regard of edifying, and profiting
others, he addeth, saying [But in the Church I wil   ♈ 19.
speake fiue wordes with my vnderstanding, that I
may also instruct others, rather then ten thousand
wordes in a tongue] He noteth also the inconuenience, and scandal, which procedeth of manie confu-
sedly speaking with strange tongues, that if [there en-   ♈. 23.
ter in (among you) vulgar persons, or infidels, wil
they not say, that you be madde? Let al chinges be   ♈ 26.
done (saith he) to edification. Whether a man speake   27.
with tongue, by two, or at most by three (at one meeting, neither al at once, but [in course, and let one interprete. But if there be not an Interpreter, let him   28.
hold his peace in the Church; and speake to himself,
and to God.] Touching this particular debate, he concluding saith [Therfore brethren be earnest to pro-   ♈. 29.
phecie (to teach & instruct) & to speake with tongues
prohibite not.] And touching al the fiue giftes before
recited, exhorting al to peace and concord, and to a-
uoide al dissention, he saith [Let al thinges be done   ♈. 40.
honestly (comely) & according to order among you.]
In al which correction of a particular abuse of certaine extraordinarie diuine giftes, amongst the
                                               Co-

In that parti-
cular exercise
he willed the
not to speake
in strange
tongue, ex-
cept it were
interrupted.

Corinthians, is no mention at al of Publique Diuine Seruice, or Administration of Sacraments, as is cleare both by that Infidels might haue accesse, and be present in these meetinges of Christians, which they could not be at the solemne Diuine Offices: and by expresse mention of the special thinges, that were abused by some, and here corrected by the Apostle. Neither was the disorder a general fault of manie, nor concerning holie Scriptures in general, nor anie Hymnes, Psalmes, Canticles, or other partes therof, in what language they must be read or song: but only of extraordinarie giftes bestowed vpon a few, and by some of them abused. And so the Apostles admonition, perteyneth specially to the direction of particular congregations, and Sodalities, how to dispose their extraordinarie exercises, to Gods more honour, and their owne, and others edification. That Protestants therfore wil applie this doctrine of S. Paul, against the Publique Diuine Seruice of the Church in the Latine tongue, in the Latine & Weast Church; and in the Greke tongue, in the Greke and East Church, procedeth of grosse ignorance in some: and of mere malice in others: who can not but see how absurdly this holie Scripture is wrested, against publique, or ordinarie priuate prayer in Latine. Wherof the Apostle here treateth not: but only by the way of example, sheweth that extraordinarie prayer, thankesgeuing, or praise to God, in a strange tongue, is good: for [the spirite prayeth. I wil pray in spirite (saith he) I wil sing in the spirite: thou in dede geuest thankes wel] Shewing that al this is good, though doctrine be better. And so notwithstanding this, and al other arguments of our Aduersaries, to the contrarie, it is sufficiently Proued, that priuate prayers may be in anie language; and that publique prayer ought to be in a sacred tongue. It resteth to see what other thinges are required vnto fruitful prayer.

v. 23.

2.26.

The Apostle speaketh not here of Publique prayer in the Church

Neither doth here discusse, In what togue holie Scripture is to be read in the Church.

v 14.
Ps. 17.

Nn 2   Faith

Faith, Hope, Humilitie, Repentance, and other vertues, are required in prayer.

ARTICLE 8.

It more importeth to be wel prepared for prayer; then in what tongue we pray.

EDification and spiritual profite of soules, being the cheefest thing, after the honour of God, which is required in euerie good worke; that our prayers may auaile both our selues, and others, it more importeth that we be rightly disposed, when we exercise this holie worke, coming thertunto with requisie vertues, then in what tongue we pray. And first of al is required true Faith in God [For how shal they inuocare (saith the Apostle) in whom they haue not beleued?] Likewise Hope is no lesse necessarie. For prayer is the proper act of hope. We must also haue repentance for our offences; gratitude for benefites; pietie, meeknes, humilitie, and other vertues, as we are amply instructed, both by examples, and testimonies of holie Scriptures.

Rom. 10. v. 14.

A notable example of a wel qualified praier. VVith Faith. Hope.

Humilitie. Gratitude.

Sinceritie.

Pietie.

2. Iacobs prayer in distresse of minde, fearing his brother Esau, was rightly qualified with manie special vertues. In most perfect faith, inuocating our Lord, he said [O God of my father Abraham, and God of my father Isaac (With confident hope he added) ô Lord that didst say to me: Returne into thy land, and into the place of thy natiuitie, and I wil doe the good, (With humilitie, and gratitude, he proceded saying) I am inferiour to al thy mercies: with my staffe I passed ouer this Iordan, and now with two troupes, I doe returne (Then in simplicitie of hart he proposed his petition, saying [Deliuer me from the hand of my brother Esau; because I am sore afraide of him: lest perhaps he come, and strike the mother with the children] So great was his pietie and solicitude, rather of his familie, then of himself. Then concluding with the same anker of Hope, wherwith he began to pray: & reposing al vpon Gods goodnes & promise, he said [Thou

Gen. 32. 9.

v. 12.

[Thou ô Lord didſt ſay, that thou wouldeſt doe good to me] Neuertheleſſe he vſed withal, his prudence in *Prudence.* diuiding his troupes, and meekenes in ſending preſents to his brother, tokens of his kinde loue: therby *Meekenes.* he mollified his brothers hart, & himſelfe was comforted by an Angel. Who alſo told him, that his name *See moe examples. ſ. 4.* ſhould be changed, from Iacob to Iſrael, and bleſſed him, and ſo al ſucceeded right wel.

3. In general, al conditions requiſite in prayer, are reduced to theſe two: Hatred of ſinne: which is the onlie thing that God hateth: and Loue of vertue, *Hatred of* which bringeth to God. Thoſe therfore which are *ſinne, and loue* burdened with anie mortal ſinne, muſt fiſt of al re- *of vertue com-* ſolue with diligent ſpede to ſeeke remiſſion therof, by *prehend al ne-* due repentance, and by the Sacrament of Penance. *paration to* Without which reſolution, al their prayers, and al *prayer.* other workes are fruitles. Becauſe remayning dead in ſoule, as rotten members, they can not receiue influence from the head, which is Chriſt our Lord, the fountaine of grace. Except therfore the ſoule of man be either free from deadlie ſinne, or penitent with purpoſe to doe al, that is neceſſarie, for remiſſion therof, his prayer, nor other worke auaileth not. But being penitent, prayer is both neceſſarie, and a ſpecial *Vntil a ſinner* meanes to receiue more mercie, and grace from God. *repet, & ceaſe* So did King Dauid crie to God, for remiſſion of greuous ſinnes, ſaying [Haue mercie on me Lord: becauſe *to continue in* I am weake; heale me Lord, becauſe my bones be *ſinne, his pray-* trubled. And my ſoule is trubled excedingly] And *er cannot be* much more in diuers places, is recorded of his earneſt, and frequent prayer, with hartie Contrition, and hate of ſinne. Teſtifying expreſly, that ſo long as anie perſon kepeth ſinne in his hart, or meaneth to continue in that ſtate, his prayers cannot be heard [If I haue beheld iniquitie in my hart (ſaith he) our Lord wil not heare] Yea he deſired and prayed, that himſelfe might be corporally puniſhed, for his owne

Pſal. 44. v. 8.
Sap. 11. v. 25
Rom. 12. v. 9.

Pſ. 49. v. 16.

Pſal. 6. v. 3. 4.
Pſ. 37. v. 4. 5.
Pſ 50. v 3. 4 5.

Pſ. 65. v. 18.

ſinne

sinne, when God punished him temporally, in striking the people, saying to our Lord [I am he that haue sinned, I haue done wickedly: these that are the sheepe, what haue they done? Let thy hand I beseech thee, be turned against me: and against my fathers house. Salomon also denounceth that [He which turneth awaie his eares from hearing]the Law, his prayer shal be execrable] An other diuine Preacher saith [Praise is not comelie in the mouth of a sinner] And the faithful man, whom our Lord cured of his blindnes, auouched confidently according to the common knowne doctrine,' saying: [We know that God doth not heare sinners] which is alwayes vnderstood of such sinners, as persist in purpose to sinne, as yet for a time, and doe not presently leaue their sinne, and detest it.

2. R'g 24: v. 17.

1. Par. 21 v. 17

Pro 28 v 9.

Eccli. 15 v. 9.

Ioan. 9 v. 31.

VVorkes of penance, aad of mercie are as winges of prayer.

Examples of fruitful prayers.

Of al the people in distresse.

Especially of Iudith for the people.

4. Those that are in state of grace, and desire to be heard in their prayers, must so loue al vertues, that they purpose to perseuer; and doe their indeuour to procede from vertue to vertue, wherin nothing is more aualable, then mortification of our selues, and workes of mercie towardes others. So the people of God hearing of Holofernes, his intention to inuade their countrie, and fearing his forces, ioyned mortification, with their prayers to God for helpe [Al the people cried to our Lord, with great instance: and they humbled their soules in fasting, and prayers, the men and their wiues. And the Priestes put on hear-cloathes; and they laide the infants prostrate against the face of the Temple of our Lord. And the High priest went about al Israel, and spake to them saying, Know ye that our Lord wil heare your prayers, if continuing you continue in fastings, and prayers in the sight of our Lord] And when the same Holofernes besieged the citie of Bethulia, the vulgar weaker people murmuring, the Ancients to appeaze them, resolued to render the citie to the enimie, [If releefe

Indith. 4.7 8.9.

v. 11. 12.

should

ch.7.v.1.2. should not come within fiue dayes] But Iudith a
11.13.25. most godlie widow, leading an austere maner of lse,
ch.8.v.1.5. in much prayer, fasting, and wearing hearecloth,
6 to.13.14. [hearing these thinges, rebuked them, for presuming
ch.9.v.1. to appoint a day vnto God, when he should send
&c. ayde. And said: Because our Lord is patient, let vs be
ch.13. penitent for this same thing; and sheding teares let
ch.14. vs desire his pardon] And she in hearecloth, and ashes
lying prostrate in her Oratorie, praying to our Lord,
obtained mercie, power, and courege, to kil Holofernes, & so deliuered al the people from distresse. Like-
Esth.4.v.16. wise Queene Esther, & Mardocheus, with al the peo- Queene Estar
ch.14 v 2. ple, in another distresse, adioyned fasting, and mour- Mardocheus.
ning, with their prayers, and so obtained Gods mer-
Dan.10.v. cie, and protection against their cruel enimies[Daniel Daniel.
2.f.12. mourned three weekes together, neither eating flesh
nor bread, nor drinking wine] And for this voluntarie affliction, his prayer was heard [Feare not Daniel
(said the Angel) because since the first day, that thou
didst set thy hart to vnderstand, to afflict thy selfe, in
the sight of thy Lord, thy words haue bene heard: & I Tobias.
Tob.12.v 8. am come for thy wordes] Holie Tobias, together with
2.Esd.1 4 prayer, exercised fasting, and workes of mercie, wher
&. upon an other Angel said: [Prayer is good with fasting & almes: rather then to lay vp treasures of gold] Esdras.
So Esdras, Nehemias, and al the Prophets, to make Nehemias.
their prayers more grateful to God, fast d, and labo- Al the Pro-
red, admonishing and instructing the people so to do, phets.
not ceasing from workes of mortification Especially
Mar.1.v.4 [S. Iohn Baptist (liued in the wildernes, with admirable abstinence, and continual meditation, and then)
preached penance, for remission of sinne] Christ for Christ and his
Act.1.v.1. our instruction [began to doe (saith S. Luke and then Precursor and
1.Cor.11.v. to teach. Be ye folowers of me (saith S. Paul) as I also his Apostles.
1. of Christ.]

§ More in particular our Lord also required, not only
faith, hope, and repentance, but also humilitie, sinceritie,

Lvc 11.v. 34 35.

Defire of The feuen giftes of the Holie Ghoſt, & the Beatitudes, anſwering therto is requiſite in prayer.

citie, with pure intention, and diligent attention [The candle of thy bodie is thyne eye (becauſe the intention directing al workes to ſome end, makech them better or worſe) If thyne eye be ſimple, thy whole bodie ſhal be light ſome: but if it be naught, thy bodie alſo ſhal be darkſome. See therfore that the light which is in thee be not darknes] So theſe groundes therfore, being fiſt laide together, muſt be ioyned diligent prayer, for obtayning of al other vertues, the ſame in ſubſtance, with the ſeuen Giftes of the Holie Ghoſt, and the ſpecial beatitudes propoſed by our B. Sauiour. The firſt of theſe is Pouertie of ſpirite

Iſa 11.v. 2.
3.

1.
The feare of our Lord, and Pouertie of ſpirite.

Bleſſed are the poore in ſpirite] vnto which rightly agreeth, the Feate of our Lord; which is the beginning of wiſdome, & the firſt gift of the Holie Ghoſt, in order of aſcending: frō the Loweſt, to the Higheſt.

Mat.5.v.3.

2.
Pietie and Meekenes.

The ſecond is Meekenes [Bleſſed are the meeke] wherto agreeth the ſecond gift of the Holie Ghoſt: which is Pietie. For thoſe that piouſly accord with others, without reſiſtance, obtaine their good deſires. The third is mourning, with patient toleration

4.

3.
Knowlege, & Mourning.

of euils in this life [Bleſſed are they that mourne] whereunto anſwereth the third gift, which is Knowlege, wherby they know that thoſe thinges, which before they ignorantly deſired, as good and profitable, are in dede, nothing, but bandes holding them captiues in miſeries. The fourth is a Feruent deſire,

5.

4.
Fortitude and Feruent deſire of iuſtice.

as hunger and thirſt of iuſtic, and perfection [Bleſſed are they that hunger, & thirſt after iuſtice [wherto anſwereth the fourth gift, which is Fortitude, through which they labour ſtrongly to ouercome al impediments: ſo to auert their loue from terrene, and temporal thinges, that they only ſeeke eternal. The fift is Mercie. [Bleſſed are the merciful] wherto anſwereth the fift gift of Counſel; aduiſing & directing to

6.

5.
Counſel and Mercie.

practiſe workes of mercie, towardes others, that themſelues may receiue mercie from God, remiſſion

7.

of

of finnes, and mitigation of punishment, with augmentation of reward. The fixth is a Cleane and pure

8. hart [Bleffed are the cleane of hart] To which anfwereth the gift of Vnderftanding: through which, God and diuine Myfteries are fene, by the eyes of faith, which otherwife no corporal eye, nor other fenfe can fee, nor perceiue. The feuenth is Pacification, or ma-

9. king peace [Bleffed are the peace makers] to which antwereth the greateft, and moft complete gift of the Holie Ghoft, called by the general name, Wifdom. By which al thinges are rightly fo difpofed in order, that no inordinate paffion, may repugne againft reafon: but al other thinges in man, obey his reafonable fpirite: and his fpirite may obey God. The eight Bea-

10. titude [Bleffed are they that fuffer perfecution, for Iuftice (& truths fake) for theirs is the kingdome of heauen] perteyneth to al the former, as an effect of the caufes, and maketh moft happie, in the kingdome of heauen. Where the bleffed fhal be happie in dede, as now they are in hope. There in *Re*, here in *fpe*. Thefe

Sap.8.v.21. feuen gittes therfore, and the anfwerable vertues, or the fincere defire of them, make prayer grateful to God; and profitable to the faithful. And in regard that none can fo much as defire thefe giftes, and vertues of themfelues, as of themfelues, but of the grace, which without merite is geuen, the holie act of prayer, is principally the worke of the Holie Ghoft, and but fecondarily (yet alfo truly) the worke of the faith-

Rom.8.v. 26. ful. Principally therfore it is afcribed to the Holie Ghoft whofe gift it is. [Becaufe (as S. Paul fpeaketh) we not knowing what we fhould aske, the Spirite himfelfe requefteth for vs (that is, maketh vs to requeft) with gronings vnfpeakable] Aud this may fuffice touching fpiritual preparation, to pray rightly. Befides which, fome preparation is alfo profitable in difpofing the bodie.

Oo	*Reuerent*

63.
Vnderftanding & Cleanes of Hart.

7.
VVifdome & Pacification.

The Holie Ghoft maketh the faithful to pray as they ought.

Reuerent, modeſt, and comelie diſpoſition of the
bodie, is alſo required, as an. help to deuotion.

ARTICLE 9

Deu 7 7.
9.10.
1 Cor. 11. 7.
10.

IN three reſpectes it behoueth to order the bodie in
ſemely maner, in the time of prayer. Firſt in regard
of the High Maieſtie of God: before whom , and the
heauenly court of innumerable glorious Angels & o-
ther Saints, we poore ſinners, as ragged beggers, and
loathſome creatures, defiled and deformed by ſinnes,
preſet our ſelues. And therfore we muſt not only prepare our mindes, as is already preſcribed, but alſo obſerue couenient & decent comelines in bodie. Otherwiſe the neglect therof , wil conuince the minde, not
to be ſo diſpoſed, as it ought to be. Secodly, that al the
external members of the bodie, may as ſeruants , attend vpon the ſoule, for better performing this holie
action of prayer. Thirdly the varietie of prayers of
times, & of places requireth diuers diſpoſitions, and
actions of the bodie. For ſomtimes, eſpecially in ſome
prayers, praiſes, or thankeſgeuing, it is moſt conuenient to change the ſituation of the bodie : to knele,
ſtand, ſitte, or walke Likewiſe diuers other geſtures
of the bodie, doe helpe to contrition , to deuotion,
to edification, to attention; and doe alſo repreſent,
and ſignifie diuine Myſteries. Al which are beſt declared, and defended to be good, and godlie (being
done in decent maner, with ſinere intention) by authentical examples recorded in holie Scriptures.

2. Iacob the Patriarch bleſſing Ioſephs two ſonnes
[croſſed his armes, and laide his handes vpon their
heades, and his right hand vpon him, that ſhould be
preferred] and promoted aboue the other. Moyſes
praying (whiles Ioſue fought againſt Amalech their
enemie, lifted vp his handes. And when he was wearie
therwith, he ſate downe vpon a ſtone, and Aaron &
Hur, ſtaide vp his handes on both ſides, & they ceaſed
not

1 Cor. 6. 7.
10.

1 Cor 14. 7
16. 40.

Gen. 48 7.
14. 17.

Exod. 17. 7
11.12.13.

Comelines in
bodie is requi-
red, in regard
of Gods High
Maieſtie.

That the body
may ſerue the
ſoule.

For varietie
of prayers,
times, and
places.

Examples of
diuers corpo-
ral actions in
prayer.

not vntil Sunne sette. Not vntil Iosue had put Amæ- | Crossing the
leeh & his people to flight, in the edge of the sword] | armes.
At an other time [Moyses bowed himselfe flatte vnto | Obseruation
the earth] Also when he prayed for Gods helpe in the | of the right
rebellion of Core, Dathan, and Abiron [he fel flatte | hand.
on his face] Iosue with the whole armie of Priestes, | Lifting vp the
and people, made a Procession round about Iericho, | handes.
euerie day once six dayes together, and the seuenth | Lying on the
day, seuen times; some Priestees carrying the holie | ground.
Arke of couenant, others sounding trumpettes, the | And on the
armed men going before, and the rest of the people | face.
folowing] and so the walles of the towne, not by | Procession
their force, but miraculously falling downe, they en- | with the holie
tred, and possessed the towne. Presently after, God | Arke, & trum-
suffering some of the Israelites to be slaine, and others | pets, seuen
to flee from their enimies [Iosue rent his garments, | dayes, the last
and fel flat on the ground, before the Arke of our | day seuē times.
Lord, vntil euening, and al the armie of Israel with | Renting of
him:& they cast dust vpon their heads] And so prayed | garments.
til God commanded them to finde out, and punish |
an offence committed: which being done [the furie | Lying prostrat
of our Lord was auerted from them] King Dauid | before the
praying for his sonnes recouerie of health, being in | Arke.
danger of death [fasted a fast, and going aside, lay | Casting dust
vpon the ground] Praying for remission of sinnes [he | on their heads
labored in sighing euerie night, washed his bed, and | Fasting.
watered his couch with his teares] Interrupting |
sometimes his nighlie repose [He was minful of God | Sighing.
vpon his bedde, and in the morning, meditated on |
him. And in prayer stretched forth his handes] King | Weeping.
Salomon in his long prayer, in the Dedication of the | Long watch-
Temple, sometime [stood before the Altar of our | ing.
Lord, in the sight of the Assemblie of Israel: and ex- | Stretching out
tended his handes towardes heauen: praised God | the handes.
with thankes for al benefitee] Then adding petiti- |
ons for himselfe and the people, as wel then liuing, | Standing.
as to succede: sometime [he fastned both knees on | Kneeling.

Left margin references:
ch.34.v.5.
Num.16.v.4.

Iosue 6.v.3.
6.13.15.20.

ch.7.v.4.5.
6.19.26.

2.Reg.12.v.10.
Psal.6 v.7.
Ps.62.v 7.

Ps.142.v.6.
3.Reg.8.v.22.&c. ad 55.

2.Par.6.v.12.13.14.
&c.

O o 2   the

the ground,: againe ſpreading his handes towardes 2.*Par.* 6.7.
heauen] Finally [bleſſed al the Aſſemblie, with a loud 12 13, 14.
voice] By which and other like examples, Superiors *&c.*
eſpecially ſpirituall Superiours, bleſſe their ſubiectes.
For Ioſue, Dauid, & Salomon, were both Princes, and 4. *Reg.* 6.7.
Prophets. King Ioram being beſieged in Samaria, by 30.
the King of Syria [rent his garments, and paſſed by
the wal. And al the people ſaw the hearcloth, which *Iudith.* 6.
he ware next vpon his fleſh] So Iudith, and the people ⱱ 14.
in Bethulia. Alſo Heathen people in Niniue, ioyned *ch.7.ⱱ.*4 14
[faſting, aſhes hearcloth (& other penal workes) with *Iona* 3. ⱱ.
prayers to God, for grace and mercie.] 5.6.

Higher and Lower voice. (margin)
Sackcloth. Ashes, &c. (margin)

3. Chriſt our Lord intending to raiſe Lazarus from *Ioan.*11. ⱱ.
death, which he could haue done with one word, or 33.35.
one thought [groned in ſpirite, and trubled himſelf,
(that is, altered his countenance, or voice, like to 38.
one trubled in mind, for he was not at al ſubiect to a-
nic paſſion) and he wept. Againe, groning in him ſelf
he came to the graue. And lifling vp his eyes vpward 41.42.
ſaid: Father, I geue thee thankes, that thou haſt heard
me, and I know that thou doeſt alwayes heare me, 43.
&c. And when he had ſaid theſe thinges, he cried
with a lowde voice. Lazarus come forth] In the gar-
den of Gethſemani, the night before his death, he re- *Mat.* 26. ⱱ.
tyring himſelfe from his diſciples [as it were a ſtones 39.
caſt, fel vpon his face flatte vpon the ground, ſome- *Mar.*14.ⱱ.
time alſo he kneled, he repeted the ſame prayer thriſe: 35.
being in an agonie, he prayed the longer] At the in- *Luc.* 22.ⱱ.
ſtant of his Aſcenſion, when he had brought his diſ- 41.43.
ciples into Bethania [lifting vp his handes, he bleſſed *ca.*24.ⱱ.49.
them. And whiles he bleſſed them, he departed from 50.51.
them, and was caried into heauen] Al which doubtles *Act.*1.ⱱ.2.
are for our inſtruction: and ſo much the more for imi- 9.
tation, as our infirmities require ſenſible ſignes, to
ſturre vp our affections. Beſides which, more proportionable to our weaknes, we may obſerue, that the
penitent [publicane going vp into the Temple to *Luc.*18.ⱱ.
pray, 10.

Chriſt groned in ſpirite. (margin)
VVept. (margin)
Lift vp his eyes. (margin)
Eleuated his voice. (margin)
Lay proſtrate Kneeled. Repeted the ſame prayer. (margin)
Lift vp his Handes. Bleſſed. (margin)
Penitents vſe geſture of hu-miliation. (margin)

v.13. pray: ſtood a farre of, and would not ſo much as lift *Decline their* vp his eyes towardes heauen : but he knocked his *eyes.* breaſt, ſaying : God be merciful to me a ſinner] And *Strike their* [The multitude of them that were preſent together, *breaſtes.*

ch. 23. v. 48. (at the death of our Lord vpon the Croſſe) & ſaw the thinges that were done ; returned knocking their breaſtes] S. Paul exhorteth al to obſerue not only

1. Cor. 11. v. 4.5. decencie in their ſpiritual exerces : and that men

ch.6. v. 20. pray barehead, wemen with their heades couered:

ch.9. v. 17. and the like, but alſo [to glorifie God, and beare God

2 Cor. 12. v. in our bodie] Yea further by his example, that toge-

7. ther with prayer, we puniſh the bodie. For ſo he pray-ing, that the pricke of the fleſh might depart from *S. Paul chaſti-* him [chaſtiſed his bodie, to bring it into ſeruitude, *ſed his Bodie:* that the fleſh might not rebel, but ſerue the ſpirite-Farre more like, that he chaſtiſed his bodie by whip ping his backe, then only by ſtriking his breaſt.

4. According therfore to theſe examples, and in- *Al external* ſtructions, Holie Church, and her faithful children, *Rites and ge-* with ſpecial care diſpoſe external Rites, and corporal *ſtures are done* actions, with comelie varietie: ſometimes kneeling *that the mind* vpon their knees, ſometimes proſtrate on the ground, *may be more* ſometimes ſtanding, ſometimes fitting, ſometimes go- *attentiue.*

Mat.21. v. ing, and otherwiſe agreable to the varietie of Myſte-

8.9. ries, times, places, and other circumſtances, as wel in publique, as in priuate prayers: al to the more honour of God, & to helpe our owne infirmitie, to more per-fect attention, wherin conſiſteth the eſpecial efficacie of al faithful prayers. As we ſhal yet further declare.

Attention is ſo neceſſarie, that the more or leſſe it is, the more or leſſe is the fruite of prayer.

ARTICLE 10.

FOrſomuch as prayer is an act of the mind, it conſi- *None doe* ſteth noin the vttering of words with the tongue, *pray, vnleſſe* but in the cogitation of the wil, intending to aske *they intend* *to pray.*

ſome-

some thing of God, or to praise or thanke him. Without which intention of the minde , wordes are no
prayer at al. (for some birdes, and other brute creatures, may pronounce wordes) but a reasonable creature intending to pray, must actually applie his wil
therto, with purpose to be attentiue vnto this holie
exercise, that is , to haue at least one of these three
kindes of attention. The first and least is, to attend in
vocal prayer, to pronounce al the wordes distinctly
which those also may doe that vnderstand them not.
The second is, to attend to the sense of the wordes,
which none can do, vnles they vnderstand them. The
third and best attention is, to attend vnto some good
cogitation, perteyning to Gods honour, or health of
soules, which al may haue, whether they pronounce
wordes or no. And those that vnderstand the wordes,
may haue al the three attentions together in vocal
prayer: And in mental prayer, the last attention alone
sufficeth.

2. But concerning vocal prayer, wherto we are
bound by anie precept, vow, or other promise , the
first attention is most necessarie. For in such prayers,
we are especially obliged so to pronounce the words
that we doe not willingly omitte, nor grosely corrupt anie word. And so hauing once actual purpose
to discharge this dutie, if we doe in deede recite the
wordes, though in the meane time, through humane
infirmitie, our minde be carried away by distraction
in to other thoughtes, yet it is not transgression of
precept, vow, or other obligatiõ (for so to iudge, were
to kil the soules that dye not) but only it is more or
lesse sinne of negligéce, because we ought with more
diligence to performe this dutie. In such Vocal
prayer, it also helpeth much to attend to the sense of
the wordes, because therby we shal be more secure,
that we pronounce the wordes rightly; and our mind
may be also directed, to thinke vpõ the good thinges,
signi-

Marginal notes (left):
Three kindes of inteation.
To the words.
To the sense of the words.
To other good desire.
In vocal prayer of obligation, the first attention is most necessarie.
The second is very profitable.

Marginal notes (right):
Mat.6. 7. 5.
7.
I.Cor. 14. 7.
14.15.
Joan. 4. 7.
24.

Ezech. 13. 7.
19.

Pro.30. 7.
33.

signified by the wordes. Which is the best attention, so there be no grosse errour in reciting the wordes. And in mental prayer there is no necessitie of words to be vttered, but of good thoughtes only: which neuerthelesse are better directed by the helpe of words. So that in al sortes of prayer, as wel of obligation, as otherwise voluntarie, vocal, or only mental, albeit euerie euagation of the minde from actual attention, maketh the prayer lesse fruitful, yet not altogether fruitles: so long as there remaineth virtual attention: that is, vntil we intend to cease for that time, from prayer, and to doe some other different thing. But if perceiuing our selues to be distracted, we doe willingly thinke vpon other thinges, we lose the merite of prayer, vntil we correct the distraction, and renew our intention, to be attentiue, because voluntarie consent of the minde, to thinke vpon other affayres, is in deede an intermission of prayer; and is an other action, good or euil, according to the qualitie therof: and so is to be iudged, as the mind is otherwise wel or euil imployed For as of wordes, so also of thoughtes, account is to be rendred.

And the third is the best.

Euerie distraction in prayer diminisheth the fruite, but doth not wholie destroy it.

Mat 12. v. 10.

3. Here in further confirmation of the necessitie, and great vtilitie of attention in prayer, we may remember these especial examples, and aduertisements. Holie Anna the mother of Samuel, praying to God in her hart, [only her lippes moued, but voice there was not heard at al. And she powred out her soule, in the sight of our Lord] The Royal Prophete said in his sprite to God [To thee ô Lord I haue lifted vp my soule. My mouth shal speake wisdome, and the meditation of my hart prudence. To him haue I cried with my mouth, and haue exulted vnder my tongue] For of the abundance of the hart, the tongue speaketh. So King Ezechias. Manasses, Iosias, Daniel, Susanna, prayed with diligent attentions. Salomon wel considering, that without attention, no man can pray at al:

Examples of diligent attention in prayer.

Holie Anna.

King Dauid.

King Salomon & other Prophets admonish the same.

See Artic. 4.
1. Reg. 1. v. 13.
Psal. 14 v. 2.
Psal. 48 v. 4
Ps 65 v. 17.
Ps. 85. v. 4.

pray at al, prayed our Lord, that he wil vouchfafe to
heare the prayers of thofe that shal doe penance in
their hart, returning to God in al their hart, and al
their foule]E cclefiafticus faith, that he which prepareth not his foule before prayer[tempteth God]Of al
such as pretend to pray, without attention of the
mind[Our Lord faith by his Prophete Ifaias. [This
people approcheth with their mouth, and with their
lippes glorifieth me: but their hart is farre from me]
For in dede negligent prayer, without attention, ar-
gueth, that the intention is not fo fincere as it ought
to be. Of which maner of praying, the Prophete Ieremie faith [Cursed be he that doth the worke of God
fraudulently] or negligently, as the Seuentie Interpreters tranflate. And our Sauiour in the Gofpel alleageth the fame prophecie of Ifaias, againft the
Scribes and Pharifees, who were both fraudulent in
their intentions, and negligent in attention, when
they pretended to pray, or praife God; ftil thinking
how to make their temporal profite.

3.Reg 8. v.
33.47.48 49

Eccli. 18. v.
23.

Ifa 29.v.1.

Iere.48.v.
10.

Mat.15.v.8.
v.5 6t
ch.23.v.14.

4. Our Lord therfore requireth both pure intention, & careful attention in prayer [When thou shalt
pray, enter into thy chamber, and hauing shutte the
doore, pray to thy Father in fecrete]Which diuine inftruction, coteyneth two fpecial precepts:the firft co-
cerning fincere intention, to auoide nypocrifie, vain-
glorie, and filthie lucre. The fecond, concerning
internal and hartie attention, to exclude al extraua-
gant thonghts of other affayres, in the time of prayer:
fo fequeftring the mind from al fuch cogitations, that
it may wholly attend to thofe onlie thinges, which
perteyne to the prefent action of praying. For whether the prayer be publique or priuate; mental or vocal, of thankes, praifes, or petitions to God: it ought
to be with diligent attention of the hart, (speaking in
fecrete to God, & free, fo much as may be, from other
thoughts. [And then wil thy heauenly Father, which
feeth in fecrete, repay thee]a ful reward.

Mat 6.v.6.

Chrift teach-
eth his fer-
nants to pray
with pure In-
tention, and
diligent At-
tention.

Prayer vvith due conditions, is meritorious.
And is alvvayes granted by God.

ARTICLE II.

OF the assured effect of prayer, which is made
with requisite conditions. We haue very manie
testimonies, and examples in holie Scriptures. So
Abraham obtayned the safetie of Lot, and his familie,
and had obtained for more if they had bene rightly
disposed. [For when God subuerted the cities of Sodom, Gomorrhe, and others of that countrie, he remembring Abraham, deliuered Lot out of the sub-
uersion of the cities, wherin he had dwelt] Abrahams
seruant being sent by his master into Mesopotamia,
prayed that God would prosper his busines, and also
by a special meanes, direct him therin [when he had
scarse ended his prayer within himselfe, al succeeded
according to his good desire. Isaac besought our Lord
for his wife Rebecca, because she was barren, who
heard him, and made her to conceiue] When the
people of Israel had by their sinne of idolatrie, deserued to be vtterly destroyed, our Lord God preuenting Moyses his prayer, which he would make for
them, said to him [Suffer me that my furie may be
angrie against them, and that I may destroy them, and
I wil make thee into a great nation] Neuerthelesse so
potent is the prayer of the iust, that God suffered himselfe to be hindered by Moyses, his intercission from
doing that which he had so iustly threatned, and they
had most iustly deserued. It is wonderful also that
Moyses durst presume to intreate in this case. But as
S. Paul instructeth vs: Albeit [the sensual man per-
ceiueth not those things, that are the Spirite of God;
for it is foolishnes to him, & he can not vnderstand:
yet the spiritual man iudgeth (discerneth) al thinges.]
For euen so Moyses a right spiritual, and most intelli-
gent seruant of God, notwithstanding that God said

Marginal notes (left):
Gen.18.v. 22.23.32. &c. ch.19.v.12. 15.29.

ch.24.v.12. 25.18.48.

ch.25.v.21.

Exod.32.v. 10.11.12. 13.14.

1.Cor.2.7. 14.15.

Marginal notes (right):
Examples of the effect of prayers; of Abraham.

Abrahams seruant.

Isaac.

Moyses ob-tained, though God himselfe willed him not to aske.

Spiritual men know Gods wil, when sen-sual men vn-derstand it not.

Pp — vnto

vnto him, [Suffer me, that my furie may be angie
againſt them, and that I may deſtroy them; and I wil
make thee into a great nation]yet for the cõſeruation
of the ſame people [he beſought our Lord his God, Exod ; 2.
ſaying : Why Lord is thy furie angrie againſt thy peo- v. 1.
ple, whom thou haſt brought forth of the land of
Ægyt, in a geeat power, and ſtrong hand:Let not the
Ægyptiás ſay,I beſeech thee:He hath craftely brought v.12.
them forth , that he might kil them in the mountaines, and deſtroy them from the earth.Remember v.13.
Abraham , Iſaac, and Iſrael thy ſeruants , to whom
thou ſwareſt by thyne owne ſelfe,that thou wouldeſt v 31.32.
multiplie, and proſper them] Againe he added[Lord
I beſeech thee, either forgeue them this treſpaſſe, or
if thou doe not,ſtrike me out of the booke that thou
haſt written] Thus holie Moyſes prayed [And our
Lord was pacified , from doing that euil which he
had ſpoken againſt his people.]

2.   That holie Moyſes praying for the ſinful people
Gods ſeruants committed to his charge, did in ſuch maner vrge his
conceiue rea-
ſons to moue petition,as it were alleaging reaſons,why God ſhould
themſelues to grant his requeſt , was not to moue God , who is im-
confidence in mutable, and of himſelf moſt merciful : but it was to
God, though ſturre vp himſelf more and more, and to fortiſie his
God himſelfe, owne faith and confidence in God: and alſo his chari-
is immutable. tie towards God (ſeeking principally his honour) and
toward the people, ſeeking their ſafetie in ſoules and
bodies. His firſt reaſon to this purpoſe, was his conſideration of Gods honour, by mitigating his iuſt furie,
and conſeruing his peculiar people , whom he had
choſen, protected, and proſpered thus farre,whom if
he ſhould now deſtroy,he ſhould ſeme to ouerthrow
his owne worke and to fruſtrate his owne wil , and
good pleaſure. And therfore he ſaid [Why Lord is thy
furie angrie? &c.] His ſecond plea was alſo grounded v.11.
vpon Gods honour, leſt the wicked enimies round
about, should calumniouſly ſay: that God could not,

of

or would not conserue his owne people, nor aduance them as he had purposed. Wherupon Moyses said [let not the Ægyptians say, I besech thee, &c.] Thirdly he proposed the sanctitie of the Patriarches their next progenitours, to whom God for reward of their merites, had promised prosperitie to their seede. Therfore he said [Lord remember Abraham Isaac, & Israel thy seruants, &c.] Fourthly wheras God had proposed to Moyses to preferre, and aduance him otherwise, ouer a greater nation then this: he for his great charitie towards them, being his proper charge, desired rather to be punished himself in stead of them, then that they should be destroyed, and he otherwise promoted, and so prayed God, saying [Either forgene them this trespasse, or strike me out of the booke, which thou hast written, &c.] As if he should say. Separate not them and me asunder, but either pardon, & saue them with me; or punish me with them. By this worthie example, among manie others, true Christians are alwayes moued with al confidence to pray for the whole Church of Christ, his inheritance, most deerly purchased with his owne bloud: that albeit the greatnes, and multitude of sinnes committed by Christians, iustly deserue our vtter destruction from the face of the earth; or to be depriued of Gods grace, and suffered to fal into Turcisme, Paganisme & Atheisme, wherinto Heresie tendeth: yet must we assuredly confide, and confidently pray, that Gods furie wil not be angrie according to our iniquities: nor suffer that his enimies may truly say; Christ hath lost his inheritance in earth, but that he wil both remember his owne purchase, and the intercession also of al his glorious Martyrs, and other Sainctes, & accept of the charitie of such, as imitated [Moyses estiming more of the reproch of Gods seruants in his Church, then of the riches of Ægypt] & haue geuen their liues, that others may be pardoned, and saued.

v 12.
v 13.

p.31.12.

Act.10.7.

Heb.11.7.
14.15.16.
40.

So it is cer-
taine, that the
like prayers,
for the whole
Church shal
stil be heard.

And therfore it is moſt certaine that ſuch prayers ſhal
be heard, and granted, eſpecially for the whole viſible
Church in general.

3. Concerning alſo the aſſured efficacie of confident prayer, for particular good cauſes: Ioſue in his
great confidence lifting vp his hart vnto God [ſaid
before al the people : Thou Sunne againſt Gabaon
moue not: and thou Moone againſt the valley of
Aialon. And the Sunne, and the Moone ſtood ſtil, til
the people reuenged themſelues of their enimies: our
Lord obeying the voice of a man : and fighting for
Iſrael] As likewiſe before, in the ſiege and taking of
Iericho:& after in the conqueſt of al the land of Chanaan, they preuailed more by faithful prayer, confi-
ding in God, then by force of armes. And al other
faithful Captaines, Iudges, Kinges, and ſeruants of
God, adioyning prayer with their induſtrious endeuours, knowing that otherwiſe [mans helpe is vaine]
& truſting in the name of our Lord, ouercame kingdomes, turned away the forces of foreners, and obtayned their godlie requeſtes, in prayer made with
faith, hope, and other vertues. You may number a-
mongſt manie the examples, of Anna, Ezechias, Manaſſes, Suſanna and others.

4. Amongſt other holie Prophetes, the Royal Pſalmiſt very often teſtifieth the aſſured fruite of deuour
prayer [They that ſeke after our Lord (ſaith he) ſhal
not be diminiſhed of anie good. Becauſe in thee ô
Lord I haue hoped, thou wilt heare me, ô Lord, my
God. The God of hoſts is with vs: the God of Iacob
is our defender. Thou my God haſt heard my prayer.
Dilate thy mouth (ſaith God to al that rightly ſerue
him) & I wil fil it] Breefly this Prophete compriſeth
in few words the ſpecial cauſes, why God wil grant al
that is demanded with right conditions, praying and
teaching others to pray in this forme, or the like [In-
cline thyne eare ô Lord, and heare me : becauſe I am
needie

*Alſo in parti-
cular cauſes
God heareth
al prayers
rightly made.*

ch.6.3.4.2⊕
ch.8.9. ad
13.
Iudic.4 ⑥.
12 14 15.
16.

Pſal 59.⑦.
13.
Heb.11.⑦.
3⑥.

*Teſtimonies,
that God grā-
teth al good
petitions.*

Pſal 33. ⑦.
11.Pſal⑦.
⑦.16
Pſ.45.7.12.
Pſ.66 ⑦.6.

Pſ 80 ⑦ 11.

Pſ.85.⑦⑦.

2. needie, and poore. Kepe my foule, becaufe I am holie, faue thy feruant my God, that hopeth in thee. Haue

3. mercie on me ô Lord, becaufe I haue cried to thee, al

4. the day. Make ioyful the foule of thy feruant, becaufe to thee ô Lord haue I lifted vp my foule. Becaufe

5. thou ô Lord art fwete: & milde: and of much mercie to al that inuocate thee}The firft requifite condition here expreffed is Humilitie: acknowleging our owne neede, and pouertie, being in want of manie neceffarie thinges, not able of our felues to procure them;

v.1. faying [Heare me, ô Lord, becaufe I am needie, and poore.]The fecond condition is to deteft finne, and

2. profeffe vertue, faying [keepe my foule, becaufe (in defire, and good purpofe) I am Holie] The third con-

3. dition, is Hope and confidence in God, faying [Saue thy feruant, my God, that hopeth in thee] The fourth

4. is conftant perfeuering in prayer, faying[Haue mercie on me, ô Lord, becaufe I haue cried to thee al the day] The fifth is due attention of mind, faying [Make ioyful the foule of thy feruant, becaufe to thee, ô Lord, haue I lifted vp my foule] Thefe fiue conditions being in competent maner, according to good wil and defire performed, are grateful caufes in the fight of our merciful Lord & Maker: Why he wil grant our petitions. To which fiue (with others of mans part implied therein, al being of Gods gift) are adioyned three other greater caufes of Gods owne part: which infinitely excel the former. So the fixt caufe why God heareth his feruants prayers, is his owne natural Benignitie; alwayes readie to beftow benefites. The feuenth his Diuine Meeknes, euer prone to remitte offences. The eight is his infinite Mercie (Which is ouer al his workes) mitigating punifhments, and augmen-

v.5. ting rewardes to al that ferue him, and inuocate his name [Becaufe thou ô Lord, art fwete, and milde, and of much mercie to al that inuocate thee] For al which caufes we may with affured confidence pray in thefe,

Eight fpecial caufes; why God granteth faithful prayers.

1. Mans neceffitie.

2. Repentance with purpofe to liue wel.

3. Confidence.

4. Perfeuerance.

5. Attention.

6. Gods owne Benignitie.

7. His Meeknes

8. His Mercie.

or like wordes, as it foloweth in the same Pſalme [Re- *v.6.*
ceiue my prayer with thyne eares; and attend to the *7.*
voice of my petition. In the day of my tribulation, I *8.*
haue called to thee, becauſe thou haſt heard me. There *Pſ.101.v.*
is not the like to thee amongſt goddes, ô Lord: and *8.18.19.*
there is not according to thy workes. Our Lord hath
reſpected to the prayer of the humble; & he hath not
deſpiſed their petition. Let theſe thinges be written
vnto an other generation: and the people, that ſhal be
created, ſhal praiſe our Lord] This therfore is the perpetual teſtimonie of the Royal Prophete, which he *Pſal.106.*
writte for al generations to remember [that the faith- *v.6.13.19.*
28.
ful ſeruants of God cryed to our Lord, when they *Pſ.118.v.*
were in tribulation, and he deliuered them out of *26.&c.*
their neceſſities] Foure times repeted in the ſame
God neuer Pſalme, and very often elſewhere in the ſame ſenſe. *Pſ.33 v.16.*
granteth the Salomon likewiſe teſtifieth, that God wil heare the
petition of a- iuſt and penitent: and wil not heare the obſtinate im- *Pro.15 v.*
nie perſiſting penitent, ſaying [Our Lord is farre from the impious: *29.*
wilful immor- and he wil heare the prayer of the iuſt.]
tal ſinne.

5. Scarſe anie other doctrine is oftner repeted: by *Mat.7.v. 8.*
God is more our B. Sauiour, then the neceſſitie, and the aſſured *9.*
careful, and effect of daylie prayer. [Which of you (ſaith he to *Luc. 11.v.*
willing to thoſe that aske, ſeke, and knocke) if his childe ſhal *11.*
grant good re- aske bread, wil he geue him a ſtone? Or if he ſhal *12.*
queſts, then a- aske him fiſh, wil he geue him a ſerpent? Or if he ſhal *v.13.*
nie earthly aske an egge, wil he reach him a ſcorpion? If you then
father. being naught, know now to geue good thinges to
your children: how much more wil your Father,
which is in heauen, geue good thinges to them that
aske him?] In his laſt Sermon the night before his
Paſſion, our Lord exhorting al to pray, promiſed to
grant whatſoeuer ſhal be rightly asked in his name
[Becauſe (ſaid he) I goe to the Father, whatſoeuer *Ioan.14.*
you ſhal aske in my name, that wil I doe: that the Fa- *v.13.)*
ther may be glorified in the Sonne. If you ſhal aske
me anie thing in my name (ſaith he againe) that wil

I doe

I doe] This his readines to grant al reasonable petitions, our Lord manifested often by fact, both in this
life, and after his Ascension [He presently turned water into Wine. When his blessed Mother did but in-
sinuate others want, and her owne desire to haue it
supplied. He presently cleansed the Leper, which
professed his beleefe, that he could if he would, make
him cleane. He healed the Centurions seruant, which
acknowleged himselfe vnworthie, that our Lord
should come into his house. He remitted Marie Mag-
dalens sinnes; because she was hartely penitent: and
loued God much. He healed the womans daughter of
Chanaan, perseuering in her suite. He came to the
house of Zacheus, who was so desirous to see him,
that being litle of stature, and not able to see him, for
presse of the multitude, he climed into a tree, that so
he might looke vpon him. And manie the like. Also
after his Ascension, he granted abundance of grace,
and constancie to his Apostles, and other faithful, for
which they [with one accord prayed] He granted the
general prayer of the Church, for S. Peters deliuerie,
forth of prison. He granted to S. Paul the safetie of
himself, and of al that were with him in danger of
drowning. And continually innumerable petitions
were dayly obtayned, through Gods owne Benignitie, Meekenes, and Mercie. Yea he is not only most
readie to grant as a father, al the good petitions of his
children, but also preuenteth al petitions, geuing
grace to aske; without which grace none at al could
aske anie thing rightly. And therfore S. Paul diuinely
demonstrateth, that for so much [as when we were
sinners, Christ died for vs: and wheras we can not
thinke a good thought of our selues, as of our selues,
he geueth grace to thinke good thoughtes, and to
aske good thinges: much more, being iustified by his
blood: and of enimies being made freindes: yea his
children

Margin left references:
Ioan.2.v.
3.5.7.8.9.

Mat.8.v.2.
3 8.13.

Luc.7 v.37.
47.

Mat.15.v.
27.

Luc.19.v.2.
9.

Act.4.6.24.
29.30.

ch.12.v.5.

ch.27.v.24.

Rom.5.v.8.
9.
2.Cor 3.v.5.

Margin right notes:
God is speci-
ally glorified
by granting
petitions in
Christs name.

God preuen-
ting, maketh
his children to
aske good
thinges.

children, we shal be saued from wrath by him, and be
heard of him in al conuenient petitions.

6. And as the holie Apostles had experience in
themselues: so they teach others, that the effect of
prayer is assured in al thinges, that are duly asked
[Euerie creature of God is sanctified (saith S. Paul) by
the word of God, and prayer. The continual prayer
of a iust man (saith S. Iames) auaileth much. The eyes
of our Lord are vpon the iust (saith S. Peter, according
to the Psalmist) and his eare vnto their prayers: but
the countenance of our Lord (his wrath) vpon them
that doe euil thinges. If our hart doth not reprehend
vs (saith S. Iohn) we haue confidence toward God.
And whatsoeuer we shal aske, we shal receiue of him:
because we kepe his commandments: and doe those
thinges which are pleasing to him.] S. Iude also exhorting al to pray, assured vs of good effect, saying
[You my dearest, building your selues vpon our most
holie faith, praying in the Holie Ghost, kepe your
selues in the loue of God; expecting the mercie of our
Lord Iesus Christ, vnto life euerlasting.]

7. Neither is the assured good effect of prayer to
be doubted of, because God oftentimes granteth not
the very thing, which in particular is desired, and
asked, as health of bodie, deliuerie from vniust persecution, or the like: for then in place therof, he geueth
that which is farre better: to wit, increase of grace to
beare affliction with patience, and strongly to resist
tentations, with good contentment to want the fulfilling of our proper wil; and to resigne the same to
Gods wil. So our Lord answered S. Paul [My grace
sufficeth thee: for power is perfited in infirmitie.
Gladly therfore (said the same Apostle) wil I glorie in
myne infirmitie, that the power of God may dwel in
me. For the which cause I please mytelfe, in infirmities; in contumelies; in necessities; in persecutions; in
distresses for Christ: for when I am weake, then am I
mightie]

Marginal notes:

The Apostles inculcate the same doctrine.

1.Tim.4 v.5.
Iac.5.v.16.
1.Pet.3.v.1.
Psal 33. v. 16.17.
1.Ioan 3. v. 21.22.

Iudic..v. 20.21.

VVhen our heauenly Father granteth not that which is rightly asked, he geueth that which is better.

2.Cor.12.v. 9.10.

mightie] And our Sauiours inſtruction is alwayes to be remembred, ſaying to al his children[Your Father knoweth what is needful for you] And therfore as al the aboue recited holie Scriptures abundantly proue, God our heauenlie Father, always heareth the prayers of the iuſt. And wil grant their petitions, when, and in what maner is moſt expedient.

Mat. 6. v. 8.

VVe are bond to pray for the VVhole militant Church. And particularly for the ſpiritual Paſtors therof.

ARTICLE 12.

IT foloweth now , hauing declared the diuers kindes, qualities, and affect of holie prayer , to ſhew brefely for whom eſpecially we are bond to pray. And firſt it is cleare , that c aritie of euerie one beginneth with him ſelfe. And therfore al are moſt ſtrictly bond to pray for themſelues: & conſequently for others : becauſe we muſt loue our neighbours as ourſelues. It is cleare alſo by the Law of nature, that as euerie member of a whole bodie, muſt in ſome ſort ſerue and helpe the other partes; ſo eſpecially the inferior parts muſt ſerue the ſuperiour, or more excellent: and al the reſt muſt ſerue the head, for better conſeruation of the whole bodie. Agreable wherto it was ordained in the written Law of God, to offer Sacrifice (which is the moſt principal kind of prayer) for ai the people in general; alſo for Prieſtes in ſpecial, and ſingularly for the Highprieſt, and in like maner for the Temporal Prince. And for particular perſons, according to diuers occaſions; & al in diuers maners. Practiſe wherof is recorded in the Conſecration of Aaron the Highprieſt, and of other Prieſtes. Likewiſe of Leuites. Agaıne in the ſubſtitution of Eleazarus to ſuccede Aaron; and of Ioſue to ſuccede Moyſes in temporal regiment; and in manie other occaſions.

Euerie one is bound to pray for himſelfe. And for the whole church.

Sec Art. 1. §. 1.

Leuit. 4. v. 13. 22. 27.

ch. 8. v. 14.

Nu t. v. 9 ch. 10 v. 16. ch. 27. v. 1. 18.

2. The Royal Prophete prayed in general for the whole Church, saying [Deale fauorably ô Lord in *Pfal 50.* thy good wil, with Sion] He inuiteth alfo al men to *v. 10.* pray for the fame caufe, faying[Aske the thinges that are for the peace of Ierufalem, and namely for the *Pf. 101. v. 6* Clergie [Let thy Prieftes be clothed with iuftice] and particularly for the chefe Superior, becaufe grace *Pf. 31. v. 9.* procedeth by the head to the members) faying[As *Pf. 132. v. 2.* ointment on the head, which ranne downe vnto the hemmes of his garment] In fpecial maner likewife he prayed for euerie Superior fpiritual, or temporal, adioyning his owne prayer, with the fame Superiors *Pf. 19. v. 2.* prayer, faying [Our Lord heare thee in the day of *3. 4. 5.* tribulation: the name of the God of Iacob protect thee. Send he ayde to thee, from the holie place: and from Sion defend he thee. Be he mindful of thy Sacrifice; and be thy Holocauft made fatte. Geue he vn- *.6* to thee according to thy hart, and confirme he al thy counfel. We shal reioyce in thy faluation : and in the *7.* name of our God, we shal be magnified : Our Lord accomplish al thy petitions.]

3, Chrift our Lord paffed the whole night in the prayer of God: before he conftituted his twelue Apoftles. He bade al his difciples to pray that the Church *Luc 6. v 12.* might haue fpiritual Paftors [The harueft truly is *ch. 10 v. 2.* much (faid he) but the workemen few: Defire therfore the Lord of the harueft, that he feud workemen into his harueft.] When an Apoftle was to be chofen to fupplie the place, from which Iudas was fallen, the other Apoftles, with the reft of the Church, prayed for a good election, faying[Thou Lord that kuow *A.7. 1. v. 24.* eft the hartes of al men; shew of thefe two, one, whom *25.* thou haft chofen, to take the place of this Minifterie, *26.* and Apoftleship] they had in their iudgements felected two of the whole companie, whom they fuppofed to be fitte, Iofeph and Matthias.[And (after their prayer) the lotte (by Gods direction) fel vpon Matthias

Proued by holie Scriptures.

Chrift and his Apoftles teach that al are bónd to pray for the Clergie.

Matthias; and he was numbred with the eleuen Apoſtles] When the perſecuters punished and threatned the Apoſtles, they and others[with one accord lifted vp their voice to God, praiſing and praying him, for the gift of ſtrength, and of miracles, againſt their enimies forces [And when they had prayed, the place was moued, where they were gathered, & they were al replenished with the Holie Ghoſt: and they ſpake the word of God, with confidence.] Shortly after S. Peter the Supreme viſible head, being apprehended, and King Herod intending to put him to death, as he had already killed S. Iames [prayer was made of the Church, without intermiſſion vnto God for him.] And he was miraculoufly deliuered out of priſon by an Angel. In the conſecrating of S. Paul & S. Barnabas Bishopes, other Apoſtles together with them, & others[faſted and prayed, & ſo impoſing handes vpon them, ſent them vnto the worke, wherto the Holie Ghoſt had taken them.] From al which examples; not only ſolemne prayers, but alſo certaine ordinarie faſtes are inſtituted, and obſerued, when Clergimen are ordayned, at ſpecial times, called the *Ember dayes*, or *Temper dayes*: in Latine *Quatuor tempora*. The reaſon wherof is the abſolute neceſſitie of ſpiritual Paſtors, to teach, and gouerne the people, in thoſe thinges, which perteyne to God, and to miniſter Holie Sacramenss, and other Rites of Religion. in which ſtate of men, al vertues are eſpecially, yea and eminently required. Becauſe [according to the Iudge of the people, ſo alſo are the miniſters: and what maner of man the Ruler of a citie is, ſuch alſo are the inhabitants therin] And therfore not only at thoſe ſpecial times more eſpecially, but alſo at al times, both Prieſtes and other Clergimen, and alſo al other Chriſtians, muſt pray particularly [that the Lord of the harueſt wil ſend workemen into his harueſt] And that our Lord wil alwayes direct the guides, whom he hath

ch. 4. v.3.]
21. 24.
29. 30. 31.

ch. 12. v.3.4.
5. &c.

ch. 13. v 2 3.

See Part. 3.
Art. 24.

Eccli. 10.
v. 2.

Luc. 10. v. 16

The Ember dayes were inſtituted by example of faſting, when S. Paul and S. Barnabas were conſecrated Bishops.

com-

commanded the flocke to heare, and to folow. [For *Ioan.10.v.*
that, al mortal Prieftes haue nede (as S. Paul admoni- 4.
fheth) to pray firft for them felues, & then for others] *Heb.7.v.*
and confequently al others for them. And fo the fame 27.
great Apoftle, requefted fuch prayers for himfelf, and
other Prelates [Pray for vs (faid he) for we haue con- *ch.13.v.18.*
fidence, that we haue a good confcience, willing to 19.
conuerfe wel in al. And I befech you the more to doe
this, that I may the more fpedyly be reftored to you] *v.24.*
He was then in Italie, where he writte this Epiftle to *Rom.15.v.*
30.
the Hebrewes in Iurie. And generally in al his Epi- *2.Cor.1.*
ftles, he requefted the prayers of them to whom he *v.11.*
writ, that his labours might be to al more profitable.

VVe are alfo bond to pray for al Chriftian Princes, and Magiftrates. Efpecially for thofe vnder vuhom vve liue.

ARTICLE. 13.

The obligation of obedience, induceth a bond to pray that Superiours may gouerne wel.

N Ext after fpiritual Paftors, which haue charge of foules, al Chriftians are bond to obey temporal Princes, and other Magiftrates; and therfore are alfo bond to pray for them: that they may be dire- *Rom.13.v.* cted by God, fo to gouerne in temporal affayres, as the *1.&c.* fpiritual may therby be more promoted, and profper. In regard wherof the true feruants of God, whether they liue vnder Catholique Princes, or vnder Ethniques, or other Infidels, doe both dutifully obey them, in al lawful caufes, and diligently pray for their good eftate, health, long life, and in al occafions refpect, honour, and ferue them, as Gods Minifters, be-

Examples of praying for Heathen Kinges.

caufe [al power is of God] Holie Iofeph the Patriarch, being gouernour of Ægypt vnder King Pharao, fo much honoured and eftemed the fame King, that [he *Gen.41.* fware by his health] which he could not lawfully haue *15.* done, vnleffe he had finceerely defired his profperitie,

Like-

Likewise Mordocheus a faithful Iew being in captiuitie, vnder King Assuerus in the citie of Susan, vnderstanding that certaine men had conspired to kil

Est.2.v. 22. the King, told it to his Neece Queene Esther, that's she
might reueale it to the King in his name) shewing
therin their dutiful allegeance, and care of the Kings

Dan.1.v.8. safetie, and of the whole kingdome. So Daniel the
20, Prophet, and those that were with him captiues in
ch.2.v.18. Babylon, stil honoured, and dutifully serued the
ch.6.v.4.5. Kinges, in al temporal causes: professing neuertheles
22.28. their faith and religion towardes God. And generally
al Prophets, and good Priestes, and faithful people   The common
3.Reg.1.v. honored, duly serued, and prayed for their kinges, of- salutation to
31.&c. ten repeting, besides other prayers, the solemne salu- al Kinges.
tation [God saue my Lord: God saue the king.]

2. In the Psalmes, and other Prophets, are special
formes of prayers, for al sortes of the Clergie, and   The Prophets
Ar.ic.12.§. Laitie (as is noted before) and namely for Kinges and prayed, and
2. other Princes, and Magistrates [Lord saue the King   admonished
Psa.19.v.10 (say the faithful people) and heare vs in the day,   others to pray
Ps.27.v.8. that we shal inuocate thee; To thee ô Lord (said   for Kinges.
9. Dauid) I wil crie. My God kepe not silence from me;
lest at anie time thou hold thy peace from me, and
I shal be like to them that goe downe into the lake]
Our Lord also by his Prophete Ieremie commanded
his people, that were captiues in Babylon, to pray for
Iere.29.v.7 the king, & kingdome, saying: [Seke the peace of the
citie, to which I haue transported you; and pray for it
to the Lord, because in the peace therof, there shal be
peace to you] And the Prophet Baruch repeted the
Bar.1.v.11. same admonition, saying [Pray ye for the life of Na-
12. buchodonosor the King of Babylon: and for the life
of Balthasar his sonne, that their dayes may be as the
dayes of heauen, vpon the earth: and our Lord geue
vs strength, and illuminate our eyes, that we may liue
vnder the shadow of Nabuchodonosor the King of
Babylon, & vnder the shadow of Balthasar his sonne:

and

and may ſerue them manie dayes: and may finde
grace in their ſight]

Chriſt, and his   3. Neither is our Sauiours precept commanding   *Mat 22 7.*
Apoſtles teach   [to render the thinges that are Cæſars, to Cæſar]li-   21.
the ſame.   mited to the paying of tribute, and doing of temporal ſeruice, but is extended alſo to ſpiritual dutie in
praying for him, and his ſtate, eſpecially for his ſoules
health. Becauſe not only al men are our neighbours,
but alſo becauſe he is a Prince amongſt men, vpon
whoſe eſtate manie depend. And therfore S. Paul
teaching that we muſt [render to al men their dew]   *Rom.13. v.*
includeth a duble obligation, to pray for the Prince,   7.
as wel for his particular good, as for the whole communitie, ouer which he ruleth. Eſpecially for our
owne Princes. And more expreſly he declareth this
dutie of al Chriſtians, writing thus to S. Timothee:
[I deſire firſt of al thinges, that obſecrations, prayers,
poſtulations, and thankeſgeuing be made for al men: *1.Tim.2. v.*
for Kinges; and al that are in preeminence; that we   1 2.
may lead a quiet and peaceable life in al pietie.]   *1.Pet. 2.1 ς*

VVe are bond to pray for the ſoules in Purga-
torie. Eſpecially for our parents, benefactors,
and other neereſt freindes.

ARTICLE 14.

Diuers points   LEſt we ſhould be ouer tedious in repeting the
being proued   ſame thing often, we remitte you (Courteous
already, it ne-   Reader) for the groundes of this doctrine vnto di-   *Part.1.*
ceſſarily folo-   uers Articles, formerly proued in this worke. For   *Art.24.*
weth, that the   firſt againſt the denial of more places of ſoules de-
faithful in   parted from their bodies, then only heauen of eter-
earth are bond   nal glorie, and hel of euerlaſting torments: wherto pray for   upon Proteſtants denie that there can be anie ſuch
the ſoules in   place as Purgatorie, it is clearly ſhewed that Chriſts
Purgatorie.   bleſſed ſoule deſcended into a place called Hel.
which can neither be the Empyrial heauen, nor hel
of

of torments: and therfore there were more places
then two: and consequently this ground of Protestants is false. And seing there was then a place for
holie, & perfite soules, out of heauen, into the which
Christ descended, there might also be, and may be
stil a place, where other inst soules, not so perfect, are
purged and perfected, that they may enter into heauen. It is also further proued, that after the remission
of actual sinnes, there remayneth most commonly
some temporal punishment due for satisfaction.
Whichif it be not discharged in this life, must be payed
after death. Which necessarily conuinceth, that there
is a place of Purgatorie in the other world. Moreouer
it is proued, that soules being departed in the state of
grace, doe perteyne to the Communion of Saintes:
and so are capable of the good, which others doe in
the whole Church of God. Likewise it is declared by
the general precept of louing our neighbours as our
selues, that al are bond in charitie: (and some also in
iustice) to pray for their neighbours, that haue neede
therof. And therfore seeing there are some faithful
soules in Purgatorie, and that they haue neede of releefe by prayers, and are capable of this benefite; it
foloweth by al these groundes, that al good Christi-
stians are bound of charitie, to pray for al the soules
which are in Purgatorie. And more particularly of
iustice, al are bond to pray for their parents; benefactors, and special freindes (that are in that place) according to their special obligations.

2. Which is further confirmed, both by authentical examples, and euident testimonies in holie Scriptures. The general custome of the Patriarches, in
mourning and celebrating Obsequies for the dead,
with funeral solemnities, in choise places; And some
times fasting for the same cause, doe euidently shew
both the ordinarie neede, which some soules haue of
helpes and the dutie of their freindes to performe,
such

Marginal notes (left):
Par t.2.
A t.31.
A t.36.

Part 1.
A t.44.

Part.3.
A t 18.
36. 43.

v d.s v.v.
11.
Ro n.13.v 8

Gen.23.v.
2.2.
ch 25.v.9.
ch. s 4.8.

Marginal notes (right):
It is further
proued by ex-
amples.

fuch works for them. So Abraham mourned for Sara *ch.47.v.* his wife: prouiding a fpecial place for her burial, and *30.* for him felfe and his famirlie. And accordingly his *ch.49.v.31.* fonnes Ifaac & Ifmael buried him in the fame place. *2 Reg.1.v.* And afterwards manie others were alfo buried there. *12.* And although fome holie perfect foules needed not prayers after their death: yet the ordinarie cuftom was obferued, and the fruite redounded to others, which had neede: participating of the Communion of Sainctes. For fo both quicke and dead participate *Pf.118.v.* of each others good workes. As the Holie Pfalmift *63.* fignifieth, faying [I am partaker of al that feare our Lord, and kepe his commandements] The charitie of *2.Mach.12.* Iudas Machabeus moft plainly fheweth this general *v 42 &c.* godlie cuftome of praying, and offering Sacrifice for *Part 2.* the dead. As is noted in an other place. *Art 36.§.* *5.&c.*

3 Where the fame doctrine is alfo proued by the iudgement of a diuine Preacher, exhorting amongft other good workes, to be mindful of foules departed,

And deduced from other textes of holie Scriptures. faying [The grace of a gift is in the fight of al the li *Eccli.7.v.* uing: and from the dead ftay not grace. Sonne vpon *37.* the dead fhede teares, and begine to wepe, as hauing *ch.38.v.16.* fuffered doleful thinges: and according to iudgement couer his bodie : and neglect not his burial] Which external actes of mourning, and burying the dead, efpecially require affection of the mind, and good defire towardes their foules. Which is a perfect prayer for them. S. Iohn exhorting to pray for fuch finners as repented before their death, prefuppofeth that the fame is a worke of mercie, perteyning to al faithful Chriftians : and alfo prefuppofeth that there may be fome faithful foules in that ftate after their *1.Io.5.v.* departure from their bodies, that they may nede, and *16.* may be holpen by fuch prayers. [He that knoweth

Some foules departed are not capable of releefe. his brother(faith he) to finne a finne not to death, let him aske, and life fhal be geuen him, finning not to death. There is a finne to death: for that I fay not, that

that anie man aske] According to which Apostolicall doctrine, as the Church neither prayeth for glorified Sainctes, because they nede not anie prayers, nor for such sinners as dye obstinate in heresie, schisme, or other enormious crime, because no prayer can profite them : so the same Holie Church piously prayeth for al those soules departed, which both haue nede, and be capable of relese, by the prayers of others. And from hence commeth the vsual godlie practise of Masses, Diriges, and other prayers for the dead. And of the concluding of most prayers, with this versicle [*Fidelium animæ per misericordiam Dei requiescant in pace*] or in English : God haue mercie vpon al Christian soules.

Some nede it not.

Very manie both are capable, & haue nede.

Artic. 1.2. 3.4.6.7. 11.12.

Hitherto is shewed in general, the necessitie of prayer as wel direct Petitions, as Thankesgeuinges, and Praises to God : both Mental and Vocal. That Priuate prayer may be in anie language; Publique must be in a sacred tongue. Also what conditions are requisite; with the Effect: and for whom we are bond to pray. Now it is further to be declared, to whom we must pray: and what we must aske. And first it is cleare, that al religious prayers are made to God [from whom only al good thinges procede] But for somuch as some doe imagine, that supplicants must alwayes pray immediatly to God, and that it is not lawful to pray by mediation of others, we shal in due place, shew that the Catholique doctrine, & practise of praying to God by intercession, as wel of glorious Sainctes in heauen; as of other faithful seruants of God in earth, is both lawful and profitable. In the meane time concerning good thinges to be asked, and the maner, how to aske them, the most common forme of praying, called Our Lords Prayer, (The Pater noster) is here especially explicated: as that which excelleth al other set formes of praying in diuers respects

The conexion of the Articles precedent and folowing.

Iac. 1.7. 17.

Art. 41. 46.

The Pater noster excelleth

R r

al other Pray-ers, in
Auctoritie,
Perfection,

Vtilitie,

spectes, of Auctoritie, Perfection, Vtilitie, Necessitie, Breuitie, and Order. For the Auctor is Iesus Christ; The Eternal wisdom of God. who hath made it so Perfect, that it conteyneth al thinges needful to mankind. It is a most Profitable prayer, because it is most gratful to God, as being composed by his onlie begotten Sonne: & because in it we not only speake to Almightie God in the name of Christ, his Sonne our Lord (as in al other prayers) but also in his very

Necessitie,

Breuitie,

and Order.

wordes. It is also most Necessarie of al prayers, because it is expresly ordained, and commanded by the same our Lord & Sauiour. The Breuitie is admirable, for in very few wordes, we aske al thinges that may be rightly desired: and we may very easyly lerne it, & with facilitie often recite it. Finally, it is diuinely disposed in most conuenient Order: directing vs first to aske our heauenlie Father, that which perteyneth to his owne most honour: secondly al spiritual thinges belonging to our selues, and al the elect in future glorie: then spiritual good thinges in earth.   After which we aske also temporal and corporal necessaries: And withal to be disburdened of al sinnes: and deliuered from al other euils, spiritual and tem-

The contents,

Diuided into nine partes.

poral: present, and in danger to come; which might hurt vs in soule, or bodie. Al which we must aske with constant hartie desire. And so this most excellent Prayer, consisteth of a Preface, and seuen Petitions, with a Conclusion. As wil more particularly appeare in the Articles folowing.

In the Preface of our Lords Prayer, vve in-uocate Almightie God, Father of al men by creation, conseruation, and redemption.

ARTICLE 15.

Prefaces in speach to mortal men are to

Secular Orators, and discrete Clients, desirous to obtaine their requests of other men, comonly vse some Preface, before they propose their suits. For

that

Act.16. v.
3.4.10.
ch.25.6.2.3.
that it might seme an arrogant demand, which is abruptly vttered in commanding termes, without anie word of supplication. As if in bare wordes, the needie shal say to a rich man: Geue me meate, clothes, &c. he shal rather auert the others affection from him, then moue him to compassion. Wheras the due maner of asking with submissiue humilitie, and shew of gratful acceptance of desired benefite, procureth beneuolence. So in prayer to God, examples of Holie men teach vs, to vse some preface before we expresse the thinges, which we desire. Yet not to the same end,

Rom 5. v. 8.
when we pray to God, as when we are suiters to mortal persons. For we neede not by preuention to craue Gods beneuolence towards vs. Who alwayes preuenteth vs with his grace. Without which we can neither

2. Cor.3. v. 5.
aske, nor desire anie good thing, nor thinke a good thought. Neither must we endeuour to change Gods wil: which is immutable: but we must make such prefaces in our prayers, which we offer to God, as are fitte to sturre vp, and to moue in our selues, assured confidence of Gods perpetual good wil, to doe that which is best, both for vs, and others, for whom we pray. So Abraham prayed six times without intermis-

Gen 18 v.
23.27.,8.31.
32.
sion, for the saftie of Sodom, interposing special prefaces, not to moue God to vse mercie, which needeth not, for he is alwayes most merciful: but to moue himselfe to more confidence, and other vertues by actual profession of his Faith, and Hope in Gods Goodnes. With such a preface also Moyses begane his prayer for the children of Israel, confessing their

Exod.32. v.
31.
mon [heinous sinne, in making to themselues goddes of gold.] praised Gods infinite mercie, saying [Dominatour Lord God, Merciful and Clement, Patient, and of much compassion, and true; which kepest mercie vnto thousandes (bowing withal flatte vnto the earth, and adorning) then proposing his petition,

ch.34.7.6 7
8.9.
he said: [If I haue found grace in thy sight, ô Lord, I

moue them to beneuolence; But in prayer to God, they are to moue the suppliants vnto a right disposition mind.

Rr 2   beseech

beseech thee, that thou wilt goe with vs (for it is a stiffe necked people) and take away our iniquities, and sinnes, and posseste vs] Salomon in the Dedication of the Temple, begane his deuout prayer, with a preface of praises, and thankes to God, for his benefites, formerly bestowed , and for promises made, saying [Bleste be our Lord the God of Israel, who spake by his mouth to Dauid my father , and in his owne handes hath perfected it, &c.] And by acknowleging great benefites receiued , and confidently expected, confirmed his owne hart, & others in God, and so made their prayers more acceptable.

3. Reg. 8. v. 15.16.20.25

Christ commandeth to vse a Preface in our prayers.

2. Aboue al other examples, is Our Lords owne practise, and precept. He for our instruction vsed to make prefaces in his prayers. As when he raised Lazarus , when he prayed in presence of his Apostles: (the night before his Passion.) And he taught his Disciples, and in them al Christians, to beginne the most ordinarie prayer , with a preface, saying [Thus shal you pray: Our Father which art in heauen] By which few wordes, if we rightly consider them, our confidence may be strongly confirmed , in that we are warranted to cal God, our Father, seeing we doe it by Gods commandment. For otherwise it were extreme presumption , that a lumpe of earth, a base seruant, a guiltie offender, should cal our Lord God Almightie (the Lord of heauen & earth : the Iudge of the whole world) by the honorable, and amiable name of Father. But [we being admonished by wholsome precepts , and taught by diuine institution, are emboldned to say (without which precept and warrant, no creature might presume to say) Our Father] Wherfore seing we may and must so speake to our Lord God: our confidence is therby exceedingly strengthened: because by this title of Father, faithful supplicants may wel conceiue assured hope, that God of his fatherlie affection, by which he wil be called our Father, wil

Ioan.11.v. 41. ch.17.v.1. Luc. 22. v. 41. Mat.6.v. 9. Luc.11.v. 2.

No creature especially a sinner might presume to cal God his father vnles we were so commanded.

Rom.8.v. 25. Gal. 4. v. 6.

By this title we conceiue assured hope.

alle

wil also as a Father, heare the prayers of those whom
he voutfafeth to make, and acknowlege to be his
children. For children euen by filial right, often obtaine their requests from paternal affection, when
feruants are refufed, and strangers repelled. Likewife,
by this name FATHER, we are put in minde to reuerence and honour God, not only for feare, but also
with filial loue [For the fonne (faith the Prophet Ma-

Mal.1.v.6.
lachias) honoreth the father. If I then be the father
faith the Lord of Hostes: Where is my honour? And if
I be the Lord, where is my feare?] By this name of Father, we are also admonished to imitate God in doing good to al. For the fonnes ought in al good
thinges to folow their fathers example. Otherwife it
wil be iustly reproched vnto them by their father [I

Ifa.1.v.2.
haue brought vp children, and exalted them, but they
haue defpifed me,] And our Lord exprefly chargeth

Mat.5.v.17
v.48.]
Luc.6.v.36.
al his children, faying [Let your light fo shine before
men, that they may fee your good workes, and glorifie your Father which is in heauen. Be ye perfect, as
your heauenlie Father is perfect. Be ye merciful, as alfo your Father is merciful.]

  3. Moreouer this word [Father] is fo largely extended, that in regard of al men yet liuing in this

Gen.1.v
26.
world, God is Father (in a general fenfe) not only by
creation, côferuation, & redemption of al, but alfo by
fatherlie affection. For [he would haue al to be faued,

1.Tim.2.v.4
& to come to the knowlege of truth] Al are his creatures, ordayned to his glorie, and (if themfelues wil

Deut. 32.v.
6.
c operate) to their owne good. [Is not our Lord thy
Father (faid Moyfes to al the people iuft or vniuft)
that poffeffed thee; and made thee, and created thee?

Pfal. 103.v.
27.28.29.
Al expect of thee (faith the Pfalmift to God) that thou
geue them meate in feafon. Thou geuing, they shal
gather it, thou opening thy hand, al shal be filled
with bountie. But thou turning away the face they
shal be trubled: thou shalt take away their fpirite,

  R r 3   and

Margin notes (right):
VVe are ad-
monished to
reuerence,
feare, and loue
God.

And to imitate
God.

God would
haue al to be
faued.

And wil hane
his feruants
to pray for al
to him, as our
common Fa-
ther.

and they shal faile, and shal returne into their dust]
For as God alone created al, so he only conserueth al.
And concerning redemption of al mankind, without
limiting or excluding anie, our Lord saith by his Prophete Osee [Out of the hand of death, I wil deliuer   *Osee. 13. 7*
them : from death I wil redeme them: I wil be thy   14.
death ô death : thy bitte wil be ô hel]Conformably   *Mal. 2. 7.*
therto saith Malachias [Is there not one father of vs   10.
al; hath not one God created vs?] There is one God
(saith S. Paul) the father of al.] This our one God,
common father of al, as Holie Scripture often wit-   *Eph. 4. 7. 8.*
nesseth [Hath geuen commandment to euerie one   *Eccli. 17. 7.*
concerning his neighbonr] In which regard, and in   12.
this general sense al hauing one Father, Gods seruants
doe pray for al, euen for the most wicked, that they
may be conuerted, excluding none in the common
prayer, when we say [OurFather which art in heauen]

God is more particularly the Father of the
faithful. And most especially of the iust.

ARTICLE 16.

That God is
more peculi-
atly called the
father of the
faithful, is
proued by ho-
lie Scriptures.
In the old Te-
stament.

BY the holie Scriptures it is no lesse cleare, that as
God in a general sense, is Father of al men : so in a
stricter sense, he is the Father of the peculiar people,
whom he hath selected to serue him in true Faith
and Religion? and yet more especially, he is the Father
of the iust, who are more neerely ioyned vnto him, by
sanctifying grace. Of the former sorte are al the mem-   *Rom. 8. 7.*
bers of the militant Church: of the other are those   15. 17.
only, Who are ioyned vnto him, not only in faith, but   *Gal. 4. 7. 5.*
also in charitie. So in the old Testament and Law of
Moyses, as S. Paul describeth their state [Al the children of Israel were vnder the cloud, al passed through   *1. Corio. 7.*
the sea: but in the more part of them, God was not   1. 5.
wel pleased, for they were ouerthrowne in the desert]

2. For distinction sake therfore of the faithful from
Infidels, in the beginning of the world, some were
                                                    called

called [the fonnes of God] and confequently God was their father, in more fpecial maner, then of others defcribed by the title of the fonnes and [daughters of men] God himfelfe not only would be peculiarly called the God of Abraham, God of Ifaac, and God of Iacob, but alfo the father of the whole people of ifrael, for he called them his fonnes, faying [My firft begotten fonne is Ifrael.] And faid to King Pharao [Difmiffe my fonne, that he may ferue me] Our Lord alfo faid to the fame people by his Prophete Ieremie [Cal me thy Father. And I faid : Thou shalt cal me, Father: and shalt not ceafe to walke after me. I am become a father to Ifrael, and Ephraim is my firft begotten] And by Malachias he expoftulateth with his people their ingratitude, for this title of Father, faying [If I be your father , where is my honour] fignifying, that it was a fingular contempt not to efteme his loue, in that he would be their Father.

Gen. 6. v. 1.
2.

Exo 3. v. 6.
ch. 4. v. 22.
23.

Ie. 3. v. 4.
19.
ch. 31. v. 9.

Mal. 1. v. 6.

3. Chrift our Lord doth very often admonish the faithful, that God is their Father in more fpecial forte, then he is of other peoples, and perfons, which beleue not in him [Be not like to the heathen, for your Father knoweth what is needful for you] plainly calling God otherwife father of the faithful, then of the heathen. [Let your light shine before men, that they may glorifie your Father] Your father is perfect, your father is merciful] and the like. S. Paul alfo declareth the fame difference by the title of adoption, faying to the Chriftian Romanes [You haue receiued the fpirite of adoption of children, in which we crie: Abba. Father] but in greater grace of the Law of Chrift, then the Iewes could doe, by the Law of Moyfes. And of this Paternitie of God, in refpect of his Chriftian children, the fame Apoftle fpeaketh in moft of his Epiftles: where moft commonly he wisheth [Grace and peace from our Father [God the Bleffed Trinitie) and from our Lord Iefus Chrift] as he is Man, our Redemer and

Mat. 6. v.
8.
ch. 5. v. 17.
45. 48.
Luc. 6. v. 36.

Rom. 8. v. 7.
1. Cor. 1. v. 3
&c.

Gal. 4. v. 6.

By Chriftes teftimonie.

By S. Paul.

Saui-

Sauiour, Who also in his manhood is our Father, in that he bought vs, by his death, regenerate vs. And as S. Peter writeth, hath begotte vs againe [according to his great mercie, hath regenerated vs vnto a liuely hope, by the Resurrection of Iesus Christ] whom also the Prophete Isaias, amongst other titles, calleth [The Father of the world to come.]

1. Pet.1.v.
3.
Isa.9.v.6.

God being euery vvhere; Heauen as the most excellent place, is called his Seate, & Kingdom.

ARTICLE 17.

HEauen is my Seate, and the earth is my foote-stoole, saith our Lord. Doe not I fil heauen, and earth?] Not that God is conteyned in heauen & in earth, or in one, or in manie, or in al places. For he is Immense, and can not be conteyned in place, nor in time, but he conteyneth and excedeth al places, al times, and al other thinges. He is incomprehensible, eternal, and is euerywhere, according to his Power, Presence, and Essence, infinitely more powerable then anie King in his Kingdome: more present, then the Sunne at clearest noone day: more essential then the Soule in a liuing man. But why then is God said to be in heauen, rather then els where? We answere: Because God in heauen, as in his splendent court, sheweth his glorie to the blessed Angels, and other Saintes, in whom he visibly reigneth: and by communicating of himselfe, maketh them glorious,

Isa.66..v.1.
Iere 23.v.
24.

2 Which his special maner of being in heauen, much excelleth his being in other places. And therfore more frequent mention is made therof, then of his being elswhere [I lift vp my hand (said Abraham) to my Lord God most High, possessor of heauen and earth. You haue sene (said God himselfe) that from heauen I haue spoken to you. From heauen he made thee to heare his voice (said Moyses to the people) that he might teach thee. Heauen is the Lords thy God, & the heauen of heauens. Looke from thy sanctuarie, and

Gen.14.v.
22.

Exod.20.v.
22.

Deut 4.v.
36.

and thy high habitation of heauen, and bleſſe thy people Iſrael , and the land which thou haſt geuen vs.]So prayed Moyſes. So al other Prophets,good Prieſtes and Leuites ,ſo al the faithful prayingto God often expreſſe his being in heauen.Signifying therby, that ne is in more excellent maner there , then in o- ther places.Who neuertheleſſe is euerywhere, & in euerie thing ,otherwiſe nothing could conſiſt.

3. Why ſo often mention is made , in the holie Scriptures, and particularly in this our moſt dayly common prayer , of Gods ſpecial and glorious reſi dence in heauen ,there be manie great reaſons,moſt worthie of our conſideration. Firſt we are here to meditate Gods moſt high Maieſtie, who reigneth in incomprehenſible glorie ; and our owne baſeneſſe in miſeries[God is in heauen , and thou art vpon earth] and yet wil he make vs partakers of the ſame glorie; in ſuch meaſure , as is vnmeaſurable. Secondly we muſt remember that earth is the place of our pere- grination, heauen is our home [We haue not here a permanent citie : but we ſeeke that which is to come]Thirdly we muſt deſire the thinges that are in heauen,& contemne this world[If you be riſen with Chriſt,ſeek the thinges that are aboue?where Chriſt is ſitting on the right hand of God.Minde the thinges that are aboue, not the thinges that are vpon the earth.]Fourthly remember that if we gaine not hea- uen, we muſt eternally be damned in hel.There are
no moe but two places,to which al ſhal be finally, and eternally adiudged. Al ſhal be either on the right hand, or on the left hand of Chriſt our Iudge,To the one ſort he wil ſay [Come ye bleſſed, poſſeſſe you the kingdome prepared for you] To the other he wil ſay[Get ye away from me, you curſed into fire euer- laſting: And theſe ſhal goe into puniſhment euerla- ſting: but the iuſt into life euerlaſting.] Euer liuing with our Father,which is in heauen.

Points ofme- ditation vpon the word hea- uen.

1.

2.

3.

4.

In the first petition vve pray, that Gods name may be honored by al: & dishonored by none.

ARTICLE 18.

Gods honour is first of al to be desired.

AS in al other actions, so especially in prayer, 1 Cor. 10. Gods honour is to be desired in the first place, v. 31. 32. before al other thinges. And therfore hath the Eternal wisdome, our B. Sauiour taught vs, first of al to pray our heauenlie Father, that he wil voutsafe to power out his abundant grace vpon al which liue in this transitorie world, that his owne holie name may be honoured by al, and dishonored by none. Which thing as none must be wanting to desire: so neither must anie faithful person omitte to aske it of God, neither must anie despare that it can not be done, but must know, that it is possible on the behalf of God: who offereth sufficient grace to al, and wil geue it effectually to manie, whom himself knoweth. And finally this desire shal be fulfilled in al the elect, and blessed children of God, who shal eternally praise him, not only for his owne in comparable excellencies, and for his gracious, & glorious giftes bestowed vpon his true seruants, al his Sainctes; but also in respect of the damned, for his mercies towards them, and his grace sometimes offered vnto them, and for his iustice, executed vpon them; because they would not cooperate with his grace, nor participate of his goodnes.

Apoc. 19. v. 1. 2.

The same was also taught in the old Testament.

2. This our obligation to desire & pray that Gods name may be halowed and glorified aboue al, was also intimated vnto vs by himselfe, in the first of the tenne commandments, as a preface to the whole Law: when he said [I am the Lord thy God, mightie, ielous. In other places (he saith) his name is Ielous. God is an emulatour. I the Lord: this is my name: I wil not geue my glorie to an other] and the like. In zele of Gods honour, that infidels should not take

Exo. 20. v. 5.
ch. 33. v. 14.
Isa. 42. v. 8.

occa-

occaſion to blaſpheme Gods name, Moyſes prayed
for the people, when they deſerued to haue bene deſtroyed, [leſt the Ægyptians ſhould haue ſaid, that he
had brought them forth, that he might kil them in
the mountaines.]

3. Examples of ſuch, as before al other deſires,
ſought the honour of Gods name, are inuumerable in
holie Scriptures; we wil here only touch two or three
Phinees the ſonne of Eleaſar, the ſonne of Aaron, was
highly commended and rewarded, for his zele of
Gods honour, by our Lord himſelfe, ſaying [He hath
auerted my wrath from the children of Iſrael. And
becauſe he was moued with the zele (againſt the carnal and ſpiritual adulterers) that my ſelf my not deſtroy the children of Iſrael in myne owne zele: there
ſhal be to him the couenant of Prieſthood for euer:
becauſe he hath bene zelous for his God; and hath
expiated the wicked fact of the children of Iſrael] the
great Prophete Elias, moued with feruent true zele
of Gods honour, feared not to preſent him ſelf before
Achab King of Iſrael, an Idolater, who ſought to kil
him. To whom he boldly auouched, that [not he, but
Achab himſelf trubled al Iſrael: by forſaking the commandment of our Lord, and folowing Baalim] He
forthwith for edifiation of the ſtaggering people, hal-
ting betwen God, and Baal (God miraculouſly concurring) conuinced four hundred & fiftie falſe prophets of Baal, and cauſed them al to be ſlaine] according to the Law of God. And the ſame King Achab,
and Iezabel ſtil perſecuting him, he ſincerely ſaid of
himſelf, euen to an Angel ſent to him from God [with
zele haue I bene zelous for our Lord, the God of
Hoſts: becauſe the children of Iſrael (of the ſchiſmatical tribes) haue forſaken thy couenant.] An other example of great zele alſo, but not ſo pure, yet commendable & rewarded by God, is recorded of Iehu king of
Iſrael. Who being annointed King by the ſame ordi-

Exod 32.*v.*
12.

Num. 25. *v.*
11.

v. 13.

3. *Reg.* 18. *v.*
3 15
v. 2.
36 40.
Deut 13.
v. 5. 6.
14.
15.

3. *Reg.* 19. *v.*
10. 14. 16.

Examples of
ſpecial zele of
Gods honour

Phinees the
Prieſt.

Elias the Pro-
phete.

Iehu King of
Iſrael,

Sſ 2   nance

nance of God: and meeting with Ionadab, the sonne
of Rechab (a zelous religious man) and agreing by
mutual promise, each to other, to promote Religion
against Idolaters, Iehu said to him [Come with me,
and see my zele for our Lord] Which in fact performing [he slew al that were left of Achab in Samaria,
til there was not one] then by a stratageme, gathered
and inurroned al the worshipers of Baal, that could
be found: and so destroyed them, together with Baals
temple, and in the place where it stood, made a common iakes. And our Lord said to Iehu: Because
thou hast diligently done that which was right, and
that pleased in myne eyes, and done al thinges that
were in my hart, against the house of Achab: thy children, shal sitte vpon the throne of Israel, to the fourth
generation] Loe this was the temporal reward, for a
good and zelous worke, done by an euil man. For as
the sacred historie expresly reporteth [Iehu obserued
not to walke in the Law of our Lord, the God of Israel in al his hart: for he departed not from the sinnes
of Ieroboam, neither forsooke he the golden calues,
that were in Bethel, and Dan]

4. Conformable to these examples; & the decrees
of diuine Law, al the Prophets doe also teach that the
honour of Gods name, is to be desired first in order
of al petitions, euen before mans saluation. For whatsoeuer is most estimed and most desired, the same to
euerie one is their god: and if it be not God the Creator, it is a false god. Therfore sayth the Royal Prophete to God our Lord [There is not the like to thee,
amongst goddes, ô Lord; and there is not according to
thy workes. Al nations shal glorifie thy name. Poure
out thy wrath vpon the Gentiles, that haue not
knowen thee, & vpon the kingdomes, that haue not
Inuocated thy name. Fil their faces with ignomie, and
they wil seeke thy name ô Lord, and let them know,
that L o r d, is thy name, Thou onlie the Highest in

al

(marginal notes:)
He had tem-
poral reward,
not being ca-
pable of eter-
nal.

The Holie
Prophets of-
ten admoni-
shed the Iewes
to honour the
name of God
aboue al.

4. Reg 9. v.
6.7.
cb.10. v. 15.
16.17.
23.25.
26.27.

v.10.

v.29.31.

Psal. 85. 7.
8 9.
Ps 78. v.4.

Ps. 82. v. 17.
19.

Pſ 8.v.10.
Pſ.19.v.6.
Pſ 28.v.2.
Pſ.43.v.26.
Pſ.144.v.1.
v.21.

al the earth. O Lord our Lord, how meruelous is thy name in the whole earth! In the name of our Lord we ſhal be magnified. Bring to our Lord glorie and honour: bring to our Lord glorie vnto his name. Ariſe Lord, helpe vs; & redeme vs for thy name. I wil bleſſe thy name for euer and for euer. Let al fleſh bleſſe his holie name for euer, and for euer and euer] Iſaias

Iſa.11. v. 4. forſheweth that Chriſtians eſpecially ſhal preferre Gods name abone al other deſires [You ſhal ſay

And foreſhew that Chriſtiaus ſhal deſire the ſame in the firſt place.

ch.24.v.15. in that day, Confeſſe ye to our Lord, and inuocate his name. Remember that his name is High. In al the Iles of the ſea, the name of our Lord the God

ch. 25. v 1.
ch. 26. v. 8.
y 13.

of Iſrael (ſhal be knowne) ô Lord thou art my God, I wil exalt thee, and confeſſe to thy name. Thy name, and thy memortal are in the deſire of the ſoule, My ſoule hath deſired thee. Only in thee, let vs remember thy name. Euerie one that inuocateth my name (ſaith

ch. 43. v. 7.
ch 48. v. 9.

our Lord) for my glorie haue I created him, formed him, and made him. For my names ſake I wil make

ch. 52. v. 6.

my furie far of, and for my praiſe I wil bridle thee. For this cauſe ſhal my people know my name in that

ch. 57. v. 15. day. Becauſe thus ſaith the High and eminent, that inhabiteth eternitie, and his name is holie, dwelling in the high, and holie place] Likewiſe Ieremie prophe

Iere 10. v.
25.
ch. 14. v. 9.

cieth that God wil [poure out his indignation vpon the peoples, that ſhal not inuocate his name. Thou Lord art in vs, and thy name is inuocated vpon vs, forſake vs not.] Our Lord ſaith by his Prophete Eze

Ezech. 20.
v. 22, 39.
Dan. 3. v. 34.
43. & c.
Oſee. 2 v. 16.
Ioel. 2. v. 26.
Amos 4 v.
v. 13.
ch 5 v 8.
Mich. 4. v 5
Soph. 1. v. 4.

chiel [I turned away my hand, and did for my names ſake, that it might not be violated before the Gentiles. But if in this alſo you feare me not, and ſhal pollute my Holie name any more, &c.] So Daniel and the other Prophetes teſtifie, that God requiring that his name be honoured aboue al, alſo rewardeth them that performe it, & puniſh thoſe that neglect it.

5. No meruel therfore, that Chriſt our Sauiour expreſly teacheth, and commandeth al his children

VVe muſt both pray, and

endeuour,that in the firſt petition to pray our heauenlie Father,that *Ma..6..v 9.*
Gods name [his name may be ſanctified, loued, and honored by *Luc.11.v 2.*
may be hono- al, yea alſo by thoſe, by whom it is as yet blaſphemed, *Mat 12.v.*
red by al. hated, and manie wayes dishonored. Which docu- *21.*
ment is often inculiated, as wel by our Lord himſelf, *Rom.2.v.*
as by his Apoſtles , admonishing al to beware of *24.*
ſcandalizing the weake, by whom God may be diſ- *1.Cor 10.*
honored, or blaſphemed : but to edifie others , that *v.31*
God may be honored, and his name ſanctified . For *I.Tim.I. v.*
that implicitely the honoring or d shoringing of *17.*
Gods name, is the acknowleging, or denying of God. *ch.6.v.1.*
Eſpecially the aſcribing of the name of God to anie
creature is direct blaſphemie, againſt God. As S. Luke
in his ſacred Hiſtorie, of the primitiue Church , hath
recorded the terrible example of King Herod , who
for admitting the flatterie of vaine people , accoun- *Act.12.v.*
ting him as a God, and [not geuing honour to God, *22.23.*
was ſtrooken by an Angel , and being conſumed of
wormes, gaue vp the ghoſt] So he perished , and the
people moſt greuouſly ſinned , in preſuming to honour a wicked man with the name of God.

*VVe pray more particularly , that yve,
vvhich beleue in God , may euer haue
grace to glorifie his name.*

ARTICLE 19.

Al being bond **B**Y the recited holie Scriptures it is ſufficiently
to honour cleare, that we are bond to deſire & to pray, that
Gods name, al men may praiſe the holie name of God . And be-
we muſt pray cauſe ourſelues are eſpecially obliged to doe the
for grace to ſame, we muſt pray for grace to performe it. Remem-
performe it. bring that as without Gods eſpecial grace [we can
doe nothing that is good: ſo we can doe al thinges *Philip. 4.v.*
(neceſſarie) in Chriſt that ſtregthneth vs] When ther- *13.*
fore we recite theſe holie wordes, [Halowed by thy
name] we muſt deſire in hart, and ſincere minde that
the

the fame, through Gods fpecial gracious gift, be now
and euer done by our felues. Which is the fecond, &
more particular fenfe of the fame facred wordes.

2. And for fo much as mention is here made, of
the name of our heauenlie Father, when we fay [Ha-
lowed be thy name] we muft confider in our cogitation, that no name nor names can fufficiently expreffe
or notifie vnto vs, the immenfe great excellent, and
incomprehenfible Diuine Maieftie. Which otherwife
for mans fmal capacitie, is commonly propofed by
thefe ordinarie names & titles: God; Our Lord: The
Lord of hofts: The Omnipotent, The higheft, Lord
God: Lord of Lords: God of heauen: God of mercie:
God of peace: and the like. Al fo proper to our Lord
God only, that they agree to no creature whatfoeuer.
Yet are they al fo improper to the diuine nature itfelf,
that they are infufficient to declare the fame, as a Definition, or effential Etymologie therof.

3. The nereft name (though alfo improper, & infuf-
cient) is the name which himfelf reuealed to Moyfes
[HE WHICH IS] importing the moft abfolute
perfect being: becaufe he onlie, and nothing els is
without beginning. Is of himfelf eternal, without
mutation. Without limitation, confifting only, of, by,
and in himfelf. And fo this name fignifieth to vs, the
very infinite Immenfitie of Gods fubftance. To vs,
I fay, it fo infinuateth, but fo that we can only perfectly know: that he is, but not perfectly know, what
he is: and that he excedeth, and excelleth the knowlege and capacitie of al more creatures. This is God,
our onlie God, whofe name we muft honour & fanctifie. And pray, that by his fpecial grace we may duly
honoure, his name, faying [Halowed be thy name.]
Thefe in chariottes, thefe in horfes, but we wil inuocate in the name of the Lord, our God. Who fhal
not feare thee o Lord, and magnifie thy name; becaufe thou onlie art holie] of thy felf: al others that
are holie, are holie by thee.

Marginal notes (left):
Gen.1.v 1.
2. & c.
ch 2.v.5.
Exod.15.v.
3 & c.

Exo.3.v.14.
15. ch. 6.v.3.

Pfal.19.v.
3.
Apoc.15.v.
4.

Marginal notes (right):
God is fignifi-
ed to vs by ma-
nie names.

His moft pro-
per name re-
uealed to vs, is,
HE WWHICH
is.

VVe know
that God is:
but not, what
he is.

Al

Al true Christians doe also pray, that them-
selues and al others, may loue, honour, and
inuocate the holie name, I E S V S.

ARTICLE 20.

The Holie
name I E S V S
is to be especially hono-
red.

BEsides al other names of God perteyning to his eternal Deitie, the holie name I E S V S, which is proper to his Humanitie, and signifieth SAVIOVR, is to be singularly honored of al mankind. And therfore we are bond to pray that by vs, and al others it may be honored. For it is a general rule, stil to be remembred, that we are bond to pray for grace to performe, what thing soeuer we are bond to doe, because of ourselues without Gods special grace, we can not doe the very least good thing. And that this name I E S V S is, and ought to be of singular estimation, especially amongst Christians, is proued by manie holie Scriptures.

Mat. 1. v 21.
Sap 8, v. 21.
2, Cor 3. v, 5.

It was prefi-
gured, and
prophecied
in the old Te-
stament.

2. First this holie renowmed name was prefigured by the new name geuen to Ioseph the Patriarch, called [The Sauiour of the world] for that he saued al Ægypt, and the countries adioyning from perishing by famine. Which figure is more excellently fulfilled by our B. Sauiour Iesus Christ, sauing men from sinnes. It was also prefigured by changing [the name of Osee(who was cheefe temporal Assistant, & Successor to Moyses) into Iosue] Which in Hebrew is the same that Iesus. As appeareth by the same Hebrew letters: only differing in the pointes, which were added long after, And S. Steuen in his Sermō, called the same Iosue Iesus, saying to the Iewes, that [their fathers entred, into the promised land of Chanaan vnder the conduct of Iesus] Likewise S. Paul writing to the Hebrews, calleth him by the same name, Iesus. Moreouer the Prophete Isaias, foreshewed this holie name, and office of a Sauiour, saying to future Christians] You shal draw

Gen, 41, v, 42. 45.
Num, 13, v. 17.
Act 7, v. 45.
Heb, 4, v. 8.
Isa. 12. v. 3

waters

watets in ioy, out of the Sauiours fountaines] Also
Abacuc in an other prophetical Canticle, expresseth
this ioyful holie name, saying in the person of the
Christian Church [I wil reioyce in our Lord, and wil
reioyce in God my I E S V S] S A V I O V R, in the
Chaldee Bible, R E D E M E R.

3. More clearly in the new Testament. The Archangel Gabriel, immediatly before Christs Incarnation
declared this holie name to the B. Virgine, saying,
[Thou shalt cal his name I E S V S.] Againe God also
by an Angel reuealed the same to Ioseph, the holie
Spouse of the immaculate Virgin Mother, with the
interpretation and reason therof saying [Thou shalt
cal his name I E S V S. For he shal saue his people
from their sinnes,] And accordingly when he was
circumcised the eight day from his birth. [His name
was called I E S V S, which was called by the Angel
(saith the Euangelist) before that he was conceiued
in the Wombe]

4. S. Peter with great fortitude and magnanimitie, auouched to the persecuters of the Christian
Church, that [there is no other name vnder heauen
geuen to men, wherin we must be saued] but this most
holie name I E S V S, which is S A V I O V R) in this
therfor al the holie Apostles gloried, when [they
went from the sight of the (Iewish) counsel, reioycing, because they were accounted worthie to suffer
reproche, for the name of I E S V S] By this potent
most holie name, diuels were cast out of men, and
therupon [The name of our Lord I E S V S was mag-
nified]

5. S. Paul also testifieth that a part of Christs glorie, which he merited by his Passion, consisteth in the
honour of this name, I E S V S, saying [Because he
humbled himself; made obedient vnto death, euen
the death of the Crosse: For the which thing, God, also hath exalted him, & hath geuen him a name, which

Margin notes (left):
Isa.12.v.3.
Abac 3.v.
18.
Luc 1.v.31.
Mat 1.v.11.
Luc.2.v.21
Act.4.v.12.
ch 5.v.41.
ch.19.v.12.
13.17.
Phil.2.v 8.
9,
10,

Margin notes (right):
It was impo-
sed to Christ
by Gods com-
mandment.

Our saluation
is by I E S V S
our onlie Sa-
uiour.

Part of Christs
glorie consi-
steth in the
honour of this
name I E S V S.

T t   is

is aboue al names: that in the name of I E S V S, euerie knee bow of the celestials, terrestrials, and infernals] This Apostle also expresly prayeth [That the name of our Lord I E S V S Christ, may be glorified in Christians: and they in him: according to the grace of our God, and of our Lord I E S V S Christ] Neither is is to be sleightly passed ouer, without due consideration, that this most glorious name I E S V S, is so diligently recited, againe, and againe repeted, by the holie Euangelistes, and Apostles, farre more often (as the Christian reader may easily obserue) for honour sake, then for necessarie explication of the thinges vttered. In so much that in the new Testament of I E S V S Christ, this most blessed name I E S V S, * is neere a thousand times recited. Wherfore seing it hath pleased the Eternal Creator of heauen and earth, and of al thinges that are in them, to make vs poore creatures, his adopted children, by Christ I E S V S, his onlie Begotten Sonne : we hartely pray, and besech him, that through his special grace, as wel by al men in the whole world, as particularly by vs, which professe him our heauenlie Father, his name, the Omnipotent One God, the most blessed Trinitie, the Father, and the Sonne, and the Holie Ghost, with Christ I E S V S God & Man, euer be sanctified world without end.

*1.Thes.1.v.
II.12.*

9 49.

*Rom.1.v.
7.&c.*

This name IEsvs is often repeted, rather for honour sake, then for declaration of other doctrine.

(marginal note:) This name IEsvs is often repeted, rather for honour sake, then for declaration of other doctrine.

Jn the second petition vve pray, that God vvil accomplisb bis glorious kingdome of al the Elect.

ARTICLE 21.

Ovr cheefe desire, and first prayer must be that God may be glorified aboue al, which is the summe of the fist petition. In the next place we are to desire and aske life euerlasting, which is the Kingdome of heauen, prepared for al the Elect of God, where he reigneth with al his Saintes. Therfore

(marginal note:) Next after Gods glorie in himself, we must pray for the acomplish-

V s

we pray our heauenlie Father, that as he hath decreed, and in part fulfilled the same in the holie Angels, and other his glorious seruants, already reigning with him in heauen: so he wil wholly accomplish it in al the rest, that al may be consummate in him. For wheras God in himselfe most perfect, euer from al eternitie, is most glorious, not needing anie other, yet of his infinite goodnes, he created the vniuersal world, & therin ordained Angels, and men, his rational creatures, to be participant of his glorie, that he reigning in them they also may reigne with him [Behold the tabernacle of God with men, & he wil dwel with them and they shal be his people.]

ment of his glorious Kingdome.

Apoc. 21. 7 1.2.3.

2. The accomplishment of which glorious Kingdome the Prophets of God haue foreshewed. Moyses saying in his Canticle of thankes, and praises to God for the Israelites deliuerie from Ægypt, and passage through the sea [thou ô Lord in thy mercie hast bene a guide vnto the people, which thou hast redemed, & in thy strength thou hast carried them vnto thy holie habitation. Our Lord shal reigne for euer and euermore.] In like maner the Royal Prophete often foreshewed, and desired the accomplishment of the heauenlie Kingdome [Our Lord (saith he) shal reigne for euer and for euer and euer. I beleeue to see the good thinges of our Lord, in the land of the liuing. Our Lord shal sitte King for euer. Our Lord wil blesse his people in peace. Euen as the Hart desireth after the fountaines of waters; so doth my soule desire after thee o God. My soule hath thirsted after God the strong, the liuing: when shal I come, and appeare before the face of God. How beloued are thy tabernacles o Lord of hosts! My soule coueteth, and fainteth vnto the courtes of our Lord. My hart, and my flesh haue reioyced towards the liuing God. Woe is to me that my seiourning is prolonged. My soule hath bene long a seiourner. I haue cried to thee o Lord, I haue said: Thou art my hope: my portion in the land of

The Prophets forshewed & desired the final establishment of the glorious Kingdome.

Exo. 15, v. 13. 18.

Psa. 9 v. 37.

Psa. 16. v. 11. Psa. 23. v. 10.

Psa. 41. v. 23.

Psa. 83. v. 23.

Psa. 119. v. 5. 6.

Psa. 141. v. 6. 7

the

the leuing. Attend to my petition: Thy kingdom is a kingdom of al worldes: and thy dominion in al ge- *Pf,144.*, neration, and generation. Our Lord wil reigne for 13, *Pfal,145,* euer. thy God o Sion in generation and: generation] *v,10,* Thus the Pfalmist in the perfon of al the iust vttereth his defire of the eternal glorious Kingdom of God. For which we Chriftians pray to our heauenlie Father, faying [Thy kingdom come] of which kingdom alfo the wifeman fpeaking, teacheth that al the iuft shal there reigne as kinges faying: [the iuft shal iudge nations, and shal haue dominion ouer peoples, and their Lord shal reigne for euer (& fo they shal reigne with him in the fame bleffed kingdom) If therfore *Sap.3.v.8,* (faith he) you be delighted with thrones, and with fcepters, o ye Kinges of the people, loue wifedom *cb,6.v,22,* that you may reigne for euer.]

3. Not anie worldlie Kingdom, nor worldlie Dominion, Princedom, nor Prelacie, nor other temporal power, or office is intended by our Sauiour in this petition [Thy kingdom come] but only the kingdom of heauen. This is it which S. Iohn Baptift. Chrift himfelf, and his Apoftles preached, requiring for the gayning therof, Penance, and other good workes. [Doe penance (faith S. Iohn) for the kingdom of *Mat 3,v,2.* heauen is at hand] Our Sauiour preached the very *ch.4 v,17,* fame [Doe penance, for the kingdom of heauen is *Luc:9, v.2.* at hand] Euen fo he fent his Difciples [to preach the kingdom of God] which is properly the kingdom of iuftice in this life, & of glorie in heauen. And withal our Lord admonisheth, not to be ouer folicitous for *Mat,6.v.33* worldlie neceffities, but promifeth that to thofe which firft feeke iuftice, and therby feeke heauen, he wil geue alfo other thinges, fo farre as they are neceffarie. The kingdom of heauen is it, which our Lord promifed to his holie Apoftles (when Iudas the traifor was parted from them, immediatly before his *Luc,22.v.* Paffion, faying [I doe difpofe vnto you, as my Father 29, 30,

hath

Al other temporal powers are trublefome tranfitorie and dangours.

hath diſpoſed to me, a Kingdom, that you may eate & drinke (enioy al ſpiritual good deſires) vpō my table, in my kingdom; and ſitte vpon thrones, iudging the twelue tribes of Iſrael.] When this kingdom ſhal be complete, then wil al that ſhal enioy the ſame, render al thankes inceſſantly ſaying [we thanke thee o Lord, God Omnipotent, which art, and which waſt, and which ſhal come : becauſe thou haſt receiued thy great power, and haſt reigned . I heard a voice (ſaith S. Iohn the Apoſtle) as the voice of a great trumpette, and as the voice of manie waters, and as the voice of great thunders ſaying. Alleluia: becauſe our Lord God Omnipotent reigneth. Let vs be glad, and reioyce, and geue glorie to him: becauſe the Mariage of the lambe is come : and his wife (the glorious Church) hath prepared herſelf] This is that vnſpeakable eternal, bliſſe, glorie, & euerlaſting life of al the elect, to be aſſembled in heauen, and there to reigne with God: for the which our B. Sauiour teacheth & commandeth vs to pray, to our heauenlie Father [Let thy kingdom come] Complete thy Church militant: make it al triumphans.

VVe alſo pray that God vvil ſtil propagate,
and euer conſerue his militant Church,
to the end of this vvorld.

ARTICLE. 22.

BVt forſomuch as it is impoſſible for anie to attaine vnto the kingdome of glorie, vnles they firſt enter into the kingdome of grace (for grace is the feede, and glorie is the fruite) and forſomuch as both grace and glorie, are the proper giftes of God (for our Lord geueth grace and glorie) grace in this life, in the militant Church , and glorie in heauen, in the triumphant. We muſt alſo deſire and pray that the militant Church, may ſtil be conſerued and increaſed, euen to
Tt 3 the

The Militant Church is Gods kingdome in earth.

Apoc.11.v. 17.
Ih 19.v.6. 7.

Mat.6.v. 10.

Pſal.83.v. 11.

the end of this word, by the conuersion of al sortes of
Infidels, so long as there remaine anie Heretikes,
Scismatikes, Iewes, Turkes, or Paganes.

The Pro-
phetes fore-
shewed and
desired pro-
sperous suc-
cesseste of the
same militant
Church.

2. Of this kingdome of God, the Royal Prophete
speaketh, foreshewing the great enlargement therof
by Chrifts merite, God saying to his Sonne Incarnate
Aske of me, & I wil geue thee, the Gentiles for thyne
inheritance: and the possession of the endes of the
earth.] For which increase the same Prophete congratulating, saith to Chrift [Be gyrded with thy sword
vpon thy thigh, ô most mightie. With thy beauter, &
fairenes intend, procede prosperously, and reigne]
Againe he saith [God shal reigne ouer the Gentiles.
Mount Sion is founded, with the exaltation of the
whole earth: The saides of the North, the citie of the
great king] For the prosperous propagation therfore
of this Christiau kingdom, the militant Church; al
the faithful must praise God, and stil pray, that it
alwayes procede accordingly [Let thy Sainctes blesse
thee (said the same Psalmist in his praise, and prayer
to God) they shal tel the glorie of thy kingdom, and
shal speake thy might] And with al praises, & thankes
for benefites, either receiued or expected, conformable desire, and prayer, is also required. For as it foloweth in the same Psalme [our Lord is nere to al that
inuocate him, to al that inuocate him in truth] So
Isaias firft prayed to God for Ezechias the king and
the same Ezechias, prayed for himself, and then it
was reuealed which before was decreed that Ezechias should recouer health of bodie, & liue longer,
and also be deliuered from the immenent great danger of his enimie, the king of Assirians. So did al the
Prophetes pray to God, for the accomplishing of
whatsoeuer God hath decreed. Whether they knew
or no, by prophetical spirite, what was decreed. Albeit therfore we most assuredly know, by the gift of
faith, that the Church of Chrift shal stil be propaga-
                                        ted,

Psf. 2. v. 2.

Psf. 44. v. 4.

Psf. 46. v. 9.
Psf 47. v. 3.

Psf. 144. v.
10. 11.

v. 19.

Isa. 37. v. 2.
3. &c
ch. 38. v. 2. 4.
Reg. 19. v.
15.
ch. 20. v. 3. 4.
&c.

Dan 9.v.15.
16.&c. ted, and conſerued, yet muſt we ſtil pray for the ſame, adioyning our deſires, and prayers, which God alſo reſpecteth, amongſt other cauſes, for which he granteth the ſame thinges, which he for manie cauſes decreeth.

3. Of this Kingdome of Chriſt, the militant viſible Church, the Archāgel Gabriel declared to the B. Virgine Mother, that [our Lord God wil geue to him the Luc.1.v.32. 33. ſeate of Dauid his father : and he ſhal reigne in the houſe of Iacob for euer : and of his kingdom there ſhal be no end] This his owne kingdome, and the greatnes and perpetual continuance therof, our Lord himſelf deſcribeth, by manie parables, reſembling it to ſeede ſowne in the fielde, of this world : which bringeth forth fruite diuerſly multiplied, ſome thirtiefold, ſome threeſcore, ſome an hundredfold. Alſo to good ſeede, wherwith cockle ſpringeth vp, whiles men doe ſlepe. To muſtardſeede, which being ſmal groweth very great. To a litle leauen, which leaueneth a great quantitie of dough. To hidden treaſure, and to a precious ſtone, eſteemed worth al, that anie man hath. To a nette that geathereth diuers ſortes of fishes, profitable and vnprofitable] By al which & other his documēts we are aſſured that the Chriſtian true Church can not faile, to be alwayes viſible, to the end of this world: yet doth our Lord inſtruct and command vs to repete dayly in our deſire, and prayer this petitiō, amongſt others [Let thy kingdom come] Himſelf ſent his Apoſtles, ſent his ſeuentie two diſciples, ſendeth continually Paſtors, and Preachers into his owne harueſt; neuertheles he biddeth vs withal [to deſire the Lord of the harneſt, to ſend men into his harueſt.]

Though we know by light of faith that the viſible Church ſhal euer cōtinue; yet we pray for the ſame, conforming our deſires thereunto.

Dau.7.v. 14.27. Mat.13.v. 24 31 33 44. 45 47. Mar 4. Luc 8.

Ephel.4.v.ß 11.

Luc 10.v.2.

We likewiſe pray that God wil reigne in vs, by his ſanctifying grace.
ARTICLE 23.

Here

Euerie iuſt
ſoule is alſo
the habitacle,
and kingdome
of God.

HEre we muſt alſo deſire in particular, and pray
that God, the King of heauen, and earth, wil
voutſafe to reigne in our ſoules, to direct, and ſanctifie, rule, and gouerne our hartes, and bodies, ſenſes,
ſpeaches, and actions in his Law, and in the workes
of his commandmēts, that here, & for euer we may
by his grace, be ſafe, and free from al dominion of
the euil ſpirite, and of ſinne: becauſe otherwiſe it
ſufficeth not to beleue only, and [to crie, Lord, Lord] Mat.7 v.21.
for al ſuch as be in ſtate if mortal ſinne; that is, al thoſe
in whom ſinne reigneth, are as dead members in a
bodie, and by ſuch ſinne, the enimie reigneth, and
poſſeſſeth the ſoules. And therfore we muſt pray, that
God himſelf wil reigne in our hartes, and beſech our
heauenlie Father; there to confirme his dominion.
Not only to exclude al poſſeſſion of the inueterate
deſtroying enimie, but alſo al the force of naughtie
concupiſcence, deſiring & praying God, the mightie
warier to come, and reigne in vs, to binde the enimie
and to take away his weapons, and make vs his ſpiri- Luc.11. v.
tual kingdom, furniſhed with al munition of ſpiri- [...]
tual armour in this life, that we may attaine vnto the
kingdom of glorie.

VVe muſt pray
that God wil
make your
ſoules his par-
ticular king-
dome.

2. This dominion of God, ruling and directing the
hartes of the iuſt, the Royal Prophete, and with him
al Gods true ſeruants, deſire, and pray for, in this or
like maner, ſaying [Direct me o Lord, my King, & my Pſal.5.v 3.
God, in thy truth: and teach me, becauſe thou art
God my Sauiour: & thee haue I expected al the day.
Thou art the ſame my King, and my God. The ſeate o Pſal.24.v 5
God for euer and euer: and of direction the rodde of
thy kingdom (not force of men, horſes, or armes, but
rule and direction of Gods grace in mans hart, is his
ſpiritual kingdom) Becauſe our protection is of our Pſ 88. v 19.
Lord, and of the holie one of Iſrael our king. L t
(therfore) the brightnes of our Lord God (his illumi- Pſ.89.v.17.
nating grace) be vpon vs. And direct thou (o God)
the

the workes of our handes ouer vs: and the worke of
our handes doe thou direct] To signifie more clearly
this point that God as King of al, not only doth rule
exteriorly in the effects of conquests and victories,
but more especially internally gouerning the faithful
soules of men, to doe that is good and iust. Isaias the
Prophete saith expresly [Behold the king shal reigne
in iustice: and the princes (Ministers of God, Angeles
Apostles, and other Pastors) shal rule in iudgement]
doing that which is right and iust. Which is the effect
of Gods grace reigning in faithful soules.

3.   Christ himself plainly teacheth the same, not
only to seeke the kingdom of heauen, in glorie euerlasting: Which is commonly called the kingdom of
God, but also he biddeth vs before al thinges [first to
seeke the kingdome of God (in this life as appeaneth
by his wordes adioyned.) And the iustice of him]that
is, the iustice which God requireth in the faithful: signifying that without iustice by which God reigneth
in faithful soules in this life, they can not be his spiritual kingdome, and that by iustice they haue his
kingdom, and gouernment within them, wherof he
said to his disciples [Loe the kingdom of God is
within you] This he further declareth by [the ghest
inuertained vnto a kings feast, at a Mariage: & found
to be without a wedding garment] in whom that
king reigned not, and therfore[commanded to cast
him into vtter darknes, where shal be weeping and
gnashing of teeth.]

4.   To the same purpose of attaining this spiritual
kingdom of Christ reigning in the hart by his grace,
S. Paul exhorteth saying[Let not sinne reigne in your
mortal bodie, that you obey the cocupiscences therof]
To others that thought themselues spiritually riche
he said [Now you are filled, now you are become
riche (as you thinke) without vs you reigne: and
would to God, you did reigne, that we also might
V v   reigne

Isa. 32. v. 1.

Luc. 17. v. 21.

Mat. 22. v. 12.

Rom. 6. v. 12

2 Cor. 4. v. 8.

And that he wil reigne in vs by his grace of iustice.

The holie A-postles teach the same to be necessarie.

reigne with you] Touching mortificatiõ of vntamed passions, which reigne in the vnperfect, he saith that [Flesh and bloud can not possesse the kingdom of God, neither shal corruption possesse incorruption] In respect also of this spiritual kingdom , where God reigneth by his grace, S. Peter calleth good Christiãs [A kinglie Priesthood] kinges in that they rule their passions, and priestes in that they offer good prayers, and other workes to Gods honour. The plainest summarie literal sense therfore, of this petition [Let thy kingdom come] or [Make that thy kingdome come] is, that we desire, and pray our heauenlie Father, to make complete, according to his eternal Decree, the perfect glorious kingdom of al his elect: & for the accomplishing therof to propagate, conserue, and prosper his militant Church , and spiritual kingdom in earth, vntil the consummation of this world: and that he wil voutsafe to reigne in vs, and al faithful particular soules by his sanctifying grace, that so we may perseuere liuing members in his militant Church, and be made partakers of glorie in the triumphant.

ch.15. v.50.

1.Pet.2.v.9.

Art. 21.

Art. 22.

Art. 23.

The summarie literal sense of this petition.

In the third petition vve pray, that Gods vvil (not our ovvne proper vvil) be so fulfilled in earth, as it is in heauen.

ARTICLE 24.

Gods wil, and good pleasure is alwayes fulfilled.

Iuc.11.v.9.

VVE must stil obserue in al prayers, & particularly in this, that when we aske anie thing of God (as he commandeth vs to recurre vnto him by prayer, for whatsoeuer is needeful) we must not thinke, that God is mutable, or wil doe otherwise then according to his diuine good pleasure. But therfore his diuine goodnes teacheth, & cõmandeth vs to pray, that therby (acknowleging our owne necessitie, and his fatherlie care of vs) we may

may sturre vp ourselues to right affections, and so become capable of his purposes, and promises, which infinitely excel al our best desires [For what we should pray, as we ought (saith S. Paul) we know not: but the Spirite himself requesteth for vs, with gronings vnspeakable. And he that searcheth the hartes, knoweth wha the Spirite desireth: because according to God he requesteth for the sainctes.] The faithful not knowing what, nor how to aske, yet resigning their willes to Gods wil, their demand is according to God: it is in deede Gods wil, and therfore gratful to God, and most profitable to them that so pray. And therfore in euerie prayer it is either to be expressed, as here it is, or necessarily to be implied, that we must alwayes aske with condition, if it be Gods wil; and with resignation expresly, or implicitely to say from the hart [ô God. Thy wil be done.]

2. Which perfect resignation is further proued to be necessarie, by manie examples and testimonies of holie Scriptures. Blessed Iob vnderstanding of the losse of al his goodes, & children, said [Our Lord gaue, and our Lord hath taken away: as it hath pleased our Lord, so is it done. The name of our Lord be blessed.] Being also strooken with a very sore boyle, from the sole of the foote, euen to the toppe of his head: and skornefully reuiled by his wife, he said [If we haue receiued good thinges of the hand of God, euil thinges whyshould we not receiue?] King Dauid hauing a wil to build a Temple to God, and being informed by Nathan a Prophete, that God would not haue it done by him, but by his sonne; conforming his owne wil to Gods wil: with thankes for al Gods benefites, he said [Now therfore ô Lord God, raise vp for euer the word that thou hast spoken vpon thy seruant, and vpon his house; and doe as thou hast spoken: that thy name may be magnified for euer.] The same Royal Prophete, often confirmeth this necessa-

Rom.8.v.26

v.27.

Iob,1.v,21.

ch.2.v.9.10

2.Reg.7.v. 2,4.12.13. 25.26.

Psl.1.v.2,

Al are bond to resigne their proper wil to Gods wil.

Proued by examples, and instructions of holie Scriptures.

rie rule of refigning al our defires to Gods wil [Bleſ- Pſ 50. v. 10.
fed is the man (ſaith he) whoſe wil is in the way of
our Lord. Deale fauourably ô Lord in thy good wil
with Sion. Conduct me into the path of thy cōmand- Pſ.128. v. 35.
ment, becauſe I would it. Teach me to doe thy wil, Pſ 142. v. 10
becauſe thou art my God. There is no wiſdome (ſaith Pro.21. v. 30
Salomon) there is no prudence, there is no counſel
againſt our Lord] Iſaias admoniſhed the people that
[God did not reſpect their faſting, becauſe they were Iſa.58. v. 5.
addicted to their proper wil, contrarie to Gods wil]
Holie Tobias deſiring rather to dye, then to liue longer, yet prayed not for the ſame abſolutely, but with
refignation to Gods wil: ſaying, [Now Lord accor- Tob 3. v. 6.
ding to thy wil doe with me] So did Iudith profeſſe
that often mans wil is different from Gods wil; and Iudith 8. v.
then muſt be refigned to Gods wil. Wherupon ſhe 17.
exhorted others ſaying: [Let vs ſay weeping to our
Lord: that according to his wil, ſo he doe his mercie
with vs] Valiant Iudas Machabeus prayed alſo thus 1.Mach. 3 v.
[As it ſhal be the wil in heauen: ſo be it done] So 60.
other faithful Iewes in Ieruſalem writing to their 2.Mach.1.
brethren in Ægypt [prayed God to geue vnto them v.3.
al, an hart to worſhip him, and to doe his wil, with a
valiant hart, and a willing mind.]

Chriſt eſpe-   3. Aboue al other proofes, our Bleſſed Sauiours
cially requi- cleareſt doctrine and practiſe aſſureth vs, how necef-
reth reſigna- ſarie it is both to ſubmitte our wil to Gods wil, and
tion if mans   alſo to pray ſincerely that Gods wil may be done.
wil to the wil [Thus you ſhal pray (ſaith he) Our Father, Thy wil Mat.6. v. 9.
if God.   be done, as in heauen, in earth alſo] propoſing the 10.
example of the glorified in heauen, that the faithful
may imitate them in deſire, For though it be not ſo
perfect: yet muſt it be according to the ſimilitude in
ſome ſort: and ſo this clauſe of ſimilitude, is to be vnderſtood in both the former petitions, that we muſt
deſire to ſanctifie Gods name, and deſire his dominion
in al the earth, and particularly in our owne ſoules

as it is in heauen, in al the glorious. Confider alfo our Lords practife, and often affeueration [I feeke not (faith he) my wil, but the wil of him that fent me, I defcended from heauen, not to doe myne owne wil, but the wil of him that fent me.] And in the agonie of his Paffion he prayed thus [My Father if it be poffible, al thinges are poffible to thee, let this chalice paffe from me. Neuertheles not as I wil, but as thou wilt. If this chalice may not paffe, but I muft drinke it, thy wil be done] And fo our Sauiour biddeth vs abfolutely to pray, that in al thinges, not our proper wil, but the wil of God be done.

4. With this refignation Chriftes Apoftles tempered al their defires, willes, and purpofes [I wil returne to you againe (faid S. Paul to the people of Ephefus) God willing] S. Luke and other freindes, when they could not diffwade S. Paul, from returning to Ierufalem, refigning their wil to Gods, faid [The wil of our Lord be done] It is S. Pauls vfual phraife in his purpofes and promifes to fay with expreffe conditions] If God wil: by the wil of God; If our Lord wil] And S. Iames expreffely reprehendeth thofe that omitted this condition in ordinarie fpeach [Behold now (faith he) you that fay to day, or to morow, we wil goe into that citie, and there certes wil fpende a yeare, and wil trafficke and make our gaine: for that you should fay: If our Lord wil, and if we shal liue, we wil doe this, or that] And S. Peter perfwadeth to patience, in regard of Gods wil. [It is better (faith he) to fuffer as doing wel, if the wil of God, wil haue it fo: then doing il: for they alfo that fuffer according to the wil of God: let them commend their foules to the faithful Creator in good deedes.]

His Apoftles inculcate the fame.

Marginal notes:
Ioan.5.v. 30.
ch.6.v.38.
Mat.26.v. 39.42.
Act.18.v. 21.
ch.21.v.14
Rom.1.v. 10.
ch.15.v.32.
1.Cor.4.v. 19.
Iac.4.v.13. 14.15.
1.Pet 3,v. 17.
ch.4.v.19.

Gods abfolute vvil, called his good pleafure, is euermore fulfilled.

ARTICLE 25.

V v 3

AI

AL thinges in God are God himſelf, his very ſub- *see Part.* ſtance, and nature. In him there are no Acci- *1, Artic. 8.* dents, as there be in creatures. So his pure and proper *§ 3.* wil (as his Goodnes, Power, Wiſdome, Iuſtice, and euerie Attirbute) is himſelfe, and therfore is immutable, and is alwayes fulfilled, as manie holie Scriptures doe clearly witneſſe. But becauſe manie other holie Scriptures doe alſo teſtifie, that Gods wil is often tranſgreſſed by ſinners: for acclaration of this ſeeming contradiction, Chriſtian ſchooles doe explicate the ſame holie Scriptures, by a neceſſarie diſtinction, calling Gods wil, as it is perfectly performed, his abſolute proper wil (which is *voluntas beneplaciti*) otherwiſe it is his conditional wil, which alwayes ought, but is not alwayes fulfilled, which is called *voluntas ſigni*, becauſe it appeareth by his Law, of commanding, or prohibiting, as by a ſigne, to be Gods wil. For confirmation of which doctrine, & for explication of theſe diuine wordes, in our Lords prayer, wherby we deſire, that [The wil of our heauenly Father may be done] we ſhal here breefely recite ſome euident diuine teſtimonies, affirming that Gods wil (to witte his proper abſolute wil) is alwayes fulfilled. And afterwardes the like teſtimonies, that Gods wil (which is *Art. 26.* therfore called conditional) alwayes ought to be performed, but often is tranſgreſſed by ſinners.

2. Holie Ioſeph the Patriarch ſaid to his brethren *Gen. 50. v.* [Feare not: Can we reſiſt the wil of God?] Euidently *19. 20.* ſhewing that Gods abſolute proper wil can not be hindered, but is alwayes fulfilled. Which he alſo explicated, ſaying [You thought euil againſt me. But *Exo. 21. v.* God turned that into good, that he might exalt me; as *16.* preſently you ſee, & might ſaue manie peoples [Their wil was, by ſelling their brother vnto ſtrangers, to hinder his aduancement, which was a greueous ſinne, & a tráſgreſſion of Gods wil: yet Gods abſolute wil was fulfilled, which was to draw good out of this euil, and

Gods abſolute wil is alwaies fulfilled: his conditional wil ought to be fulfilled, but ofteo is not.

Proued by teſtimonies.

and by this meanes to exalt Ioseph, for al their good, and the good of Ægypt, and other nations adioyning: for the saftie of manie peoples, in the scarsitie of bread, and danger of famine. Rabsaces a heathen Infidel: the general captaine of Assirians, beseging Ierusalem, knew the essicacie of Gods wil: when threatning the Inhabitants of that citie, he said to them [Why, am I come hither without the wil of the Lord, to destroy it ? The Lord said to me; Goe vp to this land, and destroy it] which he auouched hauing vnderstood that the Prophets had so told them. And acknowleged truly that the wil of God, can not be hindered; but he erred, not knowing that God in deede would haue him to come, and only to assault them, but not to destroy them.

3. More assuredly the Royal Prophete affirmeth, that Gods absolute wil is euer fulfilled [Our Lord saued me(saith he) becaufe he would me. The workes of our Lord are exquisite (exactly performed) according to al his willes] Al thinges whatsoeuer our Lord would, he hath done in heauen and in earth, in the sea, and in al the depthes. Manie cogitations (saith Salomon) are in the hart of a man : but the wil of our Lord shal be permanent. Al that he pleaseth, he wil doe] God himselfe saith by his Prophete Isaias [My counsel shal stand : and al my wil shal be done. The High one (saith Daniel) ruleth in the Kingdome of men: and to whomsoeuer it shal please him; he wil geue it. For he doth according to his wil: &c.]

4. A poore Leper faithfully beleuing, and professing the Omnipotencie of Chrifts wil , sayed to him [Lord if thou wilt: thou canst make me cleane.] Our Lord in confirmation therof, said vnto the Leper [I wil (and addeth withal) Be thou made cleane. And forthwith his Leprosie was made cleane] Further that Chrifts wil is omnipotent, and alwayes fulfilled, as he is God. S. Paul saith [Who resisteth his

wil

4 Reg 18. v. 35.

Psal. 17. v. 20.

Ps. 110. v. 2.

Pro. 19. v. 21.

Isa. 46. v. 10.

Dan. 4. v. 14. 32.

Mat. 8. v. 2. 3.

Rom. 9. v. 19.

By other testimonies of the Prophets.

By Chrift and his Apostles.

wil?] signifying that none can. [In Christ (saith the
same Apostle of himselfe and others)we are called by *Ephes.1.v.*
lotte, predestinate , according to the purpose of 11,
him that worketh al thinges,according to the counsel of his wil] The whole glorious court of heauen, *Apoc.4.9.*
adoring God,say[Thou art worthie ô Lord our God, 11.
to receiue glorie,and honour,& power,becaufe thou
haft created al thinges:and for thy wil they were,and
haue bene created.]

Gods conditional vvil, vvhich is knovvne by signes, is often not fulfilled.

ARTICLE 26.

Distinctions
are neceſſarie
to explaine
holie Scrip-
tutes;which
otherwise
might ſeme
contrarie.

Gods Com-
mandmenes,
Connſels,Pro-
miſes,Prohi-
bitions,and
Threates,are
ſignes of his
wil.

Other holie Scriptures doe alſo clearly shew that
Gods wil is often tranſgreſſed and not fulfilled:
which muſt needes be vnderſtood in an other ſenſe,
then the former, becauſe otherwiſe there should be
(which is vnpoſſible) contradiction in the word of
God. And therfore for explication of this ſeming *Artis.25.*
contrarietie(as is noted before) we muſt conſider that §.4.
ſomewhere the holie Scripture ſpeaketh of Gods ab-
ſolut wil,which is alwayes fulfilled, & ſome where of
his côditional wil,which men may fulfil,but often do
not.As when God comandeth,counſeleth,promiſeth
reward;or els forbiddeth,or threatneth punishment:
theſe be ſignes what God would haue to be done, or
not done, yet leaueth reaſonable creatures to their
free wil (wherwith they are endued) either to doe
his wil(as in heauen al doe perfectly fulfil it),or not to
doe it,as in this life,ſome doe his wil,ſome doe againſt
his wil. Not againſt Gods abſolute wil, for ſo none
can, as is proued in the precedent Article:but againſt
his conditional wil, as by theſe examples, and teſtimonies (and by others the like) it is moſt euident.
    2.   God our Lord did prohibide our firſt parent,
from eating of the fruite of a certaine tree in Paradiſe

Gen. 2. v. 17.
ch. 3. v. 6.

dife, with threatning that if he should eate therof, he should dye the death] By which prohibition, and threatning, it is cleare that God would haue had Adam, to haue abstained from eating of that fruite. And it is no lesse euident that Adam did contrarie to Gods wil, by eating of the forbidden fruite, and for the same was iustly punished. Our Lord admonished, and threatned Cain, saying to him [Why art thou angrie, and why is thy countenance fallen. If thou doe wel shalt thou not receiue againe? but if thou doest il, shal not thy sinne forthwith be present at the doore?] therby signifying to be his wil, that Cain should haue subdued his disordered passion of anger; which he not subduing, as God admonishind him, but murthering his brother, sinned greuously against Gods wil, and was iustly punished for the same crime. To al the Israelites our Lord said in general touching his wil, and al his Law [If you walke contrarie to me, and wil not heare me: I wil increafe your plagues vntil seuenfold, for your sinnes] And that manie did refift his wil made knowne to them by his Lawes, is manifest by innumerable testimonies. Brefely al sinners doe against Gods wil [because God would not haue iniquitie.]

v. 17, 18.
19.
ch. 4. v. 6. 7.

Leuit. 26.
v. 21.
Num 11 v.
1. 2 &c.

Iudic. 2. v. 2.
&c.
Psal. 5. v. 5.

Examples of not fulfilling Gods wil.

Adam.

Cain.

Al transgressors of Gods commandments, doe contrarie to his wil.

3. So the holie Prophets often admonish, that sinne and death are against Gods wil, [Wrath is in his indignation (saith the Psalmist) and life in his wil] God would in his conditional wil, that al should kepe his Law, and liue eternally: which is not fulfilled: but his absolute wil is, to reward the good, and to punish the euil. He made his wayes knowne to Moyses: his willes to the children of Israel]His willes saith the Prophete, not only his absolute wil (by his works which are the effectes therof) but also of his conditional wil, by his Law, that is, of that which appeareth by signes to be his wil. Againe, of the wil of God not fulfilled, Isaias also speaketh, saying to some:

Psal. 29. v. 6.

Psal. 102. v. 7.

Proued by other holie Scriptures.

W w

Be-

[Behold in the day of your faſt , your owne wil is ſt ..
found] ſignifying that they tranſgreſſed Gods wil, ſ ſ.
which was, that they should haue obſerued al his
commandements , and then their faſt had bene gratful. Likewiſe of Gods wil not fulfilled, him ſelf ſaith
byhis Prophete Ezechiel [Why, is the death of a ſin-   Eze h. 18. ꝟ
ner my wil, ſaith our Lord God, and not that he con   23
uert from his waues , and liue? I would cleanſe thee,   ch 24. ꝟ 13.
and thou art not cleanſed from thy filthines] Againe,
by his Prophete Oſee [When I would heale Iſrael, the   Oſee 7. ꝟ. 1.
iniquitie of Ephraim was reuea=led, and the malice of
Samaria : becauſe they haue wrought lying] And ſo
the wil of God was not done.

4. Omitting more of the Law and Prophetes,
Chriſt our Lord teſtifieth , that Gods wil is not alwaies fulfilled,by his expoſtulation with Ieruſalem,   Mat. 23. ꝟ.
ſaying [How often would I gather together thy chil-   37.
dren, as the hen doth gather together her chickines,
vnder her winges, & thou wouldeſt not] And therfore he teacheth vs to deſire, and to pray our heauenlie Father that [his wil be done as in heauen, ſo   ch. 6. ꝟ. 10.
in earth alſo] Which prayer is moſt neceſſarie , becauſe
without ſpecial grace, none can doe his wil, neither
according to the ſubſtance of the thinges, which
he commandeth, much leſſe in perfect maner, which
we are bond to deſire, that [euen in earth his wil may
be done, as it is in heauen.] And to pray that he wii
geue vs effectual grace to kepe al his comandments,
doing al we ought to doe, and auoiding al which is
prohibited. For as our Lord ſaith in one place [He
that doth the wil of my Father, ſhal enter into the
Kingdom of heauen.] So he ſaith in other wordes the   Mat 7. ꝟ.
ſame thing in ſenſe [that he which wil enter into the   21.
Kingdome of heauen, muſt kepe the comandments]   ch 19. ꝟ. 17.
Againe [Whoſoeuer ſhal doe the wil of my Father,
that is in heauen, he is my brother, and ſiſter, and mother.] Yea when our owne wil agreth with Gods wil,

In this peti-
tiou we pray
for ſpecial
grace to doe
Gods wil.
VVhich is to
kepe al his
comandde-
ments.

VC

we muſt deſire and pray, that it be fulfilled, not for our proper contentment, but becauſe it is Gods wil; for ſ ſo it is fulfiled in heauen.]

5. Vpon which ground the holie Apoſtles admoniſh, and exhorte al Chriſtians to learne, and obſerue Gods wil, not for our owne comoditie, but in more perfect maner, for Gods ſeruice, becauſe it is his wil [Walke as children of the light (ſaith S. Paul) prouing what is wel pleaſing to God. Become not vnwiſe but vnderſtanding, what is the wil of God.] And alſo teacheth that our ſanctification is Gods wil. [This is the wil of God, your ſanctification] God our Lord (ſaith he) wil al men to be ſaued, and to come to the knowlege of the truth] It is the wil of God (ſaith S. Peter to al Chriſtians) that doing wel you may make the ignorance of vnwiſe men to be dumme] And He that doth the wil of God (ſaith S. Iohn) abideth for euer, Wherfore ſeing it is certaine and euident, that Gods abſolute wil is immutable, and is alwayes, and in al thinges fulfilled, and that alſo his wil is that by doing his wil, his children ſhal pleaſe him, and ſo attaine euerlſting life, and ſeeing it is cleare alſo, that Gods wil is by manie not fulfilled: it is neceſſarie, that we deſire, and pray our heauenlie Father, that [his wil be done, as it is in heauen, ſo in earth alſo] And particularly that we may obtaine his ſpecial grace to doe and ſuffer, al that is Gods wil: wholly reſigning our proper wil, to his wil, according to this breſe Rule. Take away proper wil, and you take away Hel. Doe Gods wil, and you ſhal poſſeſſe Heauen.

Epheſ 5. v. 8 10. 17.

1 Theſ 4. v. 3. 1.

1 Tim 3 v. 4

1 Pet 2. v. 15.

1 Ioan. 2 v. 17.

Christians must deſire their owne ſaluation, becauſe it is the wil of God.

And muſt pray for grace, ſo to deſire it.

A breefe Rule.

In the fourth petition, We pray our heauenlie Father, to geue vs al neceſſarie ſpiritual, and corporal food.

ARTICLE 27.

Man

MAn consisting of soule & bodie, and being in neither part able to sustaine himself without the helpe of God, must by prayer seeke from him, both spiritual and corporal foode: and that more especially, which perteyneth to the principal part. As therfore our Blessed Sauiour hath taught, and commanded vs to aske of our heauenlie Father in the three former petitions, thinges necessarie for our soules in eternal life: so in this fourth, he likewise instructeth vs to aske other thinges, necessarie for both soules and bodies : by which we may serue God in this life. And to this purpose, our Lord hath prescribed, that we shal pray our heauenlie Father, Mat 6.v [to geue vs this day, our dailie bread] Where by the 11. same wordes, we aske both heauenlie, and terrestrial Luc.11.v.3. bread.

2. For explanation whereof, we must obserue, that often in holie Scripture, by bread is signified spiritual food of the word of God, and other diuine nutriment wherwith the soule is fedde. Of which our Lord saith [Not in bread alone doth man liue, but in Deut.8.v. euerie word that procedeth from the mouth of God] 3. Of such persons as neglect this spiritual bread, holie Mat.4 v.4. Iob saith [They lead their dayes in wealth, and in a Iob.21.v. moment they goe downe to hel. Who said to God: 13.14.15. Depart from vs, we wil not the knowlege of thy wayes. Who is the Omnipotent that we should serue him? and what doth it profite vs, if we pray him?] Such people not asking spiritual bread, dye for famine: with which kinde of spiritual famine, our Lord threatned to punish sinners, saying by his Prophete Amos [Behold the dayes come, saith our Lord, and I Amos 8.v. wil send forth famine into the land; not the famine 11. of bread, nor thirst of water, but of hearing the word of the Lord] For the same famine, when it hapened to Gods people for their sinnes, Ieremie the Prophete lamented in the behalfe of the penitents, saying [The
little

After the desire of Gods glorie, and mans saluation, we must pray for spiritual helpes, & necessarie tempotals.

In holie Scripture, bread & meate sometime is signifie spiritual food of the soule.

Thren.4.v.4 litle ones haue asked bread, and there was none that brake it vnto them] Of this kinde of meate the Royal Prophete speaketh thus, exhorting the faithful. [Be delighted in our Lord, and he wil geue thee the petitions of thy hart [Our Sauiour him self faith [The bread which I wil geue, is the life of the world. The water that I wil geue him (that commeth to me) shal become in him a fountaine of water springing vp vnto life euerlasting. The grace of God (saith S. Paul) is life euerlasting, in Christ Iesus our Lord.] Blessed therfore are they that hunger and thirst iustice, which is, the spiritual foode, and neutriment of their soules, they wil hartely pray for it, crying to our heauenlie Father [Geue vs this day our daylie bread.]

Psal.34.v. 4.

Ioan.6.v. 51.

ch.4.v.14. Rom.6.v. 23.

3. By bread also in holie Scripture, is signified al maner of conuenient corporal sustinance; yea also al corporal necessarie thinges, to the conuenient state of euerie one. Our Lord said to Adam [In the sweate of thy face, shalt thou eate bread] When Iacob the Patriarch making a vow in his prayer, said [If God shal be with me, & kepe me in the way by which I walke, and shal geue me bread to eate] he doubtles vnderstood by bread, al competent corporal foode. When Eliseus the Prophete willed the King of Israel to set bread and water before certaine Syrians, that they might eate and drinke; [a great preparion of meates was set before them, and they did eate and drinke] S. Luke also calleth a feast or dinner, the eating of bread [It came to passe (saith he) when Iesus entred into the house of a certaine Prince of the Pharasees, vpon the Sabbath to eate bread] So in this petition therfore by the name of bread, we pray both for spiritual meanes (of wholsome doctrine, knowlege, holie Sacraments, Sacramentals, and other helpes, with the fruite therof) and also for al corporal necessities, wherby we may more conueniently, by vse of temporal good thinges, attaine to the eternal. But more

Gen 3.v.19

ch.28.v.20. 21.

Iob 42.v. 11.

4.Reg 6. v.22.23.

Luc.14.v.1.

Bread also signifieth al corporal food, & other necessaries.

W w 3   parti-

particularly we are to desire & to pray for the special
good fruite of the most blessed Eucharist. The Sacrifice & Sacrament of Chrifts bodie and bloud. And for
our particular temporal and corporal releefe in this
life. Of which two, we shal here adde two special
Articles.

VVe pray in particular , that vve may fruict-
fully participate of the B. Sacrifice, and Sa-
crament of the Altar.

ARTICLE 28.

The B. Sacri-
fice, & Sacra-
ment being
the principal
foode of
foules muft
principally be
desired.

A Mongft al fpiritual foode of the foule , as none
is more excellent then the heauenlie bâquette
of Chrifts owne bodie and bloud vnder the formes
of bread and wine: fo none is more to be defired, and
the ineftimable fruite therof to be fought for, by hartie & frequent prayer. And therfore when we make
this petition to our heauenlie Father: that he wil
voutfafe to geue vs, euery day, our daylie bread; our
principal cogitation ought to be vpon this moft principal bread : defiring God to grant vs his fpecial
grace, fo to honour the fame alwayes, and with fuch
deuotion at conuenient times to receiue it, as may
make vs capable of the inexplicable fruite therof,
which is abundance of grace in this life, and of cor-
refpondent glorie in life euerlafting . For it is of no
leffe power:and value, as our B. Sauiour himfelf affirmeth: faying [that he would not only geue a better
bread then Manna, but that the fame bread is himfelf, and that he would geue it vs to eate;that is, truly
and really meate; truly and really eaten : els it were
not meate in deede. As is largely declared elfwhere.

Ioan.6.v.31.
32.51.35.58.

Part. 2.
Art. 18.

Sacrifice was
offered in the
old Law like-
wife euerie
day, and very
ofté in feaftes,
& vpon other
occafions,

2.   In this place is fpecially to be confidered, with
what feruent deuotion the faithful feruants of God
repaired to the figures, and shadowes of this fingular
Myfterie : and with what diligence, and finceritie
Chriftians frequented the thing it felf, in the primitiue

tiue Church of Christ: and that the same is regiſtred
for our inſtruction, & imitation in the written word
of God. It was ſtrictly ordayned, and by very manie
faithfully performed, that the Paſchal lambe should
be immolated, and eaten, in ſpecial time, in ſpecial
maner, with ſpecial rites adioyned. Alſo that Manna
should be gratfully receiued, greatly eſteemed, as conteyning manie miraculous qualities. It was further
ſtrictly commanded and duly performed: that euerie
day Sacrifice was twiſe offered, to vitte in the morning and euening. Which was therfore called the
Daylie Sacrifice. Manie feaſtes were inſtituted, as
the Sabbath day euerie weke. Alſo the firſt day of euerie Moone. The Paſch euerie yeare, ſeuen dayes together. Likewiſe Pentecoſt. The feaſt of Trumpets.
The feaſt of Expiation, of Tabernacles; and of Col-
lects. In al which were ſpecial Sacrifices. And at ſundrie time for manie ſpecial purpoſes, vpon diuers occaſions. King Dauid in his great afflictions, moſt lamented his exile in the deſerte, becauſe he could no
haue acceſſe to the Tabernacle of God in Ieruſalem
Where he eſpecially deſired to be, for the more particular ſeruice of God: by his preſence at Sacrifices. And
in the ſame deſert he prayed, that for this ſpecial purpoſe he might be reſtored to this moſt deſired place
[O God my God (ſaid he) to thee I watch, from the
morning light. My ſoule hath thirſted to thee: in a
deſert land without water) without wonted ſpiritual
comfort. The Prophete Daniel in captiuitie, [three
times in the day: bowing his knees, towaras Ieruſalem adored, prayed, and praiſed God.]

3. After Chriſts Aſcenſion [his diſciples (ſaith S.
Luke) perſeuered in doctrine; which is one kinde of
ſpiritual bread) and in communication of the breaking of bread (which is the Sacramental bread, our
Lords owne bodie in the forme and accidents of
bread) the ſame Bleſſed Sacrifice, and Sacrament

wherof

Margin notes (left):
Exo. 12.
ch 16.

Ex 29 v. 38.
39
Leu. 23. v. 2.
3. & c.
Nu. 28. &
29.

3. Reg 21. v.
ſ. ch. 26. v. 19

Pſ. 62 v. 2 3

Dan 6. v. 10

Act. 2. v. 22

1. Cor. 11 v.
23. & c

Margin notes (right):
Dauid much
lamented his
abſence from
ſacrifice.

The Apoſtles
with other
faithful ioyned
preaching,
communica-
ting & prayer
together.

wherof the Euangeliftes, and S. Paul declare the Inftitution by Chrift, at his laft fupper. Which although
euerie Chriftian receiue not euerie day, yet al that are
liuing members of the Church(the Myftical bodie of
Chrift) participate in fpirite, if they fo defire to doe.
[The Chalice of benedictió, which we bleffe, is it not **1.Cor.10.5.**
the communication of the bloud of Chrift (faith S. **16.17.**
Paul.) And the bread which we breake, is it not the
participation of the bodie of our Lord? For being
manie we are one bread, one bodie, al that participate
of one bread.] Therfore our Sauiour hath taught vs
to pray al as one bodie, of one communitie, not to
fay: Geue me: but geue vs: fo not, my bread, but our
bread:that both each one pray for al others, and each
The bleffed one may be partaker of al others prayers. And the fame
Sacrament is is asked euerie day: Geue vs this day: and it is called
called daylie: dailie bread, becaufe the fruite therof is daily necef-
and fuperfub- farie. It is called alfo Superfubftantial bread, which
ftantial bread. fignifieth bread, aboue the natural fubftance of ordinarie bread: and a moft fingular bread, to which no
corporal fubftance is comparable. In the Hebrew,
and Chaldee tongue it is *Seg la*. In Greke *Epioufios*, or
Perioufios. Superfubftantial, or Super-excellent. Euerie **Mat.6.v.11**
way this Epitheton fuperfubftantial, or fuper excel-
lent, expreffed by the Euagelift S. Matthew, euidently sheweth, and inuincibly proueth, that in the bleffed Eucharift, there is not natural bread; but diuine
bread; the bread which came from heauen; Chrift
the Sonne of God. Bodie and foule, flesh and bloud
of Chrift. Who is God and man. The flesh, not of a **Ioan.6.v.65.**
mere man, for fuch flesh could not profite to our redemption, and faluation; but flesh of that man, who
is God: Flesh which geueth life, which profiteth infinitely. This dailie bread, and the fruite therof, we
daily pray our heauenlie Father, to grant vnto vs euerie day.

We

VVe pray alſo for al thinges neceſſarie, in this temporal life.

ARTICLE 29.

BOth approued examples, and other documents in holie Scriptures, doe shew that it is lawful to pray for temporal good thinges of this life, ſo it be with moderation. For ſo Abraham, Iſaac, and manie others prayed for children of their owne bodies, and obtayned their requeſtes. So did the parents of Samſon: and Anna the mother of Samuel, and manie others likewiſe. Iabes a renowmed holie man of the tribe of Iuda prayed for temporal proſperitie [And God granted the thinges that he prayed for] It was an ordinarie bleſſing in the old Teſtament, and a great ſigne of Gods fauour, when his ſeruants proſpered in this world. Which the Royal Prophete wel obſeruing ſaid [I haue bene young, for I am old: & I haue not ſene the iuſt forſake; nor his ſede ſeeking bread. Caſt thy care vpon our Lord, (ſaith he) and he wil nouriſh thee] But withal he admoniſheth [If riches abound, ſet not your hart vpon them] And praiſing Gods prouidēce he ſaith [The eyes of al thinges hope in thee, ô Lord: and thou geueſt them meate in time conuenient. Thou openeſt thy hand, & filleſt euerie liuing creature with bleſſing] To the ſame purpoſe Solomen ſaith [The riche and poore haue mette one an other, our Lord is the maker of both. Labour not to be riche, but ſette a meane to thy prudence] And himſelf prayed for mediocritie, ſaying to God: [Beggerie, nor riches, geue me not; geue only thinges neceſſarie, for my ſuſtinance] By al which we ſee it is mans dutie to deſire, and to pray for neceſſarie temporal thinges with moderation.

3. Our Lord and Sauiour teacheth the ſame in planeſt termes, ſaying. [Thus ſhal you pray: Geue vs to day our daylie bread. I ſay to you: Be not careful

X x   for

Gen. 15. v. 2.
ch. 25. v. 21.
Iudic. 13. v.
2. 3. &c.
I. Reg 1 v.
7. 10. 20.
I. Par. 4 v.
10.

Pſ. 36 v. 25.
Pſ. 54. 23.
Pſ. 61. v. 11.

Pſ. 144. v.
16. 17.

Pro 22. v 2.
ch. 23. v. 4.
ch. 30. v. 8.

Mat 6. v. 9.
11. v. 25. 34.

It is lawful & neceſſarie to pray for temporal thinges, but with moderation,

VVe muſt pray with diligence but without ſolicitude.

for your life what you shal eate, neither for your bodie, what rayment you shal put on. Be not careful for
the morow. For the morow day shal be careful for it
self sufficient for the day is the euil therof] Care for
necessaries is a penal euil, but not a sinne, so long as
it is moderated with reason, yet ouer much solicitude is sinne, and forbidden. Therfore the right
meane is, to aske necessaries and no more, and so to
rest, and relie vpon God [For your heauenlie Father *v.8.32.*
knoweth what is needful for you. And that you
neede manie thinges] Againe in particular our Lord
biddeth vs to pray in time of tribulation, or persecu- *ch.24.v.21.*
tion[that your flight be not in the winter, or on the
Sabbath] that it may not be in the hardest season,
but mitigated, according to our infirmities. S. Paul
requested the Christian Romans to pray for him[that *Ro.15. v.31.*
he might be deliuered from the Infideles, that were *32.*
in Iurie. That he might come to them in ioy, by the
wil of God, that I may be refreshed (said he) with
you] S. Iames exhorteth that [If anie of you be in *Iac.5.v.13.*
heauines, let him pray] for true comforth in tribulation.

VVhy we pray euerie day?
3. For these, and al other kindes of temporal good *Luc.18. v.1.*
thinges, we must pray euerie day [Geue vs to day]be- *1.Cor.4.v.7.*
cause we stil haue neede, yea though we haue present
possession of competent needful thinges, yet we must
pray that by Gods goodnes, we may vse the same
thinges, without whose bountie they doe not, nor cā
VVhy we aske for this day?
consist, neither can we consist nor vse his giftes, without his continual assistance, and power, geuing vs al
the power which we haue. And we must aske those *Exo.16 v.*
thinges only, which may suffice for the present shotte *4.19.20.21.*
time. And so the next day, yea the next meale, must *22.*
we aske againe. For being stil beggars, hauing nothing of ourselues, but al of God; of him we must stil
begge, both the needful things, & the vse therof, with
humble submission, acknowleging whose it is: and
whose

Exo.20.v 17
Pf.127.v.2.
whose seruants we are. We aske [our bread] to witte VVhy it is cal-
that bread, & those thinges which are ours by Gods led our bread?
wil, lawfully possessed, not gotten by fraude, nor anie
way vniustly: for then it were not our bread: but o-
thers bread. Finally we aske [daylie bread] that is to VVhy is it
say, ordinarie and common, conuenient sustinance, called dalie
meete for euerie sorte, and state of people: not ouer bread?
delicate, rare, nor costlie, nor with superfluitie. For
Pro.25.v.16.
Luc.16.v.
22.25.
superfluitie bringeth surfete: which is neither good
for soule nor bodie. And excessiue delicacie, bringeth
miserie to both soule and bodie.

In the fift petition vve pray God to forgeue vs our sinnes, and the debtes therof.

ARTICLE 30.

AS in the foure precedent petitions, we are After peti-
taught and commanded to pray for al good tions of good
thinges: to witte in the three first for spiritual, thinges, we
and in the fourth for both spiritual and corporal: so pray that euil
in the other three folowing we are likewise instru-
may be remo-
ued.
cted, and admonished to pray, that euil thinges may
be remoued from vs Especially al sinnes committed:
& from the guilt therof, and debt of punishment, due
for the same. Also to be deliuered from falling agane
into sinnes by tentations. And to be deliuered from
temporal euiles, that may dangerously afflict vs in
soule, or in bodie. Touching the first and greatest of Trespasse sig-
these euils, we pray in this fift petition for remission nifieth offece,
of two euil, so conioyned as the cause and the effect. and the debt
Which are the guilt of sinnes, and punishment due for offence.
for the same: by the two Enangelists called by two
Mat.6.v.12
Luc.11.v.4.
names. For that which S. Matthew calleth debtes.
S Luke calleth sinnes. In our English tongue, not vnproperly both are comprised in one word; [Trespas-
ses] Which signifieth as wel offences, as the debt
of recompence incurred therby. And so we pray our
heauenlie Father [to forgeue vs our trespasses.]

X x 2 2, For

2. For the obtayning of which most necessarie suite, we aske grace, that we may be made capable, & participant of forgeuenes, wherto are required in vs three special preparations (for God of his part is alwayes readie to forgeue) first that we acknowlege our sinnes: secondly that we be sorie for them: thirdly that we hope to haue remission. For first except we sincerely confesse, that we haue committed sinnes, we should delude ourselues, and as it were, moke God, asking that which we thinke nedeth not. But that it is most true, that we are sinners, guiltie of some sinnes, more or lesse, euerie ones owne conscience wil easily see: and the like is acknowleged by special great seruantes of God. Holie Iob answering to his freind Baldad, said [In deede I know it is so: and that no man can be iustified, compared with God] And to God himself he said [Thou in deede hast numbred my steppes: but thou wilt spare my sinnes. Thou hast sealed mine offences, as it were in a bagge, but hast cured mine iniquitie] The Royal Prophete saith generally of al mankind [No man liuing shal be iustified in thy sight, ô God. From my secrete sinnes (ô Lord) cleanse me, and from other mens sinnes spare thy seruant. The sinnes of my youth, & my ignorances doe not remember.] Salomon also speaking generally of al, demandeth [Who can say: My hart is cleane: I am pure from sinne? Seuen times (that is, often times) shal the iust fal, and shal rise againe. He that hideth his wicked deedes, shal not be directed: but he that shal confesse, and shal forsake them, shal obtaine mercie. There is no iust man in the earth, that doth good, and sinneth not] S. Paul saith, that in respect of guiltines of sinne in general [There is no distinction (of nations) For al haue sinned, and neede the glorie of God] And S. Iohn speaking of himself and other iust, saith [If we shal say that we haue no sinne, we seduce ourselues, & the truth is not in vs] This prayer

therfore

Marginal notes:

We must confesse our sinnes.

Iob.9. v.1.
ch.14. v.16.
17.

Psal.: 42. v.2.

Psal 18. v.13.

Psal 24. v.7.

Pro. 20. v.9.
ch. 24 v.16.
ch. 28. v. 13.

Eccle. 7. v. 21
3. Reg. 8. v.
46.

Ro. 3. v. 23.

1. Io. 1. v. 8.

Mat.6.v.12. therfore is prescribed by our B. Sauiour, that al shal pray to our heauenlie Father [Forgeue vs our trespasses] Yea our B. Ladie the Mother of God, being exempted, and preserued from al actual sinne, yea (as it is prously beleued) also from original, yet did she truly say in respect of the whole bodie of the militant Church, wherof she was a principal most holie pure member [Forgeue vs our trespasses] acknowleging, that in this mystical bodie of Christ, there be sinnes, which neede to be remitted: and for the remission therof she prayed.

Our B. Ladie being preserued from sinnes, prayed for sinners, as members of the same bodlie.

3. The second special preparation requisite in vs sinners, is repentance, and sorow for sinnes committed. For the onlie bare acknowlegement of sinnes committed is not sufficient, but remorse of conscience, with iust indignation against the same sinnes, and against ourselues for hauing yelded therto, is necessarie. Because we haue preferred our owne wil, or pleasure before the wil of God, before our dutie to our Lord, our Creator, and most loning Father, and Redemer. Considering how fowle, and vnworthie a thing it is, for a silie creature to rebel against his Creator, the most High incomprehensible Diuine Maiestie: the seruant redemed from captiuitie against his Lord and Redemer, the adopted childe, against his most benigne Father, for that we haue wilfully, displeased God, and pleased the diuel, declined from reason, and yelded to iniquitie: defiled the soule, which is created to the image of God; which being in state of grace, is the temple of God, but by mortal

1.Cor.3.v. 17.

sinne is made slaue to the diuel. [For the temple of God is holie, which you are. But, if anie shal violate the temple of God (saith S. Paul) God wil destroy, him.] If anie therfore be not sufficiétly moued against sinne, for the offence of God, which ought chefely to be regarded: nor for the deformitie of euerie mortal sinne, which maketh the soule fowle, and vglie in

Due repentance requireth true sorow for sinne.

Iust motiues to be sorie and angrie, for sinnes committed.

If neither the offence of God nor soulnes of sinnes, at least eternal torment may

X x 3   the

iuſtly moue
hatered of
ſinne.

the ſight of God, and his glorious Sainctes , it keſome Iſa. 46.7.
to it ſelfe, and contemptible to the diuel. At leaſt (if
theſe moue not iuſt hate againſt mortal ſinne) let the Iere. 17.7.1.
due puniſhment, which is euerlaſting torment , and EZech. 35.
priuation of eternal life, terrifie their [hard ſtonie, Zac.7.7.12.
adamentiue hartes (as the Prophetes deſcribe them)
and make them to know and ſee that it is an euil,and
a bitter thing for thee, to haue left the Lord thy
God,& that my feare is not with thee,ſaith the Lord,
the God of hoſts]for that [according to thy hardnes, Iere.2.7.19.
and impenitent hart, thou heapeſt to thy ſelfe wrath: Rom.2.7.5.
in the day of wrath , and of the reuelation of the iuſt 6.8.9.
iudgement of God:who wil render to euerie man according to his workes. To them that are of conten- 9.
tion , and that obey not the truth, but geue credite to
iniquitie; wrath, and indignation. Tribulation and
anguiſh vpon euerie ſoule of man that worketh euil.
For the ſtipeds of ſinne is death. Their part ſhal be in ch.6. 7 23.
the poole burning with fire and brimſtone: which is Ap.21.7.8.
the ſecond death.]

VVe muſt alſo
confide in
Gods mercie.

4. But let none deſpare. For the holie Scriptures
alſo teſtifie, that if ſinners wil repent , there is an aſ- Part.1.
ſured Anker of hope(which is the third eſpecial con- Artic.48.
dition, requiſite in penitents: beſides confeſſion,and
ſorow) there is mercie with God to remitte al ſinnes.
According as we profeſſe in our Crede: that we be- Heb.6.7.
lue:The remiſſion of ſinnes: And ſo our Sauiour in 19.
this forme of prayer teacheth vs to pray our heauelie
Father [that he wil forgeue vs our ſinnes] Which

Al ſinnes are
remiſsible dū-
ring this life.

ſheweth his wil and readines, if we aske the ſame
rightly, with a prepared mind and wil, to doe that
which he hath inſtituted for this purpoſe:that is ,to re.
paire to the holie Sacrament of Penance.For he that Part 2.
wil not ſo doe, hath not a wil to haue his ſinnes for- Art.25.26.
geuen, by that meanes which Chriſt hath ordained. &c.
With this purpoſe therfore of performing al that is
requiſite, muſt we pray , and ſo there is aſſured hope
of

of forgeuenes of al sinnes. Which is further also testified by these and the like holie Scriptures [With thee
(saith the Psalmist to God our Lord, there is propiciation: and for thy Law I haue exspected thee ô Lord.

Psal 129.
v.5.7.8.

My soule hath expected in thy word: my soule hath
hoped in our Lord. Because with our Lord there is
mercie, and with him is plenteous redemption. And

*Pro.28.v.
13.*

he shal redeme Israel from al his iniquitie] Likewise
Salomon saith [He that shal confesse his iniquities,

Sap 15.*v*. 1.
2.

and shal forsake them, shal obtaine mercie. Thou our
God art swete, and true. and patient: and disposing al

Eccli. 21.*v.*
2.
*ch.*38 *v.*9,
10.

things in mercie. For if we sinne, we are thyne: knowing thy greatnes. Sonne hast thou sinned, doe so no
more: but for the old also pray, that they may be forgeuen thee. As from the face of a serpent, flee from
sinnes. Sonne in thyne infirmitie, contemne not thy
selfe: but pray our Lord, and he wil cure thee. [Turne
away from sinne, & direct thy handes: and from al offence cleanse thy hart. Wash you (saith our Lord by his

*Isa.1.v.16.
17.18.*

Prophete Isaias) be cleane, take away the euil of your
cogitations from myne eyes: Cease to doe peruersly.
Learne to doe good. Seke iudgement, succour the oppressed; iudge for the pupil, defend the widow. And
come, and accuse me, saith our Lord, if your sinnes
shal be scarlette, they shal be made white as snow:
and if they be read as vermilion, they shal be white
as wool] The same our Lord againe denounceth by

Ezech 18,
*v.*21.
22, 23.

his Prophete Eze. hiel, but stil requiring true repentance [If the impious shal doe penance, from al his
sinnes, which he hath wrought, and shal kepe al my
precepts, and doe iudgement, and iustice: liuing he
shal liue, and shal not dye. Al his iniquities, which he
hath wrought, I wil not remember them: in his iustice, which he hath wrought, he shal liue. Why, is the
death of a sinner my wil, saith our Lord God, and not
that he conuert from his wayes, and liue?] In this assured hope, Daniel prayed for the people, confessing
their

their manifold finnes, and their repentance, and hope
of remiffion [incline (faid he) ô God thyne eare; and
heare: open thyne eyes and fee our defolation, and
the citie vpon which thy name is inuocated: for neither in our inftifications, doe we proftrate prayers
before thy face, but in thy manie commiferations.
Heare ô Lord, be pacified ô Lord: attend and doe: delay not for thyne owne fake my God; becaufe thy
name is inuocated vpon thy citie, and vpon thy people. And when I yet fpake (faith he) and prayed, and
confeffed my finnes, and the finnes of my people of
Ifrael, and did proftrate my prayers in the fight of my
God, for the holie mount of my God, as I was yet
fpeaking in prayer, loe the man Gabriel (an Angel in
shape of a man) whom I had fene in the vifion from
the beginning, quickly flying touched me] And fo
the holie Angel declared that his petition was granted, wherof the firft point was remiffion of finnes,
and confequently mitigation of punishment: and in
particular their reduction from captiuitie, which was
shortly after performed.

Dan. 9.v.
4.5.
v 18.19.20.
&c.

2.Paral.36.
v.22.23.
1.Efd.1.v.
2.3.

5. Confider the great mercie, and benignitie of
our Lord and Sauiour, both inwardly mouing, and
exteriorly receiuing finners approching vnto him, to
heare his word, though the Pharifees and Scribes
murmured, faying [That this man receiueth finners,
and eateth with them] Whofe calumniation he prefently confuted, by a parable of a man that feeketh
and reduceth a loft shepe: and of a woman, that feeketh and findeth a loft grote; and reioyce more therin, then in manie that were not loft. And concludeth
therupon, that [euen fo there shal be more ioy in
heauen vpon one finner, that doth penance, then
vpon manie iuft that nede not penance] more ioy for
the conuerfion of finful men, then for the holie Angels, that perfeuered in grace, and are confirmed in
glorie. Or for one finner that doth penance, then for

Luc. 15. v.1.
2.

v.7,10.

nine:

Remiffion of
finnes muft be
fought, before
remiffion of
punishment
may be expe.
&ed.

Chrifts moft
benigne mer-
cie towardes
penitent fin-
ners.

nine : yea then for ninetie nine, which thinke themfelues to be iuſt, and not to nede penance] Chriſt in
dede [receiueth ſinners, and eateth with them] maketh them partners of al excellent ſpiritual banquets,
& coheyres of heauen. But what ſinners? not Scribes
and Phariſees, that hold themſelues to be iuſt by only
faith, or by only conceipt that they are iuſt; but [he
receiueth ſinners, and eateth with them, that doe penance.] For theſe there is great ioy in heauen, before
the Angels of God. And in the militāt viſible Church,
there is ſingular ioy for the conuerſion of S. Marie
Madgalen, who was famouſly knowen to be a ſinner
in the citie, where ſhe dwelt. Alſo of S. Matthew, &
Zacheus, who were publicans, addicted to couetouſ-
nes. And of S. Paul, who being peruerted in opinion,
was a hote, and notorious perſecutor of Chriſtians.
In which three ſpecial examples (amongſt manie o-
thers) al penitents may be comforted, what ſinnes
ſoeuer they haue committed, ſeing ſuch renowmed
Sainctes were reduced, from their ſeueral offences,
which proceded from the three capital Concupiſ-
cences of the fleſh, and of the eyes, and of pride of
life] Only of the ſinners part is required, to cooperate
by penance, with Gods grace, which is offered to al,
[For if we confeſſe our ſinnes (ſaith S. Iohn) our heauenlie Father is faithful, and iuſt to forgeue vs our
ſinnes, and to cleanſe vs from al iniquitie.]

Examples of ſinners reduced from the three general con-cupiſcences of the fleſh, of the eyes & of pride.

For obtaining remiſſion of ſinnes, vve muſt
forgeue in our hartes, al iniures done vnto vs.

ARTICLE 31.

Ovr Lord and Sauiour in his diuine Sermon
made in the mount, amongſt other precepts,
teacheth, yea ofté in the ſame Sermon, & elſwhere repeteth, that we muſt not ſeke reuenge, by priuate or
other

Priuate re-uenge is for-bidden.

Margin notes:
v.2.
v.7.10.
1.Io.2.v.16.
1.Ioan.1.v. 9.
Mat.5.v. 38.&c. ch.6.v.11 13

Y v

other vnlawful meanes. In which point the Scribes
and Pharifees corrupted the Law. For wheras it was
ordayned, that [whofoeuer did vniuftly hurt, or en-
damage an other, should render life for life; eye for
eye,&c.]Thefe corrupters held,and taught it for lawful, that euerie one might in this maner priuatly reuenge himself. So catching fome wordes of the Law
(as al Sectaries vfe to doe) neglecting other places,by
which the true fenfe is explaned. For it was alfo thus
commanded in the fame Law [Seke not reuenge,nor
be mindful of the iniurie of thy citizens. Thou shalt
loue thy freind (euerie neighbour) as thy felfe. I the
Lord, kepe ye my Lawes. Reuenge is myne,and I wil
repay them in time] By conference of which places,
it is eafy to fee that the prefcript forme of iuftice,by
rendring like paine for the wrong done perteyned to
Iudges, and publique iuftice, not to priuate perfons,
to reuenge themfelues. Neither ought priuate perfons to defire reuenge, otherwife then for publique
good, to terrifie offenders, and others,not to doe the
like. But al were commanded, to loue al,and to hate
none [Thou shalt not hate thy brother in thy hart,
but controle him openly , left thou incurre finne
through him]This is the true fenfe of the Law:which
is further explaned by examples of the beft forte of
men,and by manie other facred textes.

2. King Dauid excelled in the vertues of meekenes,and patience,in fuffering , & remitting wronges.
For when King Saul did vniuftly perfecute him , and
when he might (efpecially at two feueral times)moft
eafyly, and fecurely haue flaine Saul, he would not
hurt him: but only , at the former time [cutte of the
hemme of his cloke foftly : and let him paffe fafe a-
way] At the other time [only caried away from
Saul his fpeare, and a cuppe of water, which were at
his head ,& left him fleeping. And anfwered his owne
man,that would haue killed Sauld,that he should not
extend

v.23. extend his hand vpon the Anointed King] He also
rendered the speare to Saul, that he might see his
owne fault, and Dauids innocent hart. Neither would
this meeke King Dauid, suffer iust reuenge to be done

2.R 16. 16. vpon a traiterous priuate felow. Semei [who in most
v 5. malipert and scornful maner cursed, & threw stones
6. against him, and his seruants, crying also vnto him,
7. [Come forth, come forth, thou man of bloud, and
8. man of Belial] Yea when some would haue strooke
9. of the head of the insolent trayror : the meeke King
v.10. said [Let him alone, that he may curse Dauid: perhaps
our Lord may respect myne affliction, and our Lord
may render me good, for this dayes cursing] In confidence also of this meekenes, Dauid prayed vnto
Ps.131. v.1 God, for his continual protection, saying [Remem- His and others
Ps.7.v.2.4. ber Dauid, ô Lord, and al his meekenes. Lord my God doctrine a-
5.6.7. I haue hoped in thee, saue me from al that persecute gainst priuate
me, and deliuer me ô Lord my God. If I haue done reuenge.
this (wherwith myne enimies charge me) if there be
iniquitie in my handes. If I haue rendred to them, that
repayd me euils, let me worthyly fal emptie from
myne enimies] that is, Let me not haue victorie ouer
them. Salomon also commendeth this vertue of meke-
Pro.12.v. nes, amongst other principal vertues, saying [He that
16. dissembleth iniuries is wise. A soft answere breaketh
ch.15.v.1. anger: and a hard word raiseth vp furie. He that con-
ch.17.v.9. cealeth offence, seeketh freindshippes. He that wil be
reuenged (saith an other wise man) shal finde reuenge
of our Lord. Forgeue thy neighbour hurting thee,
and then shal thy sinnes be loosed to thee when thou
prayest] And to shew it to be vnpossible for him to be
forgeuen, that wil not forgeue, he proposeth the ab-
Eccli.28.v. surditie of such concept, saying: [Man to man reser-
1.2.3.4.5. ueth anger, and wil he seke remedie of God? He hath
not mercie on a man, like vnto himselfe, and doth he
intreate for his owne sinnes? Himselfe wheras he is
flesh, reserueth anger, and doth he aske propitiation

(forgeuenes) of God?] signifying that in vaine such doe aske a thing absurde, and vnpossible.

3. Our Lord therfore correcting the Scribes and Pharisees false doctrine, teacheth, that we must [not resist euil, but if one strike thee on thy right cheeke, turne to him also the other. Be so disposed in preparation of minde, rather then to strike againe. And therfore in this general forme of daylie prayer, our Sauiour hath expresly inserted, this clause, that we shal not otherwise aske forgeuenes of trespasses, then [as we forgeue them, that trespasse against vs.] And after the whole prayer, he repeteth this point, declaring both the fruite therof, & the necessitie. [For (saith he) if you wil forgeue men their offences, your heauenlie Father wil forgeue you your offences. Bnt if you wil not forgeue men: neither wil your Father forgeue you your offences] Moreouer our Lord geueth a general rule to be obserued, as a necessarie preparation, before both Sacrifice and other prayers, that [If thou offer thy gift at the Altar, and there thou remember, that thy brother hath ought against thee, thou must first be reconciled] Wherin is included, that we must forgeue in our hart, al iniuries] before we offer our gift. [And when you shal stand to pray, forgeue if you haue ought against anie man, that also your Father which is in heauen, may forgeue you your sinnes] Where againe he repeteth the necessitie of this condition, saying [If so be that you wil not forgeue, neither wil your Father, that is in heauen, forgeue you your sinnes] Neither is this Rule limited to anie time, nor number of times: but how often so euer occasion occurreth, so often we must forgeue in our hart. For a conuenient remedie, he prescribeth this Rule: saying [If thy brother sinne against thee rebuke him: and if he doe penance, forgeue him. And if he sinne against thee, seuen times in a day, and seuen times in a day be conuerted vnto thee, saying, It ~repen-

Our Sauiour teacheth both the great fruit, and the necessitie of forgeuing al iniuries from the hart.

Mat 5.v. 39. ch.6.v.12.

v.14.

v.15.

ch.5.v.24. 25.

Mar.11.v. 25.

v.26.

Luc.17.v. 3.4.

Mat.18.6. 21.22.

repenteth me, forgeue him.] Anſwering alſo to S. Peters demand, touching this point, he ſaid [that not only vntil ſeuen times, but vntil ſeuentie times ſeuen times thou ſhalt forgeue] Concluding, and declaring by a parable, that albeit ſinnes ſeeme to be remitted, yet becauſe this condition (of remitting to others, al iniuries)ſemed, but was not fulfilled, they are in dede not remitted in the ſight of God; but remaining are to be iuſtly punished, [becauſe the ſinner did not forgeue his brother from his hart.]

v.34.

4. Where, by theſe wordes [if you forgeue not from your hart] two particular documents may be obſerued, Firſt that forgeuenes be ſincerely from the hart, not only externally in wordes from the tongue, but in deede, and in truth of which perfect forgeuenes procedeth the prouerb, To forgeue and to forget, that is, wholly to forgeuer not reſeuing either wil or deſire of priuate reuenge. Secondly, that it be from the hart, with deſire of the offenders true repentance. And therfore muſt not be declared by word, but with caution, that ſo farre as in vs lyeth, we freely forgeue: with ſpecial deſire that the offender may ſincerely repent. For ſo long as the offender perſiſteth obſtinate in ſinne; either in falſe opinion, or in wicked intention to perſiſt as yet in that ſtate, it were againſt charitie, and rather great crueltie to omitte either neceſſatie admonition, or due correction, ſo farre as to euerie one belongeth: becauſe ſuch ſilence, or conniuence, by yelding to their il diſpoſition, doth nouriſh their ſinne, and putteth them further into the ſtate & danger of eternal damnation, remaning in mortal ſinne. And therfore in ſuch caſes it is cleare in holie Scripture (as is partly noted before) that al are bond, at leaſt in charitie; and manie alſo in iuſtice to haue care of their neighbour, eſpecially of his ſoules health. And our Sauiours rule is cleare, ſaying [If thy brother ſhal offend, goe and rebuke him, betwen

1.Io.3.v. 18.

Leuit. 19.v. 17.

§.3.

Mat.18.v. 15.

Sincere forgeuenes excludeth al deſire of reuenge

VVe mnſt alwayes forgeue in hart. But not in word, vntil the offender be penitent.

To rebuke ſinners is a neceſſarie worke of charitie.

Yy 3   thee

thee and him alone. If he shal heare thee, thou shalt
gaine thy brother (thou shalt gaine him to God) And
if he wil not heare thee, ioyne with thee besides, one
or two, that in the word of two or three witnesses,
euerie word may stand. And if he wil not heare them,
tel the Church. And if he wil not heare the Church,
let him be to thee as the heathen, and the publicane.]
Neuertheles in our harts, & from our harts, we must
forgeue euerie one our brother, and so desire and
pray that al aduersaries, & sinners may be conuerted.

16.

Deut.19.v.
15.

*Jt is necessarie to loue our enemies; doing good
to them for euil.*

ARTICLE 32.

It was also
commanded
in the Law of
Moyles, to
loue their eni-
mies.

HE that came not to breake the law, but to fulfil it, Iesus Christ our Lord, assuring vs that
not one iotte, or tittle therof shal perish] or passe vn-
filled, hath expresly commanded not only to forgeue
al iniuries from our hart (as is shewed) but also to
loue our enimies, to wish their conuersion to God,
to pray for them, and as occasion shal serue, to doe
them good. And this rule of Christian perfection
may not seme to be ouer hard, or vnpossible. For it
pleased God to geue grace to some also in the old
Testament, to performe this degree of charitie, & in
special cases, he gaue expresse precepts to his people,
concerning this point saying [If thou meete thyne
enimies oxe, or asse going astray, bring it back to
him. If thou see the asse of him that hateth thee; lie s-
vnderneth his burden, thou shalt not passe by, but
shalt lift him vp with the same] Much more al were
bond, in distresse to assist the persons themselues,
though they were their enimies. And accordingly
good men did performe in occasions diuersly occurring.

Mat.5.v.
18.19.

Exo.23.v.4.

2. Of King Dauid are already recited some examples,
shewing his great meeknes in forgeuing iniuies.

And

2.Reg.1.v. And he no leſſe excelled in perfect loue and charitie
11.12.17. towards the ſame and other enimies. For he not only
ch.2.v 5.6. ſpared the life of King Saul, and others, but alſo
mourned, wept, and faſted for him when he was
ſlaine; commended, and promiſed to reward the men
of Iabes Galaad, for their worke of mercie, in fetch 9.v.1.3. ching away, and burying the bodies of King Saul, &
4.7. his ſonnes] He diligently inquired, and found ſome
of kings Saules kinred, and nouriſhed them with
bountiful charitie. So was this moſt charitable King,
Pf.119. v.7. as himſelf ſincerely witneſſeth[Peaceable with them
Pf 138.v.21. that hated peace] Neuertheles againſt others, in that
22. they were, the enimies of God, he had holie zele, and
perfect hatred [Did not I (ſaith he) hate them, that
hate thee ô Lord: and pined away, becauſe of thyne
enimies. With perfect hatred I hated them: and they
P10.25.v. 21 (for this) are become enimies to me.] Salomon like-
Ro.12.v.20. wiſe teacheth [If thyne enimies ſhal hunger, geue
him meate: if he thirſt, geue him drinke. For ſo thou
ſhalt heape hote coales vpon his head (which may
Part.3. molifie his ſtonie hart, through thy burning charitie)
Artic.28. and our Lord wil reward thee] In like ſorte other
Prophetes, wherof ſee more in the third part. Brefely
conſider, that either he who is now thyne enimie
ſhal be conuerted to God, & ſaued, & then why wilt
thou in the meane while, hate that perſon, with
whom thou ſhalt be ioyned for euer in the glorie of
heauen? or els he ſhal be damned, & then, how canſt
thou be ſo ſtonie harted, as to deſire vnto him increaſe of tormentes in hel? It is only ſinne, which we
muſt hate, but ſtil loue the perſon, and wiſh his ſaluation ſo long as there is poſſibilitie therof, that is, ſo
long as he is in this life.

3. Foolish therfore and wicked is the corrupt doctrine of the Scribes, and Phariſees. Who by their
curſed gloſſe peruerting the text ſaid[thou ſhalt loue
thy neighbour: and hate thine enimie] conioyned
wicked

King Dauid
by fact, and
word taught
this perfe-
ction.

He impugned
none as his
owne enimies,
but as eni-
mies to God.

Mat.5.v.43.
44 45.

Gods Law, both in the old an i new Teftament bindeth al his feruants to loue their enimies. wicked falshood with diuine Law. Therfore our merciful Redemer, who payed one price for al mankind [faith to al loue your enimies: doe good to them that hate you: and pray for them, that perfecute, and abufe you: that you may be the children of your Father, which is in heauen : who maketh his funne to rife vpon good and bad : and rayneth vpon iuft and vniuft (and this, vpon condition to receiue, or not to receiue reward in heauen) For if you loue them (only) that loue you, what reward shal you haue? Doe not alfo the publicanes this ? And if you falute your brethren only, what doe you more ? Doe not alfo the heathen this ? Be you perfect therfore as alfo your heauenlie Father is perfect. [Vpon this doctrine S. Paul infifting, admonisheth al Chriftians, that they [Be not ouercome of euil, but in good to ouercome the euil] And amongft al other meanes to conuert the deceiued from their errour, none is more forcible then that thofe which are perfecuted for the truth, shal ftil vfe burning charitie towards their perfecutors, which S. Paul calleth [The powring of hate coales vpon the enimies head.] And S. Iames affirmeth that [if anie man shal make a finner to be conforted, he shal faue his foule from death, & couereth a multitude of finnes.]

46.
47.
48.

Rom.12.v.
20.21.

vt fupra.
Pro.25.
Rom. 12.
Iac.5.v.20.

The beft meãs to doe it, is to loue our perfecutors,

In the fixt petition, vve pray for ftrength of grace, to refift al tentations of finne.

ARTICLE 33.

Gen. 22.v.
1.16.

Tentation is fometimes good fometimes euil. Euil tentation is fometime profitable: often hurtful.

Tentation is fometime good, and profitable. As when God tempted Abraham to make his vertues of faith, and obedience knowne, by his readines to haue offered his fonne Ifaac in Sacrifice, vpon commandment, fo to doe. But more commonly tentation is euil, yet is not alwayes hurtful, but fometimes profitable, according as the perfons are wel or euil difpofed, to whom it happeneth. So to

holie

Iob.1.
Gen.39.v.7.
8.
Tob.12.
Dan.13.
2.Cor.12.
v.7.9.

holie Iob, Ioseph, Tobias, Susanna, S. Paul, & manie others, tentations were very profitable, through Gods grace making them able to resist the enimie. But to manie others, tentations are hurtful, as experience sheweth in the whole world: through wilful yelding consent to tentations of sinne. Seing therfore tentations are sometime profitable, and in some respect necessarie: we must not pray, that we may be wholly exempted, and free from euil tentations, because without tentation there can be no spiritual fight, without fight no victorie, without victorie no reward, nor crowne of glorie. [For (as S. Paul teacheth) whosoeuer wil liue piously in Christ Iesus, shal suffer persecution. And none is crowned, vnles he striue lawfully] But we must pray our heauenlie Father, that he mercifully granting vs remission of al our sinnes; wil also geue vs grace to resist al tentations tending to sinne. And that seing it pleaseth his diuine prouidence, for our good, to suffer tentations to happen vnto vs, that he wil strengthen, & preserue vs, by his continual grace, from being ledde into tentations, by yelding consent to sinne.

We must not praye to be freed from al tentations, but not to be ouercome by them.

2.Tim.3.v.
12.
ch.2.v.5.

2. How necessarie this prayer is, wil be more manifest, if rightly knowing our owne weaknes, we also consider the great forces, and continual assaultes made against vs by al our enimies, which are these three. The world, wherin we liue; The flesh, wherof our bodies consist: and the diuel [who as a roaring lion goeth about, seeking whom he may deuour] The world most especially tempteth by proposing vaine delectations to the eyes, and eares, of riches, and worldlie estimation, briding Pride, and Auarice The flesh especally tempteth, by desiring vnlawful pleasures of the bodie, tending to Luxurie, Glutonie, and Slouth. The diuel tempteth not only by vsing, both the world, & the flesh, alluring to sinnes aboue mentioned; but also by internal suggestions, of wicked

Our weaknes, and the enimies force shew the necessitie of Gods helpe.

Io.17.v.14.
Gal.5.v.19.
1.Pet.5.v.3.

Z z   reuenge,

How men are
tempted, to
Pride:
Auarice:
Luxurie;
Glutonie:
Slouth:
VVrath, and
Enuie.

reuenge, and of hatred, engendering wrath, and
Enuie. And by these seuen vicious head sinnes (therof
called Capital sinnes) the same three general enimies,
do tempt mens soules vnto al kinds, & sortes of sinnes,
which are innumerable. [Vnto which (to some more, *Gen. 6. v.*
to some lesse) mans sense, and cogitation are prone *12. ch. 8.*
to from their youth] from the first sinne.   *v. 21.*

3.   In regard therfore of which daylie combate,
the faithful seruants of God, knowing and often feeling the same assaults of external, & internal enimies,
worldlie, carnal, and spiritual wicked powers, haue
diligently prayed for Gods necessarie helpe, that they
may fight strongly, and gaine the victorie. So the

Diuers formes
of prayer for
grace to resist
tentations.

Royal Prophete with thankfgeuing for his often deliuerie from both temporal and spiritual dangers,
said to God in his prayer [I wil loue thee ô Lord, my
strength: our Lord is my firmament, and my refuge, &
my deliuerer. My God is my helper, and I wil hope *2. Reg. 22.*
in him. Praising I wil inuocate our Lord, and I shal be *v. 1. Pf. 17.*
saued, from myne enimies. The sorows of death haue *v. 2. 3. 4. 5.*
compassed me, and torments of iniquitie haue tru- *29.*
bled me. Because thou doest illuminate my lampe ô *30.*
Lord: my God illuminate my darkenes. Because in *Pf. 21*
thee I shal be deliuered from tentation: and in my *v. 45.*
God I shal goe ouer the wal. Although I shal walke
in the middes of the shadow of death, I wil not feare
euils; because thou art with me. Thy rodde and thy *Pf. 26. v. 1.*
staffe (thy streight Law, and strong grace) doe comforth, & strengthen me. Our Lord is myne illumination (in danger of errour) & my saluation (in supplie *Pf. 35. v.*
of my weakenes) whom shal I feare?] I feare not anie *12. 13.*

Against pride
the roote, and
quene of al
sinnes.

enimie. In particular against tentations of pride he
prayed [Let not the foote of pride come to me, & let *Pf. 54. v.*
not the hand of a sinner moue me. There (by pride) *23.*
haue they fallen, that worke iniquitie, they were expelled (diuels from heauen, and man from paradise,
pride being the first sinne, and roote of al wickednes)

Cast

Caft thy care (in al tentations) vpon our Lord : and
he wil nourifh (feede and ftrengthen) thee;he wil not
geue fluctuation (perplexe, or infuperable tentation)
to the iuft for euer] In like maner againft Auarice in
particular, which fuffocateth the feede of good cogitations, he prayed, faying [My foule hath flumbred,
for tedioufnes, confirme me in thy Law, ô God. Incline my hart into thy teftimonies, and not into Auarice. Turne away myne eyes, that they fee not vani-
tie] Againft Luxurie, & al finnes of the flefh, flight is
beft remedie. [Let it not fo much as be named, nor
thought vpon Create a cleane hart in me, ô God: and
renew a right fpirite in my bowels. Caft me not away
from thy face, and thy Holie Spirite take not from
me] Againft al finnes in general. we muft pray with
the fame Pfalmift [According to thy mercie, ô God,
quicken me, and I fhal kepe the teftimonies of thy
mouth. I am thyne faue me. Helpe me and I fhal be
faued. Pearfe my flefh with thy feare: for I am a fraide
of thy iudgements. Direct my fteppes according to
thy word: and let not anie iniuftice haue dominion
ouer me. I haue cried to thee, in my whole hart, faue
me: that I may kepe thy commandments. Let my requeft enter in thy fight, according to thy word deliuer me. Let thy hand be to faue me; becaufe I haue
chofen thy commandments.] In al which we fee, that
although men be iuftified by remiffion of finnes, and
fanctification of their foules, yet we haue nede of
fpecial grace, by which, and not of ourfelues without
it, we are enabled to refift euil tentations [Bleffed
therfore, faith Salomon) is the man, that is alwayes
fearful] And conformably faith an other wifeman
[Sonne, coming to the feruice of God, ftand in iuftice, & in feare: and prepare thy foule to tentation.]

4. For fo much then as tentation is both neceffarie, and profitable to Gods true feruants, our Sauiour hath taught vs to pray in this fpecial forme, not
that

Pf. 118.
v. 28.31.
v. 37.

Ephef.5. v.3

Pf. 50. v.
12.13.

Pf.118.v.88.
94.
116.117.

120.133.

146.

170.

173.

Prov.28.v.
14.

Eccli.2. v.1.

Againft Aua-
rice, an other
roote of ma-
nie finnes.

Againft finnes
of the flefh.

Aganift flouth
wrath, enuie,
and glutonie.

that we may be alwayes free from being tempted at
al , but that he impert his grace vnto vs , without
which we can not be able to refift , for that our enimies, the world, the flesh, and the diuel, (being ftronger then we are of ourfelues) would otherwife vndoubtedly leade vs captiue into their fnares . For except men doe hartely defire , and fincerily pray , that

God offering
grace to al,
they that ac-
cept it muft
manifeft their
defire by
asking it.

God wil ftrengthen them with his grace, which they
can not effectually haue without their owne confent and defire concurring therunto, becaufe fo long
as they remaine, addicted to their owne wil, and to
the comodities, or pleafures of this life, the diuel fo
occupieth their mindes, with fuch cogitations , that
either they geue no eare at al, to wholfome admonitions, their confciences being hardened [like the high Mat.13. v 4.
way , where the good, feede is troden vnder their 19.

Some finners
wil not heare
good aduife.

feete, & caried away by the fooles of the ayre]for the
wicked one carieth it away. Or they heare & receiue
good feede, [but are fo ftonie harted , that it taketh v. 5. 20.
no roote, and in tribulation, and perfecution for the
word, they are fcandalized]and fal from the truth:for

Some receiue
it, but fhrinke
from it.

that flesh and bloud make them to shrinke. Or they
heare good aduife , and willingly receiue it , but are v. 7. 21.
withal fo careful of worldlie wealth, riches , or honour , that the fame choketh vp al cogitation of
vertue, and they become fruitles.] Againft thefe eni-

Some are
ouerwhelmed
with greater
loue of the
world.

mies therfore we muft pray , and that from the hart,
for potent grace, that we may willingly lerne how
to ferue God truly , and breake our ftonie ftiffe wil,
mortifying our flesh:roote out al vifes:expel al fuper-
flous cares of this world : and fo refifting tentacions, v, 8. 23.
bring forth fruite, as good ground doth, fome thirtie
fold, fome threefcore , fome an hundredeed] This Mat. 26. 7.
prayer perteyneth to al , both weaker , and ftronger. 41.
Euen the moft perfect [muft watch, and pray , that Luc. 22. v. 31
they enter not into tentation [For Satan doth fift al as
wheate (as our Lord forewarned his Apoftles.) Therfore

I.Cor,10.v. 12.13. fore he that thinketh himſelf to ſtand, let him take heede (ſaith S.Paul) leſt he fal. Let not tentation apprehend you, but humane. And God is faithful who wil not ſuffer you to be tempted aboue that which you are able: but wil make alſo with tentation iſſue (euent) that you may be able to ſuſteyne]ſignifying that God ſo tempereth tentations, that none ſhal happen, but ſuch as a man, aſſiſted with his grace, may reſiſt. So that whoſoeuer reſiſteth not Gods grace, may reſiſt al tentations. And that al ſhal ſuccede to our good, if it be not hindered by ourſelues. Of the fruite alſo of tentations S. Peter ſaith [A litle now, if you muſt be made heauie, in diuers tentations, that the probation of your faith, much more precious then gold (which is proued by the fire) may be found vnto praiſe, and glorie, and honour, in the reuelation of IESVS Chriſt. Our Lord knoweth to deliuer the godlie from tentation] Stil is to be remembred, that [we muſt aske, and it ſhal be geuen.] Yea if we wil not ſhut the doore of our hart, and exclude Chriſts grace, we ſhal receiue it. [Behold (ſaith he) I ſtand at the doore, and knocke, if anie man ſhal heare my voice, and open the gate, I wil enter into him: & wil ſuppe with him, and he with me. Behold I come quickly: hold that which thou haſt, that no man take thy crowne.]

I.Pet I v 6. 7,

2.Pet.2,v,9.

Ap.3.v.20. v.11,

The fruite of reſiſting tentations is the crowne of glorie.

VVe alſo pray God, that he vvil not ſuffer vs to be aſſaulted vvith ouer great tentations.

ARTICLE 34.

ONly in this reſpect, & no other, can true Chriſtians lawfully pray to be deliuered from tentations, for that we ſee, or feare them to be ouer great to our owne, or others weaknes; and ſo we may pray that greuous perſecutions moued by the diuel againſt Catholiques for Religion, may ceaſe, leſt the weake denie their faith, or fal from God: and

Mat.24.v,6. 20.22,

VVe doe lawfully pray that ſome tentations may ceaſe in regard of mans weakenes.

that the preaching of truth may not be hindred : and
that the persecuters may be compelled also to ceafe,
from doing that euil, which they would, and to heare
the truth wherby, God lightning and molifying their
hartes, they alfo may be conuerted, and faued, Likewife concerning other great, and dangerous tentations we pray that they may be mitigated : and not
fuffered to be greater, then we shal be able to refift.
But otherwife it is not lawful to pray absolutely that *rob.1.v.'12.*
God would take away al perfecutions, & other great *ch.12. v. 13.*
tentations : for that were contrarie to Gods proui- *Iac.v.2.12.*
dence : & to exclude occafions of Gods more glorie,
and good of foules.

2. For mitigation therfore of fuch afflictions. as
feme dangerous in regard of our infirmitie, euerie
one may pray in this, or the like maner, as the Pfalmift

inftructeth vs [Haue mercie on me ô Lord : becaufe I *Pf.6.v.3.4.*
am weake, heale me Lord, becaufe my bones be tru- *5.*
bled. And my foule is trubled exceedingly, but thou
ô Lord, how long ? Turne thee ô Lord, and deliuer *Pf.9.v.22.*
my foule ; faue me for thy mercie. Why Lord haft *23.*
thou departed farre of (defpifeft me) in opportuni-
ties, in tribulations ? Whiles the impious is proud,
the poore is fet on fire (extremly afflicted) How long *Pf.12.v.1.*
ô Lord, wilt thou forgete me, vnto the end ? How *2.*
long doeft thou turne thy face farre from me ? How *3.*
long shal myne enimies be exalted ouer me ? Regard, *4.*
and heare me ô Lord my God. Illuminate myne eyes, *5.*
that I flepe not in death at anie time, left fome myne *6.*
enimie fay : I haue preuailed againft him. They that
trubled me ●l reioyce, if I be moued. But I haue
hoped in thy mercie] And with this hope, I pray that *Pf.20. v. 1.*
thou [wilt not fuffer me to be lead into tentation]
Our Lord is the Protector of my foule ; of whom shal *Ma..6.v.13.*
I be afrayde ? If campes ftand together againft me, my *Pf.26.v.1.2*
hart shal not feare. If battel rife vp againft me, in this *14.*
wil I hope. Expect our Lord (faith euerie iuft man *Pf.27.v.3.*

to

to his owne ſoule) doe manfully, and let thy hart
take corege: and expect thou our Lord. I expected
him, and he ſaued me from puſillanimitie, of ſpirite,
and tempeſt. I am humbled exccedingly, O Lord,
quicken me according to thy word. I haue cried to
thee: ſaue me, that I may kepe thy commandments.
O Lord Lord the ſtrength of my ſaluation, thou haſt
ouershadowed my head in the day of battel] Much
more might be recited out of this Royal Pſalmiſt, and
Iſaias, Ieremie, Ezechiel, Daniel, Eſdras, Nehemias,
Tobias, Iudith, Eſter, and other Prophets: praying
for the people in great diſtreſſes, in their captiuitie,
and alſo after their relaxation, by occaſion of pouertie, and other difficulties. And the like in new perſecutions in the time of the Machabees, when men fel
from God, though manie were moſt conſtant.

3. Chriſt our Lord, as he commandeth vs, to pray
our heauenlie Father [that he wil not let vs be lead
into tentation] ſo he promiſeth to reſpect mans infirmitie in al great tentations, namely, in the time of
Antichriſt [to shorten thoſe dayes, for the elects ſake.
and to cut of the cruel perſecutor, with the ſpirite of
his owne mouth] He admonisheth alſo to be watchful, becauſe himſelfe, the Sonne of God, and Sonne
of man, wil come to iudge (as wel the whole world
in the laſt day, as euerie one in particular, in the houre
of our ſeueral deathes) as the floud came when manie
expected not] We muſt therfore pray al our life, that
we then eſpecially be armed with ſtrength of grace to
reſiſt the laſt aſſaultes of our enimie, that neuer ſlee-
peth, and at our death ſeeketh to intangle vs. The
flesh alſo is within vs, and the world round about vs,
al ſtrong enimies, not to be ouercomen with idlenes,
ſoftnes, ſlight reſiſtance, nor anie temporiſing, for
that no peace, nor trewes can be made with them,
nedes we muſt fight [The kingdome of heauen ſuffereth violence, and the violent bare it away.]

We

Pſ 35. v. 12.

Pſ 54. v. 9.

Pſ. 118. v.
107.

Pſ 146.
Pſ. 119.
v. 19.
Thren. 5. v. 1.
2. &c.
Dan. 9. v.
1.
Eſ. 1. v. 3.

1. Mac. 1. v.
45.

Ma. 24. v.
22. 39.

2. Theſ. 29.
v. 8.

Mat. 11. v.
12.

Chriſtiãs muſt
pray al their
life, for a hap-
pie death.

We likevvise pray for grace, to repel first motions tending to sinne.

ARTICLE 35.

It is more easy to resist tentations at the first assault.

STrong enimies must be strongly resisted, and that with diligent speede, at the first assault : because he that wittingly permitteth another to inuade him, loseth possession of that, which might more easely haue bene defended, then can be recouered. The diuel neuer ceaseth to desire mans ruine by sinne, and therfore he often suggesteth euil cogitations, and if man being therwith allured, take delectation in them [concupiscence conceiuing bringeth forth sinne.] By which entrance the enemie is made stronger, and then striueth the more to gette ful consent, that]sinne may be consummate, which engendreth death.] But whosoeuer rightly considereth the great enormitie, and extreme miserie of sinne, wil hartely desire, and pray, with S. Paul, that [the God of peace wil crush Satan vnder our feete quickly. Remembring also the wisemans admonition. [He that loueth peril, shal perish therin. And he that contemneth smal thinges, shal fal by litle and litle.]

1. Pet. 3. v 8. 9.

Iac. 1. v. 15.

Rom. 16, v. 20 Eccli. 3. v. 17. ch. 19. v. 1.

It is a happie thing to rise from sinne, more happie to rise quickly most happie not to sinne.

2. The beginning of good life, is to depart from euil. It is a happie thing and a special grace of God that some great sinners doe not finally persist in wicked life, but repent before their death: it is more happines, not to continue long in anie sinne, but quickly to repent and turne to God: it is the greatest happines of al, neuer to consent vnto euil suggestions. These three great blessings the Royal Prophete denounceth in the first wordes of his diuine Psalter: & the greatest in the first place, saying [Blessed (or happie) is the man, that hath not gone in the counsel of the impious.] He that hath not at al yelded to euil motions but strongly resisted them. Secondly he is also happie [that hath not stood in the way of siners, who though

Ps. 1. v. 1.

he

he gaue confent, and yelded to finne: yet ftayed not
therin, but leauing that ftate returned to grace. And
laftly he is alfo happie but in the loweft degree, [that
hath not fitte in the chayre of peftilence] not perpetually remained, and died in damnable ftate. As this
laft is moft dangerous, for what thanke is it to leaue
finne, when a man can finne no longer in this world?
fo it is beft and moft fecure not to yelde to any finne
nor euil fuggeftion, for to him is affuredly promifed

Eccli.31.v.
10.
eternal glorie. For [he fhal haue eternal glorie (faith
a diuine Preacher) that could tranfgreffe and hath
not tranfgreffed: and could doe euils and hath not
done.] Againe faith the fame Pfalmift [Bleffed is he

Pf.136.v.9.
that fhal dafh the litle children (of Babylon) againft
the rocke]that is, deftroyeth leaft finnes,& motions
to finne. [If finners intife thee (faith true wifdom) cō-

Pro 1.v 10
17.ch.4 v.13
ch.6 v.27.
28.
defcend not to them. A nette is caft in vaine before
the eyes of them that haue winges. With al gard kepe
thy hart, becaufe life procedeth from it Can a man
hide fire in his bofome, that his garments burne not?
Or walke vpon hote coales, that his foales be not
burnt.!] No more can euil thoughtes be retained in
the hart, and not inflame the concupifcence of euil
thinges.

3. This necefsitie of refifting the firft euil motions
Ifaias alfo teftifieth, admonifhing the careles, of the
bad fruite which cometh from euil cogitations fug-
gufted by the malignant enemie. From the roote of

First euil mo-
tions are like
the egges of
afpes.

the ferpent (faith he) fhal iffue forth a cockatrice.

If6.14.v.
29.
ch.59.v.5.
They haue broken the egges of afpes, and wouen the
fpiders webbes. He that fhal eate of the egges fhal
die: and that which is nourifhed, fhal be hatched
into a cockatrice.] Al which il fuggeftions, fignified
by the venomous egges of afpes, are but fpiders webbes, which catch and hold weake mindes; like to
poore flies: but the ftronger feruants of God, breake
eafily through them, not yelding confent of the hart:

Aaa   with

without which no sinne is committed. Which our B. *Mat. 15.*
Sauiour teacheth most clearly, saying. [From the hart *v. 19.*
come forth euil cogitations: murders; aduoutries;
fornications; theftes; false testimonies; blasphmies.]
And so al sinnes procede from the hart where if il
suggestions be resisted, and repelled, tentations may
profite but cannot hurt vs. And therfor we pray in
this sixth Petition for special grate, that we may not
be ouercome by any euil tentation: that we may be
preserued from the more dangerous tentations: and
for grace to resist al euil motions, at the first assault, according to S. Iames expresse exhortation
saying to al Christians. [Resist the diuel, and he wil *Iac. 4. v.7.*
flee from you.]

The summe of this sixth petition, *(margin note at left)*

*In the seuenth petition vve pray our heauenlie
Father, to deliuer vs from temporal euils.
Especially from al the diuels povver.*

ARTICLE 36.

THere are in general two kindes of euiles, cal- *Amos 3.*
led *Malum culpæ*, and *Malum pœnæ*: The euil of *v. 6.*
sinne, and the euil of paine. From the euil of
sinne we pray in the two precedent Petitions to be *Psal. 77.*
deliuered, to witte in the fifth Petition to be deliue- *v. 49.*
red from al sinnes committed, by the remission therof, and in the sixth to be preserued, from falling a-
gaine, by yelding to anie euil tentation. Now in this
seuenth Petition we pray to be deliuered, and preserued from penal euils. Which are temporal afflictions
of soule, and bodie. For eternal punishment is changed, (together with remission of mortal sinnes) into
temporal. And these temporal euiles being by Gods
prouidence medicinable to al the elect, and sent, or
permitted by God for the good of soules, we may
only pray to be deliuered from them, so farre as shal
be

Sinful and pe- nal euil. *(margin note at left)*

Penal euiles are medicina- ble to the iust, & al the elect. *(margin note at left)*

be needful for our foules. Which femeth to be the proper fenfe of this feuenth Petition.

This feuenth Petition may be properly vnderftood of temporal euil.

2.   For feing in the two former petitions is expreffe mention of finnes, and of tentation tending to finne it femeth that here fome other euil is to be vnder-ftood: though otherwife this word Euil doth moft properly fignifie finne itfelf; yet it alfo comprehen-deth both finne, and al euil proceding from finne. As in the conclufion ofour B. Sauiours particular prayer made for his Church the night before his Paffion, faying to his Father [I pray not that thou take them away out of the world, but that thou preferue them from euil.] To witte from al euil, efpecially finful euil, and from penal euil, fo farre as it might in-duce to finne, or anie way hinder the progreffe in vertue.

Ioan. 17. v. 15.

It is an efpe-cial temporal euil to be pof-feffed of wic-ked fpirites.

3.   Concerning therfore temporal penal euils, from which we pray to be deliuered, the greateft in this life is the diuels power. From whofe malice we muft diligently pray to be defended, not only that he preuaile not againft vs by his tentations to finne (for which we pray in the fixth Petition) but alfo that no malignant fpirite, may poffeffe, nor obfeffe, nor anie way hurt mens bodies, nor goodnes; nor otherwife moleft them in anie forte. And for this caufe, amógft other great benefites beftowed vpon the faithful, Chrift our Lord both caft forth diuels out of mens bodies, and gaue power to his Apoftles, & Difciples to caft them out, which they performing [returned with ioy, faying: Lord the diuels alfo are fubiect to vs in thy name.] And more abundantly, after Chrifts Afcenfion, the Apoftles, and other Apoftolical men [cured difeafies, and expelled diuels; deliuering them that were vexed with wicked fpirites.] Which aucto-ritie remaineth ftil in the Church of Chrift. And God geueth effect, according to his Diuine proui-dence, as is more expedient for the health of foules.

Mat. 4. v. 32. &c. Luc. 10. v. 17

Act. 5. 1. 16 &c.

A aa2   4. Another

4. An other more ordinarie penal, and temporal euil, from which we pray to be deliuered, is the punishment due for sinnes remitted. And that this is a lawful and conuenient prayer is proued by examples, and testimonies of holie Scripture. After that [our Lord was pacified] by Moyses in prayer, for the peoples sinne of idolatrie, by their adoring the golden calues, and the guilt of that sinne being remitted,

See Part.2. Art .31.33.

Exod.32 v. 14.

Moyses and others prayed for mitigation of punishments due for Sinaes. Moyses not only destroyed the idols: and punished them by téporal death of about three thousand men] but also he prayed againe for remission of further punishment, due for the same sinne, as himselfe testifieth saying the next day to the multitude: [You haue sinned a very great sinne: I wil goe vp to our Lord: if by anie meanes I may be able to intreat him for your sinful fact] Holie Iob did pray for the mitigation of temporal punishment due to himselfe, and al mankinde in general, saying to God [Depart a little from him (spare him a litle, in his daylie afflictions) that he may rest vntil his day wished for, come; euen as the hyred man.] Like as a laborer hath some repose in his daylie trauels. Thus did the Royal Prophete pray to God [Because thou hast deliuered my soule from death, and my feete from falling, that I may please before thee (ô God) in the light of the liuing. Rise vp to mete me, ô Lord the God of power.] Likewise al the Patriarches and Prophetes, with the whole people of God, prayed to be deliuered from temporal euils: but first for remission of their sinnes, which were the cause of al other euil.

28.

v 30.

Iob.14.v.6.

Psal.55.v. 13.

Ps.58.v.6.

VVe pray also to be deliuered from euil habites gotten by sinne, and from imperfections.

ARTICLE 37.

Besides both sinne and punishment due OTher penal euils from which we must desire, and pray to be deliuered, are the euil habites or inclinations, and imperfections, contracted by sinne.

because

because thefe both make vs more prone to yelde a- for finne, there
gaine to euil tentations, and hinder the exercife of remaine euil
vertues. And therfore King Dauid, not only confef- habites, and
fed his offence, and prayed for remiffion therof in reliques of
Pfal. 50. v. thefe wordes [Haue mercie on me, ô God, according finnes.
3. to thy great mercie: And according to the multitude
of thy commifferations, take away myne iniquitie.]
but alfo prayed to be more wafhed, and cleanfed
from euiles, faying [Wafh me more amply (ô God)
v. 4. from myne iniquitie: and cleanfe me from my finne.]
Nathán the Prophete (vpon his firft acknowlegement of his fault) declared to him, that God had taken away his finne, and yet he prayed God to take it
away, and alfo to wafh him more amply, from his iniquitie, and to cleanfe him from his finne: Plainely fignifying that befides remiffion, & taking away of finne
and punifhment due for finne, a finner needeth alfo
to be more wafhed, and more cleanfed. Not from the
finne it felfe, which remayneth not, but from other
euiles pertayning to the finne, and remayning in the From which
foule, after that the finne is taken away. And thefe we muft pray
therfore muft needes be the reliques of finne, and to be deliue-
blemifhes, wrinkles, or fpottes, which remayne in red.
the foule: for which as this true penitent did fay, fo
v. 5. euerie one muft fay with him [I doe know myne iniquitie, and my finne is before me alwayes.] And muft
pray to be deliuered from it.

2, Of fuch fpottes, and imperfections, our Sauiour Proued by
alfo fpake, when he faid to S. Peter [He that is wa- Chrifts do-
Ioan. 13. v. fhed, needeth not but to wafh his feete only] mani- ctrine.
10. feftly fignifying that thofe which are baptized (and in And his Apo-
like maner, thofe which are abfolued from actual ftles.
finnes) haue fome thing that needeth to be wafhed:
which is not finne, but euil habites, and prones to
finne; carnal inclinations, and worldlie affections,
which like vnto feete, carrie the inferiour powers of
the foule, contrarie to the mind. And therfore nede

to be more amply washed, and cleansed. For correction wherof S. Paul teacheth by example, both to
chastise the bodie, that it may serue the spirite;and to   1. *Coo.9.v.*
pray that the molestation of the flesh may be taken   *27*
away, that putting of the old man, and purging the   2. *Cor.12.v*
old leauen, we may become new creatures, new paste,   *8.*
in the azimes of sinceritie and veritie.] We therfore   1. *Cor.5.v 7.*
who are subiect to manie imperfections, & possessed   *8.*
of euil habites, must labour and pray to be deliuered
from such euils: that albeit in this life, we can not be
wholly free from them, yet that their great force may   *Ro.7.v.25.*
be dimished: and that albeit [with the flesh we serue
the Law of sinne (as the same Apostle speaketh) yet
with the minde we may serue the Law of God.]

Likevvise vve pray to be deliuered from dan-
gerous afflictions, vvhich may hurt the
soule.

ARTICLE 38.

It is lawful to
pray that God
wil mitigate
tribulations,
which he per-
mitteth for
probation of
the iust.

BEsides the general penalties incurred by original
sinne (as death, infirmitie of bodie, the suffering
of heate, colde, and other difficulties , common to al   *Gen 3,v 16.*
mankinde) and besides punishments inflicted for a-   *17.*
ctual sinnes; there be manie other tribulations permitted by God, for the probation, and merite of his
faithful seruants. As Martyrdome by violent death;
spoyle of temporal goodes, imprisonment, banish.   *Ioan.9.v. 3.*
ment, &c. Concerning which kind of téporal euils,   *ch 11.v.4.*
we are taught to pray that God our heauenlie Father   *Mat.28.v.*
wil so moderate the same, proportionably to his spe-   *20.*
cial grace geuen to euerie one, that we may be deliuered from ouer great, & dangerous afflictions, which
may hurt the soules, of such as are not strong, nor able
to ouercome them.

2. It was not for anie particular sinne of Iacob the   *Gen.32.v.*
Patriarch, that he was afflicted with feare or hurt to   *9.*
him-

himself, or his familie, by his brother Esau, but for his exercise in humilitie, pietie, patience, hope in Gods protection, and of other vertues. For in this case he prayed with humble resignation of his owne wil to Gods wil: with gratful thankesgeuing for former benefites, and so obtained his desire: God so mollifying his brothers hart towards him, that he found no iniurie, but brotherlie concord, and curtesie: at Esaus hendes; and was deliuered from that temporal euil which he feared. In like maner the whole people of the same Patriarches issue, being persecuted by the Ægyptians, prayed to God for release from their temporal afflictions [And our Lord heard their gronings] and by the ministerie of Moyses, deliuered them from that penal euil. Againe very often the same people, suffering inuasions of enimies, albeit for the enormious sinnes of the greatest part, yet for probation, and more merite of the iust, who ioyntly together prayed God for his merciful remission of their sinnes, and for his deliuerance of them al, from their temporal vexations: and our Lord heard their prayers, and by certaine Iudges, or General Captaines [deliuered them from the handes of the ransakers] geuing them manie notable victories. Al these Iudges, and other general Gouernours of Gods people, besides their prudent, and valiant endeuours by way of armes, against wicked enimies, especially vsed deuour, and confident prayer to God, beseeching his bountiful Goodnes, by his mightie hand to deliuer his faithful seruants from inuasions, subiection and captiuitie of infidels.

3. Thus did the Royal Prophete pray, & hath so taught the whole Church in general tribulations, saying: [Arise Lord, let not man be strengthned: let the Gentiles be iudged in thy sight. Arise Lord God, let thy hand be exalted, forgete not the poore. Deliuer Israel ô God, out of his tribulation. In thee ô Lord haue I hoped, let me not be confounded for

euer

Marginal notes:

10. 11. &c.

Exod 1. v 6. ch. 2. v. 23. 24.

Iudic 3. v 5. ch. 4. v. 3. ch. 10. v. 10. &c.

Proued by authentical examples.

Psal 9. v. 20 33. Pl. 24. v. 22.

And by other holie Scriptures.

ouer : in thy iustice deliuer me. Let God arise, and let *Pſ.67. v. 2. 3*
his enimies be diſperſed , and let them that hate him
flee from his face. As ſmoke vaniſheth, let them va-
niſh away : as waxe melteth at the preſence of fire; ſo *Pſ.118 v.153*
let ſinners periſh, at the preſence of God. See my hu- *Pſ.119.v.*
miliation, and deliuer me. When I was in tribulation, *12.*
I cryed to our Lord, and he heard me. O Lord deliuer my ſoule from vniuſt lippes, and from a deceiptful tongue] In like maner other Prophets, prayed
that God would deliuer his people from temporal
afflictions, And expreſly teſtifie that God approueth, *Iſa.1.v 15.*
and in due time granteth ſuch prayers. [The iuſt haue *cb.41.v.17.*
cryed (ſaith the ſame Pſalmiſt) and our Lord hath
heard them; and out of their tribulations he hath de- *Pſ. 33. v 18.*
liuered them. Our Lord is nigh to them that are of a *19.20.*
contrite hart : and the humble of ſpirite he wil ſaue
(deliuer from temporal euils , ſo farre as is for their
ſpiritual good) Manie are the tribulations of the iuſt:
and out of al thoſe our Lord wil deliuer them.]

Chriſt gran-
ted ſuch pray-
ers, and tea-
cheth vs ſo to
pray.

4. Chriſt our Lord both heard the prayers of very
manie, which beſought him to cure their corporal infirmities ; and alſo commandeth al Chriſtians to pray
for al temporal neceſſarie releeſe : and namely teacheth to pray in time of perſecutions, to be defended
from aggrauating circumſtances, that the euiles may
be more tolerable [That their flight may not be in *Mat.24.v.*
the winter (as a hard time for trauel) nor in the Sab- *10. 21.*
bath (wherby they may be more hindered from Gods
ſeruice) for there ſhal be then (in the time of Antichriſt) great tribulation. (In the firſt great perſecution
of the Church, after the Martyrdome of S. Steuen,
manie fled from Ieruſalem into diuers places of Iurie, *Act.8.v. 1.*
and Samaria. And when S. Peter was taken and im- *4.5.*
priſoned [Prayer was made of the Church without
intermiſſion vnto God for him] And he was deliuered
by an Angel. S. Paul reciteth manie tribulations, fró *ch. 12.v 5.*
which by his owne & others prayers, he was deliuered. *7.*

　　　　　　　　　　　　　　　　　　S. Iames

S. Iames also admonisheth al Christians to repaire to
prayer in tribulations, saying [Is anie of you in heaui-
nesse, let him paay.] By al which, and the like examples, and instructions, it clearly appeareth to be lawful, and needful to pray vnto God, to be deliuered
from temporal euiles, discomodities, and danger. And
hereupon Holie Church ordayneth, and vseth special
prayers, and supplications, in times of contagious
sicknesses; of watres present or feared; of famine, of
great drught, or ouer much raine; & of others whatsoeuer corporal or temporal euiles. More especially
that God wil defend, and preserue vs from sudaine
death, by fire, water, lightning, or other misfortunes.
And finally from al euils, wherunto our fraile life is
subiect, according to the tenour of this last Petition,
[Deliuer vs from euil.] Not only spiritual, as we specially pray in the former Petitions: but also from the
residue of temporal paine, and punishment due for
our sinnes: from the reliques of sinnes, which rre euil
habites, and pronesse to sinne; and from dangerous
temporal tribulations.

5, Here againe especially, we must remember, that
as our Lord hath prescribed this most excellent forme
of daylie prayer: so he hath sette the same in such necessarie order, that none may presume to inuert it, or
transpose the Petitions, otherwise then here we haue
them in most perfect due order. For when being afflicted with corporal paine, or anguish of minde, feeling some vehement greefe, we first or principally desire and pray for releafe therof, not considering what
els is more necessarie, we therby make ourselues vncapable of that which we aske. To which sort of supplicants, S. Iames saith [You aske & reeeeiue not: because you aske amisse] But why amisse, some wil say:
seing we aske good thinges? We aske life, health,
peace, libertie of conscience, to be deliuered from extremitie of paine, from inuasion of enimes, from per-

*Holie Church
prayeth to be
deliuered frō
ouer great
tribulations.*

*The summe of
this last Peti-
tion.*

Art. 15.

*Due order
must be obser-
ued in praying
for necessarie
thinges.*

Iac. 4. v. 3.

fecution of infidels ? to be releeued in temporal afflictions, yet you aske amiffe, faith S. Iames, to al that
receiue not that which they aske, becaufe you aske
out of due order. You aske that in the firft place, or
you aske that more principally, which is leffe neceffarie; or you aske that abfolutely, which should
only be asked códitionaily. For reforming of which
errour, it behoueth to remember that our heauenlie
Father fendeth or permitteth afflictions for the good
of his elect; fo to reduce them vnto himfelfe, which

neglect his other admonitions and callings. So he telleth vs by his Prophete Ifaias, faying [Vexation alone **If.28.v.19.**
shalgeue vnderftáding to the hearing] becaufe we haue
often heard, but not regarding, haue not vnderftood.
And therfore that we may bemoued to regard Gods
admonitions, fo to vnderftand them, he fuffereth vs
to fal into temporal vexation, which alone geueth
that vnderftanding, which others haue not liuing in
profperitie {Loe this was the iniquitie of Sodome **Ezech.15.v.**
(faith our Lord) pride, fulnes of bread, abundance, & **49.**
idlenes] But Gods peculiar people[the children of Ifrael added to doe euil in the fight of our Lord : who
ftrengthned againft them Eglon the King of Moab, **Iudic.3.v.**
and they ferued him eightene yeares. And they cryed **12.14.**
to our Lord] For vexation geuing them vnderftanding, brought them to repentance. And fo they learned firft to pray for remiffion of their finnes, and
then prayed alfo to be deliuered from temporal tribulations. Right order therfore in praying, is no leffe **Cant.2 v.4**
neceffarie then prayer it felfe. [He that ordereth charitie in his fponfe] teacheth vs to pray, in due order.

6. Firft of al to pray that Gods name be euerie
where fanctified, his glorie preferred aboue al. That
his kingdome be propagated, and made complete in
al the elect: That not our proper wilies, but Gods wil
be done in al thinges. Then we muft pray for al neceffarie helpes. Firft fpritual, then temporal. For remif-
                                                                      fion

fion of finnes. That alfo we may refift al tentations,
tending to finne. And laftly to be deliuered from al
temporal euiles, fo farre as they may be dangerous to
our fpiritual progreffe in vertue. In this order we are
directed to pray, which againe our Sauiour repeteth
faying [Seeke therfore firft the kingdome of God (that
is, in the firft, not in the fecond, or laft place) and the

Mat.6.v.33. iuftice of God (which importeth the meanes to obtaine the kingdome of God) and in the laft place defiring other thinges conuenient [and al thefe thinges,
(meate, drinke, clothes, healthes, &c.) shal be geuen
you befides] faith our fwete Sauiour. But when we
aske relaxation from paine before remiffió of finnes,
temporal thinges before fpiritual; our owne wil before Gods wil, anie other thing beforeGods honour,
& obtaine not our requefts, we muft know, that the
denial, or delay therof proceedeth from the great
mercie of our heauenlie. Father. That we may therby
vnderftand our errour, in asking diforderly, the leffe
thing, before the greater. And if we fee not the
caufe why God femeth not to heare our prayers, his
fingular goodnes by fpecial afflictions admonisheth
his eleft againe, and againe, that at laft, [vexation

Ifa.28.v.19. may geue vs vnderftanding] And then wil the happie faithful foule, with ioyful hart confeffe, and fay
to our heauenly Father [It is good for me, ô Lord, that

Pf.118.v. thou haft humbled me: that I may lerne thy Iufti-
71. fications.]

The conclufion, Amen: is a confirmation of
our part, that vve truly defire that vvhich
vve aske in vvordes.

ARTICLE 39.

AMen is an Hebrew word: which here and in
manie other places of holie Scriprure, is not
translated into Greke, nor Latine (neither therfore into vulgar languages In Catholique Editions,

margin note: And to be deliuered from
finne, before
we aske relaxa-
tion from pu-
nifhment.

margin note: VVhy Amen
is not transla-
ted in manie
places.

Bbb 2   but

but is left in the original tongue, and by sacred vse is
made familiar to al Christians, as more significant,
then can be so breefly expressed in anie other tógue.
It is sometimes a Noone, signifying Truth, or a true
thing: as where our Sauiour saith, Amen. I say to thee *Mat 5.v.27.*
(that is an assured truth I say to thee) thou shalt not
goe out from thence, til thou repay the last farthing,

It is some-
times a
Noone, some-
times an Ad-
uerbe, some-
times a Verbe.
Amen amen I say to you (A true, a true thing, I say to
you:) If anie man kepe my word, he shal not see death *Ioan.5.v.51.*
for euer. Thus saith Amen: the faithful & true witnes] *Ap.3.v.14.*
that is Thus saith Truth the faithful and true witnes.
Sometimes it is an Aduerbe signifying Truly, or verily; as when our Lord said to the penitent theefe on
the Crosse [Amen I say to thee (that is, Truly, or assu- *Luc.23.v.43.*
redly, I say to thee) this day thou shalt be with me in
paradise] So in the end of our Crede we say [Amen]
that is, we verily, & assuredly beleue al those thinges,
which we there professe. Sometimes this word Amé
is a Verbe, signifying [Be it done; or, Be it so.] And in
this sense, it is in respect of vs that pray a word of desiring and praying that it may be so done, as is expressed: and so we ratifie al that we haue said in our prayers. And in respect of God it is a word of granting, &
commanding that the thinges be done, which are requested. And so it signifieth, that God on his part,
granteth whatsoeuer is rightly desired. Of al which
diuerse significations, and vse of this sacred word, we
haue manie examples in holie Scriptures.

2.   In a certaine forme of trial, in the case of anie
woman suspected of adultrie, it was ordained by the
Examples of
the vse of this
word. Amen.
Law of Moyses, that such a one being called into que- *Num.5.v.24.*
stion [should heare the Priests adiuration, heaping *17.22.*
terrible curses vpon a certaine water, & should say:
Amen, amen, & drinke the water] therby praying or
wittingly consenting, that those curses should fal
vpon her, if she were guiltie of the suspected crime.
It was in like maner required that [al the people
should

should heare greuous curses denounced, against al
the transgressors of certaine precepts (in al twelue)
and should answer to euerie one: Amen] Therby
praying, or yelding their consent, that if anie should
so offend, the curse should fal vpon him. King Dauid
bringing the holie Arke of God into Ierusalem [sang
an Hymne of praise to our Lord, and in the conclusion therof inuited al the people to say: Amen.] The
same King ordayning, that his sonne Salomon should
be crowned, to succede him in the Kingdom, those
that wished good successe, said : [Amen, So speake
our Lord, the God of my Lord the King] Nehemias
praying [that God would cast out of his house euerie
one, that should not accomplish his comandments,
al the multitude said: Amen] The same Nehemias
praying for himself in the end of his Booke, concludeth with [Amen] At the Mariage of young Tobias
and Sara, her Father praying for the spouses, [other
freindes said: Amen] Tobias the elder concludeth his
prophetical praises to God with [Amen.] Likewise
other Prophetes often conclude special Prophecies,
Praises, and Prayers with this word [Amen] As wel
therby affirming the assured truth of that which they
say: as desiring, and praying that Gods wil may be
fulfilled in the same : euer conforming their owne
willes to his: and so said: [Amen.]

3.   To this very purpose our Lord teacheth vs to
conclude this our most ordinarie prayer ; and by this
example also other prayers, thankesgeuinges, and
praises to God, with Amen . And so did the holie A-
postles most ordinarily conclude their Epistles with
prayers, thankes, or praises to God, and the same with
Amen [To God our Lord (saith S. Paul) be glorie for
euer. Amen. The God of peace be with you al. Amen.
The grace of our Lord Iesus Christ be with you al.
Amen. To God the onlie wise, be honour and glorie
through Iesus Christ for euer and euer; Amen. The

Marginal notes (left):
Deut.27.v.
15.&6.

1.Par.16.
v.8.

36.

3.Reg 1.v.
36.

2 Esd 5.v.13
ch.13.v.31.

Tob.9.v.12.
ch.13 v.33.

Is.25.v.1.
ch.65.v.16.

Iere.11.v.5.
ch.28.v.6.

Ro.1.v.16.
ch.15.v.33.

Marginal notes (right):
Christ tea-
cheth vs so to
conclude our
prayers. And
the Apostles
so obserued
his precept.

grace of our Lord Iesus Chrift be with your fpirite. *ch. 16. v. 17.*
Amen] So in the reft of his Epiftles. And euen fo S. *1.Cer. 16.7.*
Peter. S. Iohn, and S. Inde, conclude with prayers, *23 24.*
thankes, or praifes: and in confirmation, that they *2.Cor. 13.*
verily fo defire they finally adde [Amen.] *v. 13.*

As in the be-
ginning of
prayer, fo in
the end it moft
importeth to
haue actual at-
tention.

4. A very fpecial profite therfore we may here
reape, by adding this word. Amen: that wheras we
haue not had fo perfect attention, nor fo abfolute refignation of our proper wil, as was requifite, in euerie
petition: we may in good part, by more actual atten- *Pf. 72. v. 25.*
tion, and particular fubmiffion of our wil to Gods
wil, fupplie in this laft word. Amen, the former defect; by correcting and renewing our defire, that al,
and euerie thing may be done (and that in the fame
order, of greater thinges before the leffe) as they are
conteyned in the facred wordes, notwithftanding
our negligences and coldnes, in reciting them. For fo
in one perfect thought, we may (if we be as Daniel *Dan. 9. v. 13.*
was of right defires) really defire Gods wil in al:
which in dede conteyneth al.   And fo our hart defiring, that God wil make vs to defire, al & only thofe
thinges which pleafe him, then, and not otherwife,
we fhal receiue al that we neede, if this be our true
defire, when we fay: Amen.

This vvord Amen, is alfo a confirmation on
Gods part, that he granteth vvhatfoeuer
is duly asked in prayer.

ARTICLE   40.

It is moft cer-
taine that al
prayers rightly
made are gran-
ted.

MOreouer in this word Amen, we haue another
fingular cófolation, that if our prayer be rightly made, then God himfelfe faith Amen. in the fenfe
of granting and commanding that to be done, which
we aske. And this is fo certaine, that to hold the contrarie is heretical: againft the expreffe and manifeft
written word of God. As we haue already shewed, *Art. 11*
concerning the affured effect, on Gods part, of al
faithful

faithful good prayers. Vnto which holie Scriptures there recited, we shal adde only two or three more facred textes, in confirmation of our beleefe, and hope in this behalf.

2. Our B. Sauiour plainly faith, to euerie one that *Christ fo teacheth and promiseth.* prayeth in due maner, as he ought. [Thy Father which feeth in fecrete wil repay thee] that is wil reward this good worke: either granting that thing which is requefted, or that which he knoweth to be better for thee. Againe he faith. [Haue faith of God: Amen I fay to you, that whofoeuer shal fay to this mountaine: Be taken vp, and be caft into the fea: & shal not ftagger in hart, but baleue that whatfoeuer he faith shal be done, it shal be done vnto him] fignifying that on Gods part, there can be no want, nor defect, neither of power, nor of wil to grant, and doe anie thing: in fo much that if in cafe it were requifite, that a mountaine should be remoued, and a faithful feruant of God, should confidently aske it, it should be fo done: becaufe there neither wanteth power, nor wil in God. And the denial therof is impious infidelitie, either againft Gods power, if any dare fay, that he can not: or againft his Goodnes to fay, that he wil not, if it be needful: and againft his Truth, becaufe in fuch a cafe he hath promifed, that he wil doe it, being no defect on their part that pray. Vpon which infallible ground S. Iames expresly fayeth [If any of you lacke wifedome (or anie other neceffarie thing) let him aske of God, who geueth to al men abundantly: and vpbradeth not, and it shal be geuen. But let him aske in faith: nothing doubting] firmely beleuing, & nothing doubting that God can if he wil, and wil if it be conuenient. For this is it which the Apoftle calleth [Prayer of faith.] And this i [the faith of God.] Which our Lord requireth, in al that pray. And then is the fruite of prayer moft affured, becaufe Chrift our Lord, who is truth it felfe hath fo taught,

Mat. 6. v. 6.

Mar. 11. v. 23. 24.

Mat. 17. v. 20.

cb. 21. v. 22.

Io. 1. v. 5. 6.

cb. 5. v. 15.

Mat. 11. v. 24.

taught, and so promised. And therfore al that is preached by his true Apostles, is true & certaine. [In our preaching which was to you (said S. Paul to the Corinthians, who charged him to haue failed in his promise) there is not: It is, and it is not. For the Sonne of God Iesus Christ: who by vs was preached amóg you: by me, and Siluanus, and Timothee, was not: It is, and It is not: but, It is, was in him. For al the promises of God are in him: It is. Therfore also by him, Amen to God: vnto our glorie.] Gods truth in performing al his assertions, purposes, and promises, is to the glorie of himself, and of al his true seruants. For whereas his seruants Amen (asseueration, desire, or prayer) may erre: Gods Amen (asseueration, grant, or promise) can neuer erre, nor be frustrate, nor faile: but on his part, is alwayes most true, assured, and infallible.

3. Wherupon Holie Church representeth this no lesse certaine, then comfortable truth vnto her faithful children; especially in the holie and dailie Sacrifice (and in some other parts of the Ecclesiastical Office:) where, the Priest singing, or reading the Pater Noster, the Clerque that serueth, or the Quire, in place of the people, reciting the last Petition. [But deliuer vs from euil:] addeth not Amen, in the end: but the Priest supplieth it, at the Altar: mystically signifying, that God himselfe (if the supplicáts be rightly disposed) answereth: Amen, to al that is wel, and duly demanded. And therfore as wel the Priest, that sacrificeth, as al others that assist, and desire to be partakers of Gods benefites, both in this, & in al other prayers, must in their hart, and sincere intention, when they say Amen, desire and mentally pray to God, that his diuine Goodnes wil say: Amen.

The

Marginal notes:

It is, and, It is not, are found in men.

at Is, is always in God.

The Priest not the people sayth Amen in the end of the Pater Noster, in the holie Masse.

VVhen we say Amen, our hart must desire, that God wil say, Amen.

2. Cor. 1, v. 18.

19.

20.

Ad Primam Complet. &c.

The *Angelical Salutation of the B. Virgine, Mother of God, is lavvfully, and profitably recited by good Christians.*

ARTICLE 41.

Of the honour of our B. Ladie, fee Part. 1. Art. 21. Of al Sainctes: Part. 3 Artic. 9.

AFter the explication of our Lords Prayer, which is expresly and immediatly directed to God himselfe, the most blessed Trinitie; it resteth to shew that other prayers directed also to God our heauenlie father, by the meditation of his glorious and faithful seruants, are likewise lawful and profitable. Which because Protestants denie, as did long since Vigilantius. In this point their progenitor; against both him therfore and them, we shal, here proue the Christian beleefe, and practise of this doctrine, more euidently by the holie Scriptures, then our Aduersaries are able, by the like meanes, to disproue it, or to declare the contrarie. And because the *Aue Maria*, is often recited by Catholiques, & especially impugned, by al the Sectaries of this time, we shal here beginne with the same Angelical Salutation; and prayer adioyned. Then proue the like lawful and profitable vse of praying to God, by intercession as wel of the same most B. Virgine, as of the glorious Angels, and other Sainctes. And lastly shew that it is no derogation, but more honour to God, that we desire both his glorious Sainctes in heauen, and his faithful seruants in earth, to pray vnto him, for vs.

De. 5. v. 39.

1. Cor. 14. v. 36.

2. T. m 3. v. 16. 17.

Prayer and Inuocation of Sainctes is more clearly proued, then it can be disproued, by holie Scriptures.

2. First then concerning Prayers, and Inuocation of Sainctes, the cheefest controuersie consisteth in this doubt. How we in earth can speake vnto spiritual creatures, that are in heauen; and how the same glorious creatures can heare vs, or know our desires: For it is in deede vnpossible, that our speach in earth should be heard by the Sainctes in heauen, according to the common sense of these wordes, speaking and hearinge. Because Angels: and soules separated from their

Protestants cheefest obiection is, that Sainctes in heauen can not heare the prayers of the faithful in earth.

C c c   their

their bodies, haue not corporal eares; and are so farre distant from vs, that no mortal mans voice can be extended to them. With which common maske our Aduersaries cannot possibly delude any, but such as are wilfully blinde. For the simplest person, that beleueth the immortalitie of soules, easily knoweth, that soules being parted from their bodies (& other spirites) haue special meanes to signifie their mindes, & to vnderstand each others conceipts (Which we cal *speaking, and hearing,* that is to say, vttering and vnderstanding: which S. Paul also calleth the tongue of Angels) better then mortal men with corporal tongues, and eares. God our omnipotét Creator hath not a corporal tongue, nor eares, and he speaketh to Angels. And Angels in heauen: and diuels in hel, doe also speake, & vnderstand one an other [God also spake to Adam, and to manie other mortal men. The diuel (by a serpent) spake to Eue, and heard her speake. Good Angels spake to the Prophetes in slepe, and in visions. The diuel put into the hart of Iudas Iscariote, to betray our B. Sauiour] Manie other exemples witnesse, that spirites doe speake to spirites, and to mens soules, also whiles they are yet in their bodies. And albeit soules in their bodies can not clearly see themselues, nor other soules, yet departed from their bodies they most clearly see themselues, and other soules: and by the light of glorie doe see al that any way perteineth to themselues. Moreouer the soules of the faithful in this life, can eleuate their cogitations into heauen: and their prayers rightly made, are heard in heauen. As Salomon testifieth, saying to God. [Thou wilt heare in heauen.] And S. Paul saith of himselfe & other good Christians [Our conuersation is in heaué] Which is especially verified of hartie prayers. For it is not the external voice without intétion of mind, but the good cogitation of the soule (whether the mouth speake or no) that ascendeth into

Marginal notes (left):

Answer.

Angels, and separated soules, haue not corporal tongues: nor eares, but haue other meanes, to vnderstand each others conceipts, and willes.

Also mens soules in their bodies can eleuate their thoughtes into heauen.

Marginal notes (right):

1. Cor. 13.
v.1.

Gen 2.v.16.
ch.3.v.1.
Iob.1.v.6.
Gen.37.v.6.
&c.

Is.1.v.1.
ch 14.v.12.

Mat.1.v.20
Luc.1.v.11.
Io.13.v.2.

3.Reg.8.v.
30.
Phil.3.v.20

into heauen. And therfore, neither the great diftance of place, not lacke of corporal eares in holie Angels, and other Sainctes, can hinder the hearing of faithful prayers, directed to God by mediation of his glorious Sainctes: as the Proteftants either foolishly imagine, or malicioufly feane: and fo deceiue themfelues, or others. But let vs alfo fee what other impediments they pretend.

2. An other obiection is, that albeit fpiritual creatures doe vtter their conceipts: and vnderftand each others: & that mortal perfons doe eleuate their mindes into heauen, yet none but God only can vnderftanftand the hartes, and defires of the faithful in earth. For which, our Aduerfaries alleage thefe wordes of our Lord, faying by his Prophete Ieremie [The hart of man is peruerfe, and vnfearchable: who fhal know it? I the Lord that fearch the hart, and proue the reyners.] Therfore (fay they) no man, nor Angel can fearch, nor know the fecrete thoughtes of an other mans hart, which only God can doe, and no creature. We anfwer: that only God by his owne power, can fearch and know the fecretes, which any man referueth in his hart, & which he would conceale from al other creatures: it is in dede in mans power, if he wil, to hide the fecretes of his hart, and fo, as this facred text affirmeth [The hart of man is peruerfe] is deceiptful, and depe. Neuertheles he can, if he wil, reueale the fame fecretes of his hart, either by wordes, or other fignes, to an other mortal man: or els by voluntarie cogitation, to fuch fpiritual creatures, as haue fpiritual eares. And fo thefe wordes of the Prophete proue no more, but that naturally, and ordinarily euerie man can, if he wil, hide the fecrete cogitations of his hart: but they proue not, that a man cannot, if he wil, reueale the fecrets if his hart. For experience continually fheweth, that men can, and doe reueal their fecrete thoughts to other mortal men;

Iere.17.v.9.
10.

The Proteftants fecond obiection. That onlie God can know fecrete cogitations.

Anfwer.

Only God by his owne power knoweth the fecretes of hartes.

Sainctes can know fecretes by reuelation.

and

and can defire to reueale their fecrete thoughtes to
Sainctes in heauen : which defire and wil afcendeth
into heauen. Where (as Proteftants wil confeffe)God
feeth the fame cogitations : and therfore thofe Angels,and other Sainctes can fee them,whom God wil
haue to fee,or know them, which we fuppofe our
Aduerfaries wil not denie. If they wil denie it, we
require that they iuftifie their denial by holie Scripture. In the meane while, we auouch by holie Scriptures , that glorious Angels prefented the prayers,
& hartie defires of Daniel the Prophete,of Tobias,of $Dan.8.7.$
Cornelius,and of others,vnto God in heauen,which $15.16.$
they could not haue done, vtiles they had knowen
the thoughtes of the fupplicants hartes. Againe it is $Tob 3.7.25.$
clearly teftified in holie Scriptures , that God reuealed vnto certaine Prophetes in this life,the fecretes of $Act.10.73.$
mens hartes , which the fame men would haue con- $4.$
cealed from al men.Wherof two examples,one of the
old Teftament, an other of the new may here fuffice,
in confirmation of our anfwer to the Proteftants obiection. Elifeus the Prophete knew the fecrete of his
feruants hart , which the fame feruant denied, and
would haue concealed from his mafter : who neuertheles faid vnto him [was not my hart prefent when $4.Reg.5.7.$
the man returned out of his chariote to meete thee?] $26.$
Likewife { S. Peter knew the fecrete thoughtes, of
Ananias & Saphira , defrauding, and denying part of $Act.6.73.$
the price, which they had receiued for their land. } $8.9.$
Though therfore naturally,and ordinarily mans hart
can kepe cogitations fecrete,from al other creatures,
yet doth not this hinder Gods power,from reuealing
the fame, which man would hide,neither is the capacitie of mans vnderftanding limited , but that God
can make him, alfo in this world, to fee or know the
fecretes of others hartes , which they would côceale.
How much more like , and more ordinarie is it, that
God geueth this power to glorified Sainctes(confidering,

Either by the
light of glorie,
or by the light
of Prophecie
or by other in-
fpiration.

ring, that the light of glorie farre excelleth the light of prophecie) that they may see and know manie thinges done in earth, euen secrete cogitations, especially those, which faithful supplicants desire that they may know. And stil it is most true that only God, by his owne power [doth search the hart, & proue (or examine) the reynes.] And neuertheles by Gods gift, his seruãts can see & know (either by the light of glorie, or of Prophecie (or how soeuer God wil, that they shal know) the cogitatiõs of mortal mẽs hartes: and of their workes proceeding from their hartes.

Especially when suppli- cants desire, that Sainctes wil pray for them to God.

4. Thus much in general, for defence of the Catholike beldefe: and doctrine against Protestants cheefe obiections: that Sainctes in heauen ean, and doe vuderstand the praises, thankes, and petitions of the faithful in earth, directed to God by their intercession. Now more particularly we shal declare that the militant Church of Christ: and the faithful members therof, doe lawfully and profitable both praise: and pray the B. Virgine Mother of God (and likewise other Sainctes) to pray for vs to God, beginning our prayer, with the Angelical salutation, saying [Hayle Marie ful of grace, our Lord is with thee: blessed art thou among wemen] For as it was not impertinent to the holie Archangels purpose, coming with an embassage from the most blessed Trinitie, before he declared his message, to salute her, with these words of her singular praise: so it is also no lesse, but rather more conuenient, that we poore supplicants comming to craue her pious interciffion for vs to God, doe beginne with the same ioyful salutation, which may put vs in minde of the best tydinges, or newes, that euer came into this world, to witte of the most happie Incarnation of Christ our Redemer and Sauiour, by taking flesh of this most holie purest Virgine, ful of grace; whose soule and bodie, Almightie God, prepared to be a worthie habitacle of his

The saluta- tion of our B. Ladie pertey- neth to her praises.

Luc. 1, 7.28.

Sonne. For which purpose it was moſt requiſite, that
she should be, as the Angel pronounced, ful of grace,
and our Lord should be with her, by his ſpiritual habitation in her ſoule, alſo before she conceiued the
Sonne of God in her bodie: that she might ſo conceiue him: And therfore no maruel that S. Elizabeth,
being alſo replenished with the ſame Holie Ghoſt,
[cried out with a loud voice, & ſaid (vnto her hauing
now côceiued the ſame Sonne of God in her wombe)
Bleſſed art thou among wemen (as the Angel had
ſaid before; and further as it were expreſſing the cauſe
of her greater bleſſednes, ſaid) and bleſſed is the fruite
of thy wombe] For by this diuine fruite, she that was
before ful of grace, was now more ful: she that was
before bleſſed, was now ſuperbleſſed : she that before had our Lord God Omnipotent, dwelling with
her , now had the ſame our Lord God dwelling in
her: euen him, alſo corperatly [in whom dwelieth al
the fulnes of the Godhead corporally] as S. Paul ſpeaketh. Thus did S. Eliſabeth admiring congratulate.
How much more doe al good Chriſtians iuſtly congratulate her fulnes of grace, who is now alſo ful of
glorie, aboue al mankinde, and Angels, next after her
ſonne, the Sonne of God? By whom as she was in
this life ſuperreplenished with grace, ſo is she in heauen ſuperreplenished with glorie. She that was made
in this life, the Mother of God: is now alſo Queene
Mother in heauen: moſt truly therfore called Queene
of al Angels, Queene of al holie Patriarches, Prophetes , Apoſtles , Martyrs , Virgines, Confeſſors,
of al Sainctes, and of al mere creatures.

5. Al which her abundant grace, and glorie, being
deriued from the ſame bleſſed fruite of her wombe,
Ieſus Chriſt our Lord God, derogateth nothing from
his glorie, as Proteſtants vainly imagine, but redoundeth ſo much the more to his glorie , as it is further
extended , not only to the glorious perſon of his virgine Mother, but alſo to her pure bodie and bloude,
of which

Marginal notes (left):
She being ful of grace, before she con-
ceiued Chriſt,
was made
more ful by
conceiuing
him.

Now she is
alſo more ful
of glorie, then
anie Angel, or
other Sainct:
next after her
Sonne, our
Lord.

His glorie is
accidentally
increaſed, by

Marginal notes (right):
v 41.
42.

Coloſ. 2. v. 9.

of which he tooke his bodie : and to her sacred virginal wombe, that bare him, and to her blessed virginal breastes, which he sucked. Euen as an other deuout woman (also a figure of the Catholique Church) rightly professed, and the holie Euangelist hath recorded, that when our Lord preached afterwards to much people [A certaine woman lifting vp her voice, out of the multitude said to him: Blessed is the wōbe that bare thee: and the Pappes that thou didst sucke] Whose iust praise our Lord accepting, added, and affirmed that not only his mother was blessed, for that she bare him, and gaue him sucke, but more blessed because she heard his word, and kept it. And albeit no other creature is, or can be participant of the former blessing to be his proper Mother, and Nource, yet manie may be, and are participant of her greater blessing, for our Lord said in general: [Yea rather, blessed are they, that heare the word of God, & kepe it] that is, euerie one is blessed (more or lesse, according to their degree of grace) that heareth Gods word, and kepeth it. And so in proportion the Mother of God, most excelling in grace, was most blessed, for she best kept his diuine word. Yea and the moe in number, and the more perfectly that they heare, and kepe Gods word, the more is Christ our Lord honored, and praised by them; because al redoundeth to him, as al is deriued from him. For [Of his fulnes al we receiue.] saith S. Iohn the Baptist.

6. Moreouer al that which true Christians doe, in often reciting this Angelical Salutation, and diuers Anthémes, Hymnes, Canticles, and other praises to our B. Ladie, is iustified by her owne prophecie, (agreable to manie former Prophecies) saying [God my Sauiour hath regarded the humilitie of his hand maide (that is, hath exalted me, because I was hūble) For behold (saith she) from hence forth (since I am become the Mother of God) al generations shal call

me

Marginal notes (left):
Luc.11.v.27.

v.28.

Mat.5.v.17.

Io.1.v.16.

Luc.1.v.48, 49
Cant 2 v 2
cb.4 v.7.

Marginal notes (right):
how much it is further extended.

This maner of praising God, by praising his glorious Mother, was prophicied by herself.

ch.8. v.8.
1/7 v.14.
ch.11 v.1.
Iere.31. v.
22.
Ezech.44 v.
2.

And by other
Prophetes.

me bleff-d.] she also explaneth the reason why saying
[Becaufe he that is mightie hath done great thinges
to me.] moft plainly foreshewing, that becaufe God
Almightie hath chofen, and made her a worthie habitacle of his Sonne, the very Mother of God, who
created her, and fo endned her with al conformable
prerogatiues, priuilegies, dignities, preeminences, &
al other moft excellent graces, aboue al mere creatures, aboue al created perfons, therfore [al generations (doubtles she meant al future true feruants of
Chrift) shal cal her bleffed] shal praife, and magnifie
her. Remember her diuine giftes, moft holie life, excellent actions bleffed death, glorious Affumption
into heaue, shal celebrate her feaftes, & faftes, adorne
her Churches, and Altares, and by al meanes honour
her, next after her Sonne and Lord: our Lord Iefus
Chrift. The more we doe this, the more we fulfil her
prophecie, and the more we proue ourfelues to be of
thofe true Chriftian generations, which cal her bleffed. And thofe which difdaine, or diminish her
praifes, abrogating, her feftinities, prophaning her
Churches, and Altars dedicated to God in her name,
and memorie; abandoning her falutation, and other
praifes, euidently proue themfelues, not to be true
Chriftians.

Thofe which
difdaiue our
B.Ladies prai-
fes are not true
Ghriftians.

7. Finally reafon conuinceth, with reafonable perfons, & daylie experience teacheth, that the honour
or refpect, which is done ro feruants, or children, redoundeth to the Lord, or parets, for whofe fake it is
done. And fo al honour done to our B. Ladie, Gods
Mother, and moft excellent feruant, redoundeth to
the more honour of God, and of Chrift: becaufe
it is done to her in regard of that grace, and glorie,
which she hath with him. I know, and haue fometime heard the exception, which fome Proteftants
take againft this fimilitude, auouching that diuine &
fpiritual thinges muft not be refembled to humane; &
temporal.

Reafons
sheweth that
the praife of
Gods feruants
redoundeth to
his praife.

temporal. It is true in deede, that diuine Myſteries farre excel humane knowlege, in which reſpect comparison is not to be made, as if they were both like & equal. Neuertheles God in the old Teſtament, by humane, and temporal thinges both preſigured diuine, and ſpiritual: and Chriſt in the new Teſtament taught manie thinges by ſenſible parables. And for example in our preſent purpoſe, alſo in the old Teſtament, God Almightie reſembleth himſelf vnto a temporal Father, and Lord, ſaying by his Prophete Malachias [The Sonne honoreth the Father: and the ſeruant his Lord: If then I be the Father, where is my honour? And if I be the Lord, where is my feare? ſaith The Lord of hoſts] And Chriſt our Lord ſaith [The ſeruant is not aboue his maſter] Which prouerbe he applied to himſelf, & his diſciples. And in plaine termes ſignifieth that, whatſoeuer is done to the diſciple, or ſeruant perteyneth to the Maſter, ſaying [He that receiueth you receiueth me: and he that deſpiſeth you deſpiſeth me.] As therfore, he that deſpiſeth Gods ſeruant deſpiſeth God: euen ſo, he that honoreth Gods ſeruant, honoreth God. [And whoſoeuer gloſieth God, him God wil glorifie.]

Col.4.v.24.

God declareth diuine thinges by the ſimilitude of humane.

Mal.1.v.6.

Mat.10.v. 24.

Mat.12.v.16

2.Reg.2.v. 30.

The ſecond part of the Aue Maria: [Holie Marie Mother of God, &c.] is a godlie prayer: agreable to holie Scriptures.

ARTICLE 42.

EVen as the praiſes of out B. Ladie conteined in the Angelical ſalutation, diminiſh not Gods owne praiſes, but redound to the more honour of God, of whom ſhe receiued al her grace: ſo in like maner our prayers directed to her, not asking grace, remiſſion of ſinnes, or other diuine gift from herſelf, but by her interceſſion, from God [from whom euerie beſt, and perfect gift deſcendeth] are no leſſe, but

Our prayer is of more value by the interceſſion of Sainctes.

Iac.1.v.17.

so much more gratful to God, as her glorious intercession is of more value, then our owne onlie petition. For as we praise God not only in himself, for
his infinite Power, Wisdome, Goodnes, and other
Diuine Attributes, but also in his workes: especially
[in his Sainctes] so we pray to him not only, by immediatly inuocating his most holie name; but also by
mediation of his glorious Mother, and of other Sainctes. And that in two maners: either by praying God
to grant our desires in regard of the fauour, which
his Sainctes haue with him, and for their sakes: or by
expresly praying them to pray for vs Both which
sortes of prayer because our aduersaries generally dis-
like, and impugne, we shal therfore proue them
both.

Psal 150.
v. 1. 2.

Two waies of praying by the mediation of Sainctes.

2. God expressely promised great thinges to Abraham, and for his sake to his posteritie, saying to him
[lift vp thine eyes, and looke from the place, wherein thou now art: to the north and south; to the east
and weast: al the land which thou seest, wil I geue to
thee, & thy seede for euer. And I wil make thy seede,
as the dust of the earth: if anie man be able to
number the dust of the earth, thy seede also shal he
be able to number. Arise and walke through the land,
in the legth, & in the breadth therof: for I wil geue it
to thee.] Againe, making a couenant with Abram he
said. [To thy seede wil I geue this land, from the riuer
of Ægypt euen to the great riuer Euphrates.] Which
promise of God made for Abraham children, to be
fulfilled [after four hundred yeares] must nedes be
vnderstood, to be made for his sake, who as yet had
no childe. After this when Abraham had his soone
Isaac (by promise more then by nature) and vpon
Gods commandment was readie to sacrifice him,
being yet a childe, in whom the issue was particular-
lie promised, God not only renewed his promise but
also declared Abrahams faithful act to be the cause,

Gen. 13.
v. 14. 15.
16.
17.

God promiseth benefits for his holie seruants sakes.

Ch. 15. v. 18.

(v. 13. 16.)

Gal. 4. v. 24.
Gen. 37.
v. 21. ch. 28.
v. 12.
ch. 22. v. 14
& c. v. 16.
17. 18.

of

of so great a reward, saying. [By mine owne selfe And maketh
haue I sworne, (saith the Lord; because thou hast done such promise
this thing, and hast not spared thine onlie begotten because his
sonne for my sake ; I wil blesse thee, and wil multi- seruants did
plie thy seede, as the starres of heauen, and as the obey his com-
sand, that is by the sea shore; thy seede shal possesse mandments.
the gates of his enimies. And in thy sede shal be blessed al the nations of the earth : because thou hast
obeyed my voice.] To the same Isaac also, and to his
sonne Iacob, folowing the vertuous steppes of their
Gen.26.v. father Abraham, our Lord againe repeted the same
4. promises, saying to Isaac [I wil be with thee, and wil
blesse thee; for to thee and to thy sede, I wil geue al
these countries; accomplishing the oath, which I
sware to Abraham thy father. And I wil multiplie thy
sede as the starres of heauen : and I wil geue to thy
posteritie, al these countries. And in thy sede shal be
blessed al the nations of the earth : for because Abraham obeyed my voice : and kept my precepts, and
commandements, and obserued my ceremonies, and
lawes] Likewise the very same to Iacob saying [I am
the Lord God of Abraham thy father, and the God of
Gen.28.v.13. Isaac : the land wherin thou slepest, I wil geue to thee
14. and to thy sede. And thy sede shal be as the dust of
the earth : thou shalt be dilated to the Weast, and
to the East, and to the North, and to the South.
And in thee, and in thy sede, al the tribes of the earth
shal be blessed.] Accordingly the same Patriarch Iacob, prophetied that good thinges should be asked
Gen.48.v.16. of God by prayer in their names. [Be my name called
vpon these children (said he, when he blessed Iosephs
sonnes) the names also of my fathers Abraham, and
Isaac.] And Ioseph foretold that their whole nation
should be deliuered from Ægypt, and possesse al
Chanaan, according to Gods promise made to these
Gen.50.v.23. three most renowmed Patriarches, saying thus to his
brethren. [After my death God wil visite you, and

wil make you goe vp out of this land (of Ægypt) to
the land (of Chanaan) which he sware to Abraham,
Isaac, and Iacob.] Al which importeth that God be-
stoweth his benefites not only for his owne good
pleasure, and mere grace without any precedent merite, but also for the subsequent merites of his ser-
uants:as for secondarie causes. And for their sakes,
which are of more perfection, he respecteth their
children, and posteritie. It is true therfore that God,
protected, and prospered the children of Israël,more   ch.11 v.16.
then other nations, first of his owne mere merciful
election : he did it also for his promise sake, and yet
withal for his faithful wel deseruing seruants sakes.
Whose vertues, and good woorkes were the secon-   ch.16.v.5.
datie causes of his promise,&oath,as you see in the expresse sacred textes aboue recited [Because thou hast
done this thing. Because thou obeyedst my voice. Be-   Gen.11.v.18
cause Abraham obeyed my voice]said our Lord God.   ch.11.v.13
I haue sworne &c. And so God renewed these promi-   10.11.
ses to Isaac, and Iacob, hauing like vertues to Abra-   ch 22. v. 20.
ham. Wheras God made not these more special pro-   ch.25 v.11.
mises (but others lesse) to their brethren Nachor,
Ismael, and Esau. Whom God also temporally blessed   ch.17.v.39.
in a lower degree. And generally God promised [to   ch.36 v.9 .
doe mercie vpon thousandes, to them that loue him,   Exo.20.v.6.
and kepe his precepts.

Moyses
prayed by the
mediation of
the holie Pa-
triarches.

3. Vpon these diuine promises, and especial merites
of these more excellent Patriarches(according to the
former maner of praying, for the merites sake of
Gods holie seruantes, most vsual in the old Testament) Moyses confidently prayed for the sinful people, saying to God [Remember Abraham, Isaac, and   ch.11.v.71.
Israel thy seruants : to whom thou swarest, by thine
owne selfe &c. And our Lord was pacified.]And   Exo.32.v.13.
not only remitted part of the due punishment, but   14.
sent an Angel to bring them into the promised land,   ch.33.v.1.2.3
saying to Moyses[Goe, gette thee vp from this place,
                                                        thou

Deut 9. v 17
ch.29. v 15.
ch.30. v.20.

ch.34. v. 4.

Ex. 3. v 6.
15. 16.

Leuit. 26. v.
41.

thou and thy people, which thou haft brought out of the land of Ægypt, into the land, wherof I fware to Abraham, Ifaac, and Iacob. And I wil fend an Angel, thy precurfor, that I may caft out the Chananeite and Amorrheite, &c. and thou maift enter into the land, that floweth with milke and honey] With thefe fpecial Potriarches God would make his couenant, and would be called peculiarly their God [I am the God of thy father: the God Abraham the God of ifaac, and the God of Iacob. I wil remember my couenant which I made with Iacob, and Ifaac, and Abraham.] For this fpecial election of Abraham, Ifaac, and Iacob: for the grace geuen to them, and benefites beftowed vpon the people for their fakes, the Royal Pfalmift inviteth al the faithful to render

Pf 104. v. 1.
& 5. 10.

praifes, and thankes to God, faying [Confeffe yee to our Lord, and inuocate his name: shew forth his workes among the Gentiles. He hath bene mindful for euer of his teftamét, of the word, which he commanded to a thoufand generations. Which he difpofed to Abraham: and of his oath to Ifaac. And he appointed it to Iacob for a precept: and to Ifrael for an eternal teftament] And after rehearfal of manie great and admirable benefites concludeth, that God Almightie did al thefe thinges. [Becaufe he was mindful of his holie word, which he had vttered to Abrahã his feruant.] Not only for the promife fake, which alone is an affured confirmation, but alfo becaufe [this holie word was geuen to Abraham his feruant.] For Abrahams fake the promife was made, and for Abrahams fake it was fulfilled, yet not for Abraham otherwife, then as he was [Gods feruant] fo that al redounteth to Gods more glorie. Seing then God geueth benefites to the needie, and leffe perfect; for the more perfects fake, true faithful people may lawfully, and profitably pray God, to grant neceffarie thinges for his holie feruáts fakes. Elias the Prophete prayed

v. 42.

2. Par. 29. v.
18.
2. Par. 20.
v 7.
4 Reg. 13.
v. 21. 23.

(right margin:) God protected his peculiar people becaufe he had fo promifed, to his holie feruants.

(right margin:) And he made thefe promifes becaufe his feruants were holie.

in this maner, inuocating God for these Patriarches
sake, and by this title of their God, saying [Lord God 3.Reg. 18.7.
of Abraham, and Isaac, and Israel shew this day that 36.
thou art the God of Israel, and I thy seruant.] So he,
and other Prophetes: yea and Christ our Lord called
Almightie God [the God of Abraham, and Isaac, and Isa.29.7.23.
Iacob] And that after their temporal death, because *ch.2.*
they euer liue, in their blessed soules: and are for euer Par 30.7.6
his seruants, more perfect then they were in this life. Mat 22.7.
Further the Prophete Isaias testifieth that ʳ Because Act.3.7.13.
God called Abraham (when he had no childe) and Isa.51.7.2.3
blessed him, and multiplied him. Our Lord therfore
wil comforth Sion: and wil comforth al the ruines
therof] signifying that God geuing grace, wil also
geue reward, and not only blesse and multiplie his
seruant, but also comforth others, blessing them for
his holie seruants sake. [Because he blessed Abraham,
therfore he wil comforth Sion.] And so others by
vertue of this blessing, and diuine grace, keping Gods
precepts, that our Lord may (as himself speaketh) for
Abrahams sake, bring to effect al the thinges, that he Gen. 18.7.
hath spoken vnto him] The like promises were often 19.
made, and benefites bestowed by God Almightie ch 26 7 24.
[Because of Dauid, for Dauids sake. I wil protect this 3 Reg 11.
citie and wil sane it (saith our Lord) for my self, and ch. 5 7 4.
for Dauid my seruant] & the like. The three children 4.Reg 8.7.
also prayed in the furnace of Babylon, saying to God 19
in the name of al the people [Deliuer vs not for euer ch. 19. 7. 34.
(to our enimies) we beseech thee for thy names sake, ch 20 7.6.
and dissipate not thy testament: Neither take thou Ps.131 7.10.
away thy mercie from vs, for Abraham thy beloued, ch 45 7 4.
& Isaac thy seruaut, & Israel thy holie one, to whom Dan 3.7.34.
thou hast spoken, promising that thou wouldest mul 35.36.
tiplie their sede as the starres of heauen, and as the
sand that is in the sea shore.]

4.   Wherfore seing Moyses, Elias, and other Prophetes, and faithful people of God, for the better obtaining Gods mercie, proposed in their prayers the

And made
such promises
because his
seruants were
holie.

pious workes of ancient Patriarches, for that they were [Gods beloued and holie seruants] fortifying their petitions by mention of Gods promises made [for their sakes]it is most cleare,that the same maner of praying now in the Christian Church is both lawful and profitable. As when we thus pray in memorie of the B. Virgine Mother of God , saying [Poure into our mindes thy grace, ô Lord , we besech thee, that we which know, by the Angels Annunciation, the Incarnation of Christ thy Sonne : by his Passion, and Crosse , we may be brought to the glorie of the Resurrection : through the same Christ our Lord.] Also thus. [O God which hast ordained the rewards, of eternal saluation to mankind , the virginitie of B. Marie being made fruitful, grant we besech thee,that we may perceiue , her to intercede for vs,by whô we haue deserued to receiue the Auctor of life : through our Lord Iesus Christ thy Sonne] Likewise thus. [Omnipotēt eternal God, which by the worke of the Holie Ghost , preparedst the soule and bodie of the glorious Mother Marie , to be a worthie habitacle of thy Sonne, grant that in whose memorie we reioyce, by her pious intercession, we may be deliuered, from present euils,and from euerlasting death:through the same Christ our Lord.] In which forme are al the briefe prayers (called Collectes)which holie Church vseth in the office of the B. Virgine Mother of God, and of other Sainctes. So beseeching Almighty God in respect of the grace , which he gaue to them , and for their sakes (as formerly in memorie of the Patriarches , and for their sakes) to grant our needful petitions. Alwayes concluding [through Christ our Lord.] by whose onlie first grace, his B. Mother, and al other his Sainctes receiued their particular measures of grace. And this proof is so irrefragable that our Aduersaries can not any better way impugne it , but by auouching that God granted the petitions of

Moyses

Breuiar. Roman. post Horas Canonic.

Formes of prayers in memorie of our B. Ladie : like vnto others in memorie of the holie Patriarches.

Al prayers are concluded, asking grace through Christ, because al grace of

Sainctes is de-
riued from
Christs grace.

Moyses and others, only for his owne promise sake,
wheras both the sacred text saith expresly [for Abrahams sake, for Dauids sake] and it is also euident in Gen. 18. v. 18
like wordes, that God made thefe promises. [Because Pha. 22. v.
Abraham did the thing, which God commanded, not 16 18.
sparing his sonne Isaacs life, for Gods sake. Because 3 Reg. 15. v.
he obeyed Gods voice. Because Dauid had done 4. 5.
right in the eyes of our Lord.]

The second
maner of
praying by in-
tercession of
Sainctes is
properly In-
uocation.

5. The other maner of praying by mediation, or
intercession of Sainctes, is by expresse inuocating, and
praying them to pray for vs. As in the Aue Maria we
pray our B. Ladie, saying. [Holie Marie, Mother of
God pray for vs: &c.] Which forme was not vsual in
the old Testament praying to any holie Patriarch, or
Prophete, because none of mankind did enter into
heauen, nor to the cleare vision of God, vntil Christ 1. Cor. 15. v.
our Sauiour (the first fruites of them that sleepe) did 20.
open the way in his Ascension: but remaned in place
of ioyful rest, called *Limbus Patrum*. As is declared in Part. 1.
the first part of this worke. And so those ancient Art. 14.
Sainctes not being then in glorie, could not see, nor
ordinarily know the mindes, and desires of the faithful in this world; as now they doe, being in glorie,
and seing God, and in him whatsoeuer perteineth to
their glorie, & so amongst other thinges, they know the
prayers of the faithful, directed to their charitie:
which stil continueth more perfect, then it was in 1. Cor. 13. v. 8
earth. But the holie Angels being in glorie did al
wayes present the prayers, and other good workes
of men to God. And therfore were then inuocated: as

Inuocation of
holie Angels
was also in the
old Testamēt.

appeareth amongst other proofes, by that which Iobs
freind Eliphaz aduised him, to cal for patronage [if Iob. 5. v. 1.
anie would helpe him, and so turne to some of the
Sainctes] Which plainly sheweth, the cōmon faith, Ecclo. 5.
and practise of inuocating holie Angels. Els it had v. 5.
bene a friuolous speach, which is not to be supposed
in so sensible a man, as Eliphaz was: Who, albeit he
erred

erred in the particular cafe of holie Iob, yet knew that holie Angels would affift in a iuft caufe, & therupon prouoked Iob [to turne to fome of the Sainctes] to witte of the holie Angels, and by their helpe to iuftifie his caufe, if it were iuftifiable. The feuentie interpreters more exprefly tranflate the text thus [Inuocare if any wil anfwer thee, or if thou canft behold any of the holie Angels] which plainly importeth that holie Angels may be inuocated and be fene by the light of faith. No leffe certaine it is that Chriftians may lawfully and profitably with light of true faith, inuocate the B. Mother of God, praying thus. [Holie Marie Mother of God pray for vs finners, now and in the how of our death. Amen] In further explanation wherof: we adde the Articles eufuing concerning prayer to holie Angels, and other glorious Sainctes.

Holie Angels doe offer mens prayers to God: doe pray for men. And are profitably inuocated.

ARTICLE 43.

OF Angels, the firft and moft excellent natural creatures, we haue breefly according to our prefent purpofe declared before, conformable to the holie Scriptures, that they were created by God Almightie in the beginning, together with the vniuerfal world, and with time itfelfe, out of the treafures of his diuine and infinite power, & wifdom, diftributed into nine Orders, fubordinated in three facred Ierarchies, in al exceding manie, to vs innumerable, wherof the farre greater part, were confirmed in grace and eftablifhed in eternal glorie, continually praifing and feruing God, the Lord and Creator of al. Manie alfo fel from God, and from the ftate of grace, wherin they were created, are eternally damned diuils, calumniating enimies of God, and of the bleffed

Part. 7.
Artic. 12.

Holie Angels doe protect men, are to be honored: doe pray for vs, and are rightly inuocated.

Eee   Angels,

Angels, and particulaily, of al mankinde. And more-
uer that the holie and glorious Angels, as the Ministers of God, doe both assist in heauen, and protect
men in earth, as designed Patrones, and Protectors
of countries, kingdomes, and of publique, and priuate persons; as is also already proued. it is likewise
declared in the proper place: that due honour is to be   Bart. 1.
exhibited to holie Angels, to witte, spiritual religious   Art. 12.
honour farre more excellent then ciuil, but infinitely   Part. 3.
lesse them diuine. So here it resteth to be shewed in   Art. 5.
like maner, by the holie Scriptures, partly recited in
the former places, partly to be here added, that the
same glorious Angels, doe pray for men, and are to be
inuocated, and prayed vnto by al faithful Christians.

Iacob craued
the blessing of
an Angel.
And praved
the same An-
gel to blesse
others.

   2. Holie Iacob the Patriarch [hauing sene in vision,
Angels descending and ascending by a ladder, which
reached from the earth to heauen] and afterwards   Gen. 28.
meeting campes of Angels: and so wrestling (through   v. 12. 13.
Gods special gift of strength) with one Angel, that   Ch. 32. v. 1.
the same willed Iacob to let him goe, but he percei-   2. 24. 25. 26.
uing also (by a touch in his thigh &c.) the great vertue   28. 29
of the Angel [said vnto him: I wil not let thee goe vn-   (ch. 35. v. 10.)
les thou blesse me] Whereupon the Angel told him
[that his name should be called Israel: and blessed
him in the same place.] And againe Iacob (now cal-
led Israel) inuocated the same Angel, for his two ne-   ch. 48. v. 16.
phews, the sones of Ioseph, saying [The Angel that deliuereth me frō al euils, blesse these children:] In regard of al which diuine benefites bestowed vpon Iacob, and in him vpon al his issue (the children of Israel) the Prophete Osee saith: that [in his strength   Osea 12. v. 3.
he was directed with the Angel. And he preuailed   4.
against the Angel, and was strengthned: and he wept
(with humblest deuotion) besought him: in Bethel
he found him, and spake with vs.] The Angel spake
with Iacob concerning the future people. Either this
Angel was the proper Guardian of Iacob, which is
                                mo st

most probable: or some other by whom the same Patriarch receiued frequent protection, and by whom he confided that the two children might receiue profitable blessing: which sufficiently proueth our purpose, that Iacob did inuocate an holie Angel. No lesse certaine it is, and very cleare that God appointed an especial Angel to haue protection, and charge ouer the whole troupe of the Israelites. For as there is diuersitie in the Angels natures, and distinction of Orders, some excelling others in dignitie, and glorie: so there be also varietes of offices, & authoritie: our Lord saying to al the people by the mouth of Moyses. { Behold I wil send mine Angel, which shal goe before thee, and kepe thee in thy iourney, and bring thee into the place that I haue prepared. Obserue him, and heare his voice: neither doe thou thinke him one to be contemned: for he wil not forgeue, when thou hast sinned, and my name is in him. But if thou wilt heare his voice, and doe al that I speake, I wil be enimie, to thine enimies; and wil afflict them that afflict thee } This plaine aduertisement to the people, that God would geue an especial guide in their iourney, and this admonition (to regard and follow him, with threates that if they sinned he would punish) could by no meanes be vnderstood of any other, but of an Angel, an Angelical spirite, of that Angel { which shewed to them by a cloud in the day, and by a pillar of fire in the night, when they should moue the campe marching forward going before them: and when they should pitch their tabernacles, resting ouer thē in the places, where it remained } that Angel, which strooke the Idolators fornicators, and murmurers with death, at the place, therof called afterwards: The sepulchers of concupiscence. No other person, nor thing could the people (to whom this speach was vttered by Moyses) possibly vnderstand by this Angelse promised, but a true and proper Angel. And

the

God appointed an Augel to direct his people.

VVho protected the whole campe, and punished certaine offenders.

Exo. 23. v. 20.

Deut. 13. v. 11.

Num. 11. v. 34. ch. 33. v. 16.

Eee 2

the good and deuout amongst al the people, did accordingly regard, esteme, feare, and reuerence this
holie Angel (not the cloud and pillar of fire, otherwise then signes) but the holie Angel, that shewed
these signes, and withal they doubtles desired to be
blessed and protected by him, as Iacob had desired
the blessing of the other Angel, for himself, and the
children. Before this also in the time of Iob, and in
the countrie of Hus it was (as I likewise noted before) the beleefe of such as were faithful there, that
they receiued consolation, and assistance by holie Angels. As appeareth by the speach of Eliphaz vttered
to Iob in his effliction, saying to him [Cal therfore,
if there be that wil heare thee, and turne to some of
the Sainctes. for that freind of Iob supposing that he
should not in that case finde releefe either of God, or
Angel, sheweth plainly the common faith both of
Iob, and of himself, and others, that in some case there
is releefe, and helpe to be receiued by holie Angels.

3. This doctrine is so euident in the Booke of Tobias that our Aduersaries haue no better euasion,
then to denie this Booke to be Canouical Scripture.
And the same shift they flee vnto against the Bookes
of the Machabees. But we must neither refuse these
Bookes, which are as certaine in the Church of
Christ as anie of the others, neither omitte their
testimonies, though we haue sufficient besides them:
lest, any shal thinke, that we doubt of their diuine
auctoritie. In the Booke of Tobias the Angel Raphael, vttereth these manifest wordes vnto the same
Tobias, saying [When thou didst pray with teares,
and didst burie the dead, and left thy dinner, and didst
hide the dead by day in thy house: and by night didst
burie them: I offered thy prayer to our Lord.] Seing
therfore the Angel did offer the prayer of Tobias to
God, it is very probable, that Tobias did so request
him; at least vpon this certificate he might afterwards
                                                    with

Marginal notes:

Beut. 9.
v. 22.
1. Cor. 10.
v. 10.
Iudith. 8.
v. 25.

Faithful peo-
ple in the land
of Hus prayed
to Angels.

S Raphael the
Angel offered
the prayers
& other good
workes of To-
bias to God.

Tob. 12.
v. 12.

An holie An-
gel assisted the
Machabees.

with great confidence fo doe. And Iudas Machabeus

2.Mac.15.v.
22.23.24.
4.Reg.19.v.
35.
expreſly prayed God to ſend an Angel, to helpe him, and his armie in their diſtreſſe [inuocating in this maner Thou Lord which didſt ſend thyne Angel, in the time of Ezechias King of Iuda, and didſt kil an hundeed eightie fiue thouſand, of the campe of Sennacharib: now ô Dominatour of the heauens, ſend thy good Angel, before vs, in feare, and trembling of the greatnes of thyne arme, that they may be afraid which with blaſphemie, come againſt thyne holie people] And [they ouerthrow fiue and thirtie thouſand being greatly delighted with the preſence of

Ezec.
ek 11.v.6.8.
If 63.v.9.
Dan.10.v
11.12.
God] who ſo aſſiſted them. For a litle before there appeared before them [an horſeman in white clothing with armour of gold ſhaking a ſpeare] It is no leſſe cleare that an Angel appearing to the Prophete Daniel, inſtructed him, and aſſured him that God would ſend his Angels to defend his Church [when I ſtood trembling (ſaith he) the Angel (in forme of a man) ſaid to me. Feare not Daniel: becauſe ſince the firſt day that thou didſt ſet thy hart to vnderſtand to afflict thyſelf, in the ſight of thy God, thy wordes haue bene heard: and I am come for thy wordes.]

An other Angel inſtructed, and conforted Daniel the Prophete.

Part. 1.
Art.12.
See more, if you deſire more in the firſt part.

4.   Eſpecially remember that the very like is recorded in the Actes of the Apoſtles concerning Cornelius, which is teſtified by the holie Angel Raphael, vnto Tobias. For euen ſo ſaid an Angel to Cornelius. [Thy prayers, and thy almes deedes are aſcended

An holie Angel offered the prayers & almes deedes of Cornelius to God.

Act.10.v.4.
into remembrance in the ſight of God] Adde alſo theſe manifeſt wordes of S. Iohn in the Apocalypſe

Apoc 5.v.8.
ch.8.v.3.
[The foure liuing creatures (ſaith he) and the foure and twertie Seniors (Angels and other Saintes) fel before the lambe, hauing euerie one herpes, and golden vials ful of odores, which are the prayers of Sainctes. And an other Angel came, and ſtood before the Altar, hauing a golden cenſure, and there were geuen

Other Angels doe cõtinually the like offices for al faithful Chriſtians.

to him manie incenses, that he should geue of the prayers of sainctes (that is, of the faithful seruants of Christ) vpon the Altar of gold, which is before the throne of God. And the smoke of the incenses, of the prayers of the sainctes ascended from the hand of the Angel before God.] In consideration of which Angelical Ministerie, as wel in protecting the faithful, as in offering their prayers to God, the Church prayeth thus [O God, who in meruelous order disposest the ministeries of Angels, and men, grant merciful Lord, that of whom thou art euer serued in heauen, of them our life may be garded in earth.] Which prayer English Protestants retaine in their Communion booke, notwithstanding Puritans repining therat. And the very same reason, and the same auctoritie of holie Scriptures, côuince both Protestants and Puritanes, that not only the holie Angels, but also other glorious Sainctes both serue God in heauê, and haue charitable care of the faithful in earth., no lesse but more, then when they were in this world. For the more they loue God, the more they loue, their neighboures, and the more they know the dangerous state of mortal men, the more they desire their safe arriuing in eternal, and secure felicitie. Which shal be here further proued against our Aduersaries that denie it.

v. 4

Luc. 19. 8.
17. 19.

Some Protestants confesse that holie Angels protect men.
And pray to be continually protected by them.

Other glorious Sainctes understand the affayres of mortal men: and doe pray for them.

ARTICLE 44.

IF we doe truly beleue, and rightly consider the Communion of Sainctes, which is a part of our Crede: where we professe that there is mutual entercourse of imparting and receiuing spiritual benefites, amongst al the members of the vniuersal Church, as wel triumphant in heauen, as militant in earth, we must

See Part 1.
Art. 43.

Communion of Sainctes importe th entercourse of as-

Rom 12 v.5

1. Cor. 12. v. 39.

Ephes 3 v 6.

must also confesse, that this cōmunication consisteth in some real actes of each sorte towards others : for els it were only imaginarie, vaine. And therefore seing it is certaine, that there is a real vnion, and commu nication not only betwen Christ the head, and al his mysticall members, as wel glorious in heauen, as faithful in this world, but also amongst al the same mem bers, being [concorporate] in him : it is likewise certaine, that both the faithful in earth, by the light of faith, know in general that the Sainctes are in glorie, and in fauoure with God : and haue charitie towards vs : and that the same Sainctes, by the light of glorie know those affayres of their clients, which are com mended to them by faithful prayer : because without some reciprocal knowlege there could be no communion at al, betwen the Sainctes in heauen, and the faithful in earth. Which thing therfore whosoeuer denieth, denieth a part of our common Crede : and also gainsaith manie holie Scriptures : by which it is irrefragably proued, that as the holie Angels, so also other glorious Sainctes doe know, and offer vnto God, the prayers of the faithful.

2. Of such knowlege in glorious Sainctes, by diuine reuelation made vnto them, we haue a pregnant figure in the great Patriarch Abraham, to whom being then mortal, God reuealed his purpose to de stroy the cities of Sodome, and Gomorrhe, to the end as the euent shewed, that he should pray for the safe tie of those cities. And the reason why God Almigh tie reuealed this thing to his faithful beloued seruāt Abraham, was, as our Lord himself declareth, because he had ordayned him to be into a great nation : because in him al nations of the earth should be blessed, and because our Lord foresaw his diligence : and zele, that he would teach, & admonish al his children and successors to kepe Gods commandments. Al which reasons are expressed by holie Moyses in the

sacred

tual loue, betwen Sainctes in glorie, and the faithful in earth.

God reuealed to Abraham an especial thing, that he might pray for it.

Because he was. his especially beloued seruant.

sacred historie writing thus [Our Lord said to Abra- *Gen. 18.4.*
ham) Can I conceale from Abraham , the thinges *17. 18.*
which I wil doe? wheras he shal be into a nation
great, and very strong: and in him are to be blessed al
the natiós of the earth? For I know that he wil command his children, and his house after him, that they
kepe the way of the Lord, and doe iudgement, and
iustice] For these reasons therfore, our Lord reuealed
the particular case of Sodome & Gomorrhe to Abraham, and withal inspired into his minde to pray for
them, as he did. And though they, persisting in their
wickednes [were burut with fire and brimstone] yet *Ib. 19. v. 24,*
his prayer had effect in Lot, and his familie: as it folo- *25. v. 29.*

His prayer had effect in Lot. weth in the historie. [For when God subuerted the
cities of that countrie, he remembring Abraham, de-
liuered Lot out of the cities, wherein he had dwelt]
An other example is in Moyses, to whom God also
reuealed in mount Sinai, the idolatrie committed by *Exo. 32. v. 9.*
the people in the campe beneth. And although, our *8. 9. 10. 11.*
Lord signified that they deserued to be destroyed, yet *14.*
[Moyses besought him for them. And our Lord was
pacified] suffering himself to be ouertreated by his
seruant. Seing then our merciful Lord reuealed such
state of sinners vnto Abraham, and Moyses, being as
yet mortal, how much more doth he reueal the like
to them, and others now in glorie, and also heare
their charitable prayers, for the faithful, especially
for their deuout clients desiring the same?

5.   But because our Aduersaries, against al reason, denie that care and knowlege to be in soules departed, which they confesse, to be in Gods seruants
Prophetes de- in this life, especially in Prophetes: We haue also
parted from other examples of Prophetes, after their departure
this world, from this word. The soule of Samuel (as is most pro- *1. Reg 28. v.*
knew some se- bable) at least a spirite representing his soule, did *14. 17. 19.*
crete thinges know, and foretel that King Saul, and his sonnes *Eccli. 46. v.*
of mortal should dye the next day] Which sheweth that some *23.*
men.

in

in the other world may by Gods ordinance, know some affayres of men in this world. Likewise when [the corps of a dead man touched the bones of Eliseus the Prophete the same man reuiued, and stood vpon his feete] shal we say, that the Prophets soule knew not that this miracle was wronght by his bones? No surely, for it is farre more reasonable to thinke, that his soule knew what vertue God gaue to the Reliques of his bodie. Holie Scripture also expresly saith that [his bodie prophecied being dead] that is, did the worke of a Prophete. Wheras doubtles the sanctitie of the holie bones, or of other holie Reliques, procedeth from the sanctitie of the soule. An other sacred text saith that [There were letters brought to Ioram King of Iuda, from Elias the Prophete] which great Prophete was assumpted in a firie chariote about the eightenth yeare of Iosaphat King of Iuda, when Ioram the sonne of Achab begaue to reigne in Israel. And so Iosaphat reigned seuen yeares more, before his sonne (called also Ioram) reigned in Iuda, to whom these letters were brought, which was at the least seuen yeares after that Elias was taken from the common conuersation of mortal men. In which state, this Prophete knew that King Ioram had wickedly slaine his brethren, & committed idolatrie, as he chargeth him in the same letters, saying [Thus saith our Lord, the God of Dauid thy father. Because thou hast not walked in the wayes of Iosaphat thy Father, but hast gone by the wayes of the Kinges of Israel: moreouer also hast killed thy brethren the house of thy Father, better men then thou: behold our Lord wil strike thee with a great plagne, &c.] Againe when God said to King Ezechias, by Isaias the Prophete, [I wil protect this citie (Ierusalem) and wil saue it, for my selfe, and for Dauid my seruant: for myne owne sake, and for Dauids sake my seruant] Is it not cleare, that God heard

*Reg 13.
v. 21.
Eccli.48.v.
14.

3.Par.21.v.
12.

3.Reg.22.v.
44.

4.Reg.8.v.
11.12.
ab.4.v.1.

2.Par.21.v.
4.5.11.

v.12.
v. 14.

4.Reg.19.v.
34.
M.37.v.35.

A dead man raised to life by touch of Eliseus dead bones.

Elias seuen yeares after his translation knew the actes of King Ioram.

the prayers of this good King Ezechias, and of the holie Prophete Isaias, the rather for Dauids sake? And is it not withal to be pioufly beleued, that the foule of Dauid, then in reft, *in Limbus Patrum*, did alfo know by reuelation, the diftreffe of Ierufalem at that time, and that he defired, and prayed to God, for the fafetie of that citie? Holie Dauid fo great and deuout a Prophete in this life, could not poffibly be leffe then a Prophete after his death. And now alfo being in glorie, it is great impietie, and plaine infidelitie, to fay that he, and other Patriarches, Prophetes, Apoftles, Martyrs, or anie glorious Sainctes, haue not by the light of glorie, more knowlege of thofe thinges, which perteyne to their charitie, and pietie, then they had in this world. For Chrift our Lord teftifieth exprefly faying [Amen I fay to you there hath not rifen among the borne of wemen, a greater then Iohn the Baptift: yet he that is the leafter in the kingdom of heauen, is greater then he.] So great is the glorie of heauen, & fo great is the difference betwen the ftate of grace, and of glorie, that euerie Sainct in heauen excelleth himfelf in knowlege, power, charitie, & al other vertues, and fpiritual giftes, which he had in this tranfitorie world.

Glorious Sainctes are more perfect as wel in knowlege as in other giftes then they were in this life.

Mat.11.v. 11.

4.   Againe concerning the knowlege of glorious Angels, and other Sainctes (of whom we now efpecially fpeake) it is demonftratiuely proued by our Sauiours difcourfe, admonishing al men not to contemne his humble feruants [See that you defpife not one of thefe litle ones (faith he) for I fay to you: that their Angels in heauen doe alwayes fee the face of my Father, which is in heauen.] So threatning reuenge of wrong done to litle ones, becaufe their Angels alwayes fee the face of God. Which reafon hath this neceffarie confequence. That holie Angels by feing the face of God, know the wrong which is done to thofe, of whom they haue particular charge: and

Sainctes knowlege of thinges in this world, is by feing God in glorie.

Mat.18.v. 10.

knowing

knowing it, wil reuenge the wrong: and therfore it
behoueth not to wrong them. For vnles the Angels
knew the iniurie which is done, they could not reuenge it, and the meanes wherby they know it, is, according to our Sauiours doctrine, because they see
the face of God. And consequently other glorious
Sainctes likewise seing the face of God, which is the
proper, & essential glorie of al the blessed in heauen,
doe also therby see, and know those thinges of this
world, which perteyne to their charitie towards
their faithful freindes.

5.   Against which cleare proofes it is commonly
obiected by our Aduersaries, that the ancient Patriarches, and Prophetes knew not after their death,
the estate of their posteritie in this world : alleaging
Isa.63. v.16 for this purpose the wordes of Isaias the Prophete, An obiection out of Isaias wordes.
saying to God in the behalf of the people [Thou (o
God)art our Father: and Abraham hath not knowen
vs: and Israel hath bene ignorant of vs: thou o Lord,
art our Father, our Redemer, from the beginning is
thy name.] We answer, according to the proper sense
of these wordes, gathered by the circumstances of the
Prophetes speach, & by conference of these wordes,
with other places of holie Scripture, that at this time, We answer that the Pa-
for the greuous sinnes of the people, the holie Patri-triarches are
arches did not acknowlege them, for their children, said not to
but yet the Prophete hoped in Gods mercie: who know those,
from the beginning had called Abraham, and blessed whom they do
him (& them his seede: who had brought them out of not acknow-
● 11.Egypt, through the sea, by the ministerie of Moyses,)lege for their
11. & 6.which thing Abraham, Isaac, & Iacob could not haue children.
done, & so they prayed to God, that his mercie would
returne to his seruants, the tribes of his inheritance;
though the had suffered them to erre, and for a time
to harden their harts: that yet he would restore them
by new grace. Albeit therfore the holie Patriarches
v. 17.did not acknowlege them for their children, so long

as they were obstinate in their sinnes, yet the same
Patriarches wel knew their state, that they were very
great sinners, and this knowlege was the cause of not
acknowleging them for children. For it is cleare that
Abraham knew the rich glutton, that [he had recei-
ued good thinges in his life time, and Lazarus euil: *Luc.16.y.24.*
and therfore said [he is comforted, and thou art
tormented] which answer sheweth that Abraham
knew their estates both then, and before. And by   *y.3.4.*
manie other places of holie Scriptures already recited, it is manifest: that God bestowed benefites vpon
the same people, for the holie Patriatches sakes, as the
children of such holie Fathers: God alwayes being the
first and principal Father of them al. And so reconci-
ling and expounding one holie Scripture with an o-
ther, these wordes of Isaias are to be vnderstood, as
the like wordes in the same Prophete [Why haue we *Is.58.y.3.*
humbled ourselues (ô God)& thou hast not knowê?]
and in the Gospel, testifying that Christ shal say to
such as wil pretend to haue inuocated his name, but
haue not done his wil: And likewise to the fiue foolish virgines, bringing lampes without oyle (that is
faith without good workes,) to al which & such like
our Lord wil say[I know you not.]Which, importeth *Mat 7.y.23.*
not ignorance, but iust cause of not acknowleging *ch.25.y.12.*
them, as his children.

So Christ wil
say: I know
you not: to
those whom
he wil not
acknowlege.

6.   In further confirmation, that this is the true
sense of the Prophetes wordes: and that they make
nothing for our Aduersaries negatiue opinion (because in this Encounter with them, we alleage not
the auctoritie of Ancient Fathers, nor their interpretation of holie Scriptures) we shal adde more textes
of Gods written word, which proue our beleefe of
Sainctes prayers. And consequently, that they can
know the estates of the faithful in earth. Our Lords
owne wordes to his Prophete Ieremie saying [If
Moyses and Samuel shal stand before me: my soule is *Iere.15.y.1.*

That glorious
Sainctes doe
pray for vs: &
consequently
doe know our
estates, is fur-
ther proued.

net

not toward this people] doe neceſſarily importe, that the prayers of Moyſes, & of Samuel are of very great value. And withal doe ſufficiently proue, that ſometimes, and in ſome caſes, they did pray for the ſame people. For otherwiſe this ſuppoſition [if they ſhal ſtand before me] and pray for this people, had not bene a confirmation of Gods purpoſe, that he would for no prayers omitte to puniſh the people with captiuitie, as he ſignified to the Prophete, that they should not eſcape that puniſhment, ſaying in the next wordes [Caſt them out from my face; and let them goe forth.] where he expreſſeth alſo other afflictions, into which they should fal, ſaying [they that to death to death: and they that to ſword, to ſword: and they that to famine, to famine; and they that to captiuitie, to captiuitie] this being Gods decree at that time, and in this caſe, he declared by his Prophete that neither the prayers of anie iuſteſt men then liuing, nor of others departed this life, should preuaile to the contrarie: for that people in this caſe. Wherby is confuted the friuolous euaſion of ſome. Proteſtants, imagining without either auctoritie or reaſon: that our Lord God doth not ſpeake here of Moyſes, and of Samuels prayers, which might be made vnto him, but of anie other then liuing, if they were moued with ſo great zele towards the people as were theſe two, yet he would not grant this requeſt, for as much, as he had determined the contrarie. This is their forged gloſſe, contrarie to the text for God ſaith. [If Moyſes, & Samuel] they ſay: If anie of like zele to them, now liuing but not they: abrogating Gods word, and intruding their owne phanſie: abridging alſo the ſenſe, only to men then liuing in this world. Wheras our Lord ſpeaketh here expreſly of two renowmed Prophetes, by their proper names, who were departed from this world. And by his Prophete Ezechiel, in like maner nameth Noe, and Iob,

Ibid.

v. 2.

Their Geneua Bible 1579. 1581.

The Proteſtants gloſſe abrigeth the ſenſe, and contradicteth the text.

departed

Gods refusal to heare the prayers of his holie seruãts in some particular case, sheweth that in some other cases he doth heare them.

departed long before the others; not for want of zelous men then liuing: as our Aduersaries seme to imagine, for with these last named, our Lord ioyneth his Prophete Daniel, then liuing in captiuitie: saying [If these three men shal be in the middes of the land, Noe Daniel and Iob they by their iustice shal deliuer their owne soules, saith the Lord of hosts, but they shal deliuer neither sonnes nor daughters, and the land shal be made desolate.] Also the same Prophetes Ieremie, and Ezechiel, by whom our Lord denounced these threates, were of like zele toward the people, as Daniel then was, and as the other foure had bene in their transitorie life. And therfore this mention of Noe, Iob, Moyses, and Samuel, importeth not more zele in them whiles they were in this world, then in Ieremie, Ezechiel, Daniel, or any other then liuing; but rather more zele, greater perfection, and more forcible prayers of the same holie persons, after their deathes, then either of themselues, or any others

Ezech 14. v. 14 16 18 20.

It proueth also that the Prophetes doe pray after their departure from this life, for those that are in this world.

in this life. And it apparently proueth that they, and other holie seruants of God, doe sometimes pray for faithful people, and are heard, though in this particular case, God forbade his Prophete Ieremie to pray for them: telling him that his prayer should not be heard, saying by him to the people of Iuda [I wil cast you away from my face, as I haue cast away al your brethren, the whole seede of Ephraim] and to Ieremie himself [thou therefore pray not for this people (saith our Lord) neither take vnto thee praise, and prayer for them: and resist me not: because I wil not heare thee.] Which he repeted twise more to this Prophete, and afterward told him (as is euen now recited) that [if Moyses and Samuel shal pray for them he wil not heare them.] And the like to Ezechiel, that [if Noe, Daniel, and Iob, should pray for them, it should not preuaile] signyfying that in this case he would neither heare the prayers of his holie seruants,

Ierc. 7. v. 15. v. 16.

Ch. 11 v. 14. sb. 14. v. 11. 12. Ch. 15. v 1. vt supra.

in this

in this life, nor of others departed. Al which aboundantly confirmeth the Catholique doctrine, that the holie Patriarches, Prophetes, and other Saincts after their death, doe pray for vs, that are in this world.

7. Of the same Prophete Ieremie, and of Onias sometime High priest, it is clearly testified in a vision reuealed to Iudas Machabeus, and recorded in holie Scripture, that they prayed after their deathes for the citie of Ierusalem, and al the people. [And the vision (saith the sacred text) was in this maner: Onias who had bene the Highpriest: a good and benigne man, reuerent to behold, modest of maners, and comelie of speach, and from a childe was exercised in vertues, stretching forth the hades, prayed for al the people of the Iewes. After this, there appeared also an other mā meruelous for age, and glorie, and for the porte of great dignitie about him. And Onias answering said: This is a louer of his brethren, and of the people of Israel: this is he, that prayeth much for the people, and for the whole citie, Ieremie the Prophete of God. [Against which manifest testimonie Protestants vse two euasions, first they denie the Bookes of Machabees to be Canonical Scripture, because they are not in the Canon of the Iewes. We answer that this is no iust cause of exception against these bookes: but rather, the true cause is, why they denie these and some other bookes: because they conuince diuers of their errors: because they most clearly proue the prayer of Sainctes: and prayer for the soules departed. We accept these Bookes for Canonical vpon the iudgemēt, and testimonie of the Christian Church, as we doe the Gospel, written by the foure Euangelists: and the rest of al the holie Bible, though it be not al in the Iewes canon. Their other refuge is, their light esteeming of spiritual visions. By which especial meanes it hath pleased God to reueal very manie truthes, vnto mortal men, both in the old and new Testament.

Namely

Marginal notes (left):
2. Mach. 15.
v. 12.

v. 13.

14.

Gen. 15. v. 1.
ch. 28. v. 12.
ch. 37 b 7.9.
Ex. 3 v.3.
Is. 1. v. &c.
Dan. 1 v.17.
&c.

Marginal notes (right):
Ieremie the Prophete, and Onias sometime High priest, prayed after their deathes, for the Iewes.

We receiue the diuine Scriptures vpon testimonie of the Christian Church, not of the Iewes Synagogue.

God reuealeth manie truthes by visions.

Namely to Abraham, Iacob, Ioseph, Moyses, Samuel, and the other Prophetes. Also in our Lords Transfiguration there appeared Moyses and Elias, in such maner that the Apostles knew who they were. Likewise our Lord himself appeared in a vision to S. Paul, and by visions declared certaine assured truthes to the same Apostle directing him what to doe. Also to Cornelius a Gentile: to S. Peter; to S. Iohn, and others. Neither can Iudas Machabeus with anie reason be reiected, as vnworthie of credite, reporting that which himself saw, and heard in a vision: the euent also confirming the truth of his reporte.

Mat. 17.
v. 3. 4.
Act 9. v 4
5. 6. 7
Ch. 10. v. 3.
11.

Apoc. 1. v. 1.
10. &c.
Act. 2. v. 2.
3. ch. 7. v. 55.
56.
2. Mach. 15.
v. 27. &c.

Glorious soules are not only like to Angels in that they liue without mariage, but also are equal to Angels in glorie knowlege, power, charitie and other perfection.

8. This truth is yet further confirmed by the doctrine of Christ, and his Apostles. Our Sauiour saith, that the blessed of mankinde [are as the Angels of God in heauen] which similitude not only importeth that they are there without mariage, as Angels be, which was the particular occasion of this doctrine, but also proueth their equalitie with holie Angels in other respectes, for our Lord saith likewise (as S. Luke witnesseth) that [neither can they dye anie more, for they are equal to Angels.] To witte in equal immortalitie, and glorie, which importeth, to be like in knowlege in power, in like fauour with God, in like charitie towardes faithful persons in earth, and in other vertues, and in the whole state of glorie. Seing therfore it is cleare that holie Angels reioyce for the conuersion of sinners, it can not be but that other Sainctes, of our owne humane nature, doe likewise reioyce: and consequently doe know, when some sinners are conuerted, for els they could not reioyce. And the meanes wherby they know, is by seing God: which is the self same essential beatitude in al the blessed, both of Angelical and humane kinde. As is noted before. S. Paul further describing the excellencie of knowlege in eternal glorie, aboue knowlege in this life, saith [In part we know, and in

Mat. 22.
v. 30.
Luc. 20.
v. 36.

Luc. 19.
v. 17. 19.

1. Cor. 15.
v. 42.
Luc. 15. v. 7.
10.

Mat. 18.
v. 10.
6. 4.

1. Cor. 13.
v. 9. 10.

part

part we prophecie. But when that shal come, that is perfect, that shal be made voide, that is in part.] Whereby it is euident that both the light of faith, and of prophecie, shal be changed into the greater light of glorie [we see now (saith he) by a glasse, in a darke sorte: but then face to face. Now I know in part, but then I shal know, as also I am knowen.] Which excellent difference betwen the state of grace, and of glorie. S. Iohn likewise testifieth, saying [My dearest, now we are the sonnes of God: and it hath not yet appeared what we shal be, we know that when he shal appeare, we shal be like to him: because we shal see him as he is.] The reason therfore of Sainctes knowlege, is because they see God, as he is, & therby are in a kinde of resemblance, like to God [like to him] saith S. Iohn, and equal to Angels. In the meane time the faithful in earth, are of the same Communion of Sainctes, members of the same bodie, vnder Christ the head. As S. Paul teacheth, saying to the Christian Hebrewes [You are come to mount Sion, and the citie of the liuing God, heauenlie Ierusalem, and the assemblie of manie thousand Angels: and the Church of the first borne (holie Patriarches, and Prophetes) which are written in the heauens: & the Iudge of al God: and the spirites (or soules) of the iust made perfect (by glorie) and the Mediator of the new Testament, Iesus.] To al these the iust in this life are ioyned in felowshipe [being iustified (by Christs blond] remitting our sinnes] Why then shal we not beleue, that the glorious Sainctes can and wil assist vs vnder Christ, & through Christ, by their intercession?

9. Which very thing it semeth S. Peter promised in this life, to performe after his death, saying in his Epistle [I thinke it meete as long as I am in this tabernacle, to stirre you vp by admonition: being certaine that the laying away of my tabernacle is at hand: according as our Lord Iesus Christ also signified to me.

Margin notes:

7.12.

1.Ioan.3.v.2

Heb.12.v.22

23.

24.

2.Pet.1.v.13.14.15.

By seing God, the glorified Sainctes are made like to God, & equal to Angels. And the iust in earth are of the same felowshipe.

As grace cometh by meanes of holie

Angels; fo by
other Sainctes.

S. Peter pro-
mifed to haue
care of the
faithful after
his death.

And I wil doe my diligence, to haue you often after
my deceafe alfo; that you may kepe a memorie of
thefe thinges] fo the facred letter is fomewhat obfcure, but by connexion of the whole fentence, this
femeth to be the fenfe: That as the holie Apoftle during his temporal life, omitted not to put Chriftians
in mind of the thinges which he had taught them: fo
after his death he would endeuour, that they might
be mindful of the fame. And that, by his promifed
care after his deceafe, he meaneth his interceffion to
Chrift, is probably confirmed, by manie other textes
already recited:& by S. Iohns moft manifeft wordes,
praying that grace, and peace might be geuen, to the
feuen Churches (vnto which he writte in Afia) not
only from Chrift, from whom it is alwayes principally deriued, but alfo from holie Angels, faying
[Iohn to the feuen Churches which are in Afia, Grace
to you, and peace from him that is, and that was, and
that fhal come:and from the feuen fpirites, which are
in the fight of his throne.] Againe the fame Apoftle

Both Angels &
other Sainctes
do offer the
prayers of the
faithful to
Chrift.

euidently teftifieth, that other Sainctes in heauen doe
offer to Chrift the prayers of the faithful in earth,
faying [When he (Chrift the Lambe of God) had opened the booke, the foure liuing creatures, and the
foure and twentie feniors (the holie, and glorious
Sainctes) fel before the lambe, hauing euerie one,
harpes, and golden vials ful of odours, which are the
prayers of fainctes] that is, of the faithful commonly
called fainctes, in the new Teftament. More particularly concerning holie Martyrs, he fayeth [I faw

Martyrs pray
for iuft reuēge
and are heard.

vnder the Altar the foules of them, that were flaine
for the word of God, and for the teftimonie, which
they had (rendred) and they cried with a loud voice,
faying: How long, Lord, holie, and true, iudgeft thou
not, and reuengeft thou not our bloud, vpon them
that dwel on the earth?] What can be faid more euidently, then here the Apoftle faith: that Martyrs crie

with

Dabo au-
tem operam
& frequen-
ter habere
vos poft obi-
tum meum.

Apoc.1.v.4.

ch 5. v.8.
ch. 8. v.3.4.

Act. 9. v.13.
32.41.
ch 26. v.10.
18.
Rom. 1. v.7.
ch.8 v.27.
28
ch.12. v.13.
&c.
ch.15.v.26.
Apoc.6.v.9.
10.

with a loud voice, with zele of Gods honour, for iuſt See Pſal. 149.
reuenge againſt obdurate perſecuters. Which hinder v.6.7.8.9.
the progreſſe of true Religion. Whoſe petition is alſo
granted, and ſhal be fulfilled in due time. For [it was
ſaid to them, that they ſhould reſt yet a litle time, til
their felow ſeruants be complete, and their brethren,
that are to be ſlaine euen as they.] A litle time, ſaith
our Lord. And in an other place[I ſay to you (ſaid the
ſame Ieſus Chriſt our Lord) that God wil quickly reuenge them] for al the time of this world is paſſing
ſhorte, not a minute, or crochet in compariſon of e-
ternitie. Al which teſtimonies, and proofes (yea ſome
ſmal part thereof) may abundantly ſuffice, in defence
and confirmation of the Catholique doctrine, that
glorified Sainctes in heauen doe pray for the faithful
in earth.

Luc.18.7.8.
v.11.

It is lavvful and profitable to pray the glori-
fied Sainctes, that they vvil pray for
vs to God.

ARTICLE 45.

NOw concerning direct Inuocation of Sainctes, Vpon the pre-
& praying to them, which Catholiques vſe; & miſſes already
Proteſtants denie to be either profitable, or lawful: proued, it
the Catholique beleefe and doctrine, in this point, is is neceſſarlie
euidently deduced from the former groundes, con- concluded,
firmed by the holie Scriptures, in the precedent Ar- to be law-
ticles. Where we haue clearly ſhewed, that the me- ful and profi-
morie, and praiſes of Gods bleſſed Mother : and other table, to pray
holie ſeruants, redundeth to his owne more praiſe, to Sainctes.
& glorie. Likewiſe by expreſſe, and moſt authentical
examples, we haue declared that prayers were both
lawfully, and fruitfully made to God by mediation of
his holie ſeruãts departed from this world, God granting ſuch requeſtes, for the ſame his holie ſeruants
ſakes. Where alſo we haue ſhewed by the like diuine

Art. 41.
Art. 42.

Scriptures, that not only holie Angels, but also other *Art. 43. 44.*
glorified Sainctes can and sometime doe know the
affaires of mortal persons, can also heare (that is to
say, vnderstand) the prayers of the faithful, and that
they doe offer the same prayers to God, and so pray
for the faithful: especially since the Ascension of
Christ, being with him in glorie, which farre excelleth the light of faith, and of prophecie. Al which
being euidently proued by the holie Scriptures, we
therupon firmely conclude, that seeing our imperfection nedeth helpe, of the more perfect, to pray with
vs, and for vs: seeing the glorious Sainctes in heauen
can heare (or vnderstand) our prayers, & are willing
to assist vs, & are more worthie to be heard; the same
also redounding to the more honour of God, it is
therfore, both lawful, & very needful as wel to pray
God Almightie, to extend his grace and mercie vnto
vs, for his glorious seruants sakes: as also to inuocate
directly the same blessed Sainctes, according to the
accustomed maner, saying: Holie Marie, Mother of
God, pray for vs. Sainct Michael, S. Peter, S. Paul,
Al Sainctes of God pray for vs. For hauing mani- *Art. 42.*
festly confuted the Protestants imagined impossibi- *§. 2. 3.*
litie, that Sainctes in heauen could not heare, nor vn- *Art. 44.*
derstand the prayers of the faithful in earth, & withal *§. 4. 8.*
conuinced their incredulitie in other pointes, concerning this present controuersie, there remaineth
no other impediment, why we should not directly

Other obie
ctions: espe-
cially of Puri-
tanes.

pray the glorious Sainctes to pray for vs to God, but
either proud presumption of such as wil nedes thinke
themselues so absolutely secure of their owne both
present, and future iustice, and infallible saluation, *Iob. 21. 7. 8.*
that they neede not the prayer of anie other: or els an *12. 13.*
impious disdaine of anie Sainctes intercession, as *Luc. 18. 7.*
though, forsooth, their owne prayers were as good, *11. 12.*
as anie Sainctes: or finally an imagined derogation *Isa. 58. 7. 2.*
from Christ, by vsing anie other Intercessor to him.

That

That nothing therfore may be left vnsolued, we shal yet further declare by the like holie Scriptures, that al these pretended impediments are false, & absurde.

2. Touching the first of these impediments, we answer: that if anie were so assured of their owne saluation, as they wil needes perswade themselues: then it were needles (according to their owne conceipt) either to pray for themselues, or to desire the prayers of others. But seing according to the holie Scriptures [Man knoweth not whether he be worthie of loue, or hatred.] And that al ought [with feare and trembling to worke their saluation. And that we must labour by good workes to make sure our vocation, & election] we must both pray for remission of sinnes, & that we fal not into tentations [for he that perseuereth to the end, shal be saued] And also it is needful to desire others prayers: as S. Iames aduiseth, saying [Pray one for an other, that you may be saued] Especially al must desire the prayers of the more holie, & more perfect. As Iobs freind willed him [to turne to some of the Sainctes] And God sent the same man & his felowes to Iob, saying to them [Goe to my seruant Iob: and he shal pray for you: his face I wil receiue: that the follie be not imputed to you.]

3. The second pretended impediment, that anie mortal persons should either esteme so much of their owne prayers, or so litle of the glorious Sainctes assistance, is no lesse absurde, then the former. And yet some smal there be in these sinful times, whose foule mouthes haue darred to say, that the prayer of anie beleuing person of their faithful (they should say, faithlesse) congregation, is as good as the prayer of the Virgine Marie. Which blasphemous comparison as al modest eares abhorre to heare: so al true Christians not only preferre the preeminent excellencie of the euer blessed, most glorious Virgine Mother of God, before al other Sainctes. [Because our Lord God hath

Eccle 9. v 1.
Philo.2.v.12
2.Pet.1.v.10.
Mat.6.v.9.12
ch.16.v.41.
ch.20.v.22.
ch.24.v.13.
Iac 5.v.16.
Part 3.
Aart.1.
§ 9.
Iob.5 v 11.
ch.42.v.9.

Luther Ser.
de Natali
Virg.Mar.

Luc.1.v.48.
49.

Particular perswasion of some, that they are assured of their owne saluation, maketh as much against al prayers, as praying to Sainctes.

It is absurde to preferre priuate prayer of mortal persons, before the Intercession of glorified Sainctes.

Ggg 3

hath regarded the humilitie of his handmaide : for behold from hence forth (faith she) al generations shal cal me blessed . Because he that is Mightie hath done great thinges to me.] But also they acknowlege with the Royal Psalmist, that al the glorified [freindes *Pf.138.v.1* of God are become honorable exceedingly : their principalitie is exceedingly strenghtned.] And as the *v.18.* number of Gods Sainctes, which are & dayly shal be glorified, is to vs innumerable : so is their glorie, power, and fauour with God to al mans conceipt in

The glorie of Sainctes ex-eeedeth al mortal mans conceipt.

this world incomprehensible [From the beginning of *Is.64.v.4.* the world they haue not heard (faith Isaias) nor re-*1.Cor.2.v.9* ceiued with eares: the eye hath not seene , ô God be-side thee, what thinges thou hast prepared for them that expect thee.] But now in heauen they heare, see, and enioy that glorie , which we know by faith in general, to be farre more excellent, then anie mortal man can conceiue in particular , wherfore seing of what great valure the prayers of holie men were (as is shewed before) of Noe, Abraham, Isaac, Iacob, Iob, *Art.44.* Moyses, Dauid, Elias, Eliseus, Isaias, Ieremias , Da-niel, & others, partly whiles they liued in this world, and more , when they were in *Limbo Patrum*; of how much more force are the prayers of the same Sainctes, now being with Christ in eternal glorie? And of the like inexplicable vertue are the prayers , of al Christs Apostles, Martyrs; and other Sainctes , to be estee-med, according to the merites of euerie one: & aboue al of the most humble, most immaculate Virgine Mo-ther of God.

4.   For better consideration of whose singular most eminent sanctitie in this life, & glorie in heuen: let vs here againe remember what testimonie the

By considera-tion of S. Eli-sabeths special vertues, we may conceiue

holie Euangelist geueth of S. Elisabeth, and withal obserue the sincere iudgement of the same commen-dable person, concerning the pearlesse Virgine Mo-ther of our Lord. [There was (saith S. Luke) a certaine *Luc.1.v.5.6.* Priest

Prieſt named Zacharie, of the courſe of Abia: and his wife of the daughters of Aaron, and her name Eliſabeth. And they were both iuſt before God : walking in al the commandments, and iuſtifications of our Lord, without blame.] This worthie matron a perfect obſeruer of al Gods commandments, without blame, and therby made iuſt (not before the world only, but as the Holie Euangeliſt here affirmeth) before God: did by the ſpecial fauour of God, conceiue and beare an excellent Soone, S. Iohn the Baptiſt, Chriſts Precurſour: who was replenishad with the Holie Ghoſt euen from his mothers wombe] Which diuine woike, the ſame holie Archangel Gabriel reuealed alſo to the B. Virgine Marie : when he imperted to her the greateſt Myſterie of Gods owne Sonne incarnate, and made Man, ſaying [Behold Eliſabeth, thy cuſine, she alſo hath conceiued a ſonne, in her old age, &c.] Wherupon the B. Virgine going with ſpeede, viſited Eliſabeth. By al which, & much more in the ſacred Goſpel wee ſee, that S. Eliſabeth ſo highly commended before God, richly indued with moſt godlie iſſue of an admirable ſonne, viſited by the moſt holie Virgine, was of very great eſtimation: and yet she, alſo newly more [replenished with the Holie Ghoſt] in this preſent viſitation (as the Euangeliſt recordeth) knew, and preſently acknowleged the exceeding greater excellencie in the moſt bleſſed, Virgine, aboue herſelf, and aboue al wemen that euer were or can be ; as witneſſeth the ſame Euangeliſt ſaying, that [As Eliſabeth heard the ſalutation of Marie, the infant did leape in her wombe; and she was replenished with the Holie Ghoſt; and she cried out, with a loud voice, and ſaid· Bleſſed art thou among wemen: and bleſſed is the fruite of thy wombe. And whence is this to me, that the Mother of my Lord, doth come to me!] O wonderful knowlege in S. Eliſabeth: For who told her, that her coſine the

B. Virgine

Side notes (right margin):

that the B Virgine, Mother of God, farre excelleth the ordinarie ſtate of Gods true ſeruants.

7. 13.

14.

15.

7. 36.

7. 39.

Betwen whom & the wicked there can be no compariſon.

7. 41.

7. 42.

43.

S. Eliſabeth by ſpecial inſpiration knew very great Myſteries.

B. Virgine had now fruite in her wombe, within so
few dayes, after the diuine Incarnation? For immediatly after the Archangels Annunciation. [The B. v.39.
Virgine went with speede: to visite S. Elisabeth] And
behold she knew this diuine Mysterie, at their first
meeting, and mutual salutation. Who also told her
that this fruite, was so singularly blessed, that it made
the mother most blessed of al wemen, which either
conceiued, or not conceiued fruite? Who told her
that this is the promised, & expected Messias, Christ,
the Annointed, the Redemer of mankind? Who told
her, that this fruite, is the natural Sonne of God: who
taught her this Christian doctrine, before Christ was
yet borne: that because the B. Virgins Sonne, is also
the very Sonne of God, the Second Person of the
most blessed Trinitie; therfore the same B. Virgine is
the Mother of God? Which point of faith she also
firmely beleued, and expresly professed, saying with
admiration of the B. Virgins most admirable humilitie [Whence is this to me, that the Mother of my v.43.
Lord doth come to me?] Very great therfore was S.
Elisabeth in al vertues, very blessed with much grace.
And incomparably greatter was the B. Virgine, by
how much it excelleth to be Gods Mother, more
then to be onlie his seruant. S. Elisabeth was his faithful true seruant, and so were manie others: The B.
Virgine was his most faithful, true seruant aboue al
others: and also his worthie, true, & natural Mother,
which no other can be. Thus we see by the true
iudgement of S. Elisabeth, testified by the holie Euangelist in the sacred written word of God, that we
ought much more to esteme the great sanctitie of
Gods special seruants, aboue our poore selues, and
other common sorte of faithful people: & amongst
al, that the B. Virgine Mother of God, farre excelled
other iust holie persons, euen whiles she was in this
world, and so according to right proportion of grace
in this

Though S. Eli-
sabeth was ad-
mirably illu-
minated with
grace, yet the
excellencie of
the Mother of
God farre sur-
passed her, and
al others.

in this life, & glorie in heauen she excelleth al in eternal blisse. And therfore as the sanctitie, and glorie of anie persons is greater: so in like degree of iust comparison their prayers are of more worth, and more to be estemed, desired, and with al humble deuotion to be requested. By this holie text then, we may sufficiently lerne, that the faithful [become iust, before God; by walking without blame in al his commandments.] That the iust doe humbly, and truly acknowlege, that others are of greater excellencie in grace, then themselues: and shal be in greater glorie; And withal to detest the Luciferian pride of those, that dare compare themselues, either in the worth of their prayers, or in anie other thing, with the most worthie incomparable Mother of God.

5. We may againe meditate in like maner, as wel concerning the same most eminent glorie of the B. Virgine Mother, as the excellent blessednes of al glorious Sainctes of God, vpon an other passage in the holie Gospel where it is written, that whiles our B. Sauiour preached. [A certaine deuout woman lifting vp her voice out of the multitude said to him: Blessed is the wombe that bare thee: and blessed are the breastes, that thou didst sucke] Which praise of Christ vttered to himselfe, and redounding most especially to himselfe, importeth also not only the great praises of our B. Ladie, in her whole person, because she was made worthie, to conceiue and bare Christ our Lord in her wombe, and to geue him sucke (as is declared before, but also this blessednes deriued from Christ, is extended to her sacred bodie, & respectiuely to those special partes of the same most pure, virginal bodie, which particularly serued to the effecting of this diuine worke. [Blessed is the wombe that bare thee (ô Lord our Sauiour) & blessed are the breastes, which thou didst sucke.] Euen so likewise: Blessed are the handes that touched thee: Blessed are the armes

v.6.
42, 43.

Special pointes to be obserued in the text recited.

The same is declared by an other passage of the holie Gospel.

Luc. 11. v. 27

Art 45.
§. 5.

ch. 1. v. 22.

Hhh

mes

mes that carried thee: yea the further that this bleffednes is extended, the more is Chrift our Lord ho-
noied. From hence therfore it is, that he Church
(wh. rof this deuout woman was a pregnant figure)
profeffeth that al the true feruants of Chrft are bleffed, becaufe they (fome more fome leffe) ferued him.
Bleffed is holie Iofeph, his fuppofed father: becaufe
he not being his father, yet with al fatherly care ferued him in his infancie, & childhood. Bleffed in holie
Simeon, who fo ioyfully receiued him into his armes,
in the Temple. Bleffed is S. Iohn the Baptift, who was
his Precurfour. Bleffed as S. Peter, whom he made his
General Vicare in earth. Bleffed is S. Paul, whom he
made the Apoftle of the Gentiles. Bleffed are al his
Apoftles, Euangeliftes, Martyrs, holie Bifhoppes, Do-

Al bleffednes and fanctitie is deriued from Chrift.

ctors, Virgins, Widowes, Confeffors, al godlie men,
wemen, and children: Not for any thing they doe, or
can doe [of themfelues: as of themfelues.] but for the
feruice which they haue done to Chrift; and that by 2. Cor. 3. v. 5.
his grace, [of whom is al our fufficiencie] Breefly,
Bleffed are al that rightly beleue, and confidently
hope in Chrift, louing him aboue al, and their neighbours as themfelues, which confifteth in keping his
commandments. For fo himfelfe teftifieth, both els Io. 14. v. 11.
where, and in this very place, faying: that not neer
ues in bloud, or kinred aloue [but rather, bleffed are Luc. 11. v. 28
they, that heare the word of God, and kepe it] which
perteineth to al the iuft in this world.

Great diffe- rence betwen the ftaies of the faithful, and glorious.

6. But betwen the iuft in this life, and the glorified
in heauen is fo great difference, as betwen hope and
poffeffion, betwen hoping with danger of lofing before death, and hauing, with infallible affurance of
holding for al eternitie. The one forte are *Beati in fpe*,

Viatores & Comprehenfores.

the other are *Beati in re*. The one forte are *in Via*; the
other in *Patria*. The one forte called therfore *Viatores*,
the other *Comprehenfores*. And befides this great difference betwen iuft feare, and infallible fecuritie,

their

their ftates differ no leffe, but in deede much more: for in this life al are inuironed with imperfections, Faith it felf is vnperfect, yea Prophecie is vnperfect.

2. Cor. 13. [For in part we know (to witte by faith) and in part v.9. we prophecie] faith S. Paul. In heauen al are perfect. And therfore happie death, farre excelleth happie life. Happie life maketh bleffed in hope, becaufe without good life there is litle, or no hope : happie death maketh bleffed in deede. And therfore concer-

Pfal. 1.v.2. ning al fuch, S. Iohn teftifieth faying [I heard a voice 5.6 f.14.6. from heauen, faying to me: Write: Bleffed are the t.4. dead, which die in our Lord : from henceforth now, Apoc. 14. faith the Spirite, that they reft from their laboures : v.13. For their workes folow them.] Al confifteth in that they [dye in our Lord] in the ftate of grace, accom-panied with good workes. Then faith Gods Spirite: They reft fecure, being affured to receiue their reward, reft from laboures of tentations, in ioy, honour, and Io.14.v.25. al good, that can be defired. According as our Lord 26. els where alfo exprefly promifeth, faying,[If any man Sainctes in minifter to me; let him folow me, and where I am, heauen haue there alfo fhal my minifter be, if anie man minifter to more know-me; my Father wil honour him.] wil geue him more lege, by feing God then the grace in this life, and perfect glorie in heauen. There greateft fer-Mat. 11. v. 11. al the bleffed by the fruition of God, are indued with uant of God more knowlege: and are more confirmed in zele, in this life. pietie, and charitie, both towards God, and al mankind, then they were in this world. And therfore moft abfurde is their follie, that compare the ftate of men yet liuing in flefh, with the glorious Sainctes : which are in heauen : or the prayers of mortal per-fons yet fubiect to finne, or tentation, with the pray-ers of glorified Sainctes.

7. The laft pretended excufe, why Proteftants wil not pray to Sainctes, (if we may thinke that they are fo fcrupulous) is their feare, left they should therby The third ob-detract from Chrifts Souereigntie, or derogate from iection againft

his singular honour. But doe ye not see gentle Aduersaries, that whiles you charge vs with derogation from Christ, by our praying to Sainctes, as to intercessors for vs to him : yourselues would depriue him, of that seruice, which the glorious citizens of heauen cōtinually doe him, for the good of his faithful in earth: as is testified by S. Iohn: that [the foure liuing creatures, and twentie four seniors sal downe before him offering the prayers of the faithful] For by your iudgement, none must offer prayers to Christ, but we only that are in earth. And if we vse any intercessor betwen ourselues, & him, then, say you, we dishonour Christ; we doe him great iniurie, we committe an hainous crime, if we suppose that anie glorious Sainct shal sowner be heard then ourselues. So that al your pretence of Chrifts honour rather detecteth a proud presumption of your owne worth, with vntolerable disdaine of glorious Sainctes, then anie true zele of Chrifts honour. For [true zele is according to knowlege] but this zele of yours is without knowlege, of the great difference betwen Gods seruants in heauen, and in earth. You can not be ignorant that God granteth the requestes of his faithful seruants, for their sakes that were more faithful, and more holie, and yet yon wil not pray by mediation of any but of Christ only. But what text haue you, for this your pretext of Chrifts dishonour, by our praying the glorious Sainctes to pray for vs? The cheefest which you alleage is: Because Christ saith to al true penitents. [Come ye to me al that labour, and are burdened : and I wil refresh you] Therfore say you, we must not pray Sainctes to goe to him for vs, nor to pray him in our behalf. As if this were going from him to others. We answer, that this is going to him: because thus we goe to him, by others who are more worthie to be heard, then our selues without them. When [a certaine Centurion sent the Ancients of the Iewes. vnto

Christ,

Marginal notes (left):

praying to Sainctes is pretended derogation from Christ.

Glorious Sainctes doe honour Christ, by offering the prayers of the faithful to him.

A particular obiection answered.

Marginal notes (right):

Apoc 5. v. 9.

Rom. 10. v. 2.

Matt. 11. v. 28.

Luc. 7. v. 2. 3. 4. 5.

Chrift, defiring him to come and heale his feruant.
And they befought him earneftly: as S.Luke relateth
Mat.8. v.5. it: S.Matthew faith [There came to Chrift a Centu-
6. rion befeeching him.] By conference therfore of the
two Euangeliftes, it is neceffarie to fay; that they
which come by others, are truly faid to come to
Chrift. becaufe they come to him by wil and affection, and fo coming to him by his glorious Sainctes,
Luc.7. v.6. they come with more humilitie, then by themfelues
7. alone. As is cleare in this example of the Centurion,
who confeffing his owne vnworthines, faid [Lord,
I am not worthie, that thou shouldeft enter vnder my
roofe. For the which caufe, neither did I thinke my
felfe worthie to come to thee: but fay the word, and
my feruant fhal be made whole] So we fee the precept of Chrift bidding al, come to him, is obferued,
when we repaire to him by interceffion of Sainctes.
And that with our more confidence, & more honour
to Chrift. And fo this maner of coming is no deroga-
Iac.3. v.14. tion, but more honorable to him.
15.

8. If you wil be pleafed in like maner, [with mildnes
cafting out al bitter zele, & contention] to conferre,
and confider the facred text of Gods word in thofe
places, where mention is made of Redemer, Mediator, Aduocate, Adiutor, Protector, Sauiour, and the
like, you fhal clearly fee, that as thefe titles, in their
principal fignification, and in the moft excellent
degree, doe perteyne only to Chrift Iefus our Lord;
fo in an other fenfe, and farre lower degree, they alfo
perteyne, and are afcribed in the holie Scriptures, to
Gods feruants, as wel glorious in heauen, as faithful
in earth. Alwayes with this incomparable difference,
that Chrift our Lord doth thefe excellent offices for
men, by his owne power, in his owne name, and
through his owne merites. Al others dee them, as his
Iob 19. v.25. Minifters: through his power, name, and merites. So
holie Iob profeffed that onlie God is his Redemer;

VVe repaire to Chrift not only by our owne prayer, but alfo by the prayers of Sainctes.

And therin is more humili-tie in vs. And more honour to Chrift.

Titles and of-fices pertey-ning princi-pally to Chrift are afcribed alfo, in a true fenfe, to his feruants.

Who shal raise him from death. The Royal Psalmist
acknowlegeth onlie God to be our absolute Redemer, saying that [neither a mans owne brother (nor
anie other) shal redeme him: neither anie man can Pl.48.v.8,9
redeme himself. He shal not gene vnto God, his reconciliation. And the price of redemption, of his Pf.129.v.
owne soule.] Much lesse for an other mans soule. 7.8.
[But with our Lord there is mercie: and with him
plenteous redemption. And he shal redeme Israel
from al his iniquities.] Our Lord saith vnto al his
people, by his Prophete Isaias [Returne to me, be- If.44.v.22.
cause I haue redemed thee, you were sold for ch.5.v.3.
nought, and without siluer you shal be redemed. ch.62.v.12.
Behold thy Sauiour cometh: behold his reward is
with him, and his worke before him. And they shal
eat them: The holie people: the redemed of our
Lord.] Nothing is more frequent in the Prophetes, See Part.1.
then the necessitie of a Redeemer, onlie Christ, God Art.15.
and Man is the same Redeemer of al mankinde: which
Christ himself also plainly affirmeth, saying. [The Mat.20.v.
Sonne of man is come, to geue his life a redemption 28.
for manie.] His Apostles teach the very same [God, Act 3.v.18.
who foreshewed by the mouth of al the Prophetes
(said S. Peter) that his Christ should suffer, hath so
fulfilled it. There is not saluation in anie other, for ch.4.v.12.
neither is there anie other name vnder heauen, geuen
to men (but Iesus Christ) wherin we must be saued.]
The same Apostle in his Epistle, admonisheth al
Christians [to liue in feare: knowing (saith he) that 1.Pet 1.v.
not with corruptible thinges, gold, or siluer, you are 17.18.19.
redemed from your vaine conuersation, of your fathers tradition, but with the precious bloud, as it
were, of an immaculate, & vnspotted lambe, Christ]
S. Paul likewise testifieth the same to the Christian
Iewes and Gentils, saying [Now without the Law (of Rom. 3 v.
Moyses) the iustice of God is manifested: testified by 21. 23.
the Law, and the Prophetes. For al haue sinned; and 24.

*In the princi-
pal sense onlie
Christ s our
Redemer.*

nede

Gal 3 v.13. nedeth glorie of God. Iuſtified gratis, by his grace: by the redemption that is in Chriſt Ieſus. Chriſt hath
Coloſ. 1.
v.14
1. Tim. 2.
v.6.
redemed vs, from the curſe of the Law. In Chriſt we haue redemptiō the remiſſion of ſinnes. He gaue himſelf a redemptiō for al, a teſtimonie in due times. He gaue himſelf for vs, that he might redeme vs from

Tit.2. v. 14. al iniquitie, and might cleanſe to himſelf a people acceptable, a purſuer of good woikes. Ieſus Chriſt

1.Io.2. v.2. (ſaith S. Iohn) is the propitiation for our ſinnes: not for ours only, but alſo for the whole worlds] whereupon al the glorified Sainctes ſing vnto him this

Apoc 5.
v.9. 10.
Canticle, ſaying [Thou art worthie ô Lord to take the booke, and to open the ſeales therof: becauſe thou waſt ſlaine, and haſt redemed vs to God, in thy bloud, out of euerie tribe, and tongue, and people, and nation.

9. In the ſame principal ſignification, Chriſt our onlie abſolute Redemer is alſo our onlie Mediator, Aduocate, Protector, Helper, and Sauiour, and no other in the ſame ſenſe. So Melchiſedech king and Prieſt titleth God Almightie Proteſtor his ſeruants

Gen. 14.
v. 20.
Ch.15. v.1.
ſaying to Abraham [Bleſſed be God the Higheſt, by whoſe protection the enimies are in thy hand] God himſelfe confirmed the ſame title ſaying alſo to Abra-

Exo.15 v 2. ham [Feare not Abram I am thy Protector] Moyſes withal the people in their Canticle of thankes ſpeake

1.Reg. 10.
v.19.
to God by the like titles, ſaying, [My Strength, and my Praiſe is our Lord, and he is made vnto me a Saluation] Samuel conteſted to al the people that [God only ſaueth them out of al euils, and tribulations]

ch.17. v.46. Dauid as yet young, but moſt confident ſaid to great Goliath [Nor in ſword and ſpeare doth our Lord

2. Reg. 22.
v.1.
ſaue, but he wil deliuer thee into my hand] The ſame king and Prophete in al his life ſette forth Gods ſingular power, & abſolute goodnes, with moſt proper titles, of [Rock, Strength, Shielde, Strong one, Sauiour, Horne of ſaluatō. Lifter vp: Refuge, Deliuerer, Helper,

Marginal notes (right column):

Only Chriſt is our Protector, Strength, Mediator, Aduocate, Helper, SauiourHope, Refuge, Deliuerer &c. abſolutely of himſelfe.

His holie ſeruants haue the ſame titles by participation.

Helper, Protector, Redemer, Illumination, Salua- *Pf.17.v.2.3.*
tion, Protection, and, Al in al. Becaufe he alone can *Pf 7.v.11.*
doe al thinges: without him none at al can doe anie *Pf 9.v.10.*
thing. Al other Prophetes, and Apoftles, and Chrift *Pf.16.v.9.*
himfelf confirme the fame. There is no God but one, *Pro.2.v.7*
no Chrift but one, no Medeator, no Aduocate, no *If.12.v.2.*
Interceffor, but Iefus Chrift; in the eminent, moft *Mat.1.v.11*
proper abfolute fenfe, as thefe titles are appropriated *ch.10.v.28.*
to him, and therfore fo to afcribe them to anie other, *&c.*
were to make an other Chrift, and an other God. It is
only Iefus Chrift, that died for al mankinde.

The denial of　10.　Which cleare truth confeffed by al, that wil
the fame titles feme to be Chriftians, needeth no more côfirmation.
(in way of par- But for fo much as our Aduerfaries calumniate our
ticipation) is praying to Sainctes, charging vs, that therby we
dishonour to robbe Chrift of his honour, we ftil tel them, that they
God, and con- robbe him both of power, and honour, in denying
trarie to his the power and honour, which he geueth to his holie
diuine word. feruants, & that they plainly gainfay the holie Scri-
tures, which teftifie that God, & our Sauiour Chrift
geue the fame titles, & offices, in a true fignification,
to their feruants, and minifters. [Moyfes was made *En.7.v.1.*
the God of Pharao.] without preiudice to God Almightie; yea to Gods more honour. And [his brother
Aaron was appointed his Prophete] Neuertheles
they both were Gods owne Prophetes. The fame
Moyfes was [Moyfes, was Arbiter, and Mediator betwixt our *Deut 5 v.5.*
called God. Lord, and the people] Wherupon S. Paul faith, that
And Media- [The Law was ordayned by Angels, in the hand of a *Gal.3.v.19.*
tor. Mediator] Exprefly teaching that Moyfes was a Mediator, betwen the Angels, and the people: and fo the
Angels are Angels were likewife Mediators betwen God and
Mediators. Moyfes: without al confufion of order, or preiudice
to Superiors. For how manie Mediators foeuer there
be, they are al in order fubiect to Superiors, and al
fubordinate Superiors are al fubiect to God, the only
Supreme. So euerie good fpiritual Paftor is a
Mediator,

Mediator, in that he intreateth God, by offering Sacrifice, with other prayers to God, crauing his mercie, for himfelf, and the people: and by exhorting the people to cooperate with Gods grace, by freely accepting it, being in their power, to refufe it. And this excludeth not Chrifts Mediatió, but includeth it, for al petitions are concluded: Through Chrift our Lord. And whenfoeuer we pray a glorious Sainct, to intercede for vs, it is in the fame fubordination, as Moyfes receiued the Law, by the Angels. And when he, and Daniel, and Tobias, and Cornelius, & others prayed, and Angels offered their prayers, the fame Angels were Mediators.

11.   It may feme perhaps, fomewhat harder to a vulgar Proteftant, that the title of Redemer is alfo afcribed to Moyfes (and by that example, may in like maner be geuen to fome other fpiritual Paftors) which thing is euidently recorded in the holie Scripture, where S. Steuen calleth Moyfes a Redemer, *Act.7. v.35.* faying [This Moyfes whom they (the Ifraelites in Ægypt) denied: him God fent Prince, and Redemer, with the hand of the Angel, that appeared to him in the bush.] Yet as Moyfes was not God in the proper fenfe of God Omnipotent: fo he was not a Redemer, as Chrift is by his owne power, and merites, but by doing his function, in pleading their caufe with Pharao, by working miracles, by guiding the people through the read fea, and by praying for them: and fo in a fecondarie fenfe, redemed them from the bondage of Ægypt: & from the rigour of due punishmét for their finnes. According to which fenfe Salomon *Prou.16. v 6* faith, that [By mercie and truth iniquitie is redemed, and in the feare of our Lord euils are auoided] In the fame fenfe Daniel fpake to Nabuchodonofor *Dan 4. v.24* faying [O King, let me counfel thee: And redeme thou thy finnes with almes: and thyne iniquities with the mercies of the poore.] Signifying that he might

Moyfes was alfo called Redemer,

Mortal men may in a true fenfe, redeme their finnes.

by almes deedes procure diminution of due punishment, or longer continuance of his prosperous temporal
poral state. Which is a kinde of redemption, that may
be wrought by euerie one: especially by the faithful,
cooperating with Gods grace, and may be much fur-
thered by the prayers of glorious Sainctes.

In like sense
Gods seruants,
as wel glo-
rious as faith-
ful may be cal-
led Aduocates.

Intercessors.

12.   Likewise our most proper and principal Aduocate, is onlie Christ our Lord: of whom S. Iohn
saith [We haue an Aduocate with the Father, Iesus
Christ the iust] In an other sense, and degree holie Iob
was an Aduocate for his trublesome freindes, after
their dispute against him, and that by Gods appointment, bidding them [goe to his seruant Iob, and offer
holocausts for themselues. And my seruant Iob (said
our Lord) shal pray for you. His face I wil receiue,
that the follie be not imputed to you (and declaring
the reason why his prayer was better then theirs for
themselues, he saith) For you haue not spoken right
thinges before me, as my seruant Iob.] Iob then liuing in this world was an Aduocate for others. And
they did accordingly as our Lord had spoke to them.
And our Lord receiued the face of Iob, when he did
penance, and prayed for his freindes.] And long after
his departure, from this life, Our Lord by his Prophete Ezechiel nameth Iob, with Noe (also deceassed
long before) and with Daniel then liuing, as special
Aduocates, more worthie to be heard then ordinarie
faithful people. Which is also to be remembred concerning other Patriarches, Abraham, Isaac, Iacob, &
Dauid [for whose sakes, God both promised protection, and did protect his people, & the citie of Ierusalem.] Christ as Man is our principal Intercessor.

Christ our
principal In-
tercessor
goeth by him-
selfto God,
Al other In-
tercessors goe
by him.

[Who (saith S. Paul) is on the right hand of God, who
also maketh intercession for vs. Going by himself to
God alwayes liuing to make intercession for vs] by
which wordes [Goying by himself to God.] The Apostle teacheth vs euidently, the great differéce betwen

(margin notes:) I. Io. 2. v. 1.

Iob. 42. v. 8.

v. 9. 10.

Ezech. 14. v.
14.

4. Reg. 19. v.
24.
Isa. 37. v. 35.
ch. 63. v, 15.

Rom. 8. v. 34

Christ

Heb.7 v.25.

Act.7.v.56. 60.

Io.4. v.51.
Mat.8.v 12
ch.9 v.18.25
ch.15.v.23. 25.

Chrift & other Interceffors. For he goeth by himfelf, pleading his owne merites : al others goe by him, pleading his merites, not their, owne: otherwife then as deriued from his grace. And fo glorious Sainctes pray to him, and by him to God for the faithful , and are fubordinate Interceffors. Mortal perfons alfo are Interceffors, approued by Chrifts warrant, accepting the interceffions of a certaine Lord praying for his fonne: of a Centurion (with the Ancients of the Iewes) for his feruant : of the Archifynagogue, for his daughter : of the woman of Chanaan (together with his owne difciples) for her daughter: and the like . Chrift is the onlie Helper, by his owne po- wer : Which is proper to him: but through him others alfo are helpers, by participation of his

Ifa.41.v.13.
Pro.18. v 19
Eft.14 v.3. 14.

power.] Brother that is holpé of brother, is as aftrong citie] faith Salomon. Holie Quene Efther [befought our Lord the God of Ifrael faying ; My Lord which only art our king, helpe me folitarie woman , and which haue no other helper befides thee. Deliuer vs in thy hand, and helpe me, hauing no other helpe, but thee ô Lord] Yet was this holy woman a fubordinate helpe vnder God , for the fafetie of the fame Iewes,

Others are alfo truly cal- led Helpers,

Coadiutors.

ch.15 v 11.
ib.4.v.15.

in their danger of ruine. As the whole hiftorie repor- teth. By whofe meanes [God turned the kings fpi- rite(the furie of his breaft) into mildnes] towards her, and then by her true declaration, and fuite to the King, the cruel Edict made againft the whole nation of the Iewes, was turned againft their enimies. Which prouidence of God Mardocheus prefaging, vrged Efther to put herfelf into peril, faying to her. [Who

ch.8.v.3.
ib.4.v.14.

Exo.13.v 21
ch.14.v.2.
Nu.14. v 14

knoweth whether thou cameft to the kingdome that in fuch a time thou mighteft be readie.] to helpe, and faue thy nation. Their fafting, & other penance, with earneft prayer, did alfo helpe them. God alwayes the principal helper, worketh his wil by fecundarie meanes. God protecteth his people , and [his cloude

Protectors.

protected

protected them.] In the hand of my seruant Dauid *2. Reg. 3.*
(said our Lord) I wil saue my people Israel, from the *v. 18.*
handes of the Philistims, and of al their enimies. The *ch. 19. v 9.*
King (said al the people) hath deliuered vs, out of
the hand of our enimies. He hath saued vs, from the
head of the Philistims. Of the helpe and protection *Exod 23.*
of nolie Angels, as ministerial causes is abundantly *v 20.*
declared before in the examples of the whole people *Ios. v. 3.*
in the desert: and of Iosue: of the Iudges: of others in *Iudic 2. v 1.*
diuers occasions. So that it is most truly said: God de- *&c.*
Art. 43.
liuered, protected, saued them: and also truly said: *4. Reg. 19.*

Angels Prote-
ctors, and
Princes, of
countries.

[The Angel of his face saued them.] Whereupon An- *v. 35.*
gels were called the Princes of certaine Kingdomes, *Is. 63. v 9.*
and countries, which they protected [the Prince of *Dan. 10.*
the Kingdome of the Persians (said the Angel Gabriel *v. 13. 21.*
to Daniel the Prophete) resisted me one and twentie
daies. And none is my helper in al these, but Michael
your Prince. S. Paul saw in a vision by night at *Act. 16. v. 8.*
Troas, a certaine man of Macedonia (an Angel in *9.*
shape of a man) standing and beseeching him, saying: *Rom 16.*
Passe into Macedonia, and helpe vs] that is, helpe our *v. 9.*
countrie of Macedonia by preaching Christ, for the *1. Cor. 3.*
spiritual health of soules. Of which kind of ministe- *v. 9. 21.*
rial helpe and helpers, the same Apostle speaketh of- *2. Cor. 1.*
ten in his Epistles [Salute (saith he) Vrbanus our hel- *v. 24.*

Apostles are
Gods coadiu-
tors.

per in Christ Iesus. Timothee my Coadiutor saluteth *Phil. 4. v. 3.*
you: We are Gods Coadiutors: you are Gods husban-
drie: you are Gods building: We are helpers of your
ioy. I beseech thee my sincere companion, helpe those *Colos. 4.*
wemen. Clement and the rest of my Coadiutors. *v. 10. 11.*
Marcus, Aristarchus, Demas, and Luke, my Coad- *Phil. v. 26.*
iutors.]

The title of
Sauiour is also
in a true sense
geuen to Gods
seruants.

13. Finally the title of Sauiour, and termes of sauing,
and saluation are in this secondarie sense, ascribed to
Christs Ministers, and their ministerie, to his more
honour, and without al derogation to his absolute
Principalitie. Who is Auctor and fountaine of al. This

Title

Title was geuen to some, as to Prophetical figures of
Iesus Christ, our only absolute Lord and Sauiour. Holie Ioseph the Patriarch (by Gods special prouidence)
was called in the Ægyptian tongue: The Sauiour of the
world.] The Iudges, whom God raised vp extraordinarily (betwen the time of Iosue and the Kinges) as
general Capitanes, to deliuer, and defend his people
from their enimies, were also called Sauiours. [Our
Lord raised them vp a Sauiour, Othoniel. Againe he
raised vp a Sauiour, called Aod.] and others. Afterwards also the Kingdome of the tenne tribes, being
distressed [Ioachas their King besought the face of our
Lord, and our Lord heard him; and gaue a Sauiour to
Israel, and they were deliuered out of the hand of
their enimie.] Esdras, Nehemias, and others, in their
thankes to God, acknowleged that he [from heauen
gaue them Sauiours] as wel Angels sent from heauen,
as men indued with heauenlie grace, to succour and
saue themselues and others. S. Peter exhorting penitent persons, saied. [Saue yourselues from this peruerse generation.] Signifying that through Gods
grace they must concurre to their owne saluation:
which he calleth [sauing themselues] but al in the
grace of our Sauiour Christ Iesus. S. Paul saith [With
the hart we beleue vnto iustice: but with the mouth
confession is made to saluation. The sorow that is
according to God, worketh penance vnto saluation,
that is stable. For we are Gods worke, created in
Christ Iesus, which God hath prepared, that we
should walke in them.] Of himself he saith [I know
that this (emulation of aduersaries) shal fal out to
me, vnto saluation: by your prayer, & the submini-
stration of the Spirite of Iesus Christ.] To others he
said [My dearest, with feare and trembling worke
your saluation. For God hath not appointed vs vnto
wrath, but vnto the purchasing of saluation, by our
Lord Iesus Christ] Speaking of things to be done

The faithful doe helpe to saue them-selues, and others.

Marginal references:
Gen. 41.
v. 45.

Iudic. 2.
v 16. 18.
ch 3. v. 9.
v 15.

4. Reg. 13.
v. 3. 4. 5.

2. Esd. 9.
v. 27.

Act 7.
v. 25.
Ex 5 v. 10.
Act 2. v. 40.

Rom. 10.
v. 10.

2. Cor. 7.
v. 10.

Philip. 1.
v. 19.
ch .. v 12.
1 Thes 5
v. 9.

by

by faithful wemen, he saith, that [A **woman** (doing her dutie also in other respects)shalbe saued by generation of children.] To S. Timothee he saith [Attend to thy self, and to doctrine: be earnest in them. For this doing thou shalt saue both thy selfe, and them that heare thee. To the Hebrewes he saith. We confidently trust of you, my best beloued better thinges, and nerer to saluation.] S. Iames vseth this word sauing, in the very same sense, affirming saluation to be the effect of good workes.[Confesse your sinnes one to another (saith he) and pray one for another, that you may be saued.] Againe he saith [He which maketh a sinner to be conuerted from the errour of his way, shal saue his soule from death, and couereth a multitude of sinnes.] Much more can glorious Sainctes, by their intercession helpe forwards the saluation of their clients in earth: the same being no more derogation to Chtist our Sauiour, then the helpe, which one faithful person receiueth by another. As we shal yet further demonstrate.

1 Tim 2.
v. 15.
ch 4.v.16.
Heb. 6. v 9.

Iac.5. v.16.
20.

Iude v. 23.

It is no derogation to Christ: and is very prō-
fitable to mortal persons, that one pray
for an other.

ARTICLE 46.

Most Protestants confessing that the intercession of one mortal person for an other is good and lawful, say that the inter- cession of glo-

AS wel in more abundant confirmation, that it is lawful to inuocate glorious Sainctes: as in confutation of a new rising errour,that it should not be lawful to request the prayers of faithful persons in this life, we further adde, against al Aduersaries, which pretend that praying to Sainctes doth derogate from Christ, this one other pregnant proofe. To pray the glorious Sainctes, to pray for vs to God, is no more derogation to Christ, then to request our mortal neighbour, to pray for vs. For both in the one & the other, we vse an other mediator to Christ.

But

But so to request the prayer of a mortal person, is ^{rious Sainctes} lawful, and without any derogation to Christ. ^{is derogation} For it is euident, that the faithful haue in al times of ^{to Christ.} the old and new Testament, prayed one for an other, which God hath both approued, & sometimes commanded: & most Protestants allow, & in their maner practise it. Ergo to request glorious Sainctes to pray for vs to God, is no derogation to Christ. In stead of answering to this demonstration, our Aduersaries commonly flee from the point, which before they vrged, touching their imagined derogatiō from Christ, by praying to Sainctes: and rather stand vpon their other obiections, That Sainctes can not heare vs: Can not helpe vs, &c. Neuertheles in their pulpites, & vulgar talke they crie, that praying to Sainctes is derogation to Christ. And we prouing the contrarie, & pressing them (amongst other proofes) to answer directly to the Premisses of the here proposed perfect Syllogisme, then the most part of Protestants, denie the Maior proposition, saying: That albeit we vse other intercessors in earth, without derogation to Christ, yet to vse anie other intercessor in heauen, is derogation to Christ. But when they are demanded; Why ^{Protestants} the mediation of Sainctes should derogate from ^{can not yelde} Christ, seing the mediation of mortal persons doth ^{anie reason,} not derogate from him? They can yeelde no reason at ^{why they de-} al of difference. And we clearly shew, that neither ^{ne the Ma-} the one, nor the other is anie derogation, but both ^{ior proposi-} are lawful. For the Catholique faith, and doctrine ^{tion.} is, that the B. Virgine Mother, and al other Intercessors, both in heauen, and in earth doe pray vnto Christ, and through Christ his merits, beseech the Diuine Goodnes to grant the petitions of the faithful, principally for Christs sake, and secondarily also for Christs more beloued, and more perfect seruants, who haue better deserued, and haue more fauour with God, then the imperfect. And so the more perfect,

fect, to witte, the glorious Sainctes in heauen, must needes be more grateful to Christ, when they intercede to him for mortal persons in earth, and neither their mediation, nor the mediation of the faithful is anie way iniurious, or vngratful to him, but most grateful, and most agreable to his wil.

Others confessing the necessarie consequence that if one mediation be lawful, both are lawful, denie both alike.

2. Others seing the euident truth of the Maior proposition (that it is no more derogation to Christ, to request the prayers of glorious Sainctes, then of mortal persons) do confesse it to be true. But rather then they wil confesse the conclusion, they denie the Minor proposition: holding opinion, that to request the prayers of anie other person whosoeuer, is derogation to Christ. Which is a new deuised Paradox, false, & absurde. Which though it be a desperate shift, yet of the two is more sincere, then confessing mortal mens intercession to be lawful, to say that glorious Sainctes intercession is derogation to Christ. Albeit therfore none (for anie thing I know) hath vttered in writing their conceipt, that it is derogation to Christ, to request the prayers of mortal persons, yet some auouching it by word of mouth, being vrged by the necessarie cōsequence (for it necessarily conuinceth) that if requesting the prayers of Sainctes were derogation to Christ, then to request our mortal freind were also derogation to him: both admitting mediation of others to him) we shal shew the manifest truth, by holie Scriptures: And first by the Law of nature: then by the practise of the faithful in the written Law: and by Christs precept: and his Apostles doctrine, and al true Christians practise.

Prayer of one mortal person for an other, is proued to be lawful by examples in the Law of nature.

3. Abimelech King of Gerara, being admonished Gen 20. v. 7
by God in a dreame, to restore Sara the wife of Abra- 8.
ham to her husband [because (said our Lord) he is a 14.
Prophete, & he shal pray for thee, & thou shalt liue] 17.
estemed so much of Abrahams prayer, that he presently rose in the night, and restored her vntouched.]

And

And Abraham praying, God healed Abimelech, and
his wife, and his handmades.] Whom he had before ‿ punished with barennes. God said to Eli-
phas, and the two other Aduerfaries of Iob [My feruant Iob shal pray for you:His face I wil receiue. And
our Lord receiued the face of Iob. King Pharao requested Moyfes and Aaron, to pray for him, and his
people, that they might be freede from the plagne of
frogges. They fo prayed our Lord, and the frogges
dyed. The like for the remouing of fome other
plagues. [The people in the defert being inuironed
with fire, and fome deuoured therwith, for their
murmuring: they cried to Moyfes; and Moyfes
prayed to our Lord: and the fire was quenched.]
Againe the people being ftrooken with firie ferpents, Moyfes prayed, & our Lord appointed them
to make a brafen ferpent, for a remedie againft the
fame affliction.

*Iob.*42.*v.*8.
9.

Exo 8 *v.*8.
10.13.29 30.
ch 9.*v.*28.

*Nam.*11.*v.*
1.2.

*ch.*21.*v.*6.7.
8 9.

4. In the time of Saul, firft reigning in Ifrael [al
the people, being excedingly terrified with fudaine
noyfes of thunder, faid to Samuel: Pray for thy feruants to our Lord thy God, that we dye not. And he
anfwered (togeth'er with wholfome admonitions,
that they should be penitent for their finnes, & confident in Gods mercie) Be this finne farre from me in
our Lord (faith he) that I should ceafe to pray for
you] Ieroboam being fuddainly ftrooken lame of his
arme, for his obftinacie, againft an holie Prophete
of God, befought the fame Prophete to pray for him,
that his hand might be reftored to him [And the man
of God befought the face of our Lord, and the Kings
hand was reftored to him, and it became as it was before] The good King Ezechias, befought Ifaias the
Prophete to pray for him, and with him to God, in
the time of the Kings ficknes; And God granted him
health of bodie, with longer life: and alfo promifed
him victorie againft the Affirians. An other very
good

1.*Reg.*12.*v.*
18 19.

v. 20.

23.

*By other examples, and teftimonies in
the written
Law of
Moyfes.*

*3 Reg.*13.*v.*
4.6.

*4.Reg.*19.*v.*
2.4.&c.

*2 Par.*32.*v.*
10

K k k

good King Iosias requested the prayers of the Priests, ch,34. v.28. and Leuites. The Highpriest, and Ancients, in their common distresse, requested holie Iudith the widow, Iudith.8. v. to pray, for the whole people: & she requested them 19 31. mutually to pray for her, that her intention might haue happie successe. Esdras and others receiued 1.Eld.6.v. licence, and meanes, of King Darius, to build the 10. Temple agane in Ierusalem, with a special códition, that they should pray for the life of the King] And innumerable like examples testifie, that by the Law of God, and nature, al reasonable persons desire the prayers of others, knowing the same to be very profitable; and necessarie.

5.   Christ our Lord, in regard of this necessitie, and great profite of mutual prayer of each one for

The same is manifest by Christs doctrine, and his Apostles.

others, ordayned our most ordinarie daylie Prayer, Mat.6 v.9. in forme of asking for al the faithful members of 10. Christs mystical bodie: saying (as is explained before) Art.12.15. Our Father; Geue vs; Forgeue vs, &c.] Not My Fa- 27.30. ther, Geue me. Forgeue me, with exclusion of others. Act.1.v.54. Al the Apostles, with the rest of the faithful ioyned themselues in prayer, each one for others, and al for al. S. Paul continually in the end of his Epistles desire'd, and expresly requested the prayers of others for himself. [I beseech you bretheren (saith he) by our Rom.15.v. Lord Iesus Christ, and by the charitie of the Holie 30. Ghost, that you helpe in your prayers, for me to God.] And in like sorte in manie other places. It is 2 Cor.1.v 11 wonder that anie should be so senseles, as either to Col.4 v.3. say, that to request other mortal persons to pray for 1.Thes.5. v. vs, is derogation to Christ; or granting that it is no 25. derogation to him, yet say that to request the prayers Phil.1.v.22. of glorious Sainctes is derogatió to Christ our Lord. Heb.13.v.18. That neither therfore the one nor the other is anie derogation to our Lord and Sauiour, is cleare by the holie Scriptures recited, in this & in the former Articles. Wherby is also manifest to what desperate ab-

surditie

surditie they are driuen, that wil needes denie, and reiect the prayers of glorious Sainctes. Not only imagining it to be vnpossible, that they can know our desires, or anie way helpe vs by their prayers to God (which conceipts we haue largely confuted) but also pretending that it is derogation to Christ: rather then they wil acknowlege their errour, doe either contradict themselues, denying mediation of glorious Sainctes in heauen, and vsing mediation of mortal persons in earth: or els denying this also to be lawful, (because of the ineuitable consequence, that either both the meditions are lawful, or neither can be lawful) they doe euidently contradict the rest of the whole world, and most expresse holie Scriptures. Their next shift (vnles they wil reiurne to the Catholique truth) must be, to denie the holie Scriptures: which so plainly conuince them: and so shew themselues plaine Infidels: and finally become Hethnish, & Atheists: not allowing anie Diuine Auctoritie aboue their owne phantasies.

6.   But vpon this certaine truth, which most Protestants acknowlege: that we doe lawfully, and profitably desire other mortal persons to pray for vs to Christ: we pray them to consider, and vrge them to answer: How it can be iniurious to Christ, that we pray glorious Sainctes to pray for vs to him: seing it is no iniurie to request the same of a mortal person? Againe, why it should be erronious to beleue that glorious Sainctes in heauen, do by the light of Glorie wherin they liue, know our good desires, and prayers, seing they are like, & equal to holie Angels, both in power, & knowlege? and seing some mortal men knew the secretes of other mens hartes, by the light of Prophecie? Thirdly, why doe you denie or doubt, that holie Angels doe know mens affayres in earth, seing they haue protection of countries, and of mortal persons: and seing they reioice, when sinners

Demandes proposed to our Aduersaries.

1.

2.

Luc. 20. v. 36

3. Reg. 14. v. 6.
4. Reg 8 v. 26.
Dan. 10. v. 13. 21.

3.

ners repent: and doe offer the prayers of deuout per- Mat.13.v.
sons to God? Fourtly, how dare anie that beareth the 10.
name of a Christian denie, that holie Angels, & other Apoc 5. v.8.
glorious Sainctes, doe know mens necessities; or
denie that they pray for the faithful: seing it can not
be denied, that wicked spirites, damned diuels, the
inueterate enimies of al mankind, doe know (though
they haue not corporal eyes, nor eares) manie particular deedes, and wordes of mortal men: and cease 1.Pet.5 v.8.
not by wicked suggestions (though they haue not
corporal tongues) to tempt, and allure men to sinne: Io.13,v.2.
Finally, why then shal not Christians beleue, that as
God not only by his owne omnipotent word, but
also by the ministerie of his holie Angels, cast the Apoc 12.v.
proud apostata diuels out of heauen: so by the me- 7.8.
diation of the same holie Angelical Spirites, & other
glorious Sainctes, his Diuine Goodnes bringeth faithful iust soules through this world of tentations, vnto
eternal glorie in heauen? For [Are not the glorious
Angels, ministring spirites: sent to minister for them, Heb.1.v.14.
which shal receiue the inheritance of saluation?] Al,
through the merites of Christ our onlie SAVIOVR.
To whom with the Father, and the Holie Ghost, be
al honour, and glorie for euer.   Amen.

4.

5.

Not only to
these deman-
des, but also
to the whole
worke, we de-
sire our Aduer-
saries answers:
if they be not
satisfied.

Epilogus Auctoris ad benignum Lectorem.

PRudenterne fecerim an imprudenter, cum ijs conatus sim satisfacere,
qui nullam in rebus Fidei, ac Religionis discutiendis, auctoritatem a-
liam, præter solum scriptum Dei verbum, admittunt, nescio. Id tamen
scio, iuuandarum animarum causâ hunc me subijsse laborem. Arduam
sanè suscepi prouinciã, qui iniusta petentibus, ex abundanti liberalitate mo-
rem gerere voluerim. Equidem spero bonos boni consulturos. Quod ad Ad-
uersarios spectat, illos semper meminisse oportet, nos hac potissimum, con-
ditione istud cum eis certamen inijsse, vt ipsi quoque intra eosdem sacra-
rum Scripturarum limites se contineant. Vt tandem aliquando perspiciant;
vtrum ipsi, an nos, solis sanctarum Scripturarum armis fortiores simus.
     Qui

Qui vero plenissimam totius Doctrinæ Christianæ volunt confirmationem, admittere etiam debent, vnâ cum scripto Dei Verbo, Verbum Dei sine scripto traditum: atque de occurrentibus insuper dubijs, Iudicium Ecclesiæ audire tenentur. Ecclesiæ siquidem declaratione: Quæ sint sacræ Scripturæ, quisnam earum sensus: & quæ sint diuinæ Traditiones non scriptæ: nobis innotescit. Hic autem triplex, Dogmata Christiana docendi, & confirmandi modus (ex sacris Scripturis; ex diuinis Traditionibus agraphis, & ex Ecclesiæ, ac Ecclesiasticorum virorum, præsertim Summorum Pontificum ex Cathedra loquentium testificatione, contextus) Murus est inexpugnabilis: fortissimus hic funiculus triplex: qui nunquam dissoluitur, nunquam infringitur. Quia & pars quæuis funiculi istius, duabus alijs fulcitur, ac corroboratur partibus. Nam inprimis sacra Scriptura testimonium habet, tum quænam illa sit, tum quis illarum sensus, ab omnium præcedentium temporum traditione; atque ab Ecclesiæ Præsulibus, qui eam pro tali recipiunt, & fidelibus pro Dei verbo commendant. Deinde, quod aliquæ sint Traditiones non scriptæ necessariò credendæ, sacræ Scripturæ clarissimè testantur; & tam vetus, quam præsens Ecclesia iudicat: ipsique Aduersarij aliquas agnoscunt. Denique quòd necessarius sit Iudex aliquis, qui viuæ vocis oraculo, sententiam iuridicè quandoque ferat, cui omnes obedire debent, sacræ etiam Scripturæ apertè testantur; ac Traditiones omnium sæculorum docent: & perpetua praxis confirmat. Cum ergo ex tribus istis certissimæ veritatis fundamentis, vnum solum ab Aduersarijs hodiè, in plerisque omnibus Controuersijs, agnoscitur; vtpote purum Dei verbum scriptum, per illud solum disputatum est hic cum illis: vt hoc saltem pacto, importunitati eorum satisfiat: vtque (siue per singula, siue per omnia simul tria propugnacula) veritas innotescat: & qui errant, in veritatis viam reducantur. Qui scopus est huiusce cum Aduersarijs initi certaminis. Finis.

Deo gratias. Beatissimaque Virgini Deiparæ:
& omnibus Sanctis, laus in æternum.

IT ſhal not be neceſſarie to collect an Alphabetical table, of the particular pointes proued, and explaned in this worke : becauſe the ſame, as in a Synopſis (or conſpicuous Summarie) are prefixed in the beginning, according to the Methode of Chriſtian Doctrine diſtributed into foure Parts: and euerie part into ſpecial Articles. in al two hundred. Becauſe alſo enerie Article is diſtinguiſſhed into Paragraphes : and in the margine is noted the ſumme of the matter, therin conteyned . The very ſame wherof the other table ſhould conſiſt: which therfore in this reſpect ſemeth needles.

Some faultes are eſcaped in printing: but ſuch (eſpecially in the two laſt Parts) as the Iudicious Reader wil eaſyly diſcerne, and correct. For example in the page 179. line 9. you wil read: *Iniuſtice committed* &c. And vſe the like corrections, where you finde other errors.

CErtaine Propositions auouched by William Cartwright: and other Puritanes, in their Admonition to the Parlament. About the year. 1574.

1. The present pretended Ecclesiastical Regiment in England, by Bishops, Chancelers, Deanes, Archdeacons, &c. is Antichristian.
2. The people must choose their Ministers: and so they nede no other ordination.
3. Al Ministers are of equal auctoritie.
4. The Presbyterie by most voices, is the supreme Iudge in spiritual causes: in euerie prouince: or shire.
5. The Article, Of Chrifts descending into hel: is foysted into the Crede.
6. No holie day is to be kept but the Sabbath day only. *VVhich is Saturday.*
7. Baptisme is nor necessarie for anie person. Not to be ministred to Infants.
8. The signe of the Crosse is in nowise to be made.
9. No surplice is to be vsed; nor cope; nor square cappe; &c.
10. It is not lawful to knele, when they receiue the communion.

Al which, with the like, were impugned by Doctor whitegift: and others. And are condemned in the Proteftants Synode, holden at Hamptoncourt. 1604.

The God of peace geue vs to be of one mind; according to IESVS CHRIST, *that vvith one mouth vve may glorifie God.*